THE GROWTH
OF MYSTICISM

A four-volume series

THE PRESENCE OF GOD:
A HISTORY OF WESTERN CHRISTIAN MYSTICISM

Vol. I. *The Foundations of Mysticism*
Vol. II. *The Growth of Mysticism*
Vol. III. *The Flowering of Mysticism*
Vol. IV. *The Crisis of Mysticism*

THE GROWTH
OF MYSTICISM

Vol. II of
The Presence of God:
A History of Western Christian Mysticism

by
Bernard McGinn

A Crossroad Herder Book
The Crossroad Publishing Company

New York

1996

The Crossroad Publishing Company
370 Lexington Avenue, New York, NY 10017

Printed in the United States of America

Library of Congress Cataloging-in-Publication Data

McGinn, Bernard, 1937–
   The growth of mysticism : Gregory the Great through the
twelfth century / Bernard McGinn.
     p. cm.–(The presence of God ; vol. 2)
   Includes bibliographical references and indexes.
   ISBN 0-8245-1450-5; 0-8245-1628-1 (pbk.)
    1. Mysticism–History–Middle Ages, 600–1500. 2. Mysticism–
Catholic Church–History. 3. Catholic Church–Doctrines–History.
I. Title. II. Series: McGinn, Bernard, 1937– Presence of God ;
vol. 2.
BV5075.M37 1994
248.2'2'0902–dc20   94-21508
                                                        CIP

Dedicated

to the memory

of my beloved sister,

Carolyn McGinn Frank

(1929–1993),

who left all too soon.

Contents

Introduction

MY FIRST ENGAGEMENT with the study of mysticism was devoted to the Cistercian mystics of the twelfth century, especially Bernard of Clairvaux. In 1970 I completed a dissertation on one of the lesser Cistercians–though lesser only in comparison with Bernard–Isaac of Stella. Some years passed, and about a decade ago, after finishing a period of research and writing on the mysticism of Meister Eckhart, I dreamed of returning to Isaac, Bernard, William of St. Thierry, and the other Cistercian mystics in order to present a general account of Cistercian mysticism and its meaning for the Western Christian mystical tradition.

But what is the meaning of Cistercian mysticism in the context of the broader Christian mystical tradition? The more I pondered this question, the more convinced I became that I had no good answer to it. This is not to say that I considered as suspect the tradition that held that the Cistercians were indeed important mystics. If the Christian tradition had identified certain figures, both of East and of West, as "contemplatives" (which is more or less what we mean when we use the term "mystics" today), this seemed to me a necessary starting point for contemporary consideration of both the nature and the theological significance of Christian mysticism. But I wanted to know why certain figures came to be hailed as contemplatives and how *contemplatio* (the Greek *theōria*) and related categories came to play the role they did in Christian life and thought. I was also puzzled over why those called contemplatives or mystics were becoming renewed subjects of intensive study (and not just academic study) during the 1980s.

This is why a book that was originally conceived as a single volume about twelfth-century Cistercian mysticism has now grown to be the

second part of a history of the entire span of Western Christian mysticism. I
am happy that the great Cistercians do finally appear in this volume. What
I have to say about them now, as forming a part of this wider project, differs in many ways from what I might have said concerning them in the un-
written book that I planned in the early 1980s.

The conviction upon which this history is being written is that an in-
depth contemporary study of the history of what the monastics called *contemplatio*, and later medieval and early modern authors often called *theologia
mystica*, is the necessary prolegomenon for thinking theologically about
what "mysticism," our modern concept, might mean today. More simply
put, we will not really know what Christian mysticism is, despite the extensive literature that has been devoted to it, until we become better informed
about the entire history of its development.

In *The Foundations of Mysticism*, the first volume in this project bearing the
overall title of *The Presence of God*, I attempted two somewhat different
tasks—an analysis of the development of Christian mysticism down to the
end of the fifth century C.E., and a survey of the study of "mysticism" as a
theological, philosophical, and comparativist category in twentieth-century
thought. In the General Introduction to that volume I set out a heuristic
notion of mysticism, one whose broad lines would guide the way in which I
was presenting the history but which would be subject to development,
clarification, and even correction by the historical account itself. Since this
heuristic tool still provides the perspective for the present volume, I will
summarize it here.

I argue that mysticism is best seen not as some distinct or independent
entity or form of religion but as an *element* in concrete religious communities and traditions. This may be a truism, but one that I see as worth repeating, given the fact that it seems so often neglected. We must remain
conscious that the mystical element is part of a larger whole, one interactive
aspect of complex and developing religious processes. This perspective
helps us understand why Christian mysticism can only be understood
through the appropriation of its history. The mystical element, while implicit in Christianity from the beginning, became explicit in concrete times
and circumstances that continued to have an impact on its later development. The diverse forms in which the mystical element has expressed itself;
the varying ways in which it has interacted with institutional, intellectual,
and social forms of religious life; even the degree to which it has or has not
been subject to explicit formulation—in other words, everything that constitutes mysticism as a tradition—must be taken into account as a necessary, if
not a totally sufficient, aspect of any contemporary theology of mysticism.

It also seems necessary to insist that the mystical element of the Christian religion be seen primarily as a *process* or way of life rather than being defined solely in terms of some experience of union with God. To be sure, contemplatives or mystics do express the desire to attain, through divine grace, the goal of an encounter with God that is different from and deeper than that available in the ordinary course of their practice of religion. Though this encounter is often expressed in terms of some form of union with God, I have argued that a more flexible understanding of this goal in terms of the consciousness of the immediate or direct presence of God–a presence that paradoxically is often expressed through such thorough going negation of all created forms of being and awareness that it appears as absence–is a better way of looking at the entire story of the Christian mystical tradition. But this essential characteristic, however described, must not be considered in isolation from the practices, both ascetical and intellectual, meant to prepare for it, nor from the transformative consequences it is intended to produce in those who experience it and the roles they take up in the Christian community. This is why I have spoken of the mystical element in Christianity as that part of its beliefs and practices that concerns the preparation for, the consciousness of, and the reaction to the immediate or direct presence of God.

The first volume of the history that I decided to give the title *The Presence of God* was initially intended to cover the whole span of the first layer of all subsequent Western Christian mysticism, the monastic contemplative tradition. The material proved so extensive, however, that I soon realized that two volumes would be needed to do anything like justice to the task. *The Foundations of Mysticism* (Crossroad, 1991) set out the first part of the story down to 500 C.E.

On the basis of the appropriation of elements from both Judaism and Hellenic philosophy, Christian authors, beginning from the second century, created an understanding of special access to God present in the study of the Bible that reached the level of explicit formulation in the great exegete Origen of Alexandria. This initial sedimentary layer in the history of Christian mysticism was inextricably linked to reading and praying the biblical message with the aim of penetrating to its mystical core. Indeed, the qualifier *mystikos* (i.e., hidden), which had become a largely Christian term by the end of the second century, fundamentally signified this concealed level, or deep structure, of the mystery of salvation. Exegesis and mysticism remained inseparable down through the twelfth century.

Origen's contemplative theology, in turn, was utilized by fourth-century monastic authors, most notably Evagrius Ponticus, to give expression to the inner significance of the new form of religious life created by the *monachoi*, or monks, whom one of their first observers, Eusebius of Caesarea, described as "the front rank of those advancing in Christ." From this point on, monastic mysticism, developed and molded in various ways, especially through the injection of a powerful form of negative theology by the mysterious figure of Dionysius around 500 C.E., was to remain foundational to the mystical tradition in both the Greek East and the Latin West through the twelfth century. A somewhat simplified form of Evagrian mystical theory was conveyed to Western monks by John Cassian in the early fifth century. Two contemporary Latin bishops, Ambrose of Milan and Augustine of Hippo, both enamored of monasticism as the highest form of pursuit of God, made rich teaching about contemplative love of God available to the wider Christian community in their teaching and preaching.

I do not mean to suggest that all Christian mysticism down to the twelfth century was explicitly monastic in origin and intention, any more than I would claim that all mystics conveyed the same message. My point is that mystical theory as a way of teaching and explaining the process whereby one reaches some form of transforming consciousness of the direct presence of God in this life found its central institutional embodiment in the monastic way of life. The majority of its foremost exponents were monastics, and its understanding and expression were so closely tied to the practices of the monastic life that these exponents, at least at times, seemed to think that direct consciousness of God was not available in any other form of life.

The Growth of Mysticism takes up the story from 500 to 1200 C.E. The nine chapters that make up this volume fall naturally into two broad sections. Part I, "Early Medieval Mysticism," deals with the period from 500 to 1100 C.E., when monasticism was the dominant religious and educational institution of the new post-Roman world, the society that by the time of Charlemagne understood itself as "Christendom." Since the mystical element should be located in its larger religious and social whole, and since the centuries between 500 and 800 saw the creation of a new such whole, the first chapter deals primarily with the cultural context for early medieval mysticism. The next chapter treats Gregory the Great, bishop of Rome from 590-604, whom many have called the first medieval pope and who was the major resource for early medieval understandings of contemplation. Gregory himself is our sole source for the life of Benedict of Nursia, the author of the rule of life for monks that eventually was to dominate in the West. In this chapter I cite the exemplary formula of a modern Benedictine, Patrick Catry, who summarized the importance of the two figures thus: "Saint Benedict gave the monks of the West a *Rule*. Gregory gave them a mysticism."

Chapter 3 is devoted to a study of the background and achievement of

John Scottus Eriugena, the ninth-century Irish scholar. Eriugena not only conveyed important aspects of Greek mystical doctrine to the West, especially the writings of Dionysius, but also created the first great Western synthesis of dialectical mystical theory. His teaching did not presume the practice of the monastic life (we do not know whether he was monk, priest, or layman), and thus constitutes something of an anomaly in the early Middle Ages. Eriugena's theory was a major intellectual achievement, one that, while not without influence in the twelfth century, was to have its greatest direct and indirect impact in the later medieval period when mystics like Meister Eckhart recreated dialectical mystical theory and gave it a new contextualization in their preaching and teaching. The final chapter in this first part of *The Growth of Mysticism* surveys how the heritage of *contemplatio* was understood by monastic writers between 800 and 1100.

Part II concerns the mysticism of the twelfth century, the age of the richest development of the monastic mystical tradition in the West. The introduction to this part attempts to give a brief overview of the changes that affected Christendom in the late eleventh and the twelfth centuries as movements of reform percolated through the papacy and the religious orders, both monastic and canonical. I here advance the suggestion that the notion of the "ordering of charity" (*ordinatio caritatis*), while not explicitly addressed by all twelfth-century mystics, provides one way of summarizing the distinctive achievement of the great mystics of the time. The greatest of these, Bernard of Clairvaux, takes up the fifth chapter. It is impossible to give a brief characterization of the argument of this long chapter here—Bernard's contributions were too rich and too important for easy summary. I would point out, however, that Bernard and the other Cistercians, though they considered themselves faithful witnesses to the ancient contemplative tradition as found in Origen, Ambrose, Cassian, Augustine, Gregory, and others, were also innovators. The abbot of Clairvaux's insistence on the role of experience, the necessity for his audience to read not only the scripture but also the "book of experience" (*liber experientiae*), marks a new and important shift in the development of Christian mysticism. Two further chapters are devoted to the other major Cistercian figures. Chapter 6 studies William of St. Thierry, Bernard's friend and biographer, whose trinitarian mystical thought must be measured with the very greatest of the Christian tradition. Other significant Cistercian authors are considered in chapter 7 under three headings: Christology; theological anthropology; and the nature and ordering of *caritas*. Twelfth-century mysticism cannot be restricted to the contributions made by the Cistercians, however massive they were, as chapters 8 and 9 try to show. Other monastic teachers, both among the traditional Benedictines and in the new eremitical reform of the Carthusians, carried on and in some cases developed the tradition of monastic *contemplatio*. Another new element appeared when some religious leaders, like Rupert of Deutz, Hildegard of Bingen, and Joachim of Fiore, begin to employ direct visionary encounters with God as modes of authentification for their theological writings. This phenomenon raises the issue of the relation between autobiographical visionary accounts and mysticism, an issue that will become much more pressing in the next volume of this history. Finally, chapter 9 concerns the Victorine authors, Hugh and Richard of St. Victor, who were members of a reformed community of canons, that is, priests living a common life. The work of these canons represents yet another significant innovation of the time, one in which the contemplative tradition encountered the new form of theology called scholasticism which was to affect Christian mysticism deeply in the centuries to come. The Victorine attempt to create systematic models of the itinerary to contemplative union with God was based on a deep knowledge of and respect for the tradition, but it was something new–an ordering of charity that was also a scientific ordering of wisdom.

The kind words, even the generosity, of the many reviewers of *The Foundations of Mysticism* have given me encouragement in the pursuit of what has proven to be a much larger and more difficult enterprise than I had ever imagined. I am particularly grateful to those reviewers who have raised serious questions about the heuristic notion of mysticism I am employing in this history, as well as the adequacy of my use of it in dealing with particular figures and movements. Among the most important issues that have been raised is that of the relation between mystical texts, understood as those that contain significant teaching about attaining immediate awareness of God's presence, and the actual experiences of some form of direct consciousness of God enjoyed (or perhaps not enjoyed) by those who wrote these texts. This problem takes one form in the patristic tradition, where autobiographical references are sparse, and quite another in the later Middle Ages when they become frequent. The twelfth century represents a transition period, one when the appeal to personal experience found among the Cistercians, as well as the autobiographical accounts of visions of God, become more prevalent.

In this Introduction it is tempting to try to reply to all the queries, suggestions, and helpful criticisms made by reviewers, but I have refrained from this temptation. I have learned a great deal from them, and I hope that some of what I have learned will be reflected in these pages. Nevertheless, this does not seem to be the proper place to attempt a full-scale response. I can say that I have seen no reason yet to abandon the broad parameters of the heuristic model of mysticism outlined in *The Foundations of Mysticism* and briefly summarized above. I have seen reason to think of qualifying, possibly even of enriching it, as the project proceeds. I still do intend, in the final part of the last volume of *The Presence of God*, to provide a theological discussion of my constructive view of the nature of Christian mysticism, and I wish to invite my readers and reviewers to continue to help me to refine the issues such an attempt must necessarily address.

I close by expressing a few brief, and insufficient, words of gratitude for those who have given me so much assistance in bringing Volume II of *The Presence of God* to publication. First, to the staff at Crossroad Publishing, who have been always helpful and (what is perhaps more difficult) always patient. Second, to my wife, Patricia, and my research assistant, Shawn Madison Krahmer. Their combined editorial skills have much to do with whatever readability this account may have. Several chapters of this volume were written during a semester at The Institute for Ecumenical Research of St. John's University at Collegeville, Minnesota. I want to thank Patrick Henry, the director of the Institute, as well as his able staff, for their kindness and support. During my time at the Institute, my colleague and friend Professor Carol Neel of Colorado College was helpful in many ways as I developed what became chapters 1 and 2.

Many of the positions advanced here have profited from being first delivered in lectures, both in classes at the Divinity School of the University of Chicago and in other venues. To my students, colleagues, and friends whose comments and reactions were a part of this process I offer sincere gratitude. In this connection, I wish to single out the Cistercian communities of St. Joseph's Abbey in Spencer, Massachusetts, and the Abbey of Gethsemani in Trappist, Kentucky. Earlier forms of the chapters on Bernard and William of St. Thierry were delivered as series of conferences to these communities, and it would be difficult for me to express in adequate fashion how much I learned from the conversation and also from the example of those who keep alive in our own time the spirit of the giants of Cîteaux.

Bernard McGinn
Chicago
March 1994

Abbreviations

AASS   *Acta Sanctorum.* Paris: Palmé, 1863–. 3rd edition.

CC   *Corpus Christianorum. Series Latina.* Turnhout: Brepols, 1954–.

CCCM   *Corpus Christianorum. Continuatio Mediaevalis.* Turnhout: Brepols, 1971–.

CCSG   *Corpus Christianorum. Series Graeca.* Turnhout: Brepols, 1970–.

CSEL   *Corpus scriptorum ecclesiasticorum latinorum.* Vienna: Hoelder-Pichler-Tempsky, 1866–.

DIP   *Dizionario degli Istituti di Perfezione.* Rome: Edizioni Paoline, 1974–.

DS   *Dictionnaire de spiritualité ascétique et mystique doctrine et histoire.* Paris: Beauchesne, 1937–.

GCS   *Die griechischen christlichen Schriftsteller der ersten drei Jahrhunderte.* Berlin: Akademie-Verlag, 1897.

LXX   Septuagint version of the Hebrew Bible. See *Septuaginta, id est Vetus Testamentum Graece iuxta LXX interpres.* Stuttgart: Deutsche Bibelgesellschaft, 1980.

MGH   *Monumenta Germaniae Historica inde ab a.C. 500 usque ad a. 1500.* Hanover and Berlin, 1826–. Various publishers and sections.

PG   *Patrologiae cursus completus. Series graeca.* Paris: J. P. Migne, 1857–66. 161 volumes.

PL   *Patrologiae cursus completus. Series latina.* Paris: J. P. Migne, 1844–64. 221 volumes.

SC   *Sources chrétiennes.* Paris: Cerf, 1940–.

Vg   Vulgate version of the Christian Bible. See *Biblia sacra iuxta Vulgatam Versionem.* Stuttgart: Deutsche Bibelgemeinschaft, 1983.

PART I

Early Medieval Mysticism

The Making
of Christendom

THE TRANSITION FROM ancient Rome to medieval Christendom had fascinated students of history for centuries even before it gave rise to the greatest historical work in the English language, Edward Gibbon's *The Decline and Fall of the Roman Empire* (1776–88). Especially over the course of the past century, the literature on the topic has grown to be immense, both that directly addressed to Gibbon, and books and essays concerning the underlying issue of Rome's fate and the beginning of the Middle Ages.[1] Gibbon thought that "the decline of Rome was the natural and inevitable effect of immoderate greatness," but this good Enlightenment principle did not preclude him from attaching blame both to the barbarians whose defeat of the emperor Valens in 378 initiated "the disastrous period of the fall of the Roman Empire," and to the Christian religion.[2] Gibbon's rather negative view of Christianity, of course, produced not a few defenses that sought to free Christianity from any blame for Rome's demise; but he was surely correct about the larger issue, as scholars such as Arnaldo Momigliano and Charles Norris Cochrane have shown.[3] There was a basic incompatibility between the ancient Roman system, in which religion and the state were fused under imperial authority, and Christianity's insistence on at least some form of autonomy for the church. As Momigliano says, "An empire built on such a dual organization of state and church was never going to be the same as the old one."[4] Without denying the importance of geography, economy, politics, war, and all the other elements that created the historical context in which the transition from the ancient world to what we call the Middle Ages took place, Gibbon was correct in giving religion an important role.

Gibbon placed the fall of Rome in a traditional place, the events of the late fourth and fifth centuries, though his recognition that ancient Rome was not really dead until the conquest of Constantinople in 1453 led him to drag the story on through ages with which he had less and less sympathy. A century and a half after he completed his masterpiece, a slimmer but no less influential appraisal of the end of the ancient world appeared, Henri Pirenne's posthumous *Mahomet et Charlemagne* (1937).[5] Pirene disagreed with Gibbon and most historians by arguing that *Romania,* or "functional Romanity" in Peter Brown's phrase, though much battered by the barbarian invasions and internal strife, survived into the sixth century and beyond because the economic and cultural unity of the Mediterranean basin, the foundation of the Roman Empire, had not been broken. It was the seventh-century irruption of Islam that really spelled the end of the ancient world, shattering Mediterranean unity, severing East from West and compelling the western part of the ancient world to create a new agrarian feudal society north of the Alps, the Carolingian empire of Charlemagne. As Pirenne summarized, "It is therefore strictly correct to say that without Mohammed Charlemagne would have been inconceivable."[6] Though Pirenne disagreed with Gibbon about the timing, he too insisted on the centrality of religion by his introduction of Islam as a crucial player in the transition.[7] Pirenne's book, much debated over more than fifty years, marked a decisive change in the way in which the relations between ancient Rome and medieval Europe have been conceived. Although he did not invent the study of late antiquity, his work has been of considerable importance in historians' increasing interest in the period ca. 400–800 C.E.[8]

Today there is certainly no need to apologize for studying the history of late antiquity on its own terms, not just as the collapse or degradation of a perhaps better and happier world.[9] Over fifty years ago, when it was still common to refer to this period as the "Dark Ages," Christopher Dawson noted that while the age might lack "the superficial attractiveness of periods of brilliant cultural expansion, . . . it was the most creative age of all, since it created not this or that manifestation of [European] culture, but the very culture itself."[10] Current scholarship has little interest in trying to establish a precise date for the fall of the Roman Empire or the beginning of the Middle Ages (by no means the same thing!).[11] But the issue of how the ancient world in its final form, even its final Christian form as the empire of Constantine and his successors, yielded to a new order remains one of the most intriguing and most difficult problems in European history. In order to understand how the Latin mysticism established in the writings of Ambrose, Cassian, and Augustine became the source for a developing early medieval Western mystical tradition that reached its maturity in the twelfth century, we need to reflect on some of the issues raised by the wider problem of the end of antiquity and the creation of medieval Christendom.

Historical periodization in triplicate (ancient-medieval-modern) is one of the less satisfactory but seemingly inescapable bequests of Renaissance humanists to Western thought—often decried and attacked, but difficult to abandon. (Christian believers have always thought of themselves as living at the end of the ages, not in a middle period, at least of secular reckoning.) But the concerns that prompted such periodization were (and are) genuine ones. No one doubts that the "real" Roman Empire, at least in the West, was no longer in existence when the Frankish ruler Charles and his advisors embarked on an ambitious program of *renovatio imperii,* which allowed western European rulers to continue to claim to be "Roman" emperors down to 1806. But when did the conviction that ancient Rome was dead emerge, especially in the light of continuing Byzantine claims to the contrary? And why did Charlemagne find it important to adopt the imperial mantle? How do such issues relate to the identification of a distinctively "medieval" period in Western history?

The premise of this chapter is that the creation of a distinctive notion of Christendom (*christianitas* in Latin; *cristendome* in Old English) reflects a new awareness of Western Christianity's identity that becomes evident by ca. 800 C.E. *Christianitas* itself is a term found in Augustine (ca. 400) and in other fifth-century texts, notably the Code of Theodosius.[12] But the early uses of the term are largely ritual in nature, referring to the proper mode of practicing the Christian religion. By the ninth century, both in papal texts and in incipient vernacular uses, *christianitas* acquired greater semantic complexity. The primary sense of religious observance took on new political and territorial dimensions, so that "Christendom" came to be understood as that territory where the population observed the practice of the Christian religion under the leadership of the proper secular and ecclesiastical leaders.[13]

Two preliminary observations about the transition from the *respublica romana* of the fifth century to the *christianitas* of the ninth may be helpful at this point. As the historians of the Annales school, especially Fernand Braudel have shown, the underlying geographical and climatic continuities of the human environment make the notion of historical "change" much more ambiguous than historians previously thought. Even on the level of the datable events that fill history books, transitions are almost always gradual, piecemeal, incomplete—attaining finality, if they do, only after great effort and with considerable temporary reversal. History proceeds not in any straight-line march, but often by a wandering path, or by taking three steps forward and two back.[14] This ambulatory ambiguity is heightened by the variety of forms of evidence that leads to rather different explanations of the process and pace of transition. The materials studied by the art historian, for example, may yield a rather different picture from those that are the concern of the economic or political historian.[15] For all our desire to present a total history, a full picture of the past, we are usually constrained to pull apart what had once been a seamless cloth strand by strand and to hold up these separate filaments to a scrutiny whose very intensity implies a degree of myopia.

Geography is as important as chronology in understanding the end of antiquity and the origins of the medieval world. In discussing the formation of Latin Christianity in *The Foundations of Mysticism,* I emphasized the linguistic and cultural divisions between Eastern and Western Christianity that become evident in the fourth and especially in the fifth century.[16] Henri Pirenne, as we have seen, emphasized the Islamic rupture of the Mediterranean world between East and West as a crucial change. But Peter Brown expands on Pirenne's insight in a helpful way when he observes: "Any divergence along the East–West spectrum of the Mediterranean was always dwarfed by the immensity of the gulf which separated the Mediterranean itself from the alien societies which flanked it."[17] From the perspective of the western half of the ancient Roman Empire, the north–south polarity gradually became at least as important as the east–west division. Charlemagne's empire was a renewal (*renovatio*) and not merely a continuation—not least because it was centered north of the Alps with an outlook more Atlantic than Mediterranean.

Any full discussion of the transformation of the ancient world between 400 and 800 C.E. would demand equal attention to the ways in which all three heirs of ancient Rome—Byzantium, Islam, and the Latin West—adapted this heritage to new elements in their situation, religious, social, economic, and cultural. Although I will not be able to neglect saying something about Byzantium and Islam, largely because of the ways in which their adaptations impinged on those in the West, the restricted scope of these volumes allows me to concentrate on the transition that took place in Latin Christianity. Three themes will organize the first section of this chapter, which attempts to give a short sketch of the political and ecclesiastical events of these centuries. The second part of the chapter will concern itself with the inner history of the time, the changes in religious attitudes.

From Imperial Rome to Christendom

From the political perspective, there can be no denial that both the western part of the Roman Empire, and to a lesser extent its eastern section experienced fragmentation, even disintegration, during the centuries between 400 and 800. Byzantium, of course, remained the empire of the Romans (Gk. *romaioi*), with a continuous, if at times tenuous, identity with Constantine's realm. Its control of at least most of the eastern part of ancient Rome, as well as its claims of distant overlordship of the West, were political realities only through the fifth and sixth centuries. Islam changed all that within a single decade between 634 and 644 C.E.

In the West, fragmentation was evident from 400 on. The barbarian incursions of 406–410, of which the famous sack of Rome by Alaric (Visigothic leader and Roman general) formed a part, led to the end of Roman rule in Britain. While most of the rest of the West remained technically under the domain of the emperor in Constantinople, the fifth and the sixth centuries saw a succession of barbarian client states gain effective control of the native Roman population. Some of these, like the Visigothic kingdom in Spain, were quite independent of the East; others, like the savage Vandals who conquered North Africa, fought against the empire (their sack of Rome in 455 was far worse than Alaric's). The Ostrogothic kingdom established by Theodoric (493–526) was perhaps more typical. Theodoric had been a hostage raised in Constantinople, and for most of his reign he remained nominally under the eastern rulers as a kind of sub-emperor while he pursued a political program that sought to combine Roman civilization with barbarian military might.

The greatest attempt to overcome the disintegration of the empire was the work of Justinian, the last Latin-speaking emperor of the East (527–565). Adopting a defensive stance in the long wars against Persia, the empire's traditional enemy to the East, Justinian concentrated on regaining the West for imperial control. His able generals crushed the Vandal kingdom, reconquered part of Spain from the Visigoths and seemed on their way to a rapid defeat of the Ostrogoths in Italy. The Mediterranean appeared to be about to become the Roman *mare nostrum* once again. But Ostrogothic resistance stiffened and the eastern Roman armies became bogged down in the twenty-year Ostrogothic war that devastated Italy. Gregory the Great (the subject of the next chapter) grew up during these years. His lugubrious evocations of the ruin of a civilization testify to the significance of the break with the past that Italy experienced in the mid-sixth century. Meanwhile, in the 540s bubonic plague broke out in the East and soon ravaged most of the Mediterranean world. Despite his energy and many achievements (especially the creation of the definitive code of Roman law), Justinian died a failure.

Roman authority continued to suffer challenges and further fragmentation after 550. With almost cruel irony, new barbarian invasions, this time of the Lombards, plunged Italy into chaos just a few years after the final defeat of the Ostrogoths. Some political stability was being achieved in Spain, where in the late sixth century the Visigothic kingdom converted to Catholic Christianity and established the rudiments of a new form of Christian monarchy that was the prototype of later medieval developments.[18] In Gaul the Frankish kingdom established by Clovis, who had been baptized into Catholic Christianity (the traditional date is 496), grew powerful in the course of the century, despite grave internal struggles typical of the Germanic kingdoms. The Visigoths remained hostile to Byzantium; the Franks were effectively independent.

In the East, the *romaioi* managed to hold their own for most of the period ca. 400–600 C.E. first against violent but generally brief incursions of the Huns and also in the endemic struggles with Persia under the revived Sassanian dynasty. The sixth century saw the beginnings of invasions of the Slavs and the Avars and the first settlement of Slavs in the Balkan domains of the empire. The conflict with Persia culminated in the early seventh century in the reign of Heraclius (610–641) when, after dramatic reversals of fortune, the warrior emperor managed to inflict a decisive defeat on the Persians in 628. Like the Ostrogothic war in Italy, however, the devastation wrought by this final Persian war destroyed much of the fabric of ancient Roman civilization in the East.

Heraclius's regaining of the East was just as ironically ephemeral as Justinian's apparent reconstitution of a large part of the empire seventy-five years before. The prophet Muhammad died in 632, ten years after his flight to Medina, which constitutes the beginning of the Muslim era. Soon after his death, the Arab armies broke upon the eastern Roman Empire, taking Damascus in 634, decisively defeating Heraclius's armies in 636, and even capturing Jerusalem in 638. Syria, Egypt, Mesopotamia, and Tripoli soon followed. Islamic raids against Constantinople raged between 674 and 678. In the second half of the seventh century, the Arabs pushed into the western part of the empire. Carthage, the ancient intellectual center of Latin Christianity, was lost in 698. In 711 the Arabs crossed the Strait of Gibraltar and rapidly defeated the Visigothic kingdom. Within a few years they had also taken over parts of southern France. Thus, by the early eighth century the political fragmentation of the ancient Roman empire was largely complete, first by a gradual process of barbarization that affected the West more than the East; second—and more decisively—by the irruption of Islam and its challenge to the Christian world.

The second major theme of the transition from ancient Rome to medieval Christendom that should be stressed is socioeconomic in nature and can be broadly, if somewhat barbarously, described as the "de-urbaniza-

tion" of the ancient Mediterranean world.[19] Gibbon was not much interested in issues of economy; Pirenne was among the most accomplished economic historians of the early twentieth century, with a special interest in
urban history.[20] The scattered evidence for economic history between 400
and 800 remains the purview of experts, but it seems as difficult to deny
that the Roman Empire really did end as it is to gainsay the importance of
the decay of cities and the social and economic structures that supported
them during this era, though it is true that the vast majority of the population of the empire, even at its height, had always lived on the land and supported a basically agrarian economy. The feudal system proper, which
characterized much of northern Europe from the tenth century to the
twelfth, had its roots, at least in part, in this slow but significant change.[21]

There is much evidence to indicate that the *curiales*, that is, the governing
class of the Roman cities, experienced a precipitous decline beginning in
the fourth century. Especially in the West, the poorer *curiales* (roughly what
we might call the middle class) were reduced to poverty, while the senator-
ial class gained in wealth relative to the entire population. Rich aristocrats
retired to their great landed estates, which were increasingly farmed by
slaves and indentured serfs, as the life of free peasants became more difficult to sustain. International trade may have lasted into the seventh century,
as Pirenne argued, but it had correspondingly less importance in an increasingly rural society.

The deemphasis on urban life was probably of little concern to the barbarian chieftains who took control of the fragmented late Roman world in
the West. As much as some of them may have appreciated the splendor of
Roman cities and made use of traditional imperial sites, such as Rome and
Ravenna, to enhance their claims, they were not city dwellers but military
wanderers who demonstrated their authority in part by their ability to
move where they were needed. Charlemagne, who must be seen as the last
and greatest of the Germanic war leaders, showed his superiority over most
of his predecessors not least by being the first to think of founding a new
imperial capital, the palace-city at Aachen.

The decline in urban life between 400 and 800 did pose a particular
problem for Christianity. Christianity had been an urban religion from the
start. Jesus himself was an itinerant preacher who conveyed his message in
rural areas, in towns, but also in the sacred city of Jerusalem where he met
his death. His earliest followers in Palestine found their center in Jerusalem,
and the Acts of Apostles (however much "real" history it records) makes it
clear that Christianity spread through missionary work in the Mediterranean cities of the Roman Empire. The structures that abetted the success
of the new religion—monarchical bishops in urban centers, dramatic and

socially cohesive rituals that all members could attend, a welfare system that tried to guarantee group support from cradle to grave (and beyond)– were dependent on an urban setting that was increasingly reduced after 400 C.E. It is almost otiose to note that the Latin word *paganus*, which in the classical era had meant a peasant or civilian in general, by the late fourth century had come to designate the nonbaptized, who were more likely to be found in the rural areas not yet seriously affected by Christianity.[22] There is perhaps no greater sign of Christianity's vitality (at least in comparison with the dead ancient Roman cults and the academic attempts to create religions found in late Neoplatonism) than its ability to adapt to this new situation and to form a new kind of Christianity between 400 and 800 C.E. But before turning to the spiritual changes that brought an end to ancient Christianity, it is important to survey the Christian religion's role in the political life of the period (though, of course, any simple distinction between internal and external aspects of Christianity is always somewhat artificial).

It is not easy to find a single word to summarize the salient features of Christianity's political effect during these four centuries. "Christianization" is a term that is often used by modern historians, but it contains inherent ambiguities and has given rise to so much argument that it seems better to avoid it in this context.[23] The era has often been termed an age of conversion and missionization as Germanic, Celtic, and in the East Slavic barbarians, both inside and outside the Roman *oikumene*, came to embrace Christianity.[24] Without gainsaying the importance of a Patrick in the fifth century, Augustine of Canterbury and the Irish monks in the sixth century, and the Anglo-Saxons on the continent in the eighth century, the projection of a modern sense of missionary activity onto the late antique world is often anachronistic. The term conversion itself, while it has an important history in late antique Latin, has been the subject of considerable debate among modern historians.[25] What do we mean by conversion, and is it the same as what was meant in late antiquity?

I do not intend to enter into these controversies in any detail, but I note them in order to explain why I have chosen neither christianization nor conversion as the third theme to describe the late antique transition, but rather the theme of the defense and dissemination of the orthodox faith. From the perspective of late antique Christian leaders themselves, orthodoxy was central to the church's role in politics and society during the centuries that marked the end of antiquity and the beginning of the Middle Ages.[26] Right belief was essential both within and without, that is, as much in the internal struggles of Christians within the old Roman world as in the attitude they took toward convincing non-Romans about what was necessary in order to become true members of what came to be called Christendom.[27] Orthodoxy involved not only those doctrinal questions about which so many of the struggles of the period revolved but also the issue of how correct belief was to be determined. It was, therefore, unavoidably connected to the question of episcopal authority, especially that of the bishop of Rome, whose role in the making of Christendom was of considerable importance.

Rome was the only patriarchal see in the western part of the empire, and it possessed unimpeachable apostolic authority, having been founded by Peter and Paul and traditionally held to be the place of their martyrdom. It also profited, at least in the centuries before Constantine moved the capital to his new city on the Bosphorus, from its situation at the center of the empire.[28] Traditional early Christian conviction that the criterion of true belief was to be found in the concord among bishops emphasized the agreement of the patriarchal sees, originally four, later five (the pentarchy) when Constantinople joined their number. While some Roman bishops, even in the third century, may have claimed an apostolic mandate to act on their own in controversial matters of belief and practice, most Roman leaders of the third and fourth centuries were second-rate figures, overshadowed even in the West by other bishops, such as Cyprian of Carthage, Ambrose of Milan, Hilary of Arles, or Augustine from the tiny see of Hippo. They made no major contributions to the great debates over orthodoxy that disturbed the fourth century.

Although one important Roman document of 382 already used the term *primatus*, or primacy, in relation to the position of the Roman church, it was not until the middle of the fifth century that the Roman bishops began to build an effective theology of Rome's premier place in the ecclesiastical hierarchy, one that soon brought them into conflict with Constantinople. The idea of Roman primacy was both a development of traditional themes and a new departure in response to the changing situation of the declining empire. The crucial figure was Pope Leo I, bishop of Rome from 440 to 461.

Though little is known of his early life, Leo appears to be a good example of the movement of the old Roman aristocracy into the government of the church. One can argue that by the mid-fifth century the bishop of Rome was the most important imperial official in Italy, even in the entire West, as is evidenced by Leo's role in political negotiations with the invading Huns and Vandals. In Leo's surviving letters we find his most important contribution—the creation of a full-fledged theology of Roman primacy based on the notion of the pope as the "vicar of Peter" and "apostolic man." Leo was not denying the role of consensus in the determination of orthodoxy, but he was giving Rome's voice a special weight, as is clear from his intervention in the controversy over the nature of Christ at the Council of Chalcedon in 451.[29]

Christology, that is, the correct way of understanding the relation of the divine and the human in Jesus Christ, was the most important issue in the struggle for orthodoxy between 400 and 700. Intense debate about Christ had disturbed the eastern Christian world since the end of the fourth century. In 431 Nestorius, the patriarch of Constantinople, was condemned for allegedly teaching that there were two separate persons in Christ, one human, the other divine. His opponents, led by Cyril, the patriarch of Alexandria, also raised controversy by their insistence that while Christ was "out of two natures" (i.e., human and divine), after the Incarnation one should use formulas that stressed "the one incarnate nature of the Word." Many thought that this position compromised the full humanity of the Redeemer. Pope Leo sent a letter (known as the *Tomus*) to patriarch Flavian of Constantinople, explaining the faith of the Roman church that "the characteristic properties of both natures and substances [i.e., the human and the divine] are kept intact and come together in one person [i.e., Jesus Christ]."[30] This was read out at Chalcedon and formed an important part of the council's affirmation of a "hypostatic" (i.e., personal) union of the divine and human in Christ. Such decisive Roman intervention in the establishment of orthodoxy was a crucial plank in the papal program.[31] The sober and deeply liturgical piety found in Leo's sermons, while not mystical in the sense being addressed in these volumes, is an outstanding late patristic witness to the christological foundation of subsequent Western mysticism.[32] His insistence on the reality of Christ present in the Church (*Christus praesens in ecclesia*) is characteristic of the classic Western mystics down through the twelfth century.

Leo's immediate successors pursued the defense of doctrinal orthodoxy and gave precision to his ideas of the role of pope as head of the ecclesiastical hierarchy in the Christian Roman Empire. There is no question that until the eighth century the bishops of Rome continued to see themselves as loyal subjects of the Roman Empire, whose head was the *basileus* who ruled at Constantinople. However, the bishops of Rome often also insisted on a typically Western Christian perception of the division of powers in the Christian empire that left "secular" affairs to the emperor but "sacred" ones to the ecclesiastical hierarchy, in which the pope was increasingly "first among equals," and not just in a honorific sense. Perhaps the most noted statement of this duality of powers within Christianity was the letter sent by Pope Gelasius to the emperor Anastasius in 494, which boldly proclaimed:

Two there are, August Emperor, by which this world is chiefly ruled, the sacred authority (*auctoritas*) of the priesthood and the royal power (*potestas*). Of these the responsibility of the priests is more weighty insofar as they will answer for the kings of men themselves at the divine judgement.

Although the emperor takes "precedence over all mankind in dignity," in religious matters he is to yield to the authority of priests, especially "to the bishop of that see which the Most High wished to be pre-eminent over all priests, and which the devotion of the whole church has honored ever since."[33]

Few areas of early medieval history have been subject to more scrutiny than the papacy, especially in its relations to both the ongoing continuity of the Roman Empire found in Constantinople and the welter of barbarian successor states of the West.[34] One reason for choosing the issue of orthodoxy as the central religio-political component in this period is that it highlights the papacy's ongoing efforts to become the arbiter of right belief, which in turn does much to explain its complex policy in relation to the East, as well as its role in bringing the barbarians of the West into the orthodox camp.

Any attempt to describe all the debates over orthodoxy after Chalcedon must be avoided here. Until the outbreak of iconoclasm in the eighth century, they are primarily christological in nature (and some would argue that the underlying issue in iconoclasm was also Christology). Viewed from the broad perspective of two and a half centuries, however, a basic dynamic emerges that tells us much about the growing differences between Eastern and Western churches: the West was content with the Chalcedonian decision and resisted any attempt to dilute it; in the East, strong elements in many Christian communities were unhappy with Chalcedon and sought to modify its decisions in one way or another. This complex reaction, called Monophysitism (i.e., "one-nature" Christology) in its early phases and Monotheletism ("one-will" Christology) in its later ones, was a major factor in determining the fate of the Christian form of the Roman Empire.[35]

The debates over Christology are puzzling to most modern Christians, not least because of the intense involvement of the Eastern emperors in the discussion. The schisms, or divisions, between Eastern and Western Christians that helped loosen the framework of the ancient empire were mostly the result of imperial decrees, conciliar or otherwise, concerning the nature of Christ, ones that westerners thought were contrary to Chalcedon. The Eastern emperors, ever the heirs of that Constantine who had summoned the first ecumenical council at Nicaea and engineered its decisions, felt compelled to make such interventions to safeguard the unity of the realm in a situation where theological divisions were inseparable from political ones. In the East, these imperial decrees expressed an attempt to find a middle-of-the-road position that rarely satisfied anyone, while in the West they were viewed as a form of illegitimate imperial interference. It was an important sign of the times that Western Christians continued to support the tradition of Chalcedon even when weak popes temporized over the issue (and created difficulties for modern beliefs in papal infallibility).

Two significant controversies over orthodox Christology, one in the sixth and one in the seventh century, illustrate this dynamic. The dispute over the Three Chapters, which may appear to be a mere theological quibble, perhaps is all the more revealing of the late antique theological world. The Emperor Justinian outdid Constantine in his confidence that he alone possessed the authority to decide all issues relating to Christian belief. Though he generally sided with the Chalcedonians, Justinian decided to placate Monophysite opinion by organizing a council in 553 (today known as the Second Council of Constantinople) to condemn three texts, or chapters, by fifth-century theologians who had been thought to favor Nestorian Christology but were cleared of this charge at Chalcedon. In the West, this condemnation was treated as an attack on Chalcedon, despite the fact that Justinian forced a weak bishop of Rome named Vigilius to agree with the decision. Many episcopal sees in the West refused to accept Rome's surrender to Eastern pressure, and, in the words of Judith Herrin, "the Fifth Oecumenical Council thus marks a significant stage in growing western disaffection from the East."[36]

Rome's weakness over the Three Chapters was made good in the seventh century when the last round in the christological disputes enhanced the Petrine see's position as the pillar of orthodoxy (though only after a pope had been guilty of heresy). The same emperor Heraclius who defeated the Persians attempted to bring uniformity of belief to the East by supporting the patriarch Sergius's formula that there was only one mode of activity (*mia energeia*) in Christ–a position that was acceptable to Monophysites and even to some Chalcedonians. The theologically unskilled pope Honorius agreed, and in 638 Heraclius issued a document known as the *Ecthesis* also affirming a single will in Christ (hence the technical name of Monothelitism). Opposition to this view was spearheaded in the East by Sophronius, the patriarch of Jerusalem, and especially by the monk Maximus (ca. 580–662), the greatest thinker of the era, later known as the Confessor for his resistance unto martyrdom in the Orthodox cause. Honorius's successors in Rome also reversed field and rejected the Monothelite position.

Pope Theodore and Maximus (now in exile from the East) prepared the Lateran Synod of 649, which strongly affirmed that the Chalcedonian position necessarily implied that Christ must have *both* human and divine wills. Heraclius's grandson Constans II continued to push the Monothelite position, even to the extent of kidnapping and banishing Pope Martin I and savagely punishing the aged Maximus, but the Monothelite theology was eventually condemned in the East at the Third Council of Constantinople in 680–81. Once again, Rome had shown itself to be the arbiter of orthodoxy and a period of closer contact between Eastern and Western Christians ensued.[37] This did not, unfortunately, put an end to the gradually building differences between the two halves of the Christian world, as is evidenced by the so-called Quini-Sext Council held in 691–92 in Constantinople, where the eastern church formulated an extensive series of canons, or rules for church life, that were never accepted by the West.

Rome was also the touchstone of correct belief in the West, where the basic problem was the Arianism of the German tribes.[38] There was no conscious missionary policy on the part of the popes of late antiquity—in this Gregory I's initiative in sponsoring the mission of Augustine to convert the Germanic invaders of England was the exception rather than the rule. There were, of course, many efforts by ecclesiastical leaders, and especially monks, to help spread orthodox Christianity to the barbarians. Some of these, such as Patrick's famous mission to the Irish of the fifth century, give witness to a pure evangelical desire to preach the gospel to all humanity before the end of the age.[39] Similar witnesses are found among the later Anglo-Saxon missionaries to Germany (some of whom had close ties with the papacy).[40] But much of the conversion of Europe was not due to what we would think of as conscious missionizing today. For example, the Celtic monks who brought Christianity to Scotland with Columba and who helped spread Christianity on the continent, both among pagans and in areas partly christianized, had the motive of *peregrinatio pro Christo*, or exile for Christ's sake, as their main inspiration,[41] though they were glad to preach, baptize, and educate wherever they wandered.

In the task of converting Arian Germans to Catholic Christianity, the bishops of Rome were rarely forward, but always supportive of what was done on the local level, as the important case of the Visigoths in Spain shows. The same is true with regard to the baptism of pagan Germans, as in the case of Clovis in Francia. Given the nature of the barbarian successor states, the spread of orthodox Christianity was a top-to-bottom movement; that is, most often the ruler's decision meant the conversion of his people. What is significant, however, is that at least in the western domains of what had once been the Roman Empire, it was the faith of the see of Peter, the touchstone of orthodoxy, that served as the rallying point for the dissemination and consolidation of Christianity.[42] Modern historians may debate in largely hypothetical fashion about how "christianized" western society actually was by the year 800, but if we take baptism into the orthodox faith of Rome as the criterion, we can well understand why ninth-century authors thought of themselves as belonging to "Christendom" (i.e., *christianitas* as a religio-territorial entity). They were aware that the western part of the Roman Empire, however much it looked back to the past, was now something else.

The creation of the concept of Christendom in the ninth century was the product of fundamental changes in western Europe in the eighth century, events that are clearly "medieval" in whatever sense may be given to that term.[43] They centered on the alliance between the papacy and the strongest of the barbarian successor states, the Frankish kingdom.[44] Through this marriage of convenience the papacy gained the protection of a fully orthodox ruler, while the Frankish monarchy acquired an eminence among the barbarian states that led to the creation of the medieval western empire—a renewal of empire, not just a continuation. Though the Frankish-Roman Christian empire was to prove short-lived, its heritage remained powerful in Europe for more than a millennium.

The alliance between the papacy and the Frankish kingdom brought about important political realignments, ones that also involved the issue of orthodoxy. A new dynasty had begun in Constantinople with the accession of the Anatolian general Leo III in 717. Leo repulsed a major Arab siege of the capital that lasted until the summer of 718, but had to face continuing Arab incursions during his long reign. The Arab threat may have had something to do with the emperor's attack on icons, the sacred images that had become so central a part of eastern Christian worship over the past two hundred years.[45] The iconoclastic position, however, which was solemnly defined by a council held in 754 under Leo's son Constantine V, was seen as heretical in the West, as well as by many elements in the eastern church. Once again, Rome came to the defense of orthodoxy against heretical and persecuting emperors.

The new emperors were not only heretical; they were also unwilling and unable to help Peter's successors in time of need. Lombard pressure against papal domains in central Italy had increased in the 720s. Pope Gregory II (715–731) appealed to Leo III for help but in vain. Gregory then condemned the emperor for his inability to defend the papacy, as well as for his attacks on images.[46] In 739, his successor, Gregory III, asked Charles Martel, the Frankish war leader whose defeat of the Arabs at Poitiers in 733 marked the turn of the tide against Islamic expansion in the West, to come to the aid of Peter against the Lombards. In 749, Zacharias, the last Greek pope, approved the transfer of kingship from the "do-nothing" Merovingian kings to Charles Martel's son, Pepin, who was acclaimed king by the Frankish nobles in 751. Finally, in 753–54 Pope Stephen II took the unprecedented step of crossing the Alps into Francia to meet with Pepin and to cement the new bond with the Frankish king, which Pepin lived up to by descending into Italy in 755 and 756 to defeat the Lombards and guarantee the independence of the *sancta Dei ecclesia, respublica Romanorum.*[47] Though there was no immediate abandonment of relations with the eastern emperor especially after the iconodule (i.e. image honorers') victory in 787, what happened in the 750s "seals the north/south axis of western Europe emphasizing one unit–Italy, the Frankish territories, and the British Isles– which constitutes the new reserve of Christianity."[48]

The heir to this situation was Charlemagne, Pepin's son, who ruled the Franks from 768 to 814 and was crowned emperor by Pope Leo III on Christmas day, 800 C.E. Charlemagne remains a figure larger than life. The formation of Christendom owes as much to him as to any other single person, but he seized an opportunity that others had made possible. We must also remember that he was an emperor in a different sense from either Constantine or Constantine's Byzantine successors. For one thing, he had been crowned emperor by the pope, and papal coronation was to remain constitutive of the imperial office in the West–an obvious mark of the sense of duality of power in Christendom that characterized the West.[49] Another significant difference that emerges, especially from such events as the great reform synod held by Charles at Frankfort in 794, is the sense of theological independence from the East found in eighth-century western Christendom.[50]

The Spiritual Climate of Christendom

The changes in Christian spirituality between 400 and 800 are especially significant for understanding the development of medieval Latin mysticism. No one disputes that these centuries saw the end of ancient Christianity, tied to the world of the late Roman city, and the birth of early medieval Christianity, more often than not rural and monastic in character. But to describe the contours of the new spiritual map of Christendom is not an easy task, despite the wealth of literature that has been devoted to this topic, especially in the last few decades.[51] Here I can only try to point to the major developments and to note their significance for the history of Western mysticism.

At the risk of possible oversimplification, we can describe the spirituality of the early Middle Ages as characterized by an all-pervasive and concrete sense of sacrality based upon clerical dominance and a monastic ethos. A number of recent investigators who have examined Christian attitudes toward the holy in the period between 400 and 800 have noted a complex and subtle shift in attitudes toward the sacred and in the role that the sacred held in relation to culture as a whole. Much has been made, and rightly so, of the fourth-century rise to power of the holy men, the great ascetics;[52] but the full implications of this changing sense of the location of the sacred became more and more evident during the following centuries. The holy man dead was, if anything, even more powerful than the holy man alive, because he (more rarely, she) was now in full communion with God in heaven and still present on earth in the shrine where his relics were kept. As Peter Brown puts it, "the cult of the saints...designated dead human beings as the recipients of unalloyed reverence, and it linked these dead and invisible figures in no uncertain manner to precise visible places and, in many areas, to precise living representatives [i.e., the bishops]."[53] The real and immediate presence (*praesentia*) by means of which the dead saint manifested the divine power (*potentia*) to cure or to curse necessarily involved a particularity of place and a concreteness of means that tended to merge the spiritual and the material realms.[54] But this particular aspect of the interpenetration of matter and spirit was part of a general shift by which the sacred and the secular, the objective and the subjective (in our terms), the religious and the profane all came together into what André Vauchez has termed an "undifferentiated sacrality."[55]

Let me give one concrete illustration from Gregory of Tours, the sixth-century Gallic writer whose works are rightly seen as a rich source for understanding early medieval spirituality.[56] In the midst of an account of the miracles of St. Martin in book 8 of his *History of the Franks*, Vulfolaic, a Lombard deacon who at one stage had tried to live the life of an Eastern stylite, or column-dweller, in the harsh northern climate tells the following tale:

> Another man was accused of having burnt down his neighbor's house. "I will go to Saint Martin's church," he said, "and swear that I am innocent, and so come home again exonerated of this charge." There was no doubt at all that he had actually burned the house down.

Vulfolaic refused him entry into the church, but looking at the sanctuary the guilty man

> ... raised his hands to heaven and cried: "By almighty God and the miraculous power of his priest Saint Martin, I deny that I was responsible for this fire." As soon as he had sworn his oath, he turned to go, but he appeared to

be on fire himself! He fell to the ground and began to shout that he was being burnt up by the saintly bishop. . . . This was a warning to many folk not to dare to perjure themselves in this place.[57]

The argument is an a fortiori one—if the saint's power can punish even outside his sanctuary, how much more so within.

This mingling of the material and spiritual realms involved not only the fixing of the most potent manifestations of the sacred to concrete places, things, and rituals, but also the expansion of the realm of the sacred through a process that R. A. Markus has described as a "de-secularization," that is, a "tendency to absorb what had previously been 'secular,' indifferent from a religious point of view, into the realm of the 'sacred'; to force the sphere of the 'secular' to contract, turning it either into 'Christian,' or dismissing it as 'pagan' or 'idolatrous.'"[58] The result, in H. I. Marrou's words, was a wholly sacral society, the Christendom of the early Middle Ages, which "appears to us as organized around a single pole, the religious, I would even say, the ecclesiastical reality."[59] This all-pervasive sacrality showed itself on every level of society, from the most general conceptions of the nature of Christendom down to the routines of everyday life where an expansive system of exorcisms and benedictions sought to sanctify every aspect of the world.

This is not the place to try to flesh out the full picture of the early medieval spirituality of undifferentiated sacrality. An abundant literature exists on many aspects, especially on the role of saints and hagiography.[60] Recent work on medieval visions, on the function of miracles, on the ordeal, and on the cult of the dead have been illuminating.[61] Other important aspects, such as relics, certainly need more investigation, despite the literature that has been devoted to them.[62] Pilgrimage has attracted many recent studies, but there is no satisfactory general account.[63] Early medieval mysticism as an element in the Christendom of the Middle Ages developed in dynamic relation to all these aspects of the total spirituality of the period.

It is not easy to say how much of this shift, or better, what elements within it, was the result of Christianity's acculturation among the Germanic and Celtic peoples whose sense of the sacred was different in many ways from that of the inhabitants of the ancient Mediterranean. It is clear, however, that the general movement that shifted the manifestation of the sacred toward the ascetic holy man in the flesh and later in his remains began within ancient Christianity itself well before the conversion of the barbarians. The same appears to be true in the case of the process of de-secularization. Nevertheless, it may well be that both movements were accelerated by the creation of Germanic and Celtic Christianity. There are, however, a number of aspects of early medieval spirituality that give more obvious evidence of the impact of the barbarian element in Christendom.[64] One of the most important of these is the shift in the liturgy to be considered below, but two others of equal significance can be taken up here.

We have already seen that Christology was the central dogmatic issue in the consolidation of orthodox faith between 400 and 700 C.E. The changes in ways of conceiving of the God-man and his relation to the believer were no less vital to the formation of the spirituality of Latin Christendom. It would be foolish to look for some kind of decisive break with the past in early medieval attitudes toward Christ, but it is no less evident that subtle, though important, changes in emphasis, as well as the introduction of new elements, made the christological piety of the early Middle Ages rather different from what Ambrose and Augustine would have known.

The death of Christ on the cross took on a centrality in the piety of the nascent Christendom that would probably have puzzled earlier Christians.[65] The earliest portrayals of Christ's passion date to about 430 C.E. and are the products of late antique Christianity. They show not the suffering savior familiar in late medieval art, but the triumphant God-man victorious over death. The popularity of this type of scene accelerated in the early medieval West, with splendid examples being found in the stylized art of the Celtic and Germanic peoples.[66] The Germanic peoples especially came to view Christ as a divine warrior king.[67]

The development of devotion to Christ's triumph in his passion is also evident in the poetry of the era. In 567 the emperor Justin II had sent a piece of the true cross to the Merovingian queen Radegund. For the reception of this priceless relic, Venantius Fortunatus, who has been described as "the first of medieval poets,"[68] composed four hymns to the tree of salvation that must count among the finest liturgical poetry both for their stately form and theological depth. The most noted is the great "Pange lingua," written in the marching meter of the Roman armies:

> Sing, my tongue, the glorious battle,
> Sing the last, the dread affray;
> O'er the Cross, the Victor's trophy,
> Sound the high triumphal lay,
> How, the pain of death enduring,
> Earth's redeemer won the day.
> . . . .
> Faithful Cross! above all other,
> One and only noble Tree!
> None in foliage, none in blossom,

None in fruit thy peer may be;
Sweetest wood, and sweetest iron!
Sweetest weight is hung on thee.[69]

The Germanic image of Christ as the triumphant young hero victorious over the forces of death through his mighty weapon, the cross, is powerfully set forth in the eighth-century Old English poem "The Dream of the Rood." The cross itself speaks:

Then the Young Warrior, God, the All-Wielder,
Put off his raiment, steadfast and strong;
With lordly mood in the sight of many
He mounted the Cross to redeem mankind.
When the Hero clasped me I trembled in terror,
But I dared not bow me nor bend to earth;
I must needs stand fast. Upraised as the Rood
I held the High King, the Lord of Heaven.[70]

A similar sense of Christ as warrior is found in the Old-Saxon "Heliand," which dates from the ninth century. In this connection, the great liturgical scholar Joseph Jungmann has shown how the struggle against the Arianism of the Germanic tribes had a decisive effect on early medieval liturgy by so stressing the divinity of the Redeemer that there was a practical neglect of his humanity—"the Savior walking this earth becomes simply the epiphany of God."[71] The paraliturgical prayers directed to the cross, which became popular from the ninth century on, also reflect this emphasis on God's triumph through the victory of the cross.[72]

Another aspect of early medieval spirituality that has much to do with Christianity's movement into the barbarian world is its moralism, that is, its concentration on adherence to an external and observable standard of behavior and consequent diminution of interest in interior intention.[73] From the start, as in Paul's letters, Christians had been concerned with strict moral behavior, but the construction of a minutely detailed moral code appropriate to the various "orders," that is, states of life, within Christendom was characteristic of this transition period. It was tied to one of the major innovations of barbarian Christianity, the spread of private penance as evidenced by the *libri penitentiales,* or "books of penance."

Penance in the early church had been a notable subject of contention, especially over the question of whether serious sins committed after baptism might be forgiven. The developing penance ritual had been an expression of the urban character of Christianity—a public ritual for all sinners, administered by the bishop during the penitential season prior to Easter.

The new situation of the declining empire—but even more, it seems, changing spiritual attitudes—led to a precipitous decline of the ancient practice in the fifth century. Its place was taken by the system of private penance that was pioneered within Celtic monasticism, a development of the master-disciple relationship found in early monasticism. The abbot of the monastery functioned as the "soul-friend" (Ir. *anmcharae*) for his monks, assigning penance for faults after confession of sins and giving spiritual advice. By the mid-sixth century, this practice had become more formalized and had given rise to the penitential books, such as those attributed to Finnian, which listed categories of sins and their appropriate penances (more serious depending on one's position in the church).[74] The practice spread to the Anglo-Saxon church in the seventh century, and, through both Irish and English missionaries, to the continent soon thereafter. Nothing was more influential—and more characteristic—of medieval Christianity than private penance. The penitential discipline, even more than preaching, was the main instrument in attempts to spread and enforce Christian moral behavior in the early Middle Ages.[75]

The concrete and undifferentiated sacrality found in medieval Christendom was directed by a clerical elite who increasingly were either monks or persons who at least shared a monastic ascetic attitude. Both the clerical and the monastic character of this spirituality are of significance.

The mention of the clerical elite, that is, the bishops, priests and other clerics whose ordination gave them the functional qualification to lead the Christian church, raises the issue of the so-called popular religion of late antiquity and the early Middle Ages. There is no doubt, of course, that the centuries between 400 and 800 saw a precipitous decline in literacy, as well as a shift to a world in which Latin, virtually the only vehicle of intellectual life, became a learned language, the province largely of the clergy as distinguished from *illiterati* or *idiotae*, that is, laymen without Latin.[76] Nor can we doubt that this clerical elite saw its task as the training of the *rusticitas* of the simple and the overcoming of *superstitio* of every kind.[77] In the West especially, the alliance between the bishop and the tomb, that is, the way in which the clergy fostered and controlled the access to sacred power found in the relics of the saints gave them an added stature not found in Eastern Christianity.[78] But the "two-tiered" model (to use Peter Brown's phrase) by which the religion of this period is understood as the product of an opposition between the respectable monotheism of the educated and the unchanging polytheistic superstition of the vulgar and according to which much of what happened between 400 and 800 consisted of either a yielding of the elite to popular superstition (as in the case of the relic cult) or else an imposition of clerical culture on a folkloric religious substratum of the barbarians has been correctly seen as insufficient to account for the significant changes in Christianity during this formative period.[79] There were certainly important differences between the clerical elite and the increasingly illiterate mass of believers, but were they religious differences?[80] Christendom was a clerical culture, but the clergy were more sharers than imposers of the new spirituality.[81] It is easy to be amused by the rustic comparison of Caesarius of Arles in the sixth century when he tells us that the priests are the cows who run about the field, feeding on the word of God to prepare spiritual milk for the laity, their calves, so that they may nourish them through the two udders of the Old and New Testaments.[82] An ideal perhaps—but cultures live as much on their ideals as on quotidian reality.

The educated clergy functioned as leaders in many ways, but three of the most potent—and most distinctively clerical—were through liturgy, education, and the Bible. Etienne Delaruelle characterized the Carolingian era as "a civilization of the liturgy."[83] This is true but needs explanation, especially in light of the immense changes in public worship between 400 and 800.[84] At the beginning of this period, the liturgy was still basically in the antique Christian mold—the communal worship (though, of course, led by the clergy) of the entire community in their own language. By the end, the liturgy was well on the way to being a sacred spectacle performed by the clergy in a sacral language no longer grasped by the community. Paradoxically, this did not make the liturgy any less important (few, if any, Christian rulers ever took a greater interest in the liturgy than Charlemagne and his successors), but it did have important repercussions on the role that liturgy took within the total complex of early medieval spirituality. Correct liturgical observances, that is, those that conformed (or were thought to conform) with what was practiced in Rome, the model of orthodoxy, became a subject of great concern in the Carolingian empire at the same time that the clerical elite took control of the entire liturgical action in a way that cemented their leadership position. As a result, the Mass was no longer seen as an actual participation in the saving mystery of Christ—past, present, and to come—but as a sacred drama that, like scripture, was to be given an allegorical reading to uncover its dogmatic and moral meaning.[85] Modern liturgists have much lamented this shift, but it may well have been inevitable, given linguistic changes, the decay of ancient urban Christianity, and other factors. This important shift did not mean that liturgy could no longer function as a favored setting for the cultivation of mystical consciousness, as it had so often in the ancient church. It did mean, though, that it was likely to do so mostly for monks and clergy, and to a lesser extent than it had in previous ages.

Societies survive through education, taken in the broad sense of how the cultural heritage is communicated to the next generation through specific social structures and experiences designed to modify and enhance the behavior of the young. In the ancient Mediterranean a highly complex form of literate education had been constructed through centuries of effort.[86] In the late Roman Empire the grammatical and rhetorical urban schools held a virtual monopoly of the educational efforts of the society, as we can see from the picture given us in Augustine's *Confessions.* The prestige of the ancient Roman educational pattern remained high, even during the troubles of the fifth century. Indeed, the Romans of the time seemed to value their traditional education more than ever as a mark of what distinguished them from the barbarians–"There is as much distance between a Roman and a barbarian as between four-footed and two-footed animals, or between dumb and speaking ones."[87]

The new world of Christendom, the world that saw the triumph of the barbarians, the decline of cities, and the consolidation of orthodoxy, meant the end of the ancient schools and the birth of new types of education dominated by the Christian clergy.[88] Augustine's *On Christian Doctrine,* written about 400, was the magna carta for medieval education. In the first three books, the bishop of Hippo laid down the rules for the proper interpretation of scripture, the true source of all real learning for the Christian. His fourth book was designed to instruct the Christian preacher (successor to the Roman orator) how to convey the saving message to his audience. Augustine encouraged the pursuit of grammar and the other liberal arts, but only in service of the higher goal of helping to understand the Bible (*On Christian Doctrine* 2.18–42). Although the bishop wrote primarily for clerics, he did not exclude the educated laity from participating in this biblically-centered education. It is also important to note that he was describing an advanced education that still presupposed the functioning of the Roman "primary" schools.

During the course of the fifth and sixth centuries, the contacts between the Latin West and the philosophic sources of classical culture in the East weakened considerably, at the same time that the fabric of society declined.[89] Further, the "desecularization" of society that we spoke about above made the ancient city schools with their dependence on pagan literature less and less an option for the good Christian. The situation was ripe for the creation of distinctive Christian educational institutions in which, according to Pierre Riché, "the monastic school would provide the model for the establishment of clerical schools."[90]

This process, to be sure, was a slow and complex one that cannot be followed in detail. But a brief look at three figures from sixth-century Italy who made powerful contributions to the new form of education will highlight its importance. In the life of Benedict which forms book 2 of Gregory the Great's *Dialogues,* there is an account of how the young Benedict, born at Nursia about 480, was sent to Rome for the standard ancient education.

> But when he saw many of his fellow students falling headlong into vice, he stepped back from the threshold of the world in which he had just set foot. For he was afraid that if he acquired any of its learning he, too, would later plunge, body and soul, into the dread abyss. In his desire to please God alone, he turned his back on further studies, gave up home and inheritance and re- solved to embrace the religious life. He took this step well aware of his igno- rance, yet wise, uneducated as he was.[91]

This passage is a good illustration of the antagonism between the develop- ing "totally sacred" culture of Christendom and remnants of the older world. While Benedict was not a pioneer in the creation of monastic schools, his famous *Rule* shows no hostility to letters and reading as long as they serve the fundamental aims of the monastic life: humility and obedi- ence, prayer and work.

A key figure in the creation of the monastic schools was Cassiodorus (ca. 485–ca. 580), a prominent senator and official in Theodoric's kingdom.[92] About 535 he attempted to establish a Christian "university" in Rome dedi- cated to the study of scripture, but this failed in the confusion of the Ostro- gothic war. Cassiodorus eventually retired to ancestral lands in Calabria, where he established a monastery at Vivarium that became the prototype for Western monastic education. Cassiodorus was not an original mind, but he recognized that what was needed in his time were means for passing on the necessary skills to understand and transmit the saving knowledge of the Bible and the Christian tradition. His *Introduction to Divine and Human Read- ings (Institutiones divinarum et saecularium litterarum)* was probably intended only for his own monastery, but, like Benedict's *Rule,* accidents of history and the requirements of Christendom gave it great subsequent influence. Book 1 is basically an annotated bibliography of key biblical commentaries, stressing the importance of the office of the monastic scribe in furthering the work of salvation.[93] Agreeing with Augustine that "the study of secular letters should not be scorned" (1.28), book 2 goes on to provide a useful, if pedestrian, guide to the seven liberal arts.

The final figure I wish to note is Boethius (ca. 480–ca. 524), the most original Western philosopher/theologian for some three centuries.[94] As "the last of the Romans" and "the father of scholasticism," this wealthy aristocrat (a layman be it noted) played a large role in medieval theology and culture. From the perspective of new forms of education, he was of central impor- tance for the nascent monastic and later the clerical schools of medieval

Europe through his translations and, where necessary, creation of the text-books that would convey knowledge of the seven liberal arts. In later periods his textbooks in logic were also important, especially in the scholastic era.

The new Christian education that was being born in the sixth century was above all a biblical education that served to enculturate the clerical and monastic elite into their roles as leaders of Christendom. The intent, of course, was not to exclude the laity from the study of the Bible. Caesarius of Arles, one of the less-known but no less important pioneers of the new culture, told his flock: "I beg and exhort you, dearly beloved, if you are educated, read through the sacred scriptures often."[95] But in the barbarized culture of the West lay literacy was to become less and less a reality. The biblical culture of the early Middle Ages built on the heritage of the past; the exegesis of the period 400–800 introduced nothing new in method and little in content, but it was successful in passing on the heritage of the patristic period.[96] Especially important in the period 600–800 was the work of Irish scholars and of the Venerable Bede (673–735), the greatest of early medieval exegetes.[97] As we shall see in the chapters that follow, mysticism, understood as the search for the immediate presence of God in this life, remained bound to the Bible and the use of the Bible as it had in the period I have called "The Foundations of Mysticism." What had changed was the role of the Bible in culture: higher culture, at least, had become totally biblicized in a way not found in the early Christian period.

The key role of monasticism in this process provides the final aspect of this sketch of the shift to medieval spirituality. According to R. A. Markus, the "ascetic take-over signals the end of ancient Christianity";[98] but "take-over" may suggest something imposed or unwelcome, while there is abundant evidence that the new monastic asceticism and its spread throughout the fabric of Christendom were, for the most part, welcome, even avidly pursued.[99]

In *The Foundations of Mysticism* I have discussed how the early monasticism of eastern Christianity served as the precipitate or reagent that allowed the mystical elements of pre-Constantinian Christianity to solidify in the fourth century.[100] Latin monasticism of the late fourth century and early fifth formed the matrix for the origins of the earliest distinctively Western mystical theorists: Ambrose, Augustine, and John Cassian, the three founders, were all "monastics" in one sense or another.[101] These three reflect different views about how far immediate contact with God may be present outside the monastic life (a continuing issue in the tradition), but there can be no question that they saw the religious values manifested in monasticism—communal poverty and asceticism, virginity, devotion to prayer, and biblical study—as essential for the attainment of the highest stages of the Christian life. In the centuries between 400 and 800, monasticism attained an even more intimate bond with mysticism conceived of as the height of Christian perfection.

The reasons are not hard to find. The monks were the main scriptural exegetes in an era when mysticism was still inseparable from reading and praying the Bible. Monasticism also provided if not the only, certainly the most effective, context within which the ideal of *contemplatio* could actually be pursued. With the exception of Gregory the Great, to be considered in the next chapter, the monks and nuns of these centuries made few major contributions to the Western mystical tradition, but merely by fulfilling the obligations of their lives—especially the copying of texts, the cultivation of prayer and the celebration of the liturgy—they did for later western mysticism what the so-called Dark Ages did for Christendom in general—they made it possible.

The foundation for all this was the institutional organization of the monastic life, surely one of the most impressive achievements of the period. Between 400 and 700 C.E. some thirty *regulae*, or "Rules of Life," appeared in Latin Christianity.[102] Their differences and complex interrelations should not be allowed to obscure the underlying unity affirmed by Adalbert de Vogüé, who concluded that "Latin cenobitism presents quite a homogeneous aspect from the end of the fourth century to the seventh. Beyond all particular models, all this tradition flows from a common source, Holy Scripture."[103] Beginning from the three classic early legislators (i.e., the translations of Pachomius's and Basil's rules, and Augustine's writings for monks and nuns), de Vogüé counts eight generations of rules, primarily composed in Italy and Gaul, but also coming from Spain and Ireland. The sixth century, constituting de Vogüé's fourth and fifth generations of rules, marked the decisive era. The *Rule of the Master* was written somewhere near Rome early in the sixth century. This text, which was influential on Benedict, witnessed to some important new developments in the cenobitic life, especially concerning the common prayer of the monks and the greater formalization of entry into the monastery.[104] But it was a product of the fifth generation, the *Rule of Benedict* (*Regula Benedicti*, or RB, as it is customarily abbreviated), which proved decisive for the future of monasticism and indirectly for western mysticism as well.[105]

The RB is the single most important document in the history of western monasticism, and arguably the most significant text from the whole late antique period. During twelve centuries it has been the subject of such intensive study and annotation that it may be said to have attained a position that is almost scriptural in the Catholic tradition. Benedict's intention, however, was not to do anything new or final. Like the many other authors of monastic rules, he saw himself not so much as a creator as someone who was handing on the tradition of the true form of Christianity, rooted in scripture and transmitted by the monastic fathers. His *Rule* is one of those works of genius that hides itself behind self-effacement. In detail, it advances little that is new, but as an ensemble it demonstrates that it was not an accident that after two centuries the RB became the "rule of choice" in the complex evolution of Western monasticism.[106]

Images of warfare (*militia*) and of ascent or journey along the "path of salvation" (*via salutis*, Prol. 48) permeate the RB. The monk is described as "fighting under a rule and an abbot" (*militans sub regula vel abbate*, 1.1), and the concluding chapter 73 is dominated by the language of hastening upward to the heavenly home (*ad celsitudinem perfectionis, recto cursu perveniamus ad patriam caelestem festinas*, 73.2, 4, 8). These two sets of images can be used to suggest the ascetic and what we might call the implicitly mystical dimensions of Benedict's document.[107]

The legislator's main concern, of course, is for the ordering of his community. Much of the RB consists of liturgical legislation (RB 8–20), disciplinary code (RB 23–30, 43–46) and interspersed rules concerning the administration, officers and daily life of the monks. The overall aim is set forth at the end of the Prologue with the clarity and *gravitas* typical of the tradition of Roman legislators:

> Therefore we intend to establish a school for the Lord's service. In drawing up its regulations, we hope to set down nothing harsh, nothing burdensome. The good of all concerned, however, may prompt us to a little strictness in order to amend faults and to safeguard love. Do not be daunted immediately by fear and run away from the road that leads to salvation. It is bound to be narrow at the outset. But as we progress in this way of life and in faith, we shall run on the path of God's commandments, our hearts overflowing with the inexpressible delight of love. Never swerving from his instructions, then, but faithfully observing his teaching in the monastery until death, we shall through patience share in the sufferings of Christ that we may deserve also to share in his kingdom. Amen. (Prol. 45–50)

This text highlights most of the elements that are characteristic of Benedict's asceticism. In contrast to the desert fathers, and also to many of his contemporaries, Benedict has no interest in physical feats of asceticism. Moderation is the leitmotif. His notion of asceticism centers on absolute obedience (RB 5), total poverty (RB 33, 55, 58), evident humility (RB 7) and the *stabilitas* by which the monk commits his hope of salvation to the patient discipline of remaining in one community for life (RB 58).[108] Insofar as there can be said to be anything like explicit theology in the RB it comes mostly in the discussions of obedience and humility.

Benedict's ascetic program, as indeed the whole operation of the monastery, depends to a great extent on the wisdom and discretion of the abbot, whose task he describes at length (see especially RB 2 and 64). The abbot "is believed to hold the place of Christ in the monastery" (2.2). "He must hate faults but love the brothers . . . " so that he should "strive to be loved rather than feared" (64.11, 15). But the abbot too is bound to keep the rule in every particular (64.20). Thus, there is a reciprocity between the abbot and the rule in the sense that the rule is an expression of tradition and the abbot represents Christ, the source of that tradition. The abbot's charge is to interpret and apply the apostolic rule of life to the present moment.[109]

Benedict's asceticism is evident in almost every one of the seventy-three chapters of the RB, but one may well ask in what sense, if any, the *Rule* can be said to be a mystical text, especially when a monastic scholar of the caliber of David Knowles can claim that "the absence of any specifically 'contemplative' element must be noted as a principal negative characteristic of the *Rule*."[110] Benedict never uses the word *contemplatio* or its derivatives, and one certainly looks in vain for any explicit mystical teaching. Yet, if we adopt the wider view of mysticism argued for in these volumes, it may not seem quite as puzzling as some have thought that Benedictine monasticism broadly understood became the institutional matrix of western mysticism down through the twelfth century.

Benedict is intensely concerned with the presence of Christ in the monastery, though in typically early medieval fashion his emphasis is on the divinity of Christ not his humanity.[111] The abbot, as we have seen, holds the place of Christ (RB 2.2) and guests are welcomed with a prostration "because Christ is indeed welcomed in them" (RB 53.7). But the most powerful manifestation of the divine presence for Benedict was to be found in the liturgy:

> We believe that the divine presence is everywhere and that in every place the eyes of the Lord are watching the good and the wicked (Prov. 15:3). But beyond the least doubt we should believe this to be especially true when we celebrate the divine office (RB 19.1–2).

Although the benedictine vision of monasticism sets forth a balanced life of communal prayer, private reading and devotion, and physical labor,[112] liturgy was the essential component: "Nothing is to be preferred to the Work of God" (*nihil operi Dei praeponitur*, RB 43.53).[113] In emphasizing the presence of God in the midst of the worshiping community, Benedict helped transmit a central value of early Christian mysticism to the medieval world.

Benedict provides no theory of prayer. He does, however, leave space for both private prayer and devout reading in the *Rule*. Chapter 48 explicitly mentions that specific periods are to be set aside for *lectio divina,* the meditative reading of the Bible and the Fathers that was to form a vital part of the contemplative practice of later centuries of Benedictines.[114] (Most of the monks in Benedict's monastery appear to have been literate, although this was not a requirement for admission.) Chapter 20 provides an important opening for individual mystical prayer in the monastery. Picking up on Cassian's famous discussion of purity of heart and pure prayer,[115] Benedict says:

> We must know that God regards our purity of heart and tears of compunction, not our many words. Prayer should therefore be short and pure (*brevis debet esse et pura oratio*), unless perhaps it is prolonged under the inspiration of divine grace (RB 20.3–4).

Taking into account the fact that Benedict closes the *Rule* by insisting that it is only "a little rule for beginners," and specifically recommending the brethren to read further in "the Conferences of the Fathers, their Institutes and their Lives" (i.e., Cassian's writings and the Apophthegmata), later followers of Benedict had little difficulty in incorporating Cassian's teaching on mystical prayer, as well as its successors, into the benedictine life.[116]

It would be anachronistic to portray the whole of the monastic permeation of early medieval culture solely through an analysis of Benedict's *Rule.* In a number of ways, as already suggested, Benedict was a-typical of monasticism between 400 and 800. Later Benedictinism absorbed many elements not found in the *Rule* and lost some that were.[117] For instance, while Benedict praised anchorites (RB 1.3–5) as practicing the highest form of monasticism, he had nothing more to say about them. Both Gregory the Great's account of Benedict's early life as a hermit and the deep tides of the monastic heritage, however, were to guarantee that the eremitical life was to remain a powerful force in the Latin West. Again, we have already noted that Benedict was not interested in severe bodily mortification, but other western monks were. Third, Benedict insisted on stability; many monks were wanderers for Christ. Benedict's daily routine was balanced between prayer and work; continuous prayer dominated in other monastic traditions and at times even among his followers. Benedict's house was solely for males, but cloistered women remained of great significance; some legislators, like Caesarius of Arles, wrote rules for them. Benedict's monastery was self-contained and separated from the world; other houses were built within cities (Rome is an important example) and often took on liturgical functions for the whole population. (The distinction between monks and canons is not always easy to maintain at this time.) Finally, Benedict envisioned a house largely of lay monks, though priests were allowed to enter (see RB 60). The subsequent centuries, however, witnessed an ongoing process of clericalization so that by the Carolingian period the choir monks were usually all priests dedicated to the performance of the liturgy while the physical labor was done by serfs belonging to the monastery. Thus, the clerical and the monastic charisms had become almost one by the time of Charlemagne. Most monks were priests, and the dominance of the monastic schools before the Carolingian revival of episcopal schools and the foundation of court schools meant that a large portion of the clerical leadership was drawn from the ranks of the monks.

Many of the major themes found in the fathers of western mysticism remained strong in the monks of the transition period. While *virginitas* is not mentioned in the RB, praise of the virgin as the bride of Christ continued to be proclaimed by monastics and nonmonastics. Caesarius of Arles, for example, often used spousal language to describe not only the union of Christ and the church but also the union of the individual soul and the Divine Lover. This is not unexpected in reference to consecrated virgins,[118] but Caesarius was also willing to extend the privilege to all chaste Christians: "The souls not only of nuns but also of all men and women, if they will guard chastity of the body and virginity of heart in the five senses mentioned above, should not doubt that they are spouses to Christ."[119] The nuptials will only be completed in heaven, according to Caesarius, but they are begun here. At the end of the sixth century, Venantius Fortunatus, courtier, bishop and chaplain to the nuns of Poitiers (who lived according to Caesarius's *Rule*), penned a lengthy and original poem in praise of virginity. Into heaven's court, where humans join with angels "singing mystical words to the Creator," the virgins enter led by Mary. Fortunatus emphasized that Christ is wed only to the virgin who knows no other lover. He was also willing to describe this union with erotic language reminiscent both of the Song of Songs and Roman love poetry:

> Victory won, he hastens triumphantly to embraces,
> Impressing chaste kisses on holy lips.
> He coaxes, revives, pays homage, honors, overshadows
> And places his pure limbs in his bridal chamber.[120]

Although Benedict did not discuss contemplation in his *Rule*, there were many who did in the century and a half between Cassian and Gregory the Great. Julianus Pomerius, a north African who moved to Gaul (where he numbered Caesarius among his pupils), served as an important link between the founders of western mysticism and the first monastic pope.[121] Julianus's popular treatise *The Contemplative Life* is in three books. The first two are addressed to bishops and, by extension, to other clergy. They concern primarily an issue that had been discussed by Augustine and Cassian and was to be central to Gregory,[122] the relation of action to contemplation. These books show us how monastic and contemplative values were coming to inform the picture of the ideal priest, a process that was furthered by Gregory. The third book of *The Contemplative Life* is directed to all Christians and treats the vices and four principal virtues–a *vade mecum* of late antique moralism.

Like Augustine, by whom he was deeply influenced (see his praise of the bishop in 3.31.6), Julianus believed that the real contemplative life could be enjoyed only in heaven but that it could be begun here below. Despite their involvement in the active life, which Julianus understood in terms of restraining the passions and performing the works of mercy (1.12.1–2), bishops could not be excluded from becoming followers of the contemplative life. The most original part of his treatise is his analysis of four components in the contemplative life and his proof of how bishops can share in these.[123] Like Gregory after him, Julianus was at great pains to work out the proper balance of action and contemplation as the ideal for bishops, and even for all Christians (see especially 3.29–30 and 33). Like Augustine before him, he insisted that ordered *caritas* was the crown jewel of the Christian life (3.13–15).

Julianus Pomerius handed on some important elements of the mystical theory of the founders of western mysticism, but that is as much as can be said for him.[124] With the exception of Gregory the Great, however, it is safe to say that there are no writers of this period who played a decisive role in the western mystical tradition. However, mystical prayer of a most impassioned sort breaks out occasionally in unlikely places. The wandering Irish monk Columbanus (ca. 543–615), almost an exact contemporary of Gregory, is an important representative of early medieval monastic spirituality in many ways, but he would usually not be thought of as a mystic, at least by anyone who ever read his harsh *Community Rule (Regula coenobialis)*. Yet his twelfth sermon, "On Compunction," contains an impassioned and beautiful personal prayer that Christ will set him afire with love.[125] This artful and yet moving passage, were it found in a Bernard or a Teresa, would probably be endlessly cited as a classic example of their "mysticism."[126]

The ancient Mediterranean world had created the term *philosophia*, the love of wisdom, to express the highest mode of human life, one dedicated to more than the ordinary tasks of survival and self-aggrandizement. Early

Christians took over the word to describe their own way of life—the love of the Wisdom who was the Incarnate Word, a commitment that was the fusion of the highest form of love and knowledge. The fathers of western mysticism had already begun to use the term *philosophia* to describe the monastic life around 400 C.E., a usage that continued through the twelfth century.[127] Cassiodorus, one of those who played a role in the making of Christendom and the creation of its monastic culture, put it in exemplary fashion: "Philosophy is to be assimilated to God insofar as this is possible for a human being."[128] This remained the goal of the mysticism of the religious culture of Latin Christendom.

Gregory the Great:
The Contemplative in Action

D URING THE DIFFICULT centuries that saw the making of Christendom, one figure stands out not only in the religious history
of the time but also in the history of western mysticism.
Gregory, the first pope of that name, reigned as bishop of Rome from
590 to 604.[1] He was born about 540 into a wealthy aristocratic family
that had long been prominent in the Roman church (his great-great-
grandfather had also been bishop of Rome, Pope Felix III). Gregory
was one of the last western leaders to be educated in the ancient
Roman school system, though he did not know Greek. His attitude
toward secular learning was much like that of Augustine and Cassiodorus: it was useful as long as it served the study of the Bible, but
was not to be indulged in for itself.

Gregory's boyhood saw the horrors of the Ostrogothic war; his
young manhood was a brief time of relative peace before the Lombard invasion that began in 568. In 573 Gregory served in the city
government of Rome, but shortly after he was converted, he abandoned secular life to become a monk, establishing seven monasteries
from his inheritance, including that of St. Andrew in the family palace
on the Caelian hill. In the brief spiritual autobiography included in the
prefatory letter to his famous *Moralia on Job*, Gregory described this
decisive event to his friend, the Spanish bishop Leander:

> I explained how I had put off the grace of conversion for such a long
> time. Even after I was filled with heavenly desire, I preferred to be
> clothed in secular garb. What I ought to seek in relation to the love of
> eternity had already been revealed to me, but long-standing habit so
> bound me that I could not change my outward life. . . . Finally, I fled all
> this with anxiety (*sollicite*) and sought the safe haven of the monastery.

Having left behind what belongs to the world (as I mistakenly thought at the time), I escaped naked from the shipwreck of this life.²

Gregory's comment about his error in thinking that he had been able to leave the world behind tells us something of significance about his spirituality.

In his early years in the monastery Gregory devoted himself to rigorous asceticism, contemplative prayer, and biblical exegesis. Looking back on these days in the preface to the first book of his *Dialogues*, he provides us with another reflection on what was so central to his own experience and his spiritual message, the painful but necessary tension between action and contemplation:

> My unhappy intellectual soul (*animus*) pierced with the wound of its own distraction, remembers how it used to be in the monastery in those days, when all time's fleeting objects (*cuncta labentia*) were beneath it because it rose high above everything temporal. It thought only about heavenly things, so that while still held in the body it had already passed beyond the prison of the flesh in contemplation. . . . But now the beauty of that spiritual repose (*quies*) is over, and the contact with worldly men and their affairs, which is a necessary part of my duties as bishop, has left my soul defiled with earthly activities. . . . Now I am tossed about on the waves of a great sea and my soul, like a ship, is buffeted by the winds of a powerful storm.³

Gregory's time for the full enjoyment of monastic *quies* was actually quite short. In 579 the vigorous new pope, Pelagius II, ordained him deacon and sent him to Constantinople as *apocrisarius*, or papal ambassador to the imperial court, where he remained until about 586. While in Constantinople, Gregory displayed his administrative and diplomatic ability, becoming friendly with the emperor Maurice (582–602) and his family. He also showed his zeal for orthodoxy, engaging the patriarch Eutychius in a dispute over the resurrection of the body. Gregory continued to live as far as possible as a monk. He brought a number of his community with him, and it was at their insistence that he began his greatest work, the massive thirty-five books of his moral commentary on Job (*Moralia on Job*).

After his recall to Rome, Gregory served in important diplomatic initiatives for Pelagius; and, when the pope died of the plague in 590, Gregory, though much unwilling, was the unanimous choice to succeed him. His personal anguish at the beginning of his pontificate is reflected in his favorite image of the storm-tossed sea:

> On all sides I am tossed about by waves of business and submerged by tempests so that I can truly say, "I have come to the depths of the sea and the tempest has overwhelmed me" (Ps. 68:3). When I want to return to my heart

after business is done, I cannot do it because I am shut out by a useless tumult of thoughts. . . . I loved the beauty of the contemplative life just as if it were the sterile Rachel—beautiful and keen of sight, though of fewer children because of her repose, but seeing the light with a keener vision. Because of some decision or other, however, I was married to Leah in the night, she of the active life, fertile but poor-sighted, the one who sees less but is more fruitful.[4]

Gregory's pontificate has been seen as a watershed in papal history. According to Walter Ullmann, for example, "During the pontificate of Gregory I the papacy laid the foundations of its later potent influence in the European West."[5] But we must beware of an anachronistic reading of the activities and significance of the first monastic pope. Gregory's pontificate did make a difference, but not so dramatic a one. Not unlike Boethius, Gregory was a figure facing both ways: backward toward the world of the late antique Christian Roman Empire and forward toward the nascent Christendom. The inscription on his tomb that spoke of him as the *consul Dei*, the "Consul of God," expressed his lifelong attempt to combine the values of *romanitas* and *christianitas* into an effective religious program, just as had his great predecessors, especially Leo I.[6] The massive disturbances of his time convinced Gregory of the imminence of the end of the world, but this very fact, as well as his typically Roman sense of responsibility and his personal fortitude, led him to efforts that would have daunted even the most vigorous (and Gregory suffered from ill-health for the whole of his pontificate).[7] His prodigious activity belies the naïve conviction that mystics and contemplatives usually have little effect on the real world of power and politics.

Not all of Gregory's initiatives were as original as has been claimed or as successful as he would have liked. His attempt to improve the administration of the Roman church by making use of monastic personnel set up a conflict between a monastic party and a traditional clerical one that was won by the latter, at least during the seventh century.[8] Gregory's attitude toward the Roman emperor in Constantinople was not different in substance from that of Leo. He was always respectful of the imperial office, believing that the order of the cosmos ordained that pope and emperor should work together for the good of the people of God, each in his own sphere.[9] Even Gregory's attitude toward the barbarian West has been misunderstood, largely because some have seen his important initiative in sending missionary monks to England as indicative of a carefully orchestrated master plan, a papal turn to the new world in formation. But a consideration of the whole of Gregory's dealings in the West shows he primarily adhered to a traditional view of Roman superiority over the barbarians and the necessity for the establishment of orthodoxy, by coercion if need be.[10] Concretely, this was most often expressed through his actions in defense of the traditional prerogatives of the see of Peter over the church and his efforts in support of what had become increasingly the papal task in Italy, maintenance of the peace and the encouragement of orthodoxy. Both of these were full-time jobs, especially during years when the heretic Lombards were besieging Rome itself. But Gregory's exercise of primacy was always tempered by his acceptance of diversity of practice within the church and by his insistence on the equality of humble service among all bishops.[11]

Gregory was among the most prolific of popes. The over 850 letters from his surviving *Register* give us a good idea of the energy and ability with which he faced a myriad of problems.[12] But it is more in his theological and spiritual writings than in his day-to-day activities that Gregory merits to be seen as the first medieval spiritual author, the one who, in Jean Leclercq's words, "bridges the gap between the patristic age and the monastic culture of the Middle Ages."[13] Almost all of these works were put in their final form in the 590s, mostly during the early years of his pontificate. Gregory, like the other great mystical authors of the early church, was above all an exegete and a preacher.[14] His massive *Moralia on Job*, among the longest patristic works, had been begun in Constantinople and was finished possibly as early as 591.[15] The twenty-two *Homilies on Ezekiel* (dealing with Ezekiel 1:1–4:3 in book 1, and Ezekiel 40, in book 2) contain some of his most profound mystical teachings. They were preached during 592–593, the years that the Lombards besieged the city (Gregory had to buy them off with 500 pounds of gold).[16] The *Forty Gospel Homilies* for the liturgical year were mostly delivered during 591 and 592 and appear to have been finished by 593.[17] Other exegetical works that survive include part of his *Commentary on the Song of Songs* and a *Commentary on 1 Kings*.[18] Gregory's works were addressed to rather different audiences. The *Moralia* were written primarily for his fellow monks, while the *Gospel Homilies* were preached to the whole Christian community. The *Homilies on Ezekiel* seem to take an intermediate position, being preached to a select group that included both monks and laity.[19]

Gregory also composed two treatises that were to be greatly influential in the Middle Ages. The work he called the *Liber regulae pastoralis* (literally, *Book of Pastoral Rule*) was probably begun before his election as pope and finished in 591. As the name suggests, what Gregory was trying to do was to provide the secular clergy, primarily the bishops, but by extension priests too, with a rule of life, equivalent to the monastic *regulae* that we examined in the previous chapter.[20] Gregory's sense of the need for such a work is shown by his efforts to disseminate it in his lifetime. Its importance for the Middle Ages was immense (it was translated into Greek at the order of Emperor Maurice and later into West Saxon by King Alfred and his clergy).

Alcuin of York, one of Charlemagne's advisors, wrote to Eanbald, archbishop of York: "Wherever you go, let the *Pastoral Book* of St. Gregory go with you. Read it and re-read it often. . . . The book is a mirror of the bishop's life and a medicine for all the wounds inflicted by the devil's deception."[21]

The other treatise of Gregory was, if anything, even more influential. Gregory's *Dialogues* recount the lives and miraculous deeds of the holy men, mostly monastic, of sixth-century Italy.[22] Filled with visions, miracles, and other marvelous manifestations of the power of the saints and their relics, the *Dialogues* were eagerly read and used for centuries (they too were translated into Greek). In modern times they have been alternately decried as evidence of the triumph of "popular" religion in late antiquity (Adolf Harnack's *Vulgärkatholizismus*) or mined for their unrivaled evidence concerning the new sacrality of the time. Like the *Pastoral Rule*, the *Dialogues* consist of four books. The first, third, and fourth are collections of stories about a variety of figures. Book 2, however, is a life of "blessed Benedict, the Lord's beloved," and was one of the most influential pieces of medieval hagiography (as well as being our only source for Benedict's life).[23] Gregory himself was not a "Benedictine" in the sense of one who used the RB in his own monastic life, but his admiration for the father of western monks was a major factor in the growing importance of the RB in the centuries to come.[24]

Fundamentals of Gregorian Spirituality

"Gregory is elusive," as Carole Straw admits in her recent book on the pope's spiritual teaching.[25] It is not just a question of the extent of his writings and their at times digressive character. It is more that Gregory is much harder to pin down and to characterize than he appears at first glance. While he does not possess the creativity of an Origen, the penetration of an Augustine, or the speculative profundity of a Dionysius, he ranks with these three in stature and influence in the history of western mysticism. His role in the classic monastic tradition of mysticism that reigned supreme down to the twelfth century was particularly prominent. As Patrick Catry puts it: "Saint Benedict gave the monks of the West a *Rule*. Gregory gave them a mysticism."[26]

Gregory was not an intellectual or a systematic theologian, but, as Jacques Fontaine said, "a spiritual man and pastor . . . , a moralist of conversion."[27] Though he has often been dismissed as a mediocre theologian, many of the attacks on him are more eloquent of theological prejudices than they are open to understanding what he was really trying to say.[28] Twentieth-century study of this greatest of the early medieval popes has vindicated the position of eminence for his spiritual teaching that it enjoyed throughout the Middle Ages.[29] One can agree with Jean Leclercq that Gregory is "more consistently mystical than St. Augustine,"[30] though it is impossible to distinguish his dogmatic from his moral and mystical teaching any more easily than with other patristic authors.

A full sketch of Gregory's theology is not possible here. The pope served as an important channel of transmission for major patristic doctrines to the Middle Ages (and not always by means of crude simplification, as Harnack thought). He was especially important for his moral teaching, which he always rooted in the matrix of scripture and tradition.[31] As his *Moralia on Job* show, the pope's major concern was not with speculation on the metaphysical implications of Christianity, but with the practical application of belief in the great mysteries, especially of Christ and the church, for individual behavior.[32] In this connection, it is noteworthy that Gregory's moral thought was, in many ways, contrary to the early medieval extrinsic moralism discussed in the previous chapter. Over and over, he stresses the necessity of plumbing beneath the surface to uncover the roots of right action.[33] This moral interiority leads us into one of the most essential features of the pope's thought. The work of Paul Aubin and Claude Dagens has shown that the categories of "within" (*interior, intus, intra,* etc.) and "without" (*exterior, foris, extra,* etc.) structure the whole fabric of Gregory's thinking,[34] as we will see throughout this chapter. According to Dagens, the two major influences on Gregory's thought, the writings of Augustine and the monastic tradition stretching back to Cassian, come together in his creation of a "morality and spirituality of interiority."[35]

The aspect of Gregory's spirituality of interiority that will especially concern us here is his teaching on the way in which Christians, while still in this life, can attain a vision of God, the vision that is contemplation. In pursuing this theme, of course, it will be necessary to look at many other aspects of his close-knit thought, though always with the central notion of contemplation in mind. We can begin with Gregory's understanding of the role of scripture.[36]

The pope's position as a major intermediary in the transmission of early western mysticism to the Christendom of the Middle Ages is nowhere better displayed than in his insistence that it is only in and through study of the Bible that contemplation is possible. "For us to search out the depths of the scriptures is to contemplate the good things of eternity," as he put it in one place.[37] In commenting on the mysterious four animals of Ezekiel's vision, Gregory compares their walking about (Ezek 1:9) with the moral interpretation of scripture and their flying upward (ibid.) with contemplative reading:

The animals are lifted up from the earth when the holy ones are suspended in contemplation. The more a saint progresses in understanding scripture, the more scripture progresses in him. . . . This is what happens—you sense that the words of sacred scripture are heavenly if you yourself, enkindled through the grace of contemplation are lifted up to heavenly things. When the reader's intellectual soul is pierced by supernal love, the wonderful and ineffable power of the sacred text is truly acknowledged.[38]

All of Gregory's major mystical texts (with one exception—his account of Benedict's vision) occur within the context of commentary on the biblical text, especially on Job and on Ezekiel, both famous visionaries.[39]

Gregory's poetic imagination is nowhere more artfully portrayed than in the multitude of images he found to convey how scripture affects the life of the believer on every level. Scripture is a door because it affords us entry into *intellegenda invisibilia* ("the invisible truths that must be understood").[40] It is also a dense forest in whose cool glades the believer finds shelter from the world's burning heat.[41] Still on the level of nature, scripture is compared to the sea, because of the multitude of its meanings and its relation to the sacrament of water, baptism.[42] One of Gregory's most noted comparisons occurs in the preface to the *Moralia on Job*, where, again in the watery vein, he says that scripture is "like a river, shallow and deep, in which lambs can walk and elephants swim."[43] But scripture is also a mountain to be climbed, one "thick with meanings and covered with allegories" (see Hab 3:3).[44] One of the most striking of his natural symbols for scripture is that of flint (*silex*), the inert rock of the letter from which the fire of spiritual understanding can be struck.[45] More typical is the comparison of scripture to both food (*cibus*) and drink (*potus*): the former indicating the hard places that must be chewed to be appropriated; the latter what can be easily taken in for nourishment.[46] He also describes scripture as the mirror (*speculum*) in which the internal mind can judge its relationship to God.[47] Gregory's poetic approach to the role of the Bible in the spiritual life is unsurpassed among the Latin fathers.

God's loving-kindness in giving humankind the gift of scripture was not meant only for the delight of the contemplative few. The Bible has the same final purpose for all: salvation. Ever attentive to the inner meaning of exegetical details, Gregory finds the repetition of the phrase "the Spirit of Life [i.e., the Holy Spirit] was in the wheels" (Ezek 1:20–21) a key to the salvific intent of both the testaments: "Sacred scripture has two testaments, both written under the command of God's Spirit, to free us from the soul's death. Surely, this is due to charity's two commands—love of God and of neighbor—through whose words sacred scripture brings us life."[48] For Gregory, "sacred scripture surpasses all knowledge and teaching without any comparison."[49] It is more than just the guide; it is the engine of salvation that powers all progress in the Christian life from its first stirrings flat on the ground of fallen nature to its tentative, brief, always unsatisfactory flights into the air of contemplation. At the beginning of his *Commentary on the Song of Songs* he says that "allegory [i.e., the spiritual sense] makes a kind of machine to lift the soul far separated from God back to him."[50]

Gregory has much to say (more than any Latin Father with the possible exception of Augustine) about the personal relation of the reader to the Bible. Because the church is founded on scripture,[51] each and every member of the Body of Christ has an obligation toward the sacred text. Much of the pope's own writing can be seen as an attempt to nourish the biblical culture of the clergy, but Gregory was also concerned both to convey the message of the scriptures to his congregation through preaching and to foster its reading among the literate laity.[52] Simple believers often reach a deeper understanding of the Bible than the learned, because it is really the measure of our good works that shows how deeply we have gone.[53] The only way to reach "the height of supernal love," as a text in the *Commentary on 1 Kings* tells us, is to eat and drink in order to "be strengthened by the plain as well as the profound meanings of the sacred scripture."[54] According to Patrick Catry, "for Gregory the perfect Christian is the one who knows how to read scripture . . . not as a purely intellectual exercise; his reading commits him to be converted to self, to God and to others."[55]

Understanding scripture, then, is more the product of a divine gift than the result of human effort. The pope is nowhere more personally revealing than when he reflects on his own experience of reading the Bible. Indeed, we may well say that for Gregory the enlightenment he was granted about the inner meaning of God's word was the equivalent of the accounts of mystical visions that would become popular six hundred years and more after his death. (For Gregory, as for the Latin Fathers in general, the qualifier *mysticus* refers almost exclusively to the hidden, deeper sense of scripture.)[56] Gregory admits that God speaks both by means of his revealed word and by private inspiration, but he claims that for the holy fathers such private inspiration was achieved through deeper insight into scripture.[57] He testifies that the same is true in his own case. An especially interesting text is found in the second homily of book 2 on Ezekiel, where he talks about two forms of divine enlightenment of the meaning of scripture that he has received. The first is communal and liturgical:

> I know that often many things in the sacred text that I was not able to understand by myself I have grasped when I stood before my brethren. On the

basis of this understanding I have tried to find out whose merits were the reason for the insight given to me. It is clear that it was given to me for the sake of those in whose presence I receive it. From this, by God's bounty, understanding grows and pride diminishes while I learn for your sake what I teach in your midst, because (I tell the truth!) I often say what I am hearing along with you.

But he immediately goes on to note another form of inspiration given in private on the basis of deep experiences of compunction.

Through the grace of the Lord Almighty it often happens that certain things in scripture are better understood when God's word is read in private (*secretius*). The soul, conscious of its faults when it recognizes what it hears, pierces itself with the dart of pain and transfixes itself with the sword of compunction so that it can do nothing but weep and wash away its stains in floods of tears. In the midst of this, the soul is at times taken up to contemplate sublime things, the desire for which tortures it with a sweet weeping. . . .

He concludes:

The progress of a single person is one thing, quite another is that of the edification of many. With God's help, in a teaching sermon we should set forth those things that instruct the life and actions of the audience.[58]

Gregory was more concerned with the practice than the theory of exegesis. There are, however, a number of texts that are significant statements of his hermeneutical principles. The pope's description of his threefold approach to the Bible from the dedicatory letter to Leander at the beginning of the *Moralia* is well known. "First, we place the foundations of history; then, through typological signification we build up the mind's framework into a citadel of faith; finally, through the grace of moral interpretation we invest the structure with color."[59] Though Gregory often uses such Origenistic triple formulas for the senses of scripture, like all the great spiritual exegetes it is really the two levels of letter/spirit, exterior/interior, history/allegory, water/wine that control his exegesis.[60] The moral and the allegorical-mystical-typical dimensions of the interior meaning often tend to meld, though Gregory, of course, will at times try to distinguish them. Ever attentive to the needs of his audience, it is the "moralities," fanciful and fatiguing as we often find them, that were his main interest. He was frequently at pains to work out the literal sense, because "just as the divine word exercises the prudent through mysteries, it often refreshes the simple with the surface meaning."[61] But, like Origen before him, Gregory admitted that sometimes the literal sense was erroneous or self-contradictory and therefore should be abandoned.[62]

Gregory often reflects on the relation between the literal and the spiritual meaning in the *Moralia,*[63] but his most impressive presentation is found in the sixth homily of the first book of the *Homilies on Ezekiel,* a short treatise on scripture that deserves to rank with the most important exegetical expositions of the patristic period.[64] Commenting on the mysterious wheel of the great vision of Ezekiel 1 (ever a source for Jewish and Christian visionary speculation),[65] Gregory interprets the rolling motion of the single wheel mentioned in Ezekiel 1:15 as the harmonization of literal and spiritual meanings serving every class of Christians (*Hom. in Ez.* 1.6.2).[66] The mention of the "wheel within the wheel" (Ezek 1:16) then signifies how the New Testament is hidden in the letter of the Old Testament by way of allegory (1.6.12; cf. 1.6.15).[67]

The unity of the Bible is realized in Christ. The rolled-up scroll "written within and without" that Ezekiel was commanded to eat (Ezek 2:9) is the "obscure speech of sacred scripture." "The Truth opens this rolled up book when he brings to birth in his disciples the saying, 'Then he opened the meaning to them so that they could understand the Scriptures' (Luke 24:25)."[68] The Christocentric nature of Gregory's exegesis is evident throughout the *Moralia.* The meaning of the book of Job only becomes evident when we recognize that Job is the type of Christ, the whole Christ of head and members, so that everything he says and suffers reveals the mystery of Christ, typologically in his life on earth and morally in the actions of his body, the church.[69] Gregory admitted what we might call a symbolic ambiguity within scripture by means of which different images (e.g., the lion) could take on different meanings according to context (e.g., either Christ or the devil),[70] but this practice enriched rather than contradicted the underlying christological unity of the two testaments.

Gregory's doctrinal use of the Bible reveals him as a champion of orthodoxy but not an innovator in its formulation. He has surprisingly little to say about the Trinity. Although his Christology is rich, as we will see below, he made no theological contribution to the speculative issues of the day, though he supported Rome's perhaps unwise surrender to Constantinople on the matter of the Three Chapters. His doctrine of grace is basically Augustinian, but of the modified Augustinian character best illustrated in the decisions of the Second Synod of Orange of 529.[71] The pope's thoughts on the nature of the church, however, and the progress of the Christian life within it, are important doctrinal underpinnings of his mystical thought.

Gregory's ecclesiology is still in need of a full evaluation. Its theological center is found in the theme of the church as "Christ's body, the organic mystery of all the saved throughout the ages."[72] In his brief *Commentary on*

the Song of Songs, which is primarily of an ecclesiological nature, the pope
sees the church not only as the Bride of Christ[73] but also as the "king's
palace" (Song 1:3b), which possesses the door of faith, stairs of hope, a din-
ing room in which all are fed with charity, and finally the bedroom of mystical encounter.[74] The pope's high estimation of the church is shown by his
willingness (following Augustine) to identify it–at least under certain conditions–with the kingdom of God proclaimed by Jesus in the Gospels.[75] But
again like Augustine, Gregory insisted that the church in this life always
remains a *corpus permixtum*, a mixture of good and evil, predestined and
damned (see, e.g., *Hom. in Evang.* 2.24 and 2.38). His ecclesial reading of
the Song of Songs, for example, highlights the continuing struggle between
good and bad forces within the collective Bride during the course of history.

Gregory's treatment of the church was especially concerned with the *concors diversitas*, the way in which Christ's body harmonized the lives and
actions of its diverse members to realize its end–the heavenly goal.[76] Augustine was the first to speak of three essential orders (*ordines*) within the
church: the order of preachers, the order of the continent (i.e., monastics),
and the order of the worthy married.[77] Gregory made this division his own,
noting that it was to be found in both the Old and New Testament stages of
the church's evolution.[78] The way in which he understood the "concordant
diversity" of the church to operate in practice is of significance for the
ecclesial context of his mysticism. For Gregory, the fundamental point is
that while the three orders are not of equal value (the *praedicatores* and the
continentes lead higher forms of life than the *coniugati*), they are of "one measure" (see Ezek 40:10), because they share the same faith and live by the
same hope of heavenly reward. Their mutual interdependence within the
kingdom of God on earth is more important than their relative standing.
"What are these orders in the spiritual edifice if not bridal chambers in
which the soul may be joined (*sociatur*) with the heavenly Spouse by
thought and meditation?"[79] Although Gregory's natural preference for the
monastic life often made him dwell, at times obsessively, on the dangers of
life in the world and the trials of the married state, and although he believed that the combination of the *vita activa* and *vita contemplativa* to which
the *praedicatores* were called was the highest and most important form of life
in the church (more on this below), his spirituality was not exclusionistic in
its theology of the *ordines* or in its practical emphasis on the way in which
whatever perfection the believer ever attains in this life is always realized
through the humble recognition of continuing imperfection.[80] Reflecting on
the preacher's role at the end of the thirtieth book of the *Moralia*, he gives a
lapidary formulation to the necessity of humility that is applicable to all:

"On humility's solid foot we ought to move ahead with seriousness and constancy, because in this life the more we recognize that our teaching is not available to us from our own resources, the more truly learned we are."[81] The notion of "true learning" mentioned here recalls the praise of the holy but unlearned priest Sanctulus in the *Dialogues*, where Gregory gave a new twist to Augustine's notion of "learned ignorance" (*docta ignorantia*) by asking the reader, "Compare, if you will, his learned ignorance with our own unlearned knowledge; his learning towers up where ours lies prone."[82]

When Gregory actually talks about the spiritual progress of individual souls, his emphasis on continuing conversion, on the necessity for constant struggle, and his use of experientially dialectical language (what Jean Leclercq called the "law of alteration")[83] give his teaching a concrete character that was important for the appeal it enjoyed in the Middle Ages.[84] Above all, he sought to balance the opposing forces found in the fallen world into what we might describe as a spirituality of equilibrium.[85]

Gregory had little interest in constructing itineraries of the soul's progress to God. In the preface to his *Commentary on the Song of Songs* he does make use of the triple pattern inherited from Origen and Ambrose, according to which we begin from fearing God as Master, move through honoring him as Father, toward the goal of loving him as Spouse; but this is applied more to the church than to the individual and does not become an important structural principle of his thought.[86] In the *Moralia on Job* Gregory also speaks of three kinds of conversion:

> There are three modes of the converted: beginning, middle and perfect. In the beginning they find the allurements of sweetness; in the mid-time the struggles with temptation; at the end the perfection of fullness. At first, things pleasant console them; then bitter things train them; finally sweet and sublime things strengthen them.[87]

One might think that this pictures three distinct stages in the Christian life; but, viewed against the whole of Gregory's thought, it is the incessant labor of conversion, of turning from the world and turning toward God, of moving from exteriority to interiority in the manner not unlike what Augustine so artfully portrayed in the *Confessions*, that is the pope's real concern.[88]

Gregory's anthropology, no more or less than the rest of his thought, is both basic and yet, at least theoretically, often so generic as to appear uninteresting. He took over many of the commonplaces of the patristic past (especially from Augustine) concerning the human being as created *ad imaginem Dei* and concerning humanity's role as *microcosmos* in the created universe, but he was not really concerned with anthropological theory in the way that either Augustine or the mystical authors of the twelfth century were. Practical anthropology was Gregory's real interest. Among his most important contributions here was his profound pessimism about the fallen world, a pessimism that, paradoxically, coexists with a conviction that for the elect even this place of trial and suffering has its purpose. How much of Gregory's pessimism was the result of personal factors, including the stressful times through which he lived and his own ill health (which gave him so much sympathy with Job),[89] and how much sprang from the coming together of traditional Roman *gravitas* and an Augustinian sense of the *massa damnata* of humanity is difficult to say.

It would be easy to heap up a mountain of lugubrious passages from Gregory's writings testifying to how terrible things are in this life from day to day. And yet Gregory retains an underlying sense of the triumph of joy and peace, if not in this world, certainly in the one to come. To love and long for this goal in the midst of suffering is what we are called to as followers of Job-Christ. The power of longing desire (*desiderium* was one of Gregory's favorite terms) is what transforms the suffering we undergo, and even the sins we continue to commit, into stages of growth on the way for those who never relinquish the urgent movement forward. Gregory is the theologian of suffering in a unique way, especially in the *Moralia*.[90] But it is a suffering of patient acceptance, not voluntary, induced suffering.

Gregory, even more than many other patristic thinkers, found it hard to bring the divergent tendencies of his thought together, especially because his genius was not so much to think abstract questions through as to present practical issues in his preaching. These unresolved tensions have much to tell us about his thought and its influence, both in its inherent ambiguities and in its experiential power to reflect what so many pious Christians in the medieval period and later found applicable to their own lives. The ambiguities are especially evident in what Gregory had to say about the role of the body and the world in the process of conversion to God.

Early Christian attitudes toward the body and its relation to the soul are complex and often misunderstood, despite the considerable attention they have recently received.[91] The scriptural sense of "flesh" (Greek *sarx;* Latin *caro*) as opposed to "spirit" (*pneuma; spiritus*), which understood flesh as the total fallen human and not as body contrasted to soul, was never forgotten in early Christianity, though it did interact in varying ways with other understandings of the body.[92] As Pierre Daubercies has suggested, Gregory the Great can be seen as the central figure in the creation of a new understanding of *caro* and *carnalis,* a monastic one centering on the opposition between this world and the world to come.[93]

As a good exegete, Gregory was well aware of the scriptural uses of *homo*,[94] and especially of *caro*. "In the sacred text," he noted, "flesh is used one way in relation to nature [Gen 2:3 and John 1:14 are cited] and another way in relation to sin and corruption" [Gen 6:3; Ps 77:39; and Rom 8:9].[95] Gregory's *Moralia* are filled with passages that not only reflect the traditional hierarchy in which soul is superior to body (e.g., *Mor.* 9.49.75–50.76), but which also talk in disparaging fashion of the body as the soul's prison (e.g., *Mor.* 9.57.86), as the weight that drags it down (e.g., *Mor.* 8.30.50, citing Wis 9:15), and as something weak, vile, and base (e.g., *Mor.* 3.7.10 and 18.33, *Mor.* 14.15.17).[96] But Gregory never forgets that the body (i.e., *caro iuxta naturam*) was created as something good, and that the flesh is integral to humanity and its salvation. Speaking of the Incarnation, he says: "What is his garment [referring to Rev 19:16] except the body he assumed from the Virgin? He is not one thing and his garment another. Our garment is also called flesh, but we ourselves are the flesh that clothes us."[97] The miracle of the union of the invisible and the visible, of spirit and earth, by which "the spirit droops when the flesh is weakened and the flesh wastes away when the spirit is afflicted,"[98] was of central importance to Gregory, so that we can agree with Carole Straw that the "body becomes a particular focus of Gregory's spirituality."[99]

Hence, it is not surprising to find Gregory intensely concerned with the relation between the body and the soul in the path to salvation. Because of Adam's fall, this relation is now sadly askew and will remain so until Christ's return and the resurrection of the body, when God's original plan for perfect harmony between *spiritus* and *limus* of the body will be triumphant.[100] In good Augustinian fashion, Gregory sees sin as originating from within, that is, from the *mens carnalis*,[101] the spirit's refusal to submit to God, which in turn grounds the disharmony and struggle between the flesh and its desires and the soul.[102] This disharmony is not the source of sin, though it is the place where sin manifests itself most directly and experientially. As we struggle forward toward the goal of reintegration, which will be completed only at the resurrection, the body and soul are meant to function as partners in what Gregory acknowledges as the supremely difficult work of overcoming sin.[103] The continuing frailty of fallen flesh (*caro iuxta corruptionem*) is both a curse and an opportunity. Sin always remains an evil, but during the course of life the inherited weakness of the flesh, the tendency toward sin, and even our faults themselves when repented become necessary parts of the suffering that purifies the soul and the humility that wears down pride, the ultimate enemy. This is why we find nothing like Evagrian *apatheia* in Gregory's thought. Equilibrium will not be attained in this life, but we must continue always to struggle toward it as a goal. Thus, pain and struggle are the mark of the human condition—*militia est vita hominis super terram*, as Job said ("Human life on earth is warfare" [Job 7.1]).[104]

This helps us to understand much of Gregory's pessimistic tone, especially the negative language he uses about the body and everything that is "carnal" (*carnalis*). The key to Gregory's monastic sense of *carnalis*, as Pierre Daubercies has shown, is to recognize that for the pope the opposition is not between body and soul as such, but between terrestrial life and celestial, between *bona temporalia* (which are not *really* good) and the *bona caelestia*.[105] Gregory was not a Manichaean: the created universe was a good creation of God. But when he speaks of this world, he almost invariably means the fallen world of sin. Though he might theoretically admit that there are limited goods in terrestrial life, practically speaking he has no interest in them. "We often," he says, "freely get involved in the things of this world. Afterward, when we would give ourselves to prayer, the mind is never able to raise itself to heavenly things, because the weight of earthly care (*pondus terrenae sollicitudinis*) sinks it in the depths."[106] In Gregory's vocabulary, *carnalis* is interchangeable with *terrenus* taken in this way. So when the pope denounces *homo carnalis* for desiring passing things (*Mor.* 6.13.16), or when he speaks of the Holy Spirit lifting the mind above *carnalis cogitatio* (*Mor.* 5.31.54), he is not expressing a disdain for the body as such, but rather a profound opposition to human involvement in the world that was collapsing about him.[107] The contrast between the *impetus carnis* and the *impetus spiritus*, which the pope discusses in *Homily* 1.5 on Ezekiel, puts it in a nutshell: "To love earthly things, to prefer temporal things to eternal, to possess external goods beyond necessary use, . . . this is the movement of the flesh."[108]

Gregory's unrelenting opposition between the present world of false values and the true values of the world to come forms the theological basis for one of his most important contributions to the later history of Western spirituality, his teaching on compunction.[109] Compunction (literally, "piercing") was a biblical and Christian term, rooted in the LXX translation of the Bible and developed out of a key New Testament text, Acts 2:37, which spoke of the auditors of Peter's speech at Pentecost as "pierced to the heart" (Greek *katenygesan ten kardian*; Latin *compuncti sunt corde*). Closely associated with *metanoia*—that is, "change of heart" or "conversion"—compunction has a rich history in both eastern and western Christianity.[110] In the Latin west, compunction was especially important in the monastic tradition, being found in Cassian and also in Benedict's *Rule* (see RB 20.3 and 49.4).[111] It was Gregory who gave it the most attention, though, and who made it a central value in Latin spirituality.

Gregory is the "Doctor of Compunction" precisely because of his deeply felt sense of the radical insufficiency of all terrestrial goods in relation to those of the heavenly world.[112] Thus, his notion of compunction is not restricted to sorrow for sin (though this is vital); it involves the whole of the Christian's attitude toward present existence in relation to the underlying desire for the stability and joy of heaven. This is evident in his major discussions of *compunctio*,[113] treatments whose precision of expression shows how important the often-digressive Gregory felt this theme to be. Central to his thought is the distinction between two kinds of *compunctio*:

> There are two main kinds of compunction, because the soul (*anima*) thirsting for God is first pierced with fear and later with love. She first is overcome with weeping because she remembers her sins and fears eternal punishment for them. Then, when fear abates through prolonged sorrow and worry, a kind of security is already born from the confidence of pardon and the intellectual soul (*animus*) is inflamed with a love for heavenly joys. . . . Thus the perfect compunction of fear draws the intellectual soul to the compunction of love.[114]

Thus, for Gregory, *compunctio* is not just sorrow for sin, as it sometimes came to be interpreted in later western sources, but it is a total commitment to the whole Christian life, one that begins with sorrow for sin but that finds its real power in the compunction of love, of which Gregory says, "To hear the Spirit's voice is to rise up into love of the invisible Creator by the power of intimate compunction."[115]

In a famous passage from the *Moralia on Job,* Gregory specifies four motives for compunction in a way that helps us understand this primary distinction between compunction of fear and compunction of love.

> There are four qualities by which the just person's soul is strongly drawn to compunction—when it remembers its own evils considering where it was (*ubi fuit*); when it seeks within itself and fears God's judgments, thinking about where it will be (*ubi erit*); or when it seriously attends to the evils of the present life and bewails where it is (*ubi est*); or when it contemplates the good things of the heavenly home, and, because it has not yet attained them, looks in mourning toward where it is not (*ubi non est*).[116]

The first two spatio-temporal locations relate to the *compunctio timoris,* or "lower tears" (*irriguum inferius*); the two latter, to the *compunctio amoris,* or "upper tears" (*irriguum superius*). As Gregory develops this theme in *Moralia* 12, the compunction of love takes on the character of a contemplative experience, showing that *compunctio* and *contemplatio* are necessarily related in the pope's thought.[117] Another text explicitly draws the two together: "When the mind is lifted up to lofty things through the engine, as it were, of compunction, it contemplates everything about itself as beneath it, with a more certain judgment."[118]

If it is impossible to attain contemplation without compunction, Gregory also insists that the latter, like the former, is not a purely private experience.

We will study the relations of contemplation and action below, but it should be noted that compunction too is meant to nourish our concern for our neighbor, especially in the case of the clergy. Preaching to his fellow bishops on their pastoral duties, Gregory allegorized the bronze basin appointed for the washing of the priests in Exodus 30:18 as the "bath of compunction," advising them, "when we feel inner compunction we must also become zealous for the lives of those entrusted to our care. The bitterness of compunction should not affect us so as to turn us away from the concerns of our neighbor."[119] Gregorian compunction, then, is a rich and unifying spiritual force involving sorrow for sin, religious awe before the divine judge, detachment from the world, intense longing for heaven, contemplative self-awareness, and even the sweet sorrow that accompanies the necessary descent from the heights of the immediate experience of God. To grasp it in its many dimensions is to be firmly grounded in Gregory's spiritual sensibility at its most vital.[120]

Contemplation

The ancient tradition of contemplation, with its roots deep in the soil of Greek religious philosophy and its rich development in Christian antiquity, found a notable exponent in Gregory the Great. The pope wrote no treatise on contemplation; he scarcely needed to, since the theme is present throughout his works.[121] There is no question that his thoughts on contemplation were much influenced by his predecessors, notably Augustine and Cassian; but Gregory's treatment is richer and more complete than that found in those who went before him, though not, of course, presented in a systematic style that would be foreign to his thought. A contemporary theology of mysticism, however, needs to attempt a systematic presentation. I will structure this account around five issues: (1) the role of contemplation in the history of salvation; (2) how contemplation becomes accessible to the believer; (3) the nature of contemplation; (4) the call to contemplation; and finally (5) contemplation and action.

Contemplation in the History of Salvation

"The human person was created to contemplate the Creator so that he might always seek his beauty and dwell in the solemnity of his love."[122] Gregory anchored his teaching on contemplation in the Christian story of creation, fall, and redemption in a more decisive way than those who went before him.[123] For Gregory, Adam was first and foremost a contemplative, and a contemplative who enjoyed continuous interior loving sight of God because he had been given *ingenita standi soliditas,* or "inborn firmness of station" *(Mor.* 8.10.19).[124] The Fall, first and foremost, was the loss of the ability to contemplate owing to Adam's turning to the exteriority of sin. "By sinning he was poured outside himself and was no longer able to see the joys of the celestial homeland that he had previously contemplated,"[125] as Gregory put it in the preface to book 4 of the *Dialogues,* one of his most succinct summaries of salvation history as the history of the stages of contemplation. We are born in the position of children of an imprisoned mother, never having seen the light of day ourselves and only having heard about it from her who remembers it. Bereft of Adam's original *ingenita standi soliditas,* we labor in the toils of *lubrica mutabilitas,* the "slippery changeableness" *(Mor.* 8.10.19) of the sinful world.[126]

Hence, Gregory's answer to the question posed by his successor, Anselm of Canterbury—*Cur Deus homo?*—can be expressed in terms of God's loving desire to restore, if only in part, Adam's contemplative vision to humanity. As he goes on to say toward the conclusion of the preface to *Dialogues* 4:

> And for this reason the very Creator of visible and invisible things, the Only-Begotten of the Father, came to redeem the human race and to send the Holy Spirit to our hearts so that, given life by him, we might believe things of which we had still no knowledge through experience *(experimento)*. . . . Anyone who is still not firm in this belief without doubt ought to put faith in what our predecessors say, believing them already to have experience through the Holy Spirit of things we cannot see.[127]

Christ himself, the God-man, possessed perfect *soliditas standi* (cf., e.g., *Mor.* 3.16.30), but this gift is not restored to his followers through the grace of redemption. What they do gain is what Gregory calls *soliditas caritatis* (see, e.g., *Hom. in Ez.* 2.5.22), the firm bond of love found in the church.[128] Therefore, whatever contemplative experience *(experimentum* is Gregory's usual term, though *experientia* appears in the *Commentary on 1 Kings)* is granted to believers in this life will be less than Adam's—a partial, imperfect, but still precious restoration to what was once enjoyed in paradise. An important passage in book 8 of the *Moralia* is especially revealing here.

Commenting on Job 7:19 ("How long will you not spare me, nor let me alone so that I can swallow my spittle?"), Gregory understands spittle as "the savor of intimate contemplation" *(sapor intimae contemplationis)* which flows down from God, the head, to the mouth. It is identified with "the taste of revelation" *(gustus revelationis).* Spittle calls to mind Christ's mixing of spit and clay to heal the man born blind (John 9:6). Blind since the expulsion

from paradise, humanity's contemplative sight is restored by the anointing
of the Redeemer's spittle, but the sacred spit cannot be fully swallowed into
the stomach or mind (*mens*) as long as we remain in this life.

> This spit flows into the mouth but it is not swallowed so as to reach the stom-
> ach, because the contemplation of divinity touches the understanding (*sensus*)
> but does not fully refresh the mind in that the intellectual soul (*animus*) is not
> able to behold what it still sees with a hasty glance (*raptim*) due to the interfer-
> ence of the dark mist of corruption.[129]

The story of contemplation, then, is told in four chapters, that is, the four
ages of the Pauline view of history—before the Fall in full but not final fashion, after the Fall not at all, and under grace as a partial foretaste of the final
and full contemplation of heaven.

Access to Contemplation

How does the believing Christian, now living in the third stage of history,
gain access to the contemplative vision of God? The answer is obvious:
contemplation is available only through Christ. But it is important to reflect
in more detail about what Gregory has to say about how Christ's saving
power, which restores contemplation, actually reaches us.

There can be no question here of trying to do more than highlight some
aspects of Gregory's Christology that directly impinge on his understanding
of contemplation. Christ, who joins God and humanity, is the necessary
center of Gregory's attempt to connect the inner and the outer, contemplation and action, in the present age of salvation. According to a text in the
Homilies on Ezekiel, "God is our wall within, but our wall without is the
God-man."[130] This cuts to the heart of Gregory's view of the economy of
redemption, for it was only in the unfallen state that the "wall within" suf-
ficed for contemplation. After the Fall, whatever taste of contemplation is restored can only be effected through the "wall without," which first brings us
to faith and then to the possibility of vision.[131] The ability to desire God, lost
in the Fall, is what Christ's victory over the devil brings back to humanity.[132]

Gregory provides effective summaries of many of the usual themes of
patristic Christology, especially those concerning Christ's roll as mediator
(e.g., *Mor.* 16.30.37, 22.17.42, and 24.2.2–3.6.), his position as the point of
convergence of all history (e.g., *Hom. in Ez.* 2.4.14–20), and the way in
which the four central mysteries of his saving work (Incarnation, Passion,
Resurrection, and Ascension) are appropriated by the elect (*Hom. in Ez.*
1.4.1–2).[133] The pope also stresses the necessity for each believer to model

his or her life on the example given by Christ, the ancient *imitatio Christi* motif, which has played such a large role in the history of Christian spirituality.[134] Gregory on occasion makes use of the theme of divinization known to Augustine but more popular among the Greek Fathers—"God suffered as a human being so that the human person might be raised up to divinity."[135] Like Augustine, Gregory contains glimmerings of a teaching on the "carnal love of Christ," that is, the way in which the pedagogy of redemption first attracts us to the human model of the selfless love of the Redeemer before we can pass on to a more spiritual appreciation.[136] All this shows how deeply rooted the pope was in the common teaching of his predecessors.

What is more specially his own comes out in the places where Gregory underlines Christ's role in the restoration of contemplation to humanity. Commenting on the obscure passage in Ezekiel 1:8 ("And the hand of a man was under the wings"), Gregory interprets the "man" as Christ. "Unless, as we said, the Omnipotent Word became human for the sake of humans, human hearts would not have been able to fly up to contemplate the excellence of the Word."[137] Indeed, as a text from the twenty-sixth *Homily on the Gospels* puts it, the measure of our love for Christ (i.e., the whole Christ) is the yardstick for "how high we ascend to behold the divine omnipotence."[138] The Christocentric nature of the restoration of contemplation to humanity is rooted in the role of the Word, the Divine Image, as the only way by which we can catch some glimpse of the invisible Father.[139] Although Gregory did not expand on this theology of the Word as medium of knowledge of the Father in the way later authors did, especially Bonaventure, he provided one patristic warrant for such subsequent developments.

What enables us actually to begin to enjoy contemplation once again as members of the total Christ is the action of the Holy Spirit in our lives. Gregory's emphasis on the role of the Spirit of Christ, the Spirit of Life (*spiritus vitae* of Ezek 1:20), is a crucial part of his teaching. One of the pope's finest sermons, the thirtieth *Homily on the Gospel*, preached for Pentecost, provides an admirable summary.[140] Gregory emphasizes the Spirit's role as the internal teacher: "Unless the Spirit is present in the hearer's heart, the teacher's word is useless."[141] After a consideration of why the Spirit is portrayed in scripture under the images of fire,[142] of tongue, and of dove, he discusses the Spirit as the giver of all charisms throughout the history of salvation (30.7–8), continuing to emphasize the theme of inner teaching: "As soon as he touches the mind, he teaches; for him to have touched is to have taught."[143] Gregory places Pentecost on a par with the Incarnation as equally necessary for salvation, asserting that "If we do not want to remain carnal in death, dearly beloved, let us love this life-giving Spirit."[144] In answer to the rhetorical question how we can love one we do not see, Gregory responds that we do indeed see the Spirit, if not directly because of his divine nature, surely indirectly in the miracles of his servants. So he concludes by reminding his listeners of the inner meaning of the two givings of the Holy Spirit recorded in the Gospel:

> First, [he was given] by the Lord while he dwelt on earth (John20:21-23), and afterward by the Lord reigning in heaven (Acts 2:2-4). On earth he was given that we may love our neighbor, from heaven that we may love God. But why first on earth and only afterward from heaven? . . . Let us love our neighbor, brethren, let us love the one who is near us, so that we can attain the love of him who is above us.[145]

Though many other passages dealing with the necessary activity of the Holy Spirit in teaching and enkindling love are scattered through Gregory's works,[146] the essentials are all available here.

The action of both Christ and the Spirit become lively in the soul through the virtues of faith, hope, and charity, as well as the effects of the seven gifts of the Holy Spirit (wisdom, understanding, counsel, fortitude, knowledge, piety, and the fear of the Lord, as understood according to Isa 11:2). Gregory's teaching on both the theological virtues (as they were later called) and the gifts (*dona septiformis gratiae* [*Mor.* 9.11.13]) were formative for the later western theological tradition.[147] True to his spiritual rendering of the story of Job as revealing the mystery of the suffering *totus Christus*, the pope finds an apt symbol for the role of the virtues and the gifts in the life of the church in the story of Job's three daughters and seven sons (see *Mor.* 1.27.38 and 32.44–33.46). The details of this typically ingenious, if tortuous, reading need not delay us. What is fundamental is how Gregory sees the virtues as the means by which we are led back from our dispersion in the distractions of the exterior world into the interior realm where God can be briefly glimpsed.[148] Both the virtues and the gifts are the *rivuli fluminis*, "the streams of water," by which God pours his life into us.[149] Thus, Franz Lieblang is not incorrect in saying that "the soul's life in the sphere of exercising the theological virtues is the mystical life."[150] The role of the seven gifts is to deepen and perfect the divine action that flows into the soul through the virtues.[151]

The extent of Gregory's writings and their characteristic digressiveness make it easy to miss items of import for his spiritual message. A case in point is his teaching on the role of the Eucharist as a vital element in the believer's appropriation of Christ's redeeming activity. Here the pope's emphasis on the role of suffering in the Christian life meshes with an important transition in early medieval spirituality that began to emphasize the Eucharist as sacrifice more than as an act of thanksgiving.[152] As Adalbert de Vogüé has shown, eucharistic devotion is particularly important in the fourth book of the *Dialogues*, which closes with a carefully constructed account of how the sacrifice of the Mass gives the most direct access to the mystery of salvation both for the living and the dead.[153] According to Gregory, "This Victim saves the soul from eternal destruction in a special way; it renews the death of the only-Begotten in a mystery."[154] Gregory is still far from the eucharistic mysticism of the later Middle Ages, but his stress on the Christian's special access to Christ the Victim in the Mass, and the corresponding obligation to accept the role of suffering victim in a fallen world, adumbrates much that was to come.

The Nature of Contemplation

We can now approach the central issue: What is contemplation for Gregory? Naturally, we should not expect any systematic definition or scholastic division of kinds of contemplation, though the pope was willing to provide brief descriptive definitions, at least of the contemplative life.[155] Those who have tried to categorize Gregory's references to *contemplatio* have found wide variety, including some that do not pertain directly to God.[156] David Hurst, in his translation of the *Forty Gospel Homilies*, renders *contemplatio* as "attentive regard," a felicitous suggestion.[157] Contemplation in the proper sense may be broadly understood as "attentive regard for God alone." Though the primary sensory analogy invoked is that of vision or sight, "regard" also allows for a notion of "respectful listening" that helps us to do justice to the many auditory images that the pope employs for describing our most intimate relation to God.[158]

Contemplative vision, as we have seen, is that for which humanity was created: "The vision of God alone is our mind's true repast."[159] If contemplation is our one goal, it is also an impossible attainment, at least in any perfect sense, given the incomprehensibility of God. Too much stress on Gregory as a "mystic of light" can slight the powerful though unsystematic negative theology that underlies his thought.[160] The pope's sense of the overwhelming divine majesty, not any developed apophatic theory, is what leads him to insist over and over again that God alone *really* contemplates himself, that our limited spirit is incapable of grasping the Unlimited Spirit (*incircumscriptus spiritus*),[161] that his Unlimited Light is too much for us,[162] and that therefore we can say nothing that is worthy of him.[163] While Gregory stays far from any form of metaphysical speculation on the hiddenness of God, the measured gravity of the passages where he explores how the divine reality encompasses and yet transcends the world are among the more moving expressions of divine transcendence in medieval theology.[164]

If contemplation is both a necessary but also an impossible ideal (at least in the sense that it can never be complete), an analogous paradox is to be found in the path of contemplation. Gregory has a good deal to say, though never in terms of a systematically laid out program, about the preparation that the Christian must engage in to get ready for contemplation, while at the same time he insists that contemplation is always a divine gift dependent on God's initiative. As he says in the *Commentary on 1 Kings*, "to enjoy the light within is not the result of our effort but of God's loving kindness."[165] Gregory's emphasis on both sides of the equation—necessary but never sufficient human effort, and totally efficacious and free divine donation—made an important contribution to the later western mystical tradition, though it would be anachronistic to read him in terms of the debates about acquired and infused contemplation that did not arise until the seventeenth century.[166]

The fundamental preparation for contemplation, of course, is the devout living of the Christian life through the power of the Holy Spirit expressed in the virtues of faith, hope, and charity and the increasing activity of the sevenfold gift. As we shall see below, Gregory considered the active life, fruitful in works of love of neighbor, as standing in reciprocal relationship with contemplation, so that active virtue was to help foster more intense contemplation. Nevertheless, there were important specific practices the pope felt were helpful to prepare the believer for the gift of contemplation.[167] These included the reading and study of scripture, as we have seen, as well as the special cultivation of humility,[168] along with other virtues, such as discretion. The recognition of our unworthiness and sinfulness implies a salutary sense of fear that helps purge the soul for the divine encounter: "The ascent of the contemplative is ordered," says the pope, "if it begins from fear."[169] However, what Gregory lays the most stress on, to such an extent that he often speaks of it as the first stage in the path of contemplation itself, is the necessity for withdrawal from exterior distractions into the interior self. As a well-known text from the *Homilies on Ezekiel* puts it:

> The first step is that one call the self back to the self; the second that one inspects what has been recollected; the third that one rise above the self by giving one's attention over to the contemplation of the invisible Maker. But you cannot recollect yourself unless you have learned to lock out the ghosts of the images of earthly and heavenly things from the mind's eyes.[170]

Gregory's stress on the necessity for interiorization is deeply Augustinian, and therefore even indirectly Plotinian;[171] but within the cadre of the oppositions and reciprocity between inner and outer that govern his thought Gregorian "recollection" (*se ad se colligere*) has many distinctive notes.[172] There is no need here to review the many terms and the multitude of texts that the saint employed to make his case.[173] It is clear that he believed that concrete practices, especially those connected with the monastic life, such as solitude (*solitudo*) and intensive prayer (he uses the term *continua meditatio* in the *Commentary on 1 Kings* 1.64) were useful. But for Gregory only one *ascesis* really counted, that by which the person turns away from the distractions of knowing about *things* to the serious, even frightening, task of reflection on the inner self.[174] It is this that leads to the state described as *quies*, *otium*, or *vacatio*, the freedom from exterior things that allows the coals of love for God to be enkindled—". . . surpassing all mutable things, [the heart], in the very tranquillity of its quiet, is in the world but outside it."[175]

The text from *Homily on Ezekiel* 2.5.9 cited above describes three broad stages in the mystical ascent, well known in late antiquity since Plotinus. But Gregory was less concerned with laying out itineraries of mystical progress than with exploring the subtle interior dynamics of the mysterious ways in which God becomes present to human awareness (*experimentum, experientia*). Thus, it comes as no surprise that along with the threefold patterns of ascent,[176] we find others expressed in terms of patterns of four and five. Each of these highlights different aspects of a process that, by definition, is beyond description since it deals with the *ineffabilia summa divina*, the "inexpressible heights of the divine" (*Mor.* 20.32.62).

In the eighth homily of the first book of the *Homilies on Ezekiel* Gregory analyzes the "voice above the firmament" (Ezek 1:25) that sounds above the four creatures of the prophet's vision in terms of four "voices" or "images" (visual and auditory images intermingle in a synaesthetic way typical of patristic teaching on the spiritual senses).[177] The first voice, the *vox carnis*, contains the images of our earthly concerns that disturb us during prayer (*Hom.* 1.8.13). When we flee these earthly images and begin to move within "we discover the intelligent spirit that lives through the Creator's power," the "voice below the firmament" (1.8.14). The "voice from the firmament" is that of the angels, who are "eternal by always contemplating eternity" (1.8.15). But it is only in passing beyond even the angelic realm that we attain to the "voice above the firmament," the voice of God "which is present everywhere, yet can scarcely be found, which we pursue as it stands firm and yet are never able to grasp."[178] That the pope is speaking about what we can call a mystical ascent, or experiential knowledge of the voice above the firmament, is demonstrated by his typical invocation here of the humility and even fear that hearing this voice induces (1.8.18).

In book 18 of the *Moralia* we find a succinct formula that provides the basis for discriminating five stages or, better, activities that lead the soul to the enjoyment of the vision of God. Commenting on the fact that scripture is full of praises that God does not need for himself but that are really to tell us about him for our own sakes, Gregory concludes, "Therefore, he directs that we praise him so that we may know him through hearing, love him through knowing, seek him through loving, gain him through seeking, and thus enjoy the vision of him in this attainment."[179] In linking hearing, knowing, loving, seeking (i.e., desire), and the attainment that is vision, this text provides a good entry into the deeper investigation of the role of love and knowledge in the progress to contemplation.[180]

The relation between love and knowledge in the path to consciousness of the immediate presence of God is one of the essential themes of western Christian mysticism.[181] Gregory the Great played a crucial role in the development of this theme, not because of any speculative contributions (as his twelfth-century successors were to make) but because of his practical teaching on the necessity for both knowing and loving in the growth of contemplation. It was Gregory who coined the famous phrase *amor ipse notitia est*, "Love itself is a form of knowledge,"[182] and although the expression appears only once in his writings, it summarizes the gist of the teaching he developed from Augustine and passed on to the medieval mystics.

As the passage from *Moralia* 18 suggests, we need to know God before we can love him and that knowing comes though the hearing that is faith. Claude Dagens has shown that although Gregory had no interest in what we would call philosophical problems of epistemology, he had a theory of practical knowing that is well expressed in a frequently used term, *interna intelligentia*.[183] "Internal understanding," which might also be called "saving knowledge," involves the whole process of turning away from exterior sensible perception to the interior knowledge that culminates in the vision of God. It includes not only the uncovering of the inner meaning of scripture, to which the pope devoted most of his preaching and writing, but also the portrayal in the *Dialogues* of the lives and miracles of the saints as exterior signs of the interior meaning of the Christian life. Hence, as Dagens puts it, "Gregory conceived of contemplation as nothing else but the archetype, the realized model and at the same time the crown of all human knowing."[184] The incipient knowledge of Christ that faith brings begins the process of interiorization and is a necessary condition for the enkindling of the love and desire that culminate in a higher form of knowing.[185]

Gregory the Great's teaching on love and desire has recently been the subject of helpful study, especially by Patrick Catry.[186] *Amor, desiderium, caritas*: often Gregory uses these terms as equivalents, but on closer investigation some differences emerge. *Caritas,* which includes both love of God and love of neighbor (always mutually reciprocal for Gregory), is the general term for all saving love as contrasted with the love of the world. It embraces both *amor* (loving delight in the presence of the beloved), and *desiderium,* which etymologically implies a longing for the absent lover.[187] Gregory, like his successors, often tends to use the two terms interchangeably, a practice encouraged by the paradoxes involved in loving and desiring the Divine Lover: that is, when we love God as present, we can never exhaust that presence (and therefore we continue to desire him), and when we desire God because we perceive his absence, the very desire itself is a form of presence: "Whoever desires God with the whole mind already has the one he loves."[188] The pope's deep sense of the incommensurability between the majesty of God and the limitations of the created spirit give the "longing/desiring" aspect of love the greater weight in his presentations. Thus, Jean Leclercq aptly spoke of Gregory as the "Doctor of Desire."[189]

Gregory calls on all the resources of his symbolic approach to theology to elucidate the various dimensions of loving desire in the path to contemplation. In order to indicate that love is the primary force behind the whole process, he speaks of it under one of his favorite images, that of the *machina,* or machine: "Anyone eager for the work of contemplation has to first question himself in a careful way about how much he loves. Love's power is the mind's machine, drawing it away from the world while it lifts it on high."[190] Love is spoken of as the hand by which God lifts us up lest we fall,[191] and Gregory also talks of the feet or footsteps of love or of the heart (*gressus amoris, passus amoris*) by which we march to God.[192] The saint often describes desire as hunger and thirst, using psalm texts that had also been dear to Augustine.[193] Desire is also spoken of as "panting" (*anhelare*).[194] But there is no question that the preferred images in Gregory's vocabulary of desire are those of fire and heat, especially a wide variety of verbal forms, such as *accendere, aestuare, ardere, ignescare, inardescere,* and *incalescere.*[195] Let one text suffice here to convey Gregory's addiction to the language of the fire of desire:

> From the love of the Lord a *fire* is found in Sion, a *furnace* in Jerusalem, because here below we *burn* to some extent with the *flames* of his love as we contemplate something about him there [in heaven]. But we will be fully *ablaze* there when we will have full vision of him whom we love.[196]

Possibly under the influence of Cassian's notion of fiery prayer (*ignea oratio*) Gregory also employs the expression "enkindled contemplation" (*succensa contemplatio*) to indicate the higher stages of contact with God.[197]

Deeper even than the language of fire is language itself. For Gregory, desire and love are the language we talk to God in. As a text from book 11 of the *Moralia* says, "We speak when we seek his face through desire; God answers speakers when he appears to us who love him."[198] The language of love in patristic mysticism, at least since the time of Origen, was much interwoven with the Song of Songs, as I have tried to show in *The Foundations of Mysticism.* While Augustine himself was chary of applying the erotic language of the Song to the description of mystical consciousness, other Latin Fathers, especially Ambrose, were not. Gregory knew both the partial Latin translation of Origen's *Commentary* and *Homilies on the Song of Songs,* as well Ambrose's writings. His use of the loving conversation between Christ and the soul described in the text of the Song can be characterized as halfway between that of Ambrose and Augustine in the sense that while he does not use the Song as often as Ambrose, some key texts play a significant role in his thought.

The pope's own fragmentary *Commentary on the Song of Songs* is notable for adhering largely to an ecclesial reading, though personal appropriation occasionally appears.[199] In his major works Gregory makes sparing but still significant use of the mystical interpretation of the Bible's poem of love, especially in his comments on four texts he used to highlight central aspects of his thought on the love encounter between God and the human person.[200]

One of these is Song 2:5, the noted passage on the "wound of love," which Gregory usually cites according to the Old Latin version, "Vulnerata caritate ego sum" rather than the Vulgate ". . . quia amore langueo." The central treatment is to be found in the sixth book of the *Moralia,* where the pope is commenting on Job 5:18, "Because he wounds and heals; he strikes and his hands will cure."[201] Gregory says that God wounds in two ways. First, he strikes the flesh, wounding the elect on the outside in order to bring interior renewal (Deut 32:39 is cited). From this ascetical piercing from without to within (Gregory found this in Ambrose),[202] he passes to a second, interior form of wound:

> Sometimes, even if the exterior blows seem to cease, he inflicts wounds within, striking our mind's insensibility with desire for him. He heals by striking, because the dart of our fear of him calls us back when it pierces us to the understanding of righteousness. Our hearts are healthy in a sick way when we are not wounded by God's love. . . . But they are wounded to be healed when God strikes insensible minds with the barbs of his love and soon renders them sensitive through the fire of charity. And so the bride of the Song of Songs says, "I am wounded by charity."[203]

Jean Doignon has demonstrated how the language of this passage, with its typically Gregorian reversals, shows considerable dependence on Augustine's *Confessions*.[204] But the pope goes on to say that the soul, "which before lay dead [with respect] to salvation, is struck by the darts of charity and wounded within by the feeling of devotion and burns with the desire of contemplation, wondrously given life by this wound. It burns, it pants and it already longs to see him whom it [formerly] fled."[205] Here, the sense of passion cannot help but evoke Origen, whose comments on this verse called forth some of his most personal language.[206]

Three other passages from the Song of Songs are used by Gregory with special reference to the love between God and the soul. Taken in order, these begin with the opening line, "Let him kiss me with the kisses of the mouth," to which he refers six times in his major works. The explicit interpretation of this verse in the *Commentary on the Song of Songs* begins ecclesiologically, being referred to the church's longing for the coming of Christ, though this work goes on to allow for a number of personal applications.[207] It is these that come to the fore in Gregory's other works, where the plea for the kisses of the mouth is seen as the request of her "alone . . . who knows as someone with experience what force of love exists in the bedchamber of the Bridegroom."[208]

Two later sections of the Song were also favored by the pope. Song 3:1–4 sketches a short dramatic narrative of the Bride's pursuit of the Lover as she seeks him upon her bed, arises to search for him through the city, is discovered by the city guards, questions them about the Lover, and eventually finds him and brings him home. Gregory uses this passage five times to show how the dialectic of absence, which increases longing, and presence, which increases love, marks the soul's ascent to the heights of contemplation.[209] The text is especially prominent in what is perhaps the most erotic passage in all of Gregory's oeuvre, the description of Mary Magdalene at the tomb found in *Gospel Homily* 25.[210] After summarizing the account of Mary's desperate seeking for Jesus in the tomb inspired by her burning love, he continues:

> Therefore, first she sought but found not at all. She persevered in her seeking and so it came to pass that she did find. This was done so that her expanding desires might grow and as they grew might take hold of what they sought. This is why it says of the Lover in the *Song of Songs*, "On my little bed night after night I sought him whom my soul loves; I sought him and did not find him."[211]

Finally, Gregory used Song of Songs 5:2 ("I sleep but my heart wakes") three times in order to stress, as Grover Zinn has put it, "the interiorization of consciousness in the development of the contemplative discipline."[212] The most detailed account is found in *Moralia* 5.31.54–55 in the midst of

what is Gregory's longest and arguably most important discussion of contemplation (*Mor.* 5.28.50–37.67). Job 4:13 begins with reference to the "hor-
ror of a vision of the night," which Gregory takes as a reference to the fear
and awe that strike the contemplative when she tastes the divine sweetness
even with "uncertain vision"(*incerta visione*, 5.30.53). The continuation of
the verse, "When sleep (*sopor*) is accustomed to fall upon humans," is interpreted as the withdrawal from all external carnal desires. Gregory notes
that sleep is used in three ways in the Bible: first, as the death of the body;
second, as negligence; and, third, as "the peacefulness of life when all carnal desires have been trodden under foot as in the Bride's voice in the Song
of Songs, 'I sleep but my heart wakes'" (*Mor.* 5.31.54). This is the kind of
sleep that had been enjoyed by Jacob at Bethel when he closed the eyes of
concupiscence (first opened in the Fall; see Gen 3:5–7), put the stone under
his head and slept. Jacob's vision (Gen 28:11–13) of the angels ascending
and descending was made possible because he rested his head on the rock
that is Christ (5.31.55). In such a condition, "Holy men work harder in their
sleep than they do when awake." The "waking sleep" of Song 5:2 is glossed
as the "stillness" of Psalm 46:10, so that Gregory concludes by underlining
the message of interiorization:

> Because internal knowledge (*notitia*) is never beheld unless external entangle-
> ment ceases, the time of the hidden word and the divine whispering is now
> rightly expressed in this text, "In the horror of a vision of the night, when
> sleep is accustomed to fall upon humans." . . . The human intellectual soul is
> lifted high by the engine (*machina*) of its contemplation so that the more it
> gazes on things higher than itself the more it is filled with terror.[213]

The *notitia* that is made possible in the sleep of love brings us back to the
larger theme, that is, the relation of love and knowledge in contemplation.[214] Like almost all Christian mystics, Gregory insisted on the priority of
love in the mystical path, but he claimed that knowing plays a necessary if
subordinate role. In analyzing Jacob as a mystical archetype, he saw the patriarch's wrestling with the angel as the knowing of God "through desire
and understanding," which results in a lameness that signifies loss of all
earthly desire.[215] The mutuality of love and knowledge is expressed in many
formulas that echo the well-known *amor ipse notitia est*, such as *amando comprehendere* (*Mor.* 6.38.58), *caritatis intellegentia* (*Mor.* 29.4.7), and *per amorem
agnoscimus* (*Mor.* 10.8.13).[216] There are texts that stress the cognitional aspect
of contemplation, as when the pope says ". . . let us stretch out, if we can,
the mind's foot to the internal threshold, that is, to the mystical understanding of intimate contemplation."[217] More often, though, Gregory highlights
the limitations of knowledge in the face of the experience of love.[218] The

pope left to his successors the problem of trying to explain, however far explanation can go, what kind of knowledge contemplative love actually brings. What he made perfectly clear for them, however, was that knowledge needed love more than love needed knowledge. Longing desire for God would expand and open *intellectus* to heights undreamed of on the human level.[219]

But what exactly is the experience of contemplation, the vision of God? It was in this area that Gregory made what were probably his most notable contributions to the Western mystical tradition, since he spoke of the experiential aspects of mystical contemplation more often and in more detail than his predecessors. Though his discussions are not autobiographical, we have no reason to doubt that the pope was speaking out of his own experience, especially given the texts cited at the beginning of this chapter, where he mentions how often he had enjoyed contemplation in his days of monastic *vacatio*.

Gregory's vocabulary is dense and undifferentiated: love, desire, seeking, knowledge, vision, contemplation–all imply each other and are often used almost interchangeably.[220] The pope's emphasis on the interiority of the experience led him to frequent qualification of the terms associated with contemplation–*contemplatio, quies, visio, lux*–by the adjectives *intimus* and *internus*.[221] The same imperative fostered his preference for expressions of secrecy: *secretum contemplationis* (*Mor.* 5.6.9 and 6.37.56; *In 1 Reg.* 5.179), *secretum silentii* (*Mor.* 30.16.54). We can also note his striking metaphors of contemplation not only as a sleep, as we have seen above, but as a tomb: "Divine contemplation is a kind of sepulcher of the mind in which the soul is hidden."[222] The hidden reality of contemplation can be suggested through images of height and ascension to mysterious upper reaches. Thus, contemplation is Jacob's ladder (e.g., *Mor.* 5.31.54; cf. 5.34.62), or the mountain that Moses ascended (e.g., *Mor.* 5.36.66; cf. 6.37.58). The expression *culmen contemplationis*, the "high point of contemplation" and its equivalents is frequent.[223] In the midst of this wealth of images and intermingling of terms one needs to be particularly attentive to the details of the saint's exposition to grasp the core of his thought. Hence, I will examine in some detail three representative passages, two from the *Moralia* and one from the *Homilies on Ezekiel*, to try to provide a taste of what only a more detailed literary and theological analysis of many passages could really demonstrate.

The first text is *Moralia* 23.21.40–43 commenting on Job 33:16 ("Then he opened the ears of men and instructed them by discipline"). The first two sections (40–41) discuss the four modes of compunction already considered earlier. The fourth mode, that concerning the piercing we experience when considering *ubi non est*, or the rest of heaven, leads to a series of scripture

quotes closing with Psalm 31:22, "I have said in my fear, I have been cast
forth from the sight of your eyes." Gregory takes the opportunity to reflect
on this casting forth of David, continuing:

> Being raised up in ecstasy,[224] which our interpreters improperly call "fear," he
> sees he is cast forth from the sight of God's eyes. After a vision of internal
> light which shone out in his soul through the grace of contemplation by a ray
> of brightness, he returned to himself. With the knowledge he had received, he
> discerned both the good things of heaven that he lacked and the bad things of
> earth that were at hand. . . . Raised on high, he saw what he lamented he
> could not behold when he fell back to himself (*relapsus*).[225]

Gregory goes on to note the positive side of the relapse experience
(23.21.42). The compunction *ubi non est* that accompanies the relapse is
what enables the soul to begin to strip away the images of this world that
impede it from the ascent. Rejecting "the imagination of a limited
vision . . . , the soul tries to gather itself together so that it may prevail by
love's great power to contemplate that being is one and incorporeal." [226]
The final section of the comment (23.21.43) represents a lengthy meditation
on the oscillation between the "unaccustomed sweetness of internal savor"
(*inusitatem dulcedinem interni saporis*, an Augustinian reference; see *Confessions* 10.40.65) and the "downward journey . . . to our familiar darkness"
(*deorsum ire . . . ad familiares tenebras*). While the language is Augustinian,
Gregory differs from Augustine on what we might call the practical level by
drawing out the value of this oscillation as a "struggle" (*certamen*) and "discipline" (*disciplina*), terms that in the light of his constant teaching emphasize
the necessity for continuing ascetic effort directed toward the endless possession of the divine vision.

The second text, the comment on Job 33:26b ("He will see his face in
jubilation") in *Moralia* 24.6.10–12, emphasizes the joyful and ineffable
nature of mystical consciousness without forgetting the needed cleansing
that prepares for this and the limitations it meets. God draws us on (*afficit*)
and gladdens us (*exhilarat*) by making himself known to us. This gladdening
is nothing other than the *compunctio amoris*, whose ineffability Gregory is
anxious to draw out. "It is called the 'shout of jubilation' (*iubilum*) when an
inexpressible joy is conceived in the mind that can neither be hidden nor
exposed in words: it is exposed by certain kinds of movements although it
is not expressed in any proper ways."[227] The *iubilum* (which in the thirteenth century was to become a technical term for mystical experiences
among the Beguines) is known in the mind or intellect (*mens, intellectus*).
"Through it we know (*sentitur*) what is beyond knowing, and since the consciousness (*conscientia*) of the one knowing is scarcely adequate to contem-

plate it, how could the speaker's tongue suffice to express it?"[228] (Here Gregory shifts from terms that invoke specifically "intellectual" powers [*mens, intellectus*] to broader terms like the verb *sentire,* which can mean either "to feel" or "to know or perceive" in a general way, and the noun *conscientia,* which we might suggest is something like Augustine's notion of *memoria,* that is, the ground of the soul prior to the discrimination of powers of knowing and of loving.)

Gregory goes on to remind the reader that the fire of tribulation is needed to cleanse the mind before, with the "rust of vices" cleaned away, "it is suddenly illuminated by the bright coruscations of unbounded Light" (24.6.11). This experience, one of light, of security, of renovation (*infusione superni roris*), is, however, also an experience of paradox, though here we might say that Gregory stresses the intellectual meaning of mystical paradox rather than its existential effect. "The closer it approaches the Truth the more it knows it is far from it, because had it not beheld it at least in some way it would never have realized that it could not behold it."[229] The final section of the passage returns to Gregory's well-known insistence, following Augustine, on the experience of *relapsus* or *reverberatio,* the "beating back" always encountered in trying to contemplate God's overwhelming majesty. In one of his most penetrating and moving passages, Gregory says,

> In the very act of directing its intention [to the Truth], the intellectual soul's effort is beaten back by the encircling gleam of its immensity. This Truth fills all things; it encircles all things. Therefore, our minds can never be expanded to comprehend the unbounded encircling (*incircumscriptam circumstantiam*), because it is hemmed in by the imperfection of its own bounded existence.[230]

Continuing in this more analytic mode, Gregory identifies this "kind of imitation of vision" with the "face of God" (*Dei facies*), distinguishing between the imperfect forms of the facial vision, such as that experienced by Jacob in his struggle with the angel (Gen 32:30), and the perfect facial vision of heaven alluded to by Paul in 1 Cor 13:12.

The final text on the experience of contemplation comes from *Homily on Ezekiel* 2.1.17–18. Once again, the pope anchors his explanation both in scriptural archetypes and in the language of experience. The opening sentence aptly summarizes much of what we have already seen:

> Often the intellectual soul, suspended in divine contemplation, rejoices that it already perceives through a kind of image something of that eternal freedom "which eye has not seen nor ear heard" (1 Cor 2:9). Nonetheless, it is beaten back by the weight of its mortality, sent down to the depths where it is held bound by the chains of its punishment.[231]

Gregory describes this experience as one of looking at the gates that enter upon true freedom but not yet being able to pass through them. This allows him to call upon Old Testament mystical archetypes, the first that of the Jewish people during the wandering in the desert who were commanded to stand at the entrances to their tents and adore the "column of cloud," the sign of the divine presence (Exod 33:8–10). "We stand where we fix our mind's eyes," as he puts it. But if we, as antitypes of the Jews, can only stand and look toward heaven, Moses was able to enter the tabernacle as the model of "any holy preacher who speaks of divine mysteries because he has in some part already entered the tabernacle of the heavenly dwelling." Contemplation for a visionary like Moses becomes the ultimate "liminal" situation, being ambiguously poised between time and eternity, as the second example Gregory adduces shows even more clearly. The prophet Elijah, when he heard the voice of the Lord behind him went to stand at the mouth of the cave and veiled his face, "because when the voice of supernal understanding comes into the mind from the grace of contemplation the total person is no longer just confined within the cave (the care of the flesh doesn't dominate the soul), but he stands at the mouth because he meditates on escaping from the constraints of mortality."[232]

Elijah's veiling his head while standing at the cave's mouth is not surprisingly read in terms of Gregory's usual insistence on the humility that comes from contemplation, as well as the need to avoid imagining anything bodily in the divine reality which is "everywhere entire and everywhere unencircled." But what this particular text adds to what we have seen only in hints thus far is its emphasis on the fulfillment of all these archetypes of contemplation in the final reality of Christ whose saving works and presence in the church enable us, like Elijah, to "long for the King, to desire the citizens we know, and while standing in this edifice of Holy Church to fix our eyes on the door."[233] Gregory's mysticism, like that of the other fathers, has a pronounced ecclesiological dimension.

These few passages give us at least a broad picture of Gregory's teaching on the experience of contemplation. They make clear what many recent students of the great pope have already emphasized, that is, the way in which alternations, polarities, and mutually interactive oppositions are used to convey the paradoxes of the Christian life, most especially with regard to the consciousness of divine presence.

Gregory's mysticism has often been spoken of as a mysticism of seeing or a mysticism of light,[234] and given the emphasis found on the vision of "uncircumscribed," or "unencircled," Light found in the texts we have examined, there is no need to deny this. But Gregory's is also a mysticism of darkness, if not the darkness of the speculative apophaticism of Dionysius, certainly the experiential obscurity of the *visio nocturna* (Job 4:13; 33:15) in which the sinful creature recoils in dark dread when confronted with the majesty of God.[235]

The light imagery in Gregory is qualified not only by the *visio nocturna* but also by one of the pope's most original images (and one that it is difficult not to think is based on his own experience)—that of the *rima contemplationis*, which we can translate as both "chink" and "flash" of contemplation.[236] In commenting on the Temple vision of Ezekiel 40, Gregory made use of a strange biblical verse that can be translated as "splayed windows in the inner chambers" (Ezek 40:16: *et fenestras obliquas in thalamis*) to advance his teaching about the flashes of Divine Light that appear to the contemplative through the narrow confines of our created *intelligentia*. "In splayed windows," he says, "the part through which the light enters is narrow, but the interior part that receives the light is wide because the minds of those contemplating, although they see only a bit of the True Light in tenuous fashion, are still enlarged (*dilatantur*) in themselves to a great breadth." He goes on to note that ". . . from that little bit the inner reaches of their minds (*sinus mentium*) are opened up in an increase of fervor and love, and they become more spacious within so that they admit Truth's Light inside through narrow openings."[237] The same teaching about the *fenestrae obliquae* or *rimae* discussed at length in *Homily in Ezekiel* 2.5.16–19 appears in two other places in the Gregorian corpus.[238] Aelred Squire has reminded us of how the kind of experience Gregory is speaking of here parallels accounts of mystical light in Islam.[239]

If light and darkness form one of the basic polarities of Gregory's account of mystical consciousness, then, according to Grover Zinn, sound and silence constitute another.[240] The notion of speaking to God and having God answer, especially in the intimate discourse of lovers, has been noted above. We also find in Gregory a verbal equivalent of the "flash of contemplation," that is, passages that speak about "the whispering of contemplation" based on Job 4:14 (see *Mor.* 5.29.51–52). In *Homily on Ezekiel* 2.1.17–18, Gregory talks of hearing the voice of supernal intelligence and of the voice of interior substance that sounded through the mind. Nevertheless, silence played a not insignificant role in Gregory's mysticism. For the pope it is not only a question of canceling the noises of the exterior world (see, e.g., *Mor.* 4.33.66, 5.6.9, 5.31.54, 22.20.37, etc.), but it is also the necessity for an interior silence that is more than just the absence of mundane noise. Commenting on the Apocalypse text, "There was silence in heaven, as it were a half-hour" (Rev 8:1), the pope notes that the half-hour signifies the imperfection of all contemplative silence in this life. Even this imperfect interior silence is hard won. Gregory advises:

> Solitude of mind is rightly given at first to those turning from the world in order to restrain the clamor of earthly desires rising from within and to stifle through the grace of supernal love the cares of the heart, boiling over into the depths.... It is like chasing away some circling flies from the mind's eyes with the hand of seriousness (*gravitas*)–as if they seek a kind of secret within between God and themselves where they can silently speak with him through internal desires when all outside rumble has ceased.[241]

Gregory concludes that "in that silence of the heart, while we keep watch within through contemplation, we are as if asleep to all things that are without."[242] These passages confirm Grover Zinn's observation that "Gregory's silence is the interiorized awareness of Absolute Reality."[243]

Other polarities found in Gregory concentrate on the human reactions to contemplative consciousness. Three of these pertain to contemplation in this life; the fourth is true here and will continue even in heaven. We have already noted the pope's insistence on the sudden onset and brevity of contemplation (*raptim*, as he often says, e.g., *Mor.* 5.33.58). The polarity between attainment, arrival, even "touching" God, if only briefly,[244] and the experience of failure (*relapsus, reverberatio*), is a key element in his teaching. While Augustine too spoke of the soul's *reverberatio* (literally, "being beaten back," e.g., *Confessions* 7.10.16), Gregory insists on the experience even more than did the bishop of Hippo.[245]

The other existential polarities that appear in Gregory's writings have been adumbrated in many of the texts already considered. These are joy/fear and elevation/temptation (both characteristic of our present experience), and satisfaction/hunger, a theme in which Gregory makes his contribution to what his predecessor Gregory of Nyssa called *epektasis*, something that in various guises has been among the most perduring themes in Christian mysticism—Can you ever get enough of God?

Part of the genius of the first monastic pope was his ability both to inspire and to intimidate. Little of the rhetorical and spiritual power of his texts can be conveyed to a modern audience because of the immense cultural differences that separate him and his style of writing from contemporary sensibility. What marks him out as the quintessential Western monastic mystic– even more than twelfth-century writers who spoke more directly to monks than he did–is the fact that his digressive and elusive style can be best appreciated only after prolonged monastic *ruminatio*, that is, meditative rereading within a measured atmosphere of prayer and penance.

Even without this context, however, careful reading finds in Gregory a paradoxical coexistence of immense joy in the glimpses of Divine Light and deep fear that is always associated with these "flashes through the chinks." This terror is not so much an intellectual recognition of the nothingness of creation in the light of the divine vision[246] as it is the frightening recognition of personal sinfulness that for Gregory seems to have been a necessary concomitant to all his contemplative experiences. His sympathy for Job, one expects, may have had less to do with Job's sickness than it did with this just man's alternations of confidence and fear before God. Any full investigation of this theme would have to deal both with the "fear of faith," which *precedes* the experience of contemplative joy, and the more powerful "fear of experience," which is the necessary dark side that *follows* all contemplation in this life.[247] It is the latter that is most characteristically Gregorian: "The more [the human soul] gazes on things higher than itself the more it is filled with terror," as we heard in a text already cited.[248]

Closely allied with the polarity of joy and fear is that of elevation and temptation, which marks another area where Gregory's existential teaching both built on Augustine (especially book 10 of the *Confessions*) and yet also broke new ground. Gregory's sense of the ambivalence of fallen humanity led him to the conviction that those who enjoyed contemplation, because they might easily yield to pride, were more rather than less likely to be tempted, if only to ensure that they maintained the humility needed to be saved. This is a special example of the *reverberatio* theme, as a text from the *Homily in Ezekiel* 2.2.3 reminds us:

> Hence it often happens that the person who is most carried away in contemplation is most bothered by temptation. And frequently in the case of those who make good progress, whose minds are touched by compunction or whom contemplation snatches above themselves, temptation also immediately follows lest they become proud over the heights to which they have been lifted. By compunction or contemplation they are raised up to God, but the weight of their temptation beats them back upon themselves, so that temptation weighs them down lest contemplation puff them up, and likewise contemplation raises them lest temptation sink them.[249]

This mutual interaction between the joy and peace given in the *raptus* of contemplation and the sting of the flesh present in temptation is a special note of Gregory's teaching.

The polarities investigated thus far are characteristic of the experience of God that can be enjoyed in this life. Another polarity, however, that of satisfaction/hunger, is true both here and in the hereafter. In a noted passage the pope had contrasted physical joys, which soon sate us, with spiritual pleasures. "Spiritual delights increase the mind's desire while they satisfy it, because the more their savor is perceived, the more it is recognized that this savor is eagerly loved."[250] Applying this principle to the experience of God in contemplation, Gregory insisted not only that the possession of God in this life always left room for more but also that the enjoyment of God in heaven could never be brought to satiety. Infinite Spirit can never be exhausted by finite spirit—"By means of eternal contemplation it will happen that Almighty God will be more fully loved the more he is seen."[251] This theme of the paradoxical fusing of desire and satiety, often repeated by the pope,[252] is implied in a number of his predecessors, though it was developed most explicitly in Gregory of Nyssa's teaching on *epektasis*, the endless pursuit of the inexhaustible God.[253] Pope Gregory gives it a larger role than other Latin Fathers, though he did so without knowledge of the other Gregory.

This survey of the multiple paradoxes that Gregory used to draw out the various dimensions of contemplation leads us to the question of what kinds of language he favored regarding the moment of contact with God. This is perhaps only another way of asking about the whole meaning of Gregory's mysticism, but I believe the question can be formulated more precisely. The texts we have examined show that the pope preferred to express himself in a general and biblical manner—general in the sense that he made such frequent use of the broad traditional term *contemplatio*, and biblical in the sense that, like his patristic predecessors, he often appealed to scriptural figures (Jacob, Moses, Mary Magdalene, Paul, etc.) and to a variety of key texts from the Old and New Testaments to convey his message.

It is significant that Gregory makes relatively sparing use of the language of union with God. Augustine spoke of union with God only in relation to heaven.[254] Gregory does the same;[255] but he goes beyond Augustine in occasionally using the language of "union by joining," that is, terms like *conjunctio, copula,* and their verbal equivalents, to express the link between God and the soul.[256] This may well be due to the relatively greater weight that the Song of Songs played in his mysticism, but he may also have been influenced by Cassian.[257] In the *Dialogues* at least, we find him employing what was later to become the biblical prooftext for union with God conceived of as a loving union of wills, that is, the Pauline verse, "Who adheres to the Lord is one spirit with him"(1 Cor 6:17).[258]

The consciousness of the presence of God, the central theme of these volumes, was something to which Gregory gave explicit attention. He seems to use the language of presence more often than most of his predecessors, though it would require a statistical survey to demonstrate the truth of this claim. We have already noted the dialectic of presence and absence that the pope often expressed by invoking Song of Songs 3:1-4,[259] but a series of texts from other biblical books found in the *Moralia* appeal to God becoming present to those who seek him with longing desire. One of the most striking of these occurs at the end of one of the *Moralia* passages analyzed above, explaining the Pauline teaching that the full knowledge of God will be attained only in heaven. Gregory says:

> "Then I will know as I am known" (1 Cor 13:12). [This is] because after hard labors, after floods of temptations, the soul is often suspended in ecstasy (*in excessu*) so that it can contemplate the knowledge of the divine presence, a presence that it can feel (*sentire*) but it cannot exhaust. And rightly after so many labors can we say of someone so tempted, "He will see God's face in jubilation."[260]

Other strong uses of presence language occur when the pope speaks of archetypal mystics, such as Moses.[261]

The investigation of the language of presence in Gregory the Great leads us to the question of the pope's mystical experience itself, especially since the words *experimentum* and, more rarely, *experientia* occur in his writings,[262] though not in the three autobiographical references to his own contemplative graces (i.e., *Hom. on Ez.* 2.2.1, *Dial. Praef.*, and Ep. 1.5). In this area Gregory appears to be a transitional figure. Although he took much from his predecessors, and though he did not depart from them in building his teaching on the biblical text, I have argued that his writings display a greater interest in the exploration of contemplative consciousness than was typical among earlier patristic authors.[263] Gregory does not talk about his own mystical visions and experiences in any detail, but he does show a concern for frequent investigation of the nature of contemplation from every angle. In this, he signals the beginning of a shift that would grow strong in the twelfth century. This shift, I believe, is also evident in the interest he took in the contemplative experience of his contemporaries, especially in the account of Benedict's vision found in the second book of the *Dialogues*, perhaps the most famous nonbiblical vision of the early Middle Ages.[264]

The text is too long to be given in full, but a translation of the essential passages will bring out how the vision both illustrates the pope's teaching on *contemplatio* found in his scriptural commentaries and also adds some elements.[265] On the occasion of a visit from the deacon Servandus, when all had retired for the night, Benedict, "standing at the window in prayer to Almighty God, in the dead of night suddenly gazed and saw light poured down from on high that cast away all night's gloom and blazed forth with such splendor that this light illuminating the darkness would have been brighter than the day." What followed was even more wonderful (*mira res*). "The whole world was brought before his eyes, gathered together, as it were, in a single ray of light." As he "fixed his gaze on this brilliant gleam of light, he saw the soul of Germanus, the bishop of Capua, carried up to heaven in a fiery sphere by angels."[266] Benedict then called Servandus, who since he was not as high in contemplation as the saint, was able to see "only a small part of the light." They then sent messengers who discovered that Germanus died just when Benedict saw him taken to heaven.

This remarkable direct account (the historical *narratio*) leads to an *explanatio*, that is, a deeper penetration of the meaning (another form of the *interna intellegentia*).[267] Deacon Peter, who is not a mystic ("I've never had such an experience," he says) asks Gregory how it is possible to see the whole world. I give Gregory's response in full, emphasizing the terms that are characteristic of his other accounts of mystical comtemplation:

> To the soul that sees the Creator every creature is *limited.* To anyone who sees even a *little of the light of the Creator* everything created will become small, because in the *very light of the intimate vision the inner reaches of the mind are opened up*. It is so expanded in God that it stands above the world. The soul of someone who sees in this way is also above itself. *When the soul is rapt above itself in God's light, it is enlarged in its interior,* while it gazes beneath it, in its high state it comprehends how small that is which it could not comprehend when it was in a lowly state. Therefore, the man who, looking at the fiery globe also saw the angels returning to heaven, without doubt was able to do so *only in the light of God.* What wonder is it then if he saw the world gathered together before him, he who was lifted up outside the world *in the light of the mind?* That the world is said to have been gathered together before his eyes is not because heaven and earth was contracted but because *the intellectual soul of the one who saw was enlarged.* He who is *rapt in God* can see everything that is beneath God without difficulty. In that light which shone on his external eyes there was *an interior light in the mind* which showed the intellectual soul or the one seeing (because he had been rapt to higher things) just how limited was everything beneath it.[268]

This remarkable text, like Augustine's famous Ostia vision or Ambrose's accounts of the soul's ascent to God in his treatise *On Isaac*,[269] fuses a rich vein of themes from classical traditions, Stoic and Platonic, with a basically Christian and deeply biblical view of ascent whose language exhibits close affinities with other mystical texts of the pope in almost every phrase.[270] Investigators beginning with Odo Casel have pointed out the sources in Hellenistic mysticism, especially the close connection with the Cicero's *Dream of Scipio* and Macrobius's noted *Commentary* on it. But to admit these should not lead to the conclusion that the vision is somehow more "Hellenic" than Christian. The same delicate process of fusion of languages evident in so many of the early fathers was still at work in Gregory the Great.

The incident needs to be seen, first of all, in its place in the careful structure of Gregory's whole life of Benedict. Here it functions as a culminating point in a portrait of three stages in the abbot's path to sanctity–the retreat to a place of solitude (*ad locum dilectae solitudinis rediit*) at the outset, the living within himself (*habitavit secum*) of the early part of his career (*Dial.* 2.3),[271] and the rapture above himself (*rapitur super se*) of this moment toward the end of his life.[272] It also comes as the middle of three heavenly ascents after death, that of Scholastica, whom Benedict sees as a dove going to heaven (*Dial.* 2.34), and the dream vision given to the two monks of the magnificent shining road that marks Benedict's way to heaven (*Dial.* 2.37).[273] Benedict's superiority as a contemplative is highlighted by the fact that he alone, on the occasion of the death of Germanus, has the heavenly experience while still in this life.[274]

While T. Delforge and P. Courcelle have shown that Gregory must have used Cicero and Macrobius for the notion of a fiery globe ascending to heaven,[275] what is significant is the way in which Gregory has adapted the image to the Christian view of God–the fire is no longer the manifestation of the immanent physical divine fire of Stoic tradition, but is the ministering creature of the divine *lumen incircumscriptum*, which always remained the pope's favored image for God's transcendence.[276] Another typically Gregorian touch is the way the account emphasizes how the exterior light of the vision formed the medium within which the interior light that produced the meaning was born–a good illustration of the interaction between interiority and exteriority in the pope's thought.[277] The notion of the expansion of the soul so often found in Gregory's writings (see especially *Hom. in Ez.* 2.5.17, where the same use of both *sinus* and *mens* is found) here takes on a rather unusual dimension. Gregory nowhere else in his writings dwells at such length on a vision of the world from the divine vantage point, and, as David Bell has pointed out, such visions are rare in medieval accounts.[278] This seems to be an argument for the "authenticity" of the vision, at least in the sense that Gregory was recounting a tradition kept alive at Monte Cassino of something that befell the saint about the year 541. What he does in the *Dialogues* is to retell that story with his own explanation of what it meant.

One further issue about this famous text deserves comment. A number of scholastics, including Thomas Aquinas, considered the question of whether or not Benedict had enjoyed direct vision of the divine essence according to Gregory's account.[279] Abbot Butler also wondered if the language employed by Gregory suggests something more than the pope's usual insistence on the limitations of all vision here below.[280] Robert Gillet thought that while Gregory ordinarily emphasized the imperfection of all vision here below, like Augustine, he allowed for miraculous exceptions and that Benedict joined Moses and Paul on that list.[281] Ambrose Schaut, in a very full investigation, is inclined to doubt this, as is David Bell.[282] This may be the wrong

kind of question to ask Gregory, who is rarely interested in speculative issues. While he does use the language of "seeing the Creator" (*animae videnti
Creatorem*) here, he also emphasizes the limitation of the light that Benedict
saw (*parvum de luce Creatoris*). If Gregory thought it was a direct vision
(which he neither says nor denies), he certainly also wished to emphasize its
continuing limitation.

The Call to Contemplation and the Relation of Action and Contemplation

Two final closely related questions remain to be explored to complete
our investigation of *contemplatio* in Gregory the Great. The first concerns
the call to contemplation: Is it universal, or restricted only to some, perhaps
only to those who lead the life of monastic *vacatio*? And finally, what is the
relation between action and contemplation?

It is not difficult to find a number of texts in Gregory that state that contemplation is open to all Christians. The most noted of these occurs in the
exegesis of the "splayed windows" of Ezekiel 40:16. Gregory says:

> The grace of contemplation is not given to the highest [clergy] and not to the
> least, but frequently the highest, frequently the least, more frequently "those
> set apart" [*remoti*, i.e., the monks], and sometimes even the married receive it.
> Therefore, there is no Christian state from which the grace of contemplation
> can be excluded. Whoever has an interior heart can be illuminated by the
> light of contemplation because inside the door the splayed windows were built
> all around so that no one might glory in this grace as a private possession.[283]

Gregory's insistence on the frequency (*saepe, saepius*) of the reception of
contemplation in this text is noteworthy, and his claim that contemplation
is also accessible to the married, if less often, is implied in other texts.[284]
Almost all students of the pope's spirituality have hailed him for his recognition that the experience of contemplation is not just the prerogative of
those removed from the world (the term *remoti* for monastics also appears
in *Hom. in Ez.* 2.4.6).[285]

There are, nevertheless, some tensions within Gregory's thought on this
issue. For one thing, toward the end of the *Moralia* Gregory states, "The active life belongs to many, the contemplative to few" (*Mor.* 32.3.4). This may
seem difficult to square with the claim that contemplation is frequently
given to clerics, but it may be that all the pope is doing is distinguishing between the experience of contemplation, which is open to all Christians who
are not completely given over to dispersion in exteriority, and the way of
life of monastics, the contemplatives *par excellence*, which of its nature is only

for the few. There is no question, of course, that Gregory considered the contemplative life to be higher than the active life, nor can it be doubted that he considered the monastic life, what he called the *ordo amantium*,[286] a life of contemplation. How, then, did Gregory understand the relation between action and contemplation and in what sense is or is not monasticism "higher" than other forms of life in the church?

The issue of the relation of what the pope called the *vita activa* to the *vita contemplativa* began before Christianity in Greek speculation about how the *bios praktikos*, that is, the life of the citizen in the *polis*, was or was not compatible with the *bios theoretikos*, the philosopher's pursuit of truth.[287] These ancient debates were taken up in Christianity when the followers of Jesus adopted the notion of *theoria/contemplatio* as one important way of expressing the goal of their desire to reach direct contact with the risen Savior. The history of *contemplatio*, as I tried to show in *The Foundations of Mysticism*, does not exhaust the story of Christian mysticism but is undeniably important to it.[288]

In using Greek *theoria* to express Christian belief, however, major shifts had to be made, not least in the understanding of the relation between action (*praktike*) and contemplation (*theoria*). Broadly put, action and contemplation moved away from being understood as alternative life-styles and became related modalities of the Christian life, so that the *vita activa* came to be conceived of as the exercise of love (*agape/caritas*) toward our neighbor, while the *vita contemplativa* described the believer's primary attitude, unrestricted desire for the vision of God. Obviously, all Christians were called on to practice both kinds of life, though they might do so in different ways depending on their status in the church.[289] This is the gist of Augustine's teaching, who set down the three main points that were to govern later Western considerations: (1) both modes of life are good; (2) contemplation is higher taken in itself; (3) nevertheless, contemplation should yield to the demands of active love when necessary.[290] The issue continued to be important in the centuries between Augustine and Gregory, as we have seen in the last chapter in discussing Julianus Pomerius's treatise *The Contemplative Life*.

Gregory's numerous discussions of the relation of the *vita activa* and the *vita contemplativa* show how important this question was to him.[291] He takes his basic premises from Augustine but advances on his master in the care with which he deals with what Nicholas Lobkowicz called the "ambiguities of action," that is, the conditions under which contemplation is required to yield to action and the reasons why this oscillation is necessary. Gregory's sense of the necessity for interaction between opposites in the Christian life enabled him to give particularly subtle accounts of this mutuality. He also worked out in greater detail than the bishop of Hippo what the higher mixed life of action and contemplation actually is—nothing less than the life of the *praedicatores*, the bishops as rulers and preachers. (On this point the pope became the standard authority for later discussions.) Ambiguities still remain, however, not least in the growing tendency, so characteristic of early medieval spirituality, to restrict real perfection to the clerical and monastic states. Though the pope allows for the possibility of contemplation among the laity (*coniugati*), as we have seen, practically speaking his treatment of the issue of perfection, like that of Julianus, is over the relative standing of preachers and monks.

Gregory's longest and most detailed treatment of action and contemplation is found in the *Homily on Ezekiel* 2.2.7–15.[292] A brief survey of this text will help frame our treatment of his teaching. As usual, the pope presents his doctrine through a complicated allegorical explanation, here an obscure passage concerning the measuring of the celestial temple in Ezekiel 40:5: "There was a measuring rod in the man's hand of six cubits and a palm." The measuring rod is scripture, which is in the hand of Jesus Christ, the Mediator; the active life is signified through the six cubits, the contemplative by the palm (2.2.7). Gregory defines the active life in terms of the works of Christian love. "The contemplative life," on the other hand, "is to retain with the whole mind love of God and neighbor, but to rest from external activity, to inhere only in desire for the Maker to such an extent that no action is now allowed save that of the soul burning to see the face of its Creator with all care being left behind."[293] A palm is only a small part of a cubit, because, as Gregory explains, "however much the love with which the soul burns, however great the force by which it stretches toward God in thought, it does not yet see perfectly what it would love, but thus far only begins to see what it does love. As the great preacher says, 'We see now through a glass darkly; then we will see face to face'" (1 Cor 13:12).[294]

Having set up the basic comparison, Gregory turns to the investigation of the traditional biblical types of the two lives: first, Mary and Martha from Luke 10 (2.2.9), a type he uses to prove the superiority of the contemplative life on the grounds that the active life will not be needed in heaven. He then turns to Leah and Rachel from Genesis 29 (2.2.10), a type that allows him to discourse on the respective advantages and limitations of the two lives. Leah is "poor-sighted" with respect to the vision of God but "fertile" in bringing forth the offspring of good works; Rachel is beautiful and clear-sighted but sterile.[295] The normal order is to exercise the active life before passing on to contemplation, but Gregory insists on a reciprocal motion between the two: "By means of the active life we ought to pass to the contemplative, and sometimes, through what we have seen within the mind, the contemplative life should better recall us to the active."[296] The grounds for this lie in the very nature of contemplative experience itself. Contemplation is a wrestling match with God, as the example of Jacob shows—one in which we can never be on top for long. *Reverberatio* will always cast us back "at once" (*protinus*; 2.2.12).

In the second half of this brief treatise on action and contemplation Gregory draws out aspects of the meaning of contemplative rapture that we have already seen. Jacob limps after his encounter with the angel because the foot that represents his love of worldly things has been weakened (2.2.13). Lengthy discussion is given to the impossibility of attaining full vision of God in this life: "Almighty God is not yet beheld in his brilliance, but the soul sees something beneath that light by which, refreshed, it may advance to reach the glory of his vision afterwards."[297] The brevity of the experience is underscored by equating the "palm" of the Ezekiel text with the "half-hour" silence in heaven of Revelation 8:1. Finally, he returns to the theme of the relation between action and contemplation, this time from the perspective of the good of the church. God speaks at once to the individual soul and to the whole church. The one cubit of length and one of breadth that the measuring rod marks out in Ezekiel 40:5 is nothing other than the relation of love of neighbor and love of God that unite the two lives:

> Breadth pertains to charity for the neighbor; height to the understanding of the Maker. The breadth and the height of the building are measured at one cubit because each soul will be as high in knowledge of God as it is broad in love of neighbor. While it enlarges itself in width through love, it lifts itself in height through knowledge, and it is as high above itself as it extends outside itself in love of neighbor.[298]

Having compassion on our neighbor in the active life is the way to be joined to God in the contemplative.[299]

Much of Gregory's concrete advice about the relation of the two lives comes in his comments on the monastic state, mostly contained in the *Commentary on 1 Kings* (but also present in the life of Benedict), and those on the pastoral life given in the *Pastoral Rule*. Monasticism was central to the pope's experience, but we must not forget that he had been called to a different form of life, and however much he lamented what he had lost, he never turned back.[300] Gregory was no Cassian, and Robert Gillet is doubtless correct to claim that the pope found the abbot too exclusively monastic in orientation.[301] But his investigation of monasticism in the *Commentary on 1 Kings* shows how highly he valued the life of the *remoti*. As Adalbert de Vogüé has shown, the pope's striking exegesis of the opening of 1 Kings provides a key to his theology of monasticism. Elcana, Samuel's father, is described as a *vir unus*, "a man who is one," which Gregory interprets thus:

"He is called a man because he is strong in his resolve; he is one because he is singular in his love. He is a man because he despises present things with great strength, but he is one because his one desire is to enjoy only the vision of God almighty."[302] As the pope expands this interpretation of the ascetic and contemplative dimensions of the monastic life, it becomes clear that he places greatest emphasis on the monk as *unus*, understood more as the one who has been unified by single-minded attention to the love of God rather than by "aloneness," or solitude. The same message is evident in the picture of St. Benedict given in *Dialogues* 2, especially in the portrayal of the saint as one who passed from ascetic renunciation to the state where "he dwelt alone within himself under the eyes of the One who looks down from on high"—a succinct Gregorian definition of the contemplative life.[303]

Given Gregory's view of the higher value of the contemplative life, and his identification of the ideal monk as the contemplative in the fullest sense, it would have been easy for him to have viewed every other form of life as second-rate, save for some miracle of grace that might raise either the preacher (and perhaps even the layperson!) to an equal state. Such is not the case. Although Gregory could at times paint the monks as models for pastors,[304] it was only with regard to one aspect of their wider obligation—namely, the imperative never to abandon dedication to the contemplative side of their calling.

Over and over again, the pope teaches that the life to which the *pastores, praedicatores,* or *rectores ecclesiae* are called is the higher life in that it is meant to combine both action and contemplation. Since he finds this imperative rooted in Christ himself, it would put the whole of Gregory's theology at risk to question it. As a text from *Moralia* 28 says, "The contemplative life is far from the active, but when our incarnate Redeemer came, showing both lives, he united them in himself. When he worked miracles in the city, he spent the night in continuous prayer on the mountain."[305] Christ's example, according to Gregory, was anticipated by his greatest predecessors, such as Moses,[306] Isaiah and Jeremiah among the prophets,[307] and followed by Paul among the gospel preachers.[308] It is also the model to which all preachers in the Church should aspire. Numerous texts throughout Gregory's writings repeat his message that it is the mixed life realized in the preachers who are called both to contemplative devotion to God alone and active love of neighbor, especially in preaching and pastoral counsel, who are given the highest rank. One of the more picturesque of these passages is another allegorical reading of an image found in Job, this time of the locusts of Job 39:20, whose hoppings are seen as a figure of the alternation between solid practice of charity and bold, if brief, flight into the upper reaches of contemplation.[309]

More theologically detailed is a passage in the *Commentary in 1 Kings* which summarizes the interdependent advantages and disadvantages of action and contemplation in commenting on Merob and Michol, Saul's daughters and images of the contemplative and active lives:

> Both are called Saul's daughters, but they are allotted different names because they both agree and disagree. They agree, because they both lovingly aim at eternal life which they cherish. They also agree, because the good works by which Merob is endlessly exercised Michol performs in every possible way. Since they both love the eternal things they behold, both desire to attain them through good action no matter what. They differ, however, because one sees more, the other does more.... They differ in seeing and in acting, because the active life possesses vision in passing, but has its work by means of its [present] intention; the contemplative life possesses its work in a transitory way (*in itinere*), while its intention rests in inner peace (*quies*).[310]

It is easy to see why it is possible to think of Gregory the Great not only as the "Doctor of Desire," but also as the "Doctor of the Mixed Life."[311] Still, the pope's personal nostalgia for the monastic life and his praise for monastic heroes in the *Dialogues* has led some to see two models of perfection in his teaching: the ascetic and contemplative model of the monk and that of the contemplative preacher.[312] I do not think this is the case. The digressive style of the great papal preacher masks an inner coherence—at least on this question—that can be understood as returning to the opening issue that framed our discussion of his teaching on contemplation: its meaning in the process of salvation history. From this perspective, we can say that the monastic life is the figure of what humanity in Adam was originally created to enjoy: oneness of contemplative attention to God. But if the monk is the living *imago* of humanity's original condition, even monks no longer live in paradise. Though monks exist to remind us of what once was, and better yet, what is to come in heaven, in the present world, whose fallenness Gregory the Great felt so keenly, it is the preacher, living out his perilous vocation to keep both his eye on the goal and his heart with suffering humanity, who is the truest mystic—the contemplative in action, like the great pope himself.[313]

The Entry of Dialectical Mysticism: John Scottus Eriugena[1]

WRITING TO THE EMPEROR Charles the Bald (Charlemagne's grandson) in 875, the papal librarian Anastasius expressed both astonishment and criticism concerning the translation of the works of Dionysius completed over a decade before by the Irish scholar John Scottus Eriugena:

> It is also cause for wonder by what means that uncultivated foreigner (*vir ille barbarus*), placed on the borders of the world, ... could grasp such matters with his intellect and translate them into another tongue: I mean John the Irishman, a man who I know by hearsay is in all things holy. But herein was the working of that creative Spirit who made this man as fervent as he was eloquent. ... For love was the master who taught this man what he accomplished for the instruction and edification of many.[2]

This Greek scholar went on to criticize aspects of Eriugena's translation, but his admiration for the learning and inspiration of this *vir ille barbarus* is unmistakable.

John the Scot (to use another of the modern renditions of his name) today is recognized as the greatest speculative mind of the early Middle Ages, the most original and subtle thinker in the West between Augustine and Anselm.[3] But why call John a mystic? Although Evelyn Underhill, in her noted book *Mysticism*, said that his name was the only one in the early Middle Ages that the history of mysticism can claim, she actually made little use of Eriugena.[4] Indeed, the distinction that Underhill and other writers make between true "experiential" mystics and those who merely reflect on mystical experience would seem to imply that the Irishman should be included in the latter category, given his lack of autobiographical witness to special experiences of God. But, as I have argued in *The Foundations of Mysticism*, this distinction may be a misleading one. The determination of whether or not a particular author enjoyed what contemporary scholars think of as mystical experience is usually difficult to make before the twelfth century and is often irrelevant to the writer's intentions, as well as to her or his place in the history of Christian mysticism. If we proceed on the basis of the claim that mysticism is *primarily* (not *solely*) an ecclesial tradition of prayer and practice nourished by scripture and liturgy in order to foster awareness of whatever direct forms of divine presence may be available in this life, then a good argument can be made that Eriugena played a key role in originating (or "erigenating," to use James Joyce's term) one of the most important traditions of later Western mysticism, the dialectical Platonic mysticism that is to be found in thinkers like Meister Eckhart and Nicholas of Cusa.[5] The Irishman's thought, from start to finish, was intended to provide an account of how the cosmos, through the mediation of the human subject, returns to its fullest possible unification (*adunatio*) with the hidden God. In this light, recent work on Eriugena has stressed that his contributions to mysticism are as important as those he made to philosophy and theology (the three are inseparable in his thought). As Dermot Moran puts it, Eriugena's negative dialectic "is a spiritual means of transcending the temporal and the created condition and gaining a timeless participation in the oneness of God's infinite nothingness."[6]

The fact that this imposing system of thought, which fused traditional Latin learning with important elements of Greek Christian speculation, was created by a "barbarian" from the farthest reaches of Christendom continues to puzzle modern scholars as much as it did Anastasius. John the Scot was a man of three cultures: Celtic, Latin, and Greek. Before taking up the investigation of his mysticism, a brief look at his life and writings, as well as a consideration of the three streams in his cultural heritage, will be helpful for establishing the context of his thought.

We know little about Eriugena's life. He was born in Ireland, probably not later than 810. We do not know at which of the Irish monastic centers of learning he studied; we are not even sure if he was priest, monk, or layman. There can be no question that when he showed up at the court of Charles the Bald about 845 C.E. he was already a learned man for the times. His polymathic grasp may have included medicine[7] and certainly embraced the liberal arts, astronomy, philosophy, and theology. He must have begun these studies in Ireland, but it is impossible to know how much he learned in his homeland and how much on the continent, though the stimulation of the learned atmosphere of the Carolingian court was essential for his writing career. If the comparison be permitted, we can say that Eriugena could not have composed his *Periphyseon* in Ireland, just as James Joyce could probably not have written *Ulysses* there, but the Irish background to both works is important, though hidden in one case and manifest in the other.

The emperor Charles the Bald became John's patron, asking him to intervene in the controversy that erupted during the 840s over Augustine's teaching on predestination. The Irishman's early treatise *Divine Predestination* already shows the daring of his mind, though not the full development of his dialectical method.[8] John's special understanding of the unity of philosophy and theology/religion is clearly set forth in its famous statement: "True philosophy is true religion and conversely true religion is true philosophy."[9] About 860 Charles called on him again, this time to retranslate the works of Dionysius the Areopagite, the patron saint of the Carolingian monarchy. (A copy of the Dionysian corpus had been sent to his father Louis the Pious by the Byzantine emperor, and Hilduin, abbot of Saint-Denis, Dionysius's supposed burial place, had tried his hand at a translation a generation before.) This encounter with Dionysius and other Greek patristic authors in the 860s was the decisive event in Eriugena's intellectual development.

John could not have learned more than the rudiments of Greek while in Ireland, so it was on the continent, probably with the help of traveling Byzantine traders and ambassadors,[10] but mostly through his own efforts of rethinking as he translated these classics of Christian thought that he became the foremost Hellenist of the early medieval West.[11] Eriugena's version of the *corpus dionysiacum* (ca. 860–862),[12] the only one available until the late twelfth century and still widely used in the later Middle Ages, was followed by translations of Gregory of Nyssa's treatise on theological anthropology, entitled *The Image*,[13] and then by versions of two of the most important speculative works of the seventh-century Byzantine monk Maximus Confessor, the *Questions to Thalassius* and the *Ambigua to John*.[14]

Up to about 862, Eriugena's writing had been mostly as a translator and commentator on handbooks of the liberal arts,[15] typical pursuits of Carolingian scholars. The encounter with Greek thought, however, launched him into a new stage of production during the last fifteen some years of his life (he died ca. 877). His works from this period have been likened to a triptych.[16] At the center stands the massive synthesis he called *Periphyseon*, or in Latin *De divisione naturae* (*The Division of Nature*), the five books of which were begun in the early 860s. It appears to have been a work-in-progress throughout the rest of his life.[17] This is the Irishman's masterpiece, the first medieval *summa*, that is, a truly systematic account of all reality, or of nature, which is defined (or better "quasi-defined") as "the general name of all things that are and those that are not."[18] Smaller in scope, but also of importance for Eriugena's mature thought, are the two wings of the triptych. On one side we have his *Commentary on the Celestial Hierarchy* of Dionysius, a work of some moment for understanding the Irishman's theory of symbolism and his view of the cataphatic aspects of the return of all things to divine unity.[19] The second wing comprises Eriugena's exegesis of John, the mystical Gospel, consisting of his *Homily on the Prologue of John* and an unfinished *Commentary on John* extending to 6:14.[20] Both these works had considerable later influence. The former survives in fifty-four manuscripts (largely because it was often attributed to Origen); the latter, though known in only two manuscripts, enjoyed the good fortune of having excerpts incorporated into the *Glossa ordinaria*, the standard scholastic reference work for biblical study. Along with his translations, commentaries, and *Periphyseon*, John the Scot left some letters and a series of poems addressed to the emperor Charles which reveal the significant role he played at the Carolingian court.[21]

Eriugena's Irish Background

The most difficult part of John's heritage to deal with is what he owed to his Irish background. Interpreting Ireland in the early Middle Ages is not an easy task. Between the Scylla of "Iromania" and the Charybdis of "Irophobia" (to borrow Johannes Duft's terms) the thin-skinned curraghs of modern scholars must advance with much caution.[22] Older views that saw Ireland as the miracle of the early Middle Ages, a place where Greek learning flourished and where access to the classics of Latin literature was widespread, have faded before close historical scutiny.[23] Even the traditional picture of the "Isle of Saints" presented in early Irish hagiography has come on hard times: As one recent commentator notes, "No longer are historians growing misty-eyed over the largely conventional and highly stylised accounts of religious life in the Celtic countries as portrayed by the masters of this literary genre."[24] But enough independent witnesses, from both early medieval England and the continent, testify to the reputation for learning and sanctity enjoyed by the Irish monks to undercut the extremes of Irophobia.

The extent of Irish classical learning in the early period appears to have been small, despite the exception of Saint Columbanus (ca. 543–615). But the Irish had considerable access to late antique literature, especially on grammar and geography, sciences particularly needed by a culture that had never been part of the Roman world.[25] Early Irish Christianity, as Joseph Kelley argues, was monastic in context, conservative in its adherence to recognized patristic authorities, and exegetical in expression. Its main lines were not theologically adventurous.[26] In order to understand something of the early Irish church and its spirituality, we need to begin with Saint Patrick, its major (though not only) founder.

Patrick (ca. 390–460) ranks among the more remarkable spiritual figures of the early stages of the transition between the late classical world and the Middle Ages.[27] His brief *Confession* written late in life in a peculiar, biblically inspired, yet effective form of Latin, provides unique access to a type of late antique spirituality that also reveals much about early Irish Christianity. There is, however, no direct evidence for the influence of his writings until the seventh century, when the growth of the Patrick legend was used to further the see of Armagh's claims to hegemony over the Irish church.[28] The *Confession* shows Patrick not only as a man of one book, the Bible, but also as a person dedicated to frequent, almost constant, prayer (e.g., *Confession* 16, 18, 34, 46). He is also an ascetic (*Conf.* 49–55) who desires martyrdom (*Conf.* 59). Although he was a bishop who ordained priests to conduct the necessary pastoral tasks of preaching and administering the sacraments (*Conf.* 38 and 50), chapters 40–43 of the *Confession* make it clear that he encouraged a free-form monasticism centering on virginity, for both men and women. Patrick's own exile for Christ (*peregrinatio pro Christo*) combined a desire to spread the gospel to all people before the imminent end of the world (*Conf.* 34, 39–40), as well as devotion to the monastic life as the epitome of true Christianity. On this basis Michael Herren has claimed that "the Patrician pattern was to become the model of all future Irish missionary activity in the middle ages."[29] Furthermore, though Patrick was deeply opposed to pagan idolatry (*Conf.* 19 and 41), we do not sense in the *Confession* any obsession with expunging the whole of native Irish culture and unduly "romanizing" his converts. It is not too much to suppose that the unusual coexistence of traditional Celtic culture—artistic, poetic, folkloric—with a learned monastic Christianity that characterized medieval Ireland goes back, at least in some sense, to Patrick himself.[30]

There is another side to Patrick's spirituality as found in the *Confession*, one that displays a mystical element. The missionary bishop recounts seven dreams, or rather dream-visions, which played key roles in his career.[31] Some of these dreams deal with angelic visitors, such as Victorinus, who bears him the letter containing the "Voice of the Irish" in *Confession* 23 (obviously based on Paul's dream in Acts 16:8–9). Two of the dreams, however, can be seen as mystical visions of an unusual character.[32]

In chapter 20 of the *Confession,* Patrick recounts a dream of his youth still vividly recalled in old age, a dream in which he was assailed by Satan:

> And he fell upon me like a great rock, and I had no power over my limbs. But what was the reason, ignorant in spirit, that I called out to Elijah? Meanwhile, I saw the sun rise in heaven, and while I was crying out "Elijah, Elijah!" with all my strength, behold, the splendor of that sun fell on me and immediately removed all the weight from me. I believe I was aided by Christ, my Lord, and his Spirit was already crying out in my place (*pro me*). . . .[33]

Much about this dream remains mysterious, as it was to Patrick.[34] The invocation of Elijah may have been an unconscious appeal to one who was famous as a man whose prayers were heard by God (cf. Jer 5:15–7), or, more likely, it refers to Christ, the true sun (Greek *helios*), whose beams of light dispel the weight of Satan's gloom (see *Conf.* 60). But what is most significant about this "threshold experience," as Noel O'Donoghue terms it, is Patrick's direct awareness of the Holy Spirit crying out within him and in his place.

Even more tantalizing is the account in *Confession* 25.[35] After a brief description of a dream in which he had heard words he could not understand but eventually recognized as words that Christ was speaking in him, Patrick goes on to tell of a second and more powerful dream-vision of the same type:

> And another time I saw him praying within me and it was as if I were within my body and I heard him above me, that is, above the interior man; there he was praying strongly with groans. And meanwhile I was amazed and in awe and I was wondering who it was that was praying within me, but at the end of the prayer he declared that he was the Holy Spirit. And thus I awoke and remembered the Apostle's saying. . . . [Rom 8:26 and 1 John 2:1 are cited.][36]

This dream experience moves from a quasi-visual perception to an audition, as well as from identification of the one within as Christ to the Spirit of Christ. Once again, Patrick conveys his puzzlement over what happened to him: Who is praying and where is he praying? Christ as Spirit is both *within* him and *above* him—to move within, in the dream, is to be drawn above in the Spirit's power. Patrick was unaware of the complex theories of mysticism of an Origen or an Augustine; his autobiographical witness to these moments of mystical consciousness of the divine presence is directly rooted in the Bible as lived by a man of constant prayer, specifically centering on the New Testament teaching about the presence of the Holy Spirit in the life of the believer.

The history of Irish Christianity between Patrick and Eriugena is imperfectly known.[37] Today the idea of a single form of Celtic Christianity is largely outmoded,[38] and there is much debate over how Christianity evolved in Ireland, a non-Roman, totally agrarian, and tribal society. Most scholars would agree with Kathleen Hughes's statement, "Ireland was odd in the early middle ages."[39] It appears that for about a century after Patrick's death the Irish church had a missionary-episcopal structure (the primary witness for this is a document called the "First Synod of Patrick," though it has nothing to do with the saint), but during the course of the sixth century monasticism emanating largely from Celtic Britain became increasingly strong.[40] The seventh century is traditionally seen, though on rather slim evidence, as the age of the growth of the great monastic *paruchiae*, confederations of monasteries owing allegiance to some holy founder and organized along tribal lines. The growing preponderance of monasticism in early Ireland did not destroy the episcopal-parochial structure, but monasticism's centrality is clear from the fact that almost all the notable figures of early Christian Ireland were monastics–Finnian, Ciaran, Brendan, Columba, Columbanus and others among the men; Bridget and Ita, for example, among the women. It was the growth of the ascetic monastic reform of the Céli Dé (Servants of God) in the late eighth century and the time of troubles associated with the Viking raids (beginning in 795 C.E.) that eventually moved the Irish church toward a totally monastic structure in which abbots (who were often also bishops) dominated the ecclesiastical structure.[41]

The contacts between Ireland and other parts of Christendom during its formative period are of importance for understanding the background to Eriugena's thought. The early Irish church received much, including some elements of Eastern Christianity, from Visigothic Spain in the sixth and seventh centuries.[42] But the Irish soon began to travel widely, impelled by the spiritual ideal of exile for Christ (*peregrinatio pro Christo*), which was so powerful in the early Middle Ages. Although these monastic wanderers were not missionaries in the modern sense, they became a potent force in the christianization of Europe during the late sixth and through the seventh and eighth centuries.[43] Columba (ca. 521–597), the founder of Iona, and Columbanus, who revived monasticism in Merovingian lands and in northern Italy between 590 and 615, are the two greatest names of this movement. So powerful was the Irish input that historians have spoken of "Hiberno-Frankish" monasticism as the dominant form in much of the West during the seventh century.[44] It is not easy to say how much learning the Irish monks brought with them, though the example of Columbanus shows that the education of at least one Irish monk was equal to that of any of his contemporaries.[45] The Irish did much to spread the writings of Isidore of Seville, the most important encyclopedist of the early Middle Ages. Their own most significant contributions came in the area of exegesis, though no early Irish monk approached the eminence of Bede as a biblical scholar.[46] The defeat of the Irish view on the question of the dating of Easter at the Synod of Whitby in 664 is often seen as marking the beginning of the decline of Irish influence and even as encouraging a more inward-looking attitude in Irish Christianity,[47] but it is difficult to prove such generalizations on the basis of our scanty evidence. The careers of Virgil, the Irish bishop of Salzburg from 767 to 784, and of John the Scot himself, to mention but two names, show that a steady stream of Irish reached the continent throughout the early Middle Ages.

Early Irish spirituality fits the general picture sketched in chapter 1 above, though with some idiosyncratic elements.[48] For example, Irish hagiography has distinctive features, but it is not basically different from what was to be found in England or on the continent. The Irish showed a devotion to martyrs as the special followers of Christ crucified (see the hymn "Most Sacred Martyrs" from the Antiphonary of Bangor of ca. 680). There was also a rich cult of relics in Ireland, though it developed late and was primarily monastic in context. Irish monasticism often stressed severe forms of asceticism more reminiscent of some of the desert fathers than of the moderation of a Benedict or a Gregory the Great. The anchoritic ideal remained strong in Ireland and among the Irish wandering monks. The Irish also had a devotion to frequent and lengthy prayer, such as the daily recitation of the entire psalter (the "three fifties") and the frequent repetition of Psalm 118 (The *Beati* or *Biait*), which was thought to possess special protective powers.[49] Along with the strong ascetical tendencies went a tender devotion to Mary and the infant Jesus that was unusual in the early medieval period. This form of spirituality appears in Old Irish lyrical poetry that is difficult to date, but whose more ancient examples probably go back to the eighth century.[50] Here is the beginning of a poem ascribed to St. Ita (sixth century), but probably dating to the late ninth century:

Ísucán [little Jesus]
I nurse him in my lonely places;
though a priest have stores of wealth,
all is lies save Íuscán.[51]

Do the scattered witnesses of early Irish spirituality display any mystical elements? The evidence is sparse. A number of hagiographical texts and some poems speak of the desire of noted saints for constant intimacy with God. St. Bridget, for example, is said to have told St. Brendan that "from the time she set her mind on God she had never taken it from him," and St. Ita is held to have continued in uninterrupted meditation on the Holy Trinity every day.[52] These, of course, are *topoi* to be found in much hagiographical literature, though they are indicative of important spiritual ideals. There are, however, also a few more direct witnesses. I have already noted in chapter 1 a text from the rigid ascetic Columbanus, unexpected in the depth of the burning desire it displays for Christ (see p. 31).

Columba, the most popular of Irish saints after Patrick and Bridget, was the object of considerable legendary material. The earliest life of the saint, written about a century after his death by Adomnan, his seventh successor as abbot of Iona, devotes its third book to Columba's angelic visions. A number of these appearances involve manifestations of fire and light in a manner not unlike tales told of the desert fathers.[53] The most significant is the account of a three-day "descent or visitation" of the Holy Spirit in the form of heavenly light that came upon the saint not long before his death. In Adomnan's description this takes on the character of mystical (in the patristic sense) illumination of the meaning of the scriptures:

> . . . he saw openly revealed many things that had been secret and hidden from the beginning of the world. The dark and most difficult passages of holy scripture were spread before the eyes of his purest heart plain and more open than the light of day.[54]

Columba's experience of the Holy Spirit's illumination revealing the depths of scripture is different from Patrick's autobiographical account of the groaning of the Spirit within during his dream-visions, but it is interesting that both saints had Spirit-centered experiences. Such visionary accounts are not found in the writings of John Scottus Eriugena; but the testimony of Anastasius quoted at the outset of this chapter underlines the action of the Spirit in John's work as a translator. So, while the mysterious Eriugena presents us with little that allows us to tie him directly to his Irish background, it would be a mistake to neglect this element in his heritage.[55]

Eriugena's Debt to Greek and Latin Sources

Relating Eriugena to the two other streams of his intellectual background is easier because of the wealth of demonstrable direct evidence, but still presents difficulties because of the problems of how to interpret the Irishman's use of his Latin and Greek reading. To be sure, the measure of Eriugena's genius is not to be found in his broad knowledge of Eastern and Western theological and philosophical authorities; but, as Goulven Madec has noted, it is impossible to appreciate the originality of any author without taking into account his cultural dependencies.[56] The following remarks on John's relation to his Greek and Latin sources will provide more background for consideration of his mystical theory later in this chapter.[57]

Eriugena's Latin philosophical authorities are mostly late antique, though he did know some Cicero. Foremost among these was the *Marriage of Mercury and Philology*, a Neoplatonic handbook of the seven liberal arts popular in the early Middle Ages. He also knew Chalcidius's *Commentary on the Timaeus*, Macrobius's *Commentary on the Dream of Scipio*, and some of the logical and theological works of Boethius. More important were Eriugena's theological authorities of the Latin tradition. He knew Gregory the Great and Isidore of Seville, but rarely cites them. The influence of two of the creators of Latin Christian Neoplatonism is much stronger–Marius Victorinus and Ambrose.[58] The impact of Victorinus on John's negative theology, especially on the key distinction between "the things that are and those that are not," is an important recent discovery.[59] Ambrose was also significant for Eriugena, particularly because his Platonizing interpretation of the return to God allowed the Irishman to claim that the Greek doctrine of the absorption of all corporeal reality into spirit was also found among the Latins (e.g., P 5 [876C, 878A–79B]).

The dominant figure in Eriugena's Latin heritage, of course, was Augustine, who is cited more often than any other author (209 explicit references according to Madec's figures).[60] There is no question of the Irishman's respect for this "master of highest authority" (P 1 [493C] and P 4 [804C]), though he treated the great doctor of Latin Christianity with a freedom unusual in the Middle Ages. So many aspects of Eriugena's teaching were developed through an ongoing conversation with Augustine that it is not possible to begin to list them here. But there are many Augustines, and John's employment of the bishop's writings reveals that outside the early treatise on *Divine Predestination*, it was primarily the more Neoplatonic side of Augustine, especially on creation and the image of the Trinity in humanity, which is to the fore in his citations. Marius Victorinus, Ambrose, and above all Augustine–all Neoplatonic in various ways–were the key Latin theological authorities that John put into dialogue with the Greeks in creating his own form of dialectical Christian Platonism.

John the Scot's study of Greek speculative thought not only gave him the stimulus to begin his great systematic work but also provided him with essential elements that formed its dynamic structure.[61] From the philosophical side, once again, the take is fairly restricted. Eriugena refers to both Plato and Aristotle, but aside from possible knowledge of Chalcidius's version of part of the *Timaeus* and Aristotle's *On Interpretation* in Boethius's translation, he had no direct contact.[62] The Irishman's philosophical heritage was basically Neoplatonic, and more the Neoplatonism of Iamblichus and Proclus than that of Plotinus, as Stephen Gersh has shown,[63] but this reached him in and through the Christian transformation it had undergone in Dionysius and Maximus Confessor.

A few Greek Christian Platonists who did not belong directly to this tradition also had influence on him. Among these we can note Origen, Basil, Epiphanius, and something of John Chrysostom.[64] Gregory of Nyssa, however, was the Irishman's main non-Proclean Greek resource (though Eriugena often appears not to distinguish him from Gregory Nazianzenus).[65] John did not know Gregory's major mystical works, the *Life of Moses* and the *Homilies on the Song of Songs*, but he translated the Cappadocian's treatise the *Making of Man*, or *The Image*, as he always called it. This remarkable work of theological anthropology helped the Irish scholar to distance himself from traditional Latin understandings of what it meant to be created in the image and likeness of God (Gen 1:26) by its stress on the double creation which saw sexual differentiation as a result of the Fall, its teaching on the negative element in the image, its spiritualized understanding of the resurrection, and finally its doctrine of the universality and unending character of the return.[66]

Since Eriugena interpreted Gregory, Dionysius, and Maximus as all teaching the same basic doctrine, he constantly sought to harmonize their views into a coherent system expressing the Neoplatonic view of emanation and return (*processio-reditus*), which he took as the touchstone of right reason's teaching about the fundamental dialectic of *natura*. In this harmonizing process Dionysius was especially important in providing the structure of the positive and negative aspects of the fundamental dynamic of *processio* and *reditus*. Maximus was significant for his christological understanding of the return; and Gregory's contribution was to highlight how human nature's status was related to that of Christ. In no case, however, was Eriugena a mere copyist—every use was a creative one.

If John Scottus Eriugena had done nothing more than translate the *corpus dionysiacum* into Latin, he still would have been accorded a place of merit in the history of Western mysticism. But Eriugena did even more for the history of both Dionysianism and mysticism, writing his own commentary on the *Celestial Hierarchy* and explaining so many passages from the *Divine Names* in *Periphyseon* that the thirteenth-century compilers of the glossed Dionysian corpus used at Paris incorporated a virtual Eriugenian commentary into this important source of mystical theology.[67] (This source for the influence of Eriugena on authors like Meister Eckhart, who never cites Eriugena directly, deserves further exploration.)

The Irishman's preface to the translation he presented to Charles the Bald gives us an idea of what he found most significant in the various treatises of the Dionysian corpus.[68] He highlights the doctrine of similar and dissimilar symbols, reading it in terms of his own fundamental division between "the things that are and those that are not," in order to stress the inner harmony he discerned between the two longest Dionysian works, the *Divine Names* and the *Celestial Hierarchy*. The mysterious Dionysius was the first to baptize and transform Proclean dialectical thought in the service of Christian theology,[69] and hence it is primarily with regard to how we are to approach God's immanent/transcendent relation to the world that Eriugena mined the riches of the *corpus dionysiacum* for the future of Western thought.[70]

It is only within the past few decades that the true stature of Maximus Confessor, the seventh-century opponent of Monothelitism, has become evident to Western scholars.[71] A complex and difficult author, Maximus composed in many genres: polemical works against christological error, liturgical and pastoral compositions such as his well-known *Mystagogia*, and speculative writings in the form of *scholia* and disputed questions designed both to explain problems in the orthodox Fathers (especially Gregory Nazianzenus and Dionysius) and to present, if somewhat indirectly, his own remarkable thought.[72] The interaction between Dionysius and Maximus in stimulating Eriugena's systematics can be best approached from the perspective of Christology. In *The Foundations of Mysticism*, I discussed the debate over Dionysian Christology, noting that a number of scholars have found problems with the way in which the mysterious Dionysius integrated the role of the Incarnate Word into the divine self-manifestation and its eventual return to the hidden heart of unknowable *eros*.[73] However one evaluates this debate, there is general agreement that Maximus, through his *scholia* on the *corpus dionysiacum* and other speculative works, "achieved the Christocentric reorientation of the Dionysian system," to quote Jaroslav Pelikan.[74]

It was through two of Maximus's most difficult works, the *Questions to Thalassius* and the *Ambigua to John* that Eriugena encountered a thinker he came to value as highly and cite as often as he did Gregory. Eriugena appears to have been led to Maximus through his study of Dionysius, recognizing the anti-Monophysite monk as the foremost expositor of "the most obscure sentences of the divine theologian Dionysius the Areopagite."[75] This was a meeting of minds interested only in the deepest issues. Eriugena made an official translation of the *Ambigua* for Charles the Bald. Its dedicatory preface gives us some sense of what he learned from Maximus: how God is both one and multiple; the nature of the *processio* of all things from

the divine source and their *reversio* to it; the way in which God is both im-
movable and yet moves all things; the unity of the Trinity; and much more
besides. Maximus played a crucial role in helping Eriugena see that it was
in and through the cosmic Christ that Proclean metaphysics could best be
employed as a foundation for Christian thought, both dogmatic and mystical.

In their mutual dependence on Dionysius, both Maximus and Eriugena
display similar understandings of creation as divine self-manifestation and
the status of the creature as "another God," that is, as an aspect of "God-
manifested-in-otherness."[76] Eriugena's stress on the formation of all things
by the Word as Creative Wisdom (*sapientia creatrix*) and the consummation
of everything in Christ ("the perfection of man is Christ in whom all things
are consummated," P 4 [743B]) is deeply Maximian. His teaching on the
return to God, especially the five general stages of its accomplishment, as
well as the important distinction between the general and the special return,
is also based on Maximus. Nevertheless, as Eric Perl points out, there are
important differences between Eriugena's western christological reading of
procession and return and that found in the Byzantine author.[77] These are
based in part on the Irishman's lack of acquaintance with Byzantine christological debates, but they also reveal important divergences between eastern
and western perspectives on the dialectical Christian Platonism, which
Eriugena "erigenated" in the West.

The explanation of these differences is a work that has just begun. What
role, for example, did Eriugena's appropriation of Gregory of Nyssa's
cosmic anthropology—his assigning to the idea of humanity a quasi-correla-
tive role with the Word in manifestation and return—have in creating his
departures from Maximus on a pan-Christic ontology? This and other questions that relate to the meeting of East and West that took place in the Irishman's thought cannot be taken up in detail here. I introduce them only to
show the kinds of problems that any survey of John's attitude to his Latin
and Greek sources seems fated to produce: an admiration soon overcome
by perplexity about how the Latin and Greek elements in the thought of
this *vir barbarus* from Ireland's wild shores are to be evaluated.

Eriugena's Mysticism:
The Biblical Basis

John Scottus Eriugena is not often thought of as an important exegete,
despite his two treatises on the Gospel of John. The fact that the Irishman's
great work was a systematic treatise on *natura* seems to qualify him most
appropriately as a philosopher and to suggest that the Bible was at best sec-

ondary to his thought. That John was a philosopher and a theologian cannot be doubted, but I would also contend that he was a major biblical scholar and that a proper understanding of his exegesis is fundamental for grasping his mystical theory.[78] *Periphyseon* itself, at least from the middle of book 2 on (545B), can be seen as a massive, if digressive, commentary on Genesis 1–3. Furthermore, Eriugena's position on the relation of *auctoritas* and *ratio*, so crucial for grasping his system, must be considered in the light of the Bible's role as a guide to truth.

Eriugena's insistence on the priority of *recta ratio*, or right reason, is well known (see, e.g., P 1 [511B–513C]). Less noted is his claim that "the authority of Holy Scripture must be followed in all things."[79] There is no contradiction here for Eriugena: since God is the source of both reason and the Bible, there can be no *real* conflict between the two. A passage at the beginning of book 4 of *Periphyseon* encourages reason "to exercise her skill in the hidden straits of the ocean of divinity" at the same time that she is commanded "to till the field of holy Scripture."[80] Scripture is God's speech about himself (cf. P 4 [757C] and EI 1.1 [5–6]), and hence it is the duty of everyone who desires knowledge of God to labor at its proper understanding. This is well expressed in the prayer that the *Alumnus* offers at the end of *Periphyseon* for enlightenment to understand the sacred text:

> O Lord Jesus, I ask of thee no other reward, no other blessedness, no other joy than this: to understand in all purity and without being led astray by faulty contemplation thy words which are inspired by the Holy Spirit. For this is the crown of my happiness, this the consummation of perfect contemplation: the rational and purified mind shall find nothing beyond it for there is nothing more. For as there is no place in which it is more proper to seek thee than in thy words, so there is no place where thou art more clearly discovered than in thy words.[81]

Like many earlier exegetes, John stressed that creation and scripture were two parallel manifestations of the hidden God, noting that scripture was only necessary in light of the Fall, which has hindered humanity's ability to read the book of creation. Therefore, scripture was made for humanity, not humanity for scripture (e.g., OI 11 [254.11–17]; CI 1.29 [156.58–62]; EI 2.1 [24.146–58]). Although he allowed for more access to God through the book of creation than others did, the world of the biblical text was the primary means of bringing fallen humanity back to its divine source through the "quasi-poetry" of theology:

> ... and so theology, like a form of poetry, shapes sacred scripture with its imaginative creations to the decision of our intellectual soul and [its] withdrawal from external corporeal senses (as from a childish imperfection) into

perfect knowledge of intelligible things, as it were into the full maturity of the interior person.[82]

For Eriugena there is an exact parallel between the book of creation and the book of scripture. A famous passage from the *Homily on the Prologue of John* compares the four senses of the "intelligible world" of the Bible with the four elements that make up the visible universe: history is like earth in the middle; ethics compares to the surrounding waters; natural science (*physike*) to the air; and "outside and beyond all is the embracing sphere, the aether and fiery heat of the empyreum of heaven, that is, of the lofty contemplation of the divine nature the Greeks call theology."[83]

The Irishman's exegetical practice, unlike that of Gregory the Great, rarely dwells on the moral meaning of the text; his interests concentrate on the physical and especially the theological meanings.[84] He does not, however, neglect the *historia*, that is, the narrative sense, because "the divine history does not lie" (*divina non mendax . . . historia*, P 5 [935D]). Following the authority of Augustine, he admitted that many passages of the Bible demand both a literal and a figurative reading (e.g., P 4 [857A]).[85] But Eriugena also shared the conviction of Christian exegetes since Origen that *some* biblical texts could not be read literally and that *all* biblical texts were capable of many meanings. Thus, the exegete's primary task was to pull back the rock of the letter from Christ's tomb, that is, the Bible, in order to reveal "the mysteries of his divinity and humanity."[86] Eriugena often used the term *transitus* ("dynamic passage from one state to another" would be a possible translation) to describe the process of how the exegete moves through the infinity of textual meanings to the hidden divine unitary source.[87]

An illustration of a passage whose literal meaning is misleading can be found in the Irishman's comment on Genesis 3:22 at the beginning of *Periphyseon* 5 (859D–862A), where he insists that what seems to be a punishment (i.e., Adam's being cast out of paradise *lest* [*ne*] he eat of the Tree of Life) is actually a promise of humanity's eventual attainment of the eschatological paradise of the *reditus* (*ne* being taken in the interrogative sense— "May he *not* at some time extend his hand and take of the Tree of Life?"). Here Eriugena argues that right reason clearly shows that the former reading conflicts both with divine goodness and human capability. More fundamentally, the message is that all local and carnal readings of paradise and its furnishings contradict "the spiritual meaning which is taught by the truth, for that is the one and only way of penetrating the approaches to the mystical writings."[88]

Truth and right reason, then, are the criteria for correct biblical interpretation. In advancing this fundamental hermeneutic Eriugena would not have thought that he was doing anything new; exegetes, both Jewish and Christian, had had to deal for centuries with the problem of contradictions and anthropomorphisms in the Bible, and many of them had appealed, explicitly or implicitly, to some principle of right reason. What makes John's formulation of this tradition special, however, is the systematic and original way in which he worked out the exegetical rules for interpretation according to right reason as a part of the larger issue of the relation between *auctoritas* and *ratio*.

Though he never explicitly formulated them as such, I believe we can isolate at least three major Eriugenian hermeneutical principles based on *recta ratio*. The first principle we have already touched on. If God is infinite and unknowable in himself, as truth demands, then his manifestation/revelation, both in the book of creation and in the Bible, must contain an infinite multiplicity of meanings (*multiplex theoria*), because "the Infinite is formed in an infinite way, especially in the minds that are most purified."[89] Throughout his writings, the Irish scholar insisted on this multiplicity, even infinity, of meanings in every biblical passage (e.g., P 2 [560A], P 3 [690BC], P 4 [749C]; CI 6.2 [332.29–40]). He also claimed, paradoxically, that although scripture's formations are multiple, "their understanding is simple and uniform," because of the "most divine simplicity of the divine understandings."[90]

Diverse understandings do not cancel each other out, "provided only that what each says is consistent with the Faith and with the Catholic Creed, whether he receives it from another, or finds it in himself, albeit enlightened by God."[91] There are, however, rules that help determine which meanings have priority, at least from the perspective of *allegoria*, the theological sense.[92] The most basic of these, Eriugena's second exegetical principle, receives its clearest formulation toward the end of book 1 of *Periphyseon*, where the Irishman discusses the relation of positive and negative theology in scripture. After insisting on the necessity of following reason and scripture, "in which truth resides as though in a retreat of its own," Eriugena underlines the priority of negation in all interpretation:

... but it [scripture] is not to be believed as a book which always uses verbs and nouns in their proper sense when it teaches us about the Divine Nature, but it employs certain likenesses and transfers in various ways the meanings of the verbs or nouns out of condescension toward our weakness and to encourage by uncomplicated doctrine our senses which are still untrained and childish.[93]

Following the authority of Dionysius (Eriugena paraphrases *Divine Names* 1.1 here), the Irishman insists that scripture is the infallible source for all positive, or cataphatic, speech about God, "while reason is wholly concerned with suggesting, and proving by the most accurate investigations into the truth, that nothing can be said properly about God ... who is better known by not knowing, of whom ignorance is the true knowledge."[94]

Recta ratio, therefore, discloses that scripture in its deepest sense tells us not what God is but what God is not. A key application of this truth underlies Eriugena's third exegetical principle, the distinction between *mysterium/sacramentum* and *symbolum*, that is, between *allegoria facti et dicti* and *allegoria dicti et non facti*.[95] A *mysterium* is something that both actually took place in history and is recorded in the Bible, e.g., Moses' construction of the tabernacle in the Old Testament, or the establishment of baptism in the New; while a *symbolum* "is established in the discourses of spiritual teaching but not in sensible deeds."[96] Many passages from the Old Testament fit this latter category (e.g., the whole Genesis account of paradise). In the New Testament, *symbola* are especially found in the parables (e.g., CI 6.5 [354–56]). It should not be surprising, given John's intellectualism, that the *symbola* are preferred to the *mysteria*. Mysteries will remain only in part when their sensible and temporal reality perishes; symbols, however, remain forever. As an example, the Irishman notes the opening verse of John, the generation of the Word that is eternally spoken but that never happened in history: "There is nothing to be understood there according to history but everything refers to theology which surpasses all thought and understanding."[97]

Though all types of scriptural allegory, like all the forms of creatures, visible and invisible, are veils of the "Paternal Ray," that is, Christ, "the greatest veil who is of the same nature as we,"[98] still, the rays constituting the *allegoria dicti et non facti* are favored ones in Eriugena's exegetical practice. A good example can be seen in the way John uses scripture to support his understanding of the *reditus* or return at the end of *Periphyseon* 5. He begins with an interpretation of the Exodus as an *allegoria dicti et facti* of the universal return (1001B–1002C),[99] but pride of place is given to the exegesis of the parables (*allegoria dicti et non facti*), which closes book 5: (1) the parable of the Prodigal Son of Luke 15:11–24 (1004C–1005C, 1008C–1010A); (2) the parable of the Lost Drachma and Lost Sheep of Luke 15:1–11 (1005D–1008A); and especially (3) the parable of the Ten Virgins of Matt 25:1–12 (1011A–1018D).[100] The role of this exegesis in disclosing the deepest meaning of the return of all things to divine unity, and the distinction that Eriugena introduces here between simple parables and those that involve "parabolic transition" (*parabolorum transitus*) where "the elements of the story change from one significance to another" (1008C) argue, as Willemien Otten suggests, that we are dealing with a form of "performative" allegorical exegesis that "communicates to its readers that the return to God is not only spiritually foreshadowed, but actually performed in the exegetical process."[101] In this regard Eriugena is not unlike the greatest of early Christian exegetes, Origen, who also believed that it was within the very exercise of interpretation that what we would call mystical transformation takes place.[102]

The role that *recta ratio* plays in determining these exegetical rules highlights its centrality in Eriugena's thought. To call the Irishman a rationalist in any of the traditional modern senses would convey a false impression, however, if only because he emphasized the priority of what reason could *not* know over what it could. There is no question, of course, that he insisted that the demands of reason must be supreme in any argument (e.g., P 3 [723BC]), but this did not mean that *ratio* and *auctoritas*, either the *auctoritas* of the Bible or of the fathers, could ever be in real opposition.[103]

Ratio, as Eriugena used it, was a general term for all mental activity. Its highest forms were the *scientia* of physics and the *sapientia* of theology (e.g., P 3 [629CD]). *Auctoritas* was present in all the truth handed on directly by Christ and the apostles to the fathers (e.g., P 1 [513BC] and P2 [529D–530A]). Because reason originated "with nature and time from the beginning of things" (P 1 [513B]), it must be prior and superior to authority; but since *recta ratio* and *auctoritas* both come from God (the latter through the mediation of the Incarnate Word), essential conflict is impossible (e.g., P 1 [499B, 511B–513C], P 3 [636AD, 641CD]). Seeming conflicts will occur, to be sure, and there are many places in *Periphyseon* where Eriugena labors to conciliate diverse authorities, especially differences between Augustine and the Greek Fathers (e.g., P 4 [804C–807C]). What is most significant about Eriugena, however, is his optimistic attitude in the face of these problems. He always tries to find a middle path, and where this seems impossible he is willing to let differences stand because, in our fallen condition, every human grasp of divine truth necessarily involves a double weakness–at once from the side of the priority of transcendent negation (God can never be known), and also from the side of the effect of the limiting negation of sin on the exercise of reason. The magnificent closing words of *Periphyseon* summarize Eriugena's generous view of this perennial problem: "Let everyone hold what opinion he will until that Light shall come which makes the light of the false philosophers a darkness and converts the darkness of those who truly know into light."[104]

Foundations of Eriugenian Mysticism

The mystical theory of John Scottus Eriugena is inseparable from the whole philosophical-theological system presented in *Periphyseon* and underlying his commentaries on John's Gospel and Dionysius's *Celestial Hierarchy*.[105] Hence it will be necessary to give a brief presentation of the foundational themes of his thought concerning *processio*, the self-manifestation of God, before turning to the more directly mystical themes mostly (but not solely) found in his treatment of *reditus*. I shall do so under three headings taken from his own words, the first two dealing primarily with *processio*, the third with *reditus*: (1) *Deus est superessentialis* (P 1 [460C])–the dialectical view of God; (2) *Omnia lumina sunt* (EI 1.1 [3.76–77])–creation as the illuminating divine self-manifestation; (3) *Donec veniamus in unum* (EI 8.2 [133.550-1])–union with God through deifying contemplation.

The Dialectical View of God

Eriugena's view of God is expressed through his adaptation of the Neoplatonic dynamic of procession and return to a Christian understanding of creation and salvation.[106] *Periphyseon* can be seen as a single massive experiment in expressing the inexpressible, that is, in using language as a form of self-consuming artifact whose limitations are more important than its advantages in the task of attaining God.[107] In his discussion in *Periphyseon* 1 (458A–462D) concerning the two modes of theology, cataphatic (positive) and apophatic (negative), John, in dependence on Dionysius, argues that while positive language about God is always metaphorical and negative language is true and proper, the most appropriate language is that of eminence, which is positive in form but negative in content, expressed in terms like *superessentialis*: "For it says that God is not one of the things that are but that he is more than the things that are, but what that 'is' is, it in no way defines."[108]

To uncover the significance found in the verbal marker *superessentialis*, it would be necessary to explore all the "hidden straits of the ocean of divinity" found throughout *Periphyseon*, a task that cannot be attempted here.[109] But it may be possible to give a sense of the whole by noting three of the most typical Eriugenian formulations of positive, negative, and eminent (i.e., dialectical) predications. Eriugena, like his predecessors and successors in the dialectical tradition, insisted that God is within the world as its deepest reality (a positive statement), but at the same time he is not in the world, being negatively *above and beyond* it. However, from the perspective of eminence, we need to try to find formulations that will express how God is simultaneously and reciprocally *within and beyond* all things.

A favorite way in which John expresses God's positive relation to the world is to speak of the divine nature as the *essentia omnium*, the essence of all things.[110] But such an affirmation always needs to be balanced not only by predications that are negative in form—for example, God is not essence; he is not goodness; he is not wisdom, and the like—but also by what we may call the central negation of the Eriugenian system, the affirmation that God is *Nothing:*

> Therefore the Divine Goodness which is called "Nothing" for the reason that, beyond all things that are and that are not, it is found in no essence, descends from the negation of all essences into the affirmation of the essence of the whole universe; from itself into itself, as though from nothing into something....[111]

Texts such as this, however, already suggest a fusing of the positive and the negative moments in expressing the God-world relation into more dialectical forms that will speak, insofar as it ever can be spoken, the mutual reciprocity, or "reciprocal multiplication," to use Stephen Gersh's phrase,[112] which is the most appropriate God-language. One of the most noted of these is to be found in the third book of John's *magnum opus.* Eriugena begins from a summary statement of the divine motion (*motus/transitus*), which is his "Paulinized" rendition of the triple pattern of Proclean metaphysics (i.e., *mone,* or God in himself; *proodos,* God as going forth; and *epistrophe,* God returning): "For the motion of the supreme and threefold and only true Goodness, immutable motion in itself, and the multiplication of its simplicity, and its unexhausted diffusion from itself in itself back to itself [cf. Rom 11:36], is the cause of all things, indeed is all things." All things, then, exist within God as theophanies or divine manifestations.[113] In a dazzling series of nineteen antitheses, Eriugena goes on to explore the coincidence of negation and affirmation that is the inner meaning of theophany:

> For everything that is understood and sensed is nothing else but (1) the apparition of what is non-apparent, (2) the manifestation of the hidden, (3) the affirmation of the negated, (4) the comprehension of the incomprehensible, (5) the utterance of the unutterable, (6) the access to the inaccessible, (7) the understanding of the unintelligible, (8) the body of the bodiless, (9) the essence of the superessential, (10) the form of the formless, (11) the measure of the measureless, (12) the number of the unnumbered, (13) the weight of the weightless, (14) the materialization [literally "thickening"] of the spiritual, (15) the visibility of the invisible, (16) the placing of the not-placed, (17) the temporality of the timeless, (18) the definition of the infinite, (19) the circumscription of the uncircumscribed....[114]

As James McEvoy has shown, in this text the opening allusion to the Proclean triad indicates that we are dealing not with objective genitives but with subjective ones in which the negative first member of each phrase in the genitive (e.g., *negati* in *negati affirmatio*) points to the hidden divinity and the positive second member in the nominative indicates God as both proceeding and returning in his theophanies. Thus, McEvoy paraphrases the first antithesis (*non apparentis apparitio*) as "coming out of the non-appearing there is the appearing, which moves ineluctably to its goal that is also its source."[115] McEvoy also notes the reciprocal negations implied in each antithesis: God negates himself as "non-appearance" in producing the theophany of his appearance, while appearance as a theophany must be transcended or negated in *epistrophe/reditus* to regain its nonappearing source.[116]

This underlying dialectical structure governs the famous divisions of nature that structure the whole *Periphyseon*. These are introduced at the beginning of book one. First is the twofold division into "the things that are and those that are not" (441A). The second is the fourfold division of the *species* of the genus *natura*: (1) "that which creates and is not created; (2) that which is created and also creates; (3) that which is created and does not create; and (4) that which neither creates nor is created" (441B). All four species are finally nothing more than aspects of God in himself (1 and 4) and God as manifest (2 and 3). The extensive literature devoted to these two forms of dividing nature, and to the five dialectical modes of interpreting the first form (see 443A–445D) make an extended discussion unnecessary here.[117] Basically, both kinds of division are modes of conceiving (*theoriae*) the dynamic process by which the unknown God manifests himself and returns to himself. From our perspective, they form multiple, though interrelated viewpoints; from the side of the hidden divine *nihil*, we cannot say that this is the case.[118]

Some reflections on this understanding of the divine nature and its implications are in order before passing on to Eriugena's teaching on creation as illuminating manifestation. First, it should be obvious that Eriugena does not present an "ontology," because it is not being or essence (or any of his other terms for manifestation) that grounds his system. God, as he says in one place, "neither was nor shall be nor has become nor becomes nor shall become, nor indeed is. . ." (fairly negative that!).[119] In this sense, Dermot Moran is correct to speak of his position in post-Heideggerian terms as "meontology" or a "hyperontology."[120]

In the later Middle Ages, as well as in the modern era, the Irishman was sometimes accused of pantheism. Certainly, if one cites out of context passages that express the immanence aspect of his dialectical view of God, it is not hard to make such an accusation.[121] But even Étienne Gilson—no metaphysical friend of Eriugena—saw that this accusation was misplaced, if only because while God is certainly the *essentia omnium*, he is always much more in the sense of eminent "Nothingness."[122] God is everything, but every *thing* is only "God-manifest." Welcoming Eriugena into the happy ranks of "panentheists," however, as some recent writers have done, is perhaps not exactly right either, not only because panentheism is obviously many things, but also because this claim tends to mute the essential differences between a ninth-century author and modern proponents of at least the process theology version of panentheism.[123] Even more complex is the question of Eriugena's idealism. There can be no doubt that Eriugena is an idealist. But of what kind? If idealism is defined quite broadly (e.g., not only in terms of the *priority* of the mental over the material world, but also as indicating the *dependence* of all reality on the mind), then Eriugena merely joins company with most medieval thinkers before the fourteenth century. If idealism is defined in a more narrowly Hegelian sense as entailing the claim that "all finite reality is understood to require infinite reality for its full intelligibility and completion," a case can also be made that Eriugena is an idealist,[124] though he defends this position in a rather different way from philosophers like Hegel.[125] To the historian, especially the historical theologian, categories like pantheism, panentheism, and idealism often seem too general to be helpful in uncovering the distinctiveness of a particular thinker.

Creation as Illuminating Divine Self-Manifestation

Eriugena's dialectical view of God led him to an unusual and complex understanding of the doctrine of creation and the significance of the cosmos.[126] If creation is nothing other than the manifestation, or theophany, of the hidden God, then not only must God create out of himself, but it will also follow that the fundamental purpose of created being is found in its ability to illuminate and reveal the hidden divine nature: "This is the reason why the entire fabric of this world is the greatest light put together from many parts as from many lamps for revealing and beholding the pure reasons (*species*) of intelligible things by the mind's highest power through the cooperation of divine grace and reason's aid in the heart of the wise and faithful."[127]

Creatio ex nihilo, as we have seen, fundamentally means creation from the *nihil* that is God; it is nothing else than the affirmation of the divine negation (*negati affirmatio*) by means of which God reveals "himself" both to himself and to what he makes. As a text from *Periphyseon* 3 puts it:

> ... he makes all things from nothing, that is, he produces from his superessentiality essences, from his supervitality lives, from his superintellectuality intel-

lects, from the negation of all things which are and which are not the affirmations of all things which are and which are not.[128]

In creation the One "extends itself into all things and that very extension is all things" (P 3 [643B]). This extension is both a self-negation and a self-creation—God, as it were, moves out from himself in a *transitus* in order to reveal himself in theophany. In a deeper sense, however, there is nothing "outside" God, so we can agree with Werner Beierwaltes when he summarizes thus: "To say that God creates himself through that which is created in him evidently means that he realizes himself as the creative principle of the other."[129]

If God both creates and is created, as the fundamental understanding of the dialectical nature of divine reality demands, then all objects in this universe paradoxically must be said to be both eternal and made, that is, we can predicate of them the contradictory assertions "there was not a time when they were not" (*non erat quando non erant*) insofar as they eternally subsist in the Word of God, and also "there was a time when they were not" (*erat quando non erant*) insofar as they become manifest in time.[130] A lengthy investigation of this *aporia* is found in book three of *Periphyseon.*

Among Eriugena's primary metaphors (and more than metaphors) for this understanding of creation are those of light and darkness.[131] Indeed, Eriugena, along with the Dionysius he introduced to western thought, may be said to be the founder of one of the two key traditions of what has been called *Lichtmetaphysik,* the metaphysics of light. (Augustine stands at the head of the other branch.)[132] It is true that John often uses light and darkness in a metaphorical and symbolic way, in accord with his principle "there is no visible or corporeal thing which is not the symbol of something incorporeal and intelligible."[133] But for the Irishman light is more than just another symbol. It is, as Werner Beierwaltes and James McEvoy have shown, an "absolute metaphor," one that presents a "universal pattern for understanding and an ontological statement," something whose revelatory meaning cannot be fully translated into another form of discourse.[134]

Two primary reasons for this emphasis on light may be suggested. First, the mutual reciprocity of light and darkness provides a phenomenological basis for the task of seeking to understand the mysterious dialectic of God hidden and revealed;[135] and, second, the very act of understanding, both in its positive and negative aspects, the heart of the Eriugenian imperative, can be experienced and expressed as simultaneously illumination and darkness. The interconnection of these two aspects is brought out by Beierwaltes's observation that "the interaction or the One-being of thinking and not-thinking is a model for the 'divine metaphor' of a darkness which is light in itself or a light which must appear dark because of its absolute-ness."[136]

It would be a complex task to survey the full range of Eriugena's treat-ment of light and darkness. The language of light pervades every stage and aspect of *processio* and *reditus*. God in himself is the dialectical coincidence of ineffable light and therefore also total darkness. When he reveals himself it is as the "Father of Lights" (*pater luminum* from James 1:17, one of Eriu-gena's favorite texts).[137] This revelation is grounded in the innertrinitarian processions, which themselves can be described in terms of light.[138] The opening chapter of Eriugena's commentary on the *Celestial Hierarchy* details how the *trina lux*, the threefold light of the Trinity—that is, the *lumen primum et intimum* of the Father, the *lumen verum* of the Son, and the *lumen dona-tivum*, of the Holy Spirit—pervades the universe, "shining in all things that exist that it may bring them back into the love and knowledge of its beauty."[139] Thus, all things are lights (*omnia quae sunt lumina sunt*) for a twofold reason: They are created by the luminous Father in his coessential Light, the Word; and their essential function is to light our way back to God by revealing him to us (EI 1.1 [3.76–106]). Even a stone or a piece of wood is a light, Eriugena asserts.

This form of argumentation is primarily theological in character, moving from the divine light to creatures; but Eriugena often also uses light in the reverse direction, beginning from our experience of light or a "physical" (i.e., natural) analysis (often involving the sun's role as universal cause) to arrive at theological truths.[140] He has a particularly rich teaching (which would make an interesting comparison with Augustine) on the role of Christ as the *lux mentium* whose inner illumination of the mind is necessary to bring us to saving truth.[141] Finally, the reciprocity of light and darkness utilized in expressing the origin of all things is also found in Eriugena's analysis of their reversion to the ground. Because God is "an ineffable light ever present to the intellectual eyes of all and known to no intellect as to what it is" (P 3 [668C]), it comes as no surprise that at the close of *Periphy-seon* Eriugena employs the arresting language of "supernatural sunset" to describe the final stage of the *reditus*:

> . . . the third and highest grade is the supernatural sunset (*supernaturaliter occa-sus*) of the most purified souls into God himself, as it were into the darkness of incomprehensible and inaccessible Light in which the causes of all things are hidden. Then the night shall shine like the day (Ps 138:12), that is, the most secret divine mysteries will in some ineffable manner be opened to blessed and enlightened intellects.[142]

Creation, for John Scottus, is not only the diffusion of invisible light in its visible form, but it is also the expression in manifest speech of the unmanifested Word of God.[143] Creation is God coming to know himself in speaking himself. It may seem strange to say that God does not know himself until he creates himself, but knowing in the sense of *cognitio* for John and other Platonists always implies grasping a thing because it is *what* it is and is not anything else–that is, because it is inherently circumscribable or limited. Something can be defined (*de-finire*) precisely insofar as it has a limit (*finis*). But God by his very nature lacks any limit. He is beyond opposed terms such as "he is this" and "he is not this" (P1 [459BC]); all such opposition which we experience in the created realm must be based on something that lies beyond it. This is the root reason why God cannot be said to know himself–he is not among the kinds of things of which conceptual, that is, inherently limited, knowledge (*cognitio, definitio*) is possible. God can, however, be said to be transcendentally conscious of his indefinable self-constitution through a form of conceptual ignorance that Eriugena calls an *ineffabilis intelligentia* (e.g., P 2 [593C]).

All forms of conceptual knowing imply the superiority of the knower to the thing known, for it is the knowing mind that sets the limits which are the basis for conceptualization. God "knows" himself, then, first of all by knowing the primordial causes (the second *species* of the genus *natura*) and all their particular possible instantiations as united in his coeternal Word, the *sapientia creatrix*. This is the foundation for the reciprocity of knowing between God and the creature. God comes to know *what* he is in his creation, and creatures come to know *that* he is through the theophanic universe that expresses and illuminates him.

The key to grasping how this reciprocal recognition takes place lies in the Irish scholar's teaching about the intimate relation between the Creative Wisdom (*sapientia creatrix*), that is, the Divine Word, and the Created Wisdom (*sapientia creata*), which is nothing else than the idea of humanity in which all things are created. Eriugena's Christology has been the subject of a number of recent studies, though not of any general monograph.[144] Deeply influenced by Maximus Confessor and Augustine as he was, Eriugena still goes his own distinctive way, especially in how he relates Christology and anthropology.

"The universal goal of the entire creation is the Word of God. Thus both the beginning and the end of the world subsist in God's Word, indeed, to speak more plainly, they are the Word itself, for it is the manifold end without end and the beginning without beginning [*anarchon*], being without beginning save for the Father."[145] This passage from *Periphyseon* 5 aptly expresses the universal role of the Word. The hidden light that is the divine

Father creates the visible lights of created nature in the coessential light of his Eternal Wisdom, as we have seen (EI 1.1). The *sapientia creatrix* is the *causa causarum* (see, e.g., P. 5 [892D]), the center in which the primordial causes find their unity. Indeed, God creates the causes in the generation of the Son, as many discussions, especially in *Periphyseon* 2, demonstrate.[146] "Christ who understands all things is the understanding of all things," and therefore it is even possible to say that "the essence of all things is nothing else but the knowledge of all in Divine Wisdom."[147] While Augustine also had a rich doctrine of creation in the Word, Eriugena's way of conceiving the relation of the Word and the *causae primordiales* is different.[148]

Maximus Confessor is one of the witnesses in the early Middle Ages to the doctrine of the absolute predestination of Christ, that is, the conviction that the Word's Incarnation was predestined from eternity irrespective of humanity's fall.[149] Eriugena, perhaps because he does not follow the Greek Father in seeing creation itself as the incarnation of God (cf. *Ambigua* 33), does not explicitly advance this position; but the way in which the Irishman connects *sapientia creatrix* and *sapientia creata* in the creative process has analogies with such understandings of absolute predestination. Both the Word and human nature are necessary in the *processio* of all things from God; the Word-made-human is equally necessary for *reditus*.

Among the primordial causes (i.e., the nature that creates and is created), there is one cause that manifests the intelligible divine nature in a special way because of its ability to know. This is the primordial cause, or the idea, of humanity defined as "a certain intellectual concept formed eternally in the Mind of God."[150] If all things are God manifested, then humanity is God manifested in the most special way. It is the true and only *imago Dei*, because, like its divine source, it does not know *what* it is (it is not a *what* at all), but it does know *that* it is—namely, it possesses self-consciousness.[151] Thus, the primacy of negative theology in Eriugena is complemented by his negative anthropology: Humanity does not know God, but God does not know God either (in the sense of knowing or defining a *what*); and humanity does not know itself, nor does God know humanity insofar as it is one with the divine mind that is the cause of itself.[152] This brilliant anthropological turn, hinted at in Gregory of Nyssa's *The Image*, was brought to full and daring systematic expression in the Irishman's writings. It is the ground for a remarkable elevation of humanity (at least the idea of humanity) to a divine and co-creative status.

In *Periphyseon* 2 Eriugena asserts that reason teaches that there is "no longer . . . any difference between the image [i.e., humanity] and its principal Exemplar except in respect of subject,"[153] so that in *Periphyseon* 5 he can conclude that "there is no other way to the most pure contemplation of the

First Cause than the certain knowledge of its image which comes after it."[154] Human subjectivity and divine subjectivity, then, are one and the same in essence, an insight that leads to some important conclusions. First, as Werner Beierwaltes has shown, God himself is the *subject* (not the object) of human knowledge of God: "It is not you who understand me, but I myself who knows myself in you through my Spirit, because you are not the substantial Light but a participation in the Light that subsists through itself."[155] The corollary is that, in knowing itself, the human mind brings to expression the negative dialectic of the divine nature, becoming intersubjectively conscious of itself and of the other-as-itself.[156] To know humanity in its deepest hidden darkness is to know God.

From the perspective of creation, this means that *homo* as primordial cause must have a correlative role with the Word in the *processio* of all things within God.[157] As the "self-conscious idea" in the Divine Mind, humanity knows, actually in its source and potentially in its manifested state, all things in the universe. Thus all things are created in it: "Furthermore, if the things themselves subsist more truly in the notions of them than in themselves, and the notions of them are naturally present in humanity, therefore in humanity are they universally created, as will no doubt be proved in due course by the return of all things into humanity."[158] Creation therefore, to speak metaphorically, occurs in two "places": first, *causaliter* in the *sapientia creatrix*, the second Person of the Trinity; and second, *effectualiter*, that is, as a thing made, in human knowledge.[159] The primordial unity that exists between these two forms of transcendental wisdom will be manifested as the identity in the Person of the God-man who restores the whole of creation to its ultimate origin. As Dermot Moran puts it, "Man and God are one in that they are dialectically united in the concealing/revealing dynamic of the Word."[160]

Union with God through Deifying Contemplation

The role of the fall of humanity and sin in Eriugena's system is important and relatively unstudied.[161] The Irishman's allegorical reading of Genesis 2 and 3, spread across *Periphyseon* books 4 and 5, makes it clear that there was no real prelapsarian state of humanity (cf. P 4 [838AB]). The garden of paradise was not a place that existed in the past; it is a pure *symbolum*. As Peter Dronke puts it, "Paradise is human nature in its divine aspect—as it was originally (not historically but in the ideal world of the divine causes) and as it will be again in the return."[162] The discussion of the fall in *Periphyseon* 4 (824B–860A) is based on an allegorical reading going back to Philo and transmitted through Origen and Ambrose in which Adam stands for intellect, Eve for the senses, and the serpent is both the devil and the lustful appetite of the carnal soul (see 849AB). But it is not always easy to see exactly what fell, why, and to what extent in Eriugena's account. It is not that the effects of the fall are nugatory, since John insists that humanity would have been in some way all powerful had it not fallen from "perfect knowledge both of itself and of its Creator" (P 4 [778BC]). Rather, since Eriugena, as a good Platonist, saw evil primarily as ignorance and illusion, the fall is really nothing more than the inability of humanity as we know and experience it to grasp its true relationship with God. Adam "falls for" Eve in that the harmony between mind and the senses has been disturbed by our own lustful appetites. It is this lack of harmony, which can also be seen as an "exteriorization " of true interior humanity (e.g., 816B–817C, 828D), that necessitates salvation history. The "historical" procession of the primordial causes into material reality that is connected with the fall of the prior and truer humanity into the humanity of disharmony, exteriority, and partial ignorance seems to have both positive and negative aspects—positive insofar as this stage still forms part of God's manifestation (matter is not evil in itself); negative insofar as it involves illusion and ignorance that can only be overcome historically by *inhumanatio*—that is, the incarnation of *sapientia creatrix* in material human nature in the person of the God-man, whose task it is to incorporate all of humanity into him and thus restore it at history's end to the Father.

This restoration, that is, the conquest of ignorance and illusion, will culminate in an immaterial state (though matter will not be totally lost) and will be universal (though a redefined hell will also survive). It is in explaining how the *reditus* is begun in our present lives and in sketching out what *ratio* tells us about its higher stages and consummation that John the Scot's mystical theory becomes explicit. I shall begin with the christological component, because that is central.

The marvelously complex universe of lights that the unknowable God creates out of his divine nothingness has as its goal and purpose the restoration of all multiplicity into the "simple unity of the concentrating and deifying Father."[163] But just as creation took place through the activity of *sapientia creatrix*, the return is possible only through the descent of this *sapientia* into the historical world of effects. In a striking passage from the *Commentary on John*, Eriugena makes use of the analogy of creation as God's speech or "outcry" (*clamor*) to draw together both aspects of the Word's activity:

God's Word cried out in the most remote solitude of divine Goodness; its cry was the establishment of all natures. He called the things that are as well as those that are not, because God the Father cried out through him, that is, he created everything he wanted to create. He cried out invisibly before the world came to be in order to have it come to be; he cried out visibly when he came into the world in order to save it. The first time he cried out in an eternal way through his divinity alone before the Incarnation; afterwards he cried out through his flesh.[164]

This dual "outcry" of the Word can serve as an introduction to the christological *reditus* in John Scottus Eriugena. The cosmic redemptive role of the incarnate Christ appears throughout John's writings, nowhere more forcefully than in the fifth book of *Periphyseon*. An analysis of a key passage (907B–913B) will bring out the essential themes.[165]

Because God made all things in the Word, insofar as they exist in that Word as causes they possess eternal life (following the reading of John 1:3–4 as *quod factum est in ipso vita erat*; see 907C–908B).[166] But what about the effects of these causes as they exist outside the Word (the things that are created and do not create)? Will they perish when the world does (909C–910B)? The *Alumnus* recognizes that the effects must also be permanent in some way, not in themselves but as returning to their causes, but he cannot explain how. The *Nutritor* supplies the explanation through a dialogue drawing out the implications of the disciple's faith in the Incarnation (910D–913C). The Eternal Word has come into the world of effects, our material universe, by taking on the human nature "in which the whole world subsists" (911A).[167] In his return to the Father he elevates the whole human race, and therefore the material universe contained in it (remember humanity is the *universal* creature), above all the heavenly powers in a twofold way: first, by a restoration to the pristine state of humanity as it was to have been before the Fall, that is, as the primordial idea of humanity in which all things are made; and, second and more sublimely, by lifting up some humans who have lived their lives for Christ to the level of divinity itself. The deification of the just, however, does not involve substantial identity with God. This highest level is realized only in the case of the humanity of the Word, as is proper to the head of the church (911BC). The effects are saved, then, by the Word's decision to descend into the material world, that is, to the furthest reaches of the theophanic *processio*, in order to restore all things to God.[168] Eriugena goes even further in saying that had the effects not been saved neither would the causes, since the salvation of one implies that of the other.

Therefore in the Only-Begotten Word of God, incarnate and made man, the whole world is restored even now in its species, but at the end of the world will return universally and in its genus. For what he specially wrought in himself he will perfect generally in all: and not only in all humanity but in every sensible creature."[169]

Eriugena closes this treatment by insisting that because the incarnate Word unites both the whole of the intelligible and sensible worlds in himself in an *incomprehensibilis harmonia* (912D), as profitable to the angels to whom it gives knowledge of the hidden *Verbum* as it is to humanity and the sensible world contained within it, then "by the Incarnation [*inhumanationem*], a word he took from Maximus) of the Son of God every creature in heaven and on earth was saved" (912D).[170]

Three aspects of Christ's work of restoration briefly mentioned in this passage deserve more detailed consideration: (1) the role of the mysteries of Christ's life; (2) the means of our incorporation into Christ through the church, the sacraments, and an intellectual *imitatio Christi*; and (3) the double nature of the reward mentioned above.

Eriugena lays great stress on the role of the salvific mysteries of Christ's life in the universal return. The Incarnation is the source of the greatest dignity of the human race (EI 4.4 [82]), and John does not forget that it was only accomplished by taking on material flesh (e.g., P 4 [745A–746B, and 777BC]). As he puts it in one place, "Without effort he created us through his divinity; with effort he recreated us through his humanity."[171] The Resurrection of the Savior has particular importance because it marks the end of human sexual differentiation and the beginning of the absorption of the material reality of flesh into its higher spiritual state free of the constraints of space and time.[172] The Ascension, the mystery by which Christ begins the uplifting of the whole of humanity to the Father, plays a significant role too. In a striking passage, Eriugena interprets the meaning of the Lord's reception into the clouds in the sight of the apostles as the ascension he effects in the lifting up of his followers' minds to God in contemplation: "He really ascended in the contemplations of those who are ascending to him; nobody can ascend to him without him."[173]

While John always directs his reader's attention to the inner meaning, the spiritual reality, of the mysteries of Christ's life and the sacraments that communicate these, it is their material reality which initially makes them available to humanity in a salvific way. "We, too, who believe in him and in his mysteries after the completion of his Incarnation and Passion and Resurrection, come to understanding, as far as it is given us, and we both immolate him in a spiritual way and also eat him in an intellectual way with the mind not with the mouth."[174]

Our incorporation into Christ takes place in two ways, just as the eventual reward will be twofold. All humans are joined to Christ through their humanity, whether they are his conscious followers or not.[175] From this perspective, all humanity will be saved by returning to the primordial form in and with the risen Lord. Those humans who, as members of his Body the church, strive to fix their contemplative gaze on him and imitate his example in their lives are called to a higher reward. Here the Irish scholar makes use of the ancient typology comparing Adam and Eve and Christ and the church to underline the special unity between the Redeemer and the "higher" saved (e.g., P 4 [836B–838B]). He often speaks in terms of the growth of the total Christ, the *vir perfectus* who is the goal of all history.[176]

This special return of the blessed also involves the motif of the birth of the Word in the soul that Eriugena, in dependence on Maximus and others, was the first to introduce into the West, at least in its more mystical aspects.[177] John tends to use this theme in an ecclesial framework, as when he refers to "the conception and birth of the Word of God" in the hearts of each of the faithful that takes place in baptism (P 2 [611CD], cf. CI 1.21 and 3.5 [98, 228]), though overtones and even possible applications to personal piety are not lacking (e.g., CI 3.3 [214]). The stress on baptism here shows that Eriugena did not neglect the role of the sacraments, especially baptism, Eucharist, and anointing, in his teaching on the return, though he did stress the necessity for their spiritual appropriation.[178]

John the Scot did not exclude more personal aspects of our incorporation into Christ from his teaching. He has his own version of the theme of *imitatio Christi*, which for him means not the kind of literal imitation found in many later Western mystics, but is rather a following of Christ's example by lifting up our minds in contemplation to enjoy spiritual food (e.g., CI 6.1 [326–28]). The first book of the *Commentary on John*, for example, includes a long paraphrase of Maximus's *Ambigua* 47, which teaches a threefold "concrucifixion" with Christ involving an intellectual ascent beginning from moral philosophy, moving through the *virtus speculativa*, to ascend to the heights of *simpla theologica scientia*.[179] This form of ascent by gradual progress through levels of knowledge is found in other Eriugenian texts (e.g., EI 2.5 [46–47]) and demonstrates the strongly intellectualist character of his mystical thought. These intellectual ascents, however, are part of a broader picture taken from Dionysius of how all the created hierarchies work together to form what might be called "the great chain of virtues" that leads humanity back to God.[180]

The work of return that Christ began and that continues in the sacraments of the church and our appropriation of the virtues and of contemplation is based on the cooperation of both nature and grace. Eriugena does not spend much effort in analyzing the nature and mode of the operation of grace in relation to the powers of fallen humanity in the manner of Augustine. He is closer to his eastern sources, even admitting that reading the Greeks caused him to abandon his earlier, typically western view that the resurrection of the body was solely a work of grace.[181] Eriugena's understanding of grace is most often presented in terms of the distinction between the divine *datum* and *donum* suggested by the wording of James 1:17–"Every best thing given (*datum*) and every perfect gift (*donum*) is from above, descending from the Father of Lights." The supreme *Bonitas* that is God gives the *datum* of existence (*esse*) to all things in the act of creation. In order for *esse* to reach the goal of *aeternaliter esse* in the perfect return, however, it is necessary for it to be linked to it, in good Platonic fashion, by an intermediary, *bene esse*. Since the Fall, *bene esse*–that is, the virtuous contemplative life–is always the joint product of both free will and the *donum* that scripture calls *gratia*, something that surpasses all natural powers.[182] Eriugena's doctrine of grace, then, hearkens back to a pre-Augustinian teaching maintained by his Greek sources.

John Scottus Eriugena's universalistic understanding of the return of all things to God in Christ highlights the unusual double-reward theory already seen in the text from *Periphyseon* 5 (907B–913B) analyzed above. This idea, which he developed from a hint in Maximus Confessor, comes up for detailed discussion toward the end of book five.[183] The basic problem is one of theodicy: If all humans are to be saved, no matter what they believe and do, what is the purpose of the practice of the Christian faith? Furthermore, what are we to do with the teaching of scripture, reiterated by the authoritative fathers, about hell? The solution to the first *aporia* is found in the distinction between the two forms of reward that Eriugena demonstrates through an ingenious allegorical reading of Genesis 2–3 (remember that the paradise account deals with the future state of humanity, not its past; cf. P 4 [809B]). All humanity will return to paradise in Christ, that is, all will be united in the primordial cause that is the *sapientia creata*, but not all will taste the tree of life, the "All-Tree" (*omne-lignum paradisi*, P 4 [823AB; cf. 844BD]), which is Christ, and through that tasting ascend to deification by means of contemplation of the highest theophanies (see, e.g., P 5 [978D–979C]). John summarized the two kinds of *reditus* as follows:

> For there is a general return and a special return. The general return is the lot of all things which shall be brought back to the principle of their creation; the special return, of those which shall not only be restored to the primordial causes of their nature, but shall achieve the consummation of their return, beyond every rank in the hierarchy of nature, in the Cause of all things, which is God.[184]

Eriugena's ingenious solution to the second *aporia*, the issue of hell, shows him at his most subtle. Briefly, hell must not be seen as a place or as any limitation on the universality of the general return. God will punish the crime not the nature, which is his good creation. After a lengthy, at times tortuous, treatment of the scriptural texts on eternal punishment and the witness of the fathers, especially Augustine, Eriugena concludes: "And this is all that is meant by the punishment of the perverted free will, namely, the prohibition imposed upon its unruly impulses which prevents it from satisfying its lusts."[185] Hell is nothing else than the continuing existence in the minds of the wicked of the fantasies of the things that misled them during their time on earth (e.g., P 5 [977AB]). What they have regained in their nature, they will not be able to enjoy in their minds.

A full treatment of the role of Christ in the mystical thought of John Scottus Eriugena would demand consideration of a number of other aspects of his presentation, not least a more careful delineation of how he uses certain scriptural images, particularly those of the tree of life (or All-Tree) and the Temple or house of God as symbols of the cosmic dimensions of the activity of the incarnate Word.[186] Even with this summary treatment, however, the profundity of John's christological vision is evident. We can now turn to humanity's appropriation of what we might call the *reditus christologicus* both in this life and in the next.[187]

The Return and Mystical Union

From a general perspective, the return of all things to God can be described, in Stephen Gersh's terms, as both a cancellation and a development of the procession out from the hidden divine ground.[188] The stages of the *reditus* receive a number of different formulations throughout *Periphyseon*. What was originally conceived of as a necessary part of an overarching metaphysical scheme more and more takes on a soteriological and mystical character as the work unfolds.[189] Gersh's careful analysis of the variations in the presentation of *reditus* distinguishes between two forms of horizontal approach, largely dependent on Maximus and of a more quasi-temporal character, and two kinds of vertical approach that are more quasi-spatial.[190] The most obvious is the major horizontal, or historical, schema consisting of five stages adapted from Maximus (see *Ambigua* 37). These progressive absorptions, reversing the pattern of divisions of *processio*, are first introduced in *Periphyseon* 2 (530A–543B) and are discussed at length in book 5. They comprise: (1) the dissolution of the body into the four elements at death; (2) the restoration of the body from the elements at the general resurrection; (3) the transmutation of the body into a spiritual reality following the model of the risen body of Christ; (4) the return of the entire human nature to the primordial causes; and (5) "finally, the universal creature shall be unified with its Creator, and shall be in him and with him one."[191] However, when Eriugena comes to summarize his teaching on the *reditus* at the end of *Periphyseon 5* (1020AD), he introduces a more complex version, first by distinguishing three general levels on a more vertical path— the return of bodies into the causes, the general return of the whole human nature into its original condition, and the special return of the elect by means of grace into oneness with God (1020AC). Those in whom this last is realized are then described as traversing a sevenfold path:

> ... the first will be the transformation of the earthly body into vital motion; the second of vital motion into sensation; the third of sensation into reason; then of reason into intellectual soul (*animus*) ... ; then this fivefold unification of the parts of our nature, ... in each case the lower nature becoming absorbed in the higher not so as to lose its existence but to become with that higher nature one, shall be followed by three more stages of the ascent: first, the transformation of the intellectual soul into the knowledge of all things which come after God; second, of that knowledge into wisdom, that is into the innermost contemplation of the Truth, insofar as that is possible to a creature; the third and highest grade is the supernatural sunset of the most purified souls into God. . . .[192]

The picture is made even more complex by the fact that some texts, basing themselves on the distinction between the general and the special return discussed above, seem to distinguish three vertical levels of returning souls: the wicked; those enjoying only natural goods (these two constituting the *generalis reditus*); and the elect of the *specialis reditus*.[193]

These variations on a set of common themes need not delay us; they are typical of the winding sinosities of Eriugena's voyage on the ocean of scripture. The basic message remains clear: Death, first Christ's death and then our own, begins the process of restoration that will proceed throughout the course of salvation history by means of a spiritualizing unification which will, nevertheless, preserve all that was good in material diversity.[194] How does this general picture of the return affect those of us who have not yet experienced death? That is, what does the Irishman teach about what later ages were to call the mystical life? We can begin with his discussion of what was to become a central way of understanding the progress of the Christian life here below (the Dionysian threefold pattern) and then conclude our investigation with a study of what he has to say about deification, contemplation, and union.

In his *Commentary on the Celestial Hierarchy*, Eriugena makes some use of the Dionysian division of the progress of the Christian life in terms of *purgatio, illuminatio*, and *perfectio*. Here he is most concerned to show how these steps are tied to the action of the angelic orders,[195] but a passage from chapter 10 suggests that the classic tripartition can also function as an excellent vehicle for the presentation of properly Eriugenian themes. Though this text refers directly to the activity of the three highest angelic orders, it could also be used to define the three aspects of uplifting activity that must be begun by humans in this life—"To be purged from all ignorance, illuminated by all wisdom, and perfected by all deification."[196] Similar passages are found in both the *Commentary on John* and *Periphyseon*.[197] The purgation from ignorance and the illumination by wisdom are the main work to which *Periphyseon* and John's other writings were dedicated—overcoming the effects of sin through the study of the scripture as guided by *recta ratio*. This was the preparation for deification, contemplation (*theoria*), and union with God, which were the work of grace. These last could—and should—be tasted in this life, but their full attainment would only be realized in the stages of *reditus* that begin with death.

John Scottus often speaks of perfection as *deificatio* or *theosis* (forms of the words appear over a hundred times in his works).[198] While the theme of deification was not a new one to western Christianity, being found in Ambrose and Augustine,[199] Eriugena, under the influence of the Greek fathers, made more of it than any previous Latin writer.[200] There is no reason to think that he restricted the application of the word to the world to come, though he insisted that what is begun here can only find its perfection there given the cosmic transpositions that will begin with the resurrection from the dead. The *Commentary on the Celestial Hierarchy* distinguishes two levels of deification: "We, indeed, still like little children, are being formed into the divine likeness within us by symbols and holy images, so that we may now be deified by this likeness through faith and (afterwards) will be deified in vision."[201] The text goes on to discuss how the second mode of "dialectical discipline," the mode called *analytike* which unites what the descending mode of *diairetike* had divided, ". . . enlightened through the variety of sacred symbols, is drawn back to the height of supernal deification" (EI 7.2 [106.576–78]). In other words, deification is an exercise that is as much philosophical as it is spiritual and theological (remember that "true philosophy is true religion, and vice versa").[202]

In most discussions it is the theological side of deification that is stressed. Deification takes place "on the mountain of theology" (CI 4.7 [318.54]). Another passage from the *Commentary on the Celestial Hierarchy* says, "The Holy Trinity itself is our *theosis*, that is, our deification" (EI 1 [18.639–40];

cf. P 4 [743A]). Eriugena consistently emphasizes that deification is a grace (e.g., P 5 [903D–904A, 906BC, 978A]), but this does not mean that nature (the divine *datum*) does not play its role (see EI 9.4 [151.614–21]). When he defines the word toward the end of book 5, the definition is resolutely theological–"the psychic and bodily transformation of the saints into God so as to become one in him and with him."[203] It is important to point out that, like Augustine and his Greek sources, he clearly distinguished between being God by nature and becoming God by the adoptive sonship of deification.[204]

Deification is intimately connected with two other key terms in the history of Christian mysticism: contemplation and union. Our consideration of these two themes will also raise the question of what kind of consciousness of God (call it deification, contemplation, or union) is possible in this life.

In an important text in *Periphyseon 5* (998B–1000A) Eriugena discusses the meaning of the Pauline verse (1 Thess 5:17) about being snatched up into the clouds to meet Christ and being always with him. According to the Irishman, these clouds refer either to the individual "cloud of contemplation" (*nube contemplationis*) in which each saint will enjoy the divine theophanies (this is Maximus's interpretation) or else to the great contemplatives of the Old and New Testaments, as Ambrose held, a reading that he finds seconded by the account of Christ's Ascension. He then goes on to distinquish three forms of contemplation figured in the three protagonists of the Transfiguration: Elijah, Moses, and Christ. Elijah is the type of those who contemplate God "while still held in the body," Moses of those who "are released from the body,"[205] while Christ represents those who will enjoy contemplation in the resurrected body. In a manner close to Augustine,[206] Eriugena holds that most contemplation in this life belongs to the first mode; but that the second mode, that in which the soul as it were dies to the world around it, is also possible here, as the rapture of Paul to the third heaven indicates (see 2 Cor 12:2–3).[207] Paul's experience, then, is conceived of as a kind of death, as were those of the other apostles who "though still in the body . . . transcended all things visible and invisible" (897B). In *Periphyseon 5* (887CD) the Irish scholar gives more detail about the exact nature of Paul's rapture. The "hidden words" (*arcana verba*) that the apostle reported he had heard when taken out of the body into the third heaven were nothing other than the "unchangeable causes of things made in God's Wisdom, according to which things visible and invisible were made."[208] In other words, Paul was miraculously raised to the level of the highest angelic hierarchies who are described in the *Commentary on the Celestial Hierarchy* as "participating immediately through themselves in divine contemplation."[209] In a text from the *Homily on the Prologue of John* the author of the Fourth

Gospel goes the apostle of the Gentiles one better by being rapt above even the third heaven, the realm of the primordial causes, to contemplate the *causa omnium*, the Word of God.[210]

In what sense might such visions be described as direct or immediate visions of God, that is, of the divine Nothingness? In no sense at all, even if, as in the case of the evangelist, they seem to be equal with what will be enjoyed in the final *adunatio*. Although John the Scot spoke of "face-to-face," or "immediate," contemplation as the goal of the human search for God,[211] his unyielding apophaticism always qualified this seemingly "direct" contemplation as meaning "more direct, but not without some mediation."[212] Thus, theophanies will always be required, both in this life and in the next. It is important to remember, however, that theophanies are not *other* than God—their essential reality is nothing else than that of God manifesting Godself.[213]

An even more complicated situation meets us when we turn to the investigation of what kind of union with God Eriugena believed would characterize the final stage of the *reditus*. Although the Irishman does not use the technical term *unio mystica*, he does speak of "ineffable unification" (*adunatio ineffabilis*–886A, 894A, 912B) and "ineffable unity" (*unitas ineffabilis*–883B). He sometimes used language that seems to suggest some form of union of identity to be achieved in the final *adunatio* (his favorite term, adopted from his translations of Maximus).[214] Eriugena is also famous for having introduced into Western mystical literature two metaphors for union with God which he found in Maximus's *Ambigua* 3: "The intellectual nature . . . does not rest until it becomes a whole in the whole beloved and is comprehended in that whole, . . . as air is wholly illuminated by light, and the whole lump of iron is liquified by the whole of the fire."[215] Future generations of Western mystics for the most part employed these classical comparisons to express the loving union of wills that was characteristic of the Augustinian-Gregorian tradition of the *unitas spiritus*.[216] Similarly, Eriugena did not intend them to point to some unqualified identity between God and human; rather, he found in them apt metaphors to express his sense of the eschatological interpenetration of the divine and the human that will always preserve difference in identity, what he referred to as "the simple unity consisting of a manifold unification of all creatures in their principles and causes, and of the principles and causes themselves in the Only Begotten Word of God."[217]

How then did Eriugena conceive of the final union when the *reditus* would be completed in Christ? A close investigation of John's view of humanity's ultimate union with God discloses something that both *is* and *is not* identity. First, we can say that the *reditus* will definitely form an identity with God because we have always possessed such identity. For John, everything, but especially human nature with its divine image constituted by self-consciousness, is identical with God in the sense that God is the *essentia omnium*, the inner reality of all things. In the final return, God can no more cease being the *essentia omnium* than God can abandon the divine *nihil* of impenetrable unknowability. This latter aspect–Eriugena's "God beyond God"–not only preserves divine transcendence but also guarantees that *really* direct contact with God is impossible. There is nothing that John insisted on more than the fact that even in heaven, in the final stage of *reditus* (however it is conceived), God will be known by all intellects below that of the incarnate Word only through theophanies, even though they will be "theophanies of theophanies" (*theophaniae theophaniarum*), things unimaginable to us in this world of lesser lights.[218] The hidden God will never be revealed, nor known nor contemplated; there is no real union/identity with the dark mystery–otherwise God would not be God.

What, then, does the Eriugenian *reditus* mean? What will change? What will the future state be like? John the Scot was always realistic enough to know what could be said and what could not be said about this final *adunatio*. The ultimate differentiating union will be a change in the awareness of all humanity. First, humanity will be absorbed back into the elements in death; then, in the general resurrection humankind will be brought to a state in which there will be no more divisions, with sexual differentiation being the first to go. Finally, after it has progressed through all the stages of sublimating unification, humanity will reach the final differentiation in unity of the cosmic Christ. The Word stands at the beginning and end. But the end is different from the beginning, and it is perhaps in this aspect of his thought that John Scottus Eriugena proves himself not just a clever synthesizer of East and West, but one of the creative minds of the Christian tradition.

In Eriugena's *reditus* (to speak somewhat blasphemously), things will be better for God insofar as he will have come to know himself through the self-manifestation of creation, fully realizing "himself as the creative principle of the other."[219] His knowledge in this mode is a "real" change or development, at least in God-manifest, because the divine Word will have brought the effects back into the source through a union of identity that surpasses what was in the manifest God "before" the *processio*. From the perspective of present humanity, the salvation-historical aspect of Eriugena's version of the Neoplatonic dialectic of *processio/reditus*, there will also be a real development because true humanity–the union in difference of all humans who have ever lived–will be raised to a higher level of the endless search that is the nature of the created *imago Dei*. Eriugena's splendid vision, like that of Gregory of Nyssa, ends on the note of *epektasis*, that is, the constant, ever-deepening movement into the divine mystery. The Irishman's version of this theme of Christian mysticism, however, has its own accents because of his insistence that God can never be attained directly, but only through theophanies:

> But since that which human nature seeks and towards which it tends, whether it moves in the right or the wrong direction, is infinite and not to be comprehended by any creature, it necessarily follows that its quest is unending, and that therefore it moves forever. And yet although its search is unending, by some miraculous means it finds what it is seeking for: and again it does not find it, for it cannot be found. It finds it through theophanies, but through the contemplation of the divine nature itself it does not find it.[220]

In the face of this infinite unfulfilled fulfillment we can appreciate the Irishman's advice to "be patient and give way before the incomprehensible power of God and honor it with your silence: for until that is attained, no reason and no mind is adequate."[221]

CHAPTER 4

Mystical Elements in
Early Medieval Monasticism

ETWEEN THE DEATH of Gregory the Great in 604 C.E. and the
accession to the papal throne of his namesake, Gregory VII, in
1073, almost five centuries intervene. Gregory VII's papacy
marked the apogee of the Great Reform movement, a watershed in
the history of Western Christianity. This papal attempt to reorganize
Christendom was an important factor in the renewal of the church and
society in the central Middle Ages. The preceding chapter has taken
up the one figure during these centuries who, I argue, made an original contribution to the development of western mysticism. Though
John Scottus Eriugena is not often thought of as a mystic, and
although his influence on later mystics was somewhat sporadic,[1] the
Irishman's creation of the first form of dialectical mystical theory in
the Latin West was of decisive importance. But in many ways John
was an exception in his age. The question we must now address is
whether these centuries contributed anything else of significance to
the history of Christian mysticism.

It must be admitted at the outset that compared to Gregory the
Great, or to the Cistercian and Victorine mystics of the twelfth century, there are no outstanding mystical authors in the early medieval
period. But, as I have argued in *The Foundations of Mysticism*, what we
call mysticism today is best seen not as a discrete entity, a special kind
of religion, but as a part or element within broader concrete religious
traditions.[2] Hence, despite the absence of classic mystics in this
period, there are certainly writers and texts that deal with mystical
themes and practices, such as solitude and silence, prayer and contemplation, and the vision of God. It may also be true that there is little
that is new or distinctive in the early medieval writers who con-

tributed to the western mystical tradition.[3] Nevertheless, even to transmit a tradition over such an extended period of time is to play a role in forming it, so that, while no single author or text of these almost five centuries—with the exception of Eriugena—marks an original departure, a significant part of the history of western mysticism would be lost if no attention were given to the monastic authors of the early medieval era. The monastic core or layer of western mysticism, which has remained an essential foundation for all that has followed it, was transmitted to posterity by the patient efforts of the generations of monks between 600 and 1100 C.E.

Again with the exception of Eriugena, it is essential to stress the monastic character of the mystical element in early medieval religion. Monasticism, as we have seen in chapter 1, became the driving religious force in the formation of medieval Christendom, and it remained so down into the twelfth century. All the figures discussed in this chapter were monastics. Indeed, as the research of Jean Leclercq has shown, the monastic life, the *ordo monasticus* of Western Christendom, came to be identifed with the contemplative life (*vita contemplativa*) during this period.[4] Not all monks were contemplatives, but their way of life was seen as characterized by its goal, which could be described either by a series of terms taken from the Greek mystical tradition (*contemplatio, speculatio, theoria*) or by a group of biblically-inspired words indicating the soul's repose in God (*quies, otium, vacatio, sabbatum*).[5] In order to understand how monasticism served as the vehicle for early medieval mysticism, it will be helpful to give a brief survey of the development of western monasticism between 600 and 1100.[6]

Early medieval monasticism was marked by the tension between the desire for flight from the world and the obligation to save and transform the world, especially a world in which other institutions—religious, political, social, and economic—were often wanting. Benedict's *Rule*, as we saw in chapter 1, laid the groundwork for a self-sufficient community of religious virtuosi whose main task was to work out their own salvation. The Irish monks and hermits briefly considered in chapter 3 often fled from their homeland and ordinary ties to seek God "in the desert," that is, in any isolated spot (even an island in the ocean). But separation was rarely successful for long. The great monasteries founded on the continent in the seventh and eighth centuries became key centers of nascent Christendom, as important for social and economic reasons as they were for religious ones. Early medieval rulers recognized the importance of monasticism by founding and supporting houses and by their utilization of monastic advisers at their courts (often the only people capable of functioning as learned bureaucrats). This was especially evident with the Carolingians, whose support of monasticism was a crucial factor in the establishment of Benedictinism as the dominant form of western monasticism.

The formative period of western monasticism had witnessed a proliferation of rules. The monasteries founded from the sixth century through the eighth often lived a form of monastic life based on an amalgam of several rules (this is sometimes referred to as the time of the "mixed rule"). Benedict's fame, especially as conveyed through Gregory the Great's popular *Dialogues,* and the desire of Charlemagne and his successors for religious and social regularization led to the triumph of the *Rule of Benedict* (RB) in the early ninth century, when Benedict of Aniane (d. 821), a monastic reformer from southern France, systematized the Benedictine form of monasticism and had this approved as the standard for all Carolingian houses at the Synod of Aachen in 817. The earliest commentaries on the RB also date from this time and are a sign of the new normative role of Benedict's document. Although this was a much-modified Benedictinism, with a greater clerical component, reduced labor for the monks and increased liturgical duties, Carolingian Benedictinism, a socially embedded and often politically powerful form of monasticism, remained essential to the later history of the Benedictines.

The danger of such engaged forms of monasticism, of course, has always been that of becoming too involved with the world, either by coming under the control of lay patrons (something that almost always involves a diminishing of religious fervor and practice), or by being so dependent on social and political structures as to suffer decline and even destruction when these structures faltered and failed. Both difficulties were evident in the eighth and ninth centuries as the Carolingian empire collapsed as a result of internal weakness and renewed barbarian attacks, especially by the Vikings. By ca. 900 C.E., monasticism in Western Europe was in a sorry state.

This was when a second dynamic in the history of monasticism came into play. No other institution in western history, religious or secular, has had the ability to reform itself from within as often and as successfully as monasticism. The oscillation between decline and renewal is one of the characteristic features of what has been called the "Benedictine centuries." At the risk of oversimplification, we can note three major waves of monastic reform between ca. 900 and 1100 C.E. The first of these began shortly after 900, when a number of monastic houses, especially the recent Burgundian foundation of Cluny, attempted to improve the level of monastic observance (usually more in line with Carolingian Benedictinism than the original RB). A surge of reform, partly dependent on Cluny, and partly based on other centers in Lorraine and Germany (e.g., Gorze, Brogne, and

Hirsau), in Normandy (e.g., Bec), and in England (e.g., Glastonbury), had important effects during the following centuries.

Cluniac monasticism and its related forms (the traditional "Black monks" of the Middle Ages) were ideal expressions of the spirituality of Christendom analyzed in chapter 1. Clerical, monastic, feudal, and liturgical, this form of monasticism sought to incorporate the undifferentiated sacrality of the early Middle Ages into powerful monastic houses and loosely organized federations.[7] The interpenetration of the sacred and the secular (at least from the modern perspective) was to be found even when these reforms sought freedom from lay control by direct association with the papacy (what was called *libertas Romana*). The success of the tenth-century reforms was responsible for much of monasticism's undeniable cultural contributions to Western civilization—from the great monastic churches and the renewal of monumental sculpture to the production of manuscripts for liturgical, educational, and even aesthetic purposes. Although this monastic reform was marked by a "triumphalist" tinge, its spiritual inspiration was often real, and, at times at least, also characterized by mystical elements.

The eleventh century, as well as the early twelfth, witnessed two other major currents of monastic reform, both beginning from dissatisfaction with perceived spiritual slackness in traditional Benedictinism.[8] The first of these began around the turn of the millennium and represented a strong reaction to the establishment monasticism that was beginning to dominate Europe. Starting in Italy (under some Greek influence), a series of ascetic hermits (e.g., Nilus, Romuald, John Gualbert, Peter Damian) renewed a more severe form of asceticism through their lives, preaching, and miracle-working. The movement later spread north of the Alps, especially to France. These new ascetics founded communities, but ones whose practice of monasticism, though often broadly Benedictine, was more austere than that found in the tenth-century reforms. They also encouraged the practice of the eremitical life.[9] The new eremiticism culminated in the career of Bruno (ca. 1030–1101), the founder of the Carthusians, an order that was to have a significant role in the later story of western mysticism. Some of these eremitical reformers, such as Peter Damian, are among the most important representatives of the traditional spirituality of early medieval monasticism.

It is perhaps artificial to divide the eremitical from the coenobitical reforms of the eleventh and early twelfth centuries. Wandering hermits eventually settled down to found communities, such as the Camaldolese, Vallombrosians, and Carthusians, as mentioned above. These houses often combined aspects of Benedictinism with new departures in piety and structure, such as greater individual austerity and the use of lay brothers (*conversi*). By the end of the eleventh century, however, we can also find reform movements that began as community efforts, with the decision of a group of monks to seek a new situation where they could live the monastic life more effectively. The most significant of these community reforms was the Cistercian order, founded in 1098. Though the Cistercian propaganda machine tried to create a charismatic founder in the person of Robert of Molesmes, abbot of the monastery from which the original group departed, it is difficult to think that he was of lasting significance, especially after his abandonment of the reform to return to Molesmes.[10] The impact of this wave of coenobitical reform, centered in France and to a lesser extent in England, was not to be evident until the twelfth century and will, therefore, be taken up in the next part of this volume.

To analyze these stages of western monasticism–the mixed rule forms, Carolingian Benedictinism, Cluny and its associated reforms, eremitical reforms and renewed coenobiticism–is not within the scope of this chapter. Despite their divergences, and the often sharp criticism they directed at each other, they shared much. In reviewing the exegesis of the early medieval monasticism (the foundation of what we call mysticism), Bernard de Vregille noted how, despite the many variations, "the tradition appears, from our point of view, astonishingly one."[11] The same can be said about almost every aspect of the spirituality of early medieval monasticism.

Monastic culture, as Jean Leclercq has shown in his noted work *The Love of Learning and the Desire for God*, had a distinctive morphology whose essential foundation was the inheritance of the ancient monastic tradition as laid out in the *Regula Benedicti*, as well as the classics of the monastic spiritual literature, especially the works of Cassian, the *Vitae Patrum* and *Verba Seniorum* (i.e., the fifth- and sixth-century Latin translations of the lives and sayings of the early Greek monks),[12] and the writings of Gregory, the first monastic pope. The monks' dedication to biblical study involved a commitment to learning and cultivation of the liberal arts–a real, if also carefully limited, form of humanism, one that often displayed considerable ambivalence about the reading of classical Latin literature at the same time that it continued to read and copy the classics.[13] Early medieval monastic culture, however, was fundamentally aimed at the cultivation of *spiritualitas*, that is, life lived according to the participation in the divine life available to Christians through the church and its sacraments.[14]

Many characteristics of this monastic spirituality were of importance for the history of mysticism. In view of the fundamental unity of monastic culture and spirituality, I will proceed by way of an analysis of key motifs and themes, rather than chronologically.[15] Because of its diffuse character, the sources for this mystical aspect of medieval monasticism are many. The hagiographical material relating to early medieval monks is of importance, if not for its historical accuracy at least for its insight into the spiritual practices and values of the time. The mass of biblical commentaries and sermons produced by the monastic authors is of vital significance. Treatises, letters, and often hymns and poems are also significant. In order to synopsize the key themes as briefly as possible, I will draw most of my evidence from a handful of monks who are both typical and also especially helpful for what they have to tell us about the components of monastic mysticism. These figures include Ambrose Autpert in the eighth century, Smaragdus and Rabanus Maurus from the ninth, Odilo of Cluny in the tenth, and a trio of important eleventh-century monks: Peter Damian, John of Fécamp, and Anselm of Canterbury. A brief introduction to their lives and writings will suggest the unity in variety that marked early medieval monasticism.[16]

Ambrose Autpert was born in Gaul in the early eighth century but migrated to Italy, where he entered the monastery of St. Vincent on the Volturno river near Beneventum in 754. He eventually became abbot and died in 778. Ambrose wrote homilies, moral treatises, and a number of works of exegesis, including a lengthy commentary on the Apocalypse that concentrates on the mystery of the Incarnation and Christ's spiritual marriage to the church.[17] Scattered through these much-read works is a typically monastic teaching on the necessity for scriptural meditation as the foundation for a life of true contemplation.[18] Smaragdus, who became abbot of the Lotharingian monastery of St. Mihiel in 814, is a good example of the monastic scholars and organizers of the early Carolingian age whose activities produced classic medieval Benedictinism.[19] The abbot's mystical teaching is found primarily in his work *Crown of Monks (Diadema Monachorum)*, a popular "mirror of monks," that is, a description of the values and duties of the monastic life, and in his *Commentary on the Rule of St. Benedict.*[20] One of the most prolific writers of the mid-Carolingian period, Rabanus Maurus was born in Mainz about 780 and died as archbishop of that city in 856 after a stormy career as abbot of the famous monastery of Fulda. Rabanus's life combined political involvment and theological controversy with a large and varied literary effort, especially in the realm of biblical commentary. This powerful churchman's writings, especially his encyclopedic *The Nature of Things (De rerum naturis,* also known as the *De universo)*, provide a summary of early medieval biblical culture.[21] His three-part treatise *On Seeing God, Purity of Heart, and the Manner of Penance,* written ca. 845, shows that questions concerning the relation between the beatific vision and the experience of God that is possible in this life were alive during the Carolingian period.[22]

Odilo (ca. 961–1049) was the third abbot of the immensely successful reform house of Cluny. During his tenure of fifty-four years (994–1049), Cluny attained an importance second to none among the great Benedictine monasteries. Cluniac spirituality was always more of an institutional achievement than the product of any single charismatic leader, including that of Odo (879–942), the major figure in the early history of the house. Odilo's spirituality, as found in his lives of the saints, hymns, sermons, and treatises, has been summarized by Jacques Hourlier under the formula "vers la contemplation par la dévotion," that is, "toward contemplation through devotion," an apt summary of the early medieval monastic search.[23]

Without minimizing the contribution of these monks of the period ca. 750–1050, it is fair to say that in the course of the eleventh century the quickening pace of societal expansion and religious reform produced spiritual writers of a more impressive range, one of whom at least, Anselm of Canterbury (ca. 1033–1109), has remained a major voice in Christian theology. The three monastic authors considered here illustrate the varieties of reform discussed above.

Peter Damian was born in Ravenna in 1007 and died in 1072. In 1035 he became a monk at Fonte Avellana, one of the communities much influenced by the example of St. Romuald (d. 1027), who had revived eremitical monasticism in northern Italy. Peter's *Life of Romuald* and his treatise *The Eremitical Order* demonstrate his continuing commitment to solitude and severe asceticism as the ultimate form of Christian life. But Peter's fame as a reformer, preacher, and publicist led to his appointment as cardinal bishop of Ostia in 1057, and for the last fifteen years of his life he was a somewhat reluctant warhorse for the reform party in the Roman curia, though a more moderate one than some of his contemporaries whose zeal for improving the moral tone of the clergy led them to quasi-Donatist positions denying the validity of sacraments performed by sinful priests.

Peter Damian's extensive writings mark a departure from many early medieval monks, especially because he wrote no biblical commentaries, preferring sermons, letters, prayers, hymns, liturgical texts, and especially brief treatises (sixty-seven survive) to present his teaching.[24] It would be incorrect to think of Peter as a mystical author in the full sense of the term; his writings are mostly ascetical, moral, homiletical, liturgical, and even speculatively theological in nature.[25] Peter's vehement reformism, at times leading to almost scabrous attacks on clerical vices, and the severity of his ascetical practices (he wrote treatises encouraging the use of the "discipline," or scourge) were combined with a tenderness of devotional language and a concern for the values of the contemplative life. It was not unfitting, then, that Dante gave the hermit-cardinal a place in the heaven of Saturn in *Paradiso* XXI, where he is described as "contento ne' pensier contemplativi" ("content in contemplative thoughts," line 117). A number of

Peter's *opuscula*, or treatises, are important sources for the mystical elements in eleventh-century spirituality.[26]

Peter's contemporary, John of Fécamp (ca. 990–1078), is clearly a mystic, if this term may be said to have any meaning prior to the creation of mysticism as a category.[27] Unlike the monks considered thus far, John's writings, especially his *Theological Confession* composed early in his monastic career, deal principally with the life of meditation and contemplation that leads toward the soul's transformation in Christ.[28] John recast the Augustinian genre of *confessio*, that is, a direct address to God that is at once admission of personal sinfulness and praise of divine mercy, in a new, more monastic mode, one in which biblical citations and reminiscences mingle with extensive quotations from the fathers, especially Augustine, to form a monastic *lectio* aimed to produce contemplative prayer. He also wrote a few treatises and letters. His "Letter to a Nun," for example, is really a brief treatise on the mystical life, the finest of the early Middle Ages.[29]

Like Peter Damian, John was born in Ravenna. Although he appears to have spent some time as a hermit and always remained attracted to the eremitical life, his monastic reformism was closely associated with the activities of his uncle, William of Volpiano, who founded a series of monasteries in northern Italy and in France, including the famous house of St. Benignus at Dijon. John became abbot of Fécamp in Normandy in 1028 and ruled there for fifty years, spreading the work of reform in Normandy and England. Excerpts from his spiritual writings in the form of *Meditationes* circulated widely in the later Middle Ages, under the names of Ambrose, Augustine, Alcuin, and Anselm.[30]

Anselm too was born in northern Italy (at Aosta) and became a monk in Normandy at the noted reform abbey of Bec (it appears that he and John of Fécamp knew each other). Anselm was elected abbot in 1078 and governed the monastery until 1093 when he was named archbishop of Canterbury. His stormy relations with both William II and Henry I during his episcopacy (1093–1109) had much to do with his attempts to implement Gregorian reforms in the English church.

Anselm's name shines so brightly in the history of medieval theology, especially for his teaching on the redemption enshrined in his *Why the God-Man?* (*Cur Deus Homo*), that it is easy to forget the role he played in the evolution of medieval spirituality. Though he cannot be called a mystic in the sense that Bernard of Clairvaux, or William of Saint-Thierry, or even John of Fécamp can, his *Prayers and Meditations*, mostly composed in his earlier monastic days, marked a turning point in the development of devotional prayer that was of importance for later medieval mysticism.[31] His two famous treatises on God, the *Monologion* (1076) and *Proslogion* (completed

1078–79), straddle the border between speculative and mystical theology in a way that subsequent scholastic differentiation of theological tasks made increasingly difficult to achieve. The former he described as "a meditation on the meaning of faith"; the latter he says was written "from the point of view of someone trying to raise his mind to the contemplation of God, and seeking to understand what he believes."[32] Though the famous "ontological" argument for the existence of God found in *Proslogion* 2–4 has attracted the attention of centuries of theological and philosophical analysis, we must not forget that the argument is framed by one of the most powerful of the saint's meditations. In the words of Benedicta Ward, it is "the longest and most subtle of Anselm's prayers."[33]

Essential Themes of Monastic Mysticism

Saint Rudesindus was a tenth-century Spanish bishop who entered the monastic life after being forced out of his see. The description of his early days in the monastery found in his *Vita*, though twelfth century in origin, provides an excellent window on the essential themes of medieval monastic mysticism: "In these times the holy man Rudesindus gave himself completely to solitude, to prayer and to contemplation to such an extent that he would pray the whole night through."[34] *Solitudo*, of course, demands silence (*silentium*); prayer, or *oratio*, as the monks always insisted, is the fruit of the form of spiritual reading called *lectio divina*, just as *contemplatio* flows from *meditatio*. Making use of this succinct summary of monastic spirituality, I will analyze the mystical elements in early medieval monasticism through a consideration of three pairs of related terms essential to the life and practice of the monks and nuns of the time: *solitudo/silentium; lectio/meditatio; oratio/contemplatio*. Each pair implies the others. Though I will consider them separately here, they were never divided in real life. As Jean Leclercq put it: "The words . . . *oratio, lectio, meditatio*, etc., designate the activities and spiritual attitudes that together constituted 'contemplative prayer.'"[35]

Solitudo/Silentium

Solitude as the monks understood it depended on separation from the world. All Christians were called to "flight from the world" (*fuga mundi*), at least in the sense of abandoning "worldly" values and undertaking minimal ascetic practices; but in the early Middle Ages true separation was thought to be possible only within the monastic life.[36] The purpose of external separation, of course, was always to facilitate the internal separation from sin. Toward the end of the RB, in discussing "The Good Zeal of Monks," Benedict put it thus: "Just as there is a wicked zeal of bitterness which separates from God and leads to hell, so there is a good zeal which separates from evil and leads to God and everlasting life."[37] Most monastics doubted that this "good zeal" could be fully achieved while still in the world.

Medieval monks and nuns therefore believed that the heights of Christian perfection (barring possible miraculous exceptions) were attainable only within the monastery.[38] The monastery was the true "paradise" in which the ravages caused by the fall might be overcome.[39] Peter Damian in his *Life of Saint Romuald* praised the holy man for never being content with the number of monastic houses he founded, "so that you would think that he wanted to convert the whole world into a hermitage and to join every mass of people to the monastic life."[40] This insistence on the superiority of monasticism, though understandable within its historical context, was one of the less happy contributions of the monastic layer to the history of Christian mysticism, and one that was to be criticized, directly and indirectly, from the thirteenth century on. Such elitism did not mean that monastic thinkers denied that non-monastics could be saved, nor did it indicate that there were not important traditions of lay piety to be found in the early medieval period.[41] Since human imagination could put no limits on God's power, it did not rule out the possibility of miracles of grace, such as the tenth-century saint, Ida of Herfeld, whose life (written by the monk Uffing) praises her for being internally inflamed with a love for heavenly things even during the act of sexual intercourse with her equally devout husband.[42] But the fact remains that the triumph of monasticism during this time generally served to restrict the mystical element in Christianity to those who had separated themselves from the world and devoted their lives to the asceticism, poverty, and continence of the *ordo monasticus*. Cassian, not Ambrose or Augustine, had won the day.[43]

Separation from the world was the mark of all varieties of monasticism, but especially of the eremitic ideal. In eremitism separation became a more rigorous solitude, the kind of *solitudo* that was thought to facilitate direct contact with God. The emphasis on meeting God in solitude, strong in the classics of early monasticism that were eagerly read in the Middle Ages, did much to qualify Benedict's preference for the coenobitical life. The strength of the eremitical ideal in the early medieval period can be seen not only in Celtic monasticism but also in such texts as Grimlac's *Rule for Solitaries* (ca. 900 C.E.), the earliest such document in the West. The eleventh-century revival noted above gave eremitism an even more significant role.

Praise of solitude reverberates throughout the monastic texts of the time. For example, the ninth-century *Life* of St. Pol, the sixth-century apostle of

Britanny (*Vita Sancti Pauli Episcopi Leonensis*), speaks of the young Pol conceiving his desire to become a hermit while lying awake one night:

> This thought fixed itself in his mind that he should make his way into the depths of the desert and there, hidden from worldly life and known to God alone, lead a first-rate life of piety and purity. The further removed he would be from worldly people, the more he would deserve to be closer to God and his angels through *theoria* alone, that is, divine contemplation.[44]

Early in the eleventh century, Bruno of Querfort's *Life of the Five Brethren* described the three advantages of the coenobitical-eremitical monastery the emperor Otto III wished to have Romuald and his followers found on the Slavic frontier in the following terms: It will provide "a desirable monastery for those who have just left the world, a golden solitude (*aurea solitudo*) for the mature who seek the living God, and a gospel of the pagans for those who seek to be dissolved and be with Christ" [i.e., those desiring martyrdom].[45]

Stress on *solitudo* as the best context for the cultivation of contemplative prayer was particularly strong in the eleventh century. In his treatise *The Perfection of Monks*, which includes a defense of the eremitical life as the highest form of monasticism, Peter Damian speaks of the monk as one who "searches for and takes pleasure in remote and lonely places; as far as he can, he avoids all human contact, so that he may the more easily stand in the presence of his Creator."[46] In the chapter on the praise of the eremitical life found in his treatise *The Book Entitled "The Lord be with You"*), Damian went further in his treatment of the connection between the solitary life of hermits and the experience of contemplation. Here he pulled out all the stops in his well-provided rhetorical organ in a performance that demonstrates mastery of the heightened style that often marked the humanistic taste of monastic culture, however ascetic and world-denying it remained. Amid a plethora of images, scriptural and natural, of the superiority of the solitary life, Damian cites Jeremiah's Lamentations (Lam 3:27–28: "It is good for a man to have borne the yoke from his adolescence; he will sit down as a solitary and will be silent because he will lift himself above himself") as a description of the ecstatic prayer to which the eremitical life is directed. "The person who dwells in you has 'lifted himself above himself,' because the soul that thirsts for God has raised himself beyond the view of terrestrial things, and, having elevated himself to the summit of contemplation, is cut off from worldly activities and hovers on high with wings of celestial desire."[47] Peter's encomium for a solitude that was no longer his, however, was also important because it held out the hope that undiminished love of solitude among those who could no longer fully enjoy it still allowed some access to the experience of God for busy monastic leaders: "Whoever makes an effort to persevere in desirous love of you, he is the 'person who dwells in you' and the one who dwells in him is God."[48]

A more intimate invocation of the necessity for solitude can be found in John of Fécamp's *Lament over Lost Leisure and Solitude*. John addresses *solitudo* as his lost bride in highly erotic terms, stronger even than those that Francis of Assisi was later to use to his Lady Poverty:

> O chaste and pure Solitude, seat of peace and repose, rejoicing in familiarity with God, so long sought and finally found! Who has stolen you away from me, my beloved? Once I embraced you with both arms and happily breathed in your very pure kiss with my soul stretched out. I used to rejoice at all times in your good things and I prefered the sweetness of your love to every joy. Who has snatched me in misery from your arms?[49]

John's small work, which recalls Jerome's letters on monasticism and the treatise *The Praise of the Desert* by the fifth-century bishop Eucher of Lyons, contrasts the delights of desert solitude and its flowers and birds with a series of nautical images of the dangerous sea of this world.[50] John concludes with a prayer asking God to free him from the "crowd of brethren" (*frequentia fratrum*) in the monastery, where he daily offends in many ways. "Give me that secret of solitude," he pleads, "and the spiritual leisure of favorable openness to you, as well as purity of heart and rejoicing in mind, so that I may be worthy to love and praise you, as sweetly as possible, perfectly and fittingly all the days of my life."[51] Solitude, at least as an ideal, has rarely received more fervent praise than it did in these early medieval monastic texts. Although the monks described *solitudo* primarily in external terms in relation to the hermit's life, the opening to internal conceptions of solitude found in these eleventh-century writers was to remain a significant part of the western mystical tradition.

Solitude was closely linked to the notion of *competens silentium*, the "fitting silence" that all forms of monasticism, both coenobitical and eremitical, looked upon as necessary for attaining mystical contemplation.[52] Silence is an important practice in many religious traditions. The role of speaking to or about God in the history of Christian thought is especially complicated: Christians claim that God lies beyond all human expression, so that any attempt at naming God seems doomed to failure, but recognition of our creaturely status also impels us to praise him and therefore to name him in some way. This paradox, adumbrated in Augustine (see, e.g., *On Christian Doctrine* 1.6), and developed in a different way in the Dionysian writings, constitutes what we might call the theoretical aspect of silence, that is to say, silence as the ultimate but never sufficient or final goal in attempting to understand the experience of the presence of God. Alongside this theoretical motif, however, we can also recognize the existence of what might be called the practical meaning of silence, that is, the monastic ascetical silence employed as both a remedy for sinful uses of the tongue and also as a necessary component of the vocalized prayer that formed the core of the monastic life. As Paul Gehl reminds us, monastic silence was orthopraxis more than orthodoxy.[53]

This silence was actually a mode of activity–not just a refraining from speaking or undue noise, but a special form of attentiveness to God. Within the monastic context, prayer, silence, and speech were inextricably connected in progressing toward contemplation. Prayer was always to begin in silence, that is, with the silencing of the world and its distractions, in order to turn to God in quiet recollection. It also proceeded through the alternation of sound and silence, like the rhythm of breathing, as psalm verses and interposed pauses succeeded one another. Finally, silence was also part of the goal, insofar as the experience of God that the monastics often spoke of as a *requies* implied both rest and quiet in God. Peter Damian seems to have had all these meanings in mind when he wrote to the empress Agnes, who in her widowhood had retired to a life of withdrawal for prayer and contemplation. Comparing Agnes, now a bride of Christ, to the Jerusalem Temple, which had been built in silence according to 3 Kings 6:7, he said: "While the rumble of human speaking ceases, the temple of the Holy Spirit is being built in you through silence."[54]

Benedict's teaching on silence (which he prefers to call *taciturnitas*) was primarily ascetical in nature.[55] But the developing Benedictine tradition, encouraged by the growing eremitism of early Christendom, drew out the theoretical implications of silence to stress its role as a foundation for what later ages would call mystical experience.[56] Gregory the Great had a rich teaching on the need for silence, especially in his *Moralia*.[57] Early medieval commentators on the RB, such as Smaragdus, began to give silence a more central role than it occupies in Benedict himself;[58] but once again it was in the eleventh century that silence received some of its most intensive consideration. John of Fécamp, Peter Damian, Anselm, and others all dwelt on it.

Peter Damian's affection for silence is evident throughout his writings.[59] John of Fécamp, following Augustine, spoke of God as "truly unsayable."[60] Like the bishop of Hippo, however, he also poured out a flood of prayer to encourage the meditative reader in a loving pursuit of Christ designed to lead "to flying away, to being silent, to being at rest, and saying: 'Who will give me the wings of a dove, that I might fly away and be at rest'" (Ps 54:7).[61] The type of prayer pioneered by John and taken up by Anselm of Canterbury was designed to lead to this form of silent rest in God.[62]

Lectio/Meditatio

Solitude and silence formed the context within which the life devoted to reading and meditation—*lectio* and *meditatio*—became a real possibility. These terms had a special range of meaning within early medieval monastic culture, one that must be now explored in order to understand monastic mysticism.

The medieval monastic practice of reading was different from what we understand reading to be today. Although silent reading was known, the common practice was an acoustical reading, that is, a reading aloud (even if quietly) within which a slow and careful speaking and hearing required the involvement of the whole person.[63] Such reading implied the accompaniment of pauses for silent reflection and for absorption of the content of the text. (Think of it as the opposite of the modern infatuation with "speed reading.") Reading in this way was not essentially different from the chanting of the office (in which silent pauses between verses were also important), or from the dictation that was the common form of composition at this time. This style of literacy was the foundation for the "aural character" of monastic culture so well described in Leclercq's *Love of Learning and the Desire for God.*

Not every kind of reading was directly connected to prayer and contemplation. Here the technical term *lectio divina*, already encountered in chapter 1, must be investigated in more detail.[64] Cassian did not speak of *lectio divina*, but his advice about the necessity of reading the Bible, especially in *Conferences* 14.9–11 (where the term *sacra lectio* does occur) and *Institutes* 11.16, was one foundation for the essential role that *lectio divina* later played. Benedict's *Rule*, as we have seen, did explicitly make *lectio divina* a part of his monastic plan: "Idleness is the enemy of the soul. Therefore, the brothers should have specified periods for manual labor as well as for prayerful reading" (*lectio divina*).[65] Gregory the Great's form of moral-mystical reading of the scriptural text, especially as set forth in the *Moralia*, was also important in providing an illustration of what *lectio divina* was supposed to be.[66]

One might easily conceive the practice of *lectio divina*—that is, prayerful, slow, and audible reading of scripture and of other classic sacred texts—as a purely private exercise. This, once again, would be a modern misunderstanding of the medieval cultural and religious ambience.[67] *Lectio divina* for the medieval monk and nun was always meant to be in harmony with the communal prayer of the whole church, the Body of Christ. It was not a higher form, or substitute for, liturgical observance; rather, it was the opportunity for the individual to implement in his of her life a personal consciousness of the inner (i.e., "mystical" in the medieval sense) meaning of the corporate prayer of the Christ's Bride, the church, performed seven times each day in the *opus Dei.*

The relation between communal prayer and personal prayer raised questions during the renewed fervor for the hermit life in the eleventh century, as Peter Damian's treatise *The Book of "The Lord be with You"* demonstrates. The question addressed by this work may seem strange today: Can hermits make use of traditional plural prayer forms in their devotional life? Peter's response is revealing, and not only because the treatise provides one of the early adaptations of what was to become the standard late medieval understanding of the meaning of the "mystical body of Christ" (*corpus Christi mysticum*). For most of the patristic period Christ's mystical (i.e., "hidden") body was the Eucharist. This meaning began to shift in the eleventh century, as the *corpus mysticum* was identified more and more with the church. Damian used this developing theological motif to show that even the isolated hermit is always praying in and for the the whole church:

> Therefore let no brother who lives alone in a cell be afraid to utter the words which are common to the whole church; for although he is separated from the congregation of the faithful yet he is bound together with them all by love in the unity of the faith; although they are absent in the flesh, they are near at hand in the mystical unity of the church.[68]

While his argument for the ecclesial significance of all prayer is new, no medieval monk would ever have thought that what was later called "private prayer" or "spiritual reading" was something meant to benefit only the individual. *Lectio divina* was created within the community of the monastery and the wider community of the church and is only understandable within that context, however much the ideal was or was not realized in real life.

Although *lectio divina* could include other types of spiritual texts, its primary focus was always the Bible. Monastic culture—indeed, the whole culture of early Christendom, as pointed out in chapter 1—was a biblical culture. The use of the Bible within *lectio divina*, however, was a special one, different from its employment in other cultural contexts because of its linking of the act of meditative reading and the experience of contemplation. Gregory the Great's emphasis on the way in which "the divine words grow along with the reader" (*divina eloquia cum legente crescunt*), that is, the creative mutuality between text and reader due to the presence of the Holy Spirit in each, made him the master of *lectio divina*, as Benedetto Calati has shown.[69] In this, to be sure, the modern author is only echoing the praise showered on the pope by medieval monks, like Peter Damian in his hymn to Gregory:

Scripturae sacrae mystica	You unravel the mystical puzzles
Mire solvis aenigmata,	Of Scripture most marvellously,
Theorica mysteria	Truth Himself teaches you
Te docet ipsa Veritas.	Contemplative mysteries.[70]

In the third chapter of his *Crown of Monks,* Smaragdus of St. Mihiel supplies us with a summary of how the early medieval monk understood the role of *lectio.* His account is typical of early medieval writings: it is a catena of quotations from Isidore of Seville and Gregory the Great. This is the way in which the mystical elements of medieval monasticism were often passed on to posterity, that is, through citation of authorities in handbook or encyclopedic format. Smaragdus begins by quoting the famous adage: "When we pray, we speak to God; when we read, God speaks to us. Every advance comes from reading and meditation."[71] In discussing the dual object of reading—that is, how to understand scripture and how to make it useful to our lives—he uses the same passage from Gregory's *Homilies on Ezekiel* cited above to show that the two tasks are one: We make progress in understanding scripture to the extent that we are advancing in love of God. The highest level in this itinerary can be described as mystical, a stage he explains in language drawn from the Gregorian text:

> It often happens that someone can grasp that the words of sacred scripture are mystical if that person himself, enflamed by the grace of heavenly contemplation, hangs upon things celestial. The marvelous and inexpressible power of the sacred text is acknowledged when the reader's intellectual soul is penetrated by love from on high.[72]

Even texts such as John of Fécamp's *Theological Confession* and its siblings, which were intended to serve as forms of *lectio divina* themselves, testify to the central position of the Bible in the monastic exercise of such reading. John describes scripture as the mirror by which we know ourselves in this life, that is, how we come to recognize our sinfulness and the one way to overcome it—surrender to the all-powerful love of God.[73] In good Augustinian fashion, his text is a dialogue in which God addresses us through the numerous biblical quotations and reminiscences with which this *Confession* abounds; and we in turn respond to him in an artful combination of the human words of the fathers ("My words are the words of the fathers," John says)[74] and our own confession comprising both admission of sin and contemplative praise of the God, who remains "unsayable" (*indicibilis*).

Smaragdus's linking of *lectio* and *meditatio* was standard in the monastic tradition. Benedict himself in RB 48 used the formula "aut . . . meditare aut legere." Here too our modern understanding of "meditation," conditioned by later developments of methodical types of silent prayer and today tinged with the aura of Transcendental Meditation and other such techniques, will be misleading for an understanding of what the monks meant by *meditatio*.[75] *Meditatio*, which translates the Greek *meletē*, was originally used to indicate the repeating of a scriptural text in order to commit it to memory. This process of repetitive absorption was likened to the "chewing the cud" of ruminant animals in early Christian literature, as an allegorical interpretation of Leviticus 11:3 and Deuteronomy 14:6 going back to the early second-century *Epistle of Barnabas* shows.[76] In early monastic writings *meditatio* was often associated with manual labor as well as with reading the Bible, indicating that both activities were seen as compatible with this task of memorization of the scriptures, especially of the Psalms. By the time of Benedict, however, *meditatio/ruminatio* was coming to be more and more associated with *lectio divina*. In the early medieval encyclopedists, such as Isidore of Seville, *meditatio* took on a more internalized significance, however, as when he advises that "what is prayed with the mouth should be meditated in the heart."[77] Many of the major sources of Latin monastic culture, especially Augustine and Caesarius of Arles, also had much to say about *meditatio/ruminatio* as the interiorization of the biblical text.

Though early medieval *meditatio* is impossible to define precisely, we can think of it as a physical exercise of repetition aimed at an internal effect, the personal appropriation of the word of God. For the medieval monk, *meditatio* was the prolongation of *lectio* and at times was scarcely distinguishable from it. *Meditatio* (and its twin, *ruminatio*) began with the slow repetition, often audible, of a portion of the sacred text as an aid for its memorization. Its goal, however, was grasping the meaning of the text so that it might serve as a springboard for contemplative prayer. In other words, *meditatio* was the link between *lectio* and *oratio*,[78] and the term was used so flexibly by the monastic authors that it can be said to partake of both its source and its goal. The monks loved to identify themselves with the "pure" ruminant animals of the Old Testament dietary laws, finding in their day-by-day mastication of the sacred text a key element of life within the monastery.[79] This is what John of Fécamp had in mind when he said, "It is altogether impossible to come to purity of heart save through constant meditation in praise of God."[80]

The meaning of *meditatio* began to shift somewhat in the late eleventh century, as can be seen in the cases of John of Fécamp and Anselm. Both authors composed prayers and "meditations" (John himself did not use the term of his compilations, but it was soon applied to them). Both John and Anselm thought of themselves as providing material for private *lectio divina*, and both of them were deeply influenced by the style of prayer found in Augustine, especially in the *Confessions* and the *Soliloquies*. It was the renewed Augustinian interiority, achieved in different ways by the two authors, that marked their departure from earlier attempts to provide summaries for *lectio divina*, as in the books of prayer (*libelli precum*) of the Carolingian period. Though their intentions were traditional, by fixing a highly intense and personalized form of *lectio-oratio* in a *written* text called a *meditatio* these authors helped initiate an important shift in the meaning of meditation that was to become more evident when some twelfth-century authors began to treat meditation as a distinct stage within a methodical map of prayer and spiritual progress. It will be helpful at this point to analyze one example of a "meditation" from each author in order to flesh out the above claim and to help introduce a consideration of our final pair of themes, that is, *oratio/contemplatio*.

John of Fécamp's lengthy title for his second book of prayers (which contains much reworking of material found in the first version, the *Theological Confession*) tells it all—*The Little Book of Writings and Words of the Fathers for the Use especially of Those who are Lovers of the Contemplative Life*, that is, for monastics. Circulating under the title *The Meditations of Saint Augustine*, the work was very popular. The last "meditation" of the third and final part is one of John's most beautiful and most mystical writings.[81] The prayer begins with an appeal to Christ, "the power and wisdom of the Father," to grant the human lover "swift wings of virtues to raise him up so that he can contemplate things eternal and celestial." A lengthy second section emphasizes the soul's desire for heaven, using a kind of inclusion formula based on two passages expressing longing for heaven through repetitions of "when" (*quando*—"When will I see you? . . . When will I appear? . . . When will you lead me? . . . When will I come?"), which frame a description of the life of the blessed in their eternal enjoyment of God.[82] The third section prays for contact with God in this life, beginning with a citation of the text so often used in western accounts of mystical union, "He who adheres to the Lord is one spirit with him" (1 Cor 6:17). Here John's address shows the influence of Augustine's Ostia vision as the following long quotation demonstrates (Augustinian passages in italics):

> Hold my heart in your hand because without you it is not rapt on high. I hasten there where the highest peace rules and tranquillity always glows. Hold and rule my spirit and lift it up according to your will so that under your lead it may ascend into *that land of fullness where you feed Israel forever with the food of truth.* There *in a flash of thought it may attain you, the highest wisdom that abides above all things,* knowing and ruling them all. But there are many things that block the soul in its flight to you. At your command, O Lord, *let all things be silent to me. Let my soul be silent to me.* Let it pass beyond everything created, even itself, and may it attain you and fix its eyes of faith in you the only Cre-

ator of everything. May it gaze upon you, be attentive to you, meditate upon you, contemplate you, place you before its eyes, and revolve you in its heart— you, the highest and true Good, the Joy abiding forever.[83]

This section concludes with an observation on the superiority of the contemplation of God alone to all other forms of contemplation. The soul can only enjoy this "little foretaste of your sweetness" (*praelibare veleat aliquatenus dulcedinem tuam*) when "it sits solitary and silent, always keeping watch day and night" (*sedet solitarius et tacet, et stat super custodiam suam jugiter nocte et die*–a reminiscence of Lam 3:28 and Isa 21:8).

The final section of the prayer is strongly christological, making use of both devotion to the Passion of Christ, the source of our salvation, and the erotic language of the Song of Songs. John begs for the "wound of love." "O elect arrow and sharpest of swords . . . pierce my heart through with the wound of your love, so that my soul may say, 'I am wounded with charity'" (Song 2:5 in the LXX and Old Latin version).[84] This wound is meant to produce the constant flow of tears, an important element in all Christian piety, but especially among monastics.[85] The resultant increasing desire for God will lead him on "until I may be worthy to see my Beloved, my dearest Spouse, my Lord and God, in the heavenly bridal chamber. . . ." John's prayer is a remarkable example of how the monastic spirituality of the early Middle Ages combined elements drawn from earlier mystical traditions, especially from Origen and Augustine, to serve in new contexts.

To turn to Anselm's famous "Meditation on Human Redemption" (one of three authentic *meditationes* ascribed to him) is to enter into a somewhat different style of prayer.[86] John's meditation was directed to contemplatives; Anselm's is directed to all. John's *meditatio* is a tissue of quotations and reminiscences from both scripture and the fathers; Anselm gives sparse direct citations from the Bible and nothing from the fathers.[87] John's prayer is a mystical text; Anselm's, primarily a meditation on the passion based on his *Cur Deus homo*, though it also represents a transposition of this theology into a different key, a prayful melody that is meant to inspire our gratitude to the Redeemer and to inflame our longing for heaven (in this like John). Unlike John, however, Anselm does not explore the question of what preliminary taste of heavenly joy can be experienced in this life.[88] Anselm begins not by addressing God but by calling on the "Christian soul" to rouse herself from slumber and meditate and contemplate the Passion. The prayer to Christ (beginning "Good Lord, living Redeemer, mighty Savior, why did you conceal such power under humility?") is really a theological consideration of three essential components of Anselm's theory of the redemption: the insufficiency of the traditional "rights of the devil" explanation of redemption; the proper understanding of the satisfaction Christ made for us; and the free obedience with which Christ redeemed us. A brief second address to the soul shifts the tone from doctrine to *meditatio* in the traditional monastic sense, that is, internalization through metaphors of chewing, sucking, and swallowing, set in a eucharistic mode.[89] This sets the stage for the emotive prayer section (ed., 89.137–91.211) that closes the meditation. Here Anselm's personal appropriation of the mystery of redemption is beautifully expressed by teasing out the implications of the paradox that we can rejoice in the sufferings by which Christ has set us free–"see what thanks you should render him, and how much love you owe him" (ed., 89.152). Thanksgiving leads on to a plea for greater experience of love: "Lord, make me taste by love what I taste by knowledge; let me know by love what I know by understanding.... Draw me to you, Lord, in the fullness of love. I am wholly yours by creation; make me all yours, too, in love."[90] Anselm's final petition for increased love (ed., 91.201–11) matches the evocations of the love theme in John of Fécamp, but the context in which the plea appears argues that we should see it more in terms of longing for heaven than as an exploration of the immediate experience of God in this life.

Oratio/Contemplatio

Such meditative prayers, whether we think of them as mystical or not, help us understand the meaning of *oratio* and *contemplatio* in the monastic spirituality of the early Middle Ages. These terms, like *meditatio* itself, are by no means to be thought of as always mystical in the sense of being directly addressed to the consciousness of the immediate presence of God, but in some of their uses at least, monastic *oratio* and *contemplatio* may reflect truly mystical dimensions of Christian experience.

The foundational text for the understanding of prayer among western monks comes from RB 20: "We must know that God regards our purity of heart and tears of compunction, not our many words. Prayer should therefore be short and pure (*brevis debet esse et pura oratio*), unless perhaps it is prolonged under the inspiration of divine grace."[91] The emphasis on brevity means that Benedict conceived of prayer not as the saying of prayers or singing of psalms, but as a relatively short period of silent intimate address to God, the fruit of the practice of *lectio/meditatio* that was institutionalized in the monastery as a silent pause after each psalm in the Divine Office.[92] The "purity" of prayer was a notion that originated with Evagrius Ponticus and that was mediated to Benedict by Cassian. In Evagrius it indicated a formless and a-conceptual direct contact with the Trinity, which Cassian expressed as a "fiery outbreak of the mind through an inexpressible rapture of the heart" by which the "mind pours itself out to God in unspeakable groans and sighs" (*Conferences* 10.11; cf. 9.3).[93] Benedict does not tell us how he understood the term (he may have meant nothing more than that prayer should be undistracted); but his stress on *oratio pura* opened the Benedictine tradition to the mystical dimension found in the earlier monastic sources. Finally, because of the Lord's injunction "to pray unceasingly" (Luke 18:1; cf. 1 Thess 5:17), the qualifier *frequens,* "frequently," was often combined with *brevis* and *pura.* Though some monks took this literally and tried to institute forms of monastic life in which continual recitation of the office took place,[94] the frequency of prayer was generally understood to mean that one should pray as often as possible and *desire* to pray at all times.

The earliest medieval monastic teaching about prayer was conveyed through handbooks of traditional sources.[95] More complete analyses of prayer begin in the Carolingian period, especially in Smaragdus of St. Mihiel's *Crown of Monks.* Jean Leclercq has emphasized Smaragdus's distinction between *oratio* and *contemplatio,* showing how the former term connotes the continuing affective impulse toward God based on reading and meditating the scripture, while *contemplatio* is the goal of the desire, "a kind of beginning ... of the joys of eternity."[96] To put it in Smaragdus's own words (which are often modeled on those of Gregory the Great): "The person who seeks to mortify himself greatly rejoices when the rest of contemplation is found. As one dead, he is hidden from the world. With every disturbance of the external world put to sleep, he can plunge into the bosom of secret love."[97] While it would be erroneous to try to reduce the early medieval language about prayer to any consistent system, we can say, following the lead of Gregory the Great, that the monks used *contemplatio* and its equivalents as the central term to point to those moments in prayer when some form of more direct contact with God was attained.

Part of the difficulty in dealing with this mystical dimension of medieval monastic life is the range of vocabulary the monks used to express it. Two basic linguistic fields interacted in a complex and rich way in the early medieval monastic writings. The first was Greek and philosophical in origin and comprised the terms *contemplatio* itself, as well as its equivalents, *theoria* and *speculatio,* and even *theologia.*[98] A whole assembly of biblical words whose root meanings center on the notion of resting in God—*quies, otium, vacatio, sabbatum*—constitute the second linguistic field. These terms were often employed synonymously with *contemplatio* and its cognates, though each word also has its own semantic resonance.[99] Occasional definitions of *contemplatio* and the *vita contemplativa* are framed, as might be expected, in terms of the vision of God and are usually very general, as when Rabanus

Maurus says that "the pure contemplative life thirsts only for the vision of the Principle."[100] Early medieval teaching on contemplation is primarily practical, not speculative; traditional, not innovative.

Like Gregory the Great, the monks situated *contemplatio* within the total development of salvation history. Adam had been created to contemplate God but had lost his ability to fulfill this end through sin.[101] Christ's redemptive action restored contemplation to humanity, but more as an object of desire than as any kind of stable achievement in this life. Jean Leclercq has rightly emphasized the fundamentally eschatological character of early medieval understandings of *contemplatio,* that is, the sense that contemplation consists not so much in the actual enjoyment of the vision of God here below as in the unceasing desire for reaching the full *visio Dei* in heaven. Peter Damian spoke for the tradition when he said, "The whole aim of one seeking God is to hope for, to aim for, some day reaching rest, and in the joy of supreme contemplation to repose as in the embrace of lovely Rachel. It is like climbing, through the word that is heard, to sight of the Principle that is sought."[102]

Early medieval monastic contemplation is best understood, then, as the "contemplation of desire."[103] Ambrose Autpert expressed this priority of love and desire well in the prayer with which he ended his *Commentary on the Apocalypse*: "When we seek to investigate you, we do not discover you as you are; you are apprehended when you are loved."[104] The priority of love did not mean that the other powers of the soul were not involved in seeking heaven. At the end of his *Theological Confession* John of Fécamp summarized that best form of contemplation in which the mind "is lifted up to the simple gaze of the pure heart in God alone." In this experience, as he puts it, "the heart burns, the intellectual soul rejoices, the memory grows strong, the intellect shines, and the whole spirit is lit up by the desire of the vision of your Beauty and sees itself rapt into the love of things invisible."[105]

Thus the fundamental aim of monastic spirituality was not so much to strive to enjoy what later ages would call mystical experience here below as to encourage *contemplatio* understood as burning desire for heaven. Nevertheless, the monks did not exclude the possibility of some share or foretaste in this life of the real *contemplatio* of heaven, though few of them before the eleventh century spent time analyzing what this might be like, especially because they could read about it in Augustine and Gregory. Like their patristic forebears, the monks emphasized the brevity of the experience of God made necessary by the weakness of the fallen condition which would "beat back" (*reverberare*) every attempt to fly too high or for too long. Peter Damian has a telling image, comparing the contemplative to the flying fish that occasionally manages to soar a bit in the air, but always falls back into the sea of this mortal and sinful life.[106] Like Augustine and Gregory, the monastics stressed the profundity of the gap between the vision of God in heaven and any brief contemplative experience that might be attained in this life.

A typical discussion can be found in Rabanus Maurus, in his treatise dealing with the goal of human life and the way to attain it entitled *Seeing God, Purity of Heart, and the Manner of Penance.* The ninth century saw a revival of an issue once discussed by Augustine: whether or not the elect will see God with corporeal eyes after the resurrection of the body.[107] The monk Candidus (also called Wizo) penned a brief tract about 800 affirming that Christ did not see God with corporeal eyes but that his human soul had enjoyed the beatific vision from the first moment of the Incarnation.[108] This work was the first of a number of discussions of the beatific vision during the century. About 845 Rabanus reaffirmed Augustine's teaching in his *Seeing God,* emphasizing the impossibility of all corporeal vision of God in this life. He added to this a second book, *Purity of Heart,* partly a pastiche of the first of Cassian's *Conferences,* in which he identified the purity of heart that leads to vision with charity. The primary aspect of charity, of course, is contemplative love of God, which Rabanus praises as the evangelical "pearl" (see Matt 13:46). Even more than his source, however, Rabanus emphasized the impossibility of prolonged contemplation in this life—"No human in this life, with the exception of our Lord and Savior, always kept the natural wandering of the mind so fixed in contemplation of God that he, rapt away by it, never sinned in delight of some worldly thing."[109] This emphasis on the unique position of Christ, typical of the christological piety of the medieval monks, prompted the Carolingian abbot to conclude his treatise with a moving evocation of devotion to the God-man, the Word made flesh, the vision of whose glory is the goal of all our effort: "Therefore our soul, which wishes to draw near to God, should raise itself up from the body and always adhere to that highest Good which is divine, which always exists, which was from the beginning, and which was with God, that is, the Word of God."[110]

In the eleventh century, especially in the writings of Peter Damian and John of Fécamp, we begin to get more explicit references and discussions of the nature of the contemplative experience possible in this life. Peter Damian, for example, portrays Romuald as enjoying special experiences of God's presence,[111] and, speaking of his days at his beloved hermitage at Fonte Avellana, he says:

> I often beheld, by an immediate perception of my mind, Christ hanging from the cross, fastened with nails, and I thirstily received his dripping blood in my

mouth. But if I were to attempt to tell you of the heights of contemplation that were vouchsafed to me, both of our Redeemer's most sacred humanity and of the indescribable glory of heaven, the day would be at an end before I finished.[112]

This form of Christ-mysticism anticipates much to come in the later Middle Ages.[113]

John of Fécamp provides more extensive treatment of the mystical side of the monastic understanding of *contemplatio*. In the manner of his major patristic sources, John does not speak autobiographically; but an analysis of his "Letter to a Nun" will show that he provides some of the most detailed discussions of the mystical life found in the early Middle Ages. The letter begins by quoting the opening verse of the Song of Songs, saying of the "kiss of the mouth":

> You who seek the kiss of divine truth in most happy love, be open and see that the Lord is sweet (Ps 45:11). This desire is not human, but belongs only to those spouses who love God chastely. If you feel that you are inflamed to divine love by all the words of sacred scripture, especially and most easily by those concerning the vision of God, you should not doubt that you are called "bride."[114]

Although John of Fécamp and Peter Damian did not use the Song of Songs as often as the Cistercian mystics of the following century did, their employment of the Song to describe the relation of the loving soul to the Divine Bridegroom shows that the mystical use of the Bible's great love poem, begun with Origen, experienced a revival in the eleventh century that presaged the return of this book to a central role in western mysticism.[115] This is also evident in contemporary mystical love poems to Christ, as we shall see below.

John's brief text begins with a description of the virtues and ascetical practices necessary for the soul who wishes to be a bride of the Word (*sponsa Verbi*). John is sending her this "little book of excerpts" (*opusculum deflorationis*) filled with "sweet words of heavenly contemplation" (*caelestis theoriae dulcia verba*) for reading and meditation–"Read these words frequently, especially when you see your mind enkindled with heavenly desire, for it is right that one who is well trained in the active life should take up the wings of contemplation."[116] The message is brief, but to the point. First, he describes mystical vision in a concise fashion, using a lapidary phrase later quoted by Bernard of Clairvaux. Although the unchangable essence of God can never be seen by humans, to those who love him fervently,

. . . he now and then allows his very self to be seen suddenly in a spiritual way, but not as he is, which we await in the future. Alas, this present glimpse, although most sweet, is rare and brief; but so excellent is the vision that the soul who is filled with it is completely drawn away from every earthly desire as far as humanly possible.[117]

A soul who has experienced this is the true light and inspiration of the community in which she lives. Borrowing phrases from one of Gregory the Great's treatises on contemplation (*Moralia* 5.33.57–34.62), John emphasizes how the *reverberatio* experience, while painful, increases the soul's desire for God. The brief treatise closes with an important discussion of three kinds of seekers of God. First, the "less proficient who construct an imaginary God for themselves . . . and do not know how to contemplate the wonderful un-circumscribed light in an intellectual way."[118] They are advised to remain with the practice of the active life of asceticism and the cultivation of virtue and not to aspire to the mountain of contemplation. The second group contains true contemplatives who are so given over to "the exercises of the spiritual life" (*spiritalis vitae exercitiis*) that the active life disgusts them. The strongest souls, however, as Gregory the Great had shown, are those who can combine the lives of both Martha and Mary, which is what John advises for the nun to whom he directed his treatise: "Having been made like a winged animal, may you advance in each life every day."[119]

There are few if any descriptions of an itinerary of the path to mystical contemplation from the early Middle Ages. Here too the situation began to change in the eleventh century, at least in the case of Peter Damian. In his work *The Perfection of Monks*, Peter briefly provided an interesting variation on the triple patterns of progress that had been initiated in the patristic period and were to become dominant in the later Middle Ages.[120] Damian experimented with a number of other itineraries. The hermit's Sermon 28 interpreted the waters flowing out of the Temple in Ezekiel's vision (Ezek 47:1–6) as an image of the gradual increase of divine wisdom in the life of St. Alexis, first to the ankles (the desire for rectitude), then to the knees (the life of good works), and on to the hips (the extinction of carnal desire), and finally to the fullness of contemplation, the overwhelming flood that cannot be plumbed in this life or the next.[121] Damian's letter-treatise on the Sabbath (Letter 2.5) uses the six days of creation as a model for the advance in virtue that leads to the soul achieving the status of a paradisiacal sabbath in which God comes to dwell in it.[122] However, the cardinal's most interesting effort in this connection (one that does not seem to have had any progeny) is to be found in his tract entitled *Lent and the Forty-Two Stations of the Hebrews*.[123] This text is unusual among medieval sketches of spiritual progress in being an original reconceiving of one of the oldest of such Christian itineraries, Origen's *Homily 27 on Numbers.*[124] As in Origen's itinerary, Damian's stations on the path to God, based on etymologies of the Hebrew names, include both ascetical and more properly mystical aspects; also as in Origen's work, the path is eminently christological.[125] The hermit's linking of the soul's advance to the Lenten experience so central to medieval piety promised more than it could deliver—an itinerary based on such ingenious interpretation of so many stages was too complex to become popular. Still, Damian's creative use of an early Christian model indicates, once again, that the second half of the eleventh century was beginning to put new wine in old wineskins in its attempts to express mystical teaching.

One final indication of these developments can be found in two late eleventh-century Latin poems that use the language of the Song of Songs to express the contemplative soul's experience of the Divine Lover in new ways. In the following century, the Song was to become the subject for memorable mystical commentaries. These mystical poems are fleeting witnesses to how monastic women and men were already beginning to channel the powers of eros into their attempts to achieve a union beyond human congress.

The poem that begins "Who is this who knocks at the door?" has been ascribed to Peter Damian, but it is not found in the early authentic lists of his writings. Anyone who has read the Latin love lyrics of the early Middle Ages, whose ambiguous simplicity and directness, sometimes tender, sometimes sexually direct, mask hidden depths of sophisticated knowledge of poetry profane and sacred, will still be surprised at how this poem and the related "Sequence on the Virgins" manage to achieve a fusion of the Latin culture created by Christendom, rooted in both the Bible and the Latin classics, and the new spiritual tendencies that were to erupt in the following century. Once again, the poets acted as prophets of what was to come.

This "Quis est hic qui pulsat ad ostium?" uses the familiar intimate encounter described in Song of Songs 5:2–7 between the soul-bride on her bed and the Divine Lover, who seeks to gain entry but then disappears. Now, however, the images of the sacred text have been appropriated in a direct personal way so that the poem may be said to represent the fruit of the encounter that the *lectio* and *meditatio* of the sacred text was intended to educe. The first two stanzas present the initial dialogue, as the soul asks "Who is this who knocks at the door?" and the Divine Bridegroom responds first by praising the bride and then announcing himself as "the Son of the Highest King." The final three stanzas describe the soul's hastening desire to open the door to love and her sorrow at the brevity and incompleteness of the encounter (*rara est hora et parva mora*, as John of Fécamp put it):

Mox ego dereliqui lectulum,	At once I rose from my bed,
cucurri ad pessulum:	ran to lift the latch,
ut dilecto tota domus pateat,	so that my whole house might be open to my lover,
et mens mea plenissime videat	and my mind see in all fullness
quem videre maxime desiderat.	him whom I most longed to see.
At ille iam inde transierat,	But he had already gone!
ostium reliquerat.	He had left the gate.
quid ergo, miserrima, quid facerem?	What could I do then, in my misery?[126]

Also from the late eleventh century comes the "Sequence on the Virgins," an even more remarkable evocation of erotic language to describe the encounter with God.[127] The praise of the "happy nuptials" (*O felices nuptie*), in which Christ sleeps with his virgins in "sweet repose" (*requies dulcis*), recalls the language of the Song of Songs (see Song 1:15; 2:6; and 5:2), but as retold with a richness and effervescence that Peter Dronke judges "is unpredictable and cannot be accounted for in terms of known sources."

Dormit in istis	In these beds
Christus cum illis:	Christ sleeps with them:
felix hic somnus,	Happy the sleep,
requies dulcis,	Sweet the rest,
quo, cum fovetur	In which, when she is cherished,
virgo fidelis	The loyal maiden,
inter amplexus	Within the embraces
sponsi celestis,	Of the heavenly Bridegroom,
Dextera sponsi—	With his right arm
sponsa—complexa,	Embracing her as a bride,
capiti leva	His left arm under her head,
dormit submissa:	She falls asleep.
pervigil corde,	Wakeful in heart,
corpore dormit	In body she sleeps,
et sponsi grato	On the Bridegroom's loving
sinu quiescit.	Breast she slumbers.[128]

This kind of recasting of the language of the Song of Songs is not unknown, but the subsequent description of the love-play between Christ the Lamb and the virgin souls is unique:

Crebro saltus	Often the Lamb
dat hic agnus,	Leaps and prances,
inter illa discurrendo,	Bounding in their midst,
Et cum ipsis	Yet with the maidens
requiescit	He rests
fervore meridiano.	In the noonday heat.
In earum pectore	Upon their bosom
cubat in meridie:	He lies at mid-day,
Inter mammas virginum	Between their breasts
collocat cubiculum.	He sets his sleeping-place.[129]

To close on this erotic note may be misleading. The monastic piety of the early Middle Ages was not all that much concerned with the erotic use of the Song of Songs. It was primarily interested in offering faithful witness to a tradition that had once been open, or at least more accessible, to the whole community of believers, but which, because of the circumstances of these difficult centuries, had become increasingly directed to a monastic audience. Many aspects of this effort of *traditio*, such as the oft-repeated considerations of the relation of action and contemplation, add nothing to what we have already seen in our treatment of Gregory the Great.[130] Other aspects, as I have tried to point out, were more original. Still, a glance at these monastic authors, especially the earlier figures such Ambrose Autpert, Smaragdus, Rabanus, and Odilo, might seem to lead to the conclusion that these centuries had little to offer to the western mystical tradition. Even in the case of writers such as Peter Damian and John of Fécamp, some might suggest that what they have to present does not weigh heavily in the light of the riches of the mystical literature of the twelfth century. However, with Jean Leclercq, I would argue that the basic substratum of all later western mysticism, though formed by the Latin Fathers, especially Augustine and Gregory, cannot be adequately understood unless these simple and sometimes pedestrian early medieval texts have been studied and appreciated.

PART II

*The Mysticism
of the Twelfth Century*

Introduction
The Ordering of Charity

Ordinavit in me caritatem (Song 2:4).
He has ordered charity in me.

THE TWELFTH CENTURY marked a new departure in the history of Latin Christianity, though there is little consensus on the best way to present exactly what that departure might be. Modern historical categories for characterizing the remarkable changes of the period began with the creation of the term "the twelfth-century Renaissance" in the 1840s,[1] and they have included a variety of sonorous, if often vague and platitudinous, descriptions over the past century and a half, invoking the concepts of creativity, variety, openness, humanism, individualism, interiorization, and the like.[2] Even the chronological parameters of twelfth-century culture are fluid, since many investigators would see it beginning in the late eleventh century, perhaps with Gregory VII, and might conclude it as late as 1215 with Innocent III's great reforming council known to history as Lateran IV.[3]

Twelfth-century religious leaders preferred the vocabulary of reform (*reformatio*) and renewal (*renovatio*) for their own efforts to improve themselves and the world around them. Writing to the emperor Henry IV at the beginning of the struggle known as the Investiture Controversy or Great Reform, Gregory VII complained that "the order of the Christian religion had long been disturbed and its chief and proper function, the redemption of souls, had fallen low." He declared that he had "returned to the teaching of the holy fathers, declaring no novelties nor any inventions of our own, but holding that the primary and only rule of discipline and the well-trodden way of the saints should again be sought and followed."[4] However much Gregory's policies in pursuit of what he called the *libertas ecclesiae* (e.g., *Reg.* 4.3, 9.3) combined innovation and tradition, it was under the banner of a return to true order and not under that of new departure that religious change was effected at the time.

The same was true with regard to changes in the religious life.[5] Gregory's successor, Urban II, sent a letter of commendation to a group of Bavarian canons in which he proclaimed: "We give thanks to Almighty God . . . that you have renewed a life so deserving of the approval of the holy fathers and practices of apostolic rule that came from the beginnings of the Church."[6] In a similar vein the *Exordium Parvum*, the account of the beginnings of the Cistercian order, notes the intention of the first monks of Cîteaux "to adhere henceforth more strictly and more perfectly to the Rule of the blessed Benedict."[7] The themes of renewal and reform embraced the whole life of the church. The Premonstratensian canon Anselm of Havelberg, writing in the 1140s, made use of the image from Psalm 102:5 of the eagle renewing itself: "Holy Church, passing through different stages that succeed each other little by little down to the present day, like the eagle's youth is renewed and always will be renewed."[8] Roughly a decade before, Bernard of Clairvaux insisted on the other pole of the process of reform and renewal—all reform must serve the personal renewal that brings us closer to Christ: "We are reformed by Christ into the spirit of freedom" (*reformamur per Christum in spiritum libertatis*), as he put with conciseness.[9] The notion of reform and its equivalents, then, is both more original and more useful as a general category for understanding twelfth-century religious culture than concepts such as renaissance.[10]

The reform movement that provided the broad context for twelfth-century mysticism began in Rome about the middle of the eleventh century, when a group of important clergy initiated a series of efforts to rid the church of perceived abuses, especially simony—that is, the buying and selling of church offices—and what was called "nicolaism," understood as clerical marriage and concubinage. Spearheaded by the monk Hildebrand, the future Gregory VII, the reformers also came to attack lay investiture, the practice whereby secular rulers invested ecclesiastical leaders with the symbols of their office. (This had become widespread in the early medieval world, where rulers depended on the loyalty of powerful bishops and abbots.) This move to purify the church from secular domination, as Karl F. Morrison has shown, rested on two fundamental principles that became clear as time went on: sacerdotalism, that is, the supremacy of the priesthood over the laity in Christian society, and papal monarchy, the insistence that "the unity of the Church consisted in the principate of Peter."[11] The Gregorian Reform, as it has been called, was only partly successful. Though it established the papacy as the central office of Latin Christianity in a more powerful way than ever before, making the popes chief lawgivers, judges, and, more importantly, the arbiters of all future reform movements until the Reformation of the sixteenth century, and although it confirmed the position of the clergy in a more organized legal fashion than hitherto, politically the reformers had to settle for a compromise with secular rulers, a solution that many have seen as the beginning of the possibility of the creation of "secular" states in a new form of *Christianitas,* where more careful distinctions between sacred and secular were possible than in the undifferentiated world of the early Middle Ages.[12] How much success the reformers had in improving the life of the clergy is difficult to measure. Some improvement seems hard to deny, at least of the more flagrant abuses; but in creating the ideal of a truly spiritual clergy that, not surprisingly, was never really fulfilled, the reformers sowed the seeds for greater discontent with unworthy priests on the part of the zealous. This was a factor in the rise of quasi-Donatist popular heresies in the twelfth century that eventually rejected both Gregorian sacerdotalism and papal monarchy in the pursuit of sectarian purity.[13]

The general climate of reform encouraged monastic reform movements, both eremitical and coenobitical. (Many of the papal reformers came from such monastic backgrounds.) The twelfth-century popes were strong supporters of the new orders, especially the Cistercians. Toward the end of the eleventh century, the popes also began to encourage the revival of a more effective canonical life. Regular canons, that is, priests living in community under a rule that required personal poverty, had been known since the origins of Latin monasticism. They generally followed the *Rule* ascribed to Augustine. A revival and reorganization of the canonical life had been attempted in Carolingian times, but this did not have lasting effect. Though the variety of the different groups of canons makes it hard to generalize about their life and piety (they were also deeply influenced by Benedictine monasticism), the role of the canons in pastoral activity, preaching, and writing gave them considerable importance in twelfth-century religious life.[14] In the case of the canonical house founded outside Paris at St. Victor in 1108, the movement made a major contribution to the history of mysticism (see chapter 9).

Nor can the laity can be excluded from the swell of reform that overtook the church in the late eleventh century and grew stronger through the course of the twelfth. Pope Gregory VII himself appealed to pious lay groups, such as the "Pataria" of Milan, in his fight against entrenched and unreformed clerical interests. The fiery pope had dreamed of himself leading an expedition of the warriors of Latin Christianity to the East to restore unity with the Eastern church and to reconquer Jerusalem from the Muslims (*Reg.* 1.46, 2.31). His successor, Urban II, launched the First Crusade in 1096, a potent form of lay piety that fused penitential pilgrimage and holy war in the service of the new conception of papal monarchy.[15] Less ambiguous forms of lay piety developed in the twelfth century among those who became fixated on two key religious values that came more and more to the fore in the religious life of Christendom—*vita apostolica* (the apostolic life) and *paupertas vitae* (poverty of life).[16]

A large literature exists on these issues, but the account found in Marie-Dominique Chenu's *La théologie au douzième siècle* (English translation, *Nature, Man, and Society in the Twelfth Century*) can still provide a good starting place.[17] Chenu's classic work seeks to relate important shifts in twelfth-century theology to wider changes in Western Christianity. The first part deals with more properly intellectual issues, such as the new attitude toward nature as an independent object of study, the revival of concern for understanding salvation history, the diffusion of varying forms of Platonism, and especially the symbolic approach, which governed most theological endeavor before the translation of Aristotle. The second part of Chenu's book suggests that the engine that powered this theological creativity was the desire to implement the living of the gospel in the world: the ideal of the *vita apostolica* that had spread to monks, canons, and even the laity.[18]

What exactly did the term *vita apostolica* imply? Here especially the twelfth century marked a transition in the spiritual ideals of Christendom. The concept of the "apostolic life," that is, living in the manner of Christ's closest followers, the apostles, had been coopted by the monastic movement in the West from at least the early fifth century (see, e.g., Cassian, *Conferences* 18.5). Monks and canons understood the apostolic life as life in a religious community, separated from the world, dedicated to prayer and the sacraments, and aiming at contemplative experience. This form of life presupposed giving up private property, though not the forswearing of institutional wealth. The description of the first Christians in Jerusalem (see Acts 2:41–47, and 4:32–35) were the oft-cited scriptural warrants.

The New Testament, however, contained other pictures of Jesus and his closest followers. During the course of the twelfth century, passages from the Synoptics, especially the description of the missionary journey of the apostles in Luke 10, began to gain favor as accounts of the *vita apostolica*. This understanding of the apostolic life was characterized primarily by poverty of life, itinerant preaching, and (implicitly) by involvement with the world rather than flight from it. Such a conception of the *vita apostolica* became increasingly strong as the century developed.[19] It reached its climax in the formation of new styles of religious life, especially the mendicants and the beguines, whose history (and whose mysticism) belongs properly to the thirteenth century and will therefore be taken up in my next volume.

From the perspective of the dominant monastic layer of mysticism that forms the subject of this volume, it is important to note how the fervor for reform helped shape the mysticism of the period. Twelfth-century religious culture faced two ways: backward toward the patristic and early medieval past, but also forward toward the more complex and differentiated world of the later Middle Ages. The great twelfth-century mystics, especially the Cistercians and Victorines, depended on past masters, especially Augustine and Gregory, but were not enslaved to them. They did more than summarize the past; they brought it to completion. The tradition of monastic mysticism that had been building in the West since the fourth century attained its classic expression in the twelfth-century writers. Through their efforts it was to remain the underlying current, a kind of religious *basso continuo*, of all later Western mysticism.

The analysis of how this was accomplished is the task of the chapters that follow. But the connection between reform and mysticism can, I believe, be helpfully framed by a glance at the role of order and ordering (*ordo* and *ordinatio*) in twelfth-century religion in general and in mysticism in particular. The term *ordo* was among the most semantically complex in the medieval vocabulary. Along with the notions of order as a measure or rule, a political system, a legal framework, a recognizable group or class (e.g., *ordo monasticus*), a discipline, a ceremony, an ecclesiastical office and its duties, etc., *ordo* could be taken in the sense of *ordinatio*, that is, the state that exists when things have been put in their proper relationship.

As R. W. Southern has shown in his *The Making of the Middle Ages*, medieval society of the eleventh and twelfth centuries was avid for order, in this sense of putting things in order, across the whole range of its creative endeavor.[20] The Great Reform movement in the papacy can be seen as essentially a reordering of the fabric of the medieval church and its institutions according to a model of papal monarchy that has remained basic to much Roman Catholicism down to the present. The statebuilders and politicians of the time, especially the able, if not always admirable, Normans, organized better-structured and more efficient political entities that have been seen as marking a new stage in the growth toward the emerging nation state. Ecclesiastical and secular leaders turned increasingly away from oral tradition toward written law to help in the process of ordering society, as the formation of a universal code of canon or church law, the revival of Roman law, and the formation of English common law all demonstrate. The growth of literacy during the eleventh and twelfth centuries, as Brian Stock has shown, produced a new kind of interdependence between oral and written culture and led to the formation of new styles of "textual communities."[21]

New forms of order were evident also in education, both from the institutional and the disciplinary point of view. The twelfth century saw the establishment of the university, the institution that still dominates our educational system, not only in Western culture but also increasingly throughout the world. Within the developing university, theology, the central intellectual discipline of the time, began to undergo a process of ordered differentiation of functions that came to be known as scholasticism. This type of theology differed from the traditional manner of appropriating the scriptures found in the monastic schools with regard to institutional location, employment of resources, genre and method of expression, and even, to some extent, general purpose.[22] If the general aim of the scholastic method concentrated on establishing a new ordering of theological tasks to better achieve the *intellectus fidei*, the famous *credo ut intelligam* (I believe in order to understand) that Augustine had striven for, the monks continued to insist that all theological effort was essentially directed to increasing our love for God – *credo ut experiar* (I believe in order to experience). The conviction that God surpasses all human knowing and therefore can only be attained by love (though not by a love that denies the role of knowing) provides an entry into the motif of the ordering of love (*ordinatio caritatis*), the theme that I will employ to suggest how twelfth-century mysticism brought the tradition it had inherited to completion, yet in a distinctively twelfth-century way.

The ordering of love and charity was scarcely a new theme in the history of Christian mysticism. Origen's exegesis of the Song of Songs had dealt with it;[23] and Augustine, though his explicit references to Song 2:4 are rare, gave the proper ordering of love an important role in his thought.[24] Although it thus possessed deep roots in the tradition, the theme of the ordering of love (or better, the "reordering" in our present fallen state of the love that should have been ours) took on a heightened importance in the twelfth century.[25] It provides a key to unlock what is central and distinctive in the major mystical authors of this rich and richly influential period.

The problem of love has been described as the "great preoccupation" of the thinkers of the twelfth century.[26] Love, sacred and profane, ordered and disordered, rational and irrational, fills the texts, both Latin and vernacular, of the age. The student of medieval literature thinks of the twelfth century as the time of the birth of the ideal of courtly love. The story of the fated love of Heloise and Abelard has remained one of the great romantic tales of the West. In the history of mysticism, the twelfth century is unsurpassed in its exploration of the experience of spousal love of Christ, *Brautmystik* as it is called in German. Bridal mysticism, however, was part of a wider concern for the *ordinatio caritatis*, the effort to energize and harmonize all the powers and relationships of individual believers and the whole body of the church toward the love and enjoyment of God, the true and final goal. To the mystics of the twelfth century, love was not only to be experienced; it was also to be set in order.

The twelfth-century mystics saw the ordering of love not as an attempt to stifle and control love, but as the only way to allow it to develop the fullness of its power and passion. To set charity in order was both a theoretical and a practical task, involving knowing both what needed to be done and how to do it. Thus, the ordering of charity depended on grasping the proper relation between love and knowledge. For the twelfth-century mystics, the experience of love is superior to the acquiring of knowledge: "Instruction makes us learned; experience makes us wise," as Bernard of Clairvaux said.[27] But Bernard never denied the necessity of learned instruction. A well-ordered charity was the crowning achievement of the dynamic potential of both *sensus*, the soul's power of knowing, and *affectus*, or *desiderium*, its appetite for love. Such an *ordinatio* was the work of an intelligence that is both affective and effective. A phrase found in Gregory the Great, *amor ipse notitia est*, that is, "love itself is a [form of] knowing,"[28] was widely used in the twelfth century, but in the significantly altered form, *amor ipse intellectus est.*[29]

The concern for relating the experience of spousal union with Christ to the total complex of affective bonds within which each believer lives helps highlight the social role of mysticism in the *renovatio* of Latin Christianity in the twelfth century. Mystics have often been thought of as private, almost solipsistic, religious figures, interested only in their experience of God. This stress on inner experience has also led to the view that mysticism represents a danger to more structured forms of institutional religion—a threat, always implied if not actualized, to the order of the church and society. Without denying the tensions and difficulties that at times have existed between some mystics and the representatives of the institutional church (tensions that were to become more prevalent in the later Middle Ages for reasons to be investigated in the next volume), in the history of Western Christianity mysticism has more often encouraged commitment to and provided support for the institutional and social fabric of the church than called it into question.[30]

Perhaps at no time has this been more true than in the twelfth century. The Cistercians were the most successful of the monastic reformers, the valuable allies of the new papal order in a host of ways. Bernard of Clairvaux, the mystic *par excellence* of the time, was also the most important and active ecclesiastical leader of the West for almost twenty years. The canonical reform, which did so much for both the pastoral and the intellectual life of the age, gave rise to the School of St. Victor, which was as significant to the development of scholasticism as it was to the history of mysticism. The *ordo caritatis* that the mystics sought to attain was meant to be the inner meaning of all the forms of *ordinatio* present in the external reforming efforts of twelfth-century Christendom.

The major mystics of the twelfth century, especially Bernard of Clairvaux, William of St. Thierry, Hugh and Richard of St. Victor, became the *magistri* of mystical theory for the later Middle Ages and for centuries thereafter.[31] Perhaps it is because of this fact, as well as because they belonged to identifiable reformed religious orders, that it has been customary to speak of Cistercian and Victorine "schools" of mysticism.[32] There are both advantages and disadvantages to this form of expression. The Cistercians and the Victorines did conduct schools, though of rather different types. There are unmistakable similarities of interest and doctrine among the various Cistercian authors, all of whom were influenced by the dominant figure of Bernard. The relation of the thought of Hugh of St. Victor and Richard (they lived and taught in the same institution, though Richard may not have been a direct disciple) is even more obvious. But the term "school" often implies a unity of approach and conclusions that would not do justice to the variety found among the Cistercian authors and might even tend to mask the distinctive qualities of the two Victorines. On the one hand, all the mystical authors of the twelfth century, despite the differences among traditional monastics, reformed monastics, reformed canons, etc., may be said to constitute a "school" of sorts, one clearly different in a number of ways from the modes of mystical thought that will begin to become evident in the century to follow. On the other hand, the individuality of these authors, some of them among the greatest mystics of the Christian tradition, makes the notion of "school" at best a loose one. In its attempt to provide ways of guiding the believer to a heightened, indeed ultimate, experience of the indescribable divine presence, mystical theory escapes the unifying tendencies that can create doctrinal systems and schools, even among the more speculative and systematic of mystical authors. Rather than try to identify the characteristics of a Cistercian or a Victorine school of mysticism in the chapters that follow, I will endeavor to present an account of the distinctive teaching of the key authors and allow the reader to decide if it still useful to speak of schools or not.

Chapters 5, 6, and 7 deal with the foremost Cistercian authors, beginning with Bernard of Clairvaux, moving on to his friend William of St. Thierry, and closing with a chapter devoted to other prominent and influential Cistercians, especially Aelred of Rievaulx. Chapter 8 considers the mystical writers found in traditional Benedictinism and in the eremitical reformed order of the Carthusians. It will also investigate the existence of a visionary mysticism among certain twelfth-century figures. The ninth and final chapter will treat Victorine mysticism, a fusion of traditional motifs with the organizing mentality of early scholastic thought. The beguine movement, though it began in the late twelfth century, did not produce its remarkable flowering of women mystics until the following century and hence will be taken up in the next volume.

CHAPTER 5

Bernard of Clairvaux: "That Contemplative" (Quel Contemplante)

PROLOGUE: The Cistercian Miracle

T HE STORY OF TWELFTH-CENTURY mysticism cannot be restricted to the Cistercians, but the mystics of the new order played a preponderant role in their own time and in the later influence of twelfth-century mysticism. Why were the Cistercians so large a part of the story? A complete answer lies outside what any historian can provide, but a glance at the foundation and the character of the order of Cîteaux may suggest some reasons for the dominance of the new form of monasticism.[1]

In the first of his *Sermons for the Dedication of a Church*, Bernard of Clairvaux exclaims:

> What is more wonderful than when one who could scarcely for two days refrain from lust, from intoxication, drunkenness, wantonness, impurity, and other similar and dissimilar vices, now refrains from them for many years, and even for life? What greater miracle than when so many youths, adolescents, nobles—all those I see here—are bound, as in an open prison without chains, riveted only by the fear of God in order to endure penance so severe that it is beyond human power, above nature, out of the ordinary? . . . What are these save evident proofs of the Holy Spirit living within you? The body's lively movements prove the soul dwells there; spiritual life proves the Spirit dwells in the soul. The former is recognized by sight and hearing; the latter from charity, humility and the other virtues.[2]

The astonishing, even miraculous, success of the Cistercian monastic reform is as puzzling to modern historians as it was to Bernard and his contemporaries. The historical theologian, while not excluding the providential activity Bernard referred to, must begin by trying to investigate the social, economic, intellectual, and religious factors that produced the Cistercians and helped them achieve their success.

The sources, both institutional and theological, for the origins and early history of the order are suprisingly rich, though naturally not always either as complete or as clear as we should like.[3] The contribution made by the "white monks" (so called because their undyed grayish habits differed from the black habits of the traditional Benedictines) to the thought of the twelfth century has been the subject of a host of investigations over the past half-century. It would be impossible to try to review this literature here, but it is worthwhile noting some of the factors that made the Cistercian miracle possible as background to presenting the mystical theories of the greatest Cistercian.

The monks who left the monastery of Molesmes with their Abbot Robert in 1098 were one group among many of the sons of Benedict of the eleventh and twelfth centuries who were consumed by the desire to find a better, truer, more authentic form of the monastic life. In calling the foundation they established at Cîteaux some miles south of Dijon the "New Monastery," they highlighted the originality of their venture; but the official account of their mission, the text known as *Exordium parvum*, shows their action to have been a typical monastic revolution by way of a return to tradition,[4] one that emphasized the importance of the strict observance of the RB, especially in poverty of life and manual labor, and that broke with many of the ties to feudal obligations found in contemporary monasteries. In their sometimes unedifying quarrels with older forms of Benedictinism, especially the Cluniacs, the Cistercians were quick to claim that they were more "authentic" followers of Benedict than were their opponents;[5] but the Cistercian return to Benedict's *Rule* was by no means one of slavish literalism, as is clear from both their groundbreaking constitutional documents and their liturgical practices. The Cistercian effort at bringing new and more rational order to monasticism on the basis of the rigorous application of certain theological principles to all aspects of monastic life was characteristic of the ordering mentality of the twelfth century. They were not so much Benedictine literalists as Benedictines who strove to obey what they conceived to be the spirit of the *Rule* in as literal a fashion as possible.[6]

Three significant constitutional innovations of the early Cistercians had a direct effect on the success of the group, and, at least in indirect fashion, on their spirituality and mysticism. These innovations, enshrined in the document known as the *Carta caritatis* (how characteristic the name!),[7] helped make the white monks the first true religious "order" in the sense of a unified and coherent body of monastic houses bound together by a written constitutional form of government. While the Cluniac reform of the tenth and eleventh centuries had created a large confederation of monastic houses spread over Europe and more or less bound to the great Burgundian abbey, the Cluniacs were never an order in the constitutional or administrative sense. Although some Italian monastic reformers of the eleventh century had anticipated the mechanisms later adopted by the Cistercians in their order building, these were partial and local in scope. In the *Carta caritatis* we find for the first time a constitution establishing an integrated monastic order in which all houses were related by the same descending and ascending rules of responsibility and affection. The descending chain consisted in the filiation by which each mother house was responsible for its daughter houses, a responsibility expressed through the obligation of yearly visitation of the daughters by the abbot of the mother house. The ascending chain, a form of monastic representative government, required the presence of all the abbots of the order at the deliberations of the General Chapter held each September at Cîteaux. In an age of primitive communications, the greater the spread of the order the more difficult the observance of these regulations; but this does not detract from their elegance, originality, and wisdom.

Rather than utilizing peasant feudal labor, the Cistercians, like the Vallombrosan monks founded by St. John Gualbert, made use of *conversi*–that is, bearded lay monks–to till their lands. This development opened up the monastic life, albeit in a more simplified fashion than that observed by the choir monks, to a whole new social class, since the *conversi* came largely from the lower classes in distinction to the almost always aristocratic monks (though some knights "converted" to the life of the *conversi* in their later years, especially after the death of their wives). The exact contribution of the new class of monks to Cistercian spirituality is not easy to gauge, since most of the surviving products of the Cistercian writers were directed to the more elite audience, but they doubtless had an effect.[8]

Even more significant for Cistercian spirituality and mysticism was the break with the oblate system. From the outset, the Cistercians refused to accept children offered to the monastery, a common practice in traditional Benedictinism. Jean Leclercq has pointed out how this practice changed the nature of the audience addressed in monastic teaching and preaching and therefore modified the way in which Bernard and other Cistercians conceived of and communicated the fundamental message of Christian perfection.[9] The writings of the Cistercian fathers were meant for a monastic audience, and in general shared in the monastic elitism discussed in the previous chapter. But a monastic audience in which all the members had shared the experience of lay Christians in the world, at least for a part of their lives, was a different one from an audience in which almost all the monks had been raised within the monastery. This important change helps explain not only significant innova- tions in Cistercian teaching, but may also suggest why the Cistercian message proved so adaptable and powerful outside the monastic enclosure. The broad- ening of the Christian mystical tradition that will become evident in the thir- teenth century was the result of many factors, but the Cistercians cannot be excluded from playing a preparatory role.

The ethos or spirit of a movement is less easy to characterize than its in- stitutional and constitutional achievements, but is no less significant for its success. The Cistercian writers of the twelfth century exhibit a personal and theological diversity that makes it difficult to speak of a Cistercian "school," in the sense of one clear Cistercian position on all major issues. Still, the twelfth-century Cistercian fathers share many attitudes and values. R. W. Southern has noted how the new order combined three important values found, though usually in diverse contexts, in twelfth-century religious life–the desire to return to primitive simplicity, the search for system and rational organization, and a spirit of aggressive expansionism.[10] Other scholars, such as Louis Lekai, have emphasized the renewal of a clear and uncompromising monastic ideal as crucial both to the initial success and subsequent difficulties of the order as that ideal came into conflict with the realities of the medieval social order.[11] The uncompromising fixity of pur- pose that one finds in Bernard and some other Cistercians, however, was tempered by an emotional warmth and sensitivity to the feelings and needs of others that are still striking. One way to view the Cistercian ethos is to see it as paradigmatic of diverse, and not always reconcilable, values in twelfth-century religious life, tendencies that were later to be seen as mutu- ally exclusive and therefore impossible to try to hold together in vital, if often paradoxical, conjunctions.[12]

The white monks were literalists and rigorists who felt free to depart from the letter of the law in order to fulfill its spirit. Like the desert fathers whom they praised, they had fled the world only to find the world contin- ued to seek them out for a variety of reasons that often tempted them to actions that threatened to undermine their original spiritual intentions. Cistercian attacks, especially in the case of Bernard and William of St. Thierry, on some forms of the new theology of the schools at times make them seem obscurantist, even proto-inquisitorial; but in other areas of thought the Cistercians were among the most profound and profoundly original theologians of their era. In fine, the Cistercians were the last great movement of medieval monasticism, not least because they were such a clear manifestation of the paradoxes that had been present in monasticism from its origins.

The goal of the New Monastery was to create a *schola dilectionis,* or school of love,[13] which would enable the new humanity inaugurated by Christ to flourish, a humanity empowered by the Holy Spirit alive in the soul and manifesting his presence through humility and charity, as Bernard's sermon quoted above indicates. This goal was not a new one in the history of monasticism: the full realization of redeemed humanity had been a part of monastic theology from the beginning. Here, as in so many other areas, the Cistercians mixed the old and the new, or perhaps better, were able to give a new expression to an ancient theme. Not the least part of the "Cistercian miracle" was this ability to revive old wineskins with new wine.

I. An Introduction to Bernard of Clairvaux

In the thirty-first Canto of the *Paradiso* of the *Divine Comedy,* Dante is un-expectedly abandoned by Beatrice, who sends to him "un sene vestito con le genti gloriose" ("an elder clad like the folk in glory") whose eyes and cheeks are bathed in benign joy. The old man is Bernard of Clairvaux, who is to serve as the poet's supreme guide—the one who will lead him to Mary, the Mother of God and highest of created beings, and finally to the inde-scribable vision of the Trinity, "l'amor che move il sole e l'altre stelle." In the Florentine's carefully orchestrated poetic summation of the process by which the Christian attains the true freedom that reaches the goal of the vision of God, the figure of Bernard, the ideal contemplative ("quel contem-plante"), plays a crucial role.[14] Bernard is a human mirror in which Dante, like some pilgrim come to gaze on the relic of the "Veronica," the sacred image of Christ, can begin to see God himself:

> tal era io mirando la vivace
>   carità di colui, che 'n questo mondo,
>   contemplando, gustò di quella pace.

> (Such was I, gazing on the living
>   charity of him who, in this world,
>   in contemplation tasted of that peace.)
>   *Paradiso* 31, 109–111

The Cistercian mystic also serves as the poet's teacher:

> Affetto al suo piacer, quel contemplante
>   libero officio di dottore assunse,
>   e cominciò queste parole sante.

(With his love fixed on his delight, that contemplator
freely assumed the office of a teacher,
and began these holy words.)
Paradiso 32, 1–3[15]

Dante was not alone among medieval writers in considering Bernard of Clairvaux (1090–1153) the supreme guide to the heights of heavenly contemplation. This twelfth-century mystic, a many-talented man whom one can well imagine to have been capable of such alternate careers as crusader, courtly poet, or politician (ecclesiastical or lay), was a figure larger than life, both to his contemporaries and to subsequent generations. Although he won his greatest fame as a contemplative, the abbot of Clairvaux was also a man of action, deeply involved with a wide range of the issues of his time and engaged in more than a few acrimonious controversies. But Bernard does not appear a harsh and unlovable figure. His personality was so attractive, his powers of persuasion so difficult to withstand, that we are told that mothers hid their children and wives clung to their spouses lest he seduce them into the monastery. In the centuries since his death, Bernard's formidable reputation and the conviction so evident in his writings have also seduced some apologists into thinking that he was always in the right. Others, noting his involvement in the Crusades, his at times questionable political maneuvers—especially against those like Abelard and Gilbert of Poitiers whose theology he attacked—have found him a "difficult saint." But whether we judge him right or wrong on particular issues, we cannot accuse Bernard of tepidity, indifference, or of failure to shoulder what he conceived to be his responsibility.

Among the Latin authors of the Middle Ages, Bernard may possibly have equals, but surely no superiors. The sumptuous elegance of his Latinity, his genius at alternating soaring passages of complex periodic sentences with terse epigrammatic formulations summarizing key points, and, above all, the unmistakable personal tone he achieved throughout his work, mark him as the greatest stylist of an age of many distinguished Latinists.[16] Though Bernard has always been seen as a superb writer and major spiritual authority, modern research, beginning sixty years ago with Étienne Gilson's *La théologie mystique de saint Bernard*, has increasingly vindicated his position as an important theologian, though one decidedly not in the scholastic mold.[17]

The future abbot was born in 1090, the child of a pious Burgundian couple of the lower nobility.[18] His education was excellent, at least from the literary point of view.[19] In 1113, after a period of careful planning and recruiting of friends and relatives to accompany him, he entered the poor and relatively new monastery of Cîteaux. It is difficult to determine how much the subsequent success of the Cistercian movement owed to Bernard's forceful personality, and how much to the underlying "new model" of monasticism which had been worked out by the first abbots of Cîteaux, especially Alberic and Stephen Harding. There is no doubt, however, that the entry of Bernard and his companions marked a turning point in the history of the Cistercians. The flowering of Cîteaux began soon after Bernard's arrival with the foundation of the first of the four daughter houses of the New Monastery at La Ferté. In 1115, Bernard himself became abbot of Clairvaux, another of the first foundations.

Bernard's writing career began in the mid-1120s with his treatises *De gradibus humilitatis et superbiae* (*The Steps of Humility and Pride*), the *Apologia* he wrote in defense of the Cistercians against the Cluniacs, and his first letters and sermons. Given the absence of any formal theological education on his part, we can surmise that it was in the decade between 1115 and 1125 that he acquired his knowledge of the fathers and established the main lines of his theology. His most significant doctrinal work, the *De gratia et libero arbitrio* (*Grace and Free Choice*), was written about 1128, and his central mystical treatise, *De diligendo Deo* (*On Loving God*), may have been produced about the same time.[20] Bernard soon became a major figure in the religious and political life of France, and then of all Europe. His involvement in the papal schism between 1130 and 1137 gave him an international reputation that was to continue to grow.

In 1135, Bernard began his mystical masterpiece, the *Sermones super Cantica Canticorum* (*Sermons on the Song of Songs*).[21] Though the abbot did preach to his monks in chapter on the Song, the eighty-six sermons that he left at his death are polished literary works, a highly developed and richly rhetorical treatment of the mystical life on the basis of a spiritual exegesis of the most profound (for Bernard) book of the Old Testament, Solomon's song of love.[22] The abbot of Clairvaux knew what had survived of Origen's comment on the Song, as well as the Latin commentators, especially Ambrose and Gregory, but his unfinished work (it extends only to Sg. 3:4) was very much his own. Bernard's work is digressive, and to modern taste at times repetitious. The spiritual mode of exegesis of which he was the master loved to expose the meaning of the whole in each part, which helps explain why most spiritual commentaries on the Song do not progress very far: "When a spiritual author has said what he can about love (generally on a few verses) his message has been delivered," according to Jean Leclercq.[23] Despite this unfinished and digressive character, Bernard's *Sermons on the Song of Songs* are among the supreme masterpieces of Christian mysticism. Perhaps only John of the Cross's famous four treatises are comparable in scope and in influence.

Bernard the writer was, first and foremost, Bernard the preacher, that is, he preferred to cast his most important theological productions in the sermonic genre. Along with the *Sermons on the Song of Songs*, the one hundred and twenty-five *Sermones per annum*, or *Sermons on the Liturgical Year*, count as the most important part of his teaching.[24] The liturgical sermons center on the mystery of redemption conceived of as the communication of divine life to the church through her annual participation in the reliving of the saving events of Christ's life. The presentation of the church's yearly pilgrimage helps invoke important considerations relating to the personal appropriation of Christ's grace, and hence many passages relating to Bernard's mystical thought, both those making use of the Song of Songs and those that do not, are scattered through the *Sermones per annum*.[25] The abbot's *Sermones de diversis* (*Sermons on Different Topics*) are also not lacking in mystical texts.[26] Finally, some of Bernard's many letters,[27] as well as texts from his late treatises, such as *De praecepto et dispensatione* (*On Precept and Dispensation* [ca. 1141–44]) and *De consideratione* (*On Consideration* [ca. 1148–53]), must also be taken into account.[28] The student of Bernard's mysticism is confronted with a wealth of riches.

II. Doctrinal Foundations

Obtulit carnem sapientibus carnem, per quam discerent sapere et spiritum. (He offered his flesh to those who knew flesh so that through it they might come to know spirit too.)[29]

Bernard's mystical theology is solidly rooted in, indeed inseparable from, its doctrinal foundations. Although the *Sermons on the Song of Songs* concentrate on the personal meaning of the Song as telling of the love between Christ and the individual Christian, Bernard cannot help but turn again and again to the investigation of the mystery of Christ and the church that forms the ground for the proper understanding of the personal relation.[30] The *Sermons on the Liturgical Year*, primarily devoted to the exposition of the mystery of Christ and the church, contain passages concerning the soul's relation to God, as we have seen. It is not possible to understand Bernard's mystical theology without grasping the main lines of his whole theological program.

The first verse of the Song of Songs (*Osculetur me osculo oris sui*), the subject of the eight sermons that begin Bernard's great work, provide a good starting point to investigate the fruitful interplay between the dogmatic and the mystical aspects of his thought.[31] As the quotation from *Sermon* 6 given above indicates, they center on the abbot's understanding of the economy of salvation, the mystery of our redemption in Christ, a mystery whose goal is attaining union with God, partially and imperfectly in this life, more truly after death, but not fully until the resurrection of the body.[32]

The exegetical premise of Bernard's presentation, keyed to the unusual expression of the Vulgate text (i.e., why does it say "Let him kiss me *with the kiss of his mouth?*"), is that there must be multiple kisses between Christ, the Divine Bridegroom, and the bride, conceived of as both the church and the individual soul. *Sermon* 2 analyzes four kisses that comprise the whole course of salvation history–longing for Christ among the just souls of the Old Testament time, the kiss of the Incarnation, Christ bringing redemption to humanity in the present, and the heavenly kiss of the future eschatological age. This teaching provides the context for the personal appropriation of the present redemptive kiss discussed in *Sermon* 3: *Hodie legimus in libro experientiae* ("Today we read in the book of experience"). Here, Bernard interprets the multiplicity of kisses in a threefold way. The first kiss, or kiss of the feet, signifies the conversion and penance by which the soul turns from sin to righteousness through the action of prevenient grace. The kiss of the hands is the Christian life of continuing repentance and avoidance of sin. The final stage, that of the properly mystical kiss *of the kiss* of the mouth (the bride does not receive the kiss directly from the mouth, a state reserved for the union of God and human in Christ), is only hinted at in *Sermon* 3.

As often happens with Bernard, the introduction of the major theme, that of the triple kiss, becomes the pretext for a more developed treatment, both exegetically and doctrinally. Bernard begins by laying out his theology of the economy of salvation in *Sermons* 4 through 6, before returning to a more extensive treatment of the kiss of the kiss of the mouth in *Sermon* 7 (the first really mystical sermon) and concluding with a consideration of the trinitarian meaning of the kiss identified with the Holy Spirit, the bond of union between the Father and the Son, in *Sermon* 8.

How can God and human be said to kiss, or to be joined in marital union? How can the Song of Songs ascribe head, heart, feet, and other human attributes to the absolutely pure divine Spirit? In order to answer these anthropomorphic difficulties and to vindicate the use of the erotic language of the Song as the supreme mystical text, Bernard has to lay out his understanding of the dynamics of God's dealing with humanity. He does this in two stages. *Sermon* 4 advances an initial solution to the problem of anthropomorphic descriptions of God–one might be tempted to describe his answer here as a natural theology. "God has a mouth by which he teaches humanity knowledge, a hand by which he provides nourishment to all flesh, he has feet whose footstool is earth.... God has all these things, I say, not naturally, but effectively," that is, by reason of what he does.[33] *Ser-*

mons 5 and 6 provide a deeper reason for scripture's fleshly and anthropo-morphic descriptions of God's dealing with humanity, one which indicates that such language is also *literally* true.

Bernard begins with an analysis of humanity's place in the scale of spiritual beings and the effect of sin upon this hierarchical structure. There are four grades of spirits: animals, humans, angels, and God. God alone is Absolute Spirit with no need for any kind of body. (Bernard, like many of the fathers, held that angels required some sort of tenuous bodies, at least for their ministries.) "The spirit of the human being which occupies the middle place between the highest and the lowest clearly has to have a body for two reasons: without it the soul is not able to advance on its own, nor can it be of help to another."[34] The law of our creation is that we can only have access to what can lead us to truth and happiness through the body and its senses, but this God-given condition, by which we were created to use our fleshly nature in order to reach the spiritual domain, has been perverted through the fall. Rather than using knowledge acquired through the senses to reach beyond them, humans became enslaved to materiality so that they can conceive of nothing beyond the flesh.

> Woe! Thus human beings lost and changed their glory for the likeness of a grass-eating beast (Ps 105:20)! God had mercy on their errors and deigned to come forth from the shady dark mountain [i.e., of his hidden divinity] and place his tabernacle in the sun [i.e., take on flesh in the Incarnation].[35] He offered his flesh to those who knew flesh so that through it they might come to know spirit too. While he was in the flesh, through the flesh he performed works not of the flesh but of God. . . . [36]

We have, then, almost a syllogistic argument–a Bernardine equivalent of Anselm's famous proof for the necessity of the God-man in the *Cur Deus Homo?*.

> God does not have a body of any kind.
> But, humanity's fallen state means that we are all enslaved to the body.
> Therefore, salvation is impossible unless God takes on a body.[37]

God, in the person of the Word, takes on our bondage to the fallen fleshly condition in order to free us from imprisonment and restore the original human possibility of attaining spirit through what is bodily. Christ's activities while in the flesh are central to the economy of salvation, and thus all the physical descriptions of the body and the bodily activities of the bride-groom in the Song of Songs are to be read in reference to these saving works and their appropriation by the soul. God, for example, may now be

said to have feet that can be kissed not so much because the earth is his
footstool (Isa 66:1), as because the humanity of Jesus has revealed both his
present mercy and coming judgment, which we must embrace at the beginning of our conversion.[38] Anthropomorphic language about God is now not
only metaphorically but also literally true!

This central insight of Bernard's theology provides an access to the three
major components of his doctrinal theology that need to be considered in
order to understand his mystical theory—anthropology, Christology, and
ecclesiology. We can begin with the abbot's theological anthropology, both
because it is existentially prior, and because Bernard's theology always
emphasizes the experiential testing of the truth of belief.

Bernard's Theological Anthropology[39]

Anthropology was central to the thought of all the early Cistercian
authors. Some of these writers, such as William of St. Thierry, Aelred of
Rievaulx, and Isaac of Stella, wrote essays on anthropology, usually under
the title *De anima*; later authors penned more practical works, frequently on
the theme *De conscientia*.[40] Bernard himself wrote neither a *De anima* nor a
De conscientia, though his works are filled with reflections on the nature and
destiny of humanity and on the moral life. The abbot of Clairvaux's most
extended reflections on anthropology occur in the *Grace and Free Choice* and
at the end of the *Sermons on the Song of Songs*, where he investigates humanity's status as made in the image and likeness of God. There are significant
differences between these two treatments. (Bernard admitted this in confess-
ing in the latter text that what he had to say here was *diversa . . . sed, ut arbitror, non adversa* from the former, that is, "different, but not opposed, I
think.")[41] The divergences remain troubling, though modern studies of the
abbot's anthropology tend to support a basic consistency of approach, if not
of formulation, in his views.[42]

. The essential root of Bernard's anthropology, like that of all the fathers of
the East and West, is based on the Genesis account of humanity's formation
in the image and likeness of God (*faciamus hominem ad imaginem et similitudinem nostram*, Gen 1:26); but, like many others, the abbot understood the
Genesis text in terms of Paul's teaching concerning Christ's role as the
Father's perfect *imago* (Col 1:15–18) to whom fallen humanity is recon-
formed through salvation (see Rom 8:29–30; 2 Cor 3:18). Bernard provides
a rather different analysis of the meaning of the *imago* and *similitudo* in his
two main treatments. In the *Grace and Free Choice*, the image of God consists
of our inalienable freedom from necessity (*libertas a necessitate*) that is found
in the faculty of free choice (*liberum arbitrium*) by which we assent in a

self-determined manner to a course of action on the basis of a judgment of reason. The likeness (*similitudo*) of God, however, has been lost through sin. It resides in two elements: first, freedom from sin (*libertas a peccato*) or free counsel (*liberum consilium*); and, second, freedom from misery (*libertas a miseria*) or free good pleasure (*liberum complacitum*), which establishes the will in the good and makes it impossible for it to be in any way disturbed or unhappy.[43] Through original sin Adam's ability not to sin has become our inability to avoid sin. The grace brought by Christ restores the ability not to sin. Although the full likeness to be found in *liberum complacitum* is reserved for heaven, contemplatives can enjoy a rare and brief foretaste of it in this life. "Happiness and misery cannot exist together at the same time. Therefore, as often as they enjoy the former through the Spirit, they do not feel the latter. Only contemplatives are able in this life to enjoy free good pleasure in some way, and only in part–a very small part and one quite rare."[44] This is the anthropological basis for Bernard's understanding of mystical experience (see chart 1).

Bernard understood freedom essentially as the absence of external coercion, defining *liberum arbitrium* as a "self-determining habit of soul" (*Est enim habitus animi, liber sui*).[45] This is not the pure autonomy of an individual who creates his or her own meaning, as in the case of some modern existentialist philosophies. Bernard's idea of freedom, like Augustine's, was circumstantial, that is, tied to the subject's historical situation. It was also hierarchical, indeed theocentric, because it was centered on God's freedom, in which spontaneity and rectitude are so absolutely one that they could never be in conflict. From this perspective, all forms of freedom that involve even the possibility of a conflict between self-determination and upright action are limited and imperfect. The freedom to sin, which is the result of the deformation of the divine image in us, manages to keep the name of freedom because it does at least represent what the subject *wants* to do–conform the world to its own deformation rather than the *rectitudo* of the divine will. The way back from this truly miserable freedom Bernard summarizes as follows:

> Here below, we must learn from our freedom of counsel not to abuse free choice in order that one day we may be able fully to enjoy freedom of pleasure. Thus we are repairing God's image in us, and the way is being paved by grace for the retrieving of that former honor which we forfeited by sin.[46]

A different picture of image and likeness emerges when we turn to *Sermons* 80–82 of the *Sermons on the Song of Songs*.[47] Here the emphasis is on a more overtly Pauline pattern, concentrating on the soul's formation according to the image and likeness of the Word, the true and perfect *imago Dei*.

Chart I

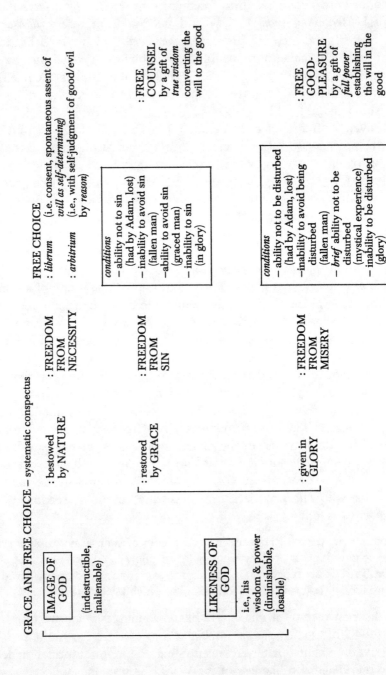

GRACE AND FREE CHOICE – systematic conspectus

IMAGE OF GOD

(indestructible, inalienable)

LIKENESS OF GOD

i.e., his wisdom & power (diminishable, losable)

: bestowed by NATURE — : FREEDOM FROM NECESSITY

: restored by GRACE — : FREEDOM FROM SIN

: given in GLORY — : FREEDOM FROM MISERY

FREE CHOICE
: *liberum* (i.e. consent, spontaneous assent of *will as self-determining*)
: *arbitrium* (i.e., with self-judgment of good/evil by *reason*)

conditions
– ability not to sin (had by Adam, lost)
– inability to avoid sin (fallen man)
– ability to avoid sin (graced man)
– inability to sin (in glory)

: FREE COUNSEL by a gift of *true wisdom* converting the will to the good

conditions
– ability not to be disturbed (had by Adam, lost)
– inability to avoid being disturbed (fallen man)
– *brief* ability not to be disturbed (mystical experience)
– inability to be disturbed (glory)

: FREE GOOD-PLEASURE by a gift of *full power* establishing the will in the good

The Word is the Father's image as *veritas, sapientia,* and *justitia;* the soul is capable of participating in these insofar as it possesses something of the greatness or dignity (*magnitudo*) and uprightness (*rectitudo*) of the Word.[48] Through sin the soul loses *rectitudo,* though it keeps something of its *magnitudo.*[49] Therefore, the image remains, but only in part. The soul's likeness (*similitudo*) to the Word consists in three elements: simplicity (*simplicitas*), the quality by which the soul's nature is identical with the act of living; immortality (*immortalitas*), which follows on this; and freedom of choice (*libertas arbitrii*).[50] Simplicity and immortality can never be lost; nor can freedom of choice. But the latter has been entrapped by sin into a position of voluntary servitude whose paradoxes Bernard explores with an intensity worthy of his masters in this teaching, Paul and Augustine.[51] Hence, in the *Sermons on the Song of Songs,* the likeness to God is not totally lost but is partly concealed,[52] just as the image is partially present in *magnitudo* and partially lost in vanished *rectitudo* (see chart 2).

The diversity in viewpoint between these two texts is not helped by the fact that other treatments of *imago* and *similitudo* in Bernard display at least two other interpretations of image theology.[53] These divergences present us with one of the characteristic features of Bernard's theology—the conscious

Chart 2

Bernard of Clairvaux, *Sermones super Cantica* 80–82
Imago et Similitudo Dei

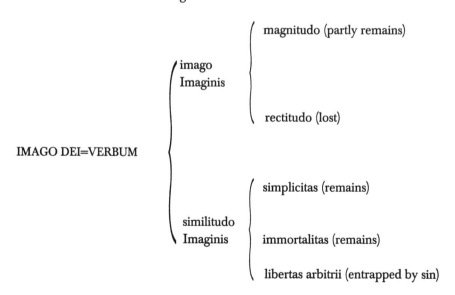

use of different presentations of the same basic doctrine, or, what is its equivalent, different interpretations of the same scriptural text. The scriptural hint may help us understand how Bernard conceived the *diversa sed non adversa* theme that characterized much of his theology. In explaining how different understandings of the same passage are perfectly legitimate, even praiseworthy, on the spiritual level, Bernard says:

> I will not be condemned by a prudent person because of a diversity of meanings as long as truth is protected in each case and the love which the scriptures should serve is more helpful to many the more true meanings it draws forth from them for its purposes. Why should what we experience time and again in using things bother us in the case of scripture? How many uses does water alone serve for our bodies? And so any single divine text will not be off the mark if it gives rise to different understandings that can be adapted to the diverse needs and purposes of souls.[54]

Maur Standaert has argued for a basic consistency underlying Bernard's variations on the *imago-similitudo* theme.[55] The abbot's intent was not to advance any single definitive treatment but to compose a set of variations on a basic triple pattern: first, *formation*, that is, humanity's inalienable similarity to God (something which for Bernard primarily centered around freedom of choice); second, *deformation*, that is, the injury done to that likeness through sin; and third, *reformation*, the possibility of the progressive restoration of the original similarity through the soul's bond with the human manifestation of the Word in Jesus Christ.

For the abbot of Clairvaux, our experience of life is one of an almost unbearable tension between what we were meant to be and what we are—between the grandeur and the misery of the human condition. The existential starting point of Bernard's anthropology, the Christian adaptation of the Delphic maxim "Know thyself" (*Scito teipsum*), was this recognition of our combined misery and majesty.[56] Like all medieval monks and good Augustinians, Bernard had a profound sense of human sinfulness and the misery of our daily experience. One can hardly read him for more than a few pages without finding a passage, pessimistic and often poignant, on the sinful situation of humanity since the fall.[57] Although the human person alone among earthly creatures is not subject to natural necessity, "nevertheless, with the interruption of sin, he too undergoes a certain coercive force (*vis*), but from the will, not from nature, so that he is not deprived of innate freedom. What is voluntary is free. Hence sin brought it about that the corruptible body weighs down the soul (Wis 9:15), but by its love not its natural weight."[58]

Bernard's view of the body and of sexuality has provoked much comment, and it is not hard to find texts that take a negative attitude even toward bodily health.[59] There are also passages in which the abbot expresses a generalized Augustinian line common in the early Middle Ages according to which sexual pleasure in fallen humanity is always in some way sinful.[60] One of his favorite scripture tags, Wisdom 9:15 (*Corpus enim quod corrumpitur aggravat animam*,"The body that decays weighs down the soul"), might seem to suggest a highly negative, almost dualistic, view of the body. But as the text from *Sermon* 81 cited above shows, Bernard claims that the body weighs down the soul not by its nature but by its false love, the *concupiscentia* that has affected the whole human person as a result of the fall. It is not the body itself but the body's infirmities (*molestiae corporis*) that drag it down.[61] Indeed, the body is central to Bernard's mysticism, since he insists that our journey toward God must begin on the carnal level and that our enjoyment of bliss will not be complete until our physical bodies are reunited with our souls at the general resurrection (how different from Eriugena).[62] Even the abbot's attitude toward the use of sex in marriage was far from negative, as the work of Jean Leclercq and others has shown.[63]

Bernard uses the terms *caro* and *carnalis* in two ways that may not always be clearly distinguished: first, to indicate the good material component of human nature as created by God; and second, to describe our fallen nature, in which the perversion of the proper relation between body and soul is most evident in the unruly bodily passions. The distinction is clear in a passage in his sermon-treatise *Conversion (De conversione)* delivered to the clerics of Paris in 1140, where he says: "As long as we are in the body, we are in exile from God, not indeed that this is the body's fault, but it is the fault of the fact that it is still a body of death, or rather that the flesh is the body of sin in which good does not exist but rather the law of sin."[64]

Self-knowledge, then, is knowledge of our sinfulness and of the predominance of "carnality" in the evil sense in our lives. The effect of this honest recognition of our plight is the necessity for humility as the essential starting point of the spiritual life (*spiritualis vita*).[65] But despite our sorry condition, we know that God "creates our minds to participate in him,"[66] and that therefore self-knowledge also brings hope for a change in our condition. This is the first step in lifelong process of conversion (*conversio*), which Bernard understood in a way close to that found in Augustine's *Confessions*.[67]

The humility and the hope that are the beginning of our journey away from sin and back to God are not our own effort, but are already the work of the Incarnate Word in us. The voluntary humbling of God in taking on flesh casts the lie in the face of all human pride,[68] and the merciful kindness

Jesus displayed throughout his life is the source of hope for all sinners, no matter how hardened. Here theological anthropology joins Christology, the centerpiece of Bernard's doctrinal message.[69]

Bernard's Teaching on Redemption

The way in which the abbot understands the communication of the message of humility and mercy is through his distinctive teaching on the "carnal" love of Christ. For Bernard, Jesus, the God-man, is lovable on the most basic level of human attraction, that of the flesh. This is why he took on humanity, since he knew "if he had not drawn near, he would not draw to himself, and if he had not drawn to himself, he would not have drawn out of sin."[70] Carnal love of Christ in the flesh and "what Christ did or ordered in the flesh" form the "main reason why the invisible God wished to be seen in the flesh and to live among humans as a human so that he might return all the affections of carnal humans, who could only love carnally, first to the saving love of his flesh, and thus, little by little, lead them to spiritual love."[71] The sweetness of carnal love of Christ is needed in order to drive out the false sweetness of illicit loves—as nail expels nail (*Sermon* 20.4). A fundamental difference between Bernard and earlier commentators on the Song of Songs, such as Origen and Gregory of Nyssa, is that the abbot of Clairvaux insists at the outset that carnal love cannot be merely denied or rejected, but that it must be accepted and redirected to the sensible or carnal love of Christ's humanity, the necessary starting point on the road to the spiritual love of his divinity.[72] Christ's "leaping" over the angels to descend from heaven to earth in order to manifest himself in the sun of his body is meant to provoke a heliotropic reaction in fallen humanity as it turns toward the source of light, heat, and nourishment.[73]

Christ's role in the reformation of the image and likeness is rooted in the function of the Word in creation and in consummation.[74] Following Paul and Augustine,[75] Bernard insisted that the Word as the true image of the Father was both the efficient and the exemplary cause of creation and therefore must play the same role in the work of reformation and consummation:

> Those who think correctly confess a triple work not so much of free choice as of divine grace in him, or from him—first, creation; second, reformation; third, consummation. For we were first created in Christ into freedom of will; second, we are reformed through Christ into the spirit of freedom; and finally, we are to be consummated with Christ into the state of eternity. What did not exist had to be created in him who did exist, and when deformed to be reformed through the Form: the members cannot be perfected save in the Head.[76]

The first two stages are summarized in one of his masterly (and untranslatable) epigrams: *In primo opere me mihi dedit, et ubi se dedit, me mihi reddidit* ("In creation he gave me myself; where he gave himself [that is, in the Passion], he gave me back myself.")[77]

Both the will and the ability to pursue the way of salvation come from the Incarnate Word, the source of all our strength.[78] Our conformation to the Word, a constant theme of Bernard's teaching,[79] is our transformation into the perfected image and likeness that the abbot found best expressed in one of his favorite biblical texts, 2 Corinthians 3:18: "All of us, gazing upon the Lord's glory with revealed face, are transformed into the same image from glory to glory, as if by the Spirit of the Lord." *Transformamur cum conformamur* ("We are transformed as we are conformed"), as he summarized this christomimetic process.[80]

There is no need to go into a detailed analysis of Bernard's Augustinian understanding of grace, especially as set forth in *Grace and Free Choice*,[81] in order to be convinced of the prevenient and subsequent role of Christ's power in the whole process of salvation.[82] In another of his epigrammatic formulas, he put the whole matter of the relation of grace and human merit in a nutshell when he said, "It is merit enough to know that merits aren't enough. But just as it is enough merit not to presume on merits, to lack merits is enough for judgment."[83]

Bernard stands in a direct line with the ancient Christian understanding of the economy of salvation first made explicit in Irenaeus—God became human so that humans might become God.[84] What is new in the abbot's development of this theology of redemption is the emphasis placed on the necessity of the carnal starting place for our appropriation of saving grace and the detailed way in which the Cistercian ties the various mysteries of Christ's life to the process of the transformation of carnal into spiritual love.[85] To be sure, the role of the saving mysteries was central to the patristic writers of both East and West, and Bernard doubtless learned much from them;[86] but the consistent and dynamic way in which he portrays the effects of the work of redemption (Bernard had little interest in the speculative problem of the metaphysical constitution of the God-man) marks him as one of the major doctrinal thinkers of the Latin Middle Ages.[87]

Bernard constantly calls up for his reader the major events of the life of Christ.

> He was incomprehensible and inaccessible, invisible and completely unthinkable. Now he wishes to be comprehended, wishes to be seen, wishes to be thought about. How, you ask? As lying in the manger, resting in the Virgin's lap, preaching on the mountain, praying through the night, or hanging on the cross, growing pale in death, free among the dead and ruling in hell, and also

as rising on the third day, showing the apostles the place of the nails, the signs of victory, and finally as ascending over heaven's secrets in their sight.[88]

It should not be thought that Bernard merely counsels some form of pious gaze upon the events of Christ's life as a means of reminding us of God's love for us. Though in our sinful carnal state we have to begin on such a level, the abbot's preaching and teaching were designed to help the reader to penetrate to the saving meaning of the mysteries and thereby to rise from a carnal to a mature spiritual love. In the one hundred and first of the *Sermons on Different Topics*, Bernard briefly outlines a progression of love tied to the great saving events of the life of Christ in a way that provides a clue to the richer and more varied development found in his preaching on the liturgical year. Love, he says, may be either carnal or spiritual, and there are two varieties of each. The passage from the lower to the higher stages of love is made possible by our coming to share in the mysteries of Christ's life. In taking on flesh, he provides us with the necessary starting point, the carnal love of the flesh of the God-man. We begin to love the spirit, though still in a carnal way, when we are struck with sorrow at the remembrance of his death for us. This can lead us on to the third stage, loving the flesh in a spiritual way when we recognize that our redemption takes place through this saving death of Christ's flesh. Finally, we love the spirit of Christ spiritually when we become one with him in his Resurrection and Ascension into heaven, the events through which his flesh became glorified and fully spiritual.[89]

Bernard's role in the development of the devotion to the sacred humanity of Christ, especially the mysteries of the nativity,[90] as well as the passion,[91] has been much stressed by students of medieval religion.[92] He is also known for fostering such affective practices as devotion to the sacred name of Jesus.[93] The account given here shows just how significant the carnal love of Christ in all its stages was for the abbot. Nevertheless, for Bernard such carnal love was always just the beginning of the itinerary that was meant to lead to spiritual love. To neglect the higher form of love would be to fail to do justice to Bernard's thought. This is why the Resurrection, and even more the Ascension, on which the abbot preached more often than any other mystery and which he honored by instituting a special liturgical procession, were such special feasts for him.[94] To cite his own words:

> To clarify what I said, if my Lord Jesus had risen from the grave but had not ascended to heaven, it could not have been said of him that he "passed beyond" (*pertransierat*), but only that he "passed from" (*transierat*). . . . Therefore, to believe in the Resurrection is to pass from; to believe in the Ascension is to pass beyond. . . . Our Head preceded both those souls [the seekers referred to

in Song 3:4] and the other members of his Body on earth in two issues–his Resurrection, as we said, and his Ascension. These are the "first fruits of Christ" (1 Cor 15:23). But if he precedes, so does our faith, for where does it not follow him?[95]

The transition from carnal to spiritual love achieved in Christ risen and ascended, as the rich argument in *Sermon on the Song of Songs* 20.6–9 shows,[96] is the center of Bernard's Christology. "Christ ascended once and for all above heaven's height in corporeal fashion, but now he ascends every day spiritually in the hearts of the elect."[97]

This transition can be conceived of as a form of imitation of Christ, but here, too, we should beware of seeing this as only a kind of literal imitation. "Through the mystery of his Incarnation the Lord ascends and descends, leaving us an example so that we might follow in his footsteps."[98] The imitation certainly involves practicing Christ's virtues,[99] especially his humility and unselfish love.[100] But detailed moral expressions of the following of Christ are secondary to the essential pattern by which we, like our Head, pass from the carnal to the spiritual level: "That carnal love through which the carnal life is excluded and the world is condemned and overcome is good. When it is also rational it advances; it is perfected when it also becomes spiritual."[101]

Bernard's Ecclesiology

The process of the communication of Christ's saving work, the restoration of humanity to the possibility of attaining its true goal, has, as its immediate subject, not the individual human person but the church, the collectivity that forms Christ's Body both here on earth and in heaven. This is evident not only in the *Sermons on the Liturgical Year,* which are primarily directed to the exposition of the mystery of Christ and the church, but also in the *Sermons on the Song of Songs,* where the emphasis is generally more personal. In *Sermon* 12 of the latter he says: "No one among us would dare to claim for himself the title of Bride of Christ for his soul, but because we belong to the church which justly glories in this name and its reality, we not unjustly appropriate a share in this glory."[102] *Sermon* 68 asks, "Who is the Bride and the Bridegroom? He is our God, and she, I dare to say, is us, along with the rest of the crowd of prisoners he acknowledged."[103] In interpreting the Song of Songs as the love song of Christ and the church, and only on this basis as applicable to the relations between Christ and the soul, Bernard, of course, was the heir to a long tradition whose major exponent, Origen, was well known to him.[104] Gregory the Great had also used this mode of interpretation, though he emphasized the ecclesiological meaning, as we have seen. The abbot of Clairvaux was less interested in breaking new ground than in renewing the tradition of melding the ecclesiological and the personal reading of the Song after many centuries in which a largely church-related meaning had predominated.[105]

Bernard's ecclesiology is not lacking in attention to the specific offices and institutions of the church, as a study of his treatise *Consideration* and his letters shows.[106] These are not directly relevant to our purpose, but the abbot's thoughts on the inner reality of the church as the Body of Christ in the history of salvation are integral to the doctrinal basis of his mystical theology. The Song of Songs provided Bernard with a key biblical foundation for interpreting the famous Pauline text describing the marital union of man and woman in relation to the *sacramentum magnum* of Christ and the church.

The true church is the preexistent reality of the heavenly Jerusalem, which Bernard describes in several texts, notably in the *Sermon on the Song of Songs* 27.4–7. The abbot interpreted the "heaven of heavens" of Psalm 67:34 as signifying the angelic world of spirits and redeemed souls, considered both collectively and individually. In comparing herself to heaven (Bernard's interpretation of Song 1:4 as worked out in *Sermon* 27.1–3), the Bride points to her origin from above, both when read as the church and when read as the individual soul. Bernard notes that John in the Apocalypse speaks of seeing the heavenly Jerusalem "descending," prepared as a Bride for her Husband (Apoc 21:2). What can this mean? According to the abbot, "He came to a Bride, but he did not come without a Bride. He was seeking a Bride, but she was with him." That is, although the Word had a Bride from all eternity in the angelic host, "it pleased him to call the church together from humanity and to unite it to the one from heaven, so that there might be one Bride and one Groom."[107] Since the two churches are absolutely one (*una . . . non duplicata*), Bernard proceeds in rather daring fashion to fuse the heavenly and earthly manifestations of the church and to underline the perfect oneness of the Bride and Groom:

> You have two from heaven, both Jesus the Bridegroom and the Bride Jerusalem. He, in order to be seen, "emptied himself taking the form of a slave and was found as man" (Phil 2:7). In what form or appearance, or in what garb, did he [i.e., John the Evangelist] who saw her descending see her? . . . He saw the Bride when he saw the Word in the flesh (John 1:14), acknowledging two in one flesh. When the holy Emmanuel brought to earth the teaching of heavenly discipline, when the visible image and beautiful appearance of that heavenly Jerusalem which is our mother became known as revealed to us in and through Christ, what did we behold except the Bride in the Bridegroom as we gazed in awe upon one and the same Lord of Glory,

both Bridegroom bedecked with crown and Bride adorned with her jewels? He who descended is the same one who ascends (Eph 4:10). No one ascends to heaven save he who descended from heaven (John 3:13)–the one and the same Lord who is both Bridegroom as Head and Bride as Body.[108]

This powerful expression of the unity of Bride and Bridegroom as a single divine reality goes further than other texts in applying to the hypostatic reality of the *Verbum-Ecclesia* the key christological passages on the Ascension that Bernard usually reserved to describe the work of the God-man.[109] The Cistercian not only revived early Christian emphasis on the preexistent reality of the church, but his fusion of the angelic and human aspects of the church into the one perfect Bride helps explain the important role that the angels play in his mystical theory, a more prominent part than that found in most of his contemporaries.[110] Bernard's emphasis on the complete cooperation found in the communion of saints is expressed throughout his works, nowhere more splendidly than in the fifth sermon for the Feast of All Saints.[111] (The abbot's stress on the supernal reality of the church provides a distant Christian analogy to the main line of Jewish mystical interpretation of the Song of Songs as dealing with the celestial union of male and female principles.) The church both exists before history and will continue after time will have come to a close: "Doesn't the goal of all things depend upon the state and consummation of the church?" he says in one place.[112]

The church called to union with Christ as the heavenly Bride is often contrasted with the synagogue, the prior betrothed. A full study of Bernard's attitude toward the Jews cannot be given here, but a few remarks drawn from the *Sermons on the Song of Songs* will shed light on this aspect of his ecclesiology. The abbot of Clairvaux did not deny that the synagogue functioned as a true, if preliminary and provisional, Bride–the Groom's left and right arms truly embraced her in her time (*Sermon* 14.4). But the synagogue rejected the Gentiles, wishing to restrict the oil of salvation to herself, whereas the church spread the saving message to all, as symbolized by the Bride's anointed breasts and garments in the Song.[113] Even though the Jews are the vineyard lost to the church (*Sermon* 30.3–4), the Bride has not forgotten her Mother. In one of the last of the *Sermons on the Song of Songs* Bernard describes how the church prays for the entry of her Mother into the Word's bridal chamber, where they both may enjoy the embraces of the Bridegroom.[114]

Bernard characterizes the church as both Bride and Mother. Following the example of the Bridegroom, who has ascended to heaven but is still with his followers until the end of the world (Matt 28:20), "So too the Bride, no matter how much she advances, how much she moves ahead, is never removed from the care, providence, and love of those she gave birth to in the Gospel; she never forgets her offspring."[115] The very fact that the church is the Bride of Christ makes her also the Mother of those souls (portrayed by the *adulescentulae* of the Song) who need her ministrations in order to enter the joy of the marriage chamber. Bernard often draws out a more personal appropriation of the message: the obligation of prelates and others in authority, especially abbots like himself, to display the motherly virtues of kindness and care, to "expose their breasts" to those in their charge.[116]

Although the church here below is always, as Augustine had argued against the Donatists,[117] a mixed body of good and evil (a fact Bernard saw expressed in the description of the Bride as "black but beautiful" in Song 1:4),[118] this does not detract from her role as the perfect Bride, "the more precious Body of Christ for which that other Body was handed over lest she taste death."[119] In a reference to the wound of love of Song 4:9 (*vulnerasti cor meum, soror mea, sponsa vulnerasti cor meum in uno oculorum tuorum et in uno crine colli tui*) found in the third of the Sermons on the Vigil of the Nativity, Bernard affirms, "She is the one who wounded his heart and sunk her eye of contemplation in the very abyss of God's secrets so that she might make her eternal dwelling in his heart and he in hers."[120] It is this total mutuality of Christ and his Body the church conceived of in primarily affective terms that makes Bernard's ecclesiology so necessary a part of the foundation upon which he constructed his mysticism.

The constant, though rarely tedious, reiteration of the message that salvation is attainable only through our participation in the church and its yearly reliving of the mystery of redemption may account for one initially surprising absence in Bernard's preaching, that is, the relative paucity of his references to the sacraments.[121] Some later medieval mystics were to find the center of their piety in contact with Christ in the sacraments, especially in the Eucharist. The abbot of Clairvaux, on the other hand, so concentrates on the *magnum mysterium*, the sacrament of the marriage of Christ and the church, of which the other sacraments serve as exemplifications (Bernard was untouched by nascent scholastic efforts to provide a conceptual definition of sacrament that allowed for the specification of seven "true" sacraments), that he did not feel compelled to discuss the latter in detail. It is through this foundational *sacramentum/mysterium* that we gain access to Christ, who united flesh to himself in a personal union without abandoning his substantial union with the Father. Bernard once summarized:

Christ the Lord is a mountain, a mountain gathered (*coagulatus*) and rich. He is a mountain in sublimity, gathered in the bringing together of a multitude, rich in charity. Now see how he draws all things to himself, how he unites all things in unity, substantial, personal, spiritual, sacramental. He has the Father in himself, with whom he is one in substance. He has the assumed humanity, with which he is one person. He has the faithful soul clinging to him, with whom he is one spirit. He has the one church of all the elect, with which he is one flesh.[122]

III. Bernard's Mystical Thought

Solus est amor ex omnibus animae motibus, sensibus atque affectibus, in quo potest creatura, etsi non ex aequo, respondere Auctori, vel de simili mutuam rependere vicem. (Of all the motions, senses, and affections of the soul, it is love alone in which the creature is able, even if not on an equal basis, to repay to its Creator what it has received, to weigh back something from the same measure.)[123]

The distinction between Bernard's dogmatic and mystical theology is not one that he makes himself, though it is reflected in the difference of emphasis found among his major works, such as the *Sermons on the Song of Songs*, where again and again he returns to detailed and cumulatively enrichening treatments of mystical contemplation,[124] and the *Sermons on the Liturgical Year*, where such considerations, while not absent, are much less frequent. The abbot's mystical theology, like all his thought, procedes in fundamentally exegetical fashion—the interpretation of the Song of Songs, and the constant invocation of certain key scriptural texts (such as Matt 11:33; 1 John 4:8, 14; 1 Cor 6.17; 2 Cor 3.18; Phil 3:20–21),[125] and, above all, his amazing ability to combine passages from the whole of the Latin Bible for the service of his teaching—all these together form the texture of Bernard's mystical theory. The emergence of crucial themes from this exegetical matrix, however, makes it possible to summarize Bernard's thought according to a systematic pattern. This is what I will attempt in the remainder of the chapter.[126]

Two things should be initally noted about the structure of the Cistercian's mystical thought—the universality of its message and the dynamism of its view of the soul's progress. At the beginning of the eighty-third of the *Sermons on the Song of Songs*, one of the most profound of the whole series, Bernard insists that every soul, no matter how weighed down by sin, "is able to find in itself not only a source from which it may seek to breathe in hope of pardon, in hope of mercy, but also whence it may dare to aspire to the nuptials of the Word."[127] This emphasis on the universality of the call to contemplation is repeated in a number of places in these sermons where Bernard's message about the delights of the bed of love seem to be directed to any person striving to advance in the Christian life.[128] Nevertheless, Bernard's immediate audience was a monastic one and his conception of the dangers of the secular world and the advantages of life in that training camp for the heavenly Jerusalem which was the monastery introduced a certain tension into his thought.[129] In the early treatise *The Steps of Humilty and Pride*, he affirmed that the two initial stages of humility could be acquired in the world, while the ten higher were only to be attained in the *schola caritatis* of the monastery.[130] Other texts, such as *Sermons on Different Topics* 22,[131] proclaim a form of spiritual elitism that was characteristic of some forms of monasticism from its origins, the model that we have seen affirmed by Cassian and generally predominant in early medieval monasticism. The evidence of Bernard's many letters to nonmonastics may also be taken into account here. Arranged as a kind of *speculum ecclesiae*, a mirror of the duties and the various states of life in the church,[132] the letters contain a wealth of moral and spiritual advice for laity and clergy struggling on the path of salvation. Many of them, however, especially those designed to convince their recipients to join or at least not to abandon the monastery, express a decidedly negative view of life in the world.[133] Bernard certainly believed that salvation was offered to all Christians, and some texts make it clear that saving grace necessarily implies at least the aspiration to the experience of loving union with the Bridegroom in this life for all Christians; but in practice the abbot seems to have thought that it was difficult, if not impossible (miraculous exceptions excluded), for anyone outside the monastery to attain the higher stages of loving union.[134]

A second characteristic of Bernard's view of the call to the delights of loving God is the dynamic and progressive view he had of this invitation. The abbot's notion of the Christian life is that of a single grand continuum of love stretching from the earthly and carnal love of fallen humanity to the heights of the heavenly spousal love in which progress comes only slowly: "I don't want to be immediately at the top; I want to advance step by step."[135] This prudent teaching about the necessity of gradual progression (often based on the image of the ladder, so dear to followers of Benedict because of its appearance in RB 7) exists in tension with the impatience of vehement love that is never satisfied short of the highest experience of union with God.[136] The coexistence of prudence and ardor gives the abbot's thought a special dynamism.

Stages on the Road to Perfection

Like so many other Christian mystics, Bernard frequently presents itineraries or descriptions of the soul's progress. These sketches are essentially pedagogical tools, road maps that the guide of souls gives to his charges to provide them some general sense of what lies ahead. They are not to be mistaken for descriptions of the actual journey itself, an experience unique to each soul and always conducted at the discretion of the Holy Spirit.

In his *The Steps of Humility and Pride* Bernard distinguishes twelve degrees in the progress of humility, the necessary ascetical preparation for the subsequent progress to mystical union.[137] In the eighteenth of the *Sermons on the Song of Songs* he mentions seven progressive stages of grace that culminate in the *plenitudo dilectionis,* or fullness of love.[138] At the end of the same series of *Sermons* a noted text summarizes seven ascending reasons why the soul seeks the Word: "... to whom she consents for her correction, by whom she is illuminated for her knowledge, to whom she owes her virtue, by whom she is reformed to wisdom, to whom she is conformed to beauty, to whom she is wed for her fruitfulness, and whom she enjoys for her bliss."[139] More frequently employed divisions are those of the various steps of love, where the abbot often uses fourfold distinctions.[140] The most noted of these is the famous distinction of four degrees of *amor* found in *On Loving God:* love of self for the sake of self, love of God for the sake of self, love of God for God's sake, and love of self for God's sake.[141] We have also already noted the alternate fourfold division found in *Sermons on Different Topics* 101: *amor carnalis carnaliter, amor carnalis spiritualiter, amor spiritualis carnaliter,* and *amor spiritualis spiritualiter.* The treatise *On Loving God* also contains a tripartition of modes of love into those of the slave, the mercenary, and the son (see *Dil* 12.34), which in the *Sermons on the Song of Songs* is expanded into four—love of slave, love of mercenary, love of son, and love of spouse.[142]

Useful and important as these enumerations are, Bernard's most frequent mode of presenting the soul's progress is through a threefold division of stages well known in Christianity since the time of Origen and whose classic form in East and West had been shaped by the writings of the Pseudo-Dionysius—the division into ascetical purification, virtuous illumination, and loving union, later canonized as the *via purgativa, via illuminativa,* and *via unitiva.* Though Bernard does not actually use these terms, his formulations are variations on this basic pattern.[143]

The abbot of Clairvaux's descriptions of the three stages of the soul's progress are most often presented through the invocation of scriptural images. Among the best known are the three kisses that he discerns in the unusual construction of the opening words of the Song of Songs: "Let him kiss me *with the kiss of the mouth.*"[144] Only after the soul has experienced the two preparatory kisses, the kiss of the feet, or penitential preparation (*Sermon* 3.2), and the kiss of the hands, the practice of virtue (the *gratia bene vivendi* of *Sermon* 3.5), is the soul ready to aspire to the kiss of the kiss of the mouth (*osculum de osculo*), or the direct encounter with the Divine Lover (*Sermon* 3.5–6). In the fourth of the *Sermons on the Song of Songs* the three stages are described as *confessio, devotio,* and *contemplatio*. "The soul finds in God reverent confession by which it lowers itself in humility, and ready devotion by which it renews and restores itself, and delightful contemplation where it rests in ecstasy."[145] Later in the same set of sermons on the three kisses Bernard refers to the three classes of souls who experience them as *confitentes, continentes,* and *contemplantes* (*Sermon* 7.6). These three stages, as we have seen, cannot be separated from the soul's participation in the saving mysteries of Christ's life. The first Sermon on the Annunciation links the testimony of Christ's Passion to the forgiveness of sins, that of the Resurrection to good works, and that of the Ascension to the hope of reward (one presumes both in this life and in heaven since Bernard always conceived of mystical experience as the brief foretaste of heaven).[146] Another version of the triple pattern appears in *Sermons* 10 and 12, which describe the three ointments of the Bride as contrition, devotion, and piety, conceived in ascending order as applied to the feet, head, and whole Body of Christ, that is, the church.[147]

In the second of the sermons for the Feast of the Ascension, Bernard speaks of the three groups of souls who will ascend to heaven—those pulled there, those led, and those rapt to the goal as Paul was (2 Cor 12:2). Each group has its own form of joy:

> The first are certainly happy because they will possess their souls in patience (cf. Luke 21:19); the second are happier because they will confess him voluntarily (cf. Ps 27:7). The third are the happiest. In God's deepest mercy, when the will's power is almost buried, they are rapt into the riches of glory in a fiery spirit, not knowing whether they are in or out of the body, only knowing that they are rapt.[148]

Another important triple category suggests not only the existence of different levels or groups within the church, but also the fact that all three levels continue to coexist within each soul. In the fifty-seventh of the *Sermons on the Song of Songs* the abbot interprets Song 2:10 (*Surge, propera, amica mea, columba mea, formosa mea*) as signifying three aspects of the soul according to its different activities. The soul is a "friend" who takes the role of Martha in Luke 10:39–40 when she preaches, advises, and serves others. The soul is a "dove," or a Lazarus, when she weeps and prays to God for forgiveness of her sins; and she is a "beautiful one," or Mary, when, "gleaming with heavenly desire, she clothes herself with the beauty of heavenly contemplation, though only for the time when this can be done properly and conveniently."[149] The abbot goes on to note, "Everyone in whose soul these three things fittingly and conveniently come together will be held perfect. He will know how to weep for himself, to rejoice in God, and at the same time he will be able to serve his neighbor's needs."[150] The same exegesis of Song 2:10 in connection with Martha, Mary, and Lazarus is richly developed in the third of the sermons for the Feast of the Annunciation.[151]

The Role of Experience and the Spiritual Senses

In entering upon the more detailed consideration of Bernard's thought on the soul's progress, especially in the third or highest stage, which is properly mystical, we must keep before our minds the words with which he began his analysis of the personal meaning of the Song of Songs: *Hodie legimus in libro experientiae* ("Today we read in the book of experience"). Autobiographical references to experiences of God's presence, while not totally lacking, were not characteristic of patristic authors. (Some important texts from Origen, Augustine, and Gregory were known to Bernard.) Many late medieval mystics, especially after the thirteenth century, had no qualms about including extensive accounts of their visions of God and other special experiences in their writings. Bernard is less reticent than most of the fathers, while also remaining less voluble than such late medieval writers. The Cistercian's *Sermons on the Song of Songs* contain several passages of a directly autobiographical character, notably a famous text in *Sermon* 74.5–7 modeled on Origen's description of the Word's visit to the soul.[152] Even more important, and indicative of significant innovation in the abbot's thought, is his constant insistence on the necessity of the personal experience of his listeners as the only way to understand his message.[153] "In matters of this kind, understanding can follow only where experience leads."[154]

Bernard's appeal to personal experience as the *sine qua non* for grasping his message should give the nonmystic interpreter pause, since it underlines the limits of any merely academic or theoretical grasp of the passionate abbot's teaching. Important as this limitation is, it need not exclude all attempts to provide summaries of a message that is meant to surpass theological reflection but that is not meant to be independent of it. (In several places Bernard reminds his readers that experience can be deceptive, always needing to be measured against the norm of faith.)[155]

Bernard's appeals to the test of personal experience point to an important dimension present in the mysticism of the twelfth century. The abbot's

use of the metaphor of the book to refer to experience is particularly pregnant. An ancient theme in Christian thought, one we have seen in a number of authors studied here, conceived of two "books" by which God
instructed his rational creatures to the supernal goal: the book of creation
and the book of scripture.[156] In humanity's unfallen state, the book of creation was fully adequate to teach the necessary truths about God and
humans' responsibility to him; but since the fall, we are no longer capable
of reading this book adequately. Therefore, God in his infinite mercy has
prepared a second book, the book of scripture, in order to convey to fallen
humanity the mystery of his being and his saving love. Scripture, as an intelligible universe, contains all knowledge and thus constitutes the proper
and complete object of all Christian teaching, as we have seen, for example,
in Origen. Although Bernard does not explicitly develop the "two books"
theme, his attitude toward scripture leaves no doubt that he shares this
basic approach. Where the abbot of Clairvaux makes a real contribution is
in adding a third book to the traditional two–the book of experience noted
in *Sermon* 3 and elsewhere.[157]

Bernard does not develop his thoughts on the book of experience in a systematic way, though recent work has shown that it is possible to construct a
theory of religious experience from his reflections.[158] What is important for
our purposes, however, is to note the role that experiential testing occupies
in his thought. The abbot puts his audience in an "intertextual" situation in
which the biblical book, especially the Song of Songs, serves as both a norm
and a guide, while the personal book of experience is meant to act as a living mirror of the same message.[159] The reader of the sermons is placed both
within and between the two books. What is essential is reciprocity of the
reading whose goal is an ever-deepening appropriation of the biblical text in
the light of mystical experience and a more profound grasp of the spiritual
meaning of the Song through a learning that is experiential, not academic.[160]

Although Bernard's emphasis on the necessity of the constant presence of
the book of experience is new, one of the ways in which he effects the translation from the book of scripture to the book of experience is through the investigation of the spiritual senses of the soul, a theme first made explicit in
Origen's commentary on the Song, and one found in various ways in many
earlier Western mystical authors, as we have seen.[161] True to his fashion in
avoiding speculation for speculation's sake, Bernard does not theorize about
the spiritual senses;[162] but his frequent evocation of a wide variety of transformed sense images, drawn both from the Song and from the whole range
of scripture, to describe how the soul is gradually conformed to the Word
shows that the spiritual senses play an important role in his thought.

As was the case with Christian mystics before him, Bernard's employment of the spiritual senses as modes of understanding the experience of the divine presence tends to be synaesthetic in nature, appealing to a wide range of sense images and sometimes deliberately mingling diverse sensory perceptions. Like all classical Christian mystics, he gives the sensation of sight, or contemplative vision, an important role. Although at times he privileges spiritual seeing as the highest of the inner sensitivities of the soul, in his usual practice he rarely paints a scene or invites his readers to visualize something for the delight of "the eyes that are the internal senses and affections."[163] Much of this has to do with his insistence that in humanity's present fallen situation hearing must precede seeing. In the twenty-eighth of the *Sermons on the Song of Songs,* he tells us that just as Adam and Eve fell through listening to the serpent, we begin to restore what was lost to us through hearing the gospel.[164] This external, physical hearing brings us to the faith that will eventually lead to the vision of God in heaven (*Sermon* 28.5). In this life, however, faith acts primarily to unlock the interior, spiritual senses, which Bernard often describes in terms of the "touching" of Christ. Mary Magdalene was forbidden to touch the risen Savior in a physical way (John 20:17). "And yet she could [touch him], but by desire not by hand, by wish not by eye, by faith not by the senses."[165] Christ promises the soul grown beautiful in the life of faith that in the "deep and mystical breast . . . , you will touch with the hand of faith, the finger of desire, the embrace of devotion; you will touch with the eye of the mind."[166] The abbot concludes with an alliterative flourish impossible to convey in English: *Talem talis taliterque tange et dic: "Dilectus meus candidus et rubicundus, electus e millibus"* ("Let such a Bride touch such a Groom in such a way and say, 'My Beloved is fair and ruddy, chosen from thousands'" [Song 5:10]).[167]

If touch predominates in the synaesthetic presentation of *Sermon* 28, in other of the Song sermons the internal senses of smell and taste are favored. In *Sermon* 67 there is an extended discussion of the Psalm text *Eructavit cor meum verbum bonum* ("My heart gave forth [literally, 'belched'] a good word" [Ps 44:2]).[168] Bernard interprets the "sacred belch," perhaps indelicately to modern tastes, as the "good odor" that comes forth from the mouths of satiated, advanced souls like Moses, David, and Paul, who have fed deep on the Lord's fare. "The just one will delight in the Lord, experiencing by taste what I sense by its smell. . . . Indeed, to behold is to taste and to see that the Lord is sweet."[169] Hence it is "through the odor of expectation that the soul attains the taste of contemplation."[170] This view agrees with a passage in *On Loving God* which affirms that it is "tasted sweetness" (*gustata suavitas*) that marks the entry into third level of love, where a person begins to love God for God's own sake.[171]

The abbot of Clairvaux, therefore, does not appear to have had a strictly established hierarchy of the spiritual senses–the delights brought by the presence of the Word are described sometimes as a mingling of smell and taste (e.g., *Sermon* 9.6), sometimes primarily in tactile fashion (e.g., *Sermon* 16.2), and sometimes more in terms of illumination or a new way of seeing (e.g., *Sermon* 41.3 and 45.5–6). At the end of the fiftieth of the *Sermons on the Song of Songs*, Bernard views the activation and development of the spiritual senses as a reordering of love, the overarching theme of so much twelfth-century mysticism:

> In tears I ask: "How long shall we smell and not taste, gazing toward our homeland but not grasping it, hailing it from afar with sighs?" O Truth, homeland of exiles and end of exile! I see you, but caught in the flesh I cannot enter you–befouled with sins, I am not worthy to be admitted. O Wisdom, you reach mightily from one end to the other in setting up and maintaining things, and you arrange all things sweetly by blessing and ordering the affections. Direct our actions as our temporal need demands and dispose our affections as your eternal truth requires, so that each of us may confidently glory in you and say, "He has ordered charity in me" (Song 2:4).[172]

To summarize what we have seen thus far of Bernard's notion of the soul's itinerary and its dependence on the gradual awakening of the spiritual senses, it may be helpful to analyze *Sermon* 23, one of the most systematically organized presentations of the mystical path in the abbot's writings. Commenting on Song 1:3 ("The King has brought me into his cellars"), Bernard uses this text to integrate the Bride's interior spiritual progress through the dynamism of the internal senses with three ways of interpreting the scriptural text.

Three places in the Divine Bridegroom's dwelling provide the topography for the introvertive journey: the garden (*hortus*) of Song 5:1, the cellars or storerooms (*cellaria*) of the verse in question, and the bed-chamber (*cubiculum*) of Song 3:4.[173] Each of these locations represents a level of reading scripture that must be personally appropriated in the book of experience through the activation of the spiritual senses. "Let the garden be the plain and simple historical sense [of scripture], the cellar the moral sense, the bridal chamber the mystery of visionary contemplation" (*theorica contemplatio*).[174] The garden of the historical sense introduces readers to the history of salvation divided into the three great works of creation, reconciliation, and restoration–that is, the coming renewal of the universe (*Sermon* 23.4). The moral sense begins the personal appropriation of salvation. It too has three divisions structured according to a spiritual reading of the "smell" of the Bridegroom's spices (*aromata*), the "feel" of his ointments (*unguenta*), and the "taste" of his wine (*vinum*). The cellar of spices represents the discipline by which we seek to tame "willfulness of character" (*insolentia morum*) through humble obedience. This leads on to the cellar of oil or ointment where humans, equal in nature from their creation, but divided by sin, learn to live together in harmony. Finally, the wine-cellar is where the soul tastes "the wine of burning zeal in charity" and learns to take charge of others through its possession of the fullness of grace (*Sermon* 23.6–8).

With regard to the delights of the bed-chamber of contemplation, Bernard does not claim exhaustive knowledge, but he admits, "If I knew nothing at all, I would say nothing."[175] Scripture teaches that there are many rooms in the Bridegroom's dwelling, just as the Song suggests various kinds of souls that enjoy this third stage of progress, when it speaks of maidens (*adulescentulae*), concubines (*concubinae*), queens (*reginae*), and the "beautiful and perfect dove" (*columba formosa, perfecta*) of Song 6:8 (*Sermon* 23.9–10). Bernard proceeds to identify three stages of contemplation. The first is where the soul experiences both delight (*delectatio*) and restlessness (*inquietudo*); this cannot be the true bed-chamber (*Sermon* 23.10). In the second stage the "fearful contemplative" (*timoratus contemplator*) beholds God's eternal judgments and is struck with fear. According to the abbot, this marks the begining of wisdom, because "instruction [as given in the first stage] makes us learned, but affection [given here] makes us wise."[176] The first stage forms a necessary preparation, but "God first begins to get a taste of the soul when he moves it (*afficit*) to fear, not when he instructs it in knowledge."[177] This, too, cannot be the true bedroom. Bernard continues:

> But there is a place where God is truly seen as at rest and giving rest—a place altogether of the Bridegroom, not of the Judge or Teacher. To me at least (I can't speak for others) this would certainly be the bed-chamber if a person at some time were given entry. But alas, rare the hour and short the stay (*rara hora et parva mora*)![178]

Though Bernard presents this noted passage in the third person, the context indicates that he is speaking of his own experience, which he claims, in rather daring fashion, consists in an experience of the soul's eternal predestination that it is numbered among the elect. "I perceived these people as if they had never sinned, because even if they seemed to have sinned to some extent in time, these sins did not appear in eternity in that the Father's love covers the multitude of their sins" (1 Pet 4:8).[179] Although "this mystery, this sanctuary of God" is certainly the bed-chamber where the King retires in private at day's end with his closest friends, Bernard concludes by wondering whether or not it is that bed-chamber in which the Bride, or unique dove, rejoices (*Sermon* 23.16). The lack of erotic language compared with other passages in the *Sermons on the Song of Songs* indicates that in this passage the abbot is speaking about a different kind of mystical experience from the bridal variety with which he is usually associated.

The Presence of God

The stages of progress outlined in *Sermon* 23 and elsewhere culminate in the encounter with the Divine King present in the hidden *cubiculum*, that is, the interior of the soul. The soul's advance in contemplation, according to Bernard, is a journey powered by the love that makes God more and more present to us. *Praesens igitur Deo est qui Deum amat in quantum amat*, that is, "A person is present to God to the extent that the person loves him."[180] The intimate relationship of love and contemplation with the divine presence brings us to the heart of Bernard's mystical theology.

The presence of God was something that Bernard reflected upon throughout his writings. While it is true that we live here below more by faith than by vision, that is, more by the memory of God's gracious gifts than by the enjoyment of his presence,[181] the Divine Lover is still present to us in a variety of ways—to all by his majesty, to some of his rational creatures by grace, and to the Bride in a special manner.[182] What exactly is this special presence the Bride enjoys, and how is it related to the presence in grace found in all virtuous Christians?

Bernard's teaching here is traditional in form, but developed in an original way. God dwells in every good soul as a special "heaven" of its own according to the capacity of its love.[183] As the soul progressively enlarges in love toward the goal of full liberty of spirit, it becomes a more commodious home for its Divine Guest (see *Sermon* 27.10–11), and it also becomes more "sensitive" to the interior experience of his presence. This is a gift given only to few, involving "the presence of the Benefactor and Giver himself as far as possible while one is in the weak body."[184] Bernard's best-known passage on the sensed presence of God in the soul describes in masterly fashion the coming of the *Verbum* as Spouse (see *Sermon* 74.5–7),[185] but it is important to begin with a look at the few passages where he stresses a trinitarian dimension to the experience of divine indwelling.

Early in the *Sermons on the Song of Songs*, Bernard devoted an entire sermon, the one that concludes the introductory set of eight exegeting the kiss of Song 1:1, to the role of the Trinity in the soul's progress. The kiss of the mouth (*osculum de ore*) is here identified with the Holy Spirit understood as the mutual kiss, or bond between the Father and the Son, who is breathed forth by the risen Christ upon the apostles (*Sermon* 8.1–2). The Bride's longing, then, is a desire for the Holy Spirit, the *amor et benignitas* of the Father and Son, whose coming brings the soul the twin gifts of knowledge and love (*agnitio et amor*) that delight the reason and the will, the soul's two spiritual lips. This coming constitutes the "kiss of the kiss" (*osculum de osculo*), that is, of the Holy Spirit.[186] Trinitarian texts like this are rare in the *Sermons on the Song of Songs*.[187] Their appearance recalls a passage found in the early *The Steps of Humility and Pride,* which provides a fuller treatment of the Trinity's role in the mystical life.[188] Here Bernard advances another version of the three stages of the soul's progress, this one tied to the work of the three divine persons in the gradual perfecting of truth–the Son brings us to "strict truth" (*veritas severa*) through the work of humility, the Holy Spirit grants "devout truth" (*veritas pia*), and the Father bestows "pure truth" (*veritas pura*) through the rapture of contemplation (*Hum* 6.19). The latter portion of this passage presents yet another understanding of the role of the Trinity in the spiritual life. The Son raises and heals reason so that it can judge itself in order to produce humility, while the Holy Spirit visits and purifies the will to give birth to charity. "Finally, the Father unites (*conglutinat*) to himself as glorious Bride the soul which is without stain through humility and without spot through charity, so that will does not war with reason nor does reason deceive will."[189] At this early stage in his career, Bernard identified union with the Father as the ultimate taste of the divine presence possible in this life.[190] His reflection on the nature of ecstasy or *raptus* in *The Steps of Humility and Pride* 8.22–23 stresses the totally gratuitous character of any ascent to the third heaven of Paul (2 Cor 2:12), the place where the Father, who has never ventured forth from the hidden recesses of the divinity, is to be found. It is interesting that the same two texts (Song 1:3 and 3:4) that Bernard later used in *Sermon* 23 to express the union between the Word as Bridegroom and his friends is employed here to describe the union between the soul and the Father.

Why did Bernard choose not to develop the trinitarian perspective in his later works?[191] He does not tell us, and so any answer is at best a conjecture. But the Bernardine spiritual program is so closely tied to the role of the Word made flesh, as we have seen, that the trinitarian aspect, while never denied, comes to be more and more muted.[192]

Most of Bernard's references to the divine presence concern the individual Persons of the Trinity. Following the lead suggested in *Sermon* 8, a number of these witness to the experience of the presence and work of the Holy Spirit in the soul. Bernard holds that some Christians at least are able to perceive (*sentire*) the Spirit within them crying "Abba, Father" (Gal 4:6; see *Sermon* 8.9). All Christians, however, are called to strive to become as sensitive as possible to the comings and goings of the Spirit in order to become more aware of how to act in accordance with the Spirit's will.[193] Sometimes, the Holy Spirit's presence also invokes that of the Son;[194] at other times, we find texts that speak of the Father and the Son as present in the soul without specific reference to the Holy Spirit.[195] But Bernard's most famous texts referring to the perception of God's presence, as we have noted, refer to the Word.

"It is not given to all to enjoy the hidden and welcome presence of the Spouse in a single place, but only as it has been prepared for each by the Father."[196] To the soul that strives to prepare itself in every way, Bernard is sure that God will not withhold the blessing of his presence, "even though he who visits in the spirit comes secretly and stealthily like a shy lover."[197] Any discourse about the fundamental virtues of the Christian life can be a reminder that the Lord is about to visit the soul. The visit's characteristic sign is the sensation of the fire of divine love, "which consumes but does not injure, burning sweetly, devastating pleasantly. . . . Therefore understand that the Lord is present in the power (*virtus*) that transforms you and the love (*amor*) that inflames you."[198]

In the seventy-fourth of the *Sermon on the Song of Songs* Bernard provides his most famous description of this experience, one modeled on a text from Origen,[199] but not less Bernardine for all that.[200] The soul that calls on the Bridegroom to "return," as the Bride does in Song 2:17, clearly demonstrates that she has already enjoyed the presence, if not the fullness, of the Divine Lover who comes and goes as he wills (*Sermon* 74.3). The "little while" (*modicum*) that Christ promised would be the extent of his absence from the apostles in John 16:17 indicates this absence, which, though brief from the divine perspective, is too long for the soul, leading her to exclaim, *O modicum et modicum! O modicum longum!* (*Sermon* 74.4). Following Paul's example (2 Cor 11–12), Bernard makes bold to recount his own experience in a passage which, despite its length, needs to be quoted in full:

> Now bear with my foolishness a little while (2 Cor 11:1). I want to tell you as I promised about my own experience of this sort of thing. Not that it is important (2 Cor 12:1), but I am relating it to be helpful. If you profit from it, I shall be consoled for my foolishness. If not, I will proclaim my foolishness. I admit that the Word has also come to me, and–I speak foolishly (2 Cor 11:17)– come often. As often as he has come to me, I have not perceived the different times of his coming. I perceived that he has been present (*adesse sensi*); I remembered that he had been there. Sometimes I was able to anticipate his coming, but I never felt it, nor his departing either. Even now I admit that I don't know whence he came into my soul and where he went after he left it, and by what way he entered and left.[201]

The Word, of course, is not perceptible to the exterior senses. If we ask where he is or from whence he has come, Bernard says we can get no answer. The Word is no-"where," that is, he is not in any place. We are rather in him. His presence can be sensed, perceived or felt only by the happy individual "in whom that Word dwells, who lives for him, who is moved by him."[202] The abbot's test for the authenticity of the visit of the *Verbum-Sponsus* is not in terms of any external experience of either normal or paranormal kind, but is based on the effect that the Word has on one's manner of life through the kindling of reforming love. "As I said, it was only from the movement of my heart that I understood (*intellexi*) his presence."[203] Similarly, the mark of his departure is the lessening of love that leaves the soul that has had "such experience of the Word" (*tale sane experimentum de Verbo*) with an ardent and increasing desire for his return (*Sermon* 74.7). Love and desire are the key.

Love as the Center of Bernard's Mysticism

Amor-caritas-desiderium: Bernard always returns to the same group of affective terms as he attempts to describe the experience of God possible in this life.[204] We must now enter in this central area of Bernard's thought in order to synthesize the many strands of his presentation. Though there are a number of texts in which the abbot summarizes his teaching on love, notably in *On Loving God* and in *Sermons* 83–85, my procedure will be to thematize the major lines of his teaching from throughout his works.

The Priority of Divine Love

Deus caritas est (1 John 4:8). No text from the whole of scripture meant more to our Cistercian than this passage. Bernard thought that it conveyed the most that we can ever really know about God—and all that we ever need to know.[205] "God also loves and has no other source save himself from which he loves. That is why he loves more ardently, because he does not so much possess love as he is love."[206] Unlike the contemporary schoolmen, Bernard did not spend much time speculating about the divine nature and analyzing the divine attributes, but in a passage in his treatise *Consideration* he does discuss the four essential characteristics of God on the basis of Ephesians 3:18, "to understand with all the saints what might be the length, the breadth, the height, and the depth."[207] God's length is his eternity; his breadth the love that "surpasses not only every affection, but also all knowledge."[208] His height is his power; his depth his wisdom. Though Bernard does not say it here, it is clear from his other writings that among these attributes *maior autem his caritas est* ("The greatest of these is charity," 1 Cor 12:13).

Love is the "law" of God's being: He cannot do other than love, though, of course, he loves from the complete and spontaneous freedom of his infinite nature. Though Bernard, like most classical Christian theologians, could not conceive of a God who could change or be affected by what lay outside his own being, God could be moved from within by his love for his creatures. "God cannot suffer, but he can suffer with, he whose nature it is always to have mercy and to spare."[209] What this means in practice is that God's love always has priority over and is the source of all other forms of love. "In this is charity, not that we have loved God, but that he loved us first" (1 John 4:10)–another text from the first Epistle of John that the abbot never tired of quoting. The absolute priority of divine love over human, of course, is a theme common to all Christian writers; but few have made as much of it as Bernard.[210] The abbot's emphasis on God's initiation of love agrees with his Pauline and Augustinian understanding of the necessity of grace. It is also the basis for the dynamism of his view of love. As the Bride comes to recognize that she is always both anticipated and surpassed in love, she is impelled to seek to grow in love more and more in order to respond to the generosity of her Divine Lover. As a text in *Sermon* 45 puts it:

> His beauty is his love, all the greater because it was prior (*praeveniens*). The more she understands that she was loved before being a lover, the more and amply she cries out in her heart's core and with the voice of her deepest affections that she must love him. Thus, the Word's speaking is the giving of the gift, the soul's response is wonder and thanksgiving. The more she grasps that she is overcome in loving, the more she loves. The more she admits that he has gone before her, the more awestruck she is.[211]

The Nature of Human Love

The soul's response to the gift of love given by the Divine Lover constitutes the reality and the stages of the love by which we ascend to God. Love (*amor-desiderium-dilectio*) is the most important of the four fundamental or attractions (*affectus*) of the human subject.[212] It is the motive power of the natural appetite (*appetitus naturalis*) that, along with the basic cognitive power or *sensus*, characterize human nature as created spirit.[213] Bernard has little interest in spelling out a detailed faculty psychology. His concern is rather with understanding the dynamics of the way in which the love that has been planted in our nature, even when that love is curved in on itself in the *cupiditas*–that is, the selfishness–of fallen humanity, calls out for its Maker and launches us on the path toward the heavenly joy and love that are its true goal. Developing Augustine's famous remark about the inability of the human heart to be fully satisfied with anything short of God,[214] Bernard says in *On Loving God*:

> ... for by that law of his cupidity according to which in all other things a person thirsts for what he does not have more than for what he has, and feels distaste more for what he has than for what he doesn't, so that everything in heaven and earth is no sooner obtained than disdained, finally, beyond the shadow of a doubt, he will run up against him who alone of all things he lacks–God.[215]

This same treatise provides us with the abbot's best known map of the stages of love, the four degrees that he first sketched out in a letter sent to the Carthusian community at Mont-Dieu (Ep. 11) and subsequently expanded in the book sent to Cardinal Humbert.

Causa diligendi Deum, Deus est; modus, sine modo diligere ("God is the reason for loving God; the measure of loving him is to love without measure"), as Bernard put it in a noted passage at the opening of *On Loving God*.[216] The problem with fallen humanity is that we can no longer directly appreciate *why* God is the only real reason for loving God, nor can we understand *how* to love without measure since our particular needs always measure our desire. Fallen humans' unending desire for more and more finite objects to satiate their hunger, as we have seen above,[217] presents a perverted image of the true unending love, the insatiable satisfaction (to coin a Bernardine phrase) which is the true love of God. As both the efficient and the final cause of love,

> God himself provides the occasion, he creates the affection, he consummates the desire.... You are good, O Lord, to the soul that seeks you. What then in the case of the one that finds you? What is wonderful in this is that no one can seek you who has not first found you. Therefore, you wish to be found so that you may be sought, to be sought that you may be found. You can indeed seek and find, but you cannot be forestalled.[218]

God's preventive, or prior, love must meet the fallen creature on the only level on which it can be found, that of selfish carnal love. Hence the reason for the Word's taking on flesh, as we have seen in our consideration of the sixth of the *Sermons on the Song of Songs*. Here in *On Loving God*, the abbot spells out the transformative stages of love's education, beginning with the "carnal love by which a person loves himself for his own sake before everything."[219] If this love did not retain at least a shadow of its divine source there would be nothing that could be done to transform it. Even carnal love, however, is the use of a basically good appetite in a wrong, or perverted, way. The humble and selfless example provided by the God-Man in his earthly career begins the expansion and reordering of our selfish love through its powerful and sweet activity in two basic ways. The first of these is through the *amor carnalis Christi*, the physical love of Christ and his saving works which we have seen played such an important role in Bernard's preaching.[220] The second is by means of the *amor carnalis socialis*, in which our recognition of our neighbor's wretchedness (both in the evil of sin and in daily needs), leads us to moderate our own pleasures and to come to each other's assistance.[221]

It is perhaps surprising that the second degree of love, that in which a person loves God for what God has done for him or her (*cum homo diligit Deum propter se*), should receive so little analysis in the treatise, since this is the place where most believers will find themselves as they come to recognize what great love God has shown them. Actually, it may be more correct to say that the audience for whom Bernard wrote was somewhere between stages 2 and 3 in a progression of the reformation of love that is mapped in only a general way by the four stages. He summarizes the relations between the two degrees at the end of the work:

> When one sees that he is not self-sufficient, he begins to seek and to love the God he needs for himself through faith. Then he loves God in the second degree—not for God's sake, but for his own. But when, on the basis of his own need, such a person begins to adore and pay attention to God—thinking, reading, praying, obeying—God slowly and gradually becomes known in the form of acquaintance and so grows sweet. In this way, having tasted that the Lord is sweet (Ps 33.9), the soul passes to the third stage in order to love God no longer for her own sake but for God's sake. It will surely be in this stage for a long time. I don't know if anyone perfectly attains the fourth stage in this life—that in which someone loves himself only for God's sake. If anyone has experienced it, speak up! It seems impossible to me.[222]

The body of *On Loving God* contains a good deal more analysis, especially of the fourth degree, the one that Bernard was not sure could ever be "perfectly" (*perfecte*) enjoyed in this life. Some students of Bernard have detected a shift or progression from the early letter to the Carthusians (written before 1125) incorporated at the end of the work, which seems to think of the fourth degree as accessible only in heaven, through the more ambivalent treatment of the possibility of earthly attainment of the fourth degree in the treatise proper (which may date from the early 1130s),[223] to the numerous mystical passages in the *Sermons on the Song of Songs* (1135–1153) in which the abbot seems to affirm the possibility of brief experiences of the highest kind during this life.[224] This may well be the case, but the rhetorical nature of Bernard's presentations are meant both to reveal and to conceal his message, making it hard to be certain about such questions. If we emphasize the adjective *perfecte* in the first account, Bernard's subsequent discussions may not be very different from the earliest one.

The abbot of Clairvaux's other enumerations of the stages in the progression of love back to God are less detailed than the four degrees of *On Loving God*, but not less significant. The fourfold pattern of *Sermons on Different Topics* 101 discussed earlier,[225] though presented in only a few lines, is revealing of the core of Bernard's thought, based as it is on the transition from the carnal to the spiritual level through our participation in Christ's mysteries. Several threefold divisions also appear in Bernard, the most noted being the triad *amor carnalis, amor rationalis,* and *amor spiritualis,*[226] a pattern that was probably taken from Origen and was much developed by William of St. Thierry.[227] A division of *affectio* into "that which the flesh begets, that which reason rules, and that which wisdom establishes" is clearly somewhat different,[228] because it specifies the first kind as blameworthy, whereas the *amor carnalis* of *Sermon* 20 and elsewhere is a carnal love that is already on the path to salvation.[229]

Another triple pattern is reflected in the theme of the three nourishments of love suggested by Song 5:1. We eat the food of love while still detained here below in the body, but our souls will begin to drink love's wine after death in heaven. However, the final inebriating draught will only be quaffed at the time of the resurrection of the body: "Eat before death, drink after death, and we will be made drunk after the resurrection."[230] Finally, we need to note again Bernard's typically ambiguous four- and fivefold enumerations of the *affectiones,* which overlap with his distinctions of loves, at times being considered modes of love,[231] at times being discriminated from true—that is, from spousal–love, as in the following succinct text in the seventh of the *Sermons on the Song of Songs:* "I set out different affections so that the one pertaining to the Bride may be clearer. A slave fears the Lord's face, a hireling hopes for his generosity. A disciple is attentive to his master; a son honors his father—but the one who seeks a kiss, she loves."[232] The complexities of Bernard's analyses of the various kinds of loves indicate that no single pattern can be taken as exhaustive of the whole.[233] The Cistercian's writings manifest a rhetorical complexity that only reluctantly and after much prayerful reading (*lectio divina*) reveals an inner message all too easily perverted if one attempts to portray it in any simple linear or discursive mode. Bernard's rhetoric, as Luke Anderson reminds us, is practical, prudential and "imperating," that is, designed to foster the reader's experience of God.[234] One thing is clear, however: the abbot was sure that the primary way to achieve this effect was through the language of bridal love.

Bridal Love

> Love is a great thing, but there are degrees in it. The Bride is at the top. Children also love, but with thought to an inheritance. . . . I am suspicious of a love which seems to be supported by hope of gaining something else. . . . Pure love has no self-interest. Pure love does not take its power from hope, nor does it feel any kind of distrust. It belongs to the Bride, because this is what a Bride is. Her reality and her hope is one single love; she is rich in it and the Bridegroom is content with it. He is not looking for anything else; she has nothing else. This is why he is a Groom and she is the Bride. That is proper to them which no one else attains, not even a son.[235]

This is how Bernard sums up the position of the Bride and points to what defines her: the pure, disinterested, and total character of her affection. God is what he has, as Bernard, following Augustine, held. God does not possess love but is completely love. No creature can ever attain this transcendent simple identification, but the Bride comes closest in her total absorption in loving without thought of self or of reward.[236] "Even though the creature loves less, because it is less, still if she loves from her whole self nothing is lacking where everything is given. Loving in this way, as I have said, is being married."[237] In several texts the abbot ascribes three qualities to this bridal love–sweetness or purity, wisdom or prudence, and strength or impetuousity. These are patterned on the example of the Word become flesh, who perfectly fulfilled the essential command, "You shall love the Lord your God with your whole heart, your whole soul and your whole mind" (Deut 6:5). As he puts it at the end of the seventy-third of the *Sermons on the Song of Songs*, "a single soul, if she loves God, sweetly, wisely and vehemently, is a Bride."[238]

Spousal, or marital, love is above all pure or sweet love, but it is also a love that has many other dimensions. It is wise and prudent, that is, not contrary to intellect and understanding, the higher dimensions of human knowing. It is also vehement and forceful in ways that may seem insane to those who have not experienced it. Such love is completely mutual, and it is perfectly satisfying in the sense that it is the highest form of vision or contemplation of God and the most exalted type of union. Finally, it sets in order all the other affections of the soul. These characteristics of bridal love will provide the structure for the analysis that follows.

Pure or Sweet Love

The problem of "pure" love has had a long history in Christian thought. Though theological debate about the nature (and even the very possibility) of pure love reached a level of explicitness in the Quietist controversy at the end of the seventeenth century that much influenced later discussion, the issue was born with Christianity itself.[239] Bernard's teaching on pure love has been attacked by modern Protestant theologians, for example, Anders Nygren, and defended by Catholic scholars such as Étienne Gilson and Martin D'Arcy.[240] Judgments about its coherence and validity doubtless depend very much on the philosophical and theological perspectives adopted by the interpreter. But any view that fails to take into account the abbot's own intentions would suffer from historical myopia.

A careful reading of the full range of Bernard's texts on pure love indicates that he tried to bring together what we might call the pyschological (or, perhaps better, "experimental") perspective of the soul so lost in love of God that she no longer has any thought beyond love with the ontological or "objective" perspective according to which a universe governed by a just God cannot allow such selfless love to go unrewarded (God must crown the merits that are nothing more than his own gifts). "God is not loved without a reward even if he is to be loved without thought of reward," as Bernard put it in *On Loving God*.[241] From the perspective of the Bride herself, love, if it is truly bridal love, *must* be its own reward—"It is its own merit, its own reward. Love has no cause or fruit beyond itself: its fruit is its use. I love because I love. I love that I may love."[242] Love, then, is the ultimate enjoyment of the Bride—her truest "sweetness"—because it is its own reward: *Amo, quia amo; amo, ut amem.* From this viewpoint, the issue of what kind of "self-love" remains in pure love is clear, as Étienne Gilson argued.[243] We do indeed continue to love ourselves in the fourth degree of the purest love—it is, after all, the stage Bernard describes as that in which "homo diligit *se* propter Deum" (*Dil* 10.27). But we do not love ourselves as discrete, independent entities, especially as fallen beings, whose love is a kind of selfishness that strives to become independent of God and others in a proud and unhappy parody of divine self-sufficiency. Rather, we love the "self" insofar as it has recovered its true reality in God, that is, as it is regaining the *imago et similitudo Dei* whose being, in its deepest reality, is nothing more than the created manifestation of the overwhelming divine love itself. Bernard was certainly aware of the subtle ways in which self-love seeks to reintroduce itself on every level of the spiritual path. From the theoretical point of view, at least, he tried with all his effort to exclude subjective self-interest. From the objective point of view, he would have insisted that his view of God's generosity to the loving soul was nothing more than the proper recognition of the essential goodness of the Creator. God loved us first, both in creating us and in redeeming us. Bernard would have thought us to be seriously failing to live the new divine life of grace if we were to try to exclude *all* love of ourselves (those selves for whom Christ died).[244] The real issue for the abbot was in learning *how* we are to love ourselves in an unselfish way.

Love and Knowledge (*amor sapiens*)

Bernard's preoccupation with love as the power that leads the soul to God has misled some investigators into easy labelings of him as an "affective" mystic.[245] The problem with such classifications is that they often forget that all Christian mystics are by definition affective mystics in the sense that they believe, on the basis of scripture, that God is love and that love is the power that leads and unites us to God in both this life and the next.[246] Such characterizations also often fail to recognize the importance of the role that intellect and understanding play in the path to God, even with supposedly "affective" mystics like Bernard. The classical Christian mystics all believed that God is Truth as well as Love. Indeed, it is because God is the Love who is identical with Truth that the bridal love which attains him must be wise (*sapiens*),[247] prudent (*prudens*), and even reasonable (*rationalis*)–as well as being sweet (*dulcis*) and violent (*vehemens*).

Bernard had little interest in technical epistemology for its own sake. He shows none of the fascination with the actual process of understanding found in Abelard and Anselm,[248] and even in his friend William of St. Thierry. But the abbot of Clairvaux accepted the major commonplaces of the Western Christian tradition, namely, that the capacities to know and to love were the essential notes of human nature and that both powers, though injured by sin, would share in the gradual restoration of the divine likeness made possible by the saving work of Christ. Although he does not explicitly say so, it is clear that Bernard thought that the intellectual power was, if anything, even more injured, more susceptible to pride, more tempted to rely on itself even after grace had intervened, than the will. Hence his suspicions about those who had more confidence in intellect, like Abelard.[249]

Reflecting on the primordial sin of the angels, Bernard engages in a wordplay on the name of *Lucifer* (light-bearer), noting that it would have been better if he had been a "fire-bearer" (*ignifer*).[250] Lucifer's false and self-centered "light-bearing" was the model for all subsequent sin. Hence, we must always beware of the temptation "to shine" with our own brilliance of mind. "Why do you hasten to shine?" he asks. "The time is not yet come in which 'The just will shine like the sun in the kingdom of their Father' (Matt 13:43). In the meantime, this appetite for shining is dangerous. It is much better to burn with love (*fervere*)."[251] There are, of course, models of virtue, like John the Baptist, who demonstrate how restored humanity joins both love and knowledge, both shining and burning. "John shone, the more brightly he burned with love, the more truly the less he desired to shine."[252] True knowledge, that is, the self-knowledge of humility, is as necessary to the foundation of the reformation of the intellectual side of human nature as the *amor carnalis Christi* is to the affective side. This balanced view is the source of Bernard's frequently pointed remarks about worldly wisdom.[253] He does not condemn it for what it does, admitting that such wisdom is the source of a real *scientia*; rather, he attacks it for what it fails to do—in its pride it refuses to be subordinated to the *affectus* or *fervor* without which "science puffs up" (*scientia inflatur*, 1 Cor 8:1).[254]

Intellect by itself, especially since the fall, represents a block to reaching God; but the *cooperation* between intellect and love is still *necessary* for attaining the goal. This is Bernard's constant teaching, especially evident in his sermons for the Feast of the Ascension. The fourth sermon ("On the Different Kinds of Ascension") emphasizes the contrast between the false ascents of pride (i.e., those of Lucifer and Adam) and the humble descent of Christ into the flesh which is the foundation for his Ascension and ours,[255] drawing the expected lesson that love is what enables us to make this arduous climb—"*affectus* becomes powerful as intellect fails."[256] But both the third and the sixth of the Ascension Sermons, entitled "De intellectu et affectu," serve as significant correctives for any views that would exclude intellect from having an important role in the path to God. Citing one of his favorite scriptural texts, Wisdom 9:15 ("The body corrupts the soul, and the earthly dwelling place weighs down the sense power (*sensum*), thinking many thoughts"), he identifies the soul with the affections and the "sense power" with the intellect. Both need to be purged so that we can know nothing but God and desire nothing save him (*Asc* 3.1–2). "Christ illumines the intellect, the Holy Spirit purifies the affection."[257] The illumination process is already well under way through the actions that Christ performed during his life on earth. Bernard pleads with his audience to allow the Spirit to go forward with the work of purifying the affections, the process that transforms carnal love of Christ into spiritual love so that "with enlightened intellect and purified affection, the Bridegroom may come to us and build his mansion among us."[258] The same message is repeated in Ascension Sermon 6, which bewails our fallen condition in which intellect and love are so often at odds (*Asc* 6.5–7), and once again analyzes Christ's activity, showing that by ascending he intended to send his Spirit upon us, "so that spiritual affection might be joined with spiritual understanding."[259] The same mutuality of love and knowledge in the highest stages of terrestrial spiritual life Bernard finds portrayed in the two middle wings of the Seraphim of Isaiah's temple vision (Isaiah 6). Nothing can fly on one wing alone, neither the wing of knowledge, nor even that of "zeal without knowledge." "But where charity accompanies understanding and devotion accompanies knowledge, any being of this sort will fly–it will fly without end, because it flies into eternity."[260]

Bernard's fundamental teaching here conforms to that of Augustine, Gregory the Great, and other major representatives of traditional Latin mystical theology. He insists that only love can attain God in this life; knowledge cannot. But knowledge does have an important, even a necessary, role to play in our ascension to God, both at the beginning of the process, where Christ enlightens the soul through his saving mysteries, gradually illuminating the intellect that has humbly recognized its fallen state, and also at the end, where knowing is lifted up into love. In a few passages Bernard even briefly describes the mode and manner of the intellectual component of loving union. In the fifty-seventh of the *Sermons on the Song of Songs*, after a passage stressing that the presence of the Bridegroom is known by the love that sets the soul aglow, he suddenly switches to a more intellectual mode. "If the conscience has been cleansed and made peaceful with every stain of sin and rust of vice consumed by this fire, a sudden and unaccustomed largeness of mind (*latitudo mentis*) will follow, as well as an infusion of light illuminating the intellect both to understand the scriptures and to know the mysteries."[261]

Bernard also speaks of specific modes of contemplative experience that partake of a more cognitive than affective character, though these are not accorded the highest status. Among these are the *cubiculum cognitionis* of *Sermon* 23 considered above. The most important text in this regard, however, occurs in the comment on Song 2:4 found in *Sermon* 49.4: "There are two forms of ecstasy (*excessus*) of divine contemplation, the one in intellect, the other in affect, the one in light, the other in heat (*fervor*), the one in knowledge, the other in devotion."[262] Although Bernard only once in his writings cites the famous dictum from Gregory the Great that *amor ipse notitia est*,[263] and though his temperament and interests did not induce him to spend much time investigating the intellectual dimension of the experience of union, there can be no question that he was sure that both love and knowledge were indispensable for union with God, however great love's priority remained.

Vehement Love

Love is not only rational-prudent-wise, that is, compatible with illuminated intellect; it is also *vehemens*, that is, forceful, powerful, even violent. What may seem like a paradox to the natural mind, Bernard would say is something well known from the book of experience to those who have actually sensed the presence of the Bridegroom. In a passage filled with the rhetorical paradoxes he loved perhaps too much, he says:

> Can the highest of all be made one with all? Who has done this? It is Love, taking no thought of dignity, rich in honor, powerful in affection, potent in persuasion. What is more violent? Love triumphs over God. But what is nonetheless so non-violent? It is love. What power is there, I ask, that is so violent to gain the victory, so vanquished by violence?[265]

This passage indicates both that God is a violent lover and that the Bride, in order to attain him, must "let go" with a similar violence. The vehemence of the Divine Lover does not appear often in Bernard (perhaps because of his emphasis on the kindness and condescension of the Word in taking on flesh), but it is certainly implied in his reference to the "wound of love" from Song 2:5 as piercing and penetrating the soul of the Virgin Mary to fill her with love.[265] "But surely it pierced her through so that it could come to us and that we might all receive from that fullness and she might become the mother of charity whose Father is God-Charity. . . ."[266] Bernard was more interested in inculcating vehement love in his readers. In pursuing the kiss of the mouth, we should be driven by desire not by reason: "headlong love (*praeceps amor*) doesn't wait for judgment, isn't tempered by advice, restrained by shame, or subject to reason."[267] We should strive "to take love's kingdom by force,"[268] to become subject to the *amor intemperans* or *amor inquietus* that drives us on and gives us no rest.[269] A passage at the beginning of the seventy-ninth of the *Sermons on the Song of Songs* summarizes:

> Have you seen him whom my soul loves?" (Song 3:3). O headlong love, vehement, burning, impetuous, which cannot think of anything besides yourself! You feel distaste for other things, condemning everything besides yourself in self-absorption. You mix up proper order, you leave ordinary usage unnoticed, you are ignorant of due measure. Everything that seems to belong to reason, shame, counsel or judgment you conquer in yourself and lead captive. Everything that the Bride thinks and speaks, sounds and smells of you and nothing else. You have claimed her heart and tongue for your own.[270]

The theme of the violence of love was an important one in twelfth-century thought and literature, both in its secular and in its spiritual manifestations.[271] Bernard shows himself much a man of his time in his exposition of this aspect of spousal love.

Love's Mutuality

The love relation of which Bernard speaks is a marriage, not a love affair, not least of all because it is founded on a mutuality and reciprocity between the lovers that finds its closest analogy in human marriage, at least human marriage considered in an ideal sense. This is, of course, one of the most paradoxical aspects of the communion of the soul and the Word: How can there be any real mutuality between the omnipotent Creator and the finite creature? Bernard recognized the problem here, and in *On Loving God* he notes how small the Bride senses her own love to be in relation to the *amor praeveniens* of the Divine Majesty (*Dil* 4.13); but in the *Sermons on the Song of Songs* much emphasis is given to the mutuality of spousal love. Where both partners give their all and share as fully as they can in one and the same reality—that is, love—even the infinite distance between Creator and creature is lost sight of in the unitive experience. Between spouses "all things are shared; they have nothing of their own, nothing to divide them."[272] Their love easily mingles because it comes from the same source (*Sermon* 45.1), the mutual charity that is the bond of perfection (*Ded* 2.4). God himself is no exception to the law of love, which makes lovers not only equal but actually one (*Sermon* 59.2).

The theme of mutual love finds its most profound treatment in sections 3 and 4 of the eighty-third of the *Sermons on the Song of Songs,* in which the abbot carefully distinguishes love as the one power in which the creature can give something back to God from the same measure, "even if not on an equal basis" (*etsi non ex aequo*).[273] He thus stresses the equality of the lovers in the one thing necessary—loving and being loved (*amari et amare*)—while at the same time maintaining the necessary divine–human distinction from another perspective.

An important text from *Sermon* 69 effects a bridge between the mutuality of spousal love and Bernard's anthropology of the *imago Dei*. In commenting on Song 2:16 (*Dilectus meus mihi et ego illi*...), the abbot notes that the mutuality of love which the soul senses is made possible by the prevenient love of the Bridegroom. This sharing, by which the Bride and the Groom can be so perfectly directed toward each other in mental attitude (*intentio*), is based on the soul's reality as *imago Dei*:

Therefore, from what she possesses that belongs to God, the soul in love recognizes and has no doubt that she is loved. This is the way it is—God's love gives birth to the soul's love and his prevenient intention makes the soul intent, full of care for him who cares for her. I do not know what closeness of nature it is that enables the soul, when once his face is revealed, to gaze upon God's glory and to be necessarily so quickly conformed to him and transformed into the same image (2 Cor 3:18). Therefore, in whatever way you get yourself ready for God, this is the way he will appear to you.[274]

The final sentence here might seem to suggest a kind of Pelagian attitude toward mystical experience in which the soul readies itself for what it desires, but the mention of the *praecurrens intentio* of the Divine Lover is crucial—God prepares us according to our own particular personalities for the many mansions of his paradise. The soul, experiencing God as always *praeveni*, or acting prior to everything she wants and does, is in awe that God seems to glory in being devoted to her alone. "The soul that sees God sees as if she alone is seen by God,"[275] a typically Bernardine version of one of the central themes of Western mystical literature.[276]

Bernard's stress on how the Bride and the Groom find their delight in mutual interaction necessarily suggests the most intimately mutual act of spouses, sexual intercourse.[277] In several texts that explore the mutuality of the lovers, Bernard (more reticent here than some of his successors) makes use of marital intercourse, by suggestion if not by description, as an apt symbol for mystical union. The Song of Songs itself, while it is lavish with descriptions of the bodily attributes of the Bride and the Groom, and of the activities leading up to the bed chamber, hints at rather than pictures intercourse itself. (The embrace of the left and right arms in Song 2:6 is one of the more direct images.) It is interesting that in *Sermon* 46, when Bernard comments on Song 1:15b, the Bride's description of the bed as *lectulus floridus noster*, he is willing to give a sensual charge to his brief exposition of the literal sense,[278] but he spends most of the sermon on an ecclesiological reading in which the "bed" signifies the monasteries, where souls can rest in Christ, and the "houses" (*tigna domorum nostrorum*) are the churches of the clergy.

An extended treatment of marital union found in *Sermon* 52, commenting on the embrace of Song 2:6–7, is one of Bernard's most developed uses of the symbol of intercourse. In the text the Bridegroom, who is embracing the Bride with his left hand under her head and his right hand about her, forbids the daughters of Jerusalem to awaken her. Bernard says that this means that some humans at least have enjoyed the experience of "supreme Godhead entering into marriage with the exiled soul."[279] The sleep in Christ's embrace is understood as "a vital and wakeful slumber illuminating the interior sense (*sensus*), driving away death and giving eternal life. It is truly a sleep that does not dull the interior sense but leads it away (*abducat*). It is also a death."[280] The abbot calls this "ecstasy" (*exstasis*) a death, because it removes the soul from life's cares, enabling it "to be snatched from itself by a holy and vehement thought (*cogitatio*) . . . so that it surpasses the common use and custom of thinking."[281] Here Bernard is obviously describing what later mystics will call a binding, or "ligature" of the exterior senses and ordinary consciousness: "The soul in ecstasy does not have the sensation of living (though it is alive), and so necessarily does not feel life's temptations."[282] The abbot goes on to state that "this kind of ecstasy (*excessus*), either alone, or principally, is called contemplation."[283] The experience is one of true rest, where "the soul, overcome by the beauty of the spot, sleeps sweetly in her beloved's embrace, that is, in spiritual ecstasy."[284] It is worth noting that while the symbolic presentation is the erotic image of sexual embrace, Bernard tends to use "intellectual" language (*sensus, cogitatio, phantasmata*, etc.) to describe the process. The richly sensuous language of the Song must be invoked with caution, subtlety, and discretion in the service of mystical transformation.

The image of the embrace of the Bride by the Bridegroom is perhaps the most important erotic image after the kiss in Bernard's writings. Since the embrace occurs in two texts (Song 2:6, and 3:4, where the Bride speaks of holding the Groom and not letting him go), the possibilities were particularly rich. No treatment is as personal and as overtly sensual as that found in *Sermon* 52.

In some places, Song 3:4 is referred to the church, who holds Christ by the two arms of faith and affection and is, in turn, held by his arms of power and mercy (e.g., *Sermon* 79.4–5). Elsewhere, reference is made to the perfect eschatological embrace to be enjoyed by the lovers after the resurrection of the dead (e.g., *Dil* 11.33). Even when the embrace is read in a more present and personal sense, it tends to be used in both a doctrinal and an erotic way. Thus, in *Sermon* 51.8–10, the left hand of the Bridegroom is interpreted as the threat of future punishment, the right as the promise of the kingdom. In the midst of these arms, the soul is able to dwell in hope, "as if supported on the soft bed of love."[285] Outside the *Sermons on the Song of Songs*, the contrast between the two arms is frequently put in terms of present and future, with the left representing the medicines of salvation or proofs of love already present in this life, and the right announcing the coming rewards of heaven, the ultimate joys of marital love.[286] Somewhat more individual and direct are two texts, one from the abbot's sermon for Wednesday in Holy Week, where he joins his two favorite images, the embrace and the kiss, once again in terms of here and hereafter:

The Lord Jesus embraced us through our labor and our sorrow. Let us also be joined to him by certain vicarious embraces through justice, his justice, that is, by directing our actions toward justice and by bearing our sufferings for justice's sake. Let us say with the Bride, "I held him and would not let him go" (Song 3:4). . . . What is left after the embrace except the kiss? If I were thus to be joined to God, how could I not be already allowed to exclaim, "Let him kiss me with the kiss of his mouth?" (Song 1:1)[287]

Finally, a brief text from *Consideration* can serve as a fitting conclusion for this theme in its appeal to the necessity of personal experience of the Divine Lover's embrace:

If you are holy, you have understood and known. If not, be holy and you will know by experience. Holy affection makes a holy person and it is twofold—holy fear of God and holy love. The soul that is perfectly affected by these two, like twin arms, grasps, embraces, binds, holds fast and says, "I have held him and will not let him go."[288]

This marital experience, as our analysis of *Sermon* 52 has shown, can be described as ecstasy (*exstasis, excessus*) and is identified with true contemplation, that is, the vision of God. These terms, each deeply embedded in the history of Christian mysticism, need to be studied to bring out further implications of Bernard's teaching about the experience of loving God in this life.[288]

Vision, Contemplation, and Ecstasy: Love and Union[289]

The abbot of Clairvaux often spoke of the contemplation of God and the vision of God, both in this life and the life to come.[291] Bernard, like all Christian mystics, insisted that such contemplation and vision do not render God any less ineffable. Although he does not often dwell on the divine unknowability in the way in which mystics of a more apophatic cast of mind do, there are a number of discussions in his writings, both early and late.[292]

Our Cistercian clearly teaches that the experience of loving union with God cannot really be communicated in rational and discursive terms. The divine *amor* that burns within the soul produces a form of expression that is not a comprehensible enunciation but an outburst of the *affectus* (*non enunciat, sed eructat*),[293] as in Song of Songs 2:16, where we encounter the ungrammatical expression *Dilectus meus mihi, et ego illi* ("My Beloved to me, and I to him"). In their rhetorical strategy, Bernard's rich and suggestive descriptions of mystical experience conceal in the very act of revealing, as Hans Urs von Balthasar noted when he said that the theologian "can clothe

the mystery in the drapery of a 'fine' style, either as an act of homage, or (as often with Bernard) in an attempt to preserve it by veiling it."[294]

What, then, constitutes the vision of God for Bernard? Perhaps the most inclusive definition makes vision another way of speaking about our loving "adherence" to God (using language favored by Augustine): "Inhering (*inhaerere*) in God is nothing else than that seeing of God which is given with special happiness only to the pure of heart (Matt 5:8) . . . 'It is good for me to adhere to God' (Ps 72:28). He adheres by seeing; he sees by adhering" (*videndo adhaerebat, et adhaerendo videbat*).[295] From a more ontological perspective, Bernard describes the kiss of the lips as a form of vision, that is, "a marvelous and somehow inseparable mingling of the heavenly light and the enlightened mind. To adhere to God is to be one Spirit" (1 Cor 6:17).[296] Such a notion of vision involves a direct experience of God in the *mens*, or deepest level of the soul. According to Augustine's triple classification of visions,[297] which Bernard is likely to have known (although to the best of my knowledge he does not cite it), this would be a vision of the third or highest type, a pure *visio intellectualis*, something that helps explain the abbot's attitude toward the lower types of vision, the corporeal and imaginary manifestations that God sent, especially to the Patriarchs and Prophets.

In his most detailed discussion of the kinds of visions in the thirty-first and thirty-second of the *Sermons on the Song of Songs*, the abbot speaks of three fundamental ways in which God can be seen in this life: first, as manifested in all creatures; second, as in the days of the patriarchs, "exteriorly, shown through external images and spoken words"; and, finally, by "a divine gaze (*inspectio*) more different than these as it is more interior when God deigns through himself to visit the soul seeking him."[298] Bernard does not despise the external visions given of old,[299] but in the current stage of salvation history we should prefer that kind of vision by which the soul "has present the one she desires, not in a bodily form, but infused, not in mere appearance, but inwardly attracting (*afficientem*), and doubtless the more pleasant the more inside, not outside."[300] Since God can never be seen here below as he is (*sicuti est*, a favorite theme of William of St. Thierry, based on 1 John 3:2), he must be seen, even in this highest form of interior vision, as he *wishes* to be seen, that is, as he adapts himself to the receptivities and needs of our souls.[301] Bernard specifies four distinct roles or ways in which Christ makes interior visits to those souls prepared for his coming (all based on the Song of Songs)—as Bridegroom, as Physician, as Partner in conversation, and as Head of the household or Ruler.[302] Each of these has its importance, but the visit of the Bridegroom is the highest.

The brief visit and vision of the Word as Bridegroom are fitting for the soul who is so full of desire "that she wishes to die and to be with Christ, with violent desire, burning thirst, frequent meditation."[303] To the soul not yet so far advanced because it is still struggling with sin, he comes as a physician, bearing oil and ointments. To the soul wearied in spiritual studies, he comes as a partner in conversation so that "when we meditate on his law day and night (Ps 1:2), we know for certain that the Bridegroom is present and is speaking to us so that our labors don't weary us as we delight in his words."[304] Finally, to those who "have been enlarged in soul from a greater freedom of spirit and purity of conscience," he appears as the powerful Householder or as the King in his full majesty.[305]

All these visions, of course, even the highest one of the Bridegroom, are only foretastes of heaven, limited both by their brevity and imperfection—there is no "face-to-face" vision in this life (see 1 Cor 13:12). "In the sleep of contemplation the sick soul dreams of God and in the meantime beholds him through a mirror and a mystery, not face to face. Although in this way God is not so much seen as guessed at, barely touched in a delicate manner, the soul is rapt and, as if with the flash of a passing little spark, burns with love."[306]

Bernard's teaching on both the supremacy of interior visions and the necessary limitations of any vision of God that can be attained in this life is expounded with great subtlety in a passage from *Sermon* 41, where he comments on why the Bride's companions tell her, "We will make you golden earrings worked with silver" (Song 1:10).[307] Here the abbot identifies the companions with the angels who act as necessary intermediaries in conveying divine visions to humans.[308] (Bernard, as we have noted, gave the angels a larger role in mystical experiences than most Latin mystics.) Gold represents the signs of divinity that the angels insert in the "internal ears of the soul." Bernard goes on to say, "I think this is nothing else than to make some spiritual likenesses (*spirituales similitudines*) and to introduce totally pure sensations (*purissima sensa*) of divine wisdom to the gaze of the contemplating soul." (Note the switch from internal hearing to internal sight, typical of Bernard's synaesthetic use of the spiritual senses.) Picking up on a favorite theme, the abbot says that for those who have not had the experience there is no way to understand how, while still in the mortal state of living by faith, "when the substance of clear internal light has not yet appeared, the contemplation of Pure Truth sometimes presumes to become active in us, at least in part." Finally, he explains why the *similitudines* accompany such a vision of Divine Truth and why the angels serve as ministers:

> When something divine shines upon the mind quickly with the swiftness of a spark of light, as the spirit goes into ecstasy (*spiritu excedenti*), imaginative likenesses of lower things are immediately present (from where I know not),

either to dampen the excessive splendor or for use in teaching. These are fittingly adapted to the divinely infused senses. Through them that completely pure and entirely brilliant ray of Truth is somewhat clouded over so that it is made more open to reception by the soul and more adaptable for those to whom it wishes to communicate God. I think that these are formed in us by the suggestion of the holy angels, just as, on the other side, there is no doubt that contrary and evil imaginings are thrust in by the evil angels.

What Bernard is suggesting here (it seems clearly on the basis of his own experience, although he does not use the first person) is that Augustine's highest, intellectual form of vision is rarely if ever experienced in a pure form in this life, but that the ray of Divine Truth is usually accompanied by *similitudines* given through the ministry of the angels that pertain more to Augustine's second kind of vision, the *visio spiritualis*, or imaginative vision.[309] This mingling of the intellectual with the imaginative, though always in an interior vision, fits the abbot's constant emphasis on the imperfection of all vision here below, and it also accords well with coherence òf the book of experience and the book of scripture. Just as the soul finds its ecstatic vision of divine light accompanied by certain necessary imaginative likenesses, so too the Bible, especially the Song of Songs, accommodated its descriptions of the divine–human encounter to the imaginative portrayal of a love match.

One final aspect of Bernard's teaching on the vision of God possible in this life needs to be considered–the relation between this vision and the transformation of the image and likeness of God in us. As we have seen, the abbot's theological anthropology as laid out in *Grace and Free Choice* identified the place of mystical experience with the foretaste of the full restoration of the *similitudo* by way of a fleeting experience of the *libertas a miseria* that will be perfectly enjoyed only in heaven. Further considerations of the same theme are present in the *Sermons on the Song of Songs*, despite the rather different understanding of *imago* and *similitudo* expounded there. In the thirty-sixth of the *Sermon,* Bernard sketches the shift in vision that takes place when we turn from the sight of our own misery in true self-knowledge to the "joyful vision of God" (*laeta visio Dei*) that gradually reveals God's mercy and even God himself to us.[310] "In this way your knowledge will be a step to knowing God, and he will become visible from his image which is being renewed in you (Col 3:8), while you confidently gaze upon the glory of the Lord when his face has been revealed, you are being transformed from glory to glory into that same image, as if by God's Spirit" (2 Cor 3:18).[311] This Pauline doctrine reappears in *Sermon* 82, which takes up the relation between *caritas/amor* and the restored *similitudo Dei.* The soul can regain its true nature not by its own efforts but only by turning to the Word (*Sermon* 82.2). As he summarizes:

> Totally admirable and wonderful is that likeness which goes with the vision of God, rather which is the vision of God. I am speaking of charity: charity is the vision and the likeness. . . . Created out of the midst of that iniquity which causes the partial unlikeness, there will come union of spirit, mutual vision and mutual love. When that which is perfect comes, what is partial will be destroyed (1 Cor 13:10)–there will be chaste consummated love one for the other, full knowledge, manifest vision, firm joining together, indivisible society, perfect likeness.[312]

The *caritas* that is the restored likeness in us forms the height of contemplative vision. Bernard, of course, realizes that *contemplatio* can be employed in a general sense, as when he differentiates between contemplation and consideration in his treatise *Consideration*: "Contemplation can be defined as the true and certain intuition of the intellectual soul about anything, the apprehension of the truth without a doubt, while consideration is thought active in investigation, or the concentration (*intensio*) of the intellectual soul pursuing truth."[313] But contemplation in the proper sense for Bernard, as for his patristic sources, was a rich term used to express a continuum of the experience of God's presence symbolized in visual form.[314] The abbot provides more than a few descriptions of various stages or degrees of contemplation, some of which we have already referred to, such as the three *cubicula* of *theorica contemplatio* in *Sermon* 23.9–17, and the four modes of seeing or sensing the Word in *Sermon* 32 and 33. Other descriptions of contemplation can be found elsewhere in the *Sermons on the Song of Songs*,[315] as well as in other of Bernard's writings.[316] But the abbot, unlike his contemporaries the Victorines, was not so much interested in detailing the kinds and stages of contemplation as he was in describing its personal dynamics through the comparison of the book of scripture and the book of experience. He never ceases appealing to the example of the great contemplatives portrayed in the Bible–Jacob, Moses, Isaiah, and David (the *maximus contemplator*) in the Old Testament,[317] and, of course, John the Baptist, Paul, and Mary Magdalene, and especially the Blessed Virgin, in the New Testament.[318]

Concerning the nature of the contemplation of God, Bernard is sure that it must always be imperfect and brief in this life, as we have seen;[319] he also notes that it is always a free gift of God. The abbot of Clairvaux is not troubled by the at times arid later debates about the form of contemplation that can be in some way acquired by human effort and that which must always be infused by a special divine gift. His profoundly Augustinian understanding of grace enabled him to grasp that every stage in the growth of contemplation was a work of purely divine initiative to which the soul was enabled to cooperate in a way that never gave it any claim in justice for a further divine reward.[320] But he was equally sure that God was above all the generous God of love, that he would not withhold his mercy from the soul who strove to follow the path of love, and that therefore the higher stages of love and contemplation were gifts of which he was not totally sparing, at least in the context of the monastic life.[321] Hence, Bernard sometimes speaks as if the soul could in some way merit or deserve this reward. But the absolute divine initiative is always highlighted by the ways in which the abbot stresses the brevity of the experience and the coming and going of the Divine Lover at his own whim.[322]

Bernard's favored term to describe the heights of contemplation is *quies* (peace, rest),[323] but he also often refers to it as an *excessus* (literally, "going or passing beyond"), or an *ecstasis* ("standing outside"), terms that he found both in the Vulgate and in his patristic sources, such as Augustine.[324] "Happy the contemplation which finds rest in going beyond" (*iucunda contemplatio, ubi excedendo quiescit*), as he put it.[325]

Another traditional term, taken from Paul's account of his ascent to the third heaven in 2 Corinthians 12:4, is *raptus*, often used in verbal form (*rapere*).[326] The frequent appearance of wine in the Song of Songs allowed Bernard to make considerable use of the notion of "sober, or sacred drunkeness" (*sobria vel sacra ebrietas*), an ancient description of the mystical experience first found in Philo and present in patristic writers.[327] As we have seen, the abbot of Clairvaux usually ascribes the full drunkenness to the perfect joy not to be realized until the resurrection of the body, but there are some texts that also employ it to describe the *excessus contemplationis* of this life.[328]

One of the most detailed and interesting discussions of the *excessus* comes at the end of *Sermon 85*, where Bernard outlines two ways of giving birth in spiritual matrimony—bearing souls by preaching and giving birth to spiritual understandings (*spirituales intelligentiae*) by meditation. Of the latter sort he says:

> In this last kind sometimes there is a passing beyond and departure (*exceditur et seceditur*) even from the corporeal senses so that she who perceives the Word does not perceive herself. This happens when the mind, attracted by the Word's ineffable sweetness, is as it were stolen away from itself—indeed, rapt and snatched from itself—in order to enjoy the Word. . . . Although the mother is happy in her offspring, the Bride is happier in her embrace. The pledge of children is dear, but kisses more delightful. It is good to save many, but to pass beyond (*excedere*) and to be with the Word is more pleasant. But

when will this be, and how long will it be? Sweet the mingling, but brief the moment, rare the experience![329]

Qui autem adhaeret Domino unus spiritus est ("One who adheres to the Lord is one spirit [with him]"). This classic passage from 1 Corinthians 6:17, though used by mystics before Bernard, became his signature text for describing the manner of union found in the love-commerce of the Bride and the Groom.[330] The abbot's abundant citation of the passage is one of the reasons for the subsequent prominence of the text in that tradition of Christian mysticism which taught that union, both in this life and in the next, does not surpass perfect loving union of wills and never involves any form of union of identity or indistinction with God.[331]

A noted presentation of this teaching is found in Bernard's treatment of the fourth degree of love in the *On Loving God*:

When a movement of love (*affectus*) of this sort is experienced so that the intellectual soul is drunk with love and forgets itself, becoming almost an empty vessel to itself, it marches right into God, and, adhering to him, becomes one spirit with him. . . . I would call a person blessed and holy to whom anything such as this very occasionally, or even just once, was granted as an experience while still in this mortal life—and that in a rapture of scarce a moment's duration![332]

After a peroration to the *amor sanctus et castus* that makes this union possible, Bernard resumes his explanation.

To be drawn in this way is to be deified (*Sic affici, deificari est*).[333] Just as a little drop of water mixed in much wine seems to lose itself totally while taking on the flavor and color of wine, and just as a burning and glowing piece of iron becomes so much like fire, having lost its pristine and proper form, and just as air suffused with sunlight is transformed into the same brightness so that it no longer seems to be illuminated but rather to be light itself, so too at that time in the saints every human affection will necessarily flow out of itself in a marvellous way and be totally transformed into God's will. Otherwise, how will God be "all in all" (1 Cor. 15:28), if anything of humanity is left in humanity? However, the substance will remain, but in another form, another glory and another power.[334]

The three comparisons that Bernard advances here have evoked a considerable literature.[335] Their history began in Greek philosophy over a thousand years before the abbot, as examples to illustrate the mixing (*krasis*) of different elements. Bernard appears to have taken them from a text of Maximus the Confessor's *Ambigua* translated by John the Scot, but there may well be a missing link as well, because the text as currently known contains only two of the three.[336] Like any metaphor, however, the three have been understood in various ways. Some later critics, like Jean Gerson, attacked Bernard for employing them.[337] The abbot certainly thought the question of union important enough to make important distinctions to underline just what he meant, as the last sentence in this text and several other passages make clear.

The preoccupation with union, especially as experientially described, was a new element in the mysticism of the twelfth century. Although twelfth-century writers were doubtless influenced by their reading of early authorities, especially the Pseudo-Dionysius, Maximus, and John the Scot, it was the flowering of new modes of mysticism in the era seeking to find more adequate modes of expression that was the driving force behind the new linguistic and theological concerns. Bernard's richest text on union is to be found in the seventy-first of the *Sermons on the Song of Songs*, a sermon that also displays the Cistercian's most developed teaching on the spiritual senses. Bernard begins his treatment here with a consideration of how while Jesus ate at Mary and Martha's house he also fed his hosts interiorly. In the present the reverse is true: "But if you saw that for him to be fed is to feed, see if now perhaps, on the contrary, to feed him is to be fed."[338] The meaning of this puzzle becomes clear in the following section as Bernard explains how eating is to be understood as a metaphor for uniting with, or being *in* the other person:

> My penance is his food, my salvation is his food, I myself am his food. . . . I am eaten when I accuse myself; I am swallowed when I am instructed; I am cooked when I am changed; I am digested when I am transformed; I am united when I am conformed. Do not be amazed at this—he eats us and we are eaten by him the more closely we are bound together with him. Otherwise, we would not be perfectly united to him. If I eat and am not eaten, it will seem that he is in me but I am not yet in him; but if I am eaten and do not eat, he has me in him, but he will not seem to be in me as well. There will be no perfect union in one or the other.[339]

The Father and the Word are in each other in perfect mutuality. So too, the soul, whose good it is to adhere to God, must feel both that it is in God and God in it. Lest anyone get the wrong idea, Bernard goes on to distinguish in *Sermon* 71.6 between the unity of the Father and the Son expressed in the text "I am in the Father and the Father in me and we are one" (*unum*, Matt 10:38 and 30), and the union of 1 Corinthians 6:17, which applies to Christ and the soul: "Who adheres to God is one spirit (*unus spiritus*) with him." The insistence on the *unus* qualifying "spirit" as against the *unum* signifying the oneness of the divine substance leads the abbot to a deeper consideration of the kinds of union in *Sermon* 71.7–10.[340] The human person is in God through *caritas* (1 John 4:16), not in any consubstantial way. "The human person and God, because they are not of the same substance or nature, cannot be said to be one thing (*unum*); but by sure and absolute power they are said to be one spirit if they inhere in each other by the glue of love. This union is made not by the coherence of essences, but by the agreement of wills."[341] In comparison with the union of the Father and the Son, where there is neither duality of essences or wills, our union of spirit with the Word is infinitely less: "A happy union, if you experience it; none, if you compare it."[342] Bernard concludes by noting that the mutuality of God in us and us in God takes place when we begin to love God after being loved by him from all eternity: *Ipse prior dilexit nos* (*Sermon* 71.10).

The abbot expanded on his concern for the proper discrimination between *unitas spiritus* and union in the Trinity by analyzing various kinds of unity in several texts.[343] Sermon 80.1 of the *Sermons on Different Topics* speaks of eight different kinds of union,[344] but the most intensive discussion, detailing no fewer than nine kinds of union, is found toward the end of *Consideration*, a work that comes from late in Bernard's life. *Unitas* can be *collectiva*, as of rocks in a pile; *constitutiva*, when many members make one body; *coniugativa* with husband and wife; *nativa*, that is, of body and soul making one person; *potestativa*, as when a person strives to act in one fashion; *consentanea* in forming one community from the agreement of many; *votiva* when the soul adheres to God and becomes one spirit with him; *dignativa* in the union of God and human in Christ; and finally *consubstantialis* in the Trinity.[345] Later mystics, such as Bonaventure, would also compile such lists in order to situate mystical union. It is not necessary to review all the appearances of 1 Corinthains 6:17 in Bernard's writings, either in the *Sermons on the Song of Songs*,[346] or in other works,[347] to vindicate the centrality of this text and the access it gives to Bernard's understanding of mystical union.

One use of the text, in the first of the sermons for the Dedication of a Church, draws it close to a theme we have seen in Augustine and also highlights its connection with Bernard's thoughts on the relation of affective and active charity to be considered below. Let us close this section with this succinct passage on the mutuality of the highest love of God and the love of neighbor:

> The stones [that is, the living stones that form the community] stick together by means of the double glue of full knowledge and perfect love. They are joined to each other by greater love the more they stand closer to that charity which is God. . . . Since "the one who adheres to God is one spirit with him," there is no doubt that those blessed ones who perfectly adhere to that Spirit with him and in him penetrate all things equally.[348]

Love as Satisfaction and Yearning

The *unitas spiritus* found in the loving embrace between the Bride and the Divine Lover is the ultimate goal, the only true satisfaction to be found in this life. But the form in which we enjoy it here below always contains an element of dissatisfaction as well. It is to this characteristic of spousal love, the relation betwen satiety and yearning, that we now turn.

Bernard, of course, believed that true satisfaction can only be found in spiritual things: the created human spirit can never attain rest in material reality.[349] "God is love and there is nothing in created things that is able to fill the creature made to God's image except the God-Love, who alone is greater than it."[350] But the fullness of the enjoyment of such love, true satiety, is not to be found on this side of heaven.[351] This is not only because of the brevity of the experience but also because, as already suggested in *Sermon* 41.3 (treated above), the experience of divine love in this life is always subject to forms of mediation that, while higher than anything else found in the created realm, are still less than the direct heavenly vision. Several sermons in the *Sermons on Different Topics* expand on this. In *Sermon* 4.3 Bernard affirms that "we cannot be immediately joined to God, but this conjunction can perhaps take place through some kind of medium."[352] He goes on to specify three bonds of increasing efficacy—ropes, i.e., the memory of Christ's Passion; nails, or the fear of the Lord; and finally, charity, "which binds us as safely as it does sweetly: adhering to God is to be one spirit."[353] Only in heaven will we see God face to face; here below we always need the help of some creaturely vehicle (see *Div* 9.1). In *Sermons on Different Topics* 19, Bernard longs for the coming of the time when "we will be sunk in the very fountain of divinity with eternal joy, where wave after wave will break without pause or alteration."[354] Here, the blessed souls "will see God's essence with naked eyes so to speak, without the deception of the images of corporeal phantasms."[355] It will be a unity without any "intervening mediator" (*medius interpres* [*Div* 110]), as is always present in this life.

This makes clear that Bernard conceived of mystical union in this life as a more immediate experience of God than anything else conceivable here below, but still needing some mediation and therefore lacking in final satisfaction. As long as we are in this life, any attainment of union with God will be fraught with as much yearning as with satisfaction or rest, however ecstatic the brief moment of absorption into the *unitas spiritus*. Our lot in this life is to be continually on the march, always reaching out for what is ahead. "Our advance in this life, as I remember I have often said, consists in this, that we never think we have taken hold, but we always reach out to what lies ahead, striving ceaselessly for the better and continually exposing our imperfection to the gaze of divine mercy."[356] The experience of God which we can enjoy in this life leaves us both satiated with wine and yet thirsty for more, as Sirach 24:29 says, "He who drinks me will thirst for more."[357]

Bernard's thoughts in this vein cannot help but remind the reader of Gregory of Nyssa's notion of *epektasis*.[358] Like the Cappadocian father, the abbot of Clairvaux made frequent use of the text in Philippians 3:13, ". . . forgetting what lies behind and stretching myself forward to what lies ahead" (*quae quidem retro sunt obliviscens ad ea vero quae sunt in priora extendens me*) to underline the fact that every encounter between God and human, must, from the human perspective, merely stretch the recipient's capacity for a greater, but continually limited infusion of Infinite Spirit.[359] This is why what can be possessed in this life, even by the great St. Paul, is never real perfection, but only, as Bernard puts it, "an imperfect perfection" (*imperfecta perfectio*).[360] Even in heaven, when we will enjoy a vision of the Trinity and a loving union with the *Verbum* beyond the dreams of this life, we will still be ever moving forward into the inexhaustible mystery of God. "What end will there be to seeking God? It says, 'Seek his face always' (Ps 104:4). I think that there will be no cessation of seeking even when he is found. God is sought by desire not by footsteps, and therefore that blessed finding will not beat out desire, but will extend it. . . . Joy will be made full, but there will be no end to desire, and for this reason not to seeking either."[361] Though Bernard does not develop this theme to the extent that Gregory does, its appearance in a number of places in his writings shows that he did not disagree with Gregory on the essential point: the role of unending yearning in the different forms of satiating union experienced in this life and the next.[362]

Spousal Love as Ordering

The final dynamic aspect of spousal love that remains for consideration is how this supreme unitive experience affects the life of the mystic in this fallen but still redeemable world. This consideration of the ordering power of love (*caritas ordinata*) involves the complex problem of Bernard's view of the relations between action and contemplation, one of the more difficult aspects of his thought. The principle of ordination, that is, the consideration of all created reality under the aspect of an order or hierarchy either already existing or in need of establishment, as Maur Standaert has shown, is one of the key elements in the abbot of Clairvaux's teaching.[363] Standaert distinguishes three levels: (1) a passive order already established by divine action; (2) an active order or ordination that humans are to establish in themselves and between themselves and God; and (3) a mixed ordination where the two levels meet and are harmonized by the action of the human will. Though these categories are not explicitly found in Bernard himself, they are not untrue to his way of thinking.

The abbot generally reserves the term *ordinatio* for the latter two activities. In the treatise *Grace and Free Choice* he describes three kinds of goods that may be predicated of the human will—the general good it possesses as something created by God, the special good it enjoys as made to God's image, and a third good that resides in its conversion to its Creator. This is *ordinatio*, which is defined as "every kind of conversion of the will to God and its total voluntary and devout subjection."[364] *Ordinatio* thus pertains to all aspects of the Cistercian's teaching on the soul's reformation to God, especially to his view of the way in which the ordering of the affections establishes solid virtues. The whole Christian life should be an *ordinata conversatio*, that is, an ordered manner of living.[365] But the most important aspect of *ordinatio* is the *ordinatio caritatis*, which is the core meaning of our conformity with Christ.

The fiftieth of the *Sermons on Different Topics* bearing the title "On the Correct Ordering of the Affection," provides us with a handy initial definition of rightly-ordered love, or *amor purgatus*, as Bernard calls it here:

> If we love the things that should be loved, if we love more the things that should be loved more, and if we do not love the things that should not be loved, love will be purged (*amor purgatus erit*). It is the same with the other affections. They are to be ordered in this way—in the beginning fear, then joy, after this sadness, love as the consummation.[366]

Two major treatments of the ordering of love help to fill out this brief description, the first from *On Loving God*, the second from *Sermons on the Song of Songs* 49 and 50.

The four degrees of love studied in Bernard's treatise are nothing more than an extended discussion of how love is purged, reformed, and set in order after the fall. In order to love our neighbor purely we must love him or her in God: that is, we must love God first, logically if not temporally.[367] Elsewhere Bernard reminds his readers that the commandment is to love our neighbors as ourselves—to love the neighbor more than the self would be a lack of due order (see *Sermon 18.4*). The lower affections, such as fear, which is the law of slaves, and self-interest (*cupiditas*), which is the law of mercenaries, are gradually lifted up and transformed into the higher law of charity:

> Charity will never exist without fear, but a chaste fear; it will never be without self-interest. Therefore, charity fulfills the slave's law when it infuses devotion; it fulfills the mercenary's law when it orders self-interest. . . . Self-interest is rightly ordered by charity coming down upon it when evil things are totally

rejected, better things are preferred to good things so that good things are sought only for the sake of better things. When this has been fully attained by God's grace, the body and all its goods will be loved only for the soul's sake, the soul for God's, God for his own.[368]

In Letter 85, which he wrote to his friend William of St. Thierry, Bernard speaks of "an ordered charity which knows and loves only what is worthy of love and in the measure that it is worthy of love and for the reasons that it is worthy of love."[369]

Ordered love, then, means not that we have to choose *between* God and creatures, or to reject totally the body and the material world, but rather that we need to put all our affections and desires in the proper relation. Whether or not we think that Bernard and his twelfth-century contemporaries, with the deep ambivalences of their views about materiality and the body, managed to create a consistent and viable order of love, we cannot deny how hard they struggled to attain this ideal. Such hopes are spelled out in his commentary on Song 2:4 (*Ordinavit in me caritatem*) found in *Sermon* 49 and 50.

The second half of *Sermon* 49 states the fundamental principle that "Zeal without knowledge is unbearable. Therefore, where there is violent striving discretion is most necessary. This is the ordering (*ordinatio*) of charity."[370] Thus, truly ordered love is the fruit of the love and knowledge that flow from the inebriating experience of the *unitas spiritus*, the brief moments of the enjoyment of the *liberum complacitum* that we are given in this life. Perhaps the most important aspect of the "content" of the love that has subsumed and transformed knowledge involves *how* to order all the loves in our lives. Without discretion, which is the "moderator and charioteer of the virtues, the orderer of the affections and the teacher of right living,"[371] virtues become vices, affections run wild, and there can be no harmony in the church, the Body of Christ. "It is necessary that one charity binds all these [church offices] and harmonizes them into the unity of Christ's Body. This would be completely impossible if charity were not ordered."[372] Bernard goes on to give the point practical application, not only with regard to his own duties as abbot but also as a counsel for not envying the achievements, virtues, and duties of others (*Sermon* 49.6–8).

Sermon 50 advances this line of argument by means of an extended discussion of love in *actus* and love in *affectus*, that is, in its active and contemplative phases. The proper relation between action and contemplation is the most important fruit of ordered charity, which is the goal of the reformation of the image of God in our lives and the principle that makes possible the harmonious functioning of the Body of Christ. Love in action is the object of the commands to love our neighbors as ourselves and to love our enemies (Deut 5:6; Luke 6:27).[373] These commands are difficult to fulfill, indeed, impossible without God's grace. Even the affective love of God has an active component: we are enjoined not only to love God but also to observe his commandments. Affective, or felt, love comprises the joy we experience in the divine presence, something that can be begun in this life but will be perfected only in heaven (*Sermon* 50.2–3).

Bernard bases his theory of the mutual interaction of active and contemplative love on a division of three kinds of *affectio*, or attraction. "There is an *affectio* which flesh begets, one which reason rules, and one which wisdom establishes."[374] The first is the product of sin, *dulcis sed turpis*. The second creates the realm of active love. Although it is "violently in love with love,"[375] it does not experience the sweetness of the Lord but lives through its firm adherence to fulfilling the often difficult tasks that love commands. The text "he ordered charity in me" (Song 2:4) pertains to both the *affectio rationalis* and the *affectio sapientialis*, but in reverse order. "For active (*actualis*) love prefers what is lower, affective love what is higher."[376] This means that while affective love always starts with the love of God, that is, contemplative experience, "in well-ordered action the opposite order is frequently, or even always, found."[377] That is, the welfare of our neighbor, especially the weaker and the more needy, comes first. Bernard gives a number of cogent examples of this law of charity at work (even that of omitting Mass when administrative needs take precedence), exclaiming, "O preposterous order, but necessity knows no law!"[378]

Affective charity, on the other hand, orders all things hierarchically in relation to God. In this mode of love we begin by tasting, or experiencing, God, not indeed as he is but insofar as we are capable of this experience (*Sermon* 50.6). In this "tasting God" we come to know ourselves as we really are (i.e., as having and being nothing apart from God) and our neighbor as ourselves (i.e., as being worthy of love only in relation to God). From this divine perspective, we can love other humans in two ways: We love as ourselves all those who love God as we love him, and we love our enemies, that is, those who do not love God, in order that they may come to love him.[379] The sermon concludes with a peroration on the wise person who has ordered charity as it relates both to all the subjects we should love–God, neighbor, enemy, parents, spiritual teachers–and to all objects in the world. Bernard ends with an impassioned prayer to the Word who is both the Truth (active love) and Wisdom (affective love): "Direct our actions as our temporal necessity demands and dispose our affections as your eternal Truth requires so that each of us may safely boast in you and say that 'He has ordered charity in me.'"[380]

Since Bernard insists that both orders of love must coexist here below, we may conclude by a look at his teaching concerning the mode of their relationship in the life of the Christian.[381] The fruit of this teaching provides the ground for how the contemplative becomes an active lover, and even an actor in the world at large.[382] Though Bernard always expressed considerable ambivalence about the tension between his commitment to the enclosed life of the monastery and the necessities thrust upon him (and all too often embraced) because of what he felt were his obligations in charity for the good of the church, the theoretical basis he sketched to understand the relation between contemplation and action is among the most nuanced in the history of Christianity. Like others, however, Bernard apparently did not always find it easy to apply his theory in the midst of life's confusions, which may be taken either as a measure of his honesty or alternately as a hint that his own loves were not always completely well-ordered.[383]

A key text for relating active and contemplative love is found in the eighteenth of the *Sermons on the Song of Songs*, where, after mentioning seven works of the Holy Spirit in us, Bernard concludes: "One and the same Spirit works all these according to the operation that is called infusion (*infusio*), so that the operation which is said to be effusion (*effusio*) may be purely and for this reason safely accomplished to the praise and glory of our Lord Jesus Christ."[385] In other words, infusion—that is, God's activity—must come first if effusion—that is, activity—is to be profitable. Not only are the two ideally correlated, but at least a rough rule of mutual cooperation can be advanced: precipitous action that would harm infusion is to be avoided, as is all attempt to try to give what one has not received.[385] On the other hand, to refuse to give what one has been granted by grace when others are in need of it is to sin against the dictates of charity. It is this latter imperative that is most often stressed in Bernard's writings, that is, his insistence that we must abandon the delights of loving union no matter how sweet when we are called to perform works of active love. *Sermon 9.8–9* insists that the breasts of the Bride flowing with the milk of preaching are better than the kisses of contemplative love, even though the young girls, or weak souls, may importune the Bride unfairly to pour out her riches.[386] The Bride wishes always to enjoy the delights of the bedchamber of contemplation, but cannot refuse the obligations of her position as Mother. The good works she performs in this role, in turn, foster a greater security in contemplation (see *Sermon 47.4*). The Divine Lover himself has no hesitation in summoning the Bride from the sleep of contemplation (Song 2:10) to "more useful things" (*utiliora*) by implanting in her "the desire for good works, the desire for bearing fruit for the Bridegroom."[387]

The fifty-first and fifty-second of the *Sermons on the Song of Songs* contain some profound reflections on the intricate ways in which the contracting and the relaxing heartbeats of ordered charity nourish each other along the path to perfection. It is one of the cornerstones of Bernard's teaching that no soul can enjoy contemplation for long in this life, as we have seen. Therefore, it is necessary (though always an imperfection from the ideal perspective of heaven) that contemplative love yield to active love when required. "As often . . . as she falls from the contemplative life she is received into the active life, from which she will surely return to her former state from nearby in a more intimate (*familiarius*) way, since these two modes of life are closely related and live together–Martha is Mary's sister."[388] It is important to emphasize that it is left up to the contemplative soul to decide when to abandon the joy of the intimate experience of the Bridegroom's visit in order to fulfill the duties of maternal love,[389] but Bernard's conviction is that every true contemplative will prove the authenticity of his or her experience of God by the alacrity with which they submit to the constraints of the call to charity. Speaking in a very personal way about the demands made upon him by his own community, the abbot of Clairvaux says, "I shall care for them as far as I am able, and in them, as long as I live, I shall serve my God in unfeigned love. I won't seek what is mine. What I judge useful to me is not what is useful *to me*, but to many."[390]

The mention of Mary and Martha as types of the contemplative and active lives in *Sermon 51.2* connects the abbot with a tradition of Christian exegesis extending back to Origen. Mary and Martha appear elsewhere in the *Sermons on the Song of Songs* (e.g., *Sermon 40.3*), and a more complete symbolic presentation, involving the two women and their brother, Lazarus, is found in *Sermon 57.9–11*. Here the three activities of preaching, prayer, and contemplation are compared with the three ways that the Bridegroom addresses the Bride (as friend, dove, and beautiful one in Song 2:10), and then to the figures of Martha, Mary, and Lazarus as representing three classes of souls (actives, contemplatives, and penitents), and finally also to three forms of activity found in each soul (see *Sermon 57.9–11*). The paradigm portrayed in the three siblings is also explored in Bernard's sermons on the Assumption, though not in a way that goes beyond the teaching of the *Sermon on the Song of Songs*. The assumption sermons stress the ongoing interaction of all three activities represented by Jesus's three friends as a form of *ordinatio caritatis*,[391] as well as the superiority of contemplation that is figured in Mary (e.g., *Asspt 3.3*). The lengthy treatment in the fifth sermon, in which Martha stands for activity (*operatio*) and Mary understanding (*intellectus*), is one of Bernard's most sustained expositions of the mystical life outside the confines of his *Sermons on the Song of Songs*.[392] In it we find another lapidary formulation of the necessity for a fruitful combination of action and contemplation in the advanced soul: "Each perfect person should have unity in his own regard and unity with regard to his neighbor–to himself through integrity, to his neighbor through conformity."[393]

Although Bernard made significant use of this traditional typology of Mary and Martha to discuss the relation between action and contemplation, in the long run, as suggested above, it was the symbol of the soul as both Bride and Mother that stands closest to the heart of his mystical theory. This language was suggested to the abbot by many passages in the Song of Songs, and he alluded to it frequently in his sermons on the text (notably in *Sermon* 41.5–6). Here Bernard provides one final striking expression of the necessity of the union of action and contemplation in the Christian soul when he says: "We learn from this that the sweet kisses are often interrupted due to the breasts flowing with milk. No one lives for himself, but all should live for him who died for all" (1 Cor 5:15).[394]

Conclusion

Dante's quotation from the *Paradiso* with which we began this chapter is a fitting expression of the traditional Latin Christian view of Bernard as the supreme guide to the delights of ecstatic contemplation. The great poet was not alone in his judgment: no mystic of the whole Middle Ages was more read and more often cited than the abbot of Clairvaux. Even those whose views were in many ways quite different from his, like Meister Eckhart, read him and learned much from him. The mystics of the later Middle Ages who elaborated on the erotic symbolization of the soul's experience of God returned again and again to Bernard's *Sermons on the Song of Songs*, even as they began to distance themselves from direct commentary on the text of the Song as the favored way to express union with God. Even in our own era, Bernard offers remarkable resources to the contemporary reader, despite the almost insurmountable loss suffered when his thought is separated from its magnificent Latin style.[395] Though Bernard can scarcely be said to have created a systematic mystical theology (nor would he have wanted to), I have tried to show that there is a pervading *integritas*, or coherent wholeness, to the way in which he strove to express the inexpressible experience of God. As he put so well, "It is God alone who can never be sought in vain, even when he cannot be found."[396]

Like his predecessors, both in the East and the West, Bernard knew the limitations, infinite in nature and number, of all that he said and that he tried to say with such passion and elegance. Where this greatest of Cistercian mystics marks a new departure (though not, of course, one *totally* new) is in how he insists that what he says is based on his own experience (*Loquor vobis experimentum meum quod expertus sum,* "I am telling you of what I myself have experienced"),[397] and in how he constantly appealed to his listeners and readers to measure his message against the book of their own experience. Bernard continues to invite us to read in the book of our hearts.

William of St. Thierry: Spirit-Centered Mysticism

WILLIAM, AT ONE TIME abbot of the Benedictine monastery of St. Thierry near Reims and later monk of the Cistercian house of Signy, is one of the major discoveries of twentieth-century medieval studies. Although three of his works were widely read in the later Middle Ages, it was under the name of his good friend Bernard of Clairvaux that they achieved their fame.[1] When the Bernardine ascription was shown to be false, these and William's lesser-known treatises and commentaries faded into obscurity.[2] William first began to attract attention again in the early part of this century.[3] In the middle decades, the work of M.-M. Davy and especially J.-M. Déchanet did much to further interest in him.[4] Over the past thirty years, a wealth of scholarship has enriched our understanding of his difficult but rewarding thought.[5] William may have been less influential in the later tradition than Bernard and the Victorines, but he yields to no twelfth-century mystic in the depth and sophistication of his theology. As a friend and admirer of the great abbot of Clairvaux, William's thought can be compared with Bernard's in many areas, some of which will be commented on below; but the fact is, that the abbot of St. Thierry is very much his own man—an independent and powerful theorist of mysticism. William also demonstrates that we should not make any sharp distinction between Cistercian mysticism and the traditional mysticism of the Benedictines. William's early writings were composed while he was still among the black monks and do not show any major break with his later Cistercian efforts.

William was born in Liège sometime in the last quarter of the eleventh century, probably at least a decade before Bernard's birth in 1090. His character, which is communicated to us especially in his deeply personal *Meditations*, has been described by Jean Leclercq as "high-strung."[6] As a young man, he attended one of the vibrant Cathedral schools of northern France (Reims more likely than Laon), which were giving birth not only to a new mode of theology—scholasticism—but also to a new educational institution of incalcuable moment in Western history, the university. William thus had an up-to-date and professional form of theological training that Bernard lacked. It affected his theology in a number of ways.

Positively, William demonstrates a deep and broad knowledge of patristic sources, including some Greek Fathers (in Latin translation, of course). Like the schoolmen he trained under, William compiled *sententiae*, or excerpts of authoritative texts, as handy pedagogical tools.[7] But he also utilized the tradition to meet current issues, both doctrinal and mystical. Like all Western theologians, the main source for his theology was Augustine of Hippo, whom he read widely and with care.[8] He was also well acquainted with Gregory the Great, as would be expected. Exaggerated claims concerning his direct access to a wide range of Greek materials (even Plotinus!) made by J.-M. Déchanet have not been borne out by subsequent research,[9] but this does not negate the fact that in several key areas of his thought Eastern fathers, especially Origen and Gregory of Nyssa, play a significant role.[10] The debates over William's sources should not blind us to what makes him worth reading today—the originality and depth of his views.

William's career in the schools before entering the cloister (a conversion not uncommon among many of the best minds of the twelfth century) appears to have had some negative effects as well. Both as abbot of St. Thierry and monk of Signy, William had a keen nose for theological error and a remarkable persistence in pursuing it for one so personally diffident. William was the one who dragged Bernard into the attack on Abelard.[11] Reading William's polemical works against Abelard and William of Conches in the light of the whole of his thought, we sense a mind paradoxically both at odds with much of the speculative efforts of the schoolmen and yet also willing to engage in profound speculation within limits of his own choosing.[12]

Sometime in the second decade of the twelfth century, William and his brother Simon entered the Benedictine monastery of St. Nicasius in Reims. About 1120 he was named abbot of the ancient monastery of St. Thierry not far from that city. Here he composed his earliest works, *On Contemplating God* and *The Nature and Dignity of Love*, both deeply Augustinian in inspiration. William had met Bernard possibly as early as 1118. In the life that he wrote of his friend, he tells us the story of how at some time in the early 1120s, when he and Bernard both lay ill in the infirmary at Clairvaux, they discoursed about the soul and Bernard disclosed the moral (i.e., personal) significance that his experience had thus far enabled him to draw from the Song of Songs.[13] Like the famous conversation of Augustine and Monica in Ostia, this colloquy was to have profound effects on the Western mystical tradition.[14]

As early as 1124, William was already importuning Bernard for permission to join the Cistercians. Bernard resisted, however, and William remained at St. Thierry, though not without serious trials as the highly personal *Meditations* he began in the late 1120's and finished after he became a Cistercian show.[15] In 1135 William was at last able to join a new Cistercian foundation near Reims at Signy as a simple monk. The hard life of the white monks caused the aging ex-abbot initial difficulties, but he soon came to enjoy the *pingue otium,* or rich leisure, that enabled him to produce his most important writings.[16] From about 1137 to early 1139 he was at work on his *Exposition on the Song of Songs,* leaving it unfinished because of the necessity of refuting Abelard. The *Exposition* is arguably William's greatest work. According to Jean Leclercq, it "has the ardor of the *Meditations,* the depth of the treatises, and the pressing tone of the *Golden Epistle,* but there is an added charm which no doubt comes from the feminine presence which the chosen theme called for."[17] William's commentary on the Song is more consistently interior in tone and more systematically organized than Bernard's digressive sermons, dividing the whole Song of Songs into four shorter poems or songs (1:1–2:7, 2:8–3:5, 3:6–8:4, and 8:5–14), each following the same structure.[18] William says that he is giving only a "moral" interpretation of the book, that is, one that concentrates on the personal application in which the Bride is read as the soul, rather than an allegorical, or doctrinal, reading interpreting the book as disclosing the mystery of Christ and the church.[19] There are many places where his reading shows affinities with that of Bernard,[20] but his main hermeneutical line is an independent one, centered on his understanding of loving union in the Holy Spirit. While William lacks the rhetorical ingenuity and epigrammatic conciseness of Bernard, the *Exposition* and the three major mystical treatises we will discuss are written in a distinctive style—complex, often knotty, capable of passion and precision, though at times bordering on opacity.

It was also apparently in the early years at Signy that William completed two important background works to his mystical compositions. The first of these, *The Nature of the Body and Soul (De natura corporis et animae,* also called the *Physica humani corporis et physica animae),*[21] uses a mass of speculative medical information (also employed by his scholastic opponent William of

Conches), as well as a theory of the soul deeply influenced by Gregory of
Nyssa's *The Making of Man (De opificio hominis)*. Using the translation of John
Scottus Eriugena,[22] William constructed an anthropology based on the harmonization of images–the human body as image (microcosm) of the universe, and the human soul as image and likeness of God.[23] William's
Exposition on the Epistle to the Romans, heavily drawn from Augustine and
Origen, is a doctrinal sketch of the bases of his mystical theory.[24] Sometime
after 1140 he composed the joint treatises called the *Mirror of Faith (Speculum fidei)* and the *Enigma of Faith (Aenigma fidei)* after the Pauline text contrasting two modes of our knowledge of God here below (*per speculum in
aenigmate*, 1 Cor 13:12) with the face-to-face vision to be enjoyed in heaven.
This contrast forms one of the central themes of William's thought, as we
shall see. Although he does not mention Abelard's name, it is clear that he
wrote the two works in the midst of the Abelardian crisis to instruct his fellow monks about the proper understanding of the role of faith in the path
to union with God, both that version of the path which leads from faith
directly to mystical contact (the *credo ut experiar* treated primarily in the *Mirror*), and that which advances by applying reason to faith (the *credo ut intelligam* that is the major concern of the *Enigma*).[25] While the *Mirror* is more
overtly mystical than the *Enigma* (which is essentially a speculative treatment of the Trinity),[26] the two treatises must be taken together in order to
get a full grasp of the complexity of William's understanding of the relation
of reason, faith, and love in the quest for the face-to-face vision of God.

The *Epistola ad fratres de Monte-Dei* was written about 1144 for the Carthusians at Mont-Dieu near Reims with whom William had spent some time.
This *Golden Letter (Epistola aurea)*, as it justly came to be called, has always
been the most popular of William's works, and not just due to its ascription
to Bernard. It is, in a sense, the treatise that Bernard should have written
but never did–a perfect guide to monastic spirituality, as balanced as it is
profound. The basic structure proceeds from a triple distinction found in
Origen (and also used by Bernard): the animal state of beginners considered in the first book, and the rational and spiritual levels of more advanced souls taken up in the second. The work is unusual among William's
oeuvre in the attention it pays to the ascetical foundation of the mystical
life.[27] The former abbot's strict and astute teaching here, coupled with the
profundity of his views on the the mystical goal found in book two, make
the *Golden Letter* one of the most important summaries of medieval mystical
teaching. William of St. Thierry and Signy, now an old monk and in ill
health, lived on a few more years, working on the life of his friend Bernard,
a task he did not complete because of his death on 8 September 1148.

William's Anthropology

O Lord, our God, who created us to your image and likeness, that is, to contemplate you and to enjoy you whom no one contemplates to the level of enjoyment save insofar as he is made like you, . . . free from the slavery of corruption that in us which ought to serve you alone: our love. Love, when it is free, is that which makes us like you to the extent that we are drawn to you by that living perception (*sensus vitae*) by means of which whoever lives from the Spirit of Life (*spiritus vitae*) has knowledge of you.[28]

This passage, from the beginning of William's *Exposition on the Song of Songs*, can serve as an introduction to the major aspects of his mysticism. None of the ideas mentioned here—image and likeness, contemplation and enjoyment, love and the Holy Spirit—is unique to the abbot of St. Thierry. They are part of the patrimony of Christian mysticism and appear in various ways in all twelfth-century spiritual writers. But the particular constellation in which William puts them already gives us a hint of his Spirit-centered mysticism. As we proceed with an analysis of the components of his thought, both those explicitly advanced here and those implied, an original, complex, and even difficult mystical theory will emerge.

It is best to begin, as we did in Bernard's case, with the anthropological foundation of the whole, that is, with William's understanding of what it means for humanity to be made in the divine image and likeness.[29] William's theological appropriation of this common property is basically Augustinian, but it was developed in an original way, partly because of his contact with Greek sources.

To be an image of anything means to participate in it, that is, to receive reality from it, but also to be distinguishable from it in some way. Although William does not advance an explicit theology of participation (as did Boethius, Aquinas, and others), there can be no doubt that this is one of the central metaphysical notions implied throughout his writings, as David Bell has shown.[30] The key to understanding William's theology of the image and likeness is to recognize that the two terms imply different, but related forms of participation—the *imago* emphasizes the essential or original share in the divine nature that makes each human person open to God, while the *similitudo* primarily concerns the participative or perfecting activity by which we do or do not resemble God in how we love and act. In a manner not unlike what we saw in Bernard of Clairvaux's *Sermons on the Song of Songs* 80-82, William teaches that both the *imago* and the *similitudo* have been damaged by sin, but the effect is far more devastating in the case of the *similitudo*.[31] The relation of the two forms of participation is well expressed in a text from the *Mirror of Faith*:

By a kind of natural affinity, eternal and divine things seem to be joined to the mind created for eternity so that it might be open to it through understanding and participate in it through enjoyment. This happens to such an extent that even if the mind has become quite dull through vice, it never loses its appetite for these things. . . . Although nature possesses an appetite in such matters on the basis of creative grace, it discerns them in a perfect way only on the basis of illuminating grace. It attains them only through God's gift.[32]

The participation based on creative grace (i.e., the *imago*) cannot be lost though it may be damaged; the participation that is likeness has been lost through sin. It is for this second mode of participation that William prays in the preface to the commentary on the Song of Song: "O Holy Spirit, we beg you to fill us with your love—O Love!—so that we may understand love's song and ourselves be made in some way participants (*efficiamur participes*) in the dialogue of the Bride and Groom. Thus, what we read we may also perform."[33] We need to investigate in more detail *imago* and *similitudo* as *originating* and *perfecting* participation, if we may use these terms, in order to grasp the full import of William's anthropology.

In the *The Nature of the Body and Soul*, and scattered throughout his works, William discusses the soul as image and likeness. We can begin with the soul as the *imago Dei* in the general sense.[34] Like Augustine and others before him, William asserts that the Divine Word, the second person of the Trinity, is the only real *imago* of the Father, so that it is always more correct to say that the human person is an *imago ad imaginem*.[35] But William, again like many others, makes more frequent use of the shorter *imago Dei* formula to describe the essence of humanity. Given the trinitarian character of William's mysticism, however, he emphasizes the human dignity of being an *imago trinitatis* as the most important aspect of our *originating* participation in God. In the twelfth of the *Meditations* he says, "The holy soul is reformed to the image of the Trinity, to the image of him who created her in the very manner of his beatitude. For a will that has been enlightened and drawn (*affecta*)—that means intellect, love and the disposition of enjoyment—is in a certain way three personal affections (*affectionum personae*), as is said and believed of God the Trinity."[36]

This is only one of the formulas that William uses to express the trinitarian nature of *originating* participation. More often he employs the traditional Augustinian psychological triad of *memoria-intellectus-amor* and its variants,[37] and in more unusual fashion he uses the three theological virtues as a trinitarian image at the beginning of the *Mirror of Faith*.[38] William was never as interested as his master, Augustine, was in exploring the theoretical intricacies of the trinitarian analogies.[39] Rather, he tended to move more quickly to the trinitarian anagogies that Augustine mostly reserved for the final book of his great *De Trinitate*. Almost all of William's explorations of the paradoxical intricacies of the Trinity are directly related to how the soul as the *imago trinitatis* is to come to regain its lost *similitudo trinitatis* through the life of prayer and contemplation.[40] Odo Brooke put it well when he said: "Whether we approach his thought from the angle of 'image' or from the angle of theological stages with their spiritual and psychological roots, we always find that these themes converge in the central one of the impetus towards resemblance through experimental knowledge given by the Holy Ghost."[41] Or, to frame it in William's own words, "Be totally present to yourself, and make total use of yourself and whose image you are so that you discern and understand what you are and what you can do in him whose image you are."[42]

Thus, William insists at the outset on calling the soul to the task of self-knowledge. But since the soul's innermost nature is to be an *imago trinitatis*, the deepest form of self-knowledge, beyond the necessary initial recognition of our sinfulness and need for reform, is the gradual awareness of the mystery of our relation to the Trinity. This implies the radical unknowability of our being–a stimulating if paradoxical insight that William found hinted at in Gregory of Nyssa. He refers to it in a brief but pregnant passage in the *The Nature of the Body and Soul*.[43]

Sin has destroyed the resemblance (*similitudo*), that is, the active or *perfecting* participation, that God originally bestowed on us in creation. We now live in the *regio dissimilitudinis*, the land of unlikeness,[44] where we have become "a laborious and wearying question" to ouselves.[45] The way in which we come to regain the *similitudo* of resemblance to God in gradual and imperfect fashion during this life and perfectly in heaven is the whole content of William's mystical theology. By way of introduction, we shall give here only a few general notions pertaining to the nature of the abbot's understanding of the *similitudo* as a guide for the more detailed analysis of the process of reappropriation to be considered in the sections that follow.

One of William's most noted texts concerning the divine likeness occurs toward the end of the *Golden Letter*:

> This is their [i.e., humanity's] whole perfection–resemblance to God. Not to wish to be perfect is to fall into sin. The will must always be nourished, love always prepared for the sake of perfection. The will must be restrained lest it lose itself in alien concerns; love protected lest it be sullied. It is for this alone that we were created and live. We were created to God's image so that we may be like God.[46]

The Cistercian goes on to analyze three levels or stages of resemblance, that is, three activities through which the soul gradually attains to perfecting participation. The first is the soul's ubiquitous presence giving life to every part of the body, a point often noted by William but one which he insists gains no merit in the quest for salvation.[47] The second likeness, closer to God because it is willed, consists in the life of virtue (*Ep frat* 261). "Beyond this there is still another likeness to God. . . . It is so expressly characteristic that it is no longer called a likeness, but a unity of spirit. It happens when a person becomes one with God, one spirit not only in the unity of willing the same thing, but by means of a more evident truth of virtue, . . . namely, the inability to will anything else."[48] Unity of spirit, one of the primary themes of William's thought, will be taken up in more detail later.

That both these higher forms of *similitudo* are expressions of the human will as it comes to be more and more conformed to the divine Will is central to William's thought.[49] But volition does not exclude cognition—we also become more like God as we come to know him or see him in more direct fashion. The First Epistle of John teaches, "We will be like him because we will see him as he is (*Similes ei erimus quoniam videbimus eum sicuti est*, 1 John 3:2), a text William loved to cite. Though the full realization of the identity of vision and likeness remains for heaven,[50] it must begin in this life if we wish to attain the celestial goal: "That likeness is in the interior person by means of which one is renewed from day to day in the recognition (*agnitio*) of God according to the image of him who created him. The more we are made like him by knowing him and loving him, the closer and more familiarly we see him."[51] This same passage from the *Enigma of Faith* goes on to discuss the transcendental divine ground for this dynamic identity of seeing and similarity:

> Just as in the Trinity, which is God, the Father and the Son see each other, and their seeing each other is for them to be one and for each of them to be what the other is, so those who are predestined to this and who have been lifted up into it will see God as he is and in seeing will be made as he is, that is, like him. There, just as in the Father and the Son vision is the unity itself, so too in God and humans the vision is that future likeness. The Holy Spirit is the unity of the Father and the Son; he is also the charity and likeness of God and humans.[52]

To love perfectly so that one is actually unable to love what God does not love, to see perfectly with the vision that constitutes the mutual knowledge of the Father and the Son is the perfection of the *similitudo Dei* and the total fruition or enjoyment of the soul. In order to understand how this perfect likeness is to be attained in heaven we must return to earth and begin with a closer look at the way in which William understood the powers and the operations of the soul.[53]

The details of William's account of the soul need not delay us here, nor his understanding of the relation of the soul to the body.[54] It is important to remember, however, that the Cistercian, like other contemporary spiritual authors, made use of an anthropology of an essentially Neoplatonic cast in which there is a distinction between two levels of the soul, one by which it vivifies the body and is directed to the things of this life (*anima* for William and many of his contemporaries), the other by which it is open to God and the realities of the divine world (William usually calls this *animus*, which I translate as "intellectual soul").[55] This distinction is paralleled, though not always in a precise way, by a discrimination between lower and higher modes of knowledge, *ratio inferior* and *ratio superior*, or *ratio* in a general sense as contrasted with *intelligentia* or *intellectus* (another of William's favorite terms).[56] Like Augustine before him, the abbot of St. Thierry had no hard and fixed terminology for these divisions, something that will seem unfortunate only to those for whom terminological exactitude is always a virtue. But the sense in which the varying expressions are being employed can usually be easily determined from the context.

A second important element in the generalized Neoplatonic anthropology William shared with his contemporaries was an insistence on the complementary roles of the cognitive and affective powers in the movement toward God.[57] William's younger contemporary, Isaac of Stella, spoke of the power of desire (*affectus*) and that of knowledge (*sensus*) as the two "feet" by which the soul journeys to God.[58] In an important passage from the *The Nature and Dignity of Love*, William affirms love's priority in the ascent, but he also insists on the necessity of accompanying reason:

> The sight for seeing God, the natural light of the soul created by nature's Author, is charity. But there are two eyes in this sight, love and reason, always throbbing with a natural intention to see the light that is God. When one makes an effort without the other, it doesn't get very far. When they help each other, they accomplish much—that is, when they become the one eye of which the Bridegroom says in the Song of Songs, "You have wounded my heart, my friend, with one of your eyes" (Song 4:9).[59]

Reason, William goes on to point out, moves toward God by discovering what he is not. Love "apprehends more by its ignorance," and "rejoices to fade away in what he is."[60] Here, at the beginning of his writing career, the abbot of St. Thierry already expresses the essence of the mutuality of love and reason that he was to investigate in such detail twenty years later in the *Mirror of Faith* and the *Enigma of Faith*. The necessary cooperation, even union, of the soul's two essential powers is the anthropological root of his distinctive teaching about the *sensus* or *intellectus amoris* to be considered below.

One final element in William's anthropology deserves consideration as part of the background to his explanation of how love and knowledge come together in effecting the restoration of our lost likeness. Léopold Malévez was the first to point out how William's understanding of the nature of sense perception helps us grasp his teaching about love becoming intellection.[61] While it is true that it is always the action of the Holy Spirit that makes possible this ultimate transformation, William uses the analogy of sensation (and, indeed, also the higher but still natural modes of perception and cognition) to suggest that this beatifying union of mystical loving and mystical knowing is not totally alien to our normal cognitive experiences. According to the *The Nature of Body and Soul*, "Every sense experience changes the one experiencing it in some way into that which is sensed or there is no sensation."[62] In the case of vision, for example, "the power of sight, leaving the brain through the rays of the eyes meets the forms or colors of visible things to which the mind conforms itself when the power brings them back to it. And vision comes about."[63] Sense perception, and by extension any form of knowing, comprises three elements: (1) an initial similarity between the knowing power and its object (like can only be known by like); (2) the joining of the interior element in the power with the similar element in the object by means of the action of the perceiving power; and (3) the transformation of the knowing power into the object. This model suggests something of how love becomes understanding in William's mystical theology, as we shall see.[64]

The Dynamics of Progress

Christian mystics, as we have seen in the case of Bernard and others, love to make use of patterns of threes in describing the stages of the soul's progress to God, not only for trinitarian reasons but also because this is a natural human way of portraying a transformation by which two extremes, such as the divine and the human, are somehow joined.[65] William of St. Thierry employs a distinctive triple pattern in two major places in his writings.

In the preface to his *Exposition on the Song of Songs* and throughout the *Golden Letter* the Cistercian uses a distinction that applies at once to three kinds of prayer, to three different kinds of souls, and to three spiritual stages to be found, at least potentially, in all Christians.[66] "It is clear that there are three states of those who pray or of kinds of prayer: animal, rational and spiritual. Each person forms for himself or proposes his own Lord God according to his mode, because the God who is prayed to appears to each according to the quality of the one who prays."[67] As the *Golden Letter* puts it: "Just as star differs from star in brightness (1 Cor 15:41), so does cell from cell in the way of life of beginners, of advanced and of perfect. The state of beginners is called animal, the state of advanced rational, the state of the perfect spiritual. . . . Every religious way of life is made up of these three kinds of persons."[68] The division, ultimately based on Paul's view of the human person as composed of body, soul and spirit (1 Thess 5:23; cf. 1 Cor 2:14), was first discussed by Origen from whom William adopted and developed it.[69]

The presentation in the *Exposition* shows how the various kinds of prayer understood as conversation with God convey growing knowledge of the Divine Lover through the action of the Word made flesh and the Holy Spirit. The carnal prayer of the animal person, who asks something from God besides God himself, is not to be found in the Song of Songs; but even on this level some contact with God is possible, especially when the soul prays in simplicity to ". . . the Lord Savior according to his human form, and, person to person, puts on a human and as it were bodily affection of prayer."[70] This mode reminds us of Bernard's *amor carnalis Christi*, a reminiscence heightened by the fact that William, like the abbot of Clairvaux, says that this manner of conceiving the Savior must eventually be withdrawn just as Christ withdrew his bodily presence from the disciples at the Ascension in order to make possible their transition to a higher spiritual level.[71] In the rational stage of prayer we begin to know God as he really is while the intellect and will are being cleansed by the action of the Holy Spirit:

> When a person aspires (*affectat*) to know God as far as permitted and to be known by him, the face of God's grace is revealed to him and God himself to his conscience, so that knowing him and known by him, he might pray to him and adore him as is fitting, "in spirit and truth" (John 4:23). He is the Groom, she the Bride, and this is their mutual conversation.[72]

Here William stresses the intimate relation of the rational and spiritual stages tied to the transition from a prayer in which some form of image or phantasm is still present in the mind to one which is dependent on a likeness that is the product of "the active purity of simple tending to God (*affectus*)."[73] The one who prays for divine sweetness "is rational as long as he depends on reason in this, but after he has attained it he is spiritual insofar as he has attained it."[74] The mystical life consists of an ongoing oscillation between the two stages—". . . the man of God ought to be always either rational in seeking or spiritual in loving" (*affectus*).[75]

In the *Golden Letter* William integrates the three stages of spiritual progress with his theological anthropology in a more detailed and systematic way. The *animales*, treated at length in the beginning (*Ep frat* 46–185), are what we might call external Christians–"... of themselves they are not led by reason or drawn by *affectus*, but are moved by authority, reminded by doctrine and inspired by example to approve what is good where they find it."[76] Their primary virtue is obedience. The *rationales* have begun the move toward interior religion. In them the *anima*, the soul as vivifying power, is already becoming the *animus*, the intellectual soul directed to the God who dwells within (see *Ep frat* 197–98). Or, from another perspective, the will or *arbitrium*, though still bound to some extent to sin, has begun to be transformed into the *libertas voluntatis* by means of which God can be freely served.[77] Though the *rationales* (treated throughout *Ep frat* 195–248) "... have knowledge and appetite for the good, they do not yet have *affectus*."[78] When "reason's judgment passes over into *affectus mentis*,"[79] the state of the *spirituales* begins (these are discussed in *Ep frat* 249–300).

Those who have reached this stage are "... the perfect who are led by the Spirit, who are more fully enlightened by the Holy Spirit. Because they taste the good whose attraction (*affectus*) draws them, they are called wise [i.e., *sapienties*, literally 'tasters']. Because the Holy Spirit puts them on, just as he once put on Gideon (Judges 6:34), they are called 'spirituals' insofar as they are the clothing of the Holy Spirit."[80] The transition from *anima* through *animus* to the divinely bestowed *spiritus* that has its fruition in our unity of spirit with God (*unitas spiritus*) governs the whole structure and exposition of William's most noted work.[81] Putting both treatments of the three stages together we also get the hint, one that will be confirmed by a study of William's related treatments of the dynamics of progress to mystical union, that the transition from *anima* to *animus* is primarily (though not solely) understood as the work of the Incarnate Word, while the soul's lifting up from *animus* to *spiritus* is ascribed to the indwelling Holy Spirit.[82]

Following the lead of J.-M. Déchanet and Odo Brooke, it is possible to discern an intimate relation between these three stages of spiritual progress and the triple formulas William employs to present the soul's journey to God in his two treatises on faith. The three theological virtues, especially faith and charity, played a major role in the Cistercian's thought.[83] At the beginning of the *Mirror of Faith*, as noted above, these virtues appear as an image of the Trinity, but one specifically invoked to express the way by which grace restores the lost likeness: "The Holy Trinity established this trinity in the faithful mind to its image and likeness. By it we are being renewed to the image of him who created us in our interior man. This is that instrument (*machina*) of human salvation for whose construction and edification in the hearts of the faithful every divinely revealed scripture has a concern."[84] The three virtues are all necessary in order that reason (here obviously the *ratio superior*) may be made just and perfect so that it can direct its gaze (*aspectus*) to the goal of the vision of God.[85] This is why anyone who seeks the divine Trinity must have this other trinity of virtues within him and strive to conform himself to them.[86] The interdependence of the three, by which ". . . faith gives birth to hope and charity proceeds from both, that is, from faith and hope," reestablishes the *similitudo trinitatis* in the soul.[87]

William's brief description of the role of the three virtues, according to which the faith and the hope that lead us on in this life will "pass over" (*transibunt*) into the reality of perfect charity in heaven does not, however, serve as the major theme of either the *Mirror of Faith* or the *Enigma of Faith*. Rather, since ". . . there is one form of the virtue of these three virtues (faith, hope and charity)," that is, because "everything in this life is based on faith,"[88] he spends most of his time in the two works trying to understand how the faith that gives birth to hope and charity works in our souls during the course of this life. From our human perspective, looking upwards from below as it were, everything comes from faith; from the divine perspective that always gazes from above, something we can only partially appropriate in this life, everything is charity, the love that draws up and gradually changes faith and hope into itself (*Spec* 10–11).

The most important summary text on the progress of faith found in the *Enigma of Faith* concerns the three degrees of understanding in faith's ascent:

> The ascent to God and knowledge of him is by means of three degrees of understanding in the progress of faith. The first degree is to investigate diligently what is to be believed about the Lord God. The second degree is how nonetheless to think and to talk correctly about what is rightly believed. The third degree is already the experience of realities in perceiving (*sentiendo*) God in goodness just as they perceive who seek him in simplicity of heart. The first is as easy for one ascending as believing is for someone who wishes to believe and to whom belief has been given. . . . The second is more difficult. . . , - although the presumptuous pretend to have it [probably a reference to Abelard]. The third belongs to the perfect who burn to love the Lord their God with their whole heart and soul and from their entire mind. . . . [89]

We may take these three degrees as homologous to the three kinds of believers and the three levels of progress in the soul discussed above. The simple faith of stage one corresponds to the *homo animalis* with his need for obedience to external authority; the effort to think and to talk correctly about faith is equivalent to the *homo rationalis*; and the stage of experiencing God is that of the *homo spiritualis*.[90] Thus, William speaks about the first degree as ". . . founded in authority, having the form of faith which has been formed from the provable testimonies of accredited authority."[91] The second level is that of *fides quaerens intellectum*, which we might translate here as "faith hoping for understanding." "It pertains to this degree to know how to think and speak about God reasonably according to the reasoning of faith (*ratio fidei*), and also how that faith may be produced where it is not found, may be nourished and aided where it exists, and how it may be defended against its enemies."[92] In the third degree, ". . . beatifying and illuminating grace puts an end to faith, or rather beatifies it into love, transferring a person from faith to vision by initiating a knowledge (*cognitio*) that is not of faith but that begins to exist in this life along with faith in the faithful person."[93]

William's conception of the relations between faith and reason, while they must be seen against the background of contemporary doctrinal disputes over the proper application of *fides quaerens intellectum*, is an essential part of his mystical theory, as Odo Brooke has demonstrated.[94] In the *Mirror of Faith*, which is more concerned with what we can call the *credo ut experiar* pattern of ascent to God,[95] we already find considerable treatment of how reason, if properly humble, can strive to fulfill its natural desire to know without overstepping the proper boundaries.[96] The Cistercian distinguishes two different kinds of faith:

> There is one faith that flesh and blood reveals; the other which the Father in heaven reveals. The one is not the other—the same faith but a different effect. The first teaches what we must believe; the second suggests its understanding of faith and also the full etymological meaning of "understanding," that is, when one who believes "reads within" in the affection of his heart what he believes.[97]

This distinction between two kinds of faith, an exterior faith grounded on authority and on the visible *sacramenta*, or mysteries of our redemption, and an interior faith written in the heart, where the *sacramentum* of the loving encounter between God and the human takes place,[98] is the foundation for the first two stages discussed in the *Enigma of Faith* passage quoted above. William suggests that some simple children of God reach the second level without effort or the necessity of exerting the power of reason (*Spec* 49–52); but others strive to understand what they believe and to give reasons for their faith. "This type, even if it often tastes the goal only with effort, nevertheless gives light and is safer against temptations."[99] It is this type that is properly called *fides quaerens intellectum* in the manner of Augustine and Anselm. It corresponds to the second degree of faith, the *ratio fidei*, found in the *Enigma* text.

The *ratio fidei* is one of William's most important theological conceptions, his answer to what he thought were the dangerous pretensions of some contemporary scholastic theologians. The *ratio fidei* is an expansion of simple faith, a movement of belief in the direction of understanding; but for William the expansion is not effected from reason's side, that is, from below, but from above, by way of the gift of faith and the truths contained in it. These instruct the believer how best to use and transform human words and terms, especially philosophical vocabulary, to indicate where and how the divine mystery surpasses understanding.[100] Its task is essentially more negative than positive as William explains it: to locate the mystery, not to probe it. Two passages from William's early writings express this well: "In matters of this sort exemplary reasons and probative arguments are to be taken from above, not from below."[101] "Faith instructs reason; reason, through faith, either improves or destroys and rejects an image. Reason does not teach faith to understand, but through faith waits on understanding from above, from the Father of lights."[102] In the *Enigma of Faith*, whose central portion is a lengthy treatise on the mystery of the Trinity, we are given numerous illustrations of how the *ratio fidei* transforms or negates ordinary philosophical terms, like substance, person and relation, when applied to the Trinity.[103] "When words are used of God, the meaning of the words is to be adapted to the realities, not vice versa,"[104] as William put it. The Cistercian's notion of the relation of faith and reason, then, is scarcely a correlational one in the modern sense of the word. Reason on its own has little or nothing to offer the work of *intellectus fidei*. We can see why he thought Abelard so dangerous.

Toward the end of the *Mirror of Faith*, William identifies two kinds of knowledge of God (*cognitio Dei*). "There is one kind of knowledge of God that belongs to faith, the other that belongs to love or charity. The one that is of faith is of this life; the one that is of charity of eternal life. . . . It is one thing to know God as a man knows his friend; another to know him as he knows himself."[105] We may ask if these two forms of *cognitio* are the same as the final two forms of the progress of faith in the passage from the *Enigma of Faith* referred to above.

There are many things that recommend such an identification, especially the description of the third stage as a *cognitio* and the contrast drawn in the *Enigma of Faith* text between a *cognitio* dependent on the *ratio fidei* (that is, on the knowledge *we* can have of God) and the *cognitio* that is God's knowledge of himself.[106] A further and comparable pattern of two kinds of knowledge of God beyond simple external faith can also be invoked here, the distinction between an illuminated faith which William places under the Pauline rubric of *ex fide in fidem* (Rom 1:17) and faith seen as the root of the possibility of attaining brief experiences of vision while still in this life, *a fide in speciem*.[107] But we should beware of making William's thought in this difficult matter too neat. The variations in his terminology and the density of his writing leave us in doubt as to whether the distinctions are to be thought of as strictly parallel or only as roughly homologous.

In his penetrating analysis of William's teaching on faith, Odo Brooke claimed that in the end the accounts of the two paths to God, the mystical ascent of the *credo ut experiar* portrayed in the *Mirror of Faith* and the more intellectual *credo ut intelligam* ascent of the *Enigma of Faith*, were only imperfectly synthesized by the Cistercian.[108] This seems borne out by certain obscurities and inconsistencies between the accounts of the various stages of each path. No presentation denies, excludes, or flatly contradicts another, just as love never rejects understanding; but the picture of faith's progress in the two treatises is primarily constructed from an intellectualist perspective while we find a more affective analysis in the *Exposition on the Song of Songs* and the *Golden Letter*. Thus, William has left us with his own illustration of what Bernard called *diversa sed non adversa* approaches to the same problem.

It is difficult to present a clear picture of the affective analysis of the restoration of the *similitudo Dei*, but a look at one of the richest sections of the *Exposition*—what Déchanet's edition identifies as William's comment on the seventh and eighth stanzas of the first song (an exegesis of Song of Songs 1:11–16)—can provide a good summary of this itinerary of love, even though it expressly deals with the purificatory stage (*actus purgatorius*). This also will give us an illustration of William's distinctive way of transforming the sensual language of the Song into the language of the soul's spiritual love.

Because of the importance of images in all human life, even the life of prayer, William argues, the Holy Spirit has clothed the message of spiritual love in a carnal form so that "... my love ... may long for the place to which it is called through images of love ... until the external parable of the drama becomes the history of truth in it."[109] For William, the two central symbols in these verses of the Song, that is, the *accubitus* or reclining of the King (Song 1:11), and the *lectulus floridus noster*, "our little flowery bed" of 1:16, signify two rather different forms of the union of the Divine Bridegroom and the human soul.

Song 1:11 ("While the King was at his reclining, my nard gave forth its odor") points to the soul's passage from initial conversion to a higher stage of self-knowledge and contemplation through the action of illuminating grace, that is, the recognition that the King is to be found within the soul and not outside it (see *Cant* 74–76). Early in his commentary, William had distinguished *accubitus*, that is, "lying near, or reclining," from *concubitus*, or "lying beside or with," as the more fitting because less sensual description of that form of *conjunctio*, or "joining," that constitutes the union of Christ and the soul, something he described as ". . . the mystical drawing together (*contractus*) of divine and human conjunction."[110] He speaks of two forms of natural *accubitus*, either to share carnal pleasure or to eat, both of which have their analogues on the spiritual level in the memory-intellect-will, or in the "heart that desires God" (*Cant* 75). But the Song of Songs does not present a picture of the Bride in constant possession of the Divine Lover; rather, it portrays a drama of pursuit, pleasure of contact, and subsequent loss, thus confirming the mystical soul's experience of the unending oscillation between pursuing and enjoying God, between absence and presence. Since our loving enjoyment of God here below can never be final, we are always caught between anxious desire and temporary fruition. But the *vehemens voluntas* for the absent Groom is itself a form of presence—the dynamic root for the mutuality of love and knowledge in both the search and the enjoyment:

> Good will is already the beginning of love. A powerful will is either desire for what is as it were absent, or love drawn to what is present when that which is loved is present in the lover's intellect. For the love of God is the very understanding of him. He is not understood unless he is loved and is not found unless understood. He is understood to the extent that he is loved and vice versa.[111]

William, like Bernard and later Pascal, knew that we would not be seeking God unless we had already in some way found him.

The initial *accubitus* of the Divine Lover with the Bride is understood as taking place when he cleanses her free choice by his prevenient grace. Because she does not yet have any experience of spiritual delight, she does not know that this is a real *accubitus*. This is why it is described as the "King's reclining," not a mutual reclining (see *Cant* 76). The remainder of the seventh stanza describes the Bride's activity in this condition, one that we may call the longing cycle of the life of love. First, her "nard gives forth its odor" (Song 1:11b), which signifies the action of humility in the soul, already a sign of God's presence. William interprets verses 12 and 13 in a twofold sense: first, to indicate the effects of the work of grace as it gradually draws the Bride into the experience of love; and second, to describe the role of the Incarnate Word and the Holy Spirit in this process. Once again, there is a mutuality of love and understanding. The *spiritualis intellectus* that ". . . melts (*resolvitur*) delightfully not knowingly into some sweet experiences of love" acts differently from the *intellectus humanus* in that it proceeds at its own initiative not ours, laying hold of us as it wills by the action of the Holy Spirit. That is, the soul remains passive (see *Cant* 79–80). The "little bundle of myrrh" (*fasciculus myrrhae*) that the Bride places between her breasts during this time of purification is the memory of Christ's saving acts, especially his Passion.[112] It is because the Son of God came down from heaven, making "from himself something similar to us in us that we can hold on to" (that is, the bundle of myrrh of his Passion), that we can be healed and lifted up.[113] The uplifting process is described in verse 13, where the Bridegroom is pictured no longer as a little bundle of myrrh, but as a "grape cluster of Cyprus in the vines of Engaddi," which William understands as a reference to the joys of Christ's Resurrection. The notice of Engaddi, famous for its balsam,[114] points to the action of the Holy Spirit drawing the memory, illuminating the intellect and inflaming the heart through the soul's meditation on the Passion and Resurrection of the Divine Lover (*Cant* 84–87). Though the details of William's spiritual reading of the text may strike us as strained in places, the rich imagery of the Song provides him with a splendid instrument for presenting the role of Christ and the Holy Spirit in the soul's search for the delights of union.

The search is crowned by the reward described in the eighth stanza, the section of the *Exposition* commenting on Song 1:14–16. This is the basis for one of William's most sustained treatments of mystical union. These verses begin with the Bridegroom's praise of the soul, who has now been purified through her long search: "Behold, you are beautiful, my beloved, and you are graceful." The Groom then praises "our little flowery bed" where the second form of reclining, the mutual *accubitus,* takes place.[115]

William begins his exposition of these verses by sketching the anthropological foundation of the journey to union. The human person's essence as image and likeness of God consists in the Augustinian interior trinity of *memoria-intelligentia-amor* understood as powers capable of being gradually directed to the God who alone is the soul's perfect fruition. Through these three powers the soul can attain the goal of full *rationalitas* in which the *ratio superior* dominates all activities. She is then truly a Bride: "For the Bride, the memory of the Bridegroom is seeking him in simplicity of heart; understanding is thinking of him in goodness; love is being drawn to him, enjoying him, existing in the way that he does."[116] When the Groom finds the Soul-Bride in this condition, with what has been discolored by sin in her repainted through the action of illuminating grace, he greets her as his "beautiful one." The "eyes that are like doves" (Song 1:14) signify reason and love, the two eyes of contemplation which work together when enlightened by grace. Indeed, these two eyes become one "... when in the contemplation of God, in which love is chiefly operative, reason passes over into love and is formed into a kind of spiritual or divine understanding which surpasses and absorbs all reason."[117] This is a lapidary expression of one of the major motifs of William's thought, the transformative understanding of the reason/ love relationship. The abbot of St. Thierry shares this with Bernard and the main tradition of Latin Christian mysticism, but his explanation is more carefully thought out, as we shall consider in detail.

The matching beauty of the Bride and the Groom enable them to hold sweet conversation in which "they begin to taste the joy of mutual joining" (*conjunctio*).[118] This converse, which is what leads the soul to the measure of perfection that will be granted to it in this life, is one in which the Groom speaks by means of operative grace and the Bride's response is the devout affection or joy that she feels in her good conscience. God truly "speaks," that is, acts, in all souls, no matter how perverse; but he speaks especially in the Bride when she is one spirit with him (1 Cor 6:17). The law that governs this process, as we have noted above, is that of the equivalence of *similitudo* and *fruitio*: the more we become like God, the more we come to enjoy him and the more he takes joy in our good.[119] "When a person is made to the likeness of the Maker, he or she becomes a 'God-affected' person, that is, becomes one spirit with God, beautiful in Beauty, good in the Good. Such a one in her own way, according to the power of faith, the light of understanding and the measure of love, exists in God through grace as what God is by nature."[120]

William proceeds with a detailed analysis of what this oneness of spirit means. First, it is a sensible or perceptible experience, at least in a transferred sense. "At times, when grace overflows to secure and manifest experience of something of God in a novel way something sensible (*sensibile*) is suddenly present to the sensation of enlightened love, something that no corporeal sense could hope for, no reason conceive, no intellect be fit for save the intellect of enlightened love."[121] William goes on to liken this strange *sensibile* to the phantasm present in every power of sensation "through which the one sensing is transformed into that which is sensed. In this way, and much more, the vision of God is at work in the *sensus amoris* by which God is seen."[122] The Cistercian's use of the model of sense perception here (which, as we have suggested, is only a distant analogy) is meant to emphasize the reality, even the concreteness, of the knowledge of God given in mystical experience.

The second point that William underscores in this section of the *Exposition* is the mutuality of the experience by which God and human are joined on *"our* little flowery bed," that is, within the human conscience. "In it takes place that wonderful joining *(conjunctio),* that mutual enjoyment of sweetness and incomprehensible joy—unthinkable even to those in which it takes place—the *conjunctio* of human to God, of created to Uncreated Spirit."[123] Finally, he draws out the trinitarian and Spirit-centered aspects of the *conjunctio.* What is realized in the soul (the *imago trinitatis*) is "the unity of the Father and the Son, their very kiss, the embrace, the love, the goodness and whatever is common to both of them in that supremely simple union. That is entirely the Holy Spirit, God, Charity, both Gift and Giver."[124] Just as human lovers share their breath or spirit in a kiss, "the created spirit pours itself out wholly for this purpose to the Spirit that creates it, and the Creator Spirit pours itself into the created spirit as it wishes and makes the human person one spirit with God."[125]

William continues by noting some of the circumstances surrounding this experience and by repeating or emphasizing points already made. If one must at times leave the delights of the internal "little bed" of conscience for the external obligations of love of neighbor, it is important to leave something of oneself within to keep the place ready for one's return.[126] Like all classical Christian mystics, the abbot insists that the perfect *conjunctio* is realized only in heaven. What takes place here on earth, the rapture that snatches the soul through the action of the Holy Spirit in the *sensus illuminatus amoris* is always brief and intermittent (see *Cant* 99). It is also the work of the entire Trinity, though one especially ascribed to the action of the Holy Spirit. God the Father, the source of all goodness, has not left us orphans. The Good Father is himself the love of those who love him. This love is nothing other than the Holy Spirit. William puts it thus:

> Rather, Love itself is what you are. It is your Holy Spirit, O Father, who proceeds from you and the Son, with whom you and the Son are one. When the human spirit has merited to be drawn to *(affici)* the Spirit, spirit to Spirit, love to Love, human love becomes *(afficitur)* divine in a way. Already in loving God a human person is the worker, but God is working.[127]

The little flowery bed of a conscience adorned with virtues is what the Bride always desires to be so that she may continue to enjoy the divine presence that accompanies, or rather is, her very likeness to God. Above all, she desires that the bed be "ours," not just her "own" on which she waits anxiously and joylessly for her Lover.[128] William closes by reading verse 16 ("The beams of our houses are of cedar and the panels of cypress") as indicating the beauty of the many virtues (i.e., houses) in which the Bride and the Groom live together and her desire to maintain unity of spirit with him.[129]

This extended interpretation of Song 1:11–16 illustrates almost all the major themes of William's understanding of how love gradually absorbs reason and leads us to the unity of spirit in which we *become* the Holy Spirit, the very oneness of the Father and the Son. William's images are the erotic ones of the Song; but his message, as compared with Bernard's reading of the Song, is less concerned with the psychology of love, and more speculative, even metaphysical in nature.[130] Bernard knew that love was a form of understanding; William tries to probe how this is so. Though the abbot of Clairvaux recognized that our union with God is union with the entire Trinity, his mysticism is primarily Christocentric. William dwells more on the action of the entire Trinity, centering his attention on the role of the Holy Spirit. These are differences in emphasis, not in fundamental belief; but they are important differences for all that.

Central Mystical Themes

Having glanced at how William presents the soul's gradual regaining of the *similitudo Dei*, both from the perspective of the faith that leads to love and the love that is transformed into a new type of understanding, we have a basis from which to begin the investigation of the major themes of the abbot's mystical theology. Odo Brooke has spoken of William's "theology of experience."[131] Although the abbot of St. Thierry did not appeal as often or as directly to his readers' experiential verification of his message as did Bernard, the description is a just one. As in the case of any experiential theology, a schematic presentation cannot be totally adequate, especially because it tends to separate themes that are woven together within the presentation of the experience itself. Still, such an account is initially useful in order to highlight the central aspects of the abbot's teaching. The following section will present William's mystical thought under the headings of Christology, the relation of love and intellect, the role of vision and union, and finally the Trinity, especially the action of the Holy Spirit.

Christ and the Economy of Salvation

To say that William's mysticism is Spirit-centered should not be understood as minimizing the essential role of the Incarnate Word. Indeed, a selection of passages could be easily drawn from William's writings which would exactly parallel much of what Bernard has to say about how the God-Man acts in our lives. But when viewed from the total perspective of his thought, William's Christology takes on a rather different hue from that of Bernard and other Cistercians.[132]

Although the historical situation brought about by Adam's sin, in which the Incarnate Word's first task is to heal and to restore our wounded nature, is the context within which our knowledge of the Word and his activity is actually found, it is clear from passages in the *Exposition on Romans* that William believed in the Word's universal predestination to take on flesh as the Head of the Body of all those destined to be united with God.[133] The innertrinitarian life of the Word as the primordial revelation or procession of the hidden Father makes this role proper to him in the eternal divine plan directed to the formation of a universe that would house human subjects formed in the image and likeness of the Trinity.[134] The Word's appearance in the flesh is thus revelatory in essence, that is, it is designed to disclose the divine mystery to humanity, a task essential in any world order, but one far more needed in a world weighed down by sin. A passage that comes at the end of the *Mirror of Faith* puts it well:

> Therefore, just as the Lord himself appearing in the flesh to humans removed the vanity of idols from the world, so too the blazing glory of his divinity took away every vain imagining from faith's thinking as he set forth the Unity in the Trinity and the Trinity in the Unity to those thinking about God. When he taught that the understanding of divinity was above humans, he taught humans to think according to his own way of thinking. All the deeds and words of the Word of God are one word for us – everything we read, hear, speak or meditate about him, either provoking love or striking fear, calls us to one thing, sends us to one thing, that about which much is said and nothing is said. There is is no way of coming to "That Which Is," unless he who is sought runs out to meet us and shines his face upon us, and brightens his face so that in its light we may know which way to proceed.[135]

This revelation of the *docta ignorantia* of the mystery of God is something that love can experience, but human knowledge cannot attain. It is the end or goal of the Word's descent. The starting point is on a more humble level, given the fact of our present sinful condition. Quoting Augustine, William insists on the necessity for a carnal beginning of humanity's path back to God. "Carnal forms into which we have fallen by consent to sin hold us back by their love. We must lean on them to rise up. Therefore, God's Son, 'who was in the form of God, emptied himself taking on the form of slave' (Phil 2:6–7), so that humans, receiving God in a man by believing, may gain the power to be made children of God."[136] The idea of carnal love of Christ as the necessary starting point in the movement toward truly spiritual love, while perhaps not as central to William as to Bernard, is fairly frequent in his writings.[137] Also like Bernard, William emphasizes the fact that the Word's coming in the flesh provides the model for the humility which humanity needs in order to begin the long climb out of the slough of sin.[138]

It is also the pattern for the transformation of love from the vicious circle of *cupiditas*, or contempt of God through love of self, to the eternal spiral that is the love of God even to the contempt of self.[139]

In his early work *The Nature and Dignity of Love*, the abbot of St. Thierry provides a summary of Christ's role as the mediator who brings God's graciousness to humanity and humanity's faith to God.[140] *On Contemplating God*, also early, has several passages that express a passionate devotion to Jesus, the loving Savior.[141] William's devotion to the Savior centers more on the Passion than on any other mystery—another contrast with Bernard. The magnificent *Meditation* 10 is surely one of the masterpieces of medieval passion-centered piety, as yet untouched by the sometimes morbid fascination with Christ's wounds often found in the later Middle Ages. Here William invokes one of his most potent themes, the universal desire for the vision of God—that is, the manifestation of the face of God—as the deepest meaning of the mystery of the cross.[142] Meditating on the *forma passionis*, William hears Christ say, "Since I have loved you, I have loved you to the end." He recognizes that it is through the image of the Passion that our thoughts about God's goodness are transformed into a love for this goodness (*Med* 10.7). He even finds in this *forma passionis* not just a reminder of God's loving face, but the reality of the face itself:

> She [the soul] seems to see you as you are while she ponders your goodness toward us in her sweet thoughts about the wonderful sacrament of your Passion. This goodness is as great as you are—it is what you are. She seems to see you as you are, face to face, when, as the face of supreme Goodness you appear to her on the Cross in the midst of your saving work. The Cross itself becomes for her the face of a mind well-disposed toward God. What better preparation, what sweeter arrangement could there be than that a person who is about to ascend to his God to offer gifts and sacrifices according to the Law's command does so, not by walking up steps to God's altar, but by way of the level path of likeness? Peacefully and with unhindered step let a human proceed to a human who is like himself, one who says to him as he enters the threshhold, "The Father and I are one" (John 10:30). Immediately, he is assumed into God through the loving action of the Holy Spirit, and he receives God coming into him and building his abode with him (John 14:23), not only spiritually but corporally through the mystery of the holy and life-giving Body and Blood of Our Lord Jesus Christ.[143]

This long quotation gives the gist of William's devotion to the Passion. Other passages provide important nuances, such as the text from the eighth *Meditation* which interprets Christ's death on the cross as a kiss of tenderness and the embrace restoring life to the dead soul (*Med* 8.2–3). In the *Exposition on Romans* William identifies Christ's death on the cross with the tree of life planted in the paradise of the church. If we die and are buried with him, we too will arise from the dead, that is, our old selves who formerly served only sin will, through Christ's cross, be free to serve God. He concludes, "Thus, our root is planted together with the root of the tree of life, that is, our love is conformed to Christ's so that from the root of his juice it can produce branches of justice and the fruit of life."[144] William, like Bernard and the other Cistercians, was a strong witness to the Pauline doctrine of our solidarity with Christ, the source of later teaching concerning the church as Christ's Mystical Body.[145] Nevertheless, William did not develop an extensive ecclesiology as a major element in his mystical thought, another important difference of emphasis between him and his friend Bernard.

The abbot of St. Thierry, both in early and later works, does pay attention to the role of the sacraments as the living links between Christ and us. William uses the term *sacramenta* in the ancient sense of all the mysteries that connect us with Christ's saving work: "The Lord's temporal actions become the wonderful sacraments of eternity in the faithful heart," as he puts it in the *Mirror of Faith.*[146] Odo Brooke has shown that there exists in William a dialectical relationship between an external and internal view of the sacraments parallel to the transition from carnal to spiritual love.[147] The abbot summarizes this in the *Mirror* as follows:

> One and the same Spirit does all these things, just as he wills, establishing the sacraments of faith, some as visible and corporeal signs of a sacred reality, as in Baptism and the sacrament of the Lord's body and blood, others only as hidden holy things to be investigated by spiritual understanding led by the Holy Spirit himself.[148]

The external sacraments, especially the Eucharist, play an important role in his writings, a larger one than they do in Bernard's works.[149] About 1127, in response to a treatise of Rupert of Deutz, William wrote an influential doctrinal treatment on the manner of Christ's presence in the Eucharist as his contribution to the ongoing debate initiated by Berengar of Tours in the late eleventh century.[150] He also discussed in several places how, through our eating of Christ's body and blood, we are transformed into what we eat.[151] It is instructive to note, however, that in the *Golden Letter* William emphasized the spiritual eating and drinking of the inner reality, the *res sacramenti*, through meditation, though he did not deny the importance of the physical celebration and reception of the Eucharist. "The reality of the mystery," as he says, "can be enacted and handled and received for salvation at every time and in every place where God rules just as it was given, that is, to the sentiment of due devotion."[152] In the explicit teaching on the *sacramenta* found in the *Mirror of Faith* and elsewhere, he emphasizes that the soul advancing from external faith to the internal loving appropriation of faith needs also to make a movement from the external sacraments to their internal reality through the action of the *sacramentum sacramentorum*,[153] the life we receive from the Holy Spirit. "With grace enlightening reason's understanding," he notes, "the assent of faith becomes the perception of love *(sensus amoris)*. This perception no longer has need of external sacraments to recognize the internal sacrament of God's will. Nonetheless, as long as we live here, our outward being is bound to these sacraments by holy religion, and even our inward being through the outward, lest it lose itself in foreign things."[154]

The final element to be considered in William's theology of the economy of salvation is that of grace, a doctrine which, as a good Augustinian he could scarce have neglected but which he handles with a some independence.[155] The most frequent category of grace found in his writings is that of *gratia illuminans*, and it will be helpful to place this oft-used term within the broad context of his views on the nature of the divine gift by which the *similitudo trinitatis* is restored to us.

A number of texts contrast *gratia creans*, creative grace, with *gratia illuminans*. "This is the state of a good mind, still sterile of the fruits of understanding and wisdom on the basis of creative grace. It awaits these from illuminating grace."[156] Without pursuing all the appearances of *gratia creans* and *gratia illuminans* in detail,[157] it is clear from even a brief sampling of texts that creative grace refers to the divine gift by which the soul is indelibly imprinted with the image of the Trinity (memory, understanding and love), while illuminating grace refers to grace in the proper Augustinian sense, that is, the special divine gift whose purpose is to begin the restoration of the *similitudo trinitatis*, the likeness that is meant to crown the image. William uses a number of other terms to describe varieties of grace. Grace is spoken of as *praeveniens*,[158] as *operans*,[159] as *cooperans*,[160] and even as *occulta*.[161] The terminology is not worked out into a strict division of the kinds of grace, but the general lines are fairly evident. According to Dominic Monti, it is possible to distinguish five, or perhaps better four, modes of grace in the soul's progress toward union.[162] The first is the creative grace by which God makes us in his image; the second the elective grace by which he enables us to assent to faith and achieve good will (e.g., *Spec* 21). The third stage would consist of the dialectical relation between two sides of the same coin: the hidden grace *(gratia occulta)* at work in the Bride as she lies on her bed alone longing for the absent lover (the first *accubitus* in the text from the *Exposition* considered above), and the illuminating grace by which God gradually and even perceptibly reveals himself to the ardent Beloved.[163] This finally leads to the divinizing grace of the *unitas spiritus,* certainly a *gratia,* but one that William prefers to call a *donum,* that is, the Holy Spirit himself. While these divisions may be neater than those found in any particular text, they are helpful for under-standing the basic thrust of William's theology.[164]

Love and Intellect [165]

Our survey of William's theological anthropology and of the dynamics of the soul's return to God has demonstrated the central importance of the teaching summarized in the formula *amor ipse intellectus est.* It is time for a more detailed look at what William says about the nature of love and the kind of "knowing" that it gives to us.

We can begin with a text from the *Mirror of Faith* in which the Cistercian lays out three stages in the progression of love:

> This process [i.e., the transformation of love] takes place more powerfully and more worthily when the Holy Spirit, he who is the substantial Will of the Father and the Son, so draws the human will to himself that
> [1] the soul loving God,
> [2] and perceiving him in the act of loving,
> [3] is transformed suddenly and totally,
> not indeed into the nature of divinity, but still into a certain form of beatitude above what is human but below what is divine, into the joy of illuminating grace and the knowledge of an enlightened conscience.[166]

This account, though not as bold as some others, is helpful in clarifying the three moments in love's path: striving or desiring, feeling or perceiving, and transformation. These moments provide us with the basic structure of William's thought about the nature of love.

"Love is a power of the soul carrying it to its place or goal by a kind of natural weight," we are told at the beginning of the *The Nature and Dignity of Love.*[167] The Augustinian notion of the gravity of love, borne upward to God by *caritas* or down to perdition by *cupiditas,* is usually employed by William in the positive ascending mode, as when he defines *amor* as a *vehemens et bene ordinata voluntas.*[168] Although the will itself is viewed as the versatile power of desire (*appetitus*),[169] one that may be turned to good or to evil, when it is strongly turned toward the good by the power of prevenient grace it should be termed love in the proper sense—that is, *amor, dilectio* or *caritas,* terms that William used interchangeably, following Augustine's ex-ample,[170] but which he also at times distinguished as different aspects of the same basic movement to God.[171]

The relations between the terms *amor* and *affectus* are complicated in detail, but not too difficult to sketch in broad lines. We have already noted the variety in the use of *affectus* (roughly, "feeling," "disposition," "desire," "attraction," etc.) and *afficio* ("to draw," "to influence," "to affect," etc.) in the writings of Bernard of Clairvaux.[172] William's employment of these and related terms is also complex (he uses *affectus* some 250 times). No single word in English could hope to cover the full range of meanings.[173] *Affectus* indicates a basic energy or disposition of an appetitive nature.[174] Thus, the power of the will itself (something we possess on the basis of *gratia creata*) can be described as an *affectus*. From this perspective, William divides the various *affectus* of the soul into the good ones directed to *caritas* and the bad ones directed to worldly loves.[175] But he also tends to use the word in a more restricted sense as applying only to those dispositions, energies or strivings placed in the soul by *gratia illuminans*. "When we love you, we are affected (*afficimur*) by you, to you, into you. . . . " Therefore, "to intend God is to be formed. Whatever is drawn (*afficitur*) to God, is not its own, but his who draws it."[176] The ascent to God, then, consists of a whole series of motions or desires (*affectus*) placed in us by God which all work together, not like separate rungs of a ladder[177] but more like the united cords of a net drawing us up to our goal. Each *affectus*, or "affect," is designed to have an *effectus*, or "effect," that is, a virtuous action that helps restore our consciences to their prelapsarian condition of true *similitudo trinitatis*, though William is aware that *affectus* does not always issue in *effectus* in this life.[178] It is in the cooperative activity by which God draws us and we let ourselves be drawn that the mutual indwelling of Christ and the believer effects the transformation from *anima* to *animus*.[179] On a higher, totally passive level, the Holy Spirit draws us up to the transformation of *animus* into *spiritus* by which we become the Love that he is.[180]

This makes it clear why William, like Bernard, insisted that we can love God only because he has loved us first (*Ipse prior dilexit nos*, 1 John 4:10). As he put it:

This is the justice of the children of men—"Love me because I love you." Rare indeed is the one who can say, "I love you so that you can love me." You, O God, have done this, because, as your love's servant has proclaimed and preached, you have loved us first. That is clearly the way it is: you have loved us first so that we might love you. It is not that you needed our love, but because we can only be what you created us for by loving you.[181]

God does not love us *affectu*, that is, by a change or movement on his part, but *effectu caritatis*, that is, by creating in us the *affectus amoris* through which we are enabled to love him.[182] The gift of this *affectus* marks the beginning of a new form of the divine presence in us.

Like his friend Bernard, William also provides the reader with a number of itineraries of love, sketches of the stages of the transformation of *affectus* into the *intellectus amoris*. One of the most interesting of these is to be found in the twelfth of the *Meditations*, an extended consideration of longing for the love of God. When asked by Christ the question once addressed to Peter, "Do you love me?" (John 21:17), William responded in honesty, "You know that I *want* to love you."[183] This indicated that he did not yet perceive God except rarely and in part; what he did possess and feel was the experience of his longing and desire: "When I sweetly perceive your love by devotion (*affectu*), I seek you by understanding of that love. I love what I perceive, I desire what I seek, and in desiring I faint away."[184] As the fire of this longing becomes enkindled in meditation, William seeks to set love in order so that he may ascend to God. "I set up the ascending steps in my heart. First, a great will (*magna voluntas*) seems necessary; then, an illuminated will (*illuminata voluntas*); and finally, an affected [or loving] will (*affecta voluntas*)."[185] The first stage is the foundation given us through the *imago Dei*; the latter stages are the work of grace in the proper sense. William is conscious of how little he shares in the two higher stages, but the part that he is given to sense or perceive gives him the ability to continue to love.[186] In this *Meditation* he, also like Bernard,[187] reflects on the way in which we are aided in the ascent of love by seeing God in the love of those who love him ardently.[188] *Amor* (in the broad sense of the soul's gravity) is in us by nature; loving God is the work of grace, and being able to feel that love is grace's manifestation.[189] William closes the *Meditation* with a plea to the Divine Lover:

> Your love, God, is always present in your poor servant's soul, but it is hidden like a flame under ashes until the Spirit who breathes where he wills is pleased to manifest it as he wills for a useful purpose. Come, Holy Spirit, come! Come, Sacred Fire! Burn the delights of our reins and our hearts (Ps 25:2). Hide your thoughts as you will in order to make more abundant fuel of the humility of your manifestation's flame. Appear when you will to manifest the glory of a good conscience and the riches it possesses in its abode.[190]

William does not actually use this threefold division as the basic structure of this *Meditation*. Nor does he generally utilize his other three- and fourfold divisions of love as structural elements, the way Bernard did with his fourfold division in the *On Loving God*. The closest he comes is in the early treatise *The Nature and Dignity of Love*, where he analyzes four stages of love at length: *voluntas, amor, caritas* and *sapientia* (a division that also appears in some later works).[191] His last mystical work, the *Golden Letter,* contains both a threefold division based on *voluntas* (slightly different from that found in *Meditation* 12),[192] and a fourfold one of *amor, dilectio, caritas* and *unitas spiritus.* This has the merit of using the crucial term *unitas spiritus,* which appears throughout his works as a description of love's ultimate transformative goal.[193] It is evident that William, like Bernard, was not so much interested in providing a single map of the stages of love's ascent as he was in trying to express different aspects of the mystery of love through the utilization of a number of models.

Many of the essential characteristics that William ascribed to transforming love are similar to those that we have already seen in Bernard of Clairvaux. Above all, William highlights the mutuality and the purity of love. The image of "our little flowery bed" investigated above provides sufficient evidence for the importance of mutuality. "Not only do we delight in God, but God also delights in our good insofar as he takes pleasure in it and deigns to account it pleasing."[194]

Our love for God can have no motive, if it is to be pure, apart from God himself: "Love is nullified or corrupt when it thinks of anything else save loving or when it loves for any other reason but God himself."[195] The reason for this, as we shall see more clearly below, is that all true love is God's love. The Bride of the Song ". . . loves you only through you who are the very life by which she loves you; she loves you to such a degree in herself that she doesn't love herself at all except in you" (an echo of Bernard's fourth degree of love from the *On Loving God*).[196] This is the definition of being a Bride.[197] So passionate a love is this, that William, like other twelfth-century mystics, though more sparingly, is willing to speak about it as a form of insanity.[198]

Love, as we have seen in the passage from the *Mirror of Faith* cited at the beginning of this section, must not only be *amans Deum* but also *amando sentiens* in order to be transformed into beatitude. But how does William describe the way in which the gift of divine love attains the level of feeling or perception. That is, how is love as *affectus* gradually drawn to the *sensus amoris* and the *intellectus amoris*?

We must ask at the outset if the abbot of St. Thierry intends to distinguish between two terms that occur frequently in his works: the *sensus amoris* and the *intellectus amoris.* Some passages might suggest that the *sensus amoris* is a preliminary stage for the higher *intellectus amoris,* which would then be identified with the soul's ultimate transformation. It seems, however, that it is best to think of the two terms as describing one and the same process but as being used to bring out different aspects, depending on the circumstances and context.[199] William's overriding concern is to try to show how love, by the action of the Holy Spirit, is lifted up and transformed into an experimental knowledge of God that conveys a real, if nondiscursive, understanding of the Trinity. When he wishes to stress the *experiential* nature of this knowledge, its directness and connaturality, William generally speaks of it as the *sensus amoris*.[200] When he wants to underline that it is a *real knowing*, he prefers to speak of it as an *intellectus amoris*, that is, the kind of knowing signified in the famous formula *amor ipse intellectus est*.[201] Some examples of both uses follow.

The term *sensus* is another of those semantically exuberant words that abound among twelfth-century mystics. From the perspective of the *power* or faculty, it can be applied both to the soul's ability to know in general (thus encompassing all the major subcategories of knowing, i.e., sense knowing, rational knowing, and suprarational knowing in various forms), as well as to each of the individual powers of sensation, such as vision, or hearing, etc. It can also be used for the *activity* of any of these powers or faculties, as well as for the effect or *product* of the activity as it exists within the power. William, as we have seen above, made use of the analogy of *sensus* (understood as the activity of sensing) in order to suggest how love can be transformed into understanding in mystical union. This was not because he thought that sense perception was the model for all understanding (medieval Neoplatonists were scarcely modern empirical philosophers) but because sensation provided a graphic and immediate way of trying to understand the homologies that bind together the structure of all forms of human knowing and point to their ultimate source—the identity of love and knowledge in the Trinity.[202]

"Love is the perceiving power (*sensus*) of the soul. Through love it perceives whatever it perceives, whether it is delighted or offended."[203] Love in the true sense, as we have seen, is an *affectus* that is properly directed to God. Therefore, what the soul is destined to perceive by means of its special power of perception is nothing other than God himself. This is spelled out in detail in the *Mirror of Faith* in one of the longer passages devoted to explaining the *sensus amoris*. Here the soul, described as thirsting for God, meets Jesus, the divine mediator, and through meditation on his love for us begins to feel (*sentit*) grace at work in her. "She loves and her love is her perception by which she perceives the one she perceives. She is somehow transformed into what she perceives, for she does not perceive him unless she is transformed into him, that is, unless he is in her and she in him."[204] William goes on to distinguish three levels of *sensus* (sensation or perception): the *sensus exterior* concerned with corporeal things; the *sensus interior* of the *intellectus* concerned with "reasonable and divine or spiritual things" (the level of *ratio fidei*); and ". . . its greater or worthier *sensus* and purer *intel-*

lectus, that is love, if it is pure."[205] It is here where we attain God. Again invoking the analogy of sense perception, William says that it is by this activity ". . . that a person is made one spirit with God to whom he is drawn."[206] In the *Exposition on the Song of Songs* the same teaching appears in many places,[207] especially in the text considered above, in which William equates the *sensus amoris* with the vision of God.[208]

It might be thought that William means nothing more by his *sensus amoris* than the traditional doctrine of the spiritual senses of the soul that we have seen in Christian mystics since the time of Origen. There is certainly a connection; but it seems, especially on the evidence of several passages where the Cistercian makes use of more traditional expressions of the role of the spiritual senses,[209] that we are dealing with something that is a development from–what we might even describe as an important deepening of–the traditional doctrine of the spiritual senses.

Transformative love, then, is both a *sensus amoris* by means of which we concretely, almost tactilely, perceive or "feel" God, and also an *intellectus amoris* by which we come to know him in a new way. The phrase *amor ipse intellectus est* occurs only four times in William's writings,[210] but the appearance of the term *intellectus amoris* and its equivalents, especially in the *Exposition on the Song of Songs,* is frequent.[211] In employing the term so often William seems to be interested in underlining at least three points about the nature of the transformation of love that takes places when the soul not only loves God with burning desire but also has begun to sense or perceive him. The first is that love of this kind advances beyond the boundaries of ordinary reason (the level of the *ratio fidei*) in its pursuit of God.[212] William, like almost all Christian mystics, believed that love had a privileged place in attaining God. This is not because reason is evil (though it has been harmed by the fall) but because it is radically insufficient in the face of the divine infinity.[213] Thus, it is necessary for reason to retreat or withdraw at a certain stage in the advance to God. Addressing the Bridegroom, the Bride says: "Then, in your light, it will appear how much the devotion of totally simple loving exceeds the prudence of the most learned reasoning in your understanding. This will happen when reason draws back and devout love itself will become its own understanding."[214] This humility of reason does not mark its death or disappearance; rather, the voluntary withdrawal is what allows reason to be subsumed or lifted up to the higher level of knowing that William usually calls *intellectus.*[215]

The second point that the Cistercian wishes to stress through the term *intellectus amoris* is the mutuality of love and knowledge in this highest stage. Speaking of the soul's love for the Bridegroom, he says: "If she had sought him through desire (*ex affectu*), she would have found him in the understanding (*in intellectu*), and she would be perfectly happy in his embrace (*in amplexu*)."²¹⁶ The image of the embrace of the Divine Lover is one of William's favorite ways of expressing this mutuality of love and knowledge:

> The Bride's head is the heart's core warmed by the Groom's left arm (Song 2:6). This happens when a well-disposed mind enjoys that which it loves through the understanding of its own love. Thus each cooperates with the other for the good. While love strengthens reason so that it can be drawn along, reason does the same for love so that it can be embraced. Love is protected by reason, reason illuminated by love. Yet more, reason "effects" love and love "affects" reason by a prevenient grace that predestines, chooses and calls. . . .²¹⁷

The notion of prevenient grace mentioned in this passage underlines the third point that William wishes to make when he speaks of the *intellectus amoris*, viz., the fact that such a state is a pure gift, a totally operative grace in other words. It is given by the Holy Spirit to whom and when he chooses. Another passage from the *Exposition* says:

> She then begins to know as she has been first known (1 Cor 13:12), and, to the extent of that knowledge, to love as she has been first loved. The prior knowledge of the Groom for the Bride was the gift of Divine Wisdom; the prior love was a free infusion of the Holy Spirit. The knowledge and the love of Bride for Groom is the same thing because in this matter love itself is understanding.²¹⁸

What kind of knowing was William talking about when he spoke of the *intellectus amoris*? There has been considerable debate on this issue over the years. Pierre Rousselot thought that William was claiming a formal or conceptual identification between the act of love and the act of understanding, but such an abstract mode of theological conceptualization is foreign to monastic authors.²¹⁹ M.-M. Davy took William to be using the term as a kind of metaphor, but this flies in the face of William's explicit statements.²²⁰ Since the time of L. Malévez's important article of 1932,²²¹ there has been a growing consensus, though one differently expressed by different authors (e.g., J.-M. Déchanet, O. Brooke, D. Bell),²²² which interprets the *intellectus amoris* as an interpenetration, not an identification, of love and knowledge in a suprarational or supradiscursive mode of knowing perhaps best described as connatural.

Such a position is well supported by a number of texts, especially the discussion in the *Golden Letter* 242–51, where the Cistercian analyzes two modes of knowing God, the way of ordinary knowledge based on reason's activation of the *imago Dei* (i.e., *memoria-intellectus-voluntas*), and the higher mode of knowing that is the *intellectus amoris.* (William does not use the term here, but there can be no doubt that is what he has in mind.)

True thinking with understanding (*cogitatio cum intellectu*)[223] requires the cooperation of three powers (will, memory, intellect) and two activities: the action of the will itself and the intention of the thinking subject (*acies cogitantis*).[224] Ordinary knowing can be directed either to the things of this life (*intellectus ex vi naturalis rationis*) or to the soul, spiritual matters and God (*intellectus ex virtute mentis rationalis*).[225] In both cases the process of thinking follows the same two steps. First, the will compels the memory (understood as the Augustinian ground of consciousness) to bring forth the *materia,* or raw data, by applying intellect to memory so that thought may be formed (*ut inde formetur*). Second, the will compels the intellect to "effect" this formation by bringing the intention of the thinker to bear on it so that actual thought may occur (*ut inde cogitetur*).[226]

The higher form of understanding God that is analyzed in paragraphs 249–51 involves the same three powers of the *imago Dei* (i.e., will, memory, intellect), but it requires four stages rather than two (two totally passive and two cooperative), as well as a new primary agent, no longer the human will but the divine *Voluntas,* the Holy Spirit. In the soul thinking upon and loving God, the *Spiritus vitae* (i.e., the Holy Spirit) gradually becomes more and more present and vivifying until suddenly "memory becomes wisdom" (*memoria efficitur sapientia*); that is, the good things of God are actually and not just potentially present in it. Then memory, under the influence of the same Holy Spirit, brings to intellect what is to be understood and formed in the *affectus* on the basis of these good things of God that it has tasted or experienced. The third stage, according to William, is when *intellectus cogitantis efficitur contemplatio amantis,* that is, when the intellect becomes, or is, or receives loving contemplation in a totally passive way. Finally, it is intellect's turn to cooperate with the Holy Spirit by forming loving contemplation ". . . into certain experiences of spiritual or divine sweetness and using them to affect the thinker's intention." The result is another reception, or passive moment (the third repetition of *efficitur* in the passage)–the intention of the thinking subject becomes the joy of one who delights in God.[227] William concludes by highlighting the differences between this way of knowing God and all other types of *cogitatio.* First of all, there is no compulsion, so it is not really a *cogitatio* in the proper sense (William follows Augustine in deriving *cogitatio* from *cogere,* to compel).[228] Though we can and should prepare our memories, intellects and wills for this higher activation, its achievement is wholly the work of the Holy Spirit. Finally, while we can analyze the various moments in the epistemological process and the roles taken by memory, intellect and will, William insists on the perfect and immediate interpenetration of the three. "When the breath of the Spirit's voice is heard, the elements that constitute thinking immediately and freely come together and cooperate for the good. They make a kind of single form (*symbolum*) for the joy of the thinker, with the will demonstrating pure affection for the joy of the Lord, the memory presenting faithful material, the intellect the sweetness of experience."[229]

William's account of the process of two different forms of human knowing, the ordinary and the mystical, is certainly not without its obscurity and problems. He does, however, highlight crucial aspects of the dynamism of knowing, especially the role of intellectual intention and affective desire. It may be possible to bracket the question of the adequacy of the mechanics of his account of human knowing while still profiting from his basic insight, that is, the insistence that in mystical knowing the same powers are at work (it is *our* knowing), but that they operate in a new fashion because they are activated by the Holy Spirit. Rather than will using intellect to bring something forth from the ground of consciousness (*memoria*) by means of intention, in mystical knowing the Holy Spirit activates the same consciousness to present to intellect a "loving contemplation" (called in other contexts *intellectus amoris* and *sensus amoris*), which intellect then forms into "experiences" that affect, change, or better transform (*afficit*) the subject's basic intentionality. Thus, mystical knowing is always transformative knowing; it alters the usual structure of the process of understanding in order to alter the subject itself. William's analysis of this process is the most detailed and the most subtle of the entire twelfth century.

What William presents in this important passage in the *Golden Letter* treats of the process of mystical knowing and not its content. Other texts address the issue of content more directly, though necessarily in ways that will not satisfy those whose view of human knowing is restricted to what can be expressed in clear and distinct conceptions. If mystical knowing as a process reverses ordinary human knowing, its "content" must also be different from the content of discursive, conceptual knowing and therefore cannot be expressed in the same way. William underlines this fact by equating *amor illuminatus* with the "learned ignorance" (*docta ignorantia*) that Augustine had spoken of.[230] The mystic does not learn more about "what God is" or even "what God has done" than can be expressed through the *ratio fidei*. Rather, he or she comes to a new kind of knowledge or awareness of "who God is," the *experientia divinae suavitatis* that William often spoke of. Modern students of William have described this as a form of connatural knowledge, or interpersonal awareness, based on the likeness or sympathy between two subjects, the transcendental exemplar of what we experience in friendship and in human love.[231] These may not be William's own terms,[232] but they are surely not far from what he intended in his accounts of the union of created and Uncreated Spirit that is realized in the *intellectus amoris*.[233]

We may note in concluding this discussion that the *intellectus amoris* brings to full awareness the new mode of the divine presence that was given, but not experienced, from the time of the first reception of *gratia illuminans*. William expresses this new interpersonal awareness especially through the language and images of the Song of Songs. "The one who is loved is present to the Lover through the understanding or the sensation of love, and then the 'little bed' is both flowery and is ours."[234] Toward the end of the *Exposition* he puts it thus: "The Truth of him who is being addressed in the lover's *affectus* becomes a clear demonstration, within the conscience of the one who addresses, of the supreme presence of him who said 'I am the Truth.'"[235] That is to say, the *intellectus* of the *intellectus amoris* is nothing more nor less than the immediate presence of Truth himself, the Divine Word.

Two final aspects of William's teaching on love need to be considered here. The first concerns the ordering of love, the *ordinatio caritatis* that was so important for virtually all twelfth-century mystics. The second concerns the goal of love, that is, whether or not love ever will reach a place of perfect rest, or whether some form of seeking will remain even in heaven. The ordering of charity plays a less extensive role in William than it does in Bernard, but still an important one. The major texts occur, as might be expected in the *Exposition on the Song of Songs*. William's basis for understanding the ordering of love is the Augustinian distinction between use and enjoyment: "When we love any creature whatsoever not to use it for you, but to enjoy it in itself, love is no longer love, but is cupidity or lust."[236] But the way in which he understands how the soul attains the ability to order all loves properly is rather unusual, stressing the role of an intermediary stage of internal turmoil or disorder as necessary to the process (see especially *Cant* 120–30). As a result of the draughts of the Bridegroom's wine (Song 2:4), the Bride becomes ill and upset, her prudence, temperence and justice (the virtues governing her obligations in this life) so out of joint that she wishes only to die and to be with Christ.[237] But she is not allowed this. The continued action of grace eventually draws her out of her confusion about how to relate the love of God, of self and of neighbor toward an *ordinatio amoris* in which "true love of self and neighbor is nothing else but love of God."[238] We must learn to pour forth the divine love within us on our neighbors and to love the divine love in them in order to achieve this goal. "The person who possesses ordered charity loves the Lord his God, and himself in God, and his neighbor like himself in the same way and to the same degree."[239] This is the reward of the *unitas spiritus*, that *conjunctio* which restores our likeness to God.[240]

Given this understanding of the *ordinatio caritatis*, very similar to that found in Bernard, we should not be surprised that William also has a characteristically western Latin way of expressing the relations between action and contemplation. In *Meditation* 11.13 this is put, again like Bernard (see *Sermon* 50 on the Song), in terms of *affectus* and *actus*. Here he says:

> The whole of love (*affectus*) is owed to God. . . . Love is enough, if there is no obligation, or no possibility to exercise action (*actus*). But when the necessity of charity demands action, the truth of charity owes it, either to God or to the neighbor. If it is not demanded, the truth of charity holds us obliged to be free for itself alone.[241]

The same traditional teaching is expressed throughout the *Exposition on the Song of Songs*.[242]

William, like all Christian mystics, sees the experience of God in this life as a real but still partial foretaste of heavenly bliss, a medium between faith and face-to-face vision. Hence, love on earth is always capable of further growth. Every enjoyment (*fruitio, gaudium*) we experience always leaves room for *desiderium*. But what about the life of the world to come? Will enjoyment there cancel out all desire? In his early *On Contemplating God* William has an interesting passage in which he advances the view that since there are different degrees of spirits in heaven, it must be possible for the lower ones to desire to love God in higher measure without detracting from the perfect joy that has been given to them in accordance with their capacities.[243] But William went even further, coming close to Gregory of Nyssa (and echoing Bernard) in emphasizing how God as Pure Love can satisfy his lovers without surfeiting them (*satietatem faciens sed sine fastidio*). Citing the same text from Philippians 3:12–13 that Gregory and Bernard loved, he expresses a similar epektetic view of heaven:

> He who desires always loves to desire, and he who loves always desires to love. For the person who both desires and loves, O Lord, you make what he desires and loves so abound that worry does not trouble him in his desire nor does his surfeit bother him in his abundance. . . . This affection is perfection. Always to advance in this way is to arrive.[244]

Vision and Union

The path that leads to the *similitudo Dei* regained through the *intellectus amoris* is also a contemplative vision bringing us to ecstatic union with God. These traditional mystical themes—*contemplatio, visio Dei, excessus, unitas spiritus*—all need to be treated in order to understand the full depth of William's mystical theology. We must also consider certain related terms more peculiar to his mysticism, such as *facies Dei* and *unitas similitudinis.*

Contemplatio is one of the most frequent words found in any medieval mystical author. William uses it extensively, especially in his *On Contemplating God* and the *Exposition on the Song of Songs,*[245] but a perusal of these uses shows that for the most part he invokes the word or its derivatives to help explain teaching whose real meat is actually found under some of his more distinctive terms. A good illustration would be in the section in the *Exposition* where he employs the word from time to time in a passage whose main message concerns the transition from rational to spiritual prayer.[246] The treatise that the abbot of St. Thierry devoted to *contemplatio* early in his writing career, despite its title (which may not be original), deals less explicitly with this topic than might be expected, since the first book concerns the soul's itinerary of love to God, and the second the Trinity as the source of the love that brings us to him.[247] William, like Bernard, does not expend much effort in trying to define the nature and various stages of contemplation, as Richard of St. Victor later did. Though the word is frequent in his writings, it serves more as a useful umbrella than as a hermeneutical key.[248]

More central to William's own forms of expression are the terms *visio Dei,* and especially *facies Dei*–the two can hardly be separated.[249] For William, the *facies* or "face" represents the inner personal reality of God and the human person. Many Old Testament texts (e.g., Pss 23:6; 26:8–9; 33:6; 43:4; Gen 32:30; Exod 3:6; 33:20; etc.) speak of seeking the "face," or the presence of the Lord. According to William, "To seek God's face, that is, his knowledge, 'face to face,' as Jacob saw it (Gen 32:30), is what the Apostle says: 'Then I will know as I am known. Now we see through a mirror and in a mystery, but then face-to-face, as it really is'" (1 Cor 13:12; cf. 1 John 3:2).[250] The passage from 2 Cor 3:18 about seeing God's glory with unveiled face (one that Bernard also often cited) was another of William's favorite sources for his reflections on face-to-face vision.[251]

Face-to-face vision is a great eschatological hope, not a real possibility in any full sense for humans in our present condition. William laments, "While the face of your goodness always hovers above me doing good, the face of my misery always gazing on the dull earth is so wrapped up in its blind cloud that it does not know how and is unable to appear before you, save insofar as it cannot be hidden from the face of your Truth that sees through everything no matter how it exists."[252] Nevertheless, the desire for a face-to-face experience of the divine presence, the need ". . . to bring before the face revealing grace the face revealing a good conscience,"[253] highlights the true goal of all human striving. "The appearance (*species*) of the

Highest Good naturally always arouses and draws every rational intellect to love and knowledge of itself."[254]

In his third *Meditation,* William provides an extended investigation of the soul's longing for the vision of God's face and her joy in briefly attaining a glimpse of this in the present life. Using the Old Testament examples of Moses and David, William begins by meditating on the existential paradox involved in our pursuit of the vision of God—we cannot see God and live, as Exodus 33:20 teaches, and yet "I seek your face through you yourself lest you turn it away from me at the end."[255] We would not be seeking God unless we had already found him or, better, unless he had already found us. This is what the *Exposition on the Song of Songs* had referred to as the first *accubitus,* when God works with us for our own good, although we are not with him, in the sense that we do not feel or see his presence (see, e.g., *Med* 3.3–4). But the soul still has flashes of the experience of God through the spiritual senses that heighten her desire for the beatific vision that can only be fully enjoyed in heaven. The soul always desires to flee *to* the face of God and not away from it.

At this point William asks, "Doesn't the soul wish to see you as you are? (1 John 3:2) And what is this 'as you are'? Is it a question about what sort of thing you are or how great you are?" None of these categories fit God. To see God as he is, then, is beyond all our powers, ". . . because to see what you are is to be what you are."[256] Here William invokes one of the key scriptural texts concerning the vision of God and its relation to the life of the Trinity: "'No one sees [knows, Vg.] the Father except the Son, and the Son except the Father' (Matt 11:27). This is what is to be the Father, that is, to see the Son, and to be the Son is to see the Father."[257] But, as William noted, Matthew goes on to say that the Son can decide to reveal this vision consisting in mutual knowledge through his Will (that is, the Holy Spirit). "Does a person see God as the Son sees the Father and the Father the Son? . . . Certainly, but not in every way."[258] As Paul Verdeyen has shown, this text on the mutual knowledge/vision between the Father and Son, as applied to the soul desiring to see God constitutes one of the scriptural foundations for William's trinitarian mysticism.[259] Though the passage had been used by many previous Christian mystics,[260] few if any before William took it at face value—we are invited to enter the mystery of the absolute mutual vision/knowledge of Father and Son by means of that mutuality itself: the Holy Spirit!

The remainder of *Meditation* 3 consists of an attempt to present what this vision of God ". . . as he is, but not in every way" might mean. William invokes the familiar analogy of how every bodily sense must be changed into what it perceives for sensation to take place. The soul's sense is love and

". . . when the soul reaches out through this toward something, it is changed into what it loves by a kind of transformation, not that it becomes the same nature but that it is conformed to the thing loved in its *affectus*."[261] Divine Charity grants us sonship and the experience of seeing God, though always briefly and partially here below.[262] The vision of God cannot be attained by reason or by rational understanding (*rationalis intelligentia*), but only by another form of *intelligentia*, ". . . which is from above and has the fragrance of what is above. It is nothing human but completely divine, and where it infuses itself it brings its own ideas with itself. . . ."[263] Though this new type of understanding provides some experience of the vision of God, it is still not the vision *sicuti est*, and thus seems close to what William later talked about under the category of the *ratio fidei* (see *Med* 3.11). Perhaps in this early work the abbot had not yet carefully distinguished between the *ratio fidei* and the *intellectus amoris*, because the conclusion of the *Meditation* describes an experience that seems closer to the latter than to the former (*Med* 3.12).

Seeing God, then, begins with a vision that is not really a vision but is God's invisible presence working within us by grace and by faith, not yet in an experiential and perceptible way.[264] Gradually, as we have seen in the last section in talking about how William speaks of the divine presence, God's action in our soul begins to become visible as we sense the effects of his grace. The Bride, William says, ". . . sees him coming when she feels him working in herself mercifully."[265] This gradual cleansing of the soul is an opening of the inner eyes by which God's prior seeing of us makes us more and more able to see him. Addressing God, William says:

> And so, you see her first and make her able to see you. Standing before her, you make her able to stand up to you until the mutual drawing together of you who have mercy and she who loves completely destroys the barriers of sin, the wall dividing you, and there is mutual vision, mutual embrace, mutual joy and one spirit.[266]

As this passage proves, for William the development of the ability to see God is one and the same as advancing in the love of God. Seeing is loving, as a host of texts remind us, and therefore everything that we have said about the dynamics of love is also applicable to the progress toward face-to-face vision.[267]

If seeing God is really loving and knowing God on a new level, it is also nothing more nor less than becoming God "though not in every way." Our gradual recapturing of the lost *similitudo trinitatis* in this life is only preparation for the full likeness to be attained in heaven.[268] "To be like God there will be to see God or to know God. He who will see or know will see or

know him to the extent that he will be like him. To see or know God there
is to be like him, and to be like him is to see or know him."[269] Almost all
the key themes in William's doctrine of the vision of God are to be found in
a passage in the *Golden Letter* in which he contrasts the differences between
vision here and vision there, praises the glimpses of heaven God grants us
in this life (". . . like a light enclosed in a person's hands which he can
reveal or hide at will"), and once again emphasizes the identity of vision
and likeness and vision and love.[270]

Perfect contemplation and the fullness of vision are also union with God.
In the Latin West, it was not until the twelfth century that explicit and
detailed treatments of the mode of union the soul can hope to enjoy with
God became a major theme in mystical literature.[271] William, even more
than Bernard, gives precise analyses of the nature of union. Although he
shares with his friend the fundamental theology of mystical union conceived of as an *unitas spiritus,* following 1 Corinthians 6:17 and Ephesians
4:3, he differs from Bernard in the way in which he concentrates on this as
an *unitas similitudinis* and ties it to the *unitas consubstantialis* of the Trinity.[272]

As we have seen in our treatment of the dynamics of the soul's progress
toward God, William uses the terminology of the Song of Songs (especially
accubitus and *conjunctio*) as one important way of describing union. When he
seeks to give a theological explanation for the meaning of these images, he
generally turns to the Pauline *unitas spiritus,* a strategy already worked out
in the *On Contemplating God,* written shortly after 1120. The love by which
God loves us cannot be anything outside himself, but it is his own Love and
Goodness, that is, the Holy Spirit who proceeds from Father and Son and
who "...unites us to God and God to us."[273] Since the Holy Spirit is the consubstantial Love who unites the Father and the Son, when the Spirit comes
into our hearts God loves himself in us: "You love yourself in us and us in
you when we love you through yourself. We are united to you insofar as we
are worthy to love you. We are made sharers in that prayer of your Son, 'I
wish that as you and I are one, so too they may be one in us'" (John 17:21–
22).[274] This union, which William calls a *conjunctio,* or an *adhaesio* (an Augustinian term), and even a *fruitio* and an *unitas,* is nothing other than the very
unity of the Trinity insofar as it is participable by humans–a beatifying
union of love. Referring to another of his central scriptural texts on the
Trinity, Matthew 11:27, the abbot says:

> . . . just as for the Father to know the Son is nothing else than being what the
> Son is and for the Son to know the Father is nothing else but being what the
> Father is . . . , and just as for the Holy Spirit knowing or comprehending the
> Father and the Son is being what they are, so too for us created in your

image . . . to love and to fear God and to obey his commands is nothing else but to be and to be one spirit with him.[275]

The *unitas spiritus* motif as expressing our participation in the Holy Spirit, the unity of the Father and the Son in the Trinity, is present in most of the works that William wrote late in life at Signy. Even the *The Nature of the Body and the Soul,* citing John 17:21 again, speaks of being "one spirit" with God–"one in love, one in beatitude, one in immortality and incorruption, one even in some way in divinity itself."[276] The *Mirror of Faith,* as might be expected, contains a number of references.[277] But it is especially in the *Exposition on the Song of Songs* and the *Golden Letter* that the most detailed considerations are to be found. Though there are no basic additions to the teaching already set forth in the *On Contemplating God,* there are some significant new nuances and some especially profound presentations. In the *Exposition,* several texts are found in the commentary on Song 1:11–16 which we have analyzed above (see pp. 240–45).[278] Other passages emphasize a theme we have also seen in Bernard, that is, that we become one spirit with God by perfect union of our wills to his. William fuses the image of the kiss, the theme of face-to-face vision, and *unitas spiritus* of wills together into a succinct formula: "Therefore, whoever is a Bride desires and loves only this, that she may always be joined to you face-to-face in the kiss of charity, that is, that she may become one spirit with you through the unity of the same will."[279] In the *Golden Letter* William identifies the *unitas spiritus* as the fourth and highest stage of the ascent of love, as we have seen (see *Ep frat* 235, 237 and 274–75). This unity is nothing else but the Holy Spirit: "The blessed conscience finds itself in a certain way in the middle of the Embrace and Kiss [i.e., the Holy Spirit] of the Father and the Son. In an ineffable and unthinkable way the godly person is found worthy to become not God but what God is–a human being becomes from grace what God is by nature."[280] The perfection of the spiritual state of life, the third and highest degree of advance toward God, is nothing else but liberty and unity of spirit, or *unitas mentis* as William calls it toward the *Epistola's* end.[281]

Toward the end of the *Golden Letter,* in the midst of an analysis of three forms of likeness or *similitudo* to God, William identifies the *unitas spiritus* with the highest form. "It makes a person one with God, one spirit not only in the unity of loving the same thing, but with a more express truth of virtue, as has been said, the inability to will anything else."[282] That William should conceive of *unitas spiritus* as the perfect form of our regaining the lost likeness to God should come as no surprise: it demonstrates once again the full coherence between his anthropology centered on *similitudo* and his mystical teaching. The notion appears often in his writings, and even the term *unitas similitudinis* is found.[283] The unity of will between the human person and the Holy Spirit can grow to the point where it becomes the inability to will anything but what the Spirit wills–a stage, like Bernard's fourth degree of love, that will only be fully realized in heaven, but which nonetheless is already begun for the predestined in this life.[284] This likeness, which is the impossibility of unlikeness, effects a divinization of the human person; but William, again like Bernard, is very careful to note the important distinctions that remain between the divine and the human subjects.[285] We become the Holy Spirit insofar as the Spirit unifies the Father and the Son in the Trinity, that is, operationally (though William does not actually use this term). We are not identical with the Holy Spirit in essence, because we only participate in the divine life. We are God by grace not by nature.[286] The distinction between essence and operation in God is, of course, a notional one, because God is what he does. In us, however, it is a real one, no matter how exalted the union to which we are raised. We do not really become the *unitas Dei*; we share in it as a *similitudo unitatis*.

Nevertheless, William's teaching on union goes beyond what Bernard of Clairvaux and many other twelfth-century mystics were willing to affirm, as several passages in the *Golden Letter* make clear. In the section in nn. 262–63 discussed above, William says that union "... makes a person one with God, one spirit" (*cum fit homo unum cum Deo, unus spiritus*). Bernard of Clairvaux, we recall, refused to allow the neuter form of the adjective (*unum*) to qualify our union with God, because it might suggest becoming "one thing."[287] William apparently had no such qualms. William also stresses how the *unitas spiritus* is realized by our share in the *unitas consubstantialis* of the Trinity, a position that Bernard would probably have felt uncomfortable with.[288] Because William emphasized that our union with God takes place on the level of person, that is, in the person of the Holy Spirit who is the bond uniting Father and Son, he was willing to use expressions that were more daring than the Latin tradition had seen thus far. For Bernard of Clairvaux, *unitas spiritus* meant "the unity *of* the Holy Spirit"; for William *unitas spiritus* meant *unitas, id est, spiritus*: the unity that *is* the Holy Spirit.[289]

David Bell has pointed out that William used the term *unitas spiritus* both to describe the state of loving oneness with God and the *affectus* or feeling of love in what we may call its ecstatic moments.[290] The Cistercian does not have a detailed theory of the ecstatic stages of prayer and contemplation, such as Richard of St. Victor possesses, but he does employ a general Augustinian approach to the study of *excessus mentis* or *exstasis* as the highest experience of love given us in this life.[291] Several discussions of this occur in the *Exposition on the Song of Songs*, as might be expected. These lay stress both on the indescribable joy and sweetness of the experience at the same time that they underline the differences between the brief ecstasies experienced in this life and the permanent joys of heaven. A key text puts it thus:

> This embrace is the Holy Spirit. He who is the communion of the Father and the Son, who is charity, who is friendship, who is the embrace, he is everything in the love of the Bride and Groom. There he is majesty of a consubstantial nature; here he is the gift of grace. There he is dignity; here he is condescension—but still absolutely the same Spirit. The embrace is begun here to be made perfect there. "The one abyss calls to the other" (Ps 41:8). This ecstasy dreams of something far different from what it sees—the one secret sighs for the other, the one joy imagines the other, the one sweetness looks forward to the other.[292]

In other places, William notes the rare and brief character of such experiences,[293] just as Bernard had done. He certainly held that these touches of divine sweetness conveyed not only real contact with God, but also a new form of knowledge of him, supraconceptual, connatural and interpersonal. From the perspective of reason's ordinary modes of operation, the soul can be described as being asleep, totally passive to the Spirit's work. But this sleep is really the supreme actuation of love and knowledge.

Can we describe this ecstasy as a form of immediate perception of the presence of God in this life? In order to answer this question it will be necessary to look into the final area of William's mystical theology, his teaching on the role of the Trinity, especially the Holy Spirit, in the mystical life. Though we have already seen many elements of this doctrine, it is necessary to try to summarize his trinitarian teaching in order to complete and to synthesize the picture and thus to conclude our presentation of the abbot of St. Thierry's teaching.

The Role of the Spirit in the Trinity and the Mystical Life

According to Odo Brooke, "the great contribution of William of St. Thierry is to have evolved a theology of the Trinity which is essentially mystical, and a mystical theology which is essentially Trinitarian."[294] This is true, but in need of qualification or explanation. First, we should note that William is by no means the first in the Western tradition to have given the Trinity an important, indeed a constitutive, role in the mystical life,[295] though he may well be thought to have expounded the necessary link between trinitarian theology and mystical theology more fully than his predecessors and contemporaries. Second, Brooke also saw William as the originator of a tradition of trinitarian mysticism that included Eckhart, Suso, Ruusbroec, and others. Though William's writings were known to Ruusbroec and had some impact upon him,[296] they do not appear to have influenced Eckhart in any decisive way. There is not *one* tradition of trinitarian mysticism in Western Christianity, but several that interacted in complex fashion in the later Middle Ages. The title of this chapter tries to express what is distinctive of William's mystical trinitarianism—its concentration on the Holy Spirit's role as the divine unity. William's was a Spirit-centered mysticism.[297]

The speculative aspect of William's trinitarian thought has been well treated by Odo Brooke;[298] our task is to summarize the mystical side of this teaching.[299] One way to begin would be by recalling some of the texts on union with the Trinity in the Holy Spirit that we have seen in the former section (e.g., *On Contemplating God* 11, *Golden Letter* 262–63, and the *Exposition on the Song of Songs* 109), realizing that they are just a sample of the many passages that could be discussed in detail to illustrate this Spirit-centered teaching.[300] But it will be perhaps more helpful in bringing our lengthy consideration of William to a close to investigate one extended passage, *Mirror of Faith* 105–110.

In contrasting the *cognitio fidei* and the *cognitio amoris*, William notes at the beginning of this text how faith knows God by way of an *affectus pietatis*, a created something in the soul that functions much as an image does in ordinary knowing. The *cognitio amoris*, on the other hand, knows God by means of the "mutual knowledge of the Father and the Son, the Unity of both, who is the Holy Spirit."[301] Those to whom this is given have within them the knowledge of Father and Son, as well as their common unity, love, and will—all identical with the Holy Spirit. William goes on to point out, as he often does, the differences between the ways in which this unity is realized in God and in us (*Spec* 107); he then draws out the implications for both our knowledge of God and the likeness to God which we regain. Following his usual contrast between the *ibi* of heaven and the *hic* of our present condition, the perfection of the experience that will be at once a seeing, a knowing and a similitude can only be partially tasted now. Despite this, the Holy Spirit does hover over all good forms of love, warming them and drawing them up to love's perfection as the sun does earthly waters. "He unites a person to himself in order that the spirit of the believer that has been accredited with God may be made one with him."[302]

William makes an important addition here, a point dependent on his discussion of the divine names in the *Enigma of Faith*.[303] The Father and the Son are called spirit, because "God is spirit" (John 3:24), but ". . . the Holy Spirit ought to be properly called this as the one who is not the Spirit of only one of them, but he in whom their community is manifested."[304] The Holy Spirit is not one *with* the Father and the Son as much as he *is their one-*

ness.[305] This understanding of the Holy Spirit as the community of the entire Trinity, a community communicated to humanity in the *unitas spiritus*, is the heart of the abbot's Spirit-centered mysticism. The ascent to God for William might be characterized as proceeding *per Filium, in Spiritu, ad Trinitatem*, in the sense that it begins with our contact with the Incarnate Word and tends toward union with all three persons by means of the unifying action of the Spirit. In a hymn to the Spirit found in the *Exposition*, William says: "You who are your Love in her, make her love you through you (O her Love!), and do you love yourself in her and through her, and make and order everything according to yourself in her and through her."[306]

The role of each of the persons in the Trinity is given a full and rigorous treatment in William's speculative trinitarian theology as found especially in the *Enigma of Faith*. Although the abbot of St. Thierry was not influenced by the Dionysian corpus and appears to have had only a very moderate acquaintance with the actual writings of Eriugena (as distinct from his translations), there are elements of Neoplatonic dialectic in his teaching about God and the divine relation to the world.[307] His insistence on the importance of the subsistent relations as the essential key to correct teaching about the Trinity and his revival of the teaching that the Father is the "source and origin of the whole divinity" further emphasized the role of the persons in our share in the inner life of God.[308] In William, even less than with other mystical authors, it is impossible to separate doctrinal teaching about the Trinity (the expression of a sober *ratio fidei*) from what we can call the mystical appropriation of this belief.

The special emphasis given to the action of the Spirit that characterizes William's mystical teaching by no means signifies that he played down the importance of the Father and the Son, the two who serve as co-principle of the Spirit. This emphasis is both innertrinitarian, in the sense that the Spirit is the one who makes the three persons truly a unity (insofar as we can ever catch a hint of how this might be so), and extratrinitarian, since it is also the Spirit who is sent to bring us where we are destined to be—inside not outside the mysterious inner life of the Three who are One. In his speculative trinitarianism William was most interested in locating the mystery through precise theological formulations that would exclude the errors of Abelard and his followers. In the more mystical works he sought to bring out the aspect of the mystery that is most profitable for the soul in her path back to God—how the Spirit functions as the essence of all uniting.

William's stress on the Father as "the source and origin of divinity," underlines a central mystical concern often noted above: namely, that the Father and Son are constituted by their mutual knowledge-vision and that therefore for us to come to know the Son, or more truly to have the Son as

Veritas present within us, is to be established in the Father, the *principium* of all. However, as we have seen, this shared knowledge, vision, and love, precisely in its shared nature, is the Holy Spirit.

The Son, the second person of the Trinity, the Only-Begotten of the Father, "... is called the Word of the One who speaks so that what can in no way be expressed might in some way be spoken in many ways."[309] Just as each human being has within her or his heart some formless word about every possible truth, and this word is capable of finding expression in a particular act of speech, so too, but in an infinitely more exalted way, the Father's Word was made flesh in order to reveal the *aenigma fidei*, the true mystery of faith, that is, the Trinity.[310]

> For this he came into the world; he accomplished this to make known God the Trinity. Nowhere in this life is divinity better comprehended by the intellect than in that by which it is understood to be more incomprehensible, that is, in preaching the Trinity. Therefore, "the Word was made flesh and dwelt amongst us" (John 1:14), so that, as our Lord Jesus Christ prayed to his Father (John 17:6), he might manifest the Father's name to humans and might pour out God's love in our hearts through the Holy Spirit whom he gave us (Rom 5:5). This is the enigma of faith, terrifying to the wicked since it frightens them and casts them away from God's face, but soothing to the pious, arousing them and moving them to seek his face forever....[311]

The Word made flesh reveals the central mystery so that we can begin to appropriate it by faith, but it is only by the action of the Holy Spirit in our hearts that we are drawn up into the mystery itself. As the *Spiritus vitae,* he vivifies and unifies all things, as we have seen.[312] "He is the anxious guest of the one who seeks well, the devoutness of the one who adores in spirit and in truth (John 4:24), the wisdom of the one who finds, the love of the one who possesses, the joy of the one who enjoys."[313] As the Kiss, Embrace, Love and Oneness of the Father and the Son, the Spirit "... becomes for a human person in relation to God, in an appropriate manner, what by consubstantial unity he is for the Son in relation to the Father and for the Father in relation to the Son."[314]

What does it mean to say that the Holy Spirit is "whatever is common to both" the Father and the Son?[315] Perhaps the best answer to this is to be found in a reflection on how William understands the nature of the Spirit as essentially intersubjective. In his *Enigma of Faith*, the Cistercian rejected the standard Boethian definition of person as "... an individual substance of a rational nature," because the use of the word "substance" seemed to signify the divine essence and therefore might imply only a single person in God.[316] He proposed instead another definition (also drawn from Boethius), defining person as "that concerning which there is sure recognition by reason of its form."³¹⁷ The advantage of this understanding is that each person in the Trinity "presents sure recognition (*agnitio*) of himself, and they also have some ability to answer the question 'What are the three?'"³¹⁸ This *personalis agnitio* is of great importance for grasping William's view of the unity of the Trinity and our participation in it. Thomas Tomasic has suggested that the term *agnitio* should be understood in a radically intersubjective way. As he puts it, "In the case of *agnoscere*, recognition implies the simultaneous grasping of the self as well as the other; in effect, it suggests the notion that one's personal identity is inaccessible to oneself unless it be recognized in the light of another's."³¹⁹ Though William does not specifically provide such an analysis of *agnitio/agnoscere*, this meaning squares with the way he analyzes the constitution of the three persons, particularly with his interpretation of Matthew 11:27 as describing the mutual knowledge of the Father and the Son (i.e., to be the Father is to *know/see* the Son, and vice versa). But, as we have seen, the mutuality of that knowledge, its character *precisely as shared*, is the Holy Spirit. This is what it means to be the Spirit, just as the definition of Bride is to be in love.³²⁰ Therefore, intersubjective union of the human with God must be the Spirit's work—this is what the Spirit is and does.³²¹ Again, it is difficult to surpass the clarity and profundity of how William himself puts it:

> I see that our dwelling in you and yours in us is heaven for us. For you the heaven of heavens is your Eternity by means of which you are what you are in yourself—the Father in the Son and the Son in the Father, and the Unity by which the Father and the Son are one, that is, the Holy Spirit. He comes not as it were from somewhere else to make himself the meeting point, but as existing for this purpose in his shared being (*coessendo*). That same Holy Spirit is the author and ordainer of the unity by which we are one in ourselves and in you. . . . ³²²

The intersubjective nature of the *unitas spiritus* sheds light on some of the puzzling issues connected with William's view of mystical union. First, it helps us see why the *intellectus amoris* must be understood as the interpenetration of love and knowledge and not their formal identification. Since the union of love and knowledge is a participation in the Holy Spirit, then, just as the Spirit unites the Father and the Son perfectly without negating the distinction of persons, so too he joins love and knowledge in us without confusing them (though in a way beyond the grasp of reason's powers). The model throughout is an intersubjective and circumincessive one found in the doctrine of the Trinity.³²³

At the end of the last section of this chapter we asked whether our union on earth was to be described as immmediate or not. This is not a question that William directly addressed, and, at first glance, two kinds of texts from his writings seem to be in conflict. The first are those that assert that the Holy Spirit becomes in us, at least in our relation to God, what he is for the Father and the Son in their relation to each other. These passages seem to imply a union as immediate as that found in the Trinity for mystical union in this life. But a second set of passages claim that the Spirit acts in us by means of the *pius affectus* he places in us, an *affectus* that draws us on and finally unites us with God.[324] It may be helpful here to make a distinction between the Spirit's mode of action and our capacity of reception. There can be no doubt that William held that the Holy Spirit is directly and immediately at work in us: "Our love toward God *is* the Holy Spirit."[325] But since we, as created beings, do not possess the absolute simplicity of God, the Spirit's unifying action in us is always participated, that is, it is received according to our mode of being, which is given both partially, and also with the mediation or involvement of the created intellect and will in this life and even hereafter, even when these interpenetrate in the gift of the *intellectus amoris*. Thus, only the three persons of the Trinity can be said to share in a truly and perfectly *immediate* union. In and through the action of the Holy Spirit, however, we do finally arrive at the *locus Dei*, the place of God (not that God has a place where he is located in any ordinary sense, but that "... this locality is the unity of the Father and the Son, the consubstantiality of the Trinity").[326] The Father is "where" the Son is, the Son "where" the Father is–and that "where" is the Holy Spirit.[327]

Being united with God in the Holy Spirit is a union that can be expressed in many ways, but always with the recognition that we are not describing its true nature, but only hinting at what language can suggest about it. Some of these linguistic formulations stress the absoluteness of the unity to which the Christian soul is called:

> All the acts and words of the Word of God are one word for us. Everything we read, hear, speak and meditate about him–either with love's provocation or fear's reminder–calls us to the One, sends us to the One about which much is said and nothing is said. . . . [328]

Other texts emphasize the Trinity of persons, each with its special inter-subjective reality, as in the prayer with which the abbot of St. Thierry closes his treatise on contemplation:

> You, therefore, God the Father,
>   by whom we live as Creator,
> You, Wisdom of the Father,
>   through whom we have been reformed and love wisely,

You, Holy Spirit,
   loving whom and in whom we live happily,
   and will live in total happiness,
Trinity of one substance,
One God from whom we are, through whom we are, in whom we
   are...,
The Principle to which we are returning,
The Form we are following,
The Grace reconciling us,
We adore and bless.
To you be glory forever. Amen.[329]

Conclusion

Although his influence on the history of Western Christian mysticism
does not rank with that of Gregory the Great or Bernard of Clairvaux,
William of St. Thierry is one of the true giants of the monastic mystical tradition. Profoundly suspicious of the role of unaided reason in the task of
theology as he was, William displays a speculative power of mind un-
matched by any mystic of his time, especially in his analysis of the relation
of love and understanding in the mystical path and in his understanding of
the role of the Holy Spirit as our union with God. Like Bernard and the
other Cistercians, he put love at the center of his consideration, especially
the notion of the ordering of love. His conception of this ordering of love,
however, was not so much concerned with explaining the effects of the ordering process itself, as understanding how such ordering is rooted in our
experience of the Trinity through the Holy Spirit. While his teaching on
love shares much with Bernard, it is far from a carbon copy, as a comparison of the two Cistercians' commentaries on the Song of Songs shows.
William lacks Bernard's passion and the psychological delicacy with which
the abbot of Clairvaux analyzes how the experience of carnal love is gradually transformed into that of spiritual love of God. On the other hand,
William has something that Bernard lacks, or perhaps that Bernard only implies (e.g., in *Sermon* 8), that is, a theoretical analysis of love's union as
grounded in a theology of the Trinity.

Odo Brooke has spoken of William's "mysticism of light rather than
darkness, of illumination rather than the way of unknowing."[330] This evaluation might seem to fly in the face of those passages where the Cistercian
insists on how little reason can know about God, and how even the *ratio
fidei* is nothing more than an exercise in the proper placing of the mystery
of God after all discursive strategies have been exhausted. The motif of

light might also seem to be at odds with William's teaching on the *docta ignorantia* noted above.[331] There is no need to deny that the abbot of St. Thierry's view of the goal of the mystical path is founded on the absolute incomprehensibility of God while still being able to admit that this apophaticism plays a rather different and less central role in his thought than "strong" negation has in the writings of more properly apophatic mystics, like the Pseudo-Dionysius, John the Scot or Meister Eckhart. William begins from the positive experience of our encounter with the Incarnate Word, and, despite the fact that the dialectic of presence and absence of the Bridegroom introduces elements of something like a "dark night" into some of his language about the Bride's search for the Divine Lover, he tends to dwell on the positive aspects of the pursuit, the gradual illumination of the intellect and the increasing fervor of love's flame within the soul. This is why for the abbot of St. Thierry, as for the abbot of Clairvaux, the Song of Songs was the mystical book *par excellence.* In it he found a rich store of positive images for love, possession, vision and enjoyment, the kind of message he summarized in more theoretical language in a text from the *Golden Letter* that may serve as a fitting conclusion to our survey:

> To see the good things of the Lord is to love them, but to love them is to possess them. Let us make every effort to see as much as we are able, so that seeing we may understand, and understanding we may love, and loving we may possess.[332]

CHAPTER 7

The Other Voices
of Cîteaux

A MID THE VARIETY of reform movements of the twelfth century the Cistercians constitute an easily recognizable group, as we have seen. The consciousness of a Cistercian identity, partly due to the structural innovations discussed in the beginning of chapter 5, was further enhanced by the sense of competition among the various *ordines* in an era of change encompassing both society and the church.[1] But the most significant factors in the remarkable success of the reform and in the influence it had in the Christian mystical tradition were those more elusive ones that comprised what has been called the "Cistercian spirit." The great modern Cistercian Thomas Merton once summarized it this way: "The Cistercian spirit is a beautiful combination of ardor, simplicity and strength."[2]

Merton's analysis of how this "ardor, simplicity, and strength" were expressed in the Cistercian authors of the twelfth century emphasized the literary culture, the intellectuality (though never an intellectuality for its own sake), and the insistence on experience that we have seen in Bernard and in William. These concerns were also true in varying degrees for the other voices of Cîteaux. According to Merton, three central theological themes of the thought of the abbot of Clairvaux and the abbot of St. Thierry formed the foundation for the other Cistercian writers—"the nature of the soul and the nature and action and degrees of charity" and, above all, "the God of Love, the God who had revealed himself to mortals in Jesus Christ, the God who deigned to make himself known in the depths of their souls by the 'visits' of mystical grace."[3] Everything that the white monks wrote about, Merton concluded, "can be reduced to these three interests which, for that matter, can be summed up in one great theme: the union of the soul with God."[4]

We can use the three themes of God in Christ, the nature of the soul, and *caritas* as keys to unlock the riches of these other voices of Cîteaux. Because I have already provided a fairly detailed investigation of Bernard and William, we need not survey the full range of the thought of each of the other major Cistercian authors.[5] Excellent surveys exist for many of them, and much of what they have to say does not differ substantially from what we have seen in Bernard. Hence, I intend to focus on the special contributions made by five of the other Cistercian writers of the twelfth century to the areas of Christology, anthropology, and the doctrine of loving union with God. All the Cistercians had something to say on each of these themes–the nature of monastic theology favored synthetic presentations of the total divine mystery rather than the articulated distinctions of nascent scholasticism within which writers might concentrate on some specialized topic. Nevertheless, it is still helpful to highlight the contributions of particular authors to specific themes within the total effort of a group of closely related monastic mystics.

For the area of Christology, I will look at the thought of Guerric of Igny, who had important links with both Bernard and William. Though all Cistercians were concerned with anthropology, and many of them wrote treatises on it, the most original Cistercian contribution to mystical anthropology was that made by Isaac of Stella, an Englishman who had studied in the French schools before entering the white monks. For explorations of the nature of love as the unifying and ordering force of all striving for God, I will consider contributions of two types. The first is the continuing emphasis on the mystical reading of the Song of Songs as *the* textbook of the love affair between God and humans. Many Cistercians were involved in this, but the English continuators of Bernard's *Sermons on the Song of Songs*, Gilbert of Hoyland and John of Ford, stand out. The second important aspect of Cistercian teaching on the love of God and neighbor is to be found in the writings of Bernard's friend and disciple, the English abbot Aelred of Rievaulx, whose concept of spiritual friendship was one of the most important aspects of the Cistercian contribution to twelfth-century mysticism.

The Christological Center: Guerric of Igny

Both Bernard of Clairvaux and William of St. Thierry built their mystical teaching on the foundation of a clear and profound doctrine concerning the role of the God-man in salvation. Though they had little interest in the technical questions of Christology that were beginning to concern the masters of the schools, these monks were original in the ways in which they revitalized patristic christological teaching and even deepened it by their emphasis on the *amor carnalis Christi*, the way by which wayward human *affectus* can be redirected to God by the "carnal" human love fostered in meditation on the mysteries of the Savior's life. Following the fathers of the ancient church, and in dependence on daily participation in the *opus Dei* of the liturgy, that central activity of monastic life, they held that it was only within the lived environment of daily and yearly reenactment of the mystery of Christ within the church's official cycles of prayer that one could encounter Christ in a more than superficial way. Liturgy and the Bible were mutually interdependent channels into the heart of the mystery of Christ.[6]

The treatises and sermons that provide the evidence for our knowledge of Cistercian mysticism can be thought of as windows, although partial ones at best, into a way of life where there was no essential divide between liturgical prayer and the personal appropriation of the meaning of the mystery through biblically grounded *lectio*, *meditatio*, and *contemplatio*. Many of the Cistercian authors of the twelfth century could be mined to show how this christological center formed the spiritual mentality of the first generations of the white monks. Isaac of Stella, for example, was notable for his theology of the Mystical Body of Christ, and Aelred of Rievaulx was unsurpassed for the evocative way in which his meditations on the boy Jesus employed natural human affection in the task of the monk's transformation. Nevertheless, no Cistercian author was more resolutely centered on the mystery of Christ than Guerric of Igny, whose surviving liturgical sermons, deceptively simple and straightforward to cursory reading, yield a remarkably coherent general presentation of Cistercian mysticism when one penetrates more deeply.[7]

Guerric was born in Tournai, probably in the 1080s. He studied in the Cathedral School there and became a *magister*, but he entered Clairvaux about 1125. His monastic formation was directly influenced by Bernard, who praises him in several letters.[8] Bernard thought so highly of Guerric that in 1137 he helped him to be elected as the second abbot of Igny, a house dependent on Clairvaux. Here Guerric ruled as abbot until his death on 19 August 1157, and it was here that he composed the fifty-four liturgical sermons that constitute his surviving works. (On his deathbed he ordered them to be destroyed, but his monks had prudently had other copies made.)[9] Guerric was also probably acquainted with William of St. Thierry, since Signy, where William spent his last days, was dependent on Igny and the abbot would likely have interviewed William during his visitations there. Although Guerric has not attracted as much attention as Bernard or William, or even Aelred, his position as the fourth member in the group sometimes called the "four evangelists of Cîteaux" is well justified. Much of the literature devoted to him has shown how his Christology, his doctrine of the community, and his description of the path of spiritual progress reflect the original Cistercian spirit.[10]

The place of the Cistercian community as a unique home for the combination of contemplative experience of God and the active love of mutual service to the brethren was well recognized by contemporaries in the twelfth century, even contemporary Benedictines. Peter of Celle (d. 1182) expressed this in traditional terms when he proclaimed: "There is true repose in the Cistercian order where Martha is joined to Mary, and where, according to the saying of the wise man, the active person should rest and the resting one act."[11] In contrast to the eremitical ideal expressed by Peter Damian and John of Fécamp in the previous century, the Cistercians, even those who appreciated the role of eremiticism, framed their teaching about the encounter with God in terms of the life of the community. Guerric forms a powerful witness to this characteristically Cistercian motif, notably because of the way in which he incorporated the traditional praise of the desert (*eremus/desertum*) and solitude (*solitudo*) into the life of the contemplative community.[12]

All monks, especially those in the twelfth century, paid homage to the necessity of inner solitude.[13] Some early Cistercians, most notably William of St. Thierry, coupled this homage with enthusiastic remarks about the revival of the "desert" both among the Carthusians and the Cistercians.[14] But Guerric seems to have been the earliest of the Cistercians to give the desert theme a central role in the identity of the Cistercian community.[15] His Fourth Sermon for Advent contains an analysis of how the paradox of desert solitude and community support form the crucial preparation for the monk's experience of the visitation of the Word.[16] Building on the Gospel text, "The voice of one crying in the desert: Prepare the way of the Lord" (Mark 1:3, citing Isa 40:3), Guerric provides an account of how the "desert," that is, any place of solitude, serves as the arena for working out our salvation, a typical theme of the monastic tradition (see *Sermon* 4.1). But he gives the tradition his own twist: "It is surely the work of a marvelous grace of divine providence that in our deserts we have the peace of solitude without any lack of the consolation of caring and holy companionship."[17] Citing the text of Ecclesiastes 4:10, which Bernard had employed as an argument against taking up the eremitical life,[18] Guerric shows how the solitary life is most properly lived in the midst of community. The mutual support found in community life is a prerequisite for perseverance, just as Cistercian insistence on exterior silence fosters the interior quiet necessary for the coming of the Word into the soul, which Guerric describes by appealing to a text in the book of Wisdom: "Now, if your inmost being holds to the silence of midnight, the Almighty Word will secretly flow into you from the Father's throne."[19]

The appeal to community support as the ambience for this interior process is not adventitious, because Guerric spends the rest of the sermon (4.2–5) giving advice about how the practices of the Cistercian life and ascetic discipline in the monastery "prepare the way of the Lord," that is, provide a necessary but not sufficient cause for the coming of the Word. Guerric's frequent teaching about silence and his other appeals to the desert motif confirm how he strove to integrate traditional eremitical themes into the Cistercian view of the contemplative community.[20] It is not necessary to go into the details of the abbot's concrete and sane advice about monastic practices and fraternal charity to understand why he is an ideal representative of the traditional themes of monastic mysticism which flowered among the Cistercians.[21]

Guerric was even less interested than Bernard and William in setting out any single itinerary of spiritual progress. In his Sermon for the Feast of All Saints, he followed a standard Cistercian pattern by appealing to the eight beatitudes as a model for "leading a person step by step from the depths to the heights of evangelical perfection until he can enter the temple to see the God of Gods in Sion."[22] As might be expected, he also speaks of three stages of progress—beginners, advanced, and perfect—in order to provide a general classification for his audience.[23] More revealing is the way in which he understood the dynamism of this familiar threefold path as a progression from faith through understanding to contemplative experience. The most succinct presentation of this aspect of his teaching can be found in his First Sermon for Our Lady's Birthday: "Unless we have believed we will not understand and we will not taste 'that the Lord is sweet.' Faith catches the scent; experience tastes and enjoys."[24] The passage from faith through understanding to what is sometimes described as taste and at other times as vision (a vision not yet fully "face-to-face," but still a real vision), is eminently christological. Making use of Pauline texts favored also by Bernard and William (1 Cor 13:12 and 2 Cor 3:18), Guerric distinguished four stages of experience of the presence of the Lord in an important passage that deserves full quotation:

> ... You will pass on, as the Bridegroom promises the Bride, going from virtue to virtue, "from splendor to splendor, as if led by the Spirit of the Lord" (2 Cor 3:18), progressing [1] from the vision which is through faith to [2] that which is through a mirror and an image, and finally from that which is in the image of the form to [3] that which will be in the very truth of the face, or the face of the truth (1 Cor 13:12). If you are always attentive to the Lord's presence through faith, even when veiled, then at some time you will "behold his glory with face unveiled" (2 Cor 3:18), even though it be through a mirror and an image. But when the days of purgation are finished and what is perfect has

come (1 Cor 13:10), [4] you will stand before the Lord in Jerusalem, dwelling with his countenance and gazing upon him "face to face" (1 Cor 13:12) forever. . . .[25]

In order to understand exactly what Guerric meant by this mysterious vision of the "truth of the face or the face of the truth," a vision that is *of* the unveiled face but still *through* a mirror and image, we need to turn to the center of his thought, what we might call his "formative" Christology.

The abbot of Igny was not a speculative thinker in the manner of William of St. Thierry or Isaac of Stella. But there is a metaphysical weight to his understanding of the word *forma* that demonstrates the doctrinal base of his practical teaching on the way to gain the vision and taste of God. The key text is to be found in his Second Sermon for Our Lady's Birthday. Reflecting on how Mary knew Christ "according to the form of flesh (*forma carnis*) in which she bore him," but not according to the *forma* in which the Father gave him birth" (Guerric is employing Phil 2:6–7 here, a text he cites nine times), the abbot proceeds to lay out what has been called his "outstanding contribution to spiritual theology," his teaching on the three forms of Christ:

> Therefore, between the form of flesh and the form of the Word, like a bridge between the two, there is a certain other form of Christ, spiritual but openly shown in the flesh. It is the form of life he lived in the body for the instruction (*informationem*) of those who were to believe in him. If Christ is formed in us according to the model of the life and action shown in this form, then we will be fit to behold not only the form formed for our sake [i.e., his body], but also the form that formed [i.e., created] us.[26]

These three forms of Christ, which Guerric refers to as the *forma corporalis* (or *forma carnis*), the *forma moralis*, and the *forma intellectualis* (in that the Son proceeds from the Father as Mind, Reason, and Wisdom), penetrate to the heart of Guerric's Christology, demonstrating both his close connection with Bernard's thought on the necessity of the God-man and the role of the *amor carnalis Christi*, as well as his originality as a mystical theologian.

The abbot of Igny's teaching on *forma*, like Bernard's Christology, is deeply Pauline and Augustinian in inspiration. The exegetical pillars for his discussions of how we are formed and reformed through Jesus Christ rest on Philippians 2:6–7 and Galatians 4:19 ("My little children with whom I am again in labor until Christ be formed in you"),[27] though many other texts from throughout the Old and New Testaments are also employed. Augustine's understanding of *forma* as expressing the causality of the Word both in the work of creation and that of re-creation was doubtless a major influence on Guerric.[28] This Augustinian background helps us grasp that the *forma moralis* includes, but is not exhausted by, the good example provided by Christ. Guerric's teaching fuses the ontological and the moral aspects of the work of the Word made flesh into a seamless whole.

Bernard of Clairvaux, as we saw in chapter 5 (pp.166–68), explained the necessity for the Incarnation through his teaching that humanity, trapped in carnality since the Fall, could only regain access to the divine Spirit by the Word taking on flesh. Guerric echoes this doctrine, especially in his Fifth Sermon for Christmas, by noting that although the Word of God could be heard in Old Testament times, this hearing was not efficacious to save us, totally carnal as we were (*qui toti sumus caro*). He had to take on flesh so that he could be seen, and even tasted and touched.[29] The eternal and unlimited *Verbum* emptied himself to become the enfleshed *Verbum abbreviatum* (see Isa 10:23 and Rom 9:28) to effect our salvation.[30] This sense contact with the *forma corporalis* of the Word allows us to begin to reflect upon and incorporate his *forma spiritualis/moralis*, the "bridge" (*medius gradus*) by which we can eventually come to behold the *forma intellectualis* of his divinity. The goal approaches as our mode of activity is gradually transformed into that of Christ, a transformation that is not mere external imitation but an interior re-forming of the self through the action of Christ, "who not only by being born but also by living and dying gave us a form to be the model of our formation."[31]

This simple but profound understanding of the dynamics of redemption is dependent in its main lines on what Guerric learned from his master Bernard, but the abbot of Igny developed it in directions that the abbot of Clairvaux often left implicit in his own writings. Rather than spend time discussing the areas where Guerric echoes Bernard, such as the importance of personal experience,[32] the role of the *amor carnalis Christi*,[33] the transition from *amor carnalis* to *amor spiritualis*,[34] or even speculating about how far his devotion to Christ's Passion may have been due to the influence of William of St. Thierry,[35] we will highlight three themes in which Guerric's Christology was original and possibly also influential on subsequent Western mystical traditions. These themes are (1) his revival of what is now called "Spirit-Christology," (2) his stress on the Christ's role as "Illuminator," and finally (3) his teaching concerning spiritual maternity after the pattern of Mary.

Déodat de Wilde, whose 1935 dissertation marked the beginning of the modern study of Guerric, was the first to note that the abbot's understanding of how the *forma moralis* of Christ opens access to his divine *forma intellectualis* is often described in terms of the action of the Holy Spirit, spoken of as the Spirit of Christ.[36] In a retrieval of basic Pauline and Johannine teachings, Guerric insisted that the Christ active in us through the *forma moralis* is Christ "the life-giving Spirit" (*spiritus vivificans*) of 1 Cor 15:45.[37]

Guerric closely identifies the activity of the Incarnate Word and of the vivi-fying Spirit in our ascent to God, as when he says, "The flesh of Christ is our food for the journey (*viaticum*), the Spirit is the vehicle. The one is the nourishment; the other is the 'chariot and charioteer of Israel' (2 Kgs 2:12)."[38] In an era in which so many careful distinctions were being made about the work of the three persons of the Trinity in the *reformatio* of the soul, Guerric's return to a form of Pauline Spirit-Christology in which it is often difficult to distinguish between the expressions *in Christo* and *in Spir-itu* may appear retrograde. This perspective certainly sets him apart from the profound trinitarian speculation of someone like William of St. Thierry. However, it also speaks to the Cistercian emphasis on the experiential char-acter of all mystical teaching. The Cistercian revival of the authentic apos-tolic life, according to Guerric, meant that the monks, like the apostles, had to be weaned from the experience of Christ in the flesh, the level of the *forma corporalis*, to that of Christ active in the Spirit. The higher transition begins from our participation in Christ's *forma moralis* and eventually allows us access to the fully "spiritual" and divine *forma intellectualis*.[39] In this expe-rience *itself*, as apart from reflection on it, Guerric could not sense any dis-tinction between Christ and the *Spiritus vivificans*.

Second, in keeping with his emphasis on the mysteries connected with Christ's birth,[40] and doubtless also under the influence of Gregory the Great,[41] Guerric emphasized Christ's role as the Illuminator. His Third Ser-mon for the Epiphany on the text "Arise, be enlightened, Jerusalem, for your Light has come" (Isa 60:1) is a powerful evocation of the light motif.[42] Christ's coming has illuminated the Jerusalem that is the church as well as the Jerusalem of the soul, though the more each of us is enlightened the more we realize how much darkness is still in us (*Sermon* 13.1–3). Guerric sketches the stages in the soul's journey of enlightenment toward the goal of beholding the *lumen incircumscriptum* (a typically Gregorian term found in 13.4). "First of all the lamp of faith is lit, by whose light we work in the night of this world" (13.4). This effort allows "justice to shine" in the sight of all even when the understanding is still in darkness (13.5). However, "the merit and experience of justice enkindle the light of knowledge," a *scientia spiritalis* that is distributed in different ways to individuals according to the grace of the "governing Spirit" (13.5–6). Through the exercise of these three–faith, justice, and knowledge–a person can advance to *sapientia* "so that he can be still and see, and while he sees taste how sweet is the Lord" (Ps 33:9) . . . (13.7). Guerric says "I would certainly call such a person mag-nificently and gloriously enlightened, like one who gazes on the Lord's glory with unveiled face (2 Cor. 3:18) and upon whom the Lord's glory often arises" (Isa 60:1).[43] He concludes by reminding his listeners that the light of wisdom is enkindled by fervent prayer (*fervens oratio*), just as that of *scientia* depends on *frequens lectio.*

The final element in Guerric's contribution concerns the birth of the Word of God, which, according to ancient Christian teaching, was not a once and forever event in the past, but was meant to take place in the hearts of the faithful throughout the course of history.[44] Guerric, according to Hugo Rahner, belongs to the Augustinian tradition of divine birth which emphasized the role of Mary in the Nativity as a model for all Christians.[45] Carolyn Bynum also notes that the abbot of Igny was second only to Bernard among the Cistercians for the frequency and complexity of his use of maternal imagery.[46] The theme of spiritual maternity after the model of Mary is especially pronounced in the Third Sermon for Christmas and the First Sermon for the Assumption. In the former homily Guerric begins by noting that prelates can be called mothers because they are charged with maternal care for their flock, but he goes on to insist that his whole audience should think of themselves as mothers "of the child who has been born for you and in you" (*Sermon 8.5: qui natus est vobis et in vobis*). Like mothers, we must undertake the responsibility of nourishing and protecting the infant to whose form we must be conformed. Mary, as the human being most closely conformed to Christ, tasted and enjoyed Jesus to the supreme degree possible in this life (*Sermon 47.1*; see *Sermon 51.4*). Hence, she is also the mother of all those in whom Christ is being formed (*Sermon 47.2*), the model for those, like the apostle Paul, who "give birth to their little ones again and again with care and loving desire until Christ be formed in them."[47] The responsibility of maternity, then, involves both the active love by which we give birth to others in Christ and the contemplative love by which we bear Christ in ourselves.

The Second Sermon for the Annunciation uses the Marian paradigm to study both the "mystical and moral conceiving of the Virgin," that is, the mystery of redemption by which the Word took on the *forma carnis* and the process whereby we attain the vision of the *forma intellectualis* through our appropriation of Christ's *forma moralis.* Few texts in the tradition express this theme as forcefully as Guerric does here:

> The God whom the entire world is not able to enclose you yourself can conceive—in heart, however, not in body. . . . Behold the inexpressible condescension of God together with the power of the incomprehensible mystery. He who created you is being created in you. As though it were not enough to have you as a father, he also wishes that you should become his mother. He says, "Whoever does my Father's will, is my brother and sister and mother" (Matt 12:50). O faithful soul, open wide your breast, stretch out your affection so that your heart won't be constrained. Conceive him whom creation cannot contain.[48]

The formation of Christ in us, according to the abbot of Igny, is a lifelong process leading to the goal of full enjoyment and vision in heaven. Like the other Cistercian authors, Guerric spoke often about the foretastes of the heavenly delight that come to advanced souls while still in this life. His teaching here reflects the common themes we have already investigated in detail in Bernard and William of St. Thierry. What he has to say about contemplation, for instance, adds nothing new.[49] Like Bernard, if in less autobiographical detail, he at times speaks of the way in which the Word comes to visit the soul.[50] He pointed to the special experience of Christ enjoyed by the great figures of the Bible as models for his community.[51] One important text also refers to the "embrace and kiss of fatherly love" (*amplexus ille et osculum paternae pietatis*) with which God draws the repentant sinner "into his very bowels and grafts them into his members, . . . so that by both charity and ineffable power he unites us not only with the body he assumed but also with his own Spirit."[52] In such discussions Guerric sometimes cites 1 Corinthians 6:17, the signature text of the monastic understanding of mystical union,[53] as well as other scriptural texts indicative of union with God here and hereafter (e.g., 1 Cor 15:28). Like the other Cistercians, he also understands the practical effect of these experiences to be the furthering of the work of "setting charity in order," the *ordinatio caritatis* that the Bride seeks from her Divine Lover in Song of Songs 2:4.[54]

Not all these texts need be thought of as explicitly "mystical" according to later categorizations in order to vindicate for Guerric the title of mystical theologian—someone whose teachings about the nature of the monastic life aimed to encourage the highest and most immediate contact with the presence of the Word. Although Guerric claims not to have had this experience himself (see *Sermon* 2.4), his accounts show that he knew members of his community had enjoyed brief direct experience of the Divine Lover. In one place, he even claims in optimistic fashion that his whole audience has enjoyed the taste of the "delicious fruits and blessed joys" of the kingdom of God.[55] Guerric's simple and sober, yet profound teaching about union with Christ is a crucial witness to the importance of Cîteaux to the history of Western Christian mysticism.

Anthropology and Mysticism: Isaac of Stella

Étienne Gilson was among the first to note the central role that anthropology played among the Cistercians, beginning with Bernard.[56] In order to attain the goal of all human striving, the Cistercians held, one needed to understand the fundamental truths about humanity: its creation as the image and likeness of God and its destiny to achieve union with the Creator.

Humanity cannot be properly known, however, if considered only in the abstract apart from its existence in time. Human history, as revealed in scripture, confirms the truth that each person can attain by introspection— we have lost our way through sin. Humanity's nature as *imago Dei* has been darkened; its *similitudo Dei* lost. How are humans to be reformed so that they may fulfill their destiny? The answer to this implies philosophical and theological questions, but inevitably goes beyond them into that area of reflection we call mystical discourse.

Cistercian theological anthropology is, therefore, inseparably bound up with Cistercian mysticism, and, because coming to know the nature of the human as *imago Dei* allows us the best channel for grasping whatever can be understood about the divine nature itself, anthropology is often linked with profound speculation about God. The common heritage of Christian thought on these issues, especially as focused in the fusion of sound doctrine and superb mystical discourse found in Bernard of Clairvaux, continued to give anthropology a central role among Cistercian thinkers.[57] For the white monks, the understanding of the human person as reflected in the *De anima* treatises was the necessary foundation for any adequate theory of mysticism.

This did not mean that all Cistercians felt called upon to pursue anthropological questions in explicit fashion. But there is a considerable twelfth-century Cistercian literature on the subject that falls into two broad groups. The first comprises the more speculative treatises that seek to classify the powers and operations of the soul (and often the body) in order to understand the basis for the ascent to God.[58] As I have noted elsewhere, the central concerns of these works are three: "the soul as mystery in itself, the soul as cosmic mystery, and the soul as divine mystery."[59] In investigating the third mystery the Cistercians followed in the wake of Bernard for whom this aspect of anthropology was always central; but with regard to the soul's mysterious constitution, its relation to the body, as well as its function as a microcosm of the universe, the more speculative writers, especially William and Isaac, took up issues that Bernard did not pursue. A second group of Cistercian treatises is represented by the popular genre of short works "On Conscience" (*De conscientia*), investigations of the moral and pastoral aspects of the introspection needed for the work of *reformatio*.[60] These are of less direct relevance for the study of Cistercian mysticism.

Not all the speculative treatises are of equal worth. Aelred's *The Soul*, for instance, left unfinished at his death, is not among his more original works.[61] In the case of William of St. Thierry we find an original anthropology whose study casts light on the abbot's trinitarian mysticism. The only Cistercian author who rivals William for the contributions he made to the anthropological foundations of Cistercian mysticism is Isaac of Stella. This English monk, living in France, also created a profound doctrine of God, one more apophatic in character than that customary among the white monks. He combined these deeply speculative interests with original reflections on the goal of the Cistercian life: the direct contact with God that takes place when the soul "ascends into the fiery brightness of the intelligence, as on Mount Tabor, . . . and beholds Jesus thus transfigured and thus glorified. . . ."[62]

Isaac was born in England probably about 1100.[63] Like many students of the day, he crossed over to France to study at the Cathedral schools in which the new scholastic theology was coming of age. It is difficult to know where he studied, but his thought shows definite connections with the Victorine tradition (not surprising given the close affinity between the Victorines and Cistercians) and (what is surprising) the "Chartrian" tradition represented by thinkers like Thierry of Chartres and William of Conches.[64] Like Guerric and others, he heeded the message that Bernard had preached to the Paris theology students in his sermons on conversion. About 1140 he abandoned the schools and entered the Cistercian order, probably at Pontigny. In 1147 Isaac was elected abbot of the small monastery of Stella outside Poitiers. At some time in his later career, most likely in 1167, he was exiled to a remote monastery on the Atlantic island of Ré, probably because of his support for the embattled Archbishop Thomas Becket. Some of his sermons reflect this brief exile "to this remote island shut in by the ocean," where, "naked and shipwrecked we few are able to embrace the naked cross of the naked Christ."[65] He returned to Stella, where we know he lived on into the 1170s because in one of his sermons he refers to once meeting with "a man who had something beyond the human," namely, "*Saint* Bernard." (The abbot of Clairvaux was canonized in 1174.)[66]

Isaac's most popular work was an allegorical commentary on the canon of the Mass. His fifty-five surviving sermons (and three sermon fragments),[67] as well as his *Letter on the Soul,* constitute his real theological contribution. Although the manuscript witness is restricted, the *Letter* exercised a significant role in later mystical speculation due to the incorporation of large sections of Isaac's work in the anthropological compendium known as the *The Spirit and the Soul,* which enjoyed the advantage of circulating under the name of Augustine and was widely used in the thirteenth century.[68]

The abbot of Stella's interest in anthropology is evident not only in his *Letter,* but also throughout his sermons.[69] The inherent tensions in the historically inescapable patristic wedding of Hellenic and Hebraic conceptions of humanity (problems easily criticized by some modern interpreters) were an important factor in the explosion of interest in theological anthropology in the twelfth century. In their efforts to revitalize traditional monasticism, the Cistercians realized that they needed to rethink the mass of inherited materials about the soul, its powers, its relation to the body, and its spiritual destiny, in order to ground their conviction that the best way to attain the goal of human life, that is, union with God, was to be found within the Cistercian monastery. Isaac of Stella's thought represents the most systematic attempt at this rethinking.[70]

"There are then three realities–the body, the soul, and God; but I profess that I do not know their essence, and that I understand less what the body is than what the soul is, and less what the soul is than what God is."[71] This surprising statement at the beginning of Isaac's *Letter* is deliberately paradoxical, especially in an author who insisted on the absolute unknowability of God. Nevertheless, it emphasizes the special character of Cistercian speculative anthropology. God is eminently knowable in himself (though not to us). Therefore, the essential reality of any nature is objectively accessible to the degree that it approaches the divine nature and to the extent that God reveals its true character to us in scripture.[72] The other noteworthy aspect of this statement is the way in which it unites knowledge of the body (and therefore of the whole material world) to that of the soul and of God. Although Isaac and his contemporaries were heirs to a long tradition of Platonizing anthropological speculation which had difficulties with the theoretical explanation of how both body and soul were integral to human nature, their understanding of creation and their faith in the resurrection of the body never allowed them to conceive of the body as merely accidental to human identity. Their sense of the damage wrought by original sin, however, encouraged them to use scriptural formulas about the body "weighing down the soul" (see Wis 9:15) and Platonizing ones about the body as the soul's prison. The fascination that William of St. Thierry took in medical and physiological material (often of a very new kind, dependent on the latest translations of Judeo-Arabic medical materials) is echoed in Isaac of Stella, both in his *Letter* and in the sermons.[73] Their attempts to understand the proper analogies between God, soul, and body reveal what the speculative Cistercian mystics were really about–the effort to anchor their mystical anthropology in both theology (i.e., doctrine of God) and cosmology (the nature of the material universe).

Isaac's desire to penetrate to the core of the issue is nowhere more evident than in his avoidance of discussion of definitions of the soul (of which there were many in his time) to concentrate on what is essential: how the human subject, understood as a spiritual reality, relates to God and the world. As a key text from *Sermon* 2 puts it:

> If you wish to know yourself, to possess yourself, do not seek yourself without, but go within.[74] You are one thing, what is yours is another, what surrounds you yet another. What surrounds you is the world; what is yours is the body; within, you are made to the image and likeness of God. . . . On the outside you are an animal in the image of the world, so that a human being is called a microcosm (*minor mundus*); within, you are a human according to the image of God, so that you are able to be deified.[75]

The centrality of the *imago Dei* theme in Cistercian writers scarcely needs repeating; what is new in Isaac is the emphasis on the other component of the human person, the body, as the *imago mundi*.

The abbot of Stella's teaching about how the interior person, that is, the soul, "images" the ultimate divine *Imago*, that is, the Word, differs from Bernard's position by returning to the mainline patristic tradition, well known from Augustine, that the image is primarily to be found in humanity's intellectual nature.[76] This intellectual image comprises both the power to know and the power to love. As he puts it in another sermon:

> This is why humanity was made to the image and likeness of God, and through these remade and reformed to the same [image and likeness]: through the power of knowledge (*sensus*) to the image; through life to the likeness. . . . Knowing the true God is eternal life, but loving with the whole heart is the true way. Charity is the way, truth is the life; charity the likeness, truth the image. . . .[77]

Isaac's teaching here reflects the common tradition of the Cistercian authors. The fundamental structure of the interior person is found in the two essential powers, identical with the soul itself, of knowing and of loving (sometimes called *sensus/affectus*, at other times *ratio/affectus*). These are the two feet by which each person, under the guiding power of grace, strides forward to encounter God.[78]

What distinguishes Isaac from the other Cistercian writers on anthropology is the systematic way in which he pursued the investigation of the powers of the soul (*vires sive potentiales partes*), as well as its functions, that is, the virtues or accidental attributes by which the soul comes to God. With customary economy he says, "The powers are able to receive the gifts [i.e., graces] which by habit become virtues."[79] Isaac's standard way of presenting the fundamental powers of the soul is through the triple pattern originating in Plato (see *Timaeus* 69D and *Republic* 439–41 and 504): rationality (*rationabilitas*), corresponding to *sensus/ratio*; and positive appetitiveness (*concupiscibilitas*) and negative appetitiveness (*irascibilitas*), both corresponding to *affectus*.

These powers are natural attributes (*naturalia*) that are identical with the soul's essence. Isaac and many who followed him insisted on this "Augustinian" position about the identity of the soul and its powers in order to safeguard the analogy between the soul and the absolutely simple divine nature. The abbot's brief analysis of *affectus* in *Letter* 5–6 provides a standard account of how the power of desire or attraction comprises four basic forms. The positive appetite (*concupiscibilitas*) either delights in a present good (*gaudium*) or hopes for a future one (*spes*), while the negative appetite (*irascibilitas*) either has sorrow (*dolor*) over a present evil or fear (*timor*) about a coming one. These four forms of *affectus* are the roots of the four cardinal virtues which Isaac, again following Augustine, sees as specifications of the supreme virtue of Christian *caritas*.[80]

In his *Letter on the Soul* and his sermons, Isaac, again unlike other Cistercian authors, was more interested in exploring how the power of *rationabilitas* takes part in the return to God than in analyzing the nature of *affectus* and *caritas*. His main concern was to show how the human capacity for knowing demonstrates both our distance from the divine nature and also our access to it. The first aspect of this paradoxical character of knowing is briefly explored in *Letter* 7 by an investigation of what we can call the temporal pattern of rationality—forethought (*ingenium*), insight (*ratio*), and memory (*memoria*) (see also *Sermon* 23.10–11). God knows all things as eternally and immovably present in his Logos, while human knowing is always imperfect because it takes place in a temporal process of this nature.

However, the abbot was more interested in what we can call the anagogic pattern of rationality, a fivefold distinction of levels by which we ascend from sense knowledge to the vision of God.[81] This schema was to have a significant influence on later mystical epistemology, especially on Bonaventure's treatise *The Mind's Journey into God*.[82] The fivefold pattern not only expresses how the soul attains true knowledge of God, but also reveals its character as the microcosm. In introducing his lengthy discussion, Isaac summarizes the cosmic and anagogic dimensions of the soul thus:

> Just as in the visible world there are as it were mounting steps: earth, water, air, ether, or firmament, and the highest heaven itself which is called the "empyrean," so too there are five stages to wisdom for the soul as it makes its pilgrimage in the world of its body: sense knowledge, imagination, reason, discernment, and understanding. For rationality is led to wisdom by five steps, just as the power of desire is led to charity by four. Through these nine stages the soul which lives in the spirit journeys into itself by the powers of knowledge and desire as if on internal feet. It advances in the spirit even unto the seraphim and cherubim, that is, to the fullness of wisdom and the consuming fire of charity.[83]

Each of these stages of knowing is specified by the object to which it is directed, its degree of corporeality, and the particular *scientia* it produces.[84] Sense knowledge (*sensus*) is purely corporeal having bodies as its object; it founds the realm of natural science (*Letter* 10). Imagination (*imaginatio*), whose object is phantasms, that is, the likeness of bodies, is also connected to natural science (*Letter* 11-14). Reason (*ratio*), discussed in *Letter* 15-16, "perceives the incorporeal forms of corporeal things" through abstraction and is the foundation for the discipline known as *mathematica*. Discernment (*intellectus*) is a somewhat anomalous power whose object is the incorporeal form of truly incorporeal beings, that is, created spirits like angels. Finally, *intelligentia*, which founds the supreme science of *theologia*, has as its object "the pure and true incorporeal being," God (*Letter* 18).

Isaac insists that the lower powers cannot rise into the higher realms of knowing by themselves, but they are, as it were, subsumed as the soul, under the action of grace, ascends toward knowledge of God. *Imaginatio* is particularly important for Isaac, since it is the "high point of the body" (*corporis supremum*) where union with the "low point of the spirit" (*infimum spiritus*) takes place, the personal union that guarantees the integrity of the human being composed of body and soul.[85] Isaac's analogy for this union is that form of *unitio personalis* that can join the intelligence or mind and the divine nature of which it is an image "without any change in the nature of the mind that has been taken up." Thus, mystical union for Isaac is the highest enactment of the central principle of his Platonic metaphysics, the law of concatenation which makes a harmony of the entire universe by joining together diverse natures at their points of greatest similarity. The abbot of Stella found apt symbols for this in both philosophy and scripture—the cosmological image of the "golden chain" (*aurea catena*) of the poet Homer (*Iliad* 8.18-27, as known through Macrobius and William of Conches), as well as the anagogical symbol of the *scala Jacob*, the ladder Jacob dreamed of in Genesis 28:12, long an important image in monastic literature. "Therefore (in a manner of speaking) by this golden chain of the poet the lowest realities hang down from the highest, or by the upright ladder of the prophet there is an ascent from the lowest to the highest."[86]

In his *Letter on the Soul* the abbot does not provide an analysis of mystical experience itself, either through autobiography or through exegesis of scripture. (He addresses mystical experience more directly in some of his sermons.) The discussion of *intelligentia* in *Letter* 18-23 is meant rather to provide the speculative foundation for understanding mystical contact with God. The soul, because it has been made according to the likeness of total Wisdom, bears the likeness of all things in itself (*Letter* 19). But due to original sin its "eyes" have been injured: the three lower eyes have been clouded; the two upper eyes almost destroyed.[87] The way in which this blinding is overcome is discussed in the final part of the treatise.

Isaac's account of this restoration of sight revolves around the traditional themes of participation, illumination, and the role of Christ and the Holy Spirit in bringing humanity back to the vision of God originally granted to *intelligentia.* All things participate in God as vestiges of the trinitarian essence, form, and gift.[88] The human spirit was originally designed to grasp this truth through its ability to know all things, though this knowledge was always contingent upon divine assistance. "The vessels that creating grace forms so that they exist, assisting grace fills so that they be not empty." Hence, "the light which departs from God illumines the mind, though remaining in God, so that the mind may see first of all that very blazing forth of light without which nothing can be seen, and in that [light the mind] may see other things."[89] Isaac's rather general reprisal of Augustinian illumination theory here leaves many unanswered questions, but his reason for invoking it is sufficiently clear: according to this universal law, illumination is necessary for all knowing, but especially for its highest form. It is necessary for "theophanies to descend from above into the understanding" in order for us to attain the wisdom found in mystical vision.[90] Such theophanies are the work of the whole Trinity,[91] but because they are gifts from God, they can be particularly ascribed to the Holy Spirit, who as the divine *donum* "seems to be closer to the creature in some way" (*Letter* 23). The Spirit is sent, Isaac continues in *Letter* 23, "that he might unite the body to the Head, that is, to Christ, and Christ to God; as it is written: 'Man is the head of woman, Christ of man, and God of Christ' (1 Cor 11:3)." This closing appeal to the doctrine of the Mystical Body of Christ, one of Isaac of Stella's most constant theological themes, shows how he sought to fix the meaning of mystical union within a broad theological program of remarkable consistency and sophistication.[92]

The second major component of Isaac's theological foundation for mysticism is found in the abbot's teaching on the divine nature contained in his Sermons for Sexagesima.[93] Since these sermons are more doctrinal than explicitly mystical, and since I have analyzed them in detail elsewhere,[94] I will not comment at length here; but I agree with Kurt Ruh who defends his treatment of the Sexagesima Sermons in volume 1 of his *Geschichte der abendländische Mystik*, with the observation, "Here theology opens itself up from within to mysticism."[95]

Isaac's doctrine of God has an impact on his mystical theory from two related perspectives: the metaphysics of God as One and its attendant apophaticism. The major Cistercian authors, even William of St. Thierry, were only generically apophatic: that is, they adhered to standard Christian teaching, often expressed in Augustinian terms, on the unknowability of God. The early white monks appear to have been aware of the name and authority of Dionysius, but there is little evidence for extensive influence of the Areopagite on their teaching.[96] Isaac of Stella is the exception. Dionysianism was an important element in his doctrine of God. It combined with aspects of Chartrian theology developed from Boethius, as well as with other twelfth-century theological currents, to form a metaphysics based on the ultimate divine One (*unum/unitas*) and its self-unfolding as the Trinity.[97]

The Sexagesima Sermons begin with an attempt to grasp the procession of the Word, which, Isaac contends, can only be approached through an exposition of the metaphysics that grounds all speech about God and proofs for his existence (*Sermons* 18–19). A consideration of the meaning of *substantia* leads to the recognition that God must be considered to be *supersubstantia*, a term that derives from Boethius rather than Dionysius in this context (*Sermon* 20.6). This form of terminology for God prompts a consideration of the essential attributes of the divine nature, which Isaac identifies as *unum-simplex-immobile*.[98] The abbot's investigation of these attributes leads him to the horizon of the language of prayer expressed in terms of desire for union with the "One-Simple-Immovable" God.[99] But the positive language of such prayer for union needs to be qualified by the limiting horizon of apophatic language, and so the heart of the Sexagesima Sermons is reached in *Sermon* 22, a heavily Dionysian reflection on the limitations of all speech about God. Though Isaac does not develop his apophaticism in the dialectical manner we have seen in John Scottus Eriugena, this sermon contains many of the elements of negative mystical discourse that were to be kindled into flame in the thirteenth century by Meister Eckhart and others. Among these are the "unapproachable light" that "itself produces our darkness" (22.5), the use of eminent terminology formed with the prefix *super* (22.8),[100] the assertion of the priority of negative language,[101] and the recognition that when "we wish to speak about the Ineffable, about whom nothing can be properly said, it is necessary to be silent, or to use altered terms."[102]

Isaac is not content, however, to invoke apophaticism as a merely speculative enterprise. Making use of the image of the seraphim in Isaiah 6:2 (an important mystical symbol throughout the Christian tradition), he invites his audience to a personal appropriation of the divine darkness in a text filled with oxymoronic formulations typical of apophatic mysticism:

> No wonder the seraphim, for all their holiness and towering nature and those wings that indicate the soaring of contemplation, are seen to cover their face and feet. It was to teach us that it was not their own ignorance that kept the beginning and the end from them; it was God's fathomless superwisdom. Just as by seeing nothing we behold invisible darkness, and by hearing nothing we

hearken to inaudible silence, so, by neither seeing nor enduring the Light that is more than superabounding and cannot be borne, we do see the Invisible, not as blind men, but as those conquered by the Light.[103]

This text indicates why the abbot of Stella deserves a place in the line of apophatic mystics of Western Christianity.

The emphasis on divine negation also appears when we turn to the texts in other sermons where Isaac reflects on the nature of the experience of God that is the goal of the monastic life. Here we find that the Abbot of Stella was a forerunner of yet another apophatic theme that was to blossom in the following century. John Scottus Eriugena, in commenting on John 1:23 (*Ego vox clamantis in deserto*, citing Isa 40:3), had daringly interpreted the desert as "the desert of the divine nature, an inexpressible height removed from all things."[104] This, the earliest identification of God as desert that I have found in Christian mystical theory, seems to have remained an anomaly for the next few centuries. Isaac appears not to have known this passage; but the abbot's Dionysian apophaticism, coupled with the power of the desert myth among the Cistercians, seems to have led him to renew the motif. Citing Hosea 2:14 (a text where the prophet speaks of God betrothing himself to Israel in the desert), he invites his monks to seek the inner solitude where God is to be found (*Sermon* 30.4). This form of appeal was not unusual among twelfth-century monks, as we have seen in discussing Guerric. But in *Sermon* 32 Isaac goes further by describing the desert of the Gospel text (Matt 4:1) as "the desert not only of place, but of spirit, or even sometimes of God, where . . . we go into ecstasy by continually meditating on his law."[105] A similar text occurs in *Sermon* 5.15, showing that Isaac is the first known witness to the linking of the divine desert and ecstatic experience.[106]

Among the passages where the abbot of Stella describes the nature of the vision of God possible in this life, two from the Sermons on the Beatitudes preached for the Feast of All Saints stand out.[107] In *Sermon* 4, Isaac comments on the "mystical" beatitude, "Blessed are the pure of heart, for they shall see God" (Matt 5:8). He invokes the Dionysian doctrine of divine darkness (4.5) to introduce a summary of his teaching on the five stages of the ascent of knowledge to God, though this time with more explicit attention to the nature of the mystical vision attained by *intelligentia*. Here, however, he says that it is the "heart" (*cor*), understood as the source of all spiritual dynamism in the subject, both intellectual and volitional,[108] that needs to be purified in the ascent to the vision of the glorified Jesus "as if on Mount Tabor" (4.9). Isaac emphasizes that the three higher powers of knowing—*ratio, intellectus*, and *intelligentia*—fall on their faces, like Peter,

James, and John, when they attempt to gaze upon "the face in which he remains equal to the Father, due to the simple form of incomprehensibility, incorporeality, and invisibility."[109] Although the purpose of purification of the heart is to attain the vision of God, the "spiritual persons (*viri spirituales*) who have trained their knowing faculties through habitual practice" are still incapable of speaking about and can scarcely remember what they have seen, tasted and perceived, "suddenly, as it were in ecstasy, in their prayer and contemplation" (*in oratione et contemplatione sua raptim, quasi in excessu mentis*).[110]

In elucidating this experience by means of an allegorical discussion of the significance of Jacob's bride Rachel (Gen 29:17–30), understood as *visum principium* ("sight of the Principle," as found in Jerome's handbook on Hebrew names), Isaac seems to hint at the nature of his own access to God. In a personal aside, he admits that his own desire has always been to investigate the inner nature of visible objects, not in themselves, but as a means to eventually beholding "their efficient, formal, and final Principle" (*Sermon* 4.13). But in whatever way each monk strives to approach the divine vision, the abbot insists that, like Jacob in the Genesis account, all must work for long years in training the soul's "positive appetite" (*concupiscibilitas*, identified with Leah) in order to be prepared to receive the grace of Rachel, the perfection of knowing which is the *contemplationis otium* (4.15).[111] In the final part of the sermon (4.16–19) Isaac shifts the gender symbolism, discussing the well-known theme of the "formation and ordering of charity" as the training of the desire (i.e., the wife) to conform to her husband or man, who is identified with reason,[112] so that the marriage of the faculties will be totally at peace ("Blessed are the peacemakers," Matt 5:9), and "the 'man' (*vir*) may be wise, and, with face unveiled, may contemplate God as himself God's image."[113]

The appeal to the marriage analogy as an intimate and personalized expression of his metaphysic of concatenation is typical of Isaac's mysticism. This can be seen in an equally rich text found in the following sermon devoted to the exegesis of "Blessed are the peacemakers." The first part of this sermon summarizes the abbot's teaching on the economy of salvation, the way in which God restores us to the peace and freedom of the children of God (*Sermon* 5.1–8).[114] After another reference to the necessity of achieving inner harmony between the "man" and the "woman" within us and the dangers of not attaining this (5.9–12), Isaac turns to the investigation of how the true peacemaker tries to bring "the God of my heart and my portion" (Ps 72:26) "home to [my] ordered attraction so that God himself may sup with me and I with him" (5.13).[115] When we enter into the "solitude of God" (*solitudinem . . . etiam Dei*), the place where he left the ninety-nine sheep (traditionally interpreted as the angels, and therefore signifying heaven or its foretaste here below), we must be careful to guard "the secret marriage" by which love and desire are subject to reason and the rational mind obedient to God's Word (5.15–16). Isaac then expands upon the marital image, citing the *unitas spiritus* text of 1 Corinthians 6:17.[116] But he goes further. The pleasure of carnal union is so powerful that it almost turns spirit into flesh, and so the union with God that he describes as "total pouring out into God" (*totum transfundens in Deum,* 5.17) must be even stronger. Citing the Johannine texts about the union Christ enjoys with his Father and wishes to share with his friends (John 17:11, 22), Isaac, like William of St. Thierry, is even willing to speak of the union we hope to attain not only as that of "one spirit" (*unus*), but also as "one reality" (*unum*) with God: ". . . from enemy to slave, from slave to friend, from friend to heir, from heir to one [spirit], even to one [reality] with the Heritage itself, so that he can no more lose himself than he can the Heritage which is God himself."[117] In speaking of four marriages later on in *Sermon 9*–that is, the marriage between man and wife, between body and soul, between the human spirit and God, and the marriage between Christ and the church that heals and makes possible the other marriages–Isaac has a similar formula:

> The third marriage brings about the greatest possible oneness between incorporeal beings. "The person who adheres to God is made one spirit with him" (1 Cor 6:17). . . . In the third marriage the spirit adhering to God is made one reality (*unum*) with him, what he is himself. Hence the Son addresses the Father on behalf of his brethren, "I wish, Father, that they may be one with us as we are one" (John. 17:21). O One before all things, One above all things, One after all things, One from which all things come, and One for which all things are! It is a strong oneness where two in one flesh are no longer two but one flesh. It is a stronger oneness where two things [i.e., body and soul] in one man are no longer two but one person. The greatest oneness is where the spirit that adheres to God is no longer two but one.[118]

In *Sermon 5* Isaac expatiates on the analogy of human marriage as a form of Dionysian "dissimilar similitude" in relation to the mystical union that unites God and the human person: "Nothing is more unlike it in truth, but nothing compares with it better" (*Nihil enim veritate dissimilius, nihil comparatione similius,* 5.20).[119] Again, he compares the self-abandonment experienced in sexual intercourse with the much greater delight in which the "entire spirit, soberly drunk, powerful in weakness, will be capable of all things in the God . . . to whom it will adhere, he who is everything in all that are his."[120] Isaac concludes this mystical sermon with comments on three of the essential themes of all Cistercian mysticism. The first is the *epektasis* by which "seeing and loving stimulate each other to form an infinite round of blessedness" (5.21). The second is the stress on the union of knowing and loving that is found in the gazing on God that is the goal of the religious life (5.22).[121] Finally, he returns to the main theme of the homily: deification, or "the full peacefulness that grants noble sonship with God" (5.23).

A more complete analysis of this exiled Englishman's teaching on the nature of union with God would demonstrate that although Isaac was less effusive than Bernard and William, and also less effective in analyzing the game of love played out between the Divine Groom and the bashful but insistent human Bride, his speculative acumen as applied both to the mystery of the human person and to our feeble attempts to understand the divine mystery, give him a special place among the other voices of Cîteaux.

Love and Friendship among the Followers of Bernard

The final component of the contribution of other twelfth-century Cistercian writers to the history of Western mysticism concentrates on the less speculative, though not less perspicacious, teaching about our affective relation to God found especially in Bernard's disciples. The fact that the great abbot died before finishing his *Sermons on the Song of Songs* encouraged other white monks to take up their pens, some to begin new commentaries (though these are on the whole less interesting), others to pick up where Bernard left off.[122] Two English abbots, Gilbert of Hoyland (d. 1172) and John of Ford (d. 1214), between them managed to complete a full comment in no fewer than 168 sermons interpreting Song of Songs 3:1 to 8:14 (these sermons comprise over two thousand pages in English translation). John of Ford's predecessor and patron, Baldwin of Ford, who became archbishop of Canterbury, also interpreted key texts from the Song in three of his theological treatises. Despite their debt to Bernard, these English interpreters testify to the ongoing vitality and creativity of Cistercian mysticism in the twelfth century.

Aelred of Rievaulx (ca. 1110–1167) was an original voice whose literary career was initiated and defended by Bernard himself. The abbot of Clairvaux gave his seal of approval to Aelred's central work, the *Mirror of Charity*, by the prefatory letter he provided for it. Aelred's understanding of the relation of love and friendship, as found both in this work and in his treatise *Spiritual Friendship*, bears interesting affinities to Bernard's teaching, though the abbot of Clairvaux might have insisted that a comparison of their respective doctrines would reveal another case of *diversa sed non adversa*, a teaching that had the same goal in mind but used other means to attain it. These two streams of Cistercian understanding of mystical love will be investigated in the remainder of this Chapter.

Commentary on the Song of Songs

The Song of Songs had played a central role in Christian mysticism since the time of Origen, who established the exegetical foundation for the transformation of *erōs* that allowed the Song to be read as both the story of God's love affair with his people in the Old and the New Testaments and the guidebook for the soul's inner encounter with the Divine Lover. The interiorized reading was creatively employed by Ambrose among the Latin Fathers; but, following the lead of Gregory the Great, the salvation-historical or ecclesiological interpretation was dominant among the early medieval monastic commentators, though never to the total exclusion of a personal application. The twelfth century witnessed a remarkable florescence of different readings of the Song, not least that found among the Cistercians.[123]

Thomas Renna, in an important article on the use of the Song among the Cistercians, has emphasized how the white monks "monasticized" the text or, perhaps better, "Cistercianized" it, that is, appropriated the Song as both an apology and "a kind of manual for *their* way of life."[124] No Cistercian ever denied the validity of the ecclesiological reading. True contemplative experience is possible only because the individual Christian belongs to the community of the church who is the Bride of Christ in the most eminent way. Nevertheless, from the 1120s on, when Bernard and William first began to discuss the meaning of the Song in their famous infirmary encounter, the white monks were to insist that the interpretation of the Song was not meant to stop with the doctrinal or "mystical" sense, as they usually called it, but was intended to move on to the level of a personal appropriation aimed at contemplative experience, what they often spoke of as the "moral," that is, tropological sense. Since true contemplation was the final aim of the Cistercian life, it is understandable why the Cistercian commentators, as Renna puts it, "associated Song exegesis explicitly with the monastic life in general, the Cistercian way in particular."[125] However much the Cistercians learned from Origen, from Ambrose, and other interpreters, their reading marked a new stage in the history of Christian transformations of *eros*.

There is, then, a distinctive program to the Cistercian commentators, at least those like Gilbert, Baldwin, and John, who walked in Bernard's footsteps. It would scarcely be fair, however, to compare Bernard's followers with the abbot himself. None of the later Cistercians could match the abbot's unique combination of ecclesiological and personal meaning in a language that conceals the mystery of the encounter with God by clothing it in the richest and most subtle rhetorical tropes. Nor did any later commentator employ the Song to present as theologically powerful and sophisticated a theory of trinitarian mysticism as we found in William of St. Thierry. But if we prescind from invidious comparisons, these later Cistercians can still take a legitimate place among the mystical readers of the Song. Though many of their favorite erotico-mystical symbols—the kiss, the breasts, the "little bed," the fire and melting of love, the wound and sickness of love, sober inebriation, the coming and going of the Bridegroom— were developed on the basis of Bernard's treatment of these images from the Song, their own, often more extensive, investigations of particular images are not without originality. It is in their poetic expatiation on some of these symbols, more than in what they have to say about the key theological themes of twelfth-century mysticism (e.g., the nature of contemplation, of rapture, or of the "oneness of spirit"), that we catch a development beyond the founding figures in directions of both enrichment and, at times, of extravagant mystical eroticism.

Gilbert of Hoyland

Little is known about Gilbert of Hoyland, aside from the fact that he was a monk of Rievaulx and a disciple of Aelred who served as abbot of Swineshead in Lincolnshire between about 1147 and his death in 1172.[126] Seven brief spiritual treatises, some letters, and forty-eight sermons commenting on Song 3:1 through 5:10 constitute his surviving oeuvre.[127] The sermons, composed in the 1160s, were fairly well known, surviving in some fifty manuscripts. Étienne Gilson, while noting that Gilbert "has a strong and well-poised mind, and his writings are still well worth reading," claimed that "Gilbert was not a great mystic, perhaps no mystic at all."[128] That Gilbert and John of Ford are not "great" mystics may be true, but to say that they are not mystics at all is another example of confusing the mystical with the autobiographical and failing to appreciate the rhetorical strategy of commentators on the Song of Songs.[129] Like Bernard and William, these English abbots constantly appealed to the experience of their audience. For example, in *Sermon* 12 Gilbert says: "If you have grasped the Bridegroom, hold him and do not let him go until you bring him home and into your mother's chamber (Song 3:4). Why should I now be persuading you of something to which your own experience of the gift of sweetness invites and attracts you so much more powerfully?"[130] It is difficult to think that the abbots meant to exclude themselves altogether from this Cistercian ideal of a taste of divine *dulcedo*.[131]

Gilbert, like William, had less interest in integrating the ecclesiological and the mystical readings of the Song than Bernard, though if questioned on this difference, he would probably have insisted that he always presupposed what his predecessors had already achieved in this regard.[132] Similarly, the English abbot was not concerned with advanced theological speculation such as one finds in William, in Isaac, and on certain topics in Bernard, too.[133] This should not be taken to mean that Gilbert was theologically naïve. Indeed, his fourth sermon combines Anselmian and Bernardine approaches in its teaching concerning two routes or rounds (*circuitus*, based on Song 3:2) to God: that of recall (*recordatio*) by which we remember what we believe or know by experience; and that of investigation or reason by which we advance from what we hold to more hidden truths (*Sermon* 4.2). Although the former is more characteristic of the Bride, Gilbert, like William of St. Thierry, would not exclude the latter from her purview: "Faith, so to say, holds and possesses correct truth; understanding beholds truth naked and revealed; reason tries to reveal it. Reason mediates between faith and understanding, being ruled by the former and lifting itself up to the latter."[134]

What makes this sermon particularly interesting is how Gilbert proceeds to identify the city through which the Bride makes her circuit first with the entire universe as the theater of God's activity and providence, perhaps hinting at cosmic concerns that his contemporary Isaac of Stella loved to investigate in his form of *intellectus fidei.* In the latter part of the homily, however, the city becomes the spiritual assembly of the saints where love manifests God directly and not under veils and concealments (*Sermon* 4.6–7). This leads into one of Gilbert's most striking passages, where, like Bernard (see chapter 5, pp. 216–17 he emphasizes that the human spirit, "stretched out on the wheel of spinning desire" (*currentis desiderii protractus rotatu*), can only find rest in the infinite God (4.8). All things give us refreshment because they originate from God; all equally produce disgust (*fastidium*), precisely because they are not God. Gilbert concludes with what may well be the most powerful evocation of the traditional Christian teaching of *epektasis* to be found in the twelfth century. In heaven our round (*circuitus*) will not be from refreshment to disgust, either by way of the movement between creatures and God, or by way of the oscillation between experiences of divine presence and those of absence.

> This circuit will have an end there, when we will have been filled with the good things of your house, O Lord. . . . O what a [new] round will be there, hastening from him into him, going out and going in—out by desire, in by delight—while his presence ever satisfies what our experience desires, so that

the mind which holds and beholds is both intent upon him by desire and content with him by satisfaction.[135]

Gilbert concludes this sermon with what seems to be an original observation on the mode of union to be enjoyed in heaven. Using the text from Apocalypse 4:26 that describes the creatures who are stationed around the throne of God as *both* in the center and on the surrounding circle (*in medio et in circuitu sedis Dei*), he interprets the centripetal image as the surcease of all desire in the perfect contemplation of God, and the centrifugal image as the difference in nature between God and humans that makes it impossible for us ever to comprehend the divine in itself. "However many eyes these blessed creatures have, God at the same time illuminates them so that they see as much as they can, and also surpasses them so that they fail to grasp the whole."[136] Gilbert was capable of both exegetical and symbolic originality in conveying the traditional themes of Christian mysticism.

Many passages in Gilbert's sermons on the Song echo standard issues discussed by Bernard and William. Among these we can number discussions of the relation of carnal and spiritual love of the God-man,[137] the generic use of *contemplatio* for a range of prayer experiences from beginning meditation to ecstatic experience,[138] the frequent use of the traditional terminology of *otium* and *sacra ebrietas*,[139] the *unitas spiritus* understanding of union with God,[140] and the stress on the proper integration of action and contemplation. Other standard themes, such as the *osculum* and the *ordo caritatis* occur relatively rarely.[141] It is not in these areas of the common heritage that Gilbert makes his contribution, however, but in introducing some new mystical imagery, especially in aspects of the erotic language of the Song.

Like Guerric and Isaac of Stella among second-generation Cistercians, Gilbert showed greater interest in the desert theme and other negative images than did Bernard. *Sermon* 15 on Song of Songs 3:6 ("Who is she who ascends through the desert like a column of smoke . . . ?") applies the desert not to God but to the soul, who is described as a "good desert" if she has not been "furrowed by the enemy's [i.e., the devil's] plough" (15.3). Mary is cited as the ideal desert, since, open to God both internally and externally, "her flesh was like a wasteland, pathless and unwatered, in which Christ appeared."[142] Comparable forms of negative symbolism appear elsewhere in Gilbert's sermons, although he lacks Isaac of Stella's speculative apophaticism. In *Sermon* 1, for example, on the text "In my little bed night after night I sought him whom my soul loves" (Song 3:1), Gilbert speaks of "the night of your unknowing, or nights of your unknowings" as the unavoidable darkness of our earthly condition in which "my Jesus is more sweetly felt by a pleasing attraction than known directly."[143] Several times he notes the need for nakedness on the part of the lovers in the mystical encounter. On the "little bed of love" the Bride, "when she is completely forgetful of herself and totally stripped of herself, passes over into him, and, as his beloved, she is, as it were, clothed with him."[144] In another sermon the grace of contemplation that comes from meditation on faith is described as an experience in which "naked Truth without the veil of speech suddenly begins to shine out for you."[145] Elsewhere, Gilbert identifies the *abyssus* of Psalm 41:8 ("Abyss calls to abyss in the noise of your cataracts") with the divine love (*affectus*) calling out to our *affectus,* and describes the ineffability of the "measureless ocean of Divine Majesty" as "the abyss of hidden light."[146] Following the lead of Dionysius (consciously or not), he refers to Moses' experience of the divine darkness (Exod 24:15) in which "the amazement, love and wonder of a light shining down from above converts the intellectual soul to itself, snatches it away in itself, hides it within itself . . . so that it is unaware of what is within it and unable to express it on the outside."[147] Taken individually, these references to apophatic motifs, many of which were to be richly developed in the next century, may not amount to much. Viewed as a group, they seem to indicate the beginnings of a shift of some moment.

The special flavor of Gilbert of Hoyland's mystical exegesis of the Song is best illustrated by the way in which he developed three key images from the poem of love—breasts, "melting away" in love, and the wound of love. Breasts (of both the Groom and the Bride) are found in no fewer than twelve verses of the Song. Bernard of Clairvaux, as we have seen, made considerable use of the symbolism of the breasts (see especially his *Sermon* 9) to indicate both Christ's inborn kindness toward us and the milky sweetness that fills the soul during some experiences of prayer. Nevertheless, Bernard most often thought of breasts as active rather than receptive. According to Carolyn Bynum, "Breasts, to Bernard, are a symbol of the pouring out toward others of affectivity or instruction and almost invariably suggest to him a discussion of the duties of prelates or abbots."[148]

Gilbert provides several extensive discussions of breasts.[149] In one place, the abbot shows the relationship among his favorite symbols from the Song when he speaks of wine as the inebriation or forgetting of the sensual perception of everyday life, the breasts as the "nourishment of the new perception" (*ubere novus nutritur*), and the ointments of the Song as "the ineffable joy which draws us to perfection" (*Sermon 32.2*). But Gilbert is scarcely systematic in the way in which he organizes his symbols. Like Bernard, he invokes breasts primarily to describe how the preacher, like Paul, must be generous in offering the milk of his spiritual knowledge to those in his care (see, e.g., *Sermons* 27.1–2, 5, and 31.3, 5–6). There are times, however, where one may be allowed to think that the erotic transformation intended in mystical commentaries on the Song has gone awry in a fairly ludicrous way. In *Sermon* 31, for example, Gilbert develops a long analogy between effective preaching and how women artfully shape their bosoms to remedy nature's shortcomings so that they achieve the goal of being "slightly prominent and moderately distended" (*paululum supereminent, et tument modice*).[150]

A more effective transformation of a sexual image is to be found in Gilbert's analysis of the Song of Song's description of the embrace of the divine and human lovers on their "little bed" (*lectulus*). His interpretation here differs in significant ways from what we have seen in William of St. Thierry. The *amplexus* of the Bridegroom and Bride (see Song 2:6 and 8:3) was a favorite theme of the Cistercian commentators. Gilbert uses it often; in his first treatise he even equates the embrace with the kiss of the lovers rather than with sexual congress.[151] In his sermons, however, Gilbert has several original passages describing the human bride enjoying the Divine Lover's embrace on the "little flowery bed" of Song 2:6. For example, *Sermon* 2 analyzes three beds. One is the Bride's alone established in hope; a second bed is shared when she and the Groom begin to find delight (this would have been William of St. Thierry's acme); and a third belongs to the Divine Lover alone, of which she says,

> In the bed that is his alone, she boils over when driven to it by the fire of the Bridegroom's love. She departs from herself, poured out and pouring herself out. She is totally transformed into him; absorbed into a similar mode of being (*qualitas*). . . . In this third [bed] she is completely in his company. We might even say that there is no one there but he alone.[152]

What is important to note here is the motif of fire and liquefaction, or melting away, which is also prominent in several other texts. For example, in *Sermon* 15.9, the abbot once again associates the bed, the embrace, fire, and melting away:

> Therefore, the bride, aglow with some gift of the blazing word of the Bridegroom's embrace, melts from the perfumer's powder into finer wisps of smoke [see Sg. 3:6], from the dust of the humbled virtues into the smoke of glory. What do you think her arrival will be like, when her ascent is so delightful? What is her destination when she ascends in such beauty? . . . Perhaps it is the bed of the Beloved.[153]

Other texts that deal with the mystery of the encounter of the divine and the human spirit in Gilbert's sermons employ the symbols of the embrace and the bed of intercourse without explicit notice of liquefaction (e.g., *Sermons* 16.8–9 and 43.6–7), or else use the images of melting and fusing that highlight his prediliction for this form of mystical discourse (e.g., *Sermons* 26.8–9 and 44.3–7).

Closely allied with this form of imagery is the abbot's treatment of the wound and sickness of love (see Song 2:5 and 4:9). The central passage here is *Sermon* 30, explicitly devoted to an address from the Groom to the Bride: "You have wounded my heart, my sister and spouse, you have wounded my heart with one of your eyes and one lock of hair of your neck" (Song 4:9). Although Christ has loved us first, so that all love we return to him "is not so much paid as repaid (*non impenditur, sed rependitur*), . . . he feels that he has been, as it were, provoked to love, as long as he allows that his heart has been wounded."[154] In a daring fashion, Gilbert invites the loving soul to wound the Spouse again and again, like a "target set up for such arrows" (*quasi signum positum ad tales sagittas*). But the wounding is mutual. Christ's loving gaze, as illustrated by the look he cast on Peter when the apostle denied him (Luke 22:61-62), pierces our sinful hearts with compunction and moves us to aspire to continue acquiring the virtues necessary for our salvation. For Gilbert, as for all Christian mystics, the loving encounter with God is inseparable from advance in the virtuous life.[155] The wound of love motif is found in three other places in Gilbert's works,[156] and the related notion of love's sickness (*quia amore langueo* of Song 5:8) occurs in several other texts.[157] What is new in the English abbot is the detailed way in which he treats the mutuality of the wounding and sickness involved in the intercourse of the Bride/Soul and Groom/Redeemer. Gilbert's sermons provide no theoretical explanation for this new, if tentatively expressed, note. Much more will be said about these issues in centuries to come as attention to the mutual depths of both God and the soul in the mystical encounter receive more detailed attention.

Baldwin of Ford and John of Ford

The fascination of the English Cistercians with the Song of Songs did not cease with the death of Gilbert of Hoyland. Baldwin, born in Exeter and educated in the schools, entered the Cistercian order and became abbot of Ford in Devon about 1175. In 1180 he was created bishop of Worchester, and from 1184 to his death in 1190 he served as a rather controversial archbishop of Canterbury. Baldwin was not a profound theologian, but he was a solid and serious one in the monastic mold.[158] He did not compose a commentary on the Song of Songs, but three of his sixteen spiritual treatises are based on verses from the Song of love.[159] *Treatise* 8, dealing with the wound the Bride inflicts on the Divine Lover (Song 4:9), is a competent though scarcely inspired piece testifying to the growing importance of the *vulnus amoris* in the later twelfth century. Baldwin also devoted a brief treatise to the seal of love mentioned in Song 8:6, which he explains in terms of the image of love Christ seals upon our hearts. The most important of Baldwin's treatises on the Song, however, is the fourteenth, which considers the *ordo caritatis*.[160] It is an able summation of Cistercian thought on this characteristically twelfth-century mystical theme.

Baldwin begins by combining two unlikely, but actually typical, twelfth-century authorities on love, Solomon (Song 2:4–5) and Ovid (*Metamorphoses* 1.153), both of whom assert that love is a sickness (*languor*), the suffering of a sick soul (*infirmi animi passio*). This is true of all the six forms of love–natural love of parents and children, social love between friends, conjugal love, impure love, the vain love of this world, and finally the pure love of God. But how can the love of God, which is *caritas,* be a sickness? The answer, of course, is that as long as we are in this life we cannot have full possession of the Bridegroom and therefore the Bride is said to "languish on the bed" (*languida lecto* in *Treatise* 14 [PL 204:540D]). The Bride is sick with the "affliction that is health" (*hic enim languor salus est* [541A]) because she has drunk of the wine of compunction and of love in the wine cellar of her heart (Song 2:3). Baldwin goes on to identify the entry into the wine cellar with the decision "to leave all things for the sake of Christ and to adhere to him alone in complete purity of heart," a scarcely veiled reference to entry into the monastic life.[161] It is this form of "sober inebriation" that allows the Bride to say, "He has set charity in order in me" (Song 2:4).

Baldwin proceeds to analyze the ordering of charity according to valuation (*aestimatio*), zeal (*aemulatio*), and choice (*electio*). We must value charity above all other virtues and gifts of God; we must desire it above everything else; and, finally, we must "seek it in such a way that we possess it and hold on to it" (542B). After a further discussion of what this entails in practical life, Baldwin provides an overview of how this ordered charity constitutes the fundamental law of the universe, governing the angels and their ministries, the mystery of our redemption, the lives and conduct of the just, and the virtues by which one becomes just. In his treatment of the relation between charity and freedom, Baldwin reveals his equivalent of Bernard's portrayal of the interaction between affective love, *amor affectualis,* and active love, *amor actualis* (see Bernard's *Sermon* 50). "Although it is true that freedom and charity are bound together," he says, "there are times that charity yields to necessity and disregards what is better so as to avoid something worse."[162] Thus, charity sometimes employs the *ordo libertatis et dignitatis* when it is free to choose what is best, especially contemplative union with God, and sometimes it must use the *ordo dispensationis et necessitatis,* when it yields to "what necessity imposes or weakness suggests," that is, service of the brethren (543D–44A). As long as charity is first in our intention, even the latter choice is ordered by it. However, this necessary selection of the lesser good, as well as the trials to which all life is subject, continue to make love a sickness here below, though one in which the Bride "acknowledges God's gifts in her tribulations" (546A). To the objection that this brief treatise is not really a mystical text because it does not concern itself directly with the consciousness of the presence of God, one can respond that it deals not so much with the experience itself as the effect which the experience, however much or little realized in this life, is meant to achieve. For the twelfth-century mystical theorists the claim to have enjoyed God in this life can only be authenticated by the measure to which the individual has reordered charity in life and affection.

John of Ford was a protégé of Baldwin who succeeded to his abbatial position in 1191. Of some importance in his day (for three years he had the unenviable position of being King John's confessor), he was almost totally forgotten in the centuries following his death in 1214. He composed 120 sermons, mostly in the first decade of the thirteenth century, to finish the Cistercian commentary on the Song of Songs. These survive in only a single manuscript, but John deserves the happier fate that has seen the recovery of his thought in the present century. His reading of the Song provides us with an admirable window onto the Cistercian experience of God.[163]

The sheer bulk of John's work precludes any attempt at summarizing the whole of his teaching. Much of what we can read in the abbot of Ford has already been seen in the other Cistercians. Several times he pays homage to the greatness of Bernard and his own unworthiness to continue his work.[164] A text in *Sermon* 24.2 praises "those companions of the Bridegroom and bridesmaids of the Bride" who "hand on to us nothing that they have not first read in their own hearts," mentioning Gregory, Augustine and Ambrose among the fathers, and "in our time" (*nostrique temporis*), Bernard, Guerric, Richard of St. Victor, and Gilbert. John was very conscious of belonging to a tradition.

Typical of this tradition is his appeal to the experience of his audience.[165] Interpreting the Bridegroom's "belly . . . studded with sapphires" (Song 5:14) as the various consolations we gain from the visit of Christ, he exclaims:

> If anyone thinks it a valuable thing to learn, let him give himself to it and experience it! Let him yearn and pray unceasingly, and exercise himself in this matter of charity. Let him give no sleep to his eyes, no rest to his eyelids (Ps 132:4). Let him give no rest by night or day to the God of peace and love, until the love of Christ comes forth to him from out of his bridal chamber, and bursts into flame before him, like a burning lamp.[166]

As might be expected, the standard erotic images of the Song are often discussed–the kiss, the embrace, and the breasts. The coming and going of the Divine Lover, so often the theme of the Song, is also a frequent subject. The Bride's sleep suggested by Song 8:3 (repeating 2:6) is equated with the *otium quietis* or *sabbati* of the monastic tradition and comes up for discussion in a number of texts, especially in *Sermons* 97–100. The wine often mentioned in the Song suggests the mystical theme of *sobria/sacra ebrietas,* which John treats in at least seven places. John has less desert imagery than we have seen in other late twelfth-century Cistercians, though he does provide one extended consideration in *Sermon* 100. We can also note the large part that the wound of love plays in his commentary (like Gilbert, he emphasizes the mutuality of the wounding between the Bride and her Lover [*Sermon* 48.9]).[167]

Many of the standard theological themes that we have come to associate with the Cistercian Song of Songs commentary tradition reappear in John. Like Bernard *Sermon* 8, and William of St. Thierry in his *Exposition on the Song of Songs,* John introduces trinitarian theology into the commentary in order to explain how all love has its source in and resembles the "fountain of love . . . where it originates" (*fons dilectionis . . . ubi oritur*).[168] John's impressive Christology would demand a separate study, particularly his consideration of the relation of the Father and the Son in the work of our salvation,[169] and his stress on Christ as both Father and Mother to us (see *Sermons* 26.7, 28.2, and 29.1). Standard mystical motifs, such as consideration of the experience of God as an *excessus mentis,*[170] the understanding of union as an *unitas spiritus* (often citing 1 Cor 6:17 as a proof text),[171] treatment of the effect of the mystical encounter as the ordering of charity,[172] and the *epektasis* motif,[173] are all present in the English abbot's long homiletic effort. Rather than pursue any of these familiar themes, we will explore John's contribution to Cistercian erotic mysticism by investigating some of the principles in his reading of the Song of love and his treatment of the master symbol of the entire Song of Songs, the soul's marriage to God, the *nuptiale sacramentum.*[174]

Although John of Ford's primary intention was to nourish the spiritual life of his community through the exposition of the moral-mystical meaning of the Song, he represents something of a return to Bernard and even to Gregory the Great in the way he combines the ecclesiological with the personal reading of the book of love. This is also evident in the concern that he shows for the Jews. Unlike Guerric of Igny, for example, who has some unpleasant anti-Jewish remarks (e.g., *Sermons* 28.1–3, 30.3, and 32.3–4), John's dominant note is one of joy in the promised return of the synagogue at the end of days (see, e.g., *Sermons* 30–32, 62, 64, 66, 95, and 103). Like Gregory and Bernard, John has a keen sense of the multivalence of scriptural symbolism: "What if the same truth is symbolized under different verbal attire?

Sacred scripture is like a queen with a very rich wardrobe, who loves to come forth from her bedchamber in varying guises to be seen by her friends."[175] The consistent ingenuity with which the abbot deals with the lush symbols of the Song across many hundreds of pages cannot be easily summarized, but it will be appreciated by anyone who makes the effort to study his entire corpus.

Like many of the early commentators, John was conscious of the need for spiritual maturity on the part of anyone who reads the Song of Songs, especially the descriptions of "the most intimate parts of the Bride's body" (*verendas dilectae suae partes* [*Sermon* 68.1]). Speaking in the Bride's voice, John says: "Where the Spirit of my Beloved is, there is liberty (2 Cor 3:17). He is the one who placed the words of this holy Song in my mouth, which are to be entrusted only to the chaste ears of those who have tasted Jesus."[176] This does not prevent John from using the erotic images of the Song in direct ways, such as in his references to the sexual intercourse (*copula coniugalis*) between the Bride and the Divine Word.[177]

A distinctive characteristic of his reading, however, is the interest that he shows in the incoherence and the lack of logic often found in the Song of Songs. Commenting on Song 7:10, "I to my Beloved, and his turning towards me" (*Ego dilecto meo, et ad me conversio eius*), John notes that "the imperfection of the expression hints at something more perfect than a complete statement."[178] The Bride is trying to "open a path to her affections" (*affectibus viam pandens*), and John reflects that when the Bride speaks to the Word mere "words" are insufficient, only "her own language, that of the affections, works."[179] The wonder is that in this converse of love God himself accommodates expressions of such human affections to himself (see *Sermon* 93.3).

Such accommodation is possible because John, like Origen and Dionysius and Bernard and other Christian mystics, believed that love, whether we call it *amor, affectus,* or its more rightful name *caritas*, reveals the ultimate mystery, the depths of the divine nature.[180] "*Caritas* is completely ineffable to humans whether one tries to suggest it or to understand it, because it is from the hidden depths of the Son and is the greatest and deepest mystery of paradise."[181] The Bride alone can utter the words of love because she is the one "who does not love in a routine way, but who burns with love, who faints, who fails, who cleaves, who chooses to know nothing at all except Jesus."[182] Such a soul marries Jesus, and it is no surprise then that the abbot's analyses of the spiritual marriage demonstrate the true depth of his mystical exegesis. A consideration of two sermons will show this.

In *Sermon* 114 the English abbot provides a summary of how the imagery of the Song of Songs reveals the progress of the soul from its childlike stage where it has no breasts and is unskilled in love, despite having had a few experiences of the Lord's sweetness, to the state of being a full-fledged Bride.[183] The soul needs to learn the art of love, which, says the abbot, "consists in this: that you seek, that you hold on, that you search anew" (*Omnis quippe haec ars in eo est, ut quaeras, ut teneas, ut requiras* [114.3]). The first verse of the Song speaks of the seeking stage, but by verses 1:6, 12, and 15 we already hear that the Bride is holding on to the Lover in the strong embrace noted in Song 3:4. Passages such as Song 2:17 and 5:8 speak of the necessity for seeking him anew when he has withdrawn. In Song 8:8–9 the angels speak on behalf of the child-soul, who develops breasts, the mark of maturity which will help her learn how to hold on to Jesus or to seek him effectively when he has slipped away (*Sermon* 114.4). "The speaking on behalf of," says John, "announces the marriage when she will become pregnant in the Holy Spirit after a richer enjoyment of the Lover. Having received the blessed seed, which is the sweet love of Christ, she will immediately have real breasts."[184] John's further comment on why Song 8:9 speaks of this address as being made "in the day" shows that he recognized what Bernard and William and others had also grasped, namely, that the images of the Song portray the history of the soul throughout this life as always in oscillation between "the night when the Spouse is sought and the day when he is found" (114.5).

The triple action of seeking, holding, and searching anew reveals the pattern of absence and presence that even the most advanced Bride can never surpass in this life. We can turn to *Sermon* 109 for a more complete discussion of what the "holding" phase, or marital union, is for the Bride. This sermon is artfully constructed around the discussion of three kinds of *caritas*: that by which God loves us; that by which we love God; and that by which we love each other in fraternal affection.[185] The analysis of the second form includes a detailed treatment of John's doctrine of the mystical marriage.[186] As is typical with the classic Cistercian commentators on the Song, John begins by rooting the individual love of each *sponsa Christi* in the love between Christ and the church.[187] All ability to love comes from God (1 John 4:19 is cited) and all true love must be perpetual, but love will only learn if it is indeed true love by overcoming the trials and temptations of this life. John's account of these trials is framed in terms of the life of the church in general. Rather than being tested now primarily by the fires of persecution and martyrdom, our love will be proven if it resists avarice, lechery, and ambition. The soul that has been brought into the wine cellar and had charity ordered in her (cf. Song 2:4) has truly learned that "love is as strong as death, jealousy as relentless as the grave; its lamps are lamps of fire and flames; many waters cannot quench love, nor can floods drown it"

(Song 8:6–7, the base text for this sermon). John says that such a soul knows the meaning of these verses from experience (*experta est*).

Analysis of this experience centers on the image of the "lamp of fire and flames." Lamps both illuminate and enflame (like Gilbert, John has a predeliction for symbols of fire as indicating the melting of the soul into God).[188] "The soul that loves Christ intimately gleams with countless lamps day and night like a noble bedchamber for the Spouse. She is exceedingly illumined by the lightning blasts of the visits of her Spouse."[189] The abbot admits that "something of this brightness at times shines on a weak soul like mine," but the brevity of his own experience of enlightenment causes him to compare it to a glass lamp rather than one of fire and flames (109.8). In the culminating section of his exegesis, he concentrates on the twofold effect the fire of love has on the Bride:

> The Lord's Bride sits by this fire and grows so warm from it that she melts like wax (Ps 21:14). Whatever is corruptible in her . . . is burned away by the heat of flaming charity. Before the face of this fire,[190] scents of myrrh and incense gently waft from her bosom. . . . From this fire, the Bride blazes out into powerful speech, either speaking of hidden and ineffable things with the Bridegroom in rejoicing and entreaty, or else taking pleasure in conversing with the maidens about the more secret dealings that the Spouse has had with her.[191]

Such ecstasies are so powerful, John asserts, that the Bride fears that "when she has been lifted above herself she will be raptured so far from herself that she may not remember to return to herself as she should" (109.9). This reflection on the vertiginous nature of the experience of rapture leads the abbot to thoughts about how the shortness and suddenness of some experiences of the Divine Lover are designed to "test" the Bride's humility (*vistans illam diliculo subito et probat illam*). Finally, the "many waters and floods" that cannot quench or drown the Bride's love are equated with the "rivers of graces and blessings" that, John claims, "terrible to say and hear as it is" (*quod dictu et auditu terribile est*), can at times flow down so heavily as to extinguish or destroy the fire itself. This obscure reference to the terror and confusion sometimes experienced in the encounter with God are not the final word, however. "Still, the Bride's soul is in her Spouse's hand; no one can take her from his hand. . . . These waters and floods will not harm one who loves Christ strongly" (109.9). In such passages John of Ford contributed his own special flavor to the Cistercian reading of *the* mystical handbook of love.

Aelred of Rievaulx

For a treatment of *amor*, *caritas*, and especially *amicitia* that was not so directly dependent on the Song of Songs, we turn to Aelred of Rievaulx, born about 1110, the son and grandson of hereditary priests from the northern English border country.[192] As a young man he had a distinguished career in the court of William of Scotland, though in his later monastic years he bewailed the sinfulness of his youth.[193] After a crisis of conscience, he joined the Cistercians at Rievaulx, a foundation of Clairvaux, in 1134. While on official business to Rome, Aelred passed through Clairvaux in 1142, where he met Bernard–a meeting of great moment for the younger monk. Bernard encouraged Aelred to put together and expand notes on the meaning of *caritas* that he had been working on. The result was the *Mirror of Charity* in three books, Aelred's central work, and one that came forearmed with a prefatory letter by Bernard himself. By 1147 Aelred was made abbot of Rievaulx, where he served until his death twenty years later.

Aelred opens his noted treatise *Spiritual Friendship*, finished in the 1160s, with the remark: "When I was still just a boy at school and the charm of my companions was a great delight, amidst the habits and vices that usually threaten that age, I gave my whole mind to affection and vowed myself to love, so that nothing seemed more pleasant to me, more delightful, more useful than 'to love and be loved.'"[194] This intense desire for love and friendship matured and deepened over the years, becoming the theme of his most noted writings as well the mainspring of the demeanor he showed to the monks under his charge. Toward the end of the *Spiritual Friendship* he speaks of how he walks the rounds of the monastic cloister, averring, "In the multitude of the brethren I found no one I did not love and by whom, I was sure, I was not also loved. I was filled with such great love that it surpassed all the delights of this world."[195] Walter Daniel's *Life of Aelred* testifies that this was not just a literary topos. According to him, "Who was there, however despised and rejected, who did not find at Rievaulx a place of rest? What weak person ever came there and did not discover fatherly love in Aelred and fitting consolation among the brethren?"[196] The monastery flourished under Aelred's leadership. Despite ill health, especially in the last decade of his life, he kept up a busy schedule of writing and political activity, as well as his duties of "fatherly love." Walter Daniel's moving description of his last days is among the finest such accounts in monastic literature.[197]

Aelred was not a literary genius in the sense that Bernard was, nor was he a profound theologian as were William of St. Thierry and Isaac of Stella. His historical writings, among them the *Genealogy of the Kings of England* and the *Tract on the Battle of the Standard*, were unusual for a Cistercian, but perhaps not for an English successor of Bede. David Knowles put it well when he said: "His unique position as a writer–wholly unique in England, and without exact parallel abroad–is due in part to the limpid sincerity with which he laid bare, in his desire to help others, the growth and progress of his own mind and heart from the human to the divine, and in part to the candid humanism of his most characteristic pages."[198] This should not be taken to mean that the abbot of Rievaulx was a mere amateur. He was a superb stylist and made a special contribution to twelfth-century mysticism. It is just that the originality of his role in the history of mysticism is restricted to a single area, the one that focused all his interests—the role of *caritas* and *amicitia* in the path to union with God. Hence, his treatises the *Mirror of Charity* and *Spiritual Friendship* will always remain the central documents for investigating his thought, although he left a considerable number of sermons and other works.[199] The power of his teaching and the geniality of his personality have resulted in an extensive modern literature devoted to this most important of English Cistercians.[200]

Like all Cistercians, Aelred rooted his spiritual teaching in a theological anthropology based on the understanding of humanity as the *imago et similitudo Dei.* The English abbot even felt compelled at the end of his life to pen a treatise on the soul in which he collected the anthropological commonplaces he used, largely dependent on Augustine and Bernard. The same basic material appears in his *Mirror of Charity*, which discusses how the soul was created as an *imago trinitatis*,[201] but suffered damage to the image (and loss of the likeness) through sin,[202] only to be given the possibility of restoration of the image and likeness through the coming of Christ.[203] The *Mirror of Charity* also contains an account of *liberum arbitrium* close to that found in Bernard, as might be expected.[204] Aelred's interest, however, is not in the exploration of faculty psychology but in the dynamics of fall and return: "Charity lifts our soul up to that for which it was created; cupidity drags it down toward that to which it was sinking of its own accord."[205]

It is not Aelred's anthropology that distinguishes him among Cistercian authors but the teaching on *affectio, amor,* and *caritas* that he rooted in it. I will begin by analyzing this doctrine and its relation to his Christology, before moving on to what he has to say about *amicitia.* I will close with a consideration of how this all affects his understanding of mystical union.

Amor is the central term in Aelred's vocabulary, but we can begin with what is existentially prior in our human experience, what Aelred calls *affectus*, which he defines as "a spontaneous and sweet inclination of the intellectual soul toward someone."[206] The abbot spends a good deal of time analyzing the five kinds of *affectus*: spiritual (which comes in two types); rational; dutiful (*officialis*); natural; and finally carnal or physical, which is not evil in itself but which can easily lead to sin (*Mirror* 3.11.31–16.39). What is important to grasp, however, is that these spontaneous movements are not love itself, but "the bases and roots of love." Being moved *by* them is neither harmful nor useful in itself; being moved *according* to them, that is, consenting to them either inwardly or outwardly, constitutes true *amor* (3.16.39). But, as Aelred immediately notes, such consent implies another cause, namely, reason (*ratio*), which is the second root of love.

Reason, which Aelred, like the other Cistercians, considers identical with the soul's essence, is used in two senses—"according to nature, by which it makes a person rational and able to discern between good and evil; . . . and according to judgment, by which it rejects what is to be rejected and approves what is to be approved."[207] Love, like reason, can also be spoken of in two ways: first, as "a power or nature of the rational soul by means of which it naturally has the faculty of loving or not loving something" (this is always good); and, secondly, as "the act of the rational soul exercising that power, employing it either for what it should do or should not do."[208] The act of "choosing to enjoy," which constitutes love in the second sense, has therefore three possible roots—*affectus* alone, which may be so powerful as to force both reason and will to go along with it (this will always be dangerous for Aelred, even when the attraction is a spiritual one); reason alone, which can rightly make the will choose a good even when there is no attraction to it present in the soul; and finally, the twin impulses of *affectus* and *ratio* when reason approves and directs a fitting natural attraction. This last constitutes *amor perfectus* (see 3.20.48).

The third book of the *Mirror of Charity* contains an extensive analysis of *caritas*, the right use of love, in terms of the choice (*electio*) that proceeds from reason, the development (*motus*) that takes place inwardly through growing desire and outwardly through action, and the fruit (*fructus*) by which it comes to enjoy what it loves. To attain the goal of "ordered love" (*amor ordinatus* [3.18.41]) the true lover must be *affectuosus, discretus, fortis,* we might say "attracted, discerning, and strong." The attracted lover will be drawn by desire for the sweetness of what is loved, but such a lover needs reason's discernment in order "not to exceed due measure in action" (*ne in actu modum excedat*). The lover also needs fortitude to overcome difficulties and temptations (3.21.51). Aelred echoes this basic teaching at the beginning of the third book of *Spiritual Friendship*.[209]

The abbot of Rievaulx's analysis is remarkable for its clarity and flexibility. Equally noteworthy is the way in which the *Mirror of Charity* anchors this teaching on human love in the love that is God and which God has suffused throughout the universe. We find this treatment in the first book of the *Mirror*. In his preface to this work, the English monk briefly outlined the subjects of its three books: first, the excellence of charity; second, a reply to inept complaints against it (really a defense of the Cistercian life as the best way of attaining charity); and, finally, a demonstration of how charity should be practiced. Charity is excellent not only because it is the way God's loved ones approach mystical experience, as "fainting away from themselves they pass over into You" (*deficientes a se, ut transeant in te* [1.1.2]); but even more because *caritas* defines the very nature of God. Aelred provides a long and digressive discussion of the excellence of charity mid way through book 1 under the general rubric of a discussion of the "Sabbath," the sevenfold mark of perfection (1.18.51–27.78). This great day of rest, without morning and evening (Gen 2:1–3), signifies God's eternity which is nothing else than his charity:

> Charity alone is his unchangeable and eternal rest, his eternal and unchangable tranquillity, his eternal and unchangable Sabbath. It was the sole cause why he created what was to be created, why he rules what is to be ruled, administers what is to be administered, moves what is to be moved, advances what is to be advanced and perfects what is to be perfected.... His charity is his very Will and also his very Goodness; all this is nothing else but his very Being.[210]

Not only is Charity identical with God's essence; it also helps us understand the mutual delight of the Father and the Son as well as "the charity and consubstantial unity of both, which is rightly called the Holy Spirit" (1.20.58).

The abbot then moves to creation, underlining how the divine Goodness which is nothing else than his Charity "contains, embraces and penetrates all things, joining the highest with the lowest, not by being poured into a place, or by being spread out through space, or by active moving about, but by the steady, incomprehensible, and permanent simplicity of its substantial presence."[211] Aelred's teaching on how universal *caritas* unites all opposites is reminiscent of Dionysius on cosmic love in *Divine Names* 4, but the language in which it is expressed, especially the stress on "the tranquillity of order which charity ordained for the universe," speaks more of Augustine.[212] In his *Spiritual Friendship* the abbot was to express this cosmic role of love in an even more original fashion, by affirming that *amicitia*, the highest form of *caritas*, is the love that unites all things in the universe.[213] In the *Mirror of Charity* passage he follows Augustine, once again, in emphasizing how all things seek their own place within the universal order of love (1.21.60–61). In terms of the created spirit, the restless desire to find its proper place will only be satisfied by reaching "what is highest and best, which has nothing above it or more excellent" (1.22.62). In the remainder of this mini-treatise on the Sabbath charity spells out the insufficiency of all created things to slake the soul's thirst for ultimate enjoyment. Only the yoke of charity, that is, *fraterna dilectio*, which "unites and does not oppress," leads to the reward (1.27.78).

The universal law of love established by God in creation was damaged, though not destroyed, by sin. As befits the centrality of love and friendship in Aelred's thought, original sin is primarily described in terms of improper *affectus*. Our distance from God is measured not by physical footsteps, but by *mentis affectus*. Echoing the language that the Cistercians developed from Augustine, the abbot says:

> Not wishing to keep my soul's substance for You, I took it for myself, and wishing to possess myself without You, I lost both You and me. I have become a burden to myself; I have made myself a place of misery and darkness, a place of horror and a region of destitution.[214]

In this *regio egestatis* we are ruled by *cupiditas* rather than *caritas*.[215] The result is that even when some measure of love is restored to us through the action of grace, reason must sometimes compel choice when *affectus* is lacking or opposed. It is also why we are bid love all people, even our enemies, although we cannot be expected to enter into friendship with all until the eschatological fulfillment of our restoration in heaven.[216]

It will come as no surprise that Aelred's teaching on the way in which the Divine Word begins the work of healing and redirecting *affectus* is through his taking on flesh and providing us with the human example of supreme love in Christ. Aelred's version of the *amor carnalis Christi* with which the work of our salvation must begin, though similar to what we have seen in Bernard, William, and others, has accents of its own that repay consideration.[217] The English abbot's short treatise called *Jesus at the Age of Twelve*, written ca. 1155 and later often taken for a work of Bernard's, is one of the classic statements of Cistercian devotion to the carnal love of Christ. Aelred begins with a treatment of the "wonderful sweetness of this most holy history," retelling the story of Jesus's boyhood from his passage from the sin of Egypt to the Nazareth of grace and then to "the most sacred of all the places in the world, the Temple at Jerusalem," where he confers with his heavenly Father about the coming mysteries of his saving work. The aim of this charming little work is to place "the sweet image of the dear boy before the eyes of the heart" (1.1), so that "affection may be aroused" (*unde affectus excitetur*. 1.11).[218] Aelred designed his account to place the reader "at the scene" in a more concrete way than we find in Bernard or the other Cistercians. But this is still the beginning not the goal. The history is lovingly recounted (and expanded upon) "in order to uncover the spiritual understanding," which Aelred develops in two parts: a treatment of the allegorical meaning, that is, how the history of salvation, especially the passing of the promise from the synagogue to the church, reveals and empowers our own spiritual progress;[219] and then an explanation of the moral sense through a consideration of the traditional three stages of spiritual development figured in the Bethlehem of beginners, the Nazareth of those advancing in the virtues, and the Jerusalem of the "contemplation of celestial secrets." In this latter section, which contains something of a precis of Aelred's teaching on mystical union (see especially 3.21–23), the emphasis is on the typical Cistercian appeal to the necessity for experiential appropriation. Aelred says that he is writing all this to his friend Ivo, "so that you may be able to make a continual study of these mystical matters (*mystica*) not so much in books as in your actions."[220]

The *amor carnalis Christi*, which the English monk once succinctly described as "extending all our affection to the sweetness of the Lord's flesh,"[221] is also central to the *Rule of Life for a Recluse* that he penned for his sister and which was to have an important influence on the history of spirituality and mysticism in later medieval England. In the third part of this work Aelred counsels his sister to practice a threefold form of meditation—on the past, the present, and the future (3.29).[222] The meditation on the past is the affective presentation of the events of the life of Jesus, in which Aelred invites his sister to accompany Mary as an actual participant in the drama of salvation. Event-by-event Aelred presents the scene and tries to arouse the appropriate *affectus* (3.29–31). For example, in recounting Jesus' visit to the house of Mary, Martha, and Lazarus, where the alabaster jar was broken to pour precious ointment over the Savior's head (Mark 14:3), he concludes: "Break the alabaster of your heart and pour everything that you have of devotion, of love, of desire, of affection over the head of your Spouse, adoring the man in God and the God in man."[223] This long meditation concludes with a summary of the purpose of Cistercian devotion to the human Christ: "And so let us pass from the remembrance of things of the past to the experience of those of the present that from these we will be able to understand how much we should love God."[224] The meditation on the present (3.32) is primarily one of thanksgiving for God's gifts in our lives; the meditation on the future (3.33) is the salutary consideration of death and the other last things. Such a program, which combines consideration of the life of Jesus with access to higher mystical experiences, is typical of Aelred's approach.[225]

The abbot of Rievaulx's personal devotion to Jesus (well-reflected in his deathbed prayer) shines through all his writings. His accounts are often most glowing when directed to the saving mysteries of Christ's birth and childhood, as we have seen, and to the mystery of the Passion. Like Peter Damian (see chapter 4, pp. 141–42), Aelred invites his reader to embrace the crucified Christ and to drink his blood.[226] Devotion to Jesus in his Passion is a model for imitation as we confront the afflictions of this life and the necessity for patient love of our enemies (see *Mirror* 2.5.8–9, and 3.5.14–15), but it is also something more: passion-centered piety cements the bond that we have with Jesus our Mother. Aelred, like Bernard, makes use of a number of maternal images of Jesus, especially how through his suffering and death he continues to feed his children in the sacrament of the Eucharist.[227]

Aelred's sustained attempts to rouse his readers to an affective but still spiritual devotion to the beauty and love of Jesus gives his mode of expressing the *amor carnalis Christi* a different flavor from what we have seen in Bernard and the other Cistercians. It has also been claimed that he differed from Bernard in rejecting any real distinction between love in the flesh and love in the spirit, that is, that he was not interested in encouraging the kind of transition from *amor carnalis Christi* to the *amor spiritualis* that Bernard felt was the true goal of the contemplative.[228] To be sure, the Englishman seems to have a stronger sense of the fact that in loving Christ's flesh we are already loving God and that this form of love is one that will always be needed in this life, but the presence of texts in which Aelred, like Bernard, speaks of spiritual love as a higher form indicate that one should beware of making any sharp distinction between the abbot of Rievaulx and the abbot of Clairvaux on this point.[229]

Among the many forms of *affectus* and *amor* that form our participation in the divine *caritas*, one stood out for the abbot of Rievaulx–that love we call friendship (*amicitia*). Aelred has been most studied for the extent and the depth of his teaching on friendship as a central aspect of our return to God. Friendship, of course, had enjoyed a long history in classical thought among philosophers such as Aristotle and Cicero. Christian adaptation of the Greco-Roman ideal of friendship was especially prominent among the Latin Fathers, beginning with Ambrose and continuing with Augustine, Paulinus of Nola, Cassian, and others. This tradition was also strong among the early medieval monks.[230] The great English scholar Alcuin of York was a predecessor of Aelred in his view of friendship in Christ as a means of access to experiencing God in this life.[231] The rhetoric (and doubtless also) the reality of friendship is found throughout the twelfth century in religious writers from every order and form of life,[232] not least in Bernard of Clairvaux.[233] Nevertheless, no one before Aelred devoted such attention to *amicitia* as the way to God.[234]

Aelred's teaching on *amicitia* is grounded in the theory of love set forth in the *Mirror of Charity*, which presents an initial version of his understanding of *amicitia* in the famous lament for his friend Simon that closes book 1 of the treatise (1.34.98–114), as well as in brief comments at the end of book 3 (3.39.107–40.112). It is in the abbot's most personal work, the treatise on *Spiritual Friendship*, that the fullness of his teaching is expressed. Because

Aelred paid testimony to Cicero's famous dialogue *Lealius*, or *On Friendship*, citing his definition of friendship,[235] adopting the dialogue form, and also using many aspects of the Roman's presentation,[236] older scholarship sometimes saw in the *Spiritual Friendship* nothing more than a revival, even a pastiche, of classical friendship theory covered with a thin Christian veneer. This view is scarcely tenable today. Despite the debt to Cicero, Aelred's work is an original transposition of ancient friendship theory into a Christian mode,[237] and one might even argue that the basically different foundation upon which the abbot builds his understanding of friendship—the definition of God as *amicitia* and the insistence that all true friendship is a gift from God realized in Christ—actually stretches the classical notion beyond all recognition and accounts for some of the interior tensions in the book.

The opening of the treatise sounds the essential theme: *Ecce ego et tu, et spero quod tertius inter nos Christus sit* ("Here we are, you and I, and I hope that Christ may be the third between us"). Basically, the work proceeds as a "how-to" book, with Aelred's younger friends (the monk Ivo in book 1, and Walter and Gratian in books 2–3) being given instruction in "how that friendship that should exist among us may be begun in Christ, preserved according to Christ, and its goal and use referred more fully to Christ."[238] Rather than follow the order of the work, based as it is on Cicero, it is better to present the Christian logic of the abbot's view of *spiritualis amicitia*.

Deus amicitia est, as the abbot affirms in *Spiritual Friendship* 1.69–70.[239] Aelred was not the first Cistercian to stress friendship with God,[240] but identifying God as friendship strikes a new note, though the abbot could offer good scriptural credentials for this unusual formulation, especially from the Johannine writings. Aelred's teaching that God can be understood as the kind of love best realized in this life through friendship constituted a new variation on the transformation of *erōs* as a key to unlocking the mystery of the divine-human relation.

When one reads what the abbot of Rievaulx says about his friendships and the role that these had in his path to God it is difficult to avoid the conclusion that *amicitia*, which for a monk like Aelred was restricted to intense friendship among males, meant something more for him than it had for his predecessors. Whether this is the result of an openness to the revelation of personal feelings characteristic of twelfth-century culture, or a product of a new kind of literary expression is not of final importance. No one before him had quite said the things that Aelred said, and the mystery of how he was able to say them to a large extent eludes the scrutiny of historians.[241] The recent discussion about how far the abbot's passionate language concerning his male friends may or may not reflect a homosexual component in his own emotional life is largely irrelevant to his primary intention of showing how *affectus* and *ratio*, with the aid of grace, can raise friendship to the level of the *spiritualis amicitia* that leads to God.[242] Aelred, as we have noted, lamented the sexual sins of his youth; but he does not tell us what kinds of sins these were. The attitude he displays toward illicit sexuality in his writings is, if anything, slightly more obsessive than that of the average twelfth-century monk;[243] but as abbot he allowed his monks signs of affection that scandalized less humane monastic leaders. The central point is that Aelred agrees with other Cistercians, especially Bernard, William, and those who completed the Cistercian commentary on the Song of Songs, in claiming that God reveals himself in *all* human forms of mutual attraction (*affectus*). Where he differs from them is in his concentration on the *affectus* named *amicitia*. If he was not the first, Aelred was certainly the foremost Christian thinker to effect a transposition of the erotic energies of *amicitia* to the service of mystical contact with God.[244]

Since God can be spoken of as *amicitia* just as legitimately as he can be named *caritas* or *amor*, then friendship is another name for the power of uniting that is spread throughout the whole universe (see *Spiritual Friendship* 1.21 and 50–61). But insofar as friendship expresses itself in the human being, the *imago Dei*, it pertains to the realm of conscious attractions and choices. "Love," as the abbot says referring to his *Mirror of Charity*, "is an attraction (*affectus*) of the rational soul through which it seeks something with desire and strives to enjoy it."[245] Within the contours of the correct forms of love called *caritas*, true friendship, that is, *amicitia spiritualis*, is that form of *caritas* which combines the highest level of *affectus* with the full perspicacity of *ratio*.[246] It is *caritas* with *benevolentia*, that is, "the very perception of loving which is inwardly moved with sweetness."[247]

In discussing the characteristics of spiritual friendship, Aelred lays great stress on its absolute purity and disinterestedness: "Its fruit and reward is nothing but itself."[248] This emphasis, plus the abbot's insistence that spiritual friendship is based on perfect equality, mutuality, and openness,[249] despite any differences in station among those who share it, shows that for Aelred *spiritualis amicitia* is the equivalent of Bernard's *amor sponsalis*, that is, it is the highest form of human love and the model for our relation to God. Indeed, in one sense Aelred's spiritual friendship has a function that Bernard's understanding of marital love does not. For the abbot of Clairvaux, human spousal love was a model for, but not a way to, the experience of loving union of the Word and the soul. Actual human marriage stood in the way of such mystical experience for Bernard. For Aelred, on the other hand, spiritual friendship is both the model of the most direct experience of God and the way to attain the goal.[250] This is evident in the way in which the abbot of Rievaulx analyzes the christocentric core of *spiritualis amicitia.*

Aelred's description of the four stages in the progress toward the perfection of friendship (*Spiritual Friendship* 3.14–118), especially what he has to say about the proofs of friendship in 3.60–82, in some ways detracts from what is central to his whole outlook: *amicitia spiritualis* is a gratuitous gift from God given in Christ. Its growth and maturation are possible only through the generosity of the Redeemer, as noted above. This core of his teaching is most evident in the discussion of three kinds of kisses friends bestow on each other in book 2. Here the abbot makes use of traditional erotic language, often taken from the Song of Songs, to indicate that spiritual friendship reaches its conclusion in friendship with Christ and, through him, friendship with God.

All the good things that friendship brings along with it "are begun in Christ, advance through Christ and reach their perfection in Christ" (2.20). "Therefore," the abbot continues:

> it doesn't seem to be too steep or unnatural an ascent from the Christ who inspires us to love our friend to the Christ who offers himself as a friend to be loved. . . . So the friend who cleaves to his friend in the spirit of Christ, is made one heart and one soul with him (Acts 4:32). Ascending to the friendship of Christ through the the stages of love, he is made one spirit with him (1 Cor 6:17) in a single kiss. The holy soul sighs for that kiss, saying "Let him kiss me with the kiss of his mouth" (Song 1:1)![251]

This key principle introduces a discussion of three forms of kisses found in friendship: an *osculum corporale,* an *osculum spiritale,* and an *osculum intellectuale.* The carnal kiss which mingles the breath of life of two persons binds their mutual *affectus;* it can be misused by lust but is legitimately employed in many human situations, including among friends (2.24–25). The spiritual kiss, which is the proper expression of spiritual friendship, is described as "the kiss of Christ, one that he does not offer from his own mouth but from that of another, breathing that most holy attraction into his lovers so that it seems to them there is but one soul in different bodies. . . ."[252] This kiss, since the soul knows that it comes from Christ, leads to longing for the intellectual kiss to be given directly by the Divine Lover "when all worldly thoughts and desires have been put to rest" (2.27). Such a grafting of the Cistercian appeal to the erotic language of the Song of Songs (both Song 1:1 and 2:6 are cited) onto the vine of spiritual friendship was unique to Aelred.

Formulations that make use of other kinds of traditional mystical language to express the inner connection between the experience of friendship and that of meeting God are found in several other places in *Spiritual Friendship*. For example, in 2.14 he says that "friendship is the step next to the perfection which consists in love and knowledge of God, so that from being a friend of his fellow a human being becomes a friend of God, according to the Savior's word in the Gospel: 'I no longer call you servants, but my friends' (John 15:15)."[253] Later in the same book he speaks of the full reward to be enjoyed by friends "when [friendship] is totally transformed into God and buries those it has united in contemplation of him."[254] Comparable texts speaking of how we ascend from the embrace of the friend to the final embrace of Christ occur also in book 3.[255]

Aelred's lofty teaching on how friendship leads to God was not just a matter of theory but was his reflection on his own experience. This is evident from the the remarkable accounts he gives of his friendships. None of these is more moving nor more revealing of his mystical doctrine than the lament for his dead friend Simon as found in book one of the *Mirror of Charity*.[256] While Aelred made use of both Augustine (*Confessions* 4.4) and Bernard (see *Sermon* 26) as sources, this text is distinctive and original. Simon was a young man who had entered the monastery with Aelred and who had died while Aelred was completing the first book of his *Mirror*. Though he rejoices that Simon is now with Jesus in heaven, Aelred cannot restrain his tears. The relationship between the *puer Iesus* and *puer Simon* is painted in the language of spiritual union—Simon became "one spirit" with him, "so that they might have the same Father, one by grace, the other by nature" (*Mirror* 1.34.100). The kind of language that Aelred applied to the boy Jesus in his *Jesus at Twelve Years of Age* here expands to include both Jesus and his alter-ego, the beloved Simon. The love triangle that binds Jesus, Simon, and Aelred is a source of both pain and pleasure to the one member still left on earth—pain in being left behind, pleasure that Simon has gone on ahead. "My soul wishes to be together with his, a part of its own, in enjoying Christ's embraces, but my infirmity resists..."(1.34.106). Aelred's memory of how Simon served as his model in the monastic life and of the "spiritual kisses" they enjoyed together (1.34.109) leads him to a painful exposure of his own bereft condition (1.34.109–112), one so deeply personal that he recognizes that some will blame him, "considering my love too carnal" (*nimis carnalem existimantes amorem meum*). He leaves judgment to God, offering his tears as "the sacrifice I offer You for my most beloved friend" (1.34.113). The lament closes with Aelred's reflection on Simon's last words, the repetition of *misericordia* (see Ps 100:1), which reminds the grieving monk of the goal that he and his friend sought together in God:

My Lord, what is it I see in this? I surely seem to behold, almost with physical eyes, his mind refreshed by the drink of this verse with an ineffable joy, as it sees its sins swallowed up in the immense sea of divine mercy. . . . It is a delight to behold that soul washed in the fountain of divine mercy after having laid aside the burden of its sins. . . . And now, o soul, return into your rest, because the Lord has been kind to you.[257]

The teaching of the abbot of Rievaulx concerning the direct contact with God in this life for which spiritual friendship prepares us has aspects of considerable originality, though in its broad lines it coheres well with what we have seen in other Cistercian authors. Aelred has little interest in constructing detailed itineraries of the soul's progress to God, though various scriptural themes and theoretical lists of stages of advance are mentioned from time to time.[258] The Englishman is also typical of other Cistercians in the generic way in which he employs the term *contemplatio*, showing none of the concern exhibited by contemporary Victorine authors, for example, in discriminating various stages and types of contemplation.[259] The abbot is more noteworthy for the way in which he employs certain scriptural images to suggest what the ineffable experience may be like.[260]

In discussing spiritual friendship above, we noted several passages in which Aelred spoke of ascending from the embraces of the friend to the embrace of Jesus himself: "Thus, ascending from that holy love in which we embrace our friend to that in which we embrace Christ, we will joyfully with open mouth pluck the spiritual fruit of friendship."[261] The image of the embrace (*amplexus*), especially as found in the Song of Songs, even more than the kiss, seems to have been Aelred's favorite way to suggest the most intimate affective contact between people and between God and humans.[262] At the end of the *Mirror of Charity* Aelred presents first a beautiful picture of spiritual friends sharing spiritual kisses and the most intimate conversation "in the embrace of charity" (*in amplexu caritatis* [3.39.109]), and then suggests its fitting conclusion by picturing John, the beloved disciple, reposing on the sacred breast of Jesus "as a special sign of love" (*in signum praecipue dilectionis* [3.39.110]). The embrace that leads to holy repose probably comes as close to expressing the inexpressible as Aelred could manage.[263]

This helps explain the English abbot's fascination with the Sabbath, the divine rest, as a central mode of expressing the soul's goal, both in this life and the next. Of course, the appeal to the Sabbath rest is found in many medieval monks, as we have seen in Peter Damian (see chapter 4, p. 143) and in some other Cistercians. But for Aelred the Sabbath was an essential symbol, one particularly revelatory of the mystery of God's *caritas*. The mystery of the Sabbath is discussed in some detail in book 1 of the

Charity (1.18.51–22.64, as well as 32.92 and 33.95). Christ himself is even identified as the true Sabbath in the same book (1.27.78). In book 3 he spells out the distinction of the three forms of Sabbath–the Sabbath of Days referring to love of self; the Sabbath of Years, meaning love of neighbor; and the Sabbath of Sabbaths referring to the love of God that leads to mystical rapture. (This outline provides the structure for the whole discussion; see the initial outline in 3.1.1–2.5).[264] The Sabbath of Sabbaths consists of the perfection of the sevenfold gift of the Spirit (7 x 7) to which has been added the "One" that represents God's unity and our union with him:

> Because there is no division in unity, may there be no mental distraction there through [attention to] differences; but let it be one in the One, with the One, through the One, about the One, knowing the One, savoring the One, and because it is always one, always being at rest, and thus enjoying a perpetual Sabbath.[265]

This desire for rest in the Absolute Unity of God not only reminds us of Isaac of Stella but is also strangely reminiscent of passages later found in a very different mystic, Meister Eckhart.[266]

We should not look to the abbot of Rievaulx for any detailed theoretical discussions of mystical union. It is not surprising that he uses the key scriptural tag of 1 Corinthians 6:17, the *unitas spiritus* text, less frequently than other major Cistercians and nowhere provides any detailed explanation of union in the manner of William of St. Thierry.[267] Like William and others (and unlike Bernard), he was willing to speak of our union with God as creating "one something" (*unum*), as well as "one spirit," but we should not press him for an explanation of what this might entail.[268] Aelred is important for his contribution to the exploration of how human affectivity, especially that of friendship, leads to and even forms a part of the experience of God, rather than for any analysis of the metaphysical and epistemological implications of mystical union.

Finally, when we turn to the question of the effect that such experience of God should have in the life of the monk or religious, we are not surprised to find a fairly standard teaching on the relation of action and contemplation,[269] which need not delay us here, as well as a variation on the ordering of charity, the major way twelfth-century mystics presented the social meaning of mysticism. It is perhaps not unusual that Aelred spoke not only of the *ordo affectus* and the *ordinatio caritatis* but also of the *ordinatio amicitiae*. The English abbot's sense of the cosmic role of *caritas* gives his teaching a somewhat different flavor from that of his fellow Cistercians, but what he has to say about the actual *ordo caritatis* does not differ substantially from what we have already seen in other twelfth-century white monks. Aelred's definition of *amor ordinatus* as that by which "a person does not love what should not be loved, loves whatever is to be loved, but not more than it should be loved . . . ," is pretty standard fare.[270] Aelred does have something to add when he discusses how our innate affections or attractions are to be ordered within the overall program where both reason and affection guide the soul to its destination. The long treatment of the six forms of *affectus* in the *Mirror of Charity* (3.11.31–30.73), despite all its digressions, can be seen as an exercise on how the affections/attractions are to be set in order so that *caritas* may find her proper balance.[271] It is also fitting that *Spiritual Friendship* expands the traditional notion of *caritas ordinata* to include *amicitia ordinata*, which the abbot defines as "reason ruling affection so that we attend not so much to the pleasure of the friends as to the benefit of the group."[272]

Aelred of Rievaulx occupies a special place among the Cistercian mystical writers of the twelfth century. No Cistercian, of course, can rival Bernard of Clairvaux for the stylistic virtuosity with which he attempts the impossible task of conveying what the experience of God may be like, but both for his style and his content, Aelred was unique. The abbot of Rievaulx was not a profound speculative theologian, like William of St. Thierry, one whose thought still challenges those who investigate the mystery of the Trinity and the nature of the kind of knowledge of God which mystics claim. Despite these limitations, Aelred is especially representative, at least to a contemporary audience, of why the Cistercians made a difference. The appeal to experience that formed the leitmotif of all Cistercian mysticism seems somehow more accessible in Aelred's personal and at times painful expressions of how he actually "felt" his friendships as part of the quest for God than it may be in Bernard's lush evocations of male–female erotic symbolization of the encounter with God.[273]

By explaining how experiential knowledge of God is rooted in the life of true friendship, that is, that *really* loving God in Christ is the product of a love that surpasses all mere human love while still subsuming it, Aelred provided a whole new dimension to the traditional understanding of mysticism as a "knowledge by connaturality."[274] His *amicitia spiritualis* takes its place alongside Bernard's *amor sponsalis* as the main contributions to the Cistercian mysticism of love. This is more than enough to guarantee the abbot of Rievaulx an honored position among the mystics of the Western tradition.

CHAPTER 8

Visionaries and Contemplatives in Twelfth-Century Monasticism

TWELFTH-CENTURY MYSTICISM has broader parameters than the contributions made by the Cistercians, just as the Cistercian reform was not the only revitalization of religious life created in the century. The renewal of the canonical order, that is, a form of communal living under the *Rule of Augustine* among priests who also usually shared pastoral duties, produced a significant body of mystical texts, especially at the Abbey of St. Victor on the outskirts of Paris. This early center of the growth of scholastic theology represents a new option in the history of Western mysticism, one based on the combination of the canonical life and the new type of scholastic theological reflection employed by the Victorines. It will be taken up in the following chapter.

Among the non-Cistercian forms of twelfth-century monastic life mystical elements were by no means lacking. None of these varieties of monasticism, even those labeled "traditional" in modern times, were merely static replicas of the monastic practices that prevailed in earlier centuries. All had been deeply touched by the tide of reform, both the renewal of the monastic life and the debate over the reform of the church. Rupert of Deutz (1077–1129), for example, though a traditional black monk, was a strong defender of the Gregorian party who suffered exile for his views. His numerous writings, largely biblical commentaries, concentrate on presenting the inner meaning of the history of salvation through the exegesis of scripture and the monastic office. As Jean Leclercq put it: "He is the source *par excellence* for traditional monastic theology."[1] But Rupert was also an innovator, especially in the way in which he related visionary experience to the task of exegesis. More traditional mystical elements centering on themes like *contemplatio-otium* are found in other twelfth-century black monks, such as Peter of Celle (ca. 1115–1182), who was an admirer of the new reformed monastic groups, as well as in the noted abbot of Cluny, Peter the Venerable (ca. 1092–1156). While Rupert and the two Peters were not mystics in the same sense as the Cistercians previously investigated, the mystical aspects of their writings cast light on how early medieval Benedictine mysticism continued to extend its life into the twelfth century. The traditional Benedictines also maintained an interest in the personal appropriation of the Song of Songs, as evidenced especially in the Middle High German poetic translation and commentary on the Song usually known as the *St. Trudpert Song of Songs*, a text that foreshadows the development of erotic mysticism in female vernacular authors in the thirteenth century.

The story of the Carthusian order also underlines the fact that twelfth-century monastic mysticism was not a Cistercian monopoly. The Carthusians made a most significant contribution to medieval Christianity by reviving eremitism. Founded by Bruno of Cologne in 1084, these hermits became a real order in the mid-1120s when Guigo I, fifth prior of the mother house of La Chartreuse, drew up the customs for the monasteries following this way of life. Their severe form of monasticism guaranteed a slow but remarkably continuous history (there were thirty-seven "Charterhouses" [*cartusiae*] by 1200). The Carthusian commitment to scribal activity gave them a special place in the copying and dissemination of mystical texts, but Carthusian authors also made their own contributions to the history of mysticism. The full impact of Carthusian mysticism came in the late Middle Ages, but the story begins here. These and the other non-Cistercian monastic mystics of the twelfth century can be placed in two broad categories—the visionary and the contemplative—both of which raise important issues for the understanding of mysticism.

The Visionary Element

The twelfth century was an age of visionaries, and visionaries of a different sort from those prevalent in the early Middle Ages. Peter Dinzelbacher's survey of medieval visionary literature argues for a significant shift in the form of visions in the twelfth century.[2] The type of vision that flourished between the sixth and the early twelfth centuries emphasized the experience of a unique and unexpected transportation, usually of considerable duration, to heaven or to hell. During this rapture the visionary, often a sinner or indifferent Christian, was given a tour of the afterlife designed to effect a personal conversion that would provide a warning to other believers. The second type of vision, which began in the twelfth century and became predominant in the later Middle Ages, tended to be a repeatable experience of shorter duration. These visions were less concerned with conversion and threat of judgment than with proving the sanctity of the seer and conveying some particular theological message. Such visions centered on an encounter with a heavenly figure; they often tended to take on a mystical character, in the sense of including or implying some form of direct experience of God. Obviously, Dinzelbacher's two categories are ideal types which cannot be sharply discriminated or chronologically divided in any simple way, but they help us think about an important and controversial issue in the history of mysticism.

Early modern investigation of mysticism, as exemplified in such studies as Johann Görries, *Die Christliche Mystik* (1836–42), treated mysticism primarily as the physical or psychological manifestation of the "supernatural" elements of religion, that is, either unexplained corporeal phenomena–such as stigmata, levitation, unusual trances, and inedia–or else claims to visions of heavenly beings. While the physical phenomena sometimes associated with mystics are no longer seen as central to mysticism (a view in which modern study accords with the predominant voice of traditional theology), the relation of visionary experience to mysticism remains ambivalent. Visions of various kinds have been important to Christian mysticism from the start.[3] But is mysticism to be identified with visionary experience? Put more precisely: Must every mystic be a visionary? Is every visionary to be considered a mystic?

If we understand vision (*visio/revelatio*) as an evident perception of some form of nonterrestrial reality, either by way of transportation to or by the irruption of these realms into the present world,[4] we can begin to grasp why it is not necessary to think that every mystic need be a visionary, in the sense of having received a visualizable perception of God. Many mystics have experienced visions of the heavenly world, often including some manifestation of God. Many others have not. Many of the mystics who have reflected on the relation between *visio Dei* as a visualizable perception of God and *visio Dei* as the conscious experience of God's immediate presence have insisted that the two are independent, if often related, phenomena. That is to say, visions, at least visions of the corporeal or imaginative types carefully delineated by Augustine, do not constitute the essence of mysticism.[5]

If every mystic need not be a visionary, we can still wonder to what extent those who have claimed to have experienced visualizable perceptions of the heavenly world and its inhabitants can be spoken of as expressing some form of mysticism. There would seem to be a *prima facie* argument that all visionaries should be thought of as also being mystics, if only because they claim to have had contact with the divine realm in special ways not available through the ordinary sacramental and liturgical channels. A close examination of visionary accounts, however, makes the relationship more ambiguous, leading to the conclusion that each case must be taken on its own merits.

For example, a number of medieval visionaries report contact with saints, angels, and especially the Blessed Virgin, but make little or no mention of "seeing" Christ or God. Others do talk about seeing God, either in his spiritual or incarnate form, but in a manner that does not seem to center on some form of immediate contact with God understood as having a transformative effect on the seer and, at least potentially, on others through the seer's teaching. Obviously, the discrimination among these ways of understanding *visio Dei* will continue to remain open to a variety of interpretations. The argument that I will try to advance, both here and in the volumes to come, is that it is not so much the employment of the category of "vision" in itself, as the way in which *visio Dei* is related to modes of expressing a sense of divine immediacy which enables us to discriminate among authors who are to be considered "mystical" and those who are not. In this discussion it may be helpful to distinguish three categories: mystics, in the sense of those who recount experiences of the immediate presence of God; mystical authors, who have not only had such experiences, but have written and taught about the process of attaining and living out lives based on mystical experience of God's presence; and visionaries, whose visions may or may not be mystical in content, depending on whether or not they involve direct contact with the divine.

A number of important twelfth-century writers provide some of the earliest test cases for the problematic of the relation between the visionary and the mystical elements in the history of Christianity. Prominent among these are Rupert of Deutz (mentioned above) and two German Benedictine nuns, Hildegard of Bingen (1098–1179) and Elisabeth of Schönau (1128–1165), as well as the Calabrian seer Joachim of Fiore (ca. 1135–1202), who was a Cistercian before founding his own Florensian order of monks. These figures were among the most influential spiritual leaders of their age. In modern times each has been claimed for the ranks of the mystics, and each provides a different perspective on the difficult task of relating visionary experience to mysticism. Elisabeth seems to me to be an example of a visionary who is clearly not a mystic in the sense in which the term is being used here. Though both Hildegard and Joachim report mystical experiences–that is, they give accounts of immediate perceptions of divine reality–their writings as such do not center on how believers attain and are affected by direct consciousness of God in this life. For this reason I prefer to distinguish their works from those of the mystical writers we examined in earlier chapters and to call them visionaries but not mystical authors. I would also argue that Rupert of Deutz is best not thought of as a mystical author, though the abbot's use of detailed mystical experiences to authenticate theological claims provides important indication of a trend that was to become more prevalent in the following century.

Rupert of Deutz

Rupert of Deutz is not only a test case for the relation between visions and mysticism but is also a fascinating example of a typically twelfth-century issue: the tension between tradition and innovation.[6] From one perspective he appears to be an arch-conservative, especially in his attacks on scholastic theology and his opposition to new forms of religious life, both those of the Cistercians and the reformed canons. But Rupert was also one of the great originators of the era: his writings constitute not only a summation of traditional monastic theology but also contain important new departures both in exegesis and in doctrine. For example, Rupert's commentary on the Apocalypse prepared the way for the more radical break with tradition later effected by Joachim of Fiore, and his thoroughgoing Marian interpretation of the Song of Songs was one of the first of its kind.[7] For the history of mysticism, however, Rupert's importance rests in the way in which he appealed to his visions as the source for his teaching.

The abbot's visionary autobiography, contained in book 12 of his commentary on Matthew entitled *The Glory and Honor of the Son of Man*, composed about 1127, is best understood against the background of his doctrine of two kinds of knowledge of God. As the result of a conversation with his friend Abbot Cuno of Siegburg in 1123, Rupert was moved to write *The Victory of the Word of God*, a treatise on the history of salvation as the epic conflict between the kingdom of the Word of God and Satan's realm. He opens this work by distinguishing between knowledge of the Word "from works" (*ex operibus*) and "from himself" (*ex semetipso*). The whole of creation, both the unseen and the seen world, reveal the Word as Creator. This knowledge is contrasted with the "experience" (*experimentum*) given only to the few, "when the Word himself is known in more splendid fashion by surpassing grace as he visits some beloved soul, strongly and sweetly attracting it by contact with his very substance."[8] Rupert's comments on such experience, which he describes as "ineffable," clearly mark this out as a form of mystical knowledge.[9]

The abbot knew whereof he spoke, as the twelfth book of *The Glory and Honor of the Son of Man* shows in detail. The first two-thirds of this book is a remarkable spiritual autobiography in which the aged abbot of Deutz, at the bidding of his confidant Cuno (now archbishop of Regensburg), describes the visionary experiences that were the foundation for his audacious literary career.[10] Though previous monastic authors, such as Othloh of St. Emmeran in the 1060s, had tied visionary experiences to vocational crises, Rupert's narrative is something new, especially for the light it casts on forms of mystical validation.[11]

From the perspective of the history of mystical narratives, we might say that Rupert, though observing a more traditional form of monasticism and a strong opponent of Cistercian novelties, was in some ways more prophetic of things to come than the major Cistercian authors. Bernard, William, and Aelred were restrained in talking about their own experiences of divine visitations, let alone in using them to authenticate the validity of their biblical interpretation. Rupert's defense of the controversial aspects of his exegesis on the basis of the charism given in his mystical visions is a forerunner of strategies often found in the later Middle Ages, especially among the women mystics. (This demonstrates, once again, how difficult it is to categorize twelfth-century figures as *either* traditional *or* innovative.)

Rupert's autobiographical narrative is remarkable for the way in which it weaves together precise descriptions of his own visions, mostly dream visions in which he is lightly sleeping,[12] with a sophisticated appeal to key biblical personalities and texts long associated with mystical consciousness of God. The account is structured around nine visions, the first five of which took place in 1100, while the final four happened eight years later in the year of his ordination.[13]

The narrative is introduced by a reference to the great chariot vision at the beginning of Ezekiel, which Gregory the Great had interpreted as signifying the inner christological meaning of the Bible (see chapter 2, p. 49). Rupert doubtless had this interpretation in mind, but invocation of the vision also allows him to create a typological parallel between his own personal crisis and that of the prophet. Like Ezekiel, Rupert finds himself in the Babylon of this world under the dominion of the tyrant Nebuchadnezzer-Satan.[14] Also like Ezekiel, divine visions will give him his true calling.

Early one morning, as he was seated behind the altar in the Mary-Chapel kissing and adoring the crucifix he had taken down from the altar, Rupert reports,

> ... my eyes were opened and I saw the Son of God; while awake I saw the living Son of Man on the cross. I saw him not with corporeal vision, but my bodily eyes suddenly vanished so that I might see, and better ones, that is, interior eyes, were opened. ... And what was his appearance like? Human tongue cannot grasp it with words.[15] It is enough to say that I there perceived in a brief fashion what he so truly said: "Learn of me, because I am meek and humble of heart" (Matt 11:29).[16]

Rupert records that this experience of *visio spiritualis* (to use Augustine's terminology) lasted only a brief moment but that the "ineffable taste of its sweetness," which he sees as an example of the consolations given by the Holy Spirit, lingered in "the mouth of the soul" a considerable time (*aliquamdiu*), reminding him of the verse, "Taste and see that the Lord is sweet" (Ps 33:9), a classic text in the monastic mystical tradition.[17]

This inaugural vision of the crucified Savior is the only fully waking experience Rupert reports, suggesting that for him it was through this form of contact with Jesus on the cross that access was given to the inner world of dream vision where both the God-man and the Trinity become visible.[18] The second vision describes how in his childish sorrow over the evil spirits that still threatened him, he went to sleep at the time of his accustomed special devotions and saw "a great light like the sun looming over him" and heard the sign summoning him to the monastery church. Still in his dream he went to the church where two choirs were singing psalms, but the Devil prevented him from entering and he awoke.[19]

The next morning the same thing happened, but this time he entered the church as Mass was being celebrated by a white-haired bishop. At the offertory procession he experienced a vision of the Trinity. "On the right at the edge of the altar stood three persons of such revered bearing and dignity that no tongue could describe them. Two were quite old, that is, with very white hair; the third was a beautiful youth of royal dignity as could be told from his garb."[20] One of the aged figures kissed him and then the beautiful youth, who is, of course, Jesus, rescued him from the demons who sought to wound him. "Then the three persons, of large and equal stature, stood around me, tiny as I was, and when a very large book had been opened they placed me on it and lifted me on high."[21] The figure who had kissed him then promised him that he would become more splendid than the golden reliquaries on the altar. When the three figures departed, Rupert noticed that he was naked, so he rushed back to his bed and there awoke. The interpretation that the monk himself supplies here emphasizes the vocational centrality of this vision in his life. Being raised up on the book indicates that God will open up the Bible to him so that his exegesis will surpass even those of the fathers whose memory is like the golden reliquaries. A potent claim indeed!

The fourth vision, which took place three days later, confirmed this special status. Here God the Father appears as the "Ancient of Days" (Dan 7:9) and commands him, "Friend, give to me what I have done to you." Rupert grasps his hand as a sign of pardon and the Father embraces him and kisses him so intensely that "the great force of holy and divine pleasure woke me from sleep."[22] Finally, on the vigil of the Feast of St. Matthew, an aged figure appeared to him in his sleep and told him that in eight years he would die.

For the next eight years Rupert meditated on the meaning of this message, which he took in a literal sense. Reading Augustine's *City of God* (specifically 1.11.10–14), however, showed him that the death referred to might well be that of constant meditation upon the last end rather than literal dying. At this juncture he prayed to the Holy Spirit to enlighten him about the issue and thereupon received a second series of dream visions that revealed to him the fullness of God's plans for him, previously hinted at in the vision of his being raised up on the open book.

The first vision of this second series concerns the Holy Spirit and thus completes the trinitarian aspect of his encounters with God.[23] Lightly asleep on his bed, he sees a multitude of evil spirits descending upon him. His invocation of the Holy Spirit at first puts them to flight, but they soon return and he is compelled to flee to a meadow enclosed with columns where he encounters "an old man bearing a staff in his hand whom I recognized as the Holy Spirit." The Spirit addresses him as "little child," in the manner of those recently baptized.[24] The purpose of the vision seems to be to signify that Rupert had undergone a second baptism, as underlined by further visionary perceptions of the Holy Spirit as "a very pure fire" (*ignis valde serenus*) and as the "shade" (*umbraculum*) created by two wings.

Rupert's desire to die and be with the Lord, as the "hart desires the fountain of waters" (Ps 41:2–3), produced three days of internal struggle over the meaning of these events that ended in a seventh vision which again occurred during "light sleep" on the night before Ash Wednesday. Here he beholds himself talking with a friend about his desire to die when suddenly, "I see, as it were, heaven above open slightly and a glowing golden mass (*talentum*) of ineffable substance swiftly descend from there upon my living substance. Heavier than gold and sweeter than honey, it fell into my breast and by its size and weight woke me up right away."[25] What follows is even stranger. Lying awake on his bed, Rupert waits to see what will happen to the golden substance that has fallen into his breast. At first, it is still, but then it begins to move in "the womb of the interior person, the soul's womb" (*uterum interioris hominis, uterum animae*), until "this living thing and true life" circulates throughout his whole interior, expanding it by its floods "until finally the ultimate pouring forth, like some vast overflowing river, led me to understand and to perceive that the whole capacity of the heart or soul was full and could hold no more."[26] Rupert seeks to behold the hidden "face" or appearance (*facies*) of this interior golden substance but to no avail. Finally, the eyes of the inner person see it flow out from the visionary's left side where it then becomes visible "liquid gold." This experience seems to be a kind of spiritual pregnancy, under the influence of the Holy Spirit, perhaps a typologically daring claim to be a new Mary who gives birth to the golden reality of the christological meaning of the biblical text.[27]

This interpretation is strengthened by the final two visions which are connected with Christ and also with Rupert's ordination to the priesthood, the institutional warrant for his career as biblical interpreter. These showings, which make considerable use of the Song of Songs (cited twice in vision 8 and three times in vision 9), are more erotic in flavor, but with an eroticism that differs from that of Bernard and William of St. Thierry in being less concerned with the feminine or bridal identity taken on by human lovers of God.

After a discussion of his reasons for putting off ordination, Rupert recounts a dream vision that came to him while he considered his unworthiness for the priesthood. He saw himself standing before the altar upon which there was placed a cross with Christ's image. Exchanging mutual gazes with the Savior, he desired to come closer to kiss and embrace the Lord. At Christ's invitation he entered the altar that opened up to receive him. Rupert continues: "As I impatiently entered, I took hold 'of him whom my soul loves' (Song 1:6). I held him, I embraced him, I kissed him for a long time. I felt how deeply he appreciated this sign of love when in the midst of the kiss he opened his mouth so that I could kiss him more deeply."[28] Upon awakening, Rupert interpreted the vision in terms of the clarity of understanding he had thereby attained of the "depths of the mysteries" (*profunda sacramentorum*), and therefore decided that he was ready to be ordained.

The final vision, which came thirty days after his ordination, was also christological and erotic. He dreamt that a prone extended human figure with hidden face descended upon him and completely filled the substance of his soul more deeply and quickly than wax fills a seal. He immediately awoke and understood the experience in terms of the Song of Songs text, "My soul has been liquified" (Song 5:6).[29] (At this point he insists that the pleasure was so great that had it not been of brief duration his soul would have left the body.) Especially noteworthy, however, is the conclusion of the account which summarizes the message repeated over and over again in the narrative: these experiences of God were the source for Rupert's writing career. "From that time on 'I have opened my mouth' (Ps 118:131), and I have never been able to stop writing. Up to the present day, I am unable to be silent, even if I wanted to."[30]

It would be difficult not to accept Rupert's visions as mystical encounters in the sense that they speak, in highly concrete terms, of direct encounters with the persons of the Trinity and the God-man. His experiences seem to be of the kind Augustine would have called *visio spiritualis*. These imaginative appearances of God not only convey ineffable sweetness, but their overall intent, as we have seen, was to grant the monk something more like an Augustinian *visio intellectualis* of the inner truth of the Bible. Indeed, the abbot of Deutz is highly traditional in his insistence that it is in relation to the biblical text itself that what we call mystical experience is both possible and actually realized. In the prefatory letter to his *Commentary on the Apocalypse* (ca. 1121), he wrote to Archbishop Frederick of Cologne, "When we read or understand scripture aren't we seeing God face-to-face? Truly, the vision of God which will be made perfect at some day is already begun here through scripture."[31]

What is peculiar about Rupert, however, is that his biblical commentaries and treatises contain almost nothing of the traditional mystical themes of monastic biblical exegesis. Meditation on scripture *is* the contemplative life for him, but he says little about *lectio, meditatio, oratio, contemplatio, otium,* and the like, as he pursues his extensive work of the christological interpretation of scripture.[32] Rupert's writings, then, with the exception of book 12 of *The Glory and Honor of the Son of Man,* are not mystical texts in the sense of writings designed to teach his audience how to attain contemplation, though they take their rise from one of the earliest detailed accounts of a series of mystical visions in Western literature. These visions mark the abbot of Deutz as the ancestor of a complex vein of authenticating mystical experiences that will grow richer in the later Middle Ages.[33]

Hildegard of Bingen and Elisabeth of Schönau

Hildegard of Bingen, the "Sibyl of the Rhine," is an even more complex example of the relationship between vision and mysticism. The German abbess, who can well be called the first great woman theologian in Christian history, was a visionary whose mode of perceiving divine mysteries escape all the inherited categories available to her, and perhaps our modern ones as well. Recent appreciation of the profundity of her theological insight has led to an extensive literature, as well as to a significant disagreement about whether or not she should be termed a mystic. One of her most sensitive readers, Peter Dronke, has said, "She is clearly of mystical disposition—her sense of the divine presence is the lodestar of her life."[34] A number of contemporary students of the German visionary, however, have seen her primarily as a prophet and apocalyptic reformer, agreeing with Caroline Bynum, who says that "Hildegard was not, technically speaking, a mystic at all."[35] These positions may not be as contradictory as they seem, if only because of the subtle qualifications each scholar introduces. Hildegard was certainly not a mystical *author* in the sense of having a major role in the tradition of Christian writing concerning the preparation for, enjoyment of, and effects produced by the consciousness of the immediate divine presence in this life.[36] Even less than Rupert (who did at least leave his readers the extended mystical autobiography studied above), did she display interest in the standard motifs of mystical teaching found in the Benedictine tradition. Nor are her writings like those of the later medieval women mystics. Still, when Hildegard discusses the mode of her visionary experience one can see why Peter Dronke can speak of her "mystical disposition."

Hildegard was not reluctant to talk about these experiences, especially because her position as a woman teacher and preacher was in need of some form of special validation. As Barbara Newman has pointed out, the German abbesses's claims for the authority of her works on the basis of her special experiences of God are, if anything, even stronger than those of the abbot of Deutz.[37] But while Rupert's visions fit into recognizable categories–traditional dream visions, although with new forms of erotic content that were to become more powerful in subsequent centuries–Hildegard's revelations are *sui generis.*[38]

The most complete account comes from the letter that she wrote late in her life to an inquisitive monk, Guibert of Gembloux, who went on to become her last secretary. In response to a series of queries Guibert addressed to her in 1175, Hildegard provided a detailed reflection on the nature of the visions she had experienced since the age of three. I quote from this important text at length:

> Since my infancy, however, when I was not yet strong in my bones and nerves and veins, I have always seen this vision in my soul, even till now, when I am more than seventy years old. And as God wills, in this vision my spirit mounts upwards, into the height of the firmament and into changing air, and dilates itself among different nations, even though they are in far-off regions and places remote from me. And because I see these things in such a manner, for this reason I also behold them in changing forms of clouds and other created things. But I hear them not with my physical ears, nor with my heart's thoughts, nor do I perceive them by bringing any of my five senses to bear–but only in my soul, my physical eyes open, so that I never suffer their failing in loss of consciousness (*exstasis*); no, I see these things wakefully, day and night. And I am constantly oppressed by illnesses, and so enmeshed in intense pains that they threaten to bring on my death; but so far God has stayed me.

Noteworthy here is the seer's insistence that her visions, unlike those of Rupert and others, have nothing to do with dream states.[39] More remarkable is her claim that they do not take place in rapture, though, as we shall see below, she admits to have been bereft of her senses at least on one occasion. These two facts alone signify that the abbesses's way of seeing was unusual. Even more original is her discrimination of two forms of seeing based on two kinds of light, a distinction that allows us insight into the central issue of how far these visions were forms of immediate perception of God:

> The brightness (*lumen*) that I see is not spatial, yet it is far, far more lucent than a cloud that envelops the sun. I cannot contemplate height or length or breadth in it;[40] and I call it "the shadow of the living brightness" (*umbra viventis lucis*).[41] And as sun, moon, and stars appear mirrored in water, so scriptures, discourses, virtues, and some works of men take form for me and are reflected radiant in this brightness....And the things I write are those I see and hear through the vision, nor do I set down words other than those I hear. . . . And the words that I see and hear through the vision are not like words that come from human lips, but like a sparkling flame and a cloud moved in pure air.

To this kind of light Hildegard contrasts a second, deeper form:

> And in that same brightness I sometimes, not often, see another light, which I call "the living light" (*lux vivens*); when and how I see it, I cannot express; and for the time I do see it, all sadness and all anguish is taken from me, so that then I have the air of an innocent young girl and not of a little old woman.[42]

The term *visio*, as used by medieval authors, indicates both the experience of seeing and the content seen. In Hildegard, because of its permanent quality, *visio* also seems to refer to a capacity of her soul.[43] Her experience of the interior vision of the *umbra viventis lucis*, however, is different from other medieval accounts.[44] Although it is characterized by the synaesthia often associated with the spiritual senses ("the words that I *see and hear* . . . are like a sparkling flame"), Hildegard perceives this vision as a quasi-physical, though internal and constant, experience of a light within which or upon which something like a movie screen, appear the complex allegorical figures, often female, and the texts that serve as the basis for her major visionary works.[45] The association of this constant light with her illnesses and her "airy" constitution, as well as the sense of the soul's elevation and dilation mentioned here, have led modern interpreters to try to find medical analogues for these descriptions. Most often they have pointed to some form of migraine of the type known as a "scintillating scotoma," but the abbesses's descriptions differ from modern examples in emphasizing the permanent character of the light.[46] Hildegard receives a message *from* God in the images she sees reflected in this light, but it does not seem that the *umbra viventis lucis* involves a direct experience *of* God in the mystical sense.

What Hildegard has to say about the experience of the *lux vivens*, how-ever, as well as some aspects of other accounts of her visions, argues for the presence of another, more properly mystical, dimension. The inexpressibil-ity and infrequency of the sight of this form of light, and the effect that it has upon her, clearly suggest that she is talking about an immediate contact with the divine source of the *umbra viventis lucis*. In the preface to the *Scivias*, she also tells how in 1141 she received "a fiery light of exceeding brilliance" from heaven that penetrated her whole brain and heart and gave her imme-diate knowledge of the meaning of the Bible. This is different from the con-stant light experience, which is also discussed here,[47] and it may well be thought of as the earliest manifestation of the more mystical vision associ-ated with the *lux vivens*.

Two other visionary accounts found in autobiographical passages in Hildegard's *Vita* present revelations that are even closer to those found else-where in the mystical tradition. During the course of one experience in 1167 the abbess confesses to have passed beyond consciousness in some form of what was often called *excessus mentis* and sometimes *exstasis*. She says:

> At last in the time that followed I saw a mystic and wondrous vision, such that all my womb was convulsed and my body's sensory powers were extin-guished, because my knowledge was transmuted into another mode, as if I no longer knew myself. And from God's inspiration as it were drops of gentle rain splashed into the knowledge of my mind, just as the Holy Spirit perme-ated John the Evangelist when he sucked supremely deep revelation from the breast of Jesus.[48]

She goes on to say that this experience allowed her to understand the Pro-logue to his Gospel, a text she commented on in book 1 of the *Book of Divine Works*. An account from the 1170s takes on a somewhat different tone. Here "the fairest and most loving man," obviously Christ, appears to her during a time of temptation, casting the demons from her as she longs to look on him forever. This is the closest that Hildegard comes to the erotic connection with Christ that was to become so popular among later female mystics.

Was Hildegard of Bingen a mystic? The evidence of some of her visions gives testimony to experiences of contact with God that would be difficult not to call mystical by the standards employed in this history. But Hilde-gard's writings are not mystical in character, neither in the sense of tradi-tional monastic mysticism centering on *contemplatio*, nor in the manner of the visionary mystics of the later Middle Ages who used their experiences as the basis for works concerned with achieving special forms of divine con-sciousness. Hildegard, poised between two worlds, is a major theological voice, but less a mystic than a prophetic teacher–truly, the "Sibyl of the Rhine."

Elisabeth, a young nun at the Benedictine priory at Schönau, was often linked with Hildegard.[49] Under the year 1158, the *Annals of Pöhlde* (a house of Premonstratensian canons) noted: "In these days also God showed the signs of his power in the frail sex, that is, in his two handmaidens Hildegard on the Rupertsberg near Bingen and Elisabeth in Schönau. He filled them with the spirit of prophecy and through the Gospel he revealed many kinds of visions to them which are extant in [their] writings."[50] Indeed, the younger visionary wrote to the elder, asking for and receiving good advice from the abbess, who described herself in the letter as "a small trumpet note from the living brightness."[51]

Elisabeth's six books were put together with the help of her brother Ekbert, who abandoned a promising ecclesiastical career to enter the male Benedictine house at Schönau about 1155. They were much more widely read in the later Middle Ages than Hildegard's writings, probably because they are less theologically challenging and more in tune with many later medieval visionary accounts.[52] While Elisabeth makes an interesting study for the history of medieval visions, she provides a good example of a type of visionary who should not be considered a mystic.[53] Although she often talks about being in rapture (*in excessu mentis*), what she experiences in these ecstatic states is not so much direct transforming contact with God,[54] as an entry into the heavenly world where messages are communicated to her, often in a mediated fashion by angels, messages meant to be proclaimed to the church through her writings. These revelations often deal with issues of reform directed against the ecclesiastical abuses of the time; others concern the defense of virginity, devotion to angels and saints, and teaching about the Eucharist and purgatory. Elisabeth is a prophet, reformer, and teacher, not a mystic.

Joachim of Fiore

The Calabrian abbot, Joachim of Fiore, provides a final twelfth-century test case for the investigation of the relation between visions and mysticism.[55] Born about 1135, Joachim lived a worldly life before undergoing a conversion experience. About 1167 he went on pilgrimage to the Holy Land, where, according to a later legend, he had a vision of God the Father on Mount Tabor. (Joachim himself never mentions this directly.) Upon his return to Italy, he first lived as a wandering preacher before joining the Cistercians about 1171. In 1183–84, Joachim visited the Cistercian monastery at Casamari south of Rome, where, with the approval of Pope Lucius III, he began writing his three major scriptural works, the *Exposition on the Apocalypse*, the *Ten-Stringed Psaltery*, and the *Book of Concordance*.

Stymied by the difficulties of the last book of the Bible, he had put down his pen for a year, when he experienced the vision he described in the following words:

> After a year, the feast of Easter came around. Awakened from sleep about midnight, something happened to me as I was meditating on this book.... About the middle of the night's silence, as I think, the hour when it is thought that our Lion of the tribe of Judah rose from the dead, as I was meditating, suddenly something of the fullness of this book and of the entire harmony of the Old and New Testaments was perceived with clarity of understanding in my mind's eye. The revelation was made when I was not even mindful of the chapter mentioned above [Apoc 1:10, which had blocked him].[56]

In form, this is an example of what Augustine would have called a *visio intellectualis*, an immediate and infallible reception of divine truth in the mind. The content of this vision, however, is distinctive of Joachim—the gift of *intellectus spiritualis*, the grasp of the presence of the Trinity in history revealed throughout the Bible, but nowhere more completely than in its final book, the Apocalypse, which Joachim described as "the key of things past, the knowledge of things to come, the opening of what is sealed, the uncovering of what is hidden."[57]

This sudden understanding of scripture given by the risen Christ was later deepened by another vision. Joachim was not an abstract thinker. He was a powerful symbolist who by virtue of his discovery of apt and original images to convey his complicated theology of history had few peers in his time, save perhaps Hildegard of Bingen.[58] These mysterious *figurae*, as the abbot called them, were later collected into a book, the noted *Book of Figures* which in many ways is the most accessible of his works. At least one of these figures, by his own testimony, was given to him in a visionary experience that took place at Pentecost in Casamari:

> In the meantime, when I had entered the church to pray to Almighty God before the holy altar, there came upon me an uncertainty concerning belief in the Trinity.... When that happened I prayed with all my might. I was very frightened and I called upon the Holy Spirit whose feast day it was to deign to show me the holy mystery of the Trinity.... I repeated this and I began to sing the psalms to complete the number I had intended. At this moment without delay the shape of a ten-stringed psaltery appeared in my mind. The mystery of the Holy Trinity shone so brightly and clearly in it that I was at once impelled to cry out, "What God is as great as our God?" (Ps 76:14).[59]

Drawing upon traditional Augustinian terminology once again, we are dealing here with an imaginative *visio spiritualis*, but one which, contrary to

Augustine's teaching, seems to provide a form of direct contact with the innermost divine mystery of the Trinity.

Joachim was traditional in tying mystical insight to scripture. The Easter vision first opened the doors to the deeper total understanding of the Bible that he called *intellectus spiritualis*. The Pentecost vision, which took place through the gift of the Holy Spirit while chanting the psalms, gave the abbot both experience of and absolute conviction about the mystery of the Trinity, the essential content of the biblical text. Joachim's notion of *intellectus spiritualis*, then, implies a form of direct contact with God. For the abbot all *intellectus spiritualis* originates in Christ and finds its fulfillment in the Spirit of Christ, that is, the Holy Spirit.

What was not traditional about Joachim, however, was the way in which he saw the growth of the spiritual understanding of the trinitarian mystery as moving forward toward a stage of perfection within history that he spoke of as the *tertius status*, the third age of history, the *status* particularly ascribed to the Holy Spirit when the church would rejoice in full possession of the *intellectus spiritualis*. From the perspective of his theology of history, Joachim's two visions can be seen as proleptic experiences of what the whole Body of Christ will enjoy on earth after the impending persecution of Antichrist, which he saw as imminent. The gift of spiritual understanding that had been given the apostles at Easter and completed in them at Pentecost would become the possession of the entire church during the third age and would serve as a prelude to perfect heavenly contemplation, as a text from Joachim's *Enchiridion on the Apocalypse*, indicates:

> It remains for us to say that the mystery is to be completed in such a way that by means of what was first given to the apostles at Easter we may receive the gift, the time of the third *status,* in which we will be admitted more fully to the contemplation which we seem to have received up to now for righteous action. Grace has been given us for the sake of the grace [to come] (cf. John 1:16). What reached its completion in the apostles at Pentecost, will be completed in all the saints after the world's last day.[60]

This conviction that a more complete contact with God lies in the future explains why the abbot of Fiore adopted many of the traditional biblical texts concerning mystical consciousness into his three-*status* explanation of the course of salvation history. For example, a text in the *Exposition on the Apocalypse* takes the account of Paul's ascension to the third heaven (2 Cor 12:1–3) as indicating the transition from the first heaven of the Old Testament, through the second heaven of the New Testament, to the third heaven of the *intelligentia spiritualis* of the third *status*. "In the first infants are taught, in the second adolescents are formed, in the third the friends are inebriated."[61]

This is not the place to attempt a detailed analysis of Joachim's notoriously complex theory of history or to try to unravel the limited and obscure comments he makes about the *ecclesia spiritualis*, the utopian monasticized "spiritual church" of the coming third *status*.[62] But the abbot's belief in a coming age of perfect contemplation to be enjoyed by the whole church does raise the issue of how far his views can be spoken of as a form of mystical teaching.

Ernesto Buonaiuti, one of the pioneers of the study of Joachim in this century, claimed the abbot for the ranks of the mystics on the basis of a distinction between "solitary mysticism" and what he called the "associative mysticism" (*misticismo associato*, perhaps better rendered as "corporate-social mysticism"), which attains God not in individual experience but in group participation in the same revealed realities.[63] Buonaiuti did not spell out the characteristics of this form of mysticism, and his distinction risks forgetting that all Christian mysticism, especially prior to the crisis of mysticism in the seventeenth century, was rooted, in one way or another, in the corporate life of the church. Still, Buonaiuti's claim that Joachim may be best understood as a mystic who stressed that the final form of access to God possible in this life lies in the future, not in the past or present, and that its perfection will be characterized not only by fullness of what is now enjoyed in part, but that this fullness must also be corporate, that is, enjoyed by the whole church, though in diverse fashion according to one's place in life (see the *Dispositio novi ordinis* figure), merits consideration. Can we speak of a new form of corporate social mysticism of an apocalyptic character that begins with the abbot of Fiore?[64]

In considering this possibility, we can first of all note how a positive answer to this question would point to a second major intersection of mysticism and apocalypticism (if I may employ these ambiguous generalizations) in the history of Christianity. In *The Foundations of Mysticism* the argument was made that the visionary component of the ancient Jewish apocalyptic tradition was an important part of the background to Christian mysticism.[65] A plausible line of interpretation even suggests that Paul's ascent to the third heaven recounted in 2 Corinthians 12 can be seen as a Christian transposition of apocalyptic ascents to the heavenly realm.[66] Joachim of Fiore never claimed to have enjoyed an ascent to heaven, and his version of apocalypticism is different from those of the Jewish and Christian ancestors of Christian mystical traditions, but it seems to me that the abbot of Fiore did indeed create a new fusion of apocalyptic and mystical traditions through his visions, figures, and writings.

It might still be argued that Joachim's distinctive form of mysticism—oriented as it is toward the coming fullness of mystical consciousness in the third *status*–is not really a significant part of the history of Western mysticism because it lacked real successors. This is only partly true. Joachim was, to be sure, an influential figure, as the research of Marjorie E. Reeves and others has shown.[67] His influence was often indirect, and even more often garbled, incorrect, and even at odds with his own intentions. What I have identified as the mystical aspect of the Calabrian's thought in most cases does seem to have been lost on his followers who concentrated on aspects of Joachim's thought that overlooked his desire for the more complete immediacy with God to be found in coming last age. Still, there were significant mystical thinkers, of whom Bonaventure was the greatest, whose theories contained elements of the Calabrian's corporate apocalyptic mysticism, elements not always appreciated by former scholarship, which has often divided the "mystical" and the "apocalyptic" dimensions of the great Franciscan. Joachim's visions, then, can be said to embody a new form of mysticism created in the twelfth century, one which will have a further history, if only a minor one, in the centuries to come.

Monastic Contemplation

The desire to attain whatever foretaste of contemplation may be possible in this life, the main goal of monks in the West, at least since the time of Cassian, continued to be strong among both reformed Benedictines and new orders like the Carthusians in the twelfth century. Though not as imposing as the Cistercians, these monastic authors take a rightful place in the Western mystical tradition.

The Black Monks

A full survey of all the Benedictine authors of the twelfth century would doubtless turn up a host of witnesses to the main themes of the monastic mysticism discussed in chapter 4. This is scarcely necessary, especially since so much of what they had to say had been said before. I wish to discuss, if briefly, only two important black monks who provide a window on the persistence of traditional Benedictine mysticism into the new era of reform.

Peter the Venerable, born to a noble family of the Auvergne, in 1122 became abbot of Cluny, the most powerful monastic house in Europe.[68] Peter's election came at a time when Cluny was in the midst of crisis, and his early days as abbot involved him in a fairly acrimonious dispute with the Cistercians in which he tried to defend the relatively lax Cluniac monastic practice against the attacks of Cistercian rigorists whom he branded as pharisaical and inhuman.[69] In the course of this monastic debate he became good friends with Bernard of Clairvaux, despite the latter's strictures against Cluniac practices. The bond that developed between these men, the most powerful monks of their age, is a fine example of those forms of twelfth-century friendship which combined exquisite literary sensitivity with profound commitment to monasticism as the only real foretaste of heaven available to humans. In the last decades of his life Peter appears as a somewhat disappointed leader who sought to inject the vast Cluniac system with a good deal of the reformism found in the newer orders. With Peter's death on Christmas day in 1156, three years after Bernard, one can say that the great age of monastic domination of Christendom was over.

Peter the Venerable does not qualify as a mystical author, at least in the sense of composing extended discussions of the major themes of monastic mysticism.[70] But the abbot of Cluny was a good witness to how fervently twelfth-century black monks still took *contemplatio/theoria* to be the true aim of their life. Throughout his works, especially in his letters, he lamented how his own involvement in the affairs of Cluny and the church precluded him from the enjoyment of the "laborious leisure and religious silence" (*negotiosum otium et religiosum silentium*) that is the monk's real task (see *Letter* 77). Though Peter lived a coenobitic life, he believed that the acme of the monastic life was to be found among the hermits. A letter he wrote to a Cluniac hermit named Gilbert provides an excellent summation of traditional teaching on the relation between eremitical monasticism and the contemplative experience possible in this life.[71]

In response to the hermit's request for advice, Peter's mini-treatise begins with praise of the silence and enclosure of the narrow cell where, like Elijah, the hermit can hear "the voice of God speaking to him in familiar fashion."[72] The cell is a true tomb in which we die and are buried with Christ, a theme that recalls one of Peter's most noted sermons, that devoted to praise of the Holy Sepulcher in Jerusalem.[73] But the enclosed life is meant only for the most advanced, especially because of the ferocity of the attacks and the deceptiveness of the wiles used by Satan against the enclosed. This is why the strictest imitation of the poverty and humility of Christ is necessary for the hermit to taste the true fruits of the contemplative life. It is by means of prayer, "the first and chief good," that temptations are overcome. "By prayer the invisible light shines into minds; by prayer the eye of the heart catches sight of things celestial while still veiled with fleshly density; by prayer the human spirit, insofar as it can, contemplates the Uncreated Spirit who creates all things."[74] Peter goes on to summarize Benedictine teaching about the relation between *lectio, meditatio,* and *oratio,* and to give a brief discussion of the three things that prepare the hermit for prayer: manual labor, especially the copying of manuscripts; the liturgy; and ascetical practice, primarily fasting and vigils. He concludes by emphasizing that the guiding principle for Gilbert's whole manner of living must always be *caritas*, the flame of divine love: "After you have been filled with this, your cell will be wider for you than the whole world; . . . nothing will be able to weigh you down, but the hope and love of things eternal will lift you up to heaven as if on two wings."[75] It is no accident that this letter appears to have been Peter the Venerable's most popular work—a classic of eremitical literature.[76] In this work at least, Peter, if not a mystic himself, is a good witness to traditional monastic mysticism.

More has been claimed for Peter of Celle, whom Jean Leclercq has defended as a monastic mystic in the manner of John of Fécamp.[77] Though a less noted figure than his friends Bernard of Clairvaux and Peter the Venerable, this son of the nobility of Champagne was an important abbot both at Celle and at Reims, ending his life as bishop of Chartres. A strong supporter of both the Cistercians and the Carthusians, Peter left an extensive list of spiritual writings. Peter's works are typical of the monastic theology of the Middle Ages, consisting of letters, sermons, exegetical works, and some treatises devoted to monastic topics—*Purity, The School of the Cloister, Affliction and Reading,* and *Conscience.*[78] Much of what Peter has to say is highly traditional, but the heightened mode of his poetical and concrete style suggests an analogy to the autumnal richness attained by great traditions in their final productive stages, one not unlike that portrayed by Johan Huizinga in his famous evocation of the late Middle Ages.[79] Unlike the visionaries discussed above, Peter adhered to the older Benedictine tradition in his reticence concerning his own experiences of God, but this need not mean that he did not speak out of personal knowledge.[80]

Peter's style is fundamentally biblical throughout, even in his nonexegetical works.[81] But the abbot of Celle was not a "scientific" exegete in the manner of some of his scholastic contemporaries; rather, in the words of Jean Leclercq, "His aim is not to explain scripture but to explain his soul's union with God on the basis of Holy Scripture: the Bible provides him with his whole vocabulary."[82] This observation marks the abbot as a biblical mystic in the tradition stretching back to Origen nine centuries before.

Despite his position as the head of coenobitical communities, Peter, like John of Fécamp, Peter Damian, Peter the Venerable, William of St. Thierry, and so many other monastic leaders of the eleventh and twelfth centuries (Bernard being an exception), praised the life of the hermit as the ideal form of dedication to God. He was also a monastic elitist. Perhaps even more strongly than many contemporaries, Peter believed that those outside the monastery might well be saved, but that their involvement in the world precluded any real access to experiencing God's presence in this life. Following the tradition established by Gregory the Great and developed by the medieval Benedictines, he emphasized the distance between all forms of contemplation given in this life and the full contemplation awaiting the saved in heaven.[83] He described the relation between the latter and the brief foretastes of heavenly joy available in this life in his work *Purity*:

> The state of contemplation by which we are conformed to the eternal God's eternity and established in his inexhaustible love is one and eternal. Thus the soul is more and more purified the more closely and strongly it is fixed on the vision of God. It does not draw near unless it is purified; it does not open to it unless glorified; it does not see unless deified. There is nothing purer in creatures than where a heart so chaste is given access to God, where a conscience so pure is rapt into God,[84] where a soul so good is filled to bursting forth to God.[85]

Peter's dedication to the life of separation from the world and ascetic discipline is especially evident in his popular work *The School of the Cloister*, or *Claustral Discipline*, where he declares, "The discipline of the cloister is the cross of Christ from which no one is taken down before death."[86] This work, written for both monks and canons, shows the abbot of Celle as a strong proponent of traditional monastic practices, especially silence and *lectio divina*, devotion and compunction. But a newer note is sounded in the emphasis Peter gives to sacramental confession and especially to the reception of the Eucharist. The twelfth century was a time of considerable discussion of the presence of Christ in the Eucharist. Peter stands out among the monastic mystics of the time for the central role he gives to the reception of Christ in the sacrament of his Body and Blood. "The Eucharist has the same place in the church's body that the heart has in the human body," as he put it.[87] His most important exegetical treatise, *The Book of Breads*, discusses twenty-four kinds of bread found in the Bible as types of the eucharistic nourishment, the basis for the believer's access to God.[88] Nevertheless, Peter does not present personal accounts of eucharistic visions or experiences of union involving the sacrament of the type often found among mystics beginning in the thirteenth century.

The abbot of Celle sees the cloister not only as the best place of discipline but also as "the royal bedchamber" (*regale cubiculum*) in which the soul is prepared for the love encounter with the Divine Bridegroom described in the Song of Songs.[89] Like the contemporary Cistercians, Peter views the purpose of the monastic life as facilitating the restoration of the *imago Dei* in fallen humanity through our gradual conformation to Christ, the true *Imago* and our divine Lover.[90] His use of the erotic images of the Song of Songs is less ubiquitous than that of Bernard or William of St. Thierry, but bridal love is still an important theme in his works. For example, at the conclusion of the treatise *Purity*, he appeals to the wound of love with which the soul pierces Christ (Song 4:9–a favorite text also among the later Cistercians, as we have seen), identifying it with purity:

> This is that special ray of which it says in the Song of Songs: "You have wounded my heart, my sister, my love, you have wounded my heart with one of your eyes and one hair of your neck." This is like saying that the eye of your contemplation is so immovably fixed in me by the penetrating point of purity that it reaches the pierced interior sanctuary of love, the chief vein of the heart, and makes it flow into the core. . . . If your eye were not so pure, no attraction and sight of "one hair of your neck" would touch me.[91]

Peter's work does not contain any real theory of mysticism, such as that found in the treatises of the contemporary Victorines, or even in the commentaries on the Song of Songs produced by the Cistercians. He instead reflects older traditions by interweaving his views on contemplation and vision within his overriding interest–the exposition of the meaning of the claustral life as preparation for heaven. The abbot's contribution to the history of mysticism, however, is of interest on several counts, especially in what he has to say about vision and about the continuing hunger found in all experience of God, both in this life and the one to come.

Peter of Celle has little to say about union with God here below, thus reflecting the pre-Cistercian and pre-Victorine emphasis of the black monks.[92] His reflections on the nature of contemplation, often discussed in the monastic language of *otium* and *quies*, are not unusual; nor is what he has to say about the relation of action and contemplation.[93] But the abbot's thoughts about the vision of God contain interesting reflections on the inherited Augustinian pattern. In his work *Purity* the abbot speaks in some detail about the vision of God to be enjoyed in heaven. "Pure vision," he says, "is where what is seen and what sees are pure."[94] Not all vision of God is to be excluded from this life, however, as he goes on to show by an original treatment of how Augustine's three kinds of visions relate to life *hic*, that is, on earth, and *ibi*, there in the eternal sabbath. "Human visions or contemplations reverse places, in order not in function, by way of a marvelous change in the present and the future."[95] Here below corporeal vision predominates, while the spiritual vision that remembers absent things and thinks of future ones by imaginary forms is rare. "More rare is the person who is capable of intellectual vision which treats of the true and highest Good without phantasm" (Leclercq, ed.: 182.3–4). In heaven, corporeal vision will still be present, but this vision will not impede the soul because it will be directed to the glorified body of Christ. Spiritual vision will not be necessary but will continue as the joy we will have in thinking of the ills of the life now past. Finally, the intellectual vision of the divine nature will be supreme: "Both corporeal and spiritual vision will pour all their illumination into one of the eyes of intellectual contemplation so that whatever corporeal vision shall have gazed upon will be subject to intellectual vision's direction and whatever spiritual vision remembers will not presumptuously expel anything from its bosom" (182.9–12).

Further developing his comparisons of the contemplative experience here and in heaven, Peter explores the paradoxical aspects of the encounter with God, a theme often found in mystical authors. Peter is unusual in employing the language of "solidity" and "liquidity," that is, hard and soft (sometimes in conjunction with the two arms of the Bridegroom of Song of Songs 2:6), to present these paradoxes. "More truly, I say that the soul liquifies (*colliquescit*) into the solid love of God and is solidified into the liquid of divinity. Everything is both solid and liquid in God: liquid because he takes us into 'the bowels of his mercy' (Luke 1:78); solid because he preserves us eternally.... "[96] It is through the liquid penetrability or divine "softness" that God reveals by sending Christ to die for us and issue forth streams of water and blood from his side (John 19:34) that we are able to gain access to the supreme and unchangeable "hardness" of the divine nature whose enjoyment will last for eternity.[97]

Finally, I have often had occasion to remark on how Christian mystical authors have struggled to show that the experience of God, even in heaven, is both totally satisfying of every human desire and yet infinitely frustrating due to the immeasurable distance between created and Uncreated Spirit. The centrality of this motif in the history of Christian thought seems largely to have been overlooked until modern scholarship uncovered it in Gregory of Nyssa's understanding of *epektasis*. The fact that the Cappadocian's sophisticated exploration of this theme, among the most subtle in the history of Christianity, was not known to Western Christian mystics demonstrates that "satisfied unsatisfaction," or whatever we may wish to call it, is among the most constant aspects of Christian mystical theory. Peter of Celle presents us with some of the most penetrating explorations of this motif in the twelfth-century, an observation that gives additional support to Jean Leclercq's claim that the abbot of Celle should be listed among the classic Benedictine mystical authors. For example, in discussing the three tables God has prepared for his people in chapter 2 of *The Book of Breads*, Peter speaks of how the *mensa mystica* of heaven will never be exhausted. "Loving totally, you will receive the whole but not consume it. Just as love is not laid waste by loving, so he who is True Love will never be exhausted when we feed on him through loving."[98] A passage in the treatise *Purity* puts the same theme with admirable conciseness in speaking of the soul's coming enjoyment of God in heaven: "You apprehend but do not comprehend; by apprehending you are satisfied, by not comprehending you avoid satiety."[99] The abbot of Celle, like Gregory of Nyssa, presents an understanding of contemplation that is fully epektetic.

Women and the Song of Songs

Cistercians such as Bernard of Clairvaux, William of St. Thierry, and their continuators pioneered the return to the mystical reading of the Song of Songs in the twelfth century. Their commentaries, however, were intended for audiences of male monastics. At the beginning of Latin Christian mystical use of the Song, Jerome had employed its images and themes for female virgins, especially in his noted *Letter* 22 written to Eustochium in 384,[100] but the use of the Song for a specifically female audience had not played a large role in the history of early medieval mystical interpretation of the text.[101] One of the earliest signs of an important shift to female identification with the Bride, and one found, significantly, in a vernacular text, is the misnamed *St. Trudpert Song of Songs.*

This Middle High German poetic translation and commentary is not the only witness to vernacular interest in the Song.[102] It is unusual, however, in being composed for a group of Benedictine nuns, either by a chaplain or possibly by a member of the community, and in presenting a strongly mystical reading of the text, which is reflected in the work's true title—*A Teaching of the Loving Knowledge of God (Ein lêre der minneclichen gotes erkennüsse).*[103] The likely place of origin was the nunnery of Admont in southern Germany; the date shortly after 1160. The book was intended to function as a *speculum virginum*, that is, a "mirror of virgins" within which, as in the Bible itself (which was often referred to as a mirror), the nun might see the virtues and the model of the love that would lead her to direct experience of Christ, the Divine Lover.[104] The author appears to have known the commentaries of Honorius Augustodunensis and Bernard of Clairvaux and made use of their Mariological and mystical motifs.[105] The work is not a slavish imitation, however, but an original contribution to twelfth-century monastic mysticism.[106]

The purpose of the poem is summarized in the Epilogue in the following way:

Now understand this:
This book began with kingly joy.
It ends with pitiful lamentation.
It began with a kingly song.
Now it closes with inner weeping.
It began with a divine kiss.
It departs in fulfilled love,
For it is a teaching of the loving knowledge of God.

In this book
shall the Brides of Almighty God have a mirror
and be attentive to their own countenance and that of
their neighbor,
and how they may please their Bridegroom.... [107]

This reference to the oscillation of experiences of presence and absence in the Song of Songs (contrasting the *osculetur me osculo oris sui* of Song 1:1 with the *fuge, dilecte mi* of 8:14) is telling. The author is insisting, like Bernard and William, that experiences of union can never be long or complete in this life and that the inner meaning of the "loving knowledge of God" shown in the mirror of the book reveals how this oscillation determines the nun's proper relationship to self, to others, and to the Divine Lover. Like William of St. Thierry, the author of the poem emphasizes that the transformation from earthly and selfish loves to divine loving takes place through activity of the Holy Spirit:

When the heat of unchaste conduct cools down,
then for the first time the love of God's Spirit
burns in you as the desire to become just.
The Spirit is your Creator, your Redeemer, your Lover.[108]

The teaching presented in the text is generally traditional, but as the first-fruits of mysticism in the German language, *A Teaching of the Loving Knowledge of God* deserves careful study. The frustrating but fascinating game played out between the inexpressibility of mystical consciousness, on the one hand, and the requirements of presenting, through written symbols, some hints about or pointers to the meaning of this consciousness, on the other, creates new possibilities when the game moves onto a different linguistic field of play—as in the case of this early vernacular commentary. Despite the studies devoted to the text, much still remains to be done on this and other representatives of the transition from the learned Latin of monks and masters to the new "vernacular" theologies which were under gestation in the twelfth century but which were not to see full light of day until the thirteenth.

The text picks up on many of the basic themes of Western monastic mysticism, though with interesting variations and new insights.[109] In contrast to contemporaries like Hildegard and Elisabeth (let alone the female mystics of the next century) there is no concern for visionary experience. *A Teaching of the Loving Knowledge of God*, theologically speaking, is founded on the Augustinian notion of the soul as the *imago trinitatis*,[110] on Gregory the Great's teaching on the role of the seven gifts of the Holy Spirit (see chapter 2, p. 54), and finally on the return to a reading of the Song of Songs that is both collective and individual (the individual interpretation having both Mariological and mystical applications). A few comments on these three aspects will show how deeply the text is rooted in the tradition.

Over and over, *A Teaching of the Loving Knowledge of God* emphasizes the fact that the soul is created in the image of the Trinity: "He created us to his image and his likeness so that our soul would be his seal."[111] The author relates the Augustinian triad of the soul's three powers (*memoria-ratio/intellectus-voluntas*, or in the Middle High German, *gehukte-uirnunste-wille*) to the three persons of the Trinity;[112] but an "Abelardian" triad of trinitarian attributes is more often employed (*potentia-sapientia-bonitas*, or *gewalt-wistuom-guote*) to emphasize how the three divine Persons are active in the work of perfecting the soul.[113] Not unlike William of St. Thierry, however, it is the Holy Spirit as the "Creator, Redeemer, and Lover" who is given the central position in the process by which the soul draws near to God.[114] Christ is the Bridegroom, but it is the Spirit who bestows the *uirnunstlichu minne*, or *amor intellectualis*, which unites us with him.[115]

The centrality of the Holy Spirit is especially evident in the prologue to the text, which, as Friedrich Ohly has shown, is structured around the place of the seven gifts of the Holy Spirit (traditionally based on Isa 11:2) in the history of salvation.[116] The opening lines provide the theme: "We wish to speak of the highest joy, the greatest grace, the most restful sweetness that is the Holy Spirit."[117] As Creator, the Holy Spirit fashions the seven parts of the human form to correspond to the seven gifts that perfect the soul (2.26–3.4). The first four gifts pertain to the active life: the left foot is the gift of fear that shuns evil, the right foot the piety that performs good works, the left hand the knowledge that protects, the right hand the fortitude that strengthens. The final three gifts belong to the contemplative life: the left eye embodies the counsel that looks upon the neighbor, the right eye corresponds to the understanding of self, and finally "the head is the wisdom that gazes constantly at God" (*dc houbet sapientia wartet allezane hin ze gote* [3.3–4]).[118] The devil injured these seven gifts by means of the seven deadly sins in the fall. The Holy Spirit's role as Redeemer consists in bestowing the gifts anew throughout each of the three ages of salvation history: before the law, under the law, and under grace (3.11–4.9). This process of re-creation (*widirbildunge*; see, e.g., 43.7–14 and 118.10–12) by the Holy Spirit is meant to be appropriated by the inner person in the present moment: "When we were created and fell, he raised us up again. He does the same today."[119] The seven gifts are compared to the seven days of creation that lead eventually to sabbath rest in God who is our life (4.17–5.12). The three basic powers of the soul, *memoria, ratio*, and *voluntas*, receive the Holy Spirit: "Then the person finally is one with God in [the gift of] wisdom" (*sô wirt der menniske denne ainez mit got in der sapientia* [5.2–21]). The virtues by which the soul strives with the help of grace to practice the Christian life, as well as the seven gifts the Holy Spirit infuses into the soul, are all central to the doctrine of *A Teaching of the Loving Knowledge of God.*[120]

The process by which the human person regains her true nature as divine image and likeness, and thus reaches whatever foretastes of heavenly union with God are available in this life, is analyzed through a detailed exegesis of the complete text of the Song of Songs (a rarity among twelfth-century mystical commentators). Although the author appears to have been familiar with a number of contemporary exegeses, the poem is a powerful and independent reading of the song of love, one far too rich to be investigated in detail here. The message is addressed to cloistered women, but the author emphasizes the universality of the call involved in the Song of Songs:

> Whoever strives earnestly toward this goal,
> even if such a one has not yet attained many virtues,
> still such a person, by reason of her good will
> and of her earnestness, will be called
> a bride of Almighty God.[121]

The bride, of course, is first of all the church through all the ages; but she is also the Virgin Mary as the archetype of all true lovers of Christ. *A Teaching of the Loving Knowledge of God* is particularly artful in weaving together the salvation-historical and Mariological with the individual mystical meaning of the Song.

The key images of the Song of Songs are employed in a variety of ways to express a form of mystical union that is quite close to that found in Bernard and in William of St. Thierry, especially in its stress on loving union of wills (*unitas spiritus*; see, e.g., 11.14–18 and 13.28–32) and in the emphasis given to the interpenetration of love and knowledge in the unitive experience. The kiss (Song 1:1, on which see 13.3–17), the leading into the garden (Song 1:3, see 18.7–19.1), and the "flowery little bed" (Song 1:15, see

26.13–27.3) are just some of the examples taken from chapter 1 that could
be analyzed in this regard. Like other mystical commentators, the author
finds in the picture of the sleeping bride's embrace by the left and right
arms of the Divine Bridegroom (see Song 2:6 and 8:3) a particularly potent
image of the experience of God. An interesting passage on this theme, one
that invokes the language of dream-vision, bears comparison with contemporary twelfth-century mystical dream-visions, such as those found in Rupert of Deutz considered above. In the midst of an explanation of the
amplexus of Song 2:6, the German commentary says:

> Whenever I sleep, then he leads
>   my soul, as if in a dream, into the fruitful meadow
>   of the Holy Spirit,
>   and my inner spirit into the brightness
>   of heavenly wisdom.
> This is the highest bliss
>   which someone still in exile can enjoy.
> Because it deals with a dark and foreign realm,
>   this bliss is more a dream than a truth.[122]

A Teaching of the Loving Knowledge of God also uses many traditional theological motifs to point to mystical union, such as those of God dwelling in
the soul (e.g., 89.12–22), or the soul becoming like God (e.g., 136.20–137.7),
that is, regaining its lost *similitudo*. Although there is no technical discussion
of the nature of union in the text, there are passages that talk about the
nature of the *wunnichlicher zart*, that is, the "wonderful delight" (see 117.28–
118.33) experienced when God visits the soul. For example, in commenting
on Song of Songs 8:2, the poem describes how God possesses the soul as
his inheritance and goes on to say:

> When the body and the soul have joy
>   in the sweetness of the Holy Spirit,
> Then the soul has drawn God into itself
>   in such a way that they will never be separated
>   either through love or fear.[123]

A favored image for this experience is that of the *brutpette*, or bridal bed
(e.g., 138.19–30), which will be given a central position in later German
female mystics, such as Mechthild of Magdeburg. Nevertheless, the basic
thrust of the commentary is not toward detailed descriptions of personal
experience, but rather toward theological exposition of the biblical ground
for the monastic life of contemplation, of which the text speaks in one place

in traditional terms as "the sweet sleep of contemplation, prayer, and read-ing" (*suozzen slâfe der contemplationis orationis lectionis* [32.14]).

This helps account for many of the typical monastic emphases to be found in the poem. Among these is the teaching that contemplative love of the Bridegroom can never afford to neglect active love for the other mem-bers of the community,[124] as well as the stress on the necessity for an *imita-tio Christi*, especially a sharing of Christ's experience of dereliction in his Passion. Such sharing is seen as a necessary part of the oscillation between presence and absence that is the lot of even the most advanced lovers of God in this life.[125] But there are certainly elements in *A Teaching of the Loving Knowledge of God* which look forward to themes to be developed in the ver-nacular mystics of the later Middle Ages. Perhaps the most significant of these is the notion that the perfected soul returns to, or "flows back into," its divine source. John Scottus Eriugena, as we have seen in chapter 3, made much of the *reditus* theme in his speculative mystical theory, and it was not absent from thinkers like William of St. Thierry. The full development of this motif, which becomes one of the controlling themes of vernacular mys-ticism in the thirteenth century (and which produced considerable contro-versy), is a story that will be pursued in detail in the next volume of this history. The fact that a text as traditional as *A Teaching of the Loving Knowl-edge of God* found it important to stress how the soul can return to its divine origin, even in this life, hints of new views of mystical union that were to be developed in later centuries. Commenting on Song of Songs 5:6 (*anima mea liquefacta est*), the author says:

> There is another kind of soul
>   that dissolves in God's love.
> That happens when the Holy Spirit illumines
>   and gives light to all our senses with his heat. . . .
> Oh, how good it is for those who dissolve in this way!
> Where do they flow?
> Back into the Godhead
>   where they were first created,
>   because we should have your image in our souls
>   although in this life the splendor and power of your Godhead
>   cannot be perfectly possessed in this life.[126]

In its teaching about how the soul flows back into God's love (see also 72.12–13) this firstfruit of vernacular mysticism lays the ground for much to come.

The Carthusians

Among the many monastic reforms of the twelfth century the Carthusians occupy a special place. Fascination with the eremitical life as the highest form of monasticism, especially evident in Western Christianity since the turn of the millennium, reached its culmination in the slow-developing but hardy stock of Carthusian monasticism.[127] The Carthusian order was a new creation in its original combination of elements of coenobitism to serve the higher hermit ideal,[128] a uniquely successful one that has continued to exercise a role in monastic mysticism over the centuries.

Bruno, the founder of the Carthusians, was born in Cologne about 1030 and became a noted teacher at the Cathedral school of Reims. Bruno's adherence to the reforming policies of Gregory VII involved him in a long struggle with Manasses, the simoniac bishop of Reims. Instead of pursuing a high ecclesiastical career, in 1083 this *magister* of the schools "converted," that is, took up the monastic life, in fulfillment of a vow that he and three friends had made a few years earlier as they discussed the true way to heaven.[129] After a brief period in Burgundy at the hermitage in Sèche-Fontaine, in 1084 Bruno and six companions were granted an extensive tract high in the Alps near Grenoble. In this difficult and remote site, they built the "Grand Chartreuse" as it came to be called, the parent monastery of the Carthusian order. Bruno himself left the mountain retreat in 1090, summoned to Rome by his former pupil, Pope Urban II. But the career of a curial official was not to his taste and he was soon allowed to retire to Calabria to found another eremitical retreat, where he died in 1101.

The extent to which the forms of the Carthusian life as found in the *Customs* written down by Guigo I, the fifth prior of the community (also called Guigo of Saint-Romain), depend on Bruno's original model is difficult to determine. But there can be no doubt that the spirit of the Carthusian order springs from Bruno, as a glance at his most revealing writing, the "Letter to Raoul," indicates. Along with Peter the Venerable's "Letter to Gilbert," it is the classic twelfth-century witness to eremitic monasticism as the most effective ambience for the cultivation of the contemplative life.[130]

Raoul "the Green" was one of the three friends who had vowed to desert the world, but he had not yet fulfilled his vow. Bruno writes to him from Calabria in praise of the solitary life, seeking to motivate him with arguments drawn from love of God, from higher "usefulness" (*utilis* is a key word in the saint's vocabulary), and even from fear of the judgment to come. Bruno's picture of the beauty of the isolated hermitage in Calabria

(1.4) has classical reminiscences, but the core of his message concerns the "advantage and divine delight" which "solitude and the silence of the desert" bestow on its admirers:

> For here it is given to the strong ones to retreat into themselves as much as they wish and to dwell within themselves,[131] to cultivate insistently the shoots of virtues and to feed in joy on the fruits of paradise. Here one searches out that eye whose calm gaze wounds the Bridegroom with love (Song 4:9) and by whose purity God is beheld (Matt 5:8). Here laborious leisure (*otium nego-tiosum*) is celebrated and one is at rest in peaceful activity. Here God rewards his athletes for the effort of the struggle with the long-desired prize, that peace which the world does not know and joy in the Holy Spirit (John 14:27 and Rom. 14:17).[132]

Bruno launches into a description of the contrast between the active and contemplative lives based on the standard scriptural archetypes (1.6–7) by way of introduction to an analysis of the higher *utilitas* of monastic solitude (1.8–11). He recalls Raoul's vow and threatens him with punishment should it not be fulfilled (1.12–14). But the deepest motivation for the Carthusian life remains love rather than fear, and Bruno's concluding peroration, with its use of the telling phrase *ex parte sentiens*, indicates that although his letter is not designed to describe the experience of divine love in detail he sees it as the apex of the life of monastic contemplation:

> What is so just and so useful, what is so engrained in human nature and so agreeable as to love the good? And what is so good as God? Indeed, what is good other than God alone? And so the holy soul, experiencing in part (*ex parte sentiens*) the incomparable grace, splendor, and beauty of this Good burns with love's flame and says: "My soul has thirsted for the strong, living God; when will I come and appear before God's face?" (Ps 41:3)[133]

Silence, solitude, and simplicity were the hallmarks of the Carthusian life, more so even than for other forms of Western monasticism. The Bene-dictine abbot, Guibert of Nogent, in the first book of his *Memoirs*, provides valuable contemporary evidence about the nature of the life at La Char-treuse ca. 1115. Guibert describes the diet, extreme poverty, and liturgical simplicity of the small community of thirteen members (the so-called *parvus numerus*, an apostolic number which became traditional among Carthu-sians). He also notes that, "Although they subject themselves to complete poverty, they are accumulating a very rich library. The less their store of worldly goods, the more they toil laboriously for that food which does not perish, but endures forever."[134] Liturgical minimalism, severe asceticism, isolation in individual cells save for a minimum of community services, and a mode of life that by its employment of lay brothers (*conversi*) was admirably suited to shield the hermits from the world, whether in isolated situations, or even, as later, within urban environments, contributed to the special flavor of the Carthusian life.[135] It is no wonder that this quintessence of the monastic ideal of the Middle Ages received the admiration of monks from every side—Bernard of Clairvaux, William of St. Thierry, Peter the Venerable, and Peter of Celle (to name only major figures studied here). William testifies to the reputation of the Carthusians as contemplatives *par excellence* in the famous *Golden Letter* that he wrote to his friends at the Charterhouse of Mont Dieu near Reims:

> Your profession is the highest, surpassing the heavens and equal to that of the angels. . . . It is for others to serve God; for you to adhere to him. It is for others to believe God, to know him, to love him, to reverence him; it is for you to taste him, to understand him, to have acquaintance of him, to enjoy him.[136]

Although the Carthusians remained dedicated to the copying of books, they were notably reticent about writing on their own during the first century of their existence, especially in comparison with the Cistercians. This makes the recovery of the mysticism of the early Carthusians a complex matter. A slim collection of letters from a handful of authors is available, but these offer little beyond the common generalizations about contemplation as the goal of the monastic life that can be found throughout the Western monastic tradition.[137] Three Carthusians, however, provide us with somewhat more ample, though still often indirect, evidence of the ways in which this new form of the eremitic life aimed to foster access to immediate experiences of God, even though these experiences were not publicized to a broad audience.[138]

Guigo I takes his place among the most remarkable monks of the twelfth century.[139] Born in 1083 near the Chateau of Saint-Romain, he entered the Grande Chatreuse in 1106. Still a young man, his abilities led him to be elected prior (the Carthusians did not employ the office of abbot) in 1109. He ruled the community until his death in 1136. It was during his priorate that the original foundation began slowly to expand, so Guigo was called upon to compose the first *Customs (Consuetudines)* of the new hermits sometime between 1121 and 1128.[140] In addition, some letters, a hagiographical piece, and his powerful *Meditations* survive—Guigo was prolix as far as the early Carthusians go.[141] He was also a spiritual leader who attracted the devotion of Bernard of Clairvaux, who visited the Grande Chatreuse probably in the 1120s and wrote several letters to Guigo.[142]

It is easy to see why Bernard of Clairvaux and Guigo I enjoyed an immediate affinity: both centered their theology on the mystery of divine love, especially as found in the Pauline letters and the writings of Augustine.[143]

Bernard seems to be referring to Guigo's *Meditations* when he writes at the beginning of his *Letter* 11: "How great a fire blazes out in these meditations to have sent out sparks like these!"[144] Nevertheless, Guigo's written expositions of this theology of love are not mystical in the sense that those of Bernard are, as a brief survey will show.

Guigo's *Customs*, as might be expected, emphasize such traditional monastic virtues as obedience (25.2–3), poverty (40.1 and 41.1), and fraternal charity (37.2 and 72.2). The hermits' devotion to the task of reading and writing books is also stressed (e.g., 7.8, 28.3–4 and 32.1). A treatment of the relation of Mary and Martha as the contemplative and active lives is found (20.2–3), but the importance of contemplation as the goal of eremiticism does not appear until the lengthy chapter 80 ("On the Praise of the Solitary Life"), which functions for the *Customs* something like Benedict's discussion of obedience (RB 7) does for the *Regula Benedicti*. In both the Old and the New Testaments Guigo notes that "the great and more subtle secrets" were never revealed in crowds, "but to God's servants when they were alone. . . and wished to meditate more carefully on something, to pray more freely, or to be snatched away from earthly matter through ecstasy of mind."[145] The list that he gives of such servants summarizes the traditional scriptural archetypes of mystical contact with God—Isaac and Jacob (80.5), Moses along with Elijah and Eliseus (80.6), Jeremiah (80.7–8), John the Baptist (80.9), and Jesus himself (80.10). The tally ends with the fathers of the monastic life who taught that solitude was the greatest support of "sweet psalmody, reading, fervent prayer, deep meditation, ecstatic contemplation, and the gift of tears." Although Guigo does not attempt to describe *excessus contemplationum* in any detail,[146] it is clear that, like Bruno, he considered it the true goal of the Carthusian life.[147]

Guigo's superb *Meditations* were written between 1109 and 1120. The *Meditations* can scarcely be described as a mystical document; they are rather a series of penetrating comments of varying length on the essential mysteries of Christian belief and on how introspection reveals the soul's failure to live according to these truths. Practical and sober throughout, they are closer to the early desert *Sayings of the Fathers* than anything else produced by Latin monasticism. Though often pessimistic in tone (Guigo is particularly negative toward "forms of bodies" as sources of sin), the goal toward which these aphorisms are directed is the traditional monastic one that Evagrius called *apatheia* and his pupil John Cassian termed *puritas cordis*. Guigo expressed this ideal best when he said of such a monk, "He will be devout toward God, kind toward neighbor, sober toward the world; the servant of God, the companion of humanity, the lord of the world; established below God, not lifted up against neighbor, not subject to the world."[148]

The practical, ascetical lessons the Carthusian draws from this fundamental teaching occupy the bulk of the *Meditations*. Self-knowledge, ever a central value of the monastic life, is emphasized throughout (e.g., #88, 303, 345, 379, etc.) Many of the aphorisms seem almost free of specifically Christian content, applicable to any form of life intent upon God conceived of as highest Good and Truth. At the outset, however, the christological perspective is briefly introduced when the prior notes that "Truth is to be adored without brilliance or beauty, fixed to the Cross" (#5: *Sine aspectu et decore crucique affixa, adoranda est veritas*), and the brief but profound treatise that closes the whole (Guigo's answer to twelfth-century question *Cur Deus homo?*) demonstrates that the Incarnation provides the sole access to recovering our true relation to divine Charity.[149] In aphorism 77 this process is described as consisting of four stages: "This is our redemption: forgiveness of sins, illumination, enkindling, immortality. Our God is all these things for us."[150] We may presume that the essential purpose of the *Meditations* concerns the first two parts. If *accensio* involves what we can call the mystical element in Christianity, Guigo does little more than allude to its possibility here.[151]

Several late twelfth-century Carthusians went further than Guigo. Under the influence of the systematic treatises about the life of perfection that were produced by the Victorines (to be taken up in the following chapter), Guigo II and Adam the Carthusian wrote compendia on the practices of the monastic life that include more explicit attention to mysticism.

Guigo II (sometimes called "the Angelic") was the ninth prior of La Chartreuse from 1174–80.[152] He died probably in 1188, leaving two works—twelve *Meditations*, in style not unlike those of William of St. Thierry, and the *Ladder of Monks* (*Scala claustralium*, also known as the *Scala paradisi*, or *Epistola de vita contemplativa*), a letter-treatise typical of monastic theology. The *Meditations* exist in only a few manuscripts, but the *Ladder of Monks*, often ascribed to Bernard of Clairvaux or even Augustine, was among the most popular of medieval spiritual works with over a hundred manuscripts known.[153] It was translated into several languages, including into Middle English under the title *A Ladder of foure ronges by the whiche men mowe wele clyme to heven.*

The *Ladder of Monks* deserved its popularity. Picking up on the ancient theme of the ladder reaching to heaven, whose scriptural warrant was found in Jacob's famous dream (Gen 28:12),[154] it deftly weaves together a rich body of traditional materials into a handbook whose usefulness does not preclude considerable originality. Guigo's carefully constructed four-step ladder witnesses to the desire to rationalize and systematize traditional spiritual practices that became evident half a century before in the writings of Hugh of St. Victor,[155] but his presentation remains deeply rooted in the monastic biblical mysticism that goes back to Cassian and Gregory the Great. What is especially evident in this classic text is the way in which it underlines that mystical consciousness (Guigo calls it *contemplatio* in traditional manner) must not be cultivated or investigated in itself, but can only be understood as the culminating element in an entire program he calls "a person's spiritual exercise" (*spirituale hominis excercitium*).[156]

The four ascending steps of this program are carefully defined according to their "properties" (*proprietates*) and "functions" (*officia*):

> Reading (*lectio*) is the careful study of the scriptures, concentrating all one's powers on it. Meditation (*meditatio*) is the busy application of the mind to seek with the help of one's own reason for knowledge of hidden truths. Prayer (*oratio*) is the heart's devoted turning to God to drive away evil and obtain what is good. Contemplation (*contemplatio*) is when the mind is in some sort lifted up to God and held above itself, so that it tastes the joys of everlasting sweetness.[157]

For his analysis of how the degrees of spiritual nourishment advance (see chap. 3), Guigo utilizes one of the basic texts of Christian mysticism, the beatitude "Blessed are the pure of heart, for they shall see God" (Matt 5:8). In chapters 3–4 he describes how reading puts this brief text in the soul's mouth like a grape, biting and chewing it to stimulate reason to investigate the meaning of such purity "on the anvil of meditation" (*in incude meditationis*). This investigation proceeds primarily through the consideration of other biblical texts that refer to purity, a typical procedure of monastic spirituality. Such an effort produces an enkindling of the soul and the activation of the spiritual sense of smell given from above.

A similar combination of the soul's effort and divine grace marks the two highest stages. In its desire for greater "sweetness of knowledge and experience" (*cognitionis et experientiae dulcedo*) the monk betakes himself to prayer, calling out to the Divine Bridegroom (chap. 6). The Lord does not wait for the soul to finish, "but breaks in upon the middle of its prayer, runs to meet it in all haste. . . . He makes the soul forget all earthly things: by making it die to itself he gives it new life in a wonderful way, and by making it drunk he brings it back to sobriety."[158] Guigo illustrates this moment of mystical contact through the analogy of sexual intercourse—just as orgasm causes the soul to lose the use of reason and become "almost wholly fleshly" (*quasi totus carnalis*), in this moment of highest contemplation all fleshly activity is overcome and absorbed "and a person becomes almost totally spiritual." The Carthusian's direct appeal to erotic analogies throughout the treatise brings him closer to Cistercian and Victorine writings than to the sober texts of earlier Carthusians.

The second half of the work contains careful theological observations on the role of grace in the process, noting especially how the necessary coming and going of the Bridegroom is a part of the divine pedagogy: "We gain something from both the drawing near and the departure" (*et de accessu et de recessu lucrum acquiris* [chap. 9]). Guigo's teaching combines both traditional elements, such as the importance of the gift of tears,[159] and twelfth-century innovations, such as the stress on personal experience (he uses the Bernardine expression of reading "in the book of experience" in chap. 8). Much of what gives his handbook its systematic character comes out in the final chapters, where he studies the causal connection of the stages, both in terms of their progressive character (chap. 12) and their necessary interconnection (chap. 13): "These steps are joined together in such a way, each one serving the other in mutual fashion, that the earlier stages are of little or no use without the latter, and those can scarcely or never be attained without the former."[160] Guigo, like Bernard and the whole monastic tradition, insisted that the experience of contemplative contact with God could never last long. The soul must move up and down the ladder of *exercitium spirituale* in due order as time and place suggest. The goal, however, is clear:

> Blessed is the one to whom it is granted to remain in this supreme degree even for a brief time. Such a person truly says: "Now I feel (*sentio*) God's grace; now along with Peter and John I contemplate his glory on the mountain; now along with Jacob I delight in the embraces of Rachel the beautiful."[161]

It may well be, as Simon Tugwell has pointed out, that Guigo's balanced presentation of the four stages in the ascent to mystical experience represents a transitional moment, "a very fragile synthesis," as Tugwell puts it, between the undifferentiated monastic mysticism of the Benedictine centuries and the changing world of late medieval piety where more rationalized attempts at presenting mystical itineraries led to significant new understandings of the traditional terms *lectio-meditatio-oratio-contemplatio*.[162] Nevertheless, the continued popularity of the *Ladder of Monks* made this monastic classic an important resource for the complex flowering of mysticism to be studied in the next volume of this history.

Guigo II's *Meditations* offer still another avenue into the thought of the Carthusian mystic. *Meditation* I is a traditional treatment of the necessity of the solitary and silent life for hearing God's whispers, but it also contains a prayer to Jesus as friend that is reminiscent of Aelred of Rievaulx.[163] *Meditation* IV is a brief but original treatise on the spiritual path structured according to the three crosses by which we attain perfect imitation of Christ: the *crux carnis,* which is mortification; the *crux animae,* or fear of God; and the *crux spiritus* which is nothing other than the love that nailed Christ to his cross. "The person who attains to this cross passes through the cloud that stands between (Lam 3:44) and pours out his prayer in God's sight." This mention of the cloud allows the Carthusian to evoke the figure of Moses ascending the mountain, the archetype of mystical meeting with God, likening his six-day ascent up the mountain through the clouds with the action of the first six gifts of the Holy Spirit. "Only on the mountain peak of wisdom does the fire of blazing charity reveal the appearance of divine glory."[164] *Meditations* V–VI form a mini-treatise exegeting the creation account of Genesis as the foundation for understanding the formation and reformation of the soul as *imago Dei. Meditations* VII–IX center on Marian teaching,[165] while X–XII stress forms of experiencing Christ in the sacrament of the altar that presage, if not yet in terms of mystical immediacy, later eucharistic mysticism.[166] Thus Guigo II, like contemporary late twelfth-century Cistercians, often hints at new forms of spirituality that became widespread after 1200.

Adam the Carthusian (as I will call him here) was born in Scotland and entered the Premonstratensian order, eventually becoming abbot of Dryburgh. About 1184 he left the Premonstratensians and joined the Charterhouse of Witham in England, where he died sometime not long after 1210.[167] Adam was a prolific author both as a Premonstratensian and as a Carthusian.[168] Although he admitted in one of his sermons that he had not himself experienced the bridal union of the soul with the Divine Lover,[169] his treatise called *The Fourfold Exercise of the Cell,* written about 1190, is a witness to how systematic treatments of the spiritual life were becoming a part of Carthusian study and writing (thus anticipating the role that Carthusian mystical treatises were to play in the later Middle Ages).[170]

Adam's treatise is longer and less well organized than that of Guigo. It is also less of a mystical text, though it does include one of the most detailed definitions of *contemplatio* found in the twelfth century. Adam is a typical twelfth-century author in his frequent appeals to the personal experience of his readers, though once again he notes that he himself has not attained the highest stages.[171] He quotes and comments on an important passage from Dionysius in an extended discussion of apophatic theology and thus provides the earliest explicit witness among the Carthusians for the order's later fascination with the *corpus dionysiacum.*[172]

Adam's four exercises are somewhat different from those of Guigo. Identifying the hermit's *cella,* the focus of Carthusian life, with paradise, he equates the four rivers that water this place of *solitudo-quies-contemplatio* with

"four exercises: the pursuit of sacred reading, the maturity of purified meditation, the devotion of pure prayer, and the vigor of useful activity."[173]
Though Adam's treatise is more complete than that of Guigo, both in detail
and in its treatment of Carthusian activity (the copying of books is again
stressed), it is less coherent, especially because *contemplatio* becomes, not
the highest goal of the process, but a wandering category treated partly
under *meditatio* and partly under *oratio*.

Adam begins with a general treatment of the Carthusian life, stressing the
role of the *quies cellae* in the history of salvation, an obvious expansion on
the final rule in Guigo I's *Customs* (see chaps. 6–9). The bulk of the work is
taken up with a consideration of the four *exercitia*, of which *oratio* is considered the highest (see PL 153:826C). *Lectio* is briefly treated in chapters
16–17; *oratio* gets five chapters (31–35), while *opus manuum* has only one.
The bulk of the discussion is given to the eight modes of *meditatio* found in
chapters 18 through 30.

Adam's eight forms of meditation sketch an itinerary from (1) consideration of the biblical picture of salvation history, through (2) fear and sorrow
for sin, (3) love and consolation based on divine mercy, (4) compassion for
others, (5) analysis of temptation, (6) the example given in the deeds of
Christ's life and that of the saints (which help to overcome the *taedium* of
the cell), (7) admiration of God in creation, finally to (8) the inner voices by
which the soul hears "spiritual and invisible things," that is, makes contact
with the three ascending forms of spiritual reality–the human soul, the angels, and the divine nature. When the Carthusian outlines these in chapter
18, his extended description of mode eight, described as *excellens contemplatio*, fuses the highest mode of Augustinian vision (i.e., the *visio intellectualis*)
with a Boethian emphasis on how this form of meditation provides a
glimpse into the supratemporal nature of God's comprehension of all
things.[174] This original definition promises more than it delivers. When
Adam treats of meditation on God in chapters 29–30, his scholastic consideration of apophatic theological themes compares with that of Isaac of
Stella's "Sermons on Sexagesima," but does little to explain how this equals
excellens contemplatio. Also confusing is the relation between this supreme
form of *meditatio* and the discussion of *oratio*. Adam's chapters on prayer
deal more with distractions to the exercise of pure prayer than they do with
prayer's nature and its relation to the height of meditation.[175]

The treatises of Guigo II and Adam reveal the degree to which the
Carthusians, despite their reticence and withdrawal, were not only an integral part of the monastic revival of the twelfth century, but also important
contributors to the monastic mystical tradition. Solitude and silence have
rarely been as effectively practiced in the history of Western monasticism.

Strict adherence to these central values may make the mystical element of the Carthusian life (for which they were famous from the outset) difficult to recover today, but enough traces remain to allow us to see why the hermits of "La Grande Chartreuse" were to take on even greater importance in the history of later Western mysticism.

The variety and creativity of twelfth-century Latin Christendom continue to elude easy generalization. Even among the monks and nuns, often seen as representing only the older, inherited tendencies in a rapidly changing world, a world where new forms of religious life, practice, and education were coming to birth, it is difficult, and often impossible, to discriminate in easy fashion between new and old elements. In framing this chapter under the rubric of visionaries and contemplatives I did not intend to suggest a division between visionaries, who looked forward to late-medieval mysticism, and hide-bound contemplatives, who did little more than mine the riches of early medieval Benedictinism. The writers and texts discussed here portray just how complex were the reactions produced by the encounter between the rich history of Christian monastic mysticism, already over seven centuries old by 1100, and the challenges offered by the developing culture of medieval Europe.

CHAPTER 9

The Victorine Ordering
of Mysticism

T
HE REGULAR CANONS belonging to the abbey of St. Victor outside Paris made notable contributions to twelfth-century mysticism. In order to understand the distinctive nature of their
mystical writings, it is necessary to glance at the development of the
canonical order and at the birth of the new form of theology practiced
by these pious academicians–scholasticism.

"Canons" (*canonici*) in the early Middle Ages were any clergy inscribed in the list (*canon*) of an episcopal see.[1] Most canons lived on
their own resources, often in private dwellings, and many were not exactly examples of higher forms of Christian devotion (later ages would
speak of them as "secular canons," in the sense they continued to live
in the world). But monasticism as the model for a specialized life of
perfection had already begun to influence the clergy in the West from
the late fourth century. Important Latin bishops, such as Augustine of
Hippo, promoted the ideal of a common life of poverty, prayer, and
asceticism for their priests. In his *Letter* 355, Augustine explains why
he wanted "to have a monastery of clerics with me in this bishop's
residence,"[2] and about 397 he wrote a series of texts that, with later
additions, eventually came to form the *Rule of St. Augustine*.[3] These
documents, which may be said to have monasticized the clergy as
much as they clericalized monasticism,[4] became the major source for
the twelfth-century conception of "regular canons." The French
bishop Ivo of Chartres (d. 1115), one of the proponents of the revival
of this form of life, says: "You are called canons, because you have
vowed to observe the canonical rules more strictly than others."[5]

Although there had been a revival of the canonical life in the Carolingian period, especially under Chrodegang of Metz (d. 766),[6] the

early medieval canons did not stress the communal poverty that became a hallmark of the "Augustinian" canonical order. About the middle of the eleventh century, first in Italy and then in France, a series of houses were founded in which the combination of the clerical state and the full common life became the norm.[7] These canons, like the somewhat later Cistercians in relation to the older types of Benedictinism, aggressively asserted their superiority to other kinds of canons, claiming to be a return to the true *vita apostolica* described in the fourth chapter of Acts. With the support of the Gregorian reformers, especially Popes Gregory VII and Urban II, the movement spread rapidly. By the early twelfth century, the *Rule* attributed to Augustine came to be the norm adopted by most of the houses of canons, providing a fitting patristic authority to equal that of the *Rule* of Benedict among monks. Besides acquiring a name and a patron, the twelfth-century spread of the canonical movement also saw growing stress on common government among the congregations of canons (often modeled on the Cistercian practice of yearly general chapters), as well as an increasing emphasis on the role of contemplation in the canonical life.[8]

The *Rule of Augustine* was brief and general, allowing considerable latitude in its adoption. Canonical houses could also be erected at less expense than Benedictine monasteries. These factors helped make the *Rule of Augustine* the most widespread of all medieval religious rules, and the variety of services performed by the Augustinian canons made them, in R. W. Southern's phrase, "ubiquitously useful."[9] Some canonical congregations, such as the Premonstratensians founded by Norbert of Xanten in 1120, were established outside cities and lived lives of ascetical separation from the world that differed little from that of the new reformed monastic groups; others, however, were created in urban environments and emphasized pastoral service and a less austere religious observance.

It is not easy to discern a specific form of spirituality characteristic of the entire canonical reform of the eleventh and twelfth centuries.[10] But while there may be no single "canonical" spirituality, given the variety of applications of the *Rule of Augustine* and the concerns the canons shared with the monks, this is not to say that there are not certain attitudes particularly associated with the canons, as well as some canonical congregations with their own distinctive approach to leading the Christian life. Caroline Walker Bynum, for example, has stressed how the canons revived Gregory I's notion of the preacher teaching "by word and example" (*docere verbo et exemplo*), a desire to edify that could be expressed both within the community and also through pastoral action. This emphasis, common to most canons, appears in the Victorine canonical reform. The Victorines also proposed a special program of spiritual, indeed even mystical, teaching.

In 1108 the learned Parisian master of theology William of Champeaux retired from the episcopal school of that city to found a house of canons at the hermitage of St. Victor outside the city walls.[11] William apparently intended to give up his scholarly pursuits, but at the urging of the noted humanist bishop of Le Mans, Hildebert of Lavardin,[12] he continued to teach in his new environment, thus setting the stage for one of the most renowned educational institutions of the twelfth century. Though the *schola* at St. Victor existed primarily for the education of canons themselves, the presence of external students, as well as the pastoral obligations taken on by the community, especially those of preaching and acting as confessors to the Paris students, assured the house direct contact with the vibrant urban context and the intellectual center of nascent scholasticism. M.-D. Chenu, the great historian of twelfth-century theology, has noted how the urban situation of the Victorines influenced their interest in the mechanical arts and perhaps even their desire for a more precise understanding of the term *meditatio*.[13] This is a concrete illustration of how twelfth-century city life, with its social freedom and diversity, provided the context for new forms of theology.[14]

In 1113 William reluctantly agreed to accept the bishopric of Chalons, where he soon became friends with the young abbot of Clairvaux, Bernard.[15] In 1114, King Louis VI made St. Victor a royal abbey with Gilduin, William's disciple, as abbot. Gilduin, who reigned until 1155, appears largely responsible for the success of St. Victor. The monastery soon became the head of a canonical order with a customary book of its own (the *Liber Ordinis*, explaining and applying the *Rule of Augustine*) and a yearly general chapter. Later abbots included the preacher and theologian Achard (1155–61), Gunther (1161–62), the weak Ervis (deposed in 1172), and Guerin (1172–93). Though it remained famous for its preaching and for its library, the great era for the Abbey of St. Victor was over by the end of the twelfth century. One late Victorine author, however, Thomas "the Frenchman" (*Gallus*, also *Parisiensis*), who was trained at St. Victor in the early thirteenth century, but left Paris in 1219 for Italy where he became abbot of the canons of St. Andrew in Vercelli, developed the traditions of the school in the context of a new era of mysticism to be considered in the next volume in this history.

The real fame of the School of St. Victor is due to the noted teacher Hugh, who entered the community perhaps around 1120. As is the case with many early twelfth-century masters, little is known about his life. He was probably born in the 1090s; his homeland may have been Lorraine, Ypres in Flanders, or Saxony, where he had connections with a canonical house at Hamersleben. Hugh's writing career began in the 1120s and continued until his death in 1141. He was a prolific author, responsible for his-

torical works, important commentaries (mostly on the Bible but also including one on Dionysius's *Celestial Hierarchies*), as well as educational handbooks, theological works (treatises and *sententiae*, or brief teaching
summaries), spiritual writings, letters, and sermons.[16] Hugh was the master,
directly or indirectly, of the other Victorine authors.[17]

Achard, who succeeded Gilduin as abbot and then became bishop of
Avranches (d. 1171), may have been a direct disciple of Hugh. His sermons
include interesting mystical teaching, especially concerning the "seven
deserts" that lead to God.[18] The literalist exegete Andrew of St. Victor, one
of the foremost Hebraists of the twelfth century, also appears to have been
a student of Hugh. Since his rediscovery by Beryl Smalley, Andrew's
numerous scriptural commentaries have attracted considerable attention,
though his mode of exegesis did not contribute to the history of mysticism.[19] Adam of St. Victor, a Breton who entered the abbey about 1130,
was the finest liturgical poet of the age, the author of some forty-five
sequences.

Other Victorine authors probably entered the community too late to be
direct pupils of Hugh, but were still influenced by the educational program
he had established. Some joined at an advanced age after careers in the
episcopal school, such as the noted master of theology, Peter Comestor,
who spent the last decade of his life at St. Victor (1169–79). Hugh's foremost indirect disciple, however, was the Scotsman Richard, who served as
teaching master at the school and then as prior of the house before his
death in 1173. While not displaying the same encyclopedic range as Hugh,
on the basis of his treatise *The Trinity* and his mystical writings, Richard can
be judged the most profound of the Victorines. Signs of debate within the
house over the value of the Hugonian educational model appear in the
writings of two late twelfth-century Victorines. Godfrey, a continuator of
the Hugonian tradition, wrote a poetic account of the seven liberal arts and
theology, *The Fountain of Philosophy*, as well as a significant though digressive anthropological treatise *The Microcosm*.[20] However, Walther, the prior
of the abbey, took quite a different tack in his virulent treatise *Against the
Four Labyrinths of France*, an attack on Peter Abelard, Peter Lombard, Peter
of Poitiers, and Gilbert of Poitiers—four of the major masters of early
scholastic thought.[21] While Hugh and Richard may not have agreed with all
the speculative innovations of a number of the early scholastics, especially
Abelard, they were solidly rooted in the theology of the schools and would
have resisted any such blanket condemnation. A grasp of the character and
significance of the new twelfth-century mode of theology we call scholasticism is necessary in order to see what helped the Victorine writers make
their special contribution to the history of Western mysticism.

The term "scholastic" as applied to theology refers initially to the context within which this innovative effort to teach and appropriate Christian faith took place. The monks, to be sure, had their schools, but scholastic theology signifies primarily the form of intellectual appropriation of faith created in the urban schools of northern Europe, which were mostly under the control of local bishops.[22] The evolution began in the eleventh century and grew exponentially during the twelfth century. By the end of that century, the episcopal school at Paris had developed to the point that it was ready to become an international institution, a true "university" (*universitas magistrorum*), whose statutes and degrees were guaranteed by papal decree in 1215.

In essence, however, scholastic theology refers not so much to a new ambiance, important as that was, as to an original modality, a new way of appropriating faith—a method, an approach, a set of operations, rather than a series of conclusions (the scholastics disagreed often and widely on their conclusions).[23] Culturally speaking, the rise of scholasticism can be seen as another expression of the drive for order that characterized all twelfth-century society. From the perspective of the history of theology, scholasticism was a novel approach to the *intellectus fidei*, the understanding of faith. The evolution of the scholastic method can be seen as a response to the question whether a scientifically differentiated and academically coordinated presentation of interrelated levels of theological operations would be profitable for deeper understanding and more adequate defense of Christian faith?[24] The scholastics and the medieval church answered a resounding yes to this query, but among the scholastics themselves, and especially between the camp of these innovators and that of the practitioners of the older forms of largely monastic theology, considerable debate ensued about the advisability of the new theology and the limits under which it was to operate. Here it is possible to focus only on a few aspects of the debates between scholastics and monastics, as well as the broadest lines of the development of the intrascholastic discussions concerning scientific differentiation.[25]

The monastic authors that have been studied thus far in this volume were fundamentally interested not so much in intellectual appropriation of Christian faith as such but in the effect that any such appropriation was supposed to have on the life of the believer. Jean Leclercq, in his study of the difference between monastic and scholastic theology, expressed the difference between the monastic and the scholastic modes in terms of the former's emphasis on *credo ut experiar* (I believe in order to experience) and the latter's concentration on *credo ut intelligam* (I believe in order to understand).[26] This was a contrast of emphasis, however, more than a divergence of goals, as Leclercq himself was always anxious to underline.[27] Monastic theology, as practiced by Anselm and by some of the Cistercian mystics considered in previous chapters, also responded to the exigence for deeper understanding of the faith, and the greatest scholastics insisted that the differentiation of theological tasks profited nothing unless it served to increase love of God and neighbor.

The monks realized that in order to be able to read the biblical text, one needed first to have mastered the seven liberal arts, the only way to produce a skilled reader. Following Augustine and Cassiodorus, they also insisted that all education was to be directed to the study of the Bible. Their advanced understanding of the biblical text was communicated through standard literary genera, especially biblical commentary and sermons based on Bible texts as found in the liturgy. These forms of teaching were undifferentiated in the sense that they were not concerned to distinguish various aspects of the appropriation of the faith. Within the same literary presentation we find the exploration of the literal meaning of scripture (often truncated), clear statements of Christian doctrine found in the tradition, speculation on its deeper meaning (the *intellectus fidei*), as well as its moral and mystical application (*tropologia*) to the Christian life. The monastics were not interested in discussing to what extent the study of the Bible was a form of *scientia* to be compared with other kinds of human knowing, convinced as they were that it was essentially *sapientia*, the wisdom sent down by God for our salvation.

The masters who taught in the cathedral and canonical schools of the twelfth century were not in disagreement with this basic agenda.[28] They too cultivated the liberal arts, though with a new sense of classroom efficiency that led to a thirst for more adequate textbooks. They were also convinced that the study of the liberal arts was not an end in itself, but was meant to serve the task of understanding the Bible. None of them would have denied that this highest form of learning, which they called by diverse names (*divina pagina, divinitas, sacra doctrina, scientia divina, theologia,* etc.) was nothing else but true *sapientia*. But the masters took up issues that had not concerned the monks, especially with regard to the scientific status and organization of the effort to understand Christian teaching. Boethius, as noted in chapter 1, had been the first in the West to pose the question of how *theologia* taken in the sense of Christian reflection on God (at least in part) related to the classification of sciences worked out by Aristotle.[29] In the urban schools and the new curriculum of the late eleventh and the twelfth centuries this issue took on an important role. The initiative of Boethius was only part of the story. The context of the new schools encouraged a revival of interest in every form of *scientia, ars,* or *disciplina,* that is, human learning in the most basic sense. Much of this interest was a turn to the past, the effort to search out, translate, and make available the scientific knowledge of antiquity that had been preserved in Jewish and Islamic cultures far more than in Christianity. The twelfth century was one of the great eras of translation in the history of Western culture. But the intellectual curiosity of the era, its concern with a more complete mastery of every form of *scientia/disciplina*, was not merely antiquarian. The twelfth-century masters were avid for new forms of knowledge and were not afraid to break with tradition in exploring them. Hugh of St. Victor was a good spokesman for the age when he said: "Learn everything; you will see later that nothing is superfluous. Meagre knowledge (*scientia*) is no fun."[30]

Augustine had expressed the goal of the study of Christian teaching as the *intellectus fidei*, citing a passage from Isaiah in the Old Latin version (7:9): "Unless you believe, you will not understand" (*Nisi credideritis, non intelligetis*).[31] Boethius, Eriugena, and even the more speculatively inclined of the monastic theologians of the early Middle Ages would not have disagreed with this. But the nature of this understanding of faith took on a new character around the year 1100. Anselm of Bec, though resolutely opposed to those he termed "the heretics of dialectic," sought the inner understanding of the deepest mysteries of the faith, such as the existence of God and the necessity of the God-Man, through his complex and still-debated "necessary reasons" (*rationes necessariae*). These epochal examples of faith seeking understanding by a monastic author constitute another warning against making any simple division between the monks and the masters in the rich theological world of the twelfth century. But the interior questioning of the intelligibility of faith found in Anselm became institutionalized in a formal way in the non-monastic schools, as the desire for a more scientific form of theology led to a differentiation of theological tasks and the literary genera that fixed them for teaching purposes. The end result of this process of differentiating theological operations produced the intellectual framework upon which the edifice of scholastic theology was erected–the distinction of *lectio, quaestio/disputatio*, and *praedicatio* as fundamental operations founding diverse genera of writings within the total task of the new organization of theology.

New attention to the academic presentation of the *lectio* produced a revival of interest in the literal meaning of scripture evidenced among the Victorines, as well as the creation of the standard academic textbook for all biblical study, the *Ordinary Gloss* (*Glosa ordinaria*). The need to resolve problems and seeming contradictions in the deposit of faith, as well as the desire to find a fruitful understanding of belief (the *intellectus fidei*), led to the isolation of the *quaestio*, the systematic investigation of such difficult issues aided by more sophisticated tools made available in new translations of Aristotle's logical works. Abelard expressed the purpose of such questioning in a nutshell in the prologue to his treatise *Yes and No (Sic et non)*: "By doubting we come to investigation; by investigation we grasp truth."[32] The disengagement of the *quaestio* from the *lectio* invited opposing views to meet in structured academic debates, the *disputationes* that became a formal school exercise and another genre of scholastic literature. The problem of how to present this scientifically differentiated *intellectus fidei* to students in accessible textbooks that would help them in the essential teaching task of all clerics, that is, *praedicatio*, became more significant as the new theology increased in subtlety and complexity. As Peter Cantor, a Paris master of the late twelfth century put it:

> Learning sacred scripture consists in three things—reading, disputation, and preaching. . . . Reading (*lectio*) is the foundation as it were, and basis for all that follows, because through it the other occupations are fitted together. Disputation (*disputatio*) is like the wall in this work and edifice, because nothing is fully understood or faithfully proclaimed unless it has first been broken up with the tooth of disputation. Preaching (*praedicatio*), which these serve, is like the roof that covers the faithful from the heat and storm of vices. Therefore, you should preach only after (not before) the reading of sacred scripture and the questioning (*inquisitionem*) of doubtful matters through disputation. Thus, "one pot will fit within the other."[33]

The possibility of a "scientific" model of theology not only offered the opportunity to work out carefully distinguished theological operations designed for specific tasks, but also called for new thought about how theology related to other forms of science and how to present the teaching of theology according to proper scientific and pedagogical requirements. Hugh of St. Victor vindicates his eminent position among early scholastics especially for the contributions he made to these two issues (he had less to do in the actual evolution of scholastic method). Hugh, as Roger Baron has emphasized, combined the functions of the *lector artium*, that is, the student of the forms of human disciplines, with the properly theological tasks of the *lector sacer* (the investigator of the literal meaning of the biblical text), and also that of the *homo interior*, the teacher of the inner significance of revelation.[34]

The investigation of the classification of sciences and the relation of this to theology was an avid concern of the first half of the twelfth century.[35] Hugh addressed the issue twice in detail, in his *Epitome of Dindimus on Philosophy* and his famous guide to learning called the *Didascalicon*, which is the most original and sustained study of the various sciences since Aristotle—one, unlike Aristotle's, that specifically addressed the integration of all forms of knowledge in the service of divine *sapientia* leading to mystical experience.[36] Though dependent on a rich early tradition stretching back to Boethius and beyond, Hugh adopted an original line in distinguishing four forms of *philosophia* understood as "the discipline that investigates in full fashion the ideas (*rationes*) of all human and divine matters," or, more theologically, as "the love and pursuit of the Wisdom . . . which is the sole primordial Reason of things. . . ."[37] The Victorine never isolates or divides *philosophia* and *theologia, scientia* and *sapientia.* All the forms of human learning serve, directly or indirectly, in a grand architectonic ensemble designed to foster the work of restoring the image of God damaged by sin. This restoration aims at contemplative experience as its true goal, the foretaste of the perfect vision of God in heaven.[38] The three fundamental forms of *philosophia*–mechanical, practical, and theoretical–are complemented by the fourth form, logical philosophy, which provides the mental tools that serve the other branches of learning (*Did.* 1.8–11). The seven mechanical arts, whose theory (not whose actual exercise) pertains to philosophy, have an indirect but still real relationship to the mystical goal insofar as they protect and nourish human life (*Did.* 2.20–27). Practical science, divided into solitary, private, and public ethics, is learning about the truth of actions (2.19). The highest form of science, theoretical science, studies the truth of things in accordance with the fundamental threefold division of Aristotle and Boethius: *theologia, mathematica,* and *physica.*[39] In the early part of the *Didascalicon,* Hugh's notion of *theologia* remains on the generic level found in Boethius (2.2), one that is applicable to any form of discussion of the divine nature in itself (3.2). In the last three books, when he turns to the treatment of scripture and Catholic tradition, he adumbrates a distinction between two kinds of theology through his employment of the term *divinitas.* "This is the whole of divinity; this is that spiritual edifice which contains as many mysteries as it has levels that lift its construction on high."[40]

This points to the distinction of theologies Hugh advanced in his commentary on Dionysius's *Celestial Hierarchies.* Here the Victorine includes *theologia* under a division of sciences into logical-ethical-theoretical, identifying it as "the height of philosophy and the perfection of truth than which there can be nothing higher to the contemplating soul."[41] His major concern here, following his patristic source, is the contrast between *theologia mundana,* the theology of the pagan philosophers, which, "by not using enough evident demonstration was not able to present incomprehensible truth without contagion of error," and the Christian *theologia divina,* which reveals "a greater declaration of divinity in the mysteries of grace, the flesh of the Word, and his hidden (*mystica*) operation."[42] The Victorine agrees with Dionysius and Augustine in stressing the contrast between the wisdom of the philosophers, useful but always flawed, and the wisdom of the true *theologia* revealed in Jesus Christ. This particular form of relating the sciences to theology was to find its true heir in another great scholastic in the thirteenth century, the Fransican doctor Bonaventure.[43]

Hugh of St. Victor also played a notable part in the evolution of the systematic side of early scholasticism, that is, its drive to more organized and pedagogically coherent presentation of Christian teaching. If theology, understood as a *scientia* that was also *sapientia*, was to form the crowning part of a total program of education, then how should it be organized and taught? To distinguish for the sake of distinction alone was useless unless the effort intended as its goal a more integrated and unified summation of the whole. Hence, the scholastic age saw the birth of many efforts to summarize *scientia divina* in textbooks often called *libri sententiarum* (i.e., "books of sentences, or positions") and later *summae*, or "summaries."[44]

Monastic authors did not write *summae*, being content to present their *intellectus fidei* through scriptural commentary, following the "order of history" (*ordo historiae*) revealed by God. Many scholastics, especially after the triumph of the full scholastic method, sought to find clear abstract schemata, or a logical order (*ordo inventionis*), to give structure to their handbooks of Christian teaching. The most popular of these in the twelfth century were based on themes found in Augustine. Thus, Peter Abelard and his followers used the bishop of Hippo's categories of faith-sacrament-charity (*fides-sacramentum-caritas*) from the *Enchiridion* to structure such early summaries as the *Introduction to Theology* (*Ysagoge in theologiam*) of ca. 1140. Peter Lombard, who had been a student at St. Victor before becoming a master at the Parisian episcopal school and eventually bishop of the city, used Augustine's distinctions of "things and signs" and "use and enjoyment" (see *Christian Doctrine* 1.2–5) as the basis for his famous *Four Books of Sentences* of ca. 1155, distinguishing between the "thing to be enjoyed" (i.e., God) treated in book 1, the "thing to be used" (creation) in book 2, the "thing that serves as medium to God" (the total Christ) of book 3, and the "signs" that makes this present (sacraments) treated in book 4.

Hugh of St. Victor adopted a middle ground in the major *summa* he produced in the third decade of the twelfth century, named *De sacramentis christianae fidei*, that is, *The Mysteries of the Christian Faith*.[45] The Victorine adhered to the *ordo historiae*, but he realized that in the new academic environment the presentation of salvation history needed to be put into a formal structure rather than merely presented through biblical commentary, that is, *lectio*. Taking a cue from Augustine's *True Religion*,[46] he structured his "brief *summa*" into two great books treating of the *opus conditionis* and the *opus restaurationis*: "The subject matter of all divine scriptures is the works of human restoration. There are two works in which everything that has been done is comprised—the first is the work of foundation; the second is the work of restoration."[47] This form of doctrinal summary, which makes moderate use of the new investigative techniques of the *quaestio* throughout, is a part of what Hugh in the *Didascalicon* called the "second foundation" (*aliud fundamentum*) of the total effort of the restoration of humanity that is the goal of all knowledge. A more detailed look at this will demonstrate how the Victorine created the first scholastic integration of human *artes*, scriptural exegesis, and the new scientific theology in the service of the goal of contemplation of God.

The last three books of the *Didascalicon* are a primer of the interpretation of scripture, the foundation for theological science (*Did.* 4.1). "Sacred scripture has three ways of being understood, that is, history, allegory, and tropology," though not all three levels are found in every text. "It is necessary," he continues, "to treat divine scripture so that we do not seek history everywhere, nor allegory, nor tropology, but we fittingly assign each to its proper places, as reason demands."[48] In discussing the order and method for studying scripture in book 6, Hugh advances the doctrine of the double foundation, which helps us understand the integration of his whole project:

> Pay attention! I have proposed something contemptible to gazers but worth imitating to the intelligent. A foundation is in the earth and doesn't always have polished stones. A building is on the earth and needs a well-proportioned structure. Thus, the divine page contains many things according to the literal sense that seem contradictory and sometimes even involve something absurd or impossible, but the spiritual understanding, in which there are many different things but no opposed ones, allows no contradiction.[49]

Hugh goes on to compare the two fundamental senses to two forms of foundation. The *historia*, or literal sense, is the underground foundation whose stones do not need to be polished but are necessary for carrying the whole building. The second foundation, which carries the building but is also a part of it, is allegory, that is, "the many mysteries contained in the divine page." The list given here (*Did.* 6.4) echoes most of the headings for the doctrinal summary found in *The Mysteries of the Christian Faith.* At the outset of this work, Hugh employs the terms "first and second teaching" (*eruditio*), rather than foundation, for these two parts of his program,[50] going on to summarize how "all the natural arts minister to divine science, and rightly ordered lower wisdom leads to higher [wisdom]."[51] History, which deals with the significance of words in relation to things, is served by grammar, rhetoric, and dialectic, that is, the trivium, or what the *Didascalicon* called *philosophia logica*. Allegory, which is here defined as the sense that consists "in the signification of things in relation to hidden deeds" (*in signifi-*

catione rerum ad facta mystica)–by which we can understand how the meaning of persons and events of the Old and New Testaments reveals the mysteries of Christian doctrine, and tropology, consisting "in the signification of things in relation to hidden things to be done" (*in significatione rerum ad facienda mystica*), are both served by the quadrivium and *physica*, that is, all knowledge of material creation. Resting upon these in the manner of the edifice analogy from the *Didascalicon*, is the "divine reality" (*divinum illud*) to which both allegory and tropology lead–"The knowledge of truth and the love of virtue are based on these things: this is the true restoration of humanity."[52]

These programmatic statements from the *Didascalicon* and *The Mysteries of the Christian Faith* reveal the inner consistency of Hugh of St. Victor's thought and locate his mystical teaching within an integrated scholastic theological program. Beryl Smalley was correct to hail the Victorine's decisive role in a new emphasis on the necessity of earnest effort at uncovering the literal sense of the Bible: "History is the foundation and beginning of sacred doctrine," as he insisted.[53] For all the lip-service to the importance of the letter found in Latin exegetes for six centuries, almost no one since Jerome had made serious effort to learn languages and wrestle with the problems of what the text really meant, especially in its complex descriptions and contradictory passages. Hugh's efforts to lay the "first foundation," as evident, for example, in his interest in Jewish exegesis,[54] as well as his consideration of the structure of Noah's ark,[55] mark a new moment in the history of medieval exegesis. Nonetheless, Hugh knew that a foundation was not a building. The *prima eruditio* was to lead to the *secunda eruditio*, the systematic presentation of the church's teaching. Like the walls of a house, this was to serve as the secure support for the higher structures or roof (Hugh himself does not appear to have used this metaphor explicitly) representing the point of contact with the divine presence in mystical contemplation.[56] As he put it with characteristic sobriety in the preface to his *Commentary on Ecclesiastes*, "They seem to me equally at fault who superstitiously try to create in sacred scripture a hidden (*mystica*) understanding and profound allegory where there is none, and who obstinately deny searching it out when it is there."[57]

For Hugh *tropologia* was a broad term that embraced moral purification, meditative illumination, and contemplative ascent to God. In *Didascalicon* 5.9 he spoke of the five steps of ascent by which the just are lifted up to future perfection: "First, reading gives understanding; second, meditation provides counsel; third, prayer makes petition; fourth, performance seeks; fifth, contemplation finds."[58] This evocation of contemplation as the goal of the process allows us to turn in more specific fashion to the Victorine's contribution to the mysticism of the twelfth century.

Hugh of St. Victor as Mystical Teacher[59]

From the perspective of its biblical foundation, Hugh of St. Victor's mystical teaching depends both on traditional tropological-anagogical texts, such as the Songs of Songs, and also on a novel use of a scriptural master-symbol which he employs to present the inner connection of history, allegory, and the soul's ascent to God.[60]

In the first homily of his *Commentary on Ecclesiastes* Hugh takes his place in a long line of Christian mystical authors stretching back to Origen in connecting Solomon's three books with the three stages of the soul's ascent to God.[61] He expresses this pattern of ascent, however, through a precise definition of stages that springs from his scholastic mentality:

> There are three visions of the rational soul: thinking, meditation, contemplation. Thinking is when the mind is touched in a passing way by the notion of things. . . . Meditation is the persistent and discerning recalling of thinking. . . . Contemplation is the attentive and free gaze (*contuitus*) of the intellectual soul poured out everywhere over the things to be discerned. . . . There are two kinds of contemplation: one prior and of beginners, treating of the consideration of creatures; the other later and of the perfect in the contemplation of the Creator. In Proverbs Solomon proceeds as if by meditating. In Ecclesiastes he ascends to the first stage of contemplation; in the Song of Songs he transports himself to the supreme level.[62]

This threefold pattern, typical of all of Hugh's teaching,[63] helps explain not only why the Victorine commented on Ecclesiastes, but also why, like many of his predecessors and contemporaries, he made so much use of the Song of Songs. This aspect of Hugh's teaching is important, but not unusual. More distinctive was the way the canon sought to integrate anagogy (*anagoge*), or ascent to God, with *simplex allegoria* (i.e., doctrine), and the *expositio historica*, the history that is its foundation.[64] This synthesis was achieved primarily through the invocation of key biblical symbols rather than by means of logical discourse.

Anagogy is defined by Hugh as "drawing above when through the visible the invisible thing that is to be done is declared."[65] This reminds us of Hugh's definition of *symbolum* found in his *Commentary on the Celestial Hierarchy*, "A symbol is a bringing together (*collatio*), that is, a fitting together of visible forms used to display something invisible."[66] Such concern for the necessity of using material images and symbols (i.e., *theophaniae*) in order to attain the invisible divine realm was something Hugh of St. Victor often discussed in his writings, and it demonstrates the importance of the Dionysian element in his thought.[67] M.-D. Chenu once remarked, in relation to Hugh's definition of *symbolum*, that the medieval period, throughout its culture, "was an era of the symbol as much as, indeed more than, an era of dialectic."[68] Symbols were not employed, as Chenu went on to emphasize, to clarify or repeat things arrived at by rational understanding, but were evoked "to give primary expression to a reality which reason could not attain and which reason, even afterwards, could not conceptualize." Still, reason and symbol could work together. In Hugh of St. Victor we can say that the symbolic expression of mystical anagogy combined in a new way with aspects of the ordering mentality of scholasticism to create a fusion in which scholastic logic brought order and clarity to rich symbolic presentations of the ineffable mystery of the divine–human encounter. This synthesis enriched rather than dissipated the symbolic power of traditional mystical themes.[69]

Hugh had a variety of ways of presenting the marriage of logic and symbol through biblical images, but it is evident from his writings that the one he especially favored was Noah's ark. Between about 1125 and 1130 he wrote three treatises on the ark–*Noah's Moral Ark*, *Noah's Mystical Ark*, and *The World's Vanity*.[70] As Grover A. Zinn has shown in a series of important articles, these three treatises "set Hugh's mystical thought within the perspective of his teaching on human nature, the effects of the fall, and the purpose and plan of the restoration of man in a more explicit manner than do any of his later mystical treatises."[71]

Noah's Moral Ark is the longest of the three works and was apparently the first written. Its four books are a harmonious fusion of the allegorical-doctrinal significance of the ark with its tropological-anagogical meaning as a symbol of the soul's transforming ascent to God. *Noah's Mystical Ark*, consisting of fifteen chapters, is a summary of the allegorical meaning which helps clarify some aspects of the presentation of the first treatise. Finally, *The World's Vanity*, also in four books, begins from a typically Hugonian evocation of the vanity and mutability of all worldly things (*Vanitas est et vanitas vanitatum* of Eccl 1:2) to advance a summary regarding "the form of the ark in the human heart," the symbol of the instrument of salvation which can save those caught on the sea of mutability. While the fundamental significance of the *arca diluvii* "is the heart's secret in which we ought to lie hid from this world's din,"[72] Hugh's teaching on this inner ark in which we meet God was based upon the description of the physical ark recounted in chapter 6 of Genesis and its polyvalent significance as a symbol of salvation history.

The literal, material, surface meaning of a symbol like the ark is a necessary aspect of its function, since it is in and through the image itself that the unknown, opaque, and anagogic aspects of mysteries that cannot be presented in purely conceptual terms make themselves present. Hugh of St.

Figure 1

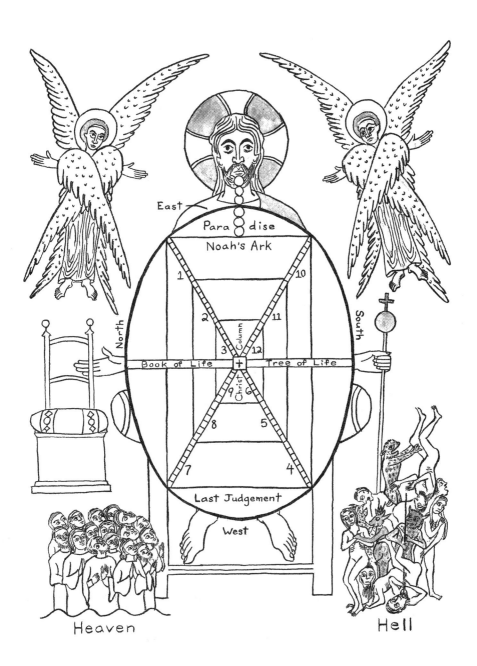

Victor illustrates this with remarkable fecundity not only because of his emphasis on the necessity for a careful literal reading of the Genesis description of the ark (see *Noah's Moral Ark* 1.3) but especially because of his presentation of its meaning through a drawing of the ark that is now lost but that can be at least partially reconstructed from the descriptions he provides (see figure 1).[73]

Hugh begins *Noah's Mystical Ark* from a traditional starting point that echoes Gregory the Great. The human person, made to contemplate God, has lost that ability through the fall.[74] Instead of stability in God, we now find ourselves with wayward hearts that cannot love God properly because he is no longer truly known. In order to know God we must seek his dwelling place, "God's house" (*domus Dei*), which can be taken in three senses. First, God dwells in the world in one way; second, he dwells in the church in another; and, finally, he is meant to dwell in the faithful soul as the Bridegroom in his wedding chamber through knowledge and love (*per cognitionem et amorem*, PL 176:621D). The Victorine invites the reader to enter the heart's secret place and "make a dwelling place for God, make a temple, make a home, make a tabernacle, make an ark of the covenant, make an ark of the flood, for whatever name you use, the Lord's house is one."[75] But Hugh does not merely invite; as a good scholastic, he also teaches how the invitation can be realized by presenting his drawing of the ark for instruction, meditation, and mystical initiation. This is the opening description of the diagram that Grover Zinn has aptly described as a kind of Christian mandala:

> The model (*exemplar*) of the spiritual edifice I will give you is Noah's ark. Your eye will see it outwardly so that your intellectual soul may be formed to its likeness inwardly. There you will see some colors, forms, and figures pleasant to behold; but you should know that they are put there so that through them you may learn wisdom, instruction, and virtue to adorn your soul. Because this ark signifies the church, and the church is Christ's body, to make the model clearer to you, I have painted the whole person of Christ, head and members, in a visible form, so that when you view the whole you can understand more easily what will be said later about [each] part. I want to represent that person to you as Isaiah testifies he saw him . . . : "I saw the Lord sitting on a throne high and lofty" (Isa. 6:1).[76]

Here the Victorine sets the ark symbol within the context of one of the classic Old Testament theophanies, a major resource for both Jewish and Christian mystical traditions—the vision of the enthroned and seraph-circled Lord (identified with Christ by most Christian authors). The point that Hugh is making is clear: the cosmos and world history manifested by the ark symbol will reveal its inner meaning only within the universal matrix of the theophany of the Word.[77]

Like some great Romanesque tympanum, Hugh's drawing portrays the enthroned Christ figure as the Lord of history embracing the created circle of the cosmos with outstretched arms.[78] In his left hand he holds a scepter; his right rests on the seat of judgment, while at his feet there is a scene of the last judgment with the ranks of the saved and the damned.[79] In contrast to the original vision of Isaiah 6, Hugh's picture of the seraphim who accompany Christ leave the Lord's face unveiled.[80] With two of their wings they cover their bodies to signify the historical sense of scripture. The two wings that reach out to cover Christ's feet and head (presumably the top of the head, leaving the face visible) indicate the allegorical sense by which we learn the "hidden things of divine scripture" (*mystica divinae scripturae*). Hugh insists that they both "reach" and "cover" Christ's head and feet "because whenever we are caught up in rapture of mind to think of his eternity we find no beginning or end in him."[81] The face, however, remains unveiled to indicate the face-to-face vision that the blessed will enjoy in heaven (1 Cor 13:12 is cited). Finally, the two wings with which they fly indicates the tropological sense by which we mount up to God through good works.

Hugh, however, is less interested in the cosmological and heavenly dimensions of the picture than in those that deal with salvation history in both its universal and its individual aspects. Although Christ's head and feet are hidden from sight, his body is visible—"This is the ark of which we propose to speak; it reaches from the head to the feet because holy church extends from the beginning to the end through the succession of generations."[82] Before embarking on his detailed study of the ark, however, Hugh reminds his readers of the polyvalent character of the symbol. The ark is both one and fourfold. It is one insofar as there is "a single likeness everywhere"; it is fourfold because this single likeness is found in the relationship between the two visible arks (that is, the historical ark of wood formed by Noah, and the allegorical ark of the church which Christ made through preachers) and the two invisible arks, namely, "that which wisdom daily builds in our hearts through constant meditation on God's law, . . . and that which mother grace works in us by joining many virtues into one charity."[83]

"History is the foundation and the beginning," as Hugh had insisted in the *Didascalicon*.[84] *Historia*, of course, for the Victorine indicated both the literal interpretation of the biblical text and the whole story of salvation set out in the Old and New Testaments. His concern for the former is evident in the efforts he makes to get right the confusing picture of the ark found in Genesis 6, especially in light of the different interpretations given by Origen and Augustine.[85] In contrast to his predecessors, Hugh argues that the only possible literal understanding of the ark was as a kind of "house-on-a-hull," in Grover Zinn's term. The drawing of this ark takes up the center of the cosmic disk covering Christ's body (indeed, it is identical with Christ's body). From the mouth of the Lord of history issue six circles representing the primordial time of the first six days of creation. Then, beginning at the eastern end of the world map, the ark is pictured from above, its length of six hundred cubits signifying the six ages of world history and its breadth of fifty cubits the multitude of all believers. Hugh understands the house structure on the ark as a pyramidal shape whose thirty cubits of height (signifying the thirty books of the Bible following his own special enumeration) contained three stories (mansiones) signifying the three orders of the faithful—the married, the clergy, and the monastics. These stories gradually slope inward until at their height they are gathered into a single cubit signifying Christ "the head of the church" (Eph 5:23).[86]

Before analyzing the details of the anagogical aspects of the ark image—that is, its properly mystical connotation—it will be helpful to note how much Hugh packs into this symbolic presentation of the ark as God's dwelling places. At the end of Noah's Moral Ark there is a summary of the treatise that begins with the remark that by now the ark must seem like a labyrinth (labyrinthus). Punning on the term, Hugh says that rather than being a labyrinthus, that is, "internal struggle" (labor intus), the ark is an "internal repose" (requies intus), one that comprises "all the works of our restoration from the beginning of the world to the end." The ark, then, is nothing else than the entire content of the history of the church, as well as "the form of human life and the sum total of perfection" (forma vitae hominis et summa perfectionis).[87] But the ark also reveals a third dimension, the domain whose eternal mode of being contrasts with the temporality and mutability of human life and the course of salvation history. The mystical diagram is meant to reveal how "that [heavenly] world is in this world," in the sense that the horizontal or temporal dimensions of the picture always contain the vertical or anagogic ones whose goal is the eternal enjoyment of the vision of God: "Eyes of flesh see the former world; the eyes of the heart contemplate the other world inwardly."[88]

The ark, then, symbolizes the presence of eternity in time, the only security and stability humanity can possess amid the dual flood of the welter of history and the interior raging of the unquiet heart. In contrast to the earlier exegetical tradition, which viewed the waters of the flood as a type of baptism (in dependence on 1 Pet 3:20–21), Hugh, very much like Gregory the Great (see chapter 2, pp. 35–36), saw the sea negatively as the symbol both for the mutability characteristic of created things and for the more terrifying disorder introduced by sin.[89] The ark treatises are filled with repeated evocations of the necessity of rising from the *diluvium* of this life to the "true and sole unchangeability which is with God."[90]

The vertical dimensions of the description of the ark in Genesis 6 reveal the tropological-anagogical content of the diagram. Hugh once again shows himself as a true disciple of Augustine and of Gregory the Great in his emphasis on the dynamic identity of introversion and ascension manifested in the symbol of the ark-dwelling, which is also a pyramid-mountain. As he puts it in *The World's Vanity*: "To ascend to God is to enter into oneself, and not only to enter the self, but in an ineffable way to pass through oneself into the interior depths."[91] The ascensional symbols invoked to understand how entering the ark allows us to ascend to God are of a rich biblical character. In book 2 of *Noah's Moral Ark* (640D) the Victorine identifies the ark with Mount Zion, "the mountain of the house of the Lord," to which all the tribes of the earth flow in order to ascend to God (see Mic 4:1–2). *Noah's Mystical Ark* invokes an even more potent mystical symbol, seeing progression up the pyramidal ark as the ascent of Sinai, with Moses, who alone reaches the top, as the type of those who "along with the perfection of work also have repose of mind."[92] The central ascensional symbol, however, is that of the column, or *axis mundi*, that supports the whole structure and whose top narrows to a single cubit:

> The column . . . is the tree of life which was planted in the midst of paradise, that is, the Lord Jesus Christ in the midst of his church. . . . He rose from the earth and pierced the heavens; he came to the depths without leaving the heights; he is both above and below, above in majesty, below in compassion. He is above to draw our desire and below to give us assistance.[93]

Hugh's master symbol is eminently christological. Without entering into an extended discussion of the Victorine's doctrinal account of the God-man (laid out in *On the Mysteries* 2.1.1–13), it would be easy to show that the spiritual teaching based on this always insisted that "without Jesus the Mediator no illumination is possible."[94]

The Victorine's symbolic ingenuity appears in the way in which he used the house-mountain of the ark to display an original itinerary of stages of ascent to God. Viewed from above, the diagram portrays the house as a series of three rectangles decreasing in size as they approach the square cubit of the central column that is Christ. The four corners of each rectangle are connected by four ascending lines, each divided into three stages as they ascend the three *mansiones*, thus making twelve ladders (*scalae*) or steps (*gradus*) in the combined ascensions (*ascensiones*) of northeast, southwest, northwest, and southeast (see figure 1).[95] The first ascent is the awakening to the spiritual life that begins from pride symbolized by the "cold of the northeast" and proceeds through the three steps of fear, sorrow, and love (see 1, 2, 3 on the figure). The second ascent, that of purgation, begins on the opposite side, that is, from the heat of the southwest (representing fleshly vices), and climbs up by the stages of patience, mercy, and compunction (4, 5, 6). The third ascent is illumination, rising up from the cold of the northwest (i.e., ignorance), when the passions have been stilled through the levels of thinking, meditation, and contemplation (7, 8, 9). This leads to the final ascent of union from the heat of the southeast, that is, from the good of contemplation through good action by way of the ascent of the virtues of temperance, prudence, and fortitude (10, 11, 12). Each ladder, like the whole structure, can only be climbed through the power of Christ, whose activity is symbolically presented under the images of the tree of life (*lignum vitae*) and the book of life (*liber vitae*). Hugh's map of the ascent looks like this in diagram form:

Figure 2

Ascent	Christ's Role	Degree
Awakening	Book corrects	Fear, Sorrow, Love
Purgation	Tree shades	Patience, Mercy, Compunction
Illumination	Book illumines	Thinking, Medit., Contemp.
Union	Tree nourishes	Temperance, Prudence, Fortitude

As Grover Zinn has shown, this program represents an original adaptation of the traditional three levels of Dionysian purgation-illumination-union.[96] Hugh's prefixing a preliminary stage of "awakening" to fill out the map of the spiritual life reflects an Augustinian emphasis on the necessity for internal recognition of sinfulness, well known through the *Confessions* but not overt in the Dionysian corpus. The Victorine's understanding of the role of purgation culminating in compunction also stresses a penitential note characteristic of Western monastic traditions. This "augustinianizing" of a basically Dionysian program complements what is elsewhere evident in his writings, especially in the *Commentary on the Celestial Hierarchy*.[97]

Hugh is supreme among twelfth-century mystical authors for the architechtonic way in which he integrated the mystical ascent of tropology-anagogy with sound Christian doctrine, or *allegoria*, based upon a careful reading of the letter. When we turn to his actual discussions of the forms of immediate contact with God possible during this life, however, we may be initially disappointed, because his teaching here is less rich and detailed than what we have seen in Cistercians such as his friend Bernard of Clairvaux, or even what will be seen in his Victorine successor, Richard. It would be unfair to describe this aspect of his teaching as jejune, or second-rate; rather, Hugh must be seen as the careful teacher whose main task is to order traditional monastic teaching on *contemplatio* within the context of the new scholastic thinking.

Hugh's doctrine of *contemplatio* is more interesting for its symbolic inclusiveness than for its analysis of mystical consciousness itself, though several key passages reflect on this latter dimension.[98] For example, in his description of the three ladders that constitute illumination (*cognitio-meditatio-contemplatio*) in *Noah's Mystical Ark* 9, he invokes the image of a shattered metal vase to illustrate how this stage of the ascent of the ark repairs the damage inflicted by sin. Thinking (*cogitatio*) is pictured as an erect female figure pointing to a broken vase, while *meditatio* sits collecting the fragments. Contemplation is the metalworker who heats the fragments to reform the image. Hugh summarizes: "The integrity of the soul which ignorance shatters, thinking discovers, meditation collects, contemplation pours by its melting action into the die of the divine likeness in order to be reformed through the fire of divine love."[99]

We should note that *contemplatio* does not constitute the final stage in the ascent of the ark. Rather, the last three ladders of temperance, prudence, and fortitude illustrate that Hugh of St. Victor, like the other mystical writers of the medieval monastic tradition, insisted that contemplation was meant to serve action by enabling virtues to be exercised in more effective ways.[100] The interrelation between contemplation and action also suggests that the twelve ladders are not meant to signify a single itinerary to be completed once and for all, but rather symbolize an ongoing process throughout the course of salvation history and the history of each life. We are always climbing all the ladders.

A similar message is found in book 3 of *Noah's Moral Ark*, where Hugh discusses fifteen degrees of growth of the tree of wisdom. This is not really a spiritual itinerary because there is no simple, straightforward progression in the fifteen steps. Rather, Hugh presents aspects of the soul's spiritual germination and growth that are all part of the process that leads eventually to eschatological *contemplatio*, that is, the perfect enjoyment of God in heaven.[101] The accounts of what might be called mystical experiences in the text (see 3.7–8) are brief and largely traditional.[102] The same is true for other parts of the ark treatises that dwell on issues related to traditional mystic themes.[103]

The three treatises on Noah's ark constitute the core of Hugh of St. Victor's distinctive ordering of the traditional monastic layer or strand of Christian mysticism in the light of the new theological model of scholasticism. It might seem to some that his thought represents a preliminary and unstable amalgam of not-easily-compatible theological visions. It is also puzzling to note how, in an age when references to one's own experience of God were becoming more acceptable in the course of mystical teaching (as in the case of Bernard of Clairvaux and in some of the visionaries treated in the last chapter), Hugh almost always refrains, except briefly in the *opusculum* entitled *The Soul's Pledge*, from any first person expression of spiritual experience.[104] Personal analysis of experience of God was clearly not Hugh's metier. We read him primarily for his ability to integrate consciousness of God into a rich symbolic synthesis and his insistence that mystical ascent is grounded in history. Hugh's attempt to manifest the inner harmony between historical process and contemplative vision was shared by some of his contemporaries, notably by Joachim of Fiore; but Joachim (as suggested in the previous chapter) worked out his version of this by breaking with the past. Hugh, on the other hand, reformulated the Augustinian and Dionysian elements of the Western mystical tradition into a new configuration that, for all its traditional sources, could not have been created in an earlier age.

Hugh's later specialized works on aspects of mystical teaching confirm this judgment, despite their limited scope.[105] To be included with them is the treatise *On Contemplation and its Forms*, one of the earliest works specifically devoted to contemplation, which appears to have been composed by students of the Victorine, possibly from classnotes based on his teaching.[106] Hugh's treatises on love may not compare in scope with those of Bernard, William, or Richard; but these works also help flesh out why the Victorine was considered by Bonaventure as the one thinker who possessed equal authority in thinking, preaching, and contemplation.[107]

Like the contemporary Cistercians, Hugh and his Victorine followers rooted their teaching about contemplative contact with God in a theological anthropology centering on the consideration of the human person as the *imago Dei*, formed according to the perfect Image who is Christ. As he put it in *Noah's Moral Ark*:

> Christ is life eternal; Christ is wisdom; wisdom is the treasure. This treasure was hidden in the field of the human heart where man was made to the image and likeness of the Creator. Because the heart of the human person was created in such a way that Divine Wisdom was to be reflected in it as in its mirror, what could not be seen in itself might become visible in its image. Great indeed is human dignity in bearing God's image, always seeing in the self the divine face and having God ever present through contemplation.[108]

This is why the Victorine, possibly under the influence of Eriugena, could describe the human creature as the *sapientia creata*, the created image of Divine Wisdom forming and containing all things.[109]

Hugh expounded the details of his *imago Dei* anthropology throughout his works, especially in the treatise he wrote on *The Union of the Spirit and the Body.*[110] In his major doctrinal work, *On the Mysteries of the Christian Faith,* he begins his treatment of the creation of humanity with a standard but significant topos: "Man was made to the image and likeness of God; . . . image according to reason, likeness according to love."[111] The loss of the contemplative presence of God through the fall affects both of the fundamental activities of the soul, the reasoning power of the *imago* and the affective power of the *similitudo.* Hugh's spiritual treatises emphasize one or the other side of this dual process of reforming the human mirror so that it can, once again, truly reflect *divina sapientia.* It is interesting to note that he could not refrain from expanding this twofold pattern into a typically Victorine triple one, as when in *Noah's Moral Ark* 1.4 he speaks of three ways of pursuing and attaining God here below: seeking him through desire, finding him through knowledge, and touching him through taste.[112] The touch of taste spoken of here (another example of the synaesthesia of the spiritual senses) can be best identified with the experiences of "liquefying love" that Hugh emphasized in his later short treatises.

The intellectual side of the ascent to God is predominant in the ark treatises and in the pseudo-Hugonian *On Contemplation and its Forms.* One of the dominant themes that the Victorine employed in presenting it was his teaching concerning the "three eyes" of the soul.[113] Inspired by Paul's teaching in 1 Corinthians 2:9–12, Hugh distinguished the "eye of flesh" (*oculus carnis*), which even fallen humans continue to possess, the "eye of reason" (*oculus rationalis,* or *oculus cordis*) that has been injured by sin, and the "eye of contemplation" (*oculus contemplationis*), extinguished by Adam's fall.[114] This triple formula was especially helpful in the Victorine program of integrating the visual images observed by the *oculus carnis* with the corrective lenses brought to the myopic *oculus rationalis* by faith in order to restore the limited vision of God possible here below through the reactivation of the *oculus contemplationis.*

The actual exposition of the intellectual aspect of the reformation of the *imago et similitudo Dei* in Hugh's treatises, however, is expressed primarily through his analyses of the orderly progress from *cogitatio* through *meditatio* to *contemplatio.*[115] In *Didascalicon* 5.9, as noted above, Hugh spoke of five steps by which the just person is raised to perfection—*lectio, meditatio, oratio, operatio,* and finally *contemplatio.*[116] The separation of *lectio* and *meditatio* evident here (originally the two terms were synonymous) had already been initiated in the eleventh century, as we saw in the previous chapter. Hugh of St. Victor marked a further stage in this development, not only in the care he took in defining *meditatio* as a distinct stage of spiritual exercise, but also in relating it not only to the traditional term *lectio*, but also to *cogitatio* as intellectual activity.[117] The Victorine underlines this in his treatise *On Meditation* where he distinguishes three kinds of *meditatio*–in creatures, in scripture, and in moral action–and where he spends the largest portion of the treatise talking about the third form.[118] Hugh would not have wished to drive any wedge between the reading of the sacred text and intellectual ascent to God, as is evident throughout his writings, but the ordering mentality of the scholastic method has here begun to introduce a concern for systematization of the forms of meditation that was to have both positive and negative results, especially on the relation between reading the biblical text and arriving at contemplation.[119]

Hugh's treatments of *cogitatio* are perfunctory, but he took care to define what he meant by *meditatio*. *Didascalicon* 3.10 says it is "assiduous thought with deliberation that investigates the cause and the source, the manner of being and the usefulness of each thing in a prudent way." Virtually the same definition is used in *On Meditation* and *On Contemplation*.[120] A more general, but not essentially different, definition occurs in the first homily *On Ecclesiastes* cited above. What the Victorine is most interested in, however, is how such "assiduous thought," whether directed to creatures as evidence of God's power,[121] to scripture as evidence of God's speaking, or to moral action as evidence of human striving for God, is essential for preparing the way for contemplation. *Meditatio* is closely linked with prayer (*oratio*) in this work, as is shown in the brief treatise *On the Manner of Praying*.[122]

Despite Hugh's systematic mentality, the term *contemplatio* maintains a good deal of its traditional ambiguous amplitude in his spiritual writings. The analyses of contemplation found in these can help to determine how much of the treatise *On Contemplation and its Forms* may be used to illuminate Hugh's teaching in this regard.[123] The Victorine sometimes used *contemplatio* in the broad etymological sense of any kind of "taking a look at something";[124] but he generally employed it in the more restricted sense as a special "regard" toward God. In the first homily on Ecclesiastes, Hugh provides his only succinct definition of contemplation as "the attentive and free gaze of the intellectual soul poured out everywhere over the things to be discerned," as we have seen above.[125] Here Hugh contrasts the way in which meditation seeks out "what is hidden from our understanding," while contemplation pursues "what is manifest either according to its nature or our capacity." This "manifest" quality appears to refer to what was originally intended by the Creator, and not to what now pertains in our fallen condition–that is, human nature was made to behold God and divine things first, and all other things through this knowledge. Now, our ability to arrive at something of the *contemplatio* which can only be fully enjoyed in heaven depends on our effort to meditate on the things we find hidden from our clouded intellects. In this same discussion the Victorine distinguishes between two forms of contemplation: the contemplation of creatures, which he calls *speculatio*; and *contemplatio* of God. "In speculation," he says, "the novelty of an unaccustomed vision lifts the mind up into admiration; in contemplation the taste of wondrous sweetness changes it totally into joy and gladness."[126] In line with the ancient monastic tradition stretching back to Gregory the Great and beyond, Hugh emphasized that real *contemplatio* was to come only in heaven (e.g., *Noah's Moral Ark* 3.15; *The Mysteries of the Christian Faith* 1.10.8) at the same time that he admitted that humans could already begin to possess the divine presence here below through forms of imperfect contemplation.[127] Although he uses the term *contemplatio* often, outside the first homily of the Ecclesiastes commentary he seems little concerned with defining it.[128]

The situation is quite different with the treatise *On Contemplation and its Forms.* Here defining *contemplatio* and providing a complex analysis of its various types has become the center of concern and contemplation is the overarching term used for all the stages of the road to God. The analysis is filled with many elements that echo and even paraphrase passages from the authentic works, as Roger Baron has shown, but how far the new organization of the material may actually reflect Hugh's own teaching is difficult to know. Two definitions of contemplation are given at the outset: "According to the principle authorities of the ancients contemplation is the departure (*digressio*) of the intellectual soul through the various roads of salvation; or contemplation is the illumination of mind that draws the intellectual soul to the invisible things of God in a saving way."[129] The four principal types or forms (*species*) of this broad definition are identified as *meditatio, soliloquium, circumspectio,* and *ascensio.* Meditation is briefly treated according to the three forms seen in *Didascalicon* 3.10, that is, in the consideration of morals, the searching out of the commandments, and in the investigation of divine works. Soliloquy, an Augustinian term that Hugh also used in the title of his dialogue *The Soul's Pledge,* represents the soul's conversation with itself through compunction, devotion, and good will. Circumspection, which Hugh had treated in a long chapter in *Noah's Moral Ark* (3.10), concerns the proper treatment of things of this world through understanding, counsel, and choice. Thus, it is the rough equivalent of the first mode of contemplation in the *Commentary on Ecclesiastes.*

The bulk of the treatise is given over to *ascensio,* a term that recalls the ladders up the ark and, like them, partakes of both moral and mystical ascent.

The three fundamental forms of ascent are in action (*in actu*), in desire (*in affectu*), and in understanding (*in intellectu*). Since the triple formulas of the treatise begin to grow complex here, a chart may be of some assistance (see figure 3).

Figure 3

I. Ascent in Action: A) confession of faults
                           B) almsgiving
                           C) despising wealth
II. Ascent in Affection: A) humility
                           B) charity
                           C) contemplation, which includes (a second divi-
                           sion of (1) in actu, (2) in affectu, and (3) in intellectu
                           (= what follows in III)
III. Ascent in Understanding: A) investigation of Creator and creature
                           B) investigation of scripture
                           C) searching out of morals

Many of these divisions contain intricate further ternaries and subternaries. These, plus the repetition of terms (as in IIC), give the treatise an artificial and often confusing complexity beyond what we find in Hugh's authentic writings. Still, *On Contemplation and its Forms* contains important discussions of mystical contemplation, primarily under IIC(2) and IIIC.

Ascent in affection concerns the soul's advance to perfect humility, to the consummation of charity, and to the purity of contemplation. This *puritas contemplationis* is directed toward our own life "in action, in affection, and in understanding" (IIC). Contemplation of our lives in affection comprises three forms of instruction—through the counsels (*consilia*) that pertain to reason, through the studies (*studia*) that illuminate the soul, and through the exercises (*exercitia*) common to both flesh and spirit. Pseudo-Hugh's lengthy discussion of these *studia* includes a consideration of the "study" by which the soul comes to glory in celestial things, one that mentions various forms of direct experiences of God's presence through what are called "sendings" (*emissiones*) and "inspirations" (*inspirationes*).[130]

The discussion of intellectual ascent (III), the longest section of the work, is somewhat confusing in that it is based on a repetition of the three forms of *meditatio*, that is, the investigation of the Creator and creature, the inquiry of scripture, and the scrutiny of morals. The third form, that is, the scrutiny of morals (which the text identifies with "knowledge of God"), expounds a complex teaching regarding forms of higher contemplation based on the invocation of a variety of biblical images in a manner reminiscent of Hugh's weaving together of scriptural motifs in the ark treatises.[131] The fourth form of knowledge of God deals with "the ray of contemplation from which the invisible things of divine contemplation (*speculatio*) are known." The text insists on God's ineffability but notes how Old Testament figures spoke of seeing God, so that it is legitimate to say that God can be seen *per excessum* through the ray of contemplation.[132] True to the triadizing technique of the text, three kinds or species of contemplation are discussed on the basis of the biblical images of (1) the throne of God mentioned in Isaiah 6:1, (2) the divine whisper heard by Elijah in 3 Kings 19:11, and (3) the palm's breadth of the measurement of the Temple in Ezekiel 40:5.[133]

Finally, the fifth form of knowledge of God, "from the joy of most happy vision," discusses how "very few happy folk in the present, . . . rapt in the abounding sweetness of the divine taste, contemplate God alone." The treatise differentiates this grade from the former, which allows for an oscillation between knowledge of self and world and the higher knowledge of invisible things, by insisting that in this form "the intellectual soul is totally enlightened by the splendor of eternal light, constantly and perfectly hates sin, disregards the world, rejects the self, and—entire, apart, naked, and pure— moves into God, never departing from God entirely, but uniting itself totally to the one God, is in every way apart from matter, naked of form, pure of limit."[134]

This description of mystical contemplation goes beyond Hugh's usual sober accounts in the direction of the analyses found in Richard's treatises. It, too, is illustrated by three kinds of biblical images: the three "suspensions" (*suspendia*) found in Job 7:15; the three silences suggested by John (Apoc. 8:1); and the three sleeps of Solomon in Song of Songs 5:2. The suspensions are presented through a paraphrase from Gregory the Great;[135] the silences and sleeps, while depending on the tradition of monastic contemplation, are treated in a more original fashion. The three silences—of mouth, mind, and reason—are necessary because of the total interior rapture of the soul in the anointing of an "ineffable joy" in God (*ineffabile gaudium*), which cannot be comprehended.[136] "Thus the sleep of heavenly sweetness seizes the fully anointed [mind] and then it dissolves and rests in the embrace of the highest light."[137] This is the sleep of the three faculties of the soul (*ratio-memoria-voluntas*), which is accomplished when the soul reaches that union with God described in 1 Corinthians 6:17, which the treatise cites at this juncture.[138] True to the endless triple formulas found throughout the treatise, this sleep has three stages: (1) the bride is led into the "house of the serving maids," to be washed by inspirations from God that induce the mind to trample on earthly things and ardently desire heavenly ones; (2) she proceeds into the "bedchamber of the young girls," where she is dressed with the "clothing of justice"; and (3) finally, she enters the banquet chamber where "she is wondrously fed by the Bridegroom himself."[139] The treatise closes by invoking a wide range of other biblical triads that symbolize the three highest forms of contemplation ascribed to the knowledge of God given in the joy of vision. Though less powerful than the treatment of the forms of rapture found in Richard's *The Mystical Ark*, the pseudo-Hugonian *On Contemplation and its Forms* is an important witness to the Victorine concern for detailed investigation of the higher states of mystical consciousness.

The images of tasting God and of melting or liquefaction, as well as the use of erotic language in this work, are authentically Hugonian elements, reminding us that the Victorine, like his Cistercian contemporaries, always stressed the inner connection between knowing and loving, between *sapientia* and *caritas*, in the experience of God. In one exemplary passage, he even insisted on their identity: "Charity itself is wisdom, because through charity we taste God, and by tasting we know, as the Psalmist said, 'Taste and see that the Lord is sweet' (Ps 23:9)."[140] Hugh's teaching on the nature of love, especially its melting and burning action, is indispensable to his mysticism. The dogmatic basis of Hugh's Augustinian doctrine of the nature of *caritas*, or love of God, is set out in *The Mysteries of the Catholic Faith* 2.13.6–12. He also wrote a number of short treatises on the nature of love, among them *The Soul's Pledge* (*De arrha animae*), which is among the most affective–and effective–of all his works. In these treatises he is concerned primarily with how charity motivates the ascent to God and how it forms the basis for the whole Christian life, rather than with trying to define the nature of love or to discriminate among the terms that describe it (*amor-caritas-dilectio*).[141] Love, as Hugh understood it (following Dionysius), is the fundamental dynamic force in the universe,[142] and therefore also the very life of the soul.[143] In this fallen world, love can be directed toward opposite goals: as *cupiditas* to the false and fleeting goods of the world; or as *caritas* to the love of God.[144] In the latter sense it is experienced as the desire (*desiderium*) by which we long for union with God in Jesus Christ.[145] Like all Christian mystics, Hugh insisted that it was love rather than knowledge or understanding that leads to God, however much the latter contributes.[146] The treatise *The Praise of Charity* is a brief summation of how charity serves as the way between God and the human person, emphasizing the message, "Through charity you make your choice, through charity you run your race, through charity you seize and enjoy."[147] It is in *The Soul's Pledge*, however, that the Victorine lays out his most complete explanation of how love brings us to God.[148]

In form the tract can be described as an Augustinian dialogue (the full title includes a reference to the bishop of Hippo's *Soliloquium*) between *homo* representing the voice of Reason and *anima* as the Soul, that is, the individual subject or person. In terms of Hugh's own distinction of stages of progress to God it is a *meditatio* that culminates in a pure prayer (*oratio pura*) that includes elements of *contemplatio*, even some spoken in an autobiographical voice.[149] The subtle literary art of the treatise demonstrates the difference between the authentic works of Hugh and those based on his classroom teaching, or merely imitating it.

The argument of the Victorine's treatise is not hard to summarize, reflecting, as it does, both his ability to analyze the love relation between God and human in abstract fashion and his conviction that this cannot really be understood apart from the history of salvation. At the outset, Reason confronts the Soul about the disordered love it has for the things of this world, arguing in good Augustinian fashion that real love is due only to God. Soul responds that it can only love what it sees (PL 176:953A). Reason then draws attention to the fact that although the Divine Bridegroom cannot be seen in this life, his pledge or down payment (*pignus/arrha*) is everywhere apparent (954D). The remainder of the work consists of a study of the meaning of this "pledge." We receive gifts that are common to everything made, gifts that are special to human nature, and gifts that are singular to each one of us as loved by God (956D–57A, 959C). The Divine Lover is found in all these gifts both "by attraction and effective presence" (*singulis quos diligit quasi omnibus affectu et effectu adsit*; 959C), but due to the fall and to our own personal history, every soul has turned away from the true Lover to become a prostitute, whoring after created attractions.

The second part of *The Soul's Pledge* takes up the salvation-historical dimensions of this Augustinian theology, emphasizing how the Word condescends to take flesh to save his unworthy bride (962BD, 963CD), and how the bride (now brought to her senses) needs to repair her fallen condition to become worthy once more for marriage with God (964B–65B). Especially noteworthy is the way in which Hugh, not unlike Bernard, utilizes the sensuous images of the Song of Songs to underline the ecclesiological, sacramental, and biblical dimensions of contemplative experience of God in this life.[150]

The Soul's Pledge has a special place among Hugh of St. Victor's writings, however, not so much for the theological sobriety of its *meditatio* as for the unique passion of the *confessio* which concludes it. Abandoning his usual mode of exposition, Hugh presents a personal prayer in the manner found in John of Fécamp and William of St. Thierry. Here *homo*, or Reason, and *anima*, or Soul-Self, seem to fuse, no longer carrying on the debate of accuser and accused. Reason praises all the gifts God has given to Hugh as the pledge that guarantees Christ's continuing devotion (967D–68B). Then

Soul responds voicing her conviction that the love that God displays for all his creation, and especially for humanity in common, does not conflict with the singular love he has for her:

> He shows that he is always present; he is always ready. No matter where I turn, he does not desert me; wherever I am, he does not depart. Whatever I do is with his help. . . . It is clear from this that though his countenance still is hid from us, his presence can never be avoided.[151]

God's omnipresence to the soul induces initial fear concerning the remnants of sin still found in the "reformed whore." But Hugh ends on a positive note. All are sinners, but all can still hope for further growth in love of God. Soul concludes with a personal testimony to the experience of the visit of the Divine Lover which can be compared with the famous passage in Bernard of Clairvaux's *Sermon on the Song of Songs* 74.5–7 (see chapter 5, pp. 192–93). The fact that this passage, like many other such mystical texts, builds upon earlier descriptions, primarily Augustine and Gregory, in no way lessens its significance for the history of twelfth-century mysticism.[152]

In the midst of the intense reflection on love that characterized the twelfth century, the sober canon Hugh, despite this rare window into his personal spiritual life, cannot compete with the lyric intensity of Bernard's rhetorical concealed-revealing of the Song of Songs, though he does demonstrate how the Augustinian-Gregorian teaching on the nature of *caritas* was capable of multiple forms of renewal, even among the scholastics. This creativity is also evident in the way in which Hugh treats images of the fire of love (*ignis amoris*) in his mystical writings.

The role of fire in human culture has given it a range of values of extraordinary richness, not least as a symbolic language for presenting the purging and transforming character of love of God. Hugh of St. Victor was fascinated with fire. As he put it in one of his teaching notes (*Miscellanea*) entitled "The Natures and Forms of Fire": "Among all visible things which bear a likeness to things invisible, fire alone has both the highest place and the richest signification."[153] Hugh distinguishes no fewer than eleven forms of fire in nature, going on to give their allegorical and tropological meanings and concluding with a survey of the opposed actions of the two primary "fireworkers" (*opifices*), the Holy Spirit and the devil. The Spirit's enkindling commences with that of compunction by which sins are purged and it proceeds to that of desire for eternal goods:

> And in some way through love's fire he melts what previously had been frozen and paralyzed, so that it already begins to flow through desire. And just as a liquified mass is poured into a mold through a tube and takes its form, so the mind, dissolved by the fire of love through the ray of contemplation, hastens on into the image of the divine likeness.[154]

Hugh returned to this image in several key passages that discuss the relation of love and contemplation. *Noah's Mystical Ark* uses the same image of the metalworker to describe the relation of thinking, meditation, and contemplation, as we have seen.[155] More extended and powerful invocations of the symbol of fire are found in two noted texts, one from the *Commentary on the Celestial Hierarchies,* the other from the *Commentary on Ecclesiastes.* The sixth book of the *Commentary on the Celestial Hierarchies,* dealing with the angelic hierarchy containing the seraphim, cherubim, and thrones, contains an analysis of the contemplation of love. The description of the seraphim as "ever moving around things divine, ceaseless, warm, piercing, and supreme heat of a motion that is always attentive and perhaps always intimate and unchanging" provides the basis for Hugh's teaching on the nature of the contemplative love that is (a) moving, (b) warm, (c) piercing, and finally (d) superheated.[156] Seraphic love is moving because it is life; it is warm because it is love and piercing because it is also wisdom (PL 175:1037A). Motion and warmth characterize the first stage of *caritas,* in which we desire the God whom we love but who is still far from us in the manner of the disciples who walked toward Emmaus with the Jesus who was still unknown to them (see Luke 24). "First warm and then penetrating" (*prius calidum, postea acutum*; 1037C) means that the vehemence of burning desire (*vehementia desiderii ardentis*) eventually carries the lover forward to the stage of penetration *into* the beloved through the desire to achieve union, or "to possess [God] as totally present" (*vel praesentissimum possidere*).

Though Hugh begins by likening this level of loving knowledge to what the disciples discovered at Emmaus as Jesus broke bread with them, he rapidly invokes an unusual mystical oxymoron in which the "sharp and penetrating" (*acutum*) aspect of love (penetrating God?), which he says might be upsetting for the fearful and timid, can be understood as what is flowing, that is, "liquid," in the "pleasing game" of love.[157] Thus the phallic image of penetration becomes the more feminine image of melting, which allows Hugh to introduce an extended reference to the love of the Bride in the Song of Songs, beginning from the passage, "My soul is dissolved, as the Beloved has said; and I have sought him" (Song 5:6, slightly altered). This artful invocation of the erotic language of the Song of Songs into the Dionysian tradition of seraphic love (which also involves subtle interchanges of gender images reminiscent of those presented by Ambrose in his treatise *On Isaac*) is the foundation for one of the major contributions of subsequent Victorine tradition to later medieval mysticism: the "affective Dionysianism" which fused the negative theology of the Areopagite with erotic motifs drawn from the Song of Songs.

The remainder of this section of Hugh's comment centers on the mutual interpenetration of the soul-bride and the Bridegroom achieved when she can go within to find him because his love has already penetrated and softened her heart (1038BC), another proof that "love is higher that knowledge and is greater than understanding" (1038D). Hugh's discussion ends with a consideration of why Dionysius refers to seraphic love as *superfervidum.* He takes the word as referring to the quality of internal heat which eventually causes it to boil over violently outside itself (1039B). The trajectory of love leads from warmth, through penetration, to bursting forth. Love is "superheated when in rejecting itself it departs from everything" (*superfervidum autem, cum etiam semetipsum contemnendo relinquit* [1039C]). This total forgetfulness of self (reminiscent of the fourth degree of ascent in Bernard's *On Loving God*) is the "boiling of the heart" that marks the final stage of love's progress (1039D).

In the first homily of his *Commentary on Ecclesiastes* Hugh once again makes use of the melting potency of divine love, this time employing the image of a burning log, which John of the Cross, quite possibly in dependence on the Victorine, was later to use with such efficacy.[158] After outlining the three stages of *cogitatio-meditatio-contemplatio* and the three books of Solomon that teach them, Hugh illustrates the struggle between knowledge and ignorance in the practice of meditation by invoking how fire struggles to be enkindled in a green log until finally "the victorious flame" (*victrix flamma*) bursts forth in triumph and then absorbs the interior of the log till all is totally aflame in contemplation. Hugh summarizes:

> The first stage, because counsel is sought amidst temptation's dangers, is that of smoke with flame, as in meditation. The second is because the heart is poured out with a pure mind to the contemplation of truth, just as in the beginning of contemplation there is flame without smoke. The third, because then truth and perfect charity have been found, seeks nothing beyond what is one. In the flame of love alone, it is sweetly driven back within (*repulsatur*) in the height of tranquility and felicity.[159]

Hugh of St. Victor's use of fire motifs is another vindication of the potency of his symbolic mystical thought.

There are other aspects of Hugh's mystical teaching that could be pursued with profit, such as his understanding of the *ordo caritatis* by which the active and contemplative aspects of charity are integrated,[160] and his teaching on the nature of the vision of God both here and hereafter.[161] It is also interesting to note that while Hugh does not explicitly discuss how broadly the invitation to contemplative ascent extends, his presentations suggest that every member of the church is called to some form of contemplation.

Finally, some may wonder what kind of contact with God the great Victorine teacher himself enjoyed. Given the perspective adopted in this volume and the paucity of the canon's autobiographical texts, this question is probably unanswerable–and, I would argue, largely otiose. Whether Hugh of St. Victor was a mystic in the restricted sense used by some modern students of mysticism is far less important than the fact that he was to remain one of the major mystical teachers for later medieval seekers after God, even those who were less reticent about recording their own experiences.

Richard and the Other Victorines

The influence of Hugh of St. Victor's thought is evident in many aspects of later medieval theology, not least in mystical theory. A number of treatises from the second half of the twelfth century take up Hugonian themes, whether or not they were written by members of his community.[162] Two of these authors, both canons of St. Victor, must be numbered among the important figures of twelfth-century mysticism–the Englishman Achard and the Scotsman Richard. Richard is by far the more significant writer, but modern research has shown that Achard, like the English Cistercians who completed Bernard's work on the Song of Songs, deserves a place among twelfth-century mystical authors.

Achard's writings were at least partly composed during his time as abbot (1155–61). They consist of fragments of his dogmatic work *The Trinity*,[163] a psychological treatise usually attributed to him called *The Discrimination of Soul, Spirit and Mind*,[164] and fifteen sermons, the last of which is really a mystical tract sometimes entitled *The Treatise on the Seven Deserts*.[165] Achard's mystical teaching is rooted in a metaphysics centering on the divine ideas/causes/forms (*rationes/causae/formae*), which seems to be dependent on Hugh's concern for philosophy as the discipline concerned with attaining the causes (see *Didascalicon* 1.4), but which also uses ideas from John Scottus Eriugena.[166] It is not necessary to go into the details of this Victorine's speculation in order to understand the relation between his mystical teaching and what we have seen in Hugh.

Several of Achard's sermons, especially *Sermon* 12 on the Transfiguration,[167] *Sermon* 13 on the Feast of the Dedication of the Abbey church of Saint Victor,[168] and *Sermon* 14 for All Saints,[169] are important for his mystical teaching. He also discusses the nature of ecstatic experience of God at the end of *The Discrimination of Soul, Spirit, and Mind*; but without doubt the best access to Achard's mysticism is to be found in *Sermon* 15. The desert motif, as we have seen, began to acquire new significance in some of the later Cistercian authors, such as Isaac of Stella. Hugh of St. Victor composed a brief *Miscellany* on the desert of the human heart,[170] which may have inspired Achard to devote attention to this theme in his sermon-treatise.[171]

This Sermon for the First Sunday of Lent is based on Mark 4:1, "Jesus was led into the desert by the Spirit," but Achard's development of the theme, while placing the desert firmly in human emptiness, is richer than other twelfth-century treatments of the desert of the heart and is also suggestive of the deeper dimensions of the divine desert theme that were to surface in the following century. According to Achard, "He was led by his Spirit into our desert, rather, into us the desert, where he left us an example to follow his footsteps so that we might be led by him and follow him into the desert. . . . "[172] Achard's seven deserts, each of which also illustrates the action of one of the seven gifts of the Holy Spirit, provide a helpful way to orchestrate one of those standard medieval monastic spiritual itineraries whose symbolic malleability, as we have seen, allowed for considerable variety within one overall pattern.

The human soul, having deserted God and therefore become a desert, or "region of unlikeness" (*Sermon* 15.1), begins to return to God through the action of Christ symbolized in the forty-day passage into the desert. The first desert is that of deserting mortal sin and Lucifer in the spirit of fear of God (15.4–7), while the second desert deserts the world in the spirit of piety, that is, it enters the religious life (15.8). The third desert, that of subduing the flesh in the spirit of knowledge, is understood as traditional ascetical practices (15.9-10). This three-day journey leads the soul to "the mountain of God, that is, its spirit. . . ; it is God's mountain because God's image and likeness are found in it, the image in reason, the likeness in will."[173] The fourth desert consists of the difficult task of leaving our own will aside in the spirit of fortitude, not because the will is evil in itself but because its proximity to the flesh leaves it suspect in fallen humanity (15.11–13).

Achard's longest discussion (15.14–33) is given over to the fifth desert, the abandonment of reason, which at first seems contradictory since giving up reason, God's image in us, appears unreasonable. But God demands the holocaust, which signifies the total offering of the self (15.15), and giving up human reason (*ratio humana*) is necessary in order to gain "God's reason, eternal truth."[174] In the spirit of counsel that empowers this abandonment Achard discusses ten mysteries revealed in scripture that demonstrate how human reason must yield to faith if it is to attain ecstatic union with God. The four wings of the seraph of Isaiah 6, two covering the enthroned Lord's head and two his feet, respectively signify the mysteries of the beginning and the end of time. The first of the prior pair points to the beginning or creation of the world; the second pertains to the state of things "before the world's beginning" (*ante principium mundi*). Here Achard invokes the mystery of the pre-existence of all things in the divine causes that seems to depend in part on Eriugena—"Who is so wise as to understand how whatever has been created in the world, whether alive or not alive in itself, before it was made was life in the Word of God?"[175] Likewise, the wings covering the feet indicate the mysteries of the end of time and what lies beyond it. The next four mysteries are based on Proverbs 30:18–19. "The path of the eagle in heaven" is an allegory for the contemplation of God in heaven,[176] while "the path of the serpent on the rock" signifies the mystery of evil. "The path of the ship in the sea" is the mystery of the church amidst the turbulence of the world (15.21–23), a clearly Hugonian theme; and, finally, "the path of the man in his adolescence" is read as the mystery of the Divine Word taking on humanity and being present in the world at one time in his corporeal body and now in his sacramental body (15.24–29).[177] The final two mysteries highlighting the contrast between faith and reason are taken from Paul's testimonies (Rom 9:20 and 11:33) regarding divine secrets and judgments.

One who seeks to fly up to God, "will surely sink, and, beaten back (*reverberatus*) by God's light, will be caught in denser darkness, unless God spread his wings and bear him up."[178] It is precisely the surrender of reason in the ten stages that makes possible the ascent to the sixth desert wherein the human person deserts both himself and even his neighbor (exteriorly at least) in mystical experience through the spirit of understanding (15.34). Achard's description of this weaves together many of the major themes and scriptural texts of the monastic mystical tradition, including 1 Corinthians 6:17:

> O happy exchange! The human leaves the human and brings in God. How joyful and grateful a guest who fills the whole house he enters with grace and rejoicing. For a person to leave self for God's sake in this way is not to go out but to go in—not leaving the house for the vestibule, but for the bedchamber. . . . This is the divine will and reason: that you keep nothing of yourself for yourself, so that when you have totally deserted yourself, the whole of God's will and reason will dwell in you—to "adhere to God" and thus with him "to be one spirit."[179]

Achard describes this experience of "contemplating the very sublimity of Christ's divinity" as a rapture (*rapitur*), an intoxication (*inebriari*), a wound of love (*medullitus caritatis transfixus sagittis*), and an ecstasy of the mind into God (*excedens Deo mente*).[180] The christocentric character of the experience recalls a passage in *Sermon* 13 where he discusses how Christ as the perfect *forma* of divine loving Justice united with the deformed matter of our human nature so that "that form is both God's and ours—God's because it is from God, ours because it is in us; expressed by God and impressed by him in us."[181] The experience of this Christ-form is achieved in the sixth desert.

There is, however, one desert more, the desert found in the spirit of wisdom in which we "desert God in certain way for the neighbor's sake." Here Achard takes his place with Bernard of Clairvaux, Richard of St. Victor, and many others, in insisting that the final goal of what we call mystical experience is not the enjoyment of God in itself, but consists in taking on Christ, and therefore, like Christ and his saints (Paul and Moses are invoked), returning from ecstasy to loving service of the neighbor. This giving up God for God's sake is the final desert because nothing surpasses God. It, too, is an *excessus* or departure. If the fifth desert can be equated with continuing meditation on God, "The sixth and the seventh are in departing to and departing from—departing to God and departing from God, going beyond the creature and going apart from God, going beyond to contemplation and going apart to astonishment."[182]

Although Hugh was the fountainhead of Victorine mysticism, and Achard was a worthy follower, Richard of St. Victor must be counted as the most significant of the Victorine mystics, both for the profundity of his thought and his subsequent influence on the later Western tradition.[183] We know little about his life save that he hailed from Scotland and served as sub-prior and prior at St. Victor during troubled years, dying on 10 March 1173. Like his great predecessor, he was an encyclopedic author, responsible for a massive handbook of biblical education, called the *Book of Selections* (*Liber Exceptionum*),[184] important scriptural commentaries, and many treatises.[185] Though he did not write a dogmatic *summa*, his treatise *The Trinity* demonstrates the originality of his theological vision.[186] Richard's mystical teaching is present in many of these works, but we shall primarily study three treatises.[187] Two of these are based on allegorical-tropological interpretations of Old Testament texts. The treatise often called *Benjamin minor*, or *The Preparation of the Intellectual Soul for Contemplation*, but more correctly entitled *The Twelve Patriarchs*, interprets Jacob, his wives, concubines, and his twelve sons as the story of how the various aspects of knowing and loving prepare the soul for the contemplative experience figured in Benjamin, the last and youngest of the patriarchs.[188] *The Mystical Ark* (also called *Benjamin major*, or *The Grace of Contemplation*) allegorizes the ark of the covenant (Exod 25) as the master symbol for the various forms of contemplation.[189] Finally, the brief tract *The Four Degrees of Violent Charity* sketches an itinerary of how vehement love leads to union with God and more perfect service of neighbor, taking up in the new language of courtly eroticism the ancient theme of the relation of contemplation and action.[190]

Richard's range of interests is reminiscent of Hugh, though he does not have Hugh's genius for combining the horizontal and the ascensional dimensions of Christian teaching, nor his amplitude of doctrinal treatment. Where he goes beyond his master, however, is in the psychological penetration (both speculative and experiential) that he brings to his ordering of Christian teaching on contemplation. In order to appreciate this fully, we have to begin by looking at Richard's theological anthropology.[191]

Hugh of St. Victor had pioneered Victorine interest in the investigation of human nature, especially the soul and its powers, and Richard often used motifs taken from the great Victorine teacher. Nevertheless, Richard's anthropology and psychology are more richly developed than Hugh's, being comparable to the major Cistercian authors. Monastic and canonical teaching about the nature of the human as made to the image and likeness of God was fundamentally a single tradition, despite individual variations and emphases, so it will not be necessary to provide minute analyses of all the details of Richard's discussions in order to grasp what is important for his mysticism.

Richard's understanding of how the human soul is made to the divine image in its rational-intellectual capacity and to the likeness in its affective ability is typical of the Victorines, the Cistercians, as well those black monks who addressed speculative questions concerning the soul. Where Richard is more interesting is in his development of a Boethian pattern of human understanding originally developed by Hugh to ground a more systematic doctrine of contemplation than any other found in the twelfth century. This systematization is not an academic flattening of the mystery of human contact with God—Richard's treatment of contemplation never displays the artificiality sometimes found in the triadic enumerations of such Victorine texts as the *On Contemplation and its Forms*. But Richard, even at his most eloquent, is still a representative of the ordering mentality of nascent scholasticism. While scarcely less profound than William of St. Thierry, and sometimes almost as rhetorically powerful as Bernard of Clairvaux, Richard provides us with a different overall flavor in his mystical texts.

In his educational manual, the *Book of Selections*, Richard begins with creation, specifically with God's creation of humanity "to his image according to reason and to his likeness according to love . . . ; to his image according to understanding, to his likeness according to attraction."[192] These are two of the three goods given in creation, the third being the natural immortality of the body that humans would have enjoyed had not Adam fallen. Ignorance now corrupts the divine image in us, as does concupiscence the like-ness. These last two can in some measure be restored in this life; the weak-ness that cancels immortality must wait for the end of time for its cure.[193] There is nothing unusual about this teaching in relation to standard twelfth-century anthropology. It is in what Richard did with the common stock, and especially in how he tied it to contemplative experience, that his origi-nality becomes clear.

As might be expected, Richard of St. Victor shows considerable variety in the ways in which he discusses the various powers contained under the two broad dynamisms of the soul–the intellectual and the affective.[194] Two patterns, however, are dominant and form the basis for his mystical teach-ing. Richard's intellectual pattern is developed from materials found in Boethius and Hugh; his affective pattern has two main components: a theory of how seven virtues help cleanse the soul's basic power of will and attraction; and a treatment of the four degrees of the progress of *caritas* found in *The Four Degrees of Violent Charity*.

In providing an answer to the puzzle of how God can know all things and yet humans still remain free, Boethius had distinguished between God's mode of total and simultaneous knowledge of all particulars and the human mode of knowing, which progresses from sense knowing (*sensus*), through imagination (*imaginatio*) and reason (*ratio*), eventually to attain some touch of understanding (*intelligentia*) which, "surpassing the whole of creation gazes on that simple form [i.e., God] by the clear point of the mind."[195] This fourfold schema was popular in the twelfth century. Richard employs it as the basis for his analysis of the progression of the knowing power to higher contemplative knowledge of God, primarily as set forth in *The Twelve Patri-archs* and *The Mystical Ark*.[196] But Richard enriched this fundamental struc-ture with another piece of Boethian epistemological theory. In his *Commentary on Porphyry's Isagoge*, the Roman had distinguished three kinds of speculative philosophy on the basis of the objects they study. "Physiol-ogy," or natural philosophy, considers *naturalia* or natural bodies; mathe-matics studies *intelligibilia*, that is, the principles of divine things found in the world represented in the numbers that can be abstracted from a consid-eration of natures; finally, theology is concerned with *intellectibilia*, a word of Boethius's coining to represent the Greek *noēta*, which he defines as "what is one and the same through itself, always consisting in its own divin-ity, and is never grasped by the sense but only by mind and intellect alone."[197] This text, which Hugh of St. Victor had quoted and commented on in *Didascalicon* 2.2–3, was to become the foundation for Richard's new map of the forms of contemplation set forth in his central mystical treatise, *The Mystical Ark*. This speculative background should not lead one to think that Richard's development of these themes is dryly pedagogical. Rather, he uses Boethian epistemology to organize traditional monastic teaching, including its emphasis on the related issues of self-knowledge and discretion (two key Ricardian themes), into a new configuration.[198]

Though it is not easy to identify the precise sources for the Victorine's treatment of how the affective-voluntaristic drive of the human likeness to God gets put back on its tracks after the derailment of original sin, it is easy to see its importance for his thought. Richard makes use of many of the commonplaces of medieval anthropology concerning *affectus*, such as the division of the four fundamental attractions into love and hate, joy and sorrow;[199] but what he mined with special enthusiasm in his mystical writings was a sevenfold affective progression of virtues beginning with fear of God and progressing through sorrow, hope, initial love of God, joy, and hatred of vice, to conclude with the perhaps surprising, but still necessary, virtue of ordered shame. This lower cleansing of the power of desire, however, is scarcely the whole story, as we shall see in turning to the major spiritual treatises of Richard of St. Victor.

Perhaps more than any other twelfth-century mystical writer, even more than William of St. Thierry in the *Golden Letter* and the Carthusian manualists surveyed in the last chapter, Richard's treatises combine the practical and the theoretical aspects of the spiritual exercise that prepares the soul for immediate contact with God, nourishes the experience itself, and enhances its effects. Some of the Victorine's treatises, such as *The Extermination of Evil and the Promotion of Good*, provide mostly practical teaching about both the ascetical and the mystical journey from the "region of unlikeness" to the contemplation that can be briefly touched in this life but which will only be fully enjoyed in heaven.[200] A more complete picture of Richard's mystical teaching in both its speculative and its practical dimensions emerges from a consideration of the three mystical treatises mentioned above.[201]

The Twelve Patriarchs is a "how-to-do-it" book of a distinctly twelfth-century form, based primarily on tropological-anagogical scriptural interpretation. Richard was not a literalist exegete in the manner of Andrew of St. Victor. Hugh's concern for rooting spiritual reading in a careful consideration of the letter was not absent from his mind, however. We see this in his brief prefatory work to *The Mystical Ark*, where he comments on the difficulties presented in a literal reading of the account of the construction of the ark in Exodus 25.[202] But Richard tends to treat the Bible more freely than did Hugh, being less concerned with literal issues in the broad sweep of his exegesis.[203] Like Hugh, Richard adhered to a fundamentally tripartite understanding of the senses of scripture—the Bible is to be read according to history, allegory, and tropology.[204] In *The Mystical Ark*, however, he expands this to a fourfold sense, distinguishing the *sensus historicus* from three forms of the *sensus mysticus*. These three "golden" senses are tropology, which deals with moral teaching, allegory, which is "the mystical teaching of mysteries," and anagogy, which is described as the "mystical understanding that leads above."[205]

The tropological structure found in *The Twelve Patriarchs* is complex. Jacob whose name became Israel (that is, "the one who sees God") is the *animus*, or intellectual soul. His marriages to Leah and Rachel, and the twelve sons he bore to them and their handmaids, Zelpha and Bala, reveal how the affective and the intellectual powers of the soul are to be trained in order to attain contemplation. This contemplation is born when Rachel (reason) dies in giving birth to Benjamin, whose identification with ecstatic contemplation is based on the text of Psalm 67:28–"There is the youth Benjamin in ecstasy of mind" (*Ibi Benjamin adulescentulus in mentis excessu*).[206] The scheme can be illustrated by in figure 4.[207]

Figure 4

LEAH (*affectio/desiderium justitiae*): seven children representing the "ordered affections" (chaps. 3–4, 60 for outline)
  1. Ruben (I. fear of punishment–chaps. 8, 28–29, 61–65)
  2. Simeon (II. grief of penance–chaps. 9, 52–59)
  3. Levi (III. hope of forgiveness–chaps. 10, 52–59)
  4. Judah (IV. love of justice–chaps. 11–12)
          BALA: Rachel's maid (*imaginatio*–chap. 5)
              5. Dan (images of material things–chaps. 19–21, 31–33)
              6. Naphtali (images of spiritual things–chaps. 22–24, 31–33)
          ZELPHA: Leah's maid (*sensualitas*–chap. 5)
              7. Gad (abstinence–chaps. 24–26, 33)
              8. Asher (patience–chaps 24–26, 33–35)

LEAH: second set of offspring
          9. Issachar (V. joy of interior sweetness–chaps. 36–39)
          10. Zabulon (VI. hatred of vices–chaps. 40–44)

Interlude (chaps. 45–59): (a) Dina (VII. ordered shame) is raped by Sichem (love of vainglory), son of Emor (love of self-excellence).
          (b) Sichem is murdered by Simeon and Levi (bad spiritual advice)

RACHEL (*ratio/studium sapientiae*): two children (chaps. 3–4)
          11. Joseph (discretion–chaps. 66–70)
          12. Benjamin (contemplative ecstasy–chaps. 71–87)

Although this personification allegory may seem artificial at first glance, and Richard's ingenuity in twisting the often tabloid-like details of the history of the twelve patriarchs recounted in Genesis 29–49 to his overriding spiritual message is at times strained, a close reading of the treatise displays a subtle understanding of the psychology of progress in the spiritual life,[208] as well as a systematic teaching about mystical ecstasy rare among twelfth-century thinkers.[209]

The purpose of the treatise is to come to know Benjamin, that is, ecstatic contemplation, at least by knowledge through teaching, if not by the higher personal experience that Richard, like the Cistercians, stresses throughout the text.[210] But the spiritual soul figured by Jacob cannot immediately enjoy the relationship with the beautiful Rachel that produces Benjamin. First, he must undergo the laborious work of acquiring the virtues symbolized by his marriage with Leah. "From reason arise correct counsels; from attraction holy desires; spiritual senses from the former, ordered affections from the latter."[211] Fear, grief, hope, and love of justice, the first four children of Leah, form the basis for the soul's journey to ecstasy. Then Bala, signifying the garrulous imagination who serves as reason's handmaid, comes to the soul's assistance, helping train our thoughts: contemplation must begin from images formed in the mind (see chaps. 5 and 14). The rational imagination is of two kinds: in one reason orders images of sensible things (this is illustrated by the birth of Dan); the other, figured in Naphtali, "rises through the form of visible things to the understanding of invisible things" (chap. 18). Richard refers to these as types of *speculatio*, which in the case of Naphtali involves a form of initial and non-ecstatic contemplation (see chaps. 23–24).

Zelpha, or sensation (*sensualitas*), is the handmaid of Leah, the soul's power of attraction or willing. Her union with Jacob is necessary in order to acquire the "rigor of abstinence" figured in Gad and the "vigor of patience" found in Asher. These provide the soul with the strength it needs to practice the obedience that will lead it on to contemplation. But before true contemplation occurs, the power of attraction (i.e., Leah) must give birth to two further virtues. Issachar, the joy of interior sweetness, is a spiritual gift that belongs to what we might call the contemplative continuum—Richard illustrates it by references to spiritual inebriation and Paul's experience of being rapt to the third heaven (see chaps. 37–38). It is accompanied by Zabulon, the last of Leah's sons, who represents firm hatred of vices, what the Victorine calls "ordered hatred" (*odium ordinatum*).

The soul still has not reached the heights of the true ecstatic contemplation of *intelligentia*, however, as is proven by the lengthy allegory of the story of Dina (Gen. 34). Dina, Leah's daughter, is the last of the affections, signifying "ordered shame" (*ordinatus pudor*). Ordered shame is not the

external shamefacedness we feel before other people for some fault or sole-
cism, but the internal judgment by which conscience accuses us because of
our continuing sinfulness. Such shame, however, is easily led astray.
Richard allegorizes the story of Dina's rape by Sichem as what happens
when one lets shame leave its interior home to compare its spiritual status
with others and thus risks being defiled by vainglory over one's own gifts.
The savage revenge on Sichem by Simeon and Levi signifies the bad spiritual advice by which grief and hope for forgiveness exacerbate the fall by
their lack of discretion (chaps. 52–59).

This crisis sets up the necessity for the intellectual virtue that plays the
decisive role in Richard's path to contemplation–Joseph, who symbolizes
the discretion that regulates the proper mode and interaction of all the prior
stages to attune the soul for achieving ecstatic contemplation. Discretion,
Rachel's first child, is really nothing other than true self-knowledge–or, perhaps more exactly, the fruit of this self-knowledge. "Believe me," he says,
"the intellectual soul makes no more tortuous demand on itself than to preserve the right measure in all its attractions."[212] It is only after laborious
progress through the virtues and disciplines of the imagination and bodily
exercise that reason, with divine aid, may finally harmonize fallen humanity for the experience of God that is the final goal.

The Twelve Patriarchs concludes with a miniature treatise contained in
chapters 71–87 dealing with Benjamin, the ecstatic contemplation born
when reason dies. Here the book shifts its exegetical ground, spending
more time with the Gospel account of the transfiguration (Matthew 17) than
its Old Testament analogues–Rachel's death (Gen 35:18–19) and Psalm 68's
reference to Benjamin's *excessus mentis*.[213] Three things stand out in this
treatment: first, the continued insistence on how contemplation must be
based on self-knowledge and discretion; second, the christological dimension introduced by the transfiguration motif; and third, the hint (to be
developed in *The Mystical Ark*) that reason's death is tied to the revelation of
the inmost divine mystery, that of the Trinity.

The intellectual soul, as the "foremost and principal mirror for seeing
God" (*praecipuum et principale speculum ad videndum Deum*), has now polished
its clouded surface sufficiently so that by gazing intently within a flash of
divine light begins to appear in it that enkindles ardent desire for seeing
God himself (chap. 72). This is always a gift of grace, though it only comes
to souls who have made intense efforts to attain it. "Benjamin is born and
Rachel dies, because when the human mind is rapt above itself all the limits
of human reasoning are surpassed. Every form of human reason succumbs
to what it beholds of the divine light when it is lifted above itself and rapt in
ecstasy."[214]

Beginning with chapter 75, Richard compares perfect self-knowledge to a "mountain great and high," which enables him not only to invoke a series of Old Testament psalms of ascent but also to bring in the transfiguration account and thus to highlight that it is only in and through the work of Christ that the ascent to the vision of light can be achieved.[215] The three apostles who accompanied Christ up the mountain are interpreted as the triple effort (*studium*) that leads to self-knowledge: the effort of works, the effort of meditation, and the effort of prayer (chap. 79). When these three fall on their faces at the sound of the divine voice proclaiming, "This is my Beloved Son in whom I am well pleased" (Matt 17:5–6), Richard reads this as the failure of all human memory, sense, and reason at the revelation of the incommunicable mystery of the Trinity's unity of substance in diversity of persons (chap. 82).

Although this experience can be described in erotic language as Benjamin's dalliance with supernal Wisdom in the bridal chamber (see chap. 85, citing Deut 33:12), Richard's major interest here is in the analysis of ecstatic contemplation as *intelligentia pura*. He closes his treatment by distinguishing between two kinds of contemplation (one to be taken up in greater detail in *The Mystical Ark*)–contemplation "above but not beyond reason" symbolized in Rachel's death, and contemplation "both above and beyond reason" which provides existential knowledge of "things which seem to contradict all human reason" (chap. 86). As long as we are in this life, of course, such pure contemplation will not be continuous. Chapter 87 interprets Benjamin's descent into Egypt, where he meets with and exchanges kisses with Joseph as the continuing interrelation of contemplation and moral meditation in the Christian life. The rich and systematic treatment of the preparation for contemplation in *The Twelve Patriarchs* thus also includes an ample consideration of the nature of ecstatic contemplation in itself.

Richard, however, did not think that this treatment was sufficient. In *The Mystical Ark* he develops his teaching on contemplation into the most complete treatment of the twelfth century. In terms of its theoretical basis in Neoplatonic epistemology, as well as its systematic extrapolation as a *summa* of contemplation, the Victorine's scholastic ordering of this central theme of the monastic tradition marks a new moment in the growth of Western mysticism. His mode of presentation, based as it is on the *intelligentia spiritualis* of a key biblical symbol of the encounter with God, namely, the construction of the ark of the covenant, is typical of the Victorine combination of the scholastic and monastic modes of theology.

It may be helpful to begin with how Richard understood the aim and audience of the work before sketching the integration of biblical symbolism and mystical speculation that provides the basic structure.[216] An aside at the end of the first book (1.12) indicates that the Victorine saw his treatise as addressed to multiple audiences. The brief summary of the whole that constitutes book 1 should suffice for busy "more learned people," presumably academic readers; but the books that follow were written "about contemplation in the manner of a contemplative and the tone of contemplation."[217] This is evident not only from the length of the treatment but also from the continuing appeal to personal experience. This typically monastic theme culminates in the final chapter, where Richard abruptly closes off an explanation of Paul's famous rapture (2 Cor 12) by appealing to the skill (*peritia*) of those who have come to the fullness of knowledge "through their own experience more than someone else's teaching."[218] Did Richard himself share in such experience? Given the fact that he compares himself with those who "sweat" to build the ark rather than those who enter into it (see 5.1[169B]), and that he insists that "few" (*pauci*) rise up to the final two levels of contemplation (see 2.15 and 4.23[94B and 167B]), this may not have been the case. Nevertheless, his teaching on contemplation is the fullest "construction" of the entire monastic tradition.

The brief treatise called *Some Allegories of the Tabernacle of the Covenant*, which appears to be a summary of the teaching of *The Mystical Ark* (though there are some differences in detail), is helpful for locating the biblical symbolism of the latter within Richard's broader spiritual program.[219] Like his master Hugh, Richard utilizes a key Old Testament account as the master symbol for describing how fallen humans return to God. The tabernacle described in Exodus 25 is the state of perfection or discipline of mind; the atrium that surrounds it is discipline of the body. Richard distinguishes between an exterior tabernacle signifying return to the self and an interior one symbolizing passage beyond the self in contemplation. This whole sacral structure houses five objects for sanctification: the exterior altar of burnt offering that signifies affliction of the body; the interior altar of incense meaning contrition; the candelabrum figuring the grace of discretion; the table, which is sacred reading; and finally the ark of the covenant itself, which is the grace of contemplation. *The Mystical Ark* treats only this last object of santification, but it does so with an exegetical ingenuity that rivals that of any of the other masters of the *intelligentia spiritualis*.

In the course of the treatise Richard employs his tropological-anagogical interpretation of the ark to illustrate an epistemology of contemplation's path to the *plenitudo scientiae*, the fullness of knowledge illustrated by the Cherubim (see, e.g., 1.12, 4.1, and 4.5). Though this epistemology is based on Boethius and has a contemporary analogue in Isaac of Stella, the richness of its development was unprecedented. Richard adopts a broad understanding of the term *contemplatio* in *The Mystical Ark*, defining it as "the free

penetration (*perspicacia*) of the mind, hovering in wonder, into the manifestations of Wisdom."[220] Since Wisdom reveals itself on every level of
creation and therefore is accessible to all modes of human knowing, contemplation represents a continuum of ways of knowing that begins on the
level of the imagination directed to *sensibilia*, advances to the level of reason, whose object is *intelligibilia*, and finally culminates on the level of the
higher understanding, which grasps *intellectibilia*.[221] The Victorine notes that
each of these three fundamental ways of knowing can be realized in two
modes: first, in a manner that keeps within the range of the power itself;
and, second, in a way that links that power with the one above it. Richard
expresses these through variations on the propositions *in* and *secundum*, and
finds them illustrated not only in the six forms of flights of birds (see 1.5)
but also in the six wings of the seraph from the vision in Isaiah 6 (1.10). It is
obvious why he insists on this doubling: it allows him to express the inner
continuity of the levels of contemplation in a manner analogous to what we
have already seen in Isaac of Stella's *Letter on the Soul*.[222] But while the Cistercian only touched on the higher levels of contemplation there, the Victorine provides a full consideration whose underlying structure can be seen
in figure 5.

Figure 5

Level of Knowing	Form of Contemplation	Object
Intelligentia directed to *intellectibilia*	(6) *praeter rationem*	Trinity
	(5) *supra sed non praeter rationem*	God
	(4) *in ratione sed non secundum rationem*	spirits (angels and human souls)
Ratio directed to *intelligibilia*	(3) *in ratione et secundum rationem*	qualities of invisible things
	(2) *in imaginatione et secundum rationem*	ideas of visible things
Imaginatio directed to *sensibilia*	(1) *in imaginatione et secundum imaginationem*	visible things

The Victorine concludes his opening presentation (1.6–10) by noting that
"whoever wishes to attain the height of knowledge must have familiar
knowledge of these six kinds of contemplation: on these six wings of contemplation we are suspended above earthly things and lifted to heavenly
ones."[223]

At the end of the first book of *The Mystical Ark* Richard turns to the more intensive analysis of the biblical images that provide his Neoplatonic schema with its symbolic power, suggesting dimensions of meaning that abstract analysis might overlook or oversimplify. The ark of the covenant is the theophany that manifests the inner meaning of each form of contemplation. The setim wood from which the ark was constructed (Exod 25:10) indicates the first type of contemplation; its gilding and other accouterments (Exod 25:11–16) the second. The crown made of wood and gold that is placed over the accompanying table for offertory bread (Exod 25:25–27) signifies the third form of contemplation, and the *propitiatorium*, or throne of mercy, described in verse 17, is the fourth kind. Finally, the pure golden figures of the two cherubim that Moses was instructed to place on either side of the throne of mercy (Exod 25:18–22) symbolize the two highest forms of contemplation, which take place in the *intelligentia.*

The actual consideration of the six levels of contemplation takes up books 2 through 4 of the treatise, with the first four levels treated in 2 and 3 and the cherubinic final levels treated in four. The fifth book is a consideration not of the structure of the ark but of its human builders and users, portrayed in the figures of Moses, Bezeleel, and Aaron–a treatment of how the reader is to appropriate contemplation in personal life. The integration of Richard's masterwork from the initial academic treatment of the theme (book 1), through an extended development of the six forms of contemplation designed to instruct contemplative theologians (books 2–4), to a final presentation of the personal meaning of ecstasy found in book 5, provides ample proof of remarkable powers of synthesis.[224] A consideration of many of the details of the six forms of contemplation, their definitions, and respective subdivisions cannot be given here.[225] The first two forms (2.1–11), where we come to admire the Creator on the basis of a consideration of his works and then move on to consider the inner meanings (*rationes*) of visible things, allow Richard (once again like Hugh) to stress the limitations of the philosophers of this world.[226] It is in the third form (2.12–27), where we begin to apprehend the "quality" and not just the mere existence of invisible things as distinct from visible ones (Rom 1:20 is cited), that divine illumination first becomes active in some existential way (see 2.13[90D– 91C]). Here Richard spends some time discussing the laws of scriptural symbolism (2.14–16).

The fourth level of contemplation, symbolically presented in the throne of mercy, is analyzed in book 3. In this stage imagination has withdrawn and reason operates in itself but already under the influence of the higher power of *intelligentia.*[227] This is the stage in which the soul through its self-knowledge, that is, through consideration of itself as made in the image and

likeness of God, begins to make the transition to truly mystical contemplation. The necessity for self-knowledge is stressed again and again,[228] being
compared to the ascent of the sun from the glimmer of light at first dawn
through the gradual rise of the sun to full illumination: "In its proper place
the sun renewing itself gradually ascends to the heights, since by self-knowledge a person ascends to contemplation of the things of heaven."[229]

The early monastics conceived of their mode of life as a human participation in the *bios angelikos*, the life of the angels. Dionysius in his *Celestial
Hierarchy* had shown how the ascending orders of angels both symbolize
and help effect the soul's anagogy into God. Richard of St. Victor provides
a new version of this motif in book 4 of *The Mystical Ark* with his teaching
on the two cherubim as signifying sanctification. Steven L. Chase has termed
this "angelization," that is, human sharing in the suspended or hovering contemplation of those angels whose name means *plenitudo scientiae*, fullness of
knowledge.[230] The Victorine expresses this through symbols of "forging" or
"hatching" (*excudere*) the angelic form in us, of putting on angelic clothing,
and of transformation into an angelic being. As he puts it at the beginning
of the book, "What ought to be represented to us under the angelic form
should be something truly great, truly excellent, above what is of earth, and
altogether more than human." The likeness (*similitudo*) that symbolizes this
level of participation must be angelic rather than human. "Therefore, so
that we may be able to hatch the form of an angelic likeness in some way in
us, it is necessary to suspend our soul with constant alacrity in awe at such
things and to fit our contemplative wings to such sublime and truly angelic
flights."[231]

These final two forms of contemplation are above human reason, though
not *ratio divina* (4.3[137AD]), and they depend on the work of grace, as
Richard earlier insisted (see 1.12[78B]). In explaining them (see 4.7–9), he
turns to the writings of Dionysius, especially to his dialectic of like and unlike symbolism (see *Celestial Hierarchy* 2). The first cherub, on the right or
open hand, represents the divine likeness found in the things that are above
but not beyond reason; the second cherub, on the left or hidden hand, is
the unlikeness found in the things that are both above and beyond reason:
"The farther they recede from human reason the more they transcend the
rational principle of any likeness connected to them."[232] Like his master
Hugh, Richard combines Augustinian and Dionysian motifs by emphasizing how the shadow of the wings of cherubinic similar dissimilarity upon
the throne of mercy (signifying human nature) indicates the humility and
moderation we must always maintain in the midst of contemplation (4.9).

In his discussion of the *excessus mentis* found in both these types of contemplation, Richard turns to Old Testament figures to illustrate his teaching.

Abraham sitting in the doorway of his tent awaiting the three visitors (Gen 18) and Elijah standing at the entrance of the cave (3 Kings 19) typify two kinds of contemplatives, as well as diverse modes of the subsequent expressibility of contemplative experience (4.10–12). The longing of the Bride of the Song of Songs provides the occasion for an extended treatment of the nature and stages of those "contemplative ecstasies" (*theorici excessus*) and "anagogic efforts" (*anagogici conatus*) that lead to mystical union.[233] Richard's description of this is reminiscent of the erotic mysticism of the Cistercians: "Finally, when the Beloved is placed between her breasts, she melts completely through desire for him into an inexpressible infusion of divine sweetness and that spirit that cleaves to the Lord becomes one spirit (1 Cor 6:17)."[234]

The final part of the fourth book (4.17–23) considers the concealed revealing of the divine mysteries symbolized by the cherubim. The Victorine's subtle exegesis of the meaning of the gaze that the angelic figures direct both at each other and at the *propitiatorium*, which represents human nature as created in the image and likeness of God, brings out important dimensions of his adaptation of Dionysian themes. As Steven Chase has shown, the positive and negative valences of the cherubim function as a dialectical symbol of the coincidence of opposites always to be found in the realization of the present absence of God—active/passive, full/empty, light/dark, revealed/hidden, moving/still, like/unlike, cataphatic/apophatic.[235] These principles, opposed on the level of reason, are fused in contemplative *intelligentia*, as symbolized by the mutual gaze of the cherubim (see 4.19). But the golden angels also look upon the *propitiatorium*, or throne of mercy, thereby signifying that the last three levels of contemplation are interrelated, because in the task of faith seeking understanding we draw our similitudes for understanding and expressing divine things - primarily from the rational spirit made to God's image and likeness (4.20). We must always remember that in finding likenesses for the Trinity "the dissimilarity is greater than the similarity,"[236] but similitudes drawn from a consideration of the rational spirit's ability to love form the basis for the Victorine's major doctrinal treatise, *The Trinity*.[237]

One of the puzzling features about *The Mystical Ark*, especially in light of an earlier exegesis of the ark of covenant which had emphasized a christological reading, is the absence of explicit reference to Christ. Chapter 21 may give a solution to this problem if, following Steven Chase's argument, we view it as suggesting an implied or apophatic Christology.[238] Here Richard exegetes Exodus 25:22 ("From whence I will give you commands and will speak to you above the throne of mercy in the midst of the two cherubim") as an invitation to the reader to take a place between the gaze of the angelic contemplations, that is, in between the first cherub signifying the divine Unity and the second signifying the Trinity. Though there is no explicit reference to the eternal generation of the Word given in the text, we must remember that it is in this silent center of the divine mystery that the Word is spoken from all eternity—*Inde loquar ad te*, that is, "From whence I will speak to you." The final chapters of book 4 introduce a discussion of the relation between the ark and three different kinds of contemplatives: Moses, who was given its form on Sinai; Bezeleel, who was commissioned to construct it; and Aaron, who, as high priest, had the power to enter it often.[239]

The fifth book of *The Mystical Ark*, a treatise on ecstasy that constitutes the fruition of Richard's mystical thought, opens by describing how these three figures represent three modes of experiencing the grace of contemplation portrayed in the ark—Moses receives contemplation from grace alone, Bezeleel receives it from the cooperation of grace and his own effort, while Aaron receives it from the instruction of someone else (5.1[167D–69D]). The structure of this final book, however, is based not on these three biblical figures as such but on the distinction between three subjective modes of appropriating contemplation and their relation to grace and human effort.

Enlargement of the mind (*dilatatio mentis*) is a work of human effort in which contemplation expands and sharpens the intellectual soul's point of concentration (*animi acies*), something that can take place by acquiring an art, exercising it, and pursuing it with attention (5.3). This is the essential but not the sole mode found in the stages of contemplation mediated by imagination and reason. Raising up of the mind (*sublevatio mentis*) combines human effort and divine grace on the level of contemplation mediated by the understanding. "Human understanding (*intelligentia*), when divinely inspired and irradiated by that heavenly light, is raised up sometimes above knowledge, sometimes above activity, sometimes even above nature."[240] This takes place by means of divine revelation, that is, it is the realm of visionary experience. Though Richard does not advert to it here, one might invoke at this point the original consideration of the four types of visions that he set forth in his *Commentary on the Apocalypse*.[241]

The primary concern of book 5 is with the third mode of experiencing contemplation, the alienation of mind (*alienatio mentis*) which Richard also describes with the traditional term *excessus mentis*. Although *The Mystical Ark* had thus far largely emphasized the intellectual side of progress to ecstatic contemplation, as had Isaac of Stella's *Letter on the Soul*, at this point the Victorine turns to the "flame of inner love" (*amoris intimi flamma*) as described in the Song of Songs in order to understand the supreme forms of mystical experience found in this life. Richard does not use the formula *amor ipse intellectus est,* but a number of passages both in this work and else-where indicate that he shared the broad view characteristic of twelfth-cen-tury mysticism that love and knowledge have reciprocal relations in the path to God, and that love (though an intellectualized love) has the domi-nant voice. As he put it in the treatise *The Extermination of Evil and Promotion of Good:* "Surely the better we come to know the grace of perfection the more ardently we also desire it, and the more fully we are inflamed to love the more perfectly we are enlightened to recognition."[242]

Alienation of mind is realized in three forms. The first is by "greatness of devotion" (*magnitudo devotionis*), when the mind is so heated by the flame of love that it liquifies and rises like smoke to God, according to the text "Who is she who comes up through the desert like a column of smoke..." (Song 3:6). The second is *magnitudo admirationis,* or "greatness of wonder," which happens when the intellectual soul is so irradiated by divine light like a flash of lightning that it loses all sense of itself in wonder and awe, driven down to the depths and then rising to the heights in its desire for God. Richard illustrates this by citing Song of Songs 6:9: "Who is she who comes forth like the dawn rising up?" Finally, "greatness of exultation"(*magnitudo exultationis*) takes place when

> ... the human mind is alienated from itself, when having drunk of the inner
> abundance of interior sweetness, indeed fully inebriated by it, the mind com-
> pletely forgets what it is and what it has been and is carried on into an ecstasy
> of alienation by the excess of its dance and is suddenly transformed into a
> form of supermundane attraction (*affectus*) under the influence of a state of
> wondrous happiness.[243]

This final state is asociated with the text "Who is she who comes up from the desert, flowing with delights, leaning upon her Beloved?" (Song 8:5).

Richard illustrates each of these modes of ecstasy by appeals to scriptural types and by detailed investigations of the nature of burning desire for God often presented through remarkable similes. The greatness of devotion (5.6–8) is compared not only to smoke but also to boiling water. It takes place in two forms: either from fervent desire alone; or from fervent desire coupled with some divine showing as in the case of Abraham, when, in the heat of the day, he saw the three men representing the Trinity and left his tent to meet them (Gen 18). The greatness of wonder treated in 5.9–13 is illustrated by the dawn's gradual transition from darkness to light and by the example of the sun's ray shining in a container of water:

> A ray of the sun pours itself into the water when divine revelation meets with
> meditation.... When the water receives the ray of supernal light into itself, it
> sends a flash of light to the heights.... Although there is a great difference

between water and light, by the ray of light that it shoots from itself water imprints something of itself on the light so that when it trembles so does the light, when it is still so is the light, when it is clear so too the light, and when it expands the light does as well.[244]

Richard finds two biblical types for this form of visionary experience that takes the soul out of itself. The first is the Queen of Sheba (3 Kings 10), who burned with love for Christ, the true Solomon. She sought him out, plied him with questions, and finally, filled with awe at what she heard and saw, fainted away in ecstasy. This is the passage from meditation, through contemplation, to alienation (5.12). The second form, illustrated by the story of St. Peter's imprisonment and freeing by angelic intervention in Acts 12, typifies how a devout soul, even in the midst of trial and temptation, and before undertaking any effort of meditation, can be lifted up to ecstasy by the grace of divine inspiration (5.13).

The final form of ecstasy described in 5.14–19 is the greatness of exultation illustrated by the love of the Bride of the Song of Songs herself. Richard's association of joy, exultation, and even jubilation *(jubilatio)*[245] with the highest stage of mystical experience is not necessarily novel, but it does point to a new note of ecstatic rejoicing that was to find increasing favor among the mystics of the later Middle Ages. The Victorine was traditional, however, in anchoring this supreme joy firmly in the text of the Bible, though once again the details of how he presents this are often ingenious and original.[246]

Richard's emphasis on the role of desire and love in the forms of ecstasy considered in the final book of *The Mystical Ark* receive an incisive and remarkable treatment in his brief tract, *The Four Degrees of Violent Charity*. *The Four Degrees*, which might be described as Richard's most personal work, represents a new understanding of yearning love as self-transcending precisely because it is rooted in the absolute transcendence of the persons of the Trinity.[247] If psychological insight is one of the defining characteristics of the Victorine's thought, it is especially evident in the way in which he examines the dynamics of loving, both love relationships between human lovers and the love betweeen finite subject and infinite subject. Richard's analysis of interpersonal relations in *The Four Degrees* was not merely an exploration of human subjectivity as such; it was grounded in the theology of intersubjectivity that he developed in his great doctrinal work, *The Trinity*.[248] *The Four Degrees* can best be seen as the mystical corollary of the doctrinal breakthrough achieved in *The Trinity*. The latter work sets out what we can know of the mystery of infinite subject loving infinite subject and thus provides the basis for understanding the violent, yet paradoxically also ordered, love with which a finite subject can express both its proper love for another finite subject and also the love it directs toward the three infinite subjects who are the Trinity.

The six books of *The Trinity* explore the mystery of Christian belief in the God who is perfectly one yet also supremely three. Like so much else in Victorine thought, Richard's achievement can be seen as an original rethinking of the mystery of the Trinity on the basis of key principles of Augustine and Dionysius, with important elements also drawn from Gregory the Great and Anselm. In order to find a "necessary reason" for the Trinity that will nourish the understanding of those who believe,[249] the Victorine turned to the Dionysian axiom *bonum est diffusivum sui*, that is, the essence of goodness is to give of itself (*Divine Names* 4.1–2).[250] But Richard personalizes the Dionysian axiom by understanding it as charity, which, following Gregory the Great, he insists is better than self-love precisely because it is reciprocal.[251] On the basis of the human experience of *caritas* as lovingly reciprocal, conferring happiness, and presupposing generosity, Richard constructs a *ratio necessaria* for Christian belief in the Trinity. In finding an analogy for the Trinity in love of neighbor, he doubtless owes something to book 8 of Augustine's own treatise on the Trinity, but he develops his own distinct ideas.

The argument, found in *The Trinity* 3.2–5, seeks to demonstrate that the three aspects of our experience of charity allow the believer to posit that God, who is perfect charity, possesses the fullness of goodness, the fullness of happiness, and the fullness of glory, and therefore must be a plurality of persons. The form of the argument is most easily seen in chapter 2, entitled "How the fullness of goodness shows from the proper character of charity that plurality of persons cannot be absent in true divinity." If God is perfect goodness, he must be charity, and charity is necessarily love for another person. It might be argued that God's love for created persons would be sufficient to fulfill this condition, but against this Richard argues that the notion of ordered love (*caritas ordinata*) makes it impossible for supreme charity to be directed to a created subject. Thus, what I have identified as the central motif in twelfth-century mystical thought, the order of charity, makes a crucial appearance at the heart of Richard's theology of love. "So that the fullness of charity can have a place in that true divinity," he says, "it is necessary that a divine person not lack a relationship to an equally worthy person, and one who is therefore divine."[252] Similar arguments are then developed from the fullness of happiness (3.3) and from the fullness of glory understood as the divine benevolence and generosity (3.4).

The middle chapters of book 3 of *The Trinity* (3.6–10) explore how rightly ordered love, here also called *amor discretus*, demonstrates the full equality of the plural persons in true divinity, but the question remains just what kind of plurality is under discussion. To answer this, Richard invokes a second key principle, the notion of the *condilectus*, that is, that true charity perfectly expressed between two subjects demands willingness to share the love that has been shown with a third, the *condilectus*. "Therefore, it is necessary that each one of those who are supremely loved and who love supremely should look with equal desire for a mutually beloved (*condilectum*) and willingly possess him in perfect sharing. You see how the consummation of charity demands a Trinity of persons."[253] Thus, there are three fundamental kinds of love: self-love (*amor privatus*) is good but limited; charity (*amor mutuus*) is superior in going out to another; but the consummation of charity (*amor consummatus*) demands the supreme and perfectly shared love found in the Trinity.

On the basis of this profound understanding of the nature of charity, the Victorine made other notable contributions to trinitarian theology in the later books of his treatise, especially in working out a new definition of divine person as "an incommunicable existence," that is, "one possessing divine existence from an incommunicable property."[254] It is also interesting to find him speaking of the "flood of divinity and the flowing abundance of supreme love" in talking about the inner relations of the three persons, language that will reappear in thirteenth-century trinitarian mysticism.[255] But while Richard's theology of *caritas* as set out in *The Trinity* is essential for understanding the dynamics of erotic love in *The Four Degrees*, his scholastic distinction of theological tasks keeps the two aspects of his thought more discrete than they were, for example, in contemporary monastic authors such as William of St. Thierry. William's treatises on faith combine trinitarian speculation and mystical appropriation in a more direct fashion. Furthermore, while Richard certainly lays the foundation for a properly trinitarian mysticism, none of his spiritual treatises develop this in an extended way.

The Four Degrees of Violent Charity takes as its major theme not the exegesis of the Song of Songs, the base text for Christian mystical erotics since the time of Origen, but rather the interpretation of the book of the experience of love, conceived of as the most basic and most forceful of all human drives. This is not to say that the Victorine neglects the Song of Songs in his treatise, but the book of experience becomes the primary text, one that, however, is continually explained by glosses drawn from the Song. Richard also broke with Origen and his tradition, as I have argued elsewhere,[256] by founding his transformation of the language of love not so much on the distinction between the inner and the outer person as on the dynamics of interpersonal relations, explored dogmatically in *The Trinity* and experientially in this work.[257]

The violence and madness of love, especially of human erotic love, was no new discovery. The sickness attendant upon yearning desire was an important theme of the courtly literature that became popular in the twelfth century.[258] If the *caritas* that is the inner life of the Trinity is the ultimate source of all love, then it is also the archetype of the violence that is destructive when love is directed to the wrong goals, though consummating when love is rightly ordered. Other twelfth-century mystics, such as Bernard of Clairvaux, as we have seen in chapter 5 (pp. 203–4), also spoke of the vehemence of love, but Richard treats the theme in a unique manner.

The Victorine begins his treatise by citing Song of Songs 2:5 in the Old Latin version—*Vulnerata caritate ego sum*. Of the many grades of *amor* and *dilectio* (Richard uses these interchangably) the highest is "that burning and fervent love which penetrates the heart and enflames the affection and pierces the soul to the very marrow so that it can truly say, 'I am wounded by charity.'"[259] In his orderly scholastic way, Richard sets up four stages of the violence of charity that will structure the brief treatise: "Behold, I see some wounded, some bound, some languishing, some fainting away, and all from charity. Charity wounds, charity binds, charity languishes [i.e., makes ill], and charity brings on a faint."[260] This fourfold distinction pertains to the violence of all loving, both sacred and profane—it speaks the inner essence of love.

The psychological state induced by each of the four levels is the same whether it is realized in sacred or profane love; the effect on the loving subject, however, will be quite different. Wounding love pierces the soul so that it burns with feverish desire for the beloved. Binding love captures the lover in a state of constant preoccupation with thoughts of the beloved. Languishing love is a state of tyranny in which the love that is experienced excludes everything else: "Whatever is done, whatever happens, seems useless, even intolerable, unless it agrees with and fosters the single goal of its desire."[261] Finally, the love that causes one to faint away or die is a state of permanent desire in which the burning soul can find no satisfaction, a form of natural *epektasis*: "It always finds something still to desire.... It thirsts and drinks, but its drinking does not extinguish its thirst."[262] What is missing in any brief survey of the four stages is the astute psychological analysis that the Victorine brings to bear in his presentation, particularly the illustrations drawn from the various stages of illness and carnal desire.

These four levels in the psychological progression of the madness of love—summarized as *amor insuperabilis, amor inseparabilis, amor singularis,* and *amor insatiabilis*—have very different effects depending on the person to whom they are directed. "In spiritual desires the greater the degree of desire the better; in fleshly desires the greater the worse."[263] The reason for this is not so much Richard's undervaluing of human love or sexual desire, however much he may have shared medieval Christian ambivalences about this, but rather the analysis of finite and infinite love objects dependent on *The Trinity.* The dynamic drive of the love planted in the human subject is our participation in the infinite love of the divine persons. Its insatiable epektetic character is our share in this infinity. When this insatiability is directed to the Divine Lover it allows a growth and ordering of love that benefits the human lover as well as all humanity; but when it is mistakenly directed to another finite person, love becomes perverted and its insatiability, unable to feed on the only truly infinite subject, eventually destroys both the lover and the human beloved.[264]

For the Victorine only the first level, *amor insuperabilis,* is healthy in human love relations. He identifies this with the highest form of human love, that which binds two people in marriage. The other forms of love, when directed to finite lovers, become increasingly destructive. *Amor inseperabilis* prevents us from fulfilling our responsibilities to other loves; *amor singularis* frustrates the lover who cannot enjoy the beloved as much as he or she would wish, while *amor insatiabilis,* as we have noted, can actually destroy both lover and beloved. When the violence of love is directed to the Divine Lover in the ascent to contemplation, however, love's logic reverses itself—the higher and more insane the love, the more satisfying and creative it becomes.

Richard illustrates the progression of sacred *eros* by a series of images and illustrations drawn from both the Bible and from human marriage considered as a progression from betrothal, through the marriage ceremony, sexual consummation, and finally the bearing of children. In the betrothal stage, the human lover deserts the world and turns away from carnal pleasure through the influence of a grace that enflames the affections but does not yet illumine the intellect.[265] The stage represented by the marriage ceremony is one of illumination in which the soul flies up on the wing of contemplation to a knowledge of heavenly mysteries.[266] The most directly erotic level is that symbolized by human sexual union, the stage in which the mind is ecstatically united with the Divine Bridegroom by being "rapt into the abyss of divine light" (*in illam rapitur divini luminis abyssum*: 38, ed. 167.5–6). "The soul," Richard says, "then thirsts to go into God, when through ecstasy of mind, she desires to pass totally into God, so that completely forgetting herself she can truly say: 'I do not know whether in the body, or out of the body; God knows'" (2 Cor 12:3).[267] Here Richard makes use of the language of fire heating and eventually liquifying a bar of iron (borrowed from Hugh), as well as standard texts from the Song of Songs, from 1 Corinthians 6:17, and from a series of other biblical books that had long been used to describe the *unitas spiritus* of Western monastic mysticism. The process is fully Christo-mimetic. In this stage the soul is melted down and reformed into the "form of the humility of Christ" (*forma humilitatis Christi*: 43, ed. 171.28).

This, however, is not the end of the process. Along with Hugh of St. Victor, with Achard, and also with the major Cistercian mystics, Richard insists that mystical experience is not just for the self but for the whole human community. Sexual congress leads to childbirth, that is, the soul passes through the ecstasy of mystical death in order to be reborn with Christ and to continue his saving work of love in the world. Like Paul, who was willing to become anathema for the sake of his brethren (Rom 9:3), such a soul abandons the delights of the mystical marriage to return to the active love symbolized by the duties of the busy mother. "Doesn't this grade of love seem to turn the intellectual soul mad since it does not allow it to keep to mode or measure in its passion?" he asks. "Doesn't it seem the height of madness to reject true life, to bring a case against the highest wisdom, to resist omnipotence? Didn't he reject life who was willing to be separated from Christ for his brethren . . . ?"[268] This is the true insanity of loving God.

Richard's remark about how such an insane soul does not preserve the proper "mode or measure" (*modum mensuramve*) might seem to indicate that the Victorine has abandoned the notion of the order of love (*ordo caritatis*) that had been so central to the mystics of the twelfth century. However, the paradoxes of mystical experience indicate that his argument is actually quite the reverse. The ordering of love, as we have seen in our treatment of *The Twelve Patriarchs*, was a crucial element in his thought. But just as the fundamental law of the Christian life is that one can only gain one's life by losing it, so too the true ordering of charity involves the insanity of love that drives the mystic to abandon even the experience of divine love itself, imitating the love by which the Divine Lover emptied himself to bring his saving love to humanity. Richard of St. Victor's evocation of this essential truth aptly summarizes the contributions of twelfth-century mystics to the great tradition that God is never sought for ourselves alone, but always for the building up of the Body of Christ.

Epilogue

B Y THE YEAR 1200, when we close this volume, Christian mysticism, at least in its explicit forms, had been in existence for a millennium. The variety of these forms, as I have suggested in the hundreds of pages contained in *The Foundations of Mysticism* and now in *The Growth of Mysticism,* was striking, but no less impressive was the inner coherence of crucial themes that gave these many expressions a form that allows the story to be presented as we have it here. Much of this coherence is due not just to the fundamentals of Christian belief but also to the institutional matrix in which most Christian mystics of this millennium lived their lives–monasticism. Even the Victorine canons considered in the final chapter, though they adopted a somewhat different form of religious life and were pioneers in the new model of scholastic theology, were, for all that, still working out of the monastic patrimony.

The same was to be only partly true for the forms of Christian mysticism that developed in the eight centuries between 1200 and 2000 C.E., which will be the subject of the remaining volumes in this history. To be sure, towering figures, especially Augustine and Gregory the Great, were to continue to be central to all later Christian mystical practice and its written expression, and the twelfth century, as I have argued in the second part of this volume, constitutes a watershed of mystical theory that was to irrigate many later traditions. The Cistercians and the Victorines were the masters of later Western mysticism just as truly as Anselm, Abelard, Peter Lombard, and the other *magistri* of the twelfth-century cathedral schools were the forebears of the rich proliferation of scholastic thought in the later Middle Ages.

To write the history of mysticism, especially from a theological perspective, is to write the history of a single element, and very much an ideal element, in the broader history of the Christian church as a human and time-bound institution where theory is inextricably bound up with the reality of day-to-day existence. Throughout the course of these two volumes I have tried to show, if only in a partial way, how aspects of mystical theory and practice must always be understood in the light of the wider context of the history of Western Christianity. But even this fragmentary attention to context has been presented from the inside not the outside—that is, not from a critical perspective that tries to measure the gap between ideals and reality or to judge the legitimacy of these ideals, but from the viewpoint of what spiritual values these Christians said they were trying to inculcate in their lives and societies. That they often failed in this task of inculcation, and even that they may have deluded themselves about their intentions, is too obvious to need underlining; but the existence and even sometimes the effects of the spiritual values of medieval monasticism are no less true. To write the history of an ideal is not to write the whole story, but that broader tale can never be understood without attention to the ideals by which particular institutions and persons expressed what was most noble in their aspirations.

For medieval monastics the goal of all their endeavors was to enjoy the presence of God in contemplative experience insofar as this might be given in this life. We have no way of knowing how far this ideal actually directed the lives of the wide range of monks of the Middle Ages. Likewise, we have no way of knowing how far any individual medieval religious writer did actually attain some form of more immediate consciousness of God. What we do have are forms of written testimony concerning that consciousness that are worthy of credence insofar as they witness to the transformative effect these writers and their lives and works had on their contemporaries and on those who came after them.

The authors we have looked at in this volume all testify to the ambiguity and difficulty of talking about this ultimate mystery. They do so under many forms, even that of the puzzling paradox of God's presence which is also his absence, the motif of these volumes. Richard of St. Victor, in discussing the penultimate mysteries in *The Mystical Ark*, that is, the contemplation of the divine nature as above but not yet beyond reason, provides a reflection on this that can form a fitting conclusion to these first two volumes of *The Presence of God.*

> Item si in omni loco est, nihil illo praesentius.
> Si extra omnem locum est, nihil illo absentius.
> Sed nunquid eo ipso absentius quo omnium praesentius,

et eo ipso praesentius quo omnium absentius cui
aliunde et aliunde non est esse omne quod est?
Sed si absentissimo nihil est praesentius,
si praesentissimo nihil est absentius,
quid illo mirabilius, quid illo incomprehensibilius?

If He is in every place, nothing is more present.
If He is outside every place, nothing is more absent.
Is anything more absent by his greater presence to all,
and anything more present by his greater absence to
all, than that One who is not one kind of being or
another as the being of all?
But if nothing is more present than that most absent One,
if nothing is more absent than that most present One,
is anything more marvelous, anything more incomprehensible?

The Mystical Ark 4.17 (PL 196:157CD)

Notes

Chapter 1

1. Two characteristically incisive and penetrating overviews of the late Arnaldo Momigliano are helpful in getting a sense of the issues: "Introduction: Christianity and the Decline of the Roman Empire," in *The Conflict between Paganism and Christianity in the Fourth Century*, ed. Arnaldo Momigliano (Oxford: Clarendon Press, 1963), pp. 1–16; and "After Gibbon's Decline and Fall," in *Age of Spirituality. A Symposium*, ed. Kurt Weitzmann (New York: The Metropolitan Museum of Art and Princeton University Press, 1980), pp. 7–16. On Gibbon, see also the papers in the special issue "Edward Gibbon and the Decline and Fall of the Roman Empire," *Daedalus* (Summer, 1976).

2. Edward Gibbon, *Decline and Fall of the Roman Empire*, 6 vols. (London: Dent; Everyman's Library, 1963), chap. 38 (4:105), Chap. 26 (3:2). As a passage from the famous chap. 38 put it: "As the happiness of a future life is the great object of religion, we may hear without surprise or scandal that the introduction, or at least the abuse of Christianity, had some influence on the decline and fall of the Roman empire" (4:106). For more on Gibbon's attitude to Christianity, see especially chaps. 20 and 28.

3. See Momigliano, "Christianity and the Decline," pp. 9–12; and "After Gibbon's *Decline and Fall,*" pp. 12–15. Perhaps the best study of the essential tensions between Roman and Christian ideas of humanity and society is the work of Charles Norris Cochrane, *Christianity and Classical Culture: A Study of Thought and Action from Augustus to Augustine* (New York: Oxford University Press, 1967).

4. Momigliano, "After Gibbon's *Decline and Fall,*" p. 14.

5. Pirenne conceived his thesis in 1916 and had presented it in article form in the 1920s. See Peter Brown, "*Mohammed and Charlemagne* by Henri Pirenne," in *Society and the Holy in Late Antiquity* (Berkeley and Los Angeles: University of California Press, 1982), pp. 63–79.

6. Henri Pirenne, *Mohammed and Charlemagne* (Cleveland and New York: World, 1957), p. 234.

7. Among the other general accounts of the transition period that have emphasized the religious dimension, see Christopher Dawson's classic, *The Making of the Middle Ages: An Introduction to the History of European Unity. 400–1000 A.D.* (London: Sheed & Ward, 1932); Peter Brown, *The World of Late Antiquity: From Marcus Aurelius to*

Muhammed (London: Thames & Hudson, 1971); and most recently, Judith Herrin, *The Formation of Christendom* (Princeton: Princeton University Press, 1987).

8. Few historians today would agree with all aspects of Pirenne's noted thesis, but none would deny his significance. As Peter Brown put it: "One can appreciate how *Mahomet et Charlemagne* is the sort of classic that can render itself unnecessary" (*"Mohammed and Charlemagne* by Henri Pirenne," p. 73).

9. This is true not only in the English-speaking literature but across the range of European historical research. Especially important contributions have been made by Henri-Irenée Marrou; see, e.g., "La place du haut moyen âge dans l'histoire du christianisme," in *Il passaggio dall'antichità al medioevo in Occidento* (Spoleto: Settimane di Studio del Centro Italiano di Studi sull'Alto Medioevo IX, 1962), pp. 595–630; idem, *Decadence romaine ou antiquite tardive? IIIe–VIe siècle* (Paris: Cerf, 1977).

10. Dawson, *Making of Europe*, p. XV.

11. Momigliano puts it well: "A date is only a symbol. Behind the question of dates there is the question of the continuity of European history. Can we notice a break in the social and intellectual history of Europe? If we can notice it, where do we place it?" ("Christianity and the Decline," p. 2).

12. Augustine, *Ep.* 53.1 (PL 33:195) talks about the *christianitas* of local Donatist areas as contrasted with "christianitas . . . totius orbis terrae."

13. The territorial dimensions of *christianitas* (Eng. "Christendom"; Fr. "chretienté"; Ger. "Kristenheit"; It. "cristianesimo") first appear in the ninth century, reflecting a distinctively medieval way of understanding the role of the Christian religion within European society. For studies of the term, see Denys Hay, *Europe: The Emergence of an Idea* (New York: Harper & Row, 1966), chap. 2, who notes that the medieval use is based on "a conviction that the brotherhood of all Christians has a political aspect no less than a sacramental" (p. 31); and especially John Van Engen, "The Christian Middle Ages as an Historiographical Problem," *American Historical Review* 91 (1986), pp. 539–41, who summarizes: "'Christendom' was the term medieval folk at every level used to identify their religious culture" (p. 541). According to H. I. Marrou, "La notion de chrétienté établit une synthèse entre les deux processus de christianisation et de civilisation" ("La place du haut moyen âge," p. 629).

14. A good example from the period in question would be the relations between the bishops of Rome and the Byzantine East, which oscillate between distancing and rapprochement, between popes ignorant of Greek and successions of Greek-speaking popes.

15. The evidence of art history is particularly significant for the defining of late antiquity and its role in preparing for the medieval world. In the telling phrase of Ernst Kitzinger, "Classical art became 'medieval' before it became Christian" (*Early Medieval Art* [Bloomington: Indiana University Press, 1966], p. 16). A major exposition at the Metropolitan Museum of Art in 1977–78 under the title *Age of Spirituality: Late Antique and Early Christian Art, Third to Seventh Century* did much to bring the importance of Late Antiquity to greater public awareness.

16. Bernard McGinn, *The Foundations of Mysticism* (New York: Crossroad, 1991), pp. 189–96.

17. Peter Brown, "Eastern and Western Christendom in Late Antiquity: Parting of the Ways," in *Society and the Holy in Late Antiquity* (Berkeley and Los Angeles: University of California Press, 1982), p. 169.

18. Recent study has stressed the importance of Visigothic Spain in the transition period, especially as a transmitter of culture to Celtic and Germanic Christians of northern Europe. For a survey, see Herrin, *Formation of Christendom*, chap. 6, "The Visigothic Alternative" (pp. 220–49).

19. Writing these lines in the summer of 1992, when we are told that for the first time the

majority of American voters now live in the suburbs, and when many are convinced that American cities, if not in decay, at least are deeply troubled, de-urbanization takes on a renewed topicality.

20. A large part of the argument of _Mohammed and Charlemagne_ concerns economic issues, especially trade. Pirenne's conclusions have been increasingly criticized over the past half century on the basis of more accurate knowledge of the economy of late antiquity. Recent research accepts the decline of urban life but emphasizes its gradual character as "a process of fragmentation which forced the ancient cities to renew themselves as religious and mercantile transmitters," in the words of S. J. B. Barnish ("The transformation of classical cities and the Pirenne debate," _Journal of Roman Archaeology_ 2 [1989]: 400).

21. See the classic work of Marc Bloch, _Feudal Society_ (Chicago: University of Chicago Press, 1961), esp. pp. 60–71, 443–52.

22. Tertullian appears to be the first to use the term in this sense. It widely found in Augustine and the Theodosian Code.

23. Who defines what it means to be Christian and on what criteria are the measurements made? Robert Markus, in the "Introduction" to _The End of Ancient Christianity_ (Cambridge: Cambridge University Press, 1990), pp. 1–17, has valuable methodological remarks on this issue. He points out (pp. 8–9) that there has been considerable confusion over whether the boundaires between pagan and Christian are set in the terms used in the period itself or on the basis of modern historical and anthropological categories. On the debate over christianization in the Middle Ages, see also Van Engen, "The Christian Middle Ages," esp. pp. 539–52.

24. For surveys of the conversion process, see _La conversione al cristianesimo nell'Europa dell'Alto Medioevo_ (Spoleto: Settimane di Studio del Centro Italiano di Studi sull'Alto Medioevo XIV, 1967); and _Die Kirche des früheren Mittelalters_, Band II/1, _Kirchengeschichte als Missionsgeschichte_, ed. Knut Schaferdiek (Munich: Kaiser, 1978). See also the annotated anthology of texts edited by J. N. Hillgarth, _Christianity and Paganism, 350–750: The Conversion of Western Europe_ (Philadelphia: University of Pennsylvania Press, 1986).

25. The classic work for the earlier period remains Arthur Darby Nock, _Conversion_ (Oxford: Clarendon, 1933). For the more recent debate on conversion, see the paper by Ramsay Macmullen, "Conversion: A Historian's View," with the responses of William S. Babcock and Mark D. Jordan, _The Second Century_ 5 (1985–86): 67–69.

26. Christianity, more than any other ancient religion, insisted on the necessity of correct belief. This is not to deny, of course, the crucial role that religious practice, especially ritual, had and still has in Christianity. Correct belief, among both educated and uneducated, always manifests itself in proper ritual observances.

27. Along with the various general histories of late antiquity, there are numerious studies devoted primarily to the history of the Christian church during this period. Note especially the survey by Henri Marrou that constitutes Part Two, "The Great Persecution to the Emergence of Medieval Christianity," in _The Christian Centuries_, Volume 1, _The First Six Hundred Years_, ed. Jean Daniélou and Henri Marrou (New York: McGraw-Hill, 1964); and _History of the Church_, Volume 2, _The Imperial Church from Constantine to the Early Middle Ages_, ed. Karl Baus, Hans-Georg Beck, Eugen Ewig, and Hermann Josef Vogt (New York: Seabury, 1980; German original, 1973–75).

28. On the relation between apostolicity and the principle of accommodation to the political structure of the empire, especially in relation to East and West, see Francis Dvornik, _Byzantium and the Roman Primacy_ (New York: Fordham University Press, 1966).

29. For a survey of the complicated and intertwined trinitarian and christological debates that culminated in Chalcedon, see Frances Young, _From Nicaea to Chalcedon: A Guide to the Literature and its Background_ (Philadelphia: Fortress, 1983).

30. For a translation, see Richard A. Norris, Jr., *The Christological Controversy* (Philadelphia: Fortress, 1980), pp. 145–55 (quotation from p. 148).

31. It is important to note also that Chalcedon highlighted Rome's growing sense of primacy. The papal delegates protested against the 28th canon of the council, affirming Constantiople's second position among the patriarchates, and Leo upheld their objection (see his *Epp.* 104–06 [PL 54:994–1009]).

32. Leo's ninety-eight surviving sermons have been given a modern edition by René Dolle in *Léon le Grand: Sermons,* 4 vols., SC 29, 49, 74, 200. For a survey of his theology, see the "Introduction" by Jean Leclercq to SC 22; and Basil Studer, "Leo the Great," in *Patrology,* Vol. 4, *The Golden Age of Latin Patristic Literature to the Council of Chalcedon,* ed. Angelo di Berardino (Westminster, MD: Christian Classics, 1986), pp. 589–612.

33. I make use here of the translation to be found in Brian Tierney, *The Crisis of Church and State 1050–1300* (Englewood Cliffs, N.J.: Prentice-Hall, 1964), pp. 13–14, an excellent annotated anthology of texts relating to medieval understandings of the church–state relations.

34. A classic of older scholarship on this period is Erich Casper, *Geschichte des Pappstums,* 2 vols. (Tübingen: Mohr, 1933). In English, see Peter Llewellyn, *Rome in the Dark Ages* (London: Faber & Faber, 1971), and esp. Jeffrey Richards, *The Popes and the Papacy in the Early Middle Ages, 476–752* (London and Boston: Routledge & Kegan Paul, 1979).

35. For an overview of the first phase, see W. H. C. Frend, *The Rise of the Monophysite Movement: Chapters in the History of the Church in the Fifth and Sixth Centuries* (Cambridge: Cambridge University Press, 1972). A detailed review of the theological discussions can be found in Aloys Grillmeier, *Christ in the Christian Tradition, Volume 2* (London: Mowbray, 1987).

36. Herrin, *Formation of Christendom,* p. 125, concluding a good summary of this complex but important quarrel.

37. Between 678 and 752 all but two of the thirteen popes were Greek-speaking in origin, some from the Eastern empire, others from Sicily.

38. The Goths had been converted to Christianity through the efforts of the Arian bishop Ulfilas, ca. 350. Some of the more remote German tribes were pagan (the Franks, the Angles and Saxons, and many Lombards), but the majority that settled in the empire adhered to Arianism, which, though primarily a trinitarian heresy, also involved christological error to the extent that it did not view Christ as fully divine.

39. As Patrick put it in his noted *Confession,* chap. 38: "Because I truly am a debtor to God, who gave me so much help that many people were reborn into God through me and afterwards were confirmed and that clergy were ordained everywhere for them, for a people who had recently come to belief whom the Lord chose from the ends of the earth (Acts 13:47)." I make use of the translation of R. P. C. Hanson in *The Life and Writings of the Historical Saint Patrick* (New York: Seabury, 1983), p. 109; cf. *Confession* 35–41, and the *Letter to Coroticus* 10, for more on Patrick's zeal to spread the gospel.

40. See *The Anglo-Saxon Missionaries to Germany,* trans. and ed. C. H. Talbot (New York: Sheed & Ward, 1954).

41. See Hans von Campenhausen, "The Ascetical Idea of Exile in Ancient and Early Medieval Monasticism," in *Tradition and Life in the Early Church* (Philadelphia: Fortress, 1968), pp. 231–51; and Jean Leclercq, "Monachisme et pérégrination," in *Aux Sources de la Spiritualité Occidentale. Étapes et Constantes* (Paris: Cerf, 1964), pp. 35–90.

42. This is evident, for instance, in the noted dispute between Celtic and Roman uses debated at the Synod of Whitby in England in 664 and described in Venerable Bede's *History of the English Church and People* 3.25. King Oswy's words deciding in favor of Rome put it succinctly: "Peter is the guardian of the gates of heaven, and I shall not contradict him. I shall obey his commands in everything to the best of my knowledge and ability; otherwise, when I come to the gates of heaven, he who holds the keys may not be willing to open them" (trans-

lation of Leo Sherley-Price, *Bede: A History of the English Church and People* [Baltimore: Penguin, 1962], p. 188).

43. The difficulties involved in modern understandings of the supposed unity of the Middle Ages are all too-evident, as John Van Engen has shown in "The Christian Middle Ages." But however much we are willing to recognize the artificiality of anachronistic views of the Middle Ages, we can scarcely deny its reality by ca. 800.

44. For an account of the forging of this alliance, see Thomas F. X. Noble, *The Republic of St. Peter: The Birth of the Papal State 680–825* (Philadelphia: University of Pennsylvania Press, 1984).

45. There is still no generally agreed-upon explanation for the motivations behind iconoclasm. The events are well described in Herrin, *Formation of Christendom*, passim. For one interesting explanation, see Peter Brown, "A Dark Age Crisis: Aspects of the Iconoclastic Controversy," in *Society and the Holy in Late Antiquity* (Berkeley and Los Angeles: University of California Press, 1982), pp. 251–301.

46. See the letter of 727 translated in Tierney, *Crisis of Church and State*, pp. 19–20.

47. I agree here with Noble (*Republic of St. Peter*, pp. 94–98) that an independent papal state had been building since the time of Gregory II and was not the result of a donation made by Pepin.

48. Herrin, *Formation of Christendom*, pp. 389.

49. It is difficult not to think that Pope Leo and his advisers were mindful of the famous *Donation of Constantine*, a forgery probably produced by the papal curia under Paul I (757–767), which assured the pope temporal control over "Rome and Italy and of the regions of the West" and put the imperial regalia at his disposal.

50. For an interesting treatment, see Herrin, *Formation of Christendom*, pp. 434–39.

52. Of particular importance are the studies of Peter Brown, especially the papers in *Society and the Holy in Late Antiquity* and *The Cult of the Saints: Its Rise and Function in Latin Christianity* (Chicago: University of Chicago Press, 1981). Two general surveys that cover respectively the beginnings and the end of the transition period are R. A. Markus, *End of Ancient Christianity*, and André Vauchez, *La spiritualité du Moyen Age occidental viii–xii siècles* (Paris: Presses universitaires de France, 1975). There are a number of helpful essays in *Christian Spirituality: Origins to the Twelfth Century*, ed. Bernard McGinn, John Meyendorff, and Jean Leclercq, WS 16 (New York: Crossroad, 1986), as well as many articles of importance scattered throughout the DS. Finally, the numerous studies of Jean Leclercq illuminate almost all aspects of early medieval spirituality. Leclercq's survey account of the period 600 to ca. 800 (written over thirty years ago) can be found in "Part One: From St. Gregory to St. Bernard," in *The Spirituality of the Middle Ages*, ed. Jean Leclercq, François Vandenbroucke, and Louis Bouyer, *History of Christian Spirituality* 2 (New York: Seabury, 1982.), pp. 3–94.

52. See Brown, "The Rise and Function of the Holy Man in Late Antiquity," originally published in 1971 and reprinted in *Society and the Holy*, pp. 103–52; cf. Brown, *The Making of Late Antiquity* (Cambridge, Mass.: Harvard, 1978).

53. Brown, *Cult of the Saints*, p. 21.

54. On *praesentia* and *potentia* as characteristics of the cult of the saints, see Brown, *Cult of the Saints*, chaps. 5 and 6.

55. Vauchez, *La spiritualité*, p. 29.

56. See P. Brown, "Relics and Social Status in the Age of Gregory of Tours," *Society and the Holy*, pp. 222–50; and Giselle de Nie, *Views from a Many-Windowed Tower: Studies of Imagination in the Works of Gregory of Tours* (Amsterdam: Rinopi, 1987). On Gregory's style and its unclassical attempt "to imitate concrete reality," see Erich Auerbach, *Mimesis: The Representation of Reality in Western Literature* (Garden City, NY: Doubleday, 1957), pp. 67–83.

57. Gregory of Tours, *The History of the Franks*, trans. Lewis Thorpe (Harmondsworth,

Middlesex: Penguin, 1974) 8.16 (pp. 448–49). On the role of light and fire in Gregory's works, see de Nie, *Views,* chap. 3.

58. Markus, *End of Ancient Christianity,* p. 16. Markus sees the transition from an Augustinian "trichotomous" model of society (sacred/Christian-secular/neutral-profane/pagan) to the dichotomous Christian-pagan one as central to the end of the ancient Christianity (see. pp. 134–35 and 175–77).

59. Marrou, "La place du haut moyen âge," p. 608.

60. A classic work, reflecting the methods of the Bollandists, is Hippolyte Delehaye, *The Legends of the Saints* (first appearing in French in 1905; Notre Dame: University of Notre Dame Press, 1961). For a recent English survey, see Thomas J. Heffernan, *Sacred Biography: Saints and Their Biographers in the Middle Ages* (New York: Oxford University Press, 1989). For the early Middle Ages, see the papers collected in *Agiografia altomedioevale,* ed. Sofia Boesch Gajano (Bologna: Il Mulino, 1976); and Claudio Leonardi, "I modelli dell'agiografia latina dall'epoca antica al medioevo," *Passaggio dal mondo antico al Medio Evo da Teodosio a San Gregorio Magno. Atti dei Convegni Lincei* 45 (Rome: Accademia Nazionale dei Lincei, 1980), pp. 435–76.

61. On medieval visions see especially Peter Dinzelbacher, *Vision und Visionsliteratur im Mittelalter* (Stuttgart: A. Hiersemann, 1981); and *"Revelationes,"* Typologie des Sources du Moyen Âge Occidental (Turnhout: Brepols, 1991). On miracles, see, e.g., Benedicta Ward, *Miracles and the Medieval Mind* (Philadelphia: University of Pennsylvania Press, 1982), though it deals mostly with a later period. On the ordeal see Robert Bartlett, *Trial by Fire and Water: The Medieval Judicial Ordeal* (Oxford: Clarendon Press, 1986). On the cult of the dead, see, e.g., the well-known work of Philip Aries, *The Hour of Our Death* (New York: Oxford University Press, 1991); also Frederick S. Paxton, *Christianizing Death: The Creation of a Ritual Process in Early Medieval Europe* (Ithaca, NY: Cornell University Press, 1990).

62. For an introduction, see Heinrich Fichtenau, "Zum Reliquienwesen im früheren Mittelalter," *Instituts für österreichische Geschichtsforschung* 60 (1952): 60–89. See also Patrick J. Geary, *Furta Sacra. Thefts of Relics in the Central Middle Ages* (Princeton NJ: Princeton University Press, 1978).

63. The writings of the anthropologist Victor Turner have been influential on much recent study of pilgrimage; see, e.g., Victor Turner and Edith Turner, *Image and Pilgrimage in Christian Culture* (New York: Columbia University Press, 1978). A helpful, if brief, overview can be found in A. Dupront, "Pèlerinage et lieux saints," in *Mélanges Fernand Braudel* (Toulouse: Privat, 1973), 2:189–206. For the beginnings of Christian pilgrimage, see the papers in *The Blessings of Pilgrimage,* ed. Robert Ousterhout (Urbana and Chicago: University of Illinois Press, 1990); for the early Middle Ages consult the collection *Pellegrinaggi e Culto dei Santi in Europa fino alla Prima Crociata,* Convegni del Centro di Studi sulla Spiritualità Medievale IV (Todi: Accademia Tudertina, 1963).

64. For an overview, see Pierre Riché, "Christianity and Cultural Diversity II: Spirituality in Celtic and Germanic Society," *Christian Spirituality: Origins to the Twelfth Century,* pp. 163–76. Helpful for England is Henry Mayr-Harting, *The Coming of Christianity to England* (New York: Schocken, 1972).

65. For a sketch of the role of the redemption in early medieval piety, see Bernard McGinn, "The Role of Christ II: Christ as Savior in the West," *Christian Spirituality: Origins to the Twelfth Century,* pp. 253–59.

66. For a survey of some examples, see Adolph Katzenellenbogen, "The Image of Christ in the Early Middle Ages," in *Life and Thought in the Early Middle Ages,* ed. Robert S. Hoyt (Minneapolis: University of Minnesota Press, 1967), pp. 66–84.

67. For aspects of the German sense of warlike Christianity, see Riché, "Spirituality in Celtic and Germanic Society," pp. 172–74.

68. F. J. E. Raby, *A History of Christian-Latin Poetry from the Beginnings to the Close of the Middle Ages* (Oxford: Clarendon Press, 1927), p. 94. On Venantius's role in medieval spirituality, see P. G. Walsh, "Venantius Fortunatus," in *Spirituality through the Centuries: Ascetics and Mystics of the Western Church,* ed. James Walsh (New York: P. J. Kenedy & Sons, n.d.), pp. 72–82.

69. I make use of the well-known translation of J. M. Neale. For the text, see *The Oxford Book of Medieval Latin Verse,* ed. F. J. E. Raby (Oxford: Clarendon, 1959), pp. 74–75.

70. Using the translation of Charles W. Kennedy, *Early English Christian Poetry* (New York: Oxford University Press, 1952), p. 94.

71. J. A. Jungmann, *Pastoral Liturgy* (New York: Herder & Herder, 1962), p. 45. Part I, "The Over-all Historical Picture (especially 1–80)," remains an important survey of medieval spirituality.

72. See Jean Leclercq, "La devotion médiévale envers le crucifié," *La Maison-Dieu* 75 (1963): 119–32.

73. Vauchez summarizes: "In the Carolingian age the practice of religion was less the expression of an interior adherence than an obligation of the social order" (*La spiritualité,* p.12). See especially his comments on "Le moralisme carolingien" (pp. 18–23).

74. The sources are translated in John T. McNeill and Helena Gamer, *Medieval Handbooks of Penance* (New York: Columbia University Press, 1938).

75. See the classic work of Cyrille Vogel, *Le pecheur et la penitence au moyen âge* (Paris: Cerf, 1969); Pierre Payer, *Sex and the Penitentials: The Development of a Sexual Code* (Toronto: University of Toronto, 1984). See also Aron Gurevich, "Popular culture in the mirror of the penitentials," *Medieval Popular Culture: Problems of Belief and Perception* (Cambridge: Cambridge University Press, 1988), pp. 78–103.

76. See Erich Auerbach, "The Western Public and Its Language," in *Literary Language and Its Public in Late Latin Antiquity and in the Middle Ages,* Bollingen Series 74 (New York: Pantheon, 1965), pp. 235–338.

77. On *rusticitas* as the absence of *reverentia* for the saints, see Brown, *Cult of the Saints,* pp. 118–24. Arnaldo Momigliano shows that the traditional Roman distinction between *religio* and *superstitio* had broken down by the fourth century among pagan authors and that Christians were more interested in the distinction between orthodoxy and heresy ("Popular Religious Beliefs and the late Roman historians," in *Popular Belief and Practice,* ed. G. J. Cuming and Derek Baker [Cambridge: Cambridge University Press, 1972], pp. 1–18). In Christian authors, *superstitio* is a very large term that can be used of Jews and heretics as well as of scrupulous practices and pagan "survivals."

78. See Brown, *Cult of the Saints,* pp. 36–49; idem, "Eastern and Western Christendom in Late Antiquity," pp. 185–90.

79. The contrast between clerical and folkloric culture argued by Jacques LeGoff is merely an "anthropologized" version of the old two-tiered model popular since the Enlightenment (see "Clerical Culture and Folklore Traditions in Merovingian Civilization," *Time, Work and Culture in the Middle Ages* [Chicago: University of Chicago Press, 1980], pp. 153–58).

80. Able attacks against the notion of "popular religion" implied in the two-tiered model have been many in recent years. For the wider methodological issue, see Brown, *Cult of the Saints,* pp. 12–22, 27–30. A devastating critique of at least one attempt to describe medieval popular religion can be found in R. C. Trexler's review of Raoul Manselli, *La religion populaire au moyen âge* (Paris and Montreal: Institut d'études médiévales, 1975) in *Speculum* 52 (1977): 1019–22. Momigliano concludes his essay "Popular Religious Beliefs and the late Roman historians" by "reporting that there were no such beliefs" [p. 18]). Even those like Aron Gurevich who continue to use the term emphasize "the connection between author and audience," concluding that "for all their erudition, the authors of Latin edifying works shared a common understanding of religion with their audience" (see his "Popular culture and

medieval Latin literature from Caesarius of Arles to Caesarius of Heisterbach," in *Medieval popular culture*, p. 35).

81. Defenders of the two-tiered model tend to forget the continuing role of the laity and the fact that many of the leaders of the clerical elite, at least until 600, came late to the clerical life. For an overview, see Jacques Fontaine, "The Practice of Christian Life: The Birth of the Laity," in *Christian Spirituality: Origins to the Twelfth Century*, pp. 453–91.

82. Caesarius of Arles, *Sermo* 4.4 (25–26) in *Césaire d'Arles: Sermons au peuple*, ed. M.-J. Delage, SC 175, pp. 298–300.

83. Etienne Delaruelle, "La Gaule chrétienne à l'epoque franque," *Revue d'histoire de l'eglise de France* 38 (1952): 64–72. See Vauchez, *La spiritualité*, pp. 14–18.

89 For a general view, see Jungmann's "The Over-all Historical Picture," in *Pastoral Liturgy*, as well as Pierre-Marie Gy, "Liturgy and Spirituality II. Sacraments and Liturgy in Latin Christianity," in *Christian Spirituality: Origins to Twelfth Century*, pp. 365–81.

85. The best expression of this view came as early as the ninth century with Amalarius of Metz, whose *Liber officialis* was widely read in the later Middle Ages.

86. See H. I. Marrou, *A History of Education in Antiquity* (New York: Sheed & Ward, 1956), which concludes with two chapters on our period.

87. Prudentius, *Contra Orationem Symmachi* 2.816–17 (LCL 2:70).

88. The standard work in this area is Pierre Riché, *Education and Culture in the Barbarian West Sixth through Eighth Centuries* (Columbia, SC: University of South Carolina Press, 1976).

89. Pierre Courcelle, *Late Latin Writers and Their Greek Sources* (Cambridge, MA: Harvard University Press, 1969) is a good account of the intellectual relations between East and West from Macrobius to Cassiodorus.

90. Riché, *Education and Culture*, p. 99; see also Riché's chapter 4, "The First Christian Schools at the Beginning of the Sixth Century" (pp. 100–35).

91. Gregory the Great, *Dialogi* 2, praef. I have used the translation of Odo John Zimmerman in FC 39:55–56. On Benedict's attitude toward the role of education for his monks, see chap. 1 in Jean Leclercq, *The Love of Learning and the Desire for God* (New York: Fordham University Press, 1961).

92. For an overview, see James J. O'Donnell, *Cassiodorus* (Berkeley: University of California Press, 1979).

93. *Institutes* 1.30 is the classic text, where Cassiodorus noted that "Every word of the Lord written by a scribe is a wound inflicted on Satan" and claimed that scribes "deserve praise too for seeming in some way to imitate the action of the Lord, who, though it was expressed figuratively, wrote his law with the use of his all-powerful finger" (cf. Exod. 31:18). I have used the translation of Leslie Webber Jones, *An Introduction to Divine and Human Readings by Cassiodorus Senator* (New York: Norton, 1969), p. 133.

94. For a good introduction, see Henry Chadwick, *Boethius: The Consolations of Music, Logic, Theology, and Philosophy* (Oxford: Clarendon, 1981).

95. *Sermo* 6.2 (33): Vos ergo, fratres, rogo et admoneo, ut quicumque litteras nostis, scripturam divinam frequentius relegatis (SC 175:322). Cf. *Sermo* 7.2(40)–5(42). On Caesarius's spirituality, see Mother Maria Caritas, "St. Caesarius of Arles," in *Spirituality through the Centuries*, pp. 42–56.

96. There are a number of introductions to early medieval exegesis. A brief overview can be found in Jean Leclercq, "From Gregory the Great to St. Bernard," in *The Cambridge History of the Bible: 2. The West from the Fathers to the Reformation*, ed. G. H. W. Lampe (Cambridge: Cambridge University Press, 1969), pp. 183–97; see also R. E. McNally, *The Bible in the Early Middle Ages* (Westminster, MD: Newman, 1959). For more detail, see the classic of Henri de Lubac, *Exégèse médiévale*, 4 vols. (Paris: Aubier, 1959–63); Bernhard Bischoff, "Wendepunckte in der Geschichte der lateinischen Exegese im Frühmittelalter," in *Mittelalterliche Studien*, vol.

1 (Stuttgart: Hiersemann, 1966), pp. 205–73; and *Bible de tous les temps:* Vol. 4, *Le Moyen Âge et la Bible,* ed. Pierre Riché and Guy Lobrichon (Paris: Beauchesne, 1984).

97. For an introduction see George Hardin Brown, *Bede the Venerable* (Boston: Twayne, 1987), esp. chap. 3, which deals with the exegetical works.

98. Markus, *End of Ancient Christianity,* p. 17; cf. chaps. 11–13 (pp. 157–211).

99. For an overview of medieval attitudes toward asceticism, see Giles Constable, *Attitudes Toward Self-Inflicted Suffering in the Middle Ages* (Brookline, MA: Hellenic College Press, 1982).

100. McGinn, *Foundations of Mysticism,* chap. 5, "The Monastic Turn and Mysticism."

101. Ibid., Part II.

102. For a survey, see Adalbert de Vogüé, "The Cenobitic Rules of the West," *Cistercian Studies* 12 (1977): 176–83.

103. Ibid., p. 182.

104. There is a large literature on *Rule of the Master* and its relation to the *Regula Benedicti.* See the English translation with extensive apparatus, *The Rule of the Master* (Kalamazoo, MI: Cistercian Publications, 1977). The other major rules from this period come from Caesarius of Arles, who wrote both for virgins and for monks.

105. The standard critical edition, with prodigious apparatus, is that of Adalbert de Vogüé and Jean Neufville, *La Reglé de saint Benoit* (SC 181–83). There is a reproduction of this text with translation and helpful apparatus in *RB 1980: The Rule of St. Benedict,* ed. Timothy Fry et al. (Collegeville, MN: Liturgical Press, 1981). I will use this translation with references to individual chapters and clauses (e.g., RB 70.4).

106. I cannot pursue here the history of how the RB (or better, the *interpreted RB*) eventually achieved a position of dominance in Latin monasticism. Although Benedict did not write just for his own house at Monte Cassino, as is sometimes asserted (see RB 62.1 and 73.1 for evidence), he certainly never thought his *regula* was to be the only one. The centuries between 400 and 800 saw much mixing of rules, even in the same community; but it seems that the advantages of the RB were becoming evident by the eighth century, especially when Charlemagne saw to it that an "authentic" copy of the text (Saint Gall ms. 914, still thought by many to be the best) was sent to the Frankish realm to help in the reform of monasticism. Paul the Deacon wrote the earliest commentary on the *Rule* ca. 775, and at the Synod of Aachen in 817 Benedict of Aniane's systematization of the RB was made the official form of monasticism for the western empire.

107. I would also note that they correspond to the two basic images of exile (=asceticism) and paradise (=mysticism) that Jean Leclercq employs to characterize the monasticism of the centuries immediately following Benedict. See "Le monachisme du haut moyen âge (VIII–Xe siècles)," in *Théologie de la vie monastique: Études sur la tradition patristique* (Paris: Aubier, 1961), pp. 437–45.

108. In this, Benedict was at odds with much contemporary monasticism, especially among the Irish, which stressed the theme of *peregrinatio pro Christo.* Nevertheless, a generation before, Caesarius of Arles had also insisted on *stabilitas.* In the description of the procedure for receiving brothers in RB 58, the novice "promises stability, fidelity to monastic life, and obedience" (58.17) before the community. This is done in a written document sworn in the names of the saints whose relics were contained in the altar–an act typical of late antique piety.

109. See Adalbert de Vogüé, "Sub regula vel abbate: A Study of the Theological Significance of the Ancient Monastic Rules," in *Rule and Life: An Interdisciplinary Symposium,* ed. M. Basil Pennington (Spencer, MA: Cistercian Publications, 1971), pp. 21–63; and, more fully, de Vogüé's *Community and Abbot in the Rule of Saint Benedict,* 2 vols. (Kalamazoo, MI: Cistercian Publications, 1979, 1988).

110. David Knowles, "St. Benedict," in *Spirituality through the Centuries,* p. 62; see p. 71,

where Knowles finds in RB 73 a possible invitation "to the higher degrees of the spiritual life."

111. See Marie-Gérard Dubois, "The Place of Christ in Benedictine Spirituality," *Cistercian Studies* 24 (1988): 105–15.

112. See especially RB 48 for *lectio divina* and *labor manuum*. Benedict's stress on the importance of physical labor, often obscured or forgotten by later Benedictines, was also not always a value to other late antique monks. See Etienne Delaruelle, "Le travail dans les régles monastiques occidentales du quatrième au neuvième siècles," *Journal de psychologie normale et pathologique* 41 (1948): 51–63.

113. For more on the importance of the *opus Dei*, see RB 22.6–8, 50.3, 58.7, etc. Benedict was not a proponent of the *laus perennis*, or perpetual prayer, that some Gaulish and Irish monks practiced in the sixth century. See Jean Leclercq, "Priere incessante. A propos de la 'Laus perennis' du moyen âge," in his *La liturgie et les paradoxes chrétiens* (Paris: Cerf, 1963), pp. 229–42.

114. *Lectio divina* will be discussed in more detail in chap. 4. For an introduction, see Jean Leclercq, *Love of Learning*, pp. 21–26; and Benedetto Calati, "La 'lectio divina' nella tradizione monastica benedittina," *Benedictina* 28 (1981): 407–38.

115. See *Foundations of Mysticism*, pp. 220–26.

116. A further impetus for strengthening the mystical element in later Benedictinism was the portrayal of Benedict's famous mystical vision recounted in Gregory the Great's *Dialogues* to be discussed in the next chapter.

117. The great Benedictine scholar Cuthbert Butler went so far as to see much of later western monasticism as a reaction against Benedict; see his *Benedictine Monachism: Studies in Benedictine Life and Rule* (London: Burns & Oates, 1924, 2nd ed.), pp. 299–300.

118. See Caesarius, *Statuta sanctarum virginum*, Prologus, in *Césaire d'Arles: Oeuvres Monastiques I*, ed. Adalbert de Vogüé and Joël Courreau, SC 345, pp. 170–72.

119. Caesarius, *Sermo* 155 in *Sancti Ceasarii Opera Omnia*, 2 vols. (Maredsous, 1937) 1.2:599.16–19: . . . non solum sanctaemonialium, sed etiam omnium virorum et mulierum animae, si et castitatem in corpore, et in illis supradictis quinque sensibus virginitatem corde servare voluerint, sponsas se Christi esse non dubitent. Cf. *Sermo* 188 (ibid., pp. 727–28).

120. Currit ad amplexus post proelia gesta triumphans,
    infigens labiis oscula casta sacris.
blanditur refovet veneratur honorat obumbrat (cf. Luke 2:35)
    et locat in thalamo membra pudica suo.
Venantius Fortunatus, "De Virginitate," *Carmina* VIII.3, lines 125–28, in MGH.AA. 4.1:184. See also Christ's address to his faithful bride in lines 188–258. There is a good summary of the poem in Walsh, "Venantius Fortunatus," pp. 79–82.

121. Julianus's treatise *De vita contemplativa* (ca. 500), was usually ascribed to the better-known Prosper of Aquitaine and thus remained popular in the medieval period. It is edited in PL 59:415–520 (see the excellent annotated translation by Sister Mary Josephine Suelzer in FC 4, which I will use here cited by book, chapter, and section). For some remarks on Julianus, see Markus, *End of Ancient Christianity*, pp. 189–92; and Aime Solignac, "Julien Pomère," DS 8:1594–1600.

122. For the treatment of action and contemplation in Cassian and Augustine, see *Foundations of Mysticism*, pp. 225–26, 256–57.

123. *De vita contemplativa* 1.13.1 (PL 59:429) claims there are four different ways of understanding the contemplative life: (a) "the knowledge of future and hidden things"; (b) "freedom from all occupations of the world"; (c) "the study of scripture"; and (d) "what is recognized as more perfect than these, the very vision of God." The first and last can be only partially attained in this life; the middle two can be more fully reached. Bishops can share in these as much as, or more than, anyone (cf. 1.25.1).

124. On the influence of Julianus, see M. L. W. Laistner, "The Influence during the Middle Ages of the Treatise *De Vita Contemplativa*," in *Miscellanea Giovanni Mercati* (Vatican City: Biblioteca Apostolica Vaticana, 1956), 2: 344–58.

125. *Instructio* 12.2–3, in *Sancti Columbani Opera*, ed. G. S. M. Walker, Scriptures Latini Hiberniae 2 (Dublin: Institute for Advanced Studies, 1970), pp. 112–14. The passage is remarkable not only for its personal devotion to Jesus (*Iesu mi*) but for the first person address it uses, e.g.: Utinam me quoque, vilem licet, suum tamen servulum, ita dignaretur de somno inertiae, ita illo divinae caritatis igne accendere, quo supra sidera exardesceret suae caritatis flamma, suae nimiae dilectionis desiderium, semperque divinus ignis intra me arderet. Utinam illud lignum haberem, quo ille ignis iugiter aleretur, pasceretur, succenderetur, et illa flamma nutrietur, quae exstingui nesciret, et augeri non nesciret (112.37–114.5).

126. On the spirituality of Columbanus, see Jean Leclercq, "The Religious Universe of St. Columban," in *Aspects of Monasticism* (Kalamazoo: Cistercian Publications, 1978), pp. 187–205; and Tomas Ò Fiaich, *Columbanus in His Own Words* (Dublin: Veritas, 1974).

127. See Jean Leclercq, "Chap. II. Philosophia," in *Études sur le vocabulaire monastique du moyen âge*, Studia Anselmiana 48 (Rome: Herder, 1961), pp. 39–79.

128. Cassiodorus, *De artibus et disciplinis* 3 (PL 70:1167D): Philosophia est assimilari Deo secundum quod possibile est homini.

Chapter 2

1. The most recent biography is Jeffrey Richards, *Consul of God: The Life and Times of Gregory the Great* (London: Routledge & Kegan Paul, 1980).

2. See *S. Gregorii Magni: Moralia in Job*,"Epistola ad Leandrum" 1. In citing the *Moralia*, I will use the edition of M. Adriaen, 3 vols. (CC 143, 143A, 143B). The *Moralia* will be cited according to book, chapter, and section with the CC volume, page, and, where needed, line numbers. All translations are my own, unless otherwise noted. This text is found in CC 143:1.5–15: . . . exposui, quoniam diu longeque conversionis gratiam distuli et postquam caelesti sum desiderio afflatus, saeculari habitu contegi melius putavi. Aperiebatur enim mihi iam de aeternitatis amore quid quaererem, sed inolita me consuetudo devinxerat, ne exteriorem cultum mutarem. . . . Quae tandem cuncta sollicite fugiens, portum monasterii petii et relictis quae mundi sunt, ut frustra tunc credidi, et huius vitae naufragio nudus evasi.

3. *Dialogi* 1, Praef.: infelix quippe animus meus occupationis suae pulsatus vulnere meminit qualis aliquando in monasterium fuit, quomodo ei labentia cuncta subter erant, quantum rebus omnibus quae volvuntur eminebat, quod nulla nisi caelestia cogitare consueverat, quod etiam retentus corpore ipsa iam carnis claustra contemplatione transiebat. . . . At nunc ex occasione curae pastoralis saecularium hominum negotia patitur, et post tam pulchram quietis suae speciem terreni actus pulvere foedatur. . . . Ecce etenim nunc magni maris fluctibus quatior, atque in navi mentis tempestatis validae procellis inlidor. In the case of the *Dialogues*, I will cite according to the edition of A. de Vogüé in SC 251, 260 and 265. This text is found in SC 260, 12.16–34. The translation is my own, but a few phrases have been adapted from the felicitous version found in *Saint Gregory the Great: Dialogues*, trans. Odo John Zimmerman, FC 39 (New York: Fathers of the Church, 1959), pp. 3–4.

4. Gregory the Great, *Epistolae* 1.5, as found in *S. Gregorii Magni: Registrum Epistularum. Libri I-VII*, ed. Dag Norberg (CC 140:6.25–34): Undique causarum fluctibus quatior ac tempestibus deprimor, ita ut recte dicam: Veni in altitudinem maris et tempestas demersit me. Redire post causas ad cor desidero, sed vanis ab eo cogitationum tumultibus exclusus redire non possum. . . . Contemplativae vitae pulchritudinem velut Rachelem dilexi sterilem, sed videntem et pulchram, quae etsi per quietem suam minus generat, lucem tamen subtilius videt.

Sed, quo iudicio nescio, Lia mihi in nocte coniuncta est, activa videlicet vita, fecunda sed lippa, minus videns quamvis amplius pariens. The letter was written to Theoctista, sister of Emperor Maurice, in October 590.

5. Walter Ullmann, *A Short History of the Papacy in the Middle Ages* (London: Methuen, 1972), p. 57. Ullmann claims that this was due to Gregory's deliberate policy of "bifurcation," by means of which he sought to avoid any trouble in the East while building up his position in the West.

6. This theme is well presented by Richards, *Consul of God*, e.g., pp. 51, 66–69, 85, 108–9, 126, 181, 189, 222–23, 226, 265.

7. Much has been written about Gregory's eschatology. For a good, brief summary, see the remarks in Jacques Fontaine, "L'expérience spirituelle chez Grégoire le Grand," *Revue d'histoire de la spiritualité* 51 (1976): 151–52.

8. See Richards, *Consul of God*, chap. 4; idem, *The Popes and the Papacy in the Early Middle Ages, 476-752* (London and Boston: Routledge & Kegan Paul, 1979), chap. 15.

9. Gregory did not hesitate to disagree with imperial encroachments on papal prerogatives, though he did so in a more discreet manner than some of his predecessors, such as Gelasius. His sense of papal primacy, as well as his fortitude, is illustrated in a quarrel over the see of Salona in Dalmatia. A phrase from a letter written during the height of this is illustrative of his character: "You know well my way of acting: I bear with things for a long time (*quia diu porto*). But once I have decided that something cannot be borne, I am happy to press on against any danger" (*Ep.* 5.6 in CC 140:271.15.17).

10. R. A. Markus puts it well in his article "Gregory the Great's Europe," in *Transactions of the Royal Historical Society*, 5th Series 31 (London, 1981), p. 29: "Gregory's Europe" fell much more easily into the mold of the traditional Byzantine representation of barbarian nations as subjected under divine providence to the universal Empire of this earthly representative, the most Christian emperor, than it does into that of a kind of anticipation of a later, Western, Latin, *imperium christianum* under the *principatus* of the Roman see" (cf. pp. 34–37).

11. For Gregory's view of diversity, see Paul Meyvaert, "Diversity within Unity, A Gregorian Theme," *Heythrop Journal* 4 (1963): 141–62. Meyvaert quotes a famous passage from *Ep.* 9.27, which aptly summarizes Gregory's view of papal primacy: Nam quod se sedi apostolicae dicit subici, si qua culpa in episcopis invenitur nescio quis ei episcopus subiectus non sit. Cum vero culpa non exigit omnes secundum rationem humilitatis aequales sunt (p. 157).

12. Gregory's letters have been most recently edited by Dag Norberg, *S. Gregorii Magni: Registrum Epistularum* (CC 140–140A).

13. Jean Leclercq, *The Love of Learning and the Desire for God* (New York: Fordham University Press, 1961), p. 33.

14. As a preacher, Gregory would make an interesting camparison with Cardinal Newman, especially in his pessimism toward the world, his insistence on interior motivation and his recognition of the necessity of living with imperfection. Newman's preaching, however, largely lacks Gregory's mystical dimension.

15. The work has been translated into English in its entirety once, *Morals on the Book of Job by S. Gregory the Great* (Oxford and London: Parker & Rivington, 1844–50), 3 vols. in 4 (1919 pp. in all!).

16. There is a recent edition by Charles Morel, *Grégoire le Grand: Homélies sur Ezechiel* (SC 327 and 360). Unfortunately, there is no English translation of this important work.

17. The two books of the *Homiliae XL in Evangelia* are found in PL 76:1075–1312. The recent translation of David Hurst is based on this edition, but he has consulted some of the better manuscripts in order to give a more accurate version and an improved order to the sermons. See *Gregory the Great: Forty Gospel Homilies*, trans. Dom David Hurst (Kalamazoo: Cistercian Publications, 1990). I will cite the traditional numeration in PL.

18. Former doubts about the fundamental authenticity of these works have been laid to rest, though they survive in "re-edited" forms. See *Sancti Gregorii Magni: Expositiones in Canticum Canticorum, In Librum Primum Regum*, ed. Patrick Verbraken (CC 144). The commentary on the Song of Songs only covers Song 1:1–8 and is primarily of an ecclesial nature. But Gregory uses other texts from the Song, often in a personal and more mystical way. In the twelfth century, William of St. Thierry put together a compendium of Gregory's interpretation (PL 180:441–74), as he had done for Ambrose.

19. On this, see the discussion in the "Introduction" in SC 327, p. 13.

20. The text can be found in PL 77:13–128. Gregory divided the work into four parts: (1) the difficulties and requirements of the pastoral office; (2) the life of the pastor; (3) how the pastor should teach the various groups in his flock (the longest section); and (4) a brief conclusion on avoiding pride. There is a good annotated English translation by Henry J. Davis, *St. Gregory the Great: Pastoral Care*, ACW 11 (Westminster: Newman, 1950).

21. Alcuin, *Ep.* 72 (PL 100:245B): . . . et quocumque vadas, liber sancti Gregorii Pastoralis tecum pergat. Seapius illum legas et relegas. . . . Speculum est enim pontificalis vitae et medicina contra singula diabolicae fraudis vulnera.

22. The most recent edition of the *Dialogi* is by A. de Vogüé in SC 251, 260, and 265. There is an English translation by O. Zimmerman, as noted above. The attack on the authenticity of the *Dialogues* by Francis Clark (*The Pseudo-Gregorian Dialogues*, 2 vols. [Leiden: Brill, 1987]) has not won favor. On the relation of the *Dialogues* to Gregory's own spiritual development, see Adalbert de Vogüé, "From Crisis to Resolutions: The *Dialogues* as the History of a Soul," *Cistercian Studies* 23 (1988): 211–21. See also Joan Petersen, *The Dialogues of Gregory the Great in their Late Antique Setting* (Toronto: University of Toronto Press, 1984).

23. The literature on book 2 is extensive. For two appreciations, see Adalbert de Vogüé, "Benoit, modéle de vie spirituelle d'après le Deuxième Livre des Dialogues de Saint Grégoire," *Collectanea Cisterciensia* 38 (1976): 147–57; and Marc Doucet, "Pédagogie et théologie dans la 'Vie de saint Benoît' par saint Grégoire le Grand," *Collectanea Cisterciensia* 38 (1976): 158–73. I have tried to reflect on the image of Benedict's sanctity as it emerges from both Gregory's *vita* and the RB in my article "St. Benedict as the Steward of Creation," *American Benedictine Review* 39 (1988): 161–76.

24. It is worth noting that the earliest direct citation of the RB is found in Gregory's *In Librum I Regum* 4.70 (CC 144:330).

25. Carole Straw, *Gregory the Great: Perfection in Imperfection* (Berkeley: University of California Press, 1988), p. 7. Straw goes on to note, "Artless and honest, he is nevertheless a mysteriously subtle personality not easily confined to conventional categories."

26. Patrick Catry, "L'Espirit-Saint et la connaissance de Dieu," as found in his *Parole de Dieu, Amour et Esprit-Saint chez Saint Grégoire-le-Grand* (Abbaye de Bellefontaine: Vie Monastiqaue, n. 17, 1984), p. 214.

27. Fontaine, "L'expérience spirituelle chez Grégoire," pp. 145, 150.

28. Perhaps the most noted attack was that of Adolph Harnack in his *History of Dogma*, 7 vols. (New York: Dover, 1961; from 3rd German ed. of 1900), 5:262, according to which, "Gregory has nowhere uttered an original thought; he has rather at all points preserved, while emasculating, the traditional system of doctrine, reduced the spiritual to the level of a coarsely material intelligence, changed the dogmatic, so far as it suited, into technical directions for the clergy, and associated it with popular religion of the second rank." For a brief survey of Gregory's theological themes, see P. Godot, "Grégoire le Grand," DTC 6:1776–81.

29. Older works of value include Cuthbert Butler, *Western Mysticism* (New York: Dutton, 1923), pp. 91–133, 213–41; Franz Lieblang, *Grundfragen der mystischen Theologie nach Gregors des Grossen Moralia und Ezechielhomilien* (Freiburg-im-Breisgau: Herder, 1934); and Marcel Viller and Karl Rahner, *Aszese und Mystik in der Väterzeit: Ein Abriss* (Freiburg: Herder, 1939),

pp. 165–77. In the second half of the century, Robert Gillet wrote two useful summaries, "Introduction," in *Grégoire le Grand: Morales sur Job. Livres 1 et 2*, SC 32, pp. 7–109; and "Grégoire le Grand (saint)" in DS 6:872–910. Jean Leclercq summarized his teaching in "Saint Gregory, Doctor of Desire," in his *The Love of Learning*, pp. 33–43; and more fully in "The Teaching of St. Gregory," in *The Spirituality of the Middle Ages*, ed. Jean Leclercq, François Vandenbroucke, Louis Bouyer, *History of Christian Spirituality* 2 (New York: Seabury Press, 1982), pp. 3–30. Among the more recent literature, along with Straw's book, see especially Claude Dagens, *Saint Grégoire le Grand: Culture et expérience chrétienne* (Paris: Etudes Agustiniennes, 1977); Patrick Catry, *Parole de Dieu, Amour et Esprit-Saint;* and the various papers in *Grégoire le Grand*, ed. Jacques Fontaine, Robert Gillet, and Stan Pellistrandi (Paris: CNRS, 1986). For the latest work on Gregory, see the review article of Robert Gooding, "Saint Grégoire le Grand à travers quelques ouvrages récents," *Analecta Bollandiana* 110 (1992): 142–57.

30. Leclercq, *Spirituality of the Middle Ages*, p. 6.

31. On Gregory's moral theology, see Leonard Weber, *Hauptfragen der Moraltheologie Gregors des Grossen* (Freiburg in der Schweiz: Universtitätsverlag, 1947).

32. Francis Clark refers to it as "a dense, unstructured compendium of lived theology" ("St. Gregory the Great, Theologian of Christian Experience," *American Benedictine Review* 39 [1988]: 264).

33. See, e.g., *Moralia* 1.35.49–36.55 (CC 143:50–57), which includes the lapidary formula: Nullum est bonum quod foris agitur, si non pro eo intus ante Dei oculos innocentiae victima in ara cordis immolatur (56.116–18).

34. See Paul Aubin, "Interiorité et exteriorité dans les Moralia in Job de Saint Grégoire le Grand," *Recherches de sciences religieuses* 62 (1974): 117–62, which studies the 2,486 uses of these terms in the *Moralia;* and especially the penetrating presentation "Interiorité," in Dagens, *Saint Grégoire le Grand,*" pp. 133–244.

35. Dagens, *Saint Grégoire le Grand,* pp. 202–3.

36. On Gregory's use of scripture, besides the discussion in standard works, such as Henri de Lubac's *Exégèse médiévale*, 4 vols. (Paris: Aubier, 1959–63), see the treatments of Bernard de Vregille in DS 4:169–76; Dietram Hofmann, *Die geistige Auslegung der Schrift bei Gregor dem Grossen* (Munsterschwarzach: Vier-Turme-Verlag, 1968); and P. Catry, "Lire l'Ecriture selon saint Grégoire le Grand," in *Parole de Dieu*, pp. 13–37.

37. *In I Reg.* 3.148 (CC 144:280.2988–89): Speculari etenim nobis est de altitudine scripturarum aeterna bona contemplari.

38. *Hom. in Ez.* 1.7.8 (SC 327:244.5–31; all references will be to this edition by book, homily number, section, and lines where necessary): Elevantur vero a terra animalia cum sancti viri se in contemplatione suspendunt. Et quia unusquisque Sanctorum quanto ipse in Scriptura sacra profecerit, tanto haec eadem Scriptura sacra profit apud ipsum. . . . Fitque ut Scripturae sacrae verba esse caelestia sentias, si accensus per contemplationis gratiam temetipsum ad caelestia suspendas. Et mira atque ineffabilis sacri eloquii virtus agnoscitur, cum superno amore legentis animus penetratur.

39. Gregory's *Homilies on Ezechiel* deal with only two of the famous theophanies of the prophet, the vision by the river Chebar of Ezekiel 1 and the vision of the temple of God's glory in Chap. 40. Job is perhaps less often thought of as a visionary, but the suffering just one not only hears God, but he also hears God speaking "in visione nocturna" (Job 33:15), an important text for Gregory (see *Moralia* 23.20.37–39).

40. *Hom. in Ez.* 2.5.3 (SC 360:230).

41. *Hom. in Ez.* 1.5.1 (SC 327:170.2–5): Hanc quoties intellegendo discutimus, quid alium quam silvarum opacitatem ingredimus ut in eius refrigerio ab huius saeculi aestibus abscondamur?

42. *Hom. in Ez.* 1.6.13 (SC 327:214).

43. *Mor. in Job* "Ad Leandrum" 4 (CC 143:6.177–78): Quasi quidem quippe est fluvius, ut ita dixerim, planus et altus, in quo et agnus ambulet et elephas natat.

44. *In Cant.* 5 (CC 144:7.96–97): Iste mons et condensus est per sententias et umbrosus per allegorias. Cf. *Hom. in Ez.* 1.9.31 (SC 327:372).

45. *Hom. in Ez.* 2.10.1 (SC 360:482).

46. On scripture as food and drink, see *Mor.* 1.21.29 (CC 143:40); *Hom. in Ez.* 1.10.3–7 (SC 327:382–90). For a somewhat different use of food, wine, and oil metaphors concerning scripture, see *Regula past.* 3.24.

47. *Mor.* 2.1.1 (CC 143:59).

48. *Hom. in Ez.* 1.7.16 (SC 327:256.8–12): . . . quia Scripturae sacrae duo sunt Testamenta, quae utraque Dei spiritus scribi voluit, ut nos ab animae morte liberaret. Vel certe quia duo sunt praecepta caritatis, delectio videlicet Dei, et dilectio proximi, per quae utraque nos sacrae Scripturae dicta vivificant. Gregory often speaks of the way in which scripture represents a communication from the divine heart to our own, e.g., *Hom. in Ez.* 1.6.6–17; 2.2.18.

49. *Mor.* 20.1.1 (CC 143A:1003.1–2) : Quamvis omnem scientiam atque doctrinam scriptura sacra sine aliqua comparatione transcendat. . . . The whole of this paragraph is one of Gregory's most striking apostrophes to the importance of the Bible.

50. *In Cant.* 2 (CC 144:3.14–15): Allegoria enim animae longe a deo positae quasi quandam machinam facit, ut per illam levetur ad deum. On this, see Rodrigue Bélanger, "Anthropologie et Parole de Dieu dans le commentaire de Grégoire le Grand sur le Cantique des Cantique," in *Grégoire le Grand,* pp. 249–51.

51. *In 1 Reg.* 1.1.48 (CC 144:80–81).

52. See, for example, the letter to Theodore, the imperial physician (*Ep.* 5.46 in CC 140:338–40). For further information, consult Grazia Rapisarda Lo Menzo, "L'écriture sainte comme guide de la vie quotidienne dans la correspondence de Grégoire le Grand," in *Grégoire le Grand,* pp. 215–25.

53. On the ability of the simple to understand scripture more deeply than the wise, see, e.g., *Mor.* 6.10.12 (CC 143:291–92).

54. *In 1 Reg.* 1.78 (CC 144:98.1743–46: Ut surgamus ergo, manducamus et bibimus: quia tunc ad altitudinem superni amoris erigimur, cum scripturae sacrae profundis ac planioribus sensibus roboramur.

55. Catry, "Lire écriture," p. 37.

56. Of twenty-six uses of *mysticus* in the *Moralia,* for example, all but one (*mystica virtute* in *Mor.* 22.24.56 [CC 143A:1135.60]) refer directly to the understanding of scripture. Of the nineteen uses I have found in the *Hom. in Ez.,* again only one is not directly tied to the deeper meaning of the text (Hom. 1.8.29 refers to Ezekiel as having enjoyed a *mystica visione* [SC 327:322.32]). Gregory often uses *mysticum, mystica et alta, mysticus sensus,* and *mysticus intellectus* to refer to the deeper meaning of scripture. Gregory uses *mysticus* and *mystice* sixty-nine times, according to the *Thesaurus Sancti Gregorii Magni* (Turnhout: Cetedoc, 1986).

57. *In 1 Reg.* 3.9 (CC 144:207–08).

58. *Hom. in Ez.* 2.2.1 (SC 360:92.5–94.34): Scio enim quia plerumque multa in sacro eloquio, quae solus intellegere non potui, coram fratribus meis positus intellexi. Ex quo intellectu et hac quoque intellegere studui, ut scirem ex quorum mihi merito intellectus daretur. Patet enim quia hoc mihi pro illis datur quibus mihi praesentibus datur. Ex qua re, largiente Deo, agitur ut et sensus crescat et elatio decrescat, dum propter vos disco quod inter vos doceo, quia–verum fatear–plerumque vobiscum audio quod dico. . . . Saepe autem per omnipotentis Domini gratiam in eius eloquio quaedam intelleguntur melius cum sermo dei secretius legitur, atque animus, culparum suarum conscius, dum recognoscit quod audierit, doloris se iaculo percutit, et compunctionis gladio transfigit, ut nihil ei nisi flere libeat, et fluentis fletuum maculas lavare. Inter quae etiam aliquando ad sublimiora contemplanda

rapitur, et in eorum desiderio suavi fletu cruciatur. . . . Sed aliud est cum de unius profectu res agitur, aliud cum de aedificatione multorum. Ea itaque doctrinae sermone, largiente Deo, proferenda sunt quae vitam audientium moresque componunt.

59. *Mor.*, "Ad Leandrum" 3 (CC 143:4.110–14): Nam primum quidem fundamenta historiae ponimus; deinde per significationem typicam in arcem fidei fabricam mentis erigimus; ad extremum quoque per moralitatis gratiam, quasi superducto aedificium colore vestimus.

60. For the two levels of scripture, see, e.g., *Hom. in Ez.* 1.6.7 and 1.9.30 (SC 327:204 and 370–72). On the senses of scripture in Gregory, see Hofmann, *Die geistige Auslegung,* pp. 15–21, 73–74. Dagens shows how Gregory's dialectic of interior/exterior makes the twofold sense the heart of this exegesis (*Grégoire le Grand,* pp. 234–37, 242).

61. *Mor.*, "Ad Leandrum" 4 (CC 143:6.173–75): Divinus etenim sermo sicut mysteriis prudentes exerciet, sic plerumque superficie simplices refovet.

62. See, e.g., *Mor.* "Ad Leandrum" 3, and 18.1.1 (CC 143: 4–5, and 143A:886).

63. E.g., *Mor. Praef.* 10.21; 1.10.21; 1.37.56; 16.19.24–20.25; 18.1.1; and 19.1.1–3.

64. *Hom. in Ez.* 1.6 (SC 327:196–232).

65. See Michael Lieb, *The Visionary Mode: Biblical Prophecy, Hermeneutics, and Cultural Change* (Ithaca, NY: Cornell University Press, 1991), who compares Jerome and Gregory (pp. 249–62).

66. Compare this account with the discussion of the two thresholds of the eastern gate of the Temple in Ezek 40:6–8 as images of the *scripturae sacrae exterius littera* and *allegoria* or *intellectum mysticum intimae contemplationis* in *Hom. in Ez.* 2.3.18 (SC 360:160–62).

67. On the relation of this to the thought of Joachim of Fiore, see Sandra Zimdars-Swartz, "A Confluence of Imagery: Exegesis and Christology according to Gregory the Great," in *Grégoire le Grand,* pp. 332–33.

68. *Hom. in Ez.* 1.9.29 (SC 327:370.25–27): Hunc involutum librum Veritas expandit quando in discipulis egit quod scriptum est: Tunc aperuit illis sensum, ut intellegerent Scripturas.

69. For a good expression of this, see *Mor.* 23.1.2 (CC 143B:1145.79–82): Beatus igitur Job, qui Mediatoris typum eo verius tenuit quo passionem illius, non loquendo tantummodo, sed etiam patiendo prophetavit, cum in dictis factisque suis expressioni Redemptoris innititur, repente ad significationem corporis aliquando derivatur. On the inner coherence of the *Moralia,* see Susan E. Schreiner, "'Where Shall Wisdom be Found?' Gregory's Interpretation of Job," *American Benedictine Review* 39 (1988): 321–42; and Paul Aubin, "Interiorité et exteriorité dans les Moralia in Job de saint Grégoire le Grand."

70. For reflections on this, see, e.g., *Mor.* 5.21.41 (CC 143:246–47), and *Hom. in Ez.* 2.7.1 (SC 360:322–24).

71. For Gregory's doctrine of grace, see, e.g., *Mor.* 16.25.30, 17.14.20, 24.10.24, 33.21.40; *Hom. in Ez.* 1.8.2, 1.9.2, 2.7.9; *Ex. in Cant.* 34; etc. On the Synod of Orange, consult Jaroslav Pelikan, *The Emergence of the Catholic Tradition (100-600)* (Chicago: University of Chicago Press, 1971), pp. 327–30.

72. E.g., *Hom. in Ez.* 2.3.17 (SC 360:158–60); and *Ex. in Cant.* 11–12 (CC 144:14–15). See Marc Doucet, "'Christus et Ecclesia una est persona,'" *Collectanea Cisterciensia* 46 (1984): 37–58.

73. The same language of church as Bride is also found at times in the *Moralia,* e.g., 4.11.19 (CC 143:176–77).

74. *Ex. in Cant.* 26–27 (CC 144:27–29). On Gregory's commentary, see E. Ann Matter, *The Voice of My Beloved: The Song of Songs in Western Medieval Christianity* (Philadelphia: University of Pennsylvania Press, 1990), pp. 92–97.

75. In *Hom. in Evang.* 1.12 (PL 76:1118CD) in reference to Matt 13:41, Gregory says, "We must be aware that often in the sacred scriptures the Church of the present time is called the

kingdom of heaven." Cf. *Hom. in Evang.* 2.32 (PL 76:1236C) and *Hom. in Evang.* 2.38 (PL 76:1282D).

76. A key text for Gregory's understanding of this Pauline teaching is *Mor.* 28.10.22–25 (CC 143B:1412–15–the phrase *concors membrorum diversitas* occurs on 1414.66–67).

77. E.g., *Enarratio in Psalmum* 132.5 (PL 17:1731–32); *De Urbis Excidio Sermo* 1.1 (PL 40:717). Augustine was also the source for seeing the three orders typified in Noe, Daniel, and Job respectively, based on the praise of the three found in Ezek 14:14. See G. Folliet, "Les trois catégories des chrétiens," in *Augustinus Magister*, 3 vols. (Paris: L'Année théologique augustinienne, 1954), 2: 631–44.

78. See, *Mor.* 1.14.20 (CC 143:34), and *Hom. in Ez* 2.1.7, 2.4.5–6 and 2.7.3 (SC 369:64–66, 192–96, and 328–30). For a survey, see R. Gillet in DS 6:882–86. For an appearance of the three orders under different symbolic terms, see *In 1 Reg.* 3.170 (CC 144:292).

79. *Hom. in Ez* 2.7.3 (SC 360:328.8–11): quid isti nisi in spiritali aedificio thalami sunt in quorum cogitatione et meditatione anima caelesti sponso sociatur?

80. This central aspect of Gregory is brought out especially well in Straw, *Gregory the Great,* e.g., pp. 25–27, 233–34, 255–56.

81. *Mor.* 30.28.83 (CC 143B:1548.53–56): sed fixo humilitatis pede, graviter et constanter incedere, quia in hac vita tanto veracius docti sumus, quanto doctrinam nobis a nobismetipsis suppetere non posse cognoscimus. Cf. *Mor.* 2.49.78 (CC 143:107).

82. *Dial.* 3.37.20 (SC 260:424.183–86): Comparemus, si placet, cum hac nostra indocta scientia illius doctam ignorantiam: ubi haec nostra iacit, ibi illius disciplina eminet. In *Dial.* 2.praef. (SC 260:126.14–15). For *docta ignorantia* in Augustine, see *Ep.* 130.14.28 (PL 33:505).

83. J. Leclercq, in *Spirituality of the Middle Ages,* p. 28; cf. *Love of Learning,* pp. 33–34. Straw also emphasizes the role of opposition and complementarity in Gregory's spirituality; see *Gregory the Great,* pp. 17–27, 30, 48, 64, 145–49, 241–43, 257–59. She summarizes: "Whatever the source, Gregory uses ideas of balance and opposition to shape Christianity in a new way" (p. 252). See also her "'Adversitas' et 'Prosperitas': une illustration du motif structurel de la complementarité," in *Grégoire le Grand,* pp. 227–88.

84. For the experiential character of Gregory's spirituality, see Francis Clark, "St. Gregory the Great, Theologian of Christian Experience," *American Benedictine Review* 39 (1988): 261–76; and especially Dagens, *Saint Grégoire le Grand.*

85. On this, see especially Straw, "'Adversitas' et 'Prosperitas'," pp. 282–84.

86. *Ex. in Cant.* 8 (CC 144:10–11). In *Ex. in Cant.* 9 (pp. 11–13) the triple pattern distinguishes three *ordines vitae . . . moralem, naturalem, et contemplativam.* Gregory, like his predecessors, sees them illustrated in Solomon's three books and in the patriarchs Abraham, Isaac, and Jacob. He also takes up the theme in *In Cant.* 18 (CC 144:19–21). For the teaching of Origen and Ambrose in this connection, see *The Foundations of Mysticism,* pp. 116–18 and 209–11, respectively.

87. *Mor.* 24.11.28 (CC 143B:1207.82–88): Tres quippe modi sunt conversorum, incohatio, medietas atque perfectio. In incohatione autem inveniunt blandimenta dulcedinis, in medio quoque tempore certamina temptationis, ad extremum vero perfectionem plenitudinis. Prius ergo illos dulcia suscipiunt, quae consolentur; postmodum amara quae exerceant; et tunc demum suavia atque sublimia quae confirment.

88. On the necessity for constant progress in the spiritual life, see esp. *Hom. in Ez* 1.3.17–18 (SC 327:142–46) and 2.7.11 (SC 360:346–50).

89. On Gregory's personal sympathy with Job, see "Ad Leandrum" 5 (CC 143:6–7). *Reg. past.* 3.12.13 contains admonitions to the sick on seeing their affliction as a mark of providence.

90. On this, see Jean Laporte, "Une théologie systematique chez Grégoire?" in *Grégoire le Grand,* pp. 235–43; Laporte speaks of the *Moralia* as a unique "théorie des *flagella Dei*" (p.

239). Dagens summarizes well: "plus l'homme souffre, plus il aspire à s'élever jusqu'à Dieu; les epreuves stimulent son désir de la contemplation" (*Saint Grégoire le Grand,* p. 186; cf. pp. 187–90). See also R. Gillet, "Spiritualité et place du moine dans l'eglise selon saint Grégoire le Grand" in *Théologie de la vie monastique* (Paris: Aubier, 1961), pp. 337–38.

91. For the body in relation to sexuality, see Peter Brown, *The Body and Society: Men, Women, and Sexual Renunciation in Early Christianity* (New York: Columbia University Press, 1988). For an interesting overview, see Gedaliahu G. Stroumsa, "*Caro salutis cardo:* Shaping the Person in Early Christian Thought," *History of Religions* 30 (1990): 25–50.

92. Pierre Daubercies argues for the existence of three strands: the scriptural; the philosophic, which identifies flesh with body non–pejoratively; and the ascetic, which does so in a pejorative way (*La Condition Charnelle: Recherches positives pour la théologie d'une realité terrestre* [Paris-Tournai: Desclée, 1958]).

93. Pierre Daubercies, "Le théologie de la condition charnelle chez les Maîtres du haut moyen âge," *Recherches de théologie ancienne et médiévale* 29–30 (1962–63): 5–54 (see esp. pp. 35–37, 41, 52–54). Also helpful is the discussion in Dagens, *Grégoire le Grand,* pp. 185–91, 204.

94. *Mor.* 4.13.25 (CC 143:180.18–20): Scriptura sacra tribus modis hominem appelat, scilicet aliquando per naturam, aliquando per culpam, aliquando per infirmitatem.

95. *Mor.* 14.56.72 (CC 143A:744.35–57): . . . in sacro eloquio aliter caro dicitur iuxta naturam atque aliter dicitur iuxta culpam, vel corruptionem. Cf. *Mor.* 9.36.58 (CC 143:498), which distinguishes the *terrenus corpus* from *desideria carnalia.* On the importance of these texts, see Daubercies, "La théologie de la condition charnelle," pp. 19–20.

96. For lists and discussion of such passages, see Daubercies, "La théologie de la condition charnelle," pp. 7–17; and Straw, *Gregory the Great,* pp. 32–34, 43–46, and 125–29.

97. *Hom. in Ez.* 2.1.9 (SC 360:68.17–21): Quid enim vestimentum eius est, nisi corpus quod assumpsit ex Virgine? Nec tamen aliud eius vestimentum, atque aliud ipse. Nam nostrum quoque vestimentum caro dicitur, sed tamen ipsi nos sumus caro, qua vestimur.

98. *Hom. in Ez.* 2.8.9 (SC 360:398.15–17): . . . ita ut in tanta convenientia misceretur spiritus et limus, ut cum caro atteritur spiritus marceat, et cum spiritus affligitur caro contabescat? Cf. *Mor.* 5.34.61 (CC 143:261), where we find the expressions *caro spiritalis* and *mens carnalis* to indicate how one element of the human unity can turn the other to its own purposes. For another text on the miracle of the union of flesh and spirit, see *Mor.* 6.15.18 (CC 143:296).

99. Straw, *Gregory the Great,* p. 127; cf. p. 12.

100. This is a large part of the reason why the physical resurrection of the body was so important for Gregory; see, e.g., *Mor.* 14.54.67–58.78 (CC 143A:739–47), and *Dial.* 4.25 (SC 265:82–86).

101. See *Mor.* 18.30.48 (CC 143A:917.38–41): Dum enim sola quae sunt visibilia diligunt, profecto invisibilia, vel si credunt esse, non diligunt, quia dum nimis se exterius sequuntur, etaim mente carnales fiunt.

102. On the interior origin of sin, see, e.g., *Mor.* 8.6.8 and 9.5.5 (CC 143:386 and 458–59). In *Mor.* 28.19.43, Gregory has a powerful passage comparing the interior tumult of the sinful heart with the surging of the sea: Quid est mare, nisi cor nostrum furore turbidum, rixis amarum, elatione superbiae tumidum, fraude malitiae obscurum? (CC 143B:1429.1–3). Straw argues for two patterns of sin in Gregory, one more external (and apparently Eastern), the other internal and Augustinian (*Gregory the Great,* pp. 131–36). I do not see any real evidence for such a distinction. Gregory's sense of sin is largely a development from Augustine, as is his doctrine of grace.

103. In this reciprocal action, the soul has a certain initiative in the sense that its submission to God is the *conditio sine qua non* for bringing the body back into some obedience; see *Mor.* 4.13.25, 5.46.85, and 6.34.53 (CC 143:180, 281–82, 322); but the body aids the soul in

acquiring virtues (e.g., *Mor.* 26.17.27–28 [CC 143A:1285–87], and 30.18.63 [CC 143B:1533–34]).

104. Significantly, in his comment on this verse, Gregory finds both the Vulgate text, which uses *militia,* and the Old Latin translation, which uses *temptatio,* as equally applicable (*Mor.* 8.6.8–11 [CC 143:385–89]). Again, Straw puts it well when she says, "More than others before him, Gregory stresses how adversity can lead to spiritual transformation" (*Gregory the Great,* p. 198).

105. See also P. Catry, "Amour du monde et amour de Dieu," in *Parole de Dieu,* pp. 61–83; and Straw, "'Adversitas' et 'Prosperitas'."

106. *Mor.* 10.15.29 (CC 143:558.81–84): Saepe curis mundi libenter occupamur. Cumque post haec studio orationis intendimus, nequaquam se mens ad caelestia erigit, quia pondus hanc terrenae sollicitudinis in profundum mersit.... See Daubercies, "La théologie de la condition charnelle," pp. 35–37, for a list of similar passages.

107. See Daubercies, "La théologie de la condition charnelle," pp. 47–52. He summarizes the difference between the scriptural and the monastic sense of "flesh" as follows: "Pour elle, la chair represente l'homme racheté ou pecheur; pour notre époque [i.e., the early Middle Ages] elle designe le pecheur, mais même tout homme interesse par ce qui touche à la vie terrestre" (p. 53).

108. *Hom. in Ez.* 1.5.2 (SC 327.172.18–21): Amare enim terrena, temporalia aeternis praeponere, exteriora bona non ad usum necessarium habere,... impetus carnis est.

109. For overviews on compunction, see Joseph de Guibert, "La componction du coeur," *Revue d'ascetique et de mystique* 15 (1934): 255–40; Joseph Pegon, "Componction," DS 2:1312–21; Kathryn Sullivan, "Compunction," *Worship* 35 (1961): 227–35; and Michael Casey, *Athirst for God: Spiritual Desire in Bernard of Clairvaux's Sermons on the Song of Songs* (Kalamazoo, MI: Cistercian Publications, 1987), pp. 120–29. For the medieval use, especially in England, see Sandra McEntire, "The Doctrine of Compunction from Bede to Margery Kempe," in *The Medieval Mystical Tradition in England: Exeter Symposium IV,* ed. Marion Glasscoe (Cambridge: Brewer, 1987), pp. 77–89.

110. The eastern Christian tradition cannot be discussed here. It is a complex one, not least because of the interaction of the two scriptural terms, *penthos* and *katanyxis* (the root of *compunctio*). See Irenée Hausherr, *Penthos: The Doctrine of Compunction in the Christian East* (Kalamazoo, MI: Cistercian Publications, 1982).

111. The most important treatment prior to Gregory, however, is by the north African bishop, Fulgentius of Ruspe (467–533 C.E.), in his *Ep. ad Probam* (PL 65:339–44).

112. The spirit of Gregorian compunction is well captured by de Guibert: "the characteristic of the Christian is that disatisfaction with actual affairs which is the essence itself of our compunction" ("La componction du coeur," p. 239).

113. The basic treatments of *compunctio* are to be found in *Mor.* 23.21.40–43, and 24.6.10–11 (CC 143B:1174–77 and 1194–96); *Hom. in Ez.* 2.10.20–21 (SC 360:524–26); *Dial.* 3.34.2–5 (SC 260:400–04); *In Cant.* 18 (CC 144:19–21); *Hom. in Ev.* 17.10–11 (PL 76:1143–44); and *Ep.* 7.23 (a copy of the *Dial.* text).

114. *Dial.* 3.34.2 (SC 260:400.6–20): Principaliter vero compunctionis genera duo sunt, quia Deum sitiens anima prius timore compungitur, post amore. Prius enim sese in lacrimis afficit, quia, dum malorum suum recolit, pro his perpeti supplicia aeterna pertimescit. At vero, cum longa maeroris anxietudine fuerit formida consumpta, quaedam iam de praesumptione veniae securitas nascitur, et in amore caelestium gaudiorum animus inflammatur.... Sicque fit, ut perfecta compunctio formidinis trahat [preferable to *tradat*] animum compunctioni dilectionis. Cf. *Mor.* 24.6.10–11; *Hom. in Ez.* 2.10.20–21; and *In 1 Regum* 5.148 (CC 144:509).

115. *Mor.* 27.21.41 (CC 143B:1361.11–13): Vocem enim spiritus audire, est vi compunctionis intimae in amore invisibilis conditoris assurgere. Michael Casey summarizes the double nature of compunction well: "Compunction is, therefore, a dual sensitivity. It places before us both the reality of our sinful condition and the urgency of our desire to be possessed totally by God" ("Spiritual Desire in the Gospel Homilies of Saint Gregory the Great," *Cistercian Studies* 16 [1981]: 309).

116. *Mor.* 23.21.41 (CC 143B:1175.25–32): Quatuor quippe sunt qualitates quibus iusti viri anima in compunctione vehementer afficitur, cum aut malorum suorum reminiscitur, considerans ubi fuit; aut iudiciorum Dei sententiam metuens et secum quaerens, cogitat ubi erit; aut cum mala vitae praesentis sollerter attendens, maerens considerat ubi est, aut cum bona supernae patriae contemplatur, quae quia necdum adipiscitur, lugens conspicit ubi non est.

117. Gregory seems to be suggesting that the "fall back" (*reverberatio*) from contemplation, to be discussed in the next section, is suffused with a deeper experience of the *compunctio amoris*. This is especially evident in *Mor.* 23.21.43 (CC 143B:1176.83–1177.112). For example: Unde aliquando ad quamdam inusitatem dulcedinem interni saporis admittitur, et raptim aliquo modo ardenti spiritu afflata renovatur; tantoque magis inhiat, quanto magis quod amet, degustat. . . . Cui inhaerere conatur, sed ab eius fortitudine sua adhuc infirmitate repellitur; et quia eius munditiae contemperari non valet, flere dulce habet, sibique ad se cadenti infirmitatis suae lacrimas sternere. . . . Proinde compuncti appetimus vitare quod fecimus, ut ad id quod facti fuimus reformemur. Cf. *Mor.* 24.6.11 (CC 143B:1195–96) and *Hom. in Ez.* 2.10.21 (SC 360:524–26) for other passages bringing out the mystical dimensions.

118. *Mor.* 1.34.48 (CC 143:50.12–15): Cum enim mens per quamdam compunctionis machinam ad alta sustollitur, omne quod ei de se ipsa est, sub se ipsa est, diiudicando certius contemplatur. See the famous account of Benedict's vision from *Dial* 2.35 discussed below (pp. 71–74).

119. *Hom. in Ev.* 17.11 (PL 76:1144B): Est autem valde necessarium ut cum de nobis in compunctione afficimus, etiam commissorum nobis vitam zelamus. Sic ergo nos amaritudo compunctionis afficiat, ut tamen a proximorum custodia non avertat. I have used the translation of D. Hurst, 142 (where this is *Homily* 19).

120. Pegon (in DS 2:1320–21) compares the traditional medieval notion of compunction coming from Gregory with Søren Kierkegaard's "concept of dread."

121. It may be helpful here to give two lists, by no means exhaustive, of major texts. First, those that deal primarily with contemplation in itself: *Mor.* 4.24.45–25.46, 4.33.67–34.68, 5.28.50–37.67, 8.30.49–50, 10.8.13–9.15, 18.54.88–93, 23.19.35.–21.43, 24.6.10–12, 30.16.52–54, 31.49.99–51.103, 35.3.4, 35.20.48; *Hom. in Ez.* 1.7.8–10, 1.8.13–17, 1.8.30–32, 2.1.16–18, 2.2.1–3, 2.2.12–15, 2.3.8–11, 2.4.15, 2.5.8–11, 2.5.17–20, 2.7.10; *Dial.* 2.3, 2.35, 4.Praef; *In 1 Reg.*. 1.61–71. The second list includes major discussions of contemplation and action: *Mor.* 6.37.56–61, 10.15.31, 18.43.69–70, 27.24.44, 28.13.33, 30.2.8, 30.13.48, 32.3.4; *Hom. in Ez.* 1.3.9–13, 1.5.12–13, 1.10.24, 2.2.7–15, 2.3.22, 2.6.5; *Hom. in Ev.* 18.3, 38.4; *In 1 Reg.* 1.64, 1.71–82, 5.177–80; *Reg. past.* 1.7, 2.5; *Ep.* 7.3–4. Important discussions of contemplation in Gregory are to be found in Butler, *Western Mysticism*, pp. 91–133; Lieblang, *Grundfragen*, pp. 99–170; Straw, *Gregory the Great*, pp. 225–31; A. Ménager, "La contemplation d'après Saint Grégoire le Grand," *La vie spirituelle* 9 (1923): 242–82; idem, "Les divers sens du mot 'contemplatio' chez saint Grégoire le Grand," *Supplément à la 'vie spirituelle'* (June 1939): 145–69; (July 1939): 39–56; and R. Gillet, "Grégoire le Grand," in DS 6:897–905.

122. *Mor.* 8.18.34 (CC 143:406.27–30): Ad contemplandum quippe Creatorem homo conditus fuerat ut eius semper speciem quaereret, atque in solemnitate illius amoris habitaret.

123. This aspect of Gregory's teaching was well brought out by Liebling (*Grundfragen*, pp. 29–43; cf. Dagens, *Saint Grégoire le Grand*, pp. 165–75; and Catry, *Parole de Dieu*, pp. 86–87).

124. On the importance of *soliditas* and its equivalent *stabilitas* in Gregory's thought, see Straw, *Gregory the Great*, chap. 3, esp. pp. 75–81.

125. *Dial.* 4.1 (SC 265:18.3–5): . . . quia peccando extra semetipsum fusus iam illa caelestis patriae gaudia, quae prius contemplabatur, videre non potuit.

126. *Lubrica mutabilitas* is treated by Straw in chap. 5 of her *Gregory the Great.*

127. *Dial.* 4.1 (SC 265:20.33–22.43): Unde factum est, ut ipse visibilium et invisibilium Creator ad humani generis redemptionem Unigenitus Patris veniret et Sanctum Spiritum ad corda nostra mitteret, quatenus, per eum vivificati, crederemus, quae adhuc scire experimento non possumus . . . . Quisquis autem in hac credulitate adhuc solidus non est, debet procul dubio maiorum dictis fidem praebere, eisque iam per Spiritum Sanctum invisibilium experimentum habentibus credere.

128. See Straw, *Gregory the Great*, chap. 4 (*"Soliditas Caritatis"*).

129. *Mor.* 8.30.49 (CC 143:421.23–28): . . . haec saliva ad os quidem labitur, ut vero ad ventrem usque perveniat non glutitur; quia divinitatis contemplatio sensum tangit, sed plene mentem non reficit, quoniam pefecte animus conspicere non valet adhuc, quia caligo corruptionis praepedit, raptim videt. Gregory underlines the message of 8.30.49 by repeating it with subtle variations in 8.30.50 (pp. 421–22).

130. *Hom. in Ez.* 2.2.5 (SC 360:102.21–22): Murus enim nobis intus est Deus, murus vero foris est Deus homo.

131. *Hom. in Ez.* 1.1.16 (SC 360:84.16–18): Propter hoc quippe incarnatus est Deus, ut nos introducat ad fidem, et reducat ad speciem visionis suae. Another important text on the relation between faith, contemplation, and heavenly vision is found in *Mor.* 18.54.93 (CC 143A:955.183–86): Quae nimirum visio nunc fide incohatur, sed tunc in specie perficitur, quando coaeternam Dei sapientiam, quam modo per ora praedicantium quasi per decurrentia flumina sumimus, in ipso fonte biberimus.

132. *Hom. in Ev.* 29.11 (PL 76:1219D).

133. For a sketch of Gregory's christological spirituality, see Straw, *Gregory the Great*, chap. 7 ("The Mediator of God and Man"), 91–196.

134. See, e.g., *Hom. in Ez.* 1.2.19–21 (SC 327:110–16); *Hom. in Ev.* 24.5 (PL 76:1187B); *Mor.* 5.31.55 (CC 143:256–58).

135. *Hom. in Ev.* 2.2 (PL 76:1082D–83A): Unde enim Deus humana patitur, inde homo ad divina sublevatur. Cf. *Hom. in Ev.* 8.2 (c. 1105B), *Hom. in Ev.* 30.9 (c. 1226BC), and *Mor.* 2.23.42 (CC 143:85). For the earlier patristic teaching, see *Foundations of Mysticism*, Subject Index under "Divinization" (p. 251 on Augustine).

136. E.g., *Mor.* 2.20.35 (CC 143:81–82); *Mor.* 20.36.69 (CC 143A:1054); and *Mor.* 27.2.3–4 (CC 143B:1332–33). The Cistercians, especially Bernard, later developed these hints into a major theme in twelfth-century mysticism.

137. *Hom. in Ez.* 1.3.14 (SC 327:138.8–11): Nisi enim, ut dictum est, omnipotens Verbum propter homines homo fieret, humana corda ad contemplandum Verbi excellentiam non volarent.

138. *Hom. in Ev.* 26.12 (PL 76:1204C): Quia tanto altius ad conspectum Dei omnipotentis pertingitis, quanto Mediatorem Dei et hominum singularius amatis. Of course, we demonstrate this love of Christ through our love of neighbor, as will be seen below.

139. See esp. *Mor.* 5.35.64 (CC 143:263.7–264.12): Cum ergo aeternitas cernitur, prout infirmitatis nostrae possibilitas admittit, imago eius mentis nostrae oculis antefertur; quia cum vere in Patrem tendimur, hunc quantum accipimus per suam imaginem, id est per Filium videmus. Et per eam speciem quae de ipso sine initio nata est, eum aliquo modo cernere, qui nec coepit nec desinit conamur. Abbot Butler contrasts this passage with one in *Mor.* 18.54.88–89 (CC 143A:952–53), which seems to teach a more direct vision of God (*Western Mysticism*, pp. 128–30), but even this is still a vision of divine *Sapientia*, that is, the Word.

140. *Hom. in Ev.* 30 (PL 76:1219–27).

141. *Hom.* 30.3: Quia nisi idem Spiritus cordi adsit audientis, otiosus est sermo doctoris (1222A). This is a common theme, e.g., *Mor.* 5.28.50 (CC 143:252–53) and 28.1.2 (CC 143A:1396–97).

142. There is also an important treatment of the Spirit as fire in the comment on Ezek 1:13 ("Et haec erat visio discurrens in medio animalium, splendor ignis, et de igne fulgur egrediens") in *Hom. in Ez.* 1.5.8–11 (SC 327:178–84).

143. *Hom.* 30.8: Mox ut tetigeret mentem, docet, solumque tetigisse docuisse est (1226A).

144. *Hom.* 30.9: Si ergo remanere carnales in morte nolumus, hunc, fratres charissimi, vivificantem Spiritum amemus (1226BC).

145. *Hom.* 30.10: . . . prius a Domino in terra degente, postmodum a Domino coelo praesidente. In terra quippe datur ut diligatur proximus, e coelo vero ut diligatur Deus. Sed cur prius in terra, postmodum e coelo. . . . Diligamus ergo proximum, fratres, amemus eum qui iuxta nos est, ut pervenire valeamus ad amorem illius qui super nos est (1227B). The same teaching is found in *Hom. in Ev.* 26.2–3 (PL 76:1197–99).

146. Among other texts of note, see *Hom. in Ev.* 24.6; *Mor.* 5.36.65, 9.53.80, 10.8.13, 18.28.45, 27.17.34 and 27.38.63. For a summary of Gregory's teaching on the Holy Spirit, see Patrick Catry, "Les voies de l'Espirit chez Grégorire," in *Grégoire le Grand,* pp. 207–14.

147. The fullest account, despite the rather rigid Neoscholastic terms in which it is framed, is to be found in Lieblang, *Grundfragen,* pp. 52–99. For the general context, see Jacques de Blic, "Pour l'histoire de la théologie des dons avant Saint Thomas," *Revue d'ascetique et de mystique* 22 (1946): 117–79 (pp. 143–52 on Gregory).

148. Significantly, the most important discussion of the virtues is to be found in *Hom. in Ez.* 2.5.8–16 (SC 360:240–60) in the midst of one of Gregory's key treatments of contemplation. Cf. *Hom. in Ez.* 2.7.13 and 2.10.17 (SC 360:352–56, 516–18).

149. *Mor.* 15.16.20 (CC 143A:760–61). See Lieblang, *Grundfragen,* pp. 79–81.

150. Lieblang, *Grundfragen,* p. 71.

151. An important treatment of the gifts is found in *Hom. in Ez.* 2.7.7–9 (SC 360:336–44). See Gerard G. Carluccio, *The Seven Steps to Spiritual Perfection according to St. Gregory the Great* (Ottawa: University of Ottawa Press, 1949).

152. See Straw, *Gregory the Great,* chap. 9 ("The Sacrifice of a Contrite Heart"), esp. pp. 180–82.

153. A. de Vogüé, "From Crisis to Resolutions," pp. 215–18. He summarizes as follows: "What Gregory used to contemplate in the monastery, what Adam saw in paradise, all this vanished beauty is mysteriously given back to the eyes of faith in the liturgical act of the Eucharist" (p. 218).

154. *Dial.* 4.60 (SC 265:200.9–11): Haec namque singulariter victima ab aeterno interitu animam salvat, quae illam nobis mortem Unigeniti per mysterium reparat. . . .

155. See, e.g., *Hom. in Ez.* 2.2.10 (SC 360:110.5–8): . . . contemplativa vero simplex ad solum videndum principium anhelat, videlicet ipsum qui ait: *Ego sum principium, propter quod et loquor vobis* [John 8:25] ("The contemplative life is a single one devoted only to beholding the First Principle, the one who says, 'I am the Principle, this is why I speak to you'"). Cf. *Hom. in Ez.* 2.2.8 (SC 360: 106.6–14) for another example. A. Ménager calculates that in his major works Gregory uses *contemplatio* 302 times and *contemplari* 110 times ("Les divers sens du mot 'contemplatio'").

156. E.g., Lieblang specifies five different uses (*Grundfragen,* pp. 27–28) ; Ménager has five too, but of a somewhat different character ("Les divers sens").

157. Hurst, *Forty Gospel Homilies,* p. 2.

158. See the important paper of Grover A. Zinn, "Sound, Silence and Word in the Spirituality of Gregory the Great," in *Grégoire le Grand,* pp. 367–75.

159. *Mor.* 31.49.99 (CC 143B:1619.26): Sola namque eius visio vera mentis nostrae refectio est. The passage contrasts the finality of the divine vision with the lower visions we gain of the heavenly spirits.

160. On this, see Leclercq, "The Teaching of St. Gregory," in *The Spirituality of the Middle Ages*, pp. 13–15.

161. See, e.g., *Mor.* 5.33.60 (CC 143:261), 17.27.39–40 (CC 143A:873–74), 22.20.50 (CC 143A:1129–30).

162. E.g., *Mor.* 5.30.53 and 10.8.13 (CC 143: 255, 547), 27.40.67 (CC 143B:1384).

163. See *Mor.* 20.32.62 (CC 143A:1048), a passage later cited with approval by Meister Eckhart (e.g., Pr. 36a in *Deutsche Werke* II, 190). Cf. *Mor.* 2.7.8 (CC 143:64–65).

164. E.g., *Mor.* 2.12.20 and 10.9.14–15 (CC 143:72–73, 547–49). On this, see Michael Frickel, *Deus totus ubique simul: Untersuchungen zur allgemeinen Gottesgegenwart im Rahmen der Gotteslehre Gregors der Grossen* (Freiburg-im-Breisgau: Herder, 1956).

165. *In 1 Reg.* 1.65 (CC 144:91.1434–35): . . . ut intima luce fruamur, non est nostri conaminis sed divinae dignationis. The necessity of grace is strongly stressed throughout the commentary on 1 Kgs 1:1–28; see esp. 1.63 and 68–70. The theme is widespread in the pope's accounts of contemplation (e.g., *Hom. in Ez.* 2.5.18).

166. Older interpreters, such as Lieblang and Ménager, did try to interpret Gregory in light of twentieth-century Neoscholastic controversies over acquired and infused contemplation. For an introduction to this debate in the modern study of mysticism, see *Foundations of Mysticism*, pp. 278–80.

167. For a summary on preparation for contemplation, see R. Gillet in DS 6:890–95.

168. On this, see esp. *Mor.* 25.12.30 and 27.46.79 (CC 143B:1255–56 and 1392–93), and *Hom. in Ev.* 20.3 (PL 76:1161C). On Gregory on humility, see Leclercq, "The Teaching of St. Gregory," in *Spirituality of the Middle ages*, pp. 23–24.

169. *In 1 Reg.* 1.68 (CC 144:93.1524–25): Ordinatus quippe contemplantis ascensus est, si a timore incipiat.

170. *Hom. in Ez.* 2.5.9 (SC 360:242.1–6): Primus ergo gradus est ut se ad se colligat, secundus ut videat qualis est collecta, tertius ut super semetipsam surgat ac se contemplationi auctoris invisibilis intendendo subiciat. Sed se ad se nullo modo colligit, nisi prius didicerit terrenarum ac caelestium imaginum phantasmata ab oculo mentis compescere. . . . Many texts echo this call for the removal of all worldly images, e.g., *Mor.* 5.33.59 (CC 143:260), 23.21.42 and 30.10.39 (CC 143B:1176 and 1519), *Hom. in Ez.* 2.5.8 (SC 360:240), etc.

171. For Gregory's dependence on Augustine, see Butler, *Western Mysticism*, pp. 106–7; and esp. Pierre Courcelle, *Les Confessions de Saint Augustin dans la tradition littéraire* (Paris: Etudes Augustiniennes, 1963), pp. 225–31, who summarizes ". . . Gregoire utilisé sans cesse les *Confessions* mais à la manière de quelqu'un qui en est nourri, plutot qu'à la manière d'un plagaire" (p. 231). Cf. Dagens, *Saint Grégoire le Grand*, pp. 178–84. On mystical interiorization in Plotinus and Augustine, see *Foundations of Mysticism*, pp. 48–49, 233, 242.

172. On *se ad se colligere* in Gregory, see Lieblang, *Grundfragen*, 108–20.

173. For a list of terms, see Aubin, "Interiorité et exteriorité," p. 136, and the charts and indices on pp. 156–66.

174. For a good discussion and list of texts, see Dagens, *Saint Grégoire le Grand*, pp. 209–12.

175. *Mor.* 22.16.35 (CC 143A:1117.15–16): . . . et mutabilia cuncta transcendens, ipsa iam tranquillitate quietis suae in mundo extra mundum est. On the notion of *vacatio* in Gregory, often connected with the Psalm text "Vacate et videte, quoniam ego sum Dominus" (Ps 45:19), see, e.g., *Mor.* 5.11.19 (CC 143:231). The history of these key terms in the monastic mystical tradition has been studied by Jean Leclercq, *Otia Monastica: Études sur le vocabulaire de*

la contemplation au moyen âge, Studia Anselmiana 51 (Rome: Herder, 1963); see esp. pp. 56–68 on Gregory.

176. For another appearance, see *Mor.* 5.34.61–63, especially the summary formula: Hoc autem modo quasi quamdam scalam sibi exhibet semetipsam per quam ab exterioribus ascendendo in se transeat, et a se in auctorem tendat (CC 143:261.23–25).

177. *Hom. in Ez.* 1.8.12–17 (SC 327:290–98). On Gregory's teaching on the spiritual senses there is little except for the disorganized article of Gregorio Penco, "La dottrina dei sensi spirituali in San Gregorio," *Benedictina* 17 (1970): 161–201. Although Gregory does not appear to add anything of note to the development of this theme, it appears fairly often in his writings. See, e.g., *Mor.* 5.34.62–36.66, 11.32.44, 28.1.2; *Hom. in Ez.* 2.1.18, 2.2.2; *Hom. in Ev.* 36.1–2; *In Cant.* 44. On the earlier patristic development of the doctrine of the spiritual senses, see *Foundations of Mysticism,* "Senses (spiritual)" under the Subject Index.

178. *Hom. in Ez.* 1.8.16 (SC 320:296.15–16): Quod ubique praesens est, et inveniri vix potest, quod stantem sequimur, et apprehendere non valemus. The passage concludes with one of Gregory's magnificent evocations of God's relation to the world: Nec alia ex parte sustinet atque alia superexcedit, neque alia ex parte implet atque alia circumplectitur, sed circumplectendo implet, implendo circumplectitur, sustinendo superexcedit, superexcedendo sustinet (296.19–22).

179. *Mor.* 18.7.14 (CC 143A:894.45–48): Idcirco ergo laudes suas indicat ut valeamus eum audientes cognoscere, cognoscentes amare, amantes sequi, sequentes adipisci, adiscipentes vero eius visione perfrui.

180. Patrick Catry, (*Parole de Dieu,* p. 95) points out the homology between this text and one from *Hom. in Ez.* 2.7.10 (SC 360:346.13–15):

Mor.	*Hom. in Ez.*
. . . laudes suas indicat	Ut ineffabilia mysteria . . .
ut valeamus eum audientes cognoscere,	caelestis agnoscant,
cognoscentes amare,	agnoscendo sitiant,
amantes sequi,	sitiendo currant,
sequentes adipisci,	currendo perveniant,
adipiscentes . . . visione perfrui.	Et apparebo ante faciem
	Domini.

181. For an overview, see Bernard McGinn, "Love, Knowledge and *Unio Mystica* in the Western Christian Tradition," in *Mystical Union and Monotheistic Faith: An Ecumenical Dialogue,* edited Moshe Idel and Bernard McGinn (New York: Macmillan, 1989), pp. 59–86; as well as the various treatments in *Foundations of Mysticism,* s.v. "Love and knowledge" in Subject Index.

182. *Hom. in Ev.* 27.4 (PL 76:1207A).

183. Dagens, *Saint Grégoire le Grand,* Chap. III, "La théorie grégorienne de la connaissance: l'interna intelligentia'," an excellent account (pp. 205–44).

184. Ibid., p. 215.

185. On the way in which knowledge precedes and continues to measure love, see Catry, *Parole de Dieu,* pp. 106–8.

186. Catry's three papers, "Amour du monde et amour de Dieu chez saint Grégoire le Grand," "Désir et amour de Dieu chez saint Grégoire le Grand," and "L'amour du prochain chez saint Grégoire le Grand," have been helpfully collected in his *Parole de Dieu,* pp. 161–178. Also helpful is Michael Casey, "Spiritual Desire in the Gospel Homilies of Saint Gregory the Great," *Cistercian Studies* 16 (1981): 297–314.

187. See Catry, *Parole de Dieu,* pp. 88–90, and the texts gathered there.

188. *Hom. in Ev.* 30.1 (PL 76:1220C): Qui ergo mente integra Deum desiderat, profecto iam habet quem amat.

189. Leclercq, *The Love of Learning and Desire for God*, chap. 2. Michael Casey expresses it well: "At the center of his thought is the experience of longing for God, for heaven and for spiritual realities" ("Spiritual Desire in the Gospel Homilies," p. 299).

190. *Mor.* 6.37.58 (CC 143:328.116–19): Unde necesse est ut quisquis ad contemplationis studia properat, semetipsum prius subtiliter interroget, quantum amat. Machina quippe mentis est vis amoris quae hanc dum a mundo extrahit in alta sustollit.

191. *Mor.* 25.6.10 (CC 143B:1236.41–45).

192. For the *gressus amoris*, see, e.g., *Mor.* 9.62.94 (CC 1443:523.27–30); for *passus amoris* and related terms, see the texts cited in Catry, *Parole de Dieu*, p. 94 n. 66.

193. E.g., Ps 41:3, "Sitivit anima mea ad Deum vivum," is employed in *Mor.* 8.8.13 and 10.8.13 (CC 143:390–91, 546), *Mor.* 18.30.48 (CC 143A:917); *Hom. in Ez.* 1.8.27 (SC 327:316), 2.10.8–9 (SC 360:498–500); and in *Hom. in Ev.* 25.4 (PL 76:1190C). See the texts gathered in Catry, *Parole de Dieu*, pp. 101–3. On Augustine's use of Psalm 41, see *Foundations of Mysticism*, p. 239.

194. E.g., *Hom. in Ez.* 2.1.16 (SC 360:86); *Hom. in Ev.* 12.1 (PL 76:1119B).

195. For a discussion, see Catry, *Parole de Dieu*, pp. 95–101, and the lists in Jean Leclercq, "Une Centon de Fleury sur les dévoirs des moins," *Analecta Monastica,* Analecta Anselmiana 20 (Rome: Herder, 1948), p. 90; and Casey, "Spiritual Desire in the Gospel Homilies," p. 304.

196. *Hom. in Ez.* 2.9.10 (SC 360:450.22–26): Ex amore ergo Domini in Sion ignis est, in Hierusalem caminus, quia hic amoris eius flammis aliquatenus ardemus, ubi de illo aliquid contemplamur, sed ibi plene ardebimus, ubi illum plene videbimus quem amamus.

197. For *succensa contemplatio*, see *Hom. in Ez.* 2.3.13 (SC 360:148.11). Cf. Ménager, "Le mot 'contemplatio' chez S. Grégoire," pp. 46–47. On Cassian's notion of "fiery prayer" (*Conl.* 9.25–26), see *Foundations of Mysticism*, p. 223.

198. *Mor.* 11.42.57 (CC 143A:617.7–618.8): Loquimur namque cum eius faciem per desiderium postulamus. Respondet vero Deus loquentibus cum nobis se amantibus apparet.

199. See, e.g., *In Cant.* 8–9, 18, 40–41 (CC 144:10–12, 19–21, 39–40).

200. On Gregory's use of the erotic language of the Song in the mystical sense, see Straw, *Gregory the Great*, pp. 225–26: and especially Jean Doignon, "'Blessure d'affliction' et 'blessure d'amour' (*Moralia* 6.25.42): une jonction de thèmes de la spiritualité patristique de Cyprien à Augustin," in *Grégoire le Grand*, pp. 297–303; and an unpublished paper of Grover A. Zinn, "Gregorian Exegesis and the 'Song of Songs,'" for whose use I thank the author.

201. Other texts on the wound of love referring to Song 2:5 can be found in *Hom. in Ez.* 2.3.8 (SC 360:140), and *Hom. in Ev.* 25.2 (PL 76:1190D). Reference to the wound without explicit appeal to Song 2:5 can be found in *Mor.* 5.1.1 (CC 143:219), and *Hom. in Ez.* 2.4.3 (SC 360:188).

202. Doignon ("'Blessure d'affliction'") discusses the source in Ambrose, *Enarratio in psalmum* 38.

203. *Mor.* 6.25.42 (CC 143:315.10–20): Aliquando autem etiam si flagella exterius cessare videantur, intus vulnera infligit, quia mentis nostrae duritiam suo desiderio percutit, sed percutiendo sanat, quia terroris sue iaculo transfixos ad sensum nos rectitudinis revocat. Corda enim nostra male sana sunt, cum nullo Dei amore sauciantur. . . . Sed vulnerantur et sanentur, quia amoris sue spiculis mentes Deus insensibiles percutit, moxque eas sensibiles per ardorem caritatis reddit. Unde et sponsa in Canticis canticorum dicit: Vulnerata caritate ego sum.

204. Doignon, "'Blessure d'affliction,'" pp. 299–300.

205. . . . percussa autem caritatis eius spiculis, vulneratur in intimis affectu pietatis, ardet desiderio contemplationis et miro modo vivificatur ex vulnere quae prius mortua iacebit in salute. Aestuat, anhelat et iam videre desiderat quem fugiebat (CC 143:315.22–26).

206. Origen, *Comm. super Cantica* 3, and *Hom. in Cantica* 2.8 (ed. Baehrens, 194.6–13, and 53–54). On these texts, see *Foundations of Mysticism*, p. 123.

207. *In Cant.* 12–13 (CC 144:14–15) for the primarily ecclesiological reading, which is also found in *Mor.* 14.43.51 (CC 143:729). Personal applications are hinted at in the reference to the experience of Cleopas in *In Cant.* 12, and expanded on in *In Cant.* 15 (pp. 17–18), where we find an intellectualist reading applied to Moses' reception of the kiss of *intellegentia*, probably Origenist in inspiration (the application to Moses is also found in *In 1 Reg.* 1.69 [CC 144:94]). There is a more properly Gregorian personal interpretation relating to compunction in *In Cant.* 18 (pp. 20–21).

208. *In 1 Reg.* 2.2 (CC 144:121.24–25): Et idcirco illa sola haec dicit, quae experta novit, quae vis amoris sit in thalamo sponsi. In *Mor.* 27.17.34 (CC 143B:1356.46–47) the verse is interpreted as: Tangat me dulcedine praesentiae unigeniti Filii redemptoris mei.

209. See *Mor.* 5.4.6 and 8.24.41 (CC 143:222–23 and 412), *Mor.* 18.49.80 in an ecclesial sense (CC 143A:944), *Mor.* 27.2.3–4 (CC143B:1332–33); *Hom. in Ez.* 2.7.11 (SC 360:350); and in *Hom. in Ev.* 25.2 (considered below).

210. There are, of course, a number of other charged erotic passages where Gregory discusses the mystery of the bed-chamber (*thalamus*), where the Bride and her Divine Lover are joined: see *Hom. in Ez.* 2.3.8 (using Song 2:5), 2.4.13–15 (using Song 2:10–12) (SC 360:138–40, 210–16); and *Hom. in Ev.* 1.12.4, where the marriage chamber refers to heaven (PL 76:1120C–21B).

211. *Hom. in Ev.* 25.2 (PL 76:1190A): Quaesivit ergo prius, et minime invenit; perseveravit ut quaereret, unde et contigit ut inveniret, actumque est ut desideria delata crescerent, et crescentia caperent quod invenissent. Hinc est enim quod de eodem sponso Ecclesia in Canticis canticorum dicit: In lectulo meo per noctes quaesivi quem diligit anima mea; quaesivi illum et non inveni (Sg. 3:1). The passage on Mary Magdalene goes on to make considerable use of the Song of Songs, citing 3:2–4a, 2:5 and 5:6.

212. Zinn, "Gregorian Exegesis and the 'Song of Songs,'" (unpublished manuscript, p. 9).

213. *Mor.* 5.31.55 (CC 143:257.74–258.82): Quia igitur nequaquam notitia interna conspicitur, nisi ab externa implicatione cessatur, recte nunc verbi absconditi et divini susurrii tempus exprimitur, cum dicitur: In horrore visionis nocturnae, quando *solet sopor occupare homines*, . . . Sed humanus animus quadam suae contemplationis machina sublevatus, quo super se altiora conspicit, eo in semetipso terribilius contremiscit. Song 2:5 is used in a similar way in *Mor.* 23.20.37–39 (CC 143B:1171–74) in the midst of another discusion of the *visio nocturna* and *sopor* (see Job 33:15), and also in *Hom. in Ez.* 2.2.12–13 (SC 360:114–16), where Jacob as sleeping contemplative is the main subject (cf. *Mor.* 28.1.7, and *In Cant.* 11).

214. For a survey of texts, see Catry, *Parole de Dieu*, pp. 108–12.

215. *Hom. in Ez.* 2.2.13 (SC 360:114): . . . omnipotens Deus cum iam per desiderium et intellectum cognoscitur . . . .

216. The mutuality of *amor* and *cogitatio/notitia* is also expressed in sentences or passages not so easily summarized; see, e.g., *Hom. in Ez.* 1.5.12 (SC 327:186), 2.2.8 and 2.9.10 (SC 360:106–08, 448–50). An interesting text relating to Moses in *In Cant.* 15 (CC 133:17) even relates the kiss of love with the bestowal of *intellegentia* and *intellectus* and thus comes near the popular twelfth-century formula *amor ipse intellectus est.*

217. *Hom. in Ez.* 2.3.18 (SC 360:162.15–17): . . . tunc ad limen interius, id est ad intellectum mysticum intimae contemplationis, tendamus, si possimus, pedem mentis. Cf. 2.5.1 (p. 226).

218. E.g., *Mor.* 22.20.50 (CC 143A:1130.160–62): . . . humano animo plenam cognitionem negat [Sapientia], ut hanc et tangendo amet, et tamen nequaquam pertranseundo penetrat. Cf. *Hom. in Ez.* 2.6.1 and 16 (SC 360:272, 302–04).

219. See especially *Mor.* 20.31.61 (CC 143A:1047.13–17): Ad multiplicandam quippe sanctorum sapientiam proficit quod postulata tarde percipiunt, ut ex dilatione crescat desiderium, ex desiderio intellectus augeatur. Intellectus vero cum intenditur, ei in Deum ardentior affectus aperitur.

220. See Catry, *Parole de Dieu,* p. 119.

221. For lists, at least for the *Moralia,* see Aubin, "Interiorité et exteriorité," pp. 156–57, 160f.

222. *Mor.* 6.6.9 (CC 143:224.3–4): ... divina contemplatio quoddam sepulcrum mentis est quo absconditur anima. Cf. *Mor.* 6.37.56 and 59.

223. E.g., *Mor.* 5.30.53, 6.37.56, 30.26.54, 31.51.102.

224. *Extasis,* a rare word with Gregory, who usually prefers *excessus.* The Latin translation of the LXX (the *Psalterium Gallicanum*) has "in excessu mentis" here while the Vulgate has "in stupore mentis." For Gregory's teaching on *excessus,* see "Extase" in DS 4:2110–11.

225. *Mor.* 23.21.41 (CC 143B:1176.60–70): Sublevatus in ecstasi, quod nostri interpres pavorem non proprie vocaverunt [some mss. omit the non], a vultu oculorum Dei vidit se esse proiectum. Post internae quippe luminis visionem quae in eius anima per contemplationis gratiam radio claritatis emicuit, ad semetipsum rediit; et cognitione percepta, vel quibus illic bonis deesset, vel quibus malis hic adesset, invenit. ... Sublevatus quippe vidit quod se hic videre non posse ad se relapsus ingemuit.

226. ... imaginatio circumscriptae visionis ... in unum se colligere nititur, ut si magna vi amoris praevalet, esse unum atque incorporeum contempletur (1176.77–82).

227. *Mor.* 24.6.10 (CC 143B:1195.8–11): Iubilum namque dicitur, quando ineffabile gaudium mente concipitur, quod nec abscondi possit, nec sermonibus aperiri; et tamen quibusdam motibus proditur, quamvis nullis proprietatibus exprimatur.

228. Sentitur per illam quippe, quod ultra sensum est. Et cum vix ad hoc contemplandum sufficiat conscientia sentientis, quomodo ad hoc exprimendum sufficiat lingua dicentis? (1195.16–18).

229. Cui veritati tanto magis se longe existimat, quanto magis appropinquat, quia nisi illam utcumque conspiceret, nequaquam eam conspicere se non posse sentiret (1195.37–1196.40).

230. 24.6.12 (1196.41–46): Adnisus ergo animi, dum in illa intenditur, immensitatis eius coruscante circumstantia reverberatur. Ipsa quippe cuncta implens, cuncta circumstat; et idcirco mens nostra nequaquam se ad comprehendendam incircumscriptam dilatat, quia eam inopia suae circumscriptionis angustat. Henry Vaughan might have had this passage in mind when he wrote
I saw Eternity the other night
Like a great Ring of pure and endless light.

231. *Hom. in Ez.* 2.1.17 (SC 360:86.1–6): Saepe namque animus in divina contemplatione suspenditur ut iam se percipere de aeterna illa libertate quam *oculus non vidit, nec auris audivit,* aliquid per quamdam imaginem laetetur, sed tamen, mortalitatis suae pondere reverberatus, ad ima relabitur et quibusdam poenae suae vinculis ligatus tenetur.

232. The texts translated in this paragraph, all from *Hom.* 2.1.17 (ed. p. 88) are as follows: Ibi etenim stamus, ubi mentis oculos figimus. ... quia cum sanctus quisque praedicator alta de Deo loquitur, supernae habitationis iam utcumque tabernaculum ingreditur ... quia cum per contemplationis gratiam vox supernae intellegentiae sit in mente, totus homo iam intra speluncam non est, quia animum carnis cura non possidet, sed stat in ostio, quia mortalitatis angustias exire meditatur.

233. 2.1.18 (90.18–20): ... concupiscamus Regem, desideremus cives quod cognovimus, atque in hoc sanctae Ecclesiae aedificio stantes oculos in porta teneamus. ...

234. E.g., R. Gillet, "Grégoire," DS 6:895; J. Leclercq, "The Teaching of St. Gregory," p. 29. For a summary of Gregory's teaching on the Divine Light, see Butler, *Western Mysticism*, pp. 109–11.

235. Butler, *Western Mysticism*, pp. 127–28, already noted Gregory's departure from Augustine in this connection.

236. The "chink" suggests the more objective aspect, that is, the way in which the Divine Light is restricted when it has to pass through any created medium; the "flash" suggests the subjective experience of the mystic, as in a darkened room when suddenly we are struck by a gleam of light coming through an aperture. Butler, notes the importance of this (*Western Mysticism*, p. 111).

237. *Hom. in Ez.* 2.5.17 (SC 360:260.1–262.10): In fenestis obliquis pars illa per quam lumen intrat angusta porta est, sed pars interior quae lumen suscipit lata, quia mentes contemplantium quamvis aliquid tenuiter de vero lumine videant, in semetipsis tamen magna amplitudine dilatantur. . . . [E]x ipso exiguo laxatur sinus mentium in augmentum fervoris et amoris, et inde apud se amplae fiunt, unde ad se veritatis lumen quasi per angustias admittunt.

238. See *Mor.* 5.29.52 (CC 143:253.30–254.33), and *Hom. in Ez.* 1.8.17 (SC 327:298.15–19).

239. Aelred K. Squire, "Light in Gregory the Great and in the Islamic Tradition," in *Studia Patristica*, vol. 23, edited by Elizabeth A. Livingstone (Leuven: Peeters, 1989), pp. 197–202.

240. See Zinn, "Sound, Silence and Word."

241. *Mor.* 30.16.52 (CC 143B:1527.9–17): Itaque bene conversantibus primum solitudo mentis tribuitur, ut exsurgentem intrinsecus strepitum terrenorum desideriorum premant; ut ebullientes ad infima curas cordis per superni gratiam restinguant amoris . . . ; quasi quasdam circumvolantes muscas ab oculis mentis abigant manu gravitatis; et quoddam sibi cum Domino intra se secretum quaerant, ubi cum illo exteriori cessante strepitu per interna desideria silenter loquantur.

242. *Mor.* 30.16.54 (CC 143B:1528.58–60): In hoc itaque silentium cordis, dum per contemplationem interius vigilamus, exterius quasi obdormiscimus.

243. Zinn, "Sound, Silence and Work," p. 371.

244. On "touching" God, see, e.g. *Mor.* 10.8.13 (CC 143:546.5), and *Hom. in Ez.* 2.7.10 (SC 360:346.25–27). Augustine had also used such language.

245. The texts are so numerous that I cite only a selection of the more important: *Mor.* 5.33.58–60, 8.6.9, 8.30.50, 8.32.54, 9.19.29, 16.8.12, 16.31.37, 24.5.10–12; *Hom. in Ez.* 2.1.17, 2.2.3 and 12, 2.5.11, etc.

246. See, e.g., *Mor.* 18.50.82 (CC 143A:945.34–36).

247. The terms for this distinction are my own, but are based on *In 1 Reg.* 1.68 (CC 144:93.1542–44) in which the sacrifice (*immolatio*) of 1 Kgs 1:3 is interpreted as two kinds of fear, one coming before and one after contemplative experience.

248. See n. 213 above.

249. *Hom. in Ez.* 2.2.3 (SC 360:96.1–10): Hinc est etiam quod plerumque qui plus in contemplatione rapitur, contingit ut amplius in tentatione fatigetur: sicut quibusdam saepe contingere bene proficientibus solet, quorum mentem dum aut compunctio afficit, aut contemplatio super semetipsam rapit, statim etiam tentatio sequitur, ne de his ad quae rapta est extollatur. Nam compunctione vel contemplatione ad Deum erigitur, sed tentationis suae pondere reverberatur ad semetipsam, quatenus tentatio aggravet, ne contemplatio inflet; et item contemplatio elevet, ne tentatio demergat. Cf. *Mor.* 10.10.17 (CC 143:550) for another example.

250. *Hom. in Ev.* 36.1 (PL 76:1266B): Augent enim spiritales deliciae desiderium in mente, dum satiant, quia quanto magis earum sapor percipitur, eo amplius cognoscitur quod avidius ametur.

251. *Mor.* 25.8.16 (CC 143B:1241.140–42): Aeterna quippe contemplatione agitur, ut omnipotens Deus quo magis visus fuerit, eo amplius diligitur.

252. See, e.g., *Mor.* 2.7.9, 2.7.11 and 4.25.46 in an addition found in some manuscripts (CC 143:65, 66 and 191–92 apparatus); *Mor.* 18.54.91 (CC 143:953–54); *Hom. in Ez* 1.8.15 (SC 327:294), and *In 1. Reg.* 4.165 (CC 144:382–83). There is a discussion in Catry, *Parole de Dieu,* pp. 104–5.

253. For a brief comment on Gregory of Nyssa's use, see *Foundations of Mysticism,* p. 141.

254. See *Foundations of Mysticism,* pp. 242, 259.

255. E.g., *Mor.* 8.8.13 (CC 143:391.27–30) and 15.47.53 (CC 143A:782.19–26).

256. These seem to appear mostly in the *Homilies in Ezekiel* e.g., 2.2.15: Compatiamur per amorem proximo, ut *coniungamur* per cognitionem Deo (SC 360:124.39–40); 2.3.12: Hi ... qui ... fervente amore Deum videre sitiunt, eique iam per desiderium *coniungantur* (ibid., 144.6–146.8); 2.4.13: Fides corda audientium in amore Dei *copulat* (ibid., 210.10–11); 2.5.1: ... castae animae Conditori suo in amore *iunguntur* (ibid., 224.10–11). But see also *Hom. in Ev.* 1.4 (PL 76:1121AB).

257. See *Foundations of Mysticism,* p. 226.

258. See *Dial.* 2.16 (SC 260:184–90).

259. There are also texts that speak of presence and absence without the appeal to Song 3, e.g., *Mor.* 16.27.33 (CC 143A:818). For more on the Bride's experience of God's presence, see *Mor.* 27.17.34 (CC 143B:1356), and *In Cant.* 13 (CC 144:15).

260. *Mor.* 24.6.12 (CC 143B:1196.55–61): Tunc cognoscam sicut et cognitus sum. Quia ergo post laborum certamina, post temptationum fluctus, saepe in excessu anima suspenditur, ut cognitionem divinae praesentiae contempletur, quam tamen prasentiam et sentire possit, et explere non possit; recte post tot labores de hoc temptato homine dicitur: *Videbit faciem eius in iubilo.*

261. For Moses, see, e.g., *Mor.* 35.8.13 (CC 143B:1782).

262. *Experientia* occurs largely in the *Commentary on 1 Kings*; see *In 1 Reg.* 1.75 (CC 144:97.1670–73): ... perfectionem contemplationis habet in spe, quam nondum habet in virtute experientiae.

263. Gregory also appears, at least on the basis of one text, to have shown some interest in the physical phenomenon of contemplative consciousness. In *Mor.* 12.30.35 he notes the blank appearance of the face of those suspended in higher contemplation: Saepe iustorum mens ita ad altiora contemplanda suspenditur, ut exterius eorum facies obstupuisse videatur (CC 143A:649.2–4).

264. The literature on Benedict's vision is extensive, both in terms of medieval discussions and modern ones. In the modern period, see Odo Casel, "Zur Vision des hl. Benedikt," *Studien und Mitteilungen zur Geschichte des Benediktinerordens* 38 (1917): 345–48; Butler, *Western Mysticism,* pp. 123–25, 132–33, 176; Joseph Maréchal, *Études sur la psychologie des mystiques* (Paris–Bruges: C. Beyaert, 1937), 2:205–06; Ambrosius Schaut, "Die Vision des heiligen Benedikt," in *Vir Dei Benedictus: Eine Festgabe zum 1400 Todestag des hl. Benedikt,* ed. Raphael Molitor (Münster: Aschendorff, 1947), pp. 207–53; T. Delforge, "Songe de Scipion et vision de saint Benoit," *Revue Bénédictine* 69 (1959): 351–54; Pierre Courcelle, "La vision cosmique de saint Benoit," *Revue des études augustiniennes* 13 (1967): 97–117; Basilius Steidle, "Die kosmische Vision des Gottesmannes Benedikt," *Erbe und Auftrag* 47 (1971): 187–92, 298–315, 409–14; V. Recchia, "La visione di S. Benedetto e la 'compositio' del secondo libro dei 'Dialoghi' di Gregorio Magno," *Revue Bénédictine* 82 (1972): 140–55; and David N. Bell, "The Vision of the World and the Archetypes in the Spirituality of the Middle Ages," *Archives d'histoire doctrinale et littéraire du moyen âge* 44 (1977): 7–31. For medieval discussions, see J. Muller, "La vision de S. Benoit dans l'interprétation des théologiens scholastiques," in *Mélanges Bénédictines* (Saint-Wandoulle: Editions de Fontenelle, 1947), pp. 145–201; and E. Lanne, "L'inter-

prétation palamite de la vision de S. Benoit," *Le millénaire du Mont-Athos* (Venice: Fondazione Giorgio Cini, 1964), pp. 21–47.

265. The narrative of the vision itself from *Dial.* 2.35 (SC 260:236.15–238.29): Cumque vir Domini Benedictus, adhuc quiescentibus fratribus, instans vigiliis, nocturnae orationis tempora preavenisset, ad fenestram stans, et omnipotentem Dominum depraecans, subito intempesta noctis hora respiciens, vidit fusam lucem desuper cunctas noctis tenebras exfugasse, tantoque splendor clarescere, ut diem vinceret illa lux, quae inter tenebras radiasset. Mira autem valde res in hac speculatione secuta est: quia, sicut post ipse narravit, omnis etiam mundus, velut sub uno solis radio collectus, ante oculos eius adductus est. Qui venerabilis pater, dum intentam oculorum, aciem in hoc splendore coruscae lucis infigerit, vidit Germani Capuani episcopi animam in spera ignea ab angelis in caelum ferri.

266. Courcelle ("La vision cosmique," p. 105) shows that the *spera ignea*, originally a Stoic image, had already been taken over as a sign of sanctity in Sulpicius Severus, *Dialogi.* 2.2.2 (CSEL 1.181).

267. On the double form of the account, see the remarks of Recchia, "La visione di S. Benedetto," pp. 140–45 and 154–55. Could this double account contain a reminiscence of the two versions of Augustine's famous Ostia vision contained in *Confessions* 9.10.23–26? Courcelle notes that both the Ostia vision and Benedict's take place at windows ("La vision cosmique," p. 102); but Recchia draws attention to the parallel between *ad fenestram stans* of the vision and the *fenestrae obliquae* of Ezek 40:16, which were so important to Gregory's view of mystical contemplation ("La visione de S. Benedetto," pp. 145-46).

268. *Dial.* 2.35 (SC 260:240.50–71): ... quia animae videnti Creatorem angusta est omnis creatura. Quamlibet etenim parum de luce Creatoris aspexerit, breve ei fit omne quod creatum est, quia ipsa luce visionis intimae mentis laxatur sinus, tantumque expanditur in Deo, ut superior existat mundo. Fit vero ipsa videntis anima etiam super semetipsam. Cumque in dei lumine rapitur super se, in interioribus ampliatur, et dum sub se conspicit, exaltata comprehendit, quam breve sit, quod conprehendere humiliata non poterat. Vir ergo qui [intueri] globum igneum, angelus quoque ad caelum redeuntes videbat, haec procul dubio cernere non nisi in Dei lumine poterat. Quid itaque mirum, si mundum ante se collectum vidit, qui sublevatus in mentis lumine extra mundum fuit? Quod autem collectus mundus ante eius oculos dicitur, non caelum et terra contracta est, sed videntis animus dilatatus, qui, in Deo raptus videre sine difficultate potuit omne, quod infra Deum est. In illa ergo luce, quae exterioribus oculis fulsit, lux interior in mente fuit, quae videntis animum, quia ad superiora rapuit, ei quam angusta essent omnia inferiora monstravit.

269. On these texts, see *Foundations of Mysticism*, pp. 210–13 (for Ambrose), and pp. 234–35 (for Augustine).

270. For some lists of these affinities, see Butler, *Western Mysticism*, p. 124; and Courcelle, "La vision cosmique," pp. 106-7. Recchia emphasizes the scriptural basis ("La Visione de S. Benedetto").

271. See Pierre Courcelle, "'Habitare secum' selon Perse et saint Grégoire le Grand," *Revue des études anciennes* 69 (1967): 266–79.

272. See Marc Doucet, "Pédagogie et théologie dans la 'Vie de saint Benoit,'" pp. 161–65.

273. *Dial.* 2.37 (SC 260:244.17–20): Viderunt namque quia strata palliis atque innumeris corusca lampadibus via recto orientis tramite ab eius cella in caelum usque tendebatur.

274. That these three visions were meant to be taken together was obvious to the medieval reader, especially as seen in the iconographic presentations found in a late eleventh century manuscript from Monte Cassino studied by Courcelle ("La vision cosmique," pp. 114–17). This presentation of the famous vision appears on the dust jacket of this volume.

275. See Cicero, *Somnium Scipionis* 3.7; Macrobius, *Commentarium in Somnium Scipionis* 1.14.4.

276. See Courcelle, "La vision cosmique," p. 111.

277. I owe this observation to Dagens, *Grégoire le Grand*, p. 233.

278. Bell, "Vision of the World," pp. 8–13.

279. Thomas Aquinas (*Questiones Quodlibetales* 1.1), who denies the fact because Benedict was not completely alienated from his senses in "spiritual" death during the experience. Bernard also discussed the character of the vision in his *De diversis* 9.1. For background to this question, see Léopold Malevez, "Essence de Dieu (Vision de L')" in DS 4:1333–45.

280. Butler did note (*Western Mysticism*, pp. 129–30) that at least one text in *Moralia* 18.54.89 seems to allow for a direct vision of divine light: Sin vero a quibusdam potest in hac adhuc corruptibili carne viventibus, sed tamen inestimabili virtute crescentibus, quodam contemplationis acumine aeterna Dei claritas videri . . . (CC 143A:952.59–62).

281. *Saint Grégoire le Grand. Morales sur Job. Livres I et II*, ed. Robert Gillet, SC 32, "Introduction," p. 35 n. 1.

282. Schaut, "Die Vision des hl. Benedikt," pp. 217–25; Bell, "Vision of the World," pp. 7–11.

283. *Hom. in Ez* 2.5.19 (SC 360:264.1–10): Non enim contemplationis gratia summis datur et minimis non datur, sed saepe hanc summi, saepe minimi, saepius remoti, aliquando etiam coniugati percipiunt. Si ergo nullum est fidelium officium, a quo possit gratia contemplationis excludi, quisquis cor intus habet, illustrari etiam lumine contemplationis potest, quia intra portam undique per circuitum fenestrae obliquae constructae sunt, ut nemo ex hac gratis quasi de singularitate glorietur. . . .

284. See, e.g., *Mor.* 6.36.55, 6.37.57 and 7.12.14 (CC 143:325, 327, 343). Although he does not explicitly call him a contemplative, one would think that the layman, Count Theophanius of Civitavecchia, whom Gregory praises in *Hom. in Ev.* 36.13 (PL 76:1273D–74B) would fit in such a category (Theophanius is also discussed in *Dial.* 4.18).

285. E.g., Butler, *Western Mysticism*, pp. 237–41; Ménager, "Le mot 'contemplatio,'" pp. 166–67; Gillet in DS 6:881; Leclercq in *Spirituality of the Middle Ages*, p. 11; Dagens, *Saint Grégoire le Grand*, pp. 215–16.

286. *In 1 Reg.* 2.130 (CC 144:190:2715–16), where, contrasting monks with preachers, he says, "ad amantium ordinem adsumpti sunt, non ad celsitudinem praedicationis."

287. For a good short account of the history, see Nicholas Lobkowicz, *Theory and Practice: History of a Concept from Aristotle to Marx* (Notre Dame: University of Notre Dame Press, 1967).

288. For the early Greek patristic development, see *Foundations of Mysticism*, pp. 106–7, 126, 148–49, etc.; and P. T. Camelot, "Action et contemplation dans la tradition chrétienne," *La Vie Spirituel* 78 (1948): 272–301.

289. Cassian represents an exception in his restriction of the active and the contemplative lives to monasticism (*vita activa* = coenobitism; *vita contemplativa* = eremitism). See *Foundations of Mysticism*, pp. 225–26.

290. On Augustine's teaching, see *Foundations of Mysticism*, pp. 256–7. Augustine also introduced the term of the "mixed" life (*composita*).

291. For a list of texts, see n. 120.

292. The text is found in SC 360:104–24.

293. *Hom.* 2.2.8 (ibid., 106.6–10): Contemplativa vero vita est caritatem quidem Dei proximi tota mente retinere, sed ab exteriore actione quiescere, soli desiderio Conditoris inhaerere, ut nil iam agere libeat, sed, calcatis curis omnibus, ad videndam faciem sui Creatoris animus inardescat. . . .

294. Ibid., 106.16–108: . . . quantolibet amore animus ardeat, quantalibet virtute se in Deum cogitatione tetendit, non iam quod amet perfecte videt, sed adhuc inchoat videre quod amat, quia sicut fortissimus praedicator dicit: Videmus nunc per speculum in aenigmate, tunc autem facie ad faciem.

295. These two paired scriptural types were common to the tradition. See the text cited in n. 4 above. Less familiar were Gregory's use of two pairs of women from 1 Kings as images of the active and contemplative lives, that is, Phenenna and Anna, the two wives of Elcana (see *In 1 Reg.* 1.42–43 [CC 144:77–78]), and Merob and Michol, Saul's daughters (see *In 1 Reg.* 5.177–80 [CC 144:528–32]).

296. *Hom.* 2.2.11 (ibid., 112.5–8): Debet ergo nos activa ad contemplativam transmittere, et aliquando tamen ex eo quod introrsus mente conspeximus contemplativa melius ad activam revocare.

297. *Hom.* 2.2.14 (ibid., 116.4–7): Neque enim omnipotens deus iam in sua claritate conspicitur, sed quiddam sub illa speculatur anima, unde refota proficiat, et post ad visionis eius gloriam pertingat. This section constitutes Gregory's longest discussion of the impossibility of a full or direct vision of God in this life. See the discussion in Butler, *Western Mysticism*, pp. 125–33.

298. *Hom.* 2.2.15 (ibid., 122.13–20): Latitudo ergo pertinet ad caritatem proximi, altitudo ad intellegentiam Conditoris. Sed latitudo et altitudo aedificii uno calamo mensuratur, quia videlicet unaquaeque anima quantum lata fuerit in amore proximi, tantum, et alta erit in cognitione Dei. Dum enim se per amorem iuxta dilatat, per cognitionem se superius exaltat, et tantum super semetipsam excelsa fit, quantum se iuxta se in proximi amorem tendit.

299. Ibid, 124.39–40: Compatiamur per amorem proximo, ut coniungamur per cognitionem Deo.

300. On Gregory's view of monasticism, see Robert Gillet, "Spiritualité et place du moine dans l'église selon saint Grégoire le grand," in *Théologie de la vie monastique*, pp. 323–51; Adalbert de Vogüé, "The Views of St. Gregory the Great on the Religious Life in his Commentary on the Book of Kings," *Cîteaux* 17 (1982): 40–64, 212–32; idem, "Renunciation and Desire: The Definition of the Monk in Gregory the Great's Commentary on the First Book of Kings," *Cistercian Studies* 22 (1987): 221–38.

301. Gillet, "Spiritualité," p. 328.

302. *In 1 Reg.* 1.61 (CC 144:87.1275–78): Vir namque dicitur, quia proposito fortis est; unus vero, quia amore singularis. Vir namque est, quia ex magna virtute cuncta praesentia despicit; sed unus, quia sola omnipotentis dei specie frui concupiscit.

303. *Dial.* 2.3.5 (SC 260:142.38–39): . . . et solus in superni spectatoris oculis habitavit secum. My presentation here is dependent on de Vogüé, "Renunciation and Desire," pp. 223–24, 232–35.

304. As de Vogüé shows in commenting on *In 1 Reg.* 4.161–68; see "The View of St. Gregory the Great on the Religious Life," pp. 217–22.

305. *Mor.* 18.13.33 (CC 143B:1420.12–15): Ab activa enim vita longe contemplativa distat, sed incarnatus Redemptor noster veniens, dum utramque exhibuit, in se utramque sociavit. Nam cum in urbe miracula faceret, in monte vero orando continue pernoctaret. For other texts that take Christ as the model for combining contemplation and action, see, e.g., *Mor.* 6.37.56 (CC 143:325–26), *Reg. past.* 2.5 (PL 77:33C), and Ep. 1.25.

306. See, e.g., *Reg. past.* 2.5, and *Mor.* 23.20.38 (CC 143B:1172–73).

307. See, e.g., *Reg. past.* 1.7; and Ep. 7.3–4 (CC 140:475).

308. E.g., *Mor.* 8.29.48 (CC 143:419–20), 19.6.10–14 (CC 143A:962–64), where Paul is compared with Elijah; and *Reg. past.* 2.5.

309. *Mor.* 31.25.49 (CC 143B:1584–85). Cf. *Hom. in Ez.* 2.4.6 (SC 360:194–96); *Hom. in Ev.* 2.38. (PL 76:1283D–84A); and *Reg. past.* 2.7

310. *In 1 Reg.* 5.179 (CC 144:530.4357–531.4371): Ambae ergo Saul filiae dicuntur, sed nomina diversa sortiuntur: quia et differunt et conveniunt. Conveniunt quidem: quia ad aeternam vitam, quam diligunt, per amorem tendunt. Item conveniunt: quia opera bona, quibus haec indesinenter extenditur, illa quomodolibet operantur. Quia igitur ambae amant

aeterna, quae vident, ambae ad illa per bonam operationem pervenire desiderant, quomodocumque conveniunt. Differunt autem: quia plus agit una plus videt altera. . . . Videndo tamen et agendo differunt: quia activa vita visionem habet in transitu, opus vero in intentione: contemplativa vero opus in itinere, intentionem in quiete.

311. See especially Dagens, *Grégoire le Grand,* pp. 158–63.

312. See Straw, *Gregory the Great,* pp. 45–46.

313. See J. Fontaine, "L'expérience spirituelle chez Grégoire," 145: "Et l'originalité de sa doctrine spirituel consista precisement à rendre compatibles et complémentaires une vocation mystique personelle et des responsibilities ecclesiales qu'il ne put eviter."

Chapter 3

1. The final part of this chapter contains an expanded version of an earlier paper published under the title "Eriugena Mysticus" in *Giovanni Scoto nel suo tempo: L'organizzazione del sapere in età carolingia. Atti del XXIV Convegno storico internazionale* (Spoleto: Centro Italiano di Studi sull'Alto Medioevo, 1989), pp. 235–60.

2. This translation and the original Latin text may be found in Mary Brennan, "Materials for the Biography of Johannes Scottus Eriugena," *Studi Medievali* 3a serie 27 (1986): 431.

3. An extensive literature has developed on Eriugena, especially since the publication of the first major modern survey, that of Maïeul Cappuyns, *Jean Scot Érigène, sa vie, son oeuvre, sa pensée* (Louvain and Paris: Universitas Catholica Lovaniensis, 1933; reprint 1964). The most recent bibliographies are those of Mary Brennan, "A Bibliography of Publications in the Field of Eriugenian Studies 1800–1975," *Studi Medievali* 3a serie 18 (1977): 401–47; eadem *Guide des études érigeniènnes: Bibliographie commentée des publications 1930-1987/ A Guide to Eriugenian Studies: A Survey of Publications, 1930-1987* (Fribourg: Editions Universitaires; Paris: Cerf, 1989). Much of the recent interest in Eriugena has been the product of SPES, the Society for the Promotion of Eriugenian Studies, which has sponsored eight International Colloquia devoted to the Irish scholar since 1971 (published under a variety of auspices).

4. Evelyn Underhill, *Mysticism: A Study in the Nature and Development of Man's Spiritual Consciousness* (Cleveland and New York: Meridian, 1965), p. 457. Underhill refers to Eriugena only three times.

5. I use the word "dialectical" in the sense of the claim that the most adequate language about God is to be found in the *Aufhebung* of mutually opposed predications into a realm of discourse that points to a God beyond both affirmation and negation. Eriugena's version of this is developed from that found in Dionysius; see B. McGinn, *The Foundations of Mysticism: Origins to the Fifth Century,* vol 1 of *The Presence of God: A History of Western Christian Mysticism* (New York: Crossroad, 1991), pp. 157–82. This is a somewhat broader use than the Irish scholar's own sense of *dialectica.*

6. Dermot Moran, *The Philosophy of John Scottus Eriugena: A Study of Idealism in the Middle Ages* (Cambridge: Cambridge University Press, 1989), p. 240. See p. 68, where Moran speaks of John's greatest work, *Periphyseon,* as "a vehicle to traveling on the road to spiritual enlightenment." Other recent works that stress Eriugena's contribution to mysticism include Paul A. Dietrich and Donald F. Duclow, "Virgins in Paradise: Deification and exegesis in 'Periphyseon V,'" in *Jean Scot Écrivain. Actes du IVe Colloque International, Montréal,* ed. Guy Allard (Montréal: Bellarmin; Paris: Vrin, 1986), pp. 29–49; Alois M. Haas, "Eriugena und die Mystik," in *Eriugena Redivivus: Zur Wirkungsgeschichte seines Denkens im Mittelalter und im Übergang zur Neuzeit (Vorträge des V. Internationalen Eriugena-Colloquiums, 1985),* ed. Werner Beierwaltes (Heidelberg: Winter, 1987), pp. 254–78; and Kurt Ruh, *Geschichte der abendländischen Mystik:*

Band I, *Die Grundlegung durch die Kirchenväter und die Mönchstheologie des 12. Jahrhunderts* (Munich: Beck, 1990), chap. 6.

7. See Brennan, "Materials for the Biography," Testimonia 1–4.

8. On the predestination controversy and John's role in it, see Moran, *Philosophy of John Scottus*, chap. 2. The *De divina praedestinatione* has been edited by Goulven Madec in CC 50 (it will be abbreviated here as *DP*).

9. *DP* 1 (CC 50:16): ... veram esse philosophiam veram religionem, conversimque veram religionem esse veram philosophiam. On the interpenetration of philosophy and theology in Eriugena, see Werner Beierwaltes who shows how Eriugena "forms philosophical and theological tenets into an integral and mutually interdependent whole" ("Eriugena's Platonism," *Hermathena* 199 [1992]: 69).

10. For the background, see Michael McCormick, "Diplomacy and the Carolingian Encounter with Byzantium down to the Accession of Charles the Bald," in *Eriugena: East and West. Papers of the Eighth International Eriugena Colloquium*, ed. Bernard McGinn and Willemien Otten (Notre Dame: University of Notre Dame Press, 1994), pp. 15–48.

11. On John's knowledge of Greek, see Edouard Jeauneau, "Jean Scot Érigène et le grec," *Archivum Latinitatis Medii Aevi (Bulletin du Cange)* 41 (1979): 5–50.

12. Eriugena's translation is found in PL 122:1029–1194.

13. This translation has been edited and studied by M. Cappuyns, "Le *De Imagine* de Grégoire de Nysse traduit par Jean Scot Érigène," *Recherches de théologie ancienne et médiévale* 32 (1965): 205–62.

14. The *Quaestiones ad Thalassium* have been edited, both the original Greek and Eriugena's translation, by Carl Laga and Carlos Steel in CCSG 7 and 22. The *Ambigua ad Iohannem* in Eriugena's Latin version is edited by Edouard Jeauneau in CCSG 18.

15. Eriugena wrote a commentary (or commentaries) on Martianus Capella's *De nuptiis Philologiae et Mercurii*, but there is ongoing discussion about how much of the surviving ninth-century interpretation of this handbook actually belongs to him. See Moran, *Philosophy of John Scottus*, pp. 38–45.

16. See Cappuyns, *Jean Scot Érigène*, p. 182.

17. The old edition of H.-J. Floss is reprinted in PL 122:441–1022. The first three books have been reedited with a translation by I. P. Sheldon-Williams in collaboration with Ludwig Bieler, *Iohannis Scotti Eriugenae Periphyseon (De Divisione Naturae)* (Dublin: Institute for Advanced Studies, 1968, 1972, 1981). There is a complete translation of all five books, *Eriugena: Periphyseon (The Division of Nature)*, trans. I. P. Sheldon-Williams, revised by John J. O'Meara (Montréal: Bellarmin; Washington: Dumbarton Oaks, 1987). I will use this translation unless otherwise noted and will cite the text according to book and column numbers in the Migne text in parentheses since these are also found in the more recent editions and translations, e.g., P 5 (921D). The Sheldon-Williams edition has been criticized; see Paolo Lucentini, "La nuovo edizione del 'De divisione naturae (Periphyseon)' di Giovanni Scoto Eriugena," *Studi Medievali* 3a serie 17 (1976): 1–22; and Aidan Breen, "Iohannes Scottus, *Periphyseon*: The Problems of an Edition," *Proceedings of the Royal Irish Academy* 91 (1991): 21–40. Edouard Jeauneau is at work on the editing of P 4 and 5.

18. P 1 (441A): N. Est igitur natura generale nomen, ut diximus, omnium quae sunt et quae non sunt? A. Est quidem. (The work is in the form of a dialogue between the teacher [*Nutritor*] and the pupil [*Alumnus*], a feature of some importance to its dialectical structure and argument.) On the structure of *Periphyseon*, see, e.g., Guy-H. Allard, "La structure littéraire de la composition du *De divisione naturae*," in *The Mind of Eriugena: Papers of a [the First Eriugena] Colloquium, Dublin, 1970* (Dublin: Irish University Press, 1973), pp. 147–57.

19. The *Expositiones in Ierarchiam Ceolestem* have been edited by Jeanne Barbet in CC 31 and will be hereafter cited as EI with chapter and section number followed by page and line

reference where needed in parentheses—e.g., EI 2.3 (31.434–38). Eriugena appears not to have thought a commentary on the *De divinis nominibus* was needed after the extensive treatment he gave it in *Periphyseon.* A commentary on the *De mystica theologia* sometimes ascribed to him is actually by Robert Grosseteste.

20. These two works have been edited by Edouard Jeauneau, *Jean Scot Érigène: Homélie sur le Prologue de Jean* (SC 151), hereafter abbreviated as OI with section number and page and line in parenthesis, e.g., OI 3 (212.1–4); and *Jean Scot: Commentaire sur l'Évangile de Jean* (SC 180), abbreviated as CI with book and chapter number followed by page and line in parentheses, e.g., CI 1.30 (162.54–58).

21. See Paul E. Dutton, "Eriugena the Royal Poet," in *Jean Scot Écrivain,* pp. 51–80.

22. Johannes Duft, "Iromanie-Irophobie," *Zeitschrift für Schweizerische Kirchengeschichte* 50 (1956): 241–62.

23. See, e.g., Eduardo Coccia, "La cultura irlandese precarolingia: Miracolo o mito?" *Studi Medievali* 3a serie 8 (1967): 257–420 (a very negative view); and Michael Herren, "Classical and Secular Learning among the Irish before the Carolingian Renaissance," *Florilegium* 3 (1981): 118–57.

24. A. Furey, "Cross-Examining the Witness: Recent Research on Celtic Monastic History," *Monastic Studies* 14 (1983): 37.

25. See Herren, "Classical and Secular Learning," pp. 129, 137–38.

26. Joseph Kelley, "Hiberno-Latin Theology," in *Die Iren und Europa im früheren Mittelalter,* ed. Heinrich Löwe, 2 vols. (Stuttgart: Klett-Cotta, 1982), 2:549–67. For an introduction to the literature, see Thomas Finan, "Hiberno-Latin Christian Literature," in *An Introduction to Celtic Christianity,* ed. James P. Mackey (Edinburgh: T. & T. Clark, 1989), pp. 64–100.

27. Patrick's authentic writings, the *Confession* and the *Epistola ad Milites Corotici,* have been edited by Richard P. C. Hanson in collaboration with Cecile Blanc in SC 249. For studies of his career and spirituality, see R. P. C. Hanson, *The Life and Writings of the Historical St. Patrick* (New York: Seabury, 1983); and Noel Dermot O'Donoghue, *Aristocracy of Soul: Patrick of Ireland* (Wilmington: Michael Glazier, 1987).

28. See Richard Sharpe, "St. Patrick and Armagh," *Cambridge Medieval Celtic Studies* 4 (1982): 33–59; and Dorothy Ann Bray, "The Making of a Hero: The Legend of St. Patrick and the Claims of Armagh," *Monastic Studies* 14 (1983): 145–60.

29. Michael Herren, "Mission and Monasticism in the *Confessio* of Patrick," in *Sages, Saints and Storytellers: Celtic Studies in Honour of Professor James Carney,* ed. Donnchadh Ò Corrain, Liam Breatnach, and Kim McCone (Maynooth: An Sagart, 1989), p. 84.

30. As Hermann J. Vogt puts it, "In Irland ist die Christianisierung sogar die Märchenmotive, oder anders ausgedruckt, die Inkulturation des Christentums besser gelungen als sonst im Abendland und scheint nicht einmal durch das Latein behindert worden zu sein" ("Zur Spiritualität des frühen irischen Mönchtums," in *Die Iren und Europa,* 1:34. At least from the point of later legend, Patrick's policy of accommodation with native culture is presented in the picture of his good relations with Dubthach maccu Lugair, the "chief poet of Ireland," as recounted in "Fiacc's Hymn" of c. 800. See Seamus MacMathuna, "Paganism and Society in Early Ireland," in *Irish Writers and Religion,* ed. Robert Welch (Savage, MD: Barnes and Noble, 1992), pp. 1–2.

31. On these dream-visions, see O'Donoghue, *Patrick of Ireland,* chap. 1.

32. On early medieval dreams, see Lisa M. Bitel, "*In visione noctis*: Dreams in European Hagiography and Histories, 450–900," *History of Religions* 31(1991): 39–59, who briefly notes Patrick's dreams (p. 51), though without comment on their mystical character.

33. *Conf.* 20 (SC 249:92.3–94.10): . . . et cecidit super me veluti saxum ingens et nihil membrorum meorum praevalens. Sed unde me venit ignarum in spiritu ut Heliam vocarem? Et inter haec vidi in caelum solem oriri et dum clamarem "Heliam, Heliam" viribus meis,

ecce splendor solis illius decidit super me et statim discussit a me omnem gravitudinem, et credo quod a Christo Domino meo subventus sum et spiritus eius iam tunc clamabat pro me.... The text ends by quoting Matt 10:19–20 on Christ's promise that the Holy Spirit will speak in those who follow him.

34. For helpful comments, see O'Donoghue, *Patrick of Ireland,* pp. 15–19, 57–60.

35. On this dream, see O'Donoghue, *Patrick of Ireland,* pp. 43–49, 51–55.

36. *Conf.* 25 (SC 249:98.1–8): Et iterum vidi in me ipsum orantem et eram quasi intra corpus meum et audivi super me, hoc est super interiorem hominem, et ibi fortiter orabat gemitibus, et inter haec stupebam et ammirabam et cogitabam quis esset qui in me orabat, sed ad postremum orationis sic effitiatus est ut sit Spiritus, et sic expertus sum et recordatus sum apostolo dicente....

37. Still basic for the study of early Irish Christianity is James F. Kenney, *The Sources for the Early History of Ireland, Ecclesiastical: An Introduction and Guide* (New York: Columbia University Press, 1929; reprint with additions by Ludwig Bieler, 1968). Among more recent works, see Ludwig Bieler, *Ireland: Harbinger of the Middle Ages* (Oxford: Oxford University Press, 1963); *Old Ireland,* ed. Robert J. McNally (New York: Fordham University Press, 1965); Kathleen Hughes, *The Church in Early Irish Society* (Ithaca, NY: Cornell University Press, 1967); John T. McNeill, *The Celtic Churches* (Chicago: University of Chicago Press, 1974); Patrick J. Corish, *The Irish Catholic Experience: A Historical Survey* (Wilmington DE: Michael Glazier, 1985), chap. 1; and John R. Walsh and Thomas Bradley, *A History of the Irish Church 400-700 AD* (Dublin: Columba Press, 1991).

38. See Kathleen Hughes, "The Celtic Church: Is this a viable concept?" *Cambridge Medieval Celtic Studies* 1 (1981): 1–20.

39. Kathleen Hughes, "Sanctity and Secularity in the Early Irish Church," in *Secularity and Sanctity: Studies in Church History 10,* ed. Derek Baker (Cambridge: Cambridge University Press, 1973), p. 21.

40. On early Irish monasticism, see John Ryan, *Irish Monasticism: Origins and Development* (Ithaca, NY: Cornell University Press, 1973; 1st ed. Dublin, 1931); Kathleen Hughes and Ann Hamlin, *The Modern Traveler to the Early Irish Church* (New York: Seabury, 1981); and Lisa M. Bitel, *Isle of the Saints: Monastic Settlement and Community in Early Ireland* (Ithaca, NY: Cornell University Press, 1990). For the Irish monastic rules, see Eoin de Bhaldraithe, "Obedience: The Doctrine of the Irish Monastic Rules," *Monastic Studies* 14 (1993): 63–84.

41. On this reform, see Peter O Dwyer, *Célí Dé, Spiritual Reform in Ireland 750-900* (Dublin: Editions Tailliura, 1981).

42. J. N. Hillgarth has written extensively on these contacts, e.g., "Old Ireland and Visigothic Spain," in *Old Ireland,* pp. 200–227.

43. For a recent survey, See Tomás Ó Fiach, "Irish Monks on the Continent," in *Introduction to Celtic Christianity,* pp. 101–39. See also Walsh and Bradley, *History of the Irish Church,* chaps. 7–9.

44. See Ó Fiach, "Irish Monks," pp. 110–11.

45. The writings of Columbanus have been edited and translated by G. W. M. Walker, *Sancti Columbani Opera* (Dublin: Institute for Advanced Studies, 1957). See also Tomás Ó Fiach, *Columbanus in his own words* (Dublin: Veritas, 1974). It now appears that three classicizing poems often attributed to Columbanus are actually eighth century; see the summary of the debate in Herren, "Classical and Secular Learning," pp. 126–28.

46. The importance of early Irish exegesis was first noted by Bernhard Bischoff in a German article of 1954, now available in English as "Turning Points in the History of Latin Exegesis in the Early Middle Ages," in *Biblical Studies: The Medieval Irish Contribution,* ed. Martin McNamara (Dublin: Proceedings of the Irish Biblical Association, 1976), pp. 74–160.

47. For a brief summary of the traditional view, see Walsh and Bradley, *History of the Irish Church*, chap. 11.

48. On early Irish spirituality, besides K. Hughes's paper "Sanctity and Secularity in the Early Irish Church," referred to above, see Diarmuid Ó Loaghaire, "Irlande" in DS 7:1971–86 (with a rich bibliography), as well as his "Old Ireland and Her Spirituality," in *Old Ireland*, pp. 29–59. Other studies include Ó Loaghaire, "Daily Intimacy with God–an Ever New Aspect of Celtic Worship," *Studia Liturgica* 13 (1979): 46–57, and "The Celtic Monk at Prayer," *Monastic Studies* 14 (1983): 123–43; Hermann J. Vogt, "Zur Spiritualität des frühen irischen Mönchtums," *Die Iren und Europa*, 1:26–51; and the volume *Irish Spirituality*, ed. Michael Maher (Dublin: Veritas, 1981), especially the papers by Michael Curren and Martin McNamara. For a broad view in relation to other forms of early medieval spirituality, see Pierre Riché, "Spirituality in Celtic and Germanic Society," in *Christian Spirituality: Origins to the Twelfth Century*, ed. B. McGinn, and J. Meyendorff, WS 16 (New York: Crossroad, 1986), pp. 163-76.

49. See Martin McNamara, "The Psalter in Early Irish Monastic Spirituality," *Monastic Studies* 14 (1983): 179–205.

50. See James Carney, "Old Ireland and Her Poetry," in *Old Ireland*, pp. 147–72. Many of these poems are edited and translated in Carney's *Medieval Irish Lyrics* (Dublin: Dolmen Press, 1967).

51. From Carney, "Old Ireland and Her Poetry," pp. 166–67. See also the translations from the late eighth century poet Blathmac (pp. 160–72).

52. For these texts, see Ó Laoghaire, "Celtic Monk at Prayer," pp. 129, 133.

53. See *Adomnan's Life of Columba*, ed. and trans. Alan Orr Anderson and Marjorie Ogilvie Anderson (Oxford: Clarendon Press, 1991), iii.2, iii.17, iii.19–21, and iii.23 (pp. 184, 206, 210–14, 232). On the fire manifestations in earlier Christian mysticism, see *Foundations of Mysticism*, pp. 137, 205.

54. *Adomnan's Life*, iii.18 (ed. 208): Sed et multa quaedam, ut ipse post coram paucis admodum professus est, occulta ab exordio ipse post coram paucis admodum professus est, occulta ab exordio mundi arcana aperte manifestata videbat. Scripturarum quoque sacrarum obscura quaeque et difficillima plana et luce clarius aperta mundissimi cordis oculis patebant. Similar mystical visions are not lacking in other monastic figures of the era. For example, St. Wandrill (d. 672), founder of Fontanelle and deeply influenced by Columbanus's monasticism, three days before his death was "led into ecstasy, [where] he contemplated the glory of God" (*Vita Wandregiseli* 18 in MGH.SS.rer.Mer. 5:22).

55. Much work still remains to be done on relating Eriugena to early Irish Christianity. For a preliminary attempt to establish links between him and previous Irish exegesis of the Hexaemeron, see Thomas O'Loughlin, "Unexplored Irish Influence on Eriugena," *Recherches de théologie ancienne et médiévale* 59 (1992): 23–40.

56. Goulven Madec provides valuable lists of all John's explicit citations of Greek and Latin authors ("Jean Scot Érigène et ses auteurs," in *Jean Scot Écrivain*, pp. 143–86). Also useful is the "Index Auctorum" in G. H. Allard, *Johannis Scoti Eriugenae Periphyseon: Indices Generales* (Montréal and Paris: Institut des études médiévales-Vrin, 1983), pp. 619–24; and chap. 7 in Moran, *Philosophy of John Scottus*.

57. Two volumes of the Colloquia sponsored by SPES have been concerned with Eriugena's sources: *Eriugena: Studien zu seinen Quellen. Vorträge des III. Internationalen Eriugena Colloquiums, Freiburg, 1979*, ed. Werner Beierwaltes (Heidelberg: Winter, 1980); and *Eriugena: East and West* (Notre Dame: University of Notre Dame Press, 1994).

58. On Victorinus and Ambrose as mystics, see *Foundations of Mysticism*, pp. 198–200 and 202–16 respectively.

59. See Gustavo Piemonte, "L'expression 'quae sunt et quae non sunt': Jean Scot et Marius Victorinus," in *Jean Scot Écrivain*, pp. 81–113.

60. For Augustine's mysticism, see *Foundations of Mysticism*, chap. 7. There is a large literature on Eriugena's relation to Augustine. Helpful introductions are Brian Stock, "Observations on the Use of Augustine by Johannes Scottus Eriugena," *Harvard Theological Review* 60 (1967): 213–20; idem, "In Search of Eriugena's Augustine," in *Eriugena: Studien zu seinen Quellen*, pp. 86–104; and John J. O'Meara, "Eriugena's Use of Augustine," *Augustinian Studies* 2 (1980): 21–34.

61. For an introduction, see I. P. Sheldon-Williams ("Eriugena's Greek Sources," in *The Mind of Eriugena*, pp. 1–15), who summarizes: "When Eriugena is dependent on Pseudo-Dionysius, which he is most of the time explicitly or implicitly, his interpretation always carries overtones derived from one or other of these subsidiaries (Maximus and Gregory). It is the subtle harmonization of these overtones with the central melody that constitutes the virtue of Eriugena's philosophy, which is neither Augustinian nor Dionysian nor that of Maximus nor of Gregory, but a new thing" (pp. 6–7). Also helpful for an overview of Eriugena's use of Greek patristic sources is Edouard Jeauneau, "Pseudo-Dionysius, Gregory of Nyssa, and Maximus Confessor in the Works of John Scottus Eriugena," in Edouard Jeauneau, *Études Érigéniennes* (Paris: Études Augustiniennes, 1987), pp. 175–87.

62. Eriugena's knowledge of Aristotelian logic mostly comes from a pseudonymous text he thought Augustine had written on Aristotle's *Categories*, the *Categoriae decem* (e.g., P 1 [463A–93A). See John Marenbon, "John Scottus and the 'Categoriae Decem,'" in *Eriugena: Studien zu seinen Quellen*, pp. 117–34.

63. See Stephen Gersh, *From Iamblichus to Eriugena: An Investigation of the Prehistory and Evolution of the Pseudo-Dionysian Tradition* (Leiden: Brill, 1978). For some comments on the role of Proclus in Christian mysticism, see *Foundations of Mysticism*, pp. 57–61, 165–68.

64. John knew Origen in Latin translation, but he quotes Basil's *Hexaemeron* and Epiphanius's *Anchoratus* in unknown versions, which may be his own lost translations.

65. Quantitatively, Eriugena cites more texts of Gregory in *Periphyseon* than any other Greek author; but, as Jeauneau argues, he read Gregory through the eyes of Dionysius and Maximus ("Pseudo-Dionysius, Gregory of Nyssa, and Maximus Confessor," p. 182).

66. On Gregory's influence on John, see Mario Naldini, "Gregorio Nisseno e Giovanni Scoto Eriugena: Note sull'idea di creazione e sull'antropologia," *Studi Medievali* 3a serie 20 (1979): 501–33; and Edouard Jeauneau, "La division des sexes chez Grégoire de Nysse et chez Jean Scot Érigène," in *Eriugena: Studien zu seiner Quellen*, pp. 34–54.

67. See H. F. Dondaine, *Le corpus dionysien de l'université de Paris au XIIIe siècle* (Rome: Edizioni di Storia et Letteratura, 1953), pp. 84–89, 135–38. Dondaine estimates that about forty of the 580 columns of *Periphyseon* in the PL 122 edition appear in the Parisian corpus (p. 88). The corpus (as found in the Dominican manuscripts now Paris, Bibl. nat. lat. 17341) contained the translations of Eriugena and John Sarrazin, as well as the *Extractio* of Thomas Gallus, along with *scholia* and explanatory materials, including John's *Expositio in Hierarchiam Coelestem*.

68. PL 122:1031–36. For a summary and discussion, see Sheldon-Williams, "Greek Sources," pp. 8–10.

69. For my own attempt to present this central moment in the history of Christian mysticism, see *Foundations of Mysticism*, pp. 157–82.

70. The literature on the relation of Dionysius and Eriugena is large. For an overall perspective on the early development of the dialectical tradition, see especially Gersh, *From Iamblichus to Eriugena*. For an insightful study of the Dionysian basis for the logic of Eriugena's God-language, see Thomas Michael Tomasic, "The Logical Function of Metaphor and Oppo-

sitional Coincidence in the Pseudo-Dionysius and Johannes Scottus Eriugena," *Journal of Religion* 68 (1988): 361–77.

71. One of the first modern theologians to highlight the importance of Maximus was Hans Urs von Balthasar in his *Kosmische Liturgie: Das Weltbild Maximus der Bekenner* (Freiburg im Breisgau: Herder, 1941; 2nd ed. 1961). Another significant work is Lars Thunberg, *Microcosm and Mediator: The Theological Anthropology of Maximus Confessor* (Lund: Gleerup, 1965). See also the papers in *Maximus Confessor: Actes du Symposium sur Maxime le Confesseur. Fribourg 2–5 September 1980*, ed. Felix Heinzer and Christoph Schönbron (Fribourg: Editions Universitaires, 1982), especially that of Jaroslav Pelikan, "The Place of Maximus Confessor in the History of Christian Thought," pp. 387–402.

72. On Maximus's works, see Polycarp Sherwood, *An Annotated Date-List of the Works of Maximus the Confessor* (Rome: Herder, 1952). For a brief introduction, see Irenée-Henri Dalmais, "Maxime le Confesseur," DS 10:836–42.

73. See *Foundations of Mysticism*, esp. pp. 180–81.

74. Pelikan, "The Place of Maximus," p. 397.

75. See the dedicatory letter to the translation of Maximus's *Ambigua* found in CCSG 18:3–5. On the translation, see Edouard Jeauneau, "Jean l'Érigène et les Ambigua ad Iohannem de Maxime le Confesseur," in *Maximus Confessor*, pp. 343–64. Eriugena cites the *Ambigua* more often than he does the *Ad Thalassium*. The list of both explicit and implicit references to the *Ambigua* found in the Jeauneau edition (Appendice II, pp. lxxvii–lxxxiii) contains 106 notations, the most frequent being to *Ambigua* III, VI and XXXVII.

76. For a comparison of Maximus and Eriugena, see Eric D. Perl, "Metaphysics and Christology in Maximus Confessor and Eriugena," *Eriugena: East and West*, pp. 253–70. On the creature as "another God," see *Questiones ad Thalassium* 6 (CCSG 7:68–70).

77. Perl discusses three basic differences in his article: (1) for Eriugena divine self-creation is not described as God's Incarnation as it is in Maximus (see, e.g., P 3 [678CD]); (2) nor does he hold that deification is the same as Incarnation (e.g., P 1 [449AB]); and, finally, (3) Eriugena thinks there will always remain a distinction between our deification and the hypostatic union realized in Christ (see P 5 [911BC]).

78. On Eriugena's exegesis, see Cappuyns, *Jean Scot Érigène*, pp. 276–80, 291–302; René Roques, "'Valde Artificialiter': le sens d'un contresens," and "Genèse I,1–3 chez Jean Scot," in *Libres sentiers vers l'érigénisme* (Rome: Edizioni dell'Ateneo, 1974), pp. 45–98, 131–94; Guy H. Allard, "Vocabulaire érigénien relatif à la représentation de l'Ecriture," in *Eriugena: Studien zu seiner Quellen*, pp. 15–32; and E. Jeauneau, "Introduction," *Jean Scot: Commentaire sur l'Évangile de Jean*, pp. 44–48.

79. P 1 (509A): Sanctae siquidem scripturae in omnibus sequenda est auctoritas. . . .

80. P 4 (744AB): . . . cui [ratio] delectabilius est in abditis divini oceani fretibus virtutem suam exercere . . . ; *in sudore enim vultus sui panem suam* (Gen 3:19), Dei videlicet verbum, jussa est *vesci*, terramque sacrae Scripturae. . . .

81. P 5 (1010BC): O Domine Jesu, nullum aliud praemium, nullam aliam beatitudinem, nullum aliud gaudium a te postulo, nisi ut ad purum absque ullo errore fallacis theoriae verba tua quae per tuum sanctum Spiritum inspirata sunt, intelligam. Haec est enim summa felicitatis meae, finisque perfectae est contemplationis, quoniam nihil ultra rationabilis anima etiam purissima inveniet, quia nihil ultra est. Ut enim non alibi aptius quaereris, quam in verbis tuis, ita non alibi apertius inveneris, quam in eis. For some comments on this prayer, see Jeauneau, "Pseudo-Dionysius, Gregory of Nyssa, and Maximus Confesor," pp. 186–87. For another prayer in *Periphyseon* asking for enlightenment, this time without direct reference to scripture, see P 3 (650B).

82. EI 2.1 (24.146–51): . . . ita theologia, veluti quedam poetria, sanctam scripturam fictis imaginationibus ad consultum nostri animi et reductionem a corporalibus sensibus exteri-

oribus, veluti ex quadem imperfecta pueritia, in rerum intelligibilium perfectam cognitionem, tamquam in quamdam interioris hominis grandevitatem conformat. On this text, see Peter Dronke, "'Theologia velut quaedam poetria': quelques observations sur la fonction des images poétiques chez Jean Scot," in *Jean Scot Érigenè et l'histoire de la philosophie (Actes du II Colloque intérnational Jean Scot Érigène. Laon, 1975)*, ed. René Roques (Paris: CNRS, 1977), pp. 243–52.

83. OI 14 (270.5–272.17): Extra autem omnia et ultra, aetherius ille igneusque ardor empyrii caeli, hoc est, superae contemplationis divinae naturae, quam graeci theologiam nominant, circumglobatur . . . (11.14–17). In "Appendice III" of the edition (pp.327–28), E. Jeauneau finds the source for this in Maximus, *Ambigua* 17 (CCSG 18:139–41), though Eriugena's adoption is a free one.

84. E.g., in P 3 (705B–707B) Eriugena claims that his interpretation of the first three days of Genesis 1 has not been according to *allegoria* (i.e., theology) but is a *nuda solummodo physica consideratio* (707B).

85. For a good example of Eriugena's more traditional exegesis, see his typological reading of John 3:15 in CI 3.5 (226.38–228.75).

86. OI 3 (212.1–4): Monumentum Christi est divina scriptura, in qua divinitatis et humanitatis eius misteria densitate litterae veluti quadam muniuntur petra.

87. E.g., P 5 (1010AB). On *transitus* in Eriugena's thought, see E. Jeauneau's note in *Commentaire*, pp. 302–3, and his *Quatre Thèmes Érigéniens* (Montréal: Institut d'études médiévales; Paris: Vrin, 1978), pp. 84–87; as well as Werner Beierwaltes, "Language and its Object: Reflections on Eriugena's Valuation of the Function and Capacities of Language," in *Jean Scot Écrivain*, pp. 223–28.

88. P 5 (862A): . . . et ad spirituales intellectus, quos veritas edocet, promptus accedat, qua una et sola via mysticarum literarum penetrantur adita.

89. CI 1.32 (182.42–43): . . . infinitus enim infinite, etiam in purgatissimis mentibus, formatur.

90. EI 4.1 (66.26–31): Quamvis enim formationes divine scripture varie sint ac multiformes sepissimeque confuse, intellectus tamen earum simplex est et uniformis, omnique dissimilitudine alienus, in quem mentis oculum elevare inque eum infigere et in eo permanere, rationabilis nature summa ac sola beatitudo est.

91. P 3 (690C): . . . dum modo ut sane fidei catholicaeque professioni conveniat quod quisque dicat, sive aliunde accipiens sive in se ipso, a deo tamen illuminatus, inveniens. This is a good Augustinian principle; see, e.g., *De doctrina christiana* 3.10(14), and *Confessiones* 12.31(42).

92 On Eriugena's vocabulary for the theological sense of scripture, see "Appendice III: Allegoria, Mysterium, Sacramentum, Symbolum," in *Commentaire*, pp. 397–402.

93. P 1 (509A): Non tamen ita credenda est ut ipsa semper propriis verborum seu nominum signis fruatur divinam nobis naturam insinuans sed quibusdam similitudinibus varisque translatorum verborum seu nominum modis utitur infirmitati nostrae condescendens nostrosque adhuc rudes infantilesque sensus simplici doctrina erigens (translation slightly altered).

94. P 1 (510B): Ratio vero in hoc universaliter studet ut suadeat certisque veritatis investigationibus approbet nil de deo proprie posse dici . . . qui melius nesciendo scitur, cuius ignorantia vera est sapientia. . . .

95. On this distinction, see Jean Pépin, "*Mysteria* et *Symbola* dans le commentaire de Jean Scot sur l'évangile de Saint Jean," in *The Mind of Eriugena*, pp. 16–30; and the "Appendice III" in *Commentaire*, where E. Jeauneau discusses the roots of the distinction in Augustine and Dionysius.

96. CI 6.5 (352.46–48): . . . quoniam in dictis solummodo spiritualis doctrinae, non autem in factis sensibilibus constituitur.

97. See CI 6.6 (362–66 [the passage cited is 366.102–4]): . . . quoniam nil ibi est quod secundum historiam intelligatur, sed totum ad theologiam, quae omnem sensum et intellectum superat [cf. Phil. 4:7] refertur. The citation from Phil 4:7 is revealing, since this is one of Eriugena's favorite proof texts for the supremacy of negative theology. See G. Madec, "Jean Scot et ses auteurs," pp. 143–44; and E. Jeauneau in *Homélie,* p. 268 n.3.

98. EI 1.2 (12.419–25): Et ut breviter dicam, omnes species visibilis et invisibilis creature, omnesque allegorie, sive in factis sive in dictis, per omnem sanctam utriusque testamenti scripturam, velamina paterni radii sunt, et ipse radius, secundum carnem suam suimet secundum deitatem, maximum velamen est nobisque connaturale.

99. See Marta Cristiani, "'Mysticus Moyses': Escatologia ed Esodo nel 'Periphyseon' di Giovanni Scoto," *Cristianesimo nella Storia* 10 (1989): 467–84.

100. On these texts, see Dietrich and Duclow, "Virgins in Paradise"; and Willemien Otten, "The Dialectic of the Return in Eriugena's *Periphyseon,*" *Harvard Theological Review* 84 (1991): 419–21.

101. Otten, "Dialectic of the Return," p. 420.

102. See *Foundations of Mysticism,* pp. 111–12, 116–17.

103. On the relation between *ratio* and *auctoritas,* see Cappuyns, *Jean Scot Érigène,* pp. 280–91; and, more recently, J. C. Marler, "Dialectical Use of Authority in the *Periphyseon,*" and Giulio d'Onofrio, "The *Concordia* of Augustine and Dionysius: Toward a Hermeneutic of the Disagreement of Patristic Sources in John the Scot's *Periphyseon,*" in *Eriugena: East and West,* pp. 95–113, 115–40.

104. P 5 (1022C): Unusquisque in suo sensu abundet, donec veniat illa lux, quae de luce falso philosophantium facit tenebras, et tenebras recte cognoscentium convertit in lucem.

105. Eriugena, both through his translations and in his own writings, did much to popularize the terms *mysticus* and *mystice* in the new Christendom (in his own works these words appear eighty-one times). His applications do not go beyond the Greek sources, though they tend to be more varied than the traditional Latin authors. He often qualifies the objects, persons, and works of the Old Testament as "mystical" (i.e., hidden) in relation to the New Testament (e.g., P 3 [724C]–*Veteris Testamenti mystica opera*). He also likes to speak of texts or objects as "mystically signifying" something (e.g., P 2 [560D], P 4 [858D], P 5 [867C, 916A]; EI 2.2 [28.314] and 13.4 [177.418]). He can refer to "mystical actions" (P 2 [583B]) and "mystical dogmas" (EI 6.2 [89.99]). *Mysticus intellectus* is a popular term (e.g., P 4 [850B]; EI 2.5 [51.1166–7]; OI 23 [316.40–1]), and he speaks of *mysticae visiones* (EI 2.2 [30.401]). Finally, Eriugena even uses the term in a substantive sense, as when he speaks of *mysticum et allegoricum* (e.g., EI 2.2 [24.170]).

106. For an introduction to procession and return in medieval thought, see Paul Rorem, "'Procession and Return' in Thomas Aquinas and His Predecessors," *Princeton Seminary Bulletin* 13 (1992): 147–63. Rorem says ". . . it was John who most thoroughly transposed Neoplatonism's timeless procession and return into Christian salvation history, especially in terms of structuring his 'Summa'" (p. 154).

107. On the function of language in Eriugena, see Beierwaltes, "Language and Object," and a number of the papers in *Begriff und Metaphor: Sprachform des Denkens bei Eriugena. Vorträge des VII. Internationalen Eriugena-Colloquiums, 1989,* ed. Werner Beierwaltes (Heidelberg: Winter, 1990).

108. P 1 (462D): Dicit enim deum non esse aliquod eorum quae sunt sed plus quam ea quae sunt esse, illud autem esse quid sit nullo modo diffinit. On this discussion, see B. McGinn, "Negative Theology in John the Scot," *Studia Patristica XIII: Texte und Untersuchungen,* Band 116 (Berlin: Akademie, 1975), pp. 232–38; Thomas Tomasic, "The Logical

Function of Metaphor and Oppositional Coincidence"; and Dominic J. O'Meara, "The Problem of Speaking about God in John Scottus Eriugena," in *Carolingian Essays*, ed. Uta-Renate Blumenthal (Washington: Catholic University, 1983), pp. 151–67.

109. Eriugena's positive and dynamic use of the image of exploring the sea of scripture appears to be original, perhaps a reflection of his Irish background, as suggested by Edouard Jeauneau, "Le symbolisme de la mer chez Jean Scot Érigène," *Le Néoplatonisme* (Paris: CNRS, 1971), pp. 385–94, who describes *Periphyseon* as "une navigation philosophique" (p. 387).

110. E.g., P 1 (454A, 518A), P 2 (559B), P 4 (759A); EI 15.2 (194–5). See Rodolfo Rini, "Dio come 'essentia omnium' nel pensiero di Giovanni Scoto Eriugena," *Rivista di filosofia neoscolastica* 62 (1970): 101–32.

111. P 3 (681C): Divina igitur bonitas quae propterea nihilum dicitur quoniam ultra omnia quae sunt et quae non sunt in nulla essentia invenitur ex negatione omnium essentiarum in affirmationem totius universitatis essentiae a se ipsa in se ipsam descendit veluti ex nihilo in aliquid. For other appearances, see, e.g., P 2 (589B), P 3 (663CD, 683B, 686D); EI 4.1 (67.73–82). (Note how many of these appearances are to be found in the lengthy "Quaesito de Nihilo" found in P 3 [634A–690B]). Cf. Wayne Teasdale, "'Nihil' as the Name of God in John Scottus Eriugena," *Cistercian Studies* 19 (1984): 232–47. It should be pointed out here that Eriugena, like all Neoplatonists, possesses two understandings of *nihil*: privative and eminent, only the latter of which points to God (e.g., P 4 [825D], P 5 [964C]).

112. See S. Gersh, "Omnipresence in Eriugena: Some Reflections on Augustino-Maximian Elements in *Periphyseon*," in *Eriugena: Studien zu seiner Quellen*, esp. pp. 70–73.

113. The notion of theophany (*theophania*), which Eriugena took over primarily from Dionysius and Maximus, is central to his thought (see especially the discussions in P 1 [449A–451C] and P 5 [905BD, 963D–964A]). Basically, a theophany involves God's descent into created reality so that the human mind can perceive divine truth in and through the creature. In this, it is to be contrasted with *phantasia*, that is, the perceiving of a created thing without reference to the Creator (see, e.g., 962C–963C). See Tullio Gregory, "Note sulla dottrina delle 'teofanie' in Giovanni Scoto Eriugena," *Studi Medievali* 3a serie 4 (1963): 75–91; and Jean Trouillard, "Érigène et la théophanie créatrice," in *The Mind of Eriugena*, pp. 98–113. For *phantasia*, see J.-C. Foussard, "Apparence et apparition: La notion de *phantasia* chez Jean Scot," in *Jean Scot Érigène et l'histoire de la philosophie*, pp. 337–48.

114. P 3 (632D–633B): Summae siquidem ac trinae soliusque verae bonitatis in se ipsa immutabilis motus et simplex multiplicatio et inexhausta a se ipsa in se ipsa ad se ipsam diffusio causa omnium immo omnia est.... Omne enim quod intelligitur et sentitur nihil aliud est nisi non apparentis apparitio, occulti manifestatio, negati affirmatio, incomprehensibilis comprehensio, ineffabilis fatus, inaccessibilis accessus, inintellibilis intellectus, incorporalis corpus, superessentialis essentia, informis forma, immensurabilis mensura, innumerabilis numerus, carentis pondere pondus, spiritualis incrassatio, invisibilis visibilitas, illocalis localitas, carentis tempore temporalitas, infiniti diffinitio, incircunscripti circunscriptio... (translation altered in some places).

115. James McEvoy, "Biblical and Platonic Measure in John Scottus Eriugena," in *Eriugena: East and West*, 153–77. On this text, see also Werner Beierwaltes, "*Negati Affirmatio* or the World as Metaphor: A Foundation for Medieval aesthetics from the writings of John Scotus Eriugena," *Dionysius* 1 (1977): 127–59.

116. There are a number of other texts that might be analyzed here that would explicitly invoke a comparable dialectical analysis implying such reversing negations, e.g., P 4 (759AC); EI 15.2 (194.274–195.284).

117. See Willemien Otten, *The Anthropology of Johannes Scottus Eriugena* (Leiden: Brill, 1991), chap 1; and Moran, *Philosophy of John Scottus*, chap. 12.

118. Stephen Gersh puts it well: "The four species are different moments of the divine consciousness which are real to the extent that they are from the human point of view transsubjective but whose distinctness is accentuated by the defective post-lapsarian human cognition" (*From Iamblichus to Eriugena*, pp. 287–88). See also Moran, *Philosophy of John Scottus*, pp. 258–62. This interpretation invokes the difficult issue of the relation of divine and human consciousness, that is, the human being's status as *imago Dei*, which will be taken up below.

119. P 3 (682B): Et neque erat, neque erit, neque factus est, neque fit, neque fiet, magis autem neque est. . . .

120. Moran, *Philosophy of John Scottus*, pp. 100–102, 214, 285–86. In one place Moran states, "The first principle of Eriugena's system is not being, but rather, the concept of a person or consciousness who is above and before all beings of which it is the cause" (p. 230). This, however, seems to be falling back into the ontological trap Eriugena always strives to avoid–no *concept* can have foundational status.

121. E.g., his frequent claim that God and his creatures are one and not two, as in P 2 (528B) and P 3 (678C, 687BC).

122. See Étienne Gilson, *Being and Some Philosophers* (Toronto: Pontifical Institute for Medieval Studies, 1949), pp. 35–36. On the place of Eriugena in the medieval and modern debate on pantheism, see Dermot Moran, "Pantheism from John Scottus Eriugena to Nicholas of Cusa," *American Catholic Philosophical Quarterly* 64 (1990): 131–52.

123. While Eriugena's God may be said to possess both a "primordial" and a "consequent" nature in the sense of process theology, for the Irishman the primordial divine nature cannot be described as lacking fullness and perfection in its inconceivable inner "reality." On this point, see Donald Duclow, "Divine Nothingness and Self-Creation in John Scotus Eriugena," *Journal of Religion* 57 (1977): 118–19.

124. See Moran who argues throughout for such a broad idealist interpretation of Eriugena (*Philosophy of John Scottus*, p. 81).

125. In a variety of studies Werner Beierwaltes has explored the relation of Eriugena to German Idealism of the nineteenth century, though without neglecting the differences; see especially his "Eriugena–Aspekte seiner Philosophie," in *Die Iren und Europa*, 2:818 n. 67.

126. For a succinct presentation of Eriugena's doctrine of creation, see Donald Duclow, "Divine Nothingness and Self-Creation in John Scottus Eriugena," pp. 109–23.

127. EI 1.1 (4.129–34): Hinc est quod universalis huius mundi fabrica maximum lumen sit, ex multis partibus veluti ex multis lucernis compactum, ad intelligibilium rerum puras species revelandas et contuendas mentis acie, divina gratia et rationis ope in corde fidelium sapientium cooperantibus.

128. P 3 (683B): . . . ac sic de nihilo facit omnia, de sua videlicet superessentialitate producit essentias, de supervitalitate vitas, de superintelletualitate intellectus, de negatione omnium quae sunt et quae non sunt affirmationes omnium quae sunt et quae non sunt. Cf. the text from P 3 (633AB) cited above.

129. Beierwaltes, "*Negati Affirmatio*," p. 140.

130. P 3 (655BC). We see Eriugena here appealing to something very much like what we find later in Meister Eckhart's use of the *in quantum* principle, that is, distinguishing various aspects in which things may be said to be both eternal and yet made: cf. 640A.

131. Edouard Jeauneau in his article, "Jean Scot et la metaphysique de feu," in *Études Érigéniennes* (Paris: Études Augustiniennes, 1987), pp. 313–15, argues that Eriugena's "metaphysics of light" is dependent on his "metaphysics of fire," heat and illumination being the two primary characteristics of the latter.

132. There is a large literature on the subject. Still valuable is the old work of Clemens Baeumker, *Witelo, ein Philosoph und Naturforscher des zwölften Jahrhunderts*, Beiträge zur Geschichte der Philosophie des Mittelalters 3.2 (Münster: Aschendorff, 1900), pp. 357–422.

This provides a historical survey of *Lichtmetaphysik*. The article "Lumière" in DS 9:2242–83 is useful but neglects the early Middle Ages. Josef Koch ("Über die Lichtsymbolik im Bereich der Philosophie und der Mystik des Mittelalters," *Studium Generale* 13 [1960]: 653–70), gives considerable attention to Eriugena, but on the basis of an artificial distinction between *Lichtsymbolik* and *Lichtmetaphysik*. For the broad background, see especially Dieter Bremer, "Licht als universales Darstellungsmedium: Materialen und Bibliographie," *Archiv für Begriffsgeschichte* 18 (1974): 185–206; and for the medieval period, the same author's "Hinweise zum griechischen Ursprung und zur Europäischen Geschichte der Lichtmetaphysik," *Archiv für Begriffsgeschichte* 17 (1973): 7–35; and Klaus Hedwig, *Sphaera Lucis, Studien zur Intelligibilität des Seienden im Kontext der mittelalterlichen Lichtspekulation*, Beiträge zur Geschichte der Philosophie und Theologie des Mittelalters, Neue Folge 18 (Münster: Aschendorff, 1980).

133. P 5 (865D–866A): . . . nihil enim visibilium rerum corporaliumque est, ut arbitror, quod non incorporale quid et intelligibile significet. Cf. P 3 (707B).

134. See Beierwaltes, *"Negati Affirmatio,"* pp. 142–46; and "Eriugena's Platonism," pp. 66–69; and James McEvoy, "Metaphors of Light and Metaphysics of Light in Eriugena," *Begriff und Metapher*, pp. 149–67. McEvoy states that in Eriugena "metaphysics of light overtakes metaphorics of light" (p. 166). Also useful on Eriugena's teaching on light are Hedwig, *Sphaera Lucis*, chap. 2; Jeauneau, "Jean Scot et la métaphysique du feu," pp. 299–319; and Deirdre Carabine, "Eriugena's Use of the Symbolism of Light, Cloud and Darkness," in *Eriugena: East and West*, pp. 141–52.

135. McEvoy puts it well: ". . . the logic commanding his multiple and purposeful employment of light metaphors is the logic of dialectical concepts, of unity-in-multiplicity remaining unity, of essential hiddenness becoming universally manifest and understood in all reality, while remaining completely inaccessible in itself" (Metaphors of Light," p. 164).

136. Beierwaltes, "Eriugena's Platonism," p. 66. The German scholar is here comparing Eriugena to Plotinus, noting that the difference between them rests in John's "emphasis on the element of God's internal self-revelation or creative self-unfolding." The positive and negative elements in divine and human consciousness will be treated below.

137. The dialectical relation of light and dark, of course, is shared by all reality, and is more evident the closer the being approaches to the divine source. Speaking of the Seraphim, the highest order of angels, Eriugena says, "Obscurior igitur ceteris prima caelestis ierarchia quia manifestior, id est lucidior, et lucidior quia obscurior . . ." (EI 10.1 [153.54–55]).

138. For Eriugena's teaching on the Trinity, see Leo Scheffczyk, "Die Grundzüge der Trinitätslehre des Johannes Scotus Eriugena," in *Theologie in Geschichte und Gegenwart, Festschrift Michael Schmaus* (Munich: Beck, 1957), pp. 497–518; and Werner Beierwaltes, "Unity and Trinity in East and West," *Eriugena: East and West*, pp. 209–31.

139. EI 1.1 (2.54–3.75). The passage quoted is found in lines 70–73: . . . Splendens in omnibus que sunt, ut in amorem et cognitionem pulchritudinis sue convertantur omnia. . . . As Beierwaltes puts it ("Eriugena's Platonism," p. 65): "The Trinitarian self-disclosure of God does not surrender its unity, but makes of it a unity born of self-reflection."

140. See McEvoy, "Metaphors of Light," pp. 152–58, for a treatment of this. For an analysis of the physical nature of light, see P 1 (520D–521A).

141. See, e.g., P 3 (656D–657A); OI 13 and 16 (266 and 280); and CI 6.5 (350).

142. P 5 (1020D–1021A): . . . tertius, qui et summus, purgatissimorum animorum in ipsum Deum supernaturaliter occasus, ac veluti incomprehensibilis lucis tenebras [not tenebrae], in quibus causae omnium absconduntur: et tunc nox sicut dies illuminabitur, hoc est, secretissima divina mysteria beatis et illuminatis intellectibus ineffabili quodam modo aperientur (my own translation). *Occasus*, of course, could also be rendered more neutrally as "merging," but given the language of light and darkness in this highly Dionysian text, the connotation of "sunset" seems more appropriate.

143. On creation as God's speaking himself, see Beierwaltes, "*Negati Affirmatio,*" pp. 138–39; Donald Duclow, "Nature as Speech and Book in John Scotus Eriugena," *Mediaevalia* 3 (Binghamton: SUNY Press, 1977), pp. 131–40; and B. McGinn, "Do Christian Platonists Really Believe in Creation?" in *God and Creation: An Ecumenical Symposium,* ed. David B. Burrell and Bernard McGinn (Notre Dame: University of Notre Dame Press, 1990), pp. 205–8, 213–14.

144. See Brian Stock, "The Philosophical Anthropology of Johannes Scottus Eriugena," *Studi Medievali* 3a serie 8 (1967): 9–12, 46–57; René Roques, "Jean Scot (Érigène)," DS 8:754–58; Donald Duclow, "Dialectic and Christology in Eriugena's *Periphyseon,*" *Dionysius* 4 (1980): 99–117; Marcia Colish, "John the Scot's Christology and Soteriology in Relation to his Greek Sources," *Downside Review* 102 (1982): 138–51; James McEvoy, "'Reditus omnium in superessentialem unitatem': Christ as universal Saviour in Periphyseon V," in *Giovanni Scoto nel suo tempo,* pp. 365–81; and Perl, "Metaphysics and Christology," pp. 262–67.

145. P 5 (893A): Universalis quippe totius creaturae finis Dei Verbum est. Principium itaque et finis mundi in Verbo Dei subsistunt, et ut apertius dicam, ipsum Verbum sunt, quod est multiplex sine fine finis et principium anarchon, hoc est, sine principio praeter Patrem (translation altered).

146. The most detailed discussion is in P 2 (556B–562A), but see also 547BC, 551C, 552AB, 554CD and 563B–564A. Creation in the Word is also discussed at length in OI 7–13 (230–68), especially OI 10.

147. P 2 (545A): Si enim Christus qui omnia intelligit, immo est omnium intellectus . . . ; and P 2 (559B): Nil enim est aliud omnium essentia nisi omnium in divina sapientia cognitio (my translations).

148. For a comparison, see Joseph Moreau, "Le Verbe et la création selon S. Augustin et J. Scot Érigène," in *Jean Scot Érigène et l'histoire de la philosophie,* pp. 201–10.

149. See *Quaestiones ad Thalassium* 60 (CCSG 22:74.42–48): Nam propter Christum, idest in Christo mysterium, omnia secula et quae in ipsis sunt seculis in christo principium essendi et finem acceperunt. Adunatio enim adunata est ante secula diffinitionis et indiffinibilitatis, et mensure et immensurabilitatis, et finis et infinitatis, et creatoris et creature, et stationis et motionis; que adunatio in Christo in novissimis temporibus manifestata facta est, plenitudinem dans prescientie per se ipsam. . . . See J. M. Bisson, "La Tradition sur la Prédestination absolué de Jésus-Christ du VIIe au IXe siècles," *France Franciscaine* 22 (1939): 14–15.

150. P 4 (768B): . . . notio quaedam intellectualis in mente divina aeternaliter facta. Much has been written on Eriugena's anthropology. Among older works, see Brian Stock, "The Philosophical Anthropology of Johannes Scottus;" and "*Intelligo me esse*: Eriugena's *cogito,*" in *Jean Scot Érigène et l'histoire de la philosophie,* pp. 328–35; as well as my own paper, "The Negative Element in the Anthropology of John the Scot," in the same *Jean Scot Érigène,* pp. 315–25. More recently, see especially Willemien Otten, *The Anthropology of Johannes Scottus,* and her "The Universe of Nature and the Universe of Man: Difference and Identity," in *Begriff und Metapher,* pp. 202–12. See also Moran, *Philosophy of John Scottus,* chaps. 9–10.

151. The key texts for Eriugena's negative anthropology are to be found in P 4 (771AD, 776C, 788A–789A). Cf P 1 (485AB), P 2 (585AD), and CI 1.26 (128.6–13). On God's ignorance, see the long discussion in P 2 (586A–598C).

152. I have investigated the first three of these assertions in "The Negative Element in the Anthropology." Moran notes the necessity of adding the fourth (*Philosophy of John Scottus,* p. 187 n.1). See also Werner Beierwaltes, "Das Problem des absoluten Selbstbewusstseins bei Johannes Scotus Erigena," in *Platonismus in der Philosophie des Mittelalters* (Darmstadt: Wissenschaftliche Buchgesellschaft, 1969), pp. 484–516.

153. P 2 (598B): . . . nec iam cernis ut opinor ullam differentiam imaginis et principalis formae praeter rationem subiecti.

154. P 5 (941CD): Nulla quippe alia via est ad principalis exempli purissimam contemplationem praeter proximae sibi suae imaginis certissimam notitiam.

155. OI 13 (266.23–6): . . . non vos estis qui intelligitis me, sed ego ipse in vobis per spiritum meum meipsum intelligo, quia vos non estis substantialis lux, sed participatio per se subsistentis luminis. Cf. P 1 (521D–522A) and P 2 (572B). See Beierwaltes, "Absoluten Selbstbewusstseins," pp. 511–13; and "Language and Object," pp. 215–16.

156. Helpful on this aspect of Eriugena's thought is Moran, *Philosophy of John Scottus*, chaps. 8–19, esp. pp. 145, 210.

157. Naturally, this implies a correlation not only between humanity and the Word but also between humanity and the universe of nature, on which see Otten, who summarizes: "It seems as if man, by sharing in *natura*'s procession as much as in its return, in a sense comes to form his own totality. . . . In comparing the development of man and the development of nature, it seems almost impossible to disentangle them" ("Universe of Nature and the Universe of Man," p. 206).

158. P 4 (774A): Porro si res ipsae in notionibus suis verius quam in seipsis subsistunt, notitiae autem earum homini naturaliter insunt, in homine igitur universaliter creatae sunt (translation adapted). Cf. the whole discussion from 772A through 778B, as well as 763D–765C. The same teaching can be found in P 5 (893BC) and OI 19 (294–6). Also to be consulted in this connection is the teaching on the human as "universal creature," e.g., P 4 (755AB, 759A–760C).

159. On the relation between the two kinds of *sapientia*, see especially P 4 (778D–779D), which states, "Ut enim sapientia creatrix, quod est Verbum Dei, omnia, quae in ea facta sunt, priusquam fierent, vidit, ipsaque visio eorum, quae priusquam fierent, visa sunt, vera et incommutabilis aeternaque essentia est, ita creata sapientia, quae est humana natura, omnia, quae in se facta sunt, priusquam fierent, cognovit, ipsaque cognitio eorum, quae, priusquam fierent, cognita sunt, vera essentia et inconcussa est (778D–79A). The distinction between *sapientia (divina) quae creat* and *sapientia creata* goes back to Augustine, *Confessiones* 12.15.20–22 (PL 32:833–34), but Eriugena develops it in his own way.

160. Moran, *Philosophy of John Scottus*, p. 172. This relationship might be pictured in the following diagram:

IDENTICAL DIVINE NATURE   { God as Archetype (hidden aspect)
(identity includes difference)   God-Man
                                        Man as Image (manifest aspect)

161. For some consideration of the fall and sin, see Otten, *Anthropology of Johannes Scottus*, pp. 111–14; idem, "Universe of Nature and the Universe of Man," pp. 208–11.

162. Peter Dronke, "Eriugena's Earthly Paradise," in *Begriff und Metapher*, p. 218; cf. P 4 (822AB) and P 5 (895A).

163. IE 1.1 (6.202–5): . . . divinae illuminationis processio copiose nos multiplicat in infinitatem, iterum complicat et unificat et restituit in simplicem congregantis et deificantis nos Patris unitatem.

164. CI 1.27 (142.93–101): Clamat itaque verbum dei in remotissima divinae bonitatis solitudine. Clamor eius naturarum omnium conditio est. Ipse enim vocat ea quae sunt tamquam quae non sunt, quia per ipsum deus pater clamavit, id est creavit cuncta quae fieri voluit. Clamavit ille invisibiliter, priusquam fieret mundus, mundum fieri. Clamavit in mundum veniens visibiliter, mundum salvari. Prius clamavit aeternaliter per solam suam divinitatem ante incarnationem; clamavit postea per suam carnem.

165. Besides the studies of Christology mentioned above, see also René Roques, "Remarques sur la signification de Jean Scot Érigène," *Divinitas* 11 (1967): esp. 321–29; and Tullio Gregory, "L'éschatologie de Jean Scot," in *Jean Scot Érigène et l'histoire de la philosophie*, pp. 377–92.

166. On this verse, see OI 9 (240–4) along with other passages in *Periphyseon*, e.g., 559A, 641AB, 666D, and 685D.

167. John's constant stress on the necessity of the Word's descent into flesh in taking on a complete humanity (see, e.g., 745A, 894B, 910D, 937D–938A) renders suspect M. Colish's doubts about the sincerity of his Chalcedonianism in her article "John the Scot's Christology and Soteriology." On the role of the flesh in Eriugena, see R. Roques, "Jean Scot," DS 8:758.

168. Even the initial movement from the second to the third division of *natura* constitutes a "quasi-incarnation," as Donald Duclow notes in "Dialectic and Christology," p. 109, following a text in CI 1.29 (156).

169. P 5 (912B): Totus itaque mundus in Verbo unigenito, incarnato, inhumanito adhuc specialiter restitutus est, in fine vero mundi generaliter et universaliter in eodem restaurabitur, quod enim specialiter in seipso perfecit, generaliter in omnibus perficiet. Non dico in omnibus hominibus solummodo, sed in omni sensibili creatura.

170. On the unification and salvation of all things in Christ, see also P 2 (541A–542B), based on Maximus), P 5 (892C–896A, 978B–984B, 989A–990B, 1018CD); and CI 3.5 (224–26). Duclow summarizes: "The Incarnation thus constitutes a threefold turning point in John's thought. In his dialectic it marks the turn from division to analysis or reduction; in his metaphysical scheme, from procession (*exitus*) to return (*reditus*); and in his Christology proper, from the creative Logos to the saving Lord" ("Dialectic and Christology," p. 110).

171. CI 4.11 (288.26–7): Absque labore creavit nos per divinitatem, cum labore recreavit nos per humanitatem.

172. On this important teaching, which Eriugena took from Gregory of Nyssa and Maximus, see, e.g., P 2 (531C–533A, 537C–539C), and P 5 (894A–895C, 991C–995B).

173. P 5 (999B): Ipse siquidem ascendit in contemplationibus ascendentium ad se; nullus quippe ad illum sine illo potest ascendere (my translation). Eriugena may have been reflecting a text from Gregory the Great here; see *Hom. in Ev.* 25.6 (PL 76:1193AB).

174. CI 1.31 (176.73–178.77): Nam et nos, qui post peractam eius incarnationem et passionem et resurrectionem in eum credimus eiusque mysteria, quantum nobis conceditur, intelligimus, et spiritualiter eum immolamus et intellectualiter, mente non dente, comedimus.

175. The root of this, of course, is that *humanitas* was created and always subsists in the Word; e.g., P 5 (865CD, 871B).

176. E.g., P 5 (995AB): His igitur incrementis corporis Christi incipiunt, illic perficientur, quando Christus cum toto et in toto suo corpore quidam perfectus et unus vir, caput in membris et membra in capite, apparebit, quando mensura et plenitudo aetatis Christi non corporalibus oculis, sed virtute contemplationis in omnibus sanctis suo capiti adunatis clarissime videbitur, quando spiritualis aetas, hoc est virtutem plenitudo, quae in Christo et Ecclesia sua constituta est, consummabitur. . . . Cf. P 4 (743B) and EI 1.2 (11).

177. See Hugo Rahner, "Die Gottesgeburt: Die Lehre der Kirchenväter von der Geburt Christi aus dem Herzen der Kirche und der Gläubigen," in *Symbole der Kirche* (Salzburg: Otto Müller, 1964), pp. 71–76 on Eriugena.

178. Eriugena's teaching on the sacraments is especially prominent in CI. For more on this, see G. S. M. Walker, "Erigena's Conception of the Sacraments," in *Studies in Church History*, ed. G. J. Cuming (Leiden: Brill, 1966), 3:150–58; and R. Roques, "Jean Scot," DS 8:755–58.

179. CI 1.32 (178–88). See E. Jeauneau's study of this text in relation to its Greek source in "Appendice II," *Commentaire*, pp. 383–95.

180. For some texts on this "great chain of virtues," see esp. EI 10.3, 15.1 and 4 (156–57, 189–91, and 202). Cf. P 1 (449CD), and CI 6.2 and 3 (330, 338). On the uplifting role of all the hierarchies, including the human hierarchy, see EI 10.1–2 (152–56).

181. Eriugena's mature teaching insists that the resurrection of the body is a work of both nature and grace. See esp. P 5 (902CD).

182. See, e.g., P 5 (903A–905C), EI 1.1 (2), and CI 3.9 (252–54). It is interesting in this connection that Eriugena pays so little attention to what we have seen as a key issue in early medieval mystical theory, the relation between action and contemplation. Two references, however, are found in *Periphyseon.* The first in P 4 (853C), interprets the woman's bruising of the serpent's head predicted in Gen 3:15 as a promise that the fallen power of sense (= woman) will be "led to the perfection of action and contemplation by the virtues of the stronger woman which is the Word of God" (*fortioris mulieris, Dei Verbi*). The second in P 5 (1014C) notes that both action and contemplation are required for risen virgins to enjoy the paradisiacal marriage feast. In OI 2–3 (208–16) Eriugena identifies the apostle Peter with *actio virtutum* and John with *altissima veritatis contemplatio*, characteristically connecting them with the two necessary modes of understanding scripture, faith and mystical understanding.

183. P 5 (978C–1021B). See Maximus, *Quaestiones ad Thalassium* 54, scholion 18 (CCSG 7:474.137–40): Resurrectio nature est reformatio, nature in paradiso formationem copiosam faciens, generaliter quidem universali omnium inconversibilitate, specialiter vero per gratiam ineffabili sanctorum deificatione. On this, see E. Jeauneau, "Le thème du retour," in *Études Érigéniennes*, p. 375.

184. P 5 (1001B): Est enim generalis, et est specialis: generalis quidem in omnibus, qui ad principium conditionis suae redituri sunt; specialis vero in his, qui non solum ad primordia naturae revocabuntur, sed etiam ultra omnem naturalem dignitatem, in causam omnium, quae Deus est, reditus sui finem constituent.

185. P 5 (967A): Et hoc est totum, quod dicitur liberae ac perversae voluntatis arbitrium fuerit obediens; sin vero contumax superbiaque inflatum in suis perversis motibus perseverare voluerit, impetus eius libidinosus retinebitur, ne, quod illicite appetit, apprehendat. The discussion of the problem of hell extends from 922A to 978B.

186. On Christ as the tree of life, see, e.g., P 4 (818B, 823B–824A, 826A, 829C–830B), and P 5 (862D, 980D–981A, 982AB). For Christ as the Temple, see P 5 (981AD), and EI 1.3 and 7.2 (12, 109).

187. The theme of the *reditus* has attracted considerable attention in recent Eriugenian studies. Besides the already-cited paper of Donald Duclow, "Dialectic and Christology," see, E. Jeauneau, "Le thème du retour," pp. 367–94; Stephen Gersh, "The Structure of the Return in Eriugena's Periphyseon," in *Begriff und Metapher*, pp. 108–25; and Willemien Otten, "The Dialectic of the Return in Eriugena's *Periphyseon,*" *Harvard Theological Review* 84 (1991): 399–421.

188. S. Gersh, "The Structure of the Return," p. 109. The element of cancellation resides in the return to unity/identity, the development consists in the fact that this is now a unity that preserves multiplicity. As Gersh puts it later (p. 114): ". . . in classical Neoplatonic doctrine prominence is often given to a conception of the return whereby the conclusion of the process is not a unity but a mediation of unity and multiplicity, and Eriugena elevates this to a general ontological principle that the combination of unity and multiplicity achieved through the return is the inner truth of which the final unity is a surface meaning." Cf. Otten, "The Dialectic of the Return," p. 401.

189. Otten expresses it thus: "As Eriugena unfolds the theme of return, we witness the transformation of procession and return from logical and/or ontological categories into more soteriological and/or eschatological ones" ("The Dialectic of the Return," p. 415).

190. Gersh, "The Structure of the Return," pp. 117–24.

191. A key discussion is P 5 (893B–898D). The passage cited is at 893D: Postremo universalis creatura Creatori adunabitur, et erit in ipso et cum ipso unum. Cf. 876AC for a brief summary.

192. P 5 (1020C–1021A): Ac primus erit mutatio terreni corporis in motum vitalem; secundus vitalis motus in sensum; tertius sensus in rationem; dehinc rationis in

animum. . . . Post hanc quinariam veluti partium nostrae naturae adunationem, . . . inferioribus semper a superioribus consummatis, non ut non sint, sed ut unum sint, sequentur alii tres ascensionis gradus, quorum unus transitus animi in scientiam omnium, quae post Deum sunt, secundus scientiae in sapientiam, hoc est, contemplationem intimam veritatis, quantum creaturae conceditur, tertius, qui et summus, purgatissimorum animorum in ipsum Deum supernaturaliter occasus . . . (translation slightly modified).

193. See, e.g., P 5 (950BC) and the discussion in Gersh, "Structure of the Return," pp. 119–20.

194. On this, see especially the discussion in P 5 (884AC), based on Pauline texts about the resurrected body and the teaching of Gregory of Nyssa and Maximus.

195. E.g., EI 3.1 (58, 61, 63–64) and 7.2 (112–13).

196. EI 10.1 (152.23–24): Purgatur quidem omni ignorantia, illuminatur omni sapientia, perficitur omni deificatione.

197. See CI 4.7 (316–18); P 1 (449C), P 2 (574A), P 5 (981D). On the relation of these three stages to divine light, see EI 3.1 (60).

198 According to Allard's *Indices Generales* for *Periphyseon, deificatio* appears thirty-nine times, forms of the verb *deificare* nineteen times; while the latinized *theōsis* is found five times and Greek forms four times. The indices to the critical editions of the other major works provide the following figures: (1) OI–seven appearances; (2) CI–four appearances; (3) EI–thirty-four appearances. For Eriugena's teaching on deification, see Ruh, *Geschichte der abendländische Mystik*, 1:204–6.

199. For the teaching of Augustine on deification, see *Foundations of Mysticism*, p. 251. Eriugena explicitly appeals, however, to the teaching of Ambrose in P 5 (1015C), referring to the bishop's *Expositio evangelii secundum Lucam* 7.192–4 (CSEL 32.4:369–71).

200. For an overview, see the multi-author article "Divinisation" in DS 3:1370–1459 (without notice of Eriugena!).

201. EI 7.2 (105.543–6): Nos siquidem adhuc veluti parvuli in symbolis sanctisque figmentis divinam similitudinem, qua nunc in fide deificamur, et in specie deificabimur, in nobis formamur. These two stages also appear in CI 3.5 (224.28–33).

202. On this point, see Moran, *Philosophy of John Scottus*, pp. 138–39.

203. P 5 (1015C): . . . sanctorum transitum in Deum non solum anima, sed etiam et corpore, ut unum in ipso et cum ipso sint. . . .

204. E.g., EI 13.3 (173).

205. On the figure of Moses as a model for contemplation in earlier Christian mysticism, see the entries under "Moses" in the Name Index in *Foundations of Mysticism*, p. 486. For a sketch of medieval uses, see Jean Chatillon, "Moïse figure du Christ et modèle de la vie parfaite: Brèves remarques sur quelques thèmes médiévaux," in *Moïse, l'homme de l'alliance, Cahiers sioniens* 8/2-4 (Paris, 1954), pp. 305–14.

206. See Augustine, *De genesi ad litteram*, esp. 12.6.15–12.26 and 12.24.51–27.55. For the relation of Eriugena to Augustine on the vision of God, see John J. O'Meara, "Eriugena's Use of Augustine in his Teaching on the Return of the Soul and the Vision of God," in *Jean Scot Érigène et l'histoire de la philosophie*, pp. 191–200.

207. On Paul's rapture as a key biblical archetype for patristic speculation of direct experience of God, see *Foundations of Mysticism*, pp. 4, 70, 172, 205–6, 254.

208. P 5 (887C): . . . incommutabiles rerum rationes in Sapientia Dei factas, secundum quas visibilia et invisibilia condita sunt. On this text, see David Bell, "The Vision of the World and the Vision of the Archetypes in the Latin Spirituality of the Middle Ages," *Archives d'histoire doctrinale et littéraire du moyen âge* 44 (1977): 25. For another text on Paul, see EI 6.2 (90), as well as the reference to those who have been rapt to the joy of the angels while still in this life in EI 15.9 (214).

209. EI 8.2 (123.204–5): . . . per seipsos immediate divinam participant contemplationem. Cf. 8.2 (127). Eriugena is willing to call such experiences by the traditional term *excessus*, though the word is relatively rare in his vocabulary (in *Periphyseon*, see 448B, 515B [a quotation from Maximus], 759C [a quote from Dionysius]). The use of *raptus* is more common.

210. OI 4 (218.7–220.13): Iohannes omne caelum conditum omnemque creatum paradisum, hoc est omnem humanam angelicamque transgreditur naturam. In tercio caelo, o vas electionis et magister gentium, audisti verba quae non licet homini loqui. Iohannes, intimae veritatis inspector, ultra omne caelum in paradiso paradisorum, hoc est in causa omnium, audivit unum verbum per quod facta sunt omnia. . . . This text highlights an important theme in Eriugena's thought, viz., the use of the three great apostles (Peter, Paul, and John) to illustrate three modes of knowing God–that is, by faith, by rational or cataphatic theology, and by negative, or intuitive mystical knowing. See OI 2–4 (208–20), and cf., EI 2.5 (50–2).

211. E.g., P 1 (447B, which speaks of *divinae essentiae puram contemplationem atque immediatam*), P 5 (941D, 977D–978A, 1017D); OI 2 (212).

212. This is especially evident in the lengthy discussion of the beatific vision found in P 1 (447B–451C).

213. A point well brought out by Dominic J. O'Meara, "Eriugena and Aquinas on the Beatific Vision," in *Eriugena Redivivus*, pp. 230–31.

214. For some texts that seem to suggest absolute identity without qualification, see, e.g., P 4 (743A, 860BD, 863A, 875D), P 5 (906B, 953A, 983B, 1015C, 1017C, 1020C); as well as EI 1.2 and 7.4 (10, 114).

215. P 1 (515C): . . . intellectuale . . . non stat quousque fiat totum in toto amato et a toto comprehendatur . . . , sicut aer per totum illuminatur lumine et igne ferrum totum toto liquefactum. For the original text in *Ambigua* 3, see CCSG 18:25.125–26. These analogies are used by Eriugena in several other places. The light and air metaphor appears in P 1 (450A, using *Ambigua* 1), P 1 (483AB), P 3 (683C), P 5 (1021B), and in OI 13 (264.5–266.6). The dual metaphor of air/light and iron/fire recurs in P 1 (451AB) and P 5 (879A). The third metaphor added by Bernard of Clairvaux, that of the drop of water in the vat of wine, has a long philosophical history as a metaphor for mixing (Gr. *krasis*) but appears to have come from patristic speculation on the mingling of divinity and humanity in Christ. For the history of the development of these three famous comparisons, see Jean Pépin, "'Stilla aquae modica multo infuso vino, ferrum ignitum, luce perfusus aer.' L'origin de trois comparaisons familières à la théologie mystique médiévale," *Divinitas* 11 (1967): 331–75, with a consideration of the role of Maximus and Eriugena on pp. 341–44 and 372–75.

216. For an overview of medieval development on theories of mystical union, see B. McGinn, "Love, Knowledge and *Unio Mystica* in the Western Christian Tradition," in *Mystical Union and Monotheistic Faith*, ed. Moshe Idel and Bernard McGinn (New York: Macmillan, 1989), pp. 59–86.

217. P 5 (906B): . . . unitas simplex et multiplex adunatio omnium creaturarum in suis rationibus et causis, ipsarum autem causarum et rationum in Verbo Dei unigenito. . . .

218. For some texts on God's ultimate unknowability and the continuing necessity for theophanies, see P 1 (448C), P 2 (557BC), P 5 (905CD, 926CD, 945CD, 1000BD, 1010CD); CI 1.25 (118–26); EI 4.3 and 8.2 (74–75, 133). For Eriugena's teaching on the limitations of the beatific vision, see Dominic O'Meara, "Eriugena and Aquinas on the Beatific Vision," in *Eriugena Redivivus*, pp. 224–36.

219. Beierwaltes, *"Negati Affirmatio,"* p. 140.

220. P 5 (919C): Sed quoniam, quod quaerit et appetit, dum recte movetur vel non recte, infinitum est, omnique creaturae incomprehensibile, necessarieque semper quaeritur, ac per hoc semper movetur: semper quaerit, mirabiliterque pacto quodammodo invenit quod quaerit, et non invenit quia invenire non potest. Invenit autem per theophanias, per naturae

vero divinae per seipsam contemplationem non invenit. The same teaching appears in the famous prayer of the *Alumnus* in P 5 (1010CD): Quaereris enim ab eis semper, et semper inveniris, et non inveneris semper: inveneris quidem in tuis theophaniis, . . . non inveneris autem in tua superessentialitate. . . . Cf. EI 6.1 (87.34–88.42), which cites Gregory of Nyssa's *De imagine* 20–2; and CI 1.32 (182.38–43).

221. P 5 (951C): . . . patiens esto, divinaeque virtute incomprehensibili locum da, eamque silentio honorifica, quoniam, dum ad eum pervenitur, omnis ratio deficit et intellectus. . . . (translation slightly altered).

Chapter 4

1. For an introduction to Eriugena's influence in later medieval mysticism, see Kurt Ruh, *Geschichte der abendländische Mystik*. Band I, *Die Grundlegung durch die Kirchenväter und die Mönchstheologie des 12. Jahrhunderts* (Munich: Beck, 1990), pp. 176-83.

2. See *The Foundations of Mysticism* (New York: Crossroad, 1991), pp. xv-xvi.

3. It is interesting to note how often major articles on mystical themes found in the *Dictionnaire de spiritualité* neglect the early medieval period, moving from Gregory I directly to the twelfth-century authors (e.g., "Dépouillement" and "Discernement des ésprits" in DS 3; "Extase" in DS 4; "Homme Interieur," "Image et Ressemblance" and "Imitation du Christ" in DS 7; "Naissance divine" and "NOUS et MENS" in DS 11; and "Toucher, Touches" in DS 15).

4. See Jean Leclercq, *Études sur le vocabulaire monastique du moyen âge*, Studia Anselmiana 48 (Rome: Herder, 1961), pp. 93–99, 117–21.

5. Leclercq, *Études*, p. 80. Chapter 3 of Leclercq's work considers early medieval monastic use of *contemplatio, speculatio,* and *theoria.* Leclercq took up the parallel "hesychast" terminology in his *Otia Monastica: Études sur le vocabulaire de la contemplation au moyen âge*, Studia Anselmiana 51 (Rome: Herder, 1963).

6. There is no standard history of medieval monasticism. Some recent surveys which also contain bibliographical notices are the multiauthor article "Monachesimo" in DIP 5:1672-1742; "Monachisme" in DS 10:1524-1617, with cols 1557-65 and 1571-75 dealing with this period; and B. McGinn, "Christian Monasticism," in *The Encyclopedia of Religion*, ed. Mircea Eliade (New York: Macmillan, 1987), 10:44-50. The most complete account is still that of Philibert Schmitz, *Histoire de l'ordre de Saint-Benoît*, 7 vols. (Maredsous: Éditions de l'Abbaye, 1942-56). In English see especially Edward Cuthbert Butler, *Benedictine Monachism: Studies in Benedictine Life and Rule* (2nd ed.; London: Burns & Oates, 1924); and David Knowles, *The Monastic Order in England: A History of Its Development from the Time of St. Dunstan to the Fourth Lateran Council, 940-1216* (2nd ed.; Cambridge: Cambridge University Press, 1963), which contains much on the general history of early medieval monasticism. A helpful bibliography can be found in Giles Constable, *Medieval Monasticism: A Select Bibliography* (Toronto: University of Toronto Press, 1976).

7. On the spirituality of Cluniac monasticism (which also generally holds for the related forms), see, e.g., the essays in *Spiritualità Cluniacense*, Convegni del Centro di Studi sulla Spiritualità Medievale 2 (Todi: L'Accademia Tudertina, 1960); Jean Leclercq, "Un sommet: Cluny," in *Aux sources de la spiritualité occidentale. Étapes et constantes* (Paris: Cerf, 1964), pp. 91–173; Noreen Hunt, ed., *Cluniac Monasticism in the Central Middle Ages* (Hamden, CT: Archon, 1971); and Barbara H. Rosenwein, *Rhinoceros Bound: Cluny in the Tenth Century* (Philadelphia: University of Pennsylvania Press, 1982). On debates on the Cluniac liturgy, see Jean Leclercq, "Prayer at Cluny," *Journal of the American Academy of Religion* 51 (1983): 651-65.

8. For an overview of the importance of these reforms in monastic history, see Jean Leclercq, "The Monastic Crisis of the Eleventh and Twelfth Centuries," in *Cluniac Monasticism in the Central Middle Ages*, pp. 217–37. John Van Engen rightly warns against misconstruing the "crisis" motif to indicate an end to the vitality of traditional Benedictinism; see "The 'Crisis of Coenobitism' Reconsidered: Benedictine Monasticism in the Years 1050–1150," *Speculum* 61 (1986): 269–304.

9. See especially the papers in *L'eremitismo in Occidente nei secoli XI e XII: Atti della seconda Settimana internazionale di Studio Mendola. 30 agosto–6 settembre 1962* (Milan: Società editrice vite e pensiero, 1965). For an overview in English, see Henrietta Leyser, *Hermits and the New Monasticism: A Study of Religious Communities in Western Europe, 1000–1150* (London: Macmillan, 1984). Helpful for a general sketch of the eremitic tradition is Peter F. Anson, *The Quest of Solitude* (New York: Dutton, 1932); idem "Erémitisme" in DS 4:936–82 (see cols. 957–63 on the early medieval period).

10. On the relation of Cîteaux to eleventh-century reform, see Bede Lackner, *The Eleventh-Century Background of Cîteaux* (Washington: Cistercian Publications, 1972).

11. Bernard de Vregille, "Écriture saint et vie spirituelle. IIB. Du 6e au 12e siècle," DS 4:186.

12. These materials were first edited by the Bollandist Heribert Rosweyde in the early seventeenth century under the title *Vitae Patrum* and are reprinted in PL 73–74. For an introduction to this literature and recent research on it, see the articles of Aimé Solignac, "'Verba Seniorum'" and "'Vitae Patrum'" in DS 16:383–92 and 1029–35.

13. See Jean Leclercq, "Humanisme et spiritualité: II. L'humanisme des moines au moyen âge," DS 7:959–71; and (more extensively) "L'humanisme des moines au moyen âge," in *A Giuseppe Ermini* (Spoleto: Centro Italiano di Studi sull'alto Medioevo, 1970), pp. 69–113.

14. The term *spiritualitas* first appeared in the fifth century in a letter once ascribed to Jerome but probably coming either from Pelagius or one of his circle, though the word was rarely used in the early Middle Ages. See Aimé Solignac, "Spiritualité: I. Le mot et l'histoire," DS 14:1142–60; and B. McGinn, "The Letter and the Spirit: Spirituality as an Academic Discipline," *The Cresset* 56 (1993): 13–21.

15. A number of surveys of early medieval spirituality proceed on chronological lines. Many of these have been written by Jean Leclercq, whose numerous works constitute a rich resource for modern study of early medieval spirituality. See, e.g., "Contemplation. IV.B. Contemplation et vie contemplative du VIe au XIIe siècle," DS 2:1929–48 (from 1952); "Part One. From St. Gregory to St. Bernard," in *The Spirituality of the Middle Ages*, ed. Jean Leclercq, François Vandenbroucke, and Louis Bouyer (New York: Seabury, 1982), vol. 2 of *A History of Christian Spirituality* (French ed. 1961), pp. 3–220; and "France. II. Le haut moyen âge. B. Spiritualité monastique du 6e au 12e siècle," DS 5:818–47. Among older works, see especially André Wilmart, *Auteurs spirituels et textes devots du Moyen Age latin: Études d'histoire littéraire* (Paris: Études Augustiniennes, 1971; reprint of 1932 ed.); as well as Ursmer Berlière, *L'ascèse bénédictine des origines à la fin du XIIe siècle* (Paris-Maredsous: Collection in Pax, 1927); and Jean Besse, *Les Mystiques Bénédictins des origines au XIIIe siècle* (Paris-Maredsous: Lethielleux-Desclée de Brouwer, 1922). Other helpful materials can be found in Bernard de Vregille, "Écriture sainte et vie spirituelle. IIB.2. Auteurs occidentaux du 7e au 11e siècle," DS 4:176–87; the multiauthor article "Italie. II. Haut Moyen Age" in DS 7:2167–2206; and André Vauchez, *La spiritualité du Moyen Age occidental viiie–xiie siècles* (Paris: Presses universitaires de France, 1975).

16. My list excludes a number of important monastic writers of the period, such as Isidore of Seville (ca. 570–636), Bede (673–735), Alcuin (730–804), and Odo of Cluny (879–942), though I will take the liberty of using them where helpful.

17. See *Ambrosius Autpertus Expositio in Apocalypsim Libri I–X*, ed. Robert Weber (CCCM 27–27A). Ambrose's other works are edited by Weber in CCCM 27B. On his place in medieval Apocalypse exegesis, see E. Ann Matter, "The Apocalypse in Early Medieval Exegesis," in *The Apocalypse in the Middle Ages*, ed. Richard K. Emmerson and Bernard McGinn (Itahca, NY: Cornell University Press, 1992), pp. 47–49.

18. On Ambrose's spiritual teaching, see Dom J. Winandy, *Ambroise Autpert: Moine et théologien* (Paris, 1952); and Claudio Leonardi, "La spiritualità di Ambrogio Autperto," *Studi Medievali* 3a serie 9 (1968): 1–131. For the monk's teaching on contemplation, see J. Winandy, "La contemplation à l'ecole des Pères: Ambroise Autpert," *La vie spirituelle* 82 (1950): 147–55.

19. There is still debate over whether Smaragdus (the name means "Emerald") was of Irish origin, or, as is more likely, of Visigothic extraction. The most complete study is Jean Leclercq, "Smaragdus," in *An Introduction to the Medieval Mystics of Europe*, ed. Paul Szarmach (Albany: SUNY Press, 1984), pp. 37–51; cf. Reginald Grégoire, "Smaragde," DS 14:959–61.

20. The *Diadema Monachorum*, of which at least 120 manuscripts are known, can be found in PL 102:593–690. The *Expositio in Regulam S. Benedicti* is in the same volume (cols. 689–932).

21. The *De naturis rerum* appears in PL 111:9–614. This popular work is known in 45 manuscripts For an introduction to Rabanus, see Raymund Kottje, "Raban Maur," DS 13:1–10.

22. The treatise is edited in PL 112:1261–1332. For a study of the context, see Maïeul Cappuyns, "Note sur le problème de la vision béatifique au IXe siècle," *Recherches de théologie ancienne et médiévale* 1 (1929): 98–107.

23. Jacques Hourlier, "Odilon de Cluny," DS 11:612. Odilo's works are mostly to be found in PL 142.

24. For a recent introduction to his life, writings, and teaching, see Benedetto Calati ("Pierre Damien," DS 12:1551–73), who notes Peter as a predecessor of Anselm in eschewing biblical commentary (col. 1556).

25. Most of Peter's writings appear in PL 144–45. The cardinal's interesting, if extreme, treatise on divine omnipotence is one of the few of his works to be given a modern critical edition. See *Pierre Damien: Lettre sur la Toute-Puissance divine*, ed. André Cantin (SC 191). Some of Damian's spiritual writings are available in English; see *St. Peter Damian: Selected Writings on the Spiritual Life*, translated with an Introduction by Patricia McNulty (London: Faber & Faber, 1959).

26. Peter's treatises appear in PL 145. See especially #11 (*Dominus vobiscum* [cols. 231–52]), #13 (*De perfectione monachorum* [cols. 291–328]), #32 (*De quadragesima observatione* [cols. 543–60]), #48 (*De spiritualibus deliciis* [cols. 715–22]) and #56 (*De fluxa mundi gloria*, a letter to the empress Agnes [cols. 807–20]). Peter's letters and sermons, mostly found in PL 144, also contain important material, e.g., Ep. 2.5, which is actually a treatise dealing with the true meaning of *sabbatum* (cols. 260–70), and Ep. 7.6, another letter to Agnes (cols.443–45). For accounts of Peter Damian's spirituality, see O. J. Blum, *Saint Peter Damian: His Teaching on the Spiritual Life* (Washington: Catholic University, 1947); and Jean Leclercq, *Saint Pierre Damien eremite et homme d'église* (Rome: Edizioni di storia e letteratura, 1960). See also Giovanni Micoli, "Théologie de la vie monastique chez saint Pierre Damien," in *Théologie de la vie monastique* (Paris: Aubier, 1961), pp. 459–83.

27. The importance of John of Fécamp was first uncovered by André Wilmart, e. g., *Auteurs spirituels et textes dévots*, # VI, VIII and XII, who called him "le plus remarquable auteur spirituel du moyen âge avant S. Bernard" (p. 127). The fundamental work remains Jean Leclercq and Jean-Paul Bonnes, *Un maître de la vie spirituelle au XIe siècle: Jean de Fécamp* (Paris: Vrin, 1946). For a brief introduction, see J. Leclercq, "Jean de Fécamp," DS 8:509–11. In English, see Leclercq, *Spirituality of the Middle Ages*, pp. 122–26; and Gerard Sitwell, *Spiritual Writers of the Middle Ages* (New York: Hawthorn, 1961), pp. 25–34.

28. The *Confessio theologica*, modeled on Augustine's *Confessions*, has been edited by Leclercq and Bonnes in *Jean de Fécamp*, pp. 110–83. Other spiritual treatises and letters appear in the same volume on pp. 185–230. John's other major works, which are to be seen as reworkings of the *Confessio theologica*, are the *Libellus de scriptoris et verbis patrum* (parts of which appear as the *Meditationes S. Augustini* in PL 40:902–42), and the *Confessio fidei*, which appears under the name of Alcuin in PL 101:1027–98.

29. This text is edited in Leclercq and Bonnes, *Jean de Fécamp*, pp. 205–10. Such writings justify the judgment of B. de Vregille, "Ces textes sont les plus authentiquement mystiques que l'on rencontre entre l'âge de saint Grégoire et celui de saint Bernard" (DS 4:184). For a discussion of John as mystic, see Leclercq and Bonnes, *Jean de Fécamp*, pp. 100–106.

30. John's writings inspired a variety of imitations; see Jean Leclercq, "Écrits spirituels del'école de Jean de Fécamp," in *Analecta Monastica*, Studia Anselmiana 20 (Rome: Libreria Vaticana, 1948), pp. 91–114. Although he was perhaps the most widely read of early medieval spiritual writers, the fact that John's major works appeared under other names led to total forgetfulness of his achievement down to the present century.

31. Anselm's prayers and meditations have been edited by F. S. Schmitt, *Sancti Anselmi Cantuariensis Archiepiscopi Opera Omnia* (Edinburg: Nelson, 1938–61), 3:3–91. I will use the translation (with excellent introduction) by Sister Benedicta Ward, *The Prayers and Meditations of Saint Anselm* (New York: Penguin, 1973). The literature on Anselm is so extensive that only those works directly relating to particular issues in spirituality will be noted at appropriate places. For a brief introduction to his spirituality, see Benedicta Ward, "Anselm of Canterbury and His Influence," in *Christian Spirituality: Origins to the Twelfth Century,* ed. Bernard McGinn, John Meyendorff, and Jean Leclercq, WS 16 (New York: Crossroad, 1986), pp. 196–205.

32. *Proslogion*, proem. (ed. Schmitt 1:83–84): . . . sub persona conantis erigere mentem suam ad contemplandum deum et quaerentis intelligere quod credit, subditum scripsi opusculum. I am using the translation of Ward, *Prayers and Meditations*, p. 238.

33. Ward, "Anselm of Canterbury and His Influence," p. 199.

34. The *Vita Rudesinde* appears in Luc d'Achery and J. B. Mabillon, *Acta Sanctorum Ordinis Sancti Benedicti*, 9 vols. (Venice: Coleti and Bettinelli, 1735) 7:514–35. The text cited is on p. 519: Sanctus vir Rudesindus solitudini, orationi et contemplatione totum se dedit in istis temporibus, in tantum ut orans pernoctaret.

35. Jean Leclercq, "Prayer and Contemplation. II. Western," in *Christian Spirituality: Origins to the Twelfth Century*, p. 423.

36. For an overview, see Zoltan Alszeghy, "Fuite du monde (fuga mundi)," DS 5:1575–1605. Leclercq summarizes: "The ideal set before all Christians was the flight from the world, which is accomplished most fully by the martyr, the hermit or the recluse, and by others, according to their ability, by the practice of asceticism." (*Spirituality of the Middle Ages*, pp. 115–16).

37. RB 72:1–2: Sicut est zelus amaritudinis malus qui separat a Deo et ducit ad infernum, ita est zelus bonus qui separat a vitia et ducit ad Deum et ad vitam aeternam.

38. See Karl Suso Frank, whose article "Perfection. III. Moyen Âge" in DS 12:1118–31, gives a good account. Frank summarizes: ". . . en outre, l'idéal monastique devint la *norme* de toute perfection chrétienne" (col. 1119). On the depreciation of the laity in relation to monastics, see also Vauchez, *La spiritualité du moyen âge occidental*, pp. 53–58.

39. A twelfth-century anonymous sermon puts this traditional theme well: Habet etiam paradisus ecclesiae tres paradisos, paradisum scilicet heremi, paradisum claustri, paradisum reclusionis vel reclusi. Possunt quoque singula militantium Deo paradisi dici in quibus vacatur lectioni, meditationi, orationi, compunctioni, contemplationi (see Jean Leclercq "Prédicateurs bénédictins aux XIe et XIIe siècles," *Revue Mabillon* 33 [1943]: 72). There were,

of course, a variety of uses of the paradise symbol during these centuries, on which see Gabriella Lodolo, "Il tema simbolico del paradiso nella tradizione monastica dell'occidente latino (secoli VI–XII): lo spazio del simbolo," *Aevum* 51 (1977): 252–88.

40. Peter Damian, *Vita S. Romualdi* 37 (PL 144:988A): . . . adeo ut putaretur totum mundum in eremum velle convertere, et monachico ordini omnem populi multitudinem sociare.

41. Aspects of early medieval lay piety are treated in Leclercq's *Spirituality of the Middle Ages*, e.g., pp. 49–51. For more complete accounts, see Ilarino da Milano, "La spiritualità dei laici nei secoli VIII–X," in *Problemi di storia della Chiesa: L'alto Medioevo* (Milan: Vita e Pensiero, 1973), pp. 139–300; and Yves Congar, "Laïc et laïcat," DS 9:79–93. See also, André Vauchez, *The Laity in the Middle Ages: Religious Beliefs and Devotional Practices* (Notre Dame, IN: University of Notre Dame Press, 1993), chaps. 1–4.

42. Uffing, *De sancta Ida vidua* 1.6 (AASS. Sept 2:262): Quid super hoc convenientius profertur, quam duobus in carne una unam inesse Spiritus sancti indiscissam operationem, quae illis deforis connubiali iure connexos ardentiore caelestium intus inflammavit amore. On this text, see Jean Leclercq, *Monks on Marriage: A Twelfth-Century View* (New York: Seabury, 1982), pp. 48–52.

43. On Cassian's more restrictive view of mysticism as contrasted with those of Ambrose and Augustine, see *Foundations of Mysticism*, p. 218.

44. *Vita Sancti Pauli Episcopi Leonenis in Britannia Minori auctore Wormonoco*, chap. 6, ed. Dom. Fr. Plaine in *Analecta Bollandiana* 1 (1882): 223: . . . haec ei in mente adhaesit cogitatio, ut eremi deserta penetraret, ibique a consortio mundialis vitae sequestratus, Deo soli cognitam pie et immaculate vitam duceret egregiam, et quanto a seculi hominibus fieret extraneus, tanto per theoriam solam, id est, contemplationem divinam, Deo et angelis ejus mereretur esse proximus.

45. Bruno of Querfort, *Vita quinque fratrum* 2 (MGH.SS. XV:719): . . . essentque tripla commoda quaerentibus viam Domini, hoc est noviter venientibus de seculo desiderabile cenobium, maturis vero et Deum vivum sitientibus aurea solitudo, cupientibus dissolvi et esse cum Christo evangelium paganorum. . . .

46. Peter Damian, *De perfectione monachorum* 3 (PL 145:294D): . . . angulas gaudet, secreta rimatur: et ut liberius conspectui sui Creatoris assistat, in quantum praevalet, etiam colloquia humana declinet (I am using the translation of McNulty, *St. Peter Damian*, p. 86).

47. Peter Damian, *Liber qui dicitur Dominus Vobiscum* 19 (PL 145:249B): Habitator etenim tuus elevat se super se, quia Deum esuriens anima a terrenarum se rerum obtutibus erigit, et in divinae se contemplationis arce suspendit, a mundi se actionibus segregat, atque in se altum coelestis desiderii pennis librat. . . .

48. Ibid. (251A): . . . quia quisquis in amoris tui desiderio perseverare studuerit, ipse quidem habitator est tuus, sed ejus inhabitator est Deus.

49. John of Fécamp, *Deploratio quietis et solitudinis derelictae*, in Leclercq and Bonnes, *Jean de Fécamp*, p. 185.1–5: O casta et munda solitudo, sedes pacis et repausationis, gaudens familiari Deo, diu exquisita tandemque inventa! Quis te miḥ abstulit, dilectam meam? Tu quidem olim totis bracchiis amplexatus sum, laetusque prono animo inhaesi tuo purissimo osculo. Delectabar in bonis tuis iugiter et suavitatem amoris tui omnibus gaudiis praeferebam. Quis me miserum avulsit a complexibus tuis?

50. On the mystical uses of images of sea and desert, see B. McGinn, "Ocean and Desert as Symbols of Mystical Absorption in the Western Tradition," *Journal of Religion* 74 (1994): 155–81.

51. John of Fécamp, *Deploratio* (Leclerq and Bonnes, *Jean de Fécamp*, p. 195.258–62): . . . et da mihi illus solitudinis secretum et spiritale oportunae ad te vacationis otium, necnon et

cordis puritatem et mentis iubilationem, ut perfecte diligere et digne te laudare merear dulcissime cunctis diebus vitae meae.

52. The phrase *competens silentium* is found as the last of the twelve necessary monastic practices listed by Lanfranc, former abbot of Bec and Anselm's predecessor as archbishop of Canterbury, in his constitutions for the monastery of Christ Church, Canterbury. For a study, see Paul F. Gehl, "Competens Silentium: Varieties of Monastic Silence in the Medieval West," *Viator* 18 (1987): 125–60. Also useful on the role of silence in medieval monasticism are Pierre Salmon, "Le silence religieux, pratique et théorie," in *Mélanges bénédictines publiés a l'occasion du XIVe centenaire de la mort de S. Benoit* (Abbaye S. Wandrille: Éditions de Fontenelle, 1947), pp. 13–57; Jean Leclercq, "Silence et parole dans l'expérience spirituelle d'hier et d'aujourd'hui," *Collectanea Cisterciensia* 45 (1983): 185–98; and the multi-author article "Silence" in DS 14:829–59. It is interesting to note that Thomas Merton's account of the varieties of monasticism was entitled *The Silent Life* (New York: Farrar, Straus & Cudahy, 1957).

53. See Gehl, "Competens Silentium," esp. pp. 157–60.

54. Peter Damian, Ep. 8.6 (PL 144:444B): . . . dum strepitus humani cessat alloquii, construitur in te per silentium templum Spiritus sancti. See the whole passage in col. 444AC, one of the finest medieval invocations of silence.

55. See RB 6 (*De Taciturnitate*), although both *taciturnitas* and *silentium* occur elsewhere in the *Rule.* Helpful here is Ambrose Wathen, *Silence: The Meaning of Silence in the Rule of St. Benedict* (Washington, DC: Cistercian Publications, 1973).

56. Gehl puts it thus: "The *competens silentium* is that appropriate to the externals of the monastic life and it is a moral virtue among others; but it is also an intellectual approach to the quest for God himself, particularly as he can be sensed, through meditation, to be beyond reason and beyond language; reasonable and speakable but only with careful limitations of time and place; and carefully circumscribed by the attitude of the human seeker after God" ("Competens Silentium," p. 150; 125–26).

57. See the pope's comment on Job 33:33 (*Tace et docebo te sapientiam*) in *Moralia* 24.13.37 (CC143B:1214–15). Cf. the praise for the silence of Moses in *Mor.* 22.17.43, and for that of Eliu in *Mor.* 23.5.12 (CC 143A:1122–23 and CC143B:1153). For a discussion of the moral value of knowing when to speak and when to keep silence, see *Mor.* 7.27.58–61 (CC143:378–81).

58. In his *Diadema Monachorum* 84, Smaragdus says "Gloriatio monachi, mansuetudo cordis et silentium" (PL 102:678B). See also chap. 4 in his *Commentaria in Regulam S. Benedicti* (cols. 782–83).

59. Along with the texts cited above, see *De bono religioso status* (PL 145:786–88).

60. John of Fécamp, *Conf. theol.* 1.6: . . . vere indicibilis es . . . (Leclercq and Bonnes, *Jean de Fécamp*, p. 113).

61. *Conf. theol.* 2.19 (Leclercq and Bonnes, p. 142): . . . nihil dulce habet nisi gemere et flere, nisi fugere tacere et quiescere dicens: Quis dabit mihi pennas sicut columbae et volabo et requiescam? For other notices of silence in John, see, e.g., *Conf. theol.* 3.30 (Leclerq and Bonnes, p. 176), and *Med.* 37 (PL 40:935). Both texts show the influence of Augustine's Ostia vision in *Confessions* 9.10.

62. On Anselm and silence, see Gehl, "Competens Silentium," pp. 147–51.

63. See Jean Leclercq, *The Love of Learning and the Desire for God,* (New York: Fordham University Press, 1961), pp. 23–26, 78–80.

64. For an introduction to the history of *lectio divina,* see "Lectio divina et lecture spirituelle," DS 9:470–510.

65. For the reading of scripture, see RB 48.1; see also 48.4, 5, 10, 13, 14, 22–23; and 49.4. The reading of the writings of the fathers is encouraged in RB 73.

66. On this see Benedetto Calati, "La 'lectio divina' nella tradizione monastica benedittina," *Benedictina* 28 (1981): 411–29.

67. Ibid., pp. 412–20. Calati stresses the communitarian aspect as grounded in the objectivity of the story of salvation recounted in the biblical text.

68. Peter Damian, *Liber qui dicitur Dominus Vobiscum* 18 (PL 145:246C): Quisquis ergo frater in cellula singulariter habitat, communia Ecclesiae verba proferre non timeat, quem videlicet de conventu fidelium, et si locale spatium dividit, cum omnibus tamen unitas fidei in charitate conjungit: qui licet absint per moles corporum, praesto sunt tamen per unitatis ecclesiasticae sacramentum (trans., McNulty, p. 74). The doctrine of the church as the mystical body is strong throughout the work; see chaps. 5–7, 13, 16.

69. The text is found in Gregory's *Hom. in Ez.* 1.7.8 (SC 327:244.11–12). See the discussion in Calati, "La 'lectio divina,'" pp. 420–22; and above, chapter 2, p. 49.

70. Peter Damian, "Hymnus 123. De S. Gregorio papa" (PL 145:957C).

71. Smaragdus, *Diadema Monachorum* 3 (PL 102:597C): Nam cum oramus, ipsi cum Deo loquimur: cum vero legimus, Deus nobiscum loquitur. Omnis profectus, ex lectione et meditatione procedit. Smaragdus took this adage on prayer from Isidore of Seville, whose *Sententiae* 3.8.1–5 are quoted in the first part of this chapter (see PL 83:679A–80A). The adage appears often in the Latin fathers, at least as early as Ambrose, *De officiis* 1.20.88 (PL 16:54B): Illum alloquimur, cum oramus; illum audimus, cum divina legimus oracula.

72. Smaragdus, *Diadema Monachorum* 3 (PL 102:598C): Plerumque fit, ut Scripturae sacrae verba esse mystica quisque sentiat, si accensus supernae contemplationis gratia, semetipsum ad coelestia suspendat. Mira enim atque ineffabilis sacri eloquii virtus agnoscitur, cum superno amore legentis animus penetratur. See Gregory, *Hom. in Ez.* 1.7.8 (SC 367:244.27–31). Smaragdus substitutes *mystica* for Gregory's *caelestia.*

73. John of Fécamp, *Conf. theol.* 3.19 (Leclercq and Bonnes, p. 163.665–69): Nunc autem per speculum, et in aenigmate, tunc facie ad faciem (1 Cor 13:12). Speculum namque nostrum scriptura tua sacra, quae nobis lucet in nocte huius vitae *tanquam lucerna ardens in caliginoso loco* (2 Pet 1:19). The image of scripture as a mirror is also found in Gregory the Great, *Moralia in Job* 2.1.1 (CC 143:59).

74. *Conf. theol.* 2 (Leclercq and Bonnes, p. 121:6–9): Dicta mea dicta sunt patrum. Sic ista quae dicimus, lege ut putes te patrum verba relegere, et toto mentis adnisu quas vales actiones gratiarum tuo redemptori alacriter sinceriterque persolve.

75. The literature on *meditatio* is rich. For an overview, see the multiauthor article "Méditation" in DS 10:906–34; and Jean Chatillon, "Prière. IIIC. Prière au moyen âge," DS 12:2271–88. Also useful are Jean Leclercq, "Prayer and Contemplation. II. Western" in *Christian Spirituality: Origins to the Twelfth Century,* pp. 415–26 (esp. 418–19); and Adalbert de Vogüé, "Les deux fonctions de la méditation dans les Règles monastiques anciennes," *Revue d'histoire de la spiritualité* 51 (1975): 3–16; and Fidelis Ruppert, "Meditatio-Ruminatio," *Collectanea Cisterciensia* 39 (1977): 81–93.

76. See *Epistle of Barnabas* 10.11, and the discussion in Ruppert, "Meditatio-Ruminatio," pp. 82–84.

77. Isidore of Seville, *Regulae* 6.3 (PL 83:876B): Hoc meditetur in corde quod psallit in ore. A similar formula can be found in Cassian, *Institutes* 2.15.1.

78. This is well set out in some early medieval texts, e.g., Bede's letter to Bishop Acca, which prefaces his *De templo Salomonis* (PL 91:736D–38C).

79. A pale modern reflection of this usage of *meditatio/ruminatio* remains in English when we speak of "not being able to digest" a difficult personal problem or situation (not just an intellectual issue).

80. John of Fécamp, "Tuae quidem" (Leclercq and Bonnes, p. 204.161–63): Omnimodis enim impossibile est ad cordis puritatem pervenire nisi per continuam in Dei laude meditationem.

81. The text appears in PL 40:934–36.

82. This section begins with eight superlatives addressed to Christ: Dulcissime, benignissime, amantissime, charissime, pretiosissime, desiderantissime, amabilissime, pulcherrime.

83. *Med.* 37 (col. 935): Tene cor meum manu tua; quia sine te ad altiora non rapitur. Illuc festino, ubi summa pax regnat, et jugis tranquillitas rutilat. Tene et rege spiritum meum, et assume illum secundum voluntatem tuam; ut te duce ascendat in illam regionem ubertatis, ubi pascis Israel in aeternam pabulo veritatis [a reminiscence of Ezek 34:14]; ut ibi vel rapida cogitatione attingat te summam sapientiam super omnia manentem, cuncta scientem [an alternative reading is *transeuntem*], et omnia gubernantem. Sed volitanti ad te animae multa sunt quae obstrepunt: jussu tuo, Domine, conticescant mihi omnia; ipsa mihi sileat anima; transeant omnia quae creata sunt; transeat et se, et perveniat ad te, atque in te solo Creatore omnium oculos fidei figat; tibi inhiet, tibi intendat, te meditetur, te contempletur, te sibi ante oculos ponat, te sub corde revolvat summum et verum bonum, et gaudium sine fine mansurum. See *Conf. theol.* 3.6 (Leclercq and Bonnes, p. 147.150–59) for a comparable use of the Ostia vision. On the influence of the *Confessiones* on John, see Pierre Courcelle, *Les Confessions de Saint Augustin dans la tradition littéraire: Antécédents et Posterité* (Paris: Études Augustiniennes, 1963), pp. 262–64.

84. *Med.* (935): Tu sagitta electa, et gladius acutissimus, . . . confige cor meum jaculo tui amoris: ut dicat tibi anima mea, Charitate tua vulnerata sum. . . . This particular reprisal of the theme of the wound of love, combining three scriptural sources (the wound of Song 2:5, the chosen arrow of Isa 49:2, and the sword of Eph 6:17), seems to be based directly on the Latin Origen and not on any intermediary uses (e.g., Augustine in *En. in Ps.* 44.16 uses only the wound and arrows). For the use in Origen, see *Foundations of Mysticism*, p. 123, and the literature cited there.

85. For a general introduction to the theme of tears in the Christian tradition, see Pierre Adnès, "Larmes," DS 9:287–303. Among John's contemporaries, Peter Damian offers teaching on the necessity for tears that is especially rich; see, e.g., *De perfectione monachorum* 12–14 (PL 145:307–13).

86. The text of the *meditatio* can be found in *S. Anselmi . . . Opera Omnia* 3:84–91. I will make use of the translation of Benedicta Ward, *Prayers and Meditations of Saint Anselm*, pp. 230–37 (see also her remarks on the meditation on pp. 76–77 of the "Introduction"). There are a number of useful comparisons of John and Anselm. See especially Leclercq and Bonnes, *Jean de Fécamp*, pp. 78–80; and Benedicta Ward, "Introduction," in *Prayers and Meditations*, pp. 47–50.

87. John's *meditatio* contains fourteen direct scriptural quotations—nine from the Psalms. Anselm's text has only four direct quotations, three in one brief sentence referring to the obedience of Christ in the Passion (ed., 88.116–18).

88. For a denial that Anselm's writings should be thought of as mystical works, see Leclercq and Bonnes, *Jean de Fécamp*, p. 103. In this connection, it is interesting to note that while John of Fécamp is willing to use the term *fruitio* of the experience of God in this life, Anselm seems to restrict it to heaven (e.g., *Monologion* 70). See Théodore Koehler, "Fruitio Dei. II. Moyen âge latin," DS 5:1552–53.

89. *Med.* 3 (ed., 89.132–36): Hoc *mandat*, o homo, hoc *ruminet*, hoc *sugat*, hoc *glutiat* cor tuum, cum eiusdem redemptoris tui carnem et sanguinem accipit os tuum [my emphasis]. A similar reference to *ruminatio* motifs is found at the beginning (ed., 84.9–12).

90. *Med.* 3 (ed., 91.196–200): Fac precor, domine, me gustare per amorem quod gusto per cognitionem. Sentiam per affectum quod sentio per intellectum. . . . trahe tu, domine, in

amorem tuum vel hoc ipsum totum. Totum quod sum tuum est conditione; fac totum tuum dilectione.

91. For medieval understandings of prayer, see Jean Chatillon, "Prière. IIIc. Prière au moyen âge," DS 12:2271–88; and Jean Leclercq, "Prayer and Contemplation. II. Western," in *Christian Spirituality: Origins to the Twelfth Century*, pp. 415–26.

92. On this, see the summary in *RB 1980*, pp. 412–13.

93. For the teaching of Evagrius and Cassian on pure prayer, see *Foundations of Mysticism*, pp. 150–51 and 222–24 respectively, and the texts and literature cited there.

94. For an introduction to this issue, see Jean Leclercq, "Prière incessante: A propos de la 'laus perennis' du moyen âge," in *La liturgie et les paradoxes chrétiennes* (Paris: Cerf, 1963), pp. 229–42.

95. Among these were Isidore of Seville (d. 636), *Sententiae* 3.7–8 (PL 83:671–80); and Defensor of Ligugé (ca. 700), *Liber Scintillarum* 7 (SC 77:128–43). Such summaries are also found in Carolingian works, such as Rabanus Maurus, *De institutione clericorum* 2.10–12 (PL 107:329–31), and his *De universo* 6.14 (PL 111:136–37).

96. Leclercq, "Smaragdus," in *Introduction to the Medieval Mystics of Europe*, p. 41; see also Leclercq's French treatment in DS 2:1937–38.

97. Smaragdus, *Diadema Monachorum* 25 (PL 102:620D–21A): Qui enim mortificare se appetit, valde ad inventam requiem contemplationis hilarescit: ut exstinctus mundum lateat, et cunctis exteriorum rerum sopitis perturbationibus, intra sinum se intimi amoris abscondat. The chapter in which this passage appears is typical of Smaragdus's procedure in combining quotations and reminisences of Gregory the Great (*Mor.* 23.21.43 in this passage) with stories and sayings of the desert fathers (here Abbas Theonas, Arsenius, Serapion and others).

98. Bede, for example, equated *theologia* and *contemplatio*, as in his *Commentarium in Lucam* 3.10 (PL 92:455): Una ergo et sola est theologia, id est contemplatio Dei, cui merito omnia iustificationum merita, universa virtutum studia postponuntur.

99. A full exploration of this terminology, its roots in the patristic period, and its flowering in the twelfth century, will not be attempted here. The interested reader will find it well set out in Jean Leclercq's *Otia Monastica*. See also H. J. Sieben, "'Quies' et 'Otium'," DS 12:2746–56.

100. Rabanus Maurus, *In Gen.* 3.16 (PL 107:596): Contemplativa vero [vita] simplex ad solum videndum principium anhelat. See also his discussion of face-to-face vision commenting on Gen 32:30 in *In Gen.* 3.20 (PL 107:610–12).

101. E.g., Odilo, *Sermo* 1 (PL 142:991CD).

102. Peter Damian, *De perfectione monachorum* 8 (PL 145:303D–04A): Omnis enim Deum quaerentis intentio hoc sperat, ad hoc spectat, ut ad requiem quandoque perveniat; et in summae contemplationis gaudio, velut in pulchrae Rachel amplexibus requiescit; videlicet ut per verbum quod audit, scandat ad videndum principium quod quaesivit.

103. See Jean Leclercq, "Contemplation," DS 2:1946; and especially *Études sur la vocabulaire monastique*, pp. 117–21.

104. Ambrose Autpert, *In Apocalypsin* 10 (CCCM 27A:871.96–97): Qui cum a nobis investigaris, ut es non inveniris; cum amaris, adprehenderis.

105. *Conf. theol.* 3.33 (ed., 182.1261–71): . . . in te solum Deum attolit simplicem puri cordis intuitum. . . . Cor ardet: animus gaudet: memoria viget: intellectus lucet: et totus spiritus ex desiderio visionis pulchritudinis tuae accensus, *in invisibilium amorem rapi* [cf. the Christmas Preface] se videt.

106. Peter Damian, *Opusculum* 52.2 (PL 145:766D).

107. On this controversy, see Maïeul Cappuyns, "Note sur le problème de la vision béatifique au IXe siécle"; and Jean Leclercq, *Regards monastiques sur le Christ au moyen âge* (Paris: Desclée, 1992), pp. 108–12. The basic text in Augustine is Ep. 92 (PL 33:318–21).

108. Wizo, *Num Christus corporeis oculis Deum videre potuerit* (PL 106:103–8).

109. Rabanus Maurus, *De puritate cordis* (PL 112:1297AB): . . . nullusque hominum in hac vita, excepto Domino Salvatore nostro, naturalem pervagationem mentis ita defixam semper in Dei contemplatione continuit, ut numquam ab ea raptus mundanae cujusque rei delectatione peccaret. . . . Compare Rabanus's lengthy discussion in cols. 1296–98 with Cassian, *Conlatio* 1.12–13.

110. Rabanus, ibid. (1301C): . . . ergo anima nostra, quae Deo vult appropinquare, elevet se a corpore, semper illi summo adhaereat bono, quod est divinum, quod est semper, et quod erat ab initio, et quod erat apud Deum, hoc est, Dei Verbum.

111. Peter Damian, *Vita Romualdi* 31 (PL 144:983AB).

112. Peter Damian, *Opusculum* 19.5 (PL 145:432AB): . . . saepe cernebam praesentissimo mentis intuiti Christum clavis affixum, in cruce pendentem, avidusque suscipiebam stillantem supposito ore cruorem. Porro si nitar apicibus tradere quidquid mihi contemplari dabatur, vel de sacratissima nostri Redemptoris humanitate, vel de illa coelestis gloriae inenarrabili specie, ante dies elabitur quam rei series digeratur. I have used the translation of McNulty, *St. Peter Damian*, p. 32.

113. For another image of feeding on Christ in Peter, see the discussion of eating the *divinum illud ac mysticum manna* which is Christ in *Opusculum* 48.2 (PL 145:717–18). Similar mystical devotion to Christ is strong in John of Fécamp, e.g., *Conf. theol.* 2.6, 3.26–27 (ed., 128–29, 170–73).

114. Ep. ad monialem 1 (ed., 205.1–206.7): OSCULETUR ME OSCULO ORIS SUI. Quae osculum divinae veritatis felicissimo amore expetis, vaca et vide quoniam Deus est suavis. Non enim hic affectus est quorumlibet hominum, sed tantum sponsarum Deum caste amantium. Si ergo ad omnia Sacrae Scripturae eloquia, plurimum et facillime in his quae circa visionem Dei versantur, sentis te ad amorem divinum inflammari, ne dubites te sponsae nomine censeri. Large parts of this letter were also later used by John in the letter he wrote to the widowed empress Agnes (the same addressed by Peter Damian) as edited in Leclercq and Bonnes, pp. 211–17.

115. John cites the Song five more times in this letter as compared with eight citations from the Psalms. Use of the erotic language of the Song is found occasionally in the *Conf. theol.*, e.g., 3.11 and 29 (Leclercq and Bonnes, pp. 154–55, 175–76). Spousal language without explicit reference to the Song is found in 3.32 (Leclercq and Bonnes, p. 181), and at 3.12 John expresses his desire for the heavenly Jerusalem, *nobilissima sponsa Christi*, with texts taken from the Song (Leclercq and Bonnes, pp. 155–56). Peter Damian used the Song more often. A disciple put together a selection of twenty-seven excerpts of his interpretation after his death, the *Capitula de Canticis Canticorum* (PL 145:1141–54). Several of these emphasize a mystical meaning (e.g., ##7, 9, and 15) and others appear to have influenced Bernard of Clairvaux, e.g., #3 on Song 1:12, and #6 on Song 2:6. This use of the Song is fitting in a writer who often refers to the *spirituale conjugium* between Christ and the soul (e.g., PL 144:333A, 444C–45D; PL 145:305D–306C, 815B–16A, 819A–20A). Especially notable here is Peter's reference to Christ as the *mystica sponsa* of Agnes in 820A. The use of the Song of Songs in Damian and John of Fécamp has been studied by Rosemarie Herde, "Das Hohelied in der lateinischen Literatur des Mittelalters bis zum 12. Jahrhundert," *Studi Medievali* 3a ser 8 (1967): 1017–23. On Damian, see also E. Ann Matter, *The Voice of My Beloved. The Song of Songs in Western Medieval Christianity* (Philadelphia: University of Pennsylvania Press, 1990), p. 188.

116. Ep. 5 (ed., 207.54–57): Haec ergo frequenter lege, et tunc praecipue cum mentem tuam caelesti afflatam desiderio vides. Iustum namque est ut qui in actuali vita bene conversatus est contemplationis pennas assumat.

117. Ep. 6 (ed., 208.73–79): ... interdum et idipsum raptim se videndam spiritaliter exhibet, nec tamen sicuti est, quod in futurum expectamus. Heu et in hoc praesenti, quamvis dulcissimo, contuitu rara est hora et parva mora. Quae tamen visionis excellentia animam quam sic repleverit ab omni terrena concupiscentia funditus, quantum homo capax, abstrahit.

118. Ep. 9 (ed., 209.103–06): ... minus proficientes, qui Deum sibi imaginaliter fingunt, ... illam miram et incircumscriptam lucem contemplari intellectualiter nesciunt. This concern for discriminating between true and false forms of mysticism is a new and important note.

119. Ep. 12 (ed., 210.135–36): ... tamquam pennatum animal effecta, per singulos dies in utraque vita proficias. ...

120. Peter Damian, *De perfectione monachorum* 8 (PL 145:303–4) sketches three stages through which the "intellectual soul is moved through the grace of contemplation to search out the manifestation of Truth" in terms of the story of Jacob and the daughters of Laban. Jacob first cleanses himself by ascetic effort (Laban=cleansing); then he beds down with Lia in the "labor" of good works, in order to finally enjoy Rachel, his desired, who represents the "delights of divine contemplation" (*divinae contemplationis oblectamenta*). A more complete version of such an allegorical anchoring of a spiritual itinerary will be found in the works of Richard of St. Victor, on which see chapter 9.

121. Peter Damian, *Sermo* 28 (PL 144:656A–58B). The final stage is described in typical terms: ... vir quisque perfectus ad tantam plenitudinem contemplationis attolitur, ut dum non potest tam eximiam profunditatem ad liquidum comprehendere, velut excrescentis undae vadum mens non valeat humana transire (657A).

122. See Ep. 2.5 (PL 144:260–70).

123. Peter Damian, *Opusculum XXXII. De Quadragesima et Quadraginta Duabus Hebraeorum Mansionibus* (PL 145:543–60). See the synopsis in DS 12:1556–57.

124. For a consideration of this text, see *Foundations of Mysticism,* pp. 117–18.

125. Peter Damian, *De Quadragesima* 3 (PL 145:547D–48A): Porro autem, sicut illi ascenderunt per quadraginta duas mansiones, ita Salvator noster in Aegyptum mundi hujus descendit per totidem patres. Quod si jam intelligimus quantum sacramenti numerus iste contineat, humanae scilicet ascensionis, et divinae descensionis, incipiamus jam per ea quae descendit Christus ascendere. ... For the mystical stages, see especially the account of *Rethma* (col. 553AB) and *Thare-Methca-Hesmona* (col. 555AC).

126. I make use of the text as found in F. J. E. Raby, *The Oxford Book of Medieval Latin Verse* (Oxford: Clarendon Press, 1959), #115 (p. 158). The poem is discussed by Peter Dronke in his *Medieval Latin and the Rise of the European Love-Lyric,* 2 vols. (Oxford: Clarendon Press, 1968), 1:269–71 (I use his translation here; slightly adapted). On the use of the Song of Songs in medieval poetry, see Rosemarie Herde, "Das Hohelied in der lateinischen Literatur des Mittelalters bis zum 12. Jahrhundert," *Studi Medievali* 3a ser. 8 (1967): 957–1073, who discusses this poem on pp. 1018–20; and Peter Dronke, "The Song of Songs and Medieval Love-Lyric," in *The Bible and Medieval Culture,* ed. W. Lourdaux and D. Verhelst (Leuven: Leuven University Press, 1979), pp. 236–62.

127. For an edition, translation, and study of this poem, see Peter Dronke, "Virgines Caste," in *Lateinische Dichtungen des X. und XI. Jahrhunderts: Festgabe für Walther Bulst zum 80. Geburtstag* (Heidelberg: Schneider, 1981), pp. 93–117.

128. These lines constitute stanzas 7b–7c of Dronke's edition in "Virgines Caste" (pp. 94–95). I have slightly adapted Dronke's translation (p. 100) here.

129. Stanzas 10a–11b (p. 95). Again, I have slightly adapted Dronke's version to give a line-by-line rendering. Dronke emphasizes (p. 103): "... the tone of lighthearted sensuality and erotic play as he pastures in the flower-maidens or rests between their breasts; indeed the

whole development of the static image of the Lamb of God into a frolicking living being, epitomizing the joys of spring. I know of nothing quite comparable in earlier Christian tradition."

130. Almost all the authors dealt with here discuss the relation of the *vita activa* and *vita contemplativa*, arguing for the superiority of contemplation, the necessity of the return of the contemplative to active charity, and the supremacy of a mixed life. See, e.g., Isidore of Seville, *Sententiarum* 3.15 (PL 83:689–91); Ambrose Autpert, *Homelia de Transfiguratione Domini* 16 (CCCM 27B:1019–21); Smaragdus, *Diadema monachorum* 24 (PL 102:619–20); Rabanus Maurus, *In Genesim* 3.16 (PL 107:596AC); Odilo of Cluny, *Sermo* 12 (PL 142:1023–28); Peter Damian, *De perfectione monachorum* 8–9 (PL 145:303–05); and John of Fécamp, *Epistola ad monialem* (ed., 209–10). For further references, see the articles "Marthe et Marie," DS 10:664–73; "Rachel et Lia," DS 13:25–30; and "Vie active, vie contemplative, vie mixte," DS 16:592–623.

Introduction to Part II

1. The term renaissance as applied to the (French) twelfth century seems to have first appeared in Jean-Jacques Ampère, *Histoire littéraire de la France avant le douzième siècle*, published in 1839–40. It was popularized in the English-speaking world by Charles Homer Haskins in his work, *The Renaissance of the Twelfth Century* (Cambridge, MA: Harvard University Press, 1927).

2. For an overview, see B. McGinn, "Renaissance, Humanism, and the Interpretation of the Twelfth Century," *Journal of Religion* 55 (1975): 444–55.

3. Two summaries of such more extended surveys of the twelfth-century stage of the Western church have recently appeared: Colin Morris, *The Papal Monarchy: The Western Church from 1050 to 1250* (Oxford: Clarendon Press, 1989); and I. S. Robinson, *The Papacy 1073–1198: Continuity and Innovation* (Cambridge: Cambridge University Press, 1990).

4. Gregory VII, *Register* 3.10, ed. Erich Caspar, *Das Register Gregors VII* (MGH. Epistulae selectae 2:265–66): . . . videntes ordinem christiane religionis multis iam labefactum temporibus et principales ac proprias lucrandarum animarum causas diu prolapsas et suadente diabolo conculcatas concussi periculo et manifesta perditione Dominici gregis ad sanctorum patrum decreta doctrinamque recurrimus nichil novi, nichil adinventione nostra statuentes, sed primam et unicam ecclesiastice discipline regulam et tritam sanctorum viam relicto errore repetendam et sectandam esse censuimus. I am using the translation of Ephraim Emerton, *The Correspondence of Pope Gregory VII* (New York: Norton, 1969), p. 88.

5. For a survey, see Giles Constable, "Reform and Renewal in Religious Life: Concepts and Realities," in *Renaissance and Renewal in the Twelfth Century*, ed. Robert L. Benson and Giles Constable with Carol D. Lanham (Cambridge, MA: Harvard University Press, 1982), pp. 37–67.

6. Urban II, Ep. 58 (PL 151:338B): Omnipotenti autem Domino, cujus melior est misericordia super victimas, gratias agimus, quia vos estis qui SS. Patrum vitam probabilem renovatis, et apostolicae instituta disciplinae, in primordiis Ecclesiae sanctae exorta. . . .

7. The text of the *Exordium parvum* appears in Jean de la Croix Bouton and Jean-Baptiste Van Damme, *Les plus anciens textes de Cîteaux* (Achel: Abbaye Cistercienne, 1974), pp. 51–86, and has been translated by Bede K. Lackner in Louis J. Lekai, *The Cistercians: Ideals and Reality* (Kent State, OH: Kent State University Press, 1977), pp. 451–61. This phrase appears in the edition on p. 58: . . . ac regulae beatissimi Benedicti . . . artius deinceps atque perfectius inhaerere velle professos fuisse.

8. Anselm of Havelberg, *Dialogi* 1.6 (SC 118:66): . . . et sancta Ecclesia pertransiens per diversos status sibi invicem paulatim succedentes, usque in hodiernum diem, sicut juventus aquilae renovatur et semper renovabitur. . . .

9. Bernard of Clairvaux, *De gratia et libero arbitrio* 14.49.

10. Much has been written about the concept of reform and its relation to renovation and even renaissance in Christian history. See especially the classic work of Gerhart B. Ladner, *The Idea of Reform: Its Impact on Christian Thought and Action in the Age of the Fathers* (Cambridge, MA: Harvard University Press, 1959). More specifically on the twelfth-century context, see Ladner, "Reform: Innovation and Tradition in Medieval Christendom," in *Theology and Law in Islam*, ed. Gustave E. von Grunebaum (Los Angeles: UCLA Near Eastern Center, 1971), pp. 53–73; and (less successful in my view) the same author's "Terms and Ideas of Renewal," in *Renaissance and Renewal in the Twelfth Century*, pp. 1–33 (with rich bibliography). See also Karl F. Morrison, "The Church, Reform, and Renaissance in the Early Middle Ages," in *Life and Thought in the Early Middle Ages*, ed. Robert S. Hoyt (Minneapolis: University of Minnesota Press, 1967), pp. 143–59.

11. Karl F. Morrison, "The Gregorian Reform," in *Christian Spirituality: Origins to the Twelfth Century*, ed. Bernard McGinn, John Meyendorff, and Jean Leclercq, WS 16 (New York: Crossroad, 1986), pp. 177–93 (quotation on 178).

12. See the essay of Frederic L. Cheyette, "The Invention of the State," in *The Walter Prescott Webb Memorial Lectures: Essays in Medieval Civilization*, ed. Bede Karl Lackner and Kenneth Roy Philp (Austin and London: University of Texas Press, 1978), pp. 143–78.

13. The relation between reform and heresy has been much debated. See especially Jeffrey Burton Russell, *Dissent and Reform in the Early Middle Ages* (Berkeley and Los Angeles: University of California Press, 1965); and R. I. Moore, *The Origins of European Dissent* (New York: St. Martin's Press, 1977).

14. G. Ladner goes so far as to say: "the Augustinian type of a monastically living clergy was the principal practical vehicle through which, as far as the West is concerned, the patristic idea of reform was to be made a reality, and through which it was actually in some measure transmitted to the following centuries" ("Reform: Innovation and Traditions," p. 59). For introductions to the canons, see Aloysius Smith, "Chanoines réguliers," DS 2:463–77; C. Egger, "Canonici regolari," DIP 2:46–63; and, more briefly, Grover A. Zinn, "IV. The Regular Canons," *Christian Spirituality: Origins to the Twelfth Century*, pp. 218–28.

15. For the background of the crusade, see Carl Erdmann, *The Origin of the Idea of Crusade* (Princeton: Princeton University Press, 1977). On the crusade as a form of lay spirituality, see Jonathan Riley-Smith, *The First Crusade and the Idea of Crusading* (Philadelphia: University of Pennsylvania Press, 1986); and B. McGinn, "*Iter Sancti Sepulchri*: The Piety of the First Crusaders," in *The Walter Prescott Webb Memorial Lectures. Essays in Medieval Civilization*, pp. 33–71.

16. See André Vauchez, *The Laity in the Middle Ages: Religious Beliefs and Devotional Practices* (Notre Dame, IN: University of Notre Dame Press, 1993).

17. Marie-Dominique Chenu, *La théologie au douzième siècle* (Paris: Vrin, 1957); the partial English translation by Jerome Taylor and Lester K. Little was published by the University of Chicago Press in 1968.

18. See, e.g., Chenu, *Nature, Man, and Society*, p. 238.

19. André Vauchez emphasizes the centrality of the ideal of poverty in twelfth-century spirituality (*La spiritualité du Moyen Âge occidental viiie-xiie siècles* [Paris: Presses universitaires de France, 1975] e.g., pp. 87, 111–14, 167).

20. See R. W. Southern, *The Making of the Middle Ages* (New Haven and London: Yale University Press, 1953).

21. See Brian Stock, *The Implications of Literacy: Written Language and Models of Interpretation in the Eleventh and Twelfth Centuries* (Princeton: Princeton University Press, 1983). According

to Stock, the effect of Bernard's sermons on the Cistercians "provided the century's outstanding example of a 'textual community'" (p. 405).

22. The contrast between monastic and scholastic theology set forth in the works of Jean Leclercq, especially his "S. Bernard et la théologie monastique du XIIe siècle," *Saint Bernard Théologien: Analecta Sacri Ordinis Cisterciensis* 9 (1953): 7–23; and subsequently in *The Love of Learning and the Desire for God* (New York: Fordham University Press, 1961), chap. 9, have been somewhat modified by Leclercq's later picture of three interacting currents of theology (contemplative monastic theology, pastoral theology of the schools, speculative theology) in "The Renewal of Theology," *Renaissance and Renewal in the Twelfth Century*, pp. 68–87.

23. See especially the treatment of Origen's *Comm. in Cant.* 3.7 and *Hom. in Cant.* 2.9 in *Foundations of Mysticism*, p. 126.

24. For Augustine's teaching on the ordering of charity, see *Foundations of Mysticism*, p. 261.

25. Song of Songs 2:4 in the Vg. text has *ordinavit in me caritatem*, whereas the Vetus Latina text, based on the LXX, uses the imperative: *ordinate in me caritatem*. Both forms were used in the twelfth century.

26. The phrase is that of M. Corneille Halflants, in the "Introduction," to *Bernard of Clairvaux: On the Songs of Songs I* (Spencer: Cistercian Publications, 1971), p. xxix. For some viewpoints on love in the twelfth century, see John C. Moore, *Love in Twelfth-Century France* (Philadelphia: University of Pennsylvania Press, 1972); and Jean Leclercq, *Monks and Love in Twelfth-Century France* (Oxford: Clarendon Press, 1979).

27. Bernard of Clairvaux, *Sermones super Cantica Canticorum* 23.14.

28. Gregory the Great, *Hom. in Ev.* 27.4 (PL 76:1207A). See the discussion of this text in chapter 2, pp. 58 and 62.

29. For an introduction to this theme, see Robert Javelet, "Intelligence et amour chez les auteurs spirituels du XIIe siècle," *Revue d'ascetique et de mystique* 37 (1961): 273–90, 429–50.

30. Some of the reasons for this have been well set-out by Gershom Scholem, especially in his paper "Mysticism and Society," *Diogenes* 58 (1967): 1–24. For a discussion of Scholem's views, see *Foundations of Mysticism*, pp. 334–36.

31. For an introduction, see Giles Constable, "Twelfth-Century Spirituality and the Late Middle Ages," *Mediaeval and Renaissance Studies* 5 (1969): 27–60.

32. E.g., Jean Leclercq, in *The Spirituality of the Middle Ages*, entitles his chapter 8 "The School of Cîteaux."

Chapter 5

1. The literature on the Cistercians and Cistercian mysticism is large. The best general book is Louis J. Lekai, *The Cistercians: Ideals and Reality* (Kent State, OH: Kent State University Press, 1977). On Cistercian mysticism, see the introductions of Louis Bouyer, *The Cistercian Heritage* (Westminster, MD: Newman, 1958); and Edmond Mikkers, "Robert de Molesmes. II. La spiritualité cistercienne," DS 13:738–814.

2. Bernard of Clairvaux, *Sermo in dedicatione ecclesiae* 1.2, in *Sancti Bernardi Opera* (abbreviated SBOp), ed. Jean Leclercq et al., 8 vols. (Rome: Editiones Cistercienses, 1957–77), 5:371.14–372.2: Quid mirabilius, quando is qui prius vix per biduum poterat continue a luxuria, a crapula et ab ebrietate et cubilibus et impudicitis, ceterisque similibus et dissimilibus vitiis, nunc ab eis continet multis annis, tota utique vita sua? Quot maius miraculum, quando tot iuvenes, tot adolescentes, tot nobiles, universi denique quos hic video, velut in carcere aperto tenentur sine vinculis, solo Dei timore confixi, quod in tanta perseverant afflictione paenitentiae, ultra virtutem humanam, supra naturam, contra consuetudinem? . . . Quid vero sunt haec, nisi manifesta inhabitantis in vobis Spiritus Sancti argumenta? Nam habitare in corpore animam probant vitales motus corporis, habitare in anima Spiritum probat vita spiri-

tualis. Illud ex visu et auditu dignoscitur, istud ex caritate et humilitate ceterisque virtutibus. All translations for Bernard, unless otherwise noted, will be my own, though most of Bernard's works have been translated in the Cistercian Fathers Series published by Cistercian Publications. I will cite from the Leclercq edition, referring to the standard divisions of the texts and using the formula 5:371.14–372.2 to indicate volume, pages and lines. I will also make use of the standard abbreviations for the works of Bernard. Those used here are: *Adv-Sermo in adventu Domini; Ann-Sermo in annuntiatione dominica; Asc-Sermo in ascensione Domini; Asspt-Sermo in assumptione B.V.M.; Conv-Sermo ad clericos de conversione; Csi-De Consideratione; Ded-Sermo in dedicatione ecclesiae; Dil-De diligendo Deo; Div-Sermo de diversis; Ep-Epistola; Gra-De gratia et libero arbitrio; IV HM-Sermo in feria IV hebdomadae sanctae; Hum-De gradibus humilitatis et superbiae; Nat-Sermo in nativitate Domini; Nat BVM-Sermo in nativitate B.V.M.; OS-Sermo in festivitate omnium sanctorium; Palm-Sermo in ramis palmarum; Par-Parabola; Pasc-Sermo in die paschae; Pent-Sermo in die pentecostes; Pre-Liber de praecepto et dispensatione; QH-Sermo super psalmum "Qui habitat"; Quad-Sermo in quadragesima; SCC-Sermo super cantica canticorum; Sent-sententia; Sept-Sermo in septuagesima; V Nat-Sermo in vigilia nativitatis Domini.* References to *Sermon* without qualifier always indicates *SCC*.

3. The most recent edition of the early sources is to be found in J. Bouton and J.-B. van Damme, *Les plus anciennes textes de Cîteaux,* translations of which by Bede J. Lackner appear in Lekai, *The Cistercians,* pp. 442-66.

4. For the notion of monastic revolution by appeal to tradition, see Michael Hill, *The Religious Order* (London: Kegan Paul, 1973), pp. 85-103.

5. Bernard himself became involved in these debates in his *Apologia ad Guillelmum abbatem* (SBOp 3:82-108). For more on the Cluniac–Cistercian debates, see, e.g., the texts from Idung of Prüfening translated in *Cluniacs and Cistercians: The Case for Cîteaux* (Kalamazoo, MI: Cistercian Publications, 1977).

6. See especially Armand Vielleux, "The interpretation of a monastic Rule," in *The Cistercian Spirit: A Symposium,* ed. M. Basil Pennington (Spencer: Cistercian Publications, 1970), pp. 59-60; and in the same volume, Jean Leclercq, "The intentions of the founders," pp. 105-6.

7. See especially chapters 3–4 of the earliest version of the *Carta caritatis,* as translated by B. Lackner in Lekai, *The Cistercians,* pp. 451–52.

8. On the *conversi,* see Lekai, *The Cistercians,* chapter 22. Not discussed here is the role the Cistercians had as a catalyst in the growth of women's piety in the twelfth century. The Cistercian reform inspired a significant movement of women committed to adopting the Cistercian form of life to the extent that this was allowed to them. See Janet E. Summers, *"The Violent Shall Take It By Force": The First Century of the Cistercian Nuns, 1125–1228* (dissertation, University of Chicago, 1986). Cistercian nuns made a contribution to mysticism, but not until the thirteenth century, so they will not be taken up until the next volume.

9. On the importance of the Cistercian refusal of oblates, see Jean Leclercq, *Monks and Love in Twelfth-Century France* (Oxford: Clarendon Press, 1979), chapter 2.

10. R. W. Southern, *Western Society and the Church in the Middle Ages* (Baltimore: Penguin, 1970), pp. 250-72.

11. Lekai, *The Cistercians,* pp. 48-50.

12. For observations on the role of such unresolved tensions in Bernard's thought, see Karl F. Morrison, "Hermeneutics and Enigma: Bernard of Clairvaux's *De Consideratione," Viator* 19 (1988): 129-51.

13. See Bernard, *Div* 121 (SBOp 6:398-99).

14. Recently, Raymond D. DiLorenzo has argued that the poet's debt to the saint is even greater, suggesting that Bernard's doctrine of grace and freedom, especially as found in the *Gra,* lies at the basis of the whole structure of the *Commedia.* See DiLorenzo's "Dante's Saint Bernard and the Theology of Liberty in the *Commedia," in Bernardus Magister: Papers Presented*

at the *Nonacentenary Celebration of the Birth of Saint Bernard of Clairvaux, Kalamazoo, Michigan*, ed. John R. Sommerfeldt (Kalamazoo, MI: Cistercian Publications; Cîteaux: Commentarii Cistercienses, 1992), pp. 497–515.

15. The text and version of the *Paradiso* is that of Charles S. Singleton, *Dante Alighieri. The Divine Comedy. Paradiso. Text and Commentary*, Bollingen series 80 (Princeton: Princeton University Press, 1975).

16. On Bernard's style, see Christine Mohrmann, "Observations sur la langue et le style de saint Bernard," SBOp 2:ix–xxxiii. For detailed studies of the genre, construction, style, and textual problems relating to Bernard's writings, see the numerous writings of Jean Leclercq, especially *Études sur saint Bernard et le texte de ses écrits, Analecta Sacri Ordinis Cisterciensis* 9.1–2 (Rome: Editiones Cistercienses, 1953); and the three volumes of his *Receuil d'études sur saint Bernard et ses écrits* (Rome: Edizioni di storia et letteratura, 1962–69; hereafter abbreviated *Recueil*).

17. Étienne Gilson, *La théologie mystique de saint Bernard* (Paris: Vrin, 1934); translated into English as *The Mystical Theology of St. Bernard* (London: Sheed & Ward, 1940). Another important milestone in modern Bernard research was the publication of Jean Leclercq's annotated anthology, *St. Bernard mystique* (Paris and Brussels: Desclée, 1948).

18. There is no fully adequate life of Bernard. The most complete account is in the outdated work of Elphège Vacandard, *Vie de saint Bernard*, 2 vols. (Paris: Gabalda, 1894). In English, see Watkin Williams, *Saint Bernard of Clairvaux* (Manchester: Manchester University Press, 1935).

19. On Bernard's education, see G. R. Evans, *The Mind of St. Bernard* (Oxford: Clarendon Press, 1983), pp. 37–49.

20. On *Gra* (edited in SBOp 3:164–203), see B. McGinn, "Introduction," in *On Grace and Free Choice by Bernard of Clairvaux* (Kalamazoo, MI: Cistercian Publications, 1988), pp. 3–50. For recent studies of *Dil* (edited 3:119–54), see Michael Casey, "In Pursuit of Ecstasy: Reflections on Bernard of Clairvaux's De diligendo Deo," *Monastic Studies* 16 (1985): 139–56; and Ermenegildo Bertola, "Introduzione," in *San Bernardo Trattati* (Milan: Scriptorum Claravallense, 1984; vol. 1 of *Opere di San Bernardo*, ed. Ferruccio Gastaldelli), pp. 221–69.

21. The *SCC* are edited in SBOp 1–2. Over 900 manuscripts survive, attesting to the popularity of the work (a French translation was made before 1200). Essential for the study of the text is Jean Leclercq, "Recherches sur les sermons sur les Cantiques," *Receuil*, 1:175–351. There is an English translation in four volumes, *Bernard of Clairvaux on the Song of Songs I–IV* (Kalamazoo, MI: Cistercian Publications, 1971–80).

22. On the genre of the *SCC*, see Jean Leclercq, "Introduction," *Bernard of Clairvaux. On the Song of Songs II*, pp. vii–xxx; and Emero Stiegman, "The Literary Genre of Bernard of Clairvaux's *Sermones super Cantica Canticorum*," in *Simplicity and Ordinariness: Studies in Medieval Cistercian History IV*, ed. John R. Sommerfeldt (Kalamazoo, MI: Cistercian Publications, 1980), pp. 68–93, who terms them "a monastic literary sermon-series" (p. 79). The rhetorical mode of argument found in the *SCC* has been well analyzed by Luke Anderson, "The Rhetorical Epistemology in Saint Bernard's *Super Cantica*," in *Bernardus Magister*, pp. 95–128.

23. J. Leclercq, *Analecta Monastica: Première serie*, Analecta Anselmiana 20 (Rome: Herder, 1948), p. 209. For Origen and Ambrose on the Song of Songs, see *Foundations of Mysticism*, pp. 117–26, 205–15. For introductions to the use of the Song of Songs in Christian mysticism, see B. McGinn, "The Language of Love in Christian and Jewish Mysticism," in *Mysticism and Language*, ed. Steven T. Katz (New York: Oxford University Press, 1992), pp. 202–35; and Ulrich Kopf, "Hoheliedauslegung als Quelle einer Theologie der Mystik," in *Grundfragen christlicher Mystik*, ed. Margot Schmidt and Dieter R. Bauer (Stuttgart-Bad Cannstaat: Froomann-Holzboog, 1987), pp. 50–72.

24. The *Sermones per annum* are edited in SBOp 4–5. An important study is Alberich Alter-matt, "Christus pro nobis: Die Christologie Bernhards von Clairvaux in den 'Sermones per annum,'" *Analecta Sacri Ordinis Cisterciensis* 33 (1977): 1–176.

25. For some passages making use of the Song of Songs, see, e.g., *IV HM* 14; *Asspt* 3.5 and 5.6; *Nat BVM* 5, as well as 13–17; *OS* 4.2; *Ded* 6.1; and *Dominica in kalendas novembris* 1.3, 5.2, and 5.12. Important mysticial passages not using the Song include, e.g., *In epiphaniam* 3.8; *In dominica post epiphaniam* 2.2–4; *Quad* 5.6 and 6.3; and *Palm* 2.7.

26. E.g., *Div* 4, 29, 41.11–13, 80, 87, 89, 92, 101, etc. (the *Div* are edited in SBOp 6, Part 1).

27. Bernard's 547 letters are edited in SBOp 7–8. Among those of interest for his mystical teaching are, e.g., *Ep* 11, 18, 107, 113, 254, 393, etc. An improved version of the Leclercq edi-tion, along with an excellent apparatus, can be found in *Opere di San Bernardo*, ed. Ferruccio Gastaldelli (Milan: Scriptorum Claravallense, 1986–87), vol. 6.

28. *Csi* is edited in SBOp 3:393–493; *Pre* is found in 3:253–94.

29. *SC* 6.3 (1:27.14–15).

30. The ecclesial interpretation is strong in many of the sermons (the most important texts are italicized): *2, 6.1-5,* 12.7 and 10–11, *14,* 16.3, 21.1–3 and 9–11, 22.4–6, *23.1-2,* 25.3–4, 26.2, 27.3–4 and 12, 29, 30.1–5, *33.14-16,* 42.11, 46.1–4, 47.5, 51.2, 53.3, 57.1, 58.5–9, 60.8, 62.1–2 and 4–6, 64.8–10, 65, *68,* 73, 77, *78,* 79.4–6, etc. On the relation of the ecclesial and the personal, or *moralis,* meaning, see Theresa Moritz, "The Church as the Bride in Bernard of Clairvaux's *Sermons on the Song of Songs,*" in *The Chimaera of His Age: Studies on Bernard of Clairvaux,* ed. E. Rozanne Elder and John Sommerfeldt (Kalamazoo, MI: Cistercian Publica-tions, 1980), pp. 3–11; and Raffaele Fassetta, "Le mariage spirituel dans les Sermons de saint Bernard sur le Cantique des Cantiques," *Collectanea Cisterciensia* 48 (1986): 155–80, and 251–65 (esp. 254–57).

31. *SCC* 1–8 (1:3–42). For another treatment of the theme of the kiss, see *Div* 87 and 89–90 (6:329–30, 335–41). An interpretation of this verse also appears in *Brevis Commentatio in Cantica Canticorum* chap. 5, a work whose earliest stage reflects the conversations of Bernard and William of St. Thierry on the Song in the 1120s (PL 184:411C–12A). On this work, see Thomas X. Davis, "A Further Study of the *Brevis Commentatio,*" in *Bernardus Magis-ter,* pp. 187–202.

32. On these three levels, see *Dil* 30–33 (3:144–47), and *Div* 41.12 and 87.4 (6:253, 331–32).

33. *SCC* 4.4 (1:20.2–6): Sed enim et os habet Deus quo docet hominem scientiam, et manum habet qua dat escam omni carni, et pedes habet quorum terra scabellum est. . . . Haec, inquam, habet Deus omnia per effectum, non per naturam. Bernard appears depen-dent on Gregory the Great here; see, e.g., *Mor.* 14.45.53 (CC143A:729–30).

34. *SCC* 5.5 (1:23.22–24): Porro hominis spiritum, qui medium quemdam inter supremum et infimum tenet locum, usque adeo ad utrumque necessarium habere corpus manifestum est, ut absque eo nec ipse proficere, nec alteri prodesse possit.

35. This symbolic reference to the Incarnation as the manifestation of the hidden God is based on a typically Bernardine spiritual use of two biblical texts, Hab 3:3 (from a non Vg. text) and Ps 18:6, traditionally read as referring to the Incarnation (see, e.g., Augustine, *Trac-tatus in 1 Jn.* 1.2 [PL 35:1979]).

36. *SCC* 6.3 (1:27.11–15): Heu! sic homines perdiderunt et commutaverunt gloriam suam in similitudinem vituli comedentis fenum! Quorum Deus miseratus errores, de monte um-broso et condenso dignanter egrediens [Hab 3:3], in sole posuit tabernaculum suum [Ps 18:6]. Obtulit carnem sapientibus carnem, per quem discerent sapere et spiritum. Nam dum in carne et per carnem facit opera non carnis, sed Dei, . . .

37. While Bernard's formulation is new, the idea of God taking flesh in order to be seen by fallen humanity is not. E.g., Gregory the Great, *Mor.* 24.2.2 (CC143B:1189-90): Sed videri ab homine non poterat Deus; homo ergo factus est, ut videri potuisset.

38. *SCC* 6.6-8 (1:28-30). On the christological theme of the meeting of *misericordia* and *veritas/iudicium* in Christ (the reference comes from Ps 84:11), see *Ann* 1.5-14 (5:16-29), one of Bernard's key christological texts.

39. Parts of the following section on Bernard's anthropology (as well as elements of the later discussion of "Spousal Love as Ordering") have already appeared in my paper, "Freedom, Formation and Reformation: The Anthropological Roots of Saint Bernard's Spiritual Teaching," in *La dottrina della vita spirituale nelle opere di San Bernardo di Clairvaux: Atti del Convegno Internazionale. Rome, 11-15 settembre 1990, Analecta Cisterciensia* 46 (Rome: Editiones Cistercienses, 1990), pp. 91-114.

40. For a general introduction to Cistercian anthropology, see B. McGinn, "Introduction," in *Three Treatises on Man: A Cistercian Anthropology* (Kalamazoo, MI: Cistercian Publications, 1977), pp. 1-100.

41. *SCC* 81.11 (2:291.14-15). David N. Bell has suggested that the differences between the earlier and later formulations may be due to the influence of William of St. Thierry, see his "Bernard in Perspective," in *La dottrina della vita spirituale*, pp. 120-22.

42. There is a large literature on Bernard's anthropology. See especially Maur Standaert, "La doctrine de l'image chez saint Bernard," *Ephemerides Theologiae Lovanienses* 23 (1947): 70-129; Endre von Ivánka, "La structure de l'âme selon S. Bernard," in *Saint Bernard Théologien*, pp. 202-8; Wilhelm Hiss, *Die Anthropologie Bernhards von Clairvaux* (Berlin: de Gruyter, 1964); B. McGinn, "Introduction," in *On Grace and Free Choice*, pp. 3-50; Michael Casey, *Athirst for God: Spiritual Desire in Bernard of Clairvaux's Sermons on the Song of Songs* (Kalamazoo, MI: Cistercian Publications, 1988), chap. 4; and the papers of B. McGinn, David N. Bell, Dagmar Heller, and Hildegard Brem in *La dottrina della vita spirituale*, pp. 91-150.

43. *Gra* 3.6-5.15 (3:170-77); cf. 9.28-10.35 (3:185-91).

44. *Gra* 5.15 (3:177.12-15): . . . porro felicitas et miseria eodem tempore simul esse non possunt. Quoties igitur per Spiritum illam participant, toties istam non sentiunt. Itaque in hac vita soli contemplativi possunt utcumque frui libertate complaciti, et hoc ex parte, et parte satis modica, viceque rarissima.

45. *Gra* 1.2 (3:167.13).

46. *Gra* 8.27 (3:185.14-16): Discendum sane hic interim nobis est ex libertate consilii iam libertate arbitrii non abuti, ut plene quandoque frui possimus libertate complaciti. Sic profecto Dei in nobis reparamus imaginem, sic antiquo honori illi capessendo, quem per peccatum amisimus, per gratiam praeparamur.

47. For a recent study of *SCC* 80-83, see Dagmar Heller, "Die Bibel als Grundlage der Anthropologie Bernhards von Clairvaux (Beobachtungen an ausgewählten Beispielen)," in *La dottrina della vita spirituale*, pp. 123-40.

48. *SCC* 80.2-3 (2:277-79). On these sermons, see Casey, *Athirst for God*, pp. 161-70.

49. *SCC* 80.4-5 (2:279-81).

50. *SCC* 81.2-5 (2:284-87).

51. *SCC* 81.6-11 (2:287-91).

52. *SCC* 82.2-6 (2:292-96).

53. See Standaert, "L'image," pp. 74-102. The other key texts are *Ann* 1.7 (5:19-20); *In solemnia apostolorum Petri et Pauli* 2.7-8 (5:196-97); and *Div* 45.1-6 (6:262-65).

54. *SCC* 51.4 (2:86.20-27): Non sane a prudente de diversitate sensuum iudicabor, dummodo veritas utrobique nobis patrocinetur, et caritas, cui Scripturas servire oportet, eo aedificet plures, quo plures ex eis in opus suum veros eruit intellectus. Cur enim hoc displiceat in sensibus Scripturarum, quod in usibus rerum assidue experimur? In quantos, verbi causa, sola

aqua nostrorum assumitur corporum usus? Ita unus quilibet divinus sermo non erit ab re, si diversos pariat intellectus, diversis animarum necessitatibus ut usibus accomodandos. This key principle of the multiplicity of the spiritual meaning of the text shows how deeply Bernard's use of the Bible was rooted in the tradition of Augustine, Gregory the Great, and the other masters of spiritual hermeneutics. For that reason it will not be given an explicit treatment here, just as the abbot himself provides hardly any theoretical discussion of exegesis but illustrates by doing. I refer the reader to the extensive secondary literature on Bernard's exegesis, especially Henri de Lubac, *Exégèse médiévale: Les quatre sens de l'écriture*, 4 vols. (Paris: Aubier, 1959–64), esp. vol. 2, chap. 9; M. Dumontier, in *Saint Bernard et la Bible* (Paris: Desclée, 1953); Claude Bodard, "La Bible, expression d'une expérience religieuse chez s. Bernard," *Saint Bernard Théologien*, pp. 24–45; Denis Farkasfalvy, "The Role of the Bible in St. Bernard's Spirituality," *Analecta Sacri Ordinis Cisterciensis* 25 (1969): 3–13; and Dagmar Heller, *Schriftauslegung und geistliche Erfahrung bei Bernhard von Clairvaux* (Würzburg: Echter, 1990). On the Song of Songs in particular, see Jean Leclercq, "St. Bernard et la tradition biblique d'après les Sermons sur les Cantiques," *Sacris Eruditi* 2 (1960): 225–48.

55. Standaert, "L'image," pp. 118–21.

56. For a still insightful introduction see Étienne Gilson, *The Spirit of Mediaeval Philosophy* (New York: Scribner, 1940), chap. 11, "Self-Knowledge and Christian Socratism." The history of the Delphic maxim has been exhaustively studied by Pierre Courcelle, *Connais-toi toi-même. De Socrate à saint Bernard*, 3 vols. (Paris: Études Augustiniennes, 1974–75), 1:258–72 on Bernard. For more on Bernard's views, see Gilson, *Mystical Theology*, pp. 209–28; and Hiss, *Anthropologie*, pp. 31–41. Key texts include *SCC* 35–37 (1:248–55 and 2:3–14); *Div* 12.1 and 40.3 (6:127–28 and 236); *Hum* 4.15 (3:27–28). On the majesty and dignity of humanity, see, e.g., *Adv* 1.7 (4:166–67).

57. See, e.g., *Div* 45 (6:262–65), which analyzes the effects of original sin on the created trinity of *memoria, ratio, voluntas*. Cf *SCC* 11.5 (1:57–58).

58. *SCC* 81.7 (2:288.7–10): Et tamen, interveniente peccato, patitur quamdam vim et ipse, sed a voluntate, non a natura, ut ne sic quidem ingenita libertate privetur. Quod enim voluntarium, et liberum. Et quidem peccato factum, ut corpus quod corrumpitur aggravet animam, sed amore, non mole.

59. For an example of a negative passage on sexuality, see *SCC* 61.2 (2:148–49); for Bernard's attitude toward health, see *SCC* 30.10–12 (1:216–18). Passages like these, however, must be put in the full context of Bernard's thought. From this perspective, overemphasis on Bernard's negative statements about the body, as in Robert Bultot's "Spirituels et théologiens devant l'homme et le monde," *Revue Thomiste* 64 (1964): 517–48 (see pp. 530–31 on Bernard), have been rightly criticized by recent Bernardine scholarship, e.g., Emero Stiegman, "Action and Contemplation in Bernard's Sermons on the Song of Songs," in *On the Song of Songs III*, pp. vii–xix; and Casey, *Athirst for God*, pp. 171–82. See also F. Lazzari, "Le *contemptus mundi* chez S. Bernard," *Revue d'ascétique et de mystique* 4 (1965): 291–304.

60. E.g., *SCC* 82.5 (2:296.6–9); and *Ep* 174.7 (7:391–92).

61. See *Pre* 20.59 (3:292).

62. This is clear from *Dil* 8.23 and 11.30–33 (3:138–39 and 145–47). Cf. *Adv* 7.5 (4:194). On the importance of the resurrection of the body in Bernard, see Casey, *Athirst for God*, pp. 234–37.

63. On the basic goodness of sex in marriage, see *Pre* 15.42 (3:282.25–27): Nam et non tangere mulierem, meriti non est mediocris, et nullius tamen delicti propriam amplecti coniugem. For Bernard on marriage, see J. Leclercq, *Monks on Marriage: A Twelfth-Century View* (New York: Seabury, 1982), chap. 7; and Fassetta, "Le mariage spirituel," 257–61.

64. *Conv* 17.30 (4:106.18–21): Quod enim dum in hoc corpore sumus, peregrinamur a Domino, non utique corporis est culpa, sed huius quod adhuc scilicet corpus mortis, magis

autem corpus peccati sit caro, in qua bonum non est, sed potius lex peccati. A similar interpretation of Bernard's view of the body has been made by Glenn W. Olsen in his unpublished paper "Twelfth-Century Humanism Reconsidered: The Case of St. Bernard" (my thanks to the author for sending me a copy of this paper).

65. For the phrase *spiritualis vita,* see, e.g., *Div* 23.2 (6:179.10–12).

66. *Csi* 5.11.24 (3:486.23): . . . creans mentes ad se participandum.

67. For a study, see Denis Farkasfalvy, "The First Step in Spiritual Life: Conversion," in *La dottrina della vita spirituale,* pp. 65–84. Farkasfalvy identifies three meanings of *conversio* in Bernard: (1) turning away from sin; (2) joining the monastic life; and, most central, what I am calling the Augustinian sense; (3) "a beginning which persists by constantly producing new beginnings of a similar kind and thus permanently marks the whole spiritual enterprise" (p. 65).

68. See, e.g., *Hum* 3.9–12 (3:23–26); *SCC* 11.7–8, 42.7–9, 48.3–4 (1:58–59; 2:37–39 and 68–70); *In circumcisione* 2.1 (4:277–78). On this aspect of Bernard's thought, see especially Chrysogonus Waddell, "The Glorified Christ, Present and Future: The Eschatological Dynamic of the Spiritual Life," in *La dottrina della vita spirituale,* pp. 334–35.

69. The relationship between these two areas of Bernard's thought has been brought out by Roch Kereszty, "Relationship between Anthropology and Christology. St. Bernard, a Teacher for Our Age," in *La dottrina della vita spirituale,* pp. 271–99 (see also the response to this paper by M. Basil Pennington on pp. 301–6).

70. *Gra* 3.12 (3:26.3): Si non accessisset, non attraxisset; si non attraxisset, non extraxisset.

71. *SCC* 20.6 (1:118.21–26): Hanc enim arbitror praecipuam invisibili Deo fuisse causam, quod voluit in carne videri et cum hominibus homo conversari, ut carnalium videlicet, qui nisi carnaliter amare non poterant, cunctas primo ad suae carnis salutarem amorem affectiones retraherent, atque ita gradatim ad amorem perduceret spiritualem.

72. This point is well set forth by Kereszty, "Relationship between Anthropology and Christology," pp. 281–82, 288. For some other texts on the carnal love of Christ's humanity, see, e.g., *SCC* 43.3–4, 70.2 (2:42–43 and 208–09); *Dil* 8.23 and 15.39 (3:138–39 and 152–53); *Asc* 3.3 and 6.11 (5:132–33 and 156); *Div* 29.2–3 (6:211–12); etc. For general background, see the multi-author article "Humanité du Christ (Dévotion et Contemplation)," DS 7:1033–1108.

73. See Bernard's allegorical interpretation of Ps 18:6–7 as found in *SCC* 53.7–8 (2:99–101), and elsewhere.

74. St. Bernard's Christology has attracted much literature. Especially helpful are J.-M. Déchanet, "La christologie de s. Bernard," in *Saint Bernard Théologien,* pp. 78–91; A. Altermatt, "Christus pro nobis"; and a series of articles of A. van den Bosch published in *Cîteaux* 9– 10 (1958–59) and the *Collectanea Ordinis Cisterciensium Reformatorum* 21–23 (1959–61).

75. See, e.g., Augustine, *De gen. ad lit.* 1.4–5 (PL 34:249–50).

76. *Gra* 14.49 (3:201.13–19): Igitur qui recte sapiunt, triplicem confitetur operationem, non quidem liberi arbitrii, sed divinae gratiae in ipso, sive de ipso: prima, creatio; secunda, reformatio; tertia est consummatio. Primo namque in Christo creati in libertatem voluntatis, secunda reformamur per Christum in spiritum libertatis, cum Christo deinde consummandi in statum aeternitatis. Siquidem quod non erat, in illo creari oportuit qui erat, per formam reformari deformem, membra non perfici nisi cum capite.

77. *Dil* 5.15 (3:132.10–11).

78. See, e.g., *SCC* 82.7, 84.3 (2:297, 304).

79. See *In resurrectione* 1.8 and 16; *In octava paschae* 1.1; *Asc* 3.4 and 6.2–4 (5:83–84, 93, 112–13, 133, 151–52).

80. *SCC* 62.5 (2:158.20).

81. See my "Introduction" to *On Grace and Free Choice,* and the literature cited there.

82. See *SCC* 67.11–12 (2:195–96) on grace as prevenient and subsequent.

83. *SCC* 69.6 (2:200.14–16): Sufficit ad meritum scire quod non sufficiant merita. Sed ut ad meritum satis est de meritis non presumere, sic carere meritis, satis ad iudicium est.

84. *V Nat* 1.2 (4:199.11–12): Quare Filius Dei factus homo, nisi ut homines faciet filios Dei? See Irenaeus, *Adversus haereses* 3.18.7.

85. Among those who have commented on this aspect of Bernard's theology, see Jacques Blanpain, "Langage mystique, expression du désir dans les Sermons sur le Cantique des cantiques de Bernard de Clairvaux," *Collectanea Cisterciensia* 36 (1974): 45–68 and 226–47 (esp. 52–54, 63, 227); and Marsha L. Dutton, "Intimacy and Imitation: The Humanity of Christ in Cistercian Spirituality," in *Erudition at God's Service,* ed. John Sommerfeldt (Kalamazoo, MI: Cistercian Publications, 1987), pp. 33–69; eadem, "The Face and Feet of God: The Humanity of Christ in Bernard of Clairvaux and Aelred of Rievaulx," in *Bernardus Magister,* pp. 203–23.

86. Older works, such as Gilson, *Mystical Theology,* pp. 25–28; and Jean Daniélou, "S. Bernard et les Pères grecs," in *Saint Bernard Théologien,* pp. 46–55, which claimed heavy influence from a variety of Greek sources, have been modified by recent research. Despite Bernard's knowledge and use of Origen, the fundamentals of his thought are rooted in Augustine and Gregory the Great.

87. As recognized by Jaroslav Pelikan, *The Growth of Medieval Theology (600-1330)* (Chicago: University of Chicago Press, 1978), chap. 3.

88. *Nat BVM* 11 (5:282.19–25): Incomprehensibilis erat et inaccessibilis, invisibilis et inexcogitabilis omnino. Nunc vero comprehendi voluit, videri voluit, voluit cogitari. Quonam modo, inquis? Nimirum iacens in praesepio, in virginali gremio cubans, in monte pallens, liber inter mortuos et in inferno imperans, seu etiam tertia die resurgens et Apostolis loca clavorum victoriae signa demonstrans, novissime coram eis caeli secreta conscendens. Cf. *Pent* 2.5 (5:168) for a similar text.

89. *Div* 101 (6:368). Cf. *Dil* 3.10 (3:126) for another text stressing the role of the mysteries of Christ's life in our progress to God. Augustine too had insisted on the necessity of beginning on the level of carnal love in order to attain a spiritual love of Christ, though he did not give this a central role in his teaching (e.g., *De vera religione* 24.45 [PL 34:141], and *Sermo* 143.4 [PL 38:786], citing 2 Cor 5:16). Similarly, Bernard would have been familiar with the Gregorian Preface for Christmas which says ... ut dum visibiliter Deum cognoscimus, per hunc in invisibilium amorem rapiamur. Nevertheless, the abbot's development of the theme of the transition from carnal to spiritual love marks a new moment in twelfth-century mystical theology. For more on this theme in Bernard, see J.-C. Didier, "L'ascension mystique et l'union mystique par l'humanité du Christ selon saint Bernard," *La vie spirituelle, Supplement* 25 (1930): [140]–[155].

90. On the nativity, see the six sermons *V Nat* (4:197–244) and the five sermons *Nat* (4:244–70).

91. Bernard's devotion to the Passion is best seen in his sermon for the Wednesday in Holy Week, *IV HM* (5:56–67). See also *SCC* 43.3–5, 61.3, 62.1 and 7 (2:42–44, 149–50, 154–55, 159–60); and *Div* 63.1 (6:296).

92. E.g., R. W. Southern, *The Making of the Middle Ages* (New Haven and London: Yale University Press, 1953), pp. 231–34.

93. E.g., *SCC* 15 and 16.5 (1:82–88, 97–98).

94. See Jean Leclercq, "Le mystère de l'Ascension dans les sermons de saint Bernard," *Collectanea Ordinis Cisterciensium Reformatorum* 15 (1953): 81–88; B. McGinn, "Resurrection and Ascension in the Christology of the Early Cistercians," *Cîteaux* 30 (1979): 5–22; and Casey, *Athirst for God,* pp. 237–41.

95. *SCC* 79.2 (2:273.20–274.7): Et ut quod dico clarius sit, si Dominus meus Iesus surrexisset quidem a mortuis, sed ad caelos minime ascendisset, non poterat dici de eo quod pertran-

sierat, sed transierat tantum; ac per hoc sponsam illum quaerentem transire solummodo oporteret, non pertransire. . . . Igitur credere resurrectionem, transire est; credere autem ascensionem, pertransire. . . . Caput nostrum punctis praecessit duobus atque transcendit, resurrectione, ut iam diximus, et ascensione. Etenim PRIMITIAE CHRISTUS (1 Cor 15:23). Quod si ille praecessit, et fides nostra. Ubi enim illa eum non sequeretur? Cf. *Div* 123.1 (6:400). On the translation of *pertransierat* as "passed beyond" in relation to *transierat* as "passed from" [death to life], see Casey, *Athirst for God,* pp. 239–40.

96. *SCC* 20.6–9 (1:118–21).

97. *Div* 61.1 (6:293.14–16): Ascendit quidem semel Christus corporaliter super altitudinem caelorum, sed et nunc ascendit quotidie spiritualiter in cordibus electorum. Cf. *Asc* 3.4 and 6.11–12 (5:133, 156–57).

98. *Div* 60.2 (6:292.5–6): Sic per incarnationis suae mysterium descendit et ascendit Dominus, relinquens nobis exemplum ut sequamur vestigia eius. Cf. *Div* 60.3–4.

99. E.g., *SCC* 15.6, 21.2–3, 22.9, 24.8 (1:87, 122–24, 135–36, 161–62).

100. On imitating Christ's humility, see, e.g., *SCC* 42.7–8 (2:37–38); on the imitation of his love, e.g., *SCC* 18.4 and 20.3–9 (1:105–6, 115–21); and *Dil* 9.26 (3:141).

101. *SCC* 20.9 (1:120.22–24): Bonus tamen amor iste carnalis, per quem vita carnalis excluditur, contemnitur et vincitur mundus. Proficitur autem in eo, cum sit rationalis; perficitur, cum efficitur etiam spiritualis. Cf. *SCC* 75.6–9 (2:250–52). This threefold advance in love (*carnalis-rationalis-spiritualis*) will be richly developed by William of St. Thierry; see below, chapter 6, pp. 234–38. For a summary of Bernard's teaching on the imitation of Christ, see DS 7:1571–73. On this form of "ontological" imitation, see C. Waddell, "The Glorified Christ" pp. 327–42.

102. *SCC* 12.11 (1:67.22–25): Quod etsi nemo nostrum sibi arroget praesumat, ut animam suam quis audeat sponsam Domini appellare, quoniam tamen de Ecclesia sumus, quae merito hoc nomine et re gloriatur, non immerito gloriae huius participium usurpamus.

103. *SCC* 68.1 (2:196.21–22): Quae est sponsa, et quis est sponsus? Hic Deus noster est, et illa, si audeo dicere, nos sumus, cum reliqua quidem multitudine captivorum, quos ipse novit. Cf. *SCC* 57.3 and 61.2 (2:120–21 and 148–49); and *In dominica I post octavum epiphaniae* 2.2–4 (4:320–22).

104. On the relation of Bernard to Origen, see Jean Leclercq, "Origène au XIIe siècle," *Irenikon* 24 (1951): 425–39; and the same author's *Receuil,* 1:281–83.

105. On Bernard's position in the history of Song of Songs exegesis, see Friedrich Ohly, *Hoheliedstudien: Grundzüge einer Geschichte der Hoheliedauslegung des Abendlandes bis zum 1200* (Wiesbaden: Steiner, 1958), esp. pp. 136–57.

106. For an introduction to Bernard's ecclesiology, see Yves Congar, "L'ecclésiologie de S. Bernard," in *Saint Bernard Théologien,* pp. 136–90. For the institutional aspects of Bernard's ecclesiology, see Bernard Jacqueline, *Episcopat et papauté chez Saint Bernard de Clairvaux* (Saint-Lo: Editions Henri Jacqueline, 1975).

107. *SCC* 27.6 (1:186.2–8): Ad sponsam veniebat, et absque sponsa non veniebat. Quaerebat sponsam, et sponsa cum ipso erat, . . . placuit ei et de hominibus convocare Ecclesiam, atque uniri illi quae de caelo est, ut sit una sponsa et unus sponsus.

108. *SCC* 27.7 (1:186.12–26): Habes utrumque de caelo, et sponsum scilicet Iesum, et sponsam Ierusalem. Et ille quidem ut videretur, semetipsum exinanivit formam servi accipiens, et habitu inventus est homo. At illam, in quanam putamus forma seu specie, aut in quo habitu, descendentem vidit ille qui vidit? . . . Dum enim sanctus ille Emmanuel terris intulit magisterium disciplinae caelestis, dum supernae illius Ierusalem, quae est mater noster, visibilis quaedam imago et species decoris eius, per ipsum nobis et in Christo expressa, innotuit, quid, nisi in sponso sponsam, perspeximus, unum eumdemque Dominum gloriae admirantes, et sponsum decoratum corona, et sponsam ornatam monilibus suis? Ipse igitur qui descendit,

ipse est quo ascendit: ut nemo ascendat in caelum, nisi qui de caelo descendit, unus idemque Dominus, et sponsis in capite, et sponsa in corpore. On the preexistence and predestination of the church, see also *SCC* 78.4–6 (2:268–70).

109. On the importance of ascent and descent in Bernard's theology, see my paper "Resurrection and Ascension," pp. 10–13.

110. On the role of the angels in Bernard, see, e.g., *SCC* 7.4–5, 19, 31.5, 41.3–4 (on which see the discussion below, p. 210), 52.6, 76.7, 77.3–4, and 78.1–2, to cite only texts from the *Sermones super Cantica.*

111. *OS* 5.6 and 11 (5:365 and 369–70).

112. *SCC* 68.4 (2:199.9–10): Nonne de statu et consummatione Ecclesiae finis omnium pendet?

113. See esp. *SCC* 14.1–4 (1:75–78), and 60.8 (2:146–47). There is a forceful attack on the Jews in *SCC* 60.1–5 (2:142–45); and Bernard, like other medieval exegetes, often criticized the Jews for "literal" exegesis, e.g., *SCC* 73.2 (2:234).

114. See *SCC* 79.5–6 (2:275–76).

115. *SCC* 23.1 (1:139.9–11): Sic et ista, quantumvis proficiat, quamlibet promoveatur, cura, providentia atque affectu ab his, quas in Evangelio genuit, nunquam amovetur, numquam sua viscera obliviscetur.

116. See, e.g., *SCC* 23.2 and 41.6 (1:139–40, and 2:32); Sept 1.2 (4:346). On this theme, see Caroline Walker Bynum, *Jesus as Mother: Studies in the Spirituality of the High Middle Ages* (Berkeley: University of California Press, 1982), chap. 4.

117. E.g., Augustine, *De baptismo* 7.25.48 and 51.99 (PL 43:233–34 and 241).

118. See *SCC* 25.3–4 (1:164–65). This is one of the several meanings Bernard advances for Song 1:4.

119. *SCC* 12.7 (1:65.2–3): Ipsa est carius corpus Christi, quod ne mortem gustaret, morti illud alterum traditum fuisse nullus christianus ignorat. Cf. *SCC* 14.5 (1:78–79) on the Bride's perfection.

120. *V Nat* 3.1 (4:212.9–11): Nimirum ipsa est quae vulnerata cor eius, et in ipsam abyssum secretorum Dei oculum contemplationis immersit, ut et illi in suo, et sibi in eius corde perennem faciat mansionem.

121. Among the more detailed treatments, see *In cena Domini* (5:67–72). References to the Eucharist can be found, e.g., in *Palm* 3.4 (5:54) and *SCC* 31.10 (1:225).

122. *Div* 33.8 (6:227.4–10): Christus Dominus mons est, mons coagulatus et mons pinguis. Mons est sublimitate, coagulatus multorum congerie, pinguis caritate. Et nunc vide quomodo trahat ad se omnia, quomodo et omnia uniantur unitate substantiali, personali, spirituali, sacramentali. Habet in se Patrem, cum quo est una substantia; habet assumptum hominem, cum quo est una persona; habet adhaerentem sibi fidelem animam, cum qua est spiritus unus; habet sponsam Ecclesiam unam omnium electorum, cum qua est caro una.

123. *SCC* 83.4 (2:300.28–301.2).

124. Among the key sermons dealing with mystical contemplation are *SCC* 7, 20, 23, 31, 42, 45, 52, 57, 67, 69, 71, 74, 79, and 83. Almost all the *SCC* sermons, however, contain materials worth studying.

125. The importance of the texts from 1 John was first noted by Gilson, *Mystical Theology,* pp. 22–25. On 1 Cor 6:17, which is quoted by Bernard at least fifty times, see Gilson, chap. 5 passim; Casey, *Athirst for God,* pp. 201–8; and B. McGinn, "Love, Knowledge and *Unio Mystica* in the Western Christian Tradition," in *Mystical Union and Monotheistic Faith,* ed. M. Idel and B. McGinn (New York: Macmillan, 1989), passim. Perhaps the single most quoted text in Bernard's oeuvre, however, as noted by Farkasfalvy ("The First Step in the Spiritual Life: Conversion," p. 67 n.3), appearing fifty-seven times, is Matt 11:33 (*Discite a me qui mitis sum et humilis corde*), a good expression of the christological core of Bernard's mysticism. 2 Cor. 3:18

(*Nos autem vero omnes revelata facie gloriam Domini speculantes in eandem imaginem transformamur a claritate in claritatem tamquam a Domini Spiritu*) is usually employed to express the gradual, though always imperfect, vision we can enjoy in this life, while texts like 1 John 3:2 (*Scimus quoniam cum apparuerit, similes ei erimus, quoniam videbimus eum sicuti est*) indicate the immense gap that always exists between vision here and there. On Phil 3:20–21, which the abbot cites twenty-seven times, see Waddell, "The Glorified Christ, Present and Future," pp. 327–28.

126. Bernard's mysticism is so much a part of his thought that it is almost impossible to make a bibliography of it. All good studies of the abbot are useful for the topic; indifferent works, even those that include the terms "mysticism" or "mystical" in the title, need not be mentioned. The most recent attempt at a summary is to be found in Kurt Ruh, *Geschichte der abendländische Mystik: Band I, Die Grundlegung durch die Kirchenväter und die Mönchstheologie des 12. Jahrhunderts* (Munich: Beck, 1990), pp. 226-75.

127. *SCC* 83.1 (2:298.20–21): . . . non modo unde respirare in spem veniae, in spem misericordiae queat, sed etiam unde audeat adspirare ad nuptias Verbi. . . .

128. E.g., *SCC* 46.5, 57.4, 68.4, and 79.1 (2:58–59, 121–22, 198–99, 272–73).

129. On the monastery as the heavenly Jerusalem on earth, see, e.g., *SCC* 55.2 (2:112); *Ep* 459 and 544 (8:437 and 511–12).

130. *Hum*, proem (3:13.19–20). On the monastery as the *schola dilectionis*, or *schola caritatis*, see *Div* 121 (6:398–99), as well as the discussion in Gilson, *Mystical Theology*, pp. 60–84.

131. *Div* 22 (6:170–78).

132. On Bernard's letters, see Jean Leclercq, "Lettres de S. Bernard: histoire ou littérature?," *Studi medievali* 3a serie 12 (1971): 1–74; and his "Introduzione" in *Opere di San Bernardo*, 6:ix–xxxvii.

133. To cite just one example, see *Ep* 110.1 (8:282.12–13), which speaks of a new monk as "abrasa *spurcitia vitae saecularis ac terreno deterso pulvere* [my italics], caelesti mansioni fiat idoneus."

134. Still, Bernard addressed his central mystical treatise, the *Dil*, to Cardinal Haimeric; and in *Pre* 1.2 he says that the RB is of profit to those who receive it, but is "no obstacle if it is not undertaken" (*non tamen, si non suscipitur, obest* [3:255.14–15]).

135. *SCC* 3.4 (1:16.14–15): Nolo repente fieri summus: paulatim proficere volo. Cf. *In natali S. Andreae* 1.10 (5:433.22–24): Nemo repente fit summus: ascendendo, non volendo apprehenditur summitas scalae. Ascendamus ergo velut duobus quibusdam pedibus, meditatione et oratione.

136. E.g., *SCC* 9.2 (1:42–43). The tension between the desire to attain the experience of union with God and the continuing recognition of sin and the necessity for repentence–a tension so well figured in the dialectic between the presence and the absence of the Divine Lover characteristic of the Song of Songs–was often referred to by Bernard as *alternatio* or *vicissitudo*. See Casey, *Athirst for God*, pp. 54, 59–62, 251–80; and Jean Mouroux, "Sur les critères de l'expérience spirituelle d'après les Sermons sur le Cantique des Cantiques," in *Saint Bernard Théologien*, pp. 261–62.

137. For Bernard, every form of ascetic effort, especially the asceticism of humility and voluntary poverty, has a mystical aim in the context of the entire spiritual journey, as *SCC* 85.12 (2:315) and other texts make clear. See E. Stiegman, "Introduction," in *Song of Songs II*, pp. xiv-xvii.

138. *SCC* 18.6 (1:107–08). These are *compunctio, devotio, paenitentiae labor, pietatis opus, orationis studium, contemplationis otium,* and *plenitudo dilectionis*, all of which constitute the *infusio* of the Holy Spirit into the soul that prepares the way for the *effusio* of love upon our neighbor. For a study of this text, see Raffaele Fassetta, "Le rôle de l'Esprit-Saint dans la vie spirituelle selon Bernard de Clairvaux," in *La dottrina della vita spirituale*, pp. 359–87.

139. *SCC* 85.1 (*SCC* 2:307.14–17): Quaerit anima Verbum, cui consentiat ad correptionem, quo illuminetur ad cognitionem, cui innitatur ad virtutem, quo reformetur ad sapientiam, cui conformetur ad decorem, cui maritetur ad fecunditatem, quo fruatur ad iucunditatem.

140. One fourfold division not tied to the categories of love is that found in *Palm* 2.7 (5:50–51), which distinguishes four kinds of souls who accompany Christ in his entry to Jerusalem.

141. *Dil* 8.23–10.29 and the summary in 15.39 (3:138–44 and 152–53), to be treated in detail below. Cf. *Ep* 2.9 (7:58–59).

142. These four grades are suggested at several places in *SCC*, though they are not always clearly outlined as four. In *SCC* 83.5 (2:301), we hear of the love of *mercenarius, filius* and *sponsa*; in *SCC* 7.2 (1:31–32) of *servus, mercenarius, discipulus, filius* and *sponsa*. The notion that spousal love is the highest form of the varieties of loves, of course, is also found in the commentary tradition on the Song; see, e.g., Gregory the Great, *In Cant.* 8 (CC 144:10–11).

143. Bernard comes closest to the traditional formula in *In natali S. Andreae* 5: Unde et triplicem licet considerare gradum: incipientium, proficientium, perfectorum. Initium enim sapientiae, timor Domini; medium, spes; caritas, plenitudo (5:430.9–11). On the triadic formulas in Bernard, see Casey, *Athirst for God*, pp. 245–51; and M. Basil Pennington, "The Three Stages of Spiritual Growth according to St. Bernard," *Studia Monastica* 11 (1969): 315–26.

144. An earlier version of the three kisses motif appears in the *Brevis Commentatio* 5 (PL 184:411C–12A). This is basically similar, though the third kiss is described as the *osculum oris sui*, not as the *osculum de osculo oris sui* (see *SCC* 8.8 [1:41]). For the context of Bernard's interpretation of the kiss, see Aimé Solignac, "Osculum," DS 11:1012–26.

145. *SCC* 4.4 (1:20.6–8): Invenit profecto apud Deum et verecundia confessio, quo se humiliando deiciat, et prompta devotio, ubi se innovando reficiat, et iucunda contemplatio, ubi excedendo quiescat. Cf. *Hum* 2.4–5 (3:19–20), where the three foods of the soul are described as *humilitas, caritas*, and *contemplatio*.

146. *Ann* 1.4 (5:15).

147. On the first two ointments, see *SCC* 10.4–10 (1:50–64). The third ointment of *pietas*, analyzed in *SCC* 12 (1:60–67), is here not so much the contemplative experience of advanced souls as the fruit which this brings, that is, active compassion for the whole Body of Christ.

148. *Asc* 2.6 (5:130.19–23): Et primi quidem felices, qui in patientia sua possident animas suas; secundi feliciores, quia ex voluntate sua confitentur ei; tertii felicisssimi, qui in profundissima Dei misericordia, quasi quodammodo sepulta iam arbitrii potestate, in divitias gloriae in spiritu ardoris rapiuntur, nescientes sive in corpore, sive extra corpus, hoc solum scientes, quod rapti sunt (cf. 2 Cor 12:2). The first two groups are based on Song 1:3, on which see *SCC* 21 and 23 to be considered below. *Quad* 6.3 (4:378–79) also details a threefold program based on Paul's rapture described in 2 Corinthians 12.

149. *SCC* 57.9–11 (2:124–26). The passage quoted is from 125.18–20: . . . quae caelesti desiderio fulgens, supernae contemplationis decorem se induit, horis dumtaxat, quibus commode et opportune id potest.

150. *SCC* 57.9 (2:125.33–126.2): Perfecto omnis reputabitur, in cuius anima tria haec congruenter atque opportune concurrere videbuntur, ut et gemere pro se, et exsultare in Deo noverit, simul et proximorum utilitatibus potens sit subvenire. . . .

151. *Asspt* 3.4–7 (5:241–44). On the use of Mary and Martha as types of the contemplative and active lives, see below pp. 222–23.

152. *SCC* 74.5–7 (2:242–44), to be treated below. See also *SCC* 12.8, 14.6, 23.15–16, 43.3–4, 51.3, 57.5, 69.1 and 82.1 (*SBOp* 1:65, 79–80, 148–50; 2:42–43, 85–86, 122, 202 and

292). Texts like *SCC* 17.2 (1:99) are expressed in a personal way without being overtly auto-biographical.

153. Bernard's views on the nature of religious experience have been the subject of a number of studies, notably, Jean Mouroux, "Sur les critères de l'expérience spirituelle d'après les Sermons sur le Cantique des Cantiques," in *Saint Bernard Théologien*, pp. 251–67; Brian Stock, "Experience, Praxis, Work, and Planning in Bernard of Clairvaux: Observations on the *Sermones in Cantica*," in *The Cultural Context of Medieval Learning*, ed. J. E. Murdoch and E. D. Sylla (Dordrecht: Reidel, 1976), pp. 219–68, and more fully in stock, *The Implications of Literacy: Written Language and Models of Interpretation in the Eleventh and Twelfth Centuries* (Princeton: Princeton University Press, 1983), pp. 403–54; Ulrich Kopf, *Religiöse Erfahrung in der Theologie Bernhards von Clairvaux* (Tübingen: Mohr, 1980), and in summary fashion in his "Die Rolle der Erfahrung im religiösen Leben nach dem heiligen Bernhard," in *La dottrina della vita spirituale*, pp. 307–19; Bernard Bonowitz, "The Role of Experience in the Spiritual Life," in *La dottrina della vita spirituale*, pp. 321–25; and Pierre Miquel, *Le vocabulaire latin de l'expérience spirituelle* (Paris: Beauchesne, 1989), pp. 97–106.

154. *SCC* 22.2 (1:130.7–8): Porro in huiusmodi non capit intelligentia, nisi quantum experientia attingit (here I use the felicitous translation of *Song of Songs II*, p. 15). For some similar appeals to experience, see, e.g., *SCC* 4.1, 9.3 and 5 and 7, 21.4–5, 31.4, 50.6, 52.1–2, 69.6–7, 84.6–7. Also in this vein are those passages where the abbot insists that love alone can grasp the meaning of the Song of Songs, e.g., *SCC* 1.11 and 79.1 (1:7; 2:272–73). Comparable insistence on the necessity for experience is found throughout Bernard's writings, e.g., *Conv* 13.25 (4:99.16–17): Solus est Spiritus qui revelat: sine causa paginam consulis; experientiam magis require.

155. E.g., *SCC* 28.8–9 (1:197–98), and *Quad* 5.5 (4:374.20–21): Ergo iudicium fidei sequere, et non experimentum tuum, quoniam fides quidem verax, sed et experimentum fallax.

156. On the theme of the two books, see H. de Lubac, *Exégèse médiévale*, 1:121–25.

157. For a study of the term *liber experientiae*, which Bernard seems to have created, see Jean Leclercq, "Aspects spirituels de la symbolique du livre au XIIe siècle," in *L'homme devant Dieu: Mélanges offerts au Père Henri de Lubac*, 3 vols. (Paris: Aubier, 1962), 2:63–72.

158. See Kopf, *Religiöse Erfahrung*, especially his summary on pp. 224–37. A good description is given by Bonowitz ("The Role of Experience," p. 323): ". . . true experience of God is the registration in the human person of a constant divine self-communication; it is the means of educating and converting the heart by mediating to it the knowledge and the love of God; and it itself is the relationship with God at the time it is occuring, since what the person meets in his experience is not his own interiority but the Persons of the Blessed Trinity."

159. This point was grasped by Ohly, who noted how Bernard's exegesis of the Song involved a "Verinnerlichung der Heilsgeschichte" (*Hoheliedstudien*, pp. 145–49). From a different perspective, see the remarks of Brian Stock on how the relations between word, text, and experience in the *Sermones super cantica* helped form a special "textual community" (*Implications of Literacy*, pp. 405–7, 451–54).

160. Bernard, like earlier commentators, warns that the Song will be a temptation or an embarrassment unless it finds a reader who is able to translate it into the book of spiritual experience (see, e.g., *SCC* 1.8, 14.5, 23.16, 31.6, 61.2, and 75.2), but his new reading has a deeper ground for this insistence.

161. On the spiritual senses in Origen and Augustine, see *Foundations of Mysticism*, pp. 121–24, 239–40. For a general view of the development of this important aspect of the Christian mystical tradition, see now Mariette Canévet, "Sens spirituel," DS 14:598–617.

162. A brief theoretical discussion does occur in *Div* 10.2–4 (6:122–24), where the five sense are compared to five forms of love with sight equated with the highest type (*amor devotus*). Cf. *Div* 116 (6:394).

163. *SCC* 24.6 (1:158.2–3): . . . oculos, id est internos sensus atque affectus. . . .

164. *SCC* 28.5–8 (1:195–98). This is a recurring theme; see, e.g., *SCC* 53.2, 59.9–10, 76.2, etc. (2:96, 140–41, 255).

165. *SCC* 28.9 (1:198.13–14): Et utique poterit, sed affectu, non manu; voto, non oculo; fide, non sensibus.

166. *SCC* 28.9–10 (1:198.22–23 and 199.2): Denique comprehendit suo illo mystico ac profundo sinu . . . tanges manu fidei, desiderii digito, devotionis amplexu; tanges oculo mentis.

167. *SCC* 28.10 (1:199.8–9).

168. *SCC* 67.4–7 (2:190–93). On the sacred "belch" (*ructus*), see also *SCC* 49.4 (2:75.19) and *Adv* 3.2 (4.176).

169. *SCC* 67.6 (2:192.8 and 10–11): Laetabitur iustus in Domino, gustu experiens quod ego sentio odoratu. . . . Porro spectare gustare est, et videre quoniam suavis est Dominus. On the role of the good odor of the brethren in the community, see *SCC* 14.6 (1:80). For Bernard's views on community, see Jean Leclercq, "Saint Bernard of Clairvaux and the Contemplative Community," in *Contemplative Community: An Interdisciplinary Symposium*, ed. M. Basil Pennington (Washington: Cistercian Publications, 1972), pp. 61–113; and Michael Casey, "*In communi vita fratrum*: St. Bernard's Teaching on Cenobitic Solitude," in *La dottrina della vita spirituale*, pp. 243–61.

170. *SCC* 67.6 (2:192.18–19): . . . et per odorem exspectationis pervenit ad gustum contemplationis.

171. *Dil* 9.26 (3:141.3–6): Ex occasione quippe frequentium necessitatum crebris necesse est interpellationibus Deum ab homine frequentari, frequentando gustari, gustando probari quam suavis est Dominus. Ita fit, ut ad diligendum pure Deum plus iam ipsius alliciat gustata suavitas quam urgeat nostra necessitas. . . .

172. *SCC* 50.8 (2:83.8–17): Quod flens dico: quousque odoramus et non gustamus, prospicientes patriam et non apprehendentes, suspirantes et de longe salutantes? O Veritas, exsulum patria, exsilii finis! Video te, sed intrare non sinor, carne retentus, sed nec dignus admitti, peccatis sordens. O Sapientia, quae attingis a fine usque ad finem fortiter in instituendis et continendis rebus, et disponis omnia suaviter in beandis et ordinandis affectibus! Dirige actus nostros, prout tua veritas aeterna requirit, ut possit unusquisque nostrum secure in te gloriari et dicere, quia ORDINAVIT IN ME CARITATEM.

173. For another treatment of these three locations, see *Div* 92 (6:346–48). For remarks on *SCC* 23, see Stock, *Implications of Literacy*, pp. 435–38.

174. *SCC* 23.3 (1:140.19–20): Sit itaque hortus plana et simplex historia, sit cellarium moralis sensus, sit cubiculum arcanum theoricae contemplationis. On the use of *theoria* in monastic theology, see Jean Leclercq, *Études sur le vocabulaire monastique du moyen âge*, Studia Anselmiana 48 (Rome: Herder, 1961), chap. 3.

175. *SCC* 23.9 (1:144.22–23): Tamen si nihil omnino scirem, nihil dicerem.

176. *SCC* 23.14 (1:147.24): Instructio doctos reddit, affectio sapientes.

177. *SCC* 23.14 (1:148.5–6): . . . quia tunc primum animae Deus sapit, cum eam afficit ad timendum, non cum instruit ad sciendum.

178. *SCC* 23.15 (1:148.17–20): Sed est locus ubi vere quiescens et quietus cernitur Deus: locus omnino, non iudicis, non magistri, sed sponsi, et qui mihi quidem–nam de aliis nescio–, plane cubiculum sit, si quando in illum contigerit introduci. Sed, heu! rara hora et parva mora! This final phrase, as noted in chapter 4 (pp. 142–43), is taken from John of Fécamp. Bernard echoes this succinct formula in several other places, e.g., *SCC* 85.3 (2:316.8): . . . sed breve momentum et experimentum rarum!; and *Gra* 5.15 (3:177.15): . . . et hoc ex parte, et parte satis modica, viceque rarissima.

179. *SCC* 23.15 (1:149.7-10): Hos ergo adverti quasi numquam peccasse: quoniam etsi qua deliquisse videntur in tempore, non apparent in aeternitate, quia caritas Patris ipsorum cooperit multitudinem peccatorum.

180. *Pre* 19.60 (3:293.4). Cf. *Conv* 12.24 (4:98.6-9).

181. *Dil* 4.11-12 (3:127-29). Cf. *In festo S. Martini* 12 (5:407).

182. E.g., *SCC* 56.4 (2:116). Luke Anderson, "The Rhetorical Epistemology in Saint Bernard's *Super Cantica*," distinguishes between the divine presence *intentionaliter*, that is, insofar as God is known, which is always limited, and the divine presence *tendentionaliter*, that is, as he is desired, which is directed toward his very being. He concludes (citing *SCC* 83.3): "The bride's love in the form of *desiderium*, stirred up by knowledge's intentionality, follows fleetfooted toward the Bridegroom's *proprium esse*, and *tendentionaliter*" (p. 101).

183. *SCC* 27.8-10 (1:187-89), esp. 189:15-16: Ergo quantitatis cuiusque animae aestimetur de mensura caritatis quam habet. In *Res* 2.1-3 (5:95-96) Bernard distinguishes between those Christ inhabits by faith alone and those in whom he has begun to live through the active love of the Holy Spirit.

184. E.g., *SCC* 4.1 (1:19.3-5): ... aut ipsius etiam indultoris et benefactoris sui praesentiam, eo quidem modo quo in corpore fragili possibile est, obtinet intueri.

185. Bernard tends to speak of the *Verbum incarnatum* when talking of the marriage of Christ and the church, and he uses *Verbum* alone when describing the union of Christ and the soul (see Fassetta, "Le mariage spirituel," p. 255).

186. See *SCC* 8.3-6 (1:37-40). Another version of this sermon appears as *Div* 89 (6:335-36). The importance of the Holy Spirit in Bernard's mysticism is summarized by R. Fassetta, "Le rôle de l'Esprit-Saint," as follows: "La doctrine spirituelle de Bernard, malgré toute la luxuriance de ses développements, se structure et s'unifie autour de cette intuition fondamentale: l'Esprit-Saint est l'Amour" (p. 387), thus emphasizing the deep inner harmony between the mysticism of Bernard and William of St. Thierry, despite real differences in their respective development of shared themes.

187. But see, e.g., *SCC* 11.4-6 (1:57-58), where the three Persons of the Trinity, in good Augustinian fashion, perfect the soul's three faculties of *ratio, voluntas,* and *memoria.* Cf. *SCC* 42.10 and 69.2 (2:39-40 and 203), as well as *Div* 45 (6:262-65).

188. *Hum* 6.19-8.23 (3:30-35). See the translation and commentary in Gilson, *Mystical Theology,* pp. 99-106.

189. *Hum* 7.21 (3:32.16-19): ... tandem iam perfectam animam, propter humilitatem sine macula, propter caritatem sine ruga, cum nec voluntas rationi repugnat, nec ratio veritatem dissimulat, gloriosam sibi sponsam Pater conglutinat. ... The text concludes with a citation of Song 1:3.

190. See *Hum* 7.21 (3:32.27-33.7).

191. There are, of course, other passages in his writings that suggest a trinitarian mysticism, e.g., *Dil* 4.13 (3:130), and *V Nat* 2.7 (4:209-10).

192. R. Fassetta rightly says that "la mystique de S. Bernard s'achève en communion trinitaire" ("Le rôle de l'Esprit-Saint," p. 389); but Bernard is less consistently trinitarian than many other mystics, including his friend William of St. Thierry.

193. E.g., *SCC* 17.1-2 and 8 (1:98-99 and 102-03). Cf. *Div* 18.1 (6:157) on the joy experienced through the presence of the Holy Spirit.

194. E.g., *Asc* 3.2-4 (5:132-33), where Christ illumines the intellect and the Holy Spirit purges the affection.

195. E.g., *SCC* 69.2 (2:203), where approaching the Word means to be instructed with Wisdom, and the coming of the Father signifies being moved to the love of Wisdom. Cf. 69.6 (2:205-06).

196. *SCC* 29.9 (1:145.1–2): Non omnibus uno in loco frui datur grata et secreta sponsi praesentia, sed ut cuique paratum est a Patre ipsius.

197. *SCC* 57.4 (2:121.28–29): ... quantumlibet is qui in spiritu visitat, clandestinus veniat et furtivus, utpote verecundus amator. Cf. *SCC* 9.4 (1:45.3).

198. *SCC* 57.5–7 (2:122–24). The passage cited here is 123.27–124.3: At vero ignis qui Deus est consumit quidem, sed non affligit, ardet suaviter, desolatur feliciter. ... Ergo in virtute qua immutaris, et in amore quo inflammaris, Dominum praesentem intellige.

199. Origen, *Homilia in Cantica* 1.7. See the discussion of this text in *Foundations of Mysticism*, pp. 123–24.

200. *SCC* 74.2–7 (2:240–44).

201. *SCC* 74.5 (2:242.13–22): Nunc vero sustinete modicum quid insipientiae meae. Volo dicere, nam et hoc pactus sum, quomodo mecum agitur in eiusmodi. Non expedit quidem. Sed prodar sane ut prosim, et, si profeceritis vos, meam insipientiam consolabor; et si non, meam insipientiam confitebor. Fateor et mihi adventasse Verbum–in insipientia dico–et pluries. Cumque saepius intraverit ad me, non sensi aliquoties cum intravit. Adesse sensi, afuisse recordor; interdum et praesentire potui introitum eius, sentire numquam, sed ne exitum quidem. Nam unde in animam meam venerit, quove abierit denuo eam dimittens, sed et qua introierit vel exierit, etiam nunc ignorare me fateor. ...

202. Ibid. (2:243.7–8): ... sed ille beatus est, in quo est ipsum, qui illi vivit, qui eo movetur.

203. *SCC* 74.6 (2:243.19–20): ... tantum ex motu cordis, sicut praefatus sum, intellexi praesentiam eius. The whole of this magnificent passage (243.9–27) with its strophic presentation of the effects of the Word's visit on the soul deserves a larger analysis than can be given here.

204. There are a number studies of Bernard's terminology of love and desire. See especially Casey, *Athirst for God*, chap. 3; Gilson, *Mystical Theology*, chap. 5; and J. Blanpain, "Langage mystique, expression du désir," pp. 47–68.

205. See Gilson, *Mystical Theology*, pp. 22–25, on the importance of this text for Bernard.

206. *SCC* 59.1 (2:136.7–9): Amat et Deus, nec aliunde hoc habet, sed ipse est unde amat. Et ideo vehementius, quia non amorem tam habet quam hoc est ipse.

207. *Csi* 5.13–14.28–32 (3:489–93). Bernard was probably basing his discussion of Gregory the Great, *Mor.* 10.9.15 (CC 143:548–49). On Bernard's doctrine of God, see Denis Farkasfalvy, "La conoscenza di Dio secondo San Bernardo," in *Studi su San Bernardo di chiaravalle nell'ottavo centenario della canonizzazione* (Rome: Editiones Cistercienses, 1975), pp. 201–14.

208. *Csi* 5.13.28 (3:491.8–9): Omnem non modo affectionem, sed et cogitationem excedit. ...

209. *SCC* 26.5 (1:173.16–17): Porro impassibilis est Deus, sed non incompassibilis, cui proprium est misereri semper et parcere.

210. For some other key appearnaces of this theme, see, e.g., *Dil* 1.1 and 7.22 (3:120.10–14 and 137.18–21); *SCC* 20.2 (1:115), and 57.6, 67.8–10, 69.7–8, 71.10, and especially 84.1–7 (2:123, 193–94, 206–07, 221–22, 303–07). Cf. *Ep* 107.7 (7:272–73). See the discussion in Casey, *Athirst for God*, pp. 73–74.

211. *SCC* 45.8 (2:54.29–55.4): Siquidem pulchritudo illius dilectio eius, et ideo maior, quia praeveniens. Medullis proinde cordis et intimarum vocibus affectionum tanto amplius atque ardentius clamitat sibi diligendum, quanto id prius sensit diligens quam dilectum. Itaque locutio Verbi infusio doni, responsio animae cum gratiarum actione admiratio. Et idcirco plus diligit, quod se sentit in diligendo victam; et ideo plus miratur, quod praeventem agnoscit.

212. The four fundamental *affectus* are *amor et laetitia, timor et tristitia*, on which see *Div* 50.2 (6:271–72). The term *affectus* and its cognate *affectio* are among the most complex in

Bernard's vocabulary. *Affectus,* derived from *afficere* (i.e., *facere ad,* "to do something to someone") is primarily passive in connotation, indicating the effect in a recipient of some action proceeding from an agent, i.e., from an *affectio.* (Thus, God can have an *affectio* but not an *affectus.*) But because the *affectus* given us by God's prior love is the source of our own various *affectiones,* Bernard, William of St. Thierry, and other Cistercians often used the terms interchangeably. It is important to remember that *affectus* and *affectio* are primarily ontological terms for the Cistercian authors, that is, they indicate fundamental dynamisms of the soul, not our perception of them, though, of course, they are often directly experienced in a sensible way. Key texts for this teaching are found in *SCC* 50 (2:78–83), *Asc* 3 (5:131–37) and *Div* (50:270–72). For discussions, see Gilson, *Mystical Theology,* p. 101; Hiss, *Anthropologie,* pp. 99–107; Blanpain, "Langage mystique," pp. 58–68; and especially Casey, *Athirst for God,* pp. 94–110.

213. *Sensus* and *appetitus naturalis* are defined in *Gra* 2.3 (3:167). *Asc* 3.12 (5:131–32) discusses *intellectus/sensus* and *affectus/appetitus* as the soul's two fundamental powers.

214. Augustine, *Conf.* 1.1 (PL 32:661): . . . et inquietem est cor nostrum, donec requiescat in te.

215. *Dil* 7.19 (3:135.24–28): Ea namque suae cupiditatis lege, qua in rebus ceteris non habita prae habitis esurire, et pro non habitis habita fastidire solebat, mox omnibus quae in caelo et quae in terra sunt obtentis et contemptis, tandem ad ipsum procul dubio curreret, qui solus deesset omnium Deus.

216. *Dil* 1.1 (3:119.19). The notion that the measure of loving God is to love him without measure Bernard could have found in a number of sources, e.g., Origen, *Comm. in Cant.* 3 (GCS 8:186.27); Severus of Milevus in a letter to Augustine (Ep 119.2 in PL 33:419); and Gregory the Great, *Hom. in Ev.* 2.38.10 (PL 76:1288). See also *SCC* 11.4 (1:57.3–4).

217. See the whole passage in *Dil* 7.18–20 (3:134–36), of which a part is quoted above.

218. *Dil* 7.22 (3:137.18–138.2): Ipse dat occasionem, ipse creat affectionem, desiderium ipse consummat. . . . Bonus es, Domine, animae quaerenti te. Quid ergo invenisti? Sed enim in hoc est mirum, quod nemo quaerere te valet, nisi qui prius invenerit. Vis igitur inveniri ut quaeraris, quaeri ut inveniaris. Potes quidem quaeri et inveniri, non tamen praeveniri. The Latin wordplay in the final sentence cannot be captured in English.

219. *Dil* 8.23 (3:138.12–13): Et est amor carnalis, quo ante omnia homo diligit seipsum propter seipsum. On *amor carnalis,* see P. Delfgaauw, "La nature et les degrés de l'amour selon S. Bernard," in *Saint Bernard Théologien,* pp. 237–43. On the four degrees in general, see the account in Blanpain, "Langage mystique," pp. 229–36.

220. This level is not discussed in *Dil,* where Bernard is only giving an outline of his thought. See above, pp. 175–77.

221. *Dil* 8.23–25 (3:138–40). See also Bernard's reflection on *fraterna dilectio* in SC 44.4 (2:46–47). Both these modes are discussed by Gilson, *Mystical Theology,* 73–84, but in placing *amor carnalis socialis* before *amor carnalis Christi* Gilson reverses Bernard's true order. How can we obey the commandment to love our neighbor as ourselves (*Dil* 8.23), unless we have already begun to be affected by the love of Christ? As the abbot later puts it: Oportet ergo Deum diligi prius, ut in Deo possit et proximus (*Dil* 8.25 [3:139.28]).

222. *Dil* 15.39 (3:152.24–153.6): Cumque se videt per se non posse subsistere, Deum quasi sibi necessarium incipit per fidem inquirere et diligere. Diligit itaque in secundo gradu Deum, sed propter se, non propter ipsum. At vero cum ipso coeperit occasione propriae necessitatis colere et frequentare, cogitando, legendo, orando, oboediendo, quadam huiuscemodi familiaritate paulatim sensimque Deus innotescit, consequenter et dulcesit; et sic, gustato quam suavis est Dominus, transit ad tertium gradum, ut diligat Deum, non iam propter se, sed propter ipsum. Sane in hoc gradu diu statur, et nescio si a quoquam hominum quartus in hac

vita perfecte apprehenditur, ut se scilicet homo diligat tantum propter Deum. Asserant hoc si qui experti sunt; mihi, fateor, impossibile videtur.

223. *Dil* 10.27–29 (3:142–44). This text will be discussed in more detail below.

224. On this transition, see Thomas Merton, "Transforming Union in St. Bernard of Clairvaux and St. John of the Cross," papers originally published 1948–50, and now available in *Thomas Merton on St. Bernard* (Kalamazoo, MI: Cistercian Publications, 1980), esp. pp. 206–10.

225. See above, p. 176.

226. As a division of kinds of *amor*, this is found in *SCC* 20.9 (1:120–21) and *Div* 29 (6:210–14). It also is found in the *Brevis Commentatio* 1–2 (PL 184:407D–409D). T. Davis sketches the mutual development of this theme in the writings of Bernard and William of St. Thierry ("The *Brevis Commentatio*," pp. 189–92).

227. On the use of this pattern in William, see chapter 6, pp. 234–38.

228. *SCC* 50.4 (2:80.11–12): Sed est affectio quam caro gignit, et est quam ratio regit, et est quam condit sapientia.

229. Compare *SCC* 20.9 (1:120.22–23) with 50.4 (2:80.12–13 and 16–17).

230. *Dil* 7.32–33 (3:146–47); the quotation is from 147.9–10: Comedite ante mortem, bibite post mortem, inebriamini post resurrectionem. Cf. *Div* 41.12 and 87.4 (6:253 and 331–32).

231. E.g., *SCC* 83.5 (2:301), to be considered below.

232. *SCC* 7.2 (1:31.17–21): Sed pono diversas affectiones, ut ea quae proprie sponsae congruit distinctius elucescat. Si servus est, timet a facie domini; si mercenarius, sperat de manu domini; si discipulus, aurem parat magistro; si filius, honorat patrem; quae vero osculum postulat, amat.

233. See, e.g., the other fivefold pattern from *Div* 10.2–3 (6:122–23) considered above in n. 162.

234. See Anderson, "Rhetorical Epistemology," esp. pp. 126–27.

235. *SCC* 83.5 (2:301.12–22): Magna res amor; sed sunt in eo gradus. Sponsa in summo stat. Amant enim filii, sed de hereditate cogitant, quam dum verentur quoquo modo amittere, ipsum, a quo exspectatur hereditas, plus reverentur, minus amant. Suspectus est mihi amor, cui aliud quid adipiscendi spes suffragari videtur. Infirmus est, qui forte, spe subtracta, aut exstinguitur, aut minuitur. Impurus est, qui et aliud cupit. Purus amor mercenarius non est. Purus amor de spe vires non sumit, nec tamen diffidentiae damna sentit. Sponsae hic est, quia haec sponsa est, quaecumque est. Sponsae res et spes unus est amor. Hoc sponsa abundat, hoc sponsus contentus est. Nec is aliud quaerit, nec illa alius habet. Hinc ille sponsus, et sponsa illa est. Is sponsus proprius, quem alter nemo attingat, ne filius quidem.

236. *SCC* 85.12 (2:315.17–20): Ergo quam videris animam, relictis omnibus, Verbo votis omnibus adhaerere, Verbo vivere, Verbo se regere, de Verbo concipere quod pariat Verbo, ... puta coniugem Verboque maritatam.

237. *SCC* 83.6 (2:2:302.10–12): Nam etsi minus diligit creatura, quoniam minor est, tamen si ex tota se diligit, nihil deest ubi totum est.

238. *SCC* 73.10 (2:239.7–8): ... nam et una, si deum dulciter, sapienter, vehementer amat, sponsa est. ... The longest development of this theme is in *SCC* 20.3–5 (1:116–18). Cf *Div* 29.1 and 4–5; *Div* 96.6 (6:210, 212–14; 360).

239. For an introduction to the problem of pure love in the history of Christianity, see John Burnaby, *Amor Dei: A Study of the Religion of St. Augustine* (London: Hodder & Stoughton, 1938), chap. 9. See also Éphrem Boularand, "Désintéressement," DS 3:550–91 (573–75 on Bernard).

240. Anders Nygren, *Agape and Eros* (Philadelphia: Westminster, 1953), pp. 645–51; Gilson, *Mystical Theology*, pp. 141–47; Martin D'Arcy, *The Mind and Heart of Love* (New York: Meridian, 1956), chaps. 1 and 2.

241. *Dil* 7.17 (3:133.21–22): Non enim sine praemio diligitur Deus, etsi absque praemii sit intuitu diligendus. Cf. ibid., 3:134.1–6 and 14–15.

242. *SCC* 83.4 (2:300.24–26): Ipse meritum, ipse praemium est sibi. Amor praeter se non requirit causam, non fructum: fructus eius, usus eius. Amo, quia amo; amo, ut amem.

243. Gilson, *Mystical Theology*, pp. 116–18.

244. See, for instance, the passage in *Dil* 5.15 (3:132.4–14): Quod si totum me debeo pro me facto, quid addam iam et pro refecto, et refecto hoc modo? Non enim tam facile refectus, quam factus. . . . In primo opere me mihi dedit, in secundo se; et ubi se dedit, me mihi reddidit. Datus ergo, et redditus, me pro me debeo, et bis debeo. Quid Deo retribuam pro se? Nam etiam si me millies rependere possem, quid sum ego ad Deum?

245. E.g., Josef Bernhart, *Bernhardische und Eckhartische Mystik in ihren Beziehungen und Gegensätze* (Kempten, 1912), passim; and Steven Ozment, *The Age of Reform 1250-1550* (New Haven: Yale University Press, 1980), pp. 115–24.

246. For more on this issue, see McGinn, "Love, Knowledge and *Unio mystica* in the Western Christian Tradition," pp. 67–68.

247. On the role of wisdom in Bernard's mysticism, see esp. Roch Kereszty, "Die Weisheit in der mystischen Erfahrung beim hl. Bernhard von Clairvaux," *Cîteaux* 16 (1963): 6–24, 105–34, 185–201.

248. Bernard does, of course, have an epistemology of his own, a practical and prudential one, as discussed by Anderson, "The Rhetorical Epistemology in Saint Bernard's *Super Cantica*." See also John R. Sommerfeldt, "The Epistemological Value of the Mysticism in the Thought of Bernard of Clairvaux," in *Studies in Medieval Culture* (Kalamazoo, MI: Western Michigan University, 1965), pp. 48–58.

249. On the priority of *affectus* over *cognitio*, see, e.g., *SCC* 23.14 (1:47–48).

250. *Dominica in kal. nov.* 3.1 (5:311–12). Cf. *Dom. in kal. nov.* 5.8 (5:323).

251. *Dom. in kal. nov.* 3.3 (5:313.15–17): Quid lucere festinas? Nondum illud advenit tempus, in quo FULGEBUNT IUSTI SICUT SOL IN REGNO PATRIS EORUM. Interim perniciosus est appetitus iste lucendi; fervere enim multo melius.

252. Ibid., 3.2 (5:312.21–23): Lucet ergo Iohannes, tanto utique clarius quanto amplius fervet, tanto verius quanto minus appetit lucere. Cf. *In nat. S. Iohannis Baptistae* 3–5 (5:177–79).

253. E.g., *SCC* 8.5 (1:38–39); *Div* 87.2 (6:330–31); *Dom. in kal. nov.* 4.2 (5:316), etc.

254. An important text for Bernard's evaluation of the positive role of knowledge is *SCC* 36.1–4 (2:3–6). On the relation of knowledge (both necessary and unnecessary) to love, see T. Merton, "St. Bernard on Interior simplicity," in *Thomas Merton on St. Bernard*, pp. 125–36.

255. *Asc* 4.3–6 (5:139–43). On this see my paper, "Resurrection and Ascension in the Christology of the Early Cistercians," pp. 11–13.

256. *Asc* 4.14 (5:148.21–22): . . . et eo magis affectus vigeat, quo deficit intellectus.

257. *Asc* 3.2 (5:132.10): . . . sed Christus intellectum illuminat, Spiritus sanctus affectum purgat.

258. *Asc* 3.9 (5:136:22–23): . . . et intellectu clarificato, et affectu purificato, veniat ad nos et apud nos faciat mansionem.

259. Asc 6.14 (5:159.3–4): . . . ut intellectui spirituali spiritualis iungeretur affectus. . . . The type of this gift is seen in the "double spirit" that Eliseus begged from Elijah (4 Kings 2:9).

260. *Dom. in kal nov.* 4.2 (5:316.11–14): Sic et zelus absque scientia, quo vehementius irruit, eo currit gravius, impingens nimirum atque resiliens. Ubi vero intelligentiam caritas, agnitionem devotio comitatur, volet secure quisquis eiusmodi est, volet sine fine, quia volat in aeternitatem. For other texts on the necessity of both love and knowledge, see, e.g., *Hum* 7.21 (3:32), *Pre* 15.36–37 (3:279), and *SCC* 49.4 (2:75).

261. *SCC* 57.8 (2:124.7–10): . . . si, iam emundata ac serenata conscientia, sequatur subita quadam atque insolita latitudo mentis, et infusio luminis illuminantis intellectum vel ad scientiam Scripturarum, vel ad mysteriorum notitiam. . . .

262. *SCC* 49.4 (2:75.20–22): Cum enim duo sint beatae contemplationis excessus, in intellectu unus et alter in affectu, unus in lumine, alter in fervore, unus in agnitione, alter in devotione. . . . On this text, see Blanpain, "Langage mystique," pp. 66–67.

263. *Div* 29.1 (6:210.10–11): Exponit beatus Gregorius quia amor ipse notitia est.

264. *SCC* 64.10 (2:171.15–19): Itane summus omnium, unus factus est omnium? Quis hoc fecit? Amor, dignitatis nescius, dignatione dives, affectu potens, suasu efficax. Quid violentius? Triumphat de Deo amor. Quid tamen non violentum? Amor est. Quae ista vis, quaeso, tam violenta ad victoriam, tam victa ad violentiam?

265. *SCC* 29.8 (1:208.26). Bernard quotes Song 2:5 according to the Old Latin version in this passage (*Vulnerata caritate ego sum*), rather than the Vg. *quia amore langueo.*

266. *SCC* 29.8 (1:208.17–19): Aut certe pertransivit eam, ut veniret usque ad nos, et de plenitudine illa omnes acciperemus, et fieret mater caritatis cuius pater est caritas Deus. . . . The role of the Blessed Virgin Mary as a paradigmatic figure in Bernard's mystical theology is worthy of further study, as an analysis of some of his Marian sermons would demonstrate, e.g., *In laudibus Virginis Mariae* (4:13–58) and *Nat BVM* (5:275–88). For observations on Mary as mystical model, see M. B. Pranger, "The Virgin Mary and the Complexities of Love-Language in the Works of Bernard of Clairvaux," *Cîteaux* 40 (1989): 112–38. Despite older exaggerated claims about Bernard's contribution to the medieval Marian cult, the abbot's attitude toward Mary is significant both for understanding his thought and for the general culture. See H. Barre, "S. Bernard, Docteur marial," in *Saint Bernard Théologien*, pp. 92–113.

267. *SCC* 9.2 (1:43.13–15): . . . sed praeceps amor, nec iudicium praestolator, nec consilio temperatur, nec pudore frenatur, nec rationi subicitur.

268. *SCC* 27.11 (1:190.8): . . . vim facere regno caritatis. . . . Cf. *Nat BVM* 16 (5:286.13–22).

269. For *amor intemperans*, see *SCC* 73.1 (2:233.21); for *amor inquietus SCC* 74.1 (2:240.1).

270. *SCC* 79.1 (2:272.3–12): NUM QUEM DILIGIT ANIMA MEA VIDISTIS? (Song 3:3). O amor praeceps, vehemens, flagrans, impetuose, qui praeter te aliud cogitare non sinis, fastidis cetera, contemnis omnia prae te, te contentus! Confundis ordines, dissimulas usum, modum ignoras; totum quod opportunitatis, quod rationis, quod pudoris, quod consilii iudicive esse videtur, triumphas in temetipso et redigis in captivitatem. En omne quod cogitet ista, et quod loquitur, te sonat, te redolet, et alius nihil: ita tibi ipsius et cor vindicasti et linguam.

271. On the vehemence of love in Bernard, see Casey, *Athirst for God*, pp. 92–93; and, for the wider picture, especially relating to Richard of St. Victor, see chapter 9, pp. 415–18.

272. *SCC* 7.2 (1:31.25–32.1): . . . quippe quibus omnia sunt communia, nil proprium, nil a se divisum habentibus.

273. *SCC* 83.3–4 (2:300–01). Text cited is at 301.1.

274. *SCC* 69.7 (2:206.20–26): Ergo ex propriis quae sunt penes Deum agnoscit, nec dubitet se amare, quae amat. Ita est: amor Dei amorem animae parit, et illius praecurrens intentio intentam animam facit, sollicitudoque sollicitam. Nescio enim qua vicinitate naturae, cum semel revelata facie gloriam Dei speculari anima poterit, mox illi se conformari necesse est, atque in eamdem imaginem transformari. Igitur qualem te paraveris Deo, talis oportet appareat tibi Deus. . . .

275. *SCC* 69.8 (2:207.9–10): . . . animam Deum videntem haud secus videre, quam si sola videatur a Deo.

276. The notion that "the eye by which I see God is the same eye with which God sees me" is found in a number of mystics of the more directly Neoplatonic sort, such as Meister Eckhart, e.g., Vernacular Sermon 12 (see Bernard McGinn, editor and translator, *Meister Eckhart: Teacher and Preacher* [New York: Paulist Press, 1986], p. 270). For the relations

between Bernard and Eckhart, see B. McGinn, "St. Bernard and Meister Eckhart," *Cîteaux* 31 (1980): 373–86.

277. For marriage as a metaphor for union with God, see "Saint Bernard and the Metaphor of Love," in J. Leclercq, *Monks on Marriage*, pp. 73–86; and R. Fassetta, "Le mariage spirituel," pp. 262–64.

278. *SCC* 46.1 (2:56.13–15): . . . [anima] lectulumque digito monstrans, dilectum, ut dixi, invitat ad requiem . . . et secum pernoctare compellit. . . . On the use of this text in monastic literature, see Leclercq, *OTIA MONASTICA: Études sur le vocabulaire de la contemplation au moyen âge*, Studia Anselmiana 51 (Rome: Herder, 1963), p. 134.

279. *SCC* 52.2 (2:91.11–12): . . . et superna Deitas animae exsulantis inire connubia. An alternate reading from the English family of manuscripts has "exulting soul" (*animae exsultantis*).

280. *SCC* 52.3 (2:92.4–6): Magis autem istiusmodi vitalis vigilque sopor sensum interiorem illuminat et, morte propulsata, vitam tribuat sempiternam. Revera enim dormitio est, quae tamen sensum non sopiat, sed abducat. Est et mors. . . .

281. *SCC* 52.4 (2:92.12–15): . . . quoties sancta aliqua et vehementi cogitatione anima a seipsa abripitur, si tamen eousque mente secedat et avolet, ut hunc communem transcendat usum et consuetudinem cogitandi.

282. Ibid. (2:92.16–17): Excedente quippe anima, etsi non vita, certe vitae sensu, necesse est etiam ut nec vitae tentatio sentiatur. For the notion of ligature in the Spanish mystics, see Isaias Rodriguez, "Ligature des puissances," DS 9:845–50.

283. *SCC* 52.5 (2:93.1–2): Talis, ut opinor, excessus, aut tantum, aut maxime, contemplatio dicitur.

284. *SCC* 52.6 (2:93.20–22): . . . ibique prae amoenitate loci inter amplexus sponsi suaviter obdormissse, id est in spiritu excedisse. The notion of ecstasy as a spiritual sleep has a rich history in Christian mysticism. For an introduction, see Pierre Adnès, "Sommeil spirituel," DS 14:1033–53.

285. *SCC* 51.8–10 (2:88–89). The passage quoted is at 89.12.

286. E.g., *Dil* 3.10 and 4.12–13 (3:126–27 and 129–30); *V Nat* 4.1 (4:221); and *Div* 41.13 (6:253). This reading seems to be based on Peter Damian, for whom the left hand was the rejection of this present life and the right the desire for the heavenly one (*Testimonia de Canticis Canticorum* 6 in PL 145:1145C). Some readings are directly christological, e.g., *V Nat* 4.7 (4:224), where the left hand is Christ crucified and the right the glorified Christ; and *OS* 4.2 (5:356–57), which has the left hand as Christ's humanity, the right as his divinity.

287. *IV HM* 14 (5:66.22–67.4): Amplexatus est nos Dominus Iesus per laborem et dolorem nostrum; adhaeremus nos quoque ei vicariis quibusdam amplexibus per iustitiam, et iustitiam suam: actiones ad iustitiam dirigendo, passiones propter iustitiam sustinendo, dicamusque cum sponsa: TENUI EUM, NEC DIMITTAM. . . . Quid post amplexum, nisi osculum restat? Si sic adhaererem Deo, quomodo non iam exclamare liberet: OSCULETUR ME OSCULO ORIS SUI?

288. *Csi* 5.14.30 (3:492.10–14): Si sanctus es, comprehendisti et nosti; si non, esto, et tuo experimento scies. Sanctum facit affecti sancta, et ipsa gemina: timor Domini sanctus et sanctus amor. His perfecte affecta anima, veluti quibusdam duobus brachiis suis comprehendit, amplectitur, stringit, tenet et ait: TENUI EUM NEC DIMITTAM.

289. For background to Bernard's terminology on *ecstasis, excessus,* and related words, see Robert Javelet, "Extase. BIII. Au 12e siècle," DS 4:2113–20; M. Casey, *Athirst for God,* pp. 290–92; and "In Pursuit of Ecstasy," pp. 139–47.

290. There are a number of treatments of Bernard's teaching on vision and contemplation. See esp. Jean-Marie Déchanet, "Contemplation. A. V. Au XIIe siècle," DS 2:1948–66. The most recent account is that of K. Ruh, *Geschichte der abendländische Mystik,* pp. 268–75.

291. The joys of heaven will include the vision of the Trinity; see *OS* 4.2–3 (5:356–58).

292. E.g., *Hum* 7.21 (3:33.4–7); *SCC* 85.14 (2:316); *Csi* 5.13.27 (3:490); etc.

293. See *SCC* 67.3–5 (2:190–91). The phrase cited is at 190.22. See the earlier discussion of the sacred "belch" (p. 187).

294. Hans Urs von Balthasar, *The Glory of the Lord* (New York: Crossroad, 1984), 2:25.

295. *SCC* 7.7 (1:35.6–9): Neque enim aliud est inhaerere Deo, quam videre Deum, quod solis mundicordibus singulari felicitate donatur . . . MIHI AUTEM ADHAERERE DEO BONUM EST. Videndo adhaerebat, et adhaerendo videbat.

296. *SCC* 2.2 (1:9.19–20): . . . mire quaedam et quodammodo indiscreta commixtio superni luminis et illuminatae mentis. Adhaerens quippe Deus unus spiritus est.

297. Augustine, *De gen. ad lit.* 12.6.25–28.56 (PL 34:463–78). See the discussion in *Foundations of Mysticism*, pp. 253–55.

298. *SCC* 31.3–4 (1:221–22), the passage cited is found at 221.21–24: . . . sed tamen foris facta est, nimirum exhibita per imaginem extrinsecus apparentes seu voces sonantes. Sed est divina inspectio eo differentior ab his, quo interior, cum per seipsum dignatur invisere Deus animam quaerentem se. . . .

299. There were, of course, some Old Testament figures, such as Jacob, Moses and Isaiah, who, like Paul, saw God in the higher modes of vision, that is, *per excessum mentis*, as *SCC* 33.6 (1: 237–38) and *Palm* 2.7 (5:50–51), suggest. But in *SCC* 45.6 (2:53) Bernard says that Old Testament visions, even those of Moses and Isaiah insofar as they saw God as Lord, are inferior to the visions of the Bride who sees God as Lover. Cf. Bernard's remarks in *Div* 9.1 (6:118) on the famous vision of St. Benedict, recounted in Gregory the Great's *Dialogi* 2.35 and discussed above in chapter 2, pp. 71–74. The abbot expresses suspicion of contemporary visions unsupported by sound reason and good authority in *Ep* 174.6 (7:390–91).

300. *SCC* 31.6 (1:233.12–24): . . . habeatque praesto quem desiderat, non figuratum, sed infusum, non apparentem, sed afficientem; nec dubium quin eo iucundiorem, quo intus, non foris. Cf. *SCC* 2.2 (1:9.21–25).

301. *SCC* 31.2 (1:220.10–11): Itaque videtur et hic, sed sicut videtur ipsi, et non sicuti est. Cf. *SCC* 31.7 (1:223).

302. These are introduced in *SCC* 31.7–8 (1:224–25) and discussed in *SCC* 32.2–20 (1:227–33).

303. *SCC* 32.2 (1:227.7–9): . . . ut cupiat solvi et cum Christo esse, cupiat autem vehementer, ardenter sitiat, assidue meditetur. . . .

304. *SCC* 32.3–4 (1:227–29), the quotation is at 229.3–5: . . . et in lege eius meditamur die ac nocte, sciamus pro certo adesse Sponsum, atque alloqui nos, ut non fatigemur laboribus, sermonibus delectati. A long section on the discernment of spirits follows (nn. 5–7 on 1:229–31).

305. *SCC* 32.8–9 (1:231–32), the quotation is from 231.10–11: . . . qui ascendentes ad cor altum, de maiori spiritus libertate et puritate conscientiae magnanimiores facti. . . .

306. *SCC* 18.6 (1:107.15–19): Dormiens in contemplatione somniat Deum; per speculum siquidem et in aenigmate, non autem facie ad faciem interim intuetur. Tamen sic non tam spectati quam coniectati, idque raptim et quasi sub quodam coruscamine scintillulae transeuntis, tenuiter vix attracti inardescit amore. . . . On the impossibility of a face-to-face vision of God in this life, see also *Palm* 2.7 (5:50–51).

307. I provide the whole of this lengthy and important text, *SCC* 41.3 (2:30.7–29): Advertendum cuiuscemodi muraenulas ei offerunt: AUREAS, inquit, et VERMICULATAS ARGENTO. Aurum divinitatis est fulgor, aurum sapientia quae desursum est. Hoc auro fulgentia quaedam quasi veritatis signacula spondent se figuraturos hi, quibus id ministerii est, superni aurifices, atque internis animae auribus inserturos. Quod ego non puto esse alius quam texere quasdam spirituales similitudines, et in ipsis purissima divinae sapientiae sensa

animae contemplantis conspectibus importare, ut videat, saltem per speculum et in aenig-mate, quod nondum facie ad faciem valet ullatenus intueri. Divina sunt, et nisi expertis pror-sus incognita, quae effamur, quomodo videlicet in hoc mortali corpore, fide adhuc habente statum, et necdum propalata perspicui substantia luminis interni, purae interdum contempla-tio veritatis partes suas agere intra nos vel ex parte praesumit, ita ut liceat usurpare etiam alicui nostrum, cui hoc datum desuper fuerit, illud Apostoli: NUNC COGNOSCO EX PARTE; item: EX PARTE COGNOSCIMUS, ET EX PARTE PROPHETAMUS. Cum autem divini aliquid raptim et veluti in velocitate corusci luminis interluxerit menti, spiritu excedenti, sive ad temperamentum nimii splendoris, sive ad doctrinae usum, continuo, nescio unde, adsunt imaginatoriae quaedam rerum inferiorum similitudines, infusis divinitus sensis convenienter accommodatae, quibus quodam modo adumbratus purissimus ille ac splen-didissimus veritatis radius, et ipsi animae tolerabilior fiat, et quibus communicare illum voluerit capabilior. Existimo tamen ipsas formari in nobis sanctorum suggestionibus angelo-rum, sicut e contrario contrarias et malas ingeri immissiones per angelos malos non dubium est.

308. See also *SCC* 31.5 (1:222) for a similar treatment of the angels.

309. For the *visio spiritualis*, see *De gen. ad lit.* 12.7.18–9.20 and 24.50–51 (PL 34:459–61 and 474–75).

310. *SCC* 36.6 (2:7). Though the abbot does not state it here, this first vision would obvi-ously involve beginning with the Incarnate Savior and his love for us, as a text from *Dom. in kal. nov.* 1.2 (5:305.8) makes clear: ... si desideras videre sublimem, humilem prius Jesum videre curato.

311. *SCC* 36.6 (2:8.4–7): Atque hoc modo erit gradus ad notitiam Dei, tui cognitio; et ex imagine sua, quae in te renovatur, ipse videbitur, dum te quidem revelata facie gloriam Domini cum fiducia speculando, in eamdem imaginem transformaris de claritate in clari-tatem, tamquam a Domini Spiritu.

312. *SCC* 82.8 (2:297.19–29): Admiranda prorsus et stupenda illa similitudo, quam Dei visio comitatur, immo quae Dei visio est, ego autem dico in caritate. Caritas illa visio, illa similitudo est. ... Facta igitur de medio iniquitate, quae eam ex parte est dissimilitudinem facit, erit unio spiritus, erit mutua visio mutuaque dilectio. Siquidem veniente quod perfectum est, evacuabitur quod ex parte est; eritque ad alterutrum casta et consummata dilectio, agnitio plena, visio manifesta, coniunctio firma, societas individua, similitudo perfecta. Other texts also identify the regaining of the *similitudo Dei* with *visio Dei*, e.g., *SCC* 38.5 and 69.7 (2:17.23–25 and 206.23–25). Although Bernard does not use William's term *visio similitudinis*, his teaching is close to his friend's on this issue.

313. *Csi* 2.2.5 (3:414.6–8): ... potest contemplatio quidem diffiniri verus certusque intuitus animi de quacumque re, sive apprehensio veri non dubia, consideratio autem intensa ad vestigandum cogitatio, vel intensio animi vestigantis verum. Bernard, however, admits that in this general sense the two are used interchangably. Later in the treatise, in distinguishing three levels of *consideratio*, Bernard is more precise by identifying only *consideratio speculativa* with *contemplatio* in the proper sense (Csi 5.2.3–4 in 3:468–69).

314. D. Farkasfalvy puts it well: "... [conversion] is a gradual process of purification and transformation, while [contemplation] is a comprehensive term for the experience of God" ("The First Step in the Spiritual Life: Conversion," pp. 77–78). See especially John R. Som-merfeldt, who says, "Contemplation, then, is an internal experience of the soul who delights in ecstatic union with God" ("Bernard as Contemplative," in *Bernardus Magister*, p. 77).

315. E.g., the definition of the third kiss given in *SCC* 4.1 (1:19.3–5). Especially important is the discussion of two kinds of contemplation in the exegesis of Song 2:4 in *SCC* 62.3–7 (2:156–60), where the "clefts in the rock" are understood as the contemplation of Christ's sav-

ing mysteries, and the "crannies in the wall" are the contemplation of heavenly realities. Bernard adds to these the "hollows in the ground," that is, meditation on Christ's wounds.

316. E.g., *Csi* 5.14.32 (3:493) outlines four kinds of contemplation relating to the four essential attributes of God—*admiratio maiestatis, intuitio iudiciorum Dei, memoria beneficiorum* and *meditatio aeternitatis. Div* 87 (6:329–33) distinguishes the contemplation of the philosophers from true Christian contemplation that takes place *per mentis excessum.* This text is especially important for stressing the christological nature of all true *contemplatio*: Fit autem contemplatio ex condescensione Verbi Dei ad humanam naturam per gratiam, et exaltationem humanae naturae ad ipsum Verbum per divinum amorem (3:331.7–9.). *Conv* 13–14.25–27 (3:98–102) has an account of the role of the spiritual senses in contemplation.

317. See especially *SCC* 33.6–7 (1:237–38). *SCC* 23.11 (1:147.10) is where David is spoken of as the *maximus contemplator.*

318. On Mary Magdalene as a contemplative, see, e.g., *SCC* 57.10–11 (2:125–26), *Asspt* 3.1–7 and 5.5–13 (5:238–44 and 253–60). An important passage in the latter text (n. 8 on 256–57) discusses three impediments to the interior eye of contemplation.

319. For some texts, see, e.g., *SCC* 23.15, 31.2 and 7, 32.2, 34.1, 41.3, 51.2, 85.13 (1:148, 220, 223, 227, 245–46; 2:30, 85, 316); *Hum* 7.21 (3:32–33); *Palm* 2.7 (5:50).

320. On *raptus* as a free gift, see especially *Hum* 8.22–23 (3:33–34).

321. E.g., *In nat S. Andreae* 1.10 (5:433.19–20), speaking of the heights of *caritas,* Bernard says: Plus dico: et ex nobis nonnullos videre mihi videor in hoc gradu.

322. Along with *SCC* 74.5–7 (treated above), see *SCC* 54.6, 57.4–5 (2:106, 121–22), and especially *Div* 41.11 (6:252–53). On the coming and going of the Holy Spirit, see *SCC* 17.2 (1:99).

323. For a partial list of *quies* and related terms, see Casey, *Athirst for God,* p. 294 n. 175. For background, see J. Leclercq, *OTIA MONASTICA,* who treats Bernard often (see under "Index des noms").

324. For the use in Ambrose, Cassian, and Augustine, see *Foundations of Mysticism,* pp. 205–6, 223–25, and 253–55, respectively.

325. *SCC* 4.4 (1:20.8). The term *excessus* has its scriptural root in such passages as Pss 30:23; 67:28; and 115:112; Acts 10:10; 11:5; and 2 Cor 5:13. Bernard uses it frequently, e.g., *SCC* 7.6 (1:34.26–27), 31.6 (1:223.3), 33.7 (1:238.8–9), 38.3 (2:16.9), 41.3 (2:30.22), 49.4 (2:75.14–26), 52.4–6 (2:92–94), 54.8 (2:108.4–5), 62.3–4 (2: 156–58), 67.5 (2:191.16), *Gra* 5.15 (3:177.5), *Sept* 2.1 (4:349.14), *Div* 87.2 (6:330.20), etc. For Bernard's use of *excessus,* see Casey, *Athirst for God,* pp. 290–92. Bernard employs the related term *exstasis* rarely—*SCC* 52.4 (2:92.9), *Csi* 5.14.32 (3:493.8), *Officium de S. Victore* (3:505.10), and the *Vita Malachiae* 50 (3:355.4).

326. K. Ruh notes that Bernard uses *raptus* much more frequently than *excessus* and *exstasis* (*Geschichte der abendländische Mystik,* pp. 272–73). But I do not take this as evidence, as Ruh thinks, that he therefore thought the latter terms indicated a higher state.

327. For discussions, see *Foundations of Mysticism,* under "Intoxication" in the "Subject Index."

328. E.g., *SCC* 7.3, 18.5, 49.1–4 and 76.2 (1:32, 107; 2:74–75, 255); and *Ep* 3.8 (4:309).

329. *SCC* 85.13 (2:315.28–316.8): In hoc ultimo genere interdum exceditur et seceditur etiam a corporeis sensibus, ut sese non sentiat quae Verbum sentit. Hoc fit, cum mens ineffabili Verbi illecta dulcedine, quodammodo se sibi furatur, immo rapitur atque elabitur a seipsa, ut Verbo fruatur. . . . Et quidem laeta in prole mater, sed in amplexibus sponsa laetior. Cara pignora filiorum: sed oscula plus delectant. Bonum est salvare multos; excedere autem et cum Verbo esse, multo iucundius. At quando hoc, aut quamdiu hoc? Dulce commercium est, sed breve momentum et experimentum rarum!

330. The text was used by Bernard and others as the scriptural basis for their understanding of that mode of union we can call the *unitas spiritus* understanding of mystical union. See my "Love, Knowledge, and *Unio mystica* in the Western Christian Tradition," esp. pp. 62–66, 74–75, and 84–85.

331. According to R. Fassetta, n. 193, Bernard uses the text fifty-four times in his writings ("Le rôle de l'Esprit-Saint," p. 384). The abbot sometimes employs it in conjunction with two Psalm texts that speak of "adhaering" to God: *adhaesit anima mea post te* (Ps 62:9); and *mihi autem adhaerere Deo bonum est* (Ps 72:28). Love, of course, is the "glue" (*gluten amoris*, *SCC* 8.2, 71.8, and *Div* 4.3; cf. Isa 41:7), which makes the adhesion possible. On Bernard's use of 1 Cor 6:17, see Casey, *Athirst for God*, pp. 201–8; and Fassetta, "Le mariage spirituel," p. 175 n. 21.

332. *Dil* 10.27 (3:142.9–15): Quando huiuscemodi experitur affectum, ut divino debriatus amore animus, oblitus sui, factusque sibi ipsi tamquam vas perditum, totus pergat in Deum et, adhaerens Deo, unus cum eo spiritus fiat. . . . Beatum dixerem et sanctum, cui tale aliquid in hac mortali vita raro interdum, aut vel semel, et hoc ipsum raptim atque unius vix momenti spatio, experiri donatum est.

333. The appearance of the term *deificari* here reminds us that Bernard, like other Western mystics, did not shy away from using the language of divinization, though such terminology was not as central to him as it was to most Eastern Christian mystics. See *V Nat* 1.2 (4:199). For a study, consult the article "Divinisation" in DS 3 (cols. 1405–7 on Bernard).

334. *Dil* 10.28 (3:143.15–24): Sic affici, deificari est. Quomodo stilla aquae modica, multo infusa vino, deficere a se tota videtur, dum et saporem vini induit et colorem, et quomodo ferrum ignitum et candens igni simillimum fit, pristina propriaque exutum forma, et quomodo solis luce perfusus aer in eamdem transformatur luminis claritatem, adeo ut non tam illuminatus quam ipsum lumen esse videatur, sic omnem tunc in sanctis humanum affectionem quodam ineffabili modo necesse erit a semetipsa liquescere, atque in Dei penitus transfundi voluntatem. Alioquin quomodo omnia in omnibus erit Deus, si in homine de homine quidquam supererit? Manebit quidem substantia, sed in alia forma, alia gloria aliaque potentia. See the parallel passage from the letter to the Carthusians that Bernard incorporated at the end of the treatise, *Dil* 15.39–40 (3:153–54).

335. See the discussion in E. Gilson, "Maxime, Érigène, S. Bernard," in *Aus der Geisteswelt des Mittelalters (Mélanges M. Grabmann)* (Münster: Aschendorff, 1935), 1:188–92. The most complete treatment is that of Jean Pepin, "'Stilla aquae modica multo infusa vino, ferrum ignitum, luce perfusus aer': L'origine de trois comparaisons familières à la théologie mystique médiévale," in *Miscellanea André Combes (Divinitas 11)* (Rome, 1967), 1:331–75.

336. Maximus Confessor, *Ambigua* 2 (PL 122:1202B). See the discussion in chapter 3 (p. 116) of Eriugena's use of the comparisons in his *Periphyseon*. It is extremely doubtful that Bernard would have known this text. Gilson, both in the article cited in the previous note and in *The Mystical Theology* (pp. 26–28), argued that Bernard took the term *excessus* from Maximus; but, as we have seen, it is not only found in scripture, but was also popular with Augustine and other Western fathers.

337. See Jean Gerson, *De mystica theologia*, ed. André Combes (Lugano: Thesaurus Mundi, 1958), I.41 (pp. 105–6). There is an English translation in *Jean Gerson: Selections*, by Steven E. Ozment (Leiden: Brill, 1969), pp. 48–58.

338. *SCC* 71.4 (2:217.2–4): Sed si vidisti, quod pasci illi pascere sit, vide etiam nunc ne forte et, e converso, pascere sit et pasci.

339. *SCC* 71.5 (2:217.12–20): Cibus eius paenitentia mea, cibus eius salus mea, cibus eius ego ipse. . . . Mandor cum arguor, glutior cum instituor, decoquor cum immutor, digeror cum transformor, unior cum conformor. Nolite mirari hoc: et manducatur a nobis, quo arctius illi adstringimur. Non sane alias perfecte unimur illi. Nam si manduco et non manducor, videbitur in me ille esse, sed nondum in illo ego; nec erit perfecta unitio in uno quovis horum. The eating metaphor was also criticized by Gerson (see Ozment trans., p. 52).

340. *SCC* 71.7–10 (2:218–22). This long and somewhat repetitious passage, as well as the alternate version in the Morimund and Clairvaux recensions of the sermons (printed at the bottom of 2:218–19), show the concern that Bernard took with this teaching. It seems that he may have thought that some were likely to misunderstand it, though we have no evidence of disputes over the nature of union at this time. Bernard may have based his contrast between *unum* and *unus* on a passage from Augustine (*Ennaratio in Ps.* 101.1.2 [PL 37:1295]).

341. *SCC* 71.7 (2:220.5–9): Quo contra homo et Deus, quia unius non sunt substantiae vel naturae, unum quidem dici non possunt; unus tamen spiritus certa et absoluta veritate dicuntur, si sibi glutino amoris inhaereant. Quam quidem unitatem non tam essentiarum cohaerentia facit, quam conniventia voluntatum.

342. *SCC* 71.10 (2:221.11–12): Felix unio, si experiaris; nulla, si comparaveris.

343. A passage close to *SCC* 71, though discussing only spiritual and substantial union, can be found in *Dom. in kal. nov.* 5.2 (5:318–19).

344. *Div* 80.1 (6:320–21). Cf. *Div* 33.8 (6:227) for a description of four kinds of unity.

345. *Csi* 5.8.18–19 (3:482–83).

346. For some other uses in the *SCC*, see, e.g., 2.2, 3.5, 8.9, 19.5, 26.5, 31.6–7 (1:19, 17, 41–42, 111, 173, 223–24); 40.4, 59.2, 61.1, 83.3, and 83.6 (2:26, 136, 148, 299, 302).

347. For some other appearances of 1 Cor 6:17 and discussions of union, see, e.g., *Dil* 15.39 (3:153), *Csi* 5.5.12 (3:476), *Nat* 2.6 (4:256), *Asspt* 5.11 (5:258), *Ann* 1.5 and 3.8 (5:10 and 40), *Dom. in kal. nov.* 5.2 (5:319), *OS* 3.3 (5:352), *De voluntate divina* 1 (6:37), *Div* 4.3, 41.11 and 92.1 (6:96, 252–53 and 347). One unusual use is found in *In Octava Paschae* 1.8 (5:117), where the text is referred to the union of the Holy Spirit with the Father and the Son as the source for our union with God. This text is close to one of the major themes in the thought of William of St. Thierry.

348. *Ded* 1.7 (5:374.20–375.1): Duplici igitur sibi cohaerent lapides illo glutino, cognitionis plenae et perfectae dilectionis. Tanto siquidem maiori ad se invicem dilectione copulantur, quanto ipsi caritati, quae Deus est, viciniores assistunt. . . . Quoniam enim QUI ADHAERET DEO, UNUS SPIRITUS EST cum eo, nihil dubium est, quin perfecte adhaerentes ei beati Spiritus cum eo pariter et in eo penetrent universa. Cf. *Ep* 90.1 (7: 237–38) and *Ep* 324 (8:261).

349. E.g., *Dil* 7.18 (3:134–35); *Conv* 14.26–27 (4:101–2).

350. *SCC* 18.6 (1:107.27–29): Denique Deus caritas est, et nihil est in rebus quod possit replere creaturam factam ad imaginem Dei, nisi caritas Deus, qui solus maior est illa.

351. *SCC* 31.1–3 (1:219–21) has a full treatment. Cf. *SCC* 32.2 (1:227). As long as we remain in this life and experience the absence of God, our desire for him is being increased, as is emphasized in *SCC* 17.1, 51.1, and 74.7 (1:98; 2:84, 243–44).

352. *Div* 4.3 (6:95.16–17): Immediate ei iungi non possumus, sed per medium aliquod poterit fieri fortassis ista coniunctio.

353. *Div* 4.3 (6:96.3–4): Tertius vero glute ei conglutinatur, id est caritate, qui tam suaviter quam secure ligatur, adhaerens Domino spiritus est.

354. *Div* 19.1 (6:165.1–3): . . . ut perennibus gaudiis in ipso divinitatis fonte profundius immergamur, ubi unda undam sine intercapedine et interpolatione continuet?

355. *Div* 19.3 (6:163.4–5): . . . et nudis, ut ita dicam, oculis deitatis intuentur essentiam, nulla corporearum phantasmatum imaginatione decepti.

356. *In purificatione S. Mariae* 2.3 (4:340.12–15): Porro profectus noster in eo consistit, ut saepius dixisse me memini, ut numquam arbitremur nos apprehendisse, sed semper extendamur in anteriora, conemur incessanter in melius, et imperfectum nostrum divinae misericordiae obtutibus iugiter exponamus.

357. *SCC* 51.1 (2:84); cf. *Dil* 7.19 (3:135–36). It is interesting to compare Bernard's interpretation of this text with the more speculative, but still "epektatic" reading of Meister Eck-

hart in his *Sermones et Lectiones super Ecclesiastici Cap.24,23-31*, nn. 42–61 (*Meister Eckhart: Die deutschen und lateinische Werke, Lateinische Werke*, 2:270–90).

358. For Gregory's teaching, see *Foundations of Mysticism*, pp. 141–42, and the literature cited there.

359. See Denis Farkasfalvy, who notes that the abbot uses the text some 25 times. Farkasfalvy summarizes: "... in this Pauline passage, Bernard finds an expression of his understanding of authentic spiritual existence as continued self-transcendence" ("The Use of Paul by Saint Bernard as Illustrated by Saint Bernard's Interpretation of Philippians 3:13," in *Bernardus Magister*, pp. 161–68).

360. *QH* 10.1 (4:443.10). This teaching appears frequently in the abbot's writings.

361. *SCC* 84.1 (2:303.10–16): ... aut quis terminus quaerendi Deum? QUAERITE, inquit, FACIEM EIUS SEMPER. Existimo quia, nec cum inventus fuerit, cessabitur a quaerendo. Non pedum passibus, sed desideriis quaeritur Deus. Et utique non extundit desiderium sanctum felix inventio, sed extendit. ... Adimplebitur laetitia; sed desiderii non erit finis, ac per hoc nec quaerendi.

362. See also *SCC* 31.1 (1:220.2–4): Quod si aeternum extenditur videndi copia et voluntas, quomodo non plena felicitas? Nil quippe aut deest iam semper videntibus, aut superest semper volentibus. Cf. *SCC* 3.1 (1:14.15), 49.7 (2:77–78), *Dil* 4.11 and 11.33 (3:127.23–25 and 147.19–23), *Dom. in kal. nov.* 3.4 (5: 314.11–18), *Div* 15.3 (6:141.20), *Ep* 254.2–4 (8:158–59), etc., for a variety of texts on expektasis here and hereafter.

363. M. Standaert, "Le principe de l'ordination dans la théologie spirituelle de Saint Bernard," *Collectanea Ordinis Cisterciensium Reformatorum* 8 (1946): 176–216.

364. *Gra* 6.19 (3:180.19–20): Est autem ordinatio, omnimoda conversio voluntatis ad Deum, et ex tota se voluntaria devotaque subiectio.

365. See *In solemnitate apostolorum Petri et Pauli* 2.8 (5:197.12). Cf. 1.4 of the same series (5:190).

366. *Div* 50.2 (6:271.20–24): Si amamus quae amanda sunt, si magis amamus quae magis amanda sunt, si non amamus quae amanda non sunt, amor purgatus erit. Sic et de ceteris. Ordinantur autem sic: in initio timor, deinde laetitia, post hanc tristitia, in consummatione amor.

367. *Dil* 8.25 (3:139–40). The transition from carnal to spiritual love, if it takes place *recto ordine* (*Dil* 15.39 at 3:152.19–20), will lead to unity of spirit with God.

368. *Dil* 14.38 (3:152.5–17): Numquam erit caritas sine timore, sed casto; numquam sine cupiditate, sed ordinata. Implet ergo caritas legem servi, cum infundit devotionem; implet et mercenarii, cum ordinat cupiditatem. ... Deinde cupiditas tunc recte a superveniente caritate ordinatur, cum male quidem penitus respuuntur, bonis vero meliora praeferuntur, nec bona nisi propter meliora appetuntur. Quod cum plene per Dei gratiam assecutum fuerit, diligetur corpus, et universa corporis bona tantum propter animam, animae propter Deum, Deus autem propter seipsum.

369. *Ep* 85.3 (7:222.4–6): ... ordinatam in me caritatem, sciens et diligens quae diligenda sunt, et quantum, et ad quid diligenda sunt. ... I am using the translation of Bruno Scott James, *The Letters of St. Bernard of Clairvaux* (London: Burns & Oates, 1953), p. 126. For other letters discussing *caritas ordinata*, see, e.g., *Ep* 8.1 (7:48.4), and 440 (8:417–18).

370. *SCC* 49.5 (2:75.27–29): Importabilis siquidem absque scientia est zelus. Ubi ergo vehemens aemulatio, ibi maxime discretio necessaria, quae est ordinatio caritatis.

371. Ibid. (2:76.9–10): Est ergo discretio non tam virtus, quam quaedam moderatrix et auriga virtutum, ordinatrixque affectuum, et morum doctrix.

372. Ibid. (2:76.15–17): Oportet autem ut hos una omnes caritas liget et contemperet in unitatem corporis Christi: quod minime omnino facere poterit, si ipsa non fuerit ordinata.

373. Bernard, to be sure, talked about love as *actus* primarily within the context of the ascetical obligations and fraternal charity of the monastic community, not in terms of the

duties of the prelate which Gregory the Great had been concerned with (see chapter 2, pp. 74–79). Nevertheless, the abbot's teaching implies important issues about all active love. On this, see Bernardo Olivero, "Aspects of the Love of Neighbor in the Spiritual Doctrine of St. Bernard," *Cistercian Studies* 26 (1991): 107–19, 204–26.

374. *SCC* 50.4 (2:80.10–11): Sed est affectio quam caro gignit, et est quam ratio regit, et est quam condit sapientia.

375. Ibid. (80:21–22): . . . amore tamen amoris ipsius vehementer accenditur.

376. *SCC* 50.5 (2:80.29–81.1): Nam actualis inferiora praefert, affectualis superiora.

377. Ibid. (2:81.4–5): Attamen in bene ordinata actione saepe, aut etiam semper, ordo oppositus invenitur.

378. Ibid. (2:81.18–19): Ordo praeposterus; sed necessitas non habet legem.

379. *SCC* 50.7 (2:82). Proceeding logically, Bernard also mentions a third category, those who clearly will never return to God and therefore are to be hated, according to Ps 138:21; but his concluding lines on this class (2:82.23–25) seem to indicate that we can never be sure in this life that any particular person actually belongs to this group.

380. *SCC* 50.8 (2:83.14–17): Dirige actus nostros, prout nostra temporalis necessitas poscit, et dispone affectus nostros, prout tua veritas aeterna requirit, ut possit unusquisque nostrum secure in te gloriari et dicere, quia ORDINAVIT IN ME CARITATEM.

381. Still valuable on this issue is Thomas Merton, "Action and Contemplation in St. Bernard," originally published in 1953–54, and reprinted in *Thomas Merton on St. Bernard*, pp. 23–104.

382. See John R. Sommerfeldt, "Bernard of Clairvaux: The Mystic and Society," in *The Spirituality of Western Christendom*, ed. E. Rozanne Elder (Kalamazoo: Cistercian Publications, 1976), pp. 72–84; and Charles Dumont, "L'action contemplative, le temps dans l'eternité d'après saint Bernard," *Collectanea Cisterciensia* 54 (1992): 269–83.

383. See the famous reference to himself as a "chimaera" in *Ep* 250.4 (8:147.2–3): Ego enim quaedam Chimaera mei saeculi, nec clericum gero nec laicum. In *SCC* 57.9 (2:125.7–8) he speaks of the holy person, like Job, in the following manner: Vides virum sanctum inter fructum operis et somnium contemplationis graviter aestuare. (This is perhaps Bernard's own temperament speaking more than his judgment of Job–everything he did, he did *graviter aestuans*.) For an interesting letter reflecting Bernard's tensions and their resolution through the *caritas* that set him free, see *Ep* 143 (7:342–43). On Bernard's psychology, see J. Leclercq, *Nouveau visage de Bernard de Clairvaux: Approches psycho-historiques* (Paris: Editions du Cerf, 1976).

384. *SCC* 18.6 (1:108.7–9): Haec omnia operatur unus atque idem Spiritus secundum operationem, quae infusio appellatur, quatenus illa, quae effusio dicta est, pure, et ob hoc tute, iam administretur, ad laudem et gloriam Domini nostri Iesu Christi. . . . This passage summarizes a wordplay between *infusio virtutum* and *effusio donorum*, which runs through the whole sermon.

385. See the abbot's insistence that it is better to be a reservoir (*concha*) than a canal (*canalis*) in *SCC* 18.3 (1:104)

386. *SCC* 9.8–9 (1:47). Cf. *SCC* 12.1 (1:60–61), where the ointment of *pietas* (mercy for others) is higher than the other ointments of *contritio* and *devotio*.

387. *SCC* 58.1 (2:127.20–25): More igitur suo sponsus, ubi dilectam paululum sinu proprio quievisse persentit, ad ea denuo quae utiliora visa sunt, trahere non cunctatur. Non tamen quasi invitam: nec enim quod fieri vetuit, faceret ipse. Sed trahi sane a sponso, sponsae est ab ipso accipere desiderium quo trahatur, desiderium bonorum operum, desiderium fructificandi sponso, quippe cui vivere sponsus est, et mori lucrum. Cf. *SCC* 57.9 (2:24–25).

388. *SCC* 51.2 (2:85.7–10): At quoties, ut dixi, corruit a contemplativa, toties in activam se recipit, inde nimirum tamquam e vicino familiarius reditura in idipsum, quoniam sunt in-

vicem contubernales hae duae et cohabitant pariter: est quippe soror Mariae Martha. Bernard goes on in 51.5 (2:85–86) to apply this to his own preaching in a highly personal way.

389. See especially *SCC* 52.6 (2:93–94), and *Asspt* 3.2 (5:239–40).

390. *SCC* 52.7 (2:95.9–12): Geram eis morem quoad potuero, et in ipsis serviam Deo meo, quamdiu fuero, in caritate non ficta. Non quaeram quae mea sunt, non quod mihi utile est, sed quod multis, id mihi utile iudicabo.

391. E.g., *Asspt* 2.7–8 and 3.4 (5:236–37 and 241).

392. See especially *Asspt* 5.6–13 (5:254–60).

393. *Asspt* 5.12 (5:258.26–27): Debet quisque perfectus unitatem habere ad seipsum, debet et ad proximum: ad seipsum per integritatem, ad proximum per conformitatem.

394. *SCC* 41.6 (2:32.1–3): Docemur ex hoc sane intermittenda plerumque dulcia oscula propter lactantia ubera, nec quemque sibi, sed illi omnes qui mortuus est pro omnibus esse vivendum. On the soul as Bride and Mother, see *SCC* 85.13 (2:315–16). An unusual version of this is found in *SCC* 8.9 (1:41–42), where the soul is Bride and Sister.

395. See, e.g., Charles Dumont, "Reading Saint Bernard Today," *Cistercian Studies* 22 (1987): 152–71; and Jean Leclercq, "Une doctrine spirituelle pour notre temps?" *La dottrina della vita spirituale*, pp. 397–410.

396. *Csi* 5.11.24 (3:486.17–18): . . . solus est Deus qui frustra numquam quaeri potest, nec cum inveniri non potest.

397. *SCC* 51.3 (2:85.21–22).

Chapter 6

1. The three works are (1) the *Epistola aurea*, Dom Mabillon's name for what the manuscripts usually entitle *Epistola ad fratres de Monte Dei*, and sometimes *De vita solitaria* (about 280 manuscripts are known); (2) the *De natura et dignitate amoris*, sometimes called the *Liber beati Bernardi de amore*; and (3) the *De contemplando Deo*, sometimes paired with the former under the title *Liber soliloquiorum sancti Bernardi*. For a study of the dissemination of the *Epistola aurea*, see Volker Honemann, "The Reception of William of Saint-Thierry's *Epistola ad fratres de Monte Dei* during the Middle Ages," *Cistercians in the Late Middle Ages*, ed. E. Rozanne Elder (Kalamazoo: Cistercian Publications, 1981), pp. 5–18.

2. William's authentic works number eighteen and were written between ca. 1121 and 1148. For the most recent listing, see *Guillemi a Sancto Theodorico Opera Omnia: Pars I, Expositio super Epistolam ad Romanos,* ed. Paul Verdeyen (CCCM 86), pp. xxiv–xxxi. Unlike Bernard, we have no standard modern edition of William's works, but several competing and incomplete series by M.-M. Davy, R. Thomas, J.-M. Déchanet, et al. (these in the SC), and now P. Verdeyen, et al. (in the CC). Unfortunately, this means there is not even a common form of reference to divisions of the various texts. William's works will be cited according to the following editions and abbreviations (page and line number in modern editions, page and column in PL):

Contemp–De contemplando Deo (ca. 1121). Critical edition of Jacques Hourlier, *Guillaume de Saint-Thierry: La contemplation de Dieu. L'Oraison de Dom Guillaume* (SC 61). Also found in PL 184:365–80.

Nat am–De natura et dignitate amoris (ca. 1121–24). PL 184:379–408.

Sacr altar–De sacramento altaris (ca. 1127). PL 180:341–66.

Brev Cant–Brevis Commentatio in Canticum (ca. 1130 and after). PL 184:407–35.

Exp Rm–Expositio super Epistolam ad Romanos (ca. 1135–37). Edition of P. Verdeyen in CCCM 86. Also in PL 180:547–694.

Med–Meditativae Orationes (ca. 1128–37). PL 180:205–48.

Nat corp–De natura corporis et animae (ca. 1135–37). PL 180:695–726.

    Cant–Expositio super Cantica Canticorum (ca. 1137–39). Critical edition by J.-M. Déchanet, *Exposé sur le Cantique des Cantiques* (SC 82). Also in PL 180:475–546.

    Spec–Speculum fidei (1142–44). Critical edition by J.-M. Déchanet, *Le miroir de la foi* (SC 301). Also in PL 180:365–87.

    Aenig–Aenigma fidei (1142–44). The best modern edition is in M.-M. Davy, *Guillaume de Saint-Thierry: Deux traités sur la foi: Le miroir de la foi, L'enigme de la foi* (Paris: Vrin, 1959). Also in PL 180:397–440.

    Ep frat–Epistola ad Fratres de Monte Dei (1144–45). Critical edition by J.-M. Déchanet, *Guillaume de Saint-Thierry. Lettre aux Frères du Mont-Dieu (Lettre d'or)* (SC 301). Also in PL 184:307–54.

    Vita Ber–Vita sancti Bernardi (1145–48). In PL 185:225–66.

Translations of most of William's works are to be found in the Cistercian Fathers Series, but unless otherwise noted all translations are my own.

3. For example, William's views on the identification of love and knowledge were briefly studied by Pierre Rousselot, *Pour l'histoire du problème de l'amour au moyen âge*, Beiträge zur Geschichte der Philosophie des Mittelalters VI.6 (Münster: Aschendorff, 1908), pp. 96–102. More intense study began in the 1920s with A. Adam, *Guillaume de Saint-Thierry, sa vie et ses oeuvres* (Bourg, 1923); and A. Wilmart, "La serie et la date des ouvrages de Guillaume de Saint-Thierry," *Revue Mabillon* 14 (1924): 157–67. Two important treatments appeared in the early 1930s: Léopold Malévez, "La doctrine de l'image et de la connaissance mystique chez Guillaume de St.-Thierry," *Recherches des sciences religieuses* 22 (1932): 178–205, 257–79; and the "Appendix V" devoted to William in E. Gilson's *The Mystical Theology of St. Bernard* (Paris: Vrin, 1934; Eng. trans. 1940).

4. J.-M. Déchanet, *Aux sources de la spiritualité de Guillaume de Saint-Thierry* (Bruges, 1940); idem, *Guillaume de Saint-Thierry: L'homme et son oeuvre* (Bruges, 1942), available in English as *William of St. Thierry: The Man and his work*, trans. R. Strachan (Spencer: Cistercian Publications, 1972). Déchanet also authored the article on William in DS 6:1241–63. M.-M. Davy edited, translated, and wrote extensively on William. Her most important work is *Théologie et mystique de Guillaume de Saint-Thierry. I. La connaissance de Dieu* (Paris: Vrin, 1954).

5. In English, see especially the papers of Odo Brooke, conveniently collected as *Studies in Monastic Theology* (Kalamazoo, MI: Cistercian Publications, 1980); David N. Bell, *The Image and Likeness: The Augustinian Spirituality of William of St. Thierry* (Kalamazoo, MI: Cistercian Publications, 1984); and various studies by E. Rozanne Elder and Thomas Tomasic cited below. Among recent French investigations, see, e.g., Y.-A. Baudelet, *L'experience spirituelle selon Guillaume de Saint-Thierry* (Paris: Cerf, 1985); Robert Thomas, *Guillaume de Saint-Thierry: Homme de doctrine, homme de prière* (Quebec: Éditions Anne Sigier, 1989); and Paul Verdeyen, *La théologie mystique de Guillaume de Saint-Thierry* (Paris: FAC-éditions, 1990). In Italian, see Ambrogio M. Piazzoni, *Guglielmo di Saint-Thierry: Il declino dell'ideale monastico nel secolo XII* (Rome: Istituto Storico Italiano per il Medio Evo. Studi Storici 181–3, 1988); and Gabriele Manzino, *"L'uomo che vuole e che corre": La problematica antropologica nel pensiero di Guglielmo di Saint-Thierry* (dissertation, University of Genoa, 1989–90). See also the introduction by Claudio Leonardi, "Guglielmo di Saint-Thierry e la Storia del Monachesimo," *Guillaume de Saint-Thierry: La Lettera d'Oro* (Florence: Sansoni, 1983), pp. 5–42. In German the most recent general study is that of Kurt Ruh, *Die Geschichte der abendländische Mystik:* Band I, *Die Grundlegung durch die Kirchenväter und die Mönchstheologie des 12. Jahrhunderts* (Munich: Beck, 1990), chapter 9.

6. Jean Leclercq, "Toward a Spiritual Portrait of William of Saint Thierry," *William, Abbot of St. Thierry: A Colloquium at the Abbey of St. Thierry*, trans. Jerry Carfantan (Kalamazoo, MI: Cistercian Publications, 1987), p. 207: "William has appeared to us as a high-strung person

with all that this entails in weakness in character, but also in sensitivity, psychological rich-ness, and interior resources which can be placed at the service of cultural and spiritual values."

7. William's lost *Sententiae* were apparently a series of excerpts from Augustine. In addi-tion, he compiled two useful books of extracts from Ambrose and from Gregory the Great on the Song of Songs (PL 15:1849–88; PL 180:441–74). Other works of William, especially *Aenig, Exp Rm* and *Nat corp*, contain much quotation but are more independent creations. On William's two methods of using patristic sources, *florilegium* and *recapitulatio*, see Déchanet, *William of St. Thierry*, pp. 140–42.

8. This has been demonstrated by David Bell, *Image and Likeness*, who summarizes: "The Augustinian tradition provides all that could be desired to establish the basis for William's spirituality" (p. 18). See also John Anderson, "The Use of Greek Sources by William of Saint-Thierry especially in the 'Enigma fidei,'" in *One Yet Two: Monastic Traditions East and West*, ed. M. Basil Pennington (Kalamazoo, MI: Cistercian Publications, 1976), pp. 242–54; and Goul-ven Madec, "A propos des sources de Guillaume de Saint Thierry," *Revue des études augustini-ennes* 24 (1978): 302–9. This is not to say that William does not differ from Augustine in places, as we shall see below.

9. See Déchanet, *Aux sources*, passim; and especially, "Guillaume et Plotin," *Revue du moyen âge latin* 2 (1946): 241–60. For a survey of the issue of William's sources, see Gonzalo Fernan-dez, "Guillaume de Saint-Thierry: Le problème des sources," *Collectanea Cisterciensia* 45 (1983): 210–20.

10. This remains a controversial area in the interpretation of William's thought. William made direct use of Gregory of Nyssa's *De opificio hominis* in his *Nat corp*, as we will note below; but this does not appear to be *the* central source of his theological anthropology. The abbot of St. Thierry made even greater use of Origen, especially the Alexandrian's commen-taries on the Song of Songs and Romans–to the extent that he can be called the great "Ori-genist" of the twelfth century. Nevertheless, I find exaggerated the claims of Verdeyen (*La théologie mystique de Guillaume*, passim), which in effect has William breaking with the tradition of Augustine and Gregory to initiate a new Origenist mysticism to be continued in the Rhineland and Flemish mystics of the thirteenth and fourteenth centuries.

11. On William's conflict with Abelard, see especially Thomas M. Tomasic, "William of Saint-Thierry against Peter Abelard: A Dispute on the Meaning of Being a Person," *Analecta Cisterciensia* 28 (1972): 3–76. For an interesting comparison of William, Bernard and Abelard, see Leclercq, "Toward a Spiritual Portrait of William of Saint Thierry," pp. 216–20.

12. For comments, perhaps overly optimistic, on the relation between William's doctrinal conservatism and his speculative daring, see Déchanet, *William of St. Thierry*, pp. 133–51.

13. William of St. Thierry, *Vita Ber* 12.59 (PL 185:259BC): Itaque tunc disseruit mihi de Cantico canticorum, quantum tempus illud infirmitatis meae permisit, moraliter tantum, in-termissis mysteriis Scripturae illius, quia sic volebam, et sic petierem ab eo. . . . In quo cum benigne et sine invidia exponeret mihi, et communicaret sententias intelligentiae et sensus ex-perientiae suae, et multa docere niteretur inexpertum, quia nonnisi experiendo discuntur, etsi intelligere non poteram adhuc quae apponebantur mihi, plus tamen solito intelligere me faciebat quid ad ea intelligenda deesset mihi. The discussion formed the basis for the *Brevis commentatio*, which William later composed partly from his reminiscences, partly from his own throughts and partly from later works of Bernard. See Thomas X. Davis, "A Further Study of the *Brevis commentatio*," *Bernardus Magister: Papers Presented at the Nonacentenary Cele-bration of the Birth of Saint Bernard of Clairvaux, Kalamazoo, Michigan*, ed. John R. Sommerfeldt (Kalamazoo, MI: Cistercian Publications; Cîteaux: Commentarii Cistercienses, 1992) pp. 187–202; and Verdeyen, *La théologie mystique*, pp. 6–9, who speculates that part of the inspira-tion for the discussion was the reading of Origen's commentary.

14. Verdeyen, reaches the same conclusion: "Tout cela nous autorise à considérer l'entretien des deux abbés à Clairvaux comme un événement décisif dans l'histoire de la spiritualité chrétienne" (*La théologie mystique,* p. 280).

15. Twelve of the *Meditativae Orationes,* in the style of John of Fécamp and Anselm, were long known. Déchanet identified the thirteenth, which, like the fourth, must date from the Signy period.

16. William speaks of *pingue otium* in *Ep frat* 13 (SC 223:152.5). (The phrase is taken from Seneca, *Epistula ad Lucilium* 73.10.) Later in the same work, William provides a succinct comment on the difference between mental laziness and the leisure of contemplation: Summa enim mentis malitia est otium iners. . . . .Otiosum est vacare Deo? Immo negotium negotiorum hoc est" (*Ep frat* 81; SC 223:206.2–7). On William's understanding of *otium* in the context of the monastic tradition, see Jean Leclercq, *OTIA MONASTICA: Études sur le vocabulaire de la contemplation au moyen âge,* Studia Anselmiana 51 (Rome: Herder, 1963), passim ("Guillaume de Saint-Thierry" under "Index des noms").

17. Leclercq, "Toward a Spiritual Portrait," p. 212.

18. According to William, each song contains a prelude, an invitation to love (*irritamen amoris*), a purification (*actus purgatorius*), a marriage song (*epithalamium*), and a description of the union of the Bride and Bridegroom (*accubitus*). He completed the commentary on the first two songs only (minus the *accubitus* section of the second), thus, like Bernard, reaching only Song 3:4. On the use of scripture in the *Cant,* see Jacques Delesalle, "*AMOUR ET LUMIERE*: Fonctions de l'ecriture sainte dans la structure d'un texte: le premier chant de l'EXPOSITIO SUPER CANTICA CANTICORUM' de Guillaume de St. Thierry," *Kartäusermystik und-Mystiker,* ed. James Hogg (Salzburg: Institut für Anglistik und Amerkanistik Universität Salzburg, 1982), 3:1–145.

19. *Cant* 5 (SC 82:76). There are, of course, allegorical readings applied to the church in a number of places, e.g., *Cant* 30, 146, 153 (SC 82:112, 308, 324), but on the whole William stays closer to the *sensus moralis* than Bernard does.

20. Among the common themes are the mutuality of love and knowledge in the path to union and the importance of the regaining of the *similitudo Dei.* Like Bernard, William characterizes union as an *unitas spiritus,* but we shall see that he understands it in a somewhat different way. For a comparison between the interpretations of Bernard and William, see M.-M. Davy, "Le thème de l'âme-épouse chez Bernard de Clairvaux et Guillaume de Saint-Thierry," in *Entretiens sur la renaissance du 12e siècle* (Paris: Mouton, 1968), pp. 247–72; and Kurt Ruh, "Die Hoheliederklärungen Bernhards von Clairvaux und Wilhelms von St. Thierry," in *"Minnichlichui gotes erkennusse": Studien zur frühen abendländischen Mystiktradition,* ed. Dietrich Schmidtke (Stuttgart-Bad Cannstaat:Frommann-holzboog, 1990), pp. 16–27.

21. For a study of this text, see B. McGinn, "Introduction," *Three Treatises on Man: A Cistercian Anthropology* (Kalamazoo, MI: Cistercian Publications, 1977), pp. 27–47; and Michel Lemoine, *De la nature du corps et de l'âme: Texte établi, traduit et commenté par M. Lemoine* (Paris, 1988).

22. William also knew something of Eriugena's *Periphyseon,* though this should not be considered a major source. See B. McGinn, "Pseudo-Dionysius and the Early Cistercians," in *One Yet Two,* pp. 224–28; and especially David N. Bell, "William of St. Thierry and John Scot Eriugena," *Cîteaux* 33 (1982): 5–28. On the influence of Eriugena in the twelfth century, see especially Edouard Jeauneau, "Le renouveau érigénien du XIIe siècle," in *Eriugena Redivivus,* ed. Werner Beierwaltes (Heidelberg: Winter, 1987), pp. 26–46. Jeauneau cautions prudence in the face of earlier scholarship that exaggerated Eriugena's twelfth-century influence (see esp. pp. 44–46).

23. On microcosm, see *Nat corp,* prol. and 2.2 (PL 180:695 and 710CD); on image and likeness, see especially 2.5 and 11–13 (ibid.:713D–15C and 720D–22D).

24. There is a translation of this work with a full apparatus of the patristic sources used and a topical index in *William of St. Thierry: Exposition on the Epistle to the Romans*, trans. John Baptist Hasbrouck (Kalamazoo, MI: Cistercian Publications, 1980).

25. For William's comments on the purposes of the two treatises, see the important introduction to his writings that appears in the dedicatory letter to the *Ep frat* 4–8 (SC 223:132–34). Odo Brooke has provided illuminating studies of the treatises in his papers "The Speculative Development of the Trinitarian Theology of William of St. Thierry" (first published 1960–61), "William of St. Thierry's Doctrine of the Ascent to God by Faith" (1963–66), and "Faith and Mystical Experience in William of St. Thierry" (1964). I will cite these papers as reprinted in *Studies*. For a brief introduction to the two treatises, see Patrick Ryan, "William of St. Thierry's Two Treatises on Faith," *Cistercian Studies* 18 (1983): 92–105.

26. According to Brooke, "The *Speculum fidei* is no less a treatise on charity than a treatise on faith. . . . But, if this is so, it is no less true to say that the *Speculum fidei* is also a treatise on the mystical experience of the Trinity" (*Studies*, p. 170).

27. See Carolyn J. Vogt, "William of St. Thierry's 'The Golden Epistle.' Mystical Ascent Through Incarnation," *Cistercian Studies* 8 (1973): 337–54, who shows how William's notion of asceticism is designed to teach the proper love of the body within a sustained mystical program.

28. *Cant* 1 (SC 82:70): Domine Deus noster, qui ad imaginem et similitudinem tuam creasti nos, scilicet ad te contemplandum, teque fruendum; quem nemo usque ad fruendum, nisi in quantum similis tibi efficitur. . . libera a servitute corruptionis, id quod tibi soli deservire debet in nobis, amorem nostrum. Amor enim est, qui cum liber est, similes nos tibi efficit, in tantum, in quantum nos tibi afficit *sensus vitae*, quo se sentit quicumque vivit de *spiritu vitae*. . . . The *spiritus vitae*, a term William found in Ezek 1:20–21 and Rom 8:2, is one of his favorite titles for the Holy Spirit, whose effect in us, the *sensus vitae*, frees our love to make it capable of knowing God. Cf. *Cant* 67 (SC 82:168): Solum etenim lumen vultus Dei docet hoc; sensus vitae, de Spiritu vitae indicat hoc. . . . See pp. 267–73 below on the role of the Holy Spirit.

29. Bell provides a good summary of the *imago Dei* theme in William (*Image and Likeness*, chap. 3). For general background, see Robert Javelet, *Image et ressemblance au douzième siècle de Saint Anselme à Alain de Lille*, 2 vols. (Paris: Letouzey & Ané, 1967).

30. See, e.g., Bell, *Image and Likeness*, pp. 89, 96–98.

31. *Exp Rm* 7, commenting on Rom 12:1–3, explains how *rationale obsequium* restores the likeness to God and therefore helps repair the damaged image (CCCM 86.166.53–59): . . . per quod [rationale obsequium] ad similitudinem Dei proficimus, et eius recuperamus imaginem, quam contraria agendo ex parte amisimus. Non enim totam, quia si totam amisissemus, nichil maneret, unde diceretur: *Quamquam in imagine pertransit homo, verumtamen vane conturbatur* (Ps 38:). Si autem nichil omnino de eo amisissemus, non esset unde diceretur: *Reformamini in novitate sensus vestri* (Rom 5:5).

32. *Spec* 79 (SC 301:146.1–148.12): Menti siquidem ad aeternitatem creatae, ut eius per intelligentiam sit capax, per fruitionem particeps, quasi naturali quadam affinitate conjuncta videntur quae aeterna sunt ac divina; in tantum, ut etsi stolidior facta forte fuerit ex vitio, numquam tamen eorum privetur appetitu. . . . In quibus tamen et si habet natura appetitum ex gratia creante, non tamen ea perfecte dinoscit, nisi ex gratia illuminante, nec apprehendit, nisi Deo donante.

33. *Cant* 4 (SC 82:74): . . . sancte Spiritus, te invocamus, ut amore tuo repleamur, o amor, ad intelligendum canticum amoris; ut et nos colloquii sancti Sponsi et Sponsae, aliquatenus efficiamur participes; ut agatur in nobis quod legitur a nobis.

34. For some treatments, see, e.g., *Contemp* 11 (SC 61:106); *Med.* 4.6 (PL 180:216CD); *Nat corp* 1.6, 2.5 and 2.7 (PL 180:702CD, 713D–15C and 717BC); *Ep frat* 199 (SC 223:308); *Cant* 19, 22, 64 and 66 (SC 82:92, 98, 162 and 166).

35. See *Nat am* 11.34 (PL 184:401B).

36. *Med* 12.14 (PL 180:246D): Reformatur enim anima sancta ad imaginem Trinitatis, ad imaginem eius qui creavit eam, etiam ipso modo beatitudinis suae. Nam illuminata voluntas et affecta, id est intellectus et amor, et fruendi habitus, sicut de Trinitate Deo dicitur et creditur, quodammodo tres sunt affectionum personae. . . .

37. *Memoria-intellectus-amor* can be found in Augustine, *De Trinitate* 14.8.11 (PL 42:1044–45). In William we find it, e.g., in *Nat am* 2.3 (PL 184:382BD) in the form *memoria-ratio-voluntas*. This triad also occurs in *Cant* 86, 88, 122 (SC 82:204, 208, 264). In *Nat corp* 2.11 (PL 180:721BD) we find *mens-cogitatio-voluntas*, while *Nat corp* 2.13 (722B) has *memoria-consilium-voluntas*. Cf. *Aenig* 26 (ed. Davy: 114), and *Ep frat* 210 (SC 223:314).

38. See *Spec* 1 and 7–9 (SC 301:60 and 66–68). This is really a form of the second type of participation and will be taken up below.

39. It would be a mistake, of course, to exclude trinitarian anagogy from Augustine's aim, as *De Trin.* 14.12.15 (PL 42:1048) shows; but there is certainly a difference in emphasis between the bishop of Hippo and the Cistercian. See Brooke, *Studies*, p. 191, n.57, for a balanced appreciation.

40. See Brooke, *Studies*, pp. 14–17. William's doctrine of the Trinity has been most recently treated by Verdeyen, *La théologie mystique*, chap. 2.

41. Brooke, *Studies*, p. 24.

42. *Cant* 66 (SC 82:166): Adesto ergo tota tibi, et tota te utere ad cognoscendum te, et cujus imago sis, quid possis in eo cujus imago es.

43. *Nat corp* 2.5 (PL 180:714B): Quin etiam in hoc ipso quod neque sui ipsius perfectam apprehendit scientiam rationalis animus, divinae incomprehensibilitatis naturam per quamdam similitudinem videtur characterizare. Cf. Gregory of Nyssa, *De hominis opificio* 8. William knew this text in the translation of John the Scot, as mentioned above; see M. Cappuyns, "Le *De Imagine* de Grégoire de Nysse, traduit par Jean Scot Érigène," *Recherches de théologie ancienne et médiévale* 32 (1965): 205–62 (see p. 219 for chap. 8). For John the Scot's more extensive development of this negative anthropology in *Periphyseon*, see above, chapter 3, pp. 105–6.

44. On the *regio* or *locus dissimilitudinis*, a term that William, like Bernard (e.g., *Div* 43.3), took from Augustine (*Conf.* 7.10.16); see *Cant* 65 (SC82:164), *Med* 4.6 (PL 180:216D) and *Nat corp* 2.15 (PL 180:725C). Cf. *profundum dissimilitudinis* in Cant 83 (SC 82:200).

45. *Contemp* 4 (SC 61:68): . . . factus sum michiipsi de meipso laboriosa et taediosa quaestio.

46. *Ep frat* 259 (SC 223:350): Et haec est omnis eorum perfectio, similitudo Dei. Perfectum autem nolle esse, delinquere est. Et ideo huic perfectioni nutrienda est semper voluntas, amor praeparandus; voluntas cohibenda, ne in aliena dissipetur; amor servandus, ne inquinetur. Propter hoc enim solum et creati sumus et vivimus, ut Deo similes simus. Ad imaginem enim Dei creati sumus.

47. *Ep frat* 260 (SC 223:350–52). Cf. *Nat corp* 2.3 and 11 (PL 180:712BC and 721A).

48. *Ep frat* 262 (SC 223:352–54): Super hanc autem alia adhuc est similitudo Dei . . . in tantum proprie propria, ut non jam similitudo, sed unitas spiritus nominetur; cum fit homo unum cum Deo, unus spiritus, non tantum unitate idem volendi, sed expressiore quadam veritate virtutis, sicut jam dictum est, aliud velle non valendi.

49. E.g., *Cant* 132 (SC 223:278): . . . ut semper tibi [i.e., God] jungatur similitudine idem volendi, a quo non receditur, nisi dissimilem volendi.

50. *Spec* 107 (SC 301:178.17–19): Videre namque ibi seu cognoscere Deum, similem est esse Deo; et similem ei esse, videre seu cognoscere eum est. Cf *Ep frat* 210 (SC 223:316). On this theme, see below pp. 262–65.

51. *Aenig* 6 (ed. Davy: 96): In interiore ergo homine similitudo ista est, qua renovatur homo de die in diem in agnitione Dei, secundum imaginem ejus qui creavit eum . . . et in tantum eum propinquius ac familiarius videmus, in quantum cognoscendo eum ac diligendo efficimur ei similiores.

52. Ibid.: Ibi enim sicut in Trinitate que Deus est, mutuo se vident Pater et Filius et mutuo se videre, unum eos esse est, et hoc alterum esse quod alter est; sic qui ad hoc predestinati sunt, et in hoc assumpti fuerint videbunt Deum sicuti est, et videndo efficientur sicut ipse est, similes ei. Ubi etiam sicut in Patre et in Filio, que visio, ipsa unitas est; sic in Deo et homine, que visio, ipsa et similitudo futura est. Spiritus sanctus unitas Patris et Filii, ipse etiam caritas es similitudo Dei et hominis. Cf. *Med* 3.6 and 6.8 (PL 180:212D–13B, 224CD). We will see more on this below.

53. On the *similitudo Dei* and its perfection, see Bell, *Image and Likeness*, pp. 108–23.

54. William's interest in the body and his stress on its need for harmonious cooperation with the soul is given theoretical exposition in *Nat corp*, especially the first part. The first book of the *Ep frat* contains many wise remarks on the proper cultivation of the *legitimum foedus* between body and soul, e.g., *Ep frat* 74, 88, 127–28, etc. (SC 223:200–02, 212, 242–44).

55. Another favored term for the higher dimension of the soul is *mens*, a word William often used, once defining it as a *vis quaedam animae, qua inhaeremus Deo et fruimur* (*Nat am* 10.28; PL 184:397C). See *Ep frat* 206 (SC 223:312), where it is equated with *animus*, and *Nat am* 7.20 (392C) where it is called the *caput animae*. Cf *Nat corp* 2.10 (PL 180:720A), and the discussion in Bell, *Image and Likeness*, p. 96 n. 34.

56. For further dicussion on the background to the terms *intellectus* and *intelligentia*, see Bernard McGinn, *The Golden Chain* (Washington: Cistercian Publications, 1972), chap. 4.

57. For an introduction to this central issue in western mysticism, let me refer once again to my paper, "Love, Knowledge and *Unio mystica* in the Western Christian Tradition," pp. 63–64 on William.

58. Isaac of Stella, *Epistola de anima* (PL 194:1880B). On Isaac, see below, chapter 7, pp. 284–96.

59. *Nat am* 3.8 (PL 184:393A): Visus ergo ad videndum Deum naturale lumen animae, ab auctore naturae creatus, charitas est. Sunt autem duo oculi in hoc visu, ad lumen quod Deus est videndum naturali quadam intentione semper palpitantes, amor et ratio. Cum alter conatur sine altero, non tantum proficit; cum invicem se adjuvant, multum possunt, scilicet cum unus oculus efficiuntur, de quo dicit Sponsus in Canticis: Vulnerasti cor meum, o amica mea, in uno oculorum tuorum. On the two becoming one, see *Ep frat* 196 (SC 223:304–06); and *Cant* 92 (SC 82:212). On the two eyes of the soul, see Verdeyen, *La théologie mystique*, pp. 31–34; and Aimé Solignac, "Oculus (Animae, Cordis, Mentis)," DS 11:591–601 (596–98 on William).

60. *Nat am* 8.21 (PL 184:393B): . . . amor autem suo defectu plus proficit, sui ignorantia plus apprehendit, . . . amor postponens quod non est, in eo quod est gaudet deficere.

61. See Malévez, "La doctrine de l'image," esp. pp. 183–88.

62. *Nat corp* 1.8 (PL 180:705D–06A): Omnis enim sensus sentientiem transmutat quodammodo in id quod sentitur, alioquin non est sensus.

63. *Spec* 97 (SC 301:168.10–12): . . . vis visibilis a cerebro per radios oculorum egressa, offendit in formas vel colores visibilium; quas cum menti renuntiat, conformatur eis mens ipsa, et fit visus. The passage goes on to make an explicit comparison with the *intellectus amoris*. For comparable texts, see *Med* 3.7–8 (PL 180:213BC) and *Cant* 21 and 94 (SC 223:96 and 218).

64. Two crucial qualifications to the analogy may be noted here. First, while love plays an active role in searching for the Divine Lover, it does so not on its own but only as first activated by God's gift of *caritas*. Second, God, unlike the sense object, is not to be thought of as an "object" outside our love, but is its immanent and intersubjective source.

65. Philosophically, this "law of mean terms" was first expressed by Plato in *Timaeus* 31B: "It is not possible that two things alone should be conjoined without a third; for there must needs be some intermediary bond to connect the two."

66. *Ep frat* 140 (SC 223:254) summarizes the different dimensions of the triple division.

67. *Cant* 13 (SC 223:84–86): Tres ergo status esse orantium, vel orationum, manifestum est: animalem, rationalem, spiritualem. Unusquisque secundum modum suum, format sibi, vel proponit Dominum Deum suum, quia qualis est ipse qui orat, talis ei apparet Deus quem orat. The notion that God appears to each person according to the manner in which we pray to him also is found in Bernard; see *SCC* 69.7 (SBOp 2:206.25–27): Igitur qualem te paraveris Deo, talis oportet appareat tibi Deus: cum sancto sanctus erit, et cum viro innocente innocens erit.

68. *Ep frat* 41–42 (SC 223:176): . . . sicut stella differt a stella in claritate, sic cella a cella in conversatione, incipientium scilicet, proficientium, et perfectorum. . . . Et cum ex his tribus hominum generibus constet omnis status religionis. . . .

69. Origen, *De principiis* 4.11 (PG 11:365A) applied the distinction to three classes of readers of scripture, and it is found as a distinction of three states of souls in his homilies *In Jeremiam* 14.10 (PG 13:415AB) and *In Romanos* 1.18 and 6.14 (PG 14:866A and 1102). All of these texts were available in the library at Clairvaux. The three stages appear in the *Brevis commentatio* 1–3 as three forms of love: Tres sunt status amoris Dei in anima christiana. Primus, sensualis vel animalis; secundus, rationalis; tertius, spiritualis vel intellectualis (PL 184:407D). It is difficult to know whether this is their earliest appearance in William's work, or we are dealing with a later insertion, as argued by T. Davis in "The *Brevis commentatio*," pp. 189–92. On this triadic division in William, see Déchanet, *William of St. Thierry*, pp. 99–101; Louis Bouyer, *The Cistercian Heritage*, (Westminster, MD: Newman, 1958), pp. 94–102; Brooke, *Studies*, pp. 22–23; and Verdeyen, *La théologie mystique*, pp. 147–48.

70. *Cant* 16 (SC 82:88): Et aliquando quidem qui sic est, proponit mentis suae oculis Dominum Salvatorem, secundum formam humanam, et sicut homo ad hominem humanam quamdam, et quasi corpoream induit orationis affectionem. . . .

71. E.g., *Cant* 17 (SC 82:90): Sed tamen usque hodie dicit Jesus discipulis suis: Expedit vos ut ego vadam (John 16:7), hoc est subtraham aspectibus vestris humanitatis meae personam; nisi enim abiero, Paraclitus non venerit ad vos. . . .

72. *Cant* 19 (SC 82:92): . . . cum affectat homo cognoscere Deum, in quantum fas est, et cognosci ab eo, revelari sibi faciem ejus gratiae, ipsum vero conscientiae suae, ut cognoscens eum, et cognitus ab eo, oret eum et adoret, sicut oportet, in spiritu et veritate. On God revealing himself in the human conscience, see *Spec* 119 (SC 301:188).

73. *Cant* 21 (SC 82:94): . . . hoc in ea absque omni phantastica imaginatione, agente puritate simplicis affectus et illuminati sensu amoris. . . . This teaching on the development of prayer in three stages, ending with imageless contemplative love, was prepared for by a discussion on prayer found in *Exp Rm* 5 (CCCM 86:122–23) based on Gregory the Great's *Hom in Ez* 2.5.8–11 and 2.2.12.

74. *Cant* 22 (SC 82:96–98): Habet ergo orator iste rationalis, vel spiritualis–quamdiu quippe ratione agente nititur ad hoc, rationalis est; postquam fuerit adeptus, in quantum fuerit adeptus, jam spiritualis est. . . .

75. *Cant* 23 (SC 82:100): . . . semper tamen debet esse homo Dei, vel rationalis in appetitu, vel spiritualis in affectu.

76. *Ep frat* 43 (SC 223:178): . . . qui per se, nec ratione aguntur, nec trahuntur affectu; et tamen vel auctoritate permoti, vel doctrina commoniti, vel exemplo provocati, approbant bonum ubi inveniunt. . . .

77. *Ep frat* 200–202 (SC 223:308–10). The *animus* here is also termed *spiritus*, which indicates the same dynamic relation between stage two and stage three that we have seen in *Cant.*

78. *Ep frat* 43 (SC 223:178): . . . habent et cognitionem boni et appetitum, sed nondum habet affectum.

79. *Ep frat* 45 (SC 223:180): . . . cum in affectum mentis transit iudicium rationis.

80. *Ep frat* 43 (SC 223:178): Sunt perfecti, qui spiritu aguntur, qui a Spirito sancto plenius illuminantur; et quoniam sapit eis bonum cujus trahuntur affectu, sapientes vocantur; quia vero induit eos Spiritus sanctus, sicut induit olim Gedeonem, sicut Spiritus sancti indumentum, spirituales appellantur. This interesting text involves a typical Latin word-play between *sapit* and *sapientia*, as well as the unusual notion of the perfect as the "clothing" of the Holy Spirit, suggested to William by the Latin text of Judg 6:34.

81. Besides this text at *Ep frat* 41–45, see the other key expositions at *Ep frat* 140, 187–94 and 195–205 (SC 223:245, 296–302, 304–12).

82. On this, see Brooke, *Studies*, pp. 120–21, n. 232.

83. See Thomas Tomasic, "The Theological Virtues as Modes of Intersubjectivity in the Thought of William of St. Thierry," *Recherches de théologie ancienne et médiévale* 38 (1971): 89–120.

84. *Spec* 1 (SC 301:60.5–10): Hanc enim trinitatem constituit Trinitas sancta in mente fideli, *ad imaginem et similitudinem* suam, qua renovamur *ad imaginem eius qui nos creavit* in homine nostro interiori; et ipsa est machina illa salutis humanae, cui aedificandae ac construendae in cordibus fidelium invigilat *omnis Scriptura divinitus inspirata.*

85. *Spec* 3–6 (SC 301:62–66). For an earlier treatment of the role of the three virtues, see *Med* 9.10–12 (PL 180:234C–35B).

86. *Spec* 7–8 (SC 301:66–68). For the role of the three virtues in producing *eucrasis*, or harmony, in the well-disposed soul, see *Spec* 53 (ibid.:120–22).

87. *Spec* 9 (SC 301:68.1–3): . . . sicut fides spem gignit, sic caritas ab utroque, hoc est a fide et spe, procedit. . . .

88. *Spec* 10 (SC 301:70.3–4): Nam et trium virtutum harum, fidei, spei, et caritatis, una virtutis forma, quia tota a fide profiscisitur, in hac vita . . . .

89. *Aenig* 40 (ed. Davy: 126): Tribus enim intelligentie gradibus proficienti fidei ascendendum est ad Deum, et ad cognitionem ejus. Primus gradus est diligenter investigatum habere, quid sibi de Domino Deo suo sit credendum; secundus, quomodo de eo quod recte creditur, recte nihilominus ei cogitandum sit et loquendum; tertius, ipsa jam rerum experientia est in sentiendo de Domino in bonitate, sicut sentiunt qui in simplicitate cordis querunt illum. Primus tam facilis est ascendenti quam credere facile est volenti, sed cui datum est. . . . Secundus eo difficilior, . . . quamvis et a curiosis presumatur. Tertius perfectorum est, qui de toto corde suo, de tota anima sua, et ex omni mente sua, affectant diligere Dominum Deum suum. . . . On the three degrees, see especially Brooke, *Studies*, 23–24, 128, 135, 177–78.

90. On these comparisons, see Brooke, *Studies*, pp. 3–6.

91. *Aenig* 41 (ed. Davy: 128): . . . in auctoriate fundatus, fidei est, habens formam fidei, probate auctoritatis probabilibus testimoniis formatam.

92. Ibid.: Hujus est scire, non solum cogitare et loqui de Deo rationabiliter secundum rationem fidei; sed et quomodo fides eadem fiat ubi non est, nutriatur et adjuvetur ubi est, et qualiter contra inimicos defendatur. The *ratio fidei* will be discussed below.

93. Ibid.: Tertius jam gratie illuminantis et beatificantis est, finiens fidem, seu potius beatificans in amorem, a fide ad speciem transmittens, inchoando cognitionem non eam que fidei est, et cum fide hic incipit esse in homine fideli. . . .

94. Especially in his paper "William of St. Thierry's Doctrine of the Ascent to God by Faith," reprinted in *Studies*, pp. 134–207.

95. On this, see Brooke, *Studies*, pp. 164–70.

96. The tension between reason and faith, introduced as early as #16 (Davy: 38–40), is expanded on in ##20–24 (Davy: 42–46). The initial answer given to this tension, viz., to believe and to love without taking reason into account (see #26; Davy: 46–48), William recognizes cannot be satisfactory for all; therefore #31 (Davy: 50) begins a more detailed response.

97. *Spec* 48 (SC 301:114.1–6): Altera siquidem est fides, quam revelat *caro et sanguis*; altera quam revelat *Pater qui est in caelis*. Altera, et non altera. Eadem fides, sed alter effectus. Illa docet quid sit credendum; ista fidei suum suggerit intellectum, et plenam intellectus ethimologiam, cum qui credit, intus in affectu cordis legit quod credit. The medieval Latin etymology for *intellectus* was *intus-legere*, that is, "to read within."

98. See the discussion in Brooke, *Studies*, pp. 124–26 and 143–44.

99. *Spec* 52 (SC 301:118.5–6): Haec autem et si nonnumquam cum labore sapit, lucet tamen et est contra temptationes tutior. For more on the use of reason in helping to effect the transition from simple faith to love, see *Spec* 55–56, 58–60, 67, 116–17, etc. (SC 301:122, 124–26, 132–34, 186).

100. See Brooke, *Studies*, pp. 5, 66–68 and 92 on the *ratio fidei*. In a useful note in his article "*Certitudo Fidei*: Faith, Reason, and Authority in the Writings of Baldwin of Ford" *Bernardus Magister*, pp. 264–65, n. 56, David N. Bell discusses three basic meanings of the term *ratio fidei* in medieval theology: (1) reasoning *for* the faith, that is, arguments for belief; (2) reasoning *within* the faith, that is, the use of reason within the boundaries established by belief; and (3) reasoning *from* the faith, that is, on the basis of belief, through the exercise of reason and love, to arrive at both experiential awareness of the truths believed as well as deeper insight into them. It is this third type that William is discussing.

101. *De sacramento altaris* (PL 180:345BC): In hujusmodi enim de sursum non de deorsum trahenda sunt rationum exempla vel probationum argumenta.

102. *Med* 2.8 (PL 180:210D): . . . fides instruit rationem, ratio per fidem erudit, vel destruit et abjicit imaginationem; fidem vero non instruit ipsa ad intelligentiam, sed per fidem desursum eam exspectat a Patre luminum. . . .

103. E.g., *Aenig* 38 (ed. Davy: 124–26) on *persona*; *Aenig* 50 (ibid.: 134) on *substantia*; and *Aenig* 75–77 (ibid.: 156–60) on *relatio*.

104. *Aenig* 64 (ed. Davy: 146): Idcirco cum de Deo verbis agitur, rationes verborum rebus coaptande sunt, non ille illis. For other important texts on the *ratio fidei*, see *Aenig* 43, 45, 47 and 50 (ibid.:130–32).

105. *Spec* 105 (SC 301:174.1–6): Cognitio autem haec Dei, alia fidei est, alia amoris vel caritatis. Quae fidei, hujus vitae est; quae vero caritatis, vitae aeterne. . . . Aliud quippe est cognoscere Deum sicut cognoscit vir amicum suum; aliud cognoscere eum sicut ipse cognoscit semetipsum.

106. *Aenig* 42–43 (ed. Davy: 128–30). William compares them to the difference between "night-to-night" and "day-to-day" knowledge in Ps 18:3.

107. On the latter type, see *Spec* 118 (SC 301:188). The contrast between two types of vision does not become a standard formula in William's writings, but Brooke argues that such a division is central to the two faith treatises (*Studies*, pp. 168–69).

108. Brooke, *Studies*, pp. 177–78 and 210–11.

109. *Cant* 144 (SC 82:304): Interim egenus et pauper amor meus . . . suspiret quo vocatur, per figuras amatorias, et imperfectum suum, ad perfectum tuum. . . . Cf. *Cant* 23–24 (ibid.: 98–100) for William's reflections on how the Holy Spirit uses the language of profane love for his own purposes. Like Bernard, Origen, and all the spiritual interpreters, William insists that

only the spiritual lover can discern the true meaning of the Song of Songs; see, e.g., *Cant* 4 (ibid.:74–76).

110. *Cant* 7 (SC 82:78–80), for the distinction, and #8 for the unusual phrase *mysticum contractum divinae et humanae conjunctionis* (ibid.:80). Cf. *Cant* 30 (ibid.:112) for more on *conjunctio*. The term *accubitus* does not seem to occur outside *Cant*, and uses of *conjunctio* in other treatises are rare (see *Contemp* 11 in SC 61:100). *Mysticus* is also of sparse appearance in William though there are some interesting uses. See, e.g., *Spec* 81 (SC 301:148.6): *mysticas interpretationes*; and *Exp Rm* 1 (CCCM 86.13.281–14.283): Maxime autem spiritualis gratia sunt sive in moralibus sive in mysticis spiritualis intelligentiae charismata. . . . In *Cant* the terms *accubitus* and *conjunctio* are both crucial, and here the "Table des mots latins" in the edition of the text by M.-M. Davy (*Guillaume de Saint-Thierry: Commentaire sur le Cantique des Cantiques* [Paris: Vrin, 1958], pp. 211–41) is more valuable than the meager apparatus in Déchanet's edition in SC 82. A study of the many uses of both terms in *Cant* indicates that William wished to place severe restrictions on the use of erotic terms in describing our union with God–another illustration of how the *ratio fidei* is meant to transform human language. Cf., e.g., the unusual use of the verb *copulari* in a mystical sense in *Cant* 187 (SC 82:378): . . . et virgo copuletur Sponso. . . .

111. *Cant* 76 (SC 82:188): Sed bona voluntas, jam initium amoris est. Vehemens autem voluntas, vel quasi ad absentem, desiderium est, vel affecta circa praesentem amor est; cum amanti id quod amat in intellectu praesto est. Amor quippe Dei, ipse intellectus ejus est; qui non nisi amatus intelligitur, nec nisi intellectus amatur, et utique tantum intelligitur quantum amatur, tantumque amatur in quantum intelligitur. The dialectic of the presence and absence, as we have seen, is also powerful in Bernard of Clairvaux. For remarks on its importance in William, see especially T. Tomasic, "William of St. Thierry against Peter Abelard," pp. 10–12 and 19, where Tomasic summarizes, "Recalling that the self is experienced as the absence of the One in Whom alone it is possible to recover self-identity, the self grasps its ownmost structure as the necessity of reciprocity to the invitation of the Other." Also useful on this aspect of William's mysticism is K. Ruh, *Die Geschichte der abendländische Mystik*, 1:301–05.

112. *Cant* 81–82 (SC 82:198–200). A similar interpretation is found in Bernard *SCC* 43.1 (SBOp 2:41–42) and in Peter Damian, *Testimonia de Canticis Canticorum* 2 (PL 145:1144C–45A).

113. *Cant* 83 (SC 82:200): Sed venit Filius Dei, aeterna sapientia, et inclinavit coelos suos et descendit, et fecit de semetipso quiddam in nobis, quod simile esset nobis, quod apprehenderemus. . . .

114. This is also the interpretation of Bernard; see *SCC* 44.2–3 (SBOp 2:45–46).

115. The symbol of the bed in medieval monastic literature has been studied by Jean Leclercq, "Sommeil Vigilant," chapter 10 in *Chances de la spiritualité occidentale* (Paris: Cerf, 1966), pp. 297–311.

116. *Cant* 89 (SC 82:210): Sponsae namque memoria de Sponso est, in simplicitate cordis Sponsum quaerere; intellectus sentire de eo in bonitate; amor ipse affici, ipso frui, esse sicut ipse est.

117. *Cant* 92 (SC 82:212): Fiuntque saepe duo isti oculi unus oculus, cum fideliter sibi cooperantur, cum in contemplatione Dei, in qua maxime amor operatur, ratio transit in amorem et in quemdam spiritualem vel divinum formatur intellectum, qui omnem superat et absorbet rationem. William also uses this same interpretation of Song 4:9 in *Nat am* 3.8 (PL 184:393A), as we have seen above (p. 233).

118. *Cant* 93 (SC 82:214): . . . praelibant gaudium mutuae conjunctionis. . . .

119. On the importance of *fruitio* in William, see Theodore Koehler, "Thème et vocabulaire de la 'Fruition divine' chez Guillaume de Saint-Thierry," *Revue d'ascétique et de mystique* 40 (1964): 139–60; and his article "Fruitio Dei" in DS 5:1546–69 (1555–59 on William).

120. *Cant* 94 (SC 82:216–18): Cumque efficitur ad similitudinem facientis, fit homo Deo affectus; hoc est cum Deo unus spiritus; pulcher in pulchro, bonus in bono; idque suo modo secundum virtutem fidei, et lumen intellectus et mensuram amoris, existens in Deo per gratiam, quod ille est per naturam.

121. Ibid. (SC 82:218): Nam et cum nonnumquam superabundat gratia usque ad certam de Deo et manifestam experientiam rei, fit repente sensui illuminati amoris modo quodam novo sensibile, quod nulli sensui corporis sperabile, nulli rationi cogitabile, nulli intellectui extra intellectum illuminati amoris fit capabile.

122. Ibid.: . . . per quam transformatur sentiens in id quod sentitur; sic et multo magis idem operatur visio Dei in sensu amoris quo videtur Deus.

123. *Cant* 95 (SC 82:220): In hoc siquidem fit conjunctio illa mirabilis, si mutua fruitio suavitatis, gaudiique incomprehensibilis et incogitabilis, illis etiam in quibus fit, hominis ad Deum, creati spiritus ad increatum. . . .

124. Ibid. (SC 82:220–22): . . . quae non est alia quam unitas Patris et Filii Dei, ipsum eorum osculum, ipse amplexus, ipse amor, ipsa bonitas, et quidquid in unitate illa simplicissima commune est amborum; quod totum est Spiritus Sanctus, Deus, caritas, idem donans, idem et donum.

125. Ibid. (SC 82:222): . . . et sicut solet in amantium osculis, suavi quodam contractu mutuo sibi spiritus suos transfundentium, creatus spiritus in hoc ipsum creanti eum Spiritus totum se effundit; ipsi vero Creator Spiritus se infundit, prout vult, et unus spiritus homo cum Deo efficitur.

126. *Cant* 97 (SC 82:224). William speaks of the *caritas veritatis*, a term he uses elsewhere in discussing the necessary relation of contemplation (*caritas veritatis*) and action (*veritas caritatis*). E.g., *Nat am* 11.32 (PL 184:400A), *Contemp* 1 (SC 61:58), *Med* 11.13 (PL 180:241BC), *Ep frat* 18 (SC 223:158). We will return to this below.

127. *Cant* 100 (SC 82:228–30): Quin potius amor ipse hoc est, quod tu es; Spiritus Sanctus tuus, o Pater, qui a te procedit et Filio, cum quo tu et Filius unum es. Cui cum meretur affici spiritus hominis, spiritus Spiritui, amor Amori, amor humanus divinus quodammodo efficitur; et jam in amando Deum homo quidem est in opere, sed Deus est qui operatur.

128. *Cant* 101–4 (SC 82:230–32). The *lectulus floridus noster*, one of William's favored images, appears in *Cant* 115, 130, 142 (SC 82:252, 276, 300). The *Brevis commentatio* 29 also speaks of the *lectulus*: interim dum in lectulo purae conscientiae perfruar conjunctione dulcedinis tuae (PL 184:430CD).

129. *Cant* 105–6 (SC 82:232–36). The interlaced panels are read as the mutual charity and connection of all the virtues in *sapientia*.

130. See J.-M. Déchanet, "Introduction," in *William of St. Thierry: The Golden Epistle* (Spenser: Cistercian Publications, 1971), pp. xxiv–xxvi.

131. See Brooke, *Studies*, p. 30; and Baudelet, *L'experience spirituelle*, esp. pp. 256–83. Pierre Miquel summarizes William's teaching on religious experience under these headings: progressive, incommunicable, gratuitous, certain, joyful and nuptial (*Le vocabulaire latin de l'expérience spirituelle*, [Paris: Beauchesne, 1989], pp. 107–18). William often provides analyses of the experience of receiving divine gifts, e.g., *Nat am* 8.21 and 9.26 (PL 184:393C and 396D); *Med* 12.16 (PL 180:248A); *Spec* 112 (SC 301:180–82); *Aenig* 40 (ed. Davy:126); *Ep frat* 194 (SC 223:302); *Cant* 66 and 94 (SC 82:166 and 218), etc. More rare are the references to his own experiences of the taste of God, though these do occur, e.g., *Contemp* 12 (SC 61:112–16).

132 On William's Christology, see E. Rozanne Elder, "The Image of the Invisible God: the Evolving Christology of William of St. Thierry" (dissertation, University of Toronto, 1972); and, more recently, "The Christology of William of Saint Thierry," *Recherches de théologie ancienne et médiévale* 58 (1991): 79–112. Also useful are Thomas Tomasic, "William of St.

Thierry on the Phenomenon of Christ: The Paradigm of Human Possibilities," *Analecta Cisterciensia* 31 (1975): 213–45; and P. Verdeyen, *La théologie mystique,* chapter 3.

133. *Exp Rm* 1 (CCCM 86:8.76–80): Haec autem eius praedestinatio, ipsa est ipsius claritas, quam qui in mundo natus est homo, habuit apud Patrem, *priusquam mundus fieret* (John 17:5). Ubi sicut ipse praedestinatus est, ut esset caput nostrum, sic et in ipso praedestinati sumus, ut membra eius essemus. On Christ's universal predestination in William, see Tomasic, "Phenomenon of Christ," pp. 220–25, 228.

134. William's analysis of the procession, the properties and the mission of the *Verbum* is found in detail in *Aenig* 90–96 (ed. Davy: 170–74). See the discussion of christological exemplarism in Verdeyen, *La théologie mystique,* pp. 137–42.

135. *Spec* 120–21 (SC 301:190): Ideo ipse Dominus apparens in carne hominibus, sicut de mundo abstulit vanitatem ydolorum, sic dum cogitantibus Deum proposuit in Trinitate unitatem, Trinitatem in unitate, fulgurans choruscatio divinitatis omnem tulit a cogitatione fidei de Deo vanitatem imaginationis. Cum enim divinitatis intellectum docuit esse supra homines, suo inde modo docuit cogitare homines. Omnia ergo facta vel verba Verbi Dei unum nobis verbum sunt; omnia que de eo legimus, audimus, loquimur, meditamur, sive provocando amorem, sive incutiendo timorem, ad unum nos vocant, ad unum nos mittunt, de quo multa dicuntur et nichil dicitur quia ad id quod est non pervenitur, nisi occurat ipse qui queritur, et *illuminet vultum suum super nos,* et illustret faciem suam, ut *in lumine vultus eius* sciamus qua gradiamur.

136. *Aenig* 13 (ed. Davy:102): Forme carnales amore suo nos detinent, in quem per consensum peccati cecidimus, ipsis innitendum est, ut surgamus. Idcirco Filius Dei "qui in forma Dei erat, exinanivit semetipsum formam servi accipiens" (Phil. 2:6–7), ut homines in homine Deum credendo recipientes, accepta potestate, efficerentur filii Dei. The first two sentences are drawn from Augustine's *De vera religione* 24.45 (PL 34:141).

137. E.g., *Nat am* 11.34 (PL 184:401B); *Orat* (SC 61:126); *Med* 10.3–5 (PL 180:235C–36B); *Cant* 15–18 and 157 (SC 82:88–92 and 332); *Ep frat* 174–75 (SC 223:282–86), etc.

138. E.g., *Nat am* 11.34 (PL 184:401B); *Aenig* 11 (ed. Davy: 100); *Ep frat* 272 (SC 223:362). On the imitation of Christ in the monastic life, see Rozanne Elder, "William of St. Thierry: The Monastic Vocation as an Imitation of Christ," *Cîteaux* 26 (1975): 9–30.

139. *Spec* 74 (SC 301:142.16–19): Diligens enim hominem quodammodo usque ad contemptum sui, docuit hominem Deum diligere usque ad contemptum sui; qui nesciebat miser diligere nisi semetipsum, etiam usque ad contemptum Dei. This language is remniscent of Bernard's four degress of love in the *De diligendo Deo.*

140. See *Nat am* 11.33–12.37 (PL 184:400C–403A). On Christ's role as mediator, see especially *Spec* 64–66, 75–77 and 94 (SC 301:130–32, 142–46 and 162–64).

141. E.g., *Contemp* 3, 10 and 12 (SC 61:62–66, 90–92 and 110).

142. On this theme, which is particularly strong in the *Meditationes,* see Soeur Monique Simon, "Le 'face à face' dans les méditations du Guillaume de Saint-Thierry," *Collectanea Cisterciensia* 35 (1975): 121–36.

143. *Med* 10.7–8 (PL 180:237AB): . . . videtur sibi videre te sicuti es, dum de mirabili passionis tuae sacramento cogitandi dulcedine ruminat bonum tuum circa nos, tantum, quantus ipse es, vel quod ipse es: videtur sibi videre te facie ad faciem, cum summi boni facies appares ei in cruce et opere salutis tuae, et ipsa crux efficitur ei ad Deum facies mentis bene affectae. Quid enim melius praeparatum, quid suavius potuit esse dispositum, quam quod ascensuro homini ad Deum suum, offerre dona et sacrificia secundum praeceptum legis, non sit ei ascendendum per gradus ad altare ejus, sed per planum similitudinis, placide et pede inoffenso eat homo ad hominem similem sibi, in primo ingressu limine dicentem sibi: "Ego et Pater unum sumus" (John 10:30): statimque per Spiritum sanctum affectu assumptus in Deum, et ipse Deum in seipsum excipiat venientem, et mansionem apud eum facientem, non

tantum spiritualiter, sed etiam corporaliter per mysterium sancti et vivifici corporis et sanguinis Domini nostri Jesu Christi? Devotion to the Passion is especially marked in William's *Meditationes;* see, e.g., *Med* 3.4, 5.1–7, 6.11–12 and 7.2–3 (ibid.:211AB, 218D–20C, 225C–26C, 229D–30B).

144. *Exp Rm* 3 (CCCM 86:82.809–12): Sic enim radici ligni vitae radix nostra complantatur, id est amori Christi amor noster conformatur, ut de succo radicis eius producat ramos iustitiae et fructus vitae.

145. Emile Mersch in his classic, *Le corps mystique du Christ,* 2 vols. (Paris: Desclée, 1933), 2:142–48, was among the first to recognize William's importance here.

146. *Spec* 85 (SC 301:154.1–2): Ex quo fiunt temporalia Domini opera in corde fideli aeternitatis mira quaedam sacramenta. . . .

147. Brooke, *Studies,* pp. 126–27, 164–66, 173–74.

148. *Spec* 60 (SC 301:126.7–12): *Omnia* enim *haec operatur unus idem Spiritus, sicut vult* (1 Cor 12:11); constituens sacramenta fidei, alia ut sint sacrae rei signa corporalia et visibilia, sicut in baptismo, sicut in sacramento corporis et sanguinis Domini; alia ut sint tantum sacra recondita, spirituali intellectu, ipso Spiritu sancto praeduce investiganda. . . . The whole discussion of sacraments in *Spec* 60–70 (SC 302:126–36) is of importance.

149. On the role of the Eucharist in William's mystical theory, see Verdeyen, *La théologie mystique,* pp. 167–74.

150. For an introduction to the Eucharistic controversies of the late eleventh and early twelfth centuries, see J. Pelikan, *The Growth of Medieval Theology* (Chicago: University of Chicago Press, 1978), pp. 184-204.

151. E.g., *Nat am* 13.38 (PL 184:403B); *Med* 8.5 (PL 180:237B).

152. *Ep frat* 117 (SC 223:236): . . . rem vero mysterii, in omni tempore, et in omni loco dominationis Dei, modo quo traditum est, hoc est pietatis affectu, agere et tractare, et sumere sibi in salutem. . . . See the whole discussion in *Ep frat* 115–19 (ibid.: 234–38).

153. *Spec* 61 (SC 301:128.1–2) describes God's Will, that is, the Holy Spirit as follows: Occultum enim voluntatis Dei, et altissimum est, et omnium sacramentorum sacramentum. . . .

154. *Spec* 67 (SC 301:134.8–14): . . . cum illuminante gratia intellectum rationis, fidei assensus efficietur amoris sensus; qui ad sacramentum cognoscendum internae Dei voluntatis, iam non habeat opus exterioribus sacramentis. Quorum tamen sacrosancta religione, quamdiu hic vivitur, religantur exteriora nostra, et per ea interiora nostra, ne in aliena diffluant. . . . Cf. *Nat am* 15.44 (PL 184:406C).

155. Bernard's *De gratia et libero arbitrio* has a far more explicitly Augustinian view of grace than William's usual teaching, though it would be incorrect to say that William disagrees with the bishop of Hippo.

156. *Cant* 174 (SC 82:356): Ipse est bonae mentis status ex gratia creante, sterilis adhuc ad intelligentiae et sapientiae fructibus; quos expectat ex gratia illuminante. The two kinds of grace appear frequently in *Cant,* as a glance at the "Table des mots latins" in the Davy edition shows.

157. For other appearances of these, see, e.g., *Contemp* 3 (SC 61:66); *Med.* 12 (PL 180:246A); *Aenig* 41 (ed. Davy: 128); *Spec* 27, 30, 38, 41, 52, 67, 79–80, 103 (SC 301:92, 94, 102, 106, 118–20, 134, 146–48, 174); *Ep frat* 176, 244 (SC 223:286, 338), etc.

158. *Gratia praeveniens:* e.g., *Nat am* 2.4 (PL 184:382D–83A); *Spec* 17 and 121 (SC 301:80 and 190); *Aenig* 22 (ed. Davy:110); *Ep frat* 298 (SC 223:382); *Cant* 10, 136, 163, 202 (SC 82:82–84, 290, 340, 398).

159. *Gratia operans:* e.g., *Cant* 170 (SC 82:352); *Aenig* 83 (ed. Davy: 164).

160. *Gratia cooperans:* e.g., *Nat am* 2.4 and 5.12 (PL 184:382D–83A and 388C); *Ep frat* 251 (SC 223:344).

161. *Gratia occulta*: e.g., *Cant* 76 (SC 82:190).

162. Dominic Monti, "The Way Within: Grace in the Mystical Theology of William of St. Thierry," *Citeaux* 28 (1975): 31-47.

163. On this, see Monti, ibid., pp. 40-43.

164. William, like Bernard, taught that at least from one perspective the saints who are predestined to glory (e.g., David and Peter) never lose the grace of charity even when they sin; see *Nat am* 5-6.13-14 (PL 184:388D-90A). David Bell finds the roots of this teaching in Augustine's doctrine of predestination, especially in the *De correptione et gratia (Image and Likeness*, pp. 191-95).

165. For the broad context to this theme, I refer the reader once again to my essay "Love, Knowledge, and *Unio mystica* in the Western Christian Tradition," as well as to Robert Javelet, "Intelligence et amour chez les auteurs spirituels du XIIe siècle," *Revue d'ascétique et de mystique* 37 (1961): 273-450. More specifically on William, see especially J.-M. Déchanet, "*AMOR IPSE INTELLECTUS EST*: La doctrine de l'amour-intellection chez Guillaume de Saint-Thierry," *Revue du moyen âge latin* 1 (1945): 349-74; Jacques Hourlier, "S. Bernard et Guillaume de Saint-Thierry dans le 'Liber de Amore,'" in *Saint Bernard Théologien*, pp. 223-33; E. Rozanne Elder, "William of St. Thierry: Rational and Affective Spirituality," in *The Spirituality of Western Christendom*, ed. E. Rozanne Elder (Kalamazoo, MI: Cistercian Publications, 1976), pp. 85-105; David Bell, *Image and Likeness*, chapters 4-6; Jacques Delesalle, "Amour et Connaissance: 'Super Cantica Canticorum' de Guillaume de Saint-Thierry," *Collectanea Cisterciensia* 49 (1987): 339-46; P. Verdeyen, *La théologie mystique*, pp. 242-73; and K. Ruh, *Die Geschichte der abendländische Mystik*, 1:280-94.

166. *Spec* 101 (SC 301:170.1-7): Quod multo potentius digniusque agitur, cum ipse qui est substantialis voluntas Patris ac Filii, Spiritus Sanctus, voluntatem hominis sic sibi afficit, ut Deum amans anima, et amando sentiens, tota repente transmutetur, non quidem in naturam divinitatis, sed tamen in quandam supra humanam, citra divinam formam beatitudinis; in gaudium illuminantis gratiae, et sensum illuminatae conscientiae....

167. *Nat am* 1.1 (PL 184:379C): Est quippe amor vis animae naturali quodam pondere ferens eam in locum vel finem suum. Cf. *Nat corp* 2.11 (PL 180:720D-21A). The source, of course, is in Augustine's comments on love as the weight of the soul in *Conf.* 13.9.10 (PL 32:848-49).

168. *Contemp* 11 (SC 61:96): Nichil enim aliud est amor: quam vehemens et bene ordinata voluntas. See also *Nat am* 2.4 (PL 184:383A): Nihil est enim aliud amor quam vehemens in bono voluntas. Cf. *Med* 12.12 (PL 180:246A), and *Spec* 19 (SC 301:82.6-7).

169. *Ep frat* 234 (SC 223:330): Voluntas naturalis quidam animi appetitus est, alius ad Deum, et circa interiora sua, alius circa corpus et exteriora corporalia.

170. E.g., *Spec* 11 (SC 301:70.1-5). Cf. Augustine, *De div quaest 83*, q. 35.2 (PL 40:24); and *De civ Dei* 14.7.2 (PL 41:410).

171. *Cant* 6 (SC 82:78): Agit enim de amore Dei, vel quo Deus amatur, vel quo ipse Deus Amor dicitur; qui utrum *amor* dicatur, an *caritas*, an *dilectio*, non refert, nisi quod in *amoris* nomine, tener quidem amantis indicari videtur affectus, tendentis vel ambientis; in nomine vero *caritatis*, spiritualis quaedam affectio, vel gaudium fruentis; in *dilectione* autem, rei delectantis appetitus naturalis; quae tamen omnia, in amore Sponsi et Sponsae, unus atque idem Spiritus operatur. Cf. *Ep frat* 235 and 257 (SC 223:332 and 348), as well as the distinction between *amor desiderii* and *amor fruitionis* in such texts as *Contemp* 5 (SC 61:74).

172. See above in chapter 5, pp. 194-95.

173. For discussion of the meaning of these terms in William, see Wolfgang Zwingmann, "Ex affectu cordis: Über die Vollkommenheit menschlicher Handelns und menschlicher Hingabe nach Willhelm von St. Thierry," and "Affectus illuminatus amoris: Über die Offenbarwerden der Gnade und die Erfahrung von Gottes," in *Citeaux* 18 (1967): 5-37, 193-226.

See also Bell, *Image and Likeness*, pp. 128–33; and the "Appendix" by Thomas X. Davis in *William of St. Thierry: The Mirror of Faith* (Kalamazoo, MI: Cistercian Publications, 1979), pp. 93–95.

174. William distinguishes *affectus* from *affectio* in *Nat am* 6.14 (PL 184:389AB): Alius quippe est affectus, aliud affectio. Affectus est qui generali quadam potentia et perpetua quadam virtute firma et stabili mentem possidet, quam per gratiam obtinuit. Affectiones vero sunt quas varias varius rerum et temporum affert eventus. In practice, however, he tends to use the two terms interchangeably.

175. On will as a natural *affectus*, see *Nat am* 2.4 (PL 184:383A). On *affectus* as well or badly directed, see *Nat am* 2.4 and 7.22–23 (ibid.:383AB and 393C–95B).

176. Conflating *Contemp* 7 (SC 61:82): Nos autem a te, ad te vel in te afficimur cum te amamus . . . ; and *Nat corp* 2.13 (PL 180:722C): Ipsum [Deum] enim intendere, formari est. Quidquid enim ad Deum afficitur, non est suum, sed eius a quo afficitur.

177. *Nat am* 15.45 (PL 184:407B–08B). On the four primary *affectus*, see *Nat am* 10.28 (397C).

178. William loves to play verbal games with the relation between *affectus* and *effectus*, e.g., *Nat am* 3.6 and 5.13 (PL 184:384A and 388D); *Med* 11.13 (PL 180:241B), etc.

179. *Spec* 95 (SC 301:164.9–12): Quem [Christum] etiam aliter vident per fidem cogitando, qui digni sunt, cum soli sibi sunt; aliter cum per afficientem gratiam, ipse est in eis, et illi in ipso per affectum devotionis.

180. Bell helpfully distinguishes three kinds of *affectus*: active, based on *gratia creans*; cooperative based on *gratia illuminans*; and passive, based on the action of the Holy Spirit alone (*Image and Likeness*, pp. 131–32). This is not explicitly formulated in William, but it does reflect his thinking.

181. *Contemp* 10 (SC 61:92): Haec est justitia filiorum hominum: Ama me: quia amo te. Rarus autem est qui dicere possit: Amo te: ut ames me. Hoc tu fecisti: qui sicut clamat et praedicat servus amoris tui, prior nos dilexisti. Et sic plane sic est, amasti nos prior, ut amaremus te; non quod egeres amari a nobis, sed quia id ad quod nos fecisti esse non poteramus nisi amando te.

182. *Aenig* 100 (ed. Davy: 176). Cf. *Contemp* 11 (SC 61:94). The theme of the priority of God's love is especially strong in *Contemp*, e.g., 2, 4, 5, 7, 8, etc. (ibid.:62, 70, 74, 82, 86–88); it is also found throughout the later works, e.g., *Med* 3.9, 6.4 and 12.9 (PL 180:213CD, 223AB and 245AB); *Spec* 120–22 (SC 301:188–92); *Ep frat* 16 (SC 223:156).

183. *Med* 12.9 (PL 180:245A): Unde si quaeras hodie a me quod olim a B. Apostolo tuo quaerebas, "Amas me?" respondere trepido, "scis quia amo te," sed alacri et secura conscientia respondeo, "Tu scis quia volo te amare."

184. Ibid. (245B): Nam cum amorem tuum suaviter sentio affectus, te autem quaero ipsius amoris intellectu, amo quod sentio, desidero quod quaero, et in desiderando languens deficio.

185. *Med* 12.10 (245C): Dispono ergo in corde mihi ascensiones istas. Primum necessaria videtur voluntas magna, deinde illuminata, deinde affecta.

186. *Med* 12.12 (246B): . . . tamen interim quod ex parte sentio, ex parte amo: quod nisi aliquatenus sentirem, nullatenus amarem.

187. See Bernard of Clairvaux, *SCC* 14.6 (SBOp 1:80).

188. E.g., *Med* 12.13–16 (246C–48B): Istos cum video, in amorem amoris tui, qui hoc in eis operatur, totus afficior, quem in eis deprehendo certa quadam experientia cognita amantibus (this passage is at 248A). For similar observations on how by enjoying others in God we come to enjoy him in them, see *Cant* 123 and 199 (SC 82:268, 396).

189. *Med* 12.18 (248B): Ut video amor naturae est; amare te gratiae est; affectus gratiae manifestatio est. . . .

190. *Med* 12.18 (248C): Semper ergo in anima pauperis tui Deus amor tuus est; sed latens sicut ignis sub cinere, donec Spiritus qui ubi vult spirat, placitum habuerit, sicut et quantum voluerit illum ad utilitatem manifestare. Adesto ergo, adesto, sancte amor adesto, sacer ignis; ure delectationes renum et cordium, cogitationes late sicut vis, ad faciendam flammae manifestationis tuae copiosiorem humilitatis materiam; appare quando vis ad manifestandam bonae conscientiae gloriam, et divitias quas habet in domo sua.

191. *Nat am* 2.3–5, 10.28 and 15.45 (PL 184:382A–83D, 397CD and 407A–08B). *Sapientia* is not divorced from *caritas* but is seen as the higher dimension by which *caritas* actually enjoys God. On this division, see D. Bell, "Introduction," in *William of St. Thierry: The Nature and Dignity of Love* (Kalamazoo, MI: Cistercian Publications, 1981), pp. 9–13.

192. *Ep frat* 49 (SC 223:184): Vel simplicitas, sola est ad Deum voluntas, scilicet nondum ratione formata, ut amor sit, id est formata voluntas, nondum illuminata, ut sit caritas, hoc est amoris jocunditas.

193. *Ep frat* 235 (SC 223:332), where the final two seem fused; and 257 (ibid.:348), where they are distinct: Sic enim diligendus est Deus. Magna enim voluntas ad Deum, amor est; dilectio, adhaesio sive conjunctio; caritas, fruitio. Unitas vero spiritus cum Deo, homini sursum cor habenti, proficientis in Deum voluntatis est perfectio. . . .

194. *Cant* 94 (SC 82:216): Non solum etenim nos fruimur Deo; sed et Deus fruitur bono nostro, in quantum delectatur et gratum illud habere dignatur.

195. *Cant* 122 (SC 82:264): . . . amor nullus vel corruptus, scilicet cum cogitatur propter aliud quam ut ametur, vel amatur propter aliud quam propter semetipsum Deus. . . .

196. *Cant* 54 (SC 82:148): Diligit enim te, non nisi de te, qui es ipsa dilectio, qua diligit te; et in tantum diligit te in se, ut se ipsam in nullo diligit, nisi in te. Cf. *Contemp* 7 and 9 (SC 61:84, 90). This is William's answer to the problem of disinterested love briefly raised in *Contemp* 4 (SC 61:70). On this issue, see also *Exp Rm* 7 (CCCM 86:175.404–06): Qui autem se propter habendum Deum diligunt, ipsi se diligunt. Ego ut se diligant, Deum diligunt.

197. *Cant* 60 (SC 82:154): Nullum adhuc amat, praeter Sponsum. Si enim alium amaret, sponsa non esset.

198. E.g., *Nat am* 2.5–3.6 (PL 184:383B–84B), where William, like Richard of St. Victor (see chapter 9, p. 418), connects this primarily with love's willingness to sacrifice all to bring Christ to others, using the example of St. Paul.

199. William seems to say as much in *Cant* 105 (SC 82:236): . . . sic ad ipsum verus ac vivens amor est, cum qui amatur amanti per intellectum, seu sensum amoris ipsius, praesto est; et tunc lectulus et noster, et floridus est. On the *sensus amoris*, see Brooke, *Studies*, pp. 165, 175–76; and Bell, *Image and Likeness*, pp. 16–65.

200. A parallel formula underlines that the understanding given in love is a "tasting." Speaking of the delights to be gained in heaven (of which we gain a foretaste here below in the understanding of love), William says: Vita ista ex illo gustu est, quia gustare, hoc est intelligere (*Nat am* 11.31 [PL 184:399C]).

201. William also uses the term *cognitio amoris*, e.g., *Spec* 105 (SC 301:174.1–2): Cognitio autem haec Dei, alia fidei est, alia amoris vel caritatis.

202. Déchanet, in his article *"AMOR IPSE INTELLECTUS EST,"* was the first to insist that it is the doctrine of the Holy Spirit as the mutual love-knowledge of the Father and the Son which is the primary analogate, not sense knowledge, its pale–but for us more immediate– participation. See also his "Introduction," in *The Golden Letter*, pp. xxvii–xxx; and Bell, *Image and Likeness*, p. 243.

203. *Med* 3.8 (PL 180:213C): Sensus enim animae amor est, per hunc sive cum mulcetur, sive cum offenditur, sentit quidquid sentit. William proceeds by drawing out the analogy to sense perception.

204. *Spec* 96 (SC 301:186.10–14): Amat enim, et amor suus sensus suus est quo sentit eum quem sentit, et quodammodo transformatur in id quod sentit, non enim eum sentit, nisi in eum transformetur, hoc est nisi ipse in ipsa, et ipsa in ipso sit. As a gloss on this text we can quote the sentence immediately following that quoted in the previous note from *Med* 3.8 (PL 180:213C): Cum per hunc [amorem] in aliquid anima extenditur, quadam transformatione in id quod amat transmutatur.

205. *Spec* 97 (SC 301:166–68): . . . sic et interior ad similia sibi, id est rationabilia ac divina vel spiritualia. Interior vero animae sensus, intellectus eius est. Maior tamen et dignior sensus eius, et purior intellectus, amor est, si fuerit ipse purus.

206. *Spec* 99 (SC 301:170.8–9): . . . et *unus spiritus* efficitur homo cum Deus, cui afficitur. For other appearances of the *sensus amoris* in the *Spec*, see, e.g., 49, 67, 75, 83, 120 (ibid.: 116.13, 134.9–10, 144.6, 152.8, 190.4–5). Cf. *Aenig* 22 (ed. Davy: 110). The *sensus amoris* also appears in *Ep frat* 292 and 294 (SC 82:378 and 380).

207. E.g., *Cant* 80, 110, 141 (SC 82:192–94, 242–44, 296–300). *Cant* 20 (ibid.:94) uses the term *sensus amantis*.

208. *Cant* 94 (SC 82:218): . . . sic et multo magis idem operatur visio Dei in sensu amoris quo videtur Deus.

209. E.g., especially *Nat am* 6.15–7.20 (PL 184:390B–93A), where five different senses or forms of love (physical, social, natural, spiritual and love of God) are compared to the five senses of the body, as in Bernard's *Div* 10.2 (SBOp 6:122–23). (It is difficult to say who depends on whom in this case.) In *Nat am* 10.29–31 (398A–99D) we find an unusual application of the five senses both to the Body of Christ, i.e., the church of the Old and the New Testaments, and to the individual soul. For more on the spiritual senses in William, see James Walsh, "Guillaume de Saint-Thierry et les sens spirituels," *Revue d'ascétique et de mystique* 35 (1959): 27–42; as well as Pierre Adnès, "Gout spirituel," DS 6:626–44 (632–33 on William).

210. *Cant* 57 and 76 (SC 82:152 and 188); *Ep frat* 173 (SC 223:282); and the *Disputatio adversus Petrum Abaelardum* (PL 180:252C). The phrase is derived from Gregory the Great's *amor ipse notitia est*, as noted above (*Homilia in Evangelia* 27.4 [PL 76:1207A]). For the use in William, see especially Bell, *Image and Likeness*, pp. 239–40, n. 59; McGinn, "Love, Knowledge and *Unio mystica*, pp. 63–64; and Verdeyen, *La théologie mystique*, pp. 257–66.

211. The term *intellectus amoris* and its cognates (e.g., *cognitio amoris*) appear at least twenty times in William's writings.

212. As P. Verdeyen puts it, "L'intelligence de l'amour, c'est sa réponse définitive aux objections rationalistes formulée par la nouvelle école dialectique" (*La théologie mystique*, p. 257).

213. A passage from *Contemp* 11 (SC 61:104) provides an insight on the reason for love's superiority, that is, its comprehensivity: Licet enim nullus sensus animae cujuslibet vel spiritus te comprehendat, tamen totum te quantus es comprehendit amor amantis, qui totum te amat, quantus es . . . Cf. *Ep frat* 294 (SC 223:380). Cf. *Cant* 100 (SC 82:228): Sed amoris dilatatus sinus, secundum magnitudinem tuam se extendens, dum amat te, vel amare affectat quantus es, incapabilem capit, incomprehensibilem comprehendit.

214. *Cant* 144 (SC 82:304): Tunc parebit in lumine tuo quantum in intellectu tuo praecedit pietas simplicissimi amantis, prudentiam eruditissimi ratiocinantis; cum retroacta ratione amor pius ipse efficietur intellectus suus.

215. *Intellectus*, as E. Rozanne Elder has pointed out, can be used in two ways—either to indicate the higher faculty or dimension of the soul in which love and knowledge are united, or to designate the state when this faculty has been activated; see "Introduction," *The Mirror of Faith*, pp. xx–xxi. But *intellectus* remains a form of *our* capacity to know, and this explains why, contrary to his usual practice, William at times speaks of the union of *ratio* and *amor* rather than *intellectus* and *amor*, e.g., *Ep frat* 196 (SC 223:304) and *Cant* 136 (SC 82:290):

... ratio efficit amorem, amor autem afficit rationem. ... In one passage, William distinguishes a lower from a higher *intellectus* in a manner similar to the Augustinian discrimination of *ratio inferior* and *ratio superior*, see *Ep frat* 244–45 (SC 223:338).

216. *Cant* 190 (SC 82:382): Si enim quaesisset ex affectu, invenisset eum in intellectu; et optime illi fuisset in ejus amplexu.

217. *Cant* 136 (SC 82:290): Caput vero Sponsae, hoc est principale cordis, in laeva fovetur, cum mens bene affecta, eo quod amat, per intellectum amoris ipsius fruitur. Sicque alterum alteri cooperatur in bonum, dum amor rationem confortat ad attrahendum, ratio amorem ad amplectandum, amor ratione munitur, ratio vero ab amore illuminatur. Quin potius, praeveniente gratia praedestinationis, et eligentis et vocantis, ratio efficit amorem, amor autem afficit rationem. ... Cf. *Cant* 132 (ibid.:282–84) on the *amplexus*.

218. *Cant* 57 (SC 82:152): Jam enim incipit cognoscere, sicut prior cognita est; et in quantum cognoscit, diligere, sicut prior dilecta est. Prior enim Sponsi ad Sponsam cognitio divinae fuit sapientiae donatio; prior dilectio, sancti Spiritus gratuita infusio; cognitio vero Sponsae ad Sponsum et amor idem est; quoniam in hac re amor ipse intellectus est. Cf. *Ep frat* 251 (SC 223:344) on the gratuity of the *intellectus amoris*.

219. Pierre Rousselot, *Pour l'histoire du problème de l'amour*, pp. 96–97.

220. M.-M. Davy, *Théologie et mystique de Guillaume de Saint-Thierry*, pp. 207–16.

221. L. Malévez, "La doctrine de l'image," pp. 277–79.

222. J.-M. Déchanet, "*AMOR IPSE INTELLECTUS EST*," pp. 349–74; Brooke, *Studies*, pp. 27–30; D. Bell, *Image and Likeness*, pp. 234–49.

223. William allows for a kind of empty and undisciplined thinking (*cogitatio sine intellectu*), or daydreaming, that while not morally evil, is certainly dangerous for contemplatives; see *Ep frat* 246–47 (SC 223:338–40).

224. *Acies cogitantis*, a term William probably took from Augustine, *De Trin.* 10.11–12 (PL 42:982–84), is the equivalent of *intentio cogitantis*, as in *Ep frat* 246–48 (SC 223:338–40).

225. *Ep frat* (SC 223:338). The latter type of *intellectus* corresponds to what is elsewhere called the *ratio fidei*.

226. *Ep frat* 242 (SC 223:336): Tria enim sunt quae cogitationem faciunt: voluntas ipsa, memoria, et intellectus. Voluntas cogit memoriam, ut proferat materiam; cogit intellectum ad formandum quod profertur, adhibens intellectum memoriae, ut inde formetur, intellectui vero aciem cogitantis, ut inde cogitetur. In *Ep frat* 248 (ibid.:340), William seems to reverse the second stage by having *intellectus* rather than *voluntas* apply what has been formed to the *acies cogitantis*. I understand this as dealing with primary and secondary causality, i.e., will activates the whole process; but intellect, once it has become active in forming the *materia*, itself takes on an active role in the encounter with the *acies cogitantis*.

227. I provide the whole passage from *Ep frat* 249 (SC 223:342): Cum vero de eis quae de Deo, vel ad Deum sunt cogitatus, et voluntas eo proficit ut amor fiat, continuo per viam amoris infundit se Spiritus sanctus, spiritus vitae, et omnia vivificat, adjuvans seu in oratione, seu in meditatione, seu in tractatu infirmitatem cogitantis. Et continuo memoria *efficitur* sapientia, cum suaviter ei sapiunt bona Domini, et quod ex eis cogitatum est formandum in affectum, adhibet intellectui; intellectus vero cogitantis *efficitur* contemplatio amantis, et formans illud in quasdam spiritualis vel divinae suavitatis experientias, afficit ex eis aciem cogitantis, illa vero *efficitur* gaudium fruentis [my italics].

228. *Ep frat* 250 (SC 223:342–44). Cf. Augustine, *De Trin.* 11.3.6 (PL 42:988–89).

229. *Ep frat* 251 (SC 223:344): ... cum audierit vocem spiritus spirantis, ea quae cogitationem faciunt, continuo libere concurrant sibi, et cooperantur in bonum, et quasi symbolum faciant in gaudium cogitantis, voluntas exhibendo in gaudium Domini puram affectionem; memoria, materiam fidelem; intellectus, experientiae suavitatem.

230. See *Cant* 80 (SC 82:194–96): Nescit unde veniat, aut quo vadat: cui sensibile quiddam fit divini cujusdam gaudii, et illuminantis ac beatificantis gratiae, quod solus amor illuminatus sentire permittitur ... quam nescit usitatis intellectus, sed sentit affectus. ... [Q]ui sentire eum, et postulare et desiderare facit, idipsum quod sentiendo nescit, ac nesciendo sentit. ... A passage in *Exp Rm* 5 (CCCM 86:123–24) parallels this and explicitly uses the Augustinian expression *docta ignorantia* (see *Ep* 130.15.28 [PL 33:505]): Estque in eo quaedam docta ignorantia, docta a Spiritu Dei, qui adiuvat infirmitatem nostram... (CCCM 86:124.503–05). For a treatment of this, see Verdeyen *La théologie mystique*, pp. 252–57.

231. On this, see especially O. Brooke, "Toward a Theology of Connatural Knowledge," in *Studies*, pp. 232–49; and T. Tomasic, "William of St. Thierry against Peter Abelard," pp. 45–50, 56–65, 74–76, as applied to the Trinity, and by extension to the knowledge of the Trinity gained in mystical knowing.

232. For another presentation of the "content" of such intersubjective mystical knowledge, see the discussion of Aelred of Rievaulx in chapter 7, pp. 321–23.

233 An interesting comparison might be drawn between William's *intellectus amoris* and the *nous eron* of Plotinus (see *Foundations of Mysticism*, pp. 48–51). Despite some similarities, there are profound differences, especially due to William's theology of the Trinity. J.–M. Déchanet's claim (e.g., *William of St. Thierry*, p. 74) that the Cistercian adopted his conception from Plotinus can scarcely be maintained.

234. *Cant* 105 (SC 82:236): ... cum qui amatur per intellectum, seu sensum amoris ipsius, praesto est; et tunc lectulus et floridus, et noster est.

235. *Cant* 181 (SC82:368–70): Veritas enim invocandi in affectu amantis, certum fit argumentum in conscientia invocantis, praesentissime presentiae ejus qui dixit: "Ego sum veritas" (John 14:6). Cf. *Med* 2 (PL 180:208BC) and *Cant* 43 and 78 (SC 82:130 and 192).

236. *Cant* 2 (SC 82:72): Cum enim amamus quamcumque creaturam, non ad utendum ad te, sed ad fruendum in se, fit amor jam non amor, sed cupiditas, vel libido. ... Cf. *Cant* 23 (ibid.:98). On the *utor/frui* distinction in William, see Verdeyen, *La théologie mystique*, pp. 230–34.

237. William often refers to death as a good, either the death to the things of this world by which we begin to love God, e.g., *Contemp* 5 (SC 61:72) and *Nat am* 8.22 (PL 184:393C–94B), or the death by which we enter into the joys of heaven, e.g., *Nat am* 15.44 (406D–07A) and *Med* 3.1 (PL 180:211BC).

238. *Cant* 121 (SC 82:264): ... verus amor vel sui, vel proximi, non sit nisi amor Dei.

239. *Cant* 128 (SC 82:274): Sic qui ordinate caritatis est, diligit Dominum Deum suum, et in ipso seipsum, et proximum suum sicut seipsum, ipsa qualitate, ipsa quantitate.

240. For more on the ordering of charity, see the great hymn to the Holy Spirit in *Cant* 131 (SC 82:276–80), as well as *Cant* 189 (ibid.:380), *Nat am* 14.42 (PL 184:405A), *Med* 12.13 (PL 180:246D), and *Ep frat* 193 (SC 223:300).

241. *Med* 11.13 (PL 180:241BC): Totus quippe affectus debetur Deo. ... Sufficit enim affectus, si res non exigit, vel possibilitas deest, ut exerceatur actus. Si enim actum exigit necessitas charitatis, debet eum, sive Deo, sive proximo, veritas charitatis; si non exigitur, habere nos debet vacantes sibi charitas veritatis. See the whole discussion from 241B–42B, as well as the comments in M. Basil Pennington, "Abbot William–Spiritual Father of Saint Thierry," in *William, Abbot of St. Thierry*, pp. 233–35. For similar teaching in the treatises, also framed in terms of *caritas veritatis* and *veritas caritatis*, see *Contemp* 1 (SC 61:58). Cf. *Nat am* 22 (PL 184:394B), and *Ep frat* 278 (SC 223:368).

242. Two of the most important passages occur in *Cant* 59 and 97 (SC 82:154 and 222–24). The latter passage also uses the expression *caritas veritatis* that William took from 2 Thess 2:10.

243. *Contemp* 6 (SC 61:76–78). The key notion that William uses to solve the problem of the different degrees of love and the perfect satisfaction enjoyed by all is that of the unity of all love in the kingdom of heaven. In loving how the angels love God we come to share in these higher degrees.

244. Ibid. (80–82): . . . ideoque et qui desiderat semper amat desiderare, et qui amat semper desiderat amare, et desideranti et amanti quod desiderat et amat, sic facis abundare o domine: ut nec anxietas desiderantem, nec fastidium affligat abundantem. . . . Haec affectio: haec est perfectio. Sic semper ire: hoc est pervenire.

245. See the "Table des mots latins" in the Davy edition under *contemplatio* and *contemplari*. William's teaching on contemplation is treated in the standard introductions; see especially J.-M. Déchanet, "La contemplation au douzième siècle," DS 2:1948–66.

246. *Cant* 22–23 (SC 82:96–100). For some other significant appearances of *contemplatio* in the *Expositio in Cantica*, see, e.g., *Cant* 92 (ibid.:212): Duo sunt oculi contemplationis, ratio et amor; *Cant* 149 (316), on the different classes of contemplative souls; *Cant* 157 (332): Sed et animae Deum quaerenti fenestra est, qua Deum contempletur oculus rationis, per quem, illuminante gratia, spiritualia sive divina speculatur, ad hoc principaliter factus in homine, ut per eum Deus videatur ab homine.

247. For an outline of the contents, see J. Hourlier, "Introduction," *William of St. Thierry: On Contemplating God* (Spencer: Cistercian Publications, 1971), pp. 22–25.

248. Naturally, *contemplatio* and its cognates occur throughout the later works. A list would be tedious, but for one important use in a trinitarian context, see *Aenig* 88 (ed. Davy: 168) where William combines both *contemplatio* and *visio* in speaking of the Trinity: visio illius contemplationis seu contemplatio illius visionis.

249. On the subject of "face-to-face" vision, see M. Simon, "Le 'face à face' dans les méditations de Guillaume de Saint-Thierry"; and K. Ruh, *Die Geschichte der abendländische Mystik*, 1:282–83, who notes William's emphasis on the term *visio* rather than *contemplatio*.

250. *Ep frat* 26 (SC 223:164): Faciem enim Dei, hoc est cognitionem ejus quaerere, faciem ad faciem quam vidit Jacob et de qua dicit Apostolus: Tunc cognoscam sicut et cognitus sum, et nunc videmus per speculum et in aenigmate, tunc autem facie ad faciem, et sicuti est. . . . Cf. *Spec* 11 (SC 301:70–72) and *Aenig* 3 (ed. Davy: 94).

251. E.g., *Contemp* 3.35 and 6.48 (SC 61:66 and 80); *Cant* 41 (SC 82:128); *Spec* 96 (SC 301:166); *Ep frat* 45 (SC 223:180); *Med* 3 (PL 180:212C).

252. *Med* 11.1 (PL 180:232D): Ideo cum facies bonitatis tuae super me semper intendat benefaciendo, facies miseriae meae stolidam semper terrena respiciens sic caecitatis suae caligine obvolvitur, ut nec sciat, nec possit coram te apparere, nisi inquantum faciei veritatis omnia transvidentis quomodocumque sit, non potest latere. William's references to the face of God are frequent in the *Meditationes*, e.g., *Med* 2.9, 3.2–3, 4.11, 6.2, 7.1–9, 8.1, 9.5–6, 11.1–2, 12.5, etc. See the study of M. Simon, "Le 'face à face' dans les méditations" for more detail.

253. *Spec* 103 (SC 301:174.15–16): . . . ante revelatam faciem gratiae revelatam offerre bonae conscientiae?

254. *Spec* 11 (SC 301:72.13–15): Species namque summi boni ad amorem sui et cognitionem naturaliter semper suscitat et trahit omnem rationalem intellectum. . . .

255. *Med* 3.3 (PL 180:211D): . . . exquiro faciem tuam per temetipsum, ne in finem avertas eam a me.

256. *Med* 3.6 (PL 180:212D): Numquid vult te videre sicuti es? Et quid est, sicuti es? Nam qualis, aut quantus? . . . Hoc videre supra nos est; quia videre quod tu es, hoc est esse quod es.

257. Ibid. (212D–13A): Nemo autem videt Patrem, nisi Filius et Filium nisi Pater; quia hoc est esse Patri, quod videre Filium; et hoc est esse Filio, quod videre Patrem. We will see more on this important theme below. For a comparable text, see *Med* 6.6–7 (223D–24C).

258. Ibid. (213A): Sed nunquid homo videt Deum, sicut Filium Pater, vel Patrem Filius. . . . Sic omnino, sed non per omnem modum. For some other important appearances of Matt 11:27, see *Contemp* 11 (SC 61:104–06); *Exp Rm* 6 (CCCM 86:161.926–30); *Cant* 66 and 82 (SC 82:166–68 and 200); *Spec* 106 (SC 301:176); etc.

259. Verdeyen, *La théologie mystique*, pp. 87–94.

260. On Origen's use, for example, see the texts referred to in *The Foundations of Mysticism*, p. 128.

261. *Med* 3.8 (PL 180:213C): Cum per hunc in aliquod anima extenditur, quadam sui transformatione in id quod amat transmutatur: non quod idem sit in natura, sed affectu rei amatae conformatur. . . .

262. The traditional notion of being given a share in the Sonship of the Word appears in a number of places in William's early writings, e.g., *Nat am* 15.45 (PL 184:407AB); *Med* 3.9, 6.8 and 7.9 (PL 180:213CD, 223CD and 229B); *Contemp* 11 (SC 61:100); etc.

263. *Med* 3.10 (PL 180:214B): Quae vero desursum est, quod sursum est redolet; nihil humanum, sed totum divinum: et ubi se infundit, rationem secum defert sui generis. . . . William uses the term *intelligentia* rather than the more usual *intellectus* for these two types of understanding.

264. On faith as a form of vision of God, see *Aenig* 4 (ed. Davy:94).

265. *Cant* 149 (SC 82:314): Videtque venientem, cum in semetipsa misericorditer sentit operantem.

266. *Cant* 155 (SC 82:328): Sicque tu prior videns eam facis videntem te, et stans illi stabilem facis tibi, donec miserantis et amantis mutua appropinquatio, solvat omnino inimicitias peccati, medium maceriae dividentis, et fiat mutua visio, mutuus amplexus, mutuum gaudium, unus spiritus. Cf. *Cant* 157 (ibid.: 330–32).

267. For some representative passages, see *Contemp* 2 and 3 (SC 61:60 and 66), and *Nat am* 7.20 (PL 184:392AD), comparing vision and love.

268. On the differences between vision in this life and vision in heaven, see especially *Aenig* 3–5, 7 and 23 (ed. Davy: 92–96, 96–98 and 112).

269. *Spec* 107 (SC 301:178.13–17): Similem enim ibi esse Deo, videre Deum sive cognoscere erit; quem in tantum videbit sive cognoscet qui cognoscet vel videbit, in quantum similis ei erit; in tantum erit ei similis, in quantum eum cognoscet vel videbit. Cf. *Aenig* 5 and 87 (ed. Davy:96, 168), and *Ep frat* 210 (SC 223: 314–16). The equation of *visio* and *similitudo* has its roots in Augustine, e.g., *De Trin.* 14.17.23 (PL 42:1055): In hac quippe imagine tunc perfecta erit Dei similitudo, quando Dei perfecta erit visio. Cf. *De Trin.* 14.19.25, and 15.11.21 (PL 42:1055–56, 1073); and *Ep* 92.3 (PL 33:318–19).

270. *Ep frat* 267–75 (SC 223:356–64), the text cited is in #268 (ibid.:358): . . . sicut lumen clausum in manibus, quod patet et latet ad arbitrium tenentis. . . . This long passage ends with a reminiscence of the theme from *Meditatio* 10 (see above, p. 247) on how the vision of divine love appears to us as we gaze on Jesus Christ, the God–man.

271. See McGinn, "Love, Knowledge, and *Unio mystica*," esp. pp. 61–66.

272. For William's teaching on mystical union, see Jean Déchanet, "Notes doctrinales. 4. L'union avec Dieu ou l'Unité divine," in SC 223:407–14; Bell, *Image and Likeness*, p. 174 n.27; and Verdeyen, *La théologie mystique*, esp. 70–106.

273. *Contemp* 11 (SC 61:96): . . . spiritus sanctus a patre procedens et filio . . . deum nobis et nos uniens deo.

274. Ibid. (SC 61:98–100): . . . tu teipsum amas in nobis, et nos in te, cum te per te amamus, et in tantum tibi unimur, in quantum amare te meremur; et participes efficimur ut dic

tum est orationis illius Christi filii tui: Volo ut sicut ego et tu unum sumus; ita et ipsi in nobis unum sint. This Johannine passage (John 17:21–22), one of William's favorites for expressing the trinitarian reality of union, appears throughout *Contemp* 11, and is frequently cited elsewhere, e.g., *Contemp* 7 (ibid.:84–86), *Med* 8.5 (PL 180:231A), and *Ep frat* 288 (SC 223:374).

275. *Contemp* 11 (SC 61:106): . . . ut sicut non est aliud patri nosse filium, nisi hoc esse quod filius, nichil aliud filio nosse patrem, nisi hoc esse quod est pater . . . et sicut spiritu sancto nichil est aliud nosse vel comprehendere patrem et filium, quam hoc esse quod est pater et filius; ita nobis qui ad ymaginem tuam conditi sumus . . . nichil sit aliud amare et timere deum et mandata ejus observare, quam esse, et unum spiritum cum deo esse.

276. *Nat corp* 2.13 (PL 180:722D): Unum amore, unum beatitudine, unum immortalite et incorruptione, unum etiam quodammodo ipsa divinitate.

277. E.g., *Spec* 100 and 106–7 (SC 301:170 and 176–78). The latter text also uses Matt 11:27.

278. See especially *Cant* 94–95 (SC 82:216 and 220–22).

279. *Cant* 131 (SC 82:280): Ideo quaecumque Sponsa est, hoc solum desiderat, hoc affectat, ut facies ejus faciei tuae jungatur jugiter in osculo caritatis; hoc est, unus tecum spiritus fiat per unitatem ejusdem voluntatis. . . . Cf. *Cant* 130 (ibid.:276).

280. *Ep frat* 263 (SC 223:354): . . . cum in amplexu et osculo Patris et Filii, mediam quodammodo se invenit beata conscientia; cum modo ineffabili, incogitabili, fieri meretur homo Dei, non Deus, sed tamen quod est Deus: homo ex gratia quod Deus ex natura. Cf. *Ep frat* 258 (ibid.:350) for a similar treatment of divinization.

281. *Ep frat* 286–89 (SC 223:372–76). #288 uses the *unitas mentis* formula and also cites John 17:21.

282. *Ep frat* 262 (SC 223:352–54): . . . cum fit homo unum cum Deo, unus spiritus, non tantum unitate idem volendi, sed expressiore quadam veritate virtutis, sicut jam dictum est, aliud velle non valendi. Cf. *Ep frat* 289 (ibid.:376) on the identity of *unitas spiritus* and *similitudo*.

283. E.g., *Exp Rm* 5 (CCCM 86:124.506–08): . . .donec renovatus ad imaginem eius qui creavit eum, per unitatem similitudinis incipiat esse filius. . . .The same teaching, without the *terminus technicus*, can be found throughout his works, see especially *Med* 6.7 (PL 180:224C), *Spec* 107 (SC 301:176–78), *Aenig* 6 (ed. Davy: 96), etc.

284. See Bell, *Image and Likeness*, pp. 188–95.

285. On these differences, see Brooke, *Studies*, pp. 26–27.

286. For other ways of expressing this distinction, see, e.g., *Cant* 173 (SC 223:354–56): Habitatio ergo parata requirit habitatorem; . . . ipse, ait, mihi, in hoc ipsum me efficiens Deus; ego illi, in hoc ipsum effecta. Cf. *Spec* 101 (SC 301:170.4–6): . . . [anima] tota repente transmutetur, non quidem in naturam divinitatis, sed tamen in quandam supra humanam, citra divinam formam beatitudinis. . . .

287. Bernard, *SCC* 71.6 (SBOp 2:218.8–15) and 9 (2:220.12–15). The distinction is concisely expressed in the Morimond-Clairvaux recension of 71.6 (2:218: apparatus) as follows: Denique innuitur tibi unitatum diversitas per 'unus' et 'unum', quoniam nec Patri et Filio unus, nec homini et Deo 'unum' poterit convenire. The difference between Bernard and William in this matter has been noted by Verdeyen, *La théologie mystique*, pp. 74–75; followed by Ruh, *Die Geschichte der abendländische Mystik*, 1:315–17.

288. *Ep frat* 263 (SC 223:354.6–9): . . . in summa illa unitate veritatis, et in veritate unitatis, hoc idem homini, suo modo fit ad Deum, quod *consubstantiali unitate*, Filio est ad Patrem, vel Patri ad Filium . . . (my italics). On this text, see Verdeyen, *La théologie mystique*, pp. 75–76.

289. On this see Robert Thomas, "William of St. Thierry: Our Life in the Trinity," *Monastic Studies* 3(1965): 159–64.

290. Bell, *Image and Likeness*, pp. 212–13.

291. For a detailed study, see Bell, ibid., pp. 198–210. See also R. Thomas, *Guillaume de Saint-Thierry*, pp. 225–32.

292. *Cant* 132 (SC 82:282): Amplexus etenim hic Spiritus sanctus est. Qui enim Patris et Filii Dei Communio, qui Caritas, qui Amicitia, qui Amplexus est, ipse in amore Sponsi ac Sponsae ipsa omnia est. Sed ibi majestas est consubstantialis naturae, hic autem donum gratiae; ibi dignitas, hic autem dignatio; idem tamen, idem plane Spiritus. Amplexus autem iste, hic initiatur; alibi perficiendus. Abyssus haec alteram abyssum invocat; extasis ista longe aliud quam quod videt somniat; secretum hoc aliud secretum suspirat; gaudium hoc aliud gaudium imaginatur; suavitas ista aliam suavitatem praeorditur. For some other appearances of *excessus mentis* and *extasis* in the *Expositio in Cantica*, see, e.g., *Cant* 38, 46, 117, 137, 140 and 147 (ibid.:122, 134; 254, 292, 296 and 312).

293. *Cant* 99 (SC 82:226) is one of the longer treatments, but the theme is a common one.

294. Brooke, *Studies*, p. 8; cf. pp. 33–34 and pp. 37–38. These sentiments have been echoed by many interpreters of William, e.g., Verdeyen, *La théologie mystique*, p. 58: "Guillaume est le premier auteur spirituel qui ait développé les aspects dialectiques de la vie trinitaire elle-même" (see also p. 70); and Léone Reypens, "Dieu (Connaissance mystique)," DS 3:892–93.

295. On the importance of the Trinity in Augustine's mysticism, see *Foundations of Mysticism*, pp. 243–48.

296. The lines of influence have been amply studied, though perhaps also overemphasized, by L. Verdeyen in his *La théologie mystique de Guillaume de Saint-Thierry*.

297. The same point has been made by D. Bell: "If Augustine's Trinitarian mysticism was Christo-centric, William's is Spirito-centric. . . . " (*Image and Likeness*, p. 253). It is interesting to note that the two most original theologies of the Holy Spirit created in the twelfth century, though very different ones, came from the pens of Cistercians, or at least sometime Cistercians—William of St. Thierry in the first half of the century and Joachim of Fiore in the second half.

298. See O. Brooke, "The Speculative Development of the Trinitarian Theology of William of St. Thierry in the Aenigma Fidei," in *Studies*, pp. 63–122. Cf. Verdeyen, *La théologie mystique*, chapter 2.

299. Useful here is the article of R. Thomas already referred to, "William of St. Thierry: Our Life in the Trinity."

300. Among many such passage we can note the following: *Cant* 31, 54–55, 66, 80, 84–87, 95, 99–100, 116, 119, 131 and 182; *Spec* 71–73 and 101–02; *Aenig* 6; *Ep frat* 142, 169–70 and 264–67; *Med* 3.6 and 11–12, *Med* 6.7–8, *Med* 8.5 and *Med* 12.17–18.

301. *Spec* 106 (SC 301:176.1–2): Ea vero cognitio quae mutua est Patris et Filii, ipsa est unitas amborum, qui est Spiritus sanctus. . . .This mutual recognition is their very substance, as William goes on to say citing his favorite proof text (Matt 11:27).

302. *Spec* 109 (SC 301:180.7–8): . . . et unit eum sibi, ut *creditus cum Deo* (Ps 77:8), *unus* cum eo fiat *spiritus* (1 Cor 6:17) hominis credentis.

303. See especially *Aenig* 87 (ed. Davy: 166–68) on how *spiritus* is both a common and a proper name in the Trinity.

304. *Spec* 110 (SC 301:180.1–4): Quodque communiter vocantur Pater et Filius, *Spiritus* enim *est Deus* (Ps 77:8), quodque proprie vocari oportuit Spiritum Sanctum qui non tam est unius eorum quam in quo apparet communitas amborum. . . .

305. See R. Thomas, "William of St. Thierry: Our Life in the Trinity," p. 154.

306. *Cant* 131 (SC 82:278): . . . Deus qui es ipse in ea amor tuus, fac in ea ut amet te de te, o amor ejus; et tu ipse in ipsa, de ipsa ames te; et de ipsa in ipsa facias et ordines omnia secundem te. Cf. *Ep frat* 170 (SC 223:278): . . . et amans semetipsum de homine Deus, unum secum efficit et spiritum ejus et amorem ejus.

307. Particularly with regard to the nonopposition between time and eternity and place and omnipresence in the *Meditationes* (e.g., *Med* 6.5–7 [PL 180:223C–24B]). William's teaching in these areas, as well as on the mutual implication of transcendence and immanence in God, are standard Neoplatonic fare developed from aspects of Augustine's teaching. Compare, to take only one example, what William says about *locus* (Locus ergo tuus Pater est, et tu Patris; et non solum, sed etiam nos locus tuus sumus, et tu noster [224A]) with Augustine's similar teaching in *Tractatus in Iohannem* 111.3 (PL 35:1928). Hence, I disagree with the exaggerated claims for the abbot's originality advanced by Verdeyen, *La théologie mystique*, e.g., pp. 44–47 and 117–23.

308. The Eleventh Council of Toledo (675 C.E.) contained the formula: *Fons ergo ipse [Pater] et origo est totius divinitatis.* The source, of this, is ultimately found in Augustine, e.g., *De Trin* 5.13.14, and *Sermo* 71.16.26 (PL 42:920–21; and PL 38:459–60). William revives this teaching in the *Aenig* 77 and 89 (ed. Davy: 158 and 168).

309. *Aenig* 91 (ed. Davy: 170): . . . sic et Verbum dicentis, ut multis modis utcumque dicatur, quod nullo edici modo potest.

310. *Aenig* 91–92 (ed. Davy: 170–72). In the mission of the Son the *Verbum* is both the one sent and, as a member of the undivided Trinity, one of the three who send; cf. *Aenig* 94–95 (ibid.:172– 74) and *Nat am* 11.34 (PL 184:400D–01C).

311. *Aenig* 67 (ed. Davy: 150): Ad hoc enim venit in mundum, hoc effecit, ut Deus Trinitas innotesceret. Nusquam autem in hac vita divinitas melius humano intellectu comprehenditur, quam in eo quo magis incomprehensibilis esse intelligitur: hoc est in praedicatione Trinitatis. Idcirco enim *Verbum caro factum est, et habitavit in nobis*, ut, sicut ipse Dominus Jesus Christus orans dicit ad Patrem, manifestaret nomen Patris hominibus, et caritatem Dei diffunderet in cordibus nostris per Spiritum sanctum quem dedit nobis. Denique hoc est enigma fidei, terribile impiis, ad deterendos eos et fugandos a facie Domini; blandum piis, ad excitandos eos et provocandos quaere faciem ejus semper. . . .

312. The term *Spiritus vitae* for the Holy Spirit (see n. 00 above) is frequent in William; see *Cant* 1 and 67 (SC 82:70 and 168), *Nat am* 8.23 (PL 184:395A), *Spec* 75 and 97 (SC 301:144 and 168), *Aenig* 23 and 24 (ed. Davy: 112, 114), *Ep frat* 249 (SC 223: 342), etc.

313. *Ep frat* 266 (SC 223:356): Ipse tamen est et sollicitudo bene quaerentis, et pietas in spiritu et veritate adorantis, et sapientia invenientis, et amor habentis, et gaudium fruentis.

314. *Ep frat* 263 (SC82:354): . . . hoc idem homini, suo modo fit ad Deum, quod consubstantiali unitate, Filio est ad Patrem, vel Patri ad Filium. . . .

315. Ibid.: . . . quidquid commune potest esse amborum. . . . Cf. *Aenig* 97 (ed. Davy: 174–76).

316. *Aenig* 38 (ed. Davy:124). Richard of St. Victor also felt unhappy with the standard Boethian definition, and, like William, adopted a more intersubjective one. See his *De Trinitate* 4.18, in *Richard de Saint-Victor: De Trinitate*, ed. J. Ribaillier (Paris: Vrin, 1958), p. 181.

317. *Aenig* 38 (ed. Davy: 124): Diffinitur autem persona a diffinientibus duobus modis: sive rationalis nature individua substantia: sive cujus pro sui forma, certa sit agnitio. John Anderson was the first to find the source of this second definition in Boethius's *Liber de persona* (PL 64:1343D–44A). See *William of St. Thierry: The Enigma of Faith* (Washington: Cistercian Publications, 1974), pp. 65–66 n. 150.

318. Ibid. (ed. Davy: 126): . . . certam sui preferentes agnitionem: ad respondendum quid tres, aliquam habent facultatem.

319. See T. Tomasic, "William of St. Thierry against Peter Abelard," p. 43 (see the whole section pp. 40–44).

320. Ibid., pp. 37–40. Tomasic also discusses the intersubjective character of the relation of the *Sponsus* and *Sponsa* in the *Expositio in Cantica*, laying emphasis on the mutual "insinuation" (etymologically, "to be placed in the bosom [*sinus*] of") described in such passages as

Cant 93 (SC 82:214): . . . jam Sponsus et Sponsa amico consortio, familiari colloquio, invicem se sibi insinuantes, invicem placentes, invicem laudantes, praelibant gaudium mutuae conjunctionis.

321. Tomasic, "William of St. Thierry against Peter Abelard," p. 49: "It would seem, then, that the Unity of the Godhead consists essentially in the Communitarian or Intersubjective Personal Structure revealed as Spirit, and is constituted by that perfectly Intersubjective Consciousness and Liberty." Cf. pp. 50–56.

322. *Med* 6.7 (PL 180:224AB): Nostra ergo, ut video, in te, vel tua in nobis habitatio, nobis coelum est: coelum vero coeli tibi aeternitas est, qua es, quod es in teipso, Pater in Filio, et Filius in Patre; et unitas qua Pater et Filius unum estis, id est, Spiritus sanctus, non quasi aliunde veniens et medium se faciens, sed coessendo in hoc ipsum existens. Unitatis vero, qua in nobis vel in te unum sumus, auctor et ordinator est idem Spiritus sanctus. . . .

323. On circumincession in William, see Brooke, *Studies*, p. 86; and Tomasic, "William of St. Thierry against Peter Abelard," pp. 63–65.

324. E.g., *Cant* 20 (SC 82:94): . . . [Deus] collocat in sensu amantis, et commendat aliquam cognitionis suae effigiem, non praesumpti phantasmatis, sed piae cujusdam affectionis. . . . On this text, see Bell, *Image and Likeness*, pp. 228–29.

325. *Exp Rm* 3 (CCCM 86:66.202–3): . . . sed amor eius ad nos est bonitas; amor noster ad ipsum Spiritus sanctus. . . .

326. *Orat* (SC 61:124): Ista localitas, unitas est patris et filii, consubstantialitatis trinitatis.

327. On William's teaching on the "place" (*locus*) of God, see, e.g., *Spec* 119 (SC 301:188), and the passage in *Med* 6.5–7 (PL 180:223C–24A) referred to above in n. 322. The meaning of such texts as ways of expressing the intersubjective circumincession of the Persons of the Trinity now becomes clear.

328. *Spec* 121 (SC 301:1–6): Omnia ergo facta vel verba Verbi Dei unum nobis verbum sunt; omnia quae de eo legimus, audimus, loquimur, meditamur, sive provocando amorem, sive incutiendo timorem, ad unum nos vocant, ad unum nos mittunt, de quo multa dicuntur, et nichil dicitur. . . .

329. *Contemp* 13 (SC 61:118–20): Te igitur deum patrem, quo creatore vivimus, te sapientia patris, per quem reformati sapienter vivimus, te sancte spiritus quem et in quo diligentes beate vivimus, et beatissime vivemus, unius substantiae trinitatem, unum deum a quo sumus, per quem sumus, in quo sumus, . . . principium ad quod recurrimus, forma quam sequimur, gratia qua reconciliamur, adoramus et benedicimus: tibi gloria in saecula. Amen. Cf. *Med* 2.7–8 (PL 180:210AB) for another passage on adoring the Trinity without neglecting the Unity. On the difficulty of speaking of number in the Trinity, see *Aenig* 32–35 (ed. Davy: 118–22).

330. Brooke, *Studies*, p. 33.

331. See also *Med* 3.12 (PL 180:214D): . . . ut pio et sobrio intellectu comprehendat non comprehendendo majestatem divinae incomprehensibilitatis. Cf. *Med* 7.7 (ibid.:228D), *Nat am* 8.21 (PL 184:393AC), *Cant* 80 (SC 82:192–94), *Spec* 115–17 (SC 301:184–86), *Aenig* 67 (ed. Davy: 150), etc.

332. *Ep frat* 194 (SC 223:302): Bona enim Domini videre amare est. Amare vero habere est. Ideo nitamur, quantum possumus, ut videamus; videndo intelligamus, intelligendo amemus, ut amando habeamus.

Chapter 7

1. On this question, see Jean Leclercq, "Consciousness of Identification in 12th Century Monasticism," *Cistercian Studies* 14 (1979): 217–31.

2. Thomas Merton, "St. Aelred of Rievaulx and the Cistercians," *Cistercian Studies* 20 (1985): 214. It is significant that the memorial for Merton issued among the first volumes of Cistercian Publications was entitled *The Cistercian Spirit: A Symposium* (Spencer, MA: Cistercian Publications, 1970).

3. The first two of Merton's five posthumously published articles appearing under the title "St. Aelred of Rievaulx and the Cistercians," *Cistercian Studies* 20 (1985): 212–23; 21 (1986): 30–42, constitute an introduction to the major lines of twelfth-century Cistercian thought. The analysis summarized here can be found on pp. 216–21.

4. Merton, St. Aelred," 222.

5. For a recent survey with bibliographies, see Edmond Mikkers, "Robert de Molesmes. II. La spiritualité cistercienne," DS 13:738–78.

6. Jean Leclercq expresses it well: "The liturgy develops men's inclination to read the Bible in order to discover yet more of the spiritual treasure which it contains, while the cycle of mysteries which is re-lived through the liturgy illuminates the most vital content of the sacred texts" ("From Gregory the Great to St. Bernard," in *The Cambridge History of the Bible: 2, The West from the Fathers to the Reformation*, ed. G. W. H. Lampe [Cambridge: Cambridge University Press, 1969], p. 189).

7. Guerric's sermons have been edited by John Morson and Hilary Costello, *Guerric d'Igny: Sermons*, 2 vols., SC 166, 202 (Paris: Cerf, 1970, 1973). A translation by the same authors was published under the title *Guerric of Igny: Liturgical Sermons*, 2 vols. (Spenser, MA: Cistercian Publications, 1970, 1971). I have consulted this translation with profit, but will use my own versions unless otherwise noted. The translation lists the fifty-four sermons in order, while the edition lists them only according to the number for each feast. I will follow the numeration of the translation, but cite the place in the edition for all significant texts. A treatise known as the *Liber amoris*, sometimes ascribed to Guerric, is actually an anonymous Cistercian work heavily influenced by Bernard's *SCC* 9 and 21; see J. Morson and H. Costello, "*Liber amoris*: Was it Written by Guerric of Igny?" *Cîteaux* 16 (1965): 114–35 (with edition).

8. E.g., Bernard, *Ep* 89.3 and 90.2 (SBOp 7:236 and 238).

9. The editors and translators have argued that Guerric's sermons, while obviously not verbatim transcriptions of his preaching to the Igny community, have been less reworked than most of Bernard's sermons and thus give us a more direct sense of what early Cistercian preaching was like. See "Introduction," *Liturgical Sermons 1*, pp. xx–xxii.

10. Among the works devoted to Guerric, see Déodat de Wilde, "The Formation of Christ in Us: Bl. Guerric of Igny," *Monastic Studies* 2 (1964): 29–45; [J. Morson and H. Costello], "Introduction," *Liturgical Sermons I*, pp. vii–lxi (this is closely related to the "Introduction" in SC 166:7–84); John Morson, *Christ the Way: The Christology of Guerric of Igny* (Kalamazoo, MI: Cistercian Publications, 1978); and M. Basil Pennington, *The Last of the Fathers: The Cistercian Fathers of the Twelfth Century* (Still River, MA: St. Bede's Publications, 1983), pp. 181–219, a reprint of three essays on Guerric originally published elsewhere. The most recent survey of Guerric's place in Western mysticism is in Kurt Ruh's *Geschichte der abendländische Mystik: Band I, Die Grundlegung durch die Kirchenväter und die Mönchstheologie des 12. Jahrhunderts* (Munich: Beck, 1990), pp. 321–29.

11. Peter of Celle, *Ep.* 176 (PL 202:635A): Vera enim quies est in ordine Cisterciensi, ubi Martha Mariae jungitur, ubi, iuxta verbum Sapientis, et agenti quiescendum, et quiescenti agendum. Guerric followed Bernard in his own teaching about the interaction of action and contemplation in the monastic life. See, e.g., *Sermones* 23.6, 33.2, 35.4–5, 45.3, 49.2, 50.3–4 and 53.2.

12. See B. Pennington, "Together Unto God: Contemplative Community in the Sermons of Guerric of Igny," in *The Last of the Fathers*, pp. 192–206. This paper originally appeared in *Contemplative Community: An Interdisciplinary Symposium*, ed. M. Basil Pennington (Washing-

ton, DC: Cistercian Publications, 1972), a volume that constitutes a rich resource for this aspect of Cistercian mysticism.

13. See Giles Constable, "The Ideal of Inner Solitude in the Twelfth Century," in *Horizons marins: Itinéraires spirituels (Mélanges Michel Mollat)*, ed. Henri Dubois, Jean-Clause Hocquet, and André Vauchez (Paris, 1976), 1:27–34.

14. William of St. Thierry, *Ep frat* 13 and 70 for the Carthusians, and *Vita Ber* 1.35 for the Cistercians.

15. For Cistercian views of the desert, see Benedicta Ward, "The Desert Myth: Reflections on the Desert Ideal in Early Cistercian Monasticism," in *One Yet Two: Monastic Traditions East and West*, ed. M. Basil Pennington (Kalamazoo, MI: Cistercian Publications, 1976), pp. 183–99; and B. McGinn, "Ocean and Desert as Symbols of Mystical Absorption in the Christian Tradition," *Journal of Religion* 74 (1994): 155–81.

16. Guerric, *Sermo* 4 (SC 166:134–48).

17. *Sermo* 4.2 (SC 166:136.46–49): Illud sane mirabili gratia provisum est divinae dispensationis, ut in his desertis nostris et quietem habeamus solitudinis, nec tamen consolatione careamus gratae et sanctae societatis.

18. Citing Eccl. 4:10 in a non-Vulgate form (*Vae soli, quoniam si ceciderit, non habet sublevantem*), Bernard attacked the temptation of some monks to undertake the dangers of solitary living in *SCC* 33.10 (SBOp 1:240). Bernard, of course, did not condemn the eremitical life as such, but he obviously thought it was meant for the *very* few.

19. *Sermo* 4.2 (SC 166:138.58–60): Et nunc quoque, si medium silentium teneant omnia interiora tua, omnipotens sermo tibi secretus illabetur de sede paterna. This text paraphrases Wis 18:4–5, a passage the liturgy uses to refer to the coming of Christ at the Nativity.

20. For Guerric's doctrine of silence, see, e.g., *Sermones* 10.2 (SC 166:226–28, also using Wis 18:14–15); and 22.5–6 and 28.5–6 (SC 202:50 and 156–60). Guerric also emphasizes the desert of Cîteaux in *Sermo* 43.1 (SC 202:352–54).

21. See especially his lapidary formulation in the First Sermon for the Feast of St. Benedict (SC 202:46.114–17): Beati et vos, fratres mei, qui in disciplinam sapientiae et christianae scholam philosophiae nomina dedistis, si perseveranter in sapientia moriemini. . . . Guerric would probably not have considered direct experience of Christ possible outside the monastic community, though he never says so explicitly. His comments about the world tend to be at least as negative as other Cistercian Fathers.

22. Guerric, *Sermo* 53.1 (SC 202:500.25–27): . . . gradatim de imis ad summa perducens virum evangelicae perfectionis, donec ad videndum Deum deorum in Sion ingrediatur templum. . . . Bernard of Clairvaux was the first to use the beatitudes in this sense in his OS 1 (SBOp 5:327–41). Aelred and Isaac of Stella have similar treatments.

23. The three gifts of the Magi figure these three stages in *Sermo* 11.5 (SC 166:248.140–43): Existimo enim, sine praeiudicio tamen melioris intellectus, myrrham esse primam oblationem incipientium, deinde thus proficientium, demumque aurum perfectorum. . . . Cf. *Sermo* 12.4 (ibid.:262). The threefold pattern is also applied to the history of salvation in *Sermo* 9.3 (ibid.:214–16).

24. *Sermo* 51.4 (SC 202:480.94–6): . . . nisi crediderimus, non intelligemus (Isa. 7:9), nec gustabimus quoniam suavis est Dominus (Ps 33:9). Fides siquidem est quae odoratur, experientia quae gustat et fruitur. Comparable and more complete analyses of the transition from faith through understanding to vision can be found in *Sermones* 12.3 and 5 (SC 166:260 and 262); 13.3–7 (ibid.:276–86, which expands the triple pattern to a fourfold one of *fides, iustitia, scientia, sapientia*). Both these texts make heavy use of 1 Cor 13:12 and 2 Cor 3:18. *Sermo* 35.5 (SC 202:258.163–66) has a somewhat different triple pattern: Primus ergo calor vitae redeuntis est cum bonus exercetur actus; secundus resurrectionis profectus cum per orationem dilatatur affectus; perfectio autem cum ad contemplandum illuminatur intellectus. . . .

25. *Sermo* 19.6 (SC 166:382.179–384.191): . . . pertransibitis, sicut Sponsus sponsae pollice-tur, euntes de virtute in virtutem, *a claritate in claritatem tamquam a Domini Spiritu*, proficientes de visione quae est per fidem ad illam quae est per speculum et imaginem; ac postremo de illa quae est in imagine speciei ad eam quae erit in ipsa veritate faciei, seu facie veritatis. Si enim iugiter praesentiam Domini, licet velatam, intendatis per fidem, aliquando etiam *revelata facie gloriam* eius speculabimini, licet per speculum et imaginem. Cum autem, impletis diebus purgationis, venerit quod perfectum est, assistetis Domino in Ierusalem, habitantes cum vultu eius ac sine fine contuentes eum facie ad faciem. . . . 1 Cor 13:10–12 appears seven times in Guerric, while 2 Cor 3:18 is used eight times.

26. *Sermo* 52.1 (SC 202:486.24–488.33): Igitur inter formam carnis et formam Verbi quasi medius de ista ad illam gradus est, quaedam alia forma Christi, spiritalis quidem sed quam in carne palam exhibuit, forma scilicet vitae quam in corpore gessit ad informationem eorum qui erant credituri. Si enim secundum exemplar vitae et morum, quod in eo monstratum est, formatus fuerit in nobis Christus, tunc demum idonei erimus videre non solum formam, quae formata est propter nos, sed etiam illam quam formavit nos. The description of this teaching as Guerric's outstanding contribution is found in the note to this passage in *Liturgical Sermons II*, p. 199. For Guerric's teaching on *forma*, see De Wilde, "The Formation of Christ in Us," pp. 29–35; and *Liturgical Sermons I*, pp. xxxi–xxxiv.

27. Guerric uses Gal 4:19 seven times. For the occurrences of these and other texts, see the useful "Index scripturaire" in SC 202:533–57.

28. For Augustine's teaching on how the Word, the *forma non formata* "informs" all cre-ation, see, e.g., *De Genesi ad litteram* 1.4.9–5.11 (PL 34:249–50), and *Sermo* 172.2–3 (PL 38:662–63).

29. Guerric, *Sermo* 10.1 (SC 166:222–24).

30. *Sermo* 10.3–4 (ibid.:228–32). The use of Isa 10:22–23 (LXX) and Rom 9:28 as christo-logical texts is probably taken from Bernard, *Nat* 1.1 (SBOp 4:244–45).

31. *Sermo* 8.5 (SC 166:200.200–02): . . . qui non solum nascendo, sed vivendo et moriendo, formam cui informemur tradidit nobis. . . . I am using the translation from *Liturgical Sermons I*, p. 53. For another significant passage on this informing process, see *Sermo* 47.1–3 (SC 202:414–20).

32. E.g., *Sermones* 2.3 and 4, 19.6, 35.2, and 53.5 (SC 166:110 and 114–16, 382–84; SC 202:248 and 508–10).

33. In keeping with his emphasis on the Nativity (to be discussed below), Guerric often spoke of our carnal love for the infant Jesus; see, e.g., *Sermones* 6.4 and 8.2 (SC 166:172–74 and 188–92). For an expression of carnal love not tied to the Nativity, see *Sermo* 27.4 (SC 202:136–38).

34. See, e.g., *Sermones* 35.2, 39.5, and 52.1 (SC 202:250, 308–10 and 486). Guerric often cites 2 Cor 5:16 in this connection.

35. E.g., especially the powerful passage on hiding in Christ's wounds in *Sermo* 32.5–6 (SC 202:210–14). On this aspect of Guerric's teaching, see the discussion in Morson, *Christ the Way*, chapter 10.

36. Portions of this dissertation, published in French in 1934–35, are translated in "The Formation of Christ in Us." On Spirit-Christology, see pp. 39–44.

37. E.g., *Sermo* 33.4 (SC 202:222.96–101): *Spiritus* enim *est, qui testificatur* (John 14:6) apud sanctorum corda et per eorum ora *quoniam Christus est veritas* (1 John 5:6), vera resurrectio et vita. Ideo et apostoli, qui prius dubitabant etiam post intuitum corporis viventis, post gustum Spiritus vivificantis (1 Cor 15:45) *virtute magna reddebant testimonium resurrectionis* (Acts 4:33). This passage provides a good example of how Guerric can create his own theologoumenon out of a concentrated fusion of scriptural texts (a quarter of the passage is direct citation).

38. *Sermo* 33.6 (SC 202:228.157–59): Caro Christi est viaticum, Spiritus vehiculum. Ipse est cibus, ipse *currus Israel et auriga eius.*

39. This is forcefully put in the passage from *Sermo* 33.4 partially cited above in n. 37 (see SC 202:222.96–224.107). For other passages on the role of the Holy Spirit in our sanctification, see, e.g., *Sermones* 17.2 and 44.3–4 (SC 166:344, and SC 202:370–74).

40. Guerric devotes nineteen *sermons* to the Christmas season—five for Advent, five for the Nativity, four for Epiphany, and five for the Purification.

41. On this see the "Introduction" in *Liturgical Sermons I*, pp. xxxviii–xlvi.

42. *Sermo* 13 (SC 166:270–86). For other appearances of the illumination theme, see, e.g., *Sermones* 12.6–7, 15.2 and 5, 31.5, 33.3 and 44.3–4.

43. *Sermo* 13.7 (SC 166:284.199–202): . . . hunc omnino dixerim illuminatum magnifice et gloriose, tamquam qui gloriam Domini revelata facie speculetur, et super quem gloria Domini saepius oriatur.

44. For an introduction to the theme, see Dietmar Mieth, "Gottesschau und Gottesgeburt: Zwei Typen Christlicher Gotteserfahrung in der Tradition," *Freiburger Zeitschrift für Philosophie und Theologie* 27 (1980): 204–23. There is a good historical sketch in Hugo Rahner, "Die Gottesgeburt: Die Lehre der Kirchenväter von der Geburt Christi aus dem Herzen der Kirche und der Gläubigen," in *Symbole der Kirche: Die Ekklesiologie der Väter* (Salzburg: Müller, 1964), pp. 11–87, which treats Guerric on pp. 67–68.

45. The theme is also found in other Cistercians, especially Bernard, *Adv* 3.4, and *V Nat* 6.10–11 (SBOp 4:177–78, 241–44); and Isaac of Stella, *Sermones* 7.16, 10.11, 42.16–19, and 45.2 (SC 130:190, 228–30, and SC 339:50–54, and 96–98). Guerric's development, however, is the richest among the white monks. See the discussion in Ruh, *Geschichte der abendländische Mystik*, pp. 323–26.

46. Carolyn Bynum, "Jesus as Mother and Abbot as Mother: Some Themes in Twelfth-Century Cistercian Writing," in *Jesus as Mother: Studies in the Spirituality of the High Middle Ages* (Berkeley: University of California Press, 1982), pp. 120–22. For a brief sketch of the development of this theme in the history of Christian piety, see André Cabassut, "A Medieval Devotion to 'Jesus Our Mother,'" *Cistercian Studies* 21 (1986): 345–55 (the article was originally published in French in 1949).

47. *Sermo* 47.3 (SC 202:420.73–75): . . . filiolos suos iterum atque iterum parturit cura et desiderio pietatis, donec formetur in eis Christus. . . .

48. *Sermo* 27.5 (SC 202:138.163–140.184): . . . Deum quem totus orbis non potest capere possis et ipse concipere, concipere autem corde non corpore. . . . Vide ineffabilem dignationem Dei simulque virtutem incomprehensibilis mysterii. Qui creavit te creatur in te, et quasi parum esset teipsum habere Patrem, vult etiam te sibi fieri matrem. *Quicumque*, inquit, *fecerit voluntatem Patris mei ipse meus et frater et soror et mater est.* O fidelis anima, expande sinus, dilata affectum, ne angustieris in visceribus tuis (cf. 2 Cor 6:12), concipe quem creatura non capit. For other appearances of this theme, see *Sermones* 49.3 and 52.3–4 (SC 202:446–48 and 490–94). See also the Second Sermon for Saints Peter and Paul (ibid.:380–94), a fascinating discussion of the maternal breasts of the apostles.

49. Like all the Cistercians, Guerric used the term *contemplatio* in a generic sense that included everything from meditative prayer to what we would call mystical experience. For some uses, see *Sermones* 2.4, 23.6, 25.3, 35.5, 37.5, 41.1 and 5, 45.3 and 5, 49.1, 53.2, and 54.3. For an introduction to some of the terms related to Cistercian teaching on contemplation (especially *otium, quies, requies, sabbath, vacare*), see Edith Scholl, "The Cistercian Vocabulary: A Proposal," *Cistercian Studies* 27 (1992): 77–92.

50. See, for example, *Sermones* 2.3–4 (which shows the influence of Bernard's *SCC* 74.5–7), 3.4, 7.3, 16.3, 35.4, 46.7, and 54.3 (SC 166:108–16, 128–32, 184, 326–30; SC 202:254–56, 412 and 520–22).

51 Especially Mary (*Sermones* 48.5–6 and 51.4) and Paul (*Sermones* 37.5, 45.5 and 54.4).

52. *Sermo* 21.2 (SC 202:30.60–64): In ipsa sua eos viscera trahit suisque inserit membris . . . et sicut caritate sic virtute ineffabili non solum assumpto corpori sed etiam ipsi couniret spiritui. See the entire passage in *Sermo* 21.2–3 (ibid.:28–32).

53. For references, direct and indirect, to 1 Cor 6:17, see *Sermones* 2.4, 21.2, 23.2, 24.2, and 48.6 (SC 166:116; SC 202:30, 58, 78, 440).

54. On the *ordinatio caritatis* in Guerric, see, e.g., *Sermones* 18.6, 24.3–4, 50.2, and 52.5 (SC 166:368; SC 202:80–84, 462, 494–96).

55. *Sermo* 53.5 (SC 202:508.142): . . . fructus suavissimos et beata gaudia. . . .

56. See E. Gilson, *The Mystical Theology of Saint Bernard* (London: Sheed & Ward, 1940), chap. 2; and *The Spirit of Mediaeval Philosophy*, chap. 11.

57. I have tried to provide an overview of the sources and significance of twelfth-century Cistercian anthropology in the "Introduction" to *Three Treatises on Man. A Cistercian Anthropology*, ed. Bernard McGinn (Kalamazoo, MI: Cistercian Publications, 1977), pp. 1–100. See also G. Webb, *An Introduction to the Cistercian De Anima*, Aquinas Paper 36 (London: Aquin Press, 1962).

58. These works include: (1) William of St. Thierry's *Nat corp* (PL 180:695–726); (2) Isaac of Stella's *Epistola de anima* (hereafter abbreviated *Ep an* and found in PL 194:1875–90); (3) Aelred of Rievaulx, *De Anima* (CCCM 1:685–754); (4) Nicholas of Clairvaux, *Epistolae* 63 and 65 (PL 202:491–95 and 498–505); and (5) Arnold of Bonneval's *De Paradiso animae* (PL 189:1515–70).

59. "Introduction," *Three Treatises*, pp. 83f.

60. Among these works are (1) the anonymous four-volume *De anima* often ascribed to either Bernard or Hugh of St. Victor (see the account in *Three Treatises*, pp. 64–65); (2) the anonymous *Tractatus de conscientia (Petis a me)* (found in both PL 213:903–12 and PL 184:551–60); (3) Helinand of Froidmont, *De cognitione sui* (PL 212:721–30). On these and related works, see Philippe Delehaye, "Dans le sillage de S. Bernard: trois petits traités *De conscientia*," *Cîteaux* 5 (1954): 92–103.

61. For a study of the work and its sources, see the "Introduction" by C. H. Talbot to his edition, *Ailred of Rievaulx: De Anima* (London: The Warburg Institute, 1952), pp. 1–62. There is an English translation by Talbot, *Aelred of Rievaulx: Dialogue on the Soul* (Kalamazoo, MI: Cistercian Publications, 1981).

62. Isaac of Stella, *Sermo* 4.9 in *Isaac de l'Étoile: Sermons Tome I* (SC 130:136.70–73): . . . in intelligentiae igneum candorem ascendat, tamquam in montem Thabor, . . . sicque transfiguratum, sic glorificatum Iesum oculis cernat. . . . This same devotion to Jesus is even more powerfully expressed in a passage found in *Sermo* 7.15: O beata anima, quae numquam obliviscitur, nec dimittit puerum Iesum! Magis beata, quae semper meditatur grandem Iesum; maxime beata, quae contemplatur semper immensum Iesum (ibid.:188.137–190.140).

63. For Isaac and his thought, general introductions can be found in Gaetano Raciti, "Isaac de l'Étoile," DS 7:2011–38; and Bernard McGinn, "Introduction," in *Isaac of Stella: Sermons on the Liturgical Year. Volume One*, trans. by Hugh McCaffrey (Kalamazoo, MI: Cistercian Publications, 1979), pp. ix–xxx. I have tried to present the main lines of Isaac's anthropology in my *The Golden Chain: A Study in the Theological Anthropology of Isaac of Stella* (Washington, DC: Cistercian Publications, 1972). For his teaching on God, see B. McGinn, "*Theologia* in Isaac of Stella," *Cîteaux* 21 (1970): 219–35; and "Isaac of Stella on the Divine Nature," *Analecta Cisterciensia* 29 (1973): 1–53. The most recent discussion of Isaac's place in medieval mysticism can be found in Kurt Ruh, *Geschichte der abendländische Mystik*, pp. 343–54. Isaac's sermons have been edited in three volumes in the SC Series by Anselm Hoste, Gaston Salet, and Gaetano Raciti, *Isaac de l'Étoile: Sermons* (SC 130, 207 and 339). I will use this edition and my own translations.

64. William of Conches had been attacked by William of St. Thierry. The difficulties encountered by him and other Chartrians may be reflected by Isaac's *Sermo* 48, known as the *ysaac abbatis stelle apologia*, which apologizes for his departure from speculation by noting the criticisms directed at unnamed figures he refers to as *spectabilis ingenii homines et exercitationis mire* (*Sermo* 48.5 in SC 339:156.44).

65. Isaac, *Sermo* 18.2 (SC 207:8.12–14): . . . in hanc semotam et inclusam Oceano insulam, nudi ac naufragi, nudam nudi Christi crucem amplexi, pauci evasimus. This formula first appeared in Jerome, *Ep.* 58.2 (PL 22:580).

66. *Sermo* 52.15 (SC 339:232–34).

67. A number of these sermons actually constitute treatises on theological topics that use the readings of the liturgy as starting points. Prominent among these are *Sermones* 1–5, a discussion of the stages of spiritual progress based on the Beatitudes; *Sermones* 18–26, Isaac's treatise on God, One and Three; and *Sermones* 33–37, a treatment of predestination.

68. The *De spiritu et anima* appears under the works of Augustine in PL 40:779–832. There is a translation with apparatus in *Three Treatises on Man*, pp. 181–288. See also Leo Norpoth, *Der pseudo-augustinische Traktat: De Spiritu et Anima* (Cologne-Bochum:Institut für Geschichte der Medizin, 1971). The compilation appears to be the work of a Cistercian and probably dates from the 1170s.

69. Among the sermons containing significant materials on anthropology, see especially 2–4, 6, 8–10, 14, 16–17, 20, 23, 25–27, 32, 35, 44, 46, 51–52 and 54–55.

70. Having investigated the sources of Isaac's anthropology in some detail in *The Golden Chain*, I will restrict myself to notices on only the most significant sources in what follows.

71. *Ep an* 2 (PL 194:1875C): Tria itaque sunt, corpus, anima et Deus. Sed horum me fateor ignorare essentiam, minusque quid corpus, quam quid anima; et quid anima, quam quid sit Deus, intelligere. I will use my translation of the *Ep an* from *Three Treatises on Man*, pp. 155–77.

72. However much Isaac and William mined the *physici*, or natural philosophers, for information about the body and soul, they were convinced that revelation alone provided the proper perspective from which to integrate this material into a true picture of the nature and destiny of humanity. Isaac criticizes the *sapientes saeculi huius de anima et de Deo per multa tractantes* in *Sermo* 10.10 (SC 130:228).

73. Isaac's interest in medicine appears in many places, e.g., *Ep an* (1879C and 1882AB), as well as *Sermones* 17.9–10, 34.5, 35.10, 42.22–24, and 52.12.

74. The theme of self-knowledge was as important to Isaac as it was to the other Cistercian authors. See Kathleen O'Neill, "Isaac of Stella on Self-knowledge," *Cistercian Studies* 19 (1984): 122–38.

75. Isaac, *Sermo* 2.13 (SC 130:106.99–106): Si vis teipsum cognoscere, te possidere, intra ad teipsum nec te quaesieris extra. Aliud tu, aliud tui, aliud circa te. Circa te mundus, tui corpus, tu ad imaginem et similitudinem Dei factus intus. . . .Foris pecus es ad imaginem mundi, unde et minor mundus dicitur homo; intus homo ad imaginem Dei, unde et potes deificari. For a discussion of humanity as *imago Dei* and *minor mundus*, see *The Golden Chain*, pp. 115–33.

76. Bernard, as we have seen in chapter 5 (pp. 168–72) placed the essence of the *imago Dei* in human freedom, the *liberum arbitrium*. Isaac too is concerned with the proper understanding of *liberum arbitrium* and was influenced by Bernard's teaching (see, e.g., *Sermones* 10.17, 26.4–10, 35.11–14, and 46.9–15), but he does not make it central to his *imago Dei* teaching. For a general sketch of the development of *imago Dei* theology in the Latin West, see B. McGinn, "The Human Person as Image of God. II. Western Christianity," in *Christian Spirituality: Origins to the Twelfth Century*, ed. Bernard McGinn, John Meyendorff, and Jean Leclercq, WS 16 (New York: Crossroad, 1986), pp. 312–30.

77. *Sermo* 16.16 (SC 130:304.163–306.172): Propter haec enim factus est homo ad imaginem et similitudinem Dei, ac per haec reficitur et reformatur ad easdem, per sensum ad imaginem, per vitam ad similitudinem. . . . Ut cognoscat verum Deum, aeterna est vita, sed ut toto corde diligat, vera est via. Caritas ergo via, veritas vita; caritas similitudo, veritas imago. . . .

78. See, e.g., *Ep an* 8 (1880B) and *Sermo* 10.1 (SC 130:220.7–14). Isaac's discussions of the *imago* understood as *sensus/ratio* and the *similitudo* as *affectus* are frequent throughout his works. For some key passages, see *Ep an* 5 (1878CD), *Sermones* 3.19, 4.2 and 16, 12.1, 17.1–2, 32.10, and 46.10–11. As we have seen, Bernard of Clairvaux also used this common psychological theme under the form *intellectus* and *affectus*, e.g., *Asc* 3.1.2–4 (SBOp 5:132–33).

79. *Ep an* 4 (1877C): Vires etenim susceptivae sunt donorum, quae habitu virtutes fiunt.

80. A similar discussion of *affectus* and the *virtutes* also is found in *Sermo* 17.10–13 (SC 130:316–20). Isaac's doctrine of the virtues uses the ancient Stoic themes adopted by the fathers, but within the context of an anagogic understanding of virtue based on the Dionysian writings. See Robert Javelet, "La vertu dans l'oeuvre d'Isaac de l'Étoile," *Cîteaux* 11 (1960): 252–67; and *The Golden Chain*, pp. 143–52.

81. The ultimate source of this important analysis of how human knowing rises to God is Boethius's *Consolation of Philosophy* as reworked by Hugh of St. Victor. It was later taken over into the pseudo-Augustinian *The Spirit and the Soul*, especially chaps. 4–5 and 12. For a study of the sources of the doctrine, see *The Golden Chain*, chap. 4.

82. For a study of how Bonaventure's *Itinerarium* utilized Isaac's ascensional schema together with one dependent on Richard of St. Victor, see B. McGinn, "Ascension and Introversion in the *Itinerarium mentis in Deum*," *San Bonaventura: 1274–1974*, 5 vols. (Grottaferrata: Collegio San Bonaventura, 1974), 3:535–52.

83. *Ep an* 8 (1880AB): Sicut ergo sursum versus quinquepertita quadam distinctione mundus iste visibilis gradatur, terra, aqua, aere, aethere, sive firmamento, ipso quoque coelo supremo, quod empyreum vocatur; sic et animae in mundo sui corporis peregrinanti quinque sunt ad sapientiam progressus: sensus, imaginatio, ratio, intellectus, intelligentia. Quinque etenim progressionibus rationabilitas exercetur ad sapientiam, sicut ipse affectus, seu voluntas quatuor ad charitatem, quatenus in novem istis progressibus anima in semetipsa proficiens, sensu et affectu quasi internis pedibus, quae spiritu vivit, spiritu ambulet, usque ad cherubim et seraphim, id est plenitudinem scientiae, et rogum charitatis. . . . Isaac subsequently mentions how easy it would be to compare these nine steps with the nine choirs of angels, a sign of Dionysian influence.

84. Isaac was unique among the Cistercians in grounding his thought in a discussion both of the kinds of *scientia* in general (based on Boethius), and also in a Dionysian analysis of three forms of *theologia*, the highest science—*divina*, *rationalis*, and *symbolica*. For the divisions of *scientia*, see *Ep an* 16 and 20 (1884CD and 1886D–87A) and *Sermo* 19.8–10 (SC 207:28–30). On the forms of *theologia*, see *Sermones* 22.9 and 23.9 (SC 207:68 and 88). For a discussion, see B. McGinn, "*Theologia* in Isaac of Stella." Isaac's thought on these divisions appears to show the influence of John Scottus Eriugena's *Periphyseon*. Compare, for example, the emphasis on the divine nature as *numerus sine numero, mensura sine mensura, pondus sine pondere*, etc., in *Sermo* 22.8 (PL 207:68.59 ff.) with the dialectical passage from *Periphyseon* 2 (ed. Sheldon-Williams 2:144.34–146.5 [590B]). Eriugena's translation of the Dionysian corpus does not speak of a *rationalis theologia*, but in *Periphyseon* 1 he says of cataphatic theology that *rationabiliter enim per causativa causale potest significari* (ed. Sheldon-Williams 1:74.6 [458B]).

85. On Isaac's efforts to understand the union of body and soul, see *The Golden Chain*, pp. 160–65.

86. *Ep an* 18 (1885C): Hac igitur quasi aurea catena poetae, vel ima dependent a summis, vel erecta scala prophetae ascenditur ad summa de imis. The *aurea catena* also appears in

Sermo 54.15 (SC 339:260), and the *scala Jacob* in *Sermo* 12.4 (SC 130:252). On the history and function of these symbols, see *The Golden Chain*, chap. 2.

87. Isaac's doctrine of the blinding of the soul's eyes through concupiscence (*Ep an* 20), appears close to that found in Hugh of St. Victor. See *The Golden Chain*, pp. 181–85.

88. This ontological trinitarian analogy of *essentia (aeternitas)-species-usus* originated in Hilary of Poitiers, *De Trinitate* 2.1 (PL 10:50–51) and was developed by Augustine, *De Trinitate* 6.10.11 (PL 42:931–32). It also appears in Isaac's *Sermo* 24.18–19 (SC 207:110–12).

89. *Ep an* 21 (1887D–88A): Vasa ergo, quae creatrix gratia format, ut sint, adjutrix gratia replet, ne vacua sint . . . ita manens in Deo lux quae exit ab eo, mentem irradiat, ut primum ipsam coruscationem lucis, sine qua nihil videtur, videat, et in ipsa caetera videat. Isaac's doctrine of grace, which should not be thought of according to the scholastic distinction between natural and supernatural, has been treated in *The Golden Chain*, pp. 186–88; and Franco Mannarini, "La grazia in Isaaco della Stella," *Collectanea Ordinis Cisterciensium Reformatorum* 16 (1954): 137–44, 207–14.

90. The full text of this passage in *Ep an* 22, mentioning both *theophaniae* and *phantasiae* is quite close to a passage in Eriugena's *Periphyseon* and forms another piece of evidence for the Cistercian's direct knowledge of that work, whether in whole or in extracts. Compare:

Isaac, *Ep an* 23 (1888B):	Eriugena, *Periphyseon* 2:
Itaque sicut in imaginationem phantasiae surgunt,	Ut enim ex inferioribus desubtus sensibilium rerum imagines quas Greci *PHANTASIAS* vocant anima recipit
ita in intelligentiam desuper theophaniae descendunt.	ita ex superioribus, hoc est primordialibus causis, cognitiones quae a Greci *THEOPHANIAI* . . . appellari sibi ipsi infigit et per ipsas quandam de Deo notitiam percipit, (Sheldon-Williams 2:114.28–32).

91. Isaac here appeals to another Augustinian trinitarian analogy, that of *lux-lucere-illuminare* taken from *Soliloquiae* 1.8.15 (PL 32:877). This is also found in *Sermones* 24.12–14 and 26.9 (SC 207:106–08 and 132). For the influence of Augustine on Isaac, see André Fracheboud, "L'influence de Saint Augustin sur le Cistercien Isaac de l'Étoile," *Collectanea Ordinis Cisterciensium Reformatorum* 11 (1949): 1–17 and 264–78; and 12 (1950): 5–16.

92. Isaac's contribution to the development of the theology of the Mystical Body was first noted by Emile Mersch in his *Le Corps mystique du Christ*, 2 vols. (Paris: Descleé, 1933), 2:142–48, who remarked "Il est étonnant que cet homme remarquable ait été relativement peu étudie" (p. 143). For a list of passages where the abbot discusses this doctrine, see "Note complémentaire 13" in SC 130:344–45.

93. The nine *Sermones in Sexagesima* (#18–26) are edited in SC 207:8–140. There is a translation in *Isaac of Stella: Sermons, Volume One*, pp. 149–217, but I have preferred to make my own versions.

94. B. McGinn, "Isaac of Stella on the Divine Nature."

95. Ruh, *Geschichte der Mystik*, p. 348.

96. See my paper, "Pseudo-Dionysius and the Early Cistercians," in *One Yet Two*, pp. 200–241.

97. The first to study the influence of Dionysius on Isaac was André Fracheboud, "Le Pseudo-Denys l'Aréopagite parmi les sources du cistercien Isaac de l'Étoile," *Collectanea Ordinis Cisterciensium Reformatorum* 9 (1947): 328–41; 10 (1948): 19–34.

98. *Sermo* 21.3 (SC 207:50.26–27): Unum ergo ante omnia, simplex post omnia, incommutabile est super omnia. This triad of common attributes seems to reflect discussion in the schools during the period ca. 1130–1160. Similar formulations are found in Hugh and Richard of St. Victor, but the text closest to Isaac comes from the Abelardian *Sententiae Parisienses* of ca. 1140: Sola divina essentia immutabilis est et simplex et una, ad comparationem aliarum rerum (*Écrits théologiques de l'école d'Abélard*, ed. Arthur Landgraf [Louvain: Bureaux, 1934], p. 7).

99. *Sermo* 21.15 (58.127–60.135): Teneamus, fratres, sensu, teneamus affectu, teneamus conscientia, teneamus vita, teneamus ipsum propter ipsum, delectantes in ipso et conformantes nos ipsi, ut a multis collecti ad unum, uniamur uni, et in simplo simplificati, immobiles stemus quantum possumus cum immobili, *in idipsum* dormientes quiescentesque *in pace*, quam nesciunt qui *a fructu frumenti, vini et olei* non Dei sed *sui multiplicati*, id est multis distracti, intenti, distenti, turbati, *sunt* (Ps 4:8–9). The use of the word *idipsum*, that is, "the Self-Same," from Psalm 4 and elsewhere as a term for God has been studied by Jean Leclercq, "'Idipsum': Les harmoniques d'un mot biblique dans S. Bernard," in *Scientia Augustiniana: Festschrift Adolar Zumkeller*, ed. Cornelius Petrus Mayer and Willigis Eckkermann (Würzburg: Augustinus-Verlag, 1975), pp. 170–83.

100. Isaac often uses such terms (for lists, see SC 207:34, n. 1.; and McGinn, "Pseudo-Dionysius and the Early Cistercians," p. 233 n. 166). Though not all of them need be directly tied to Dionysian and Eriugenean influence, their proliferation in his writings indicate a Dionysian background.

101. *Sermo* 22.8 (SC 207 68.65–68): . . . aut si, cum omnium nihil sit, omnium remotione ponatur, de quo negationes magis verae sunt. Proprius enim de illo omnia negamus, quam omnium aliquid affirmamus. This is closely related to the famous Dionysian axiom found in *De caelesti hierarchia* 2.3, which in the translation of Eriugena reads: Si igitur negationes in divinis verae, affirmationes vero incompactae obscuritate arcanorum. . . (cf. *Dionysiaca* 2:758–59).

102. *Sermo* 22.10 (68.81–70.83): . . . qui de ineffabili fari volumus, de quo nihil proprie dici potest: tacere, aut mutatis uti verbis, necesse est.

103. *Sermo* 22.12 (70.91–99): Unde sancta illa et sublimia et pennata seraphim alis, quae volatum significant contemplationis, visa sunt velare faciem eius et pedes, quatenus non velet eis principium et finem sua ignorantia, sed Dei incomprehensibilis supersapientia. Sicut enim nihil videndo tenebras invisibiles videmus, et inaudibile silentium nihil audiendo audimus, sic nimirum superabundantem et intolerabilem lucem non videndo nec tolerando videmus invisibilem, non quidem caeci, sed a lumine superati. For the first part of the translation of this passage, I have adapted the version of Hugh McCaffrey in *Sermons: Volume One*, p. 182. To the mystical oxymora of the last sentence, we can add those found in *Sermo* 37.31 (SC 207:304.260–63): Nos itaque, fratres, qui ab hac subtilitate et improbitate, sapientissima irrationabilitate ac fortissimo languore sublimique casu longe adhuc sumus. . . .

104. John Scottus Eriugena, CI 1.27 (SC 180:140.80–81): Altior vero theoria desertum intelligitur divinae naturae, ab omnibus remotae, ineffabilis altitudo.

105. *Sermo* 32.19 (SC 207:218.177–80): Itaque, dilectissimi, exemplo Domini Salvatoris, ipsum in deserto non solum loci, sed et spiritus vel etiam aliquando Dei, ipsum nostrum spiritum excedentes cum angelis, secuti, meditemur iugiter in lege ipsius. . . . For a study of the development of this tradition, see my "Ocean and Desert as Symbols of Mystical Absorption in the Christian Tradition."

106. See *Sermo* 5.15 (SC 130:154.138–41). For other references to *desertum/eremus* and *solitudo* without identification with God, see *Sermones* 1.14, 14.5 and 11–12, 30.4, and 32.4–6.

107. For Isaac's teaching the vision of God, see the section on "La vision unitive" in Raciti, "Isaac de l'Étoile," DS 7:2029–31.

108. The *cor* of this passage is to be distinguished from the *cordis affectus,* a purely volitional power discussed in *Sermo* 46.10 (SC 339:124). For a sketch of the importance of the notion of the heart in Christian spirituality, see "Cor et cordis affectus" in DS 2:2278–2307. Cf. Wolf Gewehr, "Zu den Begriffen *anima* und *cor* in frühmittelalterlichen Denken," *Zeitschrift für Religions- und Geistesgeschichte* 27(1975):40–55.

109. *Sermo* 4.9 (SC 130:136.75–78): . . . faciem vero ob incomprehensibilitatis, incorporeitatis, invisibilitatis simplicem formam, in qua Patri manet aequalis, non sustineat, immo in faciem suam et ratio, et intellectus et intelligentia cadant.

110. *Sermo* 4.10 (136.83–84). Isaac uses *excessus/excedere* in a mystical sense in only one other place, *Sermo* 32.19 (the desert of God text mentioned above). *Raptus* used mystically occurs in *Sermones* 10.2, 34.28, and 37.29 (SC 130:222.20; 207:252.257 and 302.248); *ecstasis* never occurs. Like other Christian mystics, Isaac often dwells on the inexpressibility of the mystical encounter with God; see, e.g., the passage from 22.10 discussed above, and especially 37.29–30 (SC 207:302–04) which contains a long list of scriptural types for such inexpressibility.

111. Like all monastic authors, Isaac insisted that this *otium* was a paradoxical one, distinguished by the intensity of its inward activity: Sapientia quidem in otio, sed non in otiositate discitur. Nihil enim illo otio negotiosius, illa vocatione operosius; ubi sapientia discitur, ubi Dei Verbum interrogatur (*Sermo* 14.1 in SC 130:270.7–10).

112. Surprisingly, this is the only citation of Song 2:4 in Isaac's writings and the ordering of charity is here internalized to indicate the order in the soul alone. Isaac does have an equivalent doctrine to the more customary Cistercian treatment of the order of charity, but he expresses it in terms of *caritas formata,* e.g., *Sermo* 34.28–31 (SC 207:252–54), or the relation between *caritas* and *veritas* or *sapientia,* e.g., *Sermones* 16.16, 39.10, and 47.18 (SC 130:306; SC 207:324; SC 339:148).

113. *Sermo* 4.17 (SC 130:142.142–43): Ut sit vir sapiens, et revelata facie (2 Cor 3:18) contempletur tamquam ipsius imago Deum. In *Sermo* 25.15 (SC 207:124–26), also citing Matt 5:8, Isaac speaks of how the *cor contemplantis* must be purified so that the mind can see its image as the image of God.

114. I have left Isaac's Christology and doctrine of redemption out of this account, though they are among the richest aspects of his theology. Perhaps one quotation from *Sermo* 28.12 (SC 207:158.82–84) may be allowed as a summary: . . . quantum in Domino Iesu exinanitus est Deus Dei Filius ut homo fieret, tantum exaltatus est homo hominis filius ut deus fieret. For a survey of Isaac's teaching, see R. Elmer, "Die Heilsökonomie bei Isaak von Stella," *Analecta Cisterciensia* 33 (1977): 191–261.

115. *Sermo* 5.13 (SC 130:152.118–122): . . . *Deus cordis mei,* meditatio videlicet, *et pars mea,* . . . quod ordinatae affectioni domum portem, unde caenet mecum, et ego cum illa, Deus ipse. The passage continues with a succinct expression of the transcendent-immanent character of the divine: Ipsum propter ipsum super me quaero. Ipso ab ipso intus me pasco (152.123–24).

116. The abbot of Stella's references to Paul's *unitas spiritus* are restricted in comparison with other Cistercians. Used in reference to the union of the soul with God (not of the human and divine in Christ), it occurs only four times—*Sermones* 5.17, 9.8–9, 55.15; and in the *Epistola de officio missae* (PL 194:1892C), which also uses John 17:21 (on this text see the note in SC 339:46–47).

117. *Sermo* 5.18 (SC 130:156.179–81): . . . ut fiat de inimico servus, de servo amicus, de amico filius, de filio haeres, de haerede unus, immo unum etiam cum ipsa haereditate, ut sicut non poterit seipso privari, ita nec haereditate, quae Deus est ipse.

118. *Sermo* 9.8–9 (SC 130:210.81–212.94): Tertia de incorporalibus maxime unum; nam *qui adhaeret Deo, unus spiritus est.* . . . in tertiis spiritus adhaerens Deo, unum efficitur cum ipso,

et quod est ipse. Unde ad Patrem pro fratribus Filius sic loquitur: *Volo Pater, ut, sicut ego et tu unum sumus, ita et isti sint unum nobiscum.* O unum ante omnia, unum super omnia, unum post omnia, unum a quo omnia, unum propter quod omnia! Valde unum, ubi *duo in carne una* iam non duo, sed caro una; magis unum, ubi duo in homine uno iam non duo, sed persona una; maxime unum, ubi in Deo adhaerens illi spiritus iam non duo, sed unum. The apostrophe to *unum* here echoes that found in *Sermo* 5.19 (156.184–89). Isaac's formulations go beyond anything else found in the twelfth century, but need not be taken as equivalent to the notion of indistinct union, which became popular in the following century, especially in the light of other passages that seem to qualify the *unum/unus* language. See *Sermo* 42.14 (SC 339:48), and especially the texts that stress that the "concatenating" unions that take place along the chain of being between the lowest and the highest neighboring realities fuse, but do not *confuse*, the divergent natures. In terms of the union of God and the human, Isaac emphasizes this through his use of formulas such as *absque ulla demutatione naturae* (*Ep an* 11 [1881D]).

119. Isaac's use of the marriage analogy to study the unions of body and soul, Christ and the church, and the soul with God is found in a number of his *Sermones,* see, e.g., 11.9–10, 40.1–4, 42.11, 46.9–13, 47.8, 54.8, and 55.7–13. The abbot of Stella stands out among Cistercian authors in making relatively restricted use of the erotic images of the Song of Songs (e.g., kisses, breasts, embraces, wounds of love, etc.) to concentrate on the essential, we might almost say metaphysical, dimension–marriage as the uniting of two realities.

120. *Sermo* 5.20 (SC 130:158.202–05): . . . totus spiritus sobrie ebrius, fortiter enervis, in Deo omnia potens erit, . . . ei adhaerebit, qui in omnibus suis omnia erit. Isaac uses the ancient topos of "sober drunkeness" in other *sermones,* see, e.g., 37.17 (SC 207:294); 40.4, using Song 2:4; and 44.9 (SC 330:14 and 88).

121. Isaac never uses the formula *amor ipse intellectus est,* another sign of his difference from Bernard and William. Though he often speaks of the cooperation of *cognoscere* and *diligere* on the path to God and of their uniting in the supreme moment (see, e.g., *Sermones* 5.21–22, 10.1, 12.1, 16.15, 17.10–11, 26.1, 39.10, 43.14, 45.14, and *Ep an* 23), unlike William of St. Thierry, he is uninterested in analyzing how this takes place.

122. The most extensive discussion of the other Cistercian commentators on the Song remains that found in Friedrich Ohly, *Hoheliedstudien: Grundzüge einer Geschichte der Hohelied- auslegung des Abendlandes bis zum 1200* (Wiesbaden: Steiner, 1958), pp. 170–205. Among the commentaries not discussed here is the work of Thomas the Cistercian (Thomas of Perseigne), composed in the 1180s. This was somewhat of a best-seller, surviving in over sixty manuscripts and in three printed editions (one of which is found in PL 206:17–862). Thomas's fusion of traditional Cistercian and Victorine teaching had already been begun by Isaac of Stella; but in the judgment of his most recent student, David Bell, Thomas's "normal explanations are totally lacking in mystical content. . . . "("Contemplation and the Vision of God in the Commentary on the Song of Songs of Thomas the Cistercian," *Citeaux* 29 [1978]: 221). See Bell's three articles on this text found in *Citeaux* 28 (1977): 5–25, 249–67; 28 (1978): 207–27. Geoffrey of Auxerre, one of St. Bernard's secretaries, also produced a commentary that has been edited by Ferruccio Gastaldelli, *Goffredo di Auxerre: Expositio in Cantica Canticorum,* 2 vols. (Rome: Edizioni di Storia e Letteratura, 1974). Along with several anonymous commentaries that might be by Cistercians, there is also the work of Gilbert of Stanford discovered by Jean Leclercq, "Le commentaire de Gilbert de Stanford sur le Cantique des cantiques," in *Analecta Monastica I,* Analecta Anselmiana 20 (Rome: Vatican City, 1948). pp. 205–30. Finally, the well-known scholastic author Alan of Lille, who retired to a Cistercian monastery in his old age, wrote a Marian commentary on the Song (see PL 210:51–110), but this can scarcely be considered a typical Cistercian work.

123. For a stimulating attempt at an overview, see Friedrich Ohly, "Geist und Formen der Hoheliedauslegung im 12. Jahrhundert," *Zeitschrift für deutsche Altertum und deutsche Literatur*

85 (1954–55): 181–97. For a survey of some current literature on the history of the interpretation of the Song, see B. McGinn, "With 'the Kisses of the Mouth': Recent Works on the Song of Songs," *Journal of Religion* 72 (1992): 269–75. An important analysis of the history of medieval interpretation of the Song, along with an anthology of texts, is forthcoming from Cistercian Publications; see Denys Turner, *Eros and Allegory.*

124. Thomas Renna, "The Song of Songs and the Early Cistercians," *Cistercian Studies* 27 (1992): 39–49 (quotation from p. 49).

125. Ibid., p. 48.

126. For an introduction, see Jean Vuong-Dinh-Lam, "Gilbert de Hoyland," DS 6:371–74.

127. Gilbert's works, as edited by Jean Mabillon, are available in PL 184:11–298. There is a translation along with some newly edited Latin materials by Lawrence Braceland in four volumes, *Gilbert of Hoyland: Sermons on the Song of Songs, I, II, III,* and *Gilbert of Hoyland: IV, Treatises, Epistles, and Sermons* (Kalamazoo, MI: Cistercian Publications, 1978–81). The last volume of this version contains a valuable scriptural index. I have consulted Braceland's translations with profit, but prefer to make my own versions unless otherwise noted.

128. Gilson, *Mystical Theology of St. Bernard,* p. 230 n.75. Gilson cites *Sermo* 2.8 (PL 184:22A), where Gilbert says that he has not experienced the "little bed" of mystical union—Temerarius forsitan videar, qui conor inexperta exponere de sponsae lectulo, quae illum suavius forsan et secretius collocavit, quam conjectura nostra possit attingere. But, as Braceland points out (*Gilbert Sermons I,* p. 64 n.7), this is a deliberately ambiguous topos of humility (note the *forsitan/forsan*) based on Bernard himself (see *SCC* 85.14 in SBOp 2:316).

129. Gilbert has none of the rare autobiographical accounts that we find in Bernard (e.g., *SCC* 74), but this is also true of William of St. Thierry.

130. Gilbert, *Sermo* 12.3 (62C): Et tu ergo si sponsum apprehendisti, tene nec dimittas, donec introducas in domum et in cubiculum matris tuae. Quid ego nunc tibi persuadeo, ad quod te ipsa experientia perceptae dulcedinis multo magis invitat et alliciat? For a summary of Gilbert and John on spiritual experience, see Pierre Miquel, *Le vocabulaire latin de l'expérience spirituelle* (Paris: Beauchesne, 1989), pp. 133–62.

131. John of Ford provides a good example of the necessity for careful reading. The abbot of Ford often humbly admits that he has not shared in the experience of the Bride (e.g., *Sermones* 71.7, 86.1, 98.10, 118.4), but in *Sermo* 91.6 he says that he has had visitations of the Spirit of Jesus that give him insight to help interpret the spiritual progress of others: ... verumtamen ex his, quae licet raro et tenuiter, dignanter tamen mecum aliquando agit spiritus Iesu, ad introspicienda ea, quae secreto actitantur intra vos, fodi parietem mihi. See *Iohannis de Forda: Super Extremam Partem Cantici Canticorum Sermones CXX* (CCCM 18:619.134–620.136). Cf. *Sermo* 43.9–10, which contains an account of a visit of the Word to John's soul that may be based on Bernard's noted description in *SCC* 74.2–6.

132. There are, to be sure, a number of ecclesiological readings found in his sermons, e.g., *Sermones* 21.5–6, 23.2, 30.5–9, and 33.1–6.

133. The discussion of the Trinity in *Sermo* 32.6 and that of Christ's two births in *Sermo* 47.4–5, stand out as exceptions to his usual mode of exposition.

134. *Sermo* 4.2 (27A): Fides, ut sic dicam, veritatem rectam tenet et possidet; intelligentia revelatam et nudam contuetur; ratio conatur revelare. Ratio inter fidem intelligentiamque discurrens, ad illam se erigit, sed ista se regit.

135. *Sermo* 4.9 (31CD): Habebit ibi circuitus terminum, cum repleti fuerimus in bonis domus tuae, Domine; ... O qualis ibi circuitus erit, pergere ab ipso in ipsum, ire et redire: desiderio ire, delectatione redire; dum semper ejus, quod experientia desiderat, praesentia satiat: ut mens possidentis et contuentis, et illi sit per appetentiam intenta, et illo sit sufficienter contenta! Several phrases in my translation reflect the version in *Gilbert. Sermons I,* p. 83. For another text on *epektasis,* see *Sermo* 19.2.

136. Ibid. (32A): Denique quantumlibet oculata sint beata illa animalia, et illuminat illa ut quantum possunt, capiant; et excedit, ne ad totum sufficiant.

137. See, e.g., *Sermones* 20.9–10, 40.8 and 43.2.

138. This is not to say that Gilbert does not present several interesting texts on the nature of *contemplatio* and *excessus*. See especially the description of three kinds of contemplation and three actions of the bride in *Sermo* 43.6–7 (228C–29C), the analysis of Paul's rapture in *Sermo* 27.6 (144AB), and the discussion of the *visio Dei* in *Sermo* 20.4 (104B–05A).

139. Gilbert's references to *sacra ebrietas* are particularly frequent, e.g., *Sermones* 3.2, 10.2, 15.6, 31.6, 41.3 and 8, 42.1–2; *Tractatus* 1.7, 3.4 and 6.4 and 8–9.

140. The abbot refers to 1 Cor 6:17 some sixteen times in his writings.

141. On the *osculum*, see *Sermones* 24.3, 34.4; and *Tractatus* 1.6. The *ordo caritatis* occurs in *Sermo* 41.9.

142. *Sermo* 15.3 (75B): Caro ipsius sicut terra deserta, et invia, et inaquosa, in qua Christus appareat.

143. *Sermo* 1.3 (14BC): Ignorantiae tuae nox, imo noctes ignorantiarum tuarum.... Et in hac nocte potest Jesus meus magis dulci quodam affectu suaviter sentiri, quam sciri ad purum (cf. 1.1, 4 and 6 in 12A, 14C and 16AB). In Bernard's comment on the same verse (*SCC* 75 in SBOp 2:247–54) there is no comparable dwelling on the mystical significance of the night symbolism.

144. *Sermo* 2.4 (19C): ... quando sui oblita penitus, et se exuta tota transit in ipsum, et quasi induitur ipso dilecta ipsius. For another reference to the Bride's nakedness, see *Sermo* 45.3 (237D–38A).

145. *Sermo* 18.3 (93D): ... cum nuda tibi sine sermonis involucro raptim incipit coruscare veritas.

146. *Tractatus* 6.3 (273AB): ... immensum illud divinae majestatis pelagus . . . in illam secretae lucis abyssum.... See also the emphasis on the "hidden secret" of the Divine Lover in *Sermo* 22.4–5 (116C–17A, using Isa 24:16) and of the Bride in *Sermo* 25.4 (131C–32B).

147. *Tractatus* 4.4 (268BC): ... tamen stupor, et amor, et admiratio radiantis desuper luminis, . . . animum convertit ad se, rapit in se, et continet intra se, . . . ut fiat ad interiora stupidus, ad exteriora mutus.

148. Bynum, *Jesus as Mother*, p. 115.

149. See *Sermo* 27 on Song 4:5–6 (139D–145A), *Sermo* 31 on Song 4:10 (160C–65C), and *Tractatus* 6.6–9 (274D–76C), which deals with the breasts of Christ, which are identified with the wounds of his passion.

150. *Sermo* 31.4 (162D–64A). I adopt Braceland's translation from *Gilbert. Sermons II*, p. 378. A similar fixation on the shape of breasts is found in John of Ford, *Sermo* 115.11–12 (CCCM 18:779–80).

151. *Tractatus* 1.6 (255C–56A).

152. *Sermo* 2.4 (19CD): In illo qui solius est, sponsi amoris exagitata incendio ebullit, et excrescit effusa et effluens. Tota transfunditur in ipsum, et in similem absorbetur qualitatem . . . in tertio penitus est ipsa penes ipsum, et, si dici potest, non est nisi ipse.

153. *Sermo* 15.9 (80AB): Ideo quodam igniti verbi beneficio inter sponsi flagrans amplexus, de pulvere pigmentario in fumi tenuitatem liquescit: de humiliatarum pulvere virtutum in fumum gloriae. Qualis est, putas, perventio; cum tam delicatus sit ascensus? Quo tendit quae talis ascendit? . . . Lectulus forte dilecti est. I am happy to be able use the felicitous rendering of Braceland in *Gilbert: Sermons I*, p. 187.

154. *Sermo* 30.1 (155C): Quasi provocatum ad dilectionem se persentit, dum cor suum vulneratum fatetur.

155. Gilbert concludes the application of the text to the soul (30.3 in 156B–57A) with an interpretation of the one eye (indicating singleness of intention) and the one lock of hair (meaning constant meditation). The rest of the sermon applies the text to the church.

156. See *Sermones* 16.9 and 24.3 (86D–87A and 127B), as well as *Tractatus* 4.2 (267A).

157. E.g., *Sermones* 45.3 and 46.4 (237D–38A and 244A–45A).

158. See David N. Bell, "Baldwin of Ford and Twelfth-Century Theology," in *Noble Piety and Reformed Monasticism*, ed. E. Rozanne Elder (Kalamazoo, MI: Cistercian Publications, 1981), pp. 136–48.

159. Baldwin's spiritual treatises are most easily available in PL 204. There is an English translation and study by David N. Bell, *Baldwin of Ford. Spiritual Tractates*, 2 vols. (Kalamazoo: Cistercian Publications, 1986).

160. Baldwin of Ford, *Tractatus* 14, in PL 204:539B–546B. See the translation, with apparatus, in Bell, *Baldwin of Ford. Spiritual Tractates*, 2: 141–55.

161. *Tractatus* 14 (541C): . . . disponunt propter Christum omnia relinquere, eique soli in omni puritate cordis adhaerere.

162. Ibid. (543D): Licet enim libertas adjuncta sit charitati, cedit tamen charitas necessitati, dum nonnumquam praetermittit quod melius est, ut devitet quod deterius est. Here I am using the translation of Bell, *Baldwin: Spiritual Tractates*, 2: 150.

163. John's sermons have been edited by Edmund Mikkers and Hilary Costello, *Ioannis de Forda: Super Extremam Partem Cantici Canticorum Sermones CXX*, CCCM 17–18 (Turnhout: Brepols, 1970). The sermons have been translated by Wendy Mary Beckett, *John of Ford: Sermons on the Final Verses of the Song of Songs*, 7 vols. (Kalamazoo, MI: Cistercian Publications, 1977–84). I will use my own translations, unless otherwise noted. For a sketch of John's life and thought, see Hilary Costello, "Introduction," in *John of Ford: Sermons I*, pp. 3–59. The best survey of John's mystical thought is Costello's article, "John of Ford and the Quest for Wisdom," *Cîteaux* 23 (1972): 141–59.

164. E.g., *Prologus* 4, and *Sermones* 17.7, 46.1, and 52.2. See also the confession of unworthiness at the end of his long effort (*Sermo* 120.8).

165. For a dossier of texts on John's teaching concerning spiritual experience, see P. Miquel, *Le vocabulaire latin de l'expérience spirituelle*, pp. 146–62.

166. *Sermo* 29.6 (CCCM 17:237.193–99): Si cui operae pretium est nosse, det operam et experiri. Suspiriis et precibus indefessis ad negotium se caritatis exerceat. Non det somnum oculis suis, non palpebris dormitationem, non denique Deo pacis et dilectionis det ullum nocte dieque silentium, donec egrediatur ad eum caritas Christi de thalamo suo, et velut lampas luminosa ei accendatur. Here I use the translation of Beckett in *John of Ford. Sermons III*, p. 10. It would be easy to supply a list of over forty similar references.

167. The wound of love is found in *Sermones* 1.4, 4.1, 4.9, 22.1, 24.4, 29.2, 30.5, 40.2, 48.9, 49.10, 81.4, 88.7–8 and 118.1.

168. *Sermo* 14.7 (CCCM 17:130.239–42): Quis iam miretur si fons dilectionis illic sane, ubi oritur, et impetu vehementior et saltu iucundior et ebullatione profusior et gustu dulcior et puritate sincerior et virtute potentior sit? The whole of *Sermo* 14 is a mini-treatise on the Trinity. For the role of the Trinity in the mystical life, see also *Sermo* 93.4–5.

169. One important passage from *Sermo* 14.3 on the mutuality of Father and Son deserves quotation (CCCM 17:127.92–128.96): Denique se totum dedit Filio suo, quem ex se toto dilexit totum. Itaque Unigenitus Filius totus in toto Patre est, possidens cor sapientiae eius, implens animam bonitatis ipsius, replens omnia viscera virtutum ipsius, et omnem uterum aeternitatis eius complens. See also the treatment of the mutual dereliction of the Father and the Son in the crucifixion in *Sermo* 13.7 (ibid.:122).

170. There are at least eighteen important discussions; see *Sermones* 13.4, 34.2, 39.3, 46.3, 46.5–7, 56.5, 63.8, 68.2–3, 72.3, 73.10, 94.6, 94.8, 96.4, 97.5, 98.2, 98.4–5, 109.9, and 113.10. Not all of these need to be considered as referring to direct experiences of God.

171. The verse is cited or implied fifteen times in reference to mystical union: *Sermones* 7.2, 11.5, 14.4, 14.7, 46.8, 80.3, 93.5, 94.3, 97.2, 97.7, 97.8, 106.1, 110.12, 114.5, and 119.2. In 7.2 John insists that our union with God is not a union of nature–*non tamen usque ad unitatem naturae, . . . sed usque ad individuam adhaesionem atque indissolubilem nexum unionis* (CCCM 17:75.122–25). For John's formulas in relation to other Cistercians, see H. Costello, "John of Ford and the Quest for Wisdom," pp. 149–50 n. 73.

172. This theme, citing Song 2:4, is treated more rarely by John. Discussions occur in *Sermones* 46.6, 88.5, 94.8, 94.10, and 100.1.

173. See especially *Sermones* 38.5 and 93.1, which begins with the observation: Epulentissima res amor est sed tamen famelica nimis. Votis eius anhelantibus vix aliqua visitationum ubertate ad plenam satisfieri potest (CCCM 18:629.8–10).

174. See *Sermo* 80.1 (CCCM 18:552.21). For a review of John's treatment of mystical marriage, see Costello, "John of Ford and the Quest for Wisdom," pp. 146–51.

175. *Sermo* 85.7 (CCCM 18:585.203–06): Quid si alio verborum schemate id ipsum modo figuratum est? Scriptura nempe sacra ac si regina praedives plurima habet mutatoria vestium, quibus ad amicorum aspectus gratior e thalamo, quo et multiformior procedere consuevit.

176. *Sermo* 30.1 (CCCM 17:238.22–24): Ubi spiritus dilecti mei, ibi libertas. Ipse posuit verba cantici huius sacri in ore meo, castis dumtaxat credenda auribus et illorum, qui sapiunt Iesum. Cf. *Sermo* 29.4. On "tasting" Jesus, note the succinct formulation in *Sermo* 2.2 (CCCM 17:46.88–89): Et quis sapiens, nisi qui sapit Iesum, et cui Iesus sapit?

177. E.g., *Sermo* 61.4 (CCCM 17:430.78). Cf. 97.2 (*amoris copula* in CCCM 18:657.37), and 109.7 (*copula nuptialis* in ibid.:738.146).

178. *Sermo* 89.1 (CCCM 18:604.10–12): . . . verbique imperfectio perfectius aliquid innuit, quam integer sermo formaret.

179. *Sermo* 87.3 (ibid.:594.49–53): Non quaeritur consequentia verbi, non eloquii captatur ambitus; nec velut sponsa Verbi, certe et cum Verbo verba faciens de principio verbi sui saltem sollicita est, sed verborum negligens amoris negotium, de quo sola cura est ei, lingua propria, hoc est affectibus, agit. Cf. *Sermones* 88.1, 93.3 and 106.9 (ibid.:599, 630 and 720).

180. *Sermo* 93.6 (CCCM 18:631.102–05) appears to contain a reference to the Dionysian circle of love found in *De divinis nominibus* 4.17. For an overview of God's love for us and our love for God, see *Sermones* 105–6.

181. *Sermo* 45.5 (CCCM 17:323.97–99): Ineffabilis prorsus homini caritas sive ut suggeret eam sive ut intellegat, pro eo quod de arcanis Filii est et maximum paradisi altissimumque mysterium.

182. *Sermo* 81.9 (CCCM 18:562.200–563.203): Quae diligit, sponsa est, sed si non perfunctorie diligat, sed si ferveat, si langueat, si deficiat, si adheareat, nec alius quidquam quam Iesum scire se iudicet.

183. *Sermo* 114 (CCCM 18:768–74).

184. *Sermo* 114.4 (ibid.:770.68–71): Alloquium liquido praesagiunt nuptiale, cum uberius fruitura dilecto gravidanda est in Spiritu Sancto atque ex susceptione beati seminis, qui est dulcis amor Christi, ubera protinus habitura. The fruitfulness of the Bride is another of the frequent themes of John's preaching; see, e.g., *Sermones* 19.6–8, 26.5, 68.8, 70.6 (applied to Mary), 111.7, and 112.9.

185. The importance of fraternal love in community is another key element in John's thought that is shared with the other Cistercians. One especially moving passage occurs in *Sermo* 47.7 (CCCM 17:335.161–336.164): Unde nimirum iam multiformiter sit speciosa, cui in omni facie suus illucescit dilectus, suus se repraesentat speciosus, fitque in ea cumulus

decoris immensus, quae non solum placere omnibus sed etiam ex omnibus placere concupiscit.

186. *Sermo* 109.5–9 (CCCM 18:737–40). For other important discussions of this central theme of mystical marriage, see, e.g., *Sermones* 34.2, 46.8, 53.1, 55.10–12, 58.11, 62.8, 68.2, 68.8, 80.1, 80.7–9, 94.5–11, 97.7–8, 111.7–9, and 115.9–10.

187. For important treatments of the church as the Bride of Christ through all ages, see especially *Sermones* 35.7 and 98.7.

188. See, e.g., *Sermones* 4.9, 7.7 (the iron in fire motif seen in Bernard's *De dil. Deo* 10.28), 13.4, 21.1, 53.1, 97.7, 107.11–12, and especially the comment on Song 8:6 in 108.6–9.

189. *Sermo* 109.7 (CCCM 18:739.172–75): Ergo anima Christum intime diligens, innumeris die et nocte velut nobile quoddam cubiculum sponsi est corusca lampadibus, quod nimirum de sponsi sui visitationum fulgoribus illustratur.

190. The use of the phrase *ad huius faciem ignis* is meant to recall the vision of the face of God, especially in light of the powerful passage on God as fire in the previous sermon: Es, Domine, etiam ignis consumens atque in favillam et cinerem redigens, . . . (*Sermo* 108.9 in CCCM 18:734.198–99).

191. *Sermo* 109.9 (CCCM 18:740:190–200): Ad hunc ignem sponsa Domini sedens incalescit ex eo quousque ut cera liquescat; et si quid in ea est corruptibile, . . . flammeae caritatis ardor exurat. Ad huius faciem ignis aromata myrrhae et thuris de pectore sponsae sudantia spirant. . . . Hoc denique igne sponsa ignit eloquium suum vehementer, sive cum ad sponsum suum arcana et ineffabiliter loquitur in iubilationibus et obsecrationibus suis, sive cum adolescentulas libet sermocinari de iis, quae cum ipsa secretius actitantur a sponso.

192. For Aelred's life we are fortunate in having Walter Daniel's *Vita Ailredi*, which, while typically hagiographical, also contains precious eyewitness testimony. See the edition of F. M. Powicke, *The Life of Ailred of Rievaulx by Walter Daniel* (London and Edinburgh: Thomas Nelson, 1963).

193. Aelred's *Speculum caritatis* contains two accounts of the crisis of his sinful life in the world that led to his entry into the monastery; see *Speculum caritatis* (hereafter *Spec car*) 1.28.79–82, and 2.7.18, as edited by Anselm Hoste and Charles Talbot, *Aelredi Rievallensis Opera Omnia, Vol. 1, Opera Ascetica*, CCCM 1 (Turnhout: Brepols, 1971), pp. 46–48 and 74–75. This same volume includes Aelred's other treatises, especially the *De spirituali amicitia* (hereafter *Spir am*), the *De Iesu puero duodenni* (*Iesu*), the *De institutione inclusarum* (*Instit incl*), the *De anima* (*Anima*), and the *Oratio pastoralis* (*Orat*), an extended meditation in the manner of John of Fécamp, Anselm, and William of St. Thierry. Aelred also laments his sins, especially the loss of his virginity, in the rule of life he sent his anchoress sister; see the *Instit incl* 3.32 (CCCM 1:673–77).

194. *Spir am*, prol. 1 (CCCM 1:287.4–8): Cum adhuc puer essem in scholis, et sociorum meorum me gratia plurimum delectaret, et inter mores et vitia quibus aetas illa periclitari solet, totam se mea mens dedit affectui, et devovit amori; ita ut nihil mihi dulcius, nihil iucundius, nihil utilius quam *amari et amare* videretur. (All translations are my own unless otherwise noted.) The phrase in quotation marks is from Augustine's *Confessiones* 2.2.1. The deep influence that Augustine, especially the Augustine of the *Confessiones*, exerted on Aelred has been studied by Pierre Courcelle, "Ailred de Rievaulx à l'école des *Confessions*," *Revue des études augustiniennes* 3 (1975): 163–74. On the Prologue, see James McEvoy, "Notes on the Prologue of St. Aelred of Rievaulx's *De Spirituali Amicitia*," *Traditio* 37 (1981): 396–411.

195. *Spir am* 3.82 (CCCM 1:334.607–09): . . . nullum inveniens in illa multitudine quem non diligerem, et a quo me diligi non confiderem, tanto gaudio perfusus sum ut omnes mundi huius delicias superaret.

196. Walter Daniel, *Vita Ailredi* 29 (ed. Powicke, 37): Quis ibi licet abiectissimus et contemptibilis locum quietis non invenit? Quis debilis umquam venit ad eam et in Alredo non

reperit paternam dileccionem et in fratribus debitam consolacionem? *Vita* 29–30 (ed., Powicke, 36–39) paints a charming portrait of Rievaulx under Aelred. For a beautiful expression of Aelred's pastoral love for his flock, see *Orat* 7–8 (CCM 1:760–62). The role of community in Aelred's thought has been studied by Charles Dumont, "Seeking God in Community according to St. Aelred," *Cistercian Studies* 6 (1971): 289–317.

197. *Vita Ailredi* 49–60 (ed. Powicke, 56–64), especially the abbot's constantly repeated final prayer: Dicebat ergo, ut verbis eius utar, "Festinate, *for crist luve*," id est: pro Christi amore festinate (60).

198. David Knowles, *The Monastic Order in England: A History of Its Development from the Time of St. Dunstan to the Fourth Lateran Council, 940-1216* (2nd ed.; Cambridge: Cambridge University Press, 1963), p. 265.

199. Aelred's extensive letters are unfortunately lost. The spiritual treatises, as noted above, are available in CCCM 1. There are English translations for these in the Cistercian Fathers series. The two Clairvaux collections of the abbot's sermons for the liturgical year have appeared in *Aelredi Rievallensis Opera Omnia. Sermones I–XLVI* (CCCM 2A), edited by Gaetano Raciti. In addition, a series of twenty four other sermons for the liturgical year were edited by C. H. Talbot, *Sermones Inediti B. Aelredi Abbatis Rievallensis* (Rome: Curia Generalis Sacri Ordinis Cisterciensis, 1952); and the abbot's collection of thirty three *Sermones de oneribus* (Oner), an allegorical interpretation of salvation history and its application to the individual soul based on Isa 13–16, can be found in PL 195:361–500.

200. For an early account, see Anselm Le Bail, "Aelred" in DS 1:225–34. Among important monographs, see Amédée Hallier, *The Monastic Theology of Aelred of Rievaulx. An Experiential Theology* (Spencer, MA: Cistercian Publications, 1969); and Aelred Squire, *Aelred of Rievaulx: A Study* (London: SPCK, 1969). A large periodical literature also exists, some of which will be cited below. For a recent collection of papers, see *S. Aelred de Rievaulx: Le Miroir de la Charité. Hommage au P. Charles Dumont* in *Collectanea Cisterciensia* 55 (1993). The most recent general treatment of Aelred's mysticism is in Kurt Ruh, *Geschichte der abendländische Mystik*, pp. 330–41, though Ruh denies he is a mystic (p. 330)!

201. See *Spec car* 1.3.9 (CCCM 1:16 and 22), which shows how the three fundamental powers of the soul, *memoria-scientia-amor sive voluntas*, partake of the *Aeternitas-Sapientia-Dulcedo* of the three persons of the Trinity. (Hereafter Aelred's treatises, all of which are found in CCCM 1, will be cited only by page and, where directly quoted, by line number.)

202. For summary discussions at the outset, see *Spec car* 1.2.6 and 1.4.12–13 (15 and 17).

203. See *Spec car* 1.5.14–16 and 1.8.24–25 (18–19 and 22–23).

204. E.g., *Spec car* 1.10.28–15.47 (23–31). Cf. 3.7.21.

205. *Spec. car* 1.8.26 (23.376–78): Animam itaque nostram ad id quod facta est, caritas sublevat; ad id vero, ad quod illa sponte defluxit, premit cupiditas.

206. *Spec car* 3.11.31 (119:561–62): Est igitur affectus spontanea quaedam ac dulcis ipsius animi ad aliquem inclinatio. This definition occurs in the midst of Aelred's most extensive discussion of the nature and components of *amor*, that of *Spec car* 3.7.20–21.51 (114–29). Cf. *Sermo In Ypapanti Domini* (*Sermones inediti*, 48): Affectio est, ut michi videtur, spontanea quaedam mentis inclinatio ad aliquem cum delectatione. For Aelred's doctrine of *affectus*, see James McEvoy, "Les 'affectus' et la mesure de la raison dans le Livre III du 'Miroir'," *Collectanea Cisterciensia* 55 (1993): 110–25.

207. *Anima* 2.22 (714.294–98): Dicitur enim ratio secundum naturam, qua efficit ut homo rationalis sit, possitque discernere inter bonum et malum. . . . Dicitur et secundum iudicium, quo et reprobanda reprobet, et approbat approbanda.

208. *Spec car* 3.7.20 (114.372–77): Dicitur enim amor animae rationalis vis quaedam sive natura, qua ei naturaliter inest ipsa amandi aliquid, non amandive facultas. Dicitur et amor ipsius animae rationalis quidam actus vim illam exercens, cum ea utitur vel in his quae

oportet, vel in his quae non oportet. On Aelred's doctrine of love, see Raymundus Schilling, "Aelredus van Rievaulx: Deus Amicitia Est," *Cîteaux* 8 (1957): 13–26; Adele Fiske, "Aelred's of Rievaulx Idea of Friendship and Love," *Cîteaux* 13 (1962): 7–17; and M. Basil Pennington, "A Primer of the School of Love," *Cîteaux* 31 (1980): 93–104.

209. *Spir am* 3.2–3 (317) analyzes five modes of *amor: ex natura; ex officio; ex sola ratione; ex solo affectu;* and the *amor ex ratione simul et affectu* (i.e., *amicitia*).

210. *Spec car* 1.19.56 (35.850–58): Ipsa sola incommutabilis et aeterna requies eius, aeterna et incommutabilis tranquillitas eius, aeternum et incommutabilem Sabbatum eius. Ipsa sola causa cur creavit creanda, regit regenda, administrat administranda, movet movenda, promovet promovenda, perficit perficienda.... Caritas enim eius, ipsa est voluntas eius, ipsa est et bonitas eius: nec hoc totum aliud esse quam esse eius. For more on Aelred's teaching on the Sabbath, see below, pp. 321–22.

211. *Spec car* 1.21.59 (37.915–19): ... non locali infusione, non spatiosa diffusione, non mobili discursione, sed substantialis praesentiae stabili et incomprehensibili in se permanente simplicitate omnia continentem, omnia ambientem, omnia penetrantem, ima superis coniungentem....

212. Recalling Augustine's famous definition of peace (the equivalent of Aelred's Sabbath) in *De civitate Dei* 19.13.1 (PL 41:640): Pax omnium rerum tranquillitas ordinis. Ordo est parium dispariumque rerum sua cuique loca tribuens dispositio.

213. *Spir am* 1.50–61 (297–99).

214. *Spec car* 1.7.23 (21.335–22.339): Nolens enim substantiam animae meae servare ad te, accepi eam ad me, et volens meipsum possidere sine te, et te perdidi et me. Et ecce factus sum mihimetipsi gravis; factus sum mihimet locus miseriae et tenebrarum, locus horroris et regio egestatis. This last phrase reminds us of Bernard's teaching on sin as the *regio dissimilitudinis* (see chapter 5, pp. 172–74). Aelred himself uses this expression in *Puero* 3 (251.73). For the abbot's teaching on original sin and its consequences, see Hallier, *The Monastic Theology*, pp. 10–18.

215. Most of book 2 of the *Spec car* is taken up with showing how the three basic forms of *cupiditas–concupiscentia carnis, concupiscentia oculorum,* and *superbia vitae* (1 John 2:16)–block the action of *caritas.*

216. *Spec car* 3.26.62–63 (134–35) distinguishes between *amor in Deo,* the love we bear to friends, which is realized both *affectu et ratione,* and *amor propter Deum,* the love toward enemies, which is only *ex ratione.* The last part of book 3 (3.37.98–40.112) consists of a detailed and significant examination of the rules for love and enjoyment of self and of others. On the eschatological completion in heaven, where we will enjoy friendship with all, see especially *Spir am* 3.79–80 and 134 (333–34 and 349–50).

217. For an introduction to this aspect of the Cistercian program, see Marsha L. Dutton, "Intimacy and Imitation: The Humanity of Christ in Cistercian Spirituality," in *Erudition at God's Service: Studies in Medieval Cistercian History XI,* ed. John R. Sommerfeldt (Kalamazoo, MI: Cistercian Publications, 1987), pp. 33–69.

218. An example of how Aelred's almost-too-sweet style labors to this end can be seen in the following passage from *Iesu* 1.5 (253.126–34): Credo enim in illo speciosissimo vultu tantam gratiae caelestis elegantiam refulsisse, ut omnium in se converteret aspectum, auditum erigeret, excitaret affectum. Cerne, quaeso, quemadmodum a singulis rapitur, a singulis trahitur. Senes osculantur, amplectuntur iuvenes, pueri obsequuntur. Et quae lacrimae a pueris, cum diutius a viris teneretur? Quae sanctis mulieribus quaerimoniae, cum paulo plus quam patre et eius sociis moraretur? Credo singulos intimo proclamare affectu: *Osculetur me osculo oris sui* (Song 1:1).

219. The aim of this section is expressed in an admirable formula in *Iesu* 2.12 (259.42– 43): Sic tu nasceris in Christo et in te sic nascitur Christus–another example of the theme of the birth of Christ in our hearts.

220. *Iesu* 3.19 (266.8–9): . . . ut non tam in codicibus, quam in propriis moribus mystica valeas lectitare. Following Bernard, Aelred also makes use of the theme of the "book of experience," as in *Sermo in Ypapanti Domini* (*Sermones Inediti*, 49), where he says: Legite, quaeso in libro experientiae. For an anthology of the abbot's texts on spiritual experience, see P. Miquel, *Le vocabulaire latin de l'expérience spirituelle*, pp. 123–32.

221. *Spec car* 1.5.16 (112.309–10): . . . omnem affectum suum ad suavitatem Dominicae carnis extendat.

222. Threefold forms of meditation are found elsewhere among the Cistercians (see Bernard, e.g., *Div* 12.1, and *Dom. VI post Pent* 6), but Aelred's is distinctive.

223. *Instit incl* 3.31 (667.1043–46): Frange igitur alabastrum cordis tui, et quidquid habes devotionis, quidquid amoris, quidquid desiderii, quidquid affectionis, totum effunde super Sponsum tui caput, adorans in Deo hominem, et in homine Deum.

224. *Instit incl* 3.31 (673.1243–45): Unde a praeteritorum recordatione ad experientiam praesentium transeamus, ut ex his quoque quantum a nobis sit diligendus Deus intelligere valeamus.

225. On the mystical element, see, e.g., Aelred's reminder to his sister to recall the special graces she has received while at prayer; see *Instit incl* 3.32 (676.1347–54). On the mystical character of the work, see Marsha L. Dutton, "Christ Our Mother: Aelred's Iconography for Contemplative Union," in *Goad and Nail: Studies in Cistercian History X* (Kalamazoo, MI: Cistercian Publications, 1985), pp. 21–45.

226. *Spec car* 1.5.16 (19.227–28): Amplectatur te interim crucifixum, sumat tui dulcissimi sanguinis haustum. Cf. *Instit incl* 3.31 (671.1187–94).

227. On the maternal images of Christ employed by Aelred, see M. L. Dutton, "Christ Our Mother," which emphasizes three passages in the *Instit incl* that mingle breast and Eucharistic imagery (658.748–52; 668.1078–94; and 671.1187–96). There is also a brief treatment in C. Bynum, *Jesus as Mother*, pp. 122–24.

228. See Marsha L. Dutton, "The Face and Feet of God: The Humanity of Christ in Bernard of Clairvaux and Aelred of Rievaulx," in *Bernardus Magister*, pp. 203–23, esp. pp. 205–6, 213, 221–23. I find it difficult to accept the author's contention (p. 222) that Bernard's sermons are not directed to contemplatives, while Aelred's treatises are.

229. For an example of such a text, see *Instit incl* 3.31 (668.1090–94), which contrasts the carnal affection of the anchoress with the higher love exemplified in John: Iam nunc exulta, virgo, accede proprius, et aliquam tibi huius dulcedinis portionem vendicare non differas. Si ad potiora non potes, dimitte Ioanni pectus, ubi eum vinum laetitiae in divinitatis cognitione inebriet, tu currens ad ubera humanitatis, lac exprime quo nutiaris. Dutton's treatment of this text in her earlier paper "Christ Our Mother," (p. 38–39) appears to contradict what she says of Aelred in "The Face and Feet of God."

230. Major studies of the friendship tradition in patristic and early medieval Christianity include Adele Fiske, *Friends and Friendship in the Monastic Tradition* (Cuernavaca: Civoc Cuaderno, 1970), reprising a long series of articles published in the 1960s; Brian Patrick McGuire, *Friendship and Community: The Monastic Experience 350–1250* (Kalamazoo, MI: Cistercian Publications, 1988); and Carolinne White, *Christian Friendship in the Fourth Century* (Cambridge: Cambridge University Press, 1992).

231. See Adele Fiske, "Alcuin and Mystical Friendship," *Studi medievali*, 3a serie 2 (1961): 551–75, esp. pp. 566–75. In his letters Alcuin, like Aelred, uses the image of fire and the language of the Song of Songs to describe how *amicitia* transports two friends into mutual enjoyment of Christ.

232. For an introduction, see Jean Leclercq, "L'amitie dans les lettres au moyen-âge," *Revue du moyen âge latin* 1 (1945): 391–410.

233. For Bernard's teaching on friendship, see Jean de la Croix Bouton, "La doctrine de l'amitie chez saint Bernard," *Revue d'ascétique et de mystique* 29 (1953): 3–19; A. Fiske, "St. Bernard of Clairvaux," *Cîteaux* 2 (1960): 1–41; Brian McGuire, "Was Bernard a Friend?" in *Goad and Nail*, pp. 201–27; and Shawn Madison Krahmer, "Interpreting the Letters of Bernard of Clairvaux to Ermengaude, Countess of Brittany: The Twelfth-Century Context and the Language of Friendship," *Cistercian Studies* 27 (1992): 217–50.

234. The literature on this aspect of Aelred's thought is extensive. See especially, Richard Egenter, *Gottesfreundschaft: Die Lehre von der Gottesfreundschaft in der Scholastik und Mystik des 12. und 13. Jahrhunderts* (Augsburg: Filser, 1928), pp. 201–46; A. Fiske, "Aelred's of Rievaulx Idea of Love and Friendship," *Cîteaux* 13 (1962): 5–17, 97–132; Gaetano Raciti, "L'apport original d'Aelred de Rievaulx à la réflexion occidentale sur l'amitie," *Collectanea Cisterciensia* 29 (1967): 77–99; Raffaella Paolini, "La 'spiritualis amicitia' in Aelred di Rievaulx," *Aevum* 42 (1968): 455–73; A. Hallier, *The Monastic Theology of Aelred of Rievaulx*, chap. 2; A. Squire, *Aelred of Rievaulx*, chap. 5; Douglass Roby, "Introduction," *Aelred of Rievaulx: Spiritual Friendship* (Kalamazoo, MI: Cistercian Publications, 1977), pp. 3–41; Brian Bethune, "Personality and Spirituality: Aelred of Rievaulx and Human Relationships," *Cistercian Studies* 20 (1985): 98–112; B. McGuire, *Friendship and Community*, chap. 7; and Katherine M. TePas, "Spiritual Friendship in Aelred of Rievaulx and Mutual Santification in Marriage I and II," *Cistercian Studies* 27 (1992): 63–76, 153–65.

235. Aelred cites Cicero's definition in *Spir am* 1.11 (291.80–81): Amicitia est rerum humanarum et divinarum cum benevolentia et caritate consensio (cf. *De amicitia* 20), though the discussion in *Spir am* 14–17 indicates that he knew he would have to effect a change in its meaning to vindicate it for Christian use. *Spir am* 1.40 and 48, as well as 2.28 and 3.11 (296.231–32, 297.272, 308.207–08, and 319.79) also cite the definition that comes from Sallust's *Catilina* 20: idem velle et idem nolle.

236. J. Dubois in his edition and study of the text, *Aelred de Rievaulx. L'amitié spirituelle* (Bruges: Beyaert, 1948), pp. xlviii–xl, discusses Aelred's debt to Cicero and estimates that about a third of the Roman's text is cited or paraphrased in the Spir am.

237. G. Raciti, "L'apport original," p. 98, in discussing the relation of Aelred to Cicero, says, "... il nous semble que le terme le plus approprié et le moins équivoque soit, non pas christianisation, ni adaptation, mais 'transposition.'"

238. *Spir am* 1.8 (290.59–62): ... et quemadmodum ea ipsa quae inter nos oportet esse amicitia, et in Christo incohetur, et secundum Christum servetur, et ad Christum finis eius et utilitas referatur plenius edoceri.

239. *Spir am* 1.69–70 (301.403–06): IVO. O quid est hoc? Dicamne de amicitia quod amicus Iesu Ioannes de caritate commemorat: Deus amicitia est? AELREDUS. Inusitatem quidem hoc, nec ex Scripturis habet auctoritatem. Quod tamen sequitur de caritate, amicitiae profecto dare non dubito, quoniam: *Qui manet* in amicitia, *in Deo manet, et Deus in eo* (1 John 4:16).

240. E.g., Guerric of Igny in *Sermo* 24.2 (SC 202:80) emphasizes the equivalence of love and friendship in our union with God.

241. For an evaluation of Aelred's unusual position in the history of monastic friendship, see McGuire, *Friendship and Community*, pp. 329–31.

242. For the claim that "Aelred was gay and that his erotic attraction to men was the dominant force in his life," see John Boswell, *Christianity, Social Tolerance, and Homosexuality* (Chicago: University of Chicago Press, 1980), pp. 221–26. See also the discussion in McGuire, *Friendship and Community*, pp. 302–6, 331–33.

243. See, e.g., *Spec car* 1.26.72–77 and 1.29.84; and *Instit incl* 1.18–19. Aelred's abhorrence for homosexual vice is evident in his witty reference to customs at some episcopal courts where, in his words, *Procedunt quidem capillati et effeminati seminudis natibus cultu meretricio . . . (Spec car* 3.26.64 [135.1188–90]). Cf. *Spec car* 3.28.67 and *Instit incl* 1.15 (651).

244. Charles Dumont in his "Introduction" to the *Mirror of Charity* put it well: ". . . spiritual friendship is a way toward the liberation of the divine love which is in us and seeks its full and definitive object in God" (p. 39).

245. *Spir am* 1.19 (292.109–11): Est autem amor quidem animae rationalis affectus per quem ipsa aliquid cum desiderio quaerit et appetit ad fruendum. See also the summary in 3.54 (327).

246. Aelred emphasizes the role of reason throughout the treatise, e.g., *Spec car* 2.57, which summarizes: . . . numquam tamen sequendus est [affectus amicitiae] nisi eum et ratio ducat, et honestas temperet, et regat iustitia (313.371–72). There are, of course, false forms of friendship, not in accordance with reason, which *Spir am* 1.38 describes as *amicitia carnalis* and *amicitia mundialis.* The former is seen as based only on physical attraction and created by mutual harmony in vice, while the latter is undertaken for the sake of temporal advantage. But Aelred admits that even *amicitia mundialis* may lead to some degree of true friendship (1.44), and later (3.85–87) he distinguishes between carnal friendships that involve sin and must therefore be rejected and those (*maxime adolescentium*) that are primarily affective but without sin and can be tolerated in the hope that they will grow to a higher level. *Spir am* 2.57–60 (312–13) uses the slightly different terminology of *amicitia puerilis* and *amicitia utilitatis.*

247. *Spir am* 1.48 (297.269–71): . . . benevolentia autem ipse sensus amandi qui cum quadam dulcedine movetur interius exprimatur.

248. *Spir am* 1.45 (296.259–60): . . . ita ut *fructus eius* praemiumque non sit aliud quam ipsa. The idea is based on Cicero, *De amicitia* 31. See also 2.61 and 3.118 (313–14 and 345).

249. See especially the discussion in *Spir am* 3.90–91 and 97 (336–37 and 339). The theme is also beautifully expressed in the abbot's description of his friendship with Simon and an unnamed monk (Geoffrey of Dinant?) toward the end of the *Spir am* in 3.119–129 (345–48).

250. One may even argue, at least by extrapolation, that Aelred also allowed human marriage such a role. Although his own friendships were exclusively male (unlike Bernard, who appears to have had a sincere friendship with Countess Ermengarde of Brittany if the witness of *Epp.* 116–17 be allowed), he emphasized that the original intention of God's creation of Eve was to be a friend of Adam (*Spir am* 1.57 [298–99]). Although the fall injured this friendship and introduced the distinction between the *caritas* that we must have toward all and the *amicitia* we can extend only to some (1.58–61), there is no reason why *amicitia spiritualis* cannot be realized in marriage. Indeed, in several sermons, notably *In Epiphania de tribus generibus nuptiarum* and *In Ypapanti Domini* (*Sermones inediti,* 39–52), Aelred uses marriage analogies to portray Christ's union with human nature in the church, as well as the marriage between Christ and the soul. In *Spec car* 3.35.95 (151) he also notes that *coniugati sancti* truly possess *caritas.* For Aelred's view of marriage, see B. Bethune, "Personality and Spirituality," pp. 105–7, 112; and K. TePas, "Spiritual Friendship and Mutual Sanctification in Marriage."

251. *Spir am* 2.20–21 (306.147–54): Non igitur videtur nimium gravis vel innaturalis ascensus, de Christo amorem inspirante quo amicum diligimus, ad Christum semetipsum amicum nobis praebentem, quem diligamus. . . . Itaque amicus in spiritu Christi adhaerens amico, efficitur cum eo *cor unum et anima una*; et sic per amoris gradus ad Christi conscendens amicitiam, unus cum eo spiritus efficitur in osculo uno. Ad quod osculum anima quaedam sancta suspirans: *Osculetur me,* inquit, *osculo oris sui!*

252. *Spir am* 2.26 (307.190–308.194): Hoc osculum non inconvenienter osculum dixerim Christi, quod ipse tamen porrigit non ore proprio sed alieno; illum sacratissimum amantibus inspirans affectum, ut videatur illis quasi unum animam in diversis esse corporibus. . . .

253. *Spir am* 2.14 (305.104–08): . . . quidam gradus est amicitia vicinus perfectioni, quae in Dei dilectione et cognitione consistit; ut homo ex amico hominis Dei efficiatur amicus, secundum illud Salvatoris in evangelio: *Iam non dicam vos servos, sed amicos meos.*

254. *Spir am* 2.61 (313.398–400): Quae tunc plena merces erit colentibus eam, cum tota translata in Deum, in eius contemplatione sepelit quod univit.

255. E.g., *Spir am* 3.87, 127, and 134 (336.652–57, 348.1053–57 and 349.1107–350.1118).

256. *Spec car* 1.34.98–114 (56–65). For some comments on this text, see McGuire, *Friendship and Community*, pp. 311–14.

257. *Spec car* 1.34.114 (64.1976–87): Quid est quod intueor, mi domine? Videor mihi certe quasi oculis cernere mentem illam, ad huius versiculi haustum quodam ineffabili gaudio resolutam, dum cerneret peccata sua, immenso pelago divinae miserationis absorpta, nihil reliquisse quod premeret. . . . Liber intueri animam illam, fonte divinae misericordiae dilutam, deposito pondere peccatorum. . . . Eia, convertere nunc, o anima, in requiem tuam, quia Dominus benefacit tibi. . . .

258. For example, *Spec car* 1.32.90–92 (52–54) interprets the six days of the Hexaemeron as the progress in virtues from faith through the goal of charity, and in *Spec car* 2.8.20–15.39 (75–85) a lengthy discussion of three forms of *spiritualis visitatio (timor, consolatio, dilectio)* provides an itinerary of religious experience that ends in mystical experience (see, e.g., 78.481–90, 79.517–22, and 85.729–40).

259. It is enough for him to admit . . . *sunt multa genera contemplationum ac spiritalium visionum* in *Iesu* 3.25 (271.199–272.200). In a series of four articles John R. Sommerfeldt has completed a helpful study of Aelred's vocabulary of contemplation and mystical experience. See "The Vocabulary of Contemplation in Aelred of Rievaulx' *On Jesus at the Age of Twelve, A Rule of Life for a Recluse,* and *On Spiritual Friendship,*" in *Heaven on Earth: Studies in Medieval Cistercian History IX,* ed. E. Rozanne Elder (Kalamazoo, MI: Cistercian Publications, 1983), pp. 72–89; "The Vocabulary of Contemplation in Aelred of Rievaulx' *Mirror of Love,* Book I," in *Goad and Nail,* pp. 242–50; and "Images of Visitation: The Vocabulary of Contemplation in Aelred of Rievaulx' *Mirror of Love,* Book II," and "The Rape of the Soul: The Vocabulary of Contemplation in Aelred of Rievaulx' *Mirror of Love,* Book III," both in *Erudition at God's Service,* pp. 161–74.

260. While Aelred lacks anything like an apophatic theology, he has a clear sense of the ineffability of the experience of God. In his *Sermo Beate Virginis* (*Sermones Inediti,* 142), when discussing the unexpected divine visitations that sometimes come in prayer, he says: Sunt et alia quedam spiritualia experimenta que sentiri quidem possunt ac explicari minime. This can be compared with a passage in the sermon *In Ypapanti Domini* (ibid., 51) where he emphasizes the silence that is the only fitting reaction when the created and Uncreated Spirit mingle *in osculo spirituali,* citing a classic scriptural warrant, Isa 24:16, *secretum meum michi, secretum meum michi.*

261. *Spir am* 3.134 (349.1107–09): Ita a sancto illo amore quo amplectitur amicum, ad illum conscendens, quo amplectitur Christum; spiritalem amicitiae fructum pleno laetus ore carpebit. . . .

262. Full proof of this would demand a more extensive discussion than can be given here, but it is noteworthy to compare Aelred with Bernard on the relative frequency of the language of embracing (*amplexus/amplector*) and kissing (*osculum/osculare*). (I have used the word indices for the two volumes of Aelred in CCCM and the eight volumes of SBOp). Kissing outnumbers embracing in Bernard (305 to 210 uses, or roughly 3 to 2), whereas in Aelred embracing outnumbers kissing (123 to 77 uses, or somewhat more than 3 to 2).

263. It is neither possible nor necessary in this context to review all the texts in which the *amplexus* suggests what we would call a mystical experience. For some sample passages, however, see, e.g., *Spec car* 1.1.2, 2.13.32, 3.16.17 and 3.36.102.

264. For a discussion of the Sabbaths in book 3, see C. Dumont, "Introduction," *Mirror of Charity*, pp. 36–39; Sommerfeldt, "The Rape of the Soul," pp. 171–73; and Ruh, *Geschichte der abendländische Mystik*, pp. 338–41.

265. *Spec car* 3.1.1 (105.16–20): Et quia in unitate nulla divisio, nulla sit ibi per diversa mentis effusio, sed sit unum in uno, cum uno, per unum, circa unum, unum sentiens, unum sapiens; et quia semper unum, semper requiescens, et sic perenne sabbatum sabbatizans. For another passage in this vein, see *Instit incl* 26 (659.767–71). Bernard's few texts on God as *unum* do not approach this powerful evocation (e.g., *Sept* 2.3 [SBOp 4:352.7–9]).

266. For some comparable passages in Eckhart on God's absolute unity, see *Meister Eckhart: The Essential Sermons, Commentaries, Treatises, and Defense*, ed. Edmund Colledge and Bernard McGinn (New York: Paulist, 1981), pp. 221, 230, and 247. I am not claiming that Eckhart knew Aelred's writings.

267. This is not to say that Aelred does not use the text with effect in a number of places, e.g., *Spec car* 2.18.53, and *Instit incl* 3.26 (91 and 659).

268. For two examples, see *Spec car* 3.1.1 (105.14–16): . . . ut ad ipsum, qui vere unus est, veniatur, ubi totum quod sumus *unum* cum ipso efficiatur; and In *Ypapanti Domini* (*Sermones inediti*, 51): . . . quando in osculo spirituali sibi obviant sibique miscentur spiritus creatus et increatus, ut sint duo in uno, *immo dico unum*. . . . (my italics).

269. For a survey, see Aelred Squire, "Aelred of Rievaulx and the Monastic Tradition Concerning Action and Contemplation," *Downside Review* 72 (1954): 289–304. Aelred is perhaps original in the advice that he gives to his sister about how even an enclosed anchoress can practice active love. See *Instit incl* 3.31 (668.1091–94), and especially 3.28 (661–62), which says: Itaque totum mundum uno dilectionis sinu completere, ibi simul omnes qui boni sunt considera et gratulare, ibi malos intuere et luge (661.850–53).

270. *Spec car* 3.18.41 (125.773–76): Hic est enim amor ordinatus, ut nec diligat homo quod diligendum non est, diligat autem quidquid diligendum est, amplius tamen non diligat quam diligendum est. . . . Further typical discussions can be found in *Spec car* 1.33.97, 3.9.28, 3.22.52, 3.37.98, and 101 (56, 118, 130, 153 and 155); and, on the relation between self-love and love of neighbor, *Spir am* 3.69–70, and 128 (331 and 348).

271. See especially the summary in *Spec car* 1.29.72 (139.1342–45).

272. *Spir am* 3.118 (345.957–60): Haec est enim amicitia ordinata, ut ratio regat affectum, nec tam quid illorum suavitas, quam quid multorum petat utilitas attendamus. See also 3.130 (348.1073–78).

273. These judgments, of course, are made from a contemporary perspective, with full realization of the difficulty, if not impossibility, of recapturing how these texts were read by a medieval audience.

274. For Aelred's mysticism as implying a connatural knowing of God through the experience of love and friendship, see Odo Brooke's "Towards a Theology of Connatural Knowledge," *Studies in Monastic Theology*, pp. 232–39.

Chapter 8

1. Jean Leclercq, *The Love of Learning and the Desire for God* (New York: Fordham University Press, 1961), p. 219. See also John Van Engen, *Rupert of Deutz* (Berkeley and Los Angeles: University of California Press, 1983), who summarizes: "His work gave expression to the theological vision implicit in almost two hundred years of traditional Benedictine monasticism" (p. 368).

2. See Peter Dinzelbacher, *Vision und Visionsliteratur im Mittelalter,* Monographien zur Geschichte des Mittelalters 23 (Stuttgart: Anton Hiersemann, 1981), esp. chaps. 12, 16, and the "Zusammenfassung" on pp. 229–65. For the wider context, see the same author's *"Revelationes,"* Typologie des sources du moyen âge occidental fasc. 57 (Turnhout: Brepols, 1991). A more general study of Western visionaries, including Hildegard of Bingen and Elisabeth of Schönau, can be found in Ernst Benz, *Die Vision: Ehfahrungsformen und Bilderwelt* (Stuttgart: Klett, 1969).

3. Visionary accounts in Jewish apocalypticism form part of the roots of Christian mysticism, and the role of visionary experience was significant in the second-century debate over Gnosticism, as discussed in *Foundations of Mysticism,* pp. 13–15, 96–97. For more on the role of visions in early Christian mysticism, see under "Vision" in the *subject index* in *Foundations of Mysticism.*

4. Dinzelbacher restricts his study of visions to those that involve a transfer to the other world (*Vision,* e.g., pp. 29–38). This distinction, however, is not present in the medieval texts.

5. The three types of visions (corporeal, spiritual or imaginative, and intellectual) studied by Augustine in book 12 of his *De Genesi ad litteram* remained the theological basis for medieval discussion of visions, although some twelfth-century theologians, especially Richard of St. Victor (see chapter 9, p. 411), attempted new categorizations. For a discussion of Augustine's views, see *Foundations of Mysticism,* pp. 254–56.

6. For an account of Rupert's life and thought, see Van Engen, *Rupert of Deutz.* Also helpful for his theology is Mariano Magrassi, *Teologia e storia nel pensiero di Ruperto di Deutz* (Rome: Propaganda Fidei, 1959).

7. See the discussion of these two works in Van Engen, *Rupert of Deutz,* pp. 275–82 and 291–98. Friedrich Ohly stresses Rupert's significance in the history of the exegesis of the Song by entitling his section on Rupert "Der Bruch mit der Tradition" (*Hoheliedstudien: Grundzüge einer Geschichte der Hoheliedauslegung des Abendlandes bis zum 1200* [Weisbaden: Steiner, 1958], pp. 121–35). On Rupert's role in the history of Apocalypse exegesis, see Wilhelm Kamlah, *Apokalypse und Geschichtstheologie,* Historische Studien 285 (Berlin: Ebering, 1935), chap. 3; and B. McGinn, *The Calabrian Abbot: Joachim of Fiore in the History of Western Thought* (New York: Macmillan, 1985), pp. 87–88. Rupert's theory of visions, as exposed in the Apocalypse commentary, may well have influenced his autobiographical visionary narratives. See Kamlah, chap. 4 (pp. 106–8).

8. *Rupertus Tuitiensis. De Victoria Verbi Dei,* ed. Rhaban Haacke, MGH. Quellen zur Geistesgeschichte des Mittelalters 5 (Weimar: Böhlaus, 1970), 1.3: Porro ex semetipso magnificentius (ut iam dictum est) verbum ipsum cognoscitur, quando gratia precellenti dilectam cuiuslibet animam visitans fortiter atque suaviter afficit proprie substantie contactu (p. 8). Rupert's understanding of experience has been studied by Pierre Miquel in *Le vocabulaire latin de l'expérience spirituelle,* (Paris: Beauchesne, 1989), pp. 56–82. Rupert refers to his own experience of such contact, this time in relation to the Holy Spirit, in his *De Trinitate et operibus eius* 2.12 (PL 167:1617C): Nonne ipsi scimus, quod experti sumus, aut certius aliquid ab homine audire possumus, quam quod interius Spiritu sancto revelante quasi gustando didicimus?

9. What is peculiar about this account is that the distinction between knowledge *ex operibus* and *ex semetipso* seems to allow no room for the intermediate category of knowledge *ex auditu,* that is, from faith.

10. See *Ruperti Tuitiensis. De Gloria et Honore Filii Hominis super Mattheum,* ed. Hrabanus Haacke (CCCM 29), Liber Duodecimus, 363.1–386.876. (All subsequent references will use the abbreviation *Super Mt.* followed by page and line.) This visionary account has been studied by Rhaban Haacke, "Die mystischen Visionen Ruperts von Deutz," in *"Sapientiae Doctrina": Mélanges de théologie et de littératures médiévales offets à Dom Hildebrand Bascour O.S.B.*

Recherches de théologie ancienne et médiévale. Numéro Spécial 1 (Leuven, 1980), pp. 68–90; and Van Engen, *Rupert of Deutz,* pp. 48–54, 346, 349–52, and 363. See also the comments by Hubert Silvestre in the *Bulletin de théologie ancienne et médiévale* 13 (1981): 74. Rupert recalls (366.116–368.266) that he had revealed his visions to Cuno in 1124 and that his friend had commanded them to be put in writing.

11. Othloh's account is in his *Liber visionum* in PL 146:341–85. For an analysis of his personality, see J. Leclercq, "Modern Psychology and the Interpretation of Medieval Texts," *Speculum* 48 (1973): 478–79. Rupert, of course, was not the only twelfth-century monk to experience the "new" form of *visio* that often suggested personal experience of God, but his accounts seem to be the earliest. For a survey of some English examples, see Peter Dinzelbacher, "The Beginnings of Mysticism Experienced in Twelfth-Century England," in *The Medieval Mystical Tradition in England. Exeter Symposium IV,* ed. Marion Glasscoe (Cambridge: Brewer, 1987), pp. 111–31.

12. For an analysis of the role of dreaming in medieval visions, see Dinzelbacher, *Vision,* pp. 39–45, and 65–77, which discusses the criteria for distinguishing true from literary employment of the dream motif.

13. Rupert briefly hints at some of these visions in his earlier works. See his *Commentum in Cantica canticorum* 5 (CCCM 26:110–11), and *In Regulam S. Benedicti* 1 (PL 170:480C–81B). There is a discussion of these visions in Haacke, "Die mystischen Visionen," pp. 81–84. In his late work the *De glorificatione Trinitatis et processione Spiritus sancti,* written in 1128, Rupert defends the continued action of Holy Spirit in the church by appealing to the mystical graces granted both to the anchoress Waldrada and to himself; see *De glorificatione* 2.18 (PL 169:48C–49D).

14. On the role of the Ezekiel vision in Jewish and Christian literature, see Michael Lieb, *The Visionary Mode: Biblical Prophecy, Hermenutics, and Cultural Change* (Ithaca, NY: Cornell University Press, 1991), which does not, however, refer to Rupert.

15. Rupert several times insists on the inexpressibility of what he saw and experienced, despite the considerable detail with which he actually describes the events; e.g., *Super Mt. 12* (371.337–38, and 383.786–87).

16. *Super Mt. 12* (369.242–55): . . . quia aperti sunt mihi oculi et vidi Filium Dei, vidi ipsum vigilans in cruce viventem Filium hominis. Non corporali visu vidi, sed ut viderem, repente evanuerunt corporis oculi et aperti sunt meliores, id est interiores oculi. . . . Qualis autem visus est aspectus eius? Humana hoc non potest lingua verbis comprehendere, tantumque dixerim, quia sensi illic breviter, quam veraciter dicat ipse: *Et discite a me quia mitis sum et humilis corde. . . .*

17. It is beyond the scope of this brief summary to study the whole rich tapestry of allusions used by Rupert as he recounts his experiences. These include references to biblical visionaries (e.g., Jacob, Ezekiel, the Bride of the Song, Paul, and Mary), to key texts from scripture traditionally understood to speak of direct contact with God, and even to the witness of noted figures in the tradition, such as Jerome (367.160–68), Augustine (370.281–86), and Gregory the Great's *Dialogi* (374.435–41).

18. The fact that Rupert's visions occur in dreams does not mean that they must *ipso facto* be excluded from the realm of true mystical consciousness. Medieval believers could appeal to the witness of the Bible in which God often visited his faithful in dreams.

19. *Super Mt. 12* (370.301–372.324).

20. Ibid. (371.336–40): . . . et ecce iuxta dextrum cornu altaris tres personae stantes habitus valde reverendi et dignitatis, quantum nulla potest lingua verbis consequi. Duae personae multum antiquae, id est valde cani erant capitis, persona tertia ut speciosus astabat iuvenis, regia dignitate, ut ex vestitu eius poterat agnosci.

21. Ibid. (372.360–63): Tunc ipsae tres personae grandi et pari statura aequales me pusillum circumsteterunt et aperto pergrandi libro me superpositum eidem libro in sublime sustulerunt.

22. Ibid. (373.405–7): . . . sed non mora, vis magna cuiusdam sanctae ac divinae voluptatis me somno excussit.

23. Rupert's sense of the trinitarian structure of history, aptly laid out in his *De sancta Trinitate et operibus eius* (ca. 1112–16), meant that all present experience of the divine was available only through the action of the Holy Spirit. Thus, although his visions began with seeing Christ on the cross and moved on to contact with the Trinity and then the person of the Father, it is fitting that the later visions begin with one involving the Holy Spirit.

24. *Super Mt.* 12 (376.504–22).

25. Ibid. (378.605–9): . . . video quasi caelum desuper modice aperiri atque inde quasi talentum lucidum substantiae ineffabilis substantiae viventis velociter ac dicto citius demitti, quod meo illapsum pectori magnitudine vel pondere suo me protinus somno excussit, auro gravius, melle dulcius. It is interesting to note that Gerhoh of Reichersberg (1093–1169) in his *De investigatione Antichristi* written in the mid-1160s (MGH. Libelli de Lite 3:306) recounts a similar authenticating dream-vision involving a *substantia quasi talentum auri liquentis*.

26. *Super Mt.* 12 (379.618–21): . . . donec tandem ultima *infusio* veluti quoddam magnum flumen inundans, hoc mihi dabat intelligi et hoc sentire me fecit, quod totum animae vel cordis exceptorium plenum esset et plus capere non posset.

27. The same vision is repeated, word for word, in the *De glorificatione Trinitatis* 2.18, thus showing how central it was in Rupert's experience.

28. *Super Mt.* 12 (383.758–62): Quod cum festinus introissem, apprehendi *quem diligit anima mea,* tenui eum, amplexatus sum eum, diutius exosculatus sum eum. Sensi enim gratanter hunc gestum dilectionis admitteret, cum inter osculandum suum ipse os aperiret, ut profundius oscularer. The passage goes on to embellish the event through a lengthy quotation of Song 8:1–2. In the *Commentum in Cantica Canticorum,* exegeting Song 5:4 (CCCM 26:110–11), Rupert details two experiences of erotic encounter with the Divine Bridegroom given to an *adulescentula,* which can be taken as autobiographical (the *anima=adulescentula*). The first of these is an independent experience of the divine touch, the second appears to be another rendition of the experience recounted here.

29. *Super Mr.* 12 (383.781–384.797). Here Rupert also cites two standard biblical texts for mystical experience: 1 Corinthians 6:17 and Psalm 35:9. Like Bernard of Clairvaux and others, Rupert insisted that this personal erotic experience of the Word is only possible because the soul is contained in the church, the true Bride of the Word: . . . et introeam *ad altare Dei,* ad altare caelestis sanctuarii, et ibi contingat animae meae quod verus amor dicit: *Osculetur me osculo oris sui* (Song 1:1), et ipse sponsus immortalis in illo contineat me corpore sponsae suae Ecclesiae, cui amore aeterno et sempiternis copulabitur nuptiis (385.832–36).

30. Ibid. 384.805–7): . . . ego autem extunc *os meum aperui,* et cessare quin scriberem nequaquam potui, et usque nunc, etiam si velim, tacere non possum. The relation between the mystical visions and Rupert's writing is discussed in four places in *Super Mt.* 12: (1) 372.377–373.385; (2) 379.637–380.365; (3) 384.805–07; and (4) 385.839–386.876.

31. *Comm. in Apoc.,* prol. (PL 169:825–26): Nondum quidem dum Scripturas legimus aut intelligimus, facie ad faciem Dominum videmus; verumtamen ipsa Dei visio, quae quandoque perficienda est, hic jam per Scripturas inchoatur.

32. Helpful comments on this can be found in Van Engen, *Rupert of Deutz,* pp. 67–72.

33. A hint in Rupert's last finished work, the *De Incendio* 15, seems to indicate that he continued to enjoy mystical experiences throughout his life. See Herbert Grundmann, "Der Brand von Deutz 1128 in der Darstellung Abt Ruperts von Deutz: Interpretation und Text-Ausgabe," *Deutsches Archiv fr Erforschung des Mittelalters* 22 (1966): 459–60.

34. Peter Dronke, *Women Writers of the Middle Ages* (Cambridge: Cambridge University Press, 1984), p. 200 (see also pp. 171–72). For some other defenses of Hildegard as mystic, see David Baumgardt, "The Concept of Mysticism: Analysis of a Letter written by Hildegard of Bingen to Guibert of Gembloux," *Review of Religion* 12 (1948): 277–86; Christel Meier, "*Virtus* und *operatio* als Kernbegriffe einer Konzeption der Mystik bei Hildegard von Bingen," *Grundfragen Christlicher Mystik*, ed. Margot Schmidt and Dieter R. Baur (Stuttgart-Bad Cannstaat: frommann-holzboog, 1987), pp. 73–101; and Andrew Weeks, *German Mysticism from Hildegard of Bingen to Ludwig Wittengenstein: A Literary and Intellectual History* (Albany: SUNY Press, 1993), chap. 2.

35. Caroline Bynum, "Preface," in *Hildegard of Bingen: Scivias*, trans. Mother Columba Hart and Jane Bishop, introduced by Barbara Newman (Mahwah, NJ: Paulist Press, 1990), pp. 2–3. Similar views are expressed by Barbara Newman, "Hildegard of Bingen: Visions and Validation," *Church History* 54 (1985): 164–68; and Sabina Flanagan, *Hildegard of Bingen, 1098-1179: A Visionary Life* (London and New York: Routledge, 1989), p. 209.

36. This is the reason why Kurt Ruh in his *Geschichte der abendländische Mystik: Band I, Die Grundlegung durch die Kirchenväter und die Mönohstheologie des 12. Jahrhunderts* (Munich: Beck, 1990), pp. 14–15, excludes her from his account.

37. See Newman, "Visions and Validation," pp. 163–75, which contains a comparison of Hildegard with Rupert and Elisabeth of Schönau. See also Newman's *Sister of Wisdom. St. Hildegard's Theology of the Feminine* (Berkeley and Los Angeles: University of California Press, 1987), pp. 34–41.

38. For discussions of Hildegard's visions in recent literature, see Dronke, *Women Writers*, pp. 144–71; Newman, "Hildegard of Bingen: Vision and Validation," pp. 163–75; and Flanagan, *Hildegard of Bingen*, chap. 10.

39. This may be because of Hildegard's somewhat negative attitude toward the trustworthiness of dreams, especially due to possible demonic influence. See Flanagan, *Hildegard of Bingen*, pp. 196–97.

40. This is a reminiscence of Eph 3:18: *ut possitis conprehendere cum omnibus sanctis quae sit latitudo et longitudo et sublimitas et profundum*, a text traditionally ascribed to divine love and by extension the divine nature itself.

41. Barbara Newman has argued ("Visions and Validation," p. 164) that the word *umbra* here might be better translated "reflection" than "shadow."

42. I have used the translation of Peter Dronke from *Women Writers*, pp. 168–69, which is based on his own edition of the letter (ibid., pp. 252–53): Ab infantia autem mea, ossibus et nervis et venis meis nundum confortatis, visionem hanc in anima mea usque ad praesens tempus semper video, cum iam plusquam septuaginta annorum sim. Spiritus vero meus, prout deus vult, in hac visione sursum in altitudinem firmamenti et in vicissitudinem diversi aeris ascendit, atque inter diversos populos se dilatat, quamvis in longinquis regionibus et locis a me remoti sint; et quoniam hec tali modo video, idcirco etiam secundum vicissitudinem nubium et aliarum creaturarum ea conspicio. Ista autem nec corporeis auribus audio, nec cogitationibus cordis mei, nec ulla collatione sensuum meorum quinque percipio, sed tantum in anima mea, apertis exterioribus oculis, ita ut numquam in eis defectum exstasis paciar, sed vigilanter die ac nocte video. Et assidue infirmitatibus constringor, et gravibus doloribus implicata sum, adeo ut mortem inferre minentur, sed deus usque adhuc me sustentavit.

Lumen igitur quod video locale non est, sed nube que solem portat multo et multo lucidius, nec altitudinem, nec longitudinem nec latitudinem, in eo considerare valeo, illudque umbra viventis luminis michi nominatur; atque ut sol, luna et stelle in aqua apparent, ita scripture, sermones, virtutes, et quedam opera hominum formata in illo michi resplendent.

. . . Et ea qua scribo, illa invisione video et audio, nec alia verba pono quam illa que audio . . . . Atque verba que in visione ista video et audio non sunt sicut verba que ab ore hominis sonant, sed sicut flamma choruscans, et ut nubes in aere puro mota. . . .

Et in eodem lumine aliam lucem, que lux vivens michi nominata est, interdum et non frequenter aspicio, et quando et quomodo illam videam proferre non valeo, atque interim dum illam intueor, omnis tristicia et omnis angustia a me aufertur, ita ut tunc mores simplicis puelle, et non vetule mulieris, habeam.

43. See Dronke, *Women Writers,* p. 146.

44. For a more complete account, the letter to Guibert would need to be compared to the autobiographical passages found in Hildegard's *Vita.* Dronke, *Women Mystics,* pp. 144–71, studies these passages and provides an improved edition of them on pp. 231–41.

45. Hildegard's three major works, the *Scivias* (ca. 1141–51), the *Liber vitae meritorum* (ca. 1158–63) and the *Liber divinorum operum* (ca. 1163–73), may be said to consitute a trilogy dealing respectively with creation and redemption, Christian morality, and divine *caritas* as the source of cosmology and restoration. The abbesses's thought is a variation on traditional monastic theology in the sense that it is fundamentally exegetical in character. But rather than taking the biblical text as the essential basis for the interpretation of the mysteries of salvation, she uses the visions that God has given her–claiming for them an authority equal to that of scripture!

46. The identification was first made by Charles Singer, "The Scientific Views and Visions of Saint Hildegard," in *Studies in the History and Method of Science* (Oxford: Oxford University Press, 1917), 1:1–55. The most recent discussion is in Flanagan, *Hildegard of Bingen,* pp. 199–209.

47. See Hildegard of Bingen, *Scivias,* ed. Adelgundis Führkotter (CCCM 43–43A) 43:3–4. A parallel claim for charismatic understanding of the depths of scripture is found in a passage in *Vita* 2.17 (see Dronke, *Women Writers,* p. 232).

48. Again, I use Dronke's translation (*Women Writers,* p. 162), based on his edition of these autobiographical texts: Subsequenti demum tempore mysticam et mirificam visionem vidi, ita quod omnia viscera mea concussa sunt, et sensualitas corporis mei extincta est, quoniam sciencia mea in alium modum conversa est, quasi me nescirem. Et de dei inspiratione in scienciam anime mee quasi gutte suavis pluvie spargebantur, quia et spiritus sanctus Iohannem ewangelistam imbuit, cum de pectore Iesu profundissimam revelationem suxit . . . (p. 236).

49. Previous work in English on Elisabeth, never extensive, has been superseded by Anne L. Clark, *Elisabeth of Schönau: A Twelfth-Century Visionary* (Philadelphia: University of Pennsylvania Press, 1992).

50. *Annales Palidenses* in MGH.SS. 16:90: His etiam diebus in sexu fragili signa potentie sue Deus ostendit, in duabus ancillis suis, Hildegarde videlicet in monte Roperti iuxta Pinguiam, et Elisabeth in Schonaugia, quas spiritu prophetie replevit, et multa eis genera visionum que scripte habentur per euangelium revelavit.

51. Hildegard, *Ep.* 45 (PL 197:217D–18A): . . . aliquantulum velut parvus sonus tubae a vivente luminis.

52. The six books consist of three books of visions in chronological order entitled *Libri visionum*; a book of visions of moral exhortation, entitled *Liber viarum Dei*; revelations about the imaginary martyr St. Ursula and her eleven thousand companions, the *Revelatio de sacro exercitu virginum Coloniensium*; and a series of visions about the resurrection of the Virgin Mary, the *Visio de resurrectione beate virginis Mariae.* In addition, Ekbert wrote an account of Elisabeth's death, *De obitu Elisabeth.*

53. A point emphasized by Clark; see *Elisabeth of Schönau,* pp. 104–6.

54. This is not to say that Elisabeth's accounts are totally lacking in visions of God and the God-Man, including one interesting showing of the humanity of Christ in the form of a woman. See Gertrud Jaron Lewis, "Christus als Frau: Eine Vision Elisabeths von Schönau," *Jahrbuch für Internationale Germanistik* 15 (1983): 70–80. Even when she enjoys a vision of Christ crucified in heaven, the emphasis is on coming divine judgment: Vidi autem in illo excessu meo celos apertos, et dominum Jesum cum infinitis milibus sanctorum. . . . Et non erat ei species neque decor, sed tanquam recenter crucifixus fuisset, sic miserandus apparuit. . . . Clamabat voce magna ac nimium terribili dicens: Talia propter te sustinui, tu vero, quid pro me sustinuisti? See F. W. E. Roth, ed., *Die Visionen der hl. Elisabeth und die Aebte Ekbert und Emeche von Schönau* (Brünn: Verlag der Studien aus dem Benedictiner-und Cistercienser-Orden, 1884), p. 21.

55. An extensive scholarly literature devoted to Joachim has been produced in the twentieth century. For an introduction, see my book, *The Calabrian Abbot.*

56. *Expositio in Apocalypsim* (Venice, 1527. Reprint Frankfort: Minerva, 1964), f. 39rv: . . . factum est verso anni circulo diem adesse paschalem, mihique circa horam matutinam excitato a somno aliquid in libro isto meditanti occurere. . . . Circa medium (ut opinor) noctis silentium et horam qua leo noster de tribu Iuda resurrexisse extimatur a mortuis, subito mihi meditanti aliquid quadam mentis oculis intelligentie claritate percepta de plenitudine libri huius et tota veteris ac novi testamenti concordia. Revelatio facta est, et nec sic recordatus sum suprascripti capituli. . . .

57. *Expos.* f.3b: Est enim clavis veterum: notitia futurorum: signatorum apertio: detectio secretorum. For Joachim's understanding of *intellectus spiritualis,* see *The Calabrian Abbot,* chap. 4.

58. On Joachim the symbolist, see *The Calabrian Abbot,* chap. 3.

59. *Psalterium decem chordarum* (Venice, 1527. Reprint Frankfort: Minerva, 1964), f. 227rv: Interea cum ingrederer oratorium et adorarem omnipotentem Deum coram sancto altari, accidit in me velut hesitatio quedam de fide Trinitatis. . . . Quod cum accideret oravi valde, et conterritus vehementer compulsus sum invocare Spiritum Sanctum cuius sacra solemnitas praesens erat ut ipse mihi dignaretur ostendere sacrum mysterium Trinitatis. . . . Hec dicens cepi psallere ut ad propositum numerum pervenirem. Nec mora occurrit animo modo forma Psalterii decachordi et in ipsa tam lucidum et apertum sacre mysterium Trinitatis ut protinus compellerer clamare: Quis Deus magnus sicut Deus noster?

60. Joachim of Fiore, *Enchiridion super Apocalypsim,* ed. Edward K. Burger (Toronto: Pontifical Institute of Mediaeval Studies, 1986), p. 48: Restat ergo ut sacramentum istud taliter completum esse dicamus, ut tamen in die Paschae quo datum est primo apostolis munus illud, tempus tertii status accipiamus in quo accepturi sumus plenius ad contemplandum, quod ad bene operandum hactenus accepisse videmur, gratia nobis data pro gratia. Quod autem in die Pentecostes consummatum est in apostolis, post novissimum diem saeculi consummandum est in omnibus sanctis. One merit of this passage is to show that although Joachim's conception of the coming *status* is novel, he still seeks to relate it to the experience of the apostles and the ongoing work of both Christ and the Spirit.

61. *Expos.,* f. 139r: In primo erudiuntur parvuli. In secundo instituuntur adolescentes. In tertio inebriantur amici.

62. The most noted portrayal of the coming *status* is to be found in the *figura* entitled *Dispositio novi ordinis pertinens ad tertium statum ad instar superne Jerusalem* found in the *Liber figurarum.* There is a translation and illustration of this in B. McGinn, *Apocalyptic Spirituality* (New York: Paulist Press, 1979), pp. 142–48. In addition, many scattered remarks from his writings, especially from the *Expositio,* would have to be taken into account to present a complete picture.

63. Ernesto Buonaiuti, "Il misticismo di Gioacchino da Fiore," *Ricerche religiose* 5 (1929): 410: Se il misticismo, l'esperienza cioè dell'Assoluto e dell'Eterno basata sull'intuizione e sul sentimento, anzichè sul ragionamento e sul raggiungimento dialettico, se polarizza fra due attitudini profundamente diverse; se v'è cioè, un misticismo solitario, che rifuggendo da ogni contatto con il mondo e con gli uomini, celebra nel raccoglimento dello spirito individuale e il suo intimo connobio col divino, e v'è un misticismo associato che trova unicamente il divino nella partecipazione fraterna alle medesime rivelazioni carismatiche e quindi alle medesime realtà rivelate, il misticismo di Gioacchino da Fiore, come quella della letteratura profetica e di quella neotestamentaria, appartiene al secondo tipo. A more complete discussion of how Buonaiuti understood this *misticismo associato* would need to go into his central conception of the *vita associata*, on which see William Murphy, *Vita Associata and Religious Experience in the Writings of Ernesto Buonaiuti* (dissertation, Gregorian University, Rome, 1974).

64. My consideration of the nature of Joachim's mysticism has profited from the unpublished paper of Kevin L. Hughes, "Apocalyptic Mysticism: A Study of Joachim of Fiore, St. Bonaventure and Peter Olivi," which explores the usefulness of the category "social apocalyptic mysticism" to describe the three authors.

65. See *Foundations of Mysticism*, chap. 1.

66. Ibid., p. 70.

67. See especially Marjorie E. Reeves, *Prophecy in the Later Middle Ages: A Study in Joachimism* (Oxford: Clarendon Press, 1969), as well as the papers in *Il profetismo gioachimita tra Quattrocento e Cinquecento*, ed. Gian Luca Potestà (Genoa: Marietti, 1991).

68. For a brief introduction, see M. D. Knowles, "Peter the Venerable," *Bulletin of the John Rylands Library* 39 (1956): 132–45. On Peter's spirituality, the major study remains that of Jean Leclercq, *Pierre le Vénérable* (Abbaye S. Wandrille: Éditions de Fontenelle, 1946).

69. Much has been written about this famous dispute. A still useful overview can be found in David Knowles, "Cistercians and Cluniacs: The Controversy between St. Bernard and Peter the Venerable," in *The Historian and Character* (Cambridge:Cambridge University Press, 1963), pp. 50–75. See also A. H. Bredero, "The Controversy between Peter the Venerable and Saint Bernard of Clairvaux," in *Petrus Venerabilis 1156–1956. Studies and Texts commemorating the Eighth Centenary of his Death*, ed. Giles Constable and James Kritzeck, Studia Anselmiana 40 (Rome: Herder, 1956), pp. 53–71.

70. Knowles has provided a characteristically insightful summation of the man: "Humane, wise, charitable, of the type familiar in later French history—the family of François de Sales, of Fénelon, of Blosius—the aristocrat who is also a spiritual father, a man of wide education, of statesmanlike ability and of a deep piety that borders on sanctity." ("Peter the Venerable," p. 145).

71. *Letter* 20 in *The Letters of Peter the Venerable*, edited, with an introduction and notes by Giles Constable, 2 vols. (Cambridge MA: Harvard University Press, 1967), 1:27–41. On this letter, see Jean Leclercq, "Pierre le Vénérable et l'érémetisme clunisien," in *Petrus Venerabilis*, pp. 99–120, as well as *Pierre le Vénérable*, pp. 94–97, 319–21. Peter also discusses the eremitical life in *Letter* 58 sent to Peter of Poitiers (ed. Constable, 1:179–89).

72. Peter uses the famous encounter of Elijah with God in the desert recounted in 3 Kgs 19:11–14 in this initial description of the hermit's experience of God's presence: Haec Heliae quondam Ahab et Iezebel per deserta fugienti latibulum praebuit, ubi ille constitutus vocem dei sibi familiariter loquentis audivit, ubi non in spiritu, non in commotione, non in igne, sed in sibilo aurae tenuis, hoc est in suptili et paucis percaeptibili spiritus sui inspiratione hominibus eum adesse cognovit (ed. Constable, 1:29).

73. Peter tells Gilbert: Haec in Christo tuo cuius crucem portas, cuius sepulchrum inhabitas, cuius in te resurrectionem expectas specialiter effulserunt . . . (ed. Constable 1:34, cf. 41). This recalls his *Sermo* 2 "In Laudem Sepulchri Domini" (PL 189:973–92), especially where he

emphasizes, using the language of the Song of Songs, how the Christian must become the sepulcher in which Christ is lovingly buried (980B–81C). This sermon is one of the finest examples of Peter's passion-centered piety.

74. *Letter* 22 (ed. Constable, 1:37): . . . hac infulget mentibus lumen invisibile, hac cordis oculus carnali adhuc crassitudine obvelatus caelestia rimatur, hac ipsum increatum et creantem omnia spiritum humanus prout homini licet spiritus contemplatur.

75. Ibid. (ed. Constable, 1:41): Hac postquam imbutus fueris, erit tibi cella tua toto mundo latior; . . . nec quicquam te gravare poterit, quem spes amorque aeternorum velut geminis alis ad caelestia sublevabit.

76. See Leclercq, "Pierre le Vénérable et l'érémetisme," pp. 119–20.

77. Jean Leclercq, *La spiritualité de Pierre de Celle (1115–1183)* (Paris: Vrin, 1946), esp. pp. 68–69 and 119 on Peter as mystic. See also Gérard de Martel, "Pierre de Celle," DS 12:1525–32; and in English, *Peter of Celle: Selected Works*, trans. Hugh Feiss, OSB (Kalamazoo, MI: Cistercian Publications, 1987).

78. Peter's letters, sermons, and two of his most important exegetical works, the *De panibus* and the *Mosaici tabernaculi mystica et moralis expositio* are found in PL 202:405–1084, as is his noted *De disciplina claustrali* (1097–1146), a newer edition of which appears in SC 240. The treatises *De puritate*, *De conscientia*, and *De afflictione et lectione* were edited by Leclercq, *Pierre de Celle*, pp. 174–239.

79. Johan Huizinga's classic 1919 work *Hersttij der Middeleeuwen* (*The Harvest of the Middle Ages*) was translated into English in 1924 under the title *The Waning of the Middle Ages*.

80. On this issue, see Leclercq, *Pierre de Celle*, pp. 47–48.

81. Ibid, chap. 3, "La poésie biblique."

82. Ibid., p. 63: Son but n'est pas d'expliquer l'Écriture Sainte, mais d'exprimer l'union de son âme avec Dieu à propos de l'Écriture Sainte: la Bible lui fournit tout son vocabulaire.

83. The contrast between this life and the life to come, often expressed in terms of the Latin pair *hic/ibi* was widely used by monastic writers. For an introduction, see François Chatillon, "Hic, Ibi, Interim," *Mélanges Marcel Viller* (Paris: Beauchesne, 1949), pp. 194–99. For an example in Peter, see *Ep.* 41 (PL 202:458AB).

84. Peter likes the language of *rapere/raptus*, sometimes dwelling on the violence it conveys. E.g., *Sermo* 22 (708AB): Fac de nobis rapinam, ut charitate violentissima, nos a nobis exuas, et eodem loro constrictos, ad te pertrahas. . . .

85. Peter of Celle, *De puritate* (ed. Leclercq, 180.7–14): Unus et aeternus sit status contemplationis quo aeternitati aeterni Dei conformemur et amore inexplebili constabiliamur. Sic amplius atque amplius purificatur anima quo vicinius et vehementius figitur in visione divina, nec accedit nisi purificata, nec vacat nisi clarificata, nec videt nisi deificata. Hac puritate nihil in creaturis purius, ubi cor tam castum ad Deum admittitur, ubi conscientia tam pura in Deum rapitur, ubi anima tam bona usque ad eructationem Deo saginatur.

86. Peter of Celle, *De disciplina claustrali* 7 (PL 202:1112C): Disciplina claustralis est crux Christi, de qua non deponitur, nisi mortuus. The work is built upon the comparison of four forms of *disciplina*–philosophical, Jewish, Christian, and claustral.

87. *De disciplina claustrali* 25 (PL 202:1136D–37A): Eucharistia siquidem locum tenet in corpore Ecclesiae, quem humanum cor in homine.

88. *Liber de panibus* (PL 202:927–1046). Especially important are chaps. 2 and 27 (935–38 and 1044–46).

89. *De disciplina claustrali* 15 (1118D–19C).

90. On the restoration of the *imago* according to Christ, see, especially *De conscientia* 49 (ed. Leclercq, 210) and the discussion in Leclercq, 137–38. The abbot's deeply personal devotion to Jesus is expressed in many places, e.g., *Sermo* 33 (735D–38C), *De panibus* 7 and 19 (965BC and 1010D), and *De tabernaculo* 1 (1061A).

91. *De puritate* 2 (ed. Leclercq, 191.37–192.15): Hic ille singularis radius est de quo in Canticis dicitur: *Vulnerasti cor meum, soror mea, sponsa, vulnerasti cor meum in uno oculorum tuorum et in uno crine colli tui,* quasi diceret: Tam penetrabili acie puritatis oculus ille tuae contemplationis in me irreverberatus figitur, ut perforata amoris penetralia principalem cordis contingat venam et influere faciat ad medullam. . . . Nisi tam purus esset oculus, nullus me tangeret *in uno crine colli tui* affectus et aspectus. On Peter's use of the erotic language of the Song, see Leclercq, pp. 133–35.

92. Passages such as *De conscientia* 53 (ed. Leclercq, 211–22) seem to restrict true union with God to heaven (1 Cor 6:17 is cited here).

93. For a survey, see Leclercq, *Pierre de Celle,* pp. 82–90, 105–7, and the texts listed there. On action and contemplation, see the "Introduction," in *Peter of Celle. Selected Works,* pp. 29–31.

94. *De puritate* 1 (ed. Leclercq, 178.28–29): Pura visio est ubi purum est quod videtur et purum quo videtur. See the whole discussion on pp. 178–80.

95. Ibid. (180.21–22): Mira conversione alternantur in praesenti sive futuro humanae visiones seu contemplationes, ordine utique, non officio. The whole discussion goes from 180.21 to 182.32.

96. Ibid., (174.23–26): Immo verius fateor quia colliquescit in solidum amoris Dei et consolidatur in liquidum divinitatis. Totum enim est et liquidum et solidum in Deo: liquidum revera quia nos admittit ad *viscera misericordiae,* solidum quia nos conservat in aeternitate. . . .

97. Ibid. (175–76). Peter's use of the left and right arms of the Bridegroom in this discussion is typical; this passage from the Song occurs often in his works in analogous connections; e.g., *Sermo* 33 (736C–38B). The abbot's fascination with liquid images may provide a clue to his frequent appeal to the ancient theme of *vinum/sobria ebrietas,* on which see Leclercq, *Pierre de Celle,* pp. 106–7.

98. *Liber de panibus* 2 (935B): Totum diligendo, totum sumis sed non consumis. Ut enim diligendo non vastatur dilectio, sic quando a nobis sumitur amando, nequaquam finitur ille qui est vera dilectio. See the entire passage 935A–36B.

99. *De puritate* 1 (ed. Leclercq, 178.11–12): Apprehendis igitur, sed non comprehendis; apprehendo satiaris, non comprehendendo fastidium fugis. See the whole passage on 178.1–24.

100. See the discussion in *Foundations of Mysticism,* pp. 216–7.

101. Exceptions can be found in the ninth-century treatise of Paschasius Radbertus entitled *Cogitis me,* which circulated pseudonymously as *Ep.* 9 of Jerome, as well as in some of the poems using Song of Songs imagery, such as Venantius Fortunatus's "De Virginitate" (chapter 1, p. 31) and perhaps the eleventh-century sequence "Virgines Caste" (chapter 4, pp. 145–46). The *Cogitis me,* written to the nuns Theodrada and Irma, is primarily a Mariological reading of the Song in defense of the assumption, but is not lacking in personal application to the life of the nuns. See E. Ann Matter, *The Voice of My Beloved: The Song of Songs in Western Medieval Christianity* (Philadelphia: University of Pennsylvania Press, 1990), pp. 152–55.

102. The work makes use of the eleventh-century German version of Williram of Eberberg, which in turn depended on Haimo of Auxerre's ecclesiological reading. In addition, there were at least two twelfth-century Old French verse paraphrases. One is a brief imitation only some ninety-three lines long. The other, over 3,500 lines, is both a translation and a mystical commentary. This text, found in MS. 173 of the Municipal Library of Le Mans, has been ascribed to Landri of Waben between 1176 and 1181 (see, e.g., Ohly, *Hoheliedstudien,* pp. 280–302). The latest edition, that of Cedric E. Pickford, *The Song of Songs: A Twelfth-Century French Version* (London: Oxford University Press, 1974), considers this at best a hypothesis (pp. xxi, xxiv–xxv).

103. The currently available edition is that of Hermann Menhardt, *Das St. Trudperter Hohe Lied*, 2 vols. (Halle: Niemeyer, 1934). A new critical edition has been promised by Friedrich Ohly, who discusses the title in his "Eine Lehre der liebenden Gotteserkenntnis: Zum Titel des St. Trudperter Hohenlieds," *Zeitschrift für deutsches Altertum und deutsche Literatur* 121 (1992): 399–404. There is little in English on this important text, but see the discussion in Matter, *The Voice of My Beloved*, pp. 180–81.

104. The work bears comparison to the popular text known as the *Speculum virginum* composed about 1140 and surviving in some twenty-nine Latin manuscripts and twenty six Middle Netherlandish ones because of its later popularity with the adherents of the *devotio moderna*. The Latin original, sometimes attributed to Conrad of Hirsau (ca. 1070–1150), has recently been edited by Jutta Seyfarth, *Speculum Virginum* (CCCM 5, 1990). This work, however, is not really an exegesis of the Song of Songs (see Seyfarth, "Einleitung," in CCCM 5:11* and 28*) and is more parenetic and ascetic than properly mystical. See Irene Berkenbusch, "Mystik und Askese. 'Sankt Trudperter Hohes Lied' und 'Speculum Virginum' im Vergleich," in *"Minnichlichiu gotes erkennusse": Studien zur frühen abendländischen Mystiktradition. Heidelberger Mystiksymposium vom 16. Januar 1989* (Stuttgart-Bad Cannstatt: froomann-holzboog, 1990), pp. 43–60. For more on the *Speculum Virginum*, much studied by art historians because of its combination of texts and images (*mistica pictura*, CCCM 5:40.1000), see also Matthäus Bernards, *Speculum Virginum: Geistigkeit und Seelenleben der Frau im Hochmittelalter* (Cologne: Böhlau, 1955).

105. See Friedrich Ohly, "Der Prolog des St. Trudperter Hohenliedes," *Zeitschrift für deutches Altertum und deutsche Literatur* 84 (1953): 198–232. On the relation to Bernard, see Josefine Runte, "Die Gottesliebe im St. Trudperter Hohen Lied und Bernhard von Clairvaux," *Cîteaux* 8 (1957): 27–41.

106. Among the recent studies of the mysticism of the text, see Urban Küsters, *Der verschlossene Garten: Volksprachliche Hohelied-Auslegung und monastische Lebensform im 12. Jahrhundert* (Düsseldorf: Droste, 1985); Hans-Jörg Spitz, "'Speigel der Bräute Gottes': Das Modell der vita activa und vita contemplativa als struktierendes Prinzip im St. Trudperter Hohen Lied," in *Abendländische Mystik im Mittelalter. Symposium Kloster Engelberg 1984*, ed. Kurt Ruh (Stuttgart: Metzler, 1986), pp. 481–93; Roswitha Wisniewski, "Die unio mystica im 'St. Trudperter Hohen Lied'," in *"Minnichlichiu gotes erkennusse*," pp. 28–42; and especially Regine Hummel, *Mystische Modelle im 12. Jahrhundert. 'St. Trudperter Hoheslied', Bernhard von Clairvaux, Wilhelm von St. Thierry* (Göppingen: Kümmerle, 1989). A recent general study is by Hildegard Elisabeth Keller, *Wort und Fleisch. Korperallegorien, mystische Spiritualität und Dichtung des St. Trudperter Hoheliedes im Horizont der Inkarnation* (Bern: Peter Lang, 1993).

107. Ed. Menhardt 145.6–17 [all references will be by section and line of this edition]: Nû uerne[m]ent: diz bouch uiench ane mit ainir chunichlicken mandunge. iz endet sich mit aineme ellentlichen âmere. iz uiench ane mit ainime chunichlichen sange. nû gêt ez ûz mit inniklicheme wainenne. iz uiench ane mit ainime g[o]tlichen chosse. nû scaident siu sich mit ainer durnahtiger minne. wan iz ist ain lêre der minnichlichen gotes erkennusse. An disime bouche sulin die prûte des almahtigen gotis ir spiegel haben unde sulim bisihticlîche ware tun ir selbir antlutes unde ir nâhisten, wie siu geuallen ir gemahelen. On the Epilogue, see the discussion in Hummel, *Mystische Modelle*, pp. 68–70. The translations used here are my own, but I wish to acknowledge the assistance of my colleague Kenneth Northcott, who made helpful suggestions and saved me from several misreadings.

108. Ed. 145.24–27: sô chulet an dir diu hitze der unchûske. sô haizzet allir êrist diu minne des g[o]tes gaistes hine ze deme rehten charle. dc [=daz] ist dîn scephâre dîn irlôsâre dîn minnâre.

109. A full study of the sources of this work is still needed. While traditional Latin authors are certainly central, especially Augustine, Gregory, and Bernard, other influences cannot be

excluded (e.g., Dionysian ones on the basis of 18.8–11). In the absence of any convincing analysis of the structure of the whole (I am not persuaded by H.-J. Spitz's argument that the relation of the active and contemplative lives is *the* organizing principle [see "Spiegel der Bräute Gottes," pp. 486–91]), it is best to treat the poem as another example of twelfth-century commentaries on the Song of Songs in which the images of the book of love allow different themes to be repeated in a circular or spiral fashion.

110. See *Foundations of Mysticism*, pp. 243–48.

111. Ed. 8.8–10: er schuoph uns zi sîneme bilde vnde zi sîner gelîchnuschede dc unsir sêle sîn insigele wêre. Cf. 137.5, which says: diz sigilin dc ist diu gotes erchennus[s]e.

112. For the use of the Latin terms, see e.g., 1.17–18 and 5.13–20.

113. E.g., 18.26–30: dâ wirt si allein mit g[o]te. dc [ist diu] heilige guote mit uns[er]eme willin. dc ist der hôheste wistuom mit unserre uirnunste. dc ist der forhtlike gewalt mit unserre gehukte. disiu mandunge ist diu hôheste. Cf. 2.19–21, 13.4–12, 97.7–17, 105.14–22, 110.6–13, 117.28–118.22, 130.4–6, and 132.6–14. Other important texts on the role of the Trinity include 52.24–54.6, 96.27–99.11, and 130.17–132.20. For discussions of the trinitarian aspect of the mysticism of the text, see Wisniewski, "Die unio mystica," pp. 29–37; Berkenbusch, "Mystik und Askese," pp. 48–50; and Hummel, *Mystische Modelle*, pp. 33–50.

114. The Holy Spirit is also spoken of as a "mother" in the comment on Song 8:3 (see 131.15–23).

115. Ed. 29.11–15 distinguishes three kinds of love in exegeting Song 2:4, the famous *ordinatio caritatis* verse. Human effort teaches *sinniclichen minne*, and *gewizzenliche minne* is learned from scripture, but *uirnunstlichu minne* is taught only by the Holy Spirit. This final type of love, which can also be called *mînere bechennusse* (see 136.25–26), is quite close to the interpenetration of love and knowledge that William of St. Thierry expressed through the terms *amor illuminatus* and *intellectus amoris* (see chapter 6, pp. 252–60), though direct influence from the Cistercian author is not evident.

116. See Ohly, "Der Prolog," as well as the discussions in Hummel, *Mystische Modelle*, pp. 21–30; and Berkenbusch, "Mystik und Askese," pp. 53–9.

117. Ed. 1.1–3: Wir wellen kôsen uon deme oberôsten liebe, der meisten gnâde, der râwecklikesten suozi. dc ist der heilige geist.

118. On the understanding of the active and contemplative lives in the text, see Spitz, "'Spiegel der Bräute Gottes,'" as well as Küsters, *Der verschlossene Garten*, pp. 313–19.

119. Ed. 4.11–12: dô wir wrdin gischaffin unde giuielin, dô makete er uns widere. alsame duot er hiute.

120. Hummel puts it well: "Der Tugendweg und das Wirken des Hl. Geist sind wesentliche Metaphernsysteme für den mystischen Prozess" (*Mystische Modelle*, p. 95). The gifts are also discussed in the Epilogue (145.28–147.25).

121. Ed. 147.28–32: swer iz ernestlîche wirbe[t], nehât er ouch niht uile dir[r]e tugende, er haizzet ie doch uon sîneme guoten willen unde uon sîneme erneste ain brût des almahtigen gotes.

122. Ed. 30.22–29: suenne ich in[t]slâfe, sô wîset er mîne sêle in troumes wîs an die faizten weiden des heiligin geistes unde mîne inneren sinne in den schîm des himilskin wîstuomes. daz ist diu hôheste wunne die man in den ellenden gehabin mach. wan diz aber daz uinstere unde daz ellende lant ist, sô ist disiv wunne mêre ein troum denne ein wârheit. For another reference to a dream experience, see 35.10–24. The comment on the *amplexus* of Sg 8:3 is found in 130.17–132.20.

123. Ed. 128.29–33: . . . sô der lîp unde diu sêle mandunge habent in der suozze des hailigen gaistes, sô hât die sêle got in sich gezogen sô dc siu niemmer gescaiden newerdent ainweder mit minne odir mit [v]orhte.

124. See, e.g., 31.7–32.12, 79.32–80.25, and 127.11–26.

125. See, e.g., 92.12–16 and 143.31–144.19. For a discussion, see Hummel, *Mystische Modelle*, pp. 81–83.

126. Ed. 72.20–32: sô ist noch ein andir sêle, diu zerfliuzzet mit der gotis minne. daz ist sô der hailige geist entlûtet unde schînet mit sîner hitzze in alle unsere sinne, . . . ô wi[e] wol [in] wart, die alsô zerfliezzent! wa[r] fliezzent siu? hine widere an sîne gotehait, dannan siu uon [ê]rst geschaffen wurden, daz wir sîn bilde an unseren sêlen habeten, [die wîle] sich niet uirst[ê]n mugin in disime lîbe durnachteclîche die zor[ft]ele under die herschaft sîner gotehaite. For another important text on flowing back into God, see, e.g., 136.19–29, which uses the seal-and-wax motif. On this motif, see Berkenbusch, "Mystik und Askese," pp. 47–50.

127. For general accounts of the foundation and early stages of the Carthusians, see Yves Gourdel, "Chartreux," in DS 2:705–76; Bernard Bligny, "L'Érémitisme et les Chartreux," in *L'eremitismo in Occidente nei secoli XI e XII: Atti della seconda Settimana internazionale di Studio Mendola, 30 agosto–6 settembre 1962* (Milan: Società editrice vite e pensiero, 1965), pp. 248–70; J. Dubois, "Certosini" in DIP 2:782–821; and Gordon Mursell, *The Theology of the Carthusian Life in the Writings of St. Bruno and Guigo I*, Analecta Cartusiana 127 (Salzburg: Universität Salzburg, 1988).

128. The Carthusian monks live independently in cells that function as small hermitages, sharing only minimal liturgical actions and community meetings.

129. The account of this vow is found in Bruno's *Epistula ad Radulphum* 13 in *Lettres des premiers Chartreux* (SC 88): 74–76.

130. The letter, one of two that Bruno left, is edited in SC 88:66–80. See the discussion by "Un Chartreux" in the Introduction (pp. 28–34 and 42–64), as well as Bruna Veneroni, "S. Bruno e il suo elogio della vita contemplativa: Spunti et motivi classici," *Benedictina* 16 (1969): 196–212.

131. This phrase (*tam redire in se licet quamlibet et habitare secum*) is based on Gregory the Great's account of Benedict's eremitic retreat at Subiaco in *Dialogi* 2.3 (see chapter 2, p. 78).

132. *Ep.* 1.6 (SC 88:70): Hic namque viris strenuis tam redire in se licet quamlibet et habitare secum, virtutumque germina instanter excolere atque de paradisi feliciter fructibus vesci. Hic oculus ille conquiritur, cujus sereno intuitu vulneratur sponsus amore, quo mundo et puro conspicitur Deus. Hic otium celebratur negotiosum et in quieta pausatur actione. Hic pro certaminis labore repensat Deus athletis suis mercedem optatam, pacem videlicet quam mundus ignorat, et gaudium in Spiritu Sancto.

133. *Ep.* 1.16 (SC 88:78): Quid autem tam justum tamque utile, quidve humanae naturae sic insitum et congruum quam diligere bonum? Et quid aliud tam bonum quam Deus? Imo, quid aliud bonum nisi solus Deus? Unde anima sancta, hujus boni incomparabilem decorem, splendorem, pulchritudinem, ex parte sentiens, amoris flamma succensa, dicit: *Sitivit anima mea ad Deum fortem vivum; quando veniam et apparebo ante faciem Dei?*

134. Guibert of Nogent, *De vita sua* 1.11 (PL 156:854), using the translation of John F. Benton, *Self and Society in Medieval France: The Memoirs of Abbot Guibert of Nogent* (New York: Harper Torchbooks, 1970), p. 61.

135. This is also evident in the distinctive architectural form of the Charterhouses, on which see F. Macalli, "Certosini, Architettura dei," DIP 2:822–38; and Wolfgang Braunfels, *Monasteries of Western Europe. The Architecture of the Orders* (London: Thames & Hudson, 1972), pp. 111–24.

136. William of St. Thierry, *Ep frat* 15–16 (SC 223:154–56): Altissima est professio vestra, caelos transit, par angelis est. . . . Aliorum est Deo servire, vestrum est adhaerere. Aliorum est Deum credere, scire, amare, et revereri; vestrum est sapere, intelligere, cognoscere, frui. For an analysis of how William's categories apply to the life of one twelfth-century Carthusian, see Roland Maisonneuve, "L'univers mystique cartusien et Anthelme de Belley (1107–

1178)," *Kartäuserregel und Kartäuserleben: Internationaler Kongress vom 30. Mai bis 3. Juni 1984. Stift Heiligenkreuz,* Analacta Cartusiana 113.1 (Salzburg: Universität Salzburg, 1984), pp. 20–46.

137. These letters have been published in two volumes in the SC series. SC 88 (already noted) contains Bruno's two letters, nine letters of Guigo I, and two letters of Anthelme of Chignin (d. 1178). SC 274 contains a second volume of *Lettres des premiers Chartreux* comprising nine letters written by Carthusians of Porte in the 1130s.

138. Texts on the language of spiritual experience in Bruno and in the three authors investigated below are collected in P. Miquel, *Le vocabulaire latin de l'expérience spirituelle,* pp. 233–35, 239–47.

139. The most detailed study in English of Guigo I (as I shall call him hereafter) is that found in Mursell, *The Theology of the Carthusian Life.* Other treatments to be consulted include André Wilmart, "Les écrits spirituels des deux Guiges," *Revue d'ascétique et de mystique* 5 (1924): 59–79, 127–58 (reprinted in *Auteurs spirituels et textes dévots du moyen âge latin,* pp. 217–60); Maurice Laporte, "Guiges I," DS 6:1069–75; Un Chartreux, "La doctrine monastique des Coutumes de Guiges," *Théologie de la vie monastique* (Paris: Aubier, 1964), pp. 485–501; and Kurt Ruh, *Geschichte der abendländische Mystik,* pp. 210–19.

140. The *Consuetudines* are available in an excellent edition by Un Chartreux (Maurice Laporte), *Coutumes de Chartreuse* (SC 313).

141. Guigo's *Meditationes,* 476 *sententiae* that are reminiscent of the *Apophthegmata Patrum* and, perhaps even more, of the gnomic sentences found in the works of Evagrius Ponticus, were edited by André Wilmart, *Le Récueil des pensées du B. Guiges* (Paris: Vrin, 1936). The standard edition and study is now that of Un Chartreux (Maurice Laporte), *Guiges Ier: Les Méditations (Recueil de pensées)* (SC 308), which contains an excellent introduction. There is an English translation (not always accurate) of the Wilmart edition by John J. Jolin, *Meditations of Guigo, Prior of the Charterhouse* (Milwaukee: Marquette University Press, 1951). Among the many studies of this text, see Etienne Gilson, "Presentation de Guiges I le Chartreux," *La vie spirituelle* 40 (1934): 162–78; Gaston Hocquard, *Les Meditations du bienheureux Guiges de Saint Romain cinquième Prieur de Chartreuse (1109–1136),* Analecta Cartusiana 112 (Salzburg: Universität Salzburg, 1984); and Mursell, *The Theology of the Carthusian Life,* pp. 53–58.

142. See *Epp.* 11–12 in SBOp 7:52–62. *Ep.* 11 was a "trial-run" for Bernard's treatise *De diligendo Deo* and was, indeed, appended to that tract when it was completed. Peter the Venerable also corresponded with Guigo.

143. On the relation between Bernard and Guigo, see David N. Bell, "The Carthusian Connection: Guigo I of La Chartreuse and the Origins of Cistercian Spirituality," *Cistercian Studies* 27 (1992):51–62; and Gerhard B. Winkler, "Bernhard und die Kartäuser. Zur Relativierung des monastischen Asketismus durch die reine Gottesliebe," in *Kartäuserregel und Kartäuserleben,* pp. 5–19. For a study of the relation between Cistercian and Carthusian spirituality, see Edmund Mikkers, "Zisterziernser und Kartäuser: Ein Vergleich ihrer Spiritualität," in *Spiritualität Heute und Gestern: Internationaler Kongress vom 4. bis 7. August 1982,* Analecta Cartusiana 35 (Salzburg: Universität Salzburg, 1983), pp. 52–72. On Carthusian teaching on love, see Mursell, *The Theology of the Carthusian Life,* Part II.

144. *Ep.* 11.1 (SBOp 7:52.11–12): O quantus in illis meditationibus exardescit ignis, e quibus huiuscemodi evolant scintillae!

145. *Consuetudines Cartusiae* 80.4 (SC 313:288.16–19): . . . omnia pene maiora et subtiliora secreta, non in turbis tumultuosis, sed cum soli essent dei famulis revelata, ipsosque dei famulos, cum vel subtilius aliquid meditari, vel liberius orare, vel a terrenis per mentis excessum alienari cuperent. . . .

146. Ibid., 80.11 (ed., 292.78–81): . . . suavitates psalmodiarum, studia lectionum, fervores orationum, subtilitates meditationum, excessus contemplationum, baptisma lacrimarum, nulla

re magis quam solitudine posse iuvari.

147. Chap. 80 of the *Consuetudines* can be compared with Guigo's *Ep.* 1 (SC 88:142–48), "De vita solitaria ad ignotum amicum," which makes many of the same points (see especially 1.4 on contemplation).

148. *Meditationes* § 471 (SC 308:300.2–5): Devotus erit ad Deum, benignus ad proximum, sobrius ad mundum. Dei servus, hominis socius, mundi dominus. Sub Deo constitutus, erga proximum non elatus, mundo non subditus.

149. Ibid., §§ 464–76 (ed., 292–306). See the discussion in SC 308:64–68 and 309–12.

150. Ibid., § 77 (ed., 126): Haec redemptio nostra: dimissio peccatorum, illuminatio, accensio, immortalitas. Haec omnia Deus noster nobis.

151. There are, to be sure, a few aphorisms that mention important themes of mystical theology (e.g., § 360 on deification and § 473 on our conformation to Christ), but none of these are developed in any significant way.

152. For introductions to Guigo, see Maurice Laporte, "Guiges II" in DS 6:1175–76; Humphrey Pawsey, "Guigo the Angelic," *Spirituality through the Centuries: Ascetics and Mystics of the Western Church*, ed. James Walsh (New York: Kenedy, n.d.), pp. 132–43; Keith J. Egan, "Guigo II: The Theology of the Contemplative Life," in *The Spirituality of Western Christendom*, ed. E. Rozanne Elder (Kalamazoo, MI: Cistercian Pulications, 1976), pp. 106–15; and Simon Tugwell, *Ways of Imperfection. An Exploration of Christian Spirituality* (London: Darton, Longman, Todd, 1984), chaps. 9–11. The most recent treatment is in Ruh, *Geschichte der abendländische Mystik,* pp. 220–25.

153. These texts were edited by Edmund Colledge and James Walsh, *Lettre sur la vie contemplative. Douze méditations,* SC 163. The introduction to this volume (pp. 7–79) constitutes the most detailed analysis of Guigo's thought. It, as well as a translation of the texts, is available in English as *The Ladder of Monks and Twelve Meditations by Guigo II* (London: Mowbray, 1978; Reprint, Cistercian Publications, 1981). For some notes on the popularity of the text in the late Middle Ages, see Giles Constable, "Twelfth-Century Spirituality and the Late Middle Ages," in *Medieval and Renaissance Studies,* ed. O. B. Hardison (Chapel Hill: University of North Carolina Press, 1971), pp. 31, 48; and "The Popularity of Twelfth-Century Spiritual Writers in the Late Middle Ages," in *Renaissance Studies in Honor of Hans Baron,* ed. Anthony Molho and John Tedeschi (DeKalb: Northern Illinois University Press, 1971), pp. 5–28 passim.

154. For background, see Émile Bertaud and André Rayez, "Échelle spirituelle," DS 4:62–86; and B. McGinn, *The Golden Chain,* pp. 93–101.

155. On the rational aspect of Guigo's treatise, see the remarks of K. Egan, "Guigo II," pp. 111–12. On Guigo's use of Hugh of St. Victor, see the analysis of Colledge and Walsh, *The Ladder of Monks,* pp. 24–38.

156. See Tugwell, *Ways of Imperfection,* pp. 93–94.

157. *Scala claustralium* 2 (SC 163:84.32–38): Est autem lectio sedula scripturarum cum animi intentione inspectio. Meditatio est studiosa mentis actio, occultae veritatis notitiam ductu propriae rationis investigans. Oratio est devota cordis in Deum intentio pro malis removendis vel bonis adiscipendis. Contemplatio est mentis in Deum suspensae quaedam supra se elevatio, eternae dulcedinis gaudia degustans. Here I use the translation of Colledge and Walsh (*The Ladder,* p. 82). Ruh notes the appearance of the four terms in a text of Smaragdus (PL 102:691) (*Geschichte der abendländische Mystik,* p. 222).

158. *Scala* 7 (ed., 96.162–68): . . . sed medium orationis cursum interrumpens, festinus se ingerit . . . ; facit eam terrenorum oblivisci, immemorem sui mirabiliter mortificando vivificans et inebriando sobriam reddens (trans. of Colledge and Walsh, *The Ladder,* p. 87, slightly adapted).

159. For another text on the importance of tears, see *Meditatio* II (ed., 132–34).

160. Ibid., 13 (ed., 108.303–06): Hi autem gradus ita catenati sunt, et vicaria ope sibi invicem sic deserviunt quod praecedentes sine sequentibus parum aut nihil prosunt, sequentes sine praecedentes aut numquam aut raro haberi possunt. See also the reprise of this in 14 (ed., 112.349–54).

161. Ibid., 14 (ed., 114.380–84): Beatus cui in hoc supremo gradu vel modico tempore conceditur permanere, qui vere potest dicere: Ecce sentio gratiam Dei, ecce cum Petro et Johanne gloriam ejus in monte contemplor, ecce cum Jacob pulchrae Rachelis amplexibus delector.

162. Tugwell, *Ways of Imperfection,* p. 100. Chapters 10 and 11 of Tugwell's book study the "dismantling" of the four rungs of the ladder in later Christian spirituality.

163. *Meditatio* I (SC 163:126–30), see 126.16–21 on friendship with Jesus.

164. *Meditatio* IV (ed., 146.55–57): In solo enim vertice sapientiae ignis caritatis ardentissimae speciem divinae gloriae declarat. . . . Colledge and Walsh (*The Ladder,* pp. 62–63) see evidence of Dionysian influence in this meditation, but the figure of Moses was well known in many other texts and there is no overt Dionysian language here. Besides, in Dionysian mysticism the ascent is from light through cloud into darkness, whereas here the goal is that of illuminating fire that grants vision of the *species gloriae.*

165. In several places in these *Meditationes,* Mary appears as the archetypal mystic soul in whose womb Christ dwells in all fullness; see, e.g., *Med.* VIII (ed., 168.55–68) and *Med.* IX (ed., 172.4–16).

166 *Meditatio* X, devoted to eating the Body of Christ, and *Meditatio* XI to the drinking of his Blood, both follow a similar pattern–the transition from faith in the real presence, through meditation and understanding, to ardent desire to imitate Christ that leads to "adhering" and union, here and herafter. See especially X (ed., 188.146–51): Hoc est corpus Christi spiritualiter manducare: fidem in illo puram habere, et de eadem fide studiose meditando semper quaerere, et quod quaerimus intelligendo invenire, et inventum ardenter diligere, quemque diligimus pro posse nostro imitari, et imitando constanter illi adhaerere, et adharendo perenniter uniri. Cf. *Med.* XI (ed., 196.87–92).

167. On Adam, variously called Adam Scot, Adam of Dryburgh, and Adam the Carthusian, there is one monograph in English, James Bulloch, *Adam of Dryburgh* (London: SPCK, 1958). See also A. Versteylen, "Adam l'Écossais," DS 1:196–98; André Wilmart, "Maître Adam, chanoine prémontré devenu chartreux à Witham," *Analecta Praemonstratensia* 9 (1933): 209–31; M. M. Davy, "Le vie solitaire carthusienne d'après le *De quadripertito exercitio cellae* d'Adam le Chartreux," *Revue d'ascétique et de mystique* 14 (1933): 124–45; and Humphrey Pawsey, "Adam of Dryburgh," *The Month,* n.s. 29 (1963): 261–77. There is a contemporary sketch of Adam in the *Magna Vita Sancti Hugonis: The Life of St. Hugh of Lincoln,* ed. Decima L. Douis and David Hugh Farmer, 2 vols. (Oxford: Clarendon Press, 1985), 2:52–54 (Bk. 4.11).

168. The most up-to-date list of his works known to me is found in Albert Gruys, *Cartusiana: Bibliographie générale. Auteurs cartusiens* (Paris: Éditions du Centre National de la Recherche Scientifique, 1976), pp. 37–39.

169. *Sermo* 45 (PL 198:414D): De qua conjunctione loqui non parum fortitudo, quia de ea digne loqui non potest, qui eam in semetipso adhuc expertus non est.

170. Adam the Carthusian, *Liber de quadripertito exercitio cellae* in PL 153:799–884, where it appears under the works of Guigo II.

171. See *Liber,* chap. 32 (868C) and chap. 35 (877A) for his own lack of experience. For the appeal to his reader's experience, see, e.g., 820B, 822C, 826B, 828B, 840B, 862C, 866A, 868D, 870C, 876A, and especially 824BC: Itaque quando vidit tunc scivit, quia quando expertus est, et quantum expertus est, nimirum tunc et tantum scivit. In tanta quippe talique re, tantam et non amplius comprehendi scientiam, quantum sentit ipsa experientia.

172. *Liber,* 29 (PL 153:855C–58D). The quotation from *De coelesti hierarchia* 2 is at 856AC.

173. Ibid., Prologus (802A): Sunt autem quatuor exercitia illa, studium sacrae lectionis, maturitas defecatae meditationis, devotio purae orationis, strenuitas utilis actionis. Cf. 806CD, 819D, 826B ff., 828B, etc.

174. Ibid., chap. 18 (831cd): Hic purae mentis beatus fit excelsus in Deum, qui jam non simplex meditatio, sed excellens valet contemplatio vocari. In ea namque pia et succensa mens, omne corpus, omnesque corporeas imagines similitudinesque transcendens, in ipsa luce Veritatis, in qua vere et vera sunt omnia praeterita, praesentia et futura; nec aliter praeterita, quam futura vel praesentia; nec aliter praesentia, quam praeterita vel futura; nec aliter futura, quam praeterita vel praesentia; sed simul, et semper, et eodem modo omnia, quaecunque ei Veritas revelavit simplici intuitu contemplatur. The text goes on to consider this in the light of the traditional three Augustinian categories of vision.

175. Ibid., chap. 35 (875D–80B) approaches aspects of mystical prayer under the fourfold category of (1) *quem oras*, (2) *per quem oras*, (3) *quod oras*, and (4) *teipsum qui oras* (876C). The comments under (1) come closest to ones that might be taken as applicable to the higher stages of contemplation (876CD).

Chapter 9

1. On the devlopment of the canonical life, see Charles Dereine, "Chanoines réguliers," *Dictionnaire d'histoire et géographie ecclésiastiques* (Paris: Letouzey et Ané, 1912–), 12:353–405; J. C. Dickinson, *The Origins of the Austin Canons and their Introduction into England* (London: SPCK, 1950), pp. 1–90; and C. Egger, "Canonici Regolari," DIP 2:46–63.

2. Augustine, *Ep.* 355.1 (PL 39:1570): Et ideo volui habere in ista domo episcopi mecum monasterium clericorum.

3. For a survey of these texts and their development into a *regula*, see George Lawless, O.S.A., *Augustine of Hippo and His Monastic Rule* (Oxford: Clarendon Press, 1987).

4. The characterization is from Lawless, *Augustine,* p. 62.

5. Ivo of Chartres, *Ep.* 69 (PL 162:89): Ideo canonici appellati estis, quod canonicas regulas vos velle observare ceteris arctius devovistis.

6. See William D. Carpe, *The "Vita Canonica" in the "Regula Canonicorum" of Chrodegang of Metz* (dissertation, University of Chicago, 1975).

7. For surveys, besides Dickinson, *The Origins of the Austin Canons,* chap. 1, see R. W. Southern, *Western Society and the Church in the Middle Ages* (Harmondsworth: Penguin Books, 1970), pp. 241–50; and Lester K. Little, *Religious Poverty and the Profit Economy in Medieval Europe* (Ithaca, NY: Cornell University Press, 1978), chap. 7.

8. On these developments, see Dickinson, *The Origins,* chap. 2.

9. Southern, *Western Society and the Church,* p. 248.

10. On the spirituality of the canons, see Jean Leclercq, "La spiritualité des chanoines reguliers," in *La Vita comune del clero nei secoli XI e XII,* 2 vols. (Milan: Miscellanea del Centro di Studi Medioevali III, 1962), 1:117–35; Caroline Walker Bynum, *Docere Verbo et Exemplo: An Aspect of Twelfth-Century Spirituality* (Missoula, MT: Scholars Press, 1979), and "The Spirituality of Regular Canons in the Twelfth Century," in *Jesus as Mother: Studies in the Spirituality of the High Middle Ages* (Berkeley: University of California Press, 1982), pp. 22–58; and Grover A. Zinn, "The Regular Canons," in *Christian Spirituality I: Origins to the Twelfth Century,* ed. Bernard McGinn, John Meyendorff, and Jean Leclercq, WS 16 (New York: Crossroad, 1986), pp. 218-28.

11. The standard history of the abbey is F. Bonnard, *Histoire de l'abbaye royale et de l'ordre de St. Victor de Paris,* 2 vols. (Paris, 1907). For general surveys, see the articles of Jean Chatillon, especially "De Guillaume de Champeaux à Thomas Gallus: Chronique d'histoire littéraire et doctrinale de l'école de Saint-Victor," *Revue du moyen âge latin* 8 (1952): 139–62 and 247–72;

"La culture de l'école de Saint-Victor au 12e siècle," *Entretiens sur la renaissance du 12e siècle,* ed. Maurice de Gandillac and Edouard Jeauneau (Paris: Mouton, 1965), pp. 147–78; and "Canonici regolari di San Vittore," DIP 2:125–34.

12. See Hildebert's *Ep.* 1 (PL 171:141–43). Hildebert praises William's conversion to true "philosophy" (*Hoc vere philosophari est; sic vivere, magnum jam cum superis est inire consortium* [141B]), but counsels him to continue teaching for pastoral reasons (*Noli ergo claudere rivos doctrinae tuae* [143A]).

13. Marie-Dominique Chenu, "Civilisation urbaine et théologie. L'École de Saint-Victor au XIIIe siècle," *Annales: Économies. Sociétés. Civilisations* 29 (1974): 1253–63.

14. On this, see John W. Baldwin, *The Scholastic Culture of the Middle Ages 1000–1300* (Lexington: D.C. Heath, 1971), chap. 2.

15. For William's friendship with Bernard, see *Vita Prima Bernardi* 7 (PL 185:245C–46C). Bernard also had amicable relations with Hugh of St. Victor as indicated by the lengthy *Ep.* 77, which he wrote in response to questions sent him by the canon (SBOp 7:184–200). About 1136 Bernard wrote a letter to Hugh's abbot, Gilduin of St. Victor, recommending the visiting Italian scholar, Peter Lombard, who was to become one of the greatest figures of early scholasticism (*Ep.* 410 in SBOp 8:391). The relationship between Cistercian and Victorine thought would repay further study, as the influence of Hugh on Isaac of Stella shows (see chapter 7, pp. 289–91).

16. These are the six categories of works found in Damien van den Eynde, *Essai sur la succession et la date des écrits de Hugues de Saint-Victor* (Rome: Apud Pontificium Athenaeum Antonianum, 1960), which is the standard authority in this matter. I will use van den Eynde's abbreviations in citing Hugh's works.

17. The literature on Hugh is extensive. For introductions, see Roger Baron, "Hugues de Saint-Victor," in DS 7:901–39; and Patrice Sicard, *Hugues de Saint-Victor et son école: Introduction, choix de texte, traduction et commentaires* (Turnhout: Brepols, 1991). Among other studies, see the many works of R. Baron, especially *Science et sagesse chez Hugues de Saint-Victor* (Paris: Lethielleux, 1957), and *Études sur Hugues de Saint-Victor* (Angers: Desclée, 1963). In English, the most helpful accounts are in *The Didascalicon of Hugh of St. Victor,* translated from the Latin with an Introduction and Notes by Jerome Taylor (New York and London: Columbia, 1961); and in the various articles of Grover A. Zinn listed in subsequent notes. On Hugh's influence, see R. Baron, "L'influence de Hugues de Saint-Victor," *Recherches de théologie ancienne et médiévale* 22 (1955): 56–71.

18. The best study of Achard is that of Jean Chatillon, *Théologie, spiritualité et métaphysique dans l'oeuvre oratoire d'Achard de St. Victor* (Paris: Vrin, 1969).

19. See Beryl Smalley, *The Study of the Bible in the Middle Ages* (Notre Dame: University of Notre Dame, 1964), chap. 4 (the first edition of this ground-breaking work was published in 1940).

20. This has been edited and studied by Philippe Delhaye, *Le Microcosmos de Godefroy de Saint-Victor: Étude théologique. Texte,* 2 vols. (Lille: Facultés catholiques, 1951).

21. Edited by Pierre Glorieux, "Le 'Contra quatuor Labyrinthos Franciae' de Gauthier de Saint-Victor," *Archives d'histoire doctrinale et littéraire du moyen âge* 27 (1952): 187–335.

22. The basic work on medieval schools and education remains Hastings Rashdall, ed. F. M. Powicke and A. B. Emden, *The Universities of Europe in the Middle Ages* (Oxford: Oxford University Press, 1936), 3 vols. For the twelfth century, see also Gérard M. Paré, A. Brunet, and M. Tremblay, *La renaissance du XIIe siècle: Les écoles et l'enseignement* (Paris and Ottawa: Publications de l'Institut des études médiévales d'Ottawa, 1933).

23. A standard account of the evolution of the method remains that of Martin Grabmann, *Die Geschichte der Scholastischen Methode,* 2 vols. (Freiburg-im-Breisgau: Herder, 1909).

24. For the significance of this new differentiation in the history of theology, see Bernard Lonergan, *Method in Theology* (New York: Herder, 1972), pp. 309–12. For a general picture of the development of the term *theologia*, see Yves M.-J. Congar, *A History of Theology* (Garden City, NY: Doubleday, 1968); and "Le moment 'economique' et le moment 'ontologique' dans la sacra doctrina (révélation, théologie, somme théologique)," *Mélanges offerts à M.-D. Chenu* (Paris: Vrin, 1967), pp. 135–87. On the many currents of twelfth-century theology, see the classic account of Marie-Dominique Chenu, *La théologie au douzième siècle* (Paris: Vrin, 1957), with a partial English translation by Jerome Taylor and Lester K. Little, *Nature, Man, and Society in the Twelfth Century* (Chicago: University of Chicago, 1968).

25. For a more complete picture of the background, see G. R. Evans, *Old Arts and New Theology: The Beginnings of Theology as an Academic Discipline* (Oxford: Clarendon Press, 1980). Still useful is Arthur Landgraf, *Einführung in die Geschichte der theologischen Literatur der Früh-scholastik unter dem Gesichtspunkt der Schulenbildung* (Regensburg: Pustet, 1948). An excellent brief survey is in chap. 8, "The Masters of the Theological 'Science'," of Chenu's *Nature, Man, and Society*, pp. 270–309.

26. J. Leclercq, *The Love of Learning and the Desire for God* (New York: Fordham University Press, 1961), p. 213. In chaps. VIII and IX, Leclercq contrasts monastic and scholastic theology in terms of sources, object, method, and literary genera.

27. See especially, Leclercq's later paper "The Renewal of Theology," in *Renaissance and Renewal in the Twelfth Century*, ed. Robert L. Benson and Giles Constable with Carol D. Lanham (Cambridge, MA: Harvard University Press, 1982), pp. 68–87, where he puts forward a more nuanced model of the "theology of the cloister" and two forms of "theology of the schools" (pastoral and speculative), while insisting that "speaking of several theologies and comparing them does not imply opposing one to another; their enrichment was reciprocal" (p. 71).

28. We must beware of making too easy a distinction between the personnel of the monastic and the scholastic establishments. Many masters had doubtless received their education in the monastic schools; some early scholastics, like the Victorines, lived a quasi-monastic style of life; many masters, like William of Champeaux and Peter Comestor, were converted to monastic-canonical *philosophia* early or more often late in their careers.

29. On the influence of Boethius in the twelfth century, see Chenu, *La théologie au douzième siècle*, chap. VI, "Aetas Boetiana" (pp. 142–58).

30. Hugh of St. Victor, *Didascalicon* 6.3: omnia disce, videbis postea nihil esse superfluum. coartata scientia iucunda non est. In citing this text, I will use the edition of Henry Buttimer, *Hugonis de Sancto Victore. Didascalicon. De Studio Legendi* (Washington, DC: Catholic University Press, 1939), 115.19–20 (using the abbreviation *Did.*, along with book and chapter, with page and line in parentheses.) There is an excellent translation by Jerome Taylor, *The Didascalicon of Hugh of St. Victor*, especially helpful for its notes, though I will use my own versions unless otherwise noted.

31. See, e.g., *De Trinitate* 15.2.2 (PL 42:1058), and *De libero arbitrio* 1.2.4 (PL 32:1224).

32. *Peter Abailard. Sic et Non. A Critical Edition*, ed. Blanche B. Boyer and Richard McKeon (Chicago: University of Chicago Press, 1976–77), 103.338–39: Dubitando quippe ad inquisitionem venimus; inquirendo veritatem percipimus.

33. Peter Cantor, *Verbum abbreviatum* 1 (PL 205:23B): In tribus igitur consistat exercitium sacrae Scripturae: circa lectionem, disputationem et praedicationem.... Lectio autem est quasi fundamentum, et substratorium sequentium; quia per eam ceterae utilitates comparantur. Disputatio quasi paries est in hoc exercitio et aedificio; quia nihil plene intelligitur, fideliterve praedicatur, nisi prius dente disputationis frangatur. Praedicatio vero, cui subserviunt priora, quasi tectum est tegens fideles ab aestu, et a turbine vitiorum. Post lectionem igitur

sacrae Scripturae, et dubitabilium, per disputationem, inquisitionem, et non prius, praedicandum est; ut sic cortina cortinam trahat et caetera.

34. R. Baron in DS 7:915.

35. The most comprehensive treatment is still Joseph Mariéton, *Le Problème de la classification des sciences de Aristote à Saint-Thomas* (Paris: Alcan, 1901). See also J. A. Weisheipl, "Classification of the Sciences in Medieval Thought," *Mediaeval Studies* 27 (1965): 54–90; Evans, *Old Arts and New Theology*, pp. 15–19, with handy charts; and B. McGinn, "*Theologia* in Isaac of Stella," *Cîteaux* 31 (1970): 219–35.

36. See the characterization of the work by Jerome Taylor in his "Introduction" to *The Didascalicon of Hugh of St. Victor*, 4: ". . . the *Didascalicon* set forth a program insisting on the indispensability of a whole complex of the traditional arts and on the need for their scientific pursuit in a particular order by all men as a means both of relieving the physical weaknesses of earthly life and of restoring that union with the divine Wisdom for which man was made."

37. Hugh, *Did.* 1.4 (Buttimer, 11.14–20): Philosophia est disciplina omnium rerum humanarum atque divinarum rationes plene investigans . . . diximus philosophiam esse amorem et studium sapientiae . . . quae sola rerum primaeva ratio est. Cf. the definition of philosophy in *Epitome Dindimi in Philosophiam*, lines 50–59.

38. See especially *Did.* 2.1. On this see Baron, *Science et sagesse*, pp. 221–23.

39. See *Did.* 2.2–16. Hugh further subdivides *mathematica* into the four sciences of the quadrivium (*arithmetica-musica-geometria-astronomia*). The trivium of *grammatica* and *dialectica* and *rhetorica* (comprising what Hugh calls the probable aspect of argument, i.e., *ratio disserendi*) is found under *philosophia logica*.

40. *Did.* 6.4 (Buttimer, 119.24–26): Hic est tota divinitas, haec est illa spiritualis fabrica, quae, quot continet sacramenta, tot quasi ordinibus constructa in altum extollitur.

41. Hugh of St. Victor, *In Hierarchiam celestem commentaria* (hereafter *In Hier.*), Prol. (PL 175:928A): Hic autem summa philosophiae est, et veritatis perfectio, qua nihil altius esse potest animo contemplanti. This more traditional threefold division of sciences, ultimately of Platonic-Stoic origin, is also found in a number of Hugh's contemporaries and students, such as Clarembald of Arras.

42. Hugh of St. Victor, *In Hier.*, prol. (PL 175:927A): Major autem, ut diximus, declaratio divinitatis in sacramentis gratiae, et carne Verbi, et mystica operatione ipsius ostenditur, quam naturali rerum specie praedicetur. Et idcirco mundana theologia parum evidenti demonstratione utens, non valuit incomprehensibilem veritatem sine contagione erroris educere . . . (see also the discussion in 925D–26B). *Theologia divina* can be taken as the equivalent of the *divinitas* mentioned in *Did.* 6.4, and the terms *scientia divina* and *sapientia superior* found in *De sac.* 1, prol. 6 (PL 176:185C). On the commentary on Dionysius, see René Roques, "Connaissance de Dieu et théologie symbolique d'après l'*In Hierarchiam Caelestem Sancti Dionysii* de Hugues de Saint-Victor," in *Structures théologiques de la Gnose à Richard de Saint-Victor* (Paris: Presses universitaires de France, 1962), pp. 294–364. See also McGinn, "*Theologia* in Isaac of Stella," pp. 232–34.

43. For discussions of the relation between reason and faith in Hugh (which should not be understood in Thomistic terms according to a clear division between the natural and supernatural), see, e.g., *De sac.* 1.4.30 and 1.10.2 (PL 176:231C–32B, 327C–31B).

44. On the systematic organization of treatises in early scholasticism, see Henri Cloes, "La systématisation théologique pendant la première moitié du XIIe siècle," *Ephemerides Theologicae Lovanienses* 34 (1958): 277–329.

45. The *De sacramentis* is found in PL 176:173A–618B. There is an English translation by Roy J. Deferrari, *Hugh of Saint Victor: On the Sacraments of the Christian Faith* (Cambridge: The Mediaeval Academy of America, 1951). All translations are my own unless otherwise noted.

46. Augustine, *De vera religione* 7.13 (PL 34:128–29).

47. *De sac.*, prol. (PL 176:183A): Materia divinarum Scripturarum omnium, sunt opera restaurationis humanae. Duo enim sunt opera in quibus universa continentur quae facta sunt. Primum est opus conditionis. Secundum est opus restaurationis. See the further reflection on the subdivisions of these two parts, e.g., *De sac.* 1.1.28–30 (203D–206A). This distinction is central to Hugh and appears in most of his writings. To cite just one other important discussion, see *De vanitate* 2 (PL 176:716BC).

48. *Did.* 5.2 (Buttimer, 95.15–17 and 96.15–18): Primo omnium sciendum est, quod divina scriptura triplicem habet modum intelligendi, id est historiam, allegoriam, topologiam ... oportet ergo sic tractare divinam scripturam, ut nec ubique historiam, nec ubique allegoriam, nec ubique quaeramus tropologiam, sed singula in suis locis, prout ratio postulat, competenter assignare. Hugh's adoption of the threefold understanding of scripture expressed as *historia-allegoria-tropologia* goes back to Jerome by way of Gregory the Great (see the discussion of Gregory's understanding of hermeneutics in chapter 2, pp. 40–43). Hugh does not seem to slide as easily as some earlier exegetes between a twofold formula (literal/spiritual) and the threefold one, probably because of his more differentiated and articulated understanding of Christian teaching.

49. *Did.* 6.4 (Buttimer, 118.18–26): intende! rem tibi proposui intuentibus contemptibilem, sed intelligentibus imitatione dignam. fundamentum in terra est, nec semper politos habet lapides. fabrica desuper terram, et aequalem quaerit structuram. sic divina pagina multum secundum litteralem sensum continet, quae et sibi repugnare videntur et nonnunquam absurditatis aut impossibilitatis aliquid afferre. spiritualis autem intelligentia nullam admittit repugnantiam, in qua diversa multa, adversa nulla esse possunt.

50. *De sac.* prol. (PL 176:183–84): Cum igitur de prima eruditione sacri eloquii quae in historica constat lectione, compendiosum volumen prius dictassem, hoc nunc ad secundum eruditionem (quae in allegoria est) introducendis praeparavi; in quo, si fundamento quodam cognitionis fidei animum stabiliant, ut caetera quae vel legendo vel audiendo superaedificare potuerint, inconcussa permaneant.

51. *De sac.* 1, Prol., 6 (PL 176:185C): Ex quo constat quod omnes artes naturales divinae scientiae famulantur; et inferior sapientia recte ordinata ad superiorem conducit.

52. Ibid. (PL 176:185CD): Super haec ante omnia divinum illud est ad quod ducit divina Scriptura sive in allegoria, sive in tropologia, ... in quibus constat cognitio veritatis et amor virtutis: et haec est vera reparatio hominis.

53. *Did.* 6.3 (Buttimer, 116.20–21): fundamentum autem et principium doctrinae sacrae historia est. ... For Hugh's emphasis on the importance of the letter, see also *Did.* 6.10 (Buttimer, 126–28), and the *De scripturis et scriptoribus sacris praenotiuncula* 13–15 (PL 175:20B–23B; abbreviated *Praenot.*). For Smalley's analysis of Hugh's literal exegesis, see *The Study of the Bible*, pp. 83–105. She does, however, admit that Hugh's "great service to exegesis was to lay more stress on the literal interpretation *relatively* to the spiritual, and to develop the sources for it" (p. 102).

54. For an overview of Victorine relations with medieval Jewish exegesis, see Grover Zinn, "History and Interpretation: 'Hebrew Truth,' Judaism, and the Victorine Exegetical Tradition," in *Jews and Christians: Exploring the Past, Present, and Future*, ed. James H. Charlesworth (New York: Crossroad, 1994), pp. 100–126.

55. See *De arca Noe morali* 1.3 (PL 176:626D–29D).

56. On the superiority of the *sententia*, or deeper meaning of scripture, see *Did.* 6.11 (Buttimer, 128–29), where Hugh cites Augustine on attempting to find a meaning consonent with that intended by the author. Henri de Lubac, in his *Exégèse médiévale: Les quatre sens de l'écriture*, 4 vols. (Paris: Aubier, 1959-64), Seconde Partie 1, chaps. IV and V, emphasized this aspect of Hugh's exegesis against Smalley.

57. Hugh of St. Victor, *In Salomonis Ecclesiasten* (hereafter *In Eccl.*), Praef. (PL 175:115A): Mihi vero simili culpae subjacere videntur, vel qui in sacra Scriptura mysticam intelligentiam et allegoriarum profunditatem, vel inquirendam pertinaciter negant, ubi est; vel apponendam superstitiose contendunt, ubi non est.

58. *Did.* 5.9 (Buttimer, 109.23–25): . . . prima, lectio, intelligentiam dat; secunda, meditatio, consilium praestat; tertia, oratio petit; quarta, operatio quaerit; quinta, contemplatio invenit.

59. The literature specifically related to Hugh's mystical teaching is not as extensive as might be expected, given how his teaching was integrated into his total theological program. Older essays tend to only marginally helpful, e.g., K. Muller, "Zur Mystik Hugos von St. Viktor," *Zeitschrift für Kirchengeschichte* 45 (1926–27): 175–89; and Patrick Joseph Healy, "The Mysticism of the School of Saint Victor," *Church History* 1 (1932): 211–21. Among more modern works, see Jorgen Pedersen "La recherche de la sagesse d'après Hugues de Saint-Victor," *Classica et Mediaevalia* 16 (1955): 91–133; and Dionysius Lasic, O.F.M., *Hugonis de S. Victore Theologia Perfectiva. Eius Fundamentum Philosophicum et Theologicum* (Rome: Pontificum Athenaeum Antonianum, 1956); and especially the writings of J. Chatillon, R. Baron, and G. Zinn to be referred to below. Hugh's teaching is also discussed in many articles in DS (for example, "Contemplation" in 2:1961–62; "Dieu (connaissance mystique)" in 3:887; "Extase" in 4:2113, 2116, and 2118; "Feu" in 5:263; "Fruitio Dei" in 5:1559; and "Toucher, touches" in 15:1076). The latest general treatment of Hugh's mysticism is in K. Ruh, *Geschichte der abendländische Mystik*: Band I, *Die Grundlegung durch die Kirchenväter und die Mönchstheologie des 12. Jahrhunderts* (Munich: Beck, 1990), pp. 355-80.

60. The systematic coherence of Hugh's teaching has been aptly summarized by Grover A. Zinn: "Victorine ecclesiology and Victorine spirituality are oriented toward a positive appreciation of the work of restoration carried out in history. History, eschatology, and contemplation fuse in the Victorine vision." See Zinn's article *"Historia fundamentum est:* the role of history in the contemplative life according to Hugh of St. Victor," in *Contemporary reflections on the medieval Christian tradition: Essays in honor of Ray C. Petry,* ed. George H. Shriver (Durham, NC: Duke University Press, 1974), p. 137.

61. For this central theme in Origen and Ambrose, see *Foundations of Mysticism,* pp. 117, 210.

62. *Eccl.* 1 (PL 175:116D–17B): Tres sunt animae rationalis visiones, cogitatio, meditatio, contemplatio. Cogitatio est, cum mens notione rerum transitorie tangitur. . . . Meditatio est assidua et sagax retractatio cogitationis. . . . Contemplatio est perspicax et liber animi contuitus in res perspiciendas usquequaque diffusus. . . . Contemplationis autem duo sunt genera: unum quod et prius est, et incipientium: in creaturarum consideratione; alterum quod posterius, et perfectorum est: in contemplatione Creatoris. In Proverbiis Salomon quasi meditando incessit. In Ecclesiaste ad primum gradum contemplationis ascendit. In Canticis canticorum ad supremum se transtulit. For another reflection on the pedagogical import of Solomon's three books, based on Jerome and Isidore, see *Did.* 4.8 (Buttimer, 80–81).

63. Hugh was scarcely the first Christian teacher to present his doctrine in terms of three's, but the pedagogical character of his treatises lent itself in a special way to sometimes excessive ternary formulas. As B. Smalley once put it: "A Victorine was firmly persuaded that 'all good things go in threes'" (*The Study of the Bible,* p. 86).

64. The distinction of *historia, allegoria simplex,* and the form of *allegoria* called *anagoge* (merely another way of putting Hugh's standard triple formulation of senses of scripture) appears in *Praenot.* 3 (PL 175:11D–12C). According to R. Baron in DS 7:931: "Et comme ce que Hugues appelle la grande *allégorie,* c'est sa théologie se référant au comportement de l'homme chrétien et à son ascension, vers Dieu, tropologie et anagogie désignent sa spiritualité."

65. *Praenot.* 3 (col. 12B). The text of PL reads "Anagoge est sursum ductio, cum per visibile invisibile *factum* declaratur," but the sense demands *faciendum*, as used in the rest of the passage comparing *allegoria simplex* and *anagoge.* See also *In Hier* 2 (PL 175:941C): Anagoge autem ascensio sive elevatio mentis est ad superna contemplanda.

66. *In Hier.* 3 (PL 175:960D): ... symbolum, collatio videlicet, id est, coaptatio visibilium formarum ad demonstrationem rei invisibilis propositarum.

67. Hugh found the term *theophania* in the Dionysian corpus. He employs it, though rarely, in his writings outside the *In Hier.*, e.g., *De unione* (PL 177:285B), and *Misc.* I.83 (*De multiplici theophania* in PL 177:518), where we read: Si quis omnem creaturam theophaniam dixerit, non errabit. Nevertheless, he appears to have favored the terminology of *sacramentum-simulacrum*, as in the following passage from *De tribus diebus* 16 (PL 176:823D): Et credo quod illud invisibile prius in contemplatione comprehenditur, quod in suo visibili simulacro expressius et manifestius declaratur. *In Hier.* 1.1 and 2. (PL 175:926D and 941C) describes this action as a *symbolica demonstratio.* Cf. the discussion of the rules of scriptural symbolism in *Praenot.* 14–16 (PL 175:20D–24A).

68. Chenu, *Nature, Man, and Society*, p. 103. See the entire chapter 3, "The Symbolist Mentality" (pp. 99–145), as well as B. McGinn, *The Golden Chain*, pp. 56–61.

69. Hugh's fundamentally symbolic approach has been highlighted by Grover A. Zinn, especially in his article "Mandala Symbolism and Use in the Mysticism of Hugh of St. Victor," *History of Religions* 12 (1973): 317–41, which stresses how the Victorine uses symbols as "primary bearers of meaning and agents of transformation" (p. 318).

70. *De arca Noe morali* (*De arca mor.*), *De arca Noe mystica* (*De arca myst.*), and *De vanitate mundi* (*De van.*) are found in PL 176:617–740. There is an English trans. of the four books of *De arca Noe morali* and the first two books of *De vanitate mundi* in *Hugh of St. Victor: Selected Spiritual Writings*, translated by a Religious of C.S.M.V. with an Introduction by Aelred Squire, O.P. (London: Faber & Faber, 1962). All translations are my own unless otherwise noted.

71. Grover A. Zinn, "*De gradibus ascensionum*: The Stages of Contemplative Ascent in Two Treatises on Noah's Ark by Hugh of St. Victor," in *Studies in Medieval Culture V*, ed. John R. Sommerfeldt (Kalamazoo, MI: Publications of the Medieval Center, 1975), pp. 61–79 (quotation from p. 69). See also the same author's "Hugh of St. Victor and the Ark of Noah: A New Look," *Church History* 40 (1971): 261–72; "Mandala Symbolism and Use" (referred to in note 69); and "*Historia fundamentum est*," in *Contemporary reflections on the medieval Christian tradition*, pp. 135–68 (see n. 60).

72. *De arca mor.* 2.2 (636B): Arca diluvii, sicut jam dictum est, cordis nostri secretum est, in quo latere debemus a strepitu hujus mundi. For a comparable text, see the treatise *Quid vere diligendum est* 3 in *Hugues de Saint-Victor: Six Opuscules Spirituels*, ed. Roger Baron (SC 155), p. 98.

73. The actual descriptions of the drawing can be found in *De arca mor.* 1.2 and 3 (622B–26B, 629D), and *De arca myst.* 1, 9, and 15 (681A–84A, 696C–97B, and 702AC). I am grateful to Grover A. Zinn for his help concerning Hugh's diagram of the ark. The drawing that appears here by Philip Petrie is based in part on Zinn's ongoing research, though I take responsibility for its final form and any errors this provisional presentation may contain. On the drawing, see especially Grover A. Zinn, "Hugh of St. Victor, Isaiah's Vision, and *De Arca Noe*," in *The Church and the Arts*, ed. Diana Wood (Oxford: Blackwell, 1992), pp. 99–116. See also Joachim Ehlers, "*Arca significat ecclesiam.* Ein theologisches Weltmodell aus der ersten Halfte des 12. Jahrhundert," and Barbara Bronders, "Das Bild der Schöpfung und Neuschöpfung der Welt als *orbis quadratus*," both in *Frühmittelalterlichen Studien* 6 (1972): 171–87, 188–210.

74. On the way in which Hugh emphasizes Adam as the first contemplative, see Zinn, "_De gradibus ascensionum_," pp. 68–69.

75. _De arca mor._ 1.2 (621D): Ingredere ergo nunc secretum cordis tui, et fac habitaculum deo, fac templum, fac domum, fac tabernaculum, fac arcam testamenti, fac arcam diluvii, vel quocunque nomine appelles, una est domus Dei. The notion of the heart as a dwelling place, or later a cloister, has been studied by Gerhard Bauer, _Claustrum animae: Untersuchungen zur Geschichte der Metapher vom Herzen als Kloster. Band I. Entstehungsgeschichte_ (Munich: W. Fink, 1973), who discusses the influence of Hugh and of other texts pertaining to the School of St. Victor (especially the _De claustro animae_ of Hugh of Fouilloy [see PL 176:1017–1182]) in his Parts II and III (pp. 223–335).

76. _De arca mor._ 1.2 (622BC): Hujus vero spiritualis aedificii exemplar tibi dabo arcam Noe, quam foris videbit oculus tuus, ut ad ejus similitudinem intus fabricetur animus tuus. Videbis ibi colores quosdam, formas et figuras, quae delectent visum. Sed scire debes, ideo haec posita esse, ut in eis discas sapientiam, disciplinam atque virtutem, quae exornent animum tuum. Et quia haec arca ecclesiam significat, ecclesia autem corpus Christi est, id est caput cum membris, in forma visibili depinxi, ut cum totum videris, quae deinde de parte dicuntur facilius intelligere possis. Talem autem personam hanc exprimere tibi cupio qualem Isaias se videsse testabatur, . . . _Vidi Dominum sedentem super solium excelsum et elevatum._

77. Zinn notes that the description of the drawing also encompasses references to many other key biblical theophanies–Ezekiel 1, Matthew 25, and Apocalypse 4 ("Hugh of St. Victor, Isaiah's Vision," p. 111).

78. The cosmic dimensions of the picture are quite intricate, as is clear especially from _De arca myst._ 14–15 (700C–02A). The cosmic disk that covers Christ's body has the signs of the zodiac and the twelve months inscribed on its outer rim. Within the circle are images of the twelve winds, the four humors, the four seasons, the four directions, and a map of the world.

79. See _De arca myst._ 14–15 (700D and 702AB).

80. The later descriptions of the seraphim in _De arca myst._ 15 (702CD) shows that in the drawing they were accompanied by the other choirs of angels.

81. Ibid. (624D): . . . quia quoties ad ejus aeternitatem cogitandum per excessum mentis rapimur, nullum in eo principium aut finem invenimus. This is one of the very rare mentions of the technical term _excessus mentis_ in Hugh.

82. _De arca mor._ 1.2 (625D): Haec est arca, de qua loqui proposuimus, quae a capite usque ad pedes pertingit, quia a principio usque ad finem per successionem generationum sancta ecclesia se extendit.

83. Ibid. (626C): Tertia, quam sapientia quotidie aedificat in cordibus nostris ex jugi legis Dei meditatione. Quarta est, quam mater gratia operatur in nobis ex confoederatione multarum virtutum in una charitate.

84. Hugh's notion of history has been studied by R. W. Southern, "Aspects of the European Tradition of Historical Writing: 2. Hugh of St. Victor and the Idea of Historical Development," _Royal Historical Association. Transactions,_ 5th series 21 (1971): 159–79.

85. For how Hugh broke with tradition in his attempt to find a seaworthy craft in the Genesis 6 account; see G. Zinn, "Hugh of St. Victor and the Ark of Noah: A New Look," pp. 261–66.

86. _De arca mor._ 1.4 (629D–30B). Hugh reconciles his view of three stories to the ark with the traditional interpretation of five stories by imagining the three stories as external and the five as internal (see 626D–27D, 629CD, 631C–33A).

87. _De arca mor._ 4.9 (679D–80B).

88. Ibid. (680c): Ille mundus in isto mundo est. . . . Istum mundum vident oculi carnis, illum mundum intrinsecus contemplantur oculi cordis.

89. See Zinn, *"Historia fundamentum est,"* pp. 152–54, and such texts as *In Threnos Jeremiae* (PL 175:292B). For more on Hugh's attitude toward the world, see Heinz Robert Schlette, *Die Nichtigkeit der Welt. Der philosophische Horizont des Hugo von St. Viktor* (Munich: Kösel, 1961).

90. See especially the noted passage at the beginning of *De van.* 2 (711A–14A). Cf. *De arca mor.* 4.2, 4.7, and 4.8 (666BD, 672D–73C, 675AB).

91. *De van.* 2 (715B): Ascendere ergo ad Deum hoc est intrare ad semetipsum, et non solum ad se intrare, sed ineffabili quodam modo in intimis etiam seipsum transire. Augustine often speaks of how going within is at the same time to rise above, e.g., *Conf.* 7.10.16 (PL 32:742). I have tried to study some aspects of this important tradition in Christian mysticism in my article, "Ascension and Introversion in the *Itinerarium Mentis in Deum,*" *S. Bonaventura 1274–1974,* 5 vols. (Rome: Collegio S. Bonaventura, 1974), 3:535–52.

92. *De arca myst.* 7 (695B): . . . et Moyses solus super verticem montis in nube cum Domino, hic autem versus septem gradibus distinguitur, quia tales cum perfectione operis habent et requiem mentis. Later, in *De arca myst.* 10 (697B), Hugh interprets the cloud into which Moses ascends not only as the hidden God, but also as the spiritual distance between the ascending believer and all created things. This may well be the remote source of the "cloud of forgetting" motif found in late medieval Dionysian authors, especially the anonymous English author of the *Cloud of Unknowing.*

93. *De arca mor.* 2.7 (640AB): Columna . . . est lignum vitae, quod plantatum est in medio paradisi, id est Dominus Jesus Christus in medio ecclesiae suae, . . . qui de terra ortus est, et caelos penetravit, qui ad ima venit et summa non deseruit, qui sursum ipse est et deorsum, sursum majestate, deorsum compassione. Sursum ut trahat desiderium, deorsum ut praestet subsidium. See also *De arca myst.* 2 (684A–85A). Hugh's emphasis on Christ as the *lignum vitae* may well indicate the influence of Eriugena; see the treatment of Christ as the "all-tree," or tree of life in *Periphyseon* 4 (PL 122:823A–30C).

94. *In Hier.* 2.1 (PL 175:939A): Omnis quidem illuminatio a Patre est, sed sine Jesu mediatore nulla illuminatio haberi potest. For more on the centrality of the Incarnate Word in the ascent process, see, e.g., *In Hier.* 1. (926C–27A); *De tribus diebus* 24, 26, and 27 (PL 176:834AD, 836D–37C, 838AD); and *De arca mor.* 1.4 (632B). Hugh even has something reminiscent of the *amor carnalis Christi* motif found among the Cistercians, as in *De laude charitatis* (PL 176:974C–75B).

95. This intricate account of the four ascensions and twelve steps appears twice in the treatises—*De arca mor.* 2.8–10 (640D–43B) and *De arca myst.* 7–10 (692B–97D). Many of the details of the treatment cannot be pursued here, such as the personification of virtues and vices accompanying the ladders.

96. See Zinn, *"De gradibus ascensionum,"* pp. 63–79. See also "Mandala Symbolism and Use," pp. 322–23, whose diagram is the basis for the chart used here, in Figure 2.

97. On this see René Roques, "Connaissance de Dieu et théologie symbolique d'après l''In Hierarchiam Coelestem Sancti Dionysii' de Hugues de Saint-Victor." R. Baron summarizes: "D'une façon generale, on peut dire que Saint Augustin continue d'inspirer Hugues, même quand il explique Denys" (*Science et sagesse,* p. 173; cf. p. 225). Hugh, like Eriugena, displays an interpenetration of Augustinian and Dionysian motifs, but within a more western modality in which Augustine is the dominant figure. See also Roger Baron, "Le commentaire de la 'Hiérarchie céleste' par Hugues de Saint-Victor," in *Études sur Hugues de Saint-Victor,* pp. 133–213.

98. Texts concerning Hugh's language of experience have been collected by Pierre Miquel, *Le vocabulaire latin de l'expérience spirituelle* (Paris: Beauchesne, 1989), pp. 163–85.

99. *De arca myst.* 9 (697B): . . . quia integritatem animae, quam ignorantia frangit, cognitio invenit, meditatio colligit, contemplatio per ignem divini amoris liquefaciendo in monetam divinae similitudinis reformandam infundit. For the earlier treatment of these three stages,

without the image, see *De arca mor.* 2.7 (642B), which considers the triad in relation to the interpretation of scripture.

100. The final three stages are described in *De arca mor.* 2.8 (642CD), and especially in *De arca myst.* 10 (697BD). In *De arca myst.* 7 (694D–95D) the final three ladders are also compared to the three classes of animals in the ark (reptiles, quadrupeds, and birds) as signifying "those who use the world rightly" (the married), "those who flee the world" (the clergy), and "those who forget the world" (monastics and canons). This suggests that Hugh believed contemplative experience was open to all in the church. See also the reference to the three *mansiones* in *De arrha animae* (PL 176:966A).

101. This discussion takes up the whole of *De arca mor.* 3 (645D–64A). The stages are *timor-gratia-dolor-fides-devotio-compunctio-desiderium-caritas-spes-circumspectio-disciplina-virtus-patientia/perseverentia-mors-contemplatio.*

102. *De arca mor.* 3.7 (654AC) treats of "De incremento arboris sapientiae per desiderium," which, much like Gregory the Great's notion of contemplation, is a brief experience in which "the intellectual soul is raised up to the eminence of contemplation" (*animus in quamdam contemplationis speculam sublevatur*), which both fills it with wonder but also grieves it because it sees how far it still is from the heavenly home. Such a person, however, "glories inwardly in the hiddenness of the Lord's face" (*intus in abscondito faciei Domini gloriatur*). *De arca mor.* 3.8 (654CD) compares the "strengthening of the tree of wisdom by charity" to a *sacra ebrietas.* There is one other discussion in the *De arca mor.* which contains mystical elements. Book 4 is mostly a treatise on the *opus conditionis* and the *opus reparationis,* but in chap. 4 (669B–70B) there is a treatment of the "game of love" between God and the soul making extensive use of the Song of Songs.

103. See, e.g., the analysis of how the soul goes out of the ark in *De arca mor.* 2.2–5 (636B–39C).

104. See *Soliloquium de arrha animae* (hereafter *De arrha*) in PL 176:967D–68B, and 970AC. Hugh is also autobiographical in his reminiscences concerning his youthful scholarly curiosity in *Did.* 6.3 (Buttimer, 114–15).

105. The list of these writings and their dating, especially given the problem of determining authentic Hugonian minor treatises from pseudonymous ones, is complex. In line with authorities such as D. van den Eynde, *Essai sur la succession et la date,* I accept the *De arrha animae* (*De arrha*), the *De laude charitatis,* and the *De amore sponsi ad sponsam* (*De amore*), which are to be found in PL 176:951B–70D, 969D–76D, and 987B–98A respectively. In addition, see the treatises *De meditatione* (*De medit.*), the *De substantia dilectionis* (*De subst. dilect.*), and the *Quid vere diligendus sit,* edited by Roger Baron in *Hugues de Saint-Victor: Six Opuscules Spirituels* (SC 155).

106. The treatise has been edited with a lengthy and helpful apparatus by Roger Baron, *Hugues de Saint-Victor: La contemplation et ses espèces* (Tournai-Paris: Desclée, 1958). Baron also discussed the work in detail in his articles "Le Traité De la contemplation et ses espèces," *Revue d'ascetique et de mystique* 39 (1963): 137–51, 294–301, 409–18; 40 (1964): 5–30. Baron tried to vindicate the Hugonian authenticity of the treatise, but even he admitted the extensive cooperation of students. K. Ruh seems correct in describing it as an anonymous work from the Victorine circle (*Geschichte der abendländische Mystik,* pp. 370–80). Though it displays some of Hugh's creativity in dealing with biblical symbols, it often degenerates into endless triple distinctions that fail to display the master's hand.

107. Bonaventure, *De reductione artium ad theologiam* 5 (*Opera omnia* [Quaracchi: Collegium S. Bonaventurae, 1882–1902] 5:321): Circa primum insudare debet studium doctorum, circa secundum studium praedicatorum, circa tertium studium contemplativorum. Primum maxime docet Augustinus, secundum maxime docet Gregorius, tertium vero docet Dionysius–Anselmus sequitur Augustinum, Bernardus sequitur Gregorium, Richardus sequitur

Dionysium, quia Anselmus in ratiocinatione, Bernardus in praedicatione, Richardus in contemplatione–Hugo vero omnia haec.

108. *De arca mor.* 3.6 (651D–52A): Vita autem aeterna Christus est. Christus autem sapientia est, sapientia vero thesaurus est. Et hic thesaurus absconditus est in agro cordis humani, ubi factus est homo ad imaginem et similitudinem Creatoris sui. Quoniam ita conditum est cor hominis, ut in eo tamquam in speculo quodam suo divina sapientia reluceret, et quae in se videri non potuit, in sua imagine visibilis appareret. Magna prorsus dignitas hominis portare imaginem Dei, et illius in se jugiter vultum aspicere, atque eum semper per contemplationem praesentem habere. For more on the soul as *speculum*, see *De sac.* 1.3.6–7 (219AB), and especially the discussion of the difference between seeing in a mirror and face-to-face in *De sac.* 1.10.9 (341D–44A). A possible source is in Augustine, *De Trinitate* 15.23.44 (PL 42:1091). The notion of heart (*cor*) is also significant to Hugh; see the treatment in Baron, *La contemplation et ses espèces*, p. 100.

109. Hugh, *De tribus diebus* 17 (PL 176:824D): Primum ergo est ac principale sapientiae sacramentum sapientia creata, id est rationalis creatura quae, quia secundum aliquid visibilis est, secundum aliquid invisibili[s], janua contemplationis facta est pariter et via. In quantum visibilis, est janua; inquantum invisibilis, est via. See also the discussion of the relation of *sapientia creata* and *sapientia increata* in *De naturis ignis et speciebus* (PL 177:568D). For Eriugena's teaching on *sapientia creatrix* and *sapientia creata*, see chapter 3, pp. 104–6. There can be no doubt that Hugh knew Eriugena, both through his translation of Dionysius and his own works (see *Did.* 3.2 [Buttimer, 49.3–4]); but the extent of the Irishman's influence on him has not been systematically examined. Hugh did criticize Eriugena directly, especially his view of the continuing necessity of theophanic vision of God even in heaven. On this see Jean Chatillon, "Hugues de Saint-Victor critique de Jean Scot," in *Jean Scot Érigène et l'histoire de la philosophie*, (*Actes du II Colloque international Jean Scot Érigène. Laon, 1975*), ed. René Roques (Paris: CNRS, 1977), pp. 415–31.

110. The *De unione corporis et spiritus* is edited in PL 177:285–94. For a brief summary of Hugh's teaching on the soul, see L. Reypens, "Âme," DS 1:442–44. Also helpful is Roger Baron, "La situation de l'homme d'après Hugues de Saint-Victor," in *L'homme et son destin d'après les penseurs du moyen âge* (Louvain-Paris: Nauwelaerts, 1960), pp. 431–36. More complete treatments are Heinrich Ostler, *Die Psychologie des Hugo von St. Viktor*, Beiträge zur Geschichte der Philosophie des Mittelalters 6.1 (Münster: Aschendorff, 1906); and John P. Kleinz, *The Theory of Knowledge of Hugh of St. Victor* (Washington: Catholic University, 1944).

111. *De sac.* 1.6.2 (PL 175:264C): Factus est homo ad imaginem et similitudinem Dei, . . . Imago secundum rationem, similitudo secundum dilectionem. . . . Part 6 of Book 1 discusses the creation of humanity, while Part 7 treats the fall. For a comparable treatment, see the *In Pentateuchon* (PL 175:37CD).

112. *De arca mor.* 1.4 (632B): Hoc est enim ad ipsum tendere, et ad ipsum pertingere, semper eum per desiderium quaerere, et per cognitionem invenire, et per gustum tangere.

113. For the background, see Aimé Solignac, "Oculus (Animae, Cordis, Mentis)," DS 11:591–601, which discusses Hugh on cols. 598–99.

114. The classic expositions of this theme are found in *In Hier.* 3 (PL 175:975B–76A), and the *De sac.* 1.10.2 (PL 176:329C–30A). The variant formula of *oculus carnis-oculus cordis-oculus Dei* is found in *De unione* (PL 177:292BD) and *De verbo Dei* 4.2 (SC 155:72).

115. This triad appears, as we have seen, as the three stages of the ascent of illumination in the ark treatises, see *De arca mor.* 2.10 and 4.9 (642B and 679C), and *De arca myst.* 7–10 (692C, 697AB, and 697C). It is also found in *In Eccles.* 1, where it is described as the "tres . . . animae rationalis visiones" (116D–17A). On the triad, see "Meditation," in DS 10:911–12.

116. These five stages also appear in *De medit.* 2.1 (SC 155:46).

117. *Cogitatio* is a general term for almost any kind of thinking. The most complete definition is found in *In Eccles.* 1 (116D): Cogitatio est, cum mens notione rerum transitorie tangitur cum ipsa res, sua imagine animo subito praesentatur, vel per sensum ingrediens, vel a memoria exsurgens.

118. Hugh, *De medit.* (SC 155:44–58). This triple division (*in creaturis/in scripturis/in moribus*) is different from the division found in *Did.* 3.10 (Buttimer, 60.3–5): unum constat in circumspectione morum, aliud in scrutatione mandatorum, tertium in investigatione divinorum operum.

119. Simon Tugwell rightly sees Hugh as an important influence on Guigo in this connection (*Ways of Imperfection*, pp. 107–8, 114–16).

120. *De medit.* (SC 155:44), and *De contemp.* 1 (Baron, 41). On Hugh's definitions of meditation, see n. 4 in Baron, pp. 98–99.

121. Like many others, Hugh spoke of the created world as a book written by God. See especially *De tribus diebus* 3 (PL 176:814B): Universus enim mundus iste sensibilis quasi quidem liber est scriptus digito Dei, hoc est virtute divina creatus, et singulae creaturae quasi figurae quaedam sunt non humano placito inventae, sed divino arbitrio institutae ad manifestandam invisibilium Dei sapientiam.

122. *De modo orandi* 1 (PL 176:977C): Sic ergo orationi sancta meditatio necessaria est, ut omnino perfecta esse oratio nequeat, si enim meditatio non comitetur aut praecedat. Hugh's discussion of the relation between *meditatio* and *oratio* in chapter 1 of this work (977C–79A) would be interesting to compare with that found later in Guigo's *Scala claustralium* discussed in the previous chapter.

123. For Hugh's teaching on *contemplatio*, at least with regard to general categories, see R. Baron, *Science et sagesse*, pp. 192–93 n. 101. The survey of "Le courant victorin" in the DS article on "Contemplation" (2:1961–66) slights Hugh in favor of Richard.

124. For a list of these uses, see Baron, *Science et sagesse*, pp. 192-93 n. 101, nos. 1–5.

125. See n. 62 above.

126. In *Eccl.* 1 (118B): In speculatione, novitas insolitae visionis in admirationem sublevat. In contemplatione, mirae dulcedinis gustus totam in gaudium, in jucunditatem commutat. *Speculatio* is also used as an equivalent of *contemplatio*, as we might expect, in the Dionysian commentary (see PL 175:1054B). *Did.* 2.18 (Buttimer, 37.18–19) describes the highest form of science as follows: solam autem theoricam, propter speculationem veritatis rerum, sapientiam nominamus.

127. *De sac.* 1.10.4 (PL 176:333C): . . . in tantum ut jam quodammodo eum per contemplationem praesentem habere incipiat. . . .

128. For some references to *contemplatio* in the ark treatises, see, e.g., *De arca mor.* (631D, 632A, 636B, 646C, 652A, 654B, 655D, 656D, 662A, 667A, 667D, 671A, and 679C); and the *De arca myst.* (692C, 694A, 697AB, and 698D), and *De van.* (704CD, 717A, 718A). See also, e.g., *In Eccl.* 10 (PL 175:178AC), *De amore sponsi ad sponsam* (PL 176:987C), *De tribus diebus* (PL 176:835D), and *De unione* (PL 177:285AC).

129. *De contemp.* (Baron, 41.3–6): Iuxta primarias veterum auctoritates, contemplatio est per multimodas salutis vias animi disgressio; vel contemplatio est ad invisibilia Dei salubriter afficiens animum mentis illuminatio. The precise sources for these two definitions have not been found.

130. *De contemp.* (Baron, 61–66). The *studia* comprise four kinds of private *revelationes*, seven *emissiones*, and four *inspirationes*. The *emissiones* (the term may be based on Song 4:13) are divided into three that proceed from the left side of the tree of life (*odium iniquitatis-puritas mentis-dulcedo contemplationis*) and three from the right side (*amor virtutis-spes immortalitatis-oscula divine suavitatis*). The *fructus sapientiae* crowns the whole. The latter two are characterized as what we can call mystical graces: . . . sexta felicem in cubiculum regni introducit, sep-

tima future felicitatis gaudium ad modicum praelibare permittit (Baron, 64.16–18). Similarly, the final *inspiratio*, the *affectus coniugii*, is described as: . . . sponsam sponso copulat et lectulo inserit.

131. This is not to say that traditional mystical terms do not also appear in the discussion of the first two forms of *scrutinium morum*: *de cognitione sui* (Baron 74.11–17); and *de cognitione proximi* (Baron, 76.7–16).

132. *De contemp.* (Baron, 82.25–26): Hec omnia per excessum diximus, ut sanctos vidisse Deum per contemplationis radium ostendamus.

133. See the description of these, with a rich development of scriptural reminiscences and citations, found in *De contemp.* (Baron, 83.11–86.21). The motifs of the *sibilum* and the *palmum* are based on Gregory the Great (see chapter 2, pp. 67 and 76).

134. *De contemp.* (Baron, 87.1–3 and 7–13): Felicissima visio est qua perpauci in presenti felices fruuntur, in qua, nimia divini gustus dulcedine rapti, Deum tantum contemplantur. . . . In hoc vero animus splendore lucis eterne totus illustratur, constanter et perfecte peccatum odit, mundum postponit, seipsum abicit, et totus, solus, nudus, et purus, in Deum tendit, totus numquam digrediens, sed uni Deo se totum uniens, solus a materia, nudus a forma, purus a [circumscriptione] omnimoda.

135. See Gregory the Great, *In Ezech.* 2.5.9 (discussed in chapter 2, p. 56).

136. Hugh is not an apophatic thinker in the strict sense of the term, though he was not unaffected by Dionysian apophaticism; see, e.g., *In Hier.* 3.2 and 6.7 (PL 175:975CD, 1040AC).

137. *De contemp.* (Baron, 88.20–21): Sic perunctam somnus eam caelestis arripit dulcedinis, et tunc quiescit liquefacta in amplexu summi luminis.

138. The text, almost in the manner of much later mystical writings from the sixteenth and seventeenth centuries, insists on the cessation, or "binding," of the soul's powers: Ratio anime dormit, quia, causam tante felicitatis ignorans, originem, proventum et finem apprehendere non sufficit. Memoria dormit, quia que iocunditate et suavitate ineffabili tota sopitur, nichil eorum que passa est reminiscitur. Voluntas vero dormit, quia illam ineffabilis gaudii suavitatem quam sentit, sentire se nescit (Baron, 89.2–7).

139. These stages, described in Baron, 89.9–90.19, are illustrated through a collection of texts from the Song of Songs.

140. *De arca mor.* 3.1 (647A): Charitas enim ipsa est sapientia, quia per charitatem Deum gustamus, gustando autem cognoscimus, sicut dicit Psalmista: Gustate et videte quoniam suavis est Dominus. The same doctrine is put even more succinctly in a text from *De sac.* 2.13.11 (539D): Ubi charitas est, claritas est. Cf. *In Eccl.* 10 (PL 175:179B): Quid est sapientia? Cognoscere et amare bonum.

141. Brief definitions are offered in *De subst. dilect.* 2 (SC 155:86). For an outline of Hugh's understanding of *caritas*, see Baron, *La contemplation et ses espèces*, p. 109 n.38.

142. For a brief invocation of the universal force of *amor-desiderium* in the universe, see *De van.* 2 (PL 176:713A). As the *De arrha* puts it (967B): . . . et tamen scimus quod omnium origo charitas est.

143. *De arrha* (PL 176:951D): Ego scio, quod vita tua dilectio est et scio quod sine dilectione esse non potes.

144. See *De subst. dilect.* 1 (SC 155:82–84).

145. *De arca mor.* 2.6 (640B): . . . charitas, quae nos Deo conjungit, et ideo in supremo arca ad unum colligitur; ut jam unum cogitemus, unum expectamus, unum desideremus Dominum nostrum Jesum Christum.

146. See especially, *In Hier.* 6.7 (PL 175:1038D): . . . dilectio supereminet scientiae et major est intelligentia. Plus enim diligitur, quam intelligitur, et intrat dilectio, et appropinquat, ubi scientia foris est.

147. *De laude charitatis* (PL 176:973D): Per charitatem itaque eligis, per charitatem curris, per charitatem apprehenderis et frueris.

148. The *Soliloquium de arrha animae* is edited in PL 176:951C–70D. There is an English translation by Kevin Herbert, *Hugh of St. Victor: Soliloquy on the Earnest Money of the Soul* (Milwaukee: Marquette University Press, 1965). All translations are my own unless otherwise noted.

149. The notion of *oratio pura* as mediating between *meditatio* and *contemplatio* is discussed in *De modo orandi* 2 (PL 176:980AD). What is said of pure prayer here conforms well with the *confessio* that closes the *De arrha* (967C–70D)–Ita ut pura oratio magis in jubilum convertatur, et appropinquet Deo, perveniat citius, et efficacius obtineat (980D).

150. The Victorine interweaves the story of Esther, the bride prepared for the King, with the *sponsa* of the Song of Songs in 964A–67C. The *triclinium* where the bride is readied for the heavenly *cubiculum* is, of course, the church. The means used for her beautification (*unguenta-pigmenta-vestimenta-cibus*) are the sacraments and the life of prayer and virtuous living. Scripture is the *speculum* in which the bride can gauge her renewed attraction for the Divine Lover who has rescued her from the squalor of sin.

151. *De arrha* (968C): Semper praesentem se exhibet, semper paratum se offert, quocunque vertero me, non me deserit, ubicunque fuero non recedit, quidquid egero pariter assistit. . . . Ex quo constat quod licet facies ejus adhuc a nobis non possit videri, nunquam tamen possit praesentia ejus evitari.

152. *De arrha* (970AB): . . . quid est illud dulce, quod in ejus recordatione aliquando me tangere solet, et tam vehementer atque suaviter afficere, ut jam tota quodammodo a memetipsa abalienari, et nescio quo abstrahi incipiam. Subito enim innovor et tota immutor, et bene mihi esse incipit ultra quam dicere sufficiam. . . . (J)amque alibi (nescio ubi) me esse video, et quasi quiddam amplexibus amoris intus teneo, et nescio quid illud sit, et tamen illud semper retinere, et nunquam perdere toto adnisu laboro. . . . Nunquid ille est dilectus meus? Quaeso, dic mihi, ut sciam an ille est, ut si denuo ad me venerit, obsecrem eum ne recedat, sed semper permaneat.

153. Hugh, *Miscellanea* 173, "De naturis ignis et speciebus" (PL 177:570D–71A): In omnibus autem quae videntur, et a quibus rerum invisibilium similitudo trahitur, solus ignis sicut loco supremus est, ita quoque significationibus est praecipuus. Cf. *In Hier.* 10 (PL 175:1140C): . . . videtur ignis quodammodo medius esse inter invisibilia et visibilia.

154. *Miscellanea* 173 (572A): . . . et quodammodo per amoris ignem liquefacit, ut jam per desiderium currere incipiat, quae prius frigida existens male torpebat. Et sicut massa liquefacta per fistulam in monetam funditur et formam accipit, ita mens, amoris igne soluta per radium contemplationis usque in imaginem divinae similitudinis currit.

155. *De arca myst.* 9 (697AB). A different use of the fire image is found in *De arca mor.* 3.7 (654AC) where *ignis* signifies the fire of compunction that leads to the ascent to God figured by a *virgula fumi*. The *De arrha* briefly notes the connection between fire and love in 954B: Scis quod amor ignis est, et ignis quidem fomentum quaerit ut ardeat.

156. *In Hier.* 6.7 (PL 175:1036D–39D). Hugh is using Eriugena's translation: Mobile enim semper eorum circa divina, et incessabile, et calidum, et acutum, et superfervidum intentae, et forsan intimae, et inflexibilis semper motionis. . . .

157. Ibid. (1038A): Et puto quod sponsa erat ipsa, quae loquebatur; et non oportebat durum aliquid aut asperum paventi et timidi adduci. Idcirco liquidum nominatum est pro acuto in blandimento dilectionis.

158. *In Eccl.* 1 (PL 175:117B–18B). For the relation of this image to John's frequent reprisals of the theme, see C. Sclafert, "L'allégorie de la buche enflamée dans Hugues de Saint-Victor et dans Saint Jean de la Croix," *Revue d'ascetique et de mystique* 33 (1957): 241–63, 361–86.

159. *In Eccl.* 1 (118AB): Primum ergo, quia inter pericula tentationum consilium quaeritur, quasi in meditatione fumus cum flamma est. Secundo quia mente pura cor ad contemplationem veritatis diffunditur, quasi in principio contemplationis flamma sine fumo est. Tertio, quia jam inventa veritate et perfecta charitate, nihil ultra id quod unicum est, quaeritur; in solo amoris igne, summa tranquillitate et felicitate suaviter repulsatur.

160. The notion of *caritas ordinata* is discussed at some length in the *De subst. dil.* 2–4 (SC 155:86–92), and also in the *De contemp.* (Baron, 51). On the relation of love of God and love of neighbor, see *In Hier.* 6.7 (1042AD).

161. See especially *De sac.* 2.18.16 (PL 176:613A–14C).

162. Among these are (1) the treatise *De septem septennis*, often ascribed to John of Salisbury, whose sixth section is devoted to "De septem generibus contemplationis" (PL 199:955–60); (2) Hugh of Fouilloy's allegorical *De claustro animae* (PL 176:1017–1182), which was often attributed to Hugh of St. Victor (see R. Baron, "Hugues de Fouilloy," *Revue du moyen âge latin* 2 [1946]: 25–44); and (3) the four anonymous books, especially the last two, attributed both to Bernard of Clairvaux and Hugh found in PL 177:165–91 (see Ermengildo Bertola, "Di alcuni trattati psicologici attribuiti ad Ugo da San Vittore," *Rivista di filosofia neoscolastica* 51 [1959]: 436–55).

163. These fragments were preserved by the fourteenth-century Franciscan John of Ripa, who was interested in them because of their teaching on the divine ideas. They have been edited by André Combes, *Un inédit de Saint Anselme? Le traité 'De unitate divinae essentiae et pluralitate creaturarum' d'après Jean de Ripa* (Paris: Vrin, 1944); with supplements by M.-T. d'Alverny, "Notes 2. Achard de Saint-Victor. De Trinitate-De unitate et pluralitate creaturarum," *Recherches de théologie ancienne et médiévale* 21 (1954): 299–306.

164. The latest edition is by Nicholas M. Haring, "Gilbert of Poitiers, Author of the *De discretione animae, spiritus et mentis* commonly attributed to Achard of Saint-Victor," *Mediaeval Studies* 22 (1960): 148–91. In response, the traditional ascription to Achard was defended by Jean Chatillon, "Achard de Saint-Victor et le 'De discretione animae, spiritus et mentis,'" *Archives d'histoire doctrinale et littéraire du moyen âge* 31 (1964): 7–35.

165. Edited by Jean Chatillon, *Achard de Saint-Victor: Sermons inédits* (Paris: Vrin, 1970). See also Chatillon's *Théologie, spiritualité et métaphysique*, especially chaps. IX–XI, for a summary of his spiritual teaching.

166. A full study of the role of Eriugena in Achard's thought is lacking, but there are useful remarks in Chatillon, *Théologie, spiritualité et métaphysique*, pp. 286–88, 294–99, 301–2, and 311–13.

167. *Sermo* 12 (Chatillon, 122–30). The sermon discusses nine transfigurations of Christ and fifteen transfigurations of the Christian as a spiritual itinerary embracing both this life (eleven from *penitentia* through *mors*) and four in the life to come. It ends with the "new heaven and earth" seen as a return into: . . . mundum archetipum qui in mente Dei erat antequam in hunc mundum sensibilem et visibilem prodiret (12.8, 129–all citations will be by sermon and paragraph, followed by page number to the Chatillon edition).

168. *Sermo* 13 (134–68). The sermon, as Achard admits, deals more with the building up than the dedication of the *domus sapientiae* (Prov 9:1). Christ, the Divine Wisdom, builds three dwellings in us, each with seven columns: the *domus virtutis* constructed of the squared stones of virtues; the *domus unctionis* made of the cedar wood signifying the seven interior delights of the Holy Spirit; and the *domus contemplationis* whose gold is seven forms of contemplation. Achard is obviously thinking of Hugh when he summarizes the dwelling motif: Cum autem

tres domus prefate in uno edificantur corde, ibi velut in unam jungantur domum, ut sint quodammodo et tres et una. Tres in una et una in tribus, domus una et trina, utpote domus Dei unius et trini, domus una et tamen, ut archa Noe, tripliciter distincta (13.5, 139). Especially important in this sermon is the treatment of the mutual interaction between the *delectationes*, signifying work of the Holy Spirit, and the *contemplationes* related to Christ (13.33, 166–67).

169. *Sermo* 14 (171–95). The stages of the ascent to God are here portrayed by an itinerary of five active stages represented by the saints and nine contemplative stages figured in the angelic hierarchies. These are grouped according to Achard's distinctive division of the *rationes sive causae* into *judiciales, formales atque finales* (14.21, 193), on which see Chatillon, *Théologie, spiritualité et métaphysique*, pp. 284–89. In this sermon Mary appears as the ideal contemplative in whom the divine birth as actual bearing of Christ and as ecstatic rapture in God is realized (see 14.22, 193–94).

170. Hugh of St. Victor, *Misc.* 111 (PL 177:539B–40B), based on Sg 3:6.

171. *Sermo* 15 (199–243). For a survey of the desert theme, see McGinn, "Ocean and Desert as Symbols of Mystical Absorption," which, however, neglects Achard's contribution.

172. *Sermo* 15.2 (202): A suo Spiritu ductus in desertum nostrum, immo in nos desertum, in quo et nobis reliquit exemplum ut sequamur vestigia ejus, nosque post eum et per eum in desertum ducamur....

173. *Sermo* 15.11 (211): ... pervenit ad montem dei, id est ad spiritum suum.... Is Dei mons est, quia in eo Dei consistit imago atque similitudo: imago in ratione, similitudo in voluntate. This standard Victorine teaching echoes Hugh (e.g., *De sac.* 1.6.2 [PL 176:264D]) and is also found in the *De discret.* 33 (ed. Haring, 181).

174. *Sermo* 15.15 (216): Transi ad lucem illam que est interius et lucet in tenebris, ut non tantum in eis luceat, sed et illuminet tenebras tuas. Ipsa est Dei ratio, veritas eterna....

175. *Sermo* 15.17 (220): Quis etiam sapiens, et intelliget quomodo quicquid factum est in mundo antequam fieret, sive vivens, sive non vivens in semetipso, vita fuerit in Dei Verbo? Achard's identification of the *abyssus* of Gen 1:2 with the primordial causes (ibid., 219) echoes the Irishman's teaching; see *Periphyseon* 2 (550B–51B and 563AB).

176. *Sermo* 15.19 (221): Aquilam in celo animam reor ereptam a corporis laqueo et per contemplationem libere alis quibusdam intellectualibus suspensam in Deo. Cf. *Sermo* 2.3 (40) for an extended description of the joys of heaven. This definition of heavenly contemplation utilizes the term *suspensa* that later appears in Richard's general definition–Contemplatio est libera mentis perspicacia in sapientiae spectacula cum admiratione suspensa (*De arca Moysi* 1.4 [PL 196:67D]).

177. Achard's teaching on the manner of Christ's presence in the sacrament here (*Sermo* 15.27–29) underlines the strongly eucharistic character of his spiritual teaching. See also *Sermo* 4.1–2 (55–57).

178. *Sermo* 15.33 (236–37): ... labetur profecto et, luce Dei reverberatus, densioribus implicabitur tenebris, nisi forte Deus expandat alas suas et assumat eum (cf. Deut 32:11). This use of *reverberatus* recalls the importance of this term in the mystical vocabulary of Augustine and Gregory the Great.

179. *Sermo* 15.34 (237): Felix commercium! Homo hominem exit, et Deum introducit. O quam letus et quam gratus hospes, domum quam intrat totam letitia replens et gratia. Sed sic hominem exire seipsum propter Deum non adeo est exire, quam intrare. Exit enim, non ut a domo in atrium, sed ut a domo in thalamum.... Hec etenim voluntas est et ratio divina ut de se sibi nichil retineat; unde, cum se totum deserit, voluntas Dei et ratio in eo habitat tota; *adheret Deo* et sic cum eo *unus est spiritus*. Achard also employs the verse in *Sermo* 2.3 (40) and 13.1 and 7 (134–35, 141).

180. These and a number of other traditional motifs are found in *Sermo* 15.34–35 (238–40). See the discussion in Chatillon, *Théologie, spiritualité et métaphysique*, pp. 265–74. The doctrine

of *excessus mentis,* using traditional biblical texts (e.g., Pss 67:28; 115:11), is also discussed in *De discret.* 67–71 (ed. Haring, 189–91). Achard taught that Christ enjoyed permanent *excessus mentis,* see *Sermo* 15.24 (227). The doctrine of *excessus mentis* found in these texts should be compared with what Achard has to say about the seventh and final form of *contemplatio* in *Sermo* 13.32 (166) and the treatment of Mary as the supreme contemplative in *Sermo* 14.22 (194), where Paul's rapture to the third heaven is also invoked.

181. *Sermo* 13.15 (150): Forma autem ista et Dei est et nostra: Dei est quia a Deo est, nostra est quia in nobis est; a Deo est expressa, et ab ipso nobis est impressa. See also the powerful prayer that closes this sermon (13.34, 168): Christe, magister bone, ut per tria hec inhabites in toto me et ego totus in te, simque ego totus tibi et tu totas michi, totum me trahens ad te et me totum replens in te, nec aliunde quam de ipso te, ut sic in toto me, nec solum a toto me, sed et a toto celesti domo tua sine fine lauderis pro toto me in te. Amen.

182. *Sermo* 15.37 (242): Sextum et septimum sunt excedere et excedi: excedere Deo et excedi a Deo, excedere creaturam et excedi a creatore, excedere ad contemplationem, excedi ad admirationem.

183. For an introduction to Richard's thought, see especially Jean Chatillon, "Richard de Saint-Victor," DS 13:593–654. For a survey of his contribution to mysticism, see K. Ruh, *Geschichte der abendländische Mystik,* pp. 381–406.

184. *Richard de Saint-Victor. Liber exceptionum. Texte critique avec introduction, notes et tables,* ed. Jean Chatillon (Paris: Vrin, 1958). This handbook goes beyond Hugh's *Did.* in combining an introduction to the arts, a survey of world history, a lengthy allegorical interpretation of biblical history, sermons, and other materials. See R. Roques, "Une encyclopédie du savoir médiévale: Le 'Liber exceptionum' de Richard de Saint-Victor," *Structures théologiques,* pp. 365–74.

185. Many of Richard's scriptural and theological works appear in PL 196. Among the commentaries, see especially *Mysticae adnotationes in Psalmos* (265–401), *In visionem Ezechielis* (527–600), and the *In Apocalypsim Joannis libri septem* (686–888). The *In Cantica Canticorum expositio* (405–524) is not by Richard, but belongs to the thirteenth century.

186. *Richard de Saint-Victor. De Trinitate. Texte critique avec introduction, notes et tables,* ed. Jean Ribaillier (Paris: Vrin, 1958). Much has been written on this important work. See especially A.-M. Ethier, *Le "De Trinitate" de Richard de Saint-Victor* (Paris-Ottawa: Institut d'Études Médiévales d'Ottawa, 1939); and Heinz Wipfler, *Die Trinitätsspekulation des Petrus von Poitiers und Die Trinitätsspekulation des Richard von St. Viktor. Ein Vergleich* (Münster: Aschendorff, 1965).

187. Some of the spiritual treatises not found in PL 196 have been edited in *Richard de Saint-Victor: Sermons et opuscules spirituels inédits,* ed. Jean Chatillon and William-Joseph Tulloch (Paris: Desclée, 1949).

188. *De praeparatione animi ad contemplationem. Liber dictus Benjamin minor* (PL 196:1–64), which in some manuscripts. is called *Liber de duodecim patriarchis.* (I will follow the traditional form of abbreviation in my citations as *Benj. min.* with chapter number and column in Migne.) There is a translation by Grover A. Zinn in *Richard of St. Victor: The Twelve Patriarchs, The Mystical Ark, Book Three of the Trinity* (New York: Paulist Press, 1979), pp. 53–147, though the versions are my own unless otherwise noted.

189. *De gratia contemplationis ... hactenus dictum Benjamin major (De arca mystica)* (PL 196:63–202) (I will abbreviate it as *Benj. maj.* by book, chapter, and column from PL). Although it is translated in Zinn, *Richard of St. Victor,* pp. 151–370, I will use my own versions.

190. The best edition is *Ives. Épitre à Severin sur la charité. Richard de Saint-Victor. Les quatres degrés de la violent charité,* ed. Gervais Dumeige (Paris: Vrin, 1955). For a study see G. Dumeige, *Richard de·Saint-Victor et l'idée chrétienne de l'amour.* There is an English translation in

Richard of St. Victor. Selected Writings on Contemplation, translated with an introduction and notes by Clare Kirchberger (New York: Harper, n.d.), pp. 213–33, but I will use my own versions.

191. Richard's anthropology and pyschology have been much studied. For a brief overview, see Chatillon in DS 13:632–39. More detailed treatments include Joseph Ebner, *Die Erkenntnislehre Richards von Saint-Viktor* (Münster: Aschendorff, 1917); and Carmelo Ottaviano, *Riccardo di San Vittore, La vita, le opere, il pensiero,* in *Memorie della Romana Accademia Nazionale dei Lincei,* Ser. VI, vol. iv, fasc. 5 (Rome, 1933), pp. 411–541. Considerable attention is given to Richard's psychology and mysticism in the works of Robert Javelet, especially his *Psychologie des auteurs spirituels du XIIe siècle* (Strasbourg, 1959); *Image et ressemblance au douzième siècle,* 2 vols. (Paris: Letouzey & Ané, 1967); and "La dignité de l'homme dans la pensée du XIIe siècle," in *De Dignitate Hominis: Mélanges offerts à Carlos-Josaphat Pinto de Oliveira* (Frieburg: Herder, 1987), pp. 39–87. See also Stephan Otto, *Die Funktion des Bildbegriffes in der Theologie des 12. Jahrhunderts* (Münster: Aschendorff, 1963), pp. 148–63; and Jean Ribaillier, "Richard de Saint-Victor. De statu interioris hominis," *Archives d'histoire doctrinale et littéraire du moyen âge* 34 (1967): 1–128. For general background to twelfth-century anthropology, see B. McGinn, "Introduction," *Three Treatises on Man,* pp. 1–100.

192. *Liber exceptionum* 1.1.1 (ed. Chatillon, 104): . . . ad imaginem suam secundum rationem, ad similitudinem suam secundum dilectionem. . . . Ad imaginem suam secundum intellectum, ad similitudinem suam secundum affectum. For an expanded consideration of the two powers, see, e.g., *Benj. maj.* 3.13 (122C–23C). We have already seen this teaching in Hugh (see p. 385). This does not hinder Richard from presenting a somewhat different understanding of image and likeness, influenced by Bernard of Clairvaux's *De gratia et libero arbitrio,* in *De statu interioris hominis* 3.14 (ed. Ribaillier, 78–79): Hujusmodi namque consensus cur non recte dicatur ad imaginem et similitudinem Dei factus: in quantum liber, ad imaginem, in quantum rationalis, ad similitudinem? A more complete presentation of his views on *imago Dei* anthropology would have to take into account his Dionysian insistence on the *dissimilis similitudo* that pertains between the soul and God; see *In Apoc.* 1.1 (689D).

193. Richard's teaching about the three goods given to humans, the three evils that affect them since the fall, and the three remedies given to overcome them form the basis for his discrimination of the fundamental disciplines involved in humanity's restoration—*theorica-practica-mechanica. Lib. except.* 1.1.2–5 (ed. Chatillon, 104–6).

194. There are helpful charts summarizing the Victorine's treatments in Ottaviano, *Riccardo di San Vittore,* pp. 535–38.

195. Boethius, *De consolatione philsophiae* 5.4: Intelligentiae vero celsior oculus exsistit; supergressa namque universitatis ambitum ipsam illam simplicem formam pura mentis acie contuetur. See *Boethius: The Theological Tractates and The Consolation of Philosophy,* Loeb Classical Library (Cambridge MA: Harvard University Press, 1952), p. 388.

196. For a handy summary, see *Benj. maj.* 1.3 (67AB). The same Boethian fourfold division was also the source for the fivefold division of *sensus-imaginatio-ratio-intellectus-intelligentia* found in Isaac of Stella. Isaac took this over from Hugh of St. Victor, whose *Misc.* 1.15 (PL 177:485BC) of ca. 1130 appears to be the earliest use. See McGinn, *The Golden Chain,* chap. iv.

197. Boethius, *In Isagogen Porphyrii Commenta* 1.3: est enim intellectibile quod unum atque idem per se in propria semper divinitate consistens nullis umquam sensibus, sed sola tantum mente intellectuque capitur . . . (ed. Brandt in CSEL 48:8–9).

198. In *Benj. min.* 71 (51B) Richard describes Joseph, who represents *discretio* as *plena cognitio sui.* On the importance of self-knowledge in Richard, see P. Courcelle, *Connais-toi toi-même de Socrate à Saint Bernard,* 1:242–46; and Alois Haas, "Christliche Aspekte des 'Gnothi seauton': Selbsterkenntnis und Mystik," in *Geistliches Mittelalter* (Freiburg, Schweiz: Univer-

sitätsverlag, 1984), pp. 84–87. For Richard's teaching on *discretio*, see "Discrétion," DS 3:1323–24, and the discussion below.

199. See, e.g., *De statu interioris hominis* 34 (ed. Ribaillier, 102).

200. *De exterminatione mali et promotione boni* can be found in PL 196:1073–1116. The first part deals with the ascetic level, that is, the twofold *confessio criminis* and *confessio laudis* (cf. *Benj. min.* 12 [9AC]). The second considers the relation between contemplation and the virtues and contemplation and meditation, while the third takes up a series of ancillary issues concluding with a summary chapter "De quiete contemplationis" (1113B–16C).

201. It is these three treatises that justify the claim of J. Ebner (*Die Erkenntnislehre*, p. 120) that Richard can be considered the first systematic mystical theologian (in the scholastic sense, at least).

202. See *Expositio difficultatum suborientium in expositione tabernaculi foederis* (PL 196:211–22).

203. This is the judgment of Chatillon in DS 13:630. For more on Richard's exegesis, see especially H. de Lubac, *Exégèse médiévale*, 3:387–435; and J. Chatillon, "La Bible dans les écoles du XIIe siècle," *Le moyen âge et la Bible* (Paris: Beauchesne, 1984), pp. 177–97.

204. On the three senses of scripture, see *Lib. except.* 1.2.3 (ed. Chatillon, 115–16). Richard also follows tradition in speaking of the allegorical sense as a *mystica intelligentia*, e.g., *Benj. min.* 18 (13AB), and the treatise *Ad me clamat ex Seir (De Verbo incarnato)* 8 (*Richard de Saint-Victor: Opuscules théologiques*, ed. Jean Ribaillier [Paris: Vrin, 1967], p. 266).

205. These three senses are mentioned in *Benj. maj.* 4.14 (151C), and more fully discussed in the summary of the work that Richard produced under the title *Nonnullae allegoriae taberna-culi foederis* (199D–202B), from which the quotation is taken: Quid est enim tropologia nisi moralis scientia, et quid allegoria nisi mystica mysteriorum doctrina. . . . Quid enim dicimus anagogen nisi mysticam et sursum ductivam intelligentiam? (200BC).

206. Peter Damian in the *De perfectione monachorum* 8–10 (PL 145:303–06) had already interpreted Jacob's marriages and children in this vein. For the broader history, see "Rachel et Lia," DS 13:25–30.

207. In the chart the arabic numbers represent the patriarchs, and the roman numbers signify the seven virtues that perfect the *affectio.*

208. Richard's insights as a spiritual pyschologist are especially evident in chaps. 20, 27, 29–30, 39, 41, 49, 50–59, 63, 66, and 69.

209. For a survey of the importance of the text in the history of Christian mysticism, see Grover A. Zinn, "Personification Allegory and Visions of Light in Richard of St. Victor's Teaching on Contemplation," *University of Toronto Quarterly* 46 (1977): 190–214, as well as the same author's "Introduction" in *Richard of St. Victor*, pp. 10–22.

210. *Benj. min.* 1 (1A): Quis sit Benjamin isti multi noverunt, alii per scientiam, alii per experientiam. For further texts on the necessity of experience, see, e.g., chaps. 4(3B–4A), 14(10D), 38(27D), 41(31AB), 67(48AD), 73(52B), 74(52D), 76(54D), and 81(57C). The selections on the role of experience in Richard found in P. Miquel, *Le vocabulaire latin de l'expéri-ence spirituelle*, pp. 186–200, are largely drawn from the inauthentic *Explicatio super Canticum* and are therefore not trustworthy.

211. *Benj. min.* chap. 3 (3B): Ex ratione oriuntur consilia recta; ex affectione, desideria sancta. Ex illa, spirituales sensus; ex ista, ordinati affectus. Richard defines virtue in chap. 7(6B): . . . nihil aliud est virtus quam animi affectus ordinatus et moderatus. Cf. *Benj. maj.* 3.23 (132B).

212. *Benj. min.* 69 (50B): Crede mihi, nihil a se animus difficilius extorquet, quam ut in omni affectione sua modum servet.

213. Richard explicitly equates the three in *Benj. min.* 85 (61C).

214. *Benj. min.* 73 (52D): . . . et Benjamin nascitur, et Rachel moritur, quia cum mens hominis supra seipsam rapitur, omnes humanae ratiocinationis, angustias supergreditur. Ad

illud enim quod supra se elevata, et in extasi rapta, de divinitatis luminis conspicit, omnis humana ratio succumbit.

215. The ascent up the mountain, as described in *Benj. min.* 80 (56D–57B), involves a transition from seeing Christ's seamless garment (i.e., his flesh) to beholding his glorious garment, his divinity. This is comparable to Bernard of Clairvaux's insistence on the necessity of passing from the carnal love of Christ to the spiritual love of his divinity. Richard also has an interesting reading of Moses and Elijah's presence with Christ on the mountain top in chap. 81 (57B–58A). They signify the necessity for the conformity of contemplative experience with the *intelligentia spiritualis* of scripture lest the unwary become confused by the devil, who can also transfigure himself. This is an early reference to what will become a key issue in late medieval mysticism–the importance of distinguishing between true and false ecstatic experiences.

216. Two early articles on the teaching of contemplation in the treatise retain considerable value: J.-A. Robilliard, "Les six genres de contemplation chez Richard de Saint-Victor et leur originne platonicienne," *Revue des scinces philosophiques et théologiques* 28 (1939): 229–33; and Jean Chatillon, "Les trois modes de la contemplation selon Richard de Saint-Victor," *Bulletin de littérature ecclésiastique* 41 (1940): 3–26. See also Zinn, "Personification Allegory and Visions of Light," pp. 202–8, and his "Introduction" in *Richard of St. Victor*, pp. 22–46. Also helpful is the recent dissertation of Steven L. Chase, *Into the Secret Places of Divine Incomprehensibility: The Symbol of the Cherubim in "De Arca Mystica" of Richard of St. Victor* (Fordham University, 1994). I wish to thank Dr. Chase for the opportunity to cite this work.

217. *Benj. maj.* 1.12 (78D): Contemplantis itaque more, contemplationisque tenore de contemplatione agamus. . . .

218. *Benj. maj.* 5.19 (192BC): Melius in hoc nos illorum peritia instruit, quos ad scientiae hujus plenitudinem non tam aliena doctrina quam propria experientia provexit. For texts appealing to experience in the *Benj. maj.*, see, e.g., 1.1 (63CD), 1.6 (71CD), 2.4 (82D), 2.12 (90C), 2.17 (97D), 3.4 (114D), 3.5 (116B), 3.13 (123A), 3.14 (123C), 4.3 (137BC), 4.7 (141A), 4.15 (153D), 4.16 (154D), 5.2 (170A), 5.5 (174CD), 5.13 (183D and 184C), 5.14 (185C–86B), and 5.17 (190AB).

219. *Nonnullae allegoriae tabernaculi foederis* (PL 196:191C–202B). See especially 191C–94A for what follows.

220. *Benj. maj.* 1.4 (67D): Contemplatio est libera mentis perspicacia in sapientiae spectacula cum admiratione suspensa. . . . The same passage also quotes Hugh of St. Victor's definition from *In Eccl.* 1. Later in the treatise (4.22 [164CD]), Richard admits that *excessus mentis*, or *alienatio*, is common in the final two forms of contemplation but that it can also occur on the first four levels. For considerations of Richard's definition of contemplation and his distinction of six levels and three modes in the light of the broad tradition of teaching on contemplation, see DS 2:1962–66; 3:890; 4:2116–20; and 13:640–44.

221. On the first two levels (see *Benj. maj.* 1.3–4 [66C–68C]) Richard, following Hugh, relates *contemplatio* to the lower modalities of *cogitatio*, defined as *improvidus animi respectus ad evagationem pronus*, and *meditatio*, or *providus animi obtutus in veritatis inquisitione vehementer occupatus*.

222. This is especially evident in *Benj. maj.* 1.8 (73C–74B), where Richard discusses the interactions among *imaginatio*, which is present in three of the levels of contemplation; *intelligentia*, also present in three, and *ratio*, which mediates by being found in four.

223. *Benj. maj.* 1.10 (75A): Sex iste contemplationum genera oportet illum familiariter nosse, quicunque cupit scientiae culmen attingere. His sex sane contemplationum alis a terrenis suspendimur et ad coelestia levamur.

224. J. Chatillon has useful comments on the relation of book 5 to the preceding books ("Les trois modes," pp. 23–25).

225. Handy definitions of the six punctuate the treatise: *Benj. maj.* 1 (79B), 2 (85B), 3 (89D), 4 (108D–09A), 5–6 (156AB).

226. See *Benj. maj.* 2.2 and 2.9 (80B–81C and 87A–88A). Cf. 1.10 and 3.3. This is closely related to Richard's treatment of *fides quaerens intellectum*, an important theme that cannot be pursued here. For notices in the *Benj. maj.*, see 1.7 (73BC), 2.10 (88D–89A), 3.3 (137D–38A), and 4.17 (157D–58A).

227. According to *Benj. maj.* 3.9 (118D–19A): Oculus siquidem intelligentiae est sensus ille, quo invisibilia videmus, non sicut oculo rationis. . . . Sed, sicut corporalia corporeo sensu videre solemus visibiliter, praesentialiter atque corporaliter, sic utique intellectualis ille sensus invisibilia capit, invisibiliter quidem, sed praesentialiter, sed essentialiter.

228. E.g., *Benj. maj.* 3.3 (112B–13D), 3.5 (116BD), 3.6 (116D–17C), 3.10 (120D–21B), and 3.13 (122C–23C).

229. *Benj. maj.* 3.7 (117C): In loco autem suo sol renascens paulatim ad altiora conscendit quia per sui cognitionem in coelestium contemplationem assurgit.

230. See S. Chase, *Into the Secret Places of Divine Incomprehensibility*, chap. 6.

231. The passages cited are from 4.1 (135C) and 4.2 (136D): Vere aliquid magnum, vere aliquid praeclarum, aliquid utique supermundanum, et omnino aliquid plusquam humanum esse debuit, quod sub angelica nobis forma repraesentari oportuit. . . . Ut ergo in nobis angelicae similitudinis formam qualicunque modo possimus excudere, oportet in ejusmodi rerum admiratione animum nostrum jugi celeritate suspendere, et ad sublimes et vere angelicos volatus contemplationis nostrae pennas assuescere. On the *angelica forma*, see, e.g., 4.12 and 14 (149A and 152C).

232. *Benj. maj.* 4.8 (143B): Namque caetera quidem tanto ab humana ratione longius recedunt, quanto cujuslibet adjunctae similitudinis rationem transcendunt. Cf. 4.20 (162D).

233. See *Benj. maj.* 4.13–16 (149B–56A). For the distinctive term *theorici excessus* see 155B and D as well as 190B; *anagogici conatus* occurs in 155B.

234. *Benj. maj.* 4.15 (153D): . . . donec tandem, dilecto inter ubera collocato, ad ineffabilem quamdam divinae dulcedinis infusionem tota in illius desiderium liquescat, et spiritus ille qui Domino adhaeret unus spiritus fiat. The appeal to 1 Cor 6:17 in Richard is actually rather rare: see, e.g., 5.12 (182C); *De eruditione* 2.9 (1309A); *De quatuor gradibus* (ed. Dumeige, 153, 169); *Adnotatio in Ps.* 30 (273D–74A); and *De tribus processionibus* 3 (*Sermons et opuscules spirituels*, 70).

235. See esp. *Benj. maj.* 4.17 (156A–58A); cf. S. Chase, *Into the Secret Places of Divine Incomprehensibility*, esp. chaps. 2 and 4.

236. *Benj. maj.* 4.20 (162D): . . . Vide ergo quia in his quae pro similitudine adducta sunt in rationali animo ad illam summam Trinitatem major est dissimilitudo quam similitudo.

237. R. Javelet (*La psychologie des auteurs spirituels*, pp. 62–69) argues that Richard's *De Trinitate* is both a spiritual and a doctrinal work with its first two books being an exercise in the fifth level of *contemplatio* and its last four books one of level six. On the intimate link between the *De Trinitate* and the mystical works, see especially Gaston Salet, "Les chemins de Dieu d'après Richard de Saint-Victor," *L'homme devant Dieu: Mélanges offerts au Père Henri de Lubac*, 3 vols. (Paris: Aubier, 1964), 2:73–88.

238. *Benj. maj.* 4.21 (163A–64C), which S. Chase suggests needs to be taken as a reflection on the discussion of the Word becoming flesh at the end of 4.20 (162D–63A). (*Into the Secret Places of Divine Incomprehensibility*, chap. 5).

239. 4.22–23 (164C–68C). The emphasis given here (e.g., 167A) to the coincidence of the *intimum* and *summum* of the soul echoes a theme of Augustinianism strong in Hugh (see n. 91 above). Chapter 23 also introduces the *velum oblivionis, which alienatio mentis* sets up between the mystic and created reality (see 167B–68C). In 5.2 (170B–71C) this is also called the *nebula oblivionis,* the cloud of forgetting, a theme that will have an important progeny in

the fourteenth-century text *The Cloud of Unknowing*. Richard's *nebula*, however, is different from that of the *Cloud* author insofar as it *illumines* the divine while *darkening* what is created.

240. *Benj. maj.* 5.4 (172D): . . . intelligentia namque humana divinitus inspirata, illo coelesti lumine irradiata, aliquando sublevatur supra scientia, aliquando etiam supra industriam, aliquando autem etiam supra naturam. Since this level deals with *intelligentia*, it seems restricted to the fourth, fifth, and sixth types of contemplation.

241. *In Apocalypsim* 1.1 (686B–87C) distinguishes four forms of *visiones*, two external and two internal. The external forms are (a) corporeal vision itself, and (b) when something presented to corporeal vision is understood to contain a hidden signification (*mystica significatio*: 686C). The example Richard gives is of the many meanings contained in the burning bush seen by Moses. The first mode of internal vision, given to the *oculus cordis*, takes place "quando videlicet animus per Spiritum sanctum illuminatus formalibus rerum visibilium similitudinibus, et imaginibus praesentatis quasi quibusdam figuris et signis invisibilium ducitur cognitionem" (686D). The final form, which he describes as *anagogica*, is "cum spiritus humanus per internam aspirationem subtiliter ac suaviter tactus nullis mediantibus rerum visibilium figuris sive qualitatibus spiritualiter erigitur ad coelestium contemplationem" (686D–87A). Richard's originality in medieval vision theory is evident by comparing these categories with the standard theory of three forms of vision found in Augustine, on which see *Foundations of Mysticism*, p. 254.

242. *De exterminatione mali* 2.9 (1096B): Sane perfectionis gratiam quanto melius agnoscimus, tanto ardentius et concupiscimus, et quo amplius accendimur ad amorem, eo perfectius illuminamur ad agnitionem. On the mutuality of love and knowledge in Richard, besides these chapters in *Benj. maj.* 5 (esp. 5.10 [179B]), see also *Benj. min.* 13 and 29 (10AB and 20CD); *Benj. maj.* 4.10 (145B); and *Adnotatio in Ps. CXXI* (363A–64A). For discussions, see G. Dumeige, *Richard de Saint-Victor et l'idée chrétienne de l'amour*, pp. 122–28; and Robert Javelet, "Intelligence et amour chez les auteurs spirituels du XIIe siècle," *Revue d'ascétique et de mystique* 37 (1961): 283–86.

243. *Benj. maj.* 5.5 (174BC): . . . mens hominis a seipsa alienatur, quando intima illa internae suavitatis abundantia potata, imo plene inebriata, quid sit, quid fuerit, penitus obliviscitur, et in abalienationis excessum, tripudii sui nimietate traducitur, et in supramundanum quendam affectum, sub quodam mirae felicitatis statu raptim traducitur. Richard appeals to the image of the dance of ecstasy several other times in his descriptions of mystical experience, e.g., 1.6, 5.14, and 5.18 (72BC, 186A, 187B, 190BC and 192A), as well as in *Adnotatio in Ps. CXIII* (338BC).

244. *Benj. maj.* 5.11 (180B): Ejusmodi aquae solis radius se infundit, quando divina revelatio meditationi occurit. Sed cum aqua radium in se superni luminis accipit, fulgorem quoque luminis, ut dictum est, ad superiora emittit. . . . Et cum tanta sit differentia aquae et luminis, ei tamen quem de se luminis radio emittit, nonnihil suae similitudinis imprimit, ita ut tremula tremulum, quieta quietum, purior puriorem, diffusior diffusiorem efficiat.

245. The terms *jucunditas* and *exsultatio* occur in *Benj. maj.* 5.14 (184D), and subsequently. The term *jubilatio* appears in *De quatuor gradibus* 29 (ed. Dumeige, 157), and in the *Adnotatio in Ps. CXXXVI*, in dependence on Pss 88:16, 97:4, 65:1, and Job 38:7 (375D–76B). For the wider context, see Aimé Solignac, "Jubilation," DS 8:1471–78 (1474–75 on Richard).

246. See, e.g., the exegesis of Ps 113:4 in *Benj. maj.* 5.14 (186B–87B) and the appeal to the role of jubilant music in the story of the prophet Elisha in 5.17 (189D–90B). Richard's delight in musical imagery is also evident from 3.24 (134D) and 5.18 (190D–92A).

247. I will use the edition of G. Dumeige, *Ives: Épitre à Séverin sur la charité. Richard de Saint-Victor. Les quatres degrés de la violent charité*, citing by paragraph number, with the page and where necessary line number in parentheses (translation are my own). Dumeige also edited the *Epistula ad Severinum de caritate* (known as the *De gradibus caritatis*), which older

scholars attributed to Richard, but is now known to be inauthentic, though influenced by his ideas. The most complete treatment of Richard's view of the nature of love remains, G. Dumeige, *Richard de Saint-Victor et l'idée chrétienne de l'amour*, esp. chaps. 3–4.

248. I will use the edition of Jean Ribaillier, *Richard de Saint-Victor. De Trinitate*, cited as *Trin.* with book, chapter, and page in parentheses. All translations are my own. Much has been written on *Trin.*, but see especially Ewert Cousins, "A Theology of Interpersonal Relations," *Thought* 45 (1970): 56–82.

249. Richard's concept of *ratio necessaria*, developed from Anselm, must not be thought of as a rational proof in the modern sense, but as a complex argument combining faith, reason, and personal experience. E. Cousins puts it well: "In Richard's analysis of interpersonal relations, the *ratio necessaria* is not a closed system argumentation, but the ontological necessity of the divine mystery reflected in experience and drawn partially into consciousness by reason guided by faith" ("A Theology of Interpersonal Relations," p. 64).

250. After proving God's existence in *Trin.* book 1, book 2 investigates the common attributes, including a treatment of God as *summum bonum* (2.16–19 [ed. 123–26]), which sets up the discussion of the Trinity in book 3.

251. *Trin.* 3.2 (ed. 136.8–10): Nullus autem pro privato et proprio sui ipsius amore dicitur proprie caritatem habere. Oportet itaque ut amor in alterum tendat, ut caritas esse queat. See Gregory the Great, *Hom. in Evang.* 1.17.1 (PL 76:1139A).

252. *Trin.* 3.2 (ed. 137.28–30): Ut ergo in illa vera divinitate plenitudo caritatis possit locum habere, oportuit divinam aliquam personam persone condigne, et eo ipse divine, consortio non carere. The importance of this appeal to *ordinatio caritatis* was first pointed out by Fernand Guimet, "Notes en marge d'un texte de Richard de Saint-Victor," *Archives d'histoire doctrinale et littéraire du moyen âge* 14 (1943–45): 371–94; and "*Caritas ordinata et amor discretus* dans la théologie trinitaire de Richard de Saint-Victor," *Revue du moyen âge latin* 4 (1948): 225–36.

253. *Trin.* 3.11 (ed. 147.39.42): Summe ergo dilectorum summeque diligendorum uterque oportet ut pari voto condilectum requirat, pari concordia pro voto possideat. Vides ergo quomodo caritatis consummatio personarum Trinitatem requirit. . . . See also the discussion in 3.19 (ed. 153–54). On this principle, see Cousins, "A Theology of Interpersonal Relations," pp. 77–82.

254. See *Trin.* 4.18 (ed. 181.4–5 and 10–11): . . . nichil aliud ibi est persona quam incommunicabilis existentia. . . . Et quid est persona divina, nisi habens divinum esse ex proprietate incommunicabili? In 4.21–25 (ed., 186–92) Richard provides a more extended discussion of the definition and how it applies analogously to human and divine persons.

255. *Trin.* 5.23 (ed. 222.30–34): Dicatur itaque illa divinitatis unda et summi amoris affluentia in alio tantum effluens nec infusa, in alio tam effluens quam infusa, in tertio non effluens sed solum infusa, cum sit tamen in omnibus una et eadem ipsa. On this passage, see K. Ruh, *Geschichte der abendländische Mystik*, p. 385.

256. B. McGinn, "The Language of Love in Christian and Jewish Mysticism," in *Mysticism and Language*, ed. Steven T. Katz (New York: Oxford University Press, 1992), pp. 202–35, esp. 212–15 on Richard's treatise.

257. For the fundamental principles in Origen's transformation of the language of love, see also *Foundations of Mysticism*, pp. 118–25.

258. Courtly love is a modern term, the invention of the critic Gaston Paris in the last century. Its usefulness has been much debated by students of medieval literature and culture (see, e.g., the papers in *The Meaning of Courtly Love*, ed. F. X. Newman [Albany: SUNY Press, 1968]). Still, critics such as C. S. Lewis *(The Allegory of Love* [New York: Oxford University Press, 1958], chap. 1) and philosophers such as Irving Singer *(The Nature of Love 2. Courtly and Romantic* [Chicago: University of Chicago, 1984], Part I) have found it useful insofar as it

points to a range of themes found in various medieval literary texts that emphasize an intense, ennobling, and freely given love between man and woman (often adulterous) described in a refined and stylized form of language. Much courtly literature is characterized by idealization of the beloved and a description of love as an unfulfilled yearning that brings with it suffering and sickness, and yet also a paradoxical joy. Insofar as much (not all) courtly love involves extra marital attachment, Étienne Gilson denied its relevance for the investigation of twelfth-century mysticism (*The Mystical Theology of St. Bernard*, "Appendix IV. St. Bernard and Courtly Love"); but from the perspective of descriptions of the psychology of being in love, it is difficult to deny considerable mutual interaction between courtly literature and mystical literature. The interaction will be taken up in greater detail in the next volume in this history, *The Flowering of Mysticism.*

259. *De quatuor gradibus* 2 (ed. 127.12–15): . . . amor ille ardens et fervens qui cor penetrat et affectum inflammat, animamque ipsam eousque medullitus tranfigit ut veraciter dicere possit: *Vulnerata caritate ego sum.* The violence of love had also been discussed by Richard in *Benj. maj.* 4.16 (154C–55A).

260. *De quatuor gradibus* 4 (ed. 129.1–12): Ecce video alios vulneratos, alios ligatos, alios languentes, alios deficientes; et totum a caritate. Caritas vulnerat, caritas ligat, caritas languidum facit, caritas defectum adducit.

261. Ibid. 11 (ed. 137.4–5): Quicquid agat, quicquid fiat, inutile, immo intolerabile videtur, nisi in unum desiderii sui finem concurrat atque conducat.

262. Ibid. 14 (ed. 139.28 and 141.2): . . . quia semper invenit quod adhuc concupiscere possit. . . . Sitit et bibit, bibendo tamen sitim suam non exstinguit.

263. Ibid. 18 (ed. 145.14–16): In desideriis spiritualibus quanto major tanto et melior; in desideriis carnalibus quanto est major tanto et pejor.

264. Ibid. 16 (ed., 143) Richard has some penetrating observations on the *insania amoris* of human love-hate relations on the fourth level: Diligendo itaque odiunt et odiendo diligunt, et modo mirabili, immo miserabili, crescit ex desiderio odium et ex odio desiderium.

265. Ibid. 30–33 (ed. 157–61). Here Richard also appeals to the desert theme growing popular in the late twelfth century, citing the standard proof text, Hosea 2:14.

266. Ibid. 34–37 (ed. 161–67).

267. Ibid. 28 (ed. 155.24–27): In Deum anima tunc sitit quando, per mentis excessum, tota in Deum transire concupiscit, ita ut sui penitus oblita, veraciter dicere possit: *Sive in corpore, sive extra corpus nescio, Deus scit.* The main discussion of the third level occurs in 38–43 (ed. 167–71).

268. Ibid. 46 (ed. 175.17–22): Nonne hic amoris gradus videtur animum hominis quasi in amentiam vertere, dum non sinit eum in sua emulatione modum mensuramve tenere? Nonne summe amentie videtur esse veram vitam repellere, summam sapientiam arguere, omnipotentie resistere? Nonne vitam repellit qui pro fratribus a Christo separari cupit . . . ?

Bibliography

(N.B. Full bibliographical information for volumes of essays is given under the title or name of editor.)

Adam, A. *Guillaume de Saint-Thierry, sa vie et ses oeuvres.* Bourg, 1923.

Adnès, Pierre. "Sommeil spirituel." DS 14:1033-53.

———. "Gout spirituel." DS 6:626-44.

Aelred de Rievaulx. Le Miroir de la Charité. Hommage au P. Charles Dumont in *Collectanea Cisterciensia* 55 (1993).

Allard, Guy-H, ed. *Jean Scot Écrivain.* Montréal-Paris: Institut des Etudes Médiévales, 1986.

———. "Vocabulaire érigénien relatif à la représentation de l'Ecriture," *Eriugena. Studien zu seinen Quellen,* ed. Werner Beierwaltes, 15-32.

———. "La structure litteraire de la composition du *De divisione naturae.*" *The Mind of Eriugena,* ed. John J. O'Meara and Ludwig Bieler, 145-57.

Alszeghy, Zoltan. "Fuite du monde (fuga mundi)." DS 5:1575-1605.

Altermatt, Alberich. "Christus pro nobis: Die Christologie Bernhards von Clairvaux in den 'Sermones per annum.'" *Analecta Sacri Ordinis Cisterciensis 33* (1977): 1-176.

Anderson, John. "The Use of Greek Sources by William of Saint-Thierry especially in the 'Enigma fidei.'" *One Yet Two. Monastic Tradition East and West,* ed. Basil Pennington, 242-54.

Anderson, Luke. "The Rhetorical Epistemology in Saint Bernard's *Super Cantica.*" *Bernardus Magister,* ed. John R. Sommerfeldt, 95-128.

Anson, Peter F. *The Quest of Solitude.* New York: Dutton, 1932.

Aries, Philip. *The Hour of Our Death.* New York: Oxford University Press, 1991.

Aubin, Paul. "Interiorité et exteriorité dans les Moralia in Job de Saint Grégoire le Grand." *Recherches de sciences religieuses* 62 (1974): 117-62.

Auerbach, Erich. *Mimesis. The Representation of Reality in Western Literature.* Garden City: Doubleday, 1957.

———. *Literary Language and Its Public in Late Latin Antiquity and in the Middle Ages.* New York: Pantheon, 1965. Bolingen Series LXXIV.

Baeumker, Clemens. *Witelo, ein Philosoph und Naturforscher des zwölften Jahrhunderts (Beiträge zur Geschichte der Philosophie des Mittelalters 3.2).* Münster: Aschendorff, 1900).

Baldwin, John W. *The Scholastic Culture of the Middle Ages 1000-1300.* Lexington: D.C. Heath, 1971.

Baron, Roger. *Science et sagesse chez Hugues de Saint-Victor.* Paris: Lethielleux, 1957.

———. "Hugues de Fouilloy." *Revue du moyen âge latin* 2 (1946): 25-44.

———. "Hugues de Saint-Victor." DS 7:901-39.

———. "L'influence de Hugues de Saint-Victor." *Recherches de théologie ancienne et médiévale* 22 (1955): 56-71.

———. *Études sur Hugues de Saint-Victor.* Angers: Desclée, 1963.

———. "La situation de l'homme d'après Hugues de Saint-Victor." *L'homme et son destin d'après les penseurs du moyen âge,* 431-46. Louvain-Paris: Nauwelaerts, 1960.

———. "Le Traité De la contemplation et ses espéces." *Revue d'ascetique et de mystique* 39 (1963): 137-51, 294-301, 409-18; and 40 (1964): 5-30.

Barré, H. "S. Bernard, Docteur marial." *Saint Bernard Théologien. Analecta sacri Ordinis Cisterciensis* 9 (1953): 92-113.

Baudelet, Y.-M. *L'expérience spirituelle selon Guillaume de Saint-Thierry.* Paris: Cerf, 1985.

Bauer, Gerhard. *Claustrum animae. Untersuchungen zur Geschichte der Metapher vom Herzen als Kloster. Band I. Entstehungsgeschichte.* Munich: W. Fink, 1973.

Baumgardt, David. "The Concept of Mysticism: Analysis of a Letter written by Hildegard of Bingen to Guibert of Gembloux." *Review of Religion* 12 (1948): 277-86.

Beierwaltes, Werner. ed., *Begriff und Metaphor. Sprachform des Denkens bei Eriugena. Vorträge des VII. Internationalen Eriugena-Colloquiums, 1989.* Heidelberg: Winter, 1990.

———, ed. *Eriugena. Studien zu seinen Quellen. Vorträge des III. Internationalen Eriugena Colloquiums, Freiburg, 1979.* Heidelberg: Winter, 1980.

———, ed. *Eriugena Redivivus. Zur Wirkungsgeschichte seines Denkens im Mittelalter und im Übergang zur Neuzeit (Vorträge des V. Internationalen Eriugena-Colloquiums, 1985).* Heidelberg: Winter, 1987.

———. "Eriugena–Aspekte seiner Philosophie." *Die Iren und Europa,* ed. Heinz Löwe, 2:799-818.

———. "Eriugena's Platonism." *Hermathena* 199 (1992): 53-72.

———. "*Negati Affirmatio* or the World as Metaphor. A Foundation for Medieval aesthetics from the writings of John Scotus Eriugena." *Dionysius* 1 (1977): 127-59.

———. "Language and its Object. Reflections on Eriugena's Valuation of the Function and Capacities of Language." *Jean Scot Écrivain,* ed. G.-H. Allard, 209-28.

———. "Das Problem des absoluten Selbstbewusstseins bei Johannes Scotus Erigena." *Platonismus in der Philosophie des Mittelalters,* ed. Werner Beierwaltes, 484-516. Darmstadt: Wissenschaftliche Buchgesellschaft, 1969.

———. "Unity and Trinity East and West." *Eriugena: East and West,* ed. Bernard McGinn and Willemien Otten, 209-31.

Bélanger, Rodrigue. "Anthropologie et Parole de Dieu dans le commentaire de Grégoire le Grand sur le Cantique des Cantique." *Grégoire le Grand,* ed. Jacques Fontaine, Robert Gillet, Stan Pellistrandi, 245-54.

Bell, David N. "Bernard in Perspective." *La dottrina della vita spirituale nelle opere di san Bernardo di Clairvaux,* 115-22.

———. "Contemplation and the Vision of God in the Commentary on the Song of Songs of Thomas the Cistercian." *Cîteaux* 28 (1977): 5-25 and 249-67; and 29 (1978): 207-27.

———. "*Certitudo Fidei*: Faith, Reason, and Authority in the Writings of Baldwin of Forde." *Bernardus Magister,* ed. John R. Sommerfeldt, 249-75.

———. "William of St. Thierry and John Scot Eriugena." *Cîteaux* 33 (1982): 5-28.

———. "The Carthusian Connection: Guigo I of La Chartreuse and the Origins of Cistercian Spirituality." *Cistercian Studies* 27 (1992): 51-62.

———. "The Vision of the World and the Archetypes in the Spirituality of the Middle Ages," *Archives d'histoire doctrinale et littéraire du moyen âge* 44 (1977): 7-31.

———. *The Image and Likeness. The Augustinian Spirituality of William of Saint Thierry.* Kalamazoo: Cistercian Publications, 1984.

———. "Baldwin of Ford and Twelfth-Century Theology." *Noble Piety and Reformed Monasticism,* ed. E. Rozanne Elder, 136-48. Kalamazoo: Cistercian Publications, 1981.

Benz, Ernst. *Die Vision. Ehfahrungsformen und Bilderwelt.* Stuttgart: Klett, 1969.

Berkenbusch, Irene. "Mystik und Askese. 'Sankt Trudperter Hohes Lied' und 'Speculum Virginum' im Vergleich." *"Minnichlichiu gotes erkennusse". Studien zur frhen abendländischen Mystiktradition. Heidelberger Mystiksymposium vom 16. Januar 1989,* 43-60. Stuttgart-Bad Cannstatt: froomann-holzboog, 1990.

Berlière, Ursmer. *L'ascèse bénédictine des origines à la fin du XIIe siècle.* Paris-Maredsous: Collection in Pax, 1927.

Bernard, Jacqueline. *Episcopat et papauté chez Saint Bernard de Clairvaux.* Saint-Lo: Editions Henri Jacqueline, 1975.

Bernards, Matthäus. *Speculum Virginum. Geistigkeit und Seelenleben der Frau im Hochmittelalter.* Cologne: Böhlau, 1955.

Bernhart, Josef. *Bernhardische und Eckhartische Mystik in ihren Beziehungen und Gegensätze.* Kempten, 1912.

Bertaud, Émile. "Échelle spirituelle." DS 4:62-86.

Bertola, Ermengildo. "Di alcuni trattati psicologici attribuiti ad Ugo da San Vittore." *Rivista di filosofia neoscolastica* 51 (1959): 436-55.

Besse, Jean. *Les Mystiques Bénédictins des origines au XIIIe siècle.* Paris-Maredsous: Lethielleux-Desclée, 1922.

Bethune, Brian. "Personality and Spirituality: Aelred of Rievaulx and Human Relationships." *Cistercian Studies* 20 (1985): 98-112.

Bieler, Ludwig. *Ireland: Harbinger of the Middle Ages.* Oxford: Oxford University Press, 1963.

Bischoff, Bernhard. "Wendepunckte in der Geschichte der lateinischen Exegese im Frühmittelalter." *Mittelalterliche Studien,* 3 vols., 1:205-73. Stuttgart: Hiersemann, 1966.

Bisson, J. M. "La tradition sur la prédestination absolué de Jésus-Christ du VIIe au IXe siècles." *France Franciscaine* 22 (1939): 14-15.

Bitel, Lisa M. *Isle of the Saints: Monastic Settlement and Community in Early Ireland*. Ithaca: Cornell University Press, 1990.

———. "*In visione noctis*: Dreams in European Hagiography and Histories, 450-900." *History of Religions* 31 (1991): 39-59.

Blanpain, Jacques. "Langage mystique, expression du désir dans les Sermons sur le Cantique des cantiques de Bernard de Clairvaux." *Collectanea Cisterciensia* 36 (1974): 45-68 and 226-47.

Bligny, Bernard. "L'Érémitisme et les Chartreux." *L'Eremitismo in Occidente nei Secoli XI e XII*, 248-70.

Bloch, Marc. *Feudal Society*. Chicago: University of Chicago, 1961.

Blum, O. J. *Saint Peter Damian: His Teaching on the Spiritual Life*. Washington: Catholic University, 1947.

Bodard, Claude. "La Bible, expression d'une expérience religieuse chez s. Bernard." *Saint Bernard Théologien*, 24-45.

Bonnard, F. *Histoire de l'abbaye royale et de l'ordre de St. Victor de Paris*. 2 vols. Paris, 1907.

Bonowitz, Bernard. "The Role of Experience in the Spiritual Life Life." *La dottrina della vita spirituale nelle opere di San Bernardo di Clairvaux*, 321-25.

Boswell, John. *Christianity, Social Tolerance, and Homosexuality*. Chicago: University of Chicago, 1980.

Boularand, Éphrem. "Désintéressement." DS 3:550-91.

Bouton, Jean de la Croix. "La doctrine de l'amitie chez saint Bernard." *Revue d'ascétique et de mystique* 29 (1953): 3-19.

Bouyer, Louis. *The Cistercian Heritage*. Westminster, MD: Newman, 1958.

Braunfels, Wolfgang. *Monasteries of Western Europe. The Architecture of the Orders*. London: Thames and Hudson, 1972.

Bredero, A. H. "The Controversy between Peter the Venerable and Saint Bernard of Clairvaux." *Petrus Venerabilis 1156-1956. Studies and Texts commemorating the Eighth Centenary of his Death*, ed. Giles Constable and James Kritzeck, 53-71. Rome: Herder, 1956.

Breen, Aidan. "Iohannes Scottus, *Periphyseon*: The Problems of an Edition." *Proceedings of the Royal Irish Academy* 91 (1991): 21-40.

Bremer, Dieter. "Hinweise zum griechischen Ursprung und zur Europäischen Geschichte der Lichtmetaphysik." *Archiv für Begriffsgeschichte* 17 (1973): 7-35.

———. "Licht als universales Darstellungsmedium. Materialen und Bibliographie." *Archiv für Begriffsgeschichte* 18 (1974): 185-206.

Brennan, Mary. "A Bibliography of Publications in the Field of Eriugenian Studies 1800-1975." *Studi Medievali*, 3a serie, 18 (1977): 401-47.

———. *Guide des études érigéniennes: Bibliographie commentée des publications 1930-1987/ A Guide to Eriugenian Studies: A Survey of Publications, 1930-1987*. Fribourg: Editions Universitaires. Paris: Cerf, 1989.

———. Materials for the Biography of Johannes Scottus Eriugena." *Studi Medievali*, 3a serie, 27 (1986): 413-60.

Bronders, Barbara. "Das Bild der Schöpfung und Neuschöpfung der Welt als *orbis quadratus*." *Frühmittelalterlichen Studien* 6 (1972): 171-87.

Brooke, Odo. *Studies in Monastic Theology*. Kalamazoo: Cistercian Publications, 1980.

Brown, George Hardin. *Bede the Venerable*. Boston: Twayne, 1987.

Brown, Peter. *The Body and Society. Men, Women, and Sexual Renunciation in Early Christianity*. New York: Columbia University Press, 1988.

———. *The Cult of the Saints. Its Rise and Function in Latin Christianity*. Chicago: University of Chicago, 1981.

———. *Society and the Holy in Late Antiquity*. Berkeley and Los Angeles: University of California, 1982.

———. *The World of Late Antiquity. From Marcus Aurelius to Muhammed*. London: Thames and Hudson, 1971.

Bulloch, James. *Adam of Dryburgh*. London: SPCK, 1958.

Bultot, Robert. "Spirituels et théologiens devant l'homme et le monde." *Revue Thomiste* 64 (1964): 517-48.

Buonaiuti, Ernesto. "Il misticismo di Gioacchino da Fiore." *Ricerche religiose* 5 (1929): 392-411.

Burnaby, John. *Amor Dei. A Study on the Religion of St. Augustine*. Longon: Hodder and Stoughton, 1938.

Butler, Cuthbert. *Benedictine Monachism. Studies in Benedictine Life and Rule*. London: Burns and Oates, 1924.

———. *Western Mysticism*. New York: Dutton, 1923.

Bynum, Caroline Walker. *Docere Verbo et Exemplo: An Aspect of Twelfth-Century Spirituality*. Missoula: Scholars Press, 1979.

———. *Jesus as Mother. Studies in the Spirituality of the High Middle Ages*. Berkeley: University of California, 1982.

Cabassut, André. "A Medieval Devotion to 'Jesus Our Mother.'" *Cistercian Studies* 21 (1986): 345-55.

Calati, Benedetto. "La 'lectio divina' nella tradizione monastica benedittina." *Benedictina* 28 (1981): 407-38.

Calati, Benedetto. "Pierre Damien." DS 12:1551-73.

Camelot, P. T. "Action et contemplation dans la tradition chrétienne." *La Vie Spirituel* 78 (1948): 272-301.

Canévet, Mariette. "Sens spirituel." DS 14:598-617.

Cappuyns, Maïeul. "Le *De Imagine* de Grégoire de Nysse traduit par Jean Scot Érigène." *Recherches de théologie ancienne et médiévale* 32 (1965): 205-62.

———. *Jean Scot Érigene, sa vie, son oeuvre, sa pensée.* Louvain-Paris: Universitas Catholica Lovaniensis, 1933; reprint 1964.

———. "Note sur le probléme de la vision béatifique au IXe siècle." *Recherches de théologie ancienne et médiévale* 1 (1929): 98-107.

Carabine, Deirdre. "Eriugena's Use of the Symbolism of Light, Cloud and Darkness." *Eriugena: East and West,* ed. Bernard McGinn and Willemien Otten, 141-52.

Caritas, Maria. "St. Caesarius of Arles." *Spirituality through the Centuries,* ed. James Walsh, 42-56. New York: Kenedy, n.d.

Carluccio, Gerard G. *The Seven Steps to Spiritual Perfection according to St. Gregory the Great.* Canada: University of Ottawa Press, 1949.

Carney, James. "Old Ireland and Her Poetry." *Old Ireland,* ed. Robert E. McNally, 147-72.

Carpe, William D. *The "Vita Canonica" in the "Regula Canonicorum" of Chrodegang of Metz.* University of Chicago Dissertation, 1975.

Casel, Odo. "Zur Vision des hl. Benedikt." *Studien und Mitteilungen zur Geschichte der Benediktinerordens* 38 (1917): 345-48.

Casey, Michael. *Athirst for God. Spiritual Desire in Bernard of Clairvaux's Sermons on the Song of Songs.* Kalamazoo: Cistercian Publications, 1987.

———. "*In communi vita fratrum.* St. Bernard's Teaching on Cenobitic Solitude." *La dottrina della vita spirituale nella opere di San Bernardo di Clairvaux,* 243-61.

———. "In Pursuit of Ecstasy: Reflections on Bernard of Clairvaux's *De diligendo Deo.*" *Monastic Studies* 16 (1985): 139-56.

———. "Spiritual Desire in the Gospel Homilies of Saint Gregory the Great." *Cistercian Studies* 16 (1981): 297-314.

Caspar, Erich. *Geschichte des Pappstums.* 2 vols. Tübingen: Mohr, 1933.

Catry, Patrick. "Les voies de l'Espirit chez Grégoire." *Grégoire le Grand,* ed. Jacques Fontaine, et al., 207-14.

Catry, Patrick. *Parole de Dieu, Amour et Esprit-Saint chez Saint Grégoire-le-Grand.* Abbaye de Bellefontaine: Vie Monastique, n. 17, 1984.

Chadwick, Henry. *Boethius. The Consolations of Music, Logic, Theology, and Philosophy.* Oxford: Clarendon Press, 1981.

Chase, Steven L. *Into the Secret Places of Divine Incomprehensibility: The Symbol of the Cherubim in "De Arca Mystica" of Richard of St. Victor.* Fordham University Dissertation, 1994.

Chatillon, François. "Hic, Ibi, Interim." *Mélanges Marcel Viller,* 194-99. Paris: Beauchesne, 1949.

Chatillon, Jean. "Achard de Saint-Victor et le 'De discretione animae, spiritus et mentis.'" *Archives d'histoire doctrinale et littéraire du moyen âge* 31 (1964): 7-35.

———. "La Bible dans les écoles du XIIe siècle." *Le Moyen âge et la Bible,* ed. Pierre Riché and Guy Lobrichon, 177-97. Paris: Beauchesne, 1984.

———. "Canonici regolari di San Vittore." DIP 2:125-34.

———. "La culture de l'école de Saint-Victor au 12e siècle." *Entretiens sur la renaissance du 12e siècle,* ed. Maurice de Gandillac and Edouard Jeauneau, 147-78. Paris: Mouton, 1968.

———. "De Guillaume de Champeaux à Thomas Gallus. Chronique d'histoire littéraire et doctrinale de l'école de Saint-Victor." *Revue du moyen âge latin* 8 (1952): 139-62 and 247-72.

———. "Hugues de Saint-Victor critique de Jean Scot." *Jean Scot Érigéne et l'histoire de la philosophie,* ed. René Roques, 415-31.

———. "Moïse figure du Christ et modèle de la vie parfaite. Brèves remarques sur quelques thèmes médiévaux." *Moïse, l'homme de l'alliance (Cahiers sioniens 8/2-4),* 305-14. Paris, 1954.

———. "Prière au moyen âge." DS 12:2271-88.

———. "Richard de Saint-Victor." DS 13:593-654.

———. *Théologie, spiritualité et métaphysique dans l'oeuvre oratoire d'Achard de St. Victor.* Paris: Vrin, 1969.

———. "Les trois modes de la contemplation selon Richard de Saint-Victor." *Bulletin de littérature ecclésiastique* 41 (1940): 3-26.

Chenu, Marie-Dominique. *La théologie au douzième siècle.* Paris: Vrin, 1957.

———. "Civilisation urbaine et théologie. L'École de Saint-Victor au XIIIe siècle." *Annales. Économies. Sociétés. Civilisations* 29 (1974): 1253-63.

Cheyette, Frederic L. "The Invention of the State." *The Walter Prescott Webb Memorial Lectures. Essays in Medieval Civilization,* ed. Bede Karl Lackner & Kenneth Roy Philp, 143-78. Austin & London: University of Texas Press, 1978.

Clark, Anne L. *Elisabeth of Schönau. A Twelfth-Century Visionary.* Philadelphia: University of Pennsylvania, 1992.

Clark, Francis. *The Pseudo-Gregorian Dialogues.* 2 vols. Leiden: Brill, 1987.

———. "St. Gregory the Great, Theologian of Christian Experience." *American Benedictine Review* 39 (1988): 261-76.

Cloes, Henri. "La systématisation théologique pendant la première moitié du XIIe siècle." *Ephemerides Theologicae Lovanienses* 34 (1958): 277-329.

Coccia, Eduardo. "La cultura irlandese precarolingia: Miracolo o mito?" *Studi Medievali,* 3a serie, 8 (1967): 257-420.

Cochrane, Charles Norris. *Christianity and Classical Culture. A Study of Thought and Action from Augustus to Augustine.* Oxford: Oxford University Press, 1940.

Colish, Marcia. "John the Scot's Christology and Soteriology in Relation to his Greek Sources." *Downside Review* 102 (1982): 138-51.

Congar, Yves. "L'ecclésiologie de S. Bernard." *Saint Bernard Théologien,* 136-90.

———. "Laïcat." DS 9:79-93.

Constable, Giles. *Attitudes Toward Self-Inflicted Suffering in the Middle Ages.* Brookline, MA: Hellenic College Press, 1982.

———. "The Ideal of Inner Solitude in the Twelfth Century." *Horizons marins, Itinéraires spirituels (Mélanges Michel Mollat.* 2 vols., ed. Henri Dubois, Jean-Claude Hocquet, and André Vauchez, 1:27-34. Paris, 1976.

———. *Medieval Monasticism. A Select Bibliography.* Toronto: University of Toronto, 1976.

———. "The Popularity of Twelfth-Century Spiritual Writers in the Late Middle Ages." *Renaissance Studies in Honor of Hans Baron,* ed. Anthony Molho and John Tedeschi, 5-28. DeKalb: Northern Illinois University Press, 1971.

———. "Reform and Renewal in Religious Life. Concepts and Realities." *Renaissance and Renewal in the Twelfth Century,* ed. Robert L. Benson and Giles Constable with Carol D. Lanham, 37-67. Cambridge, MA: Harvard University, 1982.

———. "Twelfth-Century Spirituality and the Late Middle Ages." *Mediaeval and Renaissance Studies* 5 (1969): 27-60.

"Contemplation." DS 2:1643-2193.

Corish, Patrick J. *The Irish Catholic Experience. A Historical Survey.* Wilmington: Michael Glazier, 1985.

Costello, Hilary. "John of Ford and the Quest for Wisdom." *Cîteaux* 23 (1972): 141-59.

Cougar, Yves M.-J. *A History of Theology.* Garden City: Doubleday, 1968.

———. "Le moment 'economique' et le moment 'ontologique' dans la sacra doctrina (révélation, théologie, somme théologique)." *Mélanges offerts à M.-D. Chenu,* 135-87. Paris: Vrin, 1967.

Courcelle, Pierre. "Ailred de Rievaulx à l'école des *Confessions.*" *Revue des études augustiniennes* 3 (1975): 163-74.

———. *Les Confessions de Saint Augustin dans la tradition littéraire.* Paris: Études Augustiniennes, 1963.

———. *Connais-toi toi-meme. De Socrate à saint Bernard.* 3 vols. Paris: Études Augustiniennes, 1974-75.

———. "'Habitare secum' selon Perse et saint Grégoire le Grand." *Revue des études anciennes* 69 (1967): 266-79.

———. *Late Latin Writers and Their Greek Sources.* Cambridge, MA: Harvard, 1969.

———. "La vision cosmique de saint Benoit." *Revue des études augustiniennes* 13 (1967): 97-117.

Cousins, Ewert. "A Theology of Interpersonal Relations." *Thought* 45 (1970): 56-82.

Cristiani, Marta. "'Mysticus Moyses.' Escatologia ed Esodo nel 'Periphyseon' di Giovanni Scoto." *Cristianesimo nella Storia* 10 (1989): 467-84.

d'Alverny, M.-Th. "Notes 2. Achard de Saint-Victor. De Trinitate-De unitate et pluralitate creaturarum." *Recherches de théologie ancienne et médiévale* 21 (1954): 299-306.

D'Arcy, Martin. *The Mind and Heart of Love.* New York: Meridian, 1956.

d'Onofrio, Giulio. "The Concord of Augustine and Dionysius: Towards a Hermeneutics of the Disagreement of Patristic Sources in the *Periphyseon.*" *Eriugena: East and West,* ed. Bernard McGinn and Willemien Otten, 115-40.

da Milano, Ilarino. "La spiritualità dei laici nei secoli VIII-X." *Problemi di storia della Chiesa. L'alto Medioevo,* 139-300. Milan: Vita e Pensiero, 1973.

Dagens, Claude. *Saint Grégoire le Grand. Culture et expérience chrétienne.* Paris: Études Augustiniennes, 1977.

Dalmais, Irenée-Henri. "Maxime le Confesseur." DS 10:836-42.

Daniélou, Jean. "S. Bernard et les Pères grecs," *Saint Bernard Théologien,* 46-55.

Daubercies, Pierre. *La Condition Charnelle. Recherches positives pour la théologie d'une realité terrestre.* Paris: 1958.

Davis, Thomas X. "A Further Study of the *Brevis Commentatio.*" *Bernardus Magister,* ed. John R. Sommerfeldt, 187-202.

Davy, M.-M. *Théologie et mystique de Guillaume de Saint-Thierry. I. La connaissance de Dieu.* Paris: Vrin, 1954.

——. "Le thème de l'âme-épouse chez Bernard de Clairvaux et Guillaume de Saint-Thierry." *Entretiens sur l' renaissance du 12e siècle*, ed. Maurice de Gandillac and Edouard Jeauneau, 247-72. Paris: Mouton, 1968.

——. "Le vie solitaire carthusienne d'après le *De quadripertito exercitio cellae* d'Adam le Chartreux." *Revue d'ascétique et de mystique* 14 (1933): 124-45.

Dawson, Christopher. *The Making of the Middle Ages. An Introduction to the History of European Unity, 400-1000 A.D.*. London: Sheed and Ward, 1932.

de Blic, Jacques. "Pour l'histoire de la théologie des dons avant Saint Thomas." *Revue d'ascetique et de mystique* 22 (1946): 117-79.

de Guibert, Joseph. "La componction du coeur." *Revue d'ascetique et de mystique* 15 (1934): 255-40.

de Lubac, Henri. *Exégèse médiévale*. 4 vols. Paris: Aubier, 1959-63.

de Martel, Gérard. "Pierre de Celle." DS 12: 1525-32.

de Nie, Giselle. *Views from a Many-Windowed Tower. Studies of Imagination in the Works of Gregory of Tours.* Amsterdam: Rinopi, 1987.

de Vregille, Bernard. "Écriture saint et vie spirituelle. IIB. Du 6e au 12e siècle." DS 4:170-87.

de Vogüé, Adalbert. *Community and Abbot in the Rule of Saint Benedict.* 2 vols. Kalamazoo, MI: Cistercian Publications, 1979, 1988.

——. "Benoit, modéle de vie spirituelle d'après le deuxième livre des Dialogues de Saint Grégoire." *Collectanea Cisterciensia* 38 (1976): 147-57.

——. "The Cenobitic Rules of the West." *Cistercian Studies* 12 (1977): 176-83.

——. "From Crisis to Resolutions: The *Dialogues* as the History of a Soul." *Cistercian Studies* 23 (1988): 211-21.

——. "Les deux fonctions de la méditation dans les Règles monastiques anciennes." *Revue d'histoire de la spiritualité* 51 (1975): 3-16.

——. "Sub regula vel abbate: A Study of the Theological Significance of the Ancient Monastic Rules." *Rule and Life: An Interdisciplinary Symposium*, ed. M. Basil Pennington, 21-63. Spencer, MA: Cistercian Publications, 1971.

——. "Renunciation and Desire: The Definition of the Monk in Gregory the Great's Commentary on the First Book of Kings." *Cistercian Studies* 22 (1987): 221-38.

——. "The Views of St. Gregory the Great on the Religious Life in his Commentary on the Book of Kings." *Cîteaux* 17 (1982): 40-64, 212-32.

de Wilde, Déodat. "The Formation of Christ in Us: B1. Guerric of Igny." *Monastic Studies* 2 (1964): 29-45.

Déchanet, J.-M. "*Amor Ipse Intellectus Est.* La Doctrine de l'amour-intellection chez Guillaume de Saint-Thierry." *Revue du moyen âge latin* 1 (1945): 349-74.

——. *Aux sources de la spiritualité de Guillaume de Saint-Thierry*. Bruges, 1942.

——. "La christologie de s. Bernard." *Saint Bernard Théologien*, 78-91.

——. "Guillaume de Saint-Thierry." DS 6: 1241-63.

——. "Guillaume et Plotin." *Revue du moyen âge latin* 2 (1946): 241-60.

——. *William of St. Thierry. The Man and his Work*, trans. R. Strachan. Spencer: Cistercian Publication, 1972.

Delaruelle, Étienne. "Le travail dans les régles monastiques occidentales du quatrième au neuvième siècles." *Journal de psychologie normale et pathologique* 41 (1948): 51-63.

Delehaye, Hippolyte. *The Legends of the Saints*. Notre Dame: University of Notre Dame, 1961.

Delehaye, Philippe. "Dans le sillage de S. Bernard: trois petits traités De conscientia." *Cîteaux* 5 (1954): 92-103.

——. *Le Microcosmos de Godfrey de Saint-Victor. Étude théologique. Texte.* 2 vols. Lille, 1951.

Delesalle, Jacques. "Amour et Connaissance. 'Super Cantica Canticorum' de Guillaume de Saint-Thierry." *Collectanea Cisterciensia* 49 (1987): 339-46.

——. "*Amour et Lumière*: Fonctions de l'ecriture sainte dans la structure d'un texte: le premier chant de l''Expositio super Cantica Canticorum' de Guillaume de St. Thierry." *Kartausermystik und- Mystiker*, ed. James Hogg, Vol. 3: 1-145. Salzburg: Institut für Anglistik und Amerikanistik. Universität Salzburg, 1982.

Delfgaauw, P. "La nature et les degrès de l'amour selon S. Bernard." *Saint Bernard Théologien*, 237-43.

Delforge, T. "Songe de Scipion et vision de saint Benoit." *Revue Bénédictine* 69 (1959): 351-54.

Dereine, Charles. "Chanoines réguliers." *Dictionnaire d'histoire et géographie ecclésiastiques.* 12:353-405. Paris: Letouzey et Ané, 1912-.

di Berardino, Angelo, ed. *Patrology*, Vol. 4. *The Golden Age of Latin Patristic Literature to the Council of Chalcedon.* Westminster, MD: Christian Classics, 1986.

Dickinson, J.C. *The Origins of the Austin Canons and their introduction into England.* London: S.P.C.K., 1950.

Didier, J.-C. "L'ascension mystique et l'union mystique par l'humanité du Christ selon saint Bernard." *La vie spirituelle. Supplement* 25 (1930), [140]-[155].

Dietrich, Paul A. "Virgins in Paradise: Deification and Exegesis in 'Periphyseon V.'" *Jean Scot Écrivain*, ed. Guy Allard, 29-49.

DiLorenzo, Raymond D. "Dante's Saint Bernard and the Theology of Liberty in the *Commedia*." *Bernardus Magister*, ed. John R. Sommerfeldt, 497-515.

Dinzelbacher, Peter. *Vision und Visionsliteratur im Mittelalter.* Stuttgart: A. Hiersemann, 1981.

———. "*Revelationes*." Turnhout: Brepols, 1991. Typologie des Sources du Moyen Âge Occidental, fasc. 57.

———. "The Beginnings of Mysticism Experienced in Twelfth-Century England." *The Medieval Mystical Tradition in England, Exeter Symposium IV*, ed. Marion Glasscoe, 111-31. Cambridge: Brewer, 1987.

"Discrétion." DS 3: 1323-24.

"Divinisation." DS 3:1370-1459.

Doignon, Jean. "'Blessure d'affliction' et 'blessure d'amour.' (*Moralia* 6.25.42): une jonction de thèmes de la spiritualité patristique de Cyprien à Augustin." *Grégoire le Grand*, ed. Jacques Fontaine et al., 297-303.

Dondaine, H. F. *Le corpus dionysien de l'université de Paris au XIIIe siècle.* Rome: Edizioni di Storia et Letteratura, 1953.

La dottrina della vita spirituale nelle opere di San Bernardo di Clairvaux. Atti del Convegno Internazionale. Rome, 11-15 settembre 1990. Analecta Cisterciensia 46. Rome: Editiones Cistercienses, 1990.

Doucet, Marc. "'Christus et Ecclesia una est persona.'" *Collectanea Cisterciensia* 46 (1984): 37-58.

———. "Pédagogie et théologie de la 'Vie de saint Benoît' par saint Grégoire le Grand." *Collectanea Cisterciensia* 38 (1976): 158-73.

Dronke, Peter. "Eriugena's Earthly Paradise." *Begriff und Metapher*, ed. Werner Beierwaltes, 213-29.

———. *Medieval Latin and the Rise of the European Love-Lyric.* 2 vols. Oxford: Clarendon Press, 1968.

———. "The Song of Songs and Medieval Love-Lyric." *The Bible and Medieval Culture*, ed. W. Lourdaux and D. Verhelst, 236-62. Leuven: Leuven University Press, 1979.

———. "'Theologia velut quaedam poetria': quelques observations sur la fonction des images poétiques chez Jean Scot." *Jean Scot Érigène et l'histoire de la philosophie*, ed. René Roques, 243-52.

———. "Virgines Caste." *Lateinische Dichtungen des X. und XI. Jahrhunderts. Festgabe für Walther Bulst zum 80. Geburtstag*, 93-117. Heidelberg: Schneider, 1981.

———. *Women Writers of the Middle Ages.* Cambridge: Cambridge University Press, 1984.

Dubois, Marie-Gérard. "The Place of Christ in Benedictine Spirituality." *Cistercian Studies* 24 (1988): 105-15.

Dubois, J. "Certosini." DIP 2:782-821.

Duclow, Donald. "Dialectic and Christology in Eriugena's *Periphyseon*." *Dionysius* 4 (1980): 99-117.

———. "Divine Nothingness and Self-Creation in John Scottus Eriugena." *Journal of Religion* 57 (1977): 109-23.

———. "Nature as Speech and Book in John Scotus Eriugena." *Mediaevalia*, Vol. 3: 131-40. Binghamton: SUNY Press, 1977.

Duft, Johannes. "Iromanie-Irophobie." *Zeitschrift für Schweizerische Kirchengeschichte* 50 (1956): 241-62.

Dumeige, Gervais. *Richard de Saint-Victor et l'idée chrétienne de l'amour.* Paris: Presses universitaires de France, 1952.

Dumont, Charles. "Seeking God in Community according to St. Aelred." *Cistercian Studies* 6 (1971): 289-317.

———. "L'action contemplative, le temps dans l'eternité d'après saint Bernard." *Collectanea Cisterciensia* 54 (1992): 269-83.

———. "Reading Saint Bernard Today." *Cistercian Studies* 22 (1987): 152-71.

Dumontier, M. *Saint Bernard et la Bible.* Paris: Desclée, 1953.

Dupront, Alphonse. "Pélérinage et lieux saints." *Mélanges Fernard Braudel.* Vol. 2: 189-206. Toulouse: Privat, 1973.

Dutton, Paul E. "Eriugena the Royal Poet." *Jean Scot Écrivain*, ed. Guy Allard, 51-80.

Dutton, Marsha L. "Christ Our Mother: Aelred's Iconography for Contemplative Union." *Goad and Nail. Studies in Cistercian History X*, 21-45. Kalamazoo: Cistercian Publications, 1985.

———. "The Face and Feet of God: The Humanity of Christ in Bernard of Clairvaux and Aelred of Rievaulx," *Bernardus Magister*, ed. John R. Sommerfeldt, 203-23.

———. "Intimacy and Imitation: The Humanity of Christ in Cistercian Spirituality." *Erudition at God's Service*, ed. John R. Sommerfeldt, 33-69. Kalamazoo: Cistercian Publications, 1987.

Dvornik, Francis. *Byzantium and the Roman Primacy.* New York: Fordham University Press, 1966.

Ebner, Joseph. *Die Erkenntnislehre Richards von Saint-Viktor.* Munster: Aschendorff, 1917.

Egan, Keith, J. "Guigo II: The Theology of the Contemplative Life." *The Spirituality of Western Christendom*, ed. E. Rozanne Elder, 106-15. Kalamazoo: Cistercian Publications, 1976.

Egenter, Richard. *Gottesfreundschaft. Die Lehre von der Gottesfreundschaft in der Scholastik Mystik des 12.und 13. Jahrhunderts.* Augsburg: Filser, 1928.

Egger, C. "Canonici regolari." DIP 2:46-63.

Ehlers, Joachim. "*Arca significat ecclesiam.* Ein theologisches Weltmodell aus der ersten Halfte des 12. Jahrhundert." *Frühmittelalterliche Studien* 6 (1972): 171-87.

Elder, E. Rozanne. "The Christology of William of Saint Thierry." *Recherches de théologie ancienne et médiévale* 58 (1991): 79-112.

——. *The Image of the Invisible God: the Evolving Christology of William of St. Thierry.* Dissertation, University of Toronto, 1972.

——, ed. *The Spirituality of Western Christendom.* Kalamazoo: Cistercian Publications, 1976.

——. "William of St. Thierry: Rational and Affective Spirituality." *The Spirituality of Western Christendom,* 85-105.

——. "William of St. Thierry: The Monastic Vocation as an Imitation of Christ." *Cîteaux* 25 (1975): 9-30.

Elmer, R. "Die Heilsökonomie bei Isaak von Stella." *Analecta Cisterciensia* 33 (1977): 191-261.

Erdmann, Carl. *The Origin of the Idea of Crusade.* Princeton: Princeton University Press, 1977.

"Erémitisme." DS 4:936-82.

L'eremitismo in Occidente nei secoli XI e XII. Atti della seconda Settimana internazionale di Studio Mendola, 1962. Milan: Società editrice vita e pensiero, 1965.

Ethier, A.-M. *Le "De Trinitate" de Richard de Saint-Victor.* Paris-Ottowa: Institut d'Études Médiévales d'Ottawa, 1939.

Evans, G.R. *The Mind of St. Bernard.* Oxford: Clarendon Press, 1983.

——. *Old Arts and New Theology. The Beginnings of Theology as an Academic Discipline.* Oxford: Clarendon Press, 1980.

Farkasfalvy, Denis. "The Role of the Bible in St. Bernard's Spirituality." *Analecta Sacri Ordinis Cistercienis* 25 (1969): 3-13.

——. "La conoscenza di Dio secondo San Bernardo." *Studi su San Bernardo di Chiaravalle nell 'ottavo centenario della canonizzazione,* 201-14. Rome: Editiones Cistercienses, 1975.

——. "The First Step in Spiritual Life: Conversion." *La dottrina della vita spirituale nella opere di San Bernard di Clairvaux,* 65-84.

——. "The Use of Paul by Saint Bernard as Illustrated by Saint Bernard's Interpretation of Philippians 3:13." *Bernard Magister,* ed. John R. Sommerfeldt, 161-68.

Fassetta, Raffaele. "Le mariage spirituel dans les Sermons de saint Bernard sur le Cantique des Cantiques." *Collectanea Cisterciensia* 48 (1986): 155-80 and 251-65.

——. "Le role de l'Espirit-Saint dans la vie spirituelle selon Bernard de Clairvaux." *La dottrina della vita spirituale nella opere di San Bernardo di Clairvaux,* 359-87.

Fernandez, Gonzalo. "Guillaume de Saint-Thierry: le problème des sources." *Collectanea Cisterciensia* 45 (1983): 210-20.

Fichtenau, Heinrich. "Zum Reliquienwesen im früheren Mittelalter." *Mitteilungen des sterreichischen Instituts für Geschichtsforschung* 60 (1952): 60-89.

Finan, Thomas. "Hiberno-Latin Christian Literature." *An Introduction to Celtic Christianity,* ed. James P. Mackey, 64-100. Edinburgh: T&T Clark, 1989.

Firey, A. "Cross-Examining the Witness: Recent Research on Celtic Monastic History." *Monastic Studies* 14 (1983): 31-49.

Fiske, Adele. "Alcuin and Mystical Friendship." *Studi medievali,* 3a serie 2 (1961): 551-75.

——. "Aelred of Rievaulx's Idea of Friendship and Love." *Cîteaux* 13 (1962): 7-17.

——. "St. Bernard of Clairvaux." *Cîteaux* 2 (1960): 1-41.

——. *Friends and Friendship in the Monastic Tradition.* Cuervaca: Civoc Cuaderno, 1970.

Flanagan, Sabina. *Hildegard of Bingen, 1098-1179. A Visionary Life.* London and New York: Routledge, 1989.

Folliet, G. "Les trois catégories des chrétiens." *Augustinus Magister.* 3 vols., 2:631-44. Paris: L'Année théologigue augustinienne, 1954.

Fontaine, Jacques. "L'experience spirituelle chez Grégoire le Grand." *Revue d'histoire de la spiritualité* 51 (1976): 141-54.

——, et al., ed., *Grégoire le Grand.* Paris: CNRS, 1986.

Foussard, J.-C. "Apparence et apparition: La notion de *phantasia* chez Jean Scot." *Jean Scot Érigène et l'histoire de la philosophie,* edited René Roques, 337-48.

Fracheboud, André. "Le Pseudo-Denys l'Aréopagite parmi les sources du cistercien Isaac de l'Étoile." *Collectanea Ordinis Cisterciensium Reformatorum* 9 (1947): 328-41 and 10 (1948): 19-34.

——. "L'influence de Saint Augustin sur le Cistercien Isaac de l'Étoile." *Collectanea Ordinis Cisterciensium Reformatorum* 11 (1949): 1-17.

"France. II. Le haut moyen âge. B. Spiritualité monastique du 6e au 12e siècle." DS 5:818-47.

Frank, Karl Suso. "Perfection. III. Moyen Âge." DS 12:1118-31.

Frend, W. H. C. *The Rise of the Monophysite Movement: Chapters in the History of the Church in the Fifth and Sixth Centuries.* Cambridge: Cambridge University Press, 1972.

Frickel, Michael. *Deus totus ubique simul: Untersuchungen zur allgemeinen Gottesgegenwart im Rahmen der Gotteslehre Gregors der Grossen.* Freiburg-im-Breisgau: Herder, 1956.

Gajano, Sofia Boesch, ed. *Agiografia altomedioevale.* Bologna: Il Mulino, 1976.

Geary, Patrick J. *Furta Sacra. Thefts of Relics in the Central Middle Ages.* Princeton University Press, 1978.

Gehl, Paul F. "Competens Silentium: Varieties of Monastic Silence in the Medieval West." *Viator* 18 (1987): 125-60.

Gersh, Stephen. *From Iamblichus to Eriugena.* Leiden: Brill, 1978.

————. "Omnipresence in Eriugena. Some Reflections on Augustino-Maximian Elements in the *Periphyseon.*" *Eriugena Studien zu seiner Quellen,* ed. Werner Beierwaltes, 55-74.

————. "The Structure of the Return in Eriugena's Periphyseon." *Begriff und Metapher,* ed. Werner Beierwaltes, 108-25.

Gewehr, Wolf. "Zu den Begriffen *anima* und *cor* in frühmittelalterlichen Denken." *Zeitschrift für Religions- und Geistesgeschichte* 27 (1975): 40-55.

Gibbon, Edward. *Decline and Fall of the Roman Empire.* 6 vols. London: Dent, 1963.

Gillet, Robert. "Spiritualité et place du moine dans l'eglise selon saint Grégoire le Grand." *Theologie de la vie monastique,* 323-51. Paris: Aubier, 1961.

————. "Grégoire le Grand (saint)." DS 6:872-910.

Gilson, Etienne. *Being and Some Philosophers.* Toronto: Pontifical Institute for Medieval Studies, 1949.

————. *The Mystical Theology of St. Bernard.* London: Sheed and Ward, 1940.

————. *The Spirit of Mediaeval Philosophy.* New York: Scribner's, 1940.

————. "Maxime, Érigène, S. Bernard." *Aus der Geisteswelt des Mittelalters (Mélanges M. Grabmann).* Vol. 1:188-92. Münster: Aschendorff, 1935.

————. "Presentation de Guiges I le Chartreux." *La vie spirituelle* 40 (1934): 162-78.

Glorieux, Pierre. "Le 'Contra quatuor Labyrinthos Franciae' de Gauthier de Saint-Victor." *Archives d'histoire doctrinale et littéraire du moyen âge* 27 (1952): 187-335.

Gooding, Robert. "Saint Grégoire le Grand à travers quelques ouvrages récents." *Analecta Bollandiana* 110 (1992): 142-57.

Gourdel, Yves. "Chartreux." DS 2: 705-76.

Grabmann, Martin. *Die Geschichte der Scholastischen Methode.* 2 vols.. Freiburg-im-Breisgau: Herder, 1909.

Grégoire, Reginald. "Smaragde." DS 14:959-61.

Gregory, Tullio. "Note sulla dottrina delle 'teofanie' in Giovanni Scoto Eriugena." *Studi Medievali,* 3a serie, 4 (1963): 75-91.

Grillmeier, Aloys. *Christ in the Christian Tradition. Volume 2.* London: Mowbray, 1987.

Grundmann, Herbert. "Der Brand von Deutz 1128 in der Darstellung Abt Ruperts von Deutz: Interpretation und Text-Ausgabe." *Deutsches Archiv für Erforschung des Mittelalters* 22 (1966): 385-471.

Gruys, Albert. *Cartusiana. Bibliographie générale. Auteurs cartusiens.* Paris: Éditions du Centre National de la Recherche Scientifique, 1976.

Guimet, Fernand. "Notes en marge d'un texte de Richard de Saint-Victor." *Archives d'histoire doctrinale et littéraire du moyen âge* 14 (1943-45): 371-94.

————. "*Caritas ordinata* et *amor discretus* dans la théologie trinitaire de Richard de Saint-Victor." *Revue du moyen âge latin* 4 (1948): 225-36.

Gurevitch, Aron. *Medieval popular culture. Problems of belief and perception.* Cambridge: Cambridge University Press, 1988.

Haacke, Rhaban. "Die mystischen Visionen Ruperts von Duetz." *"Sapientiae Doctrina". Mélanges de théologie et de littératures médiévales offets à Dom Hildebrand Bascour O.S.B..* Leuven, 1980. Recherches de théologie ancienne et médiévale. Numéro Spécial 1: 68-90.

Haas, Alois M. "Christliche Aspekte des 'Gnothi seauton.' Selbsterkenntnis und Mystik." *Geistliches Mittelalter,* ed. Alois Haas, 71-96. Freiburg, Schweiz: Universersitätsverlag, 1984.

————. "Eriugena und die Mystik." *Eriugena Redivivus,* ed. Werner Beierwaltes, 254-78.

Hallier, Amédée. *The Monastic Theology of Aelred of Rievaulx. An Experiential Theology.* Spencer: Cistercian Publications, 1969.

Hanson, R. P. C. *The Life and Writings of the Historical Saint Patrick.* New York: The Seabury Press, 1983.

Haring, Nicholas M. "Gilbert of Poitiers, Author of the *De discretione animae, spiritus et mentis* commonly attributed to Achard of Saint-Victor." *Mediaeval Studies* 22 (1960): 148-91.

Harnack, Adolph. *History of Dogma.* 7 vols. New York: Dover, 1961; from 3rd German ed. of 1900.

Haskins, Charles Homer. *The Renaissance of the Twelfth Century.* Cambridge, MA: Harvard University Press, 1927.

Hausherr, Irenée. *Penthos. The Doctrine of Compunction in the Christian East.* Kalamazoo: Cistercian Publications, 1982.

Hay, Denys. *Europe: The Emergence of an Idea.* New York: Harper and Row, 1966.

Healy, Patrick Joseph. "The Mysticism of the School of Saint Victor." *Church History* 1 (1932): 211-21.

Hedwig, Klaus. *Sphaera Lucis. Studien zur Intelligibilität des Seienden im Kontext der mittelalterlichen Lichtspekulation (Beiträge zur Geschichte der Philosophie und Theologie des Mittelalters).* Neue Folge 18. Münster: Aschendorff, 1980.

Heller, Dagmar. *Schriftauslegung und geistliche Erfahrung bei Bernhard von Clairvaux.* Wurzburg: Echter, 1990.

——. "Die Bibel als Grundlage der Anthropologie Bernhards von Clairvaux (Beobachtungen an ausgewählten Beispielen)." *La dottrina della vita spirituale nelle opere di San Bernardo di Clairvaux,* 123-40.

Herde, Rosemarie. "Das Hohelied in der lateinischen Literatur des Mittelalters bis zum 12. Jahrhundert." *Studi Medievali,* 3a ser. 8 (1967): 957-1073.

Herren, Michael. "Classical and Secular Learning among the Irish before the Carolingian Renaissance." *Florilegium* 3 (1981): 118-57.

——. "Mission and Monasticism in the *Confessio* of Patrick." *Sages, Saints and Storytellers. Celtic Studies in Honour of Professor James Carney,* ed. Donnchadh Ò Corrain, Liam Breatnach, Kim McCone, 76-85. Maynooth: An Sagart, 1989.

Herrin, Judith. *The Formation of Christendom.* Princeton: Princeton University Press, 1987.

Hill, Michael. *The Religious Order.* London: Kegan Paul, 1973.

Hillgarth, J. N. *Christianity and Paganism, 350-750. The Conversion of Western Europe.* Philadelphia: University of Pennsylvania, 1986.

——. "Old Ireland and Visigothic Spain." *Old Ireland,* ed. Robert E. McNally, 200-27.

Hiss, Wilhelm. *Die Anthropologie Bernhards von Clairvaux.* Berlin: De Gruyter, 1964.

Hocquard, Gaston. *Les Meditations du bienheureux Guiges de Saint Romain cinquième Prieur de Chartreuse (1109-1136).* Salzburg: Universität Salzburg, 1984. Analecta Carthusiana 112.

Hofmann, Dietram. *Die geistige Auslegung der Schrift bei Gregor dem Grossen.* Munsterschwarzach: Vier-Turme-Verlag, 1968.

L'Homme et son destin d'après les penseurs du moyen âge. Louvain-Paris: Éditions Nauwelaerts, 1960.

Honemann, Volker. "The Reception of William of Saint-Thierry's *Epistola ad fratres de Monte Dei* during the Middle Ages." *Cistercians in the Late Middle Ages,* ed. E. Rozanne Elder, 5-18. Kalamazoo: Cistercian Publications, 1981.

Hourlier, Jacques. "S. Bernard et Guillaume de Saint-Thierry dans le 'Liber de Amore.'" *Saint Bernard Théologien,* 223-33.

——. "Odilon de Cluny." DS 11:612.

Hughes, Kathleen. "The Celtic Church: is this a viable concept?" *Cambridge Medieval Celtic Studies* 1 (1981): 1-20.

——. *The Church in Early Irish Society.* Ithaca: Cornell University Press, 1967.

——. *The Modern Traveller to the Early Irish Church.* New York: Seabury, 1981.

——. "Sanctity and Secularity in the Early Irish Church." *Secularity and Sanctity. Studies in Church History 10,* ed. Derek Baker, 21-37. Cambridge: Cambridge University Press, 1973.

"Humanité du Christ (Dévotion et Contemplation)." DS 7:1033-1108.

Hummel, Regine. *Mystische Modelle im 12. Jahrhundert. 'St. Trudperter Hoheslied', Bernhard von Clairvaux, Wilhelm von St. Thierry.* Göttingen: Kümmerle, 1989.

Hunt, Noreen, ed. *Cluniac Monasticism in the Central Middle Ages.* Hamden, CT: Arcon, 1971.

"Italie." II. "Haut Moyen Age." DS 7:2167-2206.

Javelet, Robert. "La Dignité de l'homme dans la pensée due XIIe siècle." *De Dignitate Hominis. Mélanges offerts à Carlos-Josaphat Pinto de Oliveira,* 39-87. Freiburg: Herder, 1987.

——. "Extase. BIII. Au 12e siècle." DS 4:2113-20.

——. "Intelligence et amour chez les auteurs spirituels du XIIe siècle." *Revue d'ascétique et de mystique* 37 (1961): 283-86.

——. *Image et ressemblance au douzième siècle de Saint Anselme à Alain de Lille.* 2 vols. Paris: Letouzy & Ané, 1967.

——. *Psychologie des auteurs spirituels du XIIe siècle.* Strasbourg, 1959.

——. "La Vertu dans l'oeuvre d'Isaac de l'Étoile." *Cîteaux* 11 (1960): 252-67.

Jeauneau, Edouard. *Études érigéniennes.* Paris: Études augustiniennes, 1987.

——. "Jean Scot Erigène et le grec." *Archivum Latinitatis Medii Aevi Bulletin du Cange* 41 (1979): 5-50.

——. "Jean Scot et la metaphysique de feu." *Études érigéniennes,* 297-319.

——. "Jean l'Érigène et les Ambigua ad Johannem de Maxime le Confesseur." *Maximus Confesseur. Actes du Symposium sur Maxime le Confesseur. Fribourg, 2-5 September 1980,* ed. Felix Heinzer and Christoph Schönborn, 343-64. Fribourg: Editions Universitaires, 1982.

——. "La division des sexes chez Grégoire de Nysse et chez Jean Scot Erigene." *Eriugena. Studien zu seiner Quellen,* ed. Werner Beierwaltes, 34-54.

——. "Le renoveau érigénien du XIIe siècle," *Eriugena Redivivus,* ed. Werner Beierwaltes, 26-46.

——. "Le symbolisme de la mer chez Jean Scot Érigène." *Le Néoplatonisme,* 385-94. Paris: CNRS, 1971.

Jungmann, J. A. *Pastoral Liturgy.* New York: Herder and Herder, 1962.

Kamlah, Wilhelm. *Apokalypse und Geschichtstheologie.* Berlin: Ebering, 1935. Historische Studien 285.

Katzenellenbogen, Adolph. "The Image of Christ in the Early Middle Ages." *Life and Thought in the Early Middle Ages.* ed. Robert S. Hoyt, 66-84. Minneapolis: University of Minnesota Press, 1967.

Kelly, Joseph. "Hiberno-Latin Theology." *Die Iren und Europa,* ed. Heinrich Löwe. 2 vols., 2:549-67.

Kennedy, Charles W. *Early English Christian Poetry.* New York: Oxford University Press, 1952.

Kenney, James F. *The Sources for the Early History of Ireland, Ecclesiastical: An Introduction and Guide.* New York: Columbia, 1929; reprint with additions by Ludwig Bieler, 1968.

Kereszty, Roch. "Die Weisheit in der mystischen Erfahrung beim hl. Bernhard von Clairvaux." *Cîteaux* 16 (1963): 6-24, 105-34, 185-201.

———. "Relationship between Anthropology and Christology. St. Bernard, a Teacher for Our Age." *La dottrina della vita spirituale nelle opere di San Bernardo di Clairvaux,* 271-99.

Kitzinger, Ernst. *Early Medieval Art.* Bloomington: University of Indiana, 1966.

Kleinz, John P. *The Theory of Knowledge of Hugh of St. Victor.* Washington: Catholic University, 1944.

Knowles, David. "Cistercians and Cluniacs: The Controversy between St. Bernard and Peter the Venerable." *The Historian and Character,* 50-75. Cambridge: University Press, 1963.

———. *The Monastic Order in England: A History of Its Development from the Time of St. Dunstan to the Fourth Lateran Council, 940-1216.* Cambridge: Cambridge University Press, 2nd ed., 1963.

———. "Peter the Venerable." *Bulletin of the John Rylands Library* 39 (1956): 132-45.

Koch, Josef. "Über die Lichtsymbolik im Bereich der Philosophie und der Mystik des Mittelalters." *Stadium Generale* 13 (1960): 653-70.

Koehler, Theodore. "Fruitio Dei." *DS* 5: 1546-69.

———. "Thème et vocabulaire de la 'Fruition divine' chez Guillaume de Saint-Thierry." *Revue d'ascétique et de mystique* 40 (1964): 139-60.

Kopf, Ulrich. *Religiöse Erfahrung in der Theologie Bernhards von Clairvaux.* Tübingen: Mohr, 1980.

———. "Die Rolle der Erfahrung im religiösen Leben nach dem heiligen Bernhard." *La Dottrina della vita spirituale nelle opere di San Bernardo di Clairvaux,* 307-19.

———. "Hoheliedauslegung als Quelle einer Theologie der Mystik." *Grundfragen christlicher Mystik,* ed. Margot Schmidt und Dieter R. Bauer, 50-72. Stuttgart-Bad Cannstaat: frommann-holzboog, 1987.

Kottje, Raymund. "Raban Maur." *DS* 13:1-10.

Krahmer, Shawn Madison. "Interpreting the Letters of Bernard of Clairvaux to Ermendgaude, Countess of Brittany: The Twelfth-Century Context and the Language of Friendship." *Cistercian Studies* 27 (1992): 217-50.

Küsters, Urban. *Der verschlossene Garten. Volksprachliche Hohelied-Auslegung und monastische Lebensform im 12. Jahrhundert.* Düsseldorf: Droste, 1985.

Lackner, Bede. *The Eleventh-Century Background of Cîteaux.* Washington: Cistercian Publications, 1972.

Ladner, Gerhart B. *The Idea of Reform. Its Impact on Christian Thought and Action in the Age of the Fathers.* Cambridge, MA: Harvard University Press, 1959.

Ladner, Gerhart B. "Reform: Innovation and Tradition in Medieval Christendom." *Theology and Law in Islam,* ed. Gustave E. von Grunebaum, 53-73. Los Angeles: UCLA Near Eastern Center, 1971.

———. "Terms and Ideas of Renewal." *Renaissance and Renewal in the Twelfth Century,* ed. Robert L. Benson and Giles Constable, 1-33. Cambridge, MA: Harvard University Press, 1982

Laistner, M.L.W. "The Influence during the Middle Ages of the Treatise *De Vita Contemplativa.*" *Miscellanea Giovanni Mercati.* Vol. 2:344-58. Città del Vaticano: Biblioteca Apostolica Vaticana, 1956.

Landgraf, Arthur. *Einführung in die Geschichte der theologischen Literatur der Frühscholastik unter dem Gesichtspunkt der Schulengildung.* Regensburg: Pustet, 1948.

Lanne, E. "L'interprétation palamite de la vision de S. Benoît." *Le millénaire du Mont-Athos,* 21-47. Venice, 1964.

Laporte, Jean. "Une théologie systematique chez Grégoire?" *Grégoire le Grand,* ed. Jacques Fontaine et al., 235-43.

Laporte, Maurice. "Guiges I." *DS* 6: 1069-75.

———. ("Un Chartreux"). "La doctrine monastique des Coutumes de Guiges." *Théologie de la vie monastique,* 485-501. Paris: Aubier, 1964.

Lasic, Dionysius, OFM. *Hugonis de S. Victore Theologia Perfectiva. Eius Fundamentum Philosophicum et Theologicum.* Rome: Pontificum Athenaeum Antonianum, 1956.

Lawless, George, OSA. *Augustine of Hippo and his Monastic Rule.* Oxford: Clarendon Press, 1987.

Lazzari, F. "Le *contemptus mundi* chez S. Bernard." *Revue d'ascétique et de mystique* 4 (1965): 291-304.

Le Bail, Anselm. "Aelred." *DS* 1: 225-34.

Leclercq, Jean. *St. Bernard mystique.* Paris-Brussels: Desclée, 1948.

———. *Chances de la spiritualité occidentale.* Paris: Cerf, 1966.

———. *Études sur le vocabulaire monastique du moyen âge.* Rome: Herder, 1961. Studia Anselmiana 48.

———. *Études sur saint Bernard et le texte de ses écrits.* Rome: Editiones Cistercienses, 1953. *Analecta Sacri Ordinis Cisterciensis* 9.1-2.

———. *The Love of Learning and the Desire for God.* New York: Fordham University Press, 1961.

———, and Bonnes, Jean-Paul. *Un maitre de la vie spirituelle au XIe siècle. Jean de Fécamp.* Paris: Vrin, 1946.
———. *Monks on Marriage: A Twelfth-Century View.* New York: Seabury, 1982.
———. *Nouveau visage de Bernard de Clairvaux. Approaches psycho-historiques.* Paris: Cerf, 1976.
———. *OTIA MONASTICA. Études sur le vocabulaire de la contemplation au moyen âge.* Rome: Herder, 1963.
———. *Saint Pierre Damien eremite et homme d'eglise.* Rome: Edizioni di storia e letteratura, 1960.
———. *Pierre le Vénérable.* Abbaye S. Wandrille: Éditions de Fontenelle, 1946.
———. *Receuil d'études sur saint Bernard et ses écrits.* 3 vols. Rome: Edizioni di storia et letteratura, 1962-69.
———. *Aux Sources de la Spiritualité Occidentale. Etapes et Constantes.* Paris: Cerf, 1964.
———. *La spiritualité de Pierre de Celle (1115-1183).* Paris: Vrin, 1946.
———, ed. *The Spirituality of the Middle Ages.* New York: The Seabury Press, 1982. *A History of Christian Spirituality II.*
———. "Le commentaire de Gilbert de Stanford sur le Cantique des cantiques." *Analecta Monastica I,* 205-30. Rome: Vatican City, 1948. Analecta Anselmiana 20.
———. "La spiritualité des chanoines reguliers." *La Vita comune del clero nei secoli XI e XII,* 2 vols., 1: 117-35. Milan: Miscellanea del Centro di Studi Medioevali III, 1962.
———. "Pierre le Vénérable et l'érémetisme clunisien." *Petrus Venerabilis,* ed. Giles Constable and James Kritzek, 99-120.
———. "Consciousness of Identification in 12th Century Monasticism." *Cistercian Studies* 14 (1979): 217-31.
———. "L'amitie dans les lettres au moyen-âge." *Revue du moyen âge latin* 1 (1945): 391-410.
———. "The Intentions of the Founders of the Cistercian Order." *The Cistercian Spirit. A Symposium In Memory of Thomas Merton,* ed. M. Basil Pennington, 88-133. Spencer, MA: Cistercian Publications, 1969.
———. "The Religious Universe of St. Columban." *Aspects of Monasticism,* 187-205. Kalamazoo: Cistercian Publications, 1978.
———. "Priere incessante. A propos de la 'Laus perennis' du moyen âge." *La liturgie et les paradoxes chrétiens.* Paris: Cerf, 1963, 229-42.
———. "Le monachisme du haut moyen âge (VIII-Xe siécles)." *Théologie de la vie monastique,* 437-45. Paris: Aubier, 1961.
———. "Prayer and Contemplation. II. Western." *Christian Spirituality. Origins to the Twelfth Century,* ed. Bernard McGinn, John Meyendorff, and Jean Leclercq, 415-26. New York: Crossroad, 1985.
———. "Monastic Crisis of the Eleventh and Twelfth Centuries." *Cluniac Monasticism in the Central Middle Ages,* ed. Noreen Hunt, 217-37.
———. "Humanisme et spiritualité. II. L'humanisme des moines au moyen âge." DS 7:959-71.
———. "Silence et parole dans l'expérience spirituelle d'hier et d'aujourd'hui." *Collectanea Cisterciensia* 45 (1983): 185-98.
———. "La devotion médiévale envers le crucifié." *La Maison-Dieu* 75 (1963): 119-32.
———. "From Gregory the Great to St. Bernard." *The Cambridge History of the Bible. 2. The West from the Fathers to the Reformation,* ed. G. H. W. Lampe, 183-97. Cambridge: University Press, 1969.
———. "St. Bernard et la tradition biblique d'aprés les Sermons sur les Cantiques." *Sacris Erudiri* 2 (1960): 225-48.
———. "Aspects spirituels de la symbolique du livre au XIIe siècle." *L'homme devant Dieu. Mélanges Henri de Lubac,* 3 vols., 2:63-72. Paris: Aubier, 1962.
———. "Écrits spirituels de l'école de Jean de Fécamp." *Analecta Monastica I,* 91-114. Rome: Vatican City, 1948. Studia Anselmiana 20.
———. "Origène au XIIe siècle." *Irenikon* 24 (1951): 425-39.
———. "Smaragdus." *An Introduction to the Medieval Mystics of Europe,* ed. Paul Szarmach, 37-51. Albany: SUNY, 1984.
———. "Saint Bernard of Clairvaux and the Contemplative Community." *Contemplative Community. A Symposium,* ed. M. Basil Pennington, 61-113. Washington: Cistercian Publications, 1972.
———. "Jean de Fécamp." DS 8:509-11.
———. "Prayer at Cluny." *Journal of the American Academy of Religion* 51 (1983): 651-65.
———. "S. Bernard et la théologie monastique du XIIe siècle." *Saint Bernard Théologien,* 7-23.
———. "Predicateurs bénédictins aux XIe et XIIe siécles." *Revue Mabillon* 33 (1943): 48-73.
———. "Le mystère de l'Ascension dans les sermons de saint Bernard." *Collectanea Ordinis Cisterciensium Reformatorum* 15 (1953): 81-88.
———. "L'humanisme des moines au moyen age." *A Giuseppe Ermini,* 69-113. Spoleto: Centro Italiano di Studi sull' alto Medioevo, 1970.
———. "The Renewal of Theology." *Renaissance and Renewal in the Twelfth Century,* ed. Robert Benson and Giles Constable, 68-87.
———. "Lettres de S. Bernard: histoire ou littérature?" *Studi medievali,* 3a serie 12 (1971): 1-74.
———. "Toward a Spiritual Portrait of William of Saint Thierry." *William, Abbot of St. Thierry. A Colloquium at the Abbey of St. Thierry,* trans. Jerry Carfantan, 204-24. Kalamazoo: Cistercian Publications, 1987.
———. "Modern Psychology and the Interpretation of Medieval Texts." *Speculum* 48 (1973): 478-79.

————. "Une doctrine spirituelle pour notre temps?" *La dottrina della vita spirituale nelle opere di San Bernardo di Clairvaux*, 397-410.

————. 'Idipsum'. Les harmoniques d'un mot biblique dans S. Bernard." *Scientia Augustiniana. Festschrift Adolar Zumkeller*, ed. Cornelius Petrus Mayer and Willigis Eckkermann, 170-83. Wurzburg: Augustinus-Verlag, 1975.

LeGoff, Jacques. *Time, Work and Culture in the Middle Ages*. Chicago: University of Chicago, 1980.

Lemoine, Michel. *De la nature du corps et de l'âme. Texte établi, traduit et commentée par M. Lemoine*. Paris, 1988.

Leonardi, Claudio. "I modelli dell'agiografia latina dall'epoca antica al medioevo." *Passaggio dal mondo antico al Medio Evo da Teodosio a San Gregorio Magno. Atti dei Convegni Lincei* 45, 435-76. Rome: Accademia Nazionale dei Lincei, 1980.

Leonardi, Claudio. "La spiritualità di Ambrogio Autperto." *Studi Medievali*, 3a serie, 9 (1968): 1-131.

————. "Guglielmo di Saint-Thierry e la Storia del Monachesimo." *Guillaume de Saint-Thierry. La Lettera d'Oro*, 5-42. Florence: Sansoni, 1983.

Lewis, C. S. *The Allegory of Love*. New York: Oxford University Press, 1958.

Lewis, Gertrud Jaron. "Christus als Frau. Eine Vision Elisabeths von Schönau." *Jahrbuch für Internationale Germanistik* 15 (1983): 70-80.

Leyser, Henrietta. *Hermits and the New Monasticism. A Study of Religious Communities in Western Europe, 1000-1150*. London: Macmillan, 1984.

Lieb, Michael. *The Visionary Mode. Biblical Prophecy, Hermeneutics, and Cultural Change*. Ithaca: Cornell University Press, 1991.

Lieblang, Franz. *Grundfragen der mystischen Theologie nach Gregors des Grossen Moralia und Ezechielhomilien*. Freiburg-im-Breisgau: Herder, 1934.

Little, Lester K. *Religious Poverty and the Profit Economy in Medieval Europe*. Ithaca: Cornell, 1978.

Llewellyn, Peter. *Rome in the Dark Ages*. London: Faber and Faber, 1971.

Lo Menzo, Grazia Rapisarda. "L'écriture sainte comme guide de la vie quotidienne dans la correspondence de Grégoire le Grand." *Grégoire le Grand*, ed. Jacques Fontaine et al., 215-25.

Lobkowicz, Nicholas. *Theory and Practice: History of a Concept from Aristotle to Marx*. Notre Dame: University of Notre Dame, 1967.

Lodolo, Gabriella. "Il tema simbolico del paradiso nella tradizione monastica dell'occidente latino (secoli VI-XII): lo spazio del simbolo." *Aevum* 51 (1977): 252-88.

Löwe, Heinz, ed. *Die Iren und Europa im früheren Mittelalter*. 2 vols. Stuttgart: Klett, 1982.

Lonergan, Bernard. *Method in Theology*. New York: Herder, 1972.

Lucentini, Paolo. "La nuovo edizione del 'De divisione naturae (Periphyseon)' di Giovanni Scoto Eriugena." *Studi Medievali*, 3a serie, 17 (1976): 1-22.

Macalli, F. "Certosini, Architettura dei." DIP 2:822-38.

Madec, Goulven. "A propos des sources de Guillaume de Saint Thierry." *Revue des études augustiniennes* 24 (1978): 302-09.

————. "Jean Scot Érigène et ses auteurs." In *Jean Scot Écrivain*, ed. Guy Allard, 143-86.

Magrassi, Mariano. *Teologia e storia nel pensiero di Ruperto di Deutz*. Rome: Propaganda Fidei, 1959.

Maher, Michael, ed. *Irish Spirituality*. Dublin: Veritas, 1981.

Maisonneuve, Roland. "L'univers mystique cartusien et Anthelme de Belley (1107-1178)." *Kartäuserregel und Kartäuserleben. Internationaler Kongress vom. 30. Mai bis 3. Juni 1984*. Stift Heiligenkreuz 20-46. Analecta Carthusiana 113.1. Salzburg: Universität Salzburg, 1984.

Malévez, Léopold. "Essence de Dieu (Vision de L')." DS 4:1333-45.

————. "La doctrine de l'image et da la connaissance mystique chez Guillaume de St.-Thierry." *Recherches des sciences religieuses* 22 (1932): 178-205, 257-79.

Mannarini, Franco. "La grazia in Isaaco della Stella." *Collectanea Ordinis Cisterciensium Reformatorum* 16 (1954): 137-44 and 207-14.

Manzino, Gabriele. *"L'uomo che vuole e che corre." La problematica antropologica nel pensiero di guglielmo di Saint-Thierry*. Dissertation, University of Genoa, 1989-90.

Maréchal, Joseph. *Études sur la psychologie des mystiques*. Paris-Bruges: C. Beyaert, 1937.

Marenbon, John. "John Scottus and the 'Categoriae Decem.'" *Eriugena. Studien zu seinen Quellen*, ed. Werner Beierwaltes, 117-34.

Mariéton, Joseph. *Le Problème de la classification des sciences de Aristote à Saint-Thomas*. Paris: Alcan, 1901.

Markus, R.A. "Gregory the Great's Europe." *Transactions of the Royal Historical Society*, 5th Series, Vol. 31: 21-36. London, 1981.

————. *The End of Ancient Christianity*. Cambridge: Cambridge University Press, 1990.

Marler, J.C. "Dialectical Use of Authority in the *Periphyseon*." *Eriugena: East and West*, ed. Bernard McGinn and Willemien Otten, 95-113.

Marrou, Henri Irenée. *A History of Education in Antiquity*. New York: Sheed and Ward, 1956.

————. *Decadence romaine ou antiquité tardive? IIIe-VIe siècle*. Paris: Cerf, 1977.

——. "La place du haut moyen âge dans l'histoire du christianisme." *Il passaggio dall'antichità al medioevo in occidento*, 595-630. Spoleto: Settimane di Studio del Centro Italiano di Studi sull'Alto Medieovo IX, 1962.

"Marthe et Marie." DS 10:664-73.

Matter, E. Ann. "The Apocalypse in Early Medieval Exegesis." *The Apocalypse in the Middle Ages*, ed. Richard K. Emmerson and Bernard McGinn, 38-50. Ithaca: Cornell, 1992.

——. *The Voice of My Beloved: The Song of Songs in Western Medieval Christianity.* Philadelphia: University of Pennsylvania Press, 1990.

Maximus Confessor. Actes du Symposium sur Maxime le Confesseur. Fribourg 2-5 September 1980, ed. Felix Heinzer and Christoph Schönbron. Fribourg: Editions Universitaires, 1982.

Mayr-Harting, Henry. *The Coming of Christianity to England.* New York: Schocken Books, 1972.

McCormick, Michael. "Diplomacy and the Carolingian Encounter with Byzantium down to the Accession of Charles the Bald." *Eriugena: East and West*, ed. Bernard McGinn and Willemien Otten, 15-48.

McEntire, Sandra. "The Doctrine of Compunction from Bede to Margery Kempe." *The Medieval Mystical Tradition in England. Exeter Symposium IV*, ed. Marion Glasscoe, 77-89. Cambridge: Brewer, 1987.

McEvoy, James. "Biblical and Platonic Measure in John Scottus Eriugena." *Eriugena: East and West*, ed. Bernard McGinn and Willemien Otten, 153-77.

——. "Les 'affectus' et la measure de la raison dans le Livre III du 'Miroir.'" *Collectanea Cisterciensia* 55 (1993): 110-25.

——. "Metaphors of Light and Metaphysics of Light in Eriugena." *Begriff und Metaphor*, ed. Werner Beierwaltes, 149-67.

——. "Notes on the Prologue of St. Aelred of Reivaulx's *De Spirituali Amicitia.*" *Traditio* 37 (1981): 396-411.

——. "'Reditus omnium in superessentialem unitatem': Christ as universal Saviour in Periphyseon V." *Giovanni Scoto nel suo tempo. L'organizzazione del sapere in età carolingia. Atti del VI Colloquio Internazionale di Studi Eriugeneani*, 365-81. Spoleto: Centro Italiano di Studi sull'Alto Medioevo, 1989.

McGinn, Bernard. *The Calabrian Abbot: Joachim of Fiore in the History of Western Thought.* New York: Macmillan, 1985.

——, John Meyendorff, and Jean Leclercq, eds. *Christian Spirituality: Origins to the Twelfth Century.* WS 16. New York: Crossroad, 1985.

——. *The Foundations of Mysticism.* New York: Crossroad, 1991.

——, and Willemien Otten, eds. *Eriugena: East and West.* Notre Dame: University of Notre Dame, 1994.

——. *The Golden Chain. A Study in the Theological Anthropology of Isaac of Stella.* Washington DC: Cistercian Publications, 1979.

——. "Ascension and Introversion in the *Itinerarium mentis in Deum.*" *San Bonaventura: 1274-1974*, 5 volumes, 3:535-52. Grottaferrata: Collegio San Bonaventura, 1974.

——. "Christian Monasticism." *The Encyclopedia of Religion*, Mircea Eliade, Editor-in-Chief, 10:44-50. New York: Macmillan, 1987.

——. "Do Christian Platonists Really Believe in Creation?" *God and Creation. An Ecumenical Symposium*, ed. David B. Burrell and Bernard McGinn, 197-219. Notre Dame: University of Notre Dame, 1990.

——. "Eriugena Mysticus." *Giovanni Scoto nel suo tempo. L'organizzazione del sapere in età carolingia. Atti del VI Colloquio Internazionale di Studi Eriugeneani*, 235-260. Spoleto: Centro Italiano di Studi sull'Alto Medioevo, 1989.

——. "Freedom, Formation and Reformation: The Anthropological Roots of Saint Bernard's Spiritual Teaching." *La dottrina della vita spirituale nelle opere di San Bernardo di Clairvaux 1990*, 91-114.

——. "Introduction." *On Grace and Free Choice by Bernard of Clairvaux*, trans. Daniel O'Donovan, 3-50. Kalamazoo: Cistercian Publications, 1988.

——. "Introduction." In *Three Treatises on Man: A Cistercian Anthropology*, 1-100. Kalamazoo: Cistercian Publications, 1977.

——. "Isaac of Stella on the Divine Nature." *Analecta Cisterciensia* 29 (1973): 1-53.

——. "*Iter Sancti Sepulchri*: The Piety of the First Crusaders." *The Walter Prescott Webb Memorial Lectures. Essays on Medieval Civilization*, ed. Bede Karl Lackner and Kenneth Roy Philp, 33-71. Austin and London: University of Texas Press, 1978.

——. "Love, Knowledge and *Unio Mystica* in the Western Christian Tradition." *Mystical Union and Monotheistic Faith*, ed. Moshe Idel and Bernard McGinn, 59-86. New York: Macmillan, 1989.

——. "Negative Theology in John the Scot." *Studia Patristica XIII. Texte und Untersuchungen*, Band 116, 232-38. Berlin: Akademie, 1975.

——. "Ocean and Desert as Symbols of Mystical Absorption in the Western Tradition." *Journal of Religion* 74 (1994): 155-84.

——. "Pseudo-Dionysius and the Early Cistercians." In *One Yet Two. Monastic Tradition East and West*, ed. M. Basil Pennington, 200-41.

———. "Renaissance, Humanism, and the Interpretation of the Twelfth Century." *Journal of Religion* 55 (1975): 444-55.
———. "Resurrection and Ascension in the Christology of the Early Cistercians." *Cîteaux* 30 (1979): 5-22.
———. "St Benedict as the Steward of Creation." *American Benedictine Review* 39 (1988): 161-76.
———. "St. Bernard and Meister Eckhart." *Cîteaux* 31 (1980): 373-86.
———. "The Human Person as Image of God. II. Western Christianity." *Christian Spirituality: Origins to the Twelfth Century*, ed. Bernard McGinn, John Meyendorff, and Jean Leclercq, 312-30.
———. "The Letter and the Spirit: Spirituality as an Academic Discipline." *The Cresset* 56 (1993): 13-21.
———. "The Negative Element in the Anthropology of John the Scot." *Jean Scot Erigène et l'histoire de la philosophie (Actes du II Colloque international Jean Scot Erigène. Laon, 1975*, ed. Rene Roques, 315-25.
———. "*Theologia* in Isaac of Stella." *Cîteaux* 21 (1970): 219-35.
———. "With 'the Kisses of the Mouth': Recent Works on the Song of Songs." *Journal of Religion* 72 (1992): 269-75.
McGuire, Brian Patrick. *Friendship and Community. The Monastic Experience 350-1250.* Kalamazoo: Cistercian Publications, 1988.
McNally, Robert E. *The Bible in the Early Middle Ages.* Westminster, MD: Newman Press, 1959.
———, ed. *Old Ireland.* New York: Fordham, 1963.
McNamara, Martin, ed. *Biblical Studies: The Medieval Irish Contribution.* Dublin: Proceedings of the Irish Biblical Association, 1976.
———. "The Psalter in Early Irish Monastic Spirituality." *Monastic Studies* 14 (1983): 179-205.
McNeill, John T., and Helena Gamer. *Medieval Handbooks of Penance.* New York: Columbia University Press, 1938.
———. *The Celtic Churches.* Chicago: University of Chicago Press, 1974.
"Méditation." DS 10:906-34.
Meier, Christel. "*Virtus* und *operatio* als Kernebegriffe einer Konzeption der Mystik bei Hildegard von Bingen." *Grundfragen Christlicher Mystik*, ed. Margot Schmidt and Dieter R. Baur, 73-101. Suttgart-Bad Cannstaat: frommann-holzboog, 1987.
Ménager, A. "La contemplation d'après Saint Grégoire le Grand." *La vie spirituelle* 9 (1923): 242-82.
———. "Les diverse sens du mot 'contemplatio' chez saint Grégoire le Grand." *Supplément à la 'vie spirituelle'* (June, 1939): 145-69 and (July, 1939): 39-56.
Mersch, Émile. *Le corps mystique du Christ*, 2 vols. Paris: Desclée, 1933.
Merton, Thomas. "St. Aelred of Rievaulx and the Cistercians." *Cistercian Studies* 20 (1985): 212-23, and 21 (1986): 30-42.
———. *Thomas Merton on St. Bernard.* Kalamazoo: Cistercian Publications, 1980.
Meyvaert, Paul. "Diversity within Unity, A Gregorian Theme." *Heythrop Journal* 4 (1963): 141-62.
Micoli, Giovanni. "Théologie de la vie monastique chez saint Pierre Damien." *Théologie de la vie monastique*, 459-83. Paris: Aubier, 1961.
Mieth, Dietmar. "Gottesschau und Gottesgeburt: Zwei Typen Christlicher Gotteserfahrung in der Tradition." *Freiburger Zeitschrift für Philosophie und Theologie* 27 (1980): 204-23.
Mikkers, Edmond. "Robert de Molesmes. II. La spiritualité cistercienne." DS 13: 738-814.
———. "Zisterziernser und Kartäuser: Ein Verleich ihrer Spiritualität." *Spiritualität Heute und Gestern. Internationaler Kongress vom. 4. bis 7. August 1982*, 52-72. Analecta Cartusiana 351. Salzburg: Universität Salzburg, 1983.
Miquel, Pierre. *Le vocabulaire latin de l'expérience spirituelle.* Beauchesne: Paris, 1989.
Momigliano, Arnaldo. "After Gibbon's Fall." *Age of Spirituality. A Symposium*, ed. Kurt Weitzmann, 7-16. New York: The Metropolitan Museum of Art and Princeton University Press, 1980.
———. "Introduction. Christianity and the Decline of the Roman Empire." *The Conflict between Paganism and Christianity in the Fourth Century*, ed. Arnaldo Momigliano, 1-16. Oxford: Clarendon Press, 1963.
———. "Popular Religious Beliefs and the Late Roman Historians." *Popular Belief and Practice*, ed. G. J. Cuming and Derek Baker, 1-18. Cambridge: Cambridge University Press, 1972.
"Monachesimo." DIP 5:1672-1742.
"Monachisme." DS 10:1524-1617.
Moore, John C. *Love in Twelfth Century France.* Philadelphia: University of Pennsylvania Press, 1972.
Moore, R. I. *The Origins of European Dissent.* New York: St. Martin's Press, 1977.
Moran, Dermot. "Pantheism from John Scottus Eriugena to Nicholas of Cusa." *American Catholic Philosophical Quarterly* 64 (1990): 131-52.
———. *The Philosophy of John Scottus Eriugena. A Study of Idealism in the Middle Ages.* Cambridge: Cambridge University Press, 1989.
Moreau, Joseph. "Le Verbe et la création selon S. Augustin et J. Scot Érigène." *Jean Scot Erigène et l'histoire de la philosophie*, ed. René Roques, 201-210.

Moritz, Theresa. "The Church as the Bride in Bernard of Clairvaux's *Sermons on the Song of Songs*." *The Chimaera of His Age: Studies on Bernard of Clairvaux*, ed. E. Rozanne Elder and John R. Sommerfeldt, 3-11. Kalamazoo: Cistercian Publications, 1980.

Morris, Colin. *The Papal Monarchy. The Western Church from 1050 to 1250.* Oxford: Clarendon Press, 1989.

Morrison, Karl F. "Hermeneutics and Enigma: Bernard of Clairvaux's *De Consideratione*." *Viator* 19 (1988): 129-51.

——. "The Church, Reform, and Renaissance in the Early Middle Ages." *Life and Thought in the Early Middle Ages*, ed. Robert S. Hoyt, 143-59. Minneapolis: University of Minnesota, 1967.

——. "The Gregorian Reform." *Christian Spirituality: Origins to the Twelfth Century*, ed. Bernard McGinn, John Meyendorff, and Jean Leclercq, 177-93.

Morson, John, and Hilary Costello. "*Liber amoris*: Was it Written by Guerric of Igny?" *Cîteaux* 16 (1965): 114-35.

——. *Christ the Way. The Christology of Guerric of Igny.* Kalamazoo: Cistercian Publications, 1978.

Mouroux, Jean. "Sur les critères de l'expérience spirituelle d'après les Sermons sur le Cantique des Cantiques." *Saint Bernard Théologien*, 261-62.

Muller, J. "La vision de S. Benoit dans l'interprétation des théologiens scholastiques." *Mélanges Bénédictines.* Éditions de Fontenelle: Saint-Wandoulle, 1947.

Muller, K. "Zur Mystik Hugos von St. Viktor." *Zeitschrift für Kirchengeschichte* 45 (1926-27): 175-89.

Murphy, William. *Vita Associata and Religious Experience in the Writings of Ernesto Buonaiuti.* Dissertation, Gregorian University, Rome, 1974.

Mursell, Gordon. *The Theology of the Carthusian Life in the Writings of St. Bruno and Guigo I.* Analecta Cartusiana 127. Salzburg: Universität Salzburg, 1988.

Naldini, Mario. "Gregorio Nisseno e Giovanni Scoto Eriugena. Note sull'idea di creazione sull'antropologia." *Studi Medievali*, 3a serie, 20 (1979): 501-33.

Newman, Barbara. "Hildegard of Bingen: Visions and Validation." *Church History* 54 (1985): 163-75.

——. *Sister of Wisdom. St. Hildegard's Theology of the Feminine.* Berkeley-Los Angeles: University of California Press, 1987.

Newman, F. X., ed. *The Meaning of Courtly Love.* Albany: SUNY Press, 1968.

Noble, Thomas F. X. *The Republic of St. Peter. The Birth of the Papal State, 680-825.* Philadelphia: University of Pennsylvania, 1984.

Nock, Arthur Darby. *Conversion.* Oxford: Clarendon Press, 1933.

Norpoth, Leo. *Der pseudo-augustinische Traktat: De Spiritu et Anima.* Köln-Bochum: Institut für Geschichte der Medizin, 1971.

Nygren, Anders. *Agape and Eros.* Philadelphia: Westminster, 1953.

O'Donnell, James J. *Cassiodorus.* Berkeley: University of California Press, 1979.

O'Donoghue, Noel Dermot. *Aristocracy of Soul, Patrick of Ireland.* Wilmington: Michael Glazier, 1987.

O Dwyer, Peter. *Céli Dé, Spiritual Reform in Ireland 750-900.* Dublin: Editions Tailliura, 1981.

Ò Fiaich, Tomas. "Irish Monks on the Continent." *Introduction to Celtic Christianity*, ed. James P. Mackey, 101-39. Edinburgh: T & T Clark, 1989.

——. *Columbanus in His Own Words.* Dublin: Veritas, 1974.

Ó Loaghaire, Diarmuid. "Daily Intimacy with God—An Ever New Aspect of Celtic Worship." *Studia Liturgica* 13 (1979): 46-57.

——. "Irlande." *DS* 7:1971-86.

——. "The Celtic Monk at Prayer." *Monastic Studies* 14 (1983): 123-43.

O'Loughlin, Thomas. "Unexplored Irish Influence on Eriugena." *Recherches de théologie ancienne et médiévalle* 59 (1992): 23-40.

O'Meara, Dominic J. "Eriugena and Aquinas on the Beatific Vision." *Eriugena Redivivus*, ed. Werner Beierwaltes, 214-36.

——. "The Problem of Speaking about God in John Scottus Eriugena." *Carolingian Essays*, ed. Uta-Renate Blumenthal, 151-67. Washington, DC: Catholic University Press, 1983.

O'Meara, John J., and Ludwig Bieler, eds. *The Mind of Eriugena. Papers of a Colloquium, Dublin, 14-18 July 1970.* Dublin: Irish University Press, 1970.

——. "Eriugena's Use of Augustine in his Teaching on the Return of the Soul and the Vision of God." *Jean Scot Erigène et l'histoire de la philosophie*, ed. René Roques, 191-200.

——. "Eriugena's Use of Augustine." *Augustinian Studies* 2 (1980): 21-34.

O'Neill, Kathleen. "Isaac of Stella on Self-Knowledge." *Cistercian Studies* 19 (1984): 122-38.

Ohly, Friedrich. "Der Prolog des St. Trudperter Hohenliedes." *Zeitschrift für deutsches Altertum und deutsche Literatur* 84 (1953): 198-232.

——. "Eine Lehre der liebenden Gotteserkenntnis. Zum Titel des St. Trudperter Hohenlieds." *Zeitschrift für deutsches Altertum und deutsche Literatur* 121 (1992): 399-404.

——. "Geist und Formen der Hoheliedauslegung im 12. Jahrhundert." *Zeitschrift für deutsches Altertum und deutsche Literatur* 85 (1954-55): 181-97.

———. *Hoheliedstudien. Grundzüge einer Geschichte der Hoheliedauslegung des Abendlandes bis zum 1200.* Wiesbaden: Steiner, 1958.

Olivera, Bernardo. "Aspects of the Love of Neighbor in the Spiritual Doctrine of St. Bernard." *Cistercian Studies* 26 (1991): 107-19 and 204-26.

Ostler, Heinrich. *Die Psychologie des Hugo von St. Viktor.* Münster: Aschendorff, 1906.

Ottaviano, Carmelo. "Riccardo di San Vittore, La vita, le opere, il pensiero." *Memorie della Romana Accademia Nazionale dei Lincei,* Ser. VI, vol. IV, fasc. 5, 411-541. Rome, 1933.

Otten, Willemien. *The Anthropology of Johannes Scottus Eriugena.* Leiden: Brill, 1991.

———. "The Dialectic of the Return in Eriugena's *Periphyseon.*" *Harvard Theological Review* 84 (1991): 399-421.

———. "The Universe of Nature and the Universe of Man: Difference and Identity." *Begriff und Metapher,* ed. Werner Beierwaltes, 202-12.

Otto, Stephan. *Die Funktion des Bildbegriffes in der Theologie des 12. Jahrhunderts.* Münster: Aschendorff, 1963.

Ousterhout, Robert. *The Blessings of Pilgrimage.* Urbana and Chicago: University of Illinois Press, 1990.

Ozment, Steven. *The Age of Reform 1250-1550.* New Haven: Yale, 1980.

Paolini, Raffaella. "La 'spiritualis amicitia' in Aelred di Rievaulx." *Aevum* 42 (1968): 455-73.

Paré, Gérard M., A. Brunet, and M. Tremblay. *La renaissance du XIIe siècle: Les écoles et l'enseignement.* Paris-Ottawa: Publications de l'Institut des études médiévales d'Ottawa, 1933.

Pawsey, Humphrey. "Adam of Dryburgh." *The Month,* n.s. 29 (1963): 261-77.

———. "Guigo the Angelic." *Spirituality through the Centuries. Ascetics and Mystics of the Western Church,* ed. James Walsh, 132-43. New York: Kenedy, n.d.

Paxon, Frederick S. *Christianizing Death. The Creation of a Ritual Process in Early Medieval Europe.* Ithaca: Cornell University Press, 1990.

Payer, Pierre. *Sex and the Penitential: The Development of a Sexual Code.* Toronto: University of Toronto, 1984.

Pedersen, Jorgen. "La recherche de la sagesse d'après Hughes de Saint-Victor." *Classica et Mediaevalia* 16 (1955): 91-133.

Pegon, Joseph. "Componction." DS 2:1312-21.

Pelikan, Jaroslav. *The Emergence of the Catholic Tradition (200-600).* Chicago: University of Chicago Press, 1971.

———. *The Growth of Medieval Theology (600-1330).* Chicago: University of Chicago, 1978.

Pellegrinaggi e Culto dei Santi in Europa fino alla Prima Crociata. Convegni del Centro di Studi sulla Spiritualità Medievale IV. Todi: Accademia Tudertina, 1963.

Penco, Gregorio. "La dottrina dei sensi spirituali in San Gregorio." *Benedictina* 17 (197): 161-201.

Pennington, M. Basil, ed. *Contemplative Community. An Interdisciplinary Symposium.* Washington, DC: Cistercian Publications, 1972.

———, ed. *One Yet Two. Monastic Tradition East and West.* Kalamazoo: Cistercian Publications, 1976.

———. *The Last of the Fathers. The Cistercian Fathers of the Twelfth Century.* Still River, MA: St. Bede's Publications, 1983.

———. "A Primer of the School of Love." *Cîteaux* 31 (1980): 93-104.

———. "Abbot William–Spiritual Father of Saint Thierry." *William, Abbot of St. Thierry. A Colloquium at the Abbey of St. Thierry,* trans. Jerry Carfantan, 225-39. Kalamazoo: Cistercian Publications, 1987.

———. "The Three States of Spiritual Growth according to St. Bernard." *Studia Monastica* 11 (1969): 315-26.

———. "Together Unto God. Contemplative Community in the Sermons of Guerric of Igny." *The Last of the Fathers,* 192-206.

Pépin, Jean. *"Mysteria* et *Symbola* dans le commentaire de Jean Scot sur l'évangile de Saint Jean." *The Mind of Eriugena,* ed. John J. O'Meara and Ludwig Bieler, 16-30.

———. "'Stilla aquae modica multo infuso vino, ferrum ignitum luce perfusus aer.' L'origin de trois comparaisons familières à la théologie mystique médiévale." *Divinitas* 11 (1967): 331-75.

Perl, Eric D. "Metaphysics and Christology in Maximus Confessor and Eriugena." *Eriugena: East and West,* ed. Bernard McGinn and Willemien Otten, 258-70.

Petersen, Joan. *The Dialogues of Gregory the Great in their late Antique Setting.* Toronto: University of Toronto Press, 1984.

Piazzoni, Ambrogio M. *Guglielmo di Saint Thierry. Il declino dell'ideale monastico nel secolo XII.* Rome: Instituto Storico Italiano per il Medio Evo. Studi Storici 181-83, 1990.

Piemonte, Gustavo. "L'expression 'quae sunt et quae non sunt': Jean Scot et Marius Victorinus." *Jean Scot Écrivain,* ed. Guy Allard, 81-113.

Pirenne, Henri. *Mohammed and Charlemagne.* Cleveland and New York: World, 1957.

Potestà, Gian Luca, ed. *Il profetismo gioachimita tra Quattrocento e Cinquecento.* Genoa: Marietti, 1991.

Pranger, M.-B. "The Virgin Mary and the Complexities of Love–Language in the Works of Bernard of Clairvaux." *Cîteaux* 40 (1989): 112-38.

Raby, F. J. E. *A History of Christian-Latin Poetry from the Beginnings to the Close of the Middle Ages.* Oxford: Clarendon Press, 1927. \

———. *The Oxford Book of Medieval Latin Verse.* Oxford: Clarendon Press, 1953.

"Rachel et Lia." DS 13:25-30.

Raciti, Gaetano. "Isaac de l'Étoile." DS 7:2011-38.

———. "L'apport original d'Aelred de Rievaulx à la réflexion occidentale sur l'amitie." *Collectanea Cisterciensia* 29 (1967): 77-99.

Rahner, Hugo. "Die Gottesgeburt. Die Lehre der Kirchenväter von der Geburt Christi aus dem Herzen der Kirche und der Gläubigen." *Symbol der Kirche,* 13-87. Salzburg: Otto Müller, 1964.

Rashdall, Hastings, ed. F. M. Powicke and A.B. Emden. *The Universities of Europe in the Middle Ages.* Oxford: Oxford University Press, 1936.

Reccia, V. "La visione di S. Benedetto e la 'compositio' del secondo libro dei 'Dialoghi' di Gregorio Magno." *Revue Bénédictine* 82 (1972): 140-55.

Reeves, Marjorie E. *Prophecy in the Later Middle Ages. A Study in Joachimism.* Oxford: Clarendon Press, 1969.

Renna, Thomas. "The Song of Songs and the Early Cistercians." *Cistercian Studies* 27 (1992): 39-49.

Reypens, Léonce. "Ame." DS 1:442-44.

———. "Dieu (Connaissance mystique)." DS 3:892-93.

Ribaillier, Jean. "Richard de Saint-Victor. De statu interioris hominis." *Archives d'histoire doctrinale et littéraire du moyen âge* 34 (1967): 1-128.

Richards, Jeffrey. *Consul of God. The Life and Time of Gregory the Great.* London: Routledge & Kegan Paul, 1980.

———. *The Popes and the Papacy in the Early Middle Ages, 476-752.* London and Boston: Routledge & Kegan Paul, 1979.

Riché, Pierre, and Guy Lobrichon, eds. *Bible de tous les temps,* vol. 4. *Le Moyen Âge et la Bible.* Paris: Beauchesne, 1984.

———. *Education and Culture in the Barbarian West Sixth Through Eighth Centuries.* Columbia, SC: University of South Carolina, 1976.

———. "Spirituality in Celtic and Germanic Society." *Christian Spirituality: Origins to the Twelfth Century,* ed. Bernard McGinn, John Meyendorff, and Jean Leclercq, 163-76.

Riley-Smith, Jonathan. *The First Crusade and the Idea of Crusading.* Philadelphia: University of Pennsylvania Press, 1986.

Rini, Rodolfo. "Dio come 'essentia omnium' nel pensiero di Giovanni Scoto Eriugena." *Rivista di filosofia neoscolastica* 62 (1970): 101-32.

Robilliard, J.-A. "Les six genres de contemplation chez Richard de Saint-Victor et leur originne platonicienne." *Revue de sciences philosophiques et théologiques* 28 (1939): 229-33.

Robinson, I. S. *The Papacy 1073-1198. Continuity and Innovation.* Cambridge: Cambridge University Press, 1990.

Rodrigues, Isaias. "Ligature des puissances." DS 9:845-50.

Roques, René, ed. *Jean Scot Érigène et l'histoire de la philosophie (Actes du II Colloque intérnational Jean Scot Érigène. Laon, 1975.* Paris: CNRS, 1977.

———. "Connaissance de Dieu et théologie symbolique d'après l' *In hierarchiam Caelestem Sancti Dionysii* de Hugues de Saint-Victor." *Structures théologiques de la Gnose à Richard de Saint-Victor,* 294-364. Paris: Presses universitaires de France, 1962.

———. *Libres sentiers vers l'erigénisme.* Rome: Edizioni dell'Ateneo, 1974.

———. "Remarques sur la signification de Jean Scot Érigène." *Divinitas* 11 (1967): 245-329.

———. "Une encyclopédie du savoir médiévale: Le 'Liber exceptionum' de Richard de Saint-Victor." *Structures théologiques de la Gnose à Richard de Saint-Victor,* 365-91.

Rorem, Paul. "'Procession and Return' in Thomas Aquinas and His Predecessors." *The Princeton Seminary Bulletin* 13 (1992): 147-63.

Rosenwein, Barbara H. *Rhinoceros Bound. Cluny in the Tenth Century.* Philadelphia: University of Pennsylvania, 1982.

Rousselot, Pierre. *Pour l'histoire du problème de l'amour au moyen âge.* Münster: Aschendorff, 1908.

Ruh, Kurt. "Die Hoheliederklärungen Bernhards von Clairvaux und Wilhelms von St. Thierry." *"Minnichlichui gotes erkennnusse". Studien zur frühen abendländischen Mystiktradition,* ed. Dietrich Schmidtke, 16-27. Stuttgart-Bad Cannstaat: frommann-holzboog, 1990.

———. *Geschichte der abendländischen Mystik. Band I. Die Grundlegung durch die Kirchenväter und die Mönchstheologie des 12. Jahrhunderts.* Munich: Beck, 1990.

Runte, Josefine. "Die Gottesliebe im St. Trudperter Hohen Lied und Bernhard von Clairvaux." *Cîteaux* 8 (1957): 27-41.

Ruppert, Fidelis. "Meditatio-Ruminatio." *Collectanea Cisterciensia* 39 (1977): 81-93.

Russell, Jeffrey Burton. *Dissent and Reform in the Early Middle Ages.* Berkeley and Los Angeles: University of California Press, 1965.

Ryan, John. *Irish Monasticism: Origins and Development.* Dublin, 1931; reprint Ithaca: Cornell University Press, 1973.

Saint Bernard Théologien. Actes du Congrès de Dijon, 15-19 septembre 1953. Analecta Sacri Ordinis Cisterciensis 9 (1953).

Salet, Gaston. "Les chemins de Dieu d'après Richard de Saint-Victor." *L'homme devant Dieu. Mélanges offerts au Père Henri de Lubac,* 3 vols., 2:73-88. Paris: Aubier, 1964.

Salmon, Pierre. "Le silence religieux, pratique et théorie." *Mélanges bénédictines publiés a l'occasion du XIVe centenaire de la mort de S. Benoit,* 13-57. Abbaye S. Wandrille: Éditions de Fontenelle, 1947.

Schaut, Ambrosius. "Die Vision des heiligen Benedikt." *Vir Dei Benedictus. Eine Festgabe zum 1400 Todestag des hl. Benedikt,* ed. Raphael Molitor, 207-53. Münster: Aschendorff, 1947.

Scheffczyk, Leo. "Die Grundzüge der Trinitätslehre des Johannes Scotus Eriugena." *Theologie in Geschichte und Gegenwart (Festschrift Michael Schmaus),* 497-518. Munich: Beck, 1957.

Schilling, Raymundus. "Aelredus van Rievaulx: Deus Amicitia Est." *Cîteaux* 8 (1957): 13-26.

Schlafert, Cl. "L'allégorie de la buche enflamée dans Hughes de Saint-Victor et dans Saint Jean de la Croix." *Revue d'ascetique et de mystique* 33 (1957): 241-63 and 361-86.

Schlette, Heinz Robert. *Die Nichtigkeit der Welt. Der philosophische Horizont des Hugo von St. Viktor.* Munich: Kösel, 1961.

Schmitz, Philibert. *Histoire de l'ordre de Saint-Benoit,* 7 vols. Maredsous, 1948-56.

Scholem, Gershom. "Mysticism and Society." *Diogenes* 58 (1967): 1-24.

Scholl, Edith. "The Cistercian Vocabulary: A Proposal." *Cistercian Studies* 27 (1992): 77-92.

Schreiner, Susan E. "'Where Shall Wisdom be Found?' Gregory's Interpretation of Job." *American Benedictine Review* 39 (1988): 321-42.

Sharpe, Richard. "St. Patrick and Armagh." *Cambridge Medieval Celtic Studies* 4 (1982): 33-59.

Sheldon-Williams, I. P. "Eriugena's Greek Sources." *The Mind of Eriugena,* ed. John J. O'Meara and Ludwig Bieler, 1-15.

Sherwood, Polycarp. *An Annotated Date-List of the Works of Maximus the Confessor.* Rome: Herder, 1952.

Sicard, Patrice. *Hugues de Saint-Victor et son école. Introduction, choix de texte, traduction et commentaires.* Turnhout: Brepols, 1991.

Sieben, H.-J. "'Quies' et 'Otium.'" DS 12:2746-56.

"Silence." DS 14:829-59.

Simon, Monique. "Le 'face à face' dans les méditations du Guillaume de Saint-Thierry." *Collectanea Cisterciensia* 35 (1975): 121-36.

Singer, Charles. "The Scientific Views and Visions of Saint Hildegard." *Studies in the History and Method of Science,* 1:1-55. Oxford: Oxford University Press, 1917.

Singer, Irving. *The Nature of Love 2. Courtly and Romantic.* Chicago: University of Chicago Press, 1984.

Sitwell, Gerard. *Spiritual Writers of the Middle Ages.* New York: Hawthorn, 1961.

Smalley, Beryl. *The Study of the Bible in the Middle Ages.* Notre Dame: University of Notre Dame, 1964, 2nd ed.

Smith, Aloysius. "Chanoines réguliers." DS 2:463-77.

Solignac, Aimé. "Jubilation." DS 8:1471-78.

———. "Julien Pomère." DS 8:1594-1600.

———. "Oculus (Animae, Cordis, Mentis)." DS 11:591-601.

———. "Osculum." DS 11:1012-26.

———. "Spiritualité. I. Le mot et l'histoire." DS 14:1142-60.

———. "Vie active, vie contemplative, vie mixte." DS 16:592-623.

———. "'Verba Seniorum.'" DS 16:383-92.

———. "'Vitae Patrum.'" DS 16:1029-35.

Sommerfeldt, John R., ed. *Bernardus Magister. Papers Presented at the Nonacentenary Celebration of the Birth of Saint Bernard of Clairvaux, Kalamazoo, Michigan.* Kalamazoo: Cistercian Publications and Cîteaux: Commentarii Cistercienses, 1992.

———. "Bernard as Contemplative." *Bernardus Magister,* ed. John R. Sommerfeldt, 73-84.

———. "Bernard of Clairvaux: the Mystic and Society." *The Spirituality of Western Christendom,* ed. E. Rozanne Elder, 72-84.

———. "Images of Visitation: The Vocabulary of Contemplation in Aelred of Rievaulx' *Mirror of Love,* Book II." *Erudition at God's Service: Studies in Medieval Cistercian History XI,* ed. John R. Sommerfeldt, 169-74. Kalamazoo: Cistercian Publications, 1987.

———. "The Epistemological Value of the Mysticism in the Thought of Bernard of Clairvaux." *Studies in Medieval Culture,* 48-58. Kalamazoo: Western Michigan University, 1965.

———. "The Rape of the Soul: The Vocabulary of Contemplation in Aelred of Rievaulx' *Mirror of Love,* Book III." *Erudition at God's Service,* ed. John R. Sommerfeldt, 161-68.

———. "The Vocabulary of Contemplation in Aelred of Rievaulx' *Mirror of Love*, Book I." *Goad and Nail: Studies in Medieval Cistercian History X*, ed. E. Rozanne Elder, 241-250. Kalamazoo: Cistercian Publications, 1985.

———. "The Vocabulary of Contemplation in Aelred of Rievaulx' *On Jesus at the Age of Twelve, A Rule of Life for a Recluse*, and *On Spiritual Friendship*." *Heaven on Earth. Studies in Medieval Cistercian History IX*, ed. E. Rozanne Elder, 72-89. Kalamazoo: Cistercian Publications, 1983.

Southern, R. W. "Aspects of the European Tradition of Historical Writing: 2. Hugh of St. Victor and the Idea of Historical Development." *Royal Historical Association. Transactions*, 5th series, 21 (1971): 159-79.

———. *The Making of the Middle Ages*. New Haven & London: Yale University Press, 1953.

———. *Western Society and the Church in the Middle Ages*. Baltimore: Penguin, 1970.

Spiritualità Cluniacense. Todi: L'Accademia Tudertina. Convegni del Centro di Studi sulla Spiritualità Medievale II, 1960.

Spitz, Hans-Jörg. "'Speigel der Bräute Gottes'. Das Modell der vita activa und vita contemplative als strukierendes Prinzip im St. Trudperter Hohen Lied." *Abendländische Mystik im Mittelalter. Symposium Kloster Engelberg, 1984*, ed. Kurt Ruh, 481-93. Stuttgart: Metzler, 1986.

Squire, Aelred K. "Light in Gregory the Great and in the Islamic Tradition." *Studia Patristica*, vol. XXIII, ed. Elizabeth A. Livingston, 197-202.

———. *Aelred of Rievaulx. A Study*. London: SPCK, 1969.

———. "Aelred of Rievaulx and the Monastic Tradition Concerning Action and Contemplation." *Downside Review* 72 (1954): 289-304.

Standaert, Maur. "La doctrine de l'image chez saint Bernard." *Ephemerides Theologiae Lovanienses* 23 (1947): 70-129.

———. "Le principe de l'ordination dans la théologie spirituelle de Saint Bernard." *Collectanea Ordinis Cisterciensium Reformatorum* 8 (1946): 176-216.

Steidle, Basilius. "Die kosmische Vision des Gottesmannes Benedikt." *Erbe und Auftrag* 47 (1971): 187-92.

Stiegman, Emero. "Action and Contemplation in Bernard's Sermons on the Song of Songs." Introduction to *Bernard of Clairvaux. On the Song of Songs III*, trans. Kilian Walsh and Irene M. Edmonds, vii-xxv. Kalamazoo: Cistercian Publications, 1979.

Stiegman, Emero. "The Literary Genre of Bernard of Clairvaux's *Sermones super Cantica Canticorum*." *Simplicity and Ordinariness. Studies in Medieval Cistercian History IV*, ed. John R. Sommerfeldt, 68-93. Kalamazoo: Cistercian Publications, 1980.

Stock, Brian. "Experience, Praxis, Work, and Planning in Bernard of Clairvaux: Observations on the *Sermones in Cantica*." *The Cultural Context of Medieval Learning*, ed. J. E. Murdoch and E. D. Sylla, 219-68. Dodrecht: Reidel, 1976.

———. "In Search of Eriugena's Augustine." *Eriugena. Studien zu seinen Quellen*, ed. Werner Beierwaltes, 86-104.

———. "'Intelligo me esse'. Eriugena's *cogito*." *Jean Scot Érigène et l'histoire de la philosophie*, ed. René Roques, 328-35.

———. "Observations on the Use of Augustine by Johannes Scottus Eriugena." *Harvard Theological Review* 60 (1967): 213-20.

———. *The Implications of Literacy, Written Language and Models of Interpretation in the Eleventh and Twelfth Centuries*. Princeton: Princeton University Press, 1983.

———. "The Philosophical Anthropology of Johannes Scottus Eriugena." *Studi Medievali*, 3a serie, 8 (1967): 1-57.

Straw, Carole. "'Adversitas' et 'Prosperitas': une illustration du motif structurel de la complementarité." *Grégoire le Grand*, ed. Jacques Fontaine, et al., 277-88.

———. *Gregory the Great. Perfection in Imperfection*. Berkeley: University of California Press, 1988.

Stroumsa, Gedaliahu G. "Caro salutis cardo: Shaping the Person in Early Christian Thought." *History of Religions* 30 (1990): 25-50.

Sullivan, Kathryn. "Compunction." *Worship* 35 (1961): 227-35.

Summers, Janet E. *"The Violent Shall Take It By Force."* The First Century of the Cistercian Nuns. Dissertation, University of Chicago, 1986.

Talbot, C. H., ed. *The Anglo-Saxon Missionaries to Germany*. New York: Sheed and Ward, 1954.

Taylor, Jerome, trans. *The Didascalicon of Hugh of St. Victor*. New York and London: Columbia University Press, 1961.

Teasdale, Wayne. "'Nihil' as Name of God in John Scottus Eriugena." *Cistercian Studies* 19 (1984): 232-47.

TePas, Katherine M. "Spiritual Friendship in Aelred of Rievaulx and Mutual Sanctification in Marriage I and II." *Cistercian Studies* 27 (1992): 63-76 and 153-65.

Thomas, Robert. *Guillaume de Saint-Thierry. Homme de doctrine, homme de prière*. Quebec: Éditions Anne Sigier, 1989.

———. "William of St. Thierry: Our Life in the Trinity." *Monastic Studies* 3 (1965): 159-64.

Thunberg, Lars. *Microcosm and Mediator. The Theological Anthropology of Maximus Confessor.* Lund: Gleerup, 1965.
Tierney, Brian. *The Crisis of Church and State 1060-1300.* Englewood Cliffs, NJ: Prentice-Hall, 1964.
Tomasic, Thomas M. "The Logical Function of Metaphor and Oppositional Coincidence in the Pseudo-Dionysius and Johannes Scottus Eriugena." *Journal of Religion* 68 (1988): 361-77.
——. "The Theological Virtues as Modes of Intersubjectivity in the Thought of William of St. Thierry." *Recherches de théologie ancienne et médiévale* 38 (1971): 89-120.
——. "William of Saint-Thierry against Peter Abelard: A Dispute on the Meaning of Being a Person." *Analecta Cisterciensia* 28 (1972): 3-76.
——. "William of St. Thierry on the Phenomenon of Christ: The Paradigm of Human Possibilities." *Analecta Cisterciensia* 31 (1975): 213-45.
Trouillard, Jean. "Erigène et la théophanie créatrice." *The Mind of Eriugena,* ed. John J. O'Meara and Ludwig Bieler, 98-113.
Tugwell, Simon. *Ways of Imperfection. An Exploration of Christian Spirituality.* London: Darton, Longman, Todd, 1984.
Turner, Victor and Edith Turner. *Image and Pilgrimage in Christian Culture.* New York: Columbia University Press, 1978.
Ullman, Walter. *A Short History of the Papacy in the Middle Ages.* London: Methuen & Co., 1972.
Underhill, Evelyn. *Mysticism.* Cleveland and New York: Meridian, 1965.
Vacandard, Elphège. *Vie de saint Bernard,* 2 vols. Paris: Gabalda, 1894.
Van den Eynde, Damien. *Essai sur la succession et la date des écrits de Hugues de Saint-Victor.* Rome: Apud Pontificium Athenaeum Antonianum, 1960.
Van Engen, John. "The Christian Middle Ages as an Historiographical Problem." *American Historical Review* 91 (1986): 519-52.
——. "The 'Crisis of Ceonobitism' Reconsidered: Benedictine Monasticism in the Years 1050-1150." *Speculum* 61 (1986): 269-304.
——. *Rupert of Deutz.* Berkeley and Los Angeles: University of California Press, 1983.
Vauchez, André. *La spiritualité du moyen âge occidental viii-xii siècles.* Paris: Presses universitaires de France, 1975.
——. *The Laity in the Middle Ages. Religious Beliefs and Devotional Practices.* Notre Dame: University of Notre Dame, 1993.
Veneroni, Bruna. "S. Bruno e il suo elogio della vita contemplativa: Spunti et motivi classici." *Benedictina* 16 (1969): 196-212.
Verdeyen, Paul. *La théologie mystique de Guillaume de Saint-Thierry.* Paris: FAC-éditions, 1990.
Versteylen, A. "Adam l'Écossais." *DS* 1:196-98.
Vielleux, Armand. "The Interpretation of a Monastic Rule." *The Cistercian Spirit. A Symposium,* ed. M. Basil Pennington, 48-65. Spencer: Cistercian Publications, 1970.
Viller, Marcel, and Karl Rahner. *Aszese und Mystik in der Väterzeit. Ein Abriss.* Freiburg: Herder, 1939.
Vogel, Cyrille. *Le pecheur et la penitence au moyen âge.* Paris: Cerf, 1969.
Vogt, Carolyn J. "William of St. Thierry's The Golden Epistle. Mystical Ascent Through Incarnation." *Cistercian Studies* 8 (1973): 337-54.
Vogt, Hermann J. "Zur Spiritualität des frühen irischen Mönchtums." *Die Iren und Europa,* ed. Heinz Löwe, 26-51.
von Balthasar, Hans Urs. *Kosmische Liturgie. Das Weltbild Maximus der Bekenner.* Freiburg-im-Breisgau: Herder, 1941; 2nd edition 1961.
——. *The Glory of the Lord.* New York: Crossroad, 1984.
von Campenhausen, Hans. "The Ascetical Idea of Exile in Ancient and Early Medieval Monasticism." *Tradition and Life in the Early Church,* 231-51. Philadelphia: Fortress Press, 1968.
von Ivanka, Endré. "La structure de l'âme selon S. Bernard." *Saint Bernard Théologien,* 202-08.
Vuong-Dinh-Lam, Jean. "Gilbert de Hoyland." *DS* 6:371-74.
Waddell, Chrysogonus. "The Glorified Christ, Present and Future: The Eschatological Dynamic of the Spiritual Life." *La dottrina della vita spirituale nelle opere di San Bernardo di Clairvaux,* 327-45.
Walker, G. S. M. "Erigena's Conception of the Sacraments." *Studies in Church History,* ed. G. J. Cuming, 3:150-58. Leiden: Brill, 1966.
Walsh, James. "Guillaume de Saint-Thierry et les sens spirituals." *Revue d'ascétique et de mystique* 35 (1959): 27-42.
Walsh, John R., and Thomas Bradley. *A History of the Irish Church 400-700 AD.* Dublin: Columba Press, 1991.
Walsh, P. G. "Venantius Fortunatus." *Spirituality through the Centuries,* ed. James Walsh, 72-82.
Ward, Benedicta. "The Desert Myth: Reflections on the Desert Ideal in Early Cistercian Monasticism." *One Yet Two. Monastic Tradition East and West,* 183-99.
——. *Miracles and the Medieval Mind.* Philadelphia: University of Pennsylvania Press, 1982.

——. *The Prayers and Meditations of Saint Anselm.* New York: Penguin, 1973.

Wathen, Ambrose. *Silence: The Meaning of Silence in the Rule of St. Benedict.* Washington, DC: Cistercian Publications, 1973.

Webb, Geoffrey. *An Introduction to the Cistercian De Anima.* Aquinas Paper No. 36. London: Aquin Press, 1962.

Weber, Leonard. *Hauptfragen der Moraltheologie Gregors des Grossen.* Frieburg-in-der-Schweiz: Universtitätsverlag, 1947.

Weeks, Andrew. *German Mysticism from Hildegard of Bingen to Ludwig Wittgenstein. A Literary and Intellectual History.* Albany: SUNY Press, 1993.

Weisheiple, J. A. "Classification of the Sciences in Medieval Thought." *Mediaeval Studies* 27 (1965): 54-90.

White, Carolinne. *Christian Friendship in the Fourth Century.* Cambridge: Cambridge University Press, 1992.

Williams, Watkin. *Saint Bernard of Clairvaux.* Manchester: Manchester University Press, 1935.

Wilmart, André. *Auteurs spirituels et textes devots du moyen âge latin. Etudes d'histoire littéraire.* 1932; reprint Paris: Études Augustiniennes, 1971.

——. "La serie et la date des ouvrages de Guillaume de Saint-Thierry." *Revue Mabillon* 14 (1924): 157-67.

——. "Les écrits spirituels des deux Guiges." *Revue d'ascétique et de mystique* 5 (1924): 59-79 and 127-58.

——. "Maître Adam, chanoine prémontré devenu chartreux à Witham." *Analecta Praemonstratensia* 9 (1933): 209-31.

Winandy, J. "La contemplation à l'ecole des Pères: Ambroise Autpert." *La vie spirituelle* 82 (1950): 147-55.

Winkler, Gerhard B. "Bernhard und die Kartäuser. Zur Relativierung des monastischen Asketismus durch die reine Gottesliebe." *Kartäuserregel und Kartäuserleben. Internationaler Kongress vom. 30. Mai bis 3. Juni 1984. Stift Heiligenkreuz,* 5-19. Analecta Cartusiana 113.1. Salzburg: Universität Salzburg, 1984.

Wipfler, Heinz. *Die Trinitätsspekulation des Petrus von Poitiers und Die Trinitätsspekulation des Richard von St. Viktor. Ein Vergleich.* Münster: Aschendorff, 1965.

Wisniewski, Roswitha. "Die unio mystica im St. Trudperter Hohen Lied." *"Minnichlichiu gotes erkennusse". Studien zur frühen abendländischen Mystiktradition. Heidelberger Mystiksymposium vom 16. Januar 1989,* 28-42. Stuttgart-Bad Cannstatt: froomann-holzboog, 1990.

Young, Frances. *From Nicea to Chalcedon. A Guide to the Literature and its Background.* Philadelphia: Fortress, 1983.

Zimdars-Swartz, Sandra. "A Confluence of Imagery: Exegesis and Christology according to Gregory the Great." *Saint Grégoire le Grand,* ed. Jacques Fontaine, et al., 327-36.

Zinn, Grover A. *"De gradibus ascensionum*: The Stages of Contemplative Ascent in Two Treatises on Noah's Ark by Hugh of St. Victor." *Studies in Medieval Culture* V, ed. John R. Sommerfeldt, 61-79. Kalamazoo: Publications of the Medieval Center, 1975.

——. *"Historia fundamentum est*: the role of history in the contemplative life according to Hugh of St. Victor." *Contemporary reflections on the medieval Christian tradition. Essays in honor of Ray C. Petry,* ed. George H. Shriver, 13-50. Durham: Duke University Press, 1974.

——. "History and Interpretation: 'Hebrew Truth,' Judaism, and the Victorine Exegetical Tradition." *Jews and Christians. Exploring the Past, Present, and Future,* ed. James H. Charlesworth, 100-26. New York: Crossroad, 1994.

——. "Hugh of St. Victor and the Ark of Noah: A New Look." *Church History* 40 (1971): 261-72.

——. "Hugh of St. Victor, Isaiah's Vision, and *De Arca Noe.*" *The Church and the Arts,* ed. Diana Wood, 99-116. Oxford: Blackwell, 1992.

——. "IV. The Regular Canons." *Christian Spirituality: Origins to the Twelfth Century,* ed. Bernard McGinn, John Meyendorff, and Jean Leclercq, 218-28.

——. "Mandala Symbolism and Use in the Mysticism of Hugh of St. Victor." *History of Religions* 12 (1973): 317-41.

——. "Personification Allegory and Visions of Light in Richard of St. Victor's Teaching on Contemplation." *University of Toronto Quarterly* 46 (1977): 190-214.

——. "Sound, Silence and Word in the Spirituality of Gregory the Great." *Saint Grégoire le Grand,* ed. Jacques Fontaine et al., 367-75.

Zwingmann, Wolfgang. "Affectus illuminatus amoris. Über die Offenbarwerden der Gnade und die Erfahrung von Gottes." *Cîteaux* 18 (1967): 193-226.

——. "Ex affectu cordis. Über die Vollkommenheit menschlicher Handelns und menschlicher Hingabe nach Willhelm von St. Thierry." *Cîteaux* 18 (1967): 5-37.

Indexes

Names

Scripture References (Vg)

1:16	339	14:17	354	*Ephesians*	
1:23	293			3:18	193
3:14	179	*1 Corinthians*		4:3	264
3:24	268	2:9-12	385	4:10	179
4:23	235	2:9	65	5:23	380
4:24	270	2:14	235		
6:14	83	5:15	223	*Philippians*	
9:6	51	6:17	70, 136, 181, 208, 213,	2:6-7	246, 280
10:30	247		215, 243, 264, 284, 295,	2:7	178
14:23	247		306, 319, 322, 389, 397,	3:12-13	260
14:27	354		410, 417	3:13	217
15:15	320	8:1	201	3:20-21	181
16:17	192	11:3	291		
17:11	295	12	406	*Colossians*	
17:21-22	264	12:13	194	1:26	168
17:21	265, 295	13:10	211, 280	3:8	211
17:22	295	13:12	65, 71, 76, 209, 228, 256,		
17:6	270		261, 279, 279, 280, 379	*1 Thessalonians*	
19:34	346	14:41	235	5:17	115, 139
20:17	187	15:23	177	5:23	235
20:21-23	54	15:28	213, 284		
21:17	252	15:45	281	*James*	
				1:17	103, 110
Acts		*2 Corinthians*			
2:2-4	54	2:12	191	*1 Peter*	
2:37	48	3:17	307	3:20-21	380
2:41-47	152	3:18	168, 175, 181, 205, 211,	4:8	189
4:32-35	152		261, 279, 282		
4:32	319	11-12	192	*1 John*	
16:8-9	84	11:1	192	2:1	85
		11:17	192	3:2	208, 232, 261, 262
Romans		12	340	4:8	181, 3
1:17	240	12:1-3	339	4:10	194, 1
1:20	408	12:1	192	4:16	215
5:5	270	12:2-3	115	4:19	308
8:9	46	12:2	184		
8:26	85	12:3	417	*Apocalypse*	
8:29-30	168	12:4	212	1:10	338
9:20	397			4:26	300
9:28	281	*Galatians*		8:1	67, 77, 389
11:33	397	4:6	191	19:16	47
11:36	99	4:19	280	21:2	178

Subjects

Abbot, 29, 163, 180, 220
Absence (of God), xi, 59, 61, 192-92, 241, 249, 274, 299, 308, 348, 352, 410, 420-21. *See also* Apophatic, Nothingness.
Absolute, the, 68, 102. *See also* Principle, First
Action. *See* Contemplation
Affectus, 188, 189, 193, 194-95, 197, 198-99, 201, 202, 203, 206, 207, 208, 213, 218, 219, 220, 230, 233, 235, 236, 243, 251-52, 254, 255, 257, 259, 260, 263, 266, 268, 272, 277, 283, 288-89, 300, 301, 307, 308, 311, 312, 314, 315-16, 318, 319, 323, 388, 400, 401, 403, 412, 416, 417
Affirmation. *See* Cataphatic.
Agape. *See* Caritas, Love.
Allegory, 23, 40-43, 50, 76, 95, 96-97, 106-07, 111, 135, 227, 286, 294, 315, 335, 373-74, 375, 376, 379, 382, 392, 397, 398, 401-02, 403, 406. *See also* Bible.
Anagogy, 113, 230, 289, 290, 375-76, 380, 381, 382, 401-02, 406, 409, 410. *See also* Ascent.
Anchorites. *See* Eremiticism.
Angels, 57, 62, 71-72, 77, 84, 88, 108,

113, 115, 167, 174, 178-79, 201, 202, 209-10, 289, 290, 292, 294, 304, 308, 337, 355, 361, 379, 393, 406-07, 409, 410, 413
Anthropology, xiii, 45-48, 82, 90, 92, 104-06, 108-10, 117, 168-74, 191, 194-95, 200, 204-05, 210-11, 227-28, 229-36, 242-43, 250, 265, 276, 284-96, 311, 349, 366, 376, 384-86, 399-401. *See also* Body, Soul.
Apocalypticism, 36, 84, 333, 340-41
Apophatic (i.e., negative) language and theology, xii, 55, 66, 89, 95-100, 103-06, 115-18, 207-08, 231, 273-74, 286, 287, 291-93, 300-01, 360-61, 393, 410. *See also* Absence, Docta ignorantia, Nothingness.
Ark, Noah's, 376-83, 388, 400
Ascension (of Christ), 52, 109, 115, 176-77, 184, 201, 235
Ascent (to heaven, to God), 57, 63, 71-73, 110, 113-14, 136, 178-79, 194, 201, 202, 233, 237, 238, 240, 247, 251, 252, 269, 282, 285, 286, 293, 302, 319, 339, 340, 357-59, 360, 374, 375, 376, 381-82, 384, 385, 387-88, 390, 417
Asceticism, xi, 18, 19, 22, 26-29, 30, 35,

46, 54, 56-57, 60, 64, 78, 84, 86, 87, 122, 125, 127, 128, 129, 131, 142, 143, 144, 183, 228, 279, 343, 344, 354, 357, 363, 364, 396, 401
Authority, 11, 13, 93, 95, 97, 236, 237-38, 332-33, 334
Autobiography (and mysticism), xiv, 63, 71, 81, 85, 142, 185, 290, 298, 328-33, 391, 395

Baptism, 16, 21, 40, 96, 110, 248, 331, 380
Beatitude, 136, 183, 208, 216-17, 229, 230, 232, 242, 243, 253, 260, 265, 273, 284, 296, 299-300, 314, 346-47, 359, 380, 383, 412, 414. *See also* Epektasis.
Beauty, 50, 103, 140, 183, 194, 242, 243
Bed. *See* Symbol.
Being, 194, 313
Benedictinism, xii, xiii, 27-32, 38, 121-23, 124, 225, 324-25, 341-47, 359, 361, 399. *See also* Monasticism.
Bible (exegesis of), xi, 23-27, 34, 37, 39-43, 56, 58, 62, 70, 81, 83, 84-85, 87, 88, 93-97, 123, 132-34, 135, 154, 164, 172, 181, 186, 188-89, 210, 222, 227, 277, 280-81, 290, 306-07, 329-33, 336,